The Sporting News

THE COMPLETE
BASEBALL
RECORD BOOK

1988

The Sporting News

THE COMPLETE BASEBALL RECORD BOOK

1988

Editor/Complete Baseball Record Book
CRAIG CARTER

President-Chief Executive Officer
Richard Waters

Editor
Tom Barnidge

Director of Books and Periodicals
Ron Smith

ISSN: 0885-9183

ISBN: 0-89204-266-4

A Times Mirror
Company

CONTENTS

Regular Season

Batting
Individual 8
Club 35
League 53
Baserunning
Individual 57
Club 58
League 60
Pitching
Individual 61
Club 75
League 78
Fielding
Individual 80
Club 101
League 107
Miscellaneous
Individual 108
Club 109
League 118
Non-Playing Personnel 119
Yearly Leaders 120
Career Milestones 133
General Reference Data 142
Team Yearly Finishes & Records 159
Index 349

Championship Series

Batting
Individual 228
Club 235
Baserunning
Individual 248
Club 248
Pitching
Individual 250
Club 254

Fielding
Individual 255
Club 265
Miscellaneous 271
Non-Playing Personnel 272
General Reference Data 273
Index 350

World Series

Batting
Individual 282
Club 290
Baserunning
Individual 299
Club 300
Pitching
Individual 301
Club 305
Fielding
Individual 307
Club 315
Miscellaneous 320
Non-Playing Personnel 322
General Reference Data 323
Index 351

All-Star Game

Batting
Individual 336
Club 338
Baserunning 341
Pitching 341
Fielding
Individual 342
Club 345
Miscellaneous 346
Non-Playing Personnel 346
General Reference Data 347
Index 351

Cover Photos: Former Cincinnati Reds second baseman Joe Morgan, former Minnesota Twins and California Angels infielder Rod Carew, New York Yankees first baseman Don Mattingly and Milwaukee third baseman Paul Molitor by Rich Pilling, Photo Editor of The Sporting News.

Regular Season

including:
- ■ Batting (Individual, Club, League)
- ■ Baserunning (Individual, Club, League)
- ■ Pitching (Individual, Club, League)
- ■ Fielding (Individual, Club, League)
- ■ Miscellaneous (Individual, Club, League)
- ■ Non-Playing Personnel
- ■ Yearly Leaders
- ■ Career Milestones
- ■ General Reference Data
- ■ Team Yearly Finishes, Individual and Club Records

Individual Batting

Service
Years

Most Years Played in Major Leagues

26—James T. McGuire, Toledo, Cleveland, Rochester, Washington A. A.; Detroit, Philadelphia, Washington, Brooklyn N. L.; Detroit, New York, Boston, Cleveland A. L.; 1884 to 1912, except 1889, 1909, 1911 (4 in A. A.; 13 in N. L.; 9 in A. L.), 1781 games.

Most Years Played, League

A. L.—25—Edward T. Collins, Philadelphia, Chicago, 1906 through 1930, 2826 games.

N. L.—24—Peter E. Rose, Cincinnati, Philadelphia, Montreal, 1963 through 1986, 3562 games.

Most Consecutive Years Played, League

A. L.—25—Edward T. Collins, Philadelphia, Chicago, 1906 through 1930, 2826 games.

N. L.—24—Peter E. Rose, Cincinnati, Philadelphia, Montreal, 1963 through 1986, 3562 games.

Most Years, One Club

A. L.—23—Brooks C. Robinson, Baltimore, 1955 through 1977, 2896 games.

Carl M. Yastrzemski, Boston, 1961 through 1983, 3308 games.

N. L.—22—Adrian C. Anson, Chicago, 1876 through 1897, 2253 games.

Melvin T. Ott, New York, 1926 through 1947, 2730 games.

Stanley F. Musial, St. Louis, 1941 through 1963 (except 1945 in military service), 3026 games.

Most Consecutive Years, One Club

A. L.—23—Brooks C. Robinson, Baltimore, 1955 through 1977, 2896 games.

Carl M. Yastrzemski, Boston, 1961 through 1983, 3308 games.

N. L.—22—Adrian C. Anson, Chicago, 1876 through 1897, 2253 games.

Melvin T. Ott, New York, 1926 through 1947, 2730 games.

Stanley F. Musial, St. Louis, 1941 through 1963 (except 1945 in military service), 3026 games.

Youngest & Oldest Players

Youngest Player, Game

N. L.—15 years, 10 months, 11 days—Joseph H. Nuxhall, Cincinnati, June 10, 1944 (pitcher).

A. L.—16 years, 8 months, 5 days—Carl A. Scheib, Philadelphia, September 6, 1943, second game (pitcher).

Oldest Player, Game

A. L.—59 years, 2 months, 18 days—Leroy Paige, Kansas City, September 25, 1965 (pitched first three innings).

57 years, 10 months, 6 days—Orestes A. Minoso, October 5, 1980 (pinch-hitter).

57 years, 16 days—Nicholas Altrock, Washington, October 1, 1933 (pinch-hitter).

N. L.—52 years, 29 days—James H. O'Rourke, New York, September 22, 1904 (caught complete game).

Leagues & Clubs

Most Leagues, Played, Lifetime

4—Held by 20 players. Last Time—Lafayette N. Cross, A. A., P. L., N. L., A. L., 21 years, 2259 games, 1887 through 1907.

Most Leagues, Played, Season

3—William N. Murphy, 1884, N. L., A. A., U. A.

Walter F. Prince, 1884, N. L., A. A., U. A.

George A. Strief, 1884, A. A., U. A., N. L.

Most Clubs Played in Major Leagues

12—Charles M. Smith, Cincinnati, Cleveland, Worcester, Buffalo, Pittsburgh, Boston N. L.; Philadelphia, Baltimore, Louisville, Columbus, Pittsburgh, Washington, A. A., 1880 through 1891, 12 years, 1110 games.

James T. McGuire, Toledo, Cleveland, Rochester, Washington, A. A.; Detroit, Philadelphia, Washington, Brooklyn N. L.; Detroit, New York, Boston, Cleveland A. L.: 1884 to 1912, except 1889, 1909, 1911, 1781 games.

Most Clubs Played in Major Leagues, Since 1900

10—Robert Lane Miller, St. Louis N. L., New York N. L., Los Angeles N. L., Minnesota A. L., Cleveland A. L., Chicago A. L., Chicago N. L., San Diego N. L., Pittsburgh, N. L., Detroit A. L., 1957, 1959 through 1974 (17 years), 807 games.

H. Thomas Davis, Los Angeles N. L., New York N. L., Chicago A. L., Seattle A. L., Houston N. L., Chicago N. L., Oakland A. L., Baltimore A. L., California A. L., Kansas City A. L., 1959 through 1976 (18 years), 1999 games.

Kenneth A. Brett, Boston A.L., Milwaukee A.L., Philadelphia N.L., Pittsburgh N.L., New York A.L., Chicago A.L., California A.L., Minnesota A.L., Los Angeles N.L., Kansas City A.L., 1967, 1969 through 1981 (14 years), 349 games.

Most Clubs Played, League

N. L.—9—Dennis L. Brouthers, Troy, Buffalo, Detroit, Boston, Brooklyn, Baltimore, Louisville, Philadelphia, New York, 1879 through 1889, 1892 through 1896, 1904 (17 years).

A. L.—8—Juan J. Beniquez, Boston, Texas, New York, Seattle, California, Baltimore, Kansas City, Toronto, 1971 through 1987, except 1973 (16 years).

N. L. since 1899—7—John C. Barry, Washington, Boston, Philadelphia, Chicago, Cincinnati, St. Louis, New York, 1899 through 1908 (10 years).

Joseph C. Schultz, Sr., Boston, Brooklyn, Chicago, Pittsburgh, St. Louis, Philadelphia, Cincinnati, 1912 through 1925, except 1914, 1917 and 1918 (11 years).

Frank J. Thomas, Pittsburgh, Cincinnati, Chicago, Milwaukee, New York, Philadelphia, Houston, 1951 through 1966 (16 years).

Most Clubs Played in Majors, One Season

4—Harry E. Wheeler, St. Louis A. A., Kansas City U. A., Chicago U. A., Pittsburgh U. A., Baltimore U. A., 72 games, 1884 (Note: Pittsburgh considered part of Chicago franchise and is not considered a separate club).

Since 1900—4—Held by many players—Last player—David A. Kingman, New York N. L., San Diego N. L., California A. L., New York A. L., 132 games, 1977.

Most Clubs Played, League, One Season

N. L.—4—Thomas J. Dowse, Louisville, Cincinnati, Philadelphia, Washington, 63 games, 1892.

A. L.—4—Frank E. Huelsman, Chicago, Detroit, St. Louis, Washington, 112 games, 1904.

Paul E. Lehner, Philadelphia, Chicago, St. Louis, Cleveland, 65 games, 1951.

Theodore G. Gray, Chicago, Cleveland, New York, Baltimore, 14 games, 1955.

Most Clubs Played, One Day

N. L.—2—Max O. Flack, Chicago, St. Louis, May 30 a.m., p.m., 1922.

Clifton E. Heathcote, St. Louis, Chicago, May 30 a.m., p.m., 1922.

Joel R. Youngblood, New York, Montreal, August 4, 1982.

Positions

Most Positions Played, One Season

N. L.—9—Lewis W. McAllister, Cleveland, 110 games, 1899.

Michael T. Walsh, Philadelphia, 84 games, 1911.

E. Eugene Paulette, St. Louis, 125 games, 1918.

A. L.—9—Samuel B. Mertes, Chicago, 129 games, 1902.

John H. Rothrock, Boston, 117 games, 1928.

Dagoberto B. Campaneris, Kansas City, 144 games, 1965.

Cesar L. Tovar, Minnesota, 157 games, 1968.

Most Positions Played, One Game

A. L.—9—Dagoberto B. Campaneris, Kansas City, September 8, 1965; played 8 ⅔ innings of 13-inning game.

Cesar L. Tovar, Minnesota, September 22, 1968.

Games

Most Games, League

N. L.— 3562— Peter E. Rose, Cincinnati, Philadelphia, Montreal, 24 years, 1963 through 1986.

A. L.— 3308— Carl M. Yastrzemski, Boston, 23 years, 1961 through 1983.

Most Consecutive Games, League

A. L.— 2130— H. Louis Gehrig, New York, June 1, 1925, through April 30, 1939.

N. L.— 1207— Steven P. Garvey, Los Angeles, San Diego, September 3, 1975, through July 29, 1983, first game.

Most Consecutive Games, League, From Start of Career

N. L.— 424— Ernest Banks, Chicago, September 17, 1953, through August 10, 1957.

A. L.— 394— Aloysius H. Simmons, Philadelphia, April 15, 1924, through July 20, 1926.

Most Games Played, Season

N. L. (162-game season) —165—Maurice M. Wills, Los Angeles, 1962.

N. L. (154-game season) —160—Henry K. Groh, Cincinnati, 1915.

Thomas H. Griffith, Cincinnati, 1915.

A. L. (162-game season) —164—Cesar L. Tovar, Minnesota, 1967.

A. L. (154-game season) —162—James E. Barrett, Detroit, 1904.

Most Games Played, Season, With Two Clubs

N. L. (162-game season) —164—Franklin Taveras, Pittsburgh, New York, 1979.

N. L. (154-game season) —158—Ralph M. Kiner, Pittsburgh, Chicago, 1953.

A. L. (162-game season) —160—Julio L. Cruz, Seattle, Chicago, 1983.

A. L. (154-game season) —155—Patrick H. Dougherty, Boston, New York, 1904.

W. Edward Robinson, Washington, Chicago, 1950.

Most Games, Rookie Season

A. L. (162-game season) —162—Jacob Wood, Detroit, 1961.

Robert F. Knoop, Los Angeles, 1964.

George Scott, Boston, 1966.

A. L. (154-game season) —155—Emory E. Rigney, Detroit, 1922.

Anthony M. Lazzeri, New York, 1926.

D. Dale Alexander, Detroit, 1929.

William R. Johnson, New York, 1943.

Richard C. Wakefield, Detroit, 1943.

Albert L. Rosen, Cleveland, 1950.

Harvey E. Kuenn, Detroit, 1953.

N. L. (162-game season) —162—Richard A. Allen, Philadelphia, 1964.

Johnny C. Ray, Pittsburgh, 1982.

N. L. (154-game season) —157—Raymond L. Jablonski, St. Louis, 1953.

Most Games, Righthander, Season

N. L. (162-game season) —164—Jose A. Pagan, San Francisco, 1962.

Ronald E. Santo, Chicago, 1965.

Franklin Taveras, Pittsburgh, New York, 1979.

N. L. (154-game season) —160—Henry K. Groh, Cincinnati, 1915.

A. L. (162-game season) —164—Cesar L. Tovar, Minnesota, 1967.

A. L. (154-game season) —159—Napoleon Lajoie, Cleveland, 1910.

Derrill B. Pratt, St. Louis, 1915.

Most Games, Lefthander, Season

N. L. (162-game season) —164—Billy L. Williams, Chicago, 1965.

N. L. (154-game season) —160—Thomas H. Griffith, Cincinnati, 1915.

A. L. (162-game season) —163—Leon L. Wagner, Cleveland, 1964.

Albert Oliver, Texas, 1980.

Gregory L. Walker, Chicago, 1985.

A. L. (154-game season) —162—James E. Barrett, Detroit, 1904.

Most Games, Switch Hitter, Season

N. L. (162-game season) —165—Maurice M. Wills, Los Angeles, 1962.

A. L. (162-game season) —163—Donald A. Buford, Chicago, 1966.

O. Antonio Fernandez, Toronto, 1986.

Most Games, Season, as Pinch-Hitter

N. L. (162-game season) —94—Daniel J. Staub, New York, 1983.

N. L. (154-game season) —76—Gerald T. Lynch, Cincinnati, 1960.

A. L.— 81— Elmer W. Valo, New York, Washington, 1960.

Most Years Leading League in Most Games

A. L.—7—H. Louis Gehrig, New York, 1927, 1930 (tied), 1932, 1934 (tied), 1936 (tied), 1937, 1938 (tied).

N. L.—6—Ernest Banks, Chicago, 1954, 1955, 1957 (tied), 1958, 1959 (tied), 1960.

Steven P. Garvey, Los Angeles, 1977 (tied), 1978 (tied), 1980, 1981 (tied), 1982 (tied), San Diego, 1985 (tied).

Most Years Played All Clubs' Games

A. L.— 13—H. Louis Gehrig, New York, 1926 through 1938 (consecutive).

N. L.— 10—Peter E. Rose, Cincinnati, 1965, 1972, 1974, 1975, 1976, 1977, Philadelphia, 1979, 1980, 1981, 1982.

Most Consecutive Years Played All Clubs' Games

A. L.— 13—H. Louis Gehrig, New York, 1926 through 1938.

N. L.— 7—Steven P. Garvey, Los Angeles, 1976 through 1982.

Most Years, 150 or More Games, League

N. L.— 17—Peter E. Rose, Cincinnati, Philadelphia, 1963 through 1983, except 1964, 1967, 1968, 1981.

A. L.— 14—Brooks C. Robinson, Baltimore, 1960 through 1974, except 1965.

Most Consecutive Years, 150 or More Games, League

N. L.— 13—Willie H. Mays, New York, San Francisco, 1954 through 1966.

A. L.— 11—J. Nelson Fox, Chicago, 1952 through 1962.

Most Years, 100 or More Games, League

N. L.— 23—Peter E. Rose, Cincinnati, Philadelphia, Montreal, 1963 through 1985.

A. L.— 22— Carl M. Yastrzemski, Boston, 1961 through 1983, except 1981.

Most Consecutive Years, 100 or More Games, League

N. L.— 23— Peter E. Rose, Cincinnati, Philadelphia, Montreal, 1963 through 1985.

A. L.— 20— Carl M. Yastrzemski, Boston, 1961 through 1980.

Fewest Games, Season, for Leader in Most Games

N. L.— 152— Stanley C. Hack, Chicago, 1938.
William J. Herman, Chicago, 1938.

A. L.— 154— Held by many players.

Batting Average

Highest Average, League, Fifteen or More Seasons

A. L.—.367— Tyrus R. Cobb, Detroit, Philadelphia, 24 years, 1905 through 1928, 11,429 at-bats, 4,191 hits.

N. L.—.359— Rogers Hornsby, St. Louis, New York, Boston, Chicago, 19 years, 1915 through 1933, 8,058 at-bats, 2,895 hits.

Highest Average, Season, 100 or More Games

N. L.—.438— Hugh Duffy, Boston, 124 games, 1894.

N. L. since 1900—.424— Rogers Hornsby, St. Louis, 143 games, 1924.

A. L.—.422— Napoleon Lajoie, Philadelphia, 131 games, 1901.

Highest Average, Season, 100 or More Games, For Non-Leader

A. L.—.408— Joseph J. Jackson, Cleveland, 147 games, 1911.

N. L.—.406— Fred C. Clarke, Louisville, 129 games, 1897.

N. L. since 1900—.393— Floyd C. Herman, Brooklyn, 163 games, 1930.

Highest Average, Rookie Season, 100 or More Games

N. L.—.373— George A. Watkins, St. Louis, 119 games, 1930.

A. L.—.349— Wade A. Boggs, Boston, 104 games, 1982.

(Boggs did not have enough plate appearances to qualify for batting championship. Highest qualifying average was .343 by D. Dale Alexander, Detroit, 155 games, 1929. Watkins qualified for N.L. title in 1930 under different regulations than presently used.)

Leading Batsmen, Rookie Season

N. L.—.356— Abner L. Dalrymple, Milwaukee, 60 games, 1878.

A. L.—.323— Pedro Oliva, Minnesota, 161 games, 1964.

Highest Average, Righthander, Season, 100 or More Games

N. L.—.438— Hugh Duffy, Boston, 124 games, 1894.

N. L. since 1900—.424— Rogers Hornsby, St. Louis, 143 games, 1924.

A. L.—.422— Napoleon Lajoie, Philadelphia, 131 games, 1910.

Highest Average, Lefthander, Season, 100 or More Games

N. L.— .432— William H. Keeler, Baltimore, 128 games, 1897.

A. L.—.41979— George H. Sisler, St. Louis, 142 games, 1922.
.41962— Tyrus R. Cobb, Detroit, 146 games, 1911.

N. L. since 1900—.401— William H. Terry, New York, 154 games, 1930.

Highest Average, Switch Hitter, Season, 100 or More Games

N. L.—.373— George S. Davis, New York, 133 games, 1893.

A. L.—.365— Mickey C. Mantle, New York, 144 games, 1957.

N. L. since 1900—.353— Willie D. McGee, St. Louis, 152 games, 1985.

Highest Average, Season, 100 or More Games, First Baseman

A. L.—.420— George H. Sisler, St. Louis, 142 games, 1922; 141 games at first base.

N. L.—.401— William H. Terry, New York, 154 games, 1930; 154 games at first base.

Highest Average, Season, 100 or More Games, Second Baseman

N. L.—.424— Rogers Hornsby, St. Louis, 143 games, 1924; 143 games at second base.

A. L.—.422— Napoleon Lajoie, Philadelphia, 131 games, 1901; 130 games at second base.

Highest Average, Season, 100 or More Games, Third Baseman

A. L.—.390— George H. Brett, Kansas City, 117 games, 1980; 112 games at third base.

N. L.—.390— John J. McGraw, Baltimore, 118 games, 1899; 118 games at third base.

N. L. since 1900—.379— Fred C. Lindstrom, New York, 148 games, 1930; 148 games at third base.

Highest Average, Season, 100 or More Games, Shortstop

N. L.—.397— Hugh A. Jennings, Baltimore, 129 games, 1896; 129 games at shortstop.

A. L.—.388— Lucius B. Appling, Chicago, 138 games, 1936; 137 games at shortstop.

N. L. since 1900—.385— J. Floyd Vaughan, Pittsburgh, 137 games, 1935; 137 games at shortstop.

Highest Average, Season, 100 or More Games, Catcher

A. L.—.362— William M. Dickey, New York, 112 games, 1936; caught in 107 games.

N. L.—.358— John T. Meyers, New York, 126 games, 1912; caught in 122 games.

Highest Average, Season, 100 or More Games, Outfielder

N. L.—.438— Hugh Duffy, Boston, 124 games, 1894; 123 games in outfield.

A. L.—.420— Tyrus R. Cobb, Detroit, 146 games, 1911; 146 games in outfield.

N. L. since 1900—.398— Frank J. O'Doul, Philadelphia, 154 games, 1929; 154 games in outfield.

Highest Average, Season, Pitcher (Only for Games as Pitcher)

A. L.—.440— Walter P. Johnson, Washington, 36 games, 1925; pitched 30 games.

N. L.—.406— John N. Bentley, New York, 52 games, 1923; pitched 31 games.

Most Years Leading League in Batting Average

A. L.— 12— Tyrus R. Cobb, Detroit, 1907, 1908, 1909, 1910, 1911, 1912, 1913, 1914, 1915, 1917, 1918, 1919.

N. L.— 8— John P. Wagner, Pittsburgh, 1900, 1903, 1904, 1906, 1907, 1908, 1909, 1911.

Most Consecutive Years Leading League in Batting Average

A. L.—9— Tyrus R. Cobb, Detroit, 1907 through 1915.

N. L.—6— Rogers Hornsby, St. Louis, 1920 through 1925.

Most Years .400 or Over, 50 or More Games

N. L.—3— Jesse C. Burkett, Cleveland, St. Louis, 1895, 1896, 1899.
Rogers Hornsby, St. Louis, 1922, 1924, 1925.

A. L.—3— Tyrus R. Cobb, Detroit, 1911, 1912, 1922.

Most Consecutive Years .400 or Over, 50 or More Games

N. L.—2— Jesse C. Burkett, Cleveland, 1895, 1896.
Rogers Hornsby, St. Louis, 1924, 1925.

A. L.—2— Tyrus R. Cobb, Detroit, 1911, 1912.

Most Years .300 or Over, 50 or More Games

A. L.— 23— Tyrus R. Cobb, Detroit, Philadelphia, 1906 through 1928.

N. L.— 18— Adrian C. Anson, Chicago, 1876 to 1897, except 1877, 1879, 1891 and 1892.

N. L. since 1900—17—Stanley F. Musial, St. Louis, 1942 through 1958, and 1962 (except 1945, in military service).

Most Consecutive Years, .300 or Over, 50 or More Games

A. L.— 23— Tyrus R. Cobb, Detroit, Philadelphia, 1906 through 1928.

N. L.— 17— John P. Wagner, Louisville, Pittsburgh, 1897 through 1913.

N. L. since 1900—16—Stanley F. Musial, St. Louis, 1942 through 1958 (except 1945, in military service).

Most Consec. Years, .300 or Over, 50 or More Games, Start of Career

N. L.— 17— John P. Wagner, Louisville, Pittsburgh, 1897 through 1913.

N. L. since 1900—16—Stanley F. Musial, St. Louis, 1942 through 1958 (except 1945, in military service).

A. L.— 15— Theodore S. Williams, Boston, 1939 through 1958 (except 1943-44-45 and 1952-53, in military service).

Most Years .300 or Over, Pitcher

A. L.—8—Charles H. Ruffing, Boston, New York, 1928, 1929, 1930, 1931, 1932, 1935, 1939, 1941.

N. L.—5—John E. Stivetts, Boston, 1892, 1893, 1894, 1896, 1897.

Highest Average, Five Consecutive Seasons, 100 or More Games

N. L.—.4024— Rogers Hornsby, St. Louis, 1921 through 1925.

A. L.—.3965— Tyrus R. Cobb, Detroit, 1909 through 1913.

Highest Average, Four Consecutive Seasons, 100 or More Games

N. L.—.4039— Rogers Hornsby, St. Louis, 1922 through 1925.

A. L.—.4019— Tyrus R. Cobb, Detroit, 1910 through 1913.

Highest Average, Three Consecutive Seasons, 100 or More Games

A. L.— .4084— Tyrus R. Cobb, Detroit, 1911, 1912, 1913.

N. L.—.40647— William H. Keeler, Baltimore, 1895, 1896, 1897.
.40627— Jesse C. Burkett, Cleveland, 1895, 1896, 1897.

N. L. since 1900—.405—Rogers Hornsby, St. Louis, 1923, 1924, 1925.

Highest Average, Two Consecutive Seasons, 100 or More Games

N. L.—.417—Jesse C. Burkett, Cleveland, 1895, 1896.
A. L.—.415—Tyrus R. Cobb, Detroit, 1911, 1912.
N. L. since 1900—.413—Rogers Hornsby, St. Louis, 1924, 1925.

Lowest Average, Season, 150 or More Games

A. L.—.182—Montford M. Cross, Philadelphia, 153 games, 1904.
N. L.—.201—C. Dallan Maxvill, St. Louis, 152 games, 1970.

Lowest Average, Season, Batting Leader, 100 or More Games

A. L.—.301—Carl M. Yastrzemski, Boston, 157 games, 1968.
N. L.—.320—Lawrence J. Doyle, New York, 150 games, 1915.

Lowest Average, Season, with Most At-Bats

N. L.—.000—Robert R. Buhl, Milwaukee, Chicago, 35 games, 1962, 70 at-bats.
A. L.—.000—William R. Wight, Chicago, 30 games, 1950, 61 at-bats.

Slugging Average

Highest Slugging Average, League, 13 or More Seasons

A. L.—.692—George H. Ruth, Boston, New York, 21 years, 1914 through 1934.
N. L.—.578—Rogers Hornsby, St. Louis, New York, Boston, Chicago, 19 years, 1915 through 1933.

Highest Slugging Average, Season, 100 or More Games

A. L.—.847—George H. Ruth, New York, 142 games, 1920.
N. L.—.756—Rogers Hornsby, St. Louis, 138 games, 1925.

Highest Slugging Average, Rookie Season, 100 Games

N. L.—.621—George A. Watkins, St. Louis, 119 games, 1903.
A. L.—.618—Mark D. McGwire, Oakland, 151 games, 1987.

Highest Slugging Average, Righthander, Season, 100 Games

N. L.—.756—Rogers Hornsby, St. Louis, 138 games, 1925.
A. L.—.749—James E. Foxx, Philadelphia, 154 games, 1932.

Highest Slugging Average, Lefthander, Season, 100 Games

A. L.—.847—George H. Ruth, New York, 142 games, 1920.
N. L.—.702—Stanley F. Musial, St. Louis, 155 games, 1948.

Highest Slugging Average, Switch Hitter, Season

A. L.—.705—Mickey C. Mantle, New York, 150 games, 1956.
N. L.—.615—James A. Collins, St. Louis, 154 games, 1934.

Most Years Leading League in Slugging, 100 or More Games

A. L.—13—George H. Ruth, Boston, New York, 1918 through 1931, except 1925. (Played only 95 games in 1918, short season due to war.)
N. L.—9—Rogers Hornsby, St. Louis, Boston, Chicago, 1917, 1920, 1921, 1922, 1923, 1924, 1925, 1928, 1929.

Lowest Slugging Average, Season, 150 or More Games

N. L.—.223—C. Dallan Maxvill, St. Louis, 152 games, 1970.
A. L.—.243—George F. McBride, Washington, 156 games, 1914.

Lowest Leading Slugging Average, Season, 100 or More Games

N. L.—.436—Henry H. Myers, Brooklyn, 133 games, 1919.
A. L.—.466—Elmer H. Flick, Cleveland, 131 games, 1905.

At-Bats & Plate Appearances
Career & Season

Most At-Bats, League

N. L.—14,053—Peter E. Rose, Cincinnati, Philadelphia, Montreal, 24 years, 1963 through 1986.
A. L.—11,988—Carl M. Yastrzemski, Boston, 23 years, 1961 through 1983.

Most Plate Appearances, League

N. L.—15,890—Peter E. Rose, Cincinnati, Philadelphia, Montreal, 24 years, 1963 through 1986.
A. L.—13,990—Carl M. Yastrzemski, Boston, 23 years, 1961 through 1983.

Most At-Bats, Season

A. L. (162-game season)—705—Willie J. Wilson, Kansas City, 161 games, 1980.
A. L. (154-game season)—679—Harvey Kuenn, Detroit, 155 games, 1953.

N. L. (162-game season)—701—Juan M. Samuel, Philadelphia, 160 games, 1984.
N. L. (154-game season)—696—Forrest D. Jensen, Pittsburgh, 153 games, 1936.

Most Plate Appearances, Season

N. L. (162-game season)—771—Peter E. Rose, Cincinnati, 163 games, 1974.
N. L. (154-game season)—755—Elwood G. English, Chicago, 156 games, 1930.
A. L. (162-game season)—758—Wade A. Boggs, Boston, 161 games, 1985.
A. L. (154-game season)—757—Frank P. J. Crosetti, New York, 157 games, 1938.

Most At-Bats, Rookie Season

N. L. (154-game season)—643—Frank C. Baumholtz, Cincinnati, 151 games, 1947.
N. L. (162-game season)—701—Juan M. Samuel, Philadelphia, 160 games, 1984.
A. L. (154-game season)—679—Harvey E. Kuenn, Detroit, 155 games, 1953.

Most At-Bats, Righthander, Season

N. L. (162-game season)—701—Juan M. Samuel, Philadelphia, 160 games, 1984.
N. L. (154-game season)—672—Walter J. Maranville, Pittsburgh, 155 games, 1922.
A. L. (162-game season)—692—Robert C. Richardson, New York, 161 games, 1962.
A. L. (154-game season)—679—Harvey Kuenn, Detroit, 155 games, 1953.

Most At-Bats, Lefthander, Season

N. L. (162-game season)—698—Mateo R. Alou, Pittsburgh, 162 games, 1969.
N. L. (154-game season)—696—Forrest D. Jensen, Pittsburgh, 153 games, 1936.
A. L. (162-game season)—677—Donald A. Mattingly, New York, 162 games, 1986.
A. L. (154-game season)—671—John T. Tobin, St. Louis, 150 games, 1921.

Most At-Bats, Switch Hitter, Season

A. L.—705—Willie J. Wilson, Kansas City, 161 games, 1980.
N. L.—695—Maurice M. Wills, Los Angeles, 165 games, 1962.

Most At-Bats, Season, Pinch-Hitter

N. L. (162-game season)—81—Daniel J. Staub, New York, 94 games, 1983.
N. L. (154-game season)—72—Samuel A. Leslie, New York, 75 games, 1932.
A. L. (162-game season)—72—David E. Philley, Baltimore 79 games, 1961.
A. L. (154-game season)—66—Julio Becquer, Washington, 70 games, 1957.

Most Years Leading League in At-Bats

A. L.—7—Roger M. Cramer, Philadelphia, Boston, Washington, Detroit, 1933, 1934, 1935, 1938, 1940, 1941, 1942.
N. L.—4—Abner F. Dalrymple, Chicago, 1880, 1882, 1884, 1885.
Peter E. Rose, Cincinnati, 1965, 1972, 1973, 1977.

Most Consecutive Years Leading League in At-Bats

N. L.—3—Earl J. Adams, Chicago, 1925, 1926, 1927.
David Cash, Philadelphia, 1974, 1975, 1976.
A. L.—3—Roger M. Cramer, Philadelphia, 1933, 1934, 1935.
Roger M. Cramer, Boston, Washington, Detroit, 1940, 1941, 1942.
Robert C. Richardson, New York, 1962, 1963, 1964.

Most Years 600 or More At-Bats, League

N. L.—17—Peter E. Rose, Cincinnati, 1963 through 1978, except 1964, 1967, Philadelphia, 1979, 1980, 1982.
A. L.—12—J. Nelson Fox, Chicago, 1951 through 1962.

Most Consecutive Years, 600 or More At-Bats, League

N. L.—13—Peter E. Rose, Cincinnati, Philadelphia, 1968 through 1980.
A. L.—12—J. Nelson Fox, Chicago, 1951 through 1962.

Fewest At-Bats, Season, 150 or More Games

A. L.—389—Tommy L. McCraw, Chicago, 151 games, 1966.
N. L.—399—C. Dallan Maxvill, St. Louis, 152 games, 1970.

Fewest At-Bats, Season, for Leader in At-Bats
N. L.— 585— Porter B. Shannon, New York, 155 games, 1907.
A. L.— 588— Tyrus R. Cobb, Detroit, 152 games, 1917.

Game & Inning

Most At-Bats, Game, Nine Innings
N. L.—8—Held by 18 players. Last player—William J. McCormick, Chicago, June 29, 1897.
N. L. since 1900—7—Held by many players.
A. L.—7—Held by many players.

Most Times Faced Pitcher as Batsman, Game, Nine Innings
N. L. before 1900—8—Held by many players.
N. L. since 1900—8—Russell G. Wrightstone, Philadelphia, August 25, 1922.
　　　　　Frank J. Parkinson, Philadelphia, August 25, 1922.
　　　　　Taylor L. Douthit, St. Louis, July 6, 1929, second game.
　　　　　Andrew A. High, St. Louis, July 6, 1929, second game.
A. L.—8—Clyde F. Vollmer, Boston, June 8, 1950.

Most At-Bats, Extra-Inning Game
N. L.— 11—Carson L. Bigbee, Pittsburgh, August 22, 1917, 22 innings.
　　　　　Charles Pick, Boston, May 1, 1920, 26 innings.
　　　　　Norman D. Boeckel, Boston, May 1, 1920, 26 innings.
　　　　　Ralph A. Garr, Atlanta, May 4, 1973, 20 innings.
　　　　　David L. Schneck, New York, September 11, 1974, 25 innings.
　　　　　David Cash, Montreal, May 21, 1977, 21 innings.
A. L.— 11—John H. Burnett, Cleveland, July 10, 1932, 18 innings.
　　　　　Edward Morgan, Cleveland, July 10, 1932, 18 innings.
　　　　　Irvin Hall, Philadelphia, July 21, 1945, 24 innings.
　　　　　Robert C. Richardson, New York, June 24, 1962, 22 innings.
　　　　　Cecil C. Cooper, Milwaukee, May 8, 1984 (completed May 9), 25 innings.
　　　　　Julio L. Cruz, Chicago, May 8, 1984 (completed May 9), 25 innings.
　　　　　Carlton E. Fisk, Chicago, May 8, 1984 (completed May 9), 25 innings.
　　　　　Rudy K. Law, Chicago, May 8, 1984 (completed May 9), 25 innings.

Most Times Faced Pitcher as Batsman, Extra-Inning Game
N. L.— 12—Felix B. Millan, New York, September 11, 1974, 25 innings.
　　　　　John D. Milner, New York, September 11, 1974, 25 innings.
A. L.— 12—Harold D. Baines, Chicago, May 8, 1984 (completed May 9), 25 innings.
　　　　　Carlton E. Fisk, Chicago, May 8, 1984 (completed May 9), 25 innings,.
　　　　　Rudy K. Law, Chicago, May 8, 1984 (completed May 9), 25 innings.

Most Times Faced Pitcher, Game, No Official At-Bats
N. L.—6—Charles M. Smith, Boston, April 17, 1890; 5 bases on balls, 1 hit by pitcher.
　　　　　Walter Wilmot, Chicago, August 22, 1891. 6 bases on balls.
　　　　　Miller J. Huggins, St. Louis, June 1, 1910; 4 bases on balls, 1 sacrifice hit, 1 sacrifice fly.
　　　　　William M. Urbanski, Boston, June 13, 1934; 4 bases on balls, 2 sacrifice hits.
A. L.—6—James E. Foxx, Boston, June 16, 1938; 6 bases on balls.

Most At-Bats, Doubleheader, 18 Innings
N. L.— 13—Walter J. Maranville, Pittsburgh, August 8, 1922.
　　　　　William J. Herman, Chicago, August 21, 1935.
A. L.— 13—David E. Philley, Chicago, May 30, 1950.

Most At-Bats, Doubleheader, More Than 18 Innings
N. L.— 14—Joseph O. Christopher, New York, May 31, 1964, 32 innings.
　　　　　James L. Hickman, New York, May 31, 1964, 32 innings.
　　　　　Edward E. Kranepool, New York, May 31, 1964, 32 innings.
　　　　　Roy D. McMillan, New York, May 31, 1964, 32 innings.
　　　　　Frank J. Thomas, New York, May 31, 1964, 32 innings.
A. L.— 14—Robert J. Monday, Kansas City, June 17, 1967, 28 innings.

Ramon A. Webster, Kansas City, June 17, 1967, 28 innings.

Most Times Faced Pitcher as Batsman, Inning
A. A.—3—Lawrence P. Murphy, Washington, June 17, 1891, first inning.
N. L. before 1900—3—Held by ten players.
N. L. since 1900—3—Martin Callaghan, Chicago, August 25, 1922, fourth inning.
　　　　　William R. Cox, Harold H. Reese and Edwin D. Snider, Brooklyn, all on May 21, 1952, first inning.
　　　　　Gilbert R. Hodges, Brooklyn, August 8, 1954, eighth inning.
　　　　　Johnnie B. Baker, Atlanta, September 20, 1972, second inning.
A. L.—3—Theodore S. Williams, Boston, July 4, 1948, seventh inning; Samuel C. White, G. Eugene Stephens, Thomas M. Umphlett, John J. Lipon and George C. Kell, Boston, all on June 18, 1953, seventh inning.

Runs
Career & Season

Most Runs, League
A. L.— 2,245— Tyrus R. Cobb, Detroit, Philadelphia, 24 years, 1905 through 1928.
N. L.— 2,165— Peter E. Rose, Cincinnati, Philadelphia, Montreal, 24 years, 1963 through 1986.

Most Runs, Season
N. L.— 196— William R. Hamilton, Philadelphia, 131 games, 1894.
A. L.— 177— George H. Ruth, New York, 152 games, 1921.
N. L. since 1900—158—Charles H. Klein, Philadelphia, 156 games, 1930.

Most Runs, Rookie Season
A. A.— 152— Michael J. Griffin, Baltimore, 136 games, 1887.
N. L.— 135— Roy Thomas, Philadelphia, 148 games, 1899.
N. L. since 1900—133—Lloyd J. Waner, Pittsburgh, 150 games, 1927.
A. L.— 132— Joseph P. DiMaggio, New York, 138 games, 1936.

Most Runs, Righthander, Season
N. L.— 167— Joseph J. Kelley, Baltimore, 129 games, 1894.
N. L. since 1900—156—Rogers Hornsby, Chicago, 156 games, 1929.
A. L.— 152— Aloysius H. Simmons, Philadelphia, 138 games, 1930.

Most Runs, Lefthander, Season
N. L.— 196— William R. Hamilton, Philadelphia, 131 games, 1894.
A. L.— 177— George H. Ruth, New York, 152 games, 1921.
N. L. since 1900—158—Charles H. Klein, Philadelphia, 156 games, 1930.

Most Runs, Switch Hitter, Season
N. L.— 140— Max G. Carey, Pittsburgh, 155 games, 1922.
A. L.— 133— Willie J. Wilson, Kansas City, 161 games, 1980.

Most Years Leading League in Runs
A. L.—8—George H. Ruth, Boston, New York, 1919, 1920, 1921, 1923, 1924, 1926, 1927, 1928.
N. L.—5—George J. Burns, New York, 1914, 1916, 1917, 1919, 1920.
　　　　　Rogers Hornsby, St. Louis, New York, Chicago, 1921, 1922, 1924 (tied), 1927 (tied), 1929.
　　　　　Stanley F. Musial, St. Louis, 1946, 1948, 1951 (tied), 1952 (tied), 1954 (tied).

Most Consecutive Years Leading League in Runs
A. L.—5—Theodore S. Williams, Boston, 1940, 1941, 1942 (in military service 1943-44-45), 1946, 1947.
N. L.—3—Michael J. Kelly, Chicago, 1884, 1885, 1886.
　　　　　Charles H. Klein, Philadelphia, 1930, 1931 (tied), 1932.
　　　　　Edwin D. Snider, Brooklyn, 1953, 1954 (tied), 1955.
　　　　　Peter E. Rose, Cincinnati, 1974, 1975, 1976.

Most Years 150 or More Runs, League
A. L.—6—George H. Ruth, New York, 1920, 1921, 1923, 1927, 1928, 1930.
N. L.—4—William R. Hamilton, Philadelphia, Boston, 1894, 1895, 1896, 1897.
N. L. since 1900—2—Charles H. Klein, Philadelphia, 1930, 1932.

Most Years 100 or More Runs, League
N. L.— 15— Henry L. Aaron, Milwaukee, Atlanta, 1955 through 1970, except 1968.
A. L.— 13— H. Louis Gehrig, New York, 1926 through 1938.

Most Consecutive Years 100 or More Runs, League
A. L. — 13 — H. Louis Gehrig, New York, 1926 through 1938.
N. L. — 13 — Henry L. Aaron, Milwaukee, Atlanta, 1955 through 1967.

Fewest Runs, Season, for Leader in Runs (154-Game Schedule)
N. L. — 89 — Clifford C. Cravath, Philadelphia, 150 games, 1915.
A. L. — 92 — Harry H. Davis, Philadelphia, 149 games, 1905.

Fewest Runs, Season, 150 or More Games
A. L. — 25 — Leonard A. Cardenas, California, 150 games, 1972.
N. L. — 32 — Michael J. Doolan, Philadelphia, 151 games, 1913.

Game & Inning

Most Runs, Game
A. A. — 7 — Guy J. Hecker, Louisville, August 15, 1886, second game.
N. L. — 6 — James E. Whitney, Boston, June 9, 1883.
Adrian C. Anson, Chicago, August 24, 1886.
Michael J. Tiernan, New York, June 15, 1887.
Michael J. Kelly, Boston, August 27, 1887.
Ezra B. Sutton, Boston, August 27, 1887.
James Ryan, Chicago, July 25, 1894.
Robert L. Lowe, Boston, May 3, 1895.
Clarence H. Beaumont, Pittsburgh, July 22, 1899.
Melvin T. Ott, New York, August 4, 1934, second game; April 30, 1944, first game.
Frank J. Torre, Milwaukee, September 2, 1957, first game.
A. L. — 6 — John Pesky, Boston, May 8, 1946.
Spike D. Owen, Boston, August 21, 1986.

Most Runs, Game, by Pitcher
A. A. — 7 — Guy J. Hecker, Louisville, August 15, 1886, second game.
N. L. — 5 — George B. Cuppy, Cleveland, August 9, 1895.
N. L. since 1900 and A. L. — 4 — Held by many pitchers.
N. L. — Last Pitcher — James A. Tobin, Boston, September 12, 1940, first game.
A. L. — Last Pitcher — William F. Hoeft, Detroit, May 5, 1956.

Most Runs, Two Consecutive Games, 18 Innings
A. A. — 11 — Guy J. Hecker, Louisville, August 12, August 15, second game, 1886.
N. L. — 9 — Herman A. Long, Boston, May 30, 30, 1894.
James Ryan, Chicago, July 24, 25, 1894.
William F. Dahlen, Chicago, September 20, 21, 1894.
A. L. — 9 — Melo Almada, Washington, July 25, 25, 1937.
Mark D. McGwire, Oakland, June 27, 28, 1987.
N. L. since 1900 — 8 — Hazen S. Cuyler, Pittsburgh, June 20, 22, 1925.
John H. Frederick, Brooklyn, May 17, 18, 1929.
Melvin T. Ott, New York, August 4, second game, August 5, 1934.
Charles H. Klein, Chicago, August 21, 21, 1935.
Stanley F. Musial, St. Louis, May 19, 20, 1948.

Most Runs, Doubleheader, 18 Innings
N. L. — 9 — Herman A. Long, Boston, May 30, 1894.
A. L. — 9 — Melo Almada, Washington, July 25, 1937.
N. L. since 1900 — 8 — Charles H. Klein, Chicago, August 21, 1935.

Most Consecutive Games Scoring One or More Runs, Season
N. L. — 24 — William R. Hamilton, Philadelphia, July 6 through August 2, 1894, 35 runs.
A. L. — 18 — Robert A. Rolfe, New York, August 9 through August 25, second game, 1939, 30 runs.
N. L. since 1900 — 17 — Theodore B. Kluszewski, Cincinnati, August 27 through September 13, 1954, 24 runs.

Most Times Five or More Runs in One Game, in Major Leagues
6 — George F. Gore, Chicago N. L., 1880, 1881, 1882 (2), 1883, New York P. L. 1890.
James E. Ryan, Chicago N. L., 1887, 1089, 1891, 1894 (2), 1897.
William H. Keeler, Baltimore N. L., 1895 (2), 1897 (2), Brooklyn N. L., 1901, 1902.

Most Times Five or More Runs in One Game, League
N. L. — 6 — James E. Ryan, Chicago, 1887, 1889, 1891, 1894 (2), 1897.
William H. Keeler, Baltimore, Brooklyn, 1895 (2), 1897 (2), 1901, 1902.
A. L. — 3 — H. Louis Gehrig, New York, 1928, 1936 (2).
James E. Foxx, Philadelphia, Boston, 1932, 1935, 1939.
N. L. since 1900 — 3 — Melvin T. Ott, New York, 1934, 1944 (2).
Willie H. Mays, New York, San Francisco, 1954, 1964 (2).

Most Times Five or More Runs in One Game, Season
N. L. — 1876 through 1899 — 2 — Held by many players.
N. L. since 1900 — 2 — Hazen S. Cuyler, Pittsburgh, May 12, second game, June 20, 1925.
Melvin T. Ott, New York, April 30, first game, June 12, 1944.
Philip Weintraub, New York, April 30, first game, June 12, 1944.
Willie H. Mays, San Francisco, April 24, September 19, 1964.
A. L. — 2 — H. Louis Gehrig, New York, May 3, July 28, 1936.

Most Runs, Inning
N. L. — 3 — Thomas E. Burns, Chicago, September 6, 1883, seventh inning.
Edward N. Williamson, Chicago, September 6, 1883, seventh inning.
A. L. — 3 — Samuel C. White, Boston, June 18, 1953, seventh inning.
N. L. since 1900 — 2 — Held by many players.

Hits
Career & Season

Most Hits, League
N. L. — 4,256 — Peter E. Rose, Cincinnati, Philadelphia, Montreal, 24 years, 1963 through 1986.
A. L. — 4,191 — Tyrus R. Cobb, Detroit, Philadelphia, 24 years, 1905 through 1928.

Most Hits, League, by Pinch-Hitter
N. L. — 150 — Manuel Mota, San Francisco, Pittsburgh, Montreal, Los Angeles, 20 years, 1962 through 1982, except 1981, 599 games.
A. L. — 107 — William J. Brown, Detroit, 13 years, 1963 through 1975, 525 games.

Most Hits, Season
(Except 1887 when bases on balls counted as hits.)
A. L. — 257 — George H. Sisler, St. Louis, 154 games, 1920.
N. L. — 254 — Frank J. O'Doul, Philadelphia, 154 games, 1929.
William H. Terry, New York, 154 games, 1930.

Most Hits, Rookie Season
N. L. — 223 — Lloyd J. Waner, Pittsburgh, 150 games, 1927.
A. L. (162-game season) — 217 — Pedro Oliva, Minnesota, 161 games, 1964.
A. L. (154-game season) — 215 — Dale Alexander, Detroit, 155 games, 1929.

Most Hits, Righthander, Season
A. L. — 253 — Aloysius H. Simmons, Philadelphia, 153 games, 1925.
N. L. — 250 — Rogers Hornsby, St. Louis, 154 games, 1922.

Most Hits, Lefthander, Season
A. L. — 257 — George H. Sisler, St. Louis, 154 games, 1920.
N. L. — 254 — Frank J. O'Doul, Philadelphia, 154 games, 1929.
William H. Terry, New York, 154 games, 1930.

Most Hits, Switch Hitter, Season
N. L. — 230 — Peter E. Rose, Cincinnati, 160 games, 1973.
A. L. — 230 — Willie J. Wilson, Kansas City, 161 games, 1980.

Switch Hitters With 100 or More Hits, Both Sides of Plate, Season
N. L. — Garry L. Templeton, St. Louis, 154 games, 1979; 111 hits lefthanded, 100 hits righthanded.
A. L. — Willie J. Wilson, Kansas City, 161 games, 1980; 130 hits lefthanded, 100 hits righthanded.

Most Hits, Season, by Pinch-Hitter
N. L. (162-game season) — 25 — Jose M. Morales, Montreal, 82 games, 1976.
N. L. (154-game season) — 22 — Samuel A. Leslie, New York, 75 games, 1932.
A. L. (162-game season) — 24 — David E. Philley, Baltimore, 79 games, 1961.
A. L. (154-game season) — 20 — Parke E. Coleman, St. Louis, 74 games, 1936.

Most Years Leading League in Hits
A. L. — 8 — Tyrus R. Cobb, Detroit, 1907, 1908, 1909, 1911, 1912, 1915, 1917, 1919 (tied).
N. L. — 7 — Peter E. Rose, Cincinnati, 1965, 1968 (tied), 1970 (tied), 1972, 1973, 1976, Philadelphia 1981.

Most Consecutive Years Leading League in Hits

N. L.—3—Clarence H. Beaumont, Pittsburgh, 1902, 1903, 1904.
   Rogers Hornsby, St. Louis, 1920, 1921, 1922.
   Frank A. McCormick, Cincinnati, 1938, 1939, 1940 (tied).
   Stanley F. Musial, St. Louis, 1943, 1944 (in military service 1945), 1946.
A. L.—3—Tyrus R. Cobb, Detroit, 1907, 1908, 1909.
   John M. Pesky, Boston, 1942, 1946, 1947 (in military service 1943, 1944, 1945).
   Pedro (Tony) Oliva, Minnesota, 1964, 1965, 1966.

Most Games, One or More Hits, Season

N. L.— 135— Rogers Hornsby, St. Louis, 154 games, 1922.
   Charles H. Klein, Philadelphia, 156 games, 1930.
A. L.— 135— Wade A. Boggs, Boston, 161 games, 1985.

Most Years 200 or More Hits, League

N. L.— 10— Peter E. Rose, Cincinnati, 1965, 1966, 1968, 1969, 1970, 1973, 1975, 1976, 1977, Philadelphia, 1979.
A. L.— 9— Tyrus R. Cobb, Detroit, 1907, 1909, 1911, 1912, 1915, 1916, 1917, 1922, 1924.

Most Consecutive Years 200 or More Hits, League

N. L.—8—William H. Keeler, Baltimore, Brooklyn, 1894 through 1901.
A. L.—5—Aloysius H. Simmons, Philadelphia, Chicago, 1929 through 1933.
   Charles L. Gehringer, Detroit, 1933 through 1937.
   Wade A. Boggs, Boston, 1983 through 1987.
N. L. since 1900—5—Charles H. Klein, Philadelphia, 1929 through 1933.

200 or More Hits, Rookie Season

N. L.— 223— Lloyd J. Waner, Pittsburgh, 150 games, 1927.
   219— James T. Williams, Pittsburgh, 153 games, 1899.
   206— John H. Frederick, Brooklyn, 148 games, 1929.
   201— Richard A. Allen, Philadelphia, 162 games, 1964.
A. L.— 217— Pedro Oliva, Minnesota, 161 games, 1964.
   215— Dale Alexander, Detroit, 155 games, 1929.
   209— Harvey E. Kuenn, Detroit 155 games, 1953.
   207— Kevin L. Seitzer, Kansas City, 161 games, 1987.
   206— Joseph P. DiMaggio, New York, 138 games, 1936.
   206— Harold A. Trosky, Cleveland, 154 games, 1934.
   205— John M. Pesky, Boston, 147 games, 1942.
   201— Roy C. Johnson, Detroit, 148 games, 1929.
   200— Richard C. Wakefield, Detroit, 155 games, 1943.

Most Hits, Two Consecutive Seasons, League

N. L.— 485— Rogers Hornsby, St. Louis, 235 in 1921, 250 in 1922.
A. L.— 475— Tyrus R. Cobb, Detroit, 248 in 1911, 227 in 1912.

Fewest Hits, Season, 150 or More Games

N. L.— 80— C. Dallan Maxvill, St. Louis, 152 games, 1970.
A. L.— 82— Edwin A. Brinkman, Washington, 154 games, 1965.

Fewest Hits, Season, for Leader in Hits

N. L.— 171— Sherwood R. Magee, Philadelphia, 146 games, 1914.
A. L.— 177— Dagoberto B. Campaneris, Oakland, 159 games, 1968.

Game & Doubleheader

Most Hits, Game, Nine Innings

N. L.—7—Wilbert Robinson, Baltimore, June 10, 1892, first game, 6 singles, 1 double (consecutive).
   Renaldo A. Stennett, Pittsburgh, September 16, 1975, 4 singles, 2 doubles, 1 triple (consecutive).
N. L. since 1900—6—Held by many players.
A. L.—6—Held by many players.

Most Hits, Extra-Inning Game

A. L.—9—John H. Burnett, Cleveland, July 10, 1932, 18 innings, 7 singles, 2 doubles.
N. L.—6—Held by 13 players. Last Player—Eugene Richards, San Diego, July 26, 1977, second game, 15 innings, 5 singles, 1 double.

Most Times Reached Base, Nine-Inning Game (Batting 1.000)

N. L.—8—Frank G. Ward, Cincinnati, June 18, 1893, 2 singles, 5 bases on balls, 1 hit by pitcher.
A. L.—7—W. Benjamin Chapman, New York, May 24, 1936, 2 doubles, 5 bases on balls.
N. L. since 1900—7—Clifton E. Heathcote, Chicago, August 25, 1922, 3 singles, 2 doubles, 2 bases on balls.
   Harry A. Lavagetto, Brooklyn, September 23, 1939, first game, 4 singles, 1 double, 1 triple, 1 base on balls.

Melvin T. Ott, New York, April 30, 1944, first game; 2 singles, 5 bases on balls.
Renaldo A. Stennett, Pittsburgh, September 16, 1975, 4 singles, 2 doubles, 1 triple.

Most Times Reached Base, Extra-Inning Game (Batting 1.000)

N. L.—9—Max G. Carey, Pittsburgh, July 7, 1922, 18 innings; 5 singles, 1 double, 3 bases on balls.
A. L.—7—Cesar D. Gutierrez, Detroit, June 21, 1970, second game, 12 innings; 6 singles, 1 double.

Most Clubs, One or More Hits, One Day

N. L.—2—Joel R. Youngblood, New York, Montreal, August 4, 1982.

Most Hits, First Game in Majors

N. L.—5—Fred C. Clarke, Louisville, June 30, 1894; 4 singles, 1 triple.
A. L.—5—Cecil H. Travis, Washington, May 16, 1933, 12 innings; 5 singles.
A. L.—Nine innings—4—Raymond W. Jansen, St. Louis, September 30, 1910; 4 singles (only game in major league career).
   Charles A. Shires, Chicago, August 20, 1928; 3 singles, 1 triple.
   Russell P. Van Atta, New York, April 25, 1933; 4 singles.
   Forrest V. Jacobs, Philadelphia, April 13, 1954; 4 singles.
   W. Ted Cox, Boston, September 18, 1977; 3 singles, 1 double (consecutive).
   Kirby Puckett, Minnesota, May 8, 1984; 4 singles.
   William D. Bean, Detroit, April 25, 1987; 2 singles, 2 doubles.
N. L. since 1900—4—Charles D. Stengel, Brooklyn, September 17, 1912; 4 singles.
   Edwin C. Freed, Philadelphia, September 11, 1942; 1 single, 2 doubles, 1 triple.
   Willie L. McCovey, San Francisco, July 30, 1959; 2 singles, 2 triples (consecutive).
   Mack Jones, Milwaukee, July 13, 1961; 3 singles, 1 double.

Most Hits, Game, by Pitcher

A. A.—6—Guy J. Hecker, Louisville, August 15, 1886, second game.
N. L.-A. L.—5—Held by many pitchers.
N. L.—Last pitcher, Peter J. Donohue, Cincinnati, May 22, 1925, 4 singles, 1 home run.
A. L.—Last pitcher, Melvin L. Stottlemyre, New York, September 26, 1964, 4 singles 1 double.

Most Hits, Opening Day of Season

N. L.-A. L.—5—Held by many players.
N. L.—Last Player—William J. Herman, Chicago, April 14, 1936, 1 single, 3 doubles, 1 home run.
A. L.—Last Player—J. Nelson Fox, Chicago, April 10, 1959, 14 innings, 3 singles, 1 double, 1 home run.

Making All Club's Hits, Game (Most)

A. L.—4—Norman Elberfeld, New York, August 1, 1903, 4 singles.
A. L.—4—Billy L. Williams, Chicago, September 5, 1969, 2 doubles, 2 homers.

Most At-Bats, Extra-Inning Game, No Hits

N. L.— 11—Charles Pick, Boston, May 1, 1920, 26 innings.
A. L.— 10— George C. Kell, Philadelphia, July 21, 1945, 24 innings.

Most Times Six Hits in Six Times at Bat, Game, League

N. L.—2—James L. Bottomley, St. Louis, September 16, 1924; August 5, 1931, second game.
A. L.—2—Roger M. Cramer, Philadelphia, June 20, 1932; July 13, 1935.
Two leagues—2—Edward J. Delahanty, Cleveland, P. L., June 2, 1890; Philadelphia, N. L., June 16, 1894.

Most Times Five or More Hits in One Game, League

A. L.— 14—Tyrus R. Cobb, Detroit, Philadelphia, 1908 to 1927.
N. L.— 10— Peter E. Rose, Cincinnati, Philadelphia, 1965 to 1986.

Most Times Five Hits in One Game, by Pitcher, Major Leagues

3—James J. Callahan, Chicago N. L., 1897, Chicago A. L., 1902, 1903.

Most Times Five or More Hits in One Game, Season

N. L.—4—William H. Keeler, Baltimore, July 17, August 14, September 3, September 6, first game, 1897.
   Stanley F. Musial, St. Louis, April 30, May 19, June 22, September 22, 1948.
A. L.—4—Tyrus R. Cobb, Detroit, May 7, July 7, second game, July 12, July 17, 1922.

Most Hits, Doubleheader

A. A.—9—Fred H. Carroll, Pittsburgh, July 5, 1886.
N. L.—9—Wilbert Robinson, Baltimore, June 10, 1892.
    Joseph J. Kelley, Baltimore, September 3, 1894 (consecutive).
    Fred C. Lindstrom, New York, June 25, 1928.
    William H. Terry, New York, June 18, 1929.
A. L.—9—Ray Morehart, Chicago, August 31, 1926.
    George W. Case, Washington, July 4, 1940.
    James E. Runnels, Boston, August 30, 1960, 25 innings.
    J. Leroy Thomas, Los Angeles, September 5, 1961.

Most Hits, Doubleheader, Pinch-Hitter

N. L.-A. L.—2—Held by many pinch-hitters.

Most Hits, First Doubleheader in Majors

N. L.-A. L.—6—Held by many players.

Most Hits, Two Consecutive Doubleheaders

A. L.—14—Tyrus R. Cobb, Detroit, July 17 (7), 19 (7), 1912.
N. L.—14—William D. White, St. Louis, July 17 (8), 18 (6), 1961.

Most At-Bats, Doubleheader (9-Inning Games), No Hits

A. L.—11—Albert G. Pearson, Los Angeles, July 1, 1962.
N. L.—10—Held by many players.

Most At-Bats, Doubleheader (Over 18 Innings), No Hits

N. L.—12—Albert F. Schoendienst, St. Louis, June 9, 1947, 24 innings.
A. L.—12—Robert P. Saverine, Washington, June 8, 1966, 23 innings.

Hitting For Cycle

Hitting for Cycle, Game (single, double, triple, homer)

N. L.—106 times—Last players—Andre F. Dawson, Chicago, April 29, 1987; Candido Maldonado, San Francisco, May 4, 1987; Timothy Raines, Montreal, August 16, 1987; Albert Hall, Atlanta, September 23, 1987.
A. L.—87 times—Last players—K. Anthony Phillips, Oakland, May 16, 1986; Kirby Puckett, Minnesota, August 1, 1986.

Most Times Hitting for Cycle (single, double, triple, homer)

A. L.—3—Robert W. Meusel, New York, 1921, 1922, 1928.
N. L.—3—Floyd C. Herman, Brooklyn, 1931 (2), Chicago, 1933.
Two Leagues—3—John G. Reilly, Cincinnati A.A., 1883 (2), Cincinnati N. L., 1890.

Hitting for Cycle, Both Leagues (single, double, triple, homer)

Robert J. Watson, Houston N.L., June 24, 1977; Boston A. L., September 15, 1979.

Inning

Most Hits, Inning

N. L.—3—Thomas E. Burns, Chicago, September 6, 1883, seventh inning; 2 doubles, 1 home run.
    Fred N. Pfeffer, Chicago, September 6, 1883, seventh inning; 2 singles, 1 double.
    Edward N. Williamson, Chicago, September 6, 1883, seventh inning; 2 singles, 1 double.
A. L.—3—G. Eugene Stephens, Boston, June 18, 1953, seventh inning; 2 singles, 1 double.

Most Hits, Inning, First Game in Majors

A. L.—2—Alfred M. Martin, New York, April 18, 1950, eighth inning.
    Russell L. Morman, Chicago, August 3, 1986, fourth inning.
N. L.—1—Held by many players.

Most Times Two Hits in One Inning, Game

N. L.—2—Max Carey, Pittsburgh, June 22, 1925, first and eighth innings; 2 singles, each inning.
    Renaldo A. Stennett, Pittsburgh, September 16, 1975, first inning, single and double; fifth inning, double and single.
A. L.—2—John Hodapp, Cleveland, July 29, 1928, second and sixth innings, 2 singles, each inning.
    J. Sherman Lollar, Chicago, April 23, 1955, second inning, single and home run; sixth inning, 2 singles.

Most Times Reached First Base Safely, Inning

N. L.—3—Edward N. Williamson, Chicago, September 6, 1883, seventh inning.
    Thomas E. Burns, Chicago, September 6, 1883, seventh inning.

Fred N. Pfeffer, Chicago, September 6, 1883, seventh inning.
    Herman A. Long, Boston, June 18, 1894, a.m. game, first inning.
    Robert L. Lowe, Boston, June 18, 1894, a.m. game, first inning.
    Hugh Duffy, Boston, June 18, 1894, a.m. game, first inning.
    Harold H. Reese, Brooklyn, May 21, 1952, first inning.
A. L.—3—Samuel C. White, Boston, June 18, 1953, seventh inning.
    G. Eugene Stephens, Boston, June 18, 1953, seventh inning.
    Thomas M. Umphlett, Boston, June 18, 1953, seventh inning.

Batting Streaks

Most Consecutive Hits During Season (BBs Shown in Streak)

A. L.—12—Michael F. Higgins, Boston, June 19, 19, 21, 21, 1938. (2 B.B.)
    Walter O. Dropo, Detroit, July 14, 15, 15, 1952. (0 B.B.)
N. L.—10—Edward J. Delahanty, Philadelphia, July 13, 13, 14, 1897. (1 B.B.)
    Jacob Gettman, Washington, September 10, 11, 11, 1897. (0 B.B.)
    Edward J. Konetchy, Brooklyn, June 28, second game, June 29, July 1, 1919. (0 B.B.)
    Hazen S. Cuyler, Pittsburgh, September 18, 19, 21, 1925. (1 B.B.)
    Charles J. Hafey, St. Louis, July 6, second game, July 8, 9, 1929. (2 B.B.)
    Joseph M. Medwick, St. Louis, July 19, 19, 21, 1936. (1 B.B.)
    John A. Hassett, Boston, June 9, second game, June 10, 14, 1940. (1 B.B.)
    Woodrow W. Williams, Cincinnati, September 5, second game, September 6, 6, 1943. (1 B.B.)

Most Consecutive Times Reached Base Safely, Season

A. L.—16—Theodore S. Williams, Boston, September 17 (1), 18 (1), 20 (1), 21 (4), 22 (4), 23 (5), 1957; 2 singles, 4 home runs, 9 bases on balls, 1 hit by pitcher.
N. L.—14—Pedro Guerrero, Los Angeles, July 23 (2), 24 (4), 25 (4), 26 (4), 1985; 2 singles, 3 doubles, 2 home runs, 6 bases on balls, 1 hit by pitcher.

Most Consecutive Hits, Start of Career

A. L.—6—W. Ted Cox, Boston, September 18, 19, 1977.

Most Consecutive Hits, League, by Pinch-Hitter

N. L.—9—David E. Philley, Philadelphia, September 9 through September 28, 1958; April 16, 1959.

Most Consecutive Hits During Season by Pinch-Hitter

N. L.—8—David E. Philley, Philadelphia, September 9 through September 28, 1958.
    Daniel J. Staub, New York, June 11 through June 26, first game, 1983 (1 hit by pitch during streak).
A. L.—7—William R. Stein, Texas, April 14 through May 25, 1981.

Most Consecutive Games Batted Safely During Season

A. L.—56—Joseph P. DiMaggio, New York, May 15 through July 16, 1941.
N. L.—44—William H. Keeler, Baltimore, April 22 through June 18, 1897.
    Peter E. Rose, Cincinnati, June 14 through July 31, 1978.

Most Consecutive Games Batted Safely, Rookie Season

N. L.—34—Benito Santiago, San Diego, August 25 through October 2, 1987.
A. L.—26—Guy P. Curtright, Chicago, June 6, first game, through July 1, 1943.

Most Consecutive Games Batted Safely, Righthander, Season

A. L.—56—Joseph P. DiMaggio, New York, May 15 through July 16, 1941.
N. L.—42—William F. Dahlen, Chicago, June 20 through August 6, 1894.
N. L. since 1900—33—Rogers Hornsby, St. Louis, August 13 through September 19, 1922.

Most Consecutive Games Batted Safely, Lefthander, Season

N. L.—44—William H. Keeler, Baltimore, April 22 to June 18, 1897.
A. L.—41—George H. Sisler, St. Louis, July 27 to September 17, 1922.

N. L. since 1900—37—Thomas F. Holmes, Boston, June 6, first game, to July 8, second game, 1945.

Most Consecutive Games Batted Safely, Switch Hitter, Season

N. L.—44—Peter E. Rose, Cincinnati, June 14 through July 31, 1978.

A. L.—22—Eddie C. Murray, Baltimore, August 17 through September 10, 1984.

Most Consecutive Games Batted Safely, Start of Season

N. L.—44—William H. Keeler, Baltimore, April 22 through June 18, 1897.

A. L.—34—George H. Sisler, St. Louis, April 14 through May 19, 1925.

N. L. since 1900—25—Charles J. Grimm, Pittsburgh, April 17 through May 16, 1923.

Most Consec.-Game Batting Streaks (20 Games) Season, League

A. L.—7—Tyrus R. Cobb, Detroit, Philadelphia, 1906, 1911, 1912, 1917, 1918, 1926, 1927.

N. L.—7—Peter E. Rose, Cincinnati, Philadelphia, 1967, 1968, 1977 (2), 1978, 1979, 1982.

Most Consecutive-Game Batting Streaks (20 Games) Season

A. L.—3—Tristram E. Speaker, Boston, 1912.

N. L.—2—Held by many players. Last player—Steven P. Garvey, Los Angeles, 1978.

Most Hits, Two Consecutive Games

N. L.—12—Calvin A. McVey, Chicago, July 22 (6), 25 (6), 1876.

N. L. since 1900—10—Roberto W. Clemente, Pittsburgh, August 22 (5), 23 (5), 1970, 25 innings.
Renaldo A. Stennett, Pittsburgh, September 16 (7), 17 (3), 1975.

A. L.—11—John H. Burnett, Cleveland, July 9, second game (2), 10, (9), 1932, 27 innings.

A. L.—Nine-inning games—10—Kirby Puckett, Minnesota, August 29 (4), 30 (6), 1987.

Most Hits, Two Consecutive Games, by Pitcher

A. A.—10—Guy J. Hecker, Louisville, August 12, 15, second game, 1886.

A. L.—8—George L. Earnshaw, Philadelphia, June 9, 12, second game, 1931.

N. L. since 1900—8—W. Kirby Higbe, Brooklyn, August 11, 17, first game, 1941.

Most Hits, Three Consecutive Games

N. L.—15—Calvin A. McVey, Chicago, July 20, 22, 25, 1876.

N. L.—14—William H. Keeler, Baltimore, September 3, 4, 6, first game, 1897.

A. L.—13—Joseph E. Cronin, Washington, June 19, 21, 22, 1933.
Walter O. Dropo, Detroit, July 14, 15, 15, 1952.

N. L. since 1900—12—William H. Keeler, Brooklyn, June 19, 20, 21, 1901.
Milton J. Stock, Brooklyn, June 30, July 1, 2, 1925.
Stanley F. Musial, St. Louis, August 11, 11, 12, 1946.
Renaldo A. Stennett, Pittsburgh, September 16, 17, 18, 1975.

Most Hits, Four Consecutive Games

N. L.—17—Calvin A. McVey, Chicago, July 20, 22, 25, 27, 1876.
William H. Keeler, Baltimore, September 2, 3, 4, 6, first game, 1897.

N. L. since 1900—16—Milton J. Stock, Brooklyn, June 30, July 1, 2, 3, 1925.

A. A.—17—Guy J. Hecker, Louisville, August 8, 10, 12, 15, second game, 1886.

A. L.—15—Joseph E. Cronin, Washington, June 18, second game, 19, 21, 22, 1933.
Joseph E. Cronin, Washington, June 19, 21, 22, 23, 1933.
John K. Lewis, Jr., Washington, July 25, 25, 27, 28, 1937.
Walter O. Dropo, Detroit, July 14, 15, 15, 16, 1952.

Most Consecutive Games, Three or More Hits, Season

A. L.—6—George H. Brett, Kansas City, May 8, 9, 10, 11, 12, 13, 1976.

Singles

Most Singles, League

N. L.—3,215—Peter E. Rose, Cincinnati, Philadelphia, Montreal, 24 years, 1963 through 1986.

A. L.—3,052—Tyrus R. Cobb, Detroit, Philadelphia, 24 years, 1905 through 1928.

Most Singles, Season

N. L.—202—William H. Keeler, Baltimore, 128 games, 1898.

N. L. since 1900—198—Lloyd J. Waner, Pittsburgh, 150 games, 1927.

A. L.—187—Wade A. Boggs, Boston, 161 games, 1985.

Most Singles, Rookie Season

N. L.—198—Lloyd J. Waner, Pittsburgh, 150 games, 1927.

A. L.—167—Harvey E. Kuenn, Detroit, 155 games, 1953.

Most Singles, Righthander, Season

A. L.—174—Aloysius H. Simmons, Philadelphia, 153 games, 1925.

N. L. (162-game season)—178—Curtis C. Flood, St. Louis, 162 games, 1964.

N. L. (154-game season)—172—Nicholas J. Witek, New York, 153 games, 1943.

Most Singles, Lefthander, Season

N. L.—202—William H. Keeler, Baltimore, 128 games, 1898.

N. L. since 1900—198—Lloyd J. Waner, Pittsburgh, 150 games, 1927.

A. L.—187—Wade A. Boggs, Boston, 161 games, 1985.

Most Singles, Switch Hitter, Season

A. L.—184—Willie J. Wilson, Kansas City, 161 games, 1980.

N. L.—181—Peter E. Rose, Cincinnati, 160 games, 1973.

Most Years Leading League in Singles

A. L.—8—J. Nelson Fox, Chicago, 1952, 1954, 1955, 1956, 1957, 1958, 1959, 1960.

N. L.—4—Clarence H. Beaumont, Pittsburgh, Boston, 1902, 1903, 1904, 1907.
Lloyd J. Waner, Pittsburgh, 1927, 1928, 1929 (tied), 1931.
Richie Ashburn, Philadelphia, 1951, 1953, 1957, 1958.
Maurice M. Wills, Los Angeles, Pittsburgh, 1961 (tied), 1962, 1965, 1967.

Most Consecutive Years Leading League in Singles

A. L.—7—J. Nelson Fox, Chicago, 1954, 1955, 1956, 1957, 1958, 1959, 1960.

N. L.—3—Clarence H. Beaumont, Pittsburgh, 1902, 1903, 1904.
Lloyd J. Waner, Pittsburgh, 1927, 1928, 1929 (tied).

Fewest Singles, Season, 150 or More Games

A. L.—58—F. Gene Tenace, Oakland, 158 games, 1974.

N. L.—63—Michael J. Schmidt, Philadelphia, 160 games, 1979.

Fewest Singles, Season, Leader in Singles

A. L.—129—Donald A. Buford, Chicago, 155 games, 1965.

N. L.—127—Enos B. Slaughter, St. Louis, 152 games, 1942.

Most Singles, Game, Nine Innings

N. L.-A. A.-A. L.—6—Held by many players.

N. L.—Last player—David J. Bancroft, New York, June 28, 1920.

A. L.—Last player—Floyd A. Robinson, Chicago, July 22, 1962.

Most Singles, Extra-Inning Game

A. L.—7—John H. Burnett, Cleveland, July 10, 1932, 18 innings.

N. L.—6—Held by many players. Last player—Willie H. Davis, Los Angeles, May 24, 1973, 19 innings.

Most Singles, Game, Each Batting in Three Runs

N. L.-A. L.—1—Held by many players.

N. L.—Last player—Guillermo N. Montanez, Philadelphia, September 8, 1974, eighth inning.

A. L.—Last player—Ernest Riles, Milwaukee, June 5, 1985, third inning.

Most Singles, Doubleheader

N. L.-A. L.—8—Held by many players.

A. L.—Last player—H. Earl Averill, Cleveland, May 7, 1933.

N. L.—Last player—Kenneth D. Hubbs, Chicago, May 20, 1962.

Most Singles, Inning

N. L.-A. L.—2—Held by many players.

Doubles
Career & Season

Most Doubles, League

A. L.—793—Tristram Speaker, Boston, Cleveland, Washington, Philadelphia, 22 years, 1907 through 1928.

N. L.—746—Peter E. Rose, Cincinnati, Philadelphia, Montreal, 24 years, 1963 through 1986.

Most Doubles, Season

N.L.—67—Earl W. Webb, Boston, 151 games, 1931.
N. L.—64—Joseph M. Medwick, St. Louis, 155 games, 1936.

Most Doubles, Rookie Season

N. L.—52—John H. Frederick, Brooklyn, 148 games, 1929.
A. L. (162-game season)—47—Frederic M. Lynn, Boston, 145 games, 1975.
A. L. (154-game season)—45—Roy C. Johnson, Detroit, 148 games, 1929.
Harold A. Trosky, Cleveland, 154 games, 1934.

Most Doubles, Righthander, Season

A. L.—64—George H. Burns, Cleveland, 151 games, 1926.
N. L.—64—Joseph M. Medwick, St. Louis, 155 games, 1936.

Most Doubles, Lefthander, Season

A. L.—67—Earl W. Webb, Boston, 151 games, 1931.
N. L.—62—Paul G. Waner, Pittsburgh, 154 games, 1932.

Most Doubles, Switch Hitter, Season

N. L.—51—Peter E. Rose, Cincinnati, 159 games, 1978.
A. L.—47—John J. Anderson, Milwaukee, 138 games, 1901.

Most Doubles, Season, Catcher

A. L.—42—Gordon S. Cochrane, Philadelphia, 130 games, 1930; caught 130 games.
N. L.—40—Johnny L. Bench, Cincinnati, 154 games, 1968; caught 154 games.
Terrence E. Kennedy, San Diego, 153 games, 1982; caught 139 games (also had 2 doubles as first baseman).

Most Years Leading League in Doubles

N. L.—8—John P. Wagner, Pittsburgh, 1900, 1901 (tied), 1902, 1904, 1906, 1907, 1908, 1909.
Stanley F. Musial, St. Louis, 1943, 1944, 1946, 1948, 1949, 1952, 1953, 1954.
A. L.—8—Tristram Speaker, Boston, Cleveland, 1912, 1914, 1916 (tied), 1918, 1920, 1921, 1922, 1923.

Most Consecutive Years Leading League in Doubles

N. L.—4—John P. Wagner, Pittsburgh, 1906, 1907, 1908, 1909.
A. L.—4—Tristram Speaker, Cleveland, 1920, 1921, 1922, 1923.

Most Years 50 or More Doubles, League

A.L.—5—Tristram Speaker, Boston, Cleveland, 1912, 1920, 1921, 1923, 1926.
N. L.—3—Paul G. Waner, Pittsburgh, 1928, 1932, 1936.
Stanley F. Musial, St. Louis, 1944, 1946, 1953.

Fewest Doubles, Season, 150 or More Games

N. L.—5—C. Dallan Maxvill, St. Louis, 152 games, 1970.
A. L.—6—William P. Purtell, Chicago, Boston, 151 games, 1910.

Fewest Doubles, Season, Leader in Doubles

A. L.—32—Salvatore L. Bando, Oakland, 162 games, 1973.
Pedro Garcia, Milwaukee, 160 games, 1973.
N. L.—34—Henry L. Aaron, Milwaukee, 153 games, 1956.

Game & Inning

Most Doubles, Game

N. L.—4—18 times (Held by 18 players). Last Player—Rafael E. Ramirez, Atlanta, May 21, 1986; 13 innings.
A. L.—4—16 times (Held by 16 players). Last Player—Damaso D. Garcia, Toronto, June 27, 1986.
A. A.—4—2 times (Held by 2 players).

Most Consecutive Doubles, Game

N.L.—4—Frank J. Bonner, Baltimore, August 4, 1894.
Joseph J. Kelley, Baltimore, September 3, 1894, second game.
Richard Bartell, Philadelphia, April 25, 1933.
Ernest N. Lombardi, Cincinnati, May 8, 1935, first game.
William M. Werber, Cincinnati, May 13, 1940, 14 innings.
Willie E. Jones, Philadelphia, April 20, 1949.
Billy L. Williams, Chicago, April 9, 1969.
A. L.—4—William M. Werber, Boston, July 17, 1935, first game.
Michael A. Kreevich, Chicago, September 4, 1937.
John H. Lindell, New York, August 17, 1944.
Louis Boudreau, Cleveland, July 14, 1946, first game.
Victor W. Wertz, Cleveland, September 26, 1956.
William H. Bruton, Detroit, May 19, 1963.
David E. Duncan, Baltimore, June 30, 1975, second game.

Most Doubles, Opening Game of Season

A. L.—4—Frank Dillon, Detroit, April 25, 1901.
N. L.—4—James R. Greengrass, Cincinnati, April 13, 1954.

Most Doubles, Game, by Pitcher

N. L.—3—George E. Hemming, Baltimore, August 1, 1895.
John A. Messersmith, Los Angeles, April 25, 1975.
A. L.—3—George Mullin, Detroit, April 27, 1903.
Walter P. Johnson, Washington, July 29, 1917.
George H. Ruth, Boston, May 9, 1918, 10 innings.
George E. Uhle, Cleveland, June 1, 1923.
Charles H. Ruffing, Boston, May 25, 1929, second game.
Donald H. Ferrarese, Cleveland, May 26, 1959.

Most Doubles, Game, Each Batting in Three Runs

N. L.—2—Robert J. Gilks, Cleveland, August 5, 1890, 1 in second, 1 in eighth.
Harry H. Davis, New York, June 27, 1896, 1 in fifth, 1 in ninth.
William B. Douglas, Philadelphia, July 11, 1898, 1 in second, 1 in sixth.
Clifford C. Cravath, Philadelphia, August 8, 1915, 1 in fourth, 1 in eighth.
A. L.—1—Held by many players.

Most Doubles, Doubleheader

A. L.—6—Henry Majeski, Philadelphia, August 27, 1948.
N. L.—5—Charles J. Hafey, Cincinnati, July 23, 1933.
Joseph M. Medwick, St. Louis, May 30, 1935.
Albert F. Schoendienst, St. Louis, June 6, 1948.
Michael W. Ivie, San Diego, May 30, 1977.

Most Doubles, Two Consecutive Games

N. L.—6—Adrian C. Anson, Chicago, July 3, 4, a.m. game, 1883.
Samuel L. Thompson, Philadelphia, June 29, July 1, 1895, 22 innings.
Albert F. Schoendienst, St. Louis, June 5, 6, first game, 1948.
A. L.—6—Joseph A. Dugan, Philadelphia, September 24, 25, 1920.
Earl H. Sheely, Chicago, May 20, 21, 1926.
Henry Majeski, Philadelphia, August 27, 28, 1948.

Most Doubles, Three Consecutive Games

N. L.—8—Albert F. Schoendienst, St. Louis, June 5, 6, 6, 1948.
A. L.—7—Joseph A. Dugan, Philadelphia, September 23, 24, 25, 1920.
Earl H. Sheely, Chicago, May 20, 21, 22, 1926.

Most Doubles, Three Consecutive Games, Pinch-Hitter

N. L.—3—Berthold Haas, Brooklyn, September 18, 19, 20, 1937.
Douglas H. Clemens, Philadelphia, June 6, 6, 7, 1967.
A. L.—Never accomplished.

Most Doubles, Inning

N. L.-A. L.—2—Held by many players.
N. L.—Last player—Richard S. Schu, Philadelphia, October 3, 1985, third inning.
A. L.—Last player—Donald A. Mattingly, New York, April 11, 1987, seventh inning.

Most Doubles, Inning, by Pitcher

N. L.—2—Fred Goldsmith, Chicago, September 6, 1883, seventh inning.
Henry L. Borowy, Chicago, May 5, 1946, first game, seventh inning.
A. L.—2—Joseph Wood, Boston, July 4, 1913, a.m. game, fourth inning.
Theodore A. Lyons, Chicago, July 28, 1935, first game, second inning.

Triples
Career & Season

Most Triples in Major Leagues

312—Samuel Crawford, Cincinnati N. L., Detroit A. L., 19 years, 1899 through 1917; 62 in N. L. and 250 in A. L.

Most Triples, League

A. L.—298—Tyrus R. Cobb, Detroit, Philadephia, 24 years, 1905 through 1928.
N. L.—252—John P. Wagner, Louisville, Pittsburgh, 21 years, 1897 through 1917.
N. L. since 1900—231—John P. Wagner, Pittsburgh, 18 years, 1900 through 1917.

Most Triples With Bases Filled, League

A. L.—8—John F. Collins, Chicago, Boston, 1910, 1915, 1916, 1918 (3), 1920 (2).

N. L.—7—Stanley F. Musial, St. Louis, 1946, 1947 (2), 1948, 1949, 1951, 1954.

Most Triples, Season

N. L.—36—J. Owen Wilson, Pittsburgh, 152 games, 1912.

A. L.—26—Joseph J. Jackson, Cleveland, 152 games, 1912.
Samuel Crawford, Detroit, 157 games, 1914.

Most Triples, Rookie Season

N. L.—27—James T. Williams, Pittsburgh, 153 games, 1899.

N. L. since 1900—22—Paul G. Waner, Pittsburgh, 144 games, 1926.

A. L.—17—Russell M. Scarritt, Boston, 151 games, 1929.

Most Triples, Righthander, Season

N. L.—33—Perry W. Werden, St. Louis, 124 games, 1893.

N. L. since 1900—26—Hazen S. Cuyler, Pittsburgh, 153 games, 1925.

A. L.—23—James T. Williams, Baltimore, 125 games, 1902.

Most Triples, Lefthander, Season

N. L.—36—J. Owen Wilson, Pittsburgh, 152 games, 1912.

A. L.—26—Joseph J. Jackson, Cleveland, 152 games, 1912.
Samuel Crawford, Detroit, 157 games, 1914.

Most Triples, Switch Hitter, Season

N. L.—26—George S. Davis, New York, 133 games, 1893.

N. L. since 1900—19—Max G. Carey, 153 games, 1923.
Garry L. Templeton, St. Louis, 154 games, 1979.

A. L.—21—Willie J. Wilson, Kansas City, 141 games, 1985.

Most Triples With Bases Filled, Season

A. L.—3—John F. Collins, Chicago, 103 games, 1918.
Elmer W. Valo, Philadelphia, 150 games, 1949.
Jack E. Jensen, Boston, 151 games, 1956.

N. L.—3—George J. Burns, New York, 154 games, 1914.
Ted C. Sizemore, Los Angeles, 159 games, 1969.
Manuel de J. Sanguillen, Pittsburgh, 138 games, 1971.

Most Years Leading Major Leagues in Triples, Since 1900

6—Samuel Crawford, Cincinnati N. L., 1902; Detroit A. L., 1903, 1910, 1913, 1914, 1915.

Most Years Leading League in Triples, Since 1900

A. L.—5—Samuel Crawford, Detroit, 1903, 1910, 1913, 1914, 1915.

N. L.—5—Stanley F. Musial, St. Louis, 1943, 1946, 1948, 1949 (tied), 1951 (tied).

Most Consecutive Years Leading League in Triples, Since 1900

N. L.—3—Garry L. Templeton, St. Louis, 1977, 1978, 1979.

A. L.—3—Elmer H. Flick, Cleveland, 1905, 1906, 1907.
Samuel Crawford, Detroit, 1913, 1914, 1915.
Zoilo Versalles, Minnesota, 1963, 1964 (tied), 1965 (tied).

Most Years, 20 or More Triples in Major Leagues

5—Samuel Crawford, Cincinnati N. L., 1902; Detroit A. L., 1903, 1912, 1913, 1914.

Most Years, 20 or More Triples, League

A. L.—4—Samuel Crawford, Detroit, 1903, 1912, 1913, 1914.
Tyrus R. Cobb, Detroit, 1908, 1911, 1912, 1917.

N. L.—2—Held by many players. Last player—Stanley F. Musial, St. Louis, 1943, 1946.

Fewest Triples, Season, Most At-Bats

N. L.—0—Octavio R. Rojas, Philadelphia, 152 games, 1968, 621 at-bats.

A. L.—0—James F. Morrison, Chicago, 162 games, 1980, 604 at-bats.

Fewest Triples, Season, for Leader in Triples

A. L.—8—Delbert B. Unser, Washington, 153 games, 1969.

N. L.—10—John W. Callison, Philadelphia, 157 games, 1962.
William H. Davis, Los Angeles, 157 games, 1962.
William C. Virdon, Pittsburgh, 156 games, 1962.
Maurice M. Wills, Los Angeles, 165 games, 1962.
Richard W. Thon, Houston, 136 games, 1982.

Game & Inning

Most Triples, Game

A. A.—4—George A. Strief, Philadelphia, June 25, 1885.

N. L.—4—William Joyce, New York, May 18, 1897.

N. L. since 1900—3—Held by many players.

N. L.—Last player—G. Craig Reynolds, Houston, May 16, 1981.

A. L.—3—Held by many players.

A. L.—Last player—Kenneth F. Landreaux, Minnesota, July 3, 1980.

Most Triples, First Major League Game

A. L.—2—Edward Irwin, Detroit, May 18, 1912. (Only major league game.)
Roy Weatherly, Cleveland, June 27, 1936.

N. L.—2—Willie L. McCovey, San Francisco, July 30, 1959.
John W. Sipin, San Diego, May 24, 1969. (Only major league triples.)

Most Triples, Game, by Pitcher

N. L.—3—Jouett Meekin, New York, July 4, 1894, first game.

Most Consecutive Triples, Game, Nine Innings

N. L.-A. L.—3—Held by many players.

N. L.—Last player—Roberto W. Clemente, Pittsburgh, September 8, 1958.

A. L.—Last player—W. Benjamin Chapman, Cleveland, July 3, 1939.

Most Triples With Bases Filled, Game

N. L.—2—Samuel L. Thompson, Detroit, May 7, 1887.
Henry P. Reitz, Baltimore, June 4, 1894, 1 in third inning, 1 in seventh inning.
William Clark, Pittsburgh, September 17, 1898, second game, 1 in first inning, 1 in seventh inning.
William H. Bruton, Milwaukee, August 2, 1959, second game, 1 in first inning, 1 in sixth inning.

A. L.—2—Elmer W. Valo, Philadelphia, May 1, 1949, first game, 1 in third inning, 1 in seventh inning.
Duane E. Kuiper, Cleveland, July 27, 1978, second game, 1 in first inning, 1 in fifth inning.

Most Times Three Triples in One Game, League

N. L.—2—John G. Reilly, Cincinnati, 1890, 1891.
George S. Davis, Cleveland, New York, 1891, 1894.
William F. Dahlen, Chicago, 1896, 1898.
David L. Brain, St. Louis, Pittsburgh, 1905 (2).

A. L.—1—Held by many players.

Most Times Three Triples in One Game, Season

N. L.—2—David L. Brain, St. Louis, May 29, 1905; Pittsburgh, August 8, 1905.

A. L.—1—Held by many players.

Triple and Home Run, First Major League Game

A. L.—Henry I. Arft, St. Louis, July 27, 1948.

N. L.—Lloyd A. Merriman, Cincinnati, April 24, 1949, first game.
Frank Ernaga, Chicago, May 24, 1957.
Kenneth G. Caminiti, Houston, July 16, 1987.

Triple and Home Run With Bases Filled, Game

N. L.—Dennis L. Brouthers, Detroit, May 17, 1887.
Charles A. Nichols, Boston, September 19, 1892.
Jacob C. Stenzel, Pittsburgh, July 15, 1893.
Adelphia L. Bissonette, Brooklyn, April 21, 1930.
Edward D. Phillips, Pittsburgh, May 28, 1931.
Luis R. Olmo, Brooklyn, May 18, 1945.

A. L.—George H. Sisler, St. Louis, July 11, 1925.
Harry E. Heilmann, Detroit, July 26, 1928, second game.

Most Triples, Doubleheader

A. A.—4—William R. Hamilton, Kansas City, June 28, 1889.

N. L.—4—Michael J. Donlin, Cincinnati, September 22, 1903.

A. L.—3—Held by many players.

Most Triples, Five Consecutive Games

N. L.—6—J. Owen Wilson, Pittsburgh, June 17, 18, 19, 20, 20 (2), 1912.

Most Triples, Inning

N. L.—2—Joseph Hornung, Boston, May 6, 1882, eighth inning.
Henry Peitz, St. Louis, July 2, 1895, first inning.
William F. Shugart, Louisville, July 30, 1895, fifth inning.
John B. Freeman, Boston, July 25, 1900, first inning.
William F. Dahlen, Brooklyn, August 30, 1900, eighth inning.
W. Curtis Walker, Cincinnati, July 22, 1926, second inning.

A. A.—2—Harry Wheeler, Cincinnati, June 28, 1882, eleventh inning.
Harry D. Stovey, Philadelphia, August 18, 1884, eighth inning.

A. L.—2—Allen L. Zarilla, St. Louis, July 13, 1946, fourth inning.
Gilbert F. Coan, Washington, April 21, 1951, sixth inning.

Home Runs
Career

Most Home Runs in Major Leagues
755—Henry L. Aaron, 733 in N.L., Milwaukee, Atlanta, 21 years, 1954 through 1975 (375 at home, 358 on road), 22 in A.L., Milwaukee, 2 years, 1975, 1976. (10 at home, 12 on road).

Most Home Runs, League
N. L.— 733— Henry L. Aaron, Milwaukee, Atlanta, 21 years, 1954 through 1974, (375 at home, 358 on road).
A. L.— 708— George H. Ruth, Boston (49), New York (659), 21 years, 1914 through 1934, (345 at home, 363 on road).

Most Home Runs, One Club, League
N. L.— 733— Henry L. Aaron, Milwaukee, Atlanta, 21 years, 1954 through 1974 (375 at home, 358 on road).
A. L.— 659— George H. Ruth, New York, 15 years, 1920 through 1934 (333 at home, 326 on road).

Most Home Runs, Righthander in Major Leagues
755—Henry L. Aaron, 733 in N.L., Milwaukee, Atlanta, 21 years, 1954 through 1974; 22 in A.L., 2 years, Milwaukee, 1975, 1976.

Most Home Runs, Righthander, League
N. L.— 733— Henry L. Aaron, Milwaukee, Atlanta, 21 years, 1954 through 1974.
A. L.— 573— Harmon C. Killebrew, Washington, Minnesota, Kansas City, 22 years, 1954 through 1975.

Most Home Runs, Lefthander in Major Leagues
714—George H. Ruth, Boston A. L., New York A. L., Boston N. L., 22 years, 1914 through 1935, 708 in A. L. and 6 in N. L.

Most Home Runs, Lefthander, League
A. L.— 708— George H. Ruth, Boston, New York, 21 years, 1914 through 1934.
N. L.— 521— Willie L. McCovey, San Francisco, San Diego, 22 years, 1959 through 1980.

Most Home Runs, Switch Hitter, League
A. L.— 536— Mickey C. Mantle, New York, 18 years, 1951 through 1968.
N. L.— 180— Ted L. Simmons, St. Louis, Atlanta, 15 years, 1968 through 1980, 1986 through 1987.

Most Home Runs by Pinch-Hitter
Both Leagues—20—Clifford Johnson, Houston N. L., New York A. L., Cleveland A. L., Chicago N. L., Oakland A. L., Toronto A. L., 1974 (5), 1975 (1), 1976 (1), 1977 (3), 1978 (2), 1979 (1), 1980 (3), 1981 (1), 1983 (1), 1984 (1), 1986 (1).
N. L.— 18— Gerald T. Lynch, Cincinnati, Pittsburgh, 1957 (3), 1958 (1), 1959 (1), 1961 (5), 1962 (1), 1963 (4), 1964 (1), 1965 (1), 1966 (1).
A. L.— 16— William J. Brown, Detroit, 1963 (1), 1964 (1), 1965 (1), 1966 (2), 1968 (3), 1970 (1), 1971 (2), 1972 (1), 1974 (3), 1975 (1).

Most Home Runs as Leadoff Batter in Major Leagues
35—Bobby L. Bonds, 30 in N.L., San Francisco, 9 years, 1968 through 1974, St. Louis, 1980, Chicago, 1981; 5 in A.L., 5 years, New York, 1975, California, 1976 and 1977, Chicago and Texas, 1978, Cleveland, 1979.

Most Home Runs as Leadoff Batter, League
A. L.— 34— Rickey H. Henderson, Oakland, New York, 9 years, 1979 through 1987.
N. L.— 30— Bobby L. Bonds, San Francisco, St. Louis, Chicago, 9 years, 1968 through 1974, 1980 through 1981.

Most Home Runs in Extra Innings, League
N. L.— 22— Willie H. Mays, original New York club, San Francisco, present New York club, 22 years, 1951 through 1973 (except 1953 in military service).
A. L.— 16— George H. Ruth, Boston, New York, 21 years, 1914 through 1934.

Most Home Runs, Opening Games of Season in Major Leagues
8—Frank Robinson, Cincinnati N.L., 1959, 1961, 1963; Baltimore A.L., 1966, 1969, 1970; California A.L., 1973; Cleveland A.L., 1975: 5 in A.L., 3 in N.L.

Most Home Runs, Opening Games of Season, League
N. L.—7—Edwin Mathews, Milwaukee, 1954 (2), 1958 (2), 1959, 1961, 1965.
Willie H. Mays, New York, 1954; San Francisco, 1962, 1963, 1964 (2), 1966, 1971.
A. L.—6—George H. Ruth, Boston, 1919; New York, 1923, 1929, 1931, 1932 (2).
Brooks C. Robinson, Baltimore, 1960, 1966, 1967, 1968, 1973 (2).
Carl M. Yastrzemski, Boston, 1963, 1968 (2), 1973, 1974, 1980.

Most Home Runs, League, First Baseman
A. L.— 493— H. Louis Gehrig, New York, 17 years, 1923 through 1939.
N. L.— 439— Willie L. McCovey, San Francisco, San Diego, 22 years, 1959 through 1980.

Most Home Runs, Major Leagues, Second Baseman
266—Joe L. Morgan, 260 in N.L., Houston, Cincinnati, San Francisco, Philadelphia, 21 years, 1963 through 1983; 6 in A.L., 1 year, 1984.

Most Home Runs, League, Second Baseman
N. L.— 263— Rogers Hornsby, St. Louis, New York, Boston, Chicago, 15 years, 1916, 1919 through 1931, 1933.
A. L.— 246— Joseph L. Gordon, New York, Cleveland, 11 years, 1938 through 1950, (except 1944, 1945 in military service).

Most Home Runs, League, Third Baseman
N. L.— 491— Michael J. Schmidt, Philadelphia, 16 years, 1972 through 1987.
A. L.— 319— Graig Nettles, Minnesota, Cleveland, New York, 16 years, 1968 through 1983.

Most Home Runs, League, Shortstop
N. L.— 277— Ernest Banks, Chicago, 9 years, 1953 through 1961.
A. L.— 213— Vernon D. Stephens, St. Louis, Boston, Chicago, 10 years, 1942 through 1952, except 1951.

Most Home Runs, Major Leagues, Outfielder
692—George H. Ruth, 686 in A.L., Boston, New York, 17 years, 1918 through 1934; 6 in N.L., 1 year, Boston, 1935.

Most Home Runs, League, Outfielder
A. L.— 686— George H. Ruth, Boston, New York, 17 years, 1918 through 1934.
N. L.— 661— Henry L. Aaron, Milwaukee, Atlanta, 21 years, 1954 through 1974.

Most Home Runs, League, Catcher
N. L.— 327— Johnny L. Bench, Cincinnati, 17 years, 1967 through 1983.
A. L.— 306— Lawrence P. Berra, New York, 18 years, 1946 through 1963.

Most Home Runs, League, Pitcher
A. L.— 36— Wesley C. Ferrell, Cleveland, Boston, Washington, New York, 13 years, 1927 through 1939. (Also 1 home run as pinch-hitter, 1935; 1 home run as pitcher, Boston N.L., 1941).
N. L.— 35— Warren E. Spahn, Boston, Milwaukee, New York, San Francisco, 21 years, 1942 through 1965 (except 1943, 1944, 1945 in military service).

Most Major League Parks, One or More Home Runs, Career
32—Frank Robinson, Cincinnati N. L., Baltimore A. L., Los Angeles N. L., California A. L., Cleveland A. L., 21 years, 1956 through 1976.
Daniel J. Staub, Houston N. L., Montreal N. L., New York N. L., Detroit A. L., Texas A. L., 23 years, 1963 through 1985.
31—Henry L. Aaron, Milwaukee N. L., Atlanta N. L., Milwaukee A. L., 23 years, 1954 through 1976.

Homering in All Major League Parks (15) in Use During Career
Harry E. Heilmann, Detroit A. L., 1914, 1916 through 1929, Cincinnati N. L., 1930, 1932.
J. Geoffrey Heath, Cleveland A. L., 1936 through 1945, Washington A. L., 1946, St. Louis A. L., 1946, 1947, Boston N. L., 1948, 1949 (League Park and Municipal Stadium, Cleveland).
John R. Mize, St. Louis N. L., 1936 through 1941, New York N. L., 1942, 1946 through 1949, New York A. L., 1949 through 1953.

Most Parks, One or More Home Runs, During Career, League

N. L.— 22—Henry L. Aaron, Milwaukee, Atlanta, 21 years, 1954 through 1974.

Willie H. Mays, New York, San Francisco, 22 years, 1951 through 1973 except 1953.

Willie L. McCovey, San Francisco, San Diego, 22 years, 1959 through 1980.

A. L.— 19—Carl M. Yastrzemski, Boston, 23 years, 1961 through 1983.

Reginald M. Jackson, Kansas City, Oakland, Baltimore, New York, California, 21 years, 1967 through 1987.

Most Consecutive At-Bats Without Hitting a Home Run, League

N. L.—3,347—Thomas J. Thevenow, St. Louis, Philadelphia, Pittsburgh, Cincinnati, Boston, September 24, 1926 through October 2, 1938 (end of career).

A. L.—3,278—Edward C. Foster, Washington, Boston, St. Louis, April 20, 1916 through August 5, 1923 (end of career).

Season

Most Home Runs, Season

A. L. (162-game season) —61—Roger E. Maris, New York, 161 games, 1961.

A. L. (154-game season) —60—George H. Ruth, New York, 151 games, 1927.

N. L. (154-game season) —56—Lewis R. Wilson, Chicago, 155 games, 1930.

N. L. (162-game season) —52—Willie H. Mays, San Francisco, 157 games, 1965.

George A. Foster, Cincinnati, 158 games, 1977.

Most Home Runs, Season, for Runner-Up in Home Runs

A. L. (162-game season) —54—Mickey C. Mantle, New York, 153 games, 1961.

A. L. (154-game season) —50—James E. Foxx, Boston, 149 games, 1938.

N. L. (154-game season) —47—Theodore B. Kluszewski, Cincinnati, 153 games, 1955.

N. L. (162-game season) —47—Henry L. Aaron, Atlanta, 139 games, 1971.

Most Years Leading League in Home Runs

A. L.— 12—George H. Ruth, Boston, New York, 1918 (tied), 1919, 1920, 1921, 1923, 1924, 1926, 1927, 1928, 1929, 1930, 1931 (tied).

N. L.— 8—Michael J. Schmidt, Philadelphia, 1974, 1975, 1976, 1980, 1981, 1983, 1984 (tied), 1986.

Most Consecutive Years Leading League in Home Runs

N. L.—7—Ralph M. Kiner, Pittsburgh, 1946, 1947 (tied), 1948 (tied), 1949, 1950, 1951, 1952 (tied).

A. L.—6—George H. Ruth, New York, 1926 through 1931 (tied in 1931).

Most Home Runs, Rookie Season

A. L.—49—Mark D. McGwire, Oakland, 151 games, 1987.

N. L.—38—Walter A. Berger, Boston, 151 games, 1930.

Frank Robinson, Cincinnati, 152 games, 1956.

Most Home Runs, Righthander, Season

A. L.—58—James E. Foxx, Philadelphia, 154 games, 1932.

Henry B. Greenberg, Detroit, 155 games, 1938.

N. L.—56—Lewis R. Wilson, Chicago, 155 games, 1930.

Most Home Runs, Lefthander, Season

A. L. (162-game season) —61—Roger E. Maris, New York, 161 games, 1961.

A. L. (154-game season) —60—George H. Ruth, New York, 151 games, 1927.

N. L.—51—John R. Mize, New York, 154 games, 1947.

Most Home Runs, Switch Hitter, Season

A. L.—54—Mickey C. Mantle, New York, 153 games, 1961.

N. L.—36—Howard M. Johnson, New York, 157 games, 1987.

Most Home Runs by Pinch-Hitter, Season

N. L.—6—John H. Frederick, Brooklyn, 1932.

A. L.—5—Joseph E. Cronin, Boston, 1943.

Most Home Runs as Leadoff Batter, Season

N. L.—11—Bobby L. Bonds, San Francisco, 160 games, 1973, 39 home runs for season.

A. L.— 9—Rickey H. Henderson, New York, 153 games, 1986, 28 home runs for season.

Most Home Runs, Season, First Baseman

A. L.—58—Henry B. Greenberg, Detroit, 155 games, 1938; 154 games at first base.

N. L.—51—John R. Mize, New York, 154 games, 1947; 154 games at first base.

Most Home Runs, Season, Second Baseman

N. L.—42—Rogers Hornsby, St. Louis, 154 games, 1922; 154 games at second base.

David A. Johnson, Atlanta, 157 games, 1973; 156 games at second base (also had 1 home run as pinch-hitter).

A. L.—32—Joseph L. Gordon, Cleveland, 144 games, 1948; 144 games at second base.

Most Home Runs, Season, Third Baseman

N. L.—48—Michael J. Schmidt, Philadelphia, 150 games, 1980; 149 games at third base.

A. L.—43—Albert L. Rosen, Cleveland, 155 games, 1953; 154 games at third base.

Most Home Runs, Season, Shortstop

N. L.—47—Ernest Banks, Chicago, 154 games, 1958; 154 games at shortstop.

A. L.—40—Americo Petrocelli, Boston, 154 games, 1969; 153 games at shortstop.

Most Home Runs, Season, Outfielder

A. L.—61—Roger E. Maris, New York, 161 games, 1961; 160 games in outfield.

N. L.—56—Lewis R. Wilson, Chicago, 155 games, 1930; 155 games in outfield.

Most Home Runs, Season, Catcher

N. L.—40—Roy Campanella, Brooklyn, 144 games, 1953; caught 140 games (also had 1 home run as pinch-hitter).

(Johnny L. Bench, Cincinnati, 1970, had 38 home runs in 139 games as catcher; 6 home runs in 24 games as outfielder; 1 home run in 12 games as first baseman.)

A. L.—33—Carlton E. Fisk, Chicago, 153 games, 1985; caught 130 games (also had 4 home runs as designated hitter).

Most Home Runs, Season, Pitcher (Only those hit as pitcher)

A. L.—9—Wesley C. Ferrell, Cleveland, 48 games, 1931; pitched 40 games.

N. L.—7—Donald Newcombe, Brooklyn, 57 games, 1955; pitched 34 games.

Donald S. Drysdale, Los Angeles, 47 games, 1958; pitched 44 games.

Donald S. Drysdale, Los Angeles, 58 games, 1965; pitched 44 games.

Most Home Runs, Season, Against One Club

A. L.— 14— (8-club league) —H. Louis Gehrig, New York vs. Cleveland, 1936; 6 at New York, 8 at Cleveland.

13— (10-club league) —Roger E. Maris, New York vs. Chicago, 1961; 8 at New York, 5 at Chicago.

11— (12-club league) —Harmon C. Killebrew, Minnesota vs. Oakland, 1969; 6 at Minnesota, 5 at Oakland.

N. L.— 13— (8-club league) —Henry J. Sauer, Chicago vs. Pittsburgh, 1954; 8 at Chicago, 5 at Pittsburgh.

Joseph W. Adcock, Milwaukee vs. Brooklyn, 1956; 5 at Milwaukee, 7 at Brooklyn, 1 at Jersey City.

11— (10-club league) —Frank Robinson, Cincinnati vs. Milwaukee, 1962; 8 at Cincinnati, 3 at Milwaukee.

(12-club league) —Wilver D. Stargell, Pittsburgh vs. Atlanta, 1971; 6 at Pittsburgh, 5 at Atlanta.

(12-club league) —Dale B. Murphy, Atlanta vs. San Francisco, 1983; 6 at Atlanta, 5 at San Francisco.

Fewest Home Runs, Season, Most At-Bats

N. L.—0—Walter J. Maranville, Pittsburgh, 155 games, 1922; 672 at-bats.

A. L.—0—Roger M. Cramer, Boston, 148 games, 1938; 658 at-bats.

Fewest Home Runs, Season, for Leader (54-Game Schedule)

A. L.—7—Samuel Crawford, Detroit, 152 games, 1908.

Robert F. Roth, Chicago, Cleveland, 109 games, 1915.

N. L.—7—John J. Murray, New York, 149 games, 1909.

Home & Road

Most Home Runs, Season, at Home Grounds

A. L.— 39— Henry B. Greenberg, Detroit, 1938.

N. L.— 34— Theodore B. Kluszewski, Cincinnati, 1954.

Most Home Runs, Righthander, Season at Home Grounds

    A. L.— 39— Henry B. Greenberg, Detroit, 1938.
    N. L.— 33— Lewis R. Wilson, Chicago, 1930.

Most Home Runs, Lefthander, Season at Home Grounds

    N. L.— 34— Theodore B. Kluszewski, Cincinnati, 1954.
    A. L.— 32— George H. Ruth, New York, 1921.
            Kenneth R. Williams, St. Louis, 1922.

Most Home Runs, Switch Hitter, Season at Home Grounds

    A. L.— 27— Mickey C. Mantle, New York, 1956.
    N. L.— 22— James A. Collins, St. Louis, 1934.

Most Home Runs, Season, at Home Grounds Against One Club

    A. L.— 10— Gus E. Zernial, Philadelphia vs. St. Louis, 1951.
    N. L.— 9— Stanley F. Musial, St. Louis vs. New York, 1954.

Most Home Runs, Season on Road

    A. L.— 32— George H. Ruth, New York, 1927.
    N. L.— 31— George A. Foster, Cincinnati, 1977.

Most Home Runs, Righthander, Season on Road

    N. L.— 31— George A. Foster, Cincinnati, 1977.
    A. L.— 28— Harmon C. Killebrew, Minnesota, 1962.
            George A. Bell, Toronto, 1987.

Most Home Runs, Lefthander, Season on Road

    A. L.— 32— George H. Ruth, New York, 1927.
    N. L.— 30— Edwin L. Mathews, Milwaukee, 1953.

Most Home Runs, Switch Hitter, Season on Road

    A. L.— 30— Mickey C. Mantle, New York, 1961.
    N. L.— 23— Howard M. Johnson, New York, 1987.

Most Home Runs, Season, on Road, Against One Club

    A. L.— 10— Harry E. Heilmann, Detroit at Philadelphia, 1922.
    N. L.— 9— Joseph W. Adcock, Milwaukee at Brooklyn, 1954.
            Willie H. Mays, New York at Brooklyn, 1955.

Hitting Home Runs all Twelve Parks in League, Season

    N. L.—Willie L. McCovey, San Francisco, 1970.
            Joseph A. Pepitone, Houston, Chicago, 1970.
            Wilver D. Stargell, Pittsburgh, 1970 (13 including both Pittsburgh parks) .
            Johnny L. Bench, Cincinnati, 1972.
            George A. Foster, Cincinnati, 1977.
            Michael J. Schmidt, Philadelphia, 1979.
    A. L.—Reginald M. Jackson, Oakland, 1975.

Most Years Hitting Home Runs All Parks, League

    A. L.— 11— George H. Ruth, Boston, New York, 1919, 1920, 1921, 1923, 1924, 1926, 1927, 1928, 1929, 1930, 1931.
    N. L.— 9— Henry L. Aaron, Milwaukee, Atlanta, 1954, 1955, 1956, 1957, 1958, 1959, 1960, 1963, 1966.

50, 40, 30 & 20 In Season

Most Years, 50 or More Home Runs, League

    A. L.—4—George H. Ruth, New York, 1920, 1921, 1927, 1928.
    N. L.—2—Ralph Kiner, Pittsburgh, 1947, 1949.
           Willie H. Mays, New York, 1955; San Francisco, 1965.

Most Consecutive Years, 50 or More Home Runs, Season, League

    A. L.—2—George H. Ruth, New York, 1920, 1921 and 1927, 1928.
    N. L.—Never accomplished.

Most Years, 40 or More Home Runs, League

    A. L.— 11— George H. Ruth, New York, 1920, 1921, 1923, 1924, 1926, 1927, 1928, 1929, 1930, 1931, 1932.
    N. L.— 8— Henry L. Aaron, Milwaukee, Atlanta, 1957, 1960, 1962, 1963, 1966, 1969, 1971, 1973.

Most Consecutive Years, 40 or More Home Runs, League

    A. L.—7—George H. Ruth, New York, 1926 through 1932.
    N. L.—5—Ralph M. Kiner, Pittsburgh, 1947 through 1951.
           Edwin D. Snider, Brooklyn, 1953 through 1957.

Most Years, 30 or More Home Runs, League

    N. L.— 15— Henry L. Aaron, Milwaukee, Atlanta, 1957 through 1973, except 1964, 1968.
    A. L.— 13— George H. Ruth, New York, 1920 through 1933, except 1925.

Most Consecutive Years, 30 or More Home Runs, League

    A. L.— 12— James E. Foxx, Philadelphia, Boston, 1929 through 1940.
    N. L.— 9— Edwin L. Mathews, Milwaukee, 1953 through 1961.

Most Years, 20 or More Home Runs, League

    N. L.— 20— Henry L. Aaron, Milwaukee, Atlanta, 1955 through 1974.
    A. L.— 16— George H. Ruth, Boston, New York, 1919 through 1934.
            Theodore S. Williams, Boston, 1939, 1940, 1941, 1942, 1946, 1947, 1948, 1949, 1950, 1951, 1954, 1955, 1956, 1957, 1958, 1960.
            Reginald M. Jackson, Oakland, Baltimore, New York, California, 1968 through 1980, 1982, 1984, 1985.

Most Consecutive Years, 20 or More Home Runs, League

    N. L.— 20— Henry L. Aaron, Milwaukee, Atlanta, 1955 through 1974.
    A. L.— 16— George H. Ruth, Boston, New York, 1919 through 1934.

Two Consecutive Seasons

Most Home Runs, Two Consecutive Seasons

    A. L.— 114— George H. Ruth, New York, 60 in 1927; 54 in 1928.
    N. L.— 101— Ralph M. Kiner, Pittsburgh, 54 in 1949; 47 in 1950.

Most Home Runs, Righthander, Two Consecutive Seasons

    A. L.— 106— James E. Foxx, Philadelphia, 58 in 1932; 48 in 1933.
    N. L.— 101— Ralph M. Kiner, Pittsburgh, 54 in 1949; 47 in 1950.

Most Home Runs, Lefthander, Two Consecutive Seasons

    A. L.— 114— George H. Ruth, New York, 60 in 1927; 54 in 1928.
    N. L.— 96— Theodore B. Kluszewski, Cincinnati, 49 in 1954; 47 in 1955.

Most Home Runs, Switch Hitter, Two Consecutive Seasons

    A. L.— 94— Mickey C. Mantle, New York, 40 in 1960, 54 in 1961.
    N. L.— 61— C. Reginald Smith, Los Angeles, 32 in 1977, 29 in 1978.

Month & Week

Most Home Runs, Month (From first through last day of month)

    A. L.— 18—Rudolph P. York, Detroit, August, 1937.
    N. L.— 17— Willie H. Mays, San Francisco, August, 1965.

Most Home Runs, Righthander, One Month

    A. L.— 18—Rudolph P. York, Detroit, August, 1937.
    N. L.— 17— Willie H. Mays, San Francisco, August, 1965.

Most Home Runs, Lefthander, One Month

    A. L.— 17— George H. Ruth, New York, September, 1927.
    N. L.— 15—Fred Williams, Philadelphia, May, 1923.
            Edwin D. Snider, Brooklyn, August, 1953.

Most Home Runs, Switch Hitter, One Month

    A. L.— 16— Mickey C. Mantle, New York, May, 1956.
    N. L.— 11— James A. Collins, St. Louis, June, 1935.
            Kenneth J. Henderson, San Francisco, August, 1972.

Most Home Runs Month of April

    N. L.— 11— Wilver D. Stargell, Pittsburgh, April 1971.
            Michael J. Schmidt, Philadelphia, April 1976.
    A. L.— 11— Graig Nettles, New York, April 1974.

Most Home Runs Through April 30

    N. L.— 11— Wilver D. Stargell, Pittsburgh, 1971.
            Michael J. Schmidt, Philadelphia, 1976.
    A. L.— 11— Graig Nettles, New York, 1974.

Most Home Runs Month of May

    A. L.— 16— Mickey C. Mantle, New York, May 1956.
    N. L.— 15— Fred Williams, Philadelphia, May 1923.

Most Home Runs Through May 31

    A. L.— 20— Mickey C. Mantle, New York, 1956.
    N. L.— 19— Eric K. Davis, Cincinnati, 1987.

Most Home Runs Month of June

    A. L.— 15— George H. Ruth, New York, June 1930.
            Robert L. Johnson, Philadelphia, June 1934.
            Roger E. Maris, New York, June 1961.
    N. L.— 15— Pedro Guerrero, Los Angeles, June 1985.

Most Home Runs Through June 30

    A. L.— 30— George H. Ruth, New York, 1928; also 1930.
    N. L.— 28— Wilver D. Stargell, Pittsburgh, 1971.

Most Home Runs Month of July

    A. L.— 15— Joseph P. DiMaggio, New York, July 1937.
            Henry B. Greenberg, Detroit, July 1938.
    N. L.— 15— Joseph W. Adcock, Milwaukee, July 1956.

Most Home Runs Through July 31

A. L.— 41— George H. Ruth, New York, 1928.
James E. Foxx, Philadelphia, 1932.
N. L.— 36— Willie H. Mays, New York, 1954.
Johnny L. Bench, Cincinnati, 1970.
Wilver D. Stargell, Pittsburgh, 1971.
Michael J. Schmidt, Philadelphia, 1979.

Most Home Runs Month of August

A. L.— 18— Rudolph P. York, Detroit, August 1937.
N. L.— 17— Willie H. Mays, San Francisco, August 1965.

Most Home Runs Through August 31

A. L.— 51— Roger E. Maris, New York, 1961.
N. L.— 46— Lewis R. Wilson, Chicago, 1930.

Most Home Runs Month of September

A. L.— 17— George H. Ruth, New York, September 1927.
N. L.— 16— Ralph M. Kiner, Pittsburgh, September 1949.

Most Home Runs Through September 30

A. L.— 60— George H. Ruth, New York, 1927.
Roger E. Maris, New York, 1961.
N. L.— 56— Lewis R. Wilson, Chicago, 1930.

Most Home Runs Month of October

A. A.— 4— John Milligan, St. Louis, October 1889.
N. L.— 4— Edward N. Williamson, Chicago, October 1884.
Michael J. Schmidt, Philadelphia, October 1980.
David G. Parker, Cincinnati, October 1985.
A. L.— 4— Gus E. Zernial, Chicago, October 1950.
George H. Brett, Kansas City, October 1985.
Ronald C. Kittle, Chicago, October 1985.
Wallace K. Joyner, California, October 1987.

Most Home Runs, One Week (Sunday through Saturday)

A. L.— 10— Frank O. Howard, Washington, May 12 through 18, 1968, 6 games.
N. L.— 8— Ralph M. Kiner, Pittsburgh, September 7 through 13, 1947, 7 games.
Theodore B. Kluszewski, Cincinnati, July 1, first game, through 7, 1956, 7 games.
Nathan Colbert, San Diego, July 30, first game, through August 5, 1972, 9 games.

Game, Doubleheader & Inning

Most Home Runs, Game

N. L.— 4— Robert L. Lowe, Boston, May 30, 1894, p.m. game, consecutive.
Edward J. Delahanty, Philadelphia, July 13, 1896.
Charles H. Klein, Philadelphia, July 10, 1936, 10 innings.
Gilbert R. Hodges, Brooklyn, August 31, 1950.
Joseph W. Adcock, Milwaukee, July 31, 1954.
Willie H. Mays, San Francisco, April 30, 1961.
Michael J. Schmidt, Philadelphia, April 17, 1976, 10 innings, consecutive.
J. Robert Horner, Atlanta, July 6, 1986.
A. L.— 4— H. Louis Gehrig, New York, June 3, 1932, consecutive.
J. Patrick Seerey, Chicago, July 18, 1948, first game, 11 innings.
Rocco D. Colavito, Cleveland, June 10, 1959, consecutive.

Most Home Runs, Game, by Pitcher

A. A.— 3— Guy J. Hecker, Louisville, August 15, 1886, second game.
N. L.— 3— James A. Tobin, Boston, May 13, 1942.
A. L.— 2— Held by many pitchers. Last pitcher—Wilfred C. Siebert, Boston, September 2, 1971.

Most Home Runs, First Game in Major Leagues

A. A.— 2— Charles T. Reilly, Columbus, October 9, 1889 (on third and fifth times at bat).
A. L.— 2— Robert C. Nieman, St. Louis, September 14, 1951 (on first 2 times at bat).
Dagoberto B. Campaneris, Kansas City, July 23, 1964 (on first and fourth times at bat).
N. L.— 1— Held by many players.

Most Home Runs, Opening Game of Season

N. L.— 2— 23 times—Held by 21 players—Last player, Albert Oliver, Montreal, April 6, 1983.
A. L.— 2— 25 times—Held by 25 players—Last players, Kirk H. Gibson, Detroit, April 7, 1986; James A. Presley, Seattle, April 8, 1986; 10 innings.

Most Inside-the-Park Home Runs, Game

N. L.— 3— Thomas L. McCreery, Louisville, July 12, 1897.
N. L.-A. L. since 1900— 2— Held by many players.
N. L.— Last player—Henry C. Thompson, New York at New York, August 16, 1950.
A. L.— Last player—Gregory C. Gagne, Minnesota at Minnesota, October 4, 1986.

Most Home Runs, Game, In Extra Innings

A. L.— 2— Vernon D. Stephens, St. Louis, September 29, 1943, first game, consecutive, eleventh and thirteenth innings.
Willie C. Kirkland, Cleveland, June 14, 1963, second game, eleventh and nineteenth innings.
Michael D. Young, Baltimore, May 28, 1987, consecutive, tenth and twelfth innings.
N. L.— 2— Arthur L. Shamsky, Cincinnati, August 12, 1966, consecutive, tenth and eleventh innings.
Ralph A. Garr, Atlanta, May 17, 1971, consecutive, tenth and twelfth innings.

Home Run Winning Longest Extra-Inning Game

A. L.— Harold D. Baines, Chicago, 25 innings, 0 on base, Chicago won vs. Milwaukee, 7-6, May 8, 1984 (completed May 9) .
N. L.— Lawrence J. Doyle, New York, 21 innings, 1 on base, New York won vs. Pittsburgh, 3-1, July 17, 1914.
Mervin W. Rettenmund, San Diego, 21 innings, 2 on base, San Diego won vs. Montreal, 11-8, May 21, 1977.

Home Run Winning Longest 1-0 Game

N. L.— Charles G. Radbourn, Providence, August 17, 1882, 18 innings.
N. L. since 1900— Willie H. Mays, San Francisco, July 2, 1963, 16 innings.
A. L.— William J. Skowron, New York, April 22, 1959, 14 innings.

Home Run by Pitcher Winning 1-0 Extra-Inning Complete Game

A. L.— Thomas J. Hughes, Washington, August 3, 1906, 10 innings.
Charles H. Ruffing, New York, August 13, 1932, 10 innings.
N. L.— Never accomplished— (John C. Klippstein, Cincinnati, August 6, 1962, hit home run in 13th inning, after relieving Robert T. Purkey, who had pitched first 10 innings) .

Home Run, First Major League At-Bat
(N.L. 30 Times; A.L. 27 Times; A.A. 2 Times)
*On First Pitch †Not First Plate Appearance

A. A.— George E. Tebeau, Cincinnati, April 16, 1887.
Michael J. Griffin, Baltimore, April 16, 1887.
N. L.— William J. Duggleby, Philadelphia, April 21, 1898.
John W. Bates, Boston, April 12, 1906.
Walter J. Mueller, Pittsburgh, May 7, 1922.
E. Clise Dudley, Brooklyn, April 27, 1929.*
Gordon L. Slade, Brooklyn, May 24, 1930.
Edwin Morgan, St. Louis, April 14, 1936.*
Ernest Koy, Brooklyn, April 19, 1938.
Emmett J. Mueller, Philadelphia, April 19, 1938.
Clyde F. Vollmer, Cincinnati, May 31, 1942, second game.*
John J. Kerr, New York, September 8, 1943.
Carroll W. Lockman, New York, July 5, 1945.
Daniel P. Bankhead, Brooklyn, August 26, 1947.
Lester L. Layton, New York, May 21, 1948.
Edward R. Sanicki, Philadelphia, September 14, 1949.
Theodore N. Tappe, Cincinnati, September 14, 1950, first game.
J. Hoyt Wilhelm, New York, April 23, 1952.
Wallace W. Moon, St. Louis, April 13, 1954.
Charles W. Tanner, Milwaukee, April 12, 1955.*
William D. White, New York, May 7, 1956.
Frank Ernaga, Chicago, May 24, 1957.
Donald G. Leppert, Pittsburgh, June 18, 1961, first game.
Facundo A. Barragan, Chicago, September 1, 1961.
Benigno F. Ayala, New York, August 27, 1974.
John J. Montefusco, San Francisco, September 3, 1974.†
Jose Y. Sosa, Houston, July 30, 1975.
Johnnie L. LeMaster, San Francisco, September 2, 1975.
Timothy C. Wallach, Montreal, September 6, 1980.†
Carmelo Martinez, Chicago, August 22, 1983.†
Michael R. Fitzgerald, New York, September 13, 1983.
William N. Clark, San Francisco, April 8, 1986.
A. L.— H. Earl Averill, Cleveland, April 16, 1929.
Clarence M. Parker, Philadelphia, April 30, 1937.
Wilfred H. Lefebvre, Boston, June 10, 1938.*
James E. Miller, Detroit, April 23, 1944, second game.
Edward C. Pellagrini, Boston, April 22, 1946.
George S. Vico, Detroit, April 20, 1948.*
Robert C. Nieman, St. Louis, September 14, 1951.

J. Robert Tillman, Boston, May 19, 1962.†
John E. Kennedy, Washington, September 5, 1962, first game.
Leslie F. Narum, Baltimore, May 3, 1963.
W. Gates Brown, Detroit, June 19, 1963.
Dagoberto B. Campaneris, Kansas City, July 23, 1964.*
William A. Roman, Detroit, September 30, 1964, second game.
Garrabrant R. Alyea, Washington, September 12, 1965.*
John Miller, New York, September 11, 1966.
W. Richard Renick, Minnesota, July 11, 1968.
Joseph W. Keough, Oakland, August 7, 1968, second game.
Gene W. Lamont, Detroit, September 2, 1970, second game.
Donald G. Rose, California, May 24, 1972.*
Reginald J. Sanders, Detroit, September 1, 1974.
David L. McKay, Minnesota, August 22, 1975.
Alvis Woods, Toronto, April 7, 1977.
David R. Machemer, California, June 21, 1978.
Gary J. Gaetti, Minnesota, September 20, 1981.
Andre A. David, Minnesota, June 29, 1984, first game.
Terry L. Steinbach, Oakland, September 12, 1986.
Jay S. Bell, Cleveland, September 29, 1986.*

Home Run, First Time at Bat in Major Leagues, Pinch-Hitter

N. L.—Edwin Morgan, St. Louis, April 14, 1936, seventh inning.
Lester L. Layton, New York, May 21, 1948, ninth inning.
Theodore N. Tappe, Cincinnati, September 14, 1950, first game, eighth inning.
Charles W. Tanner, Milwaukee, April 12, 1955, eighth inning.
A. L.—Clarence M. Parker, Philadelphia, April 30, 1937, ninth inning.
John E. Kennedy, Washington, September 5, 1962, first game, sixth inning.
W. Gates Brown, Detroit, June 19, 1963, fifth inning.
William A. Roman, Detroit, September 30, 1964, second game, seventh inning.
Garrabrant R. Alyea, Washington, September 12, 1965, sixth inning.
Joseph W. Keough, Oakland, August 7, 1968, second game, eighth inning.
Alvis Woods, Toronto, April 7, 1977, fifth inning.

Most Home Runs, Doubleheader, Hitting Homers in Each Game

N. L.—5—Stanley F. Musial, St. Louis, May 2, 1954.
Nathan Colbert, San Diego, August 1, 1972.
A. L.—4—H. Earl Averill, Cleveland, September 17, 1930.
James E. Foxx, Philadelphia, July 2, 1933, 19 innings.
James R. Tabor, Boston, July 4, 1939.
Gus E. Zernial, Chicago, October 1, 1950.
Charles R. Maxwell, Detroit, May 3, 1959, consecutive.
Roger E. Maris, New York, July 25, 1961.
Rocco D. Colavito, Detroit, August 27, 1961.
Harmon C. Killebrew, Minnesota, September 21, 1963.
Bobby R. Murcer, New York, June 24, 1970, consecutive.
Graig Nettles, New York, April 14, 1974.
Otoniel Velez, Toronto, May 4, 1980, 19 innings.
Albert Oliver, Texas, August 17, 1980.

Most Home Runs, Doubleheader, Pinch-Hitter

A. L.—2—Joseph E. Cronin, Boston, June 17, 1943.
N. L.—2—Harold N. Breeden, Montreal, July 13, 1973.

Most Home Runs, Inning

N. L.—2—Charles Jones, Boston, June 10, 1880, eighth inning.
Robert L. Lowe, Boston, May 30, 1894, p.m. game, third inning.
Jacob C. Stenzel, Pittsburgh, June 6, 1894, third inning.
Lewis R. Wilson, New York, July 1, 1925, second game, third inning.
Henry Leiber, New York, August 24, 1935, second inning.
Andrew W. Seminick, Philadelphia, June 2, 1949, eighth inning.
Sidney Gordon, New York, July 31, 1949, second game, second inning.
Willie L. McCovey, San Francisco, April 12, 1973, fourth inning and June 27, 1977, sixth inning.
John D. Boccabella, Montreal, July 6, 1973, first game, sixth inning.
Lee A. May, Houston, April 29, 1974, sixth inning.
Andre F. Dawson, Montreal, July 30, 1978, third inning and September 24, 1985, fifth inning.
C. Ray Knight, Cincinnati, May 13, 1980, fifth inning.
Von F. Hayes, Philadelphia, June 11, 1985, first inning.
P. L.—2—Louis Bierbauer, Brooklyn, July 12, 1890, third inning.
A. A.—2—Edward Cartwright, St. Louis, September 23, 1890, third inning.

A. L.—2—Kenneth R. Williams, St. Louis, August 7, 1922, sixth inning.
William Regan, Boston, June 16, 1928, fourth inning.
Joseph P. DiMaggio, New York, June 24, 1936, fifth inning.
Albert W. Kaline, Detroit, April 17, 1955, sixth inning.
James R. Lemon, Washington, September 5, 1959, third inning.
Joseph A. Pepitone, New York, May 23, 1962, eighth inning.
Frederic C. Reichardt, California, April 30, 1966, eighth inning.
Clifford Johnson, New York, June 30, 1977, eighth inning.

Three & Two In Game

Most Times, Three or More Home Runs, Game, in Major Leagues

6—John R. Mize, St. Louis N. L., 1938 (2), 1940 (2), New York N. L., 1947, New York A. L., 1950.

Most Times, Three or More Home Runs, Game, League

N. L.—5—John R. Mize, St. Louis, 1938 (2), 1940 (2), New York, 1947.
A. L.—4—H. Louis Gehrig, New York, 1927, 1929, 1930, 1932.

Most Times, Three or More Home Runs, Game, Season

N. L.—2—John R. Mize, St. Louis, twice, July 13, July 20, second game, 1938; May 13, September 8, first game, 1940.
Ralph M. Kiner, Pittsburgh, August 16, September 11, second game, 1947.
Willie H. Mays, San Francisco, April 30, 4 home runs, June 29, first game, 1961.
Wilver D. Stargell, Pittsburgh, April 10, April 21, 1971.
David A. Kingman, Chicago, May 17, July 28, 1979.
A. L.—2—Theodore S. Williams, Boston, May 8, June 13, 1957.
Douglas V. DeCinces, California, August 3, August 8, 1982.

Most Times, Three Home Runs in a Doubleheader, League (Connecting in Both Games)

A. L.—7—George H. Ruth, New York, 1920, 1922, 1926, 1927, 1930, 1933 (2).
N. L.—5—Melvin T. Ott, New York, 1929, 1931, 1932, 1933, 1944.

Most Times, Three Consecutive Homers, Game, in Major Leagues

4—John R. Mize, St. Louis, N. L., 1938, 1940, New York, N. L., 1947, New York A. L., 1950.

Most Times, Three or More Consecutive Homers, Game, League

N. L.—3—John R. Mize, St. Louis, 1938, 1940, New York, 1947.
A. L.—2—Joseph P. DiMaggio, New York, 1937, 1948.
Rocco D. Colavito, Cleveland, 1959; Detroit, 1962.

Most Times, Two or More Home Runs, Game, in Major Leagues

72—George H. Ruth, Boston A. L., New York A. L., Boston N. L., 22 years, 1914-1935; 71 in A.L., 1 in N.L.

Most Times, Two or More Home Runs, Game, League

A. L.—71—George H. Ruth, Boston, New York, 21 years, 1914 through 1934.
N. L.—63—Willie H. Mays, original New York club, San Francisco, present New York club, 22 years, 1951 through 1973 (except 1953 in military service), 2 home runs, game, 60 times; 3 home runs, game, 2 times; 4 home runs, game, 1 time.

Most Times, Two or More Home Runs, Game, Season

A. L.—11—Henry B. Greenberg, Detroit, 1938.
N. L.—10—Ralph M. Kiner, Pittsburgh, 1947.

Most Times, Two Home Runs Game by Pitcher, League

A. L.—5—Wesley C. Ferrell, Cleveland, Boston, 1931, 1934 (2), 1935, 1936.
N. L.—3—Donald Newcombe, Brooklyn, 1955 (2), 1956.

Most Times, Two Home Runs, Game by Pitcher, Season

A. L.—2—Wesley C. Ferrell, Boston, 1934.
Jack E. Harshman, Baltimore, 1958.
Richard E. Donovan, Cleveland, 1962.
N. L.—2—Donald Newcombe, Brooklyn, 1955.
Tony L. Cloninger, Atlanta, 1966.
Richard C. Wise, Philadelphia, 1971.

Most Games, Switch Hitting Home Runs, League

A. L.—10—Mickey C. Mantle, New York, 1955 (2), 1956 (2), 1957, 1958, 1959, 1961, 1962, 1964.
N. L.—3—Charles T. Davis, San Francisco, 1983, 1987 (2).

Most Games, Switch Hitting Home Runs, Season

A. L.—2—Mickey C. Mantle, New York, 1955, 1956.
        Eddie C. Murray, Baltimore, 1982, 1987.
N. L.—2—Kevin C. Bass, Houston, 1987.
        Charles T. Davis, San Francisco, 1987.

Hitting Homers From Both Sides of Plate, Game
(N.L. 24 Times; A.L. 47 Times)

N. L.—August J. Galan, Chicago, June 25, 1937.
    James W. Russell, Boston, June 7, 1948.
    James W. Russell, Brooklyn, July 26, 1950.
    Albert F. Schoendienst, St. Louis, July 8, 1951, second game.
    Maurice M. Wills, Los Angeles, May 30, 1962, first game.
    Ellis N. Burton, Chicago, August 1, 1963.
    Ellis N. Burton, Chicago, September 7, 1964, first game.
    James K. Lefebvre, Los Angeles, May 7, 1966.
    M. Wesley Parker, Los Angeles, June 5, 1966, first game.
    Peter E. Rose, Cincinnati, August 30, 1966.
    Peter E. Rose, Cincinnati, August 2, 1967.
    Ted L. Simmons, St. Louis, April 17, 1975.
    C. Reginald Smith, St. Louis, May 4, 1975.
    C. Reginald Smith, St. Louis, May 22, 1976 (2 RH, 1 LH).
    Lee L. Mazzilli, New York, September 3, 1978.
    Ted L. Simmons, St. Louis, June 11, 1979.
    Alan D. Ashby, Houston, September 27, 1982.
    Charles T. Davis, San Francisco, June 5, 1983.
    J. Mark Bailey, Houston, September 16, 1984.
    Charles T. Davis, San Francisco, June 27, 1987.
    Roberto M.A. Bonilla, Pittsburgh, July 3, 1987.
    Kevin C. Bass, Houston, August 3, 1987; 13 innings.
    Kevin C. Bass, Houston, September 2, 1987.
    Charles T. Davis, San Francisco, September 15, 1987.

A. L.—Walter H. Schang, Philadelphia, September 8, 1916.
    John Lucadello, St. Louis, September 16, 1940.
    Mickey C. Mantle, New York, May 13, 1955 (1 RH, 2 LH).
    Mickey C. Mantle, New York, August 15, 1955, second game.
    Mickey C. Mantle, New York, May 18, 1956.
    Mickey C. Mantle, New York, July 1, 1956, second game.
    Mickey C. Mantle, New York, June 12, 1957.
    Mickey C. Mantle, New York, July 28, 1958.
    Mickey C. Mantle, New York, September 15, 1959.
    Mickey C. Mantle, New York, April 26, 1961.
    Mickey C. Mantle, New York, May 6, 1962, second game.
    Thomas M. Tresh, New York, September 1, 1963.
    Thomas M. Tresh, New York, July 13, 1964.
    Mickey C. Mantle, New York, August 12, 1964.
    Thomas M. Tresh, New York, June 6, 1965, second game (1 RH, 2 LH).
    C. Reginald Smith, Boston, August 20, 1967, first game.
    C. Reginald Smith, Boston, August 11, 1968, second game.
    Donald A. Buford, Baltimore, April 9, 1970.
    Roy H. White, New York, May 7, 1970.
    C. Reginald Smith, Boston, July 2, 1972, first game.
    C. Reginald Smith, Boston, April 16, 1973.
    Roy H. White, New York, August 13, 1973.
    Roy H. White, New York, April 23, 1975.
    Kenneth J. Henderson, Chicago, August 29, 1975.
    Roy H. White, New York, August 18, 1976.
    Eddie C. Murray, Baltimore, August 3, 1977.
    Roy H. White, New York, June 13, 1978.
    Lawrence W. Milbourne, Seattle, July 15, 1978.
    Willie J. Wilson, Kansas City, June 15, 1979.
    Eddie C. Murray, Baltimore, August 29, 1979, second game (2 RH, 1 LH).
    U. L. Washington, Kansas City, September 21, 1979.
    Eddie C. Murray, Baltimore, August 16, 1981.
    Eddie C. Murray, Baltimore, April 24, 1982.
    Ted L. Simmons, Milwaukee, May 2, 1982.
    Eddie C. Murray, Baltimore, August 26, 1982.
    Roy F. Smalley, New York, September 5, 1982.
    Donald M. Scott, Seattle, April 29, 1985.
    Michael D. Young, Baltimore, August 13, 1985.
    Eddie C. Murray, Baltimore, August 26, 1985 (1 RH, 2 LH).
    Nelson B. Simmons, Detroit, September 16, 1985.
    Roy F. Smalley, Minnesota, May 30, 1986.
    Antonio Bernazard, Cleveland, July 1, 1986.
    Ruben A. Sierra, Texas, September 13, 1986.
    Eddie C. Murray, Baltimore, May 8, 1987.
    Eddie C. Murray, Baltimore, May 9, 1987.
    Devon M. White, California, June 23, 1987.
    Dale C. Sveum, Milwaukee, July 17, 1987 (1 RH, 2 LH).

Consecutive & In Consecutive Games

Most Consecutive Home Runs, Game

N. L.—4—Robert L. Lowe, Boston, May 30, 1894, p.m. game.
        Michael J. Schmidt, Philadelphia, April 17, 1976, 10 innings.
A. L.—4—H. Louis Gehrig, New York, June 3, 1932.
        Rocco D. Colavito, Cleveland, June 10, 1959.

Most Consecutive Home Runs, Two Games (*also base on balls)

A. L.—4—James E. Foxx, Philadelphia, June 7 (1), 8 (3), 1933.
        Henry B. Greenberg, Detroit, July 26 (2), 27 (2), 1938.
        Charles R. Maxwell, Detroit, May 3, first game (1), 3, second game (3), 1959.
        Willie C. Kirkland, Cleveland, July 9, second game (3), 13 (1), 1961; also 2 bases on balls and 1 sacrifice hit.
        Mickey C. Mantle, New York, July 4, second game (2), 6 (2), 1962.
        *Bobby R. Murcer, New York, June 24, first game (1), 24, second game (3), 1970.
        Michael P. Epstein, Oakland, June 15 (2), 16 (2), 1971.
        *Don E. Baylor, Baltimore, July 1 (1), 2 (3), 1975.
        Larry D. Herndon, Detroit, May 16 (1), 18 (3), 1982.
N. L.—4—*William B. Nicholson, Chicago, July 22 (1), 23, first game (3), 1944.
        *Ralph M. Kiner, Pittsburgh, August 15 (1), 16 (3), 1947.
        Ralph M. Kiner, Pittsburgh, September 11 (2), 13 (2), 1949.
        *Stanley F. Musial, St. Louis, July 7, second game (1), 8 (3), 1962.
        Arthur L. Shamsky, Cincinnati, August 12 (3), 14 (1), 1966.
        Deron R. Johnson, Philadelphia, July 10, second game (1), 11 (3), 1971.
        Michael J. Schmidt, Philadelphia, July 6 (1), 7 (3), 1979.

Most Consecutive Home Runs, Three Games

A. L.—4—John E. Blanchard, New York, July 21 (1), 22 (1), 26 (2), 1961.
N. L.—Never accomplished.

Most Consecutive Home Runs, Four Games

A. L.—4—Theodore S. Williams, Boston, September 17, 20, 21, 22 1957 (4 bases on balls in streak).
N. L.—Never accomplished.

Most Home Runs, Consecutive At-Bats, Pinch-Hitter

N. L.—3—Leondaus Lacy, Los Angeles, May 2, 6, 17, 1978 (includes 1 base on balls during streak).
        Delbert B. Unser, Philadelphia, June 30, July 5, 10, 1979.
A. L.—2—Raymond B. Caldwell, New York, June 10, 11, 1915.
        Joseph E. Cronin, Boston, June 17, first game, 17, second game, 1943.
        Charles E. Keller, New York, September 12, 14, 1948.
        Delbert Q. Wilber, Boston, May 6, 10, 1953.
        Theodore S. Williams, Boston, September 17, 20, 1957 (includes 1 base on balls during streak).
        John E. Blanchard, New York, July 21, 22, 1961.
        Charles T. Schilling, Boston, April 30, May 1, 1965.
        Raymond H. Barker, New York, June 20, June 22, first game, 1965.
        Curtell H. Motton, Baltimore, May 15, 17, 1968.
        W. Gates Brown, Detroit, August 9, 11, first game, 1968.
        Gary W. Alexander, Cleveland, July 5, 6, 1980.
        Daryl A. Sconiers, California, April 30, May 7, 1983.
        Alejandro Sanchez, Detroit, July 20, 23, 1985.
        R. Randall Bush, Minnesota, June 20, 23, 1986.

Most Consecutive Games Hitting Homer Each Game

N. L.—8—R. Dale Long, Pittsburgh, May 19, 20, first game, 20, second game, 22, 23, 25, 26, 28, 1956, 8 home runs.
A. L.—8—Donald A. Mattingly, New York, July 8 (2), 9, 10, 11, 12, 16 (2), 17, 18, 1987, 10 home runs.

Most Consecutive Games Hitting Homer, Pitcher

N. L.—4—Kenneth A. Brett, Philadelphia, June 9, 13, 18, 23, 1973. (Starting pitcher).
A. L.—2—Held by many pitchers.

Most Home Runs, Two Consecutive Days

A. L.—6—George H. Ruth, New York, May 21 (3), 21 (0), 22 (2), 22 (1), 1930, 4 games.
        Anthony M. Lazzeri, New York, May 23 (1), 23 (2), 24 (3), 1936, 3 games.

N. L.—6—Ralph M. Kiner, Pittsburgh, September 11 (1), 11 (3), 12 (2), 1947, 3 games.

Most Hits, All Home Runs, Consecutive Games

N. L.—6—Frank O. Hurst, Philadelphia, July 28 through August 2, 1929, 6 games.

A. L.—5—Kenneth R. Williams, St. Louis, July 28 through August 1, 1922, 5 games.

Most Home Runs, First Two Major League Games

A. A.—3—Charles T. Reilly, Columbus, October 9 (2), 10 (1), 1889.

N. L.—3—Joseph R. Cunningham, St. Louis, June 30 (1), July 1 (2), 1954.

A. L.—2—H. Earl Averill, Cleveland, April 16 (1), 17 (1), 1929.
Robert C. Nieman, St. Louis, September 14 (2), 15 (0), 1951.
Dagoberto B. Campaneris, Kansas City, July 23 (2), 24 (0), 1964.
Curtis L. Blefary, Baltimore, April 14 (0), 17 (2), 1965.
Joseph H. Lefebvre, New York, May 22 (1), 23 (1), 1980.
David L. Stapleton, Boston, May 30 (0), 31 (1), 1980.
Timothy J. Laudner, Minnesota, August 28 (1), 29 (1), 1981.
Alvin G. Davis, Seattle, April 11 (1), 13 (1), 1984.
Samuel L. Horn, Boston, July 25 (1), 26 (1), 1987.

Most Homers, Two Straight Games, Hitting Homer Each Game

N. L.—5—Adrian C. Anson, Chicago, August 5 (2), 6 (3), 1884.
Ralph M. Kiner, Pittsburgh, August 15 (2), 16 (3), 1947, also September 11 (3), 12 (2), 1947.
Donald F. Mueller, New York, September 1 (3), 2 (2), 1951.
Stanley F. Musial, St. Louis, May 2, first game (3), 2, second game (2), 1954.
Joseph W. Adcock, Milwaukee, July 30 (1), 31 (4), 1954.
Billy L. Williams, Chicago, September 8 (2), 10 (3), 1968.
Nathan Colbert, San Diego, August 1, first game (2), second game (3), 1972.
Michael J. Schmidt, Philadelphia, April 17 (4), 18 (1), 1976.
David A. Kingman, Chicago, July 27, (2), 28 (3), 1979.
Gary E. Carter, New York, September 3 (3), 4 (2), 1985.

A. L.—5—Tyrus R. Cobb, Detroit, May 5 (3), 6 (2), 1925.
Anthony M. Lazzeri, New York, May 23, second game (2), 24 (3), 1936.
Carl M. Yastrzemski, Boston, May 19 (3), 20 (2), 1976.
Mark D. McGwire, Oakland, June 27 (3), 28 (2), 1987.

Most Homers, Three Straight Games, Homering in Each Game

A. L.—6—Anthony M. Lazzeri, New York, May 23 (1), 23 (2), 24 (3), 1936.
Gus E. Zernial, Philadelphia, May 13, second game (2), 15 (2), 16 (2), 1951.

N. L.—6—Ralph M. Kiner, Pittsburgh, August 14 (1), 15 (2), 16 (3), 1947, also September 10 (2), 11 (1), 11 (3), 1947.
Frank J. Thomas, New York, August 1 (2), 2 (2), 3 (2), 1962.
Lee A. May, Cincinnati, May 24 (2), 25 (2), 28 (2), 1969.
Michael J. Schmidt, Philadelphia, April 17 (4), 18 (1), 20 (1), 1976.

Most Homers, Four Straight Games, Homering in Each Game

N. L.—8—Ralph M. Kiner, Pittsburgh, September 10 (2), 11 (1), 11 (3), 12 (2), 1947.

A. L.—7—Anthony M. Lazzeri, New York, May 21 (1), 23 (1), 23 (2), 24 (3), 1936.
Gus E. Zernial, Philadelphia, May 13, second game (2), 15 (2), 16 (2), 17 (1), 1951.
Frank O. Howard, Washington, May 12 (2), 14 (2), 15 (1), 16 (2), 1968.

Hitting Homer in First Four Games of Season

N. L.—4—Willie H. Mays, San Francisco, April 6 (1), 7 (1), 8 (1), 10 (1), 1971.

Most Homers, Five Straight Games, Homering in Each Game

A. L.—8—Frank O. Howard, Washington, May 12 (2), 14 (2), 15 (1), 16 (2), 17 (1), 1968.
Frank O. Howard, Washington, May 14 (2), 15 (1), 16 (2), 17 (1), 18 (2), 1968.

N. L.—7—James L. Bottomley, St. Louis, July 5 (1), 6 (2), 6 (1), 8 (1), 9 (2), 1929.
Johnny L. Bench, Cincinnati, May 30 (2), 31 (1), June 1 (1), 2 (2), 3 (1), 1972.

Michael J. Schmidt, Philadelphia, July 6 (1), 7 (3), 8 (1), 9 (1), 10 (1), 1979.

Most Homers, Six Straight Games, Homering in Each Game

A. L.—10—Frank O. Howard, Washington, May 12 (2), 14 (2), 15, 16 (2), 17, 18 (2), 1968.

N. L.—7—George L. Kelly, New York, July 11, 12 (2), 13, 14, 15, 16, 1924.
W. Walker Cooper, New York, June 22 (2), 23, 24, 25, 27, 28, 1947.
Willie H. Mays, New York, September 14 (2), 16, 17, 18, 20, 20, 1955.
Graig Nettles, San Diego, August 11 (1), 12 (1), 16 (1), 17 (2), 21 (1), 22 (1), 1984.

Most Homers, Seven Straight Games, Homering in Each Game

A. L.—9—Donald A. Mattingly, New York, July 8 (2), 9, 10, 11, 12, 16 (2), 17, 1987.

N. L.—7—R. Dale Long, Pittsburgh, May 19, 20, 20, 22, 23, 25, 26, 1956.

Most Homers, Eight Straight Games, Homering in Each Game

A. L.—10—Donald A. Mattingly, New York July 8 (2), 9, 10, 11, 12, 16 (2), 17, 18, 1987.

N. L.—8—R. Dale Long, Pittsburgh, May 19, 20, 20, 22, 23, 25, 26, 28, 1956.

Grand Slams

Most Grand Slams, League

A. L.—23—H. Louis Gehrig, New York, 17 years, 1923 through 1939.

N. L.—18—Willie L. McCovey, San Francisco, San Diego, 22 years, 1959 through 1980.

Most Grand Slams, Pinch-Hitter, League

N. L.—3—Ronald J. Northey, St. Louis, September 3, 1947; May 30, 1948, second game; Chicago, September 18, 1950.
Willie L. McCovey, San Francisco, June 12, 1960; September 10, 1965; San Diego, May 30, 1975.

A. L.—3—Richard B. Reese, Minnesota, August 3, 1969, June 7, 1970, July 9, 1972.

Most Grand Slams, Season

A. L. (162-game season)—6—Donald A. Mattingly, New York, 141 games, 1987.

A. L. (154-game season)—4—George H. Ruth, Boston, 130 games, 1919.
H. Louis Gehrig, New York, 154 games, 1934.
Rudolph P. York, Detroit, 135 games, 1938.
Thomas D. Henrich, New York, 146 games, 1948.
Albert L. Rosen, Cleveland, 154 games, 1951.
Raymond O. Boone, Cleveland-Detroit, 135 games, 1953.

N. L. (154-game season)—5—Ernest Banks, Chicago, 154 games, 1955.

Most Grand Slams, Pinch-Hitter, Season

N. L.—2—David A. Johnson, Philadelphia, April 30, June 3, 1978.
Michael W. Ivie, San Francisco, May 28, June 30, first game, 1978.

A. L.—1—Held by many pinch-hitters.

Most Grand Slams, One Month

A. L.—3—Rudolph P. York, Detroit, May 16, 22, 30, first game, 1938.
James T. Northrup, Detroit, June 24 (2), 29, 1968.
Larry A. Parrish, Texas, July 4, 7, 10, first game, 1982.

N. L.—3—Eric K. Davis, Cincinnati, May 1, 3, 30, 1987.

Most Grand Slams, One Week (Sunday Through Saturday)

A. L.—3—James T. Northrup, Detroit, June 24 (2), 29, 1968.
(H. Louis Gehrig, New York, hit grand slams on Saturday, August 29, Monday, August 31, Tuesday, September 1, 1931, second game.)
Larry A. Parrish, Texas, July 4, 7, 10, first game, 1982.

N. L.—2—Held by many players. Last player—Eric K. Davis, Cincinnati, May 1, 3, 1987.

Most Grand Slams, Game

A. L.—2—Anthony M. Lazzeri, New York, May 24, 1936, second and fifth innings.

James R. Tabor, Boston, July 4, 1939, second game, third and sixth innings.
Rudolph P. York, Boston, July 27, 1946, second and fifth innings.
James E. Gentile, Baltimore, May 9, 1961, first and second innings.
James T. Northrup, Detroit, June 24, 1968, fifth and sixth innings.
Frank Robinson, Baltimore, June 26, 1970, fifth and sixth innings.
N. L.—2—Tony L. Cloninger, Atlanta, July 3, 1966, first and fourth innings.

Most Grand Slams, Pinch-Hitter, Game
A. L.-N. L.—1—Held by many players.

Most Grand Slams, First Major League Game
N. L.—1—William Duggleby, Philadelphia, April 21, 1898, second inning, on first at-bat.
Bobby L. Bonds, San Francisco, June 25, 1968, sixth inning, on third at-bat.
A. L.—Never accomplished.

Most Grand Slams, Two Straight Games (Connecting Each Game)
N. L.—2—James H. Bannon, Boston, August 6, 7, 1894.
James T. Sheckard, Brooklyn, September 23, 24, 1901.
Philip M. Garner, Pittsburgh, September 14, 15, 1978.
A. L.—2—George H. Ruth, New York, September 27, 29, 1927; also August 6, second game, August 7, first game, 1929.
William M. Dickey, New York, August 3, second game, 4, 1937.
James E. Foxx, Boston, May 20, 21, 1940.
James F. Busby, Cleveland, July 5, 6, 1956.
Brooks C. Robinson, Baltimore, May 6, 9, 1962.
Willie M. Aikens, California, June 13, second game, 14, 1979.
Gregory M. Luzinski, Chicago, June 8, 9, 1984.
Robert G. Deer, Milwaukee, August 19, 20, 1987.

Total Bases
Career & Season

Most Total Bases in Major Leagues
6856—Henry L. Aaron, National League, 6591, Milwaukee, Atlanta, 21 years, 1954 through 1974; American League, 265, 2 years, Milwaukee, 1975, 1976.

Most Total Bases, League
N. L.—6591—Henry L. Aaron, Milwaukee, Atlanta, 21 years, 1954 through 1974.
A. L.—5862—Tyrus R. Cobb, Detroit, Philadelphia, 24 years, 1905 through 1928.

Most Total Bases, Season
A. L.—457—George H. Ruth, New York, 152 games, 1921.
N. L.—450—Rogers Hornsby, St. Louis, 154 games, 1922.

Most Total Bases, Rookie Season
A. L. (154-game season)—374—Harold A. Trosky, Cleveland, 154 games, 1934.
A. L. (162-game season)—374—Pedro Oliva, Minnesota, 161 games, 1964.
N. L. (162-game season)—352—Richard A. Allen, Philadelphia, 162 games, 1964.
N. L. (154-game season)—342—John H. Frederick, Brooklyn, 148 games, 1929.

Most Total Bases, Righthander, Season
N. L.—450—Rogers Hornsby, St. Louis, 154 games, 1922.
A. L.—438—James E. Foxx, Philadelphia, 154 games, 1932.

Most Total Bases, Lefthander, Season
A. L.—457—George H. Ruth, New York, 152 games, 1921.
N. L.—445—Charles H. Klein, Philadelphia, 156 games, 1930.

Most Total Bases, Switch Hitter, Season
A. L.—376—Mickey C. Mantle, New York, 150 games, 1956.
N. L.—369—James A. Collins, St. Louis, 154 games, 1934.

Most Years Leading League in Total Bases
N. L.—8—Henry L. Aaron, Milwaukee, Atlanta, 1956, 1957, 1959, 1960, 1961, 1963, 1967, 1969.
A. L.—6—Tyrus R. Cobb, Detroit, 1907, 1908, 1909, 1911, 1915, 1917.

George H. Ruth, Boston, New York, 1919, 1921, 1923, 1924, 1926, 1928.
Theodore S. Williams, Boston, 1939, 1942, 1946, 1947, 1949, 1951.

Most Consecutive Years Leading League in Total Bases
N. L.—4—John P. Wagner, Pittsburgh, 1906, 1907, 1908, 1909.
Charles H. Klein, Philadelphia, 1930, 1931, 1932, 1933.
A. L.—3—Tyrus R. Cobb, Detroit, 1907, 1908, 1909.
Theodore S. Williams, Boston, 1942, 1946, 1947 (in military service 1943-44-45).
James E. Rice, Boston, 1977, 1978, 1979.

Most Years, 400 or More Total Bases, League
A. L.—5—H. Louis Gehrig, New York, 1927, 1930, 1931, 1934, 1936.
N. L.—3—Charles H. Klein, Philadelphia, 1929, 1930, 1932.

Most Consecutive Years, 400 or More Total Bases, League
A. L.—2—H. Louis Gehrig, New York, 1930, 1931.
James E. Foxx, Philadelphia, 1932, 1933.
N. L.—2—Charles H. Klein, Philadelphia, 1929, 1930.

Most Years, 300 or More Total Bases, League
N. L.—15—Henry L. Aaron, Milwaukee, Atlanta, 1955 through 1971, except 1964, 1970.
A. L.—13—H. Louis Gehrig, New York, 1926 through 1938.

Most Consecutive Years, 300 or More Total Bases, League
A. L.—13—H. Louis Gehrig, New York, 1926 through 1938.
N. L.—13—Willie H. Mays, New York, San Francisco, 1954 through 1966.

Fewest Total Bases, Season, 150 or More Games
N. L.—89—C. Dallan Maxvill, St. Louis, 152 games, 1970.
A. L.—114—Edwin A. Brinkman, Washington, 154 games, 1965.

Fewest Total Bases, Season, for Leader in Total Bases
N. L.—237—John P. Wagner, Pittsburgh, 140 games, 1906.
A. L.—260—George H. Stone, St. Louis, 154 games, 1905.

Game & Inning

Most Total Bases, Game, Nine Innings
N. L.—18—Joseph W. Adcock, Milwaukee, July 31, 1954; 4 home runs, 1 double.
A. L.—16—Tyrus R. Cobb, Detroit, May 5, 1925; 3 home runs, 1 double, 2 singles.
H. Louis Gehrig, New York, June 3, 1932; 4 home runs.
Rocco D. Colavito, Cleveland, June 10, 1959; 4 home runs.
Fredric M. Lynn, Boston, June 18, 1975; 3 home runs, 1 triple, 1 single.

Most Total Bases, Extra-Inning Game, Since 1900
N. L.—17—Michael J. Schmidt, Philadelphia, April 17, 1976, 10 innings; 4 home runs, 1 single.
A. L.—16—James E. Foxx, Philadelphia, July 10, 1932, 18 innings; 3 home runs, 1 double, 2 singles.
James P. Seerey, Chicago, July 18, 1948, first game, 11 innings; 4 home runs.

Most Total Bases by Pitcher, Nine-Inning Game
A. A.—15—Guy J. Hecker, Louisville, August 15, 1886, second game, 3 home runs, 3 singles.
N. L.—12—James Tobin, Boston, May 13, 1942; 3 home runs.
A. L.—10—Lewis D. Wiltse, Philadelphia, August 10, 1901, second game, 2 triples, 2 doubles.
Charles H. Ruffing, New York, June 17, 1936, first game, 2 singles, 2 home runs.
Jack E. Harshman, Baltimore, September 23, 1958, 2 home runs, 1 double.

Most Total Bases by Pitcher, Extra-Inning Game
A. L.—10—George H. Ruth, Boston, May 9, 1918, 10 innings, 1 single, 3 doubles, 1 triple.

Most Total Bases, Doubleheader, Nine-Inning Games
N. L.—22—Nathan Colbert, San Diego, August 1, 1972.
A. L.—21—Albert Oliver, Texas, August 17, 1980.

Most Total Bases, Doubleheader (More Than 18 Innings)
A. L.—21—James E. Foxx, Philadelphia, July 2, 1933, 19 innings.
N. L.—19—Ralph M. Kiner, Pittsburgh, September 11, 1947, 22 innings.

Most Total Bases, Two Consecutive Games
- A. L.—25—Tyrus R. Cobb, Detroit, May 5, 6, 1925.
- N. L.—25—Joseph W. Adcock, Milwaukee, July 30, 31, 1954.

Most Total Bases, Inning
- N. L.-A. L.—8—Held by many players.
- A. L.—Last player—Clifford Johnson, New York, June 30, 1977, eighth inning, 2 home runs.
- N. L.—Last players—Von F. Hayes, Philadelphia, June 11, 1985, first inning and Andre F. Dawson, Montreal, September 24, 1985, fifth inning, 2 home runs apiece.

Long Hits
Career & Season

Most Long Hits in Major Leagues
- 1477—Henry L. Aaron, 1429 in N.L., Milwaukee, Atlanta, 21 years, 1954 through 1974; 48 in A.L., 2 years, Milwaukee, 1975, 1976, 624 doubles, 98 triples, 755 home runs.

Most Long Hits, League
- N. L.— 1429— Henry L. Aaron, Milwaukee, Atlanta, 21 years, 1954 through 1974, 600 doubles, 96 triples, 733 home runs.
- A. L.— 1350— George H. Ruth, Boston, New York, 21 years, 1914 through 1934, 506 doubles, 136 triples, 708 home runs.

Most Long Hits, Season
- A. L.— 119— George H. Ruth, New York, 152 games, 1921; 44 doubles, 16 triples, 59 home runs.
- N. L.— 107— Charles H. Klein, Philadelphia, 156 games, 1930; 59 doubles, 8 triples, 40 home runs.

Most Long Hits, Rookie Season
- A. L.— 89— Harold A. Trosky, Cleveland, 154 games, 1934; 45 doubles, 9 triples, 35 home runs.
- N. L.— 82— John H. Frederick, Brooklyn, 148 games, 1929; 52 doubles, 6 triples, 24 home runs.

Most Long Hits, Righthander, Season
- A. L.— 103— Henry B. Greenberg, Detroit, 154 games, 1937; 49 doubles, 14 triples, 40 home runs.
- N. L.— 102— Rogers Hornsby, St. Louis, 154 games, 1922; 46 doubles, 14 triples, 42 home runs.

Most Long Hits, Lefthander, Season
- A. L.— 119— George H. Ruth, New York, 152 games, 1921; 44 doubles, 16 triples, 59 home runs.
- N. L.— 107— Charles H. Klein, Philadelphia, 156 games, 1930; 59 doubles, 8 triples, 40 home runs.

Most Long Hits, Switch Hitter, Season
- N. L.— 87— James A. Collins, St. Louis, 154 games, 1934.
- A. L.— 79— Mickey C. Mantle, New York, 150 games, 1956.

Most Years Leading League, Doubles, Triples, Homers (Same Season)
- A. A.—1—James E. O'Neill, St. Louis, 123 games, 1887, 46 doubles, 24 triples, 13 home runs. Also led in batting, .492.
- N. L.-A. L.—Never accomplished.

Twenty or More Doubles, Triples and Homers, Season
- N. L.—John F. Freeman, Washington, 155 games, 1899 (20 doubles, 26 triples, 25 home runs).
  - Frank M. Schulte, Chicago, 154 games, 1911 (30 doubles, 21 triples, 21 homers).
  - James L. Bottomley, St. Louis, 149 games, 1928 (42 doubles, 20 triples, 31 homers).
  - Willie H. Mays, New York, 152 games, 1957 (26 doubles, 20 triples, 35 homers).
- A. L.—J. Geoffrey Heath, Cleveland, 151 games, 1941 (32 doubles, 20 triples, 24 homers).
  - George H. Brett, Kansas City, 154 games, 1979 (42 doubles, 20 triples, 23 homers).

Most Years Leading League in Long Hits
- N. L.—7—John P. Wagner, Pittsburgh, 1900, 1902, 1903, 1904, 1907, 1908, 1909.
  - Stanley F. Musial, St. Louis, 1943, 1944, 1946, 1948, 1949, 1950, 1953.
- A. L.—7—George H. Ruth, Boston, New York, 1918, 1919, 1920, 1921, 1923, 1924, 1928.

Most Consecutive Years Leading League in Long Hits
- A. L.—4—George H. Ruth, Boston, New York, 1918, 1919, 1920, 1921.
- N. L.—3—Held by many players. Last player—Edwin D. Snider, Brooklyn, 1954, 1955 (tied), 1956.

Fewest Long Hits, Season, 150 or More Games
- N. L.— 7— C. Dallan Maxvill, St. Louis, 152 games, 1970, 5 doubles, 2 triples.
- A. L.— 11— Michael Tresh, Chicago, 150 games, 1945, 11 doubles.

Fewest Long Hits, Season, for Leader (154-Game Season)
- N. L.— 50— Sherwood R. Magee, Philadelphia, 154 games, 1906; 36 doubles, 8 triples, 6 home runs.
- A. L.— 54— Samuel Crawford, Detroit, 156 games, 1915; 31 doubles, 19 triples, 4 home runs.

Most Consecutive Long Hits, Season
- A. L.—7—Elmer J. Smith, Cleveland, September 4, 5, 5, 1921, 3 doubles, 4 home runs (2 bases on balls in streak).
  - Earl H. Sheely, Chicago, May 20, 21, 1926, 6 doubles, 1 home run (1 sacrifice hit in streak).
- N. L.—5—Held by many players.

Most Consecutive Games, One or More Long Hits, Season
- N. L.— 14— Paul G. Waner, Pittsburgh, June 3 through 19, 1927; 12 doubles, 4 triples, 4 home runs.
- A. L.— 10— Donald A. Mattingly, New York, July 7 through 19, 1987; 4 doubles, 10 home runs.

Game & Inning

Most Long Hits, Game
- A. A.—5—George A. Strief, Philadelphia, June 25, 1885; 4 triples, 1 double, consecutive.
- N. L.—5—George F. Gore, Chicago, July 9, 1885; 2 triples, 3 doubles, consecutive.
  - Lawrence Twitchell, Cleveland, August 15, 1889; 1 double, 3 triples, 1 home run.
  - Joseph W. Adcock, Milwaukee, July 31, 1954; 4 home runs, 1 double, consecutive.
  - Wilver D. Stargell, Pittsburgh, August 1, 1970; 3 doubles, 2 home runs.
  - Steven P. Garvey, Los Angeles, August 28, 1977; 3 doubles, 2 home runs, consecutive.
- A. L.—5—Louis Boudreau, Cleveland, July 14, 1946; first game; 4 doubles, 1 home run.

Most Long Hits, Opening Game of Season
- N. L.—4—George D. Myers, Indianapolis, April 20, 1888; 3 doubles, 1 home run.
  - William J. Herman, Chicago, April 14, 1936; 3 doubles, 1 home run.
  - James R. Greengrass, Cincinnati, April 13, 1954; 4 doubles.
- A. L.—4—Frank Dillon, Detroit, April 25, 1901; 4 doubles.
  - Don E. Baylor, Baltimore, April 6, 1973; 2 doubles, 1 triple, 1 home run.

Most Long Hits by Pitcher, Nine-Inning Game
- A. A.—4—Robert L. Caruthers, St. Louis, August 16, 1886, 2 home runs, 1 triple, 1 double.
- A. L.—4—Lewis D. Wiltse, Philadelphia, August 10, 1901, second game, 2 triples, 2 doubles.
- N. L.—3—Held by many pitchers—Last pitcher—John A. Messersmith, Los Angeles, April 25, 1975, 3 doubles.

Most Long Hits by Pitcher, Extra-Inning Game
- A. L.—4—George H. Ruth, Boston, May 9, 1918, 10 innings, 3 doubles, 1 triple.

Most Times, Four or More Long Hits, Game, League
- A. L.—5—H. Louis Gehrig, New York, 1926, 1928, 1930, 1932, 1934.
  - Joseph P. DiMaggio, New York, 1936, 1937, 1941, 1948, 1950.
- N. L.—4—Wilver D. Stargell, Pittsburgh, 1965, 1968, 1970, 1973.

Most Times, Four Long Hits, Game, Season
- A. A.—2—Henry E. Larkin, Philadelphia, June 16, July 29, 1885.
- A. L.—2—George H. Burns, Cleveland, June 19, first game, July 23, 1924.
  - James E. Foxx, Philadelphia, April 24, July 2, second game, 1933.
- N. L.—2—Joseph M. Medwick, St. Louis, May 12, August 4, 1937.
  - Billy L. Williams, Chicago, April 9, September 5, 1969.

Most Long Hits, Doubleheader, Nine-Inning Games

N. L.—6—Joseph M. Medwick, St. Louis, May 30, 1935, 5 doubles, 1 triple.

Albert F. Schoendienst, St. Louis, June 6, 1948, 5 doubles, 1 home run.

A. L.—6—John T. Stone, Detroit, April 30, 1933, 4 doubles, 2 home runs.

Henry Majeski, Philadelphia, August 27, 1948, 6 doubles.

Harold A. McRae, Kansas City, August 27, 1974, 5 doubles, 1 home run.

Albert Oliver, Texas, August 17, 1980, 1 double, 1 triple, 4 home runs.

Most Long Hits, Doubleheader (More Than 18 Innings)

N. L.—6—Charles J. Hafey, St. Louis, July 28, 1928, 21 innings, 4 doubles, 2 home runs.

Melvin T. Ott, New York, June 19, 1929, 20 innings, 4 doubles, 2 home runs.

James L. Rhodes, New York, 20 innings, August 29, 1954, 2 doubles, 2 triples, 2 home runs (played 12 innings, 7 at-bats).

A. L.—6—James E. Foxx, Philadelphia, July 2, 1933, 19 innings, 1 double, 1 triple, 4 home runs.

Most Long Hits, Two Consecutive Games

N. L.—7—Edward J. Delahanty, Philadelphia, July 13, 14, 1896, 2 doubles, 1 triple, 4 home runs.

Albert F. Schoendienst, St. Louis, June 5, 6, first game, 1948, 6 doubles, 1 home run.

Joseph W. Adcock, Milwaukee, July 30, 31, 1954, 2 doubles, 5 home runs.

A. L.—7—Earl H. Sheely, Chicago, May 20, 21, 1926, 6 doubles, 1 home run.

Most Long Hits, Three Consecutive Games

N. L.—9—Albert Schoendienst, St. Louis, June 5, 6, 6, 1948, 8 doubles, 1 home run.

A. L.—8—Earl H. Sheely, Chicago, May 20, 21, 22, 1926, 7 doubles, 1 home run.

Most Long Hits, Inning

N. L.—3—Thomas E. Burns, Chicago, September 6, 1883, seventh inning, 2 doubles, 1 home run.

A. L.-N. L. since 1900—2—Held by many players.

Most Long Hits, Inning, Pitcher

N. L.—2—Fred Goldsmith, Chicago, September 6, 1883, seventh inning, 2 doubles.

William J. Terry, Chicago, May 19, 1895, third inning, 1 home run, 1 double.

Henry L. Borowy, Chicago, May 5, 1946; first game, seventh inning, 2 doubles.

A. L.—2—Joseph Wood, Boston, July 4, 1913, a.m. game, fourth inning, 2 doubles.

J. Robert Shawkey, New York, July 12, 1923, third inning, 1 triple, 1 double.

Theodore A. Lyons, Chicago, July 28, 1935, first game, second inning, 2 doubles.

Extra Bases On Long Hits

Most Extra Bases on Long Hits, in Major Leagues

3085—Henry L. Aaron, 2991 in N. L., Milwaukee, Atlanta, 21 years, 1954 through 1974; 94 in A. L., Milwaukee, 2 years, 1975, 1976.

Most Extra Bases on Long Hits, League

N. L.—2991—Henry L. Aaron, Milwaukee, Atlanta, 21 years, 1954 through 1974.

A. L.—2902—George H. Ruth, Boston, New York, 21 years, 1914 through 1934.

Most Extra Bases on Long Hits, Season

A. L.—253—George H. Ruth, New York, 152 games, 1921.

N. L.—215—Lewis R. Wilson, Chicago, 155 games, 1930.

Most Extra Bases on Long Hits, Rookie Season

A. L.—183—Mark D. McGwire, Oakland, 151 games, 1987.

N. L.—169—Walter A. Berger, Boston, 151 games, 1930.

Most Extra Bases on Long Hits, Righthander, Season

A. L.—225—James E. Foxx, Philadelphia, 154 games, 1932.

N. L.—215—Lewis R. Wilson, Chicago, 155 games, 1930.

Most Extra Bases on Long Hits, Lefthander, Season

A. L.—253—George H. Ruth, New York, 152 games, 1921.

N. L.—199—Stanley F. Musial, St. Louis, 155 games, 1948.

Most Extra Bases on Long Hits, Switch Hitter, Season

A. L.—190—Mickey C. Mantle, New York, 153 games, 1961.

N. L.—169—James A. Collins, St. Louis, 154 games, 1934.

Most Years Leading League in Extra Bases on Long Hits

A. L.—9—George H. Ruth, Boston, New York, 1918, 1919, 1920, 1921, 1923, 1924, 1926, 1928, 1929.

N. L.—7—Michael J. Schmidt, Philadelphia, 1974, 1975, 1976, 1980, 1981, 1982, 1986.

Most Consec. Years Leading League, Extra Bases on Long Hits

A. L.—4—George H. Ruth, Boston, New York, 1918, 1919, 1920, 1921.

N. L.—3—Held by many players.

Last player—Michael J. Schmidt, Philadelphia, 1980, 1981, 1982.

Most Years 200 or More Extra Bases on Long Hits

A. L.—4—George H. Ruth, New York, 1920, 1921, 1927, 1928.

N. L.—1—Rogers Hornsby, St. Louis, 1922.

Lewis R. Wilson, Chicago, 1930.

Most Consecutive Years 200 or More Extra Bases on Long Hits

A. L.—2—George H. Ruth, New York, 1920, 1921, also 1927, 1928.

N. L.—No player with 2 consecutive years.

Most Years 100 or More Extra Bases on Long Hits

N. L.—19—Henry L. Aaron, Milwaukee, Atlanta, 1955 through 1973.

A. L.—16—Theodore S. Williams, Boston, 1939, 1940, 1941, 1942, 1946, 1947, 1948, 1949, 1950, 1951, 1954, 1955, 1956, 1957, 1958, 1960.

Most Consecutive Years 100 or More Extra Bases on Long Hits

N. L.—19—Henry L. Aaron, Milwaukee, Atlanta, 1955 through 1973.

A. L.—15—Theodore S. Williams, Boston, 1939, 1940, 1941, 1942 (in military service, 1943, 1944, 1945), 1946, 1947, 1948, 1949, 1950, 1951 (in military service, most of seasons, 1952, 1953), 1954, 1955, 1956, 1957, 1958.

14—H. Louis Gehrig, New York, 1925 through 1938.

Fewest Extra Bases on Long Hits, Season, 150 or More Games

N. L.—9—C. Dallan Maxvill, St. Louis, 152 games, 1970.

A. L.—11—Michael Tresh, Chicago, 150 games, 1945.

Fewest Extra Bases on Long Hits, Season, for Leader

N. L.—74—Harry G. Lumley, Brooklyn, 131 games, 1906.

John P. Wagner, Pittsburgh, 137 games, 1909.

A. L.—80—Samuel Crawford, Detroit, 144 games, 1907.

Most Extra Bases on Long Hits, Nine-Inning Game

N. L.—13—Joseph W. Adcock, Milwaukee, July 31, 1954; 4 home runs, 1 double.

A. L.—12—H. Louis Gehrig, New York, June 3, 1932; 4 home runs.

Rocco D. Colavito, Cleveland, June 10, 1959; 4 home runs.

Most Extra Bases on Long Hits, Extra-Inning Game

N. L.—12—Charles H. Klein, Philadelphia, July 10, 1936, 10 innings; 4 home runs.

Michael J. Schmidt, Philadelphia, April 17, 1976, 10 innings; 4 home runs.

A. L.—12—J. Patrick Seerey, Chicago, July 18, 1948, first game, 11 innings; 4 home runs.

Most Extra Bases on Long Hits, Doubleheader, 18 Innings

N. L.—15—Stanley F. Musial, St. Louis, May 2, 1954.

Nathan Colbert, San Diego, August 1, 1972.

A. L.—15—Albert Oliver, Texas, August 17, 1980.

Most Extra Bases on Long Hits, Doubleheader, Over 18 Innings

A. L.—15—James E. Foxx, Philadelphia, July 2, 1933, 19 innings.

N. L.—13—Ralph M. Kiner, Pittsburgh, September 11, 1947, 22 innings.

Most Extra Bases on Long Hits, Two Consecutive Games

A. L.—17—Anthony M. Lazzeri, New York, May 23, second game, May 24, 1936; 5 home runs, 1 triple

N. L.—17—Joseph W. Adcock, Milwaukee, July 30, July 31, 1954; 5 home runs, 2 doubles.

Most Extra Bases on Long Hits, Inning

N. L.-A. L.—6—Held by many players.

Runs Batted In
Career & Season

Most Runs Batted In, Major Leagues

2297—Henry L. Aaron, 2202 in N. L., Milwaukee, Atlanta, 21 years, 1954 through 1974; 95 in A. L., Milwaukee, 2 years, 1975, 1976.

Most Runs Batted In, League

N. L.— 2202—Henry L. Aaron, Milwaukee, Atlanta, 21 years, 1954 through 1974.

A. L.— 2192—George H. Ruth, Boston, New York, 21 years, 1914 through 1934.

Most Runs Batted In, Season

N. L.— 190— Lewis R. Wilson, Chicago, 155 games, 1930.

A. L.— 184— H. Louis Gehrig, New York, 155 games, 1931.

Most Runs Batted In, Rookie Season

A. L.— 145— Theodore S. Williams, Boston, 149 games, 1939.

N. L.— 119— Walter A. Berger, Boston, 151 games, 1930.

Most Runs Batted In, Righthander, Season

N. L.— 190— Lewis R. Wilson, Chicago, 155 games, 1930.

A. L.— 183— Henry B. Greenberg, Detroit, 154 games, 1937.

Most Runs Batted In, Lefthander, Season

A. L.— 184— H. Louis Gehrig, New York, 155 games, 1931.

N. L.— 170— Charles H. Klein, Philadelphia, 156 games, 1930.

Most Runs Batted In, Switch Hitter, Season

A. L.— 130— Mickey C. Mantle, New York, 150 games, 1956.

N. L.— 128— James A. Collins, St. Louis, 154 games, 1934.

Most Runs Batted In, Season, Catcher

N. L.— 142— Roy Campanella, Brooklyn, 144 games, 1953; caught 140 games.

A. L.— 133— William M. Dickey, New York, 140 games, 1937; caught 137 games.

Most Years Leading League, Runs Batted In

A. L.—6—George H. Ruth, Boston, New York, 1919, 1920, 1921, 1923, 1926, 1928 (tied).

N. L.—4—Rogers Hornsby, St. Louis, 1920 (tied), 1921, 1922, 1925. Henry L. Aaron, Milwaukee, Atlanta, 1957, 1960, 1963, 1966. Michael J. Schmidt, Philadelphia, 1980, 1981, 1984 (tied), 1986.

Most Consecutive Years Leading League, Runs Batted In

A. L.—3—Tyrus R. Cobb, Detroit, 1907, 1908, 1909. George H. Ruth, Boston, New York, 1919, 1920, 1921.

N. L.—3—John P. Wagner, Pittsburgh, 1907, 1908, 1909. Rogers Hornsby, St. Louis, 1920 (tied), 1921, 1922. Joseph M. Medwick, St. Louis, 1936, 1937, 1938. George A. Foster, Cincinnati, 1976, 1977, 1978.

Most Years, 100 or More Runs Batted In

A. L.—13—George H. Ruth, Boston, New York, 1919 through 1933, except 1922 and 1925. H. Louis Gehrig, New York, 1926 through 1938. James E. Foxx, Philadelphia, Boston, 1929 through 1941.

N. L.—11—Henry L. Aaron, Milwaukee, Atlanta, 1955, 1957, 1959, 1960, 1961, 1962, 1963, 1966, 1967, 1970, 1971.

Most Consecutive Years, 100 or More Runs Batted In, League

A. L.—13—H. Louis Gehrig, New York, 1926 through 1938. James E. Foxx, Philadelphia, Boston, 1929 through 1941.

N. L.— 8—Melvin T. Ott, New York, 1929 through 1936. Willie H. Mays, San Francisco, 1959 through 1966.

Most Years, 150 or More Runs Batted In, League

A. L.—7—H. Louis Gehrig, New York, 1927, 1930, 1931, 1932, 1934, 1936, 1937.

N. L.—2—Lewis R. Wilson, Chicago, 1929, 1930.

Most Consecutive Years, 150 or More Runs Batted In

A. L.—3—George H. Ruth, New York, 1929, 1930, 1931. H. Louis Gehrig, New York, 1930, 1931, 1932.

N. L.—2—Lewis R. Wilson, Chicago, 1929, 1930.

Fewest Runs Batted In, Season, 150 or More Games

N. L.—20—Richie Ashburn, Philadelphia, 153 games, 1959.

A. L.—23—Owen Bush, Detroit, 157 games, 1914.

Fewest Runs Batted In, Season, for Leader in RBIs (Since 1920)

N. L.— 94— George L. Kelly, New York, 155 games, 1920. Rogers Hornsby, St. Louis, 149 games, 1920.

A. L.— 105— Albert L. Rosen, Cleveland, 148 games, 1952.

Most Consecutive Games, Season, One or More Runs Batted In

N. L.— 17— Oscar R. Grimes, Chicago, June 27 through July 23, 1922; 27 runs batted in.

A. L.— 13— Taft S. Wright, Chicago, May 4 through May 20, 1941; 22 runs batted in.

Game & Inning

Most Runs Batted In, Game

N. L.— 12— James L. Bottomley, St. Louis, September 16, 1924.

A. L.— 11— Anthony M. Lazzeri, New York, May 24, 1936.

Most Runs Batted In, Game, Pitcher

N. L.—9—Henry E. Staley, Boston, June 1, 1893.* Tony L. Cloninger, Atlanta, July 3, 1966.

A. L.—7—Victor J. Raschi, New York, August 4, 1953.

*RBIs not officially adopted until 1920.

Batting In All Club's Runs, Game (Most)

N. L.—8—George L. Kelly, New York vs. Cincinnati, June 14, 1924; New York won, 8 to 6.

A. L.—8—Robert L. Johnson, Philadelphia vs. St. Louis, June 12, 1938; Philadelphia won, 8-3.

Most Runs Batted In, Two Consecutive Games

A. L.— 15— Anthony M. Lazzeri, New York, May 23, second game (4), May 24, (11) 1936.

N. L.— 13— Nathan Colbert, San Diego, August 1, first game (5), August 1, second game (8), 1972.

Most Runs Batted In, Doubleheader

N. L.— 13— Nathan Colbert, San Diego, August 1, 1972.

A. L.— 11— H. Earl Averill, Cleveland, September 17, 1930, 17 innings. James R. Tabor, Boston, July 4, 1939, 18 innings. John W. Powell, Baltimore, July 6, 1966, 20 innings.

Most Runs Batted In, Inning

A.A.—7—Edward Cartwright, St. Louis, September 23, 1890, third inning.*

N. L.—6—Fred C. Merkle, New York, May 13, 1911, first inning*. James R. Hart, San Francisco, July 8, 1970, fifth inning. Andre F. Dawson, Montreal, September 24, 1985, fifth inning.

A. L.—6—Robert L. Johnson, Philadelphia, August 29, 1937, first game, first inning. Thomas R. McBride, Boston, August 4, 1945, second game, fourth inning. Joseph H. Astroth, Philadelphia, September 23, 1950, sixth inning. Gilbert J. McDougald, New York, May 3, 1951, ninth inning. Sabath A. Mele, Chicago, June 10, 1952, fourth inning. James R. Lemon, Washington, September 5, 1959, third inning.

*RBIs not officially adopted until 1920.

Most Runs Batted In, Two Consecutive Innings

A. L.—8—James E. Gentile, Baltimore, May 9, 1961, first and second innings. James T. Northrup, Detroit, June 24, 1968, fifth and sixth innings. Frank Robinson, Baltimore, June 26, 1970, fifth and sixth innings.

N. L.—7—Charles A. Nichols, Boston, September 19, 1892, fifth and sixth innings. Anthony Piet, Pittsburgh, July 28, 1932, second game, second and third innings. John J. Rucker, New York, September 29, 1940, second and third innings. Delmer Ennis, Philadelphia, July 27, 1950, seventh and eighth innings. C. Earl Torgeson, Boston, June 30, 1951, seventh and eighth innings. Ralph M. Kiner, Pittsburgh, July 4, 1951, second game, third and fourth innings. Joe L. Morgan, Cincinnati, August 19, 1974, second and third innings.

Most Runners Left on Base, Game

N. L.— 12—Glenn A. Beckert, Chicago, September 16, 1972.
A. L.— 11—W. Frank Isbell, Chicago, August 10, 1901.
John A. Donahue, Chicago, June 23, 1907, 12 innings.
George D. Wright, Texas, August 12, 1984, 11 innings.

Game-Winning RBIs

Most Game-Winning RBIs, League (Since 1980)

N. L.— 120— Keith Hernandez, St. Louis, New York, 1980 through 1987.
A. L.— 109— Eddie C. Murray, Baltimore, 1980 through 1987.

Most Game-Winning RBIs, Season (Since 1980)

N. L.—24—Keith Hernandez, New York, 158 games, 1985.
A. L.—22—Harold D. Baines, Chicago, 156 games, 1983.

Most Game-Winning RBIs, Season, by Pitcher (Since 1980)

N. L.—3—Richard K. Mahler, Atlanta, 39 games, 1985.
Richard A. Rhoden, Pittsburgh, 35 games, 1985.
A. L.—Never accomplished.

Most Game-Winning RBIs, Rookie Season (Since 1980)

A. L.— 14— Jose Canseco, Oakland, 157 games, 1986.
Wallace K. Joyner, California, 154 games, 1986.
Mark D. McGwire, Oakland, 151 games, 1987.
N. L.— 13— Juan M. Samuel, Philadelphia, 160 games, 1984.
Darryl E. Strawberry, New York, 122 games, 1983.

Fewest Game-Winning RBIs, Season, 150 Games (Since 1980)

N. L.—0—Alan A. Wiggins, San Diego, 158 games, 1984.
A. L.—1—Joaquin F. Gutierrez, Boston, 151 games, 1984.
K. Anthony Phillips, Oakland, 154 games, 1984.
Stephen P. Lombardozzi, Minnesota, 156 games, 1986.

Most Game-Winning RBIs, Doubleheader (Since 1980)

N. L.-A. L.—2—Held by many players.

Most Consecutive Games With G-W RBI, Season (Since 1980)

A. L.—5—Kirk H. Gibson, Detroit, July 13 through 20, 1986.
N. L.—4—Johnny C. Ray, Pittsburgh, September 18 through 21, 1984.
Milton B. Thompson, Philadelphia, August 19 through 21, second game, 1987.

Most Consecutive Victories With G-W RBI, Season (Since 1980)

N. L.—6—Johnny C. Ray, Pittsburgh, September 13 through 21, 1984, 2 losses in streak.
A. L.—5—Kirk H. Gibson, Detroit, July 13 through 20, 1986, no losses in streak.

Bases On Balls

Most Bases on Balls in Major Leagues

2056—George H. Ruth, Boston A. L., New York A. L., Boston N. L., 22 years, 1914 through 1935; 2036 in A. L., 20 in N. L..

Most Bases on Balls, League

A. L.— 2036— George H. Ruth, Boston, New York, 21 years, 1914 through 1934.
N. L.— 1799— Joe L. Morgan, Houston, Cincinnati, San Francisco, Philadelphia, 21 years, 1963 through 1983.

Most Bases on Balls, Season

A. L.— 170— George H. Ruth, New York, 152 games, 1923.
N. L.— 148— Edward R. Stanky, Brooklyn, 153 games, 1945.
James S. Wynn, Houston, 149 games, 1969.

Most Bases on Balls, Rookie Season

A. L.— 107— Theodore S. Williams, Boston, 149 games, 1939.
N. L.— 100— James Gilliam, Brooklyn, 151 games, 1953.

Most Bases on Balls, Righthander, Season

A. L.— 151— Edward F. Yost, Washington, 152 games, 1956.
N. L.— 148— Edward R. Stanky, Brooklyn, 153 games, 1945.
James S. Wynn, Houston, 149 games, 1969.

Most Bases on Balls, Lefthander, Season

A. L.— 170— George H. Ruth, New York, 152 games, 1923.
N. L.— 147— James T. Sheckard, Chicago, 156 games, 1911.

Most Bases on Balls, Switch Hitter, Season

A. L.— 146— Mickey C. Mantle, New York, 144 games, 1957.
N. L.— 116— Miller J. Huggins, St. Louis, 151 games, 1910.

Most Bases on Balls, Season, Pinch-Hitter

A. L.— 18— Elmer W. Valo, New York, Washington, 81 games, 1960.
N. L.— 16— Harry H. McCurdy, Philadelphia, 71 games, 1933.
Mervin W. Rettenmund, San Diego, 86 games, 1977.

Most Years Leading League in Bases on Balls

A. L.— 11—George H. Ruth, New York, 1920, 1921, 1923, 1924, 1926, 1927, 1928, 1930, 1931, 1932, 1933.
N. L.— 6— Melvin T. Ott, New York, 1929, 1931, 1932, 1933, 1937, 1942.

Most Consecutive Years Leading in Bases on Balls

A. L.—6—Theodore S. Williams, Boston, 1941, 1942, 1946, 1947, 1948, 1949 (except 1943, 1944, 1945, in military service) .
N. L.— 3— George J. Burns, New York, 1919, 1920, 1921.
Melvin T. Ott, New York, 1931, 1932, 1933.
J. Floyd Vaughan, Pittsburgh, 1934, 1935, 1936.
Edwin L. Mathews, Milwaukee, 1961, 1962, 1963.
Ronald E. Santo, Chicago, 1966, 1967, 1968.
Michael J. Schmidt, Philadelphia, 1981, 1982, 1983.

Most Years, 100 or More Bases on Balls, League

A. L.— 13—George H. Ruth, Boston, New York, 1919, 1920, 1921, 1923, 1924, 1926, 1927, 1928, 1930, 1931, 1932, 1933, 1934.
N. L.— 10— Melvin T. Ott, New York, 1929, 1930, 1932, 1936, 1937, 1938, 1939, 1940, 1941, 1942.

Most Consecutive Years 100 or More Bases on Balls, League

N. L.—7—Melvin T. Ott, New York, 1936 through 1942.
A. L.—6—Theodore S. Williams, Boston, 1941 through 1949 (except 1943-44-45 in military service) .
Edwin D. Joost, Philadelphia, 1947 through 1952.

Fewest Bases on Balls, Season, 150 or More Games

N. L.— 12—Harold C. Lanier, San Francisco, 151 games, 1968.
A. L.— 12—Oswaldo J. Guillen, Chicago, 150 games, 1985.
Oswaldo J. Guillen, Chicago, 159 games, 1986.

Fewest Bases on Balls, Season, Leader in Bases on Balls

N. L.— 69—Lewis R. Wilson, Chicago, 142 games, 1926.
A. L.— 89—Lawton W. Witt, New York, 140 games, 1922.

Most Consecutive Bases on Balls, During Season

A. L.—7—William G. Rogell, Detroit, August 17, second game, August 18, August 19, first game, 1938.
N. L.— 7— Melvin T. Ott, New York, June 16, 17, 18, 1943.
Edward R. Stanky, New York, August 29, 30, 1950.

Most Consecutive Games, Season, One or More Bases on Balls

A. L.— 22— Roy J. Cullenbine, Detroit, July 2 through July 22, 1947, 34 bases on balls.
N. L.— 16— Jack A. Clark, St. Louis, July 18 through August 10, 1987, 28 bases on balls.
A. A.— 16— William H. Robinson, St. Louis, September 15 through October 2, 1888, 23 bases on balls.

Most Bases on Balls, Game

N. L.—6—Walter Wilmot, Chicago, August 22, 1891 (consecutive) .
A. L.—6—James E. Foxx, Boston, June 16, 1938 (consecutive) .
Andre Thornton, Cleveland, May 2, 1984, 16 innings.
N. L. since 1900—5—Held by many players.
N. L.—Last Player—Dale B. Murphy, Atlanta, May 23, 1987, 16 innings.

Most Bases on Balls, Game, Pitcher

A. A.—4—Joseph Miller, Philadelphia, September 13, 1886.
A. L.—4—Urban C. Faber, Chicago, June 18, 1915, consecutive.
Charles K. Stobbs, Boston, June 8, 1950, consecutive.
N. L.—3—Held by many pitchers.

Most Bases on Balls, First Major League Game

A. L.—4—Otto H. Saltzgaver, New York, April 12, 1932.
Milton Galatzer, Cleveland, June 25, 1933, first game.
N. L.—3—Held by many players.

Most Times Five Bases on Balls, Game, League

N. L.—4—Melvin T. Ott, New York, 1929, 1933, 1943, 1944.
A. L.—2—Max F. Bishop, Philadelphia, 1929, 1930.

30

Most Bases on Balls, Doubleheader

A. L.—8—Max Bishop, Philadelphia, May 21, 1930; Boston, July 8, 1934.

N. L.—6—Melvin T. Ott, New York, October 5, 1929.
John R. Mize, St. Louis, August 26, 1939.
Melvin T. Ott, New York, April 30, 1944.
Clayton E. Dalrymple, Philadelphia, July 4, 1967, 19 innings.
Cleon J. Jones, New York, June 25, 1971.
Jack A. Clark, St. Louis, July 8, 1987, 19 innings

Most Bases on Balls, Inning

N. L.-A. L.—2—Held by many players.

Most Times Two Bases on Balls, Inning, League

A. L.—4—George A. Selkirk, New York, 1936 (2), 1938, 1940.
N. L.—2—Edward R. Stanky, New York, 1950 (2).

Most Times Two Bases on Balls, Inning, Season

A. L.—2—George A. Selkirk, New York, June 24, August 28, second game, 1936.
James L. Webb, Chicago, July 30, September 3, 1940.
N. L.—2—Edward R. Stanky, New York, June 27, August 22, 1950.

Intentional

Most Intentional Bases on Balls in Major Leagues, Since 1955

293—Henry L. Aaron, 289 in N. L., Milwaukee, Atlanta, 20 years, 1955 through 1974; 4 in A. L., Milwaukee, 2 years, 1975, 1976.

Most Intentional Bases on Balls, League, Since 1955

N. L.—289—Henry L. Aaron, Milwaukee, Atlanta, 20 years, 1955 through 1974.
A. L.—190—Carl M. Yastrzemski, Boston, 23 years, 1961 through 1983.

Most Intentional Bases on Balls, Season, Since 1955

N. L.—45—Willie L. McCovey, San Francisco, 149 games, 1969.
A. L.—33—Theodore S. Williams, Boston, 132 games, 1957.

Most Intentional Bases on Balls, Rookie Season, Since 1955

A. L.—16—Alvin G. Davis, Seattle, 152 games, 1984.
N. L.—14—Guillermo N. Montanez, Philadelphia, 158 games, 1971.

Most Intentional Bases on Balls, Season, Righthander, Since 1955

N. L.—29—Adolfo E. Phillips, Chicago, 144 games, 1967.
Dale B. Murphy, Atlanta, 159 games, 1987.
A. L.—29—Frank O. Howard, Washington, 161 games, 1970.

Most Intentional Bases on Balls, Lefthander, Season, Since 1955

N. L.—45—Willie L. McCovey, San Francisco, 149 games, 1969.
A. L.—33—Theodore S. Williams, Boston, 132 games, 1957.

Most Intentional Bases on Balls, Switch Hitter, Season, Since 1955

N. L.—26—Timothy Raines, Montreal; 139 games, 1987.
A. L.—25—Eddie C. Murray, Baltimore, 162 games, 1984.

Most Years Leading League in Intentional Walks, Since 1955

N. L.—4—Frank Robinson, Cincinnati, 1961, 1962 (tied), 1963, 1964.
Willie L. McCovey, San Francisco, 1969, 1970, 1971 (tied), 1973.
A. L.—3—Theodore S. Williams, Boston, 1955, 1956, 1957.
Harmon C. Killebrew, Minnesota, 1966, 1967 (tied), 1969 (tied).
Rodney C. Carew, Minnesota, 1975, 1977, 1978.

Most Consec. Years Leading League in Int. Walks, Since 1955

N. L.—4—Frank Robinson, Cincinnati, 1961, 1962 (tied), 1963, 1964.
A. L.—3—Theodore S. Williams, Boston, 1955, 1956, 1957.

Most Years, 10 or More Intentional Bases on Balls

N. L.—16—Henry L. Aaron, Milwaukee, Atlanta, 1957 through 1973, except 1964.
A. L.—9—Pedro Oliva, Minnesota, 1965 through 1975, except 1971, 1972.

Fewest Intentional Bases on Balls, Season, Most At-Bats

A. L.—0—Kirby Puckett, Minnesota, 161 games, 1985; 691 at-bats.
N. L.—0—Lawrence R. Bowa, Philadelphia, 162 games, 1974; 669 at-bats.

Most Intentional Bases on Balls, Game

N. L.—4—Garry L. Templeton, San Diego, July 5, 1985, 12 innings.
A. L.—4—Roger E. Maris, New York, May 22, 1962, 12 innings.

Strikeouts
Career & Season

Most Strikeouts, League

A. L.—2597—Reginald M. Jackson, Kansas City, Oakland, Baltimore, New York, California, 21 years, 1967 through 1987.
N. L.—1936—Wilver D. Stargell, Pittsburgh, 21 years, 1962 through 1982.

Fewest Strikeouts, League, 14 or More Seasons, Except Pitchers

A. L.—113—Joseph W. Sewell, Cleveland, New York, 14 years, 1903 games, 1920 through 1933.
N. L.—173—Lloyd J. Waner, Pittsburgh, Boston, Cincinnati, Philadelphia, Brooklyn, 18 years, 1993 games, 1927 through 1945, except 1943.

Most Strikeouts, Season

N. L. (162-game season)—189—Bobby L. Bonds, San Francisco, 157 games, 1970.
A. L. (162-game season)—186—Robert G. Deer, Milwaukee, 134 games, 1987.
A. L. (154-game season)—138—James R. Lemon, Washington, 146 games, 1956.
N. L. (154-game season)—136—J. Francisco Herrera, Philadelphia, 145 games, 1960.

Most Strikeouts, Rookie Season

A. L. (162-game season)—185—Peter J. Incaviglia, Texas, 153 games, 1986.
A. L. (154-game season)—101—Robert J. Hoover, Detroit, 144 games, 1943.
N. L. (162-game season)—168—Juan M. Samuel, Philadelphia, 160 games, 1984.
N. L. (154-game season)—115—Edwin L. Mathews, Boston, 145 games, 1952.

Most Strikeouts, Righthander, Season

N. L. (162-game season)—189—Bobby L. Bonds, San Francisco, 157 games, 1970.
A. L. (162-game season)—186—Robert G. Deer, Milwaukee, 134 games, 1987.
A. L. (154-game season)—138—James R. Lemon, Washington, 146 games, 1956.
N. L. (154-game season)—136—J. Francisco Herrera, Philadelphia, 145 games, 1960.

Most Strikeouts, Lefthander, Season

A. L. (162-game season)—171—Reginald M. Jackson, Oakland, 154 games, 1968.
A. L. (154-game season)—121—Lawrence E. Doby, Cleveland, 149 games, 1953.
N. L. (162-game season)—154—Wilver D. Stargell, Pittsburgh, 141 games, 1971.
N. L. (154-game season)—115—Edwin L. Mathews, Boston, 145 games, 1952.

Most Strikeouts, Switch Hitter, Season

A. L. (162-game season)—135—Devon M. White, California, 159 games, 1987.
A. L. (154-game season)—126—Mickey C. Mantle, New York, 144 games, 1959.
N. L. (162-game season)—126—Vincent M. Coleman, St. Louis, 151 games, 1987.
N. L. (154-game season)—112—Samuel Jethroe, Boston, 151 games, 1952.

Most Strikeouts by Pitcher, Season, Since 1900

A. L.—65—Wilbur F. Wood, Chicago, 49 games, 1972.
N. L.—62—Jerry M. Koosman, New York, 35 games, 1968.

Most Years Leading League in Strikeouts

A. L.—7—James E. Foxx, Philadelphia, Boston, 1929, 1930 (tied), 1931, 1933, 1935, 1936, 1941.
N. L.—6—Vincent P. DiMaggio, Boston, Pittsburgh, Philadelphia, 1937, 1938, 1942, 1943, 1944, 1945.

Most Consecutive Years Leading League in Strikeouts

N. L.—4—Lewis R. Wilson, Chicago, 1927 through 1930.
Vincent P. DiMaggio, Pittsburgh, Philadelphia, 1942 through 1945.
Juan M. Samuel, Philadelphia, 1984 through 1987.
A. L.—4—Reginald M. Jackson, Oakland, 1968 through 1971.

Most Years, 100 or More Strikeouts, League

A. L.— 18—Reginald M. Jackson, Oakland, Baltimore, New York, California, 1968 through 1980, 1982 through 1986.

N. L.— 13— Wilver D. Stargell, Pittsburgh, 1965 through 1976, 1979.

Most Consecutive Years, 100 or More Strikeouts, League

A. L.— 13—Reginald M. Jackson, Oakland, Baltimore, New York, 1968 through 1980.

N. L.— 12—Wilver D. Stargell, Pittsburgh, 1965 through 1976.

Fewest Strikeouts, Season, 150 or More Games

A. L.— 4—Joseph W. Sewell, Cleveland, 155 games, 1925; 152 games, 1929.

N. L.— 5—Charles J. Hollocher, Chicago, 152 games, 1922.

Fewest Strikeouts, Rookie Season, 150 or More Games

N. L.— 17—John A. Hassett, Brooklyn, 156 games, 1936.

A. L.— 25—Thomas Oliver, Boston, 154 games, 1930.

Fewest Strikeouts, Righthander, Season, 150 or More Games

N. L.— 8—Emil M. Verban, Philadelphia, 155 games, 1947.

A. L.— 9—John P. McInnis, Boston, 152 games, 1921.
Louis Boudreau, Cleveland, 152 games, 1948.

Fewest Strikeouts, Lefthander, Season, 150 or More Games

A. L.— 4—Joseph W. Sewell, Cleveland, 155 games, 1925; 152 games, 1929.

N. L.— 5—Charles J. Hollocher, Chicago, 152 games, 1922.

Fewest Strikeouts, Switch Hitter, Season, 150 Games

N. L.— 10—Frank F. Frisch, St. Louis, 153 games, 1927.

A. L.— 23—George D. Weaver, Chicago, 151 games, 1920.

Fewest Strikeouts, Season, for Leader in Most Strikeouts

N. L.— 63—George F. Grantham, Chicago, 127 games, 1924.

A. L.— 66—James E. Foxx, Philadelphia, 153 games, 1930.
Edward Morgan, Cleveland, 150 games, 1930.

Most Years Leading League in Fewest Strikeouts, 150 Games

A. L.— 11—J. Nelson Fox, Chicago, 1952 through 1962.

N. L.— 4—Stanley F. Musial, St. Louis, 1943, 1948, 1952, 1956 (tied).
Richard M. Groat, Pittsburgh, St. Louis, 1955, 1958, 1964, 1965 (tied).

Most Consecutive Games, Season, No Strikeouts

A. L.— 115—Joseph W. Sewell, Cleveland, May 17 through September 19, 1929, 437 at-bats.

N. L.— 77—Lloyd J. Waner, Pittsburgh, Boston, Cincinnati, April 24 through September 16, 1941, 219 at-bats.

Game & Inning

Most Strikeouts, Game, Nine Innings (*Consecutive)

N. L.—5—Oscar Walker, Buffalo, June 20, 1879*.
Henry Dowling, Louisville, August 15, 1899*.
L. Floyd Young, Pittsburgh, September 29, 1935, second game*.
Robert Sadowski, Milwaukee, April 20, 1964*.
Richard A. Allen, Philadelphia, June 28, 1964, first game*.
Ronald A. Swoboda, New York, June 22, 1969, first game*.
Steve E. Whitaker, San Francisco, April 14, 1970*.
Richard A. Allen, St. Louis, May 24, 1970*.
William E. Russell, Los Angeles, June 9, 1971*.
Jose M. Mangual, Montreal, August 11, 1975*.
Franklin Taveras, New York, May 1, 1979*.
David A. Kingman, New York, May 28, 1982*.

A. L.—5—Robert M. Grove, Philadelphia, June 10, 1933, first game*.
John J. Broaca, New York, June 25, 1934*.
Chester P. Laabs, Detroit, October 2, 1938, first game*.
Lawrence E. Doby, Cleveland, April 25, 1948*.
James H. Landis, Chicago, July 28, 1957*.
W. Robert Allison, Minnesota, September 2, 1965*.
Reginald M. Jackson, Oakland, September 27, 1968*.
Raymond A. Jarvis, Boston, April 20, 1969*.
Robert J. Monday, Oakland, April 29, 1970*.
Frank O. Howard, Washington, September 19, 1970, first game*.
Donald A. Buford, Baltimore, August 26, 1971*.
Richard E. Manning, Cleveland, May 15, 1977*.
Vincent E. Jackson, Kansas City, April 18, 1987*.
Robert E. Deer, Milwaukee, August 8, 1987, first game*.

Most Strikeouts, Extra-Inning Game

A. L.—6—Carl Weilman, St. Louis, July 25, 1913, 15 innings (consecutive).
Frederic C. Reichardt, California, May 31, 1966, 17 innings.
Billy R. Cowan, California, July 9, 1971, 20 innings.
Cecil C. Cooper, Boston, June 14, 1974, 15 innings.

N. L.—6—Donald A. Hoak, Chicago, May 2, 1956, 17 innings.

Most Times, Four or More Strikeouts, Game, Major Leagues

15—Richard A. Allen, Philadelphia N. L., 1964 (2), 1966 (1), 1968 (7), 1969 (2), St. Louis N.L., 1970 (1), Chicago A.L., 1974 (2).

Most Times, Four or More Strikeouts, Game, League

N. L.— 13—Richard A. Allen, Philadelphia, 1964 (2), 1966, 1968 (7), 1969 (2), St. Louis, 1970.

A. L.— 10—Mickey C. Mantle, New York, 1952, 1954, 1959, 1964, 1965, 1966, 1967, 1968 (3).

Most Times, Four or More Strikeouts, Game, Season

N. L.—7—Richard A. Allen, Philadelphia, April 13, May 1, 9, June 29, July 16, 21, August 19, 1968.

A. L.—5—Reginald M. Jackson, Oakland, April 7, second game, April 21, May 18, June 4, September 21, first game, 1971.
A. Bobby Darwin, Minnesota, May 12-13, June 23, July 14, August 6, first game, August 10, 1972.

Most Strikeouts, First Major League Game

N. L.—4—William A. Sunday, Chicago, May 22, 1883.
Wesley O. Bales, Atlanta, August 7, 1966.

A. A.—4—Hercules H. Burnett, Louisville, June 26, 1888.

A. L.—4—Roleine C. Naylor, Philadelphia, September 14, 1917.
Samuel J. Ewing, Chicago, September 11, 1973.

Most Strikeouts, Doubleheader

A. L.—7—J. Patrick Seerey, Chicago, July 24, 1948 (19 innings).
David L. Nicholson, Chicago, June 12, 1963 (17 innings).
Frank O. Howard, Washington, July 9, 1965 (18 innings).
William E. Melton, Chicago, July 24, 1970 (18 innings).

N. L.—7—Michael L. Vail, New York, September 26, 1975 (24 innings).

Most Strikeouts, Two Consecutive Games (18 Innings)

A. L.—8—Robert J. Monday, Oakland, April 28 (3), 29 (5), 1970.
J. Gorman Thomas, Milwaukee, July 27, second game (4), 28 (4), 1975.

N. L.—8—Wayne L. Twitchell, Philadelphia, May 16 (4), 22 (4), 1973.
Ruppert S. Jones, San Diego, July 16 (4), 17 (4), 1982.

Most Strikeouts, Two Consecutive Games (More Than 18 Innings)

N. L.—9—Eric K. Davis, Cincinnati, April 24 (4), 25 (5), 1987 (21 innings).

A. L.—8—Pedro Ramos, Cleveland, August 19, 23, 1963 (22 innings).
Roy F. Smalley, Minnesota, August 28, 29, 1976 (26 innings).

Most Strikeouts, Three Consecutive Games

N. L.— 10—Adolfo E. Phillips, Chicago, June 8 (2), 10 (5), 11 (3), 1966.
Wayne L. Twitchell, Philadelphia, May 16 (4), 22 (4), 27 (2), 1973.

A. L.— 10—William E. Melton, Chicago, July 24 (4), 24 (3), 28, (3), 1970.
Richard A. Drago, Kansas City, September 5 (3), 10, second game (4), 17 (3), 1970.
James H. Fuller, Baltimore, September 25 (3), 27 (4), 28, first game (3), 1973.
J. Gorman Thomas, Milwaukee, July 27, second game (4), 28 (4), 29 (2), 1975.

Most Strikeouts, Four Consecutive Games

N. L.— 12—Adolfo E. Phillips, Chicago, June 7 (2), 8 (2), 10 (5), 11 (3), 1966.

A. L.— 12—James J. Hannan, Washington, July 24 (4), 29 (2), August 3 (3), 8 (3), 1968.
William E. Melton, Chicago, July 23 (2), 24 (4), 24 (3), 28 (3), 1970.

Ten or More Consecutive Strikeouts, Season (Consec. Plate App.)

N. L.— 12—Sanford Koufax, Brooklyn, June 24 to September 24, second game, 1955. (12 at-bats for season, 12 strikeouts.)

10—Tommie W. Sisk, Pittsburgh, July 27 (2), August 1 (3), 6 (4), 12 (1), 1966.

A. L.— 11—W. Dean Chance, Los Angeles, July 24 (1), 30 (2), August 4, first game (3), 9 (4), 13 (1), 1965.
10—Joseph C. Grzenda, Washington, April 7 (2), 22 (1), May 26 (4), June 13 (1), 16 (1), August 3 (1), 1970.

Most Consecutive Strikeouts, Season (Not Consec. Plate App.)

N. L.—14—William A. Hands, Chicago, June 9, second game through July 11, 1968, second game; also 1 base on balls and 2 sacrifice hits.
Juan T. Eichelberger, San Diego, June 30 through August 15, 1980; also 1 sacrifice hit.
A. L.—13—James J. Hannan, Washington, July 24, through August 13, 1968; also 2 bases on balls.

Most Strikeouts, Inning

N. L.—2—18 times (held by 18 players). Last player—Larry D. McWilliams, Atlanta, April 22, 1979, fourth inning.
A. L.—2—16 times (held by 16 players). Last player—Vincent E. Jackson, Kansas City, April 8, 1987, fourth inning.

Sacrifice Hits

Most Sacrifices, League

A. L.—511—Edward T. Collins, Philadelphia, Chicago, 25 years, 1906 through 1930.
N. L.—392—Jacob E. Daubert, Brooklyn, Cincinnati, 15 years, 1910 through 1924.

Most Sacrifices, Season (Including Sacrifice Scoring Flies)

A. L.—67—Raymond J. Chapman, Cleveland, 156 games, 1917.
N. L.—46—James T. Sheckard, Chicago, 148 games, 1909.

Most Sacrifices, Season (No Sacrifice Flies)

A. L.—46—William J. Bradley, Cleveland, 139 games, 1907.
N. L.—43—William Gleason, Philadelphia, 155 games, 1905.

Most Sacrifices, Rookie Season (Includes Sacrifice Scoring Flies)

A. L.—39—Emory E. Rigney, Detroit, 155 games, 1922.
N. L.—29—John B. Miller, Pittsburgh, 150 games, 1909.

Most Sacrifices, Rookie Season, Since 1931 (Excludes Sac. Flies)

A. L.—28—Robert J. Hoover, Detroit, 144 games, 1943.
N. L.—28—Jack R. Robinson, Brooklyn, 151 games, 1947.
Osborne E. Smith, San Diego, 159 games, 1978.

Most Sacrifices, Righthander, Season

A. L.—67—Raymond J. Chapman, Cleveland, 156 games, 1917 (includes a few sacrifice scoring flies).
N. L.—43—William Gleason, Philadelphia, 155 games, 1905 (does not include sacrifice flies.

Most Sacrifices, Lefthander, Season

A. L.—52—Robert S. Ganley, Washington, 150 games, 1908 (includes a few sacrifice scoring flies).
N. L.—46—James T. Sheckard, Chicago, 148 games, 1909 (includes a few sacrifice scoring flies).

Most Sacrifices, Switch Hitter, Season

A. L.—52—Owen J. Bush, Detroit, 157 games, 1909 (includes a few sacrifice scoring flies).
N. L.—35—Leo G. Magee, St. Louis, 142 games, 1914 (includes sacrifice flies).

Most Years Leading League in Sacrifices

A. L.—6—George W. Haas, Philadelphia, Chicago, 1930, 1931, 1932, 1933, 1934, 1936.
N. L.—4—Franz O. Knabe, Philadelphia, 1907, 1908, 1910, 1913.

Most Consecutive Years Leading League in Sacrifices

A. L.—5—George W. Haas, Philadelphia, Chicago, 1930 through 1934.
N. L.—2—Held by many players. N. L.—Last player—John E. Temple, Cincinnati, 1957, 1958 (tied).

Fewest Sacrifice Hits, Season, Most At-Bats

N. L.—0—Juan M. Samuel, Philadelphia, 160 games, 1984; 701 at-bats.
A. L.—0—Aloysius H. Simmons, Philadelphia, 154 games, 1932; 670 at-bats.

Fewest Sacrifices, Season, for Leader (No Sacrifice Flies) (154 or 162-Game Schedule)

A. L.—13—Alfred M. Martin, Detroit, 131 games, 1958.
Anthony C. Kubek, New York, 132 games, 1959.
James H. Landis, Chicago, 149 games, 1959.

Alfred J. Pilarcik, Baltimore, 130 games, 1959.
Victor P. Power, Minnesota, 138 games, 1963.
Paul L. Blair, Baltimore, 150 games, 1969.
Dennis D. McLain, Detroit, 42 games, 1969.
N. L.—13—Maurice M. Wills, Los Angeles, 148 games, 1961.

Most Sacrifice Hits, Game

A. L.—4—Wade H. Killefer, Washington, August 27, 1910, first game.
John J. Barry, Boston, August 21, 1916.
Raymond J. Chapman, Cleveland, August 31, 1919.
N. L.—4—Jacob E. Daubert, Brooklyn, August 15, 1914, second game.
J. Bentley Seymour, Cincinnati, July 25, 1902.

Most Sacrifice Hits, Doubleheader

N. L.—6—Jacob E. Daubert, Brooklyn, August 15, 1914.
A. L.—5—Wade H. Killefer, Washington, August 27, 1910.

Most Sacrifice Hits, Inning

A. L.—2—J. Alton Benton, Detroit, August 6, 1941, third inning.
N. L.—1—Held by many players.

Sacrifice Flies

Most Sacrifice Flies in Major Leagues

121—Henry L. Aaron, 113 in N. L., Milwaukee, Atlanta, 21 years, 1954 through 1974; 8 in A. L., Milwaukee, 2 years, 1975, 1976.

Most Sacrifice Flies, League

A. L.—114—Brooks C. Robinson, Baltimore, 23 years, 1955 through 1977.
N. L.—113—Henry L. Aaron, Milwaukee, Atlanta, 21 years, 1954 through 1974.

Most Sacrifice Flies, Season

N. L.—19—Gilbert R. Hodges, Brooklyn, 154 games, 1954.
A. L.—17—Roy H. White, New York, 147 games, 1971.
(Harold J. Traynor, Pittsburgh, N. L., 144 games, 1928, had 31 sacrifice flies, advancing runners to second base, third base and home.)

Most Sacrifice Flies, Rookie Season

N. L.—13—Guillermo N. Montanez, Philadelphia, 158 games, 1971.
A. L.—13—Gary J. Gaetti, Minnesota, 145 games, 1982.

Most Sacrifice Flies, Righthander, Season

N. L.—19—Gilbert R. Hodges, Brooklyn, 154 games, 1954.
A. L.—16—Charles A. Gandil, Washington, 145 games, 1914.

Most Sacrifice Flies, Lefthander, Season

A. L.—16—Samuel E. Crawford, Detroit, 157 games, 1914.
N. L.—13—Guillermo N. Montanez, Philadelphia, 158 games, 1971.

Most Sacrifice Flies, Switch Hitter, Season

A. L.—17—Roy H. White, New York, 147 games, 1971.
N. L.—13—C. Reginald Smith, Los Angeles, 128 games, 1978.
Thomas M. Herr, St. Louis, 159 games, 1985.

Most Years Leading League in Sacrifice Flies

A. L.—4—Brooks C. Robinson, Baltimore, 1962 (tied), 1964, 1967 (tied), 1968 (tied).
N. L.—3—Ronald E. Santo, Chicago, 1963, 1967, 1969.
Johnny L. Bench, Cincinnati, 1970, 1972, 1973 (tied).

Most At-Bats, Season, No Sacrifice Flies

N. L.—680—Peter E. Rose, Cincinnati, 160 games, 1973.
Franklin Taveras, Pittsburgh, New York, 164 games, 1979.
A. L.—680—Kirby Puckett, Minnesota, 161 games, 1986.

Most Sacrifice Flies, Game

N. L.—3—Harry M. Steinfeldt, Chicago, May 5, 1909.
Ernest Banks, Chicago, June 2, 1961.
Vincent M. Coleman, St. Louis, May 1, 1986.
Candido Maldonado, San Francisco, August 29, 1987.
A. L.—3—Robert W. Meusel, New York, September 15, 1926.
Russell E. Nixon, Boston, August 31, 1965, second game.
Donald A. Mattingly, New York, May 3, 1986.

Hit By Pitch

Most Hit by Pitch, League

A. L.—255—Donald E. Baylor, Baltimore, Oakland, California, New York, Boston, Minnesota, 18 years, 1970 through 1987.

N. L.— 243— Ronald K. Hunt, New York, Los Angeles, San Francisco, Montreal, St. Louis, 12 years, 1963 through 1974.

Most Hit by Pitch, Season

  N. L.—50—Ronald K. Hunt, Montreal, 152 games, 1971.
  A. L.—35—Donald E. Baylor, Boston, 160 games, 1986.

Most Hit by Pitch, Rookie Season

  A. A.—29—Thomas J. Tucker, Baltimore, 136 games, 1887.
  N. L.—20—Frank Robinson, Cincinnati, 152 games, 1956.
  A. L.—17—Henry E. Manush, Detroit, 109 games, 1923.

Most Hit by Pitch, Righthander, Season

  N. L.—50—Ronald K. Hunt, Montreal, 152 games, 1971.
  A. L.—35—Donald E. Baylor, Boston, 160 games, 1986.

Most Hit by Pitch, Lefthander, Season

  N. L.—31—Louis R. Evans, St. Louis, 151 games, 1910.
  A. L.—20—Harry H. Gessler, Washington, 128 games, 1911.

Most Hit by Pitch, Switch Hitter, Season

  N. L.—11—Samuel Jethroe, Boston, 148 games, 1951.
    Peter E. Rose, Cincinnati, 162 games, 1975.
  A. L.—10—Fred L. Valentine, Washington, 146 games, 1966.
    Fred L. Valentine, Washington, 151 games, 1967.

Most Years Leading League, Hit by Pitch

  A. L.—10—Orestes A. Minoso, Cleveland, Chicago, 1951, 1952, 1953, 1954, 1956, 1957, 1958, 1959, 1960, 1961.
  N. L.— 7—Ronald K. Hunt, San Francisco, Montreal, St. Louis, 1968, 1969, 1970, 1971, 1972, 1973, 1974.

Most Consecutive Years, Leading League, Hit by Pitch

  N. L.—7—Ronald K. Hunt, San Francisco, Montreal, St. Louis, 1968 through 1974.
  A. L.—6—Orestes A. Minoso, Chicago, Cleveland, 1956 through 1961.

Fewest Hit by Pitch, Season, Most At-Bats

  A. L.—0—Santos C. Alomar, California, 162 games, 1971, 689 at-bats.
  N. L.—0—Hugh M. Critz, Cincinnati, New York, 152 games, 1930, 662 at-bats.
    Granville W. Hamner, Philadelphia, 154 games, 1949, 662 at-bats.

Fewest Hit by Pitch, Season, for Leader in Hit by Pitch

  A. L.—5—Frank P. J. Crosetti, New York, 138 games, 1934.
    Frank A. Pytlak, Cleveland, 91 games, 1934.
  N. L.—6—Robert G. Blattner, New York, 126 games, 1946.
    Andre F. Dawson, Montreal, 151 games, 1980.
    Daniel Driessen, Cincinnati, 154 games, 1980.
    Timothy J. Foli, Pittsburgh, 127 games, 1980.
    Gregory M. Luzinski, Philadelphia, 106 games, 1980.
    Elliott Maddox, New York, 130 games, 1980.
    Peter E. Rose, Philadelphia, 162 games, 1980.

Most Hit by Pitch, Game, Nine Innings

  N. L.—3—13 times (held by 10 players). Last player—Rigoberto P. Fuentes, San Francisco, September 13, 1973.
  A. A.—3—5 times (held by 5 players).
  A. L.—3—4 times (held by 4 players). Last player—William A. Freehan, Detroit, August 16, 1968 (consecutive).

Most Hit by Pitch, Extra-Inning Game

  N. L.—3—Ronald K. Hunt, San Francisco, April 29, 1969, 13 innings.
  A. L.—3—J. Garland Stahl, Washington, April 15, 1904, 10 innings.
    Craig R. Kusick, Minnesota, August 27, 1975, 11 innings.

Most Times Three Hit by Pitch, Game, League

  N. L.—3—Hugh A. Jennings, Baltimore, 1894, 1896, 1898.
  N. L. since 1900—2—Frank Chance, Chicago, 1902, 1904.
  A. L.—1—Held by 5 players.

Most Hit by Pitch, Doubleheader

  N. L.—5—Frank L. Chance, Chicago, May 30, 1904.
  A. L.—3—Bertram C. Daniels, New York, June 20, 1913.
    Alphonse E. Smith, Chicago, June 21, 1961.

Most Hit by Pitch, Inning

  N. L.—2—Willard R. Schmidt, Cincinnati, April 26, 1959, third inning.
    Frank J. Thomas, New York, April 29, 1962, first game, fourth inning.
  A. L.—1—Held by many players.

Grounding Into Double Plays

Most Grounding Into Double Plays in Major Leagues

  328—Henry L. Aaron, 305 in N. L., Milwaukee, Atlanta, 21 years, 1954 through 1974; 23 in A. L., Milwaukee, 2 years, 1975, 1976.

Most Grounding Into Double Plays, League

  A. L.— 311— Carl M. Yastrzemski, Boston, 23 years, 1961 through 1983.
  N. L.— 305— Henry L. Aaron, Milwaukee, Atlanta, 21 years, 1954 through 1974.

Most Grounding Into Double Plays, Season

  A. L.—36—James E. Rice, Boston, 159 games, 1984.
  N. L.—30—Ernest N. Lgmbardi, Cincinnati, 129 games, 1938.

Most Grounding Into Double Plays, Rookie Season

  A. L.—27—William F. Johnson, New York, 155 games, 1943.
    Albert L. Rosen, Cleveland, 155 games, 1950.
  N. L. (162-game season) —20—Kenneth D. Hubbs, Chicago, 160 games, 1962.
    George A. Foster, San Francisco, Cincinnati, 140 games, 1971.
  N. L. (154-game season) —19—Robert B. Schmidt, San Francisco, 127 games, 1958.

Most Grounding Into Double Plays, Righthander, Season

  A. L.—36—James E. Rice, Boston, 159 games, 1984.
  N. L.—30—Ernest N. Lombardi, Cincinnati, 129 games, 1938.

Most Grounding Into Double Plays, Lefthander, Season

  A. L. (162-game season) —30—Carl M. Yastrzemski, Boston, 151 games, 1964.
  A. L. (154-game season) —23—Richard J. Wakefield, Detroit, 155 games, 1943.
    George S. Vico, Detroit, 144 games, 1948.
  N. L. (162-game season) —26—Guillermo N. Montanez, Philadelphia, San Francisco, 156 games, 1975.
    David G. Parker, Cincinnati, 160 games, 1985.
  N. L. (154-game season) —23—Edwin D. Snider, Brooklyn, 150 games, 1951.

Most Grounding Into Double Plays, Switch Hitter, Season

  A. L.— 29— David E. Philley, Philadelphia, 151 games, 1952.
  N. L.— 29— Ted L. Simmons, St. Louis, 161 games, 1973.

Most Years Leading League, Grounding Into Double Plays

  N. L.—4—Ernest N. Lombardi, Cincinnati, New York, 1933, 1934, 1938, 1944.
  A. L.—4—James E. Rice, Boston, 1982, 1983 (tied), 1984, 1985.

Fewest Grounding Into Double Plays, Season, 150 or More Games

  N. L.—0—August J. Galan, Chicago, 154 games, 1935.
  A. L.—0—Richard J. McAuliffe, Detroit, 151 games, 1968.

Fewest GDPs, Rookie Season, 150 or More Games

  N. L.—3—Vincent M. Coleman, St. Louis, 151 games, 1985.
  A. L.—4—Manuel J. Rivera, St. Louis-Chicago, 150 games, 1952.

Fewest GDPs, Righthander, Season, 150 or More Games

  N. L.—1—Ronald K. Hunt, Montreal, 152 games, 1971.
  A. L.—2—Cesar L. Tovar, Minnesota, 157 games, 1968.
    Mark Belanger, Baltimore, 152 games, 1975.

Fewest GDPs, Lefthander, Season, 150 or More Games

  A. L.—0—Richard J. McAuliffe, Detroit, 151 games, 1968.
  N. L.—2—Louis C. Brock, St. Louis, 155 games, 1965.
    Louis C. Brock, St. Louis, 157 games, 1969.
    William N. Clark, San Francisco, 150 games, 1987.

Fewest GDPs, Switch Hitter, Season, 150 or More Games

  N. L.—0—August J. Galan, Chicago, 154 games, 1935.
  A. L.—1—Willie J. Wilson, Kansas City, 154 games, 1979.

Fewest Grounding Into Double Plays for Leader in GDPs, Season

  N. L.— 19— Andrew W. Seminick, Philadelphia, 124 games 1946.
    George J. Kurowski, St. Louis, 146 games, 1947.
    Andrew Pafko, Chicago, 129 games, 1947.
  A. L.— 21— Brooks C. Robinson, Baltimore, 158 games, 1967.

Most Years Leading in Fewest GDPs, 150 or More Games

  N. L.—6—Richie Ashburn, Philadelphia, Chicago, 1951, 1952, 1953, 1954, 1958, 1960 (tied).

A. L.—2—Held by ten players. Last player—Willie J. Wilson, Kansas City, 1979, 1980.

Most Grounding Into Double Plays, Game, Nine Innings

A. L.—4—Leon A. Goslin, Detroit, April 28, 1934 (consecutive).
Michael A. Kreevich, Chicago, August 4, 1939 (consecutive).
N. L.—4—Joseph P. Torre, New York, July 21, 1975 (consecutive).

Most Grounding Into Double Plays, Two Consecutive Games

N. L.—5—Henry J. Bonura, New York, July 8 (3), second game, July 9 (2), 1939.
A. L.—4—Held by many players.

Most Times Grounding Into Infield Triple Play, Game or Season

N. L.—A. L.—1—Held by many players.

Reaching On Errors Or Interference

Most First on Error, Game, Fair-Hit Balls

P. L.—4—Michael J. Griffin, Philadelphia, June 23, 1890.

N. L.—3—George Gore, New York, August 15, 1887.
Alphonso R. Lopez, Boston, July 16, 1936.
Gerald W. Grote, New York, September 5, 1975.
A. L.—2—Held by many players.

Most First on Error, Inning, Fair-Hit Balls

A. L.—2—Emory E. Rigney, Detroit, August 21, 1922, sixth inning.
Fred Spurgeon, Cleveland, April 14, 1925, eighth inning.
John C. Bassler, Detroit, June 17, 1925, sixth inning.
Edgar C. Rice, Washington, July 10, 1926, eighth inning.
N. L.—2—Stuart Martin, St. Louis, June 22, 1940, sixth inning.

Most Times Reaching Base, Season, on Catcher's Interference

N. L.—7—Dale A. Berra, Pittsburgh, 161 games, 1983.
A. L.—6—G. Robert Stinson, Seattle, 124 games, 1978.

Most Times Reaching Base, Game, on Catcher's Interference

N. L.—2—Benjamin Geraghty, Brooklyn, April 26, 1936.
Patrick Corrales, Philadelphia, September 29, 1965.
A. L.—2—Daniel T. Meyer, Seattle, May 3, 1977.
G. Robert Stinson, Seattle, July 24, 1979.

Club Batting

Service

Players Used

Most Players, Season

A. L. (162-game season)—53—Seattle, 1969.
A. L. (154-game season)—56—Philadelphia, 1915.
N. L. (162-game season)—54—New York, 1967.
N. L. (154-game season)—53—Brooklyn, 1944.

Fewest Players, Season

A. L. (154-game season)—18—Boston, 1905.
A. L. (162-game season)—30—New York, 1963; Boston, 1965; Baltimore, 1969.
N. L. (162-game season)—29—Cincinnati, 1975.
N. L. (154-game season)—20—Chicago, 1905.

Most Players, Nine-Inning Game

A. L.—27—Kansas City vs. California, September 10, 1969.
N. L.—25—St. Louis vs. Los Angeles, April 16, 1959.
Milwaukee vs. Philadelphia, September 26, 1964.

Most Players, Extra-Inning Game

A. L.—30—Oakland vs. Chicago, September 19, 1972, 15 innings.
N. L.—27—Philadelphia vs. St. Louis, September 13, 1974, 17 innings.
Chicago vs. Pittsburgh, September 21, 1978, 14 innings.
Chicago vs. Houston, September 2, finished September 3, 1986, 18 innings.
Los Angeles vs. San Francisco, September 28, 1986, 16 innings.

Most Players, Nine-Inning Game, Both Clubs

N. L.—45—Chicago 24, Montreal 21, September 5, 1978.
A. L.—42—Oakland 24, Kansas City 18, September 20, 1975.

Most Players, Extra-Inning Game, Both Clubs

N. L.—53—Chicago 27, Houston 26, September 2, finished September 3, 1986, 18 innings.
A. L.—51—Oakland 30, Chicago 21, September 19, 1972, 15 innings.

Most Players Used, Doubleheader

A. L.—41—Chicago vs. Oakland, September 7, 1970.
N. L.—41—San Diego vs. San Francisco, May 30, 1977.

Most Players Used, Doubleheader, More Than 18 Innings

N. L.—42—St. Louis vs. Brooklyn, August 29, 1948, 19 innings.
Montreal vs. Pittsburgh, September 5, 1975, 19 innings.

Most Players Used, Doubleheader, Both Clubs

N. L.—74—San Diego 41, San Francisco 33, May 30, 1977.
A. L.—70—Oakland 36, Texas 34, September 7, 1975.

Most Players Used, Doubleheader, Both Clubs, Over 18 Innings

N. L.—74—Montreal 42, Pittsburgh 32, September 5, 1975, 19 innings.

A. L.—73—Washington 37, Cleveland 36, September 14, finished September 20, 1971, 29 innings.

Pinch-Hitters

Most Pinch-Hitters, Nine-Inning Game

N. L.—9—Los Angeles vs. St. Louis, September 22, 1959.
Montreal vs. Pittsburgh, September 5, 1975, second game.
A. L.—8—Baltimore vs. Chicago, May 28, 1954, first game.

Most Pinch-Hitters, Extra-Inning Game

A. L.—10—Oakland vs. Chicago, September 17, 1972, 15 innings.
N. L.—7—New York vs. Chicago, May 2, 1956, 17 innings.
Chicago vs. New York, May 2, 1956, 17 innings.

Most Pinch-Hitters, Nine-Inning Game, Both Clubs

N. L.—11—Chicago 7, Los Angeles 4, October 1, 1961.
A. L.—10—Baltimore 6, New York 4, April 26, 1959, second game.

Most Pinch-Hitters, Extra-Inning Game, Both Clubs

N. L.—14—New York 7, Chicago 7, May 2, 1956, 17 innings.
A. L.—14—Oakland 10, Chicago 4, September 17, 1972, 15 innings.

Most Pinch-Hitters, Doubleheader, Nine-Inning Games

A. L.—10—New York vs. Boston, September 6, 1954.
Baltimore vs. Washington, April 19, 1959.
N. L.—10—St. Louis vs. Chicago, May 11, 1958.
St. Louis vs. Pittsburgh, July 13, 1958.

Most Pinch-Hitters, Doubleheader, Over 18 Innings

N. L.—15—Montreal vs. Pittsburgh, September 5, 1975, 19 innings.
A. L.—9—New York vs. Washington, August 14, 1960, 24 innings.

Most Pinch-Hitters, Doubleheader, Both Clubs, 9-Inning Games

N. L.—15—Milwaukee 8, San Francisco 7, August 30, 1964.
A. L.—14—New York 10, Boston 4, September 6, 1954.

Most Pinch-Hitters, Doubleheader, Both Clubs, Over 18 Innings

N. L.—19—Montreal 15, Pittsburgh 4, September 5, 1975, 19 innings.
A. L.—17—New York 9, Washington 8, August 14, 1960, 24 innings.

Most Pinch-Hitters, Inning

N. L.—6—San Francisco vs. Pittsburgh, May 5, 1958, ninth inning.
San Diego vs. San Francisco, September 16, 1986, ninth inning.
A. L.—6—Detroit vs. New York, September 5, 1971, seventh inning.

Most Consecutive Pinch-Hitters, Inning

N. L.-A. L.—5—Made in many innings.
N. L.—Last time—New York vs. San Francisco, September 16, 1966, ninth inning.
A. L.—Last time—New York vs. Milwaukee, September 22, 1987, first game, eighth inning.

Most Pinch-Hitters, Inning, Both Clubs

A. L.—8—Chicago 5, Baltimore 3, May 18, 1957, seventh inning.
N. L.—8—Philadelphia 5, St. Louis 3, April 30, 1961, eighth inning.
New York 5, San Francisco 3, September 16, 1966, ninth inning.

Pinch-Runners

Most Pinch-Runners, Inning

A. L.—4—Chicago vs. Minnesota, September 16, 1967, ninth inning.
Texas vs. California, September 10, 1987, ninth inning.
N. L.—3—Made in many innings.

Most Pinch-Runners, Inning, Both Clubs

N. L.—5—Pittsburgh 3, New York 2, September 21, 1981, ninth inning.
A. L.—4—Made in many innings.

Years & Games

Most Years, League

N. L.—112—Chicago, 1876 to date (consecutive).
Boston-Milwaukee-Atlanta, 1876 to date (consecutive).
A. L.—87—Boston, Chicago, Cleveland, Detroit, Washington-Minnesota, 1901 to date (consecutive).

Most Games, League

N. L.—16,425—Chicago, 112 years, 1876 to date.
A. L.—13,516—Detroit, 87 years, 1901 to date.

Most Games, Season

N. L. (162-game season)—165—Los Angeles, 1962 (3 playoffs).
San Francisco, 1962 (3 playoffs).
N. L. (154-game season)—160—Cincinnati, 1915 (6 tied).
A. L. (162-game season)—164—Cleveland, 1964 (2 tied).
New York, 1964, 1968 (2 tied).
Minnesota, 1967 (2 tied).
Detroit, 1968 (2 tied).
A. L. (154-game season)—162—Detroit, 1904 (10 tied, 2 unplayed).

Fewest Games, Season

A. L. (154-game season)—147—Cleveland, 1945 (2 tied, 9 unplayed).
N. L. (154-game season)—149—Philadelphia, 1907 (2 tied, 7 unplayed), 1934 (5 unplayed).
A. L. (162-game season)—158—Baltimore, 1971 (4 unplayed).
N. L. (162-game season)—160—Cincinnati, 1966 (2 unplayed).
Atlanta, 1979 (2 unplayed).
Montreal, 1979 (2 unplayed).

Most Games, One Day

N. L.—3—Brooklyn and Pittsburgh, September 1, 1890 (Brooklyn won 3).
Baltimore and Louisville, September 7, 1896 (Baltimore won 3).
Pittsburgh and Cincinnati, October 2, 1920 (Cincinnati won 2).
A. L.—2—Made on many days.

Most Doubleheaders, Season

A. L. (154-game season)—44—Chicago, 1943. (Won 11, lost 10, split 23).
A. L. (162-game season)—29—Chicago, 1967. (Won 9, lost 5, split 15).
Kansas City, 1967. (Won 3, lost 9, split 17).
N. L. (154-game season)—43—Philadelphia, 1943. (Won 11, lost 14, split 18).
N. L. (162-game season)—30—New York, 1962. (Won 3, lost 17, split 10).

Fewest Doubleheaders, Season

A. L.—0—Seattle, 1983.
California, 1987.
N. L.—0—Chicago, 1985.

Most Consecutive Doubleheaders Played, Season

N. L.—9—Boston, September 4 through September 15, 1928.
A. L.—8—Washington, July 27 through August 5, 1909.

Most Consecutive Games Between Same Clubs, Season

A. L.—11—Detroit vs. St. Louis, September 8 through 14, 1904.
N. L.—10—Chicago vs. Philadelphia, August 7 through 16, 1907.

Most Consecutive Doubleheaders Between Same Clubs, Season

A. L.—5—Philadelphia vs. Washington, August 5, 7, 8, 9, 10, 1901.
N. L.—4—New York vs. Boston, September 10, 11, 13, 14, 1928.

Batting Average

Highest Batting Average, Season

N. L.—.343—Philadelphia, 132 games, 1894.

N. L. since 1900—.319—New York, 154 games, 1930.
A. L.—.316—Detroit, 154 games, 1921.

Highest Batting Average, Pennant Winner, Season

N. L.—.328—Baltimore, 129 games, 1894.
N. L. since 1900—.314—St. Louis, 154 games, 1930.
A. L.—.307—New York, 155 games, 1927.

Highest Batting Average, Outfield, Season

N. L.—.405—Philadelphia, 132 games, 1894.
A. L.—.367—Detroit, 156 games, 1925.
N. L. since 1900—.350—Chicago, 156 games, 1929.

Most Years Leading League in Batting Average, Since 1900

N. L.—21—Pittsburgh, 1902, 1907, 1909, 1922, 1923 (tied), 1925, 1927, 1928, 1933, 1936 (tied), 1938 (tied), 1942, 1960, 1961, 1966, 1967, 1969 (tied), 1970 (tied), 1972, 1974, 1982.
A. L.—16—Detroit, 1907, 1908, 1909, 1915, 1916, 1917, 1921, 1924, 1929, 1934, 1935, 1937, 1940 (tied), 1943, 1956, 1961 (tied).

Most Consecutive Years, Leading League in Batting Average

A. L.—5—Philadelphia, 1910, 1911, 1912, 1913, 1914.
Boston, 1938, 1939, 1940 (tied), 1941, 1942.
N. L.—4—Philadelphia, 1892 (tied), 1893, 1894, 1895.
New York, 1910, 1911, 1912, 1913.
St. Louis, 1941 (tied), 1942, 1943, 1944.

Most Players Batting .300 or Over, Season, 50 Games

A. L.—10—Philadelphia, 1927.
N. L.—10—St. Louis, 1930.

Most Players Batting .400 or Over, Season, 50 Games

N. L.—3—Philadelphia, 1894.
N. L. since 1900—1—St. Louis, 1922, 1924, 1925; New York, 1930.
A. L.—1—Philadelphia, 1901; Detroit, 1911, 1912, 1922, 1923; Cleveland, 1911; St. Louis, 1920, 1922; Boston, 1941.

Lowest Batting Average, Season

N. L.—.207—Washington, 136 games, 1888.
A. L.—.212—Chicago, 156 games, 1910.
N. L. since 1900—.213—Brooklyn, 154 games, 1908.

Lowest Batting Average, Pennant Winner, Season

A. L.—.228—Chicago, 154 games, 1906; last in batting.
N. L.—.242—New York, 162 games, 1969; tied for seventh in batting.

Lowest Batting Average, Season, Club Leader in Batting

A. L.—.240—Oakland, 163 games, 1968.
N. L.—.254—Pittsburgh, 157 games, 1907; St. Louis, 157 games, 1915.

Slugging Average

Highest Slugging Average, Season

A. L.—.489—New York, 155 games, 1927.
N. L.—.481—Chicago, 156 games, 1930.

Most Years Leading League in Slugging Average, Since 1900

A. L.—29—New York, 1920, 1921, 1923, 1924, 1926, 1927, 1928, 1930, 1931, 1936, 1937, 1938, 1939, 1943, 1944, 1945, 1947, 1948, 1951, 1953, 1954, 1955, 1956, 1957, 1958, 1960, 1961, 1962, 1986.
N. L.—18—New York-San Francisco, 1904, 1905, 1908, 1910, 1911, 1919, 1923, 1924, 1927, 1928, 1935, 1945, 1947, 1948, 1952 (tied), 1961, 1962, 1963.

Most Consecutive Years Leading in Slugging, Since 1900

N. L.—7—Brooklyn, 1949, 1950, 1951, 1952 (tied), 1953, 1954, 1955.
A. L.—6—New York, 1953, 1954, 1955, 1956, 1957, 1958.

Lowest Slugging Average, Season (150 or More Games)

A. L.—.261—Chicago, 156 games, 1910.
N. L.—.274—Boston, 155 games, 1909.

At-Bats & Plate Appearances

Most At-Bats, Season

N. L.—5767—Cincinnati, 163 games, 1968.
A. L.—5733—Milwaukee, 163 games, 1982.

Fewest At-Bats, Season
  N. L.— 4725— Philadelphia, 149 games, 1907.
  A. L.— 4827— Chicago, 153 games, 1913.

Most At-Bats, Game, Nine Innings
  N. L.— 66— Chicago vs. Buffalo, July 3, 1883.
  N. L. since 1900— 58— New York vs. Philadelphia, September 2, 1925, second game.
              New York vs. Philadelphia, July 11, 1931, first game.
  A. L.— 56— New York vs. Philadelphia, June 28, 1939, first game.

Most At-Bats, Extra-Inning Game
  A. L.— 95— Chicago vs. Milwaukee, May 8, finished May 9, 1984, 25 innings.
  N. L.— 89— New York vs. St. Louis, September 11, 1974, 25 innings.

Most Plate Appearances, Game, Nine Innings
  N. L.— 71— Chicago vs. Louisville, June 29, 1897.
  N. L. since 1900— 66— Philadelphia vs. Chicago, August 25, 1922.
              St. Louis vs. Philadelphia, July 6, 1929, second game.
  A. L.— 64— Boston vs. St. Louis, June 8, 1950.

Most Plate Appearances, Extra-Inning Game
  A. L.— 104— Chicago vs. Milwaukee, May 8, finished May 9, 1984, 25 innings.
  N. L.— 103— New York vs. St. Louis, September 11, 1974, 25 innings.

Fewest At-Bats, Game, Nine Innings
  A. L.— 23— Chicago vs. St. Louis, May 6, 1917.
              Cleveland vs. Chicago, May 9, 1961.
              Detroit vs. Baltimore, May 6, 1968.
  N. L.— 24— Cincinnati vs. Brooklyn, July 22, 1911.
              Boston vs. Cincinnati, May 15, 1951.
              Pittsburgh vs. Chicago, May 12, 1955.

Fewest At-Bats, Game, Eight Innings
  A. L.— 19— Baltimore vs. Kansas City, September 12, 1964.
  N. L.— 21— Pittsburgh vs. St. Louis, September 8, 1908.

Most At-Bats, Game, Nine Innings
  N. L.— 106— Chicago 64, Louisville 42, July 22, 1876.
  N. L. since 1900— 99— New York 56, Cincinnati 43, June 9, 1901.
              New York 58, Philadelphia 41, July 11, 1931, first game.
  A. L.— 96— Cleveland 51, Philadelphia 45, April 29, 1952.

Most At-Bats, Extra-Inning Game, Both Clubs
  N. L.— 175— New York 89, St. Louis 86, September 11, 1974, 25 innings.
  A. L.— 175— Chicago 85, Milwaukee 80, May 8, finished May 9, 1984, 25 innings.

Most Plate Appearances, Game, Both Clubs
  N. L.— 125— Philadelphia 66, Chicago 59, August 25, 1922.
  A. L.— 108— Cleveland 58, Philadelphia 50, April 29, 1952.

Most Plate Appearances, Extra-Inning Game, Both Clubs
  N. L.— 202— New York 103, St. Louis 99, September 11, 1974, 25 innings.
  A. L.— 198— Chicago 104, Milwaukee 94, May 8, finished May 9, 1984, 25 innings.

Fewest At-Bats, Game, Nine Innings, Both Clubs
  N. L.— 48— Boston 25, Philadelphia 23, April 22, 1910.
              Brooklyn 24, Cincinnati 24, July 22, 1911.
  A. L.— 46— Kansas City 27, Baltimore 19, September 12, 1964.

Most At-Bats, Doubleheader, 18 Innings
  A. L.— 99— New York vs. Philadelphia, June 28, 1939.
  N. L.— 98— Pittsburgh vs. Philadelphia, August 8, 1922.

Fewest At-Bats, Doubleheader
  A. L.— 50— Boston vs. Chicago, August 28, 1912.
  N. L.— 52— Brooklyn vs. St. Louis, July 24, 1909.

Most At-Bats, Doubleheader, 18 Innings, Both Clubs
  N. L.— 176— Pittsburgh 98, Philadelphia 78, August 8, 1922.
  A. L.— 172— Boston 89, Philadelphia 83, July 4, 1939.

Most At-Bats, Doubleheader, More Than 18 Innings, Both Clubs
  N. L.— 234— New York 119, San Francisco 115, May 31, 1964, 32 innings.
  A. L.— 215— Kansas City 112, Detroit 103, June 17, 1967, 28 innings.

Fewest At-Bats, Doubleheader, Both Clubs
  N. L.— 109— St. Louis 57, Brooklyn 52, July 24, 1909.
  A. L.— 111— Cleveland 56, Chicago 55, May 28, 1916.

Most Plate Appearances, Inning
  A. L.— 23— Boston vs. Detroit, June 18, 1953, seventh inning.
  N. L.— 23— Chicago vs. Detroit, September 6, 1883, seventh inning.
  N. L. since 1900— 21— Brooklyn vs. Cincinnati, May 21, 1952, first inning.

Most Batters Facing Pitcher, Three Times, Inning, Club
  N. L.— 5— Chicago vs. Detroit, September 6, 1883, seventh inning.
  A. L.— 5— Boston vs. Detroit, June 18, 1953, seventh inning.
  N. L. since 1900— 3— Brooklyn vs. Cincinnati, May 21, 1952, first inning.

Runs
Season & Month

Most Runs, Season
  N. L.— 1221— Boston, 133 games, 1894.
  A. L.— 1067— New York, 155 games, 1931.
  N. L. since 1900— 1004— St. Louis, 154 games, 1930.

Most Runs, Season, Pennant Winner
  N. L.— 1170— Baltimore, 129 games, 1894.
  A. L.— 1065— New York, 155 games, 1936.
  N. L. since 1900— 1004— St. Louis, 154 games, 1930.

Most Runs, Season, at Home, Since 1900
  A. L.— 625— Boston, 77 games, 1950.
  N. L.— 543— Philadelphia, 77 games, 1930.

Most Runs, Season, on Road, Since 1900
  A. L.— 591— New York, 78 games, 1930.
  N. L.— 492— Chicago, 78 games, 1929.

Most Runs, Season, Against One Club, Since 1900
  N. L.— 218— Chicago vs. Philadelphia 24 games, 1930 (117 at home, 101 at Philadelphia).
         190— St. Louis vs. Philadelphia, 22 games, 1930 (103 at home, 87 at Philadelphia).
  A. L.— 216— Boston vs. St. Louis, 22 games, 1950 (118 at home, 98 at St. Louis).

Most Players Scoring 100 or More Runs, Season
  N. L.— 7— Boston, 1894.
  A. L.— 6— New York, 1931.
  N. L. since 1900— 6— Brooklyn, 1953.

Fewest Runs, Season
  N. L.— 372— St. Louis, 154 games, 1908.
  A. L.— 380— Washington, 156 games, 1909.

Fewest Runs, Season, for Leader in Most Runs
  N. L.— 590— St. Louis, 157 games, 1915.
  A. L.— 622— Philadelphia, 152 games, 1905.

Fewest Runs, Season, Pennant Winner
  A. L.— 550— Boston, 156 games, 1916.
  N. L.— 571— Chicago, 155 games, 1907.

Most Runs, One Month, Since 1900
  A. L.— 275— New York, August 1938, 36 games.
  N. L.— 260— New York, June 1929, 33 games.

Game & Doubleheader—One Club

Most Runs, Game
  N. L.— 36— Chicago vs. Louisville (7), June 29, 1897.
  A. L.— 29— Boston vs. St. Louis (4), June 8, 1950.
              Chicago vs. Kansas City (6), April 23, 1955.
  N. L. since 1900— 28— St. Louis vs. Philadelphia (7), July 6, 1929, second game.

Most Runs, Opening Game of Season
  P. L.— 23— Buffalo vs. Cleveland, April 19, 1890 (23-2).
  A. L.— 21— Cleveland vs. St. Louis, April 14, 1925 (21-14).
  N. L.— 19— Philadelphia vs. Boston, April 19, 1900, 10 innings (19-17).

Most Runs by Infield, Game
  N. L.— 16— Chicago vs. Philadelphia, June 29, 1897.
              Chicago vs. Boston, July 3, 1945.
  A. L.— 16— Boston vs. St. Louis, June 8, 1950.

Most Runs by Outfield, Game

A. A.— 14—Kansas City vs. Philadelphia, September 30, 1888.
N. L.— 14—New York vs. Cincinnati, June 9, 1901.
     New York vs. Brooklyn, April 30, 1944, first game.
A. L.— 11—Chicago vs. Philadelphia, September 11, 1936.
     New York vs. Washington, August 12, 1953.

Most Runs, Game, to Overcome and Win

A. L.— 12—Detroit vs. Chicago, June 18, 1911, at Detroit.

Chicago	7	0	0	3	3	0	2	0	0—15
Detroit	0	1	0	0	4	3	0	5	3—16

     Philadelphia vs. Cleveland, June 15, 1925, at Phila.

Cleveland	0	4	2	2	4	2	1	0	0—15
Philadelphia	0	2	1	1	0	0	1	13	x—17

N. L.—11—St. Louis vs. New York, June 15, 1952, first game, at N.Y.

St. Louis	0	0	0	0	7	0	3	2	2—14
New York	0	5	6	0	0	0	0	0	1—12

     Philadelphia vs. Chicago, April 17, 1976, at Chi., 10 inn.

Philadelphia	0	1	0	1	2	0	3	5	3	3—18
Chicago	0	7	5	1	0	0	0	0	2	1—16

Most Runs by Two Players, Game

N. L.— 12—Boston vs. Pittsburgh, August 27, 1887; Michael J. Kelly 6, Ezra B. Sutton 6.
N. L. since 1900—11—New York vs. Brooklyn, April 30, 1944, first game; Melvin T. Ott 6, Joseph M. Medwick 5.
A. L.— 10—Cleveland vs. Baltimore, September 2, 1902; Harry E. Bay 5, William J. Bradley 5.
     Chicago vs. Kansas City, April 23, 1955; Alfonso Carrasquel 5, Orestes A. Minoso 5.

Longest Extra-Inning Game Without a Run

N. L.—24 innings— New York vs. Houston, April 15, 1968.
A. L.—18 innings— Washington vs. Detroit, July 16, 1909.
     Detroit vs. Washington, July 16, 1909.
     Chicago vs. Washington, May 15, 1918.
     Chicago vs. Washington, June 8, 1947, first game.

Most Players, Six Runs in Game

N. L.—2—Boston vs. Pittsburgh, August 27, 1887, (M. J. Kelly, Ezra B. Sutton).
N. L. since 1900—1—New York vs. Philadelphia, August 4, 1934, second game, (Melvin T. Ott).
     New York vs. Brooklyn, April 30, 1944, first game, (Melvin T. Ott).
     Milwaukee vs. Chicago, September 2, 1957, first game, (Frank J. Torre).
A. L.—1—Boston vs. Chicago, May 8, 1946, (John Pesky).

Most Players, Five or More Runs in Game

N. L.—3—Chicago vs. Cleveland, July 24, 1882.
     Boston vs. Philadelphia, June 20, 1883.
     Boston vs. Pittsburgh, August 27, 1887.
     New York vs. Brooklyn, April 30, 1944, first game.
     Chicago vs. Boston, July 3, 1945.
A. L.—2—Cleveland vs. Baltimore, September 2, 1902.
     Chicago vs. Kansas City, April 23, 1955.

Most Players, Four or More Runs in Game

N. L.—6—Chicago vs. Cleveland, July 24, 1882.
     Chicago vs. Louisville, June 29, 1897.
N. L. since 1900—4—St. Louis vs. Philadelphia, July 6, 1929, second game.
A. L.—4—Boston vs. St. Louis, June 8, 1950.

Most Players, Three or More Runs in Game

N. L.—9—Chicago vs. Buffalo, July 3, 1883.
A. L.—7—Boston vs. St. Louis, June 8, 1950.
N. L. since 1900—6—New York vs. Philadelphia, September 2, 1925, second game.

Most Players, Two or More Runs in Game

N. L.— 10—Chicago vs. Louisville, June 29, 1897.
A. L.— 9—New York vs. Cleveland, July 14, 1904.
     Cleveland vs. Boston, July 7, 1923, first game.
     New York vs. Chicago, July 26, 1931, second game.
     New York vs. Philadelphia, May 24, 1936.
     Boston vs. Philadelphia, June 29, 1950.
N. L. since 1900—9—St. Louis vs. Chicago, April 16, 1912.
     Chicago vs. Philadelphia, August 25, 1922.
     St. Louis vs. Philadelphia, July 6, 1929, second game.

Most Players, One or More Runs in Game

N. L.— 13—Cincinnati vs. Boston, June 4, 1911.

     New York vs. Boston, June 20, 1912.
     Philadelphia vs. Chicago, August 25, 1922.
     San Francisco vs. San Diego, June 23, 1986.
A. L.— 13—Washington vs. St. Louis, July 10, 1926.
     New York vs. St. Louis, August 7, 1949, first game.
     Oakland vs. Kansas City, September 20, 1975.

Most Games, League, Scoring 20 or More Runs

N. L.— 38—Chicago, 1876 to date.
A. L.— 19—New York, 1903 to date.
N. L. since 1900—15—Brooklyn, 1900 through 1957.

Most Games, Season, Scoring 20 or More Runs

N. L.—8—Boston, 1894.
N. L. since 1900—3—Philadelphia, 1900.
A. L.—3—New York, 1939.
     Boston, 1950.

Most Runs, Doubleheader

N. L.— 43—Boston vs. Cincinnati, August 21, 1894.
A. L.— 36—Detroit vs. St. Louis, August 14, 1937.
N. L. since 1900—34—St. Louis vs. Philadelphia, July 6, 1929.

Fewest Runs, Longest Doubleheader

N. L.—0—St. Louis vs. New York, July 2, 1933, 27 innings.
     New York vs. Philadelphia, October 2, 1965, 27 innings.
A. L.—0—Held by many clubs, 18 innings. Last doubleheader— Cleveland vs. Boston, September 26, 1975.

Most Runs, Two Consecutive Games

N. L.— 53—Chicago, July 22, 25, 1876.
A. L.— 49—Boston vs. St. Louis, June 7, 8, 1950.
N. L. since 1900—45—Pittsburgh, June 20, 22, 1925.

Most Runs, Three Consecutive Games

N. L.— 71—Chicago, July 20, 22, 25, 1876.
A. L.— 56—Boston vs. St. Louis, June 7, 8, 9, 1950.

Most Runs, Four Consecutive Games

N. L.— 88—Chicago, July 20, 22, 25, 27, 1876.
A. L.— 65—Boston, June 5, 6, 7, 8, 1950.

Game & Doubleheader—Both Clubs

Most Runs, Game, Both Clubs

N. L.— 49—Chicago 26, Philadelphia 23, August 25, 1922.
A. L.— 36—Boston 22, Philadelphia 14, June 29, 1950.

Most Runs, Opening Game of Season, Both Clubs

N. L.— 36—Philadelphia 19, Boston 17, April 19, 1900, 10 innings.
A. L.— 35—Cleveland 21, St. Louis 14, April 14, 1925.

Most Players, Six or More Runs in Game, Both Clubs

N. L.— 2—Boston 2 (M. J. Kelly, Ezra B. Sutton), Pittsburgh 0, August 27, 1887.
A. L.— 1—Boston 1 (John Pesky) Chicago 0, May 8, 1946.

Most Players Five or More Runs in Game, Both Clubs

N. L.— 3—Chicago 3, Cleveland 0, July 24, 1882.
     Boston 3, Philadelphia 0, June 20, 1883.
     Boston 3, Pittsburgh 0, August 27, 1887.
     New York 3, Brooklyn 0, April 30, 1944, first game.
     Chicago 3, Boston 0, July 3, 1945.
A. L.— 2—Cleveland, 2, Baltimore 0, September 2, 1902.
     Chicago 2, Kansas City 0, April 23, 1955.

Most Players, Four or More Runs in Game, Both Clubs

N. L.—6—Chicago 6, Cleveland 0, July 24, 1882.
     Chicago 6, Louisville 0, June 29, 1897.
N. L. since 1900—4—St. Louis 4, Philadelphia 0, July 6, 1929, second game.
A. L.— 4—Boston 4, St. Louis 0, June 8, 1950.

Most Players, Three or More Runs in Game, Both Clubs

N. L.—9—Chicago 9, Buffalo 0, July 3, 1883.
A. L.—7—Boston 7, St. Louis 0, June 8, 1950.
N. L. since 1900—6—New York 6, Philadelphia 0, September 2, 1925, second game.

Most Players, Two or More Runs, in Game, Both Clubs

N. L.— 16—Chicago 9, Philadelphia 7, August 25, 1922.
A. L.— 13—Boston 9, Philadelphia 4, June 29, 1950.

Most Players, One or More Runs in Game, Both Clubs

N. L.— 22—Philadelphia 13, Chicago 9, August 25, 1922.
A. L.— 18—Boston 10, Philadelphia 8, June 29, 1950.

Most Runs, Doubleheader, Both Clubs

  N. L.—54—Boston 43, Cincinnati 11, August 21, 1894.
  A. L.—54—Boston 35, Philadelphia 19, July 4, 1939.
  N. L. since 1900—50—Brooklyn 26, Philadelphia 24, May 18, 1929.
          St. Louis 34, Philadelphia 16, July 6, 1929.

Fewest Runs, Doubleheader, Both Clubs

  N. L.—1—Boston 1, Pittsburgh 0, September 4, 1902.
          Philadelphia 1, Boston 0, September 5, 1913.
  A. L.—2—Washington 1, St. Louis 1, September 25, 1904.
          Philadelphia 1, Boston 1, June 1, 1909.
          Philadelphia 1, Boston 1, September 11, 1909.
          Los Angeles 1, Detroit 1, August 18, 1964.
          Washington 1, Kansas City 1, May 2, 1967.
          Baltimore 2, Boston 0, September 2, 1974.

Inning

Most Runs, Inning

  N. L.—18—Chicago vs. Detroit, September 6, 1883, seventh inning.
  A. L.—17—Boston vs. Detroit, June 18, 1953, seventh inning.
  N. L. since 1900—15—Brooklyn vs. Cincinnati, May 21, 1952, first
          inning.

Most Runs, Inning, Both Clubs

  A. L.—19—Cleveland 13, Boston 6, April 10, 1977, eighth inning.
  A. A.—19—Washington 14, Baltimore 5, June 17, 1891, first inning.
  N. L.—18—Chicago 18, Detroit 0, September 6, 1883, seventh inning.
  N. L. since 1900—17—Boston 10, New York 7, June 20, 1912, ninth
          inning.

Most Runs, Two Consecutive Innings

  N. L.—21—Pittsburgh vs. Boston, June 6, 1894; 12 in third inning; 9
          in fourth inning.
  A. L.—19—Boston vs. Philadelphia, May 2, 1901; 9 in second inning,
          10 in third inning.
          Boston vs. Detroit, June 18, 1953; 2 in sixth inning, 17 in
          seventh inning.
  N. L. since 1900—17—New York vs. Boston, September 3, 1926; 5 in
          fourth inning, 12 in fifth inning.

Most Runs, Extra Inning

  A. L.—12—Texas vs. Oakland, July 3, 1983, fifteenth inning.
  N. L.—10—Kansas City vs. Detroit, July 21, 1886, eleventh inning.
          Boston vs. New York, June 17, 1887, a.m. game, tenth
          inning.
          Cincinnati vs. Brooklyn, May 15, 1919, thirteenth inning.

Most Runs, Extra Inning, Both Clubs

  A. L.—12—Minnesota 11, Oakland 1, June 21, 1969, tenth inning.
          Texas 12, Oakland 0, July 3, 1983, fifteenth inning.
  N. L.—11—New York 8, Pittsburgh 3, June 15, 1929, fourteenth in-
          ning.
          New York 6, Brooklyn 5, April 24, 1955, tenth inning.
          New York 6, Chicago 5, June 30, 1979, eleventh inning.

Most Runs, Start of Game, With None Out

  N. L.—10—New York vs. St. Louis, May 13, 1911, first inning.
  A. L.—8—Cleveland vs. Baltimore, July 6, 1954, first inning.
          New York vs. Baltimore, April 24, 1960, first inning.

Most Runs, Start of Inning, With None Out

  N. L.—13—Chicago vs. Detroit, September 6, 1883, seventh inning.
  A. L.—11—Detroit vs. New York, June 17, 1925, sixth inning.
  N. L. since 1900—12—Brooklyn vs. Philadelphia, May 24, 1953,
          eighth inning.

Most Runs, Inning, With Two Out

  A. L.—13—Cleveland vs. Boston, July 7, 1923, first game, sixth in-
          ning.
          Kansas City vs. Chicago, April 21, 1956, second inning.
  N. L.—12—Brooklyn vs. Cincinnati, May 21, 1952, first inning.
          Brooklyn vs. Cincinnati, August 8, 1954, eighth inning.

Most Runs, Inning, With Two Out, None on Base

  N. L.—12—Brooklyn vs. Cincinnati, August 8, 1954, eighth inning.
  A. L.—10—Chicago vs. Detroit, September 2, 1959, second game,
          fifth inning.

Most Runs, Inning, by Pinch-Hitters

  N. L.—3—Boston vs. Philadelphia, April 19, 1900, ninth inning.
          Brooklyn vs. Philadelphia, September 9, 1926, ninth inning.
          San Francisco vs. Pittsburgh, May 5, 1958, ninth inning.
  A. L.—3—Chicago vs. Philadelphia, September 19, 1916, ninth in-
          ning.

Philadelphia vs. Detroit, September 18, 1940, second
          game, ninth inning.
          Cleveland vs. Detroit, August 7, 1941, ninth inning.

Most Runs, Inning, by Pinch-Runners

  A. L.—3—Chicago vs. Minnesota, September 16, 1967, ninth inning.
          Chicago vs. Oakland, May 19, 1968, second game, fifth
          inning.
          Oakland vs. California, May 7, 1975, seventh inning.
  N. L.—2—Made in many innings.

Most Players, Two or More Runs in One Inning

  N. L.—7—Chicago vs. Detroit, September 6, 1883, seventh inning.
  N. L. since 1900—6—Brooklyn vs. Cincinnati, May 21, 1952, first in-
          ning.
  A. L.—5—New York vs. Washington, July 6, 1920, fifth inning.
          New York vs. Boston, June 21, 1945, fifth inning.
          Boston vs. Philadelphia, July 4, 1948, seventh inning.
          Cleveland vs. Philadelphia, June 18, 1950, second game,
          first inning.
          Boston vs. Detroit, June 18, 1953, seventh inning.

Most Innings Scored, Nine-Inning Game (Scoring Every Inning)

  A. A.—9—Columbus vs. Pittsburgh, June 14, 1883.
          Kansas City vs. Brooklyn, May 20, 1889.
  N. L.—9—Cleveland vs. Boston, August 15, 1889.
          Washington vs. Boston, June 22, 1894.
          Cleveland vs. Philadelphia, July 12, 1894.
          Chicago vs. Louisville, June 29, 1897.
          New York vs. Philadelphia, June 1, 1923.
          St. Louis vs. Chicago, September 13, 1964.
  A. L.—8—Boston vs. Cleveland, September 16, 1903, did not bat in
          ninth.
          Cleveland vs. Boston, July 7, 1923, first game, did not bat
          in ninth.
          New York vs. St. Louis, July 26, 1939, did not bat in ninth.
          Chicago vs. Boston, May 11, 1949, did not bat in ninth.

Most Innings Scored, Game, Nine Innings, Both Clubs

  N. L.—15—Philadelphia 8, Detroit 7, July 1, 1887.
          Washington 9, Boston 6, June 22, 1894.
  A. A.—15—Kansas City 9, Brooklyn 6, May 20, 1889.
  P. L.—15—New York 8, Chicago 7, May 23, 1890.
  A. L.—14—Baltimore 8, Philadelphia 6, May 7, 1901.
          St. Louis 7, Detroit 7, April 23, 1927.
          Detroit 7, Chicago 7, July 2, 1940.
  N. L. since 1900—14—New York 9, Philadelphia 5, June 1, 1923.
          Pittsburgh 8, Chicago 6, July 6, 1975.
          Los Angeles 8, Chicago 6, May 25, 1976.

Most Consecutive Innings Scored During Season

  A. L.—17—Boston, September 15 (last 3 innings), September 16 (8
          innings), September 17 (first 6 innings), 1903 (3
          games).
  N. L.—14—Pittsburgh, July 31 (last 5 innings), August 1 (8 innings),
          August 2 (first inning), 1894 (3 games).
          New York, July 18 (last 3 innings) July 19 (8 innings),
          July 20 (first 3 innings), 1949 (3 games).

Most Innings, League, Scoring 10 or More Runs

  N. L.—30—Chicago, 1876 to date.
  A. L.—22—Boston, 1901 to date.
  N. L. since 1900—19—Brooklyn-Los Angeles, 1900 through 1957 in
          Brooklyn, 1958 to date in Los Angeles.

Most Innings, Season, Scoring 10 or More Runs

  N. L.—5—Boston, 1894.
  A. L.—3—Washington, 1930.
  N. L. since 1900—3—Brooklyn, 1943.

Most Innings, Game, Scoring 10 or More Runs

  N. L.—2—Chicago vs. Philadelphia, August 25, 1922; 10 in second,
          14 in fourth inning.
          St. Louis vs. Philadelphia, July 6, 1929, second game; 10 in
          first, 10 in fifth inning.
          Brooklyn vs. Pittsburgh, July 10, 1943; 10 in first, 10 in
          fourth inning.
  A. L.—1—Made in many games.

**Most Innings, Game, Scoring 10+ Runs, Both Clubs (Each Club
Scoring)**

  A. L.—2—Philadelphia, 11 in third vs. New York, 10 in fifth, June 3,
          1933.
  N. L.—Never accomplished.

1st Through 26th Innings

Most Runs, First Inning

N. L.— 16—Boston vs. Baltimore, June 18, 1894, a.m. game.
N. L. since 1900—15—Brooklyn vs. Cincinnati, May 21, 1952.
A. L.— 14—Cleveland vs. Philadelphia, June 18, 1950, second game.

Most Runs, First Inning, Both Clubs

A. A.— 19—Washington 14, Baltimore 5, June 17, 1891.
N. L.— 16—Boston 16, Baltimore 0, June 18, 1894, a.m. game.
N. L. since 1900—15—Brooklyn 15, Cincinnati 0, May 21, 1952.
A. L.— 14—Cleveland 14, Philadelphia 0, June 18, 1950, second game.
　　　　　Chicago 11, Baltimore 3, August 3, 1956.

Most Runs, Second Inning

N. L.— 13—New York vs. Cleveland, July 19, 1890, first game.
　　　　　Atlanta vs. Houston, September 20, 1972.
A. L.— 13—Kansas City vs. Chicago, April 21, 1956.

Most Runs, Second Inning, Both Clubs

A. L.— 14—Philadelphia 10, Detroit 4, September 23, 1913.
　　　　　New York 11, Detroit 3, August 28, 1936, second game.
N. L.— 13—New York 13, Cleveland 0, July 19, 1890, first game.
　　　　　Chicago 10, Philadelphia 3, August 25, 1922.
　　　　　Brooklyn 11, New York 2, April 29, 1930.
　　　　　Atlanta 13, Houston 0, September 20, 1972.

Most Runs, Third Inning

N. L.— 14—Cleveland vs. Washington, August 7, 1889.
N. L. since 1900—13—San Francisco vs. St. Louis, May 7, 1966.
A. L.— 12—New York vs. Washington, September 11, 1949, first game.

Most Runs, Third Inning, Both Clubs

N. L.— 14—Cleveland 14, Washington 0, August 7, 1889.
N. L. since 1900—13—San Francisco 13, St. Louis 0, May 7, 1966.
　　　　　St. Louis 7, Atlanta 6, August 21, 1973.
A. L.— 12—Boston 8, Washington 4, August 12, 1949, second game.
　　　　　New York 12, Washington 0, September 11, 1949, first game.

Most Runs, Fourth Inning

N. L.— 15—Hartford vs. New York, May 13, 1876.
N. L. since 1900—14—Chicago vs. Philadelphia, August 25, 1922.
A. L.— 13—Chicago vs. Washington, September 26, 1943, first game.

Most Runs, Fourth Inning, Both Clubs

N. L.— 15—Hartford 15, New York 0, May 13, 1876.
　　　　　Chicago 14, Philadelphia 1, August 25, 1922.
A. L.— 13—Chicago 13, Washington 0, September 26, 1943, first game.

Most Runs, Fifth Inning

A. L.— 14—New York vs. Washington, July 6, 1920.
N. L.— 13—Chicago vs. Pittsburgh, August 16, 1890.
N. L. since 1900—12—New York vs. Boston, September 3, 1926.
　　　　　Cincinnati vs. Atlanta, April 25, 1977.
　　　　　Montreal vs. Chicago, September 24, 1985.

Most Runs, Fifth Inning, Both Clubs

N. L.— 16—Brooklyn 11, New York 5, June 3, 1890.
N. L. since 1900—15—Brooklyn 10, Cincinnati 5, June 12, 1949.
　　　　　Philadelphia 9, Pittsburgh 6, April 16, 1953.
A. L.— 14—New York 14, Washington 0, July 6, 1920.

Most Runs, Sixth Inning

P. L.— 14—Philadelphia vs. Buffalo, June 26, 1890.
A. L.— 13—Cleveland vs. Boston, July 7, 1923, first game.
　　　　　Detroit vs. New York, June 17, 1925.
N. L.— 12—Chicago vs. Cincinnati, May 8, 1890.
　　　　　Philadelphia vs. Chicago, July 21, 1923, first game.
　　　　　Chicago vs. Philadelphia, August 21, 1935, second game.

Most Runs, Sixth Inning, Both Clubs

A. L.— 15—Philadelphia 10, New York 5, September 5, 1912, first game.
　　　　　Detroit 10, Minnesota 5, June 13, 1967.
N. L.— 15—New York 10, Cincinnati 5, June 12, 1979.

Most Runs, Seventh Inning

N. L.— 18—Chicago vs. Detroit, September 6, 1883.
A. L.— 17—Boston vs. Detroit, June 18, 1953.
N. L. since 1900—12—Chicago vs. Cincinnati, May 28, 1925.
　　　　　Brooklyn vs. St. Louis, August 30, 1953.

Most Runs, Seventh Inning, Both Clubs

N. L.— 18—Chicago 18, Detroit 0, September 6, 1883.
A. L.— 17—Boston 17, Detroit 0, June 18, 1953.

Most Runs, Eighth Inning

A. L.— 13—Philadelphia vs. Cleveland, June 15, 1925.
　　　　　Cleveland vs. Boston, April 10, 1977.
N. L.— 13—Brooklyn vs. Cincinnati, August 8, 1954.

Most Runs, Eighth Inning, Both Clubs

A. L.— 19—Cleveland 13, Boston 6, April 10, 1977.
N. L.— 14—New York 11, Pittsburgh 3, May 25, 1954.
　　　　　Brooklyn 13, Cincinnati 1, August 8, 1954.

Most Runs, Ninth Inning

N. L.— 14—Baltimore vs. Boston, April 24, 1894.
N. L. since 1900—12—San Francisco vs. Cincinnati, August 23, 1961.
A. L.— 13—California vs. Texas, September 14, 1978.

Most Runs, Ninth Inning, Both Clubs

N. L.— 17—Boston 10, New York 7, June 20, 1912.
A. L.— 15—Toronto 11, Seattle 4, July 20, 1984.

Most Runs, Ninth Inning, With Two Out

A. L.— 9—Cleveland vs. Washington, May 23, 1901; won 14 to 13.
　　　　　Boston vs. Milwaukee, June 2, 1901; won 13 to 2.
　　　　　Cleveland vs. New York, August 4, 1929, second game; won 14 to 6.
N. L.— 7—Chicago vs. Cincinnati, June 29, 1952, first game; won 9 to 8.
　　　　　San Francisco vs. Pittsburgh, May 1, 1973; won 8 to 7.

Most Runs, Ninth Inning, With Two Out, None on Base

A. L.— 9—Cleveland vs. Washington, May 23, 1901; won 14 to 13.
　　　　　Boston vs. Milwaukee, June 2, 1901; won 13 to 2.
N. L.— 7—Chicago vs. Cincinnati, June 29, 1952, first game; won 9 to 8.

Most Runs, Tenth Inning

A. L.— 11—Minnesota vs. Oakland, June 21, 1969.
N. L.— 10—Boston vs. New York, June 17, 1887, a.m. game.
N. L. since 1900—9—Cincinnati vs. Philadelphia, August 24, 1947, first game.

Most Runs, Tenth Inning, Both Clubs

A. L.— 12—Minnesota 11, Oakland 1, June 21, 1969.
N. L.— 11—New York 6, Brooklyn 5, April 24, 1955.

Most Runs, Eleventh Inning

N. L.— 10—Kansas City vs. Detroit, July 21, 1886.
A. L.— 8—Philadelphia vs. Detroit, May 1, 1951.
N. L. since 1900—8—Brooklyn vs. Milwaukee, August 29, 1954, first game.
　　　　　Pittsburgh vs. Montreal, July 24, 1984.

Most Runs, Eleventh Inning, Both Clubs

A. L.— 11—Seattle 6, Boston 5, May 16, 1969.
N. L.— 11—New York 6, Chicago 5, June 30, 1979.

Most Runs, Twelfth Inning

A. L.— 11—New York vs. Detroit, July 26, 1928, first game.
N. L.— 9—Chicago vs. Pittsburgh, July 23, 1923.

Most Runs, Twelfth Inning, Both Clubs

A. L.— 11—New York 11, Detroit 0, July 26, 1928, first game.
N. L.— 9—Chicago 9, Pittsburgh 0, July 23, 1923.
　　　　　New York 8, Brooklyn 1, May 30, 1940, second game.
　　　　　Houston 8, Cincinnati 1, June 2, 1966.
　　　　　San Diego 5, Houston 4, July 5, 1969.

Most Runs, Thirteenth Inning

N. L.— 10—Cincinnati vs. Brooklyn, May 15, 1919.
A. L.— 9—Cleveland vs. Detroit, August 5, 1933, first game.

Most Runs, Fourteenth Inning

N. L.—8—New York vs. Pittsburgh, June 15, 1929.
A. L.—7—Cleveland vs. St. Louis, June 3, 1935.

Most Runs, Fifteenth Inning

A. L.— 12—Texas vs. Oakland, July 3, 1983.
N. L.— 7—St. Louis vs. Boston, September 28, 1928.

Most Runs, Sixteenth Inning

A. L.—8—Chicago vs. Washington, May 20, 1920.
N. L.—5—Cincinnati vs. New York, August 20, 1973.

Most Runs, Seventeenth Inning

N. L.—7—New York vs. Pittsburgh, July 16, 1920.
A. L.—6—New York vs. Detroit, July 20, 1941.

Most Runs, Eighteenth Inning

N. L.—5—Chicago vs. Boston, May 14, 1927.
A. L.—4—Minnesota vs. Seattle, July 19, 1969.

Most Runs, Nineteenth Inning

N. L.—5—New York vs. Atlanta, July 4, 1985.
A. L.—4—Cleveland vs. Detroit, April 27, 1984.

Most Runs, Nineteenth Inning, Both Clubs

N. L.—7—New York 5, Atlanta 2, July 4, 1985.
A. L.—5—Chicago 3, Boston 2, July 13, 1951.

Most Runs, Twentieth Inning

N. L.—4—Brooklyn vs. Boston, July 5, 1940.
A. L.—3—Boston vs. Seattle, July 27, 1969.
Washington vs. Cleveland, September 14, second game, finished September 20, 1971.

Most Runs, Twentieth Inning, Both Clubs

N. L.—4—Brooklyn 4, Boston 0, July 5, 1940.
A. L.—4—Boston 3, Seattle 1, July 27, 1969.
Washington 3, Cleveland 1, September 14, second game, finished September 20, 1971.

Most Runs, Twenty-First Inning

A. L.—4—Chicago vs. Cleveland, May 26, finished May 28, 1973.
N. L.—3—San Diego vs. Montreal, May 21, 1977.

Most Runs, Twenty-First Inning, Both Clubs

A. L.—6—Milwaukee 3, Chicago 3, May 8, finished May 9, 1984.
N. L.—3—San Diego 3, Montreal 0, May 21, 1977.

Most Runs, Twenty-Second Inning

A. L.—2—New York vs. Detroit, June 24, 1962.
N. L.—1—Brooklyn vs. Pittsburgh, August 22, 1917.
Chicago vs. Boston, May 17, 1927.

Most Runs, Twenty-Third Inning

N. L.—2—San Francisco vs. New York, May 31, 1964, second game.
A. L.—0—Boston vs. Philadelphia, September 1, 1906.
Philadelphia vs. Boston, September 1, 1906.
Detroit vs. Philadelphia, July 21, 1945.
Philadelphia vs. Detroit, July 21, 1945.

Most Runs, Twenty-Fourth Inning

A. L.—3—Philadelphia vs. Boston, September 1, 1906.
N. L.—1—Houston vs. New York, April 15, 1968.

Most Runs, Twenty-Fifth Inning

N. L.—1—St. Louis vs. New York, September 11, 1974.
A. L.—1—Chicago vs. Milwaukee, May 8, finished May 9, 1984.

Most Runs, Twenty-Sixth Inning

N. L.—0—Boston vs. Brooklyn, May 1, 1920.
Brooklyn vs. Boston, May 1, 1920.
A. L.—No twenty-six inning game.

Games Being Shut Out

Most Games Shut Out, Season

N. L.—33—St. Louis, 1908.
A. L.—30—Washington, 1909 (includes 1 tie).

Most Consecutive Games Shut Out, Season

N. L.—4—Boston, May 19 through 23, 1906.
Cincinnati, July 30 through August 3, 1908.
Cincinnati, July 31 through August 3, 1931.
Houston, June 20, 21, 22, 23, first game, 1963.
Houston, September 9, 10, 11, 11, 1966.
Chicago, June 16, 16, 19, 20, 1968.
A. L.—4—Boston, August 2 through 6, 1906.
Philadelphia, September 23 through 25, 1906.
St. Louis, August 25 through 30, 1913.
Washington, September 19, 20, 21, 22, 1958.
Washington, September 1, 2, 4, 5, 1964.

Most Games Shut Out, Season, League Champion

N. L. (154-game season)—16—New York, 1913 (includes 1 tie).
15—Philadelphia, 1915.
N. L. (162-game season)—17—Los Angeles, 1966.

A. L. (154-game season)—16—Chicago, 1906 (includes 2 ties).
14—Philadelphia, 1913.
Detroit, 1945.
A. L. (162-game season)—15—Boston, 1967.

Most Consecutive Innings Shut Out by Opponent, Season

A. L.—48—Philadelphia, September 22, last 7 innings, through September 26, first 5 innings, 1906.
N. L.—48—Chicago, June 15, last 8 innings, through June 21, first 2 innings, 1968.

Most Consecutive Games Without Being Shut Out, League

A. L.—308—New York, August 3, 1931 through August 2, 1933.
N. L.—182—Philadelphia, August 17, 1893 through May 10, 1895.

Fewest Games Shut Out, Season, 150 or More Games

A. L.—0—New York, 156 games, 1932.
N. L.—1—Brooklyn, 155 games, 1953.
Cincinnati, 162 games, 1970.

Hits
Season

Most Hits, Season

N. L.—1783—Philadelphia, 156 games, 1930.
A. L.—1724—Detroit, 154 games, 1921.

Fewest Hits, Season

N. L.—1044—Brooklyn, 154 games, 1908.
A. L.—1061—Chicago, 156 games, 1910.

Most Players, 200 or More Hits, Season

N. L.—4—Philadelphia, 1929.
A. L.—4—Detroit, 1937.

Most Players, 100 or More Hits, Season

N. L.—9—Pittsburgh, 1921, 1972, 1976; Philadelphia, 1923; New York, 1928; St. Louis, 1979.
A. L.—9—Philadelphia, 1925; Detroit, 1934, 1980; Baltimore, 1973; Kansas City, 1974, 1977, 1980, 1982; Oakland, 1975; Texas, 1976, 1978; Chicago, 1977; New York, 1977; California, 1978, 1982; Milwaukee, 1978; Toronto, 1983; Boston, 1984.

Fewest Players, 100 or More Hits, Season

N. L.—0—New York, 1972.
A. L.—2—Washington, 1965.

Game

Most Hits, Game, Nine Innings

N. L.—36—Philadelphia vs. Louisville, August 17, 1894.
N. L. since 1900—31—New York vs. Cincinnati, June 9, 1901.
A. L.—30—New York vs. Boston, September 28, 1923.

Most Hits, Game, Nine Innings, Both Clubs

N. L.—51—Philadelphia 26, Chicago 25, August 25, 1922.
A. L.—45—Philadelphia 27, Boston 18, July 8, 1902.
Detroit 28, New York 17, September 29, 1928.

Most Hits, Extra-Inning Game

N. L.—Less than nine-inning game.
N. L.—since 1900—Less than nine-inning game.
A. L.—33—Cleveland vs. Philadelphia, July 10, 1932, 18 innings.

Most Hits, Extra-Inning Game, Both Clubs

A. L.—58—Cleveland 33, Philadelphia 25, July 10, 1932, 18 innings.
N. L.—52—New York 28, Pittsburgh 24, June 15, 1929, 14 innings.

Most Hits by Pinch-Hitters, Nine-Inning Game

N. L.—6—Brooklyn vs. Philadelphia, September 9, 1926.
A. L.—4—Cleveland vs. Chicago, April 22, 1930.
Philadelphia vs. Detroit, September 18, 1940, second game.
Detroit vs. Chicago, April 22, 1953.
Kansas City vs. Detroit, September 1, 1958, a.m. game.
Cleveland vs. Boston, September 21, 1967.
Oakland vs. Detroit, August 30, 1970.
Chicago vs. Oakland, September 7, 1970, second game.

Most Hits by Infield, Game

N. L.—18—Boston vs. St. Louis, May 31, 1897.
A. L.—16—Boston vs. St. Louis, June 8, 1950.
N. L. since 1900—16—Pittsburgh vs. Chicago, September 16, 1975.

Most Hits by Outfield, Game
N. L. — 16 — New York vs. Cincinnati, June 9, 1901.
A. L. — 12 — Baltimore vs. Detroit, June 24, 1901.
    Detroit vs. Washington, July 30, 1917.
    Cleveland vs. Philadelphia, April 29, 1952.
    Boston vs. Baltimore, July 11, 1969, second game.

Most Hits in Shutout Loss
N. L. — 14 — New York vs. Chicago, September 14, 1913; lost 7 to 0,
    15 total bases.
A. L. — 14 — Cleveland vs. Washington, July 10, 1928, second game;
    lost 9 to 0, 16 total bases.

Most Hits in Extra-Inning Shutout Loss
N. L. — 15 — Boston vs. Pittsburgh, July 10, 1901, 12 innings, 16 total
    bases; lost 1 to 0.
    Boston vs. Pittsburgh, August 1, 1918, 21 innings, 15
    total bases; lost 2 to 0.
A. L. — 15 — Boston vs. Washington, July 3, 1913, 15 innings, 19 total
    bases; lost 1 to 0.

Most Consecutive Hits, Game
N. L. — 12 — St. Louis vs. Boston, September 17, 1920, fourth and fifth
    innings.
    Brooklyn vs. Pittsburgh, June 23, 1930, sixth and seventh
    innings.
A. L. — 10 — Boston vs. Milwaukee, June 2, 1901, ninth inning.
    Detroit vs. Baltimore, September 20, 1983, first inning (1
    walk during streak) .

Fewest Hits, Game
N. L., U. A., A. A., A. L. — 0 — Made in many games.

Fewest Hits, Extra-Inning Game
A. A. — 0 — Toledo vs. Brooklyn, October 4, 1884, 10 innings.
N. L. — 0 — Philadelphia vs. New York, July 4 1908, a.m. game, 10
    innings.
    Chicago vs. Cincinnati, May 2, 1917, 10 innings.
    Chicago vs. Cincinnati, August 19, 1965, first game, 10
    innings.
N. L. — 1 — Milwaukee vs. Pittsburgh, May 26, 1959, 13 innings.
A. L. — 1 — Cleveland vs. Chicago, September 6, 1903, 10 innings.
    Boston vs. St. Louis, September 18, 1934, 10 innings.
    Los Angeles vs. New York, May 22, 1962, 12 innings.

Fewest Hits, Nine-Inning Game, Both Clubs
N. L. — 1 — Los Angeles 1, Chicago 0, September 9, 1965.
A. A. — 2 — Philadelphia 1, Baltimore 1, August 20, 1886.
A. L. — 2 — Cleveland 1, St. Louis 1, April 23, 1952.
    Chicago 1, Baltimore 1, June 21, 1956.
    Baltimore 1, Kansas City 1, September 12, 1964.
    Baltimore 2, Detroit 0, April 30, 1967, first game.

Most Games Held Hitless, Season
A. A. — 2 — Pittsburgh 1884.
N. L. — 2 — Providence 1885; Boston 1898; Philadelphia 1960; Chica-
    go 1965; Cincinnati 1971.
A. L. — 2 — Cleveland 1910; Chicago 1917; Philadelphia 1923; Detroit
    1967, 1973; California 1977.

Most Consecutive Years Without Being Held Hitless, Game
N. L. — 40 — St. Louis, 1920 through 1959.
A. L. — 29 — Washington, 1918 through 1946.

Most Games Held to One Hit, Season
A. L. — 5 — St. Louis, 1910.
    Cleveland, 1915.
N. L. — 4 — New York, 1965.

Most Players, Six Hits in Game, Nine Innings
A. A. — 2 — Cincinnati vs. Pittsburgh, September 12, 1883.
N. L. — 2 — Baltimore vs. St. Louis, September 3, 1897.
A. L. — 1 — Made in many games.

Most Players, Five or More Hits in Game
N. L. — 4 — Philadelphia vs. Louisville, August 17, 1894.
N. L. since 1900 — 3 — New York vs. Cincinnati, June 9, 1901.
    New York vs. Philadelphia, June 1, 1923.
A. L. — 3 — Detroit vs. Washington, July 30, 1917.
    Cleveland vs. Philadelphia, July 10, 1932, 18 innings.
    Washington vs. Cleveland, May 16, 1933, 12 innings.
    Chicago vs. Philadelphia, September 11, 1936.

Most Players, Five or More Hits, Game, Nine Innings, Both Clubs
N. L. — 4 — Philadelphia 4, Louisville 0, August 17, 1894.
N. L. since 1900 — 3 — New York 3, Cincinnati 0, June 9, 1901.
    New York 3, Philadelphia 0, June 1, 1923.

A. L. — 3 — Detroit 3, Washington 0, July 30, 1917.
    Washington 3, Cleveland 0, May 16, 1933, 12 innings.
    Chicago 3, Philadelphia 0, September 11, 1936.

Most Players, Five or More Hits, Extra-Inn. Game, Both Clubs
A. L. — 5 — Cleveland 3, Philadelphia 2, July 10, 1932, 18 innings.

Most Players, Four or More Hits in Game, Nine Innings
N. L. — 7 — Chicago vs. Cleveland, July 24, 1882.
N. L. since 1900 — 5 — San Francisco vs. Los Angeles, May 13, 1958.
A. L. — 4 — Detroit vs. New York, September 29, 1928.
    Chicago vs. Philadelphia, September 11, 1936.
    Boston vs. St. Louis, June 8, 1950.

Most Players, Four or More Hits, Game, Nine Innings, Both Clubs
N. L. — 7 — Chicago 7, Cleveland 0, July 24, 1882.
  N. L. since 1900 — 5 — St. Louis 4, Philadelphia 1, July 6, 1929, second
    game.
    San Francisco 5, Los Angeles 0, May 13, 1958.
A. L. — 4 — Detroit 4, New York 0, September 29, 1928.
    Chicago 4, Philadelphia 0, September 11, 1936.
    Boston 4, St. Louis 0, June 8, 1950.

Most Players, Three or More Hits in Game, Nine Innings
N. L. — 8 — Chicago vs. Detroit, September 6, 1883.
N. L. since 1900 — 7 — Pittsburgh vs. Philadelphia, June 12, 1928.
A. L. — 7 — New York vs. Philadelphia, June 28, 1939, first game.
    Chicago vs. Kansas City, April 23, 1955.

Most Players, Two or More Hits in Game, Nine Innings
A. A. — 10 — Brooklyn vs. Philadelphia, June 25, 1885.
N. L. — 10 — Pittsburgh vs. Philadelphia, August 7, 1922.
    New York vs. Philadelphia, September 2, 1925, second
    game.
A. L. — 9 — Held by many clubs.

Most Players, One or More Hits in Game, Nine Innings
A. L. — 14 — Cleveland vs. St. Louis, August 12, 1948, second game.
N. L. — 14 — San Francisco vs. San Diego, June 23, 1986.

Most Players, One or More Hits, Game, Nine Innings, Both Clubs
N. L. — 23 — St. Louis 13, Philadelphia 10, May 11, 1923.
A. L. — 22 — New York 12, Cleveland 10, July 18, 1934.

Each Player, One or More Hits, Consecutive Games
N. L. — 5 — Pittsburgh, August 5, 7, 8, 9, 10, 1922.

Doubleheader & Consecutive Games

Most Hits, Doubleheader
N. L. — 46 — Pittsburgh vs. Philadelphia, August 8, 1922.
A. L. — 43 — New York vs. Philadelphia, June 28, 1939.

Most Hits, Doubleheader, Both Clubs
N. L. — 73 — Washington 41, Philadelphia 32, July 4, 1896.
    St. Louis 43, Philadelphia 30, July 6, 1929.
A. L. — 65 — Boston 35, Philadelphia 30, July 4, 1939.

Most Hits by Pitchers, Doubleheader
A. L. — 8 — New York vs. Cleveland, June 17, 1936.

Fewest Hits, Doubleheader
N. L. — 3 — Brooklyn vs. St. Louis, September 21, 1934.
    New York vs. Philadelphia, June 21, 1964.
A. L. — 3 — Chicago vs. Boston, May 27, 1945.
    California vs. Cleveland, June 8, 1969.

Fewest Hits, Doubleheader, Both Clubs
A. L. — 11 — Detroit 7, St. Louis 4, May 30, 1914.
N. L. — 12 — Chicago 6, Pittsburgh 6, September 3, 1905.
    St. Louis 6, Brooklyn 6, July 24, 1909.

Most Hits, Two Consecutive Games
N. L. — 55 — Philadelphia vs. Louisville, August 16, 17, 1894.
A. L. — 51 — Boston vs. St. Louis, June 7, 8, 1950.
N. L. since 1900 — 49 — Pittsburgh vs. Philadelphia, August 7, August
    8, first game, 1922.

Most Hits by Pitchers, Two Consecutive Games
N. L. — 9 — Chicago, May 19, 20, 1895.

Fewest Hits, Two Consecutive Nine-Inning Games
N. L. — 2 — New York vs. Providence, June 17 (1), 18 (1), 1884.
    Cincinnati vs. Brooklyn, July 5 (1), 6 (1), 1900.
    Boston vs. New York, September 28, second game (1);
    September 30, first game (1), 1916.

New York vs. Milwaukee, September 10, (1), September 11 (1), 1965.

Los Angeles vs. Houston, September 26 (0), 27 (2), 1981.

A. A.—2—Baltimore vs. St. Louis - Louisville, July 28 (1), 29 (1), 1886.

A. L.—2—New York vs. Cleveland, September 25 (1), 26 (1), 1907.

St. Louis vs. Washington, Philadelphia, September 25, second game (1), September 27, 1910 (1), first game.

Chicago vs. Washington, August 10 (1), 11 (1), 1917.

Milwaukee vs. Kansas City, June 18 (2), June 19 (0), 1974.

Inning

Most Hits, Inning

N. L.— 18—Chicago vs. Detroit, September 6, 1883, seventh inning.

A. L.— 14—Boston vs. Detroit, June 18, 1953, seventh inning.

N. L. since 1900—12—St. Louis vs. Cincinnati, April 22, 1925, first inning.

Most Hits, Inning, by Pinch-Hitters

N. L.—4—Chicago vs. Brooklyn, May 21, 1927, second game, ninth inning.

Philadelphia vs. Pittsburgh, September 12, 1974, eighth inning.

A. L.—4—Philadelphia vs. Detroit, September 18, 1940, second game, ninth inning.

Most Consecutive Hits, Inning

N. L.— 10—St. Louis vs. Boston, September 17, 1920, fourth inning.

St. Louis vs. Philadelphia, June 12, 1922, sixth inning.

Chicago vs. Boston, September 7, 1929, first game, fourth inning.

Brooklyn vs. Pittsburgh, June 23, 1930, sixth inning.

A. L.— 10—Boston vs. Milwaukee, June 2, 1901, ninth inning.

Detroit vs. Baltimore, September 20, 1983, first inning (1 walk during streak).

Most Consecutive Hits, Inning, by Pinch-Hitters

N. L. - A. L.—3—Made in many innings.

N. L.—Last time, Pittsburgh vs. San Francisco, July 2, 1961, first game, eighth inning.

A. L.—Last time, Boston vs. Chicago, June 4, 1975, ninth inning.

Most Consecutive Hits, Start of Game, With None Out

N. L.—8—Philadelphia vs. Chicago, August 5, 1975, 4 singles, 2 doubles, 2 home runs.

Pittsburgh vs. Atlanta, August 26, 1975, 7 singles, 1 triple.

A. L.—8—Oakland vs. Chicago, September 27, 1981, first game, 8 singles.

Most Batters Reaching First Base Safely, Inning

A. L.—20—Boston vs. Detroit, June 18, 1953, seventh inning.

N. L.—19—Boston vs. Baltimore, June 18, 1894, a.m. game, first inning.

Brooklyn vs. Cincinnati, May 21, 1952, first inning.

Most Consecutive Batters Reaching Base Safely, Inning

N. L.— 19—Brooklyn vs. Cincinnati, May 21, 1952, first inning.

A. L.— 13—Kansas City vs. Chicago, April 21, 1956, second inning.

Most Batters Reaching Base Safely Three Times, Inning

N. L.—3—Chicago vs. Detroit, September 6, 1883, seventh inning.

Boston vs. Baltimore, June 18, 1894, a.m. game, first inning.

N. L. since 1900—1—Brooklyn vs. Cincinnati, May 21, 1952, first inning.

A. L.—3—Boston vs. Detroit, June 18, 1953, seventh inning.

Most Players Making Two or More Hits, Inning

N. L.—6—Chicago vs. Detroit, September 6, 1883, seventh inning.

A. L.—5—Philadelphia vs. Boston, July 8, 1902, sixth inning.

New York vs. Philadelphia, September 10, 1921, ninth inning.

Singles

Most Singles, Season

N. L.— 1338—Philadelphia, 132 games, 1894.

A. L.— 1298—Detroit, 154 games, 1921.

N. L. since 1900—1297—Pittsburgh, 155 games, 1922.

Fewest Singles, Season

A. L.— 811— Baltimore, 162 games, 1968.

N. L.— 843— New York, 156 games, 1972.

Most Singles, Game

N. L.— 28—Philadelphia vs. Louisville, August 17, 1894.

Boston vs. Baltimore, April 20, 1896.

A. L.— 24—Cleveland vs. New York, July 29, 1928.

Boston vs. Detroit, June 18, 1953.

N. L. since 1900—23—New York vs. Chicago, September 21, 1931.

New York vs. Atlanta, July 4, 1985, 19 innings.

Most Singles, Game, Both Clubs

N. L.— 37—Baltimore 21, Washington 16, August 8, 1896.

N. L. since 1900—36—New York 22, Cincinnati 14, June 9, 1901.

A. L.— 36—Chicago 21, Boston 15, August 15, 1922.

Most Singles, Inning

N. L.— 11—St. Louis vs. Cincinnati, April 22, 1925, first inning.

A. L.— 11—Boston vs. Detroit, June 18, 1953, seventh inning.

Most Consecutive Singles, Inning

N. L.— 10—St. Louis vs. Boston, September 17, 1920, fourth inning.

A. L.— 8—Washington vs. Cleveland, May 7, 1951, fourth inning.

Oakland vs. Chicago, September 27, 1981, first game, first inning.

Doubles

Most Doubles, Season

N. L.— 373— St. Louis, 154 games, 1930.

A. L.— 358— Cleveland, 154 games, 1930.

Fewest Doubles, Season

N. L.— 110— Brooklyn, 154 games, 1908.

A. L.— 116— Chicago, 156 games, 1910.

Most Consecutive Years Leading League in Doubles

A. L.—8—Cleveland, 1916 through 1923.

N. L.—5—St. Louis, 1920 through 1924.

Most Doubles, Game

N. L.— 14—Chicago vs. Buffalo, July 3, 1883.

N. L. since 1900—13—St. Louis vs. Chicago, July 12, 1931, second game.

A. L.— 11—Detroit vs. New York, July 14, 1934.

Most Doubles by Pinch-Hitters, Game

A. L.— 3—Cleveland vs. Washington, June 27, 1948, first game.

Chicago vs. New York, May 7, 1971.

N. L.— 3—San Francisco vs. Pittsburgh, May 5, 1958.

Most Doubles, Game, Both Clubs

N. L.— 23—St. Louis 13, Chicago 10, July 12, 1931, second game.

A. L.— 16—Cleveland 9, New York 7, July 21, 1921.

Most Doubles, Doubleheader

N. L.— 17—St. Louis vs. Chicago, July 12, 1931.

A. L.— 14—Philadelphia vs. Boston, July 8, 1905.

Most Doubles, Doubleheader, Both Clubs

N. L.— 32—St. Louis 17, Chicago 15, July 12, 1931.

A. L.— 26—Philadelphia 14, Boston 12, July 8, 1905.

Most Doubles With Bases Filled, Game

N. L. - A. L.—2—Made in many games.

Most Doubles With Bases Filled, Game, Both Clubs

N. L. - A. L.—2—Made in many games.

Most Doubles, Inning

N. L.—7—Boston vs. St. Louis, August 25, 1936, first game, first inning.

A. L.—6—Washington vs. Boston, June 9, 1934, eighth inning.

Most Consecutive Doubles, Inning

A. L.—5—Washington vs. Boston, June 9, 1934, eighth inning.

N. L.—4—Held by many clubs.

Last time—St. Louis vs. Pittsburgh, August 30, 1952, third inning.

Most Players, Two Doubles, Inning

N. L.—3—Boston vs. St. Louis, August 25, 1936, first game, first inning.

A. L.—2—New York vs. Boston, July 3, 1932, sixth inning.

Toronto vs. Baltimore, June 26, 1978, second inning.

Triples

Most Triples, Season
N. L.— 153—Baltimore, 129 games, 1894.
N. L. since 1900—129—Pittsburgh, 152 games, 1912.
A. L.— 112—Baltimore, 134 games, 1901.
  Boston, 141 games, 1903.

Fewest Triples, Season
A. L.— 13—Baltimore, 162 games, 1986.
N. L.— 14—Los Angeles, 162 games, 1986.

Most Consecutive Years Leading League in Triples
A. L.—7—Washington, 1931 through 1937 (tied 1934).
N. L.—6—Pittsburgh, 1932 through 1937.

Most Triples, Game
N. L.—9—Baltimore vs. Cleveland, September 3, 1894, first game.
N. L. since 1900—8—Pittsburgh vs. St. Louis, May 30, 1925, second game.
A. L.—6—Chicago vs. Milwaukee, September 15, 1901; second game.
  Chicago vs. New York, September 17, 1920.
  Detroit vs. New York, June 17, 1922.

Most Triples, Game, Both Clubs
N. L.— 11—Baltimore 9, Cleveland 2, September 3, 1894, first game.
N. L. since 1900—9—Pittsburgh 6, Chicago 3, July 4, 1904, p.m. game.
  Pittsburgh 8, St. Louis 1, May 30, 1925, second game.
A. L.— 9—Detroit 6, New York 3, June 17, 1922.

Most Triples With Bases Filled, Game
N. L.—2—Detroit vs. Indianapolis, May 7, 1887.
  Pittsburgh vs. Brooklyn, September 17, 1898.
  Chicago vs. Philadelphia, May 14, 1904.
  Brooklyn vs. St. Louis, August 25, 1917, first game.
  Cincinnati vs. Brooklyn, September 25, 1925.
  Pittsburgh vs. St. Louis, September 10, 1938.
  Chicago vs. Boston, June 12, 1936.
  Brooklyn vs. Philadelphia, May 24, 1953, both in eighth inning.
  Milwaukee vs. St. Louis, August 2, 1959, second game.
  Montreal vs. Cincinnati, September 1, 1979.
A. A.—2—Kansas City vs. Philadelphia, August 22, 1889.
A. L.—2—Boston vs. St. Louis, August 16, 1926, second game.
  Philadelphia vs. Washington, April 26, 1928.
  Philadelphia vs. Washington, May 1, 1949, first game.
  Detroit vs. New York, June 9, 1950.
  Cleveland vs. New York, July 27, 1978.

Most Bases-Loaded 3Bs, Game, Both Clubs, Each Club Connecting
N. L.—2—Made in many games. Last time—Chicago 1, St. Louis 1, April 22, 1938.
A. L.—2—Made in many games. Last time—Washington 1, New York 1, July 4, 1950, first game.

Longest Extra-Inning Game Without a Triple
N. L.—26 innings—Brooklyn vs. Boston, May 1, 1920.
A. L.—25 innings—Milwaukee vs. Chicago, May 8, finished May 9, 1984.
  Chicago vs. Milwaukee, May 8, finished May 9, 1984.

Longest Extra-Inning Game Without a Triple, Both Clubs
N. L.—25 innings—New York 0, St. Louis 0, September 11, 1974.
A. L.—25 innings—Milwaukee 0, Chicago 0, May 8, finished May 9, 1984.

Most Triples, Doubleheader
N. L.—9—Baltimore vs. Cleveland, September 3, 1894.
  Cincinnati vs. Chicago, May 27, 1922.
A. L.—9—Chicago vs. Milwaukee, September 15, 1901.

Most Triples, Doubleheader, Both Clubs
N. L.— 11—Baltimore 9, Cleveland 2, September 3, 1894.
N. L. since 1900—10—Cincinnati 9, Chicago 1, May 27, 1922.
  New York 7, Pittsburgh 3, July 30, 1923.
A. L.— 10—Chicago 9, Milwaukee 1, September 15, 1901.

Most Triples, Inning
A. L.—5—Chicago vs. Milwaukee, September 15, 1901, second game, eighth inning.

N. L.—4—Boston vs. Troy, May 6, 1882, eighth inning.
  Baltimore vs. St. Louis, July 27, 1892, seventh inning.
  St. Louis vs. Chicago, July 2, 1895, first inning.
  Chicago vs. St. Louis, April 17, 1899, fourth inning.
  Brooklyn vs. Pittsburgh, August 23, 1902, third inning.
  Cincinnati vs. Boston, July 22, 1926, second inning.
  New York vs. Pittsburgh, July 17, 1936, first inning.

Most Consecutive Triples, Inning
A. L.—4—Boston vs. Detroit, May 6, 1934, fourth inning.
N. L.—3—Made in many innings. Last times—Chicago vs. Philadelphia, April 25, 1981, fourth inning; Montreal vs. San Diego, May 6, 1981, ninth inning.

Home Runs
Season & Month

Most Home Runs, Season
A.L. (162-game season)—240—New York, 163 games, 1961 (112 at home, 128 on road).
A.L. (154-game season)—193—New York, 155 games, 1960 (92 at home, 101 on road).
N.L. (154-game season)—221—New York, 155 games, 1947 (131 at home, 90 on road).
  Cincinnati, 155 games, 1956 (128 at home, 93 on road).
N.L. (162-game season)—209—Chicago, 161 games (114 at home, 95 on road).

Fewest Home Runs, Season (154 or 162-Game Schedule)
N.L.—9—Pittsburgh, 157 games, 1917.
A.L.—3—Chicago, 156 games, 1908.

Most Home Runs by Pinch-Hitters, Season
N.L.— 12—Cincinnati, 1957.
  New York, 1983.
A.L.— 11—Baltimore, 1982.

Most Home Runs, Season, at Home
A.L.— 133—Cleveland, 1970, 81 games.
N.L.— 131—New York, 1947, 76 games.

Most Home Runs, Season, on Road
A.L.— 128—New York, 1961, 82 games.
N.L.— 124—Milwaukee, 1957, 77 games.

Most Home Runs, Season, Against One Club
A.L.— 48—New York vs. Kansas City, 1956.
N.L.— 44—Cincinnati vs. Brooklyn, 1956.

Most Years Leading League in Home Runs, Since 1900
A.L.—34—New York.
N.L.—27—New York-San Francisco (24 by N.Y., 3 by S.F.).

Most Consecutive Years Leading League or Tied in Home Runs
A.L.— 12—New York, 1936 through 1947.
N.L.— 7—Brooklyn, 1949 through 1955 (1954 tied).

Most Years 200 or More Home Runs, Season
A.L.—3—Detroit, 209, in 1962; 202 in 1985; 225 in 1987.
N.L.—2—Brooklyn, 208 in 1953; 201 in 1955.
  Atlanta, 207 in 1966; 201 in 1973.
  San Francisco, 204 in 1962; 205 in 1987 (Giants also had 221 representing New York in 1947).

Most Years 100 or More Home Runs, Season, Since 1900
A.L.—62—New York.
N.L.—51—New York-San Francisco (26 by N.Y., 25 by S.F.).

Most Consecutive Years, 100 or More Home Runs, Season
A.L.—35—Boston, 1946 through 1980.
N.L.—29—New York-San Francisco, 1945 through 1957 in New York, 1958 through 1973 in San Francisco.
  Cincinnati, 1952 through 1980.

Most Home Runs by Two Players, Season
A.L. (162-game season)—115—New York, 1961, Maris 61, Mantle 54.
A.L. (154-game season)—107—New York, 1927, Ruth 60, Gehrig 47.
N.L. (154-game season)—93—Chicago, 1930, Wilson 56, Hartnett 37.
N.L. (162-game season)—91—San Francisco, 1965, Mays 52, McCovey 39.

Most Home Runs by Three Players, Season

A.L. (162-game season) —143—New York, 1961, Maris 61, Mantle, 54, Skowron, 28.

A.L. (154-game season) —125—New York, 1927, Ruth 60, Gehrig 47, Lazzeri 18.

N.L. (162-game season) —124—Atlanta, 1973, Johnson 43, Evans 41, Aaron 40.

N.L. (154-game season) —122—New York, 1947, Mize 51, Marshall 36, Cooper 35.

Most Players, 50 or More Home Runs, Season

A.L.—2—New York, 1961 (Maris 61, Mantle 54).
N.L.—1—Held by many clubs.

Most Players, 40 or More Home Runs, Season

N.L.—3—Atlanta, 1973 (Johnson 43, Evans 41, Aaron 40).
A.L.—2—New York, 1927 (Ruth 60, Gehrig 47), 1930 (Ruth 49, Gehrig 41), 1931 (Ruth 46, Gehrig 46), 1961 (Maris 61, Mantle 54).
Detroit, 1961 (Colavito 45, Cash 41).
Boston, 1969 (Petrocelli 40, Yastrzemski 40).

Most Players, 30 or More Home Runs, Season

N.L.—4—Los Angeles, 1977.
A.L.—3—New York, 1941; Washington, 1959; Minnesota, 1963, 1964, 1987; Boston, 1977; Milwaukee, 1982; Cleveland, 1987.

Most Players, 20 or More Home Runs, Season

A.L.—6—New York, 1961; Minnesota, 1964; Detroit, 1986.
N.L.—6—Milwaukee, 1965.

Most Home Runs, One Month

A.L.—58—Baltimore, May, 1987.
N.L.—55—New York, July, 1947.

Game

Most Home Runs, Game

A. L.—10—Toronto vs. Baltimore, September 14, 1987.
N. L.— 8—Milwaukee vs. Pittsburgh, August 30, 1953, first game.
Cincinnati vs. Milwaukee, August 18, 1956.
San Francisco vs. Milwaukee, April 30, 1961.
Montreal vs. Atlanta, July 30, 1978.

Most Home Runs, Game, Both Clubs

A. L.—11—New York 6, Detroit 5, June 23, 1950.
Boston 6, Milwaukee 5, May 22, 1977, first game.
Toronto 10, Baltimore 1, September 14, 1987.
N. L.—11—Pittsburgh 6, Cincinnati 5, August 12, 1966, 13 innings.
Chicago 7, New York 4, June 11, 1967, second game.
Chicago 6, Cincinnati 5, July 28, 1977, 13 innings.
Chicago 6, Philadelphia 5, May 17, 1979, 10 innings.

Most Home Runs, Night Game

A. L.— 10—Toronto vs. Baltimore, September 14, 1987.
N. L.— 8—Cincinnati vs. Milwaukee, August 18, 1956.

Most Home Runs, Night Game, Both Clubs, Nine Innings

A. L.— 11—New York 6, Detroit 5, June 23, 1950.
Toronto 10, Baltimore 1, September 14, 1987.
N. L.— 10—Cincinnati 8, Milwaukee 2, August 18, 1956.
Cincinnati 7, Atlanta 3, April 21, 1970.

Most Home Runs by Pinch-Hitters, Game

N. L.—2—Philadelphia vs. New York, May 30, 1925, second game.
Philadelphia vs. St. Louis, June 2, 1928.
St. Louis vs. Brooklyn, July 21, 1930, first game.
St. Louis vs. Cincinnati, May 12, 1951, second game.
New York vs. Brooklyn, August 5, 1952.
Chicago vs. Philadelphia, June 9, 1954, second game.
New York vs. St. Louis, June 20, 1954.
San Francisco vs. Milwaukee, June 4, 1958.
Philadelphia vs. Pittsburgh, August 13, 1958.
New York vs. Philadelphia, August 15, 1962, second game, 13 innings.
Los Angeles vs. Chicago, August 8, 1963, 10 innings.
New York vs. Philadelphia, September 17, 1963.
New York vs. San Francisco, August 4, 1966.
Montreal vs. Atlanta, July 13, 1973, first game.
Chicago vs. Pittsburgh, September 10, 1974.
Los Angeles vs. St. Louis, July 23, 1975.
Chicago vs. Houston August 23, 1975.
Los Angeles vs. Chicago, August 27, 1982.
San Francisco vs. San Diego, September 28, 1987.

A. L.—2—Cleveland vs. Philadelphia, May 26, 1937.
New York vs. Kansas City, July 23, 1955.
Cleveland vs. Minnesota, August 15, 1965, second game, 11 innings.
Baltimore vs. Boston, August 26, 1966, 12 innings.
Detroit vs. Boston, August 11, 1968, first game, 14 innings.
Seattle vs. New York August 2, 1969.
Minnesota vs. Detroit, July 31, 1970.
Minnesota vs. California, July 28, 1974, second game.
Seattle vs. New York, April 27, 1979.
Chicago vs. Oakland, July 6, 1980, second game.
Minnesota vs. Oakland, May 16, 1983.
Baltimore vs. Texas, May 5, 1984.
Baltimore vs. Cleveland, August 12, 1985.
Toronto vs. Detroit, June 14, 1986.
Texas vs. Boston, September 1, 1986.
California vs. Chicago, June 28, 1987.

Most Home Runs by Pinch-Hitters, Game, Both Clubs,

N. L.—3—Philadelphia 2, St. Louis 1, June 2, 1928.
St. Louis, 2, Brooklyn 1, July 21, 1930, first game.
A. L.—2—Made in many games. Last time—Baltimore 1, Detroit 1, June 10, 1985.

Most Home Runs, Opening Game of Season

A. L.—5—New York vs. Philadelphia, April 12, 1932.
Boston vs. Washington, April 12, 1965.
Milwaukee vs. Boston, April 10, 1980.
N. L.—5—Chicago vs. St. Louis, April 14, 1936.
San Francisco vs. Milwaukee, April 14, 1964.

Most Home Runs, Opening Game of Season, Both Clubs

A. L.—7—New York 5, Philadelphia 2, April 12, 1932.
Boston 5, Washington 2, April 12, 1965.
Milwaukee 5, Boston 2, April 10, 1980.
N. L.—6—Chicago 5, St. Louis 1, April 14, 1936.

Most Home Runs, First-Game Players, Game, Both Clubs

N. L.—2—Brooklyn 1 (Ernest Koy), Philadelphia 1 (Emmett J. Mueller), April 19, 1938 (each in first inning).

Most Home Runs, Game, No Other Runs

N. L.—5—New York vs. Chicago, June 16, 1930.
St. Louis vs. Brooklyn, September 1, 1953.
Cincinnati vs. Milwaukee, April 16, 1955.
Chicago vs. Pittsburgh, April 21, 1964.
Pittsburgh vs. Los Angeles, May 7, 1973.
A. L.—5—Oakland vs. Washington, June 16, 1971.

Most Home Runs, Game, Both Clubs, No Other Runs

N. L.—5—San Francisco 3, Milwaukee 2, August 30, 1962.
Montreal 3, San Diego 2, May 16, 1986.
A. L.—4—Cleveland 4, New York 0, August 2, 1956.
New York 4, Baltimore 0, May 13, 1973, first game.

Most Home Runs, Shutout Game, No Other Runs

A. L.—4—Cleveland vs. New York, August 2, 1956.
New York vs. Baltimore, May 13, 1973, first game.
N. L.—3—St. Louis vs. New York, July 19, 1923.
Philadelphia vs. Cincinnati, August 27, 1951, second game.
San Francisco vs. Milwaukee, August 14, 1964.
Cincinnati vs. Pittsburgh, September 25, 1968.
New York vs. Philadelphia, June 29, 1971.
New York vs. Pittsburgh, September 17, 1971.
New York vs. Cincinnati, August 29, 1972.

Most Home Runs, Nine-Inning Game, None on Bases

A. L.—7—Boston vs. Toronto, July 4, 1977 (8 home runs in game by Boston).
N. L.—6—New York vs. Philadelphia, August 13, 1939, first game (7 home runs in game by New York).
New York vs. Cincinnati, June 24, 1950 (7 home runs in game by New York).
Atlanta vs. Chicago, August 3, 1967 (7 home runs in game by Atlanta).
Chicago vs. San Diego, August 19, 1970 (7 home runs in game by Chicago).

Most Home Runs, Nine-Inning Game, Both Clubs, None on Bases

A. L.—7—Minnesota 6, Cleveland 1, April 29, 1962, second game.
Chicago 5, Cleveland 2, June 18, 1974.
California 6, Oakland 1, April 23, 1985.
Minnesota 4, Chicago 3, June 21, 1987.
Toronto 6, Baltimore 1, September 14, 1987.
N. L.—7—Chicago 6, San Diego 1, August 19, 1970.
Pittsburgh 4, Cincinnati 3, June 7, 1976.

Most Home Runs, Infield, Game
N. L.—6—Milwaukee vs. Brooklyn, July 31, 1954.
    Montreal vs. Atlanta, July 30, 1978.
A. L.—5—New York vs. Philadelphia, June 3, 1932.
    New York vs. Philadelphia, May 24, 1936.
    Cleveland vs. Philadelphia, June 18, 1941.
    Boston vs. St. Louis, June 8, 1950.

Most Home Runs, Outfield, Game
N.L.—6—Cincinnati vs. Milwaukee, August 18, 1956.
    San Francisco vs. Milwaukee, April 30, 1961.
A.L.—5—New York vs. Chicago, July 28, 1940, first game.
    Cleveland vs. New York, July 13, 1945.
    Cleveland vs. Baltimore, June 10, 1959.
    New York vs. Boston, May 30, 1961.

Most Times, Five or More Home Runs in Game, Season
A.L.—8—Boston, 1977.
N.L.—6—New York, 1947.

Most Players, Three or More Home Runs in Game, Season
N.L.—4—Brooklyn, 1950 (Snider, Campanella, Hodges, Brown).
    Cincinnati, 1956 (Bell, Bailey, Kluszewski, Thurman).
A.L.—3—Cleveland, 1987 (Snyder, Carter, Jacoby).

Most Times, Two or More Homers by One Player, Game, Season
A.L.—24—New York, 1961.
N.L.—24—Atlanta, 1966.

Most Players Two or More Home Runs, Game
N. L.—3—Pittsburgh vs. St. Louis, August 16, 1947.
    Chicago vs. St. Louis, April 16, 1955, 14 innings.
    New York vs. Pittsburgh, July 8, 1956, first game.
    Cincinnati vs. Milwaukee, August 18, 1956.
A. L.—3—Boston vs. St. Louis, June 8, 1950.
    New York vs. Boston, May 30, 1961.
    Toronto vs. Baltimore, September 14, 1987.

Most Players Two or More Homers, Nine-Inning Game, Both Clubs
N. L.—4—Pittsburgh 3, St. Louis 1, August 16, 1947.
A. L.—3—Boston 3, St. Louis 0, June 8, 1950.
    New York 2, Kansas City 1, July 28, 1958.
    New York 3, Boston 0, May 30, 1961.
    Detroit 2, California 1, July 4, 1968.
    Chicago 2, Cleveland 1, June 18, 1974.
    Seattle 2, Oakland 1, August 2, 1983.
    Toronto 3, Baltimore 0, September 14, 1987.

Most Players One or More Home Runs, Game
A. L.—7—Baltimore vs. Boston, May 17, 1967 (7 home runs in game by Baltimore).
N. L.—7—Los Angeles vs. Cincinnati, May 25, 1979 (7 home runs in game by Los Angeles).

Most Players One or More Home Runs, Game, Both Clubs
N. L.—9—New York 5, Brooklyn 4, September 2, 1939, first game.
    New York 6, Pittsburgh 3, July 11, 1954, first game.
    Chicago 5, Pittsburgh 4, April 21, 1964.
    Cincinnati 6, Atlanta 3, April 21, 1970.
    Los Angeles 5, Atlanta 4, April 24, 1977.
    Cincinnati 5, Chicago 4, July 28, 1977, 13 innings.
A. L.—9—New York 5, Detroit 4, June 23, 1950.
    Minnesota 5, Boston 4, May 25, 1965.
    Baltimore 7, Boston 2, May 17, 1967.
    California 5, Cleveland 4, August 30, 1970.
    Boston 5, Milwaukee 4, May 22, 1977, first game.
    California 5, Oakland 4, April 23, 1985.

Longest Extra-Inning Game Without a Home Run, Both Clubs
N. L. 26 innings—0—Boston 0, Brooklyn 0, May 1, 1920.
A. L. 24 innings—0—Boston 0, Philadelphia 0, September 1, 1906.
    Detroit 0, Philadelphia 0, July 21, 1945.

Doubleheader & Consecutive Games

Most Home Runs, Doubleheader
A.L.—13—New York vs. Philadelphia, June 28, 1939.
N.L.—12—Milwaukee vs. Pittsburgh, August 30, 1953.

Most Home Runs, Doubleheader, Both Cubs
N.L.—15—Milwaukee 9, Chicago 6, May 30, 1956.
A.L.—14—New York 9, Philadelphia 5, May 22, 1930.

Most Home Runs by Pinch-Hitters, Doubleheader
N.L.—3—Montreal vs. Atlanta, July 13, 1973.
A.L.—2—Made in many doubleheaders.

Most Home Runs by Pinch-Hitters, Doubleheader
N.L.—4—St. Louis 2, Brooklyn 2, July 21, 1930.
A.L.—2—Made in many doubleheaders.

Most Consecutive Games, One or More Home Runs
A.L.—25—New York, June 1, second game, through June 29, second game, 1941 (40 home runs).
N.L.—24—Brooklyn, June 18 through July 10, 1953 (39 home runs).

Most Home Runs in Consec. Games in Which Homers Were Hit
N.L.—41—Cincinnati, August 4 through August 24, 1956 (21 games).
A.L.—40—New York, June 1, second game, through June 29, second game, 1941 (25 games).

Most Consecutive Games, Start of Season, One or More Homers
N.L.—13—Chicago, April 13 through May 2, second game, 1954 (28 home runs).
A.L.—8—New York, April 12 through April 23, 1932 (20 home runs).

Most Consecutive Games, Season, Two or More Home Runs
A.L.—9—Cleveland, May 13, first game, through May 21, 1962 (28 home runs).
    Baltimore, May 8 through May 16, 1987 (29 home runs).
N.L.—8—Milwaukee, July 19 through July 26, 1956 (20 home runs).

Most Home Runs, 2 Consecutive Games (Connecting Each Game)
N. L.—13—San Francisco, April 29, 30, 1961.
A. L.—13—New York, June 28, 28, 1939.

Most Home Runs, 3 Consecutive Games
A. L.—16—Boston, June 17 through June 19, 1977.
N. L.—14—Milwaukee, August 30, 30, September 2, 1953.
    Milwaukee, May 30, 30, 31, 1956.
    San Francisco, April 29, 30, May 2, 1961.
    Milwaukee, June 8, 9, 10, 1961.

Most Home Runs, 4 Consecutive Games
A. L.—18—Boston, June 16 through June 19, 1977.
N. L.—16—Milwaukee, August 30, 30, September 2, 3, 1953.
    Milwaukee, May 28, 30, 30, 31, 1956.
    Milwaukee, June 8, 9, 10, 11, first game, 1961.

Most Home Runs, 5 Consecutive Games
A. L.—21—Boston, June 14 through June 19, 1977.
N. L.—19—New York, July 7 through July 11, first game, 1954.

Most Home Runs, 6 Consecutive Games
A. L.—24—Boston, June 17 through June 22, 1977.
N. L.—22—New York, July 6 through July 11, first game, 1954.

Most Home Runs, 7 Consecutive Games
A. L.—26—Boston, June 16 through June 22, 1977.
N. L.—24—New York, July 5, second game through July 11, first game, 1954.

Most Home Runs, 8 Consecutive Games
A. L.—29—Boston, June 14 through June 22, 1977.
N. L.—26—New York, July 5, first game through July 11, first game, 1954.

Most Home Runs, 9 Consecutive Games
A. L.—30—Boston, June 14 through June 23, 1977.
    Boston, June 16 through June 24, 1977.
N. L.—27—New York, July 4, second game through July 11, first game, 1954.

Most Home Runs, 10 Consecutive Games
A. L.—33—Boston, June 14 through June 24, 1977.
N. L.—28—New York, July 4, first game through July 11, first game, 1954.

Most Home Runs, 11 Consecutive Games
A. L.—32—Baltimore, May 8 through May 18, 1987.
    Baltimore, May 9 through May 19, 1987.
N. L.—30—New York, June 22 through July 3, 1947.

Most Home Runs, 12 Consecutive Games
A. L.—35—Baltimore, May 8 through May 19, 1987.
N. L.—31—New York, June 21 through July 3, 1947.

Most Home Runs, 13 Consecutive Games
A. L.—36—Baltimore, May 8 through May 20, 1987.
N. L.—33—New York, June 20 through July 3, 1947.

Most Home Runs, 14 Consecutive Games

    A. L.— 38— Baltimore, May 8 through May 22, 1987.
    N. L.— 34— New York, June 20 through July 4, a.m. game, 1947.

Most Home Runs, 15 Consecutive Games

    N. L.— 35— New York, June 20 through July 4, p.m. game, 1947.
    A. L.— 35— Milwaukee, June 18 through July 3, 1982.

Most Home Runs, 16 Consecutive Games

    N. L.— 37— New York, June 20 through July 5, 1947.
    A. L.— 31— New York, May 22 through June 7, 1961.

Most Home Runs, 17 Consecutive Games

    N. L.— 34— Cincinnati, August 9 through August 24, 1956.
    A. L.— 32— New York, May 22 through June 8, first game, 1961.

Most Home Runs, 18 Consecutive Games

    N. L.— 36— Cincinnati, August 8 through August 24, 1956.
    A. L.— 31— New York, June 2 through June 24, 1941.

Most Home Runs, 19 Consecutive Games

    N. L.— 38— Cincinnati, August 7 through August 24, 1956.
    A. L.— 33— New York, June 1, second game, through June 24, 1941.

Most Home Runs, 20 Consecutive Games

    N. L.— 39— Cincinnati, August 4 through August 23 (also August 6 through August 24), 1956.
    A. L.— 34— New York, June 1, second game, through June 25, 1941

Most Home Runs, 21 Consecutive Games

    N. L.— 41— Cincinnati, August 4 through August 24, 1956.
    A. L.— 35— New York, June 1, second game, through June 26, 1941.

Most Home Runs, 22 Consecutive Games

    N. L.— 39— Milwaukee, July 8 through July 31, 1956.
    A. L.— 36— New York, June 1, second game, through June 27, 1941.

Most Home Runs, 23 Consecutive Games

    N. L.— 38— Brooklyn, June 18 through July 9, 1953.
    A. L.— 37— New York, June 1, second game, through June 28, 1941.

Most Home Runs, 24 Consecutive Games

    N. L.— 39— Brooklyn, June 18 through July 10, 1953.
    A. L.— 38— New York, June 1, second game, through June 29, first game, 1941.

Most Home Runs, 25 Consecutive Games

    A. L.— 40— New York, June 1, second game, through June 29, second game, 1941.
    N. L.—Never accomplished.

Inning

Most Home Runs, Inning

    N. L.— 5— New York vs. Cincinnati, June 6, 1939, fourth inning.
           Philadelphia vs. Cincinnati, June 2, 1949, eighth inning.
           San Francisco vs. Cincinnati, August 23, 1961, ninth inning.
    A. L.— 5— Minnesota vs. Kansas City, June 9, 1966, seventh inning.

Most Home Runs by Pinch-Hitters, Inning

    N. L.— 2— New York vs. St. Louis, June 20, 1954, sixth inning (Hofman, Rhodes).
           San Francisco vs. Milwaukee, June 4, 1958, tenth inning (Sauer, Schmidt, consecutive).
           Los Angeles vs. Chicago, August 8, 1963, fifth inning (Howard, Skowron, consecutive).
           Los Angeles vs. St. Louis, July 23, 1975, ninth inning (Crawford, Lacy, consecutive).
    A. L.— 2— New York vs. Kansas City, July 23, 1955, ninth inning (Cerv, Howard).
           Baltimore vs. Boston, August 26, 1966, ninth inning (Roznovsky, Powell, consecutive).
           Seattle vs. New York, April 27, 1979, eighth inning (Stinson, Meyer).
           Minnesota vs. Oakland, May 16, 1983, ninth inning (Engle, Hatcher).
           Baltimore vs. Cleveland, August 12, 1985, ninth inning (Gross, Sheets, consecutive).
           Texas vs. Boston, September 1, 1986, ninth inning (McDowell, Porter, consecutive).

Most Home Runs, Inning, Both Clubs

    A. L.— 5— St. Louis 3, Philadelphia 2, June 8, 1928, ninth inning.
           Detroit 4, New York 1, June 23, 1950, fourth inning.
           Minnesota 5, Kansas City 0, June 9, 1966, seventh inning.
           Baltimore 4, Boston 1, May 17, 1967, seventh inning.
           Minnesota 4, Oakland 1, May 16, 1983, ninth inning.

    N. L.— 5— New York 5, Cincinnati 0, June 6, 1939, fourth inning.
           Philadelphia 5, Cincinnati 0, June 2, 1949, eighth inning.
           New York 3, Boston 2, July 6, 1951, third inning.
           Cincinnati 3, Brooklyn 2, June 11, 1954, seventh inning.
           San Francisco 5, Cincinnati 0, August 23, 1961, ninth inning.
           Philadelphia 3, Chicago 2, April 17, 1964, fifth inning.
           Chicago 3, Atlanta 2, July 3, 1967, first inning.
           Pittsburgh 3, Atlanta 2, August 1, 1970, seventh inning.
           Cincinnati 3, Chicago 2, July 28, 1977, first inning.
           San Francisco 3, Atlanta 2, May 25, 1979, fourth inning.

Most Consecutive Home Runs, Inning

    N. L.— 4— Milwaukee vs. Cincinnati, June 8, 1961, seventh inning.
    A. L.— 4— Cleveland vs. Los Angeles, July 31, 1963, second game, sixth inning.
           Minnesota vs. Kansas City, May 2, 1964, eleventh inning.

Most Home Runs, Inning, With Two Out

    N. L.— 5— New York vs. Cincinnati, June 6, 1939, fourth inning.
    A. L.— 3— Cleveland vs. Philadelphia, June 25, 1939, first game, seventh inning.
           New York vs. Philadelphia, June 28, 1939, first game, third inning.
           Minnesota vs. Kansas City, June 9, 1966, seventh inning.
           Washington vs. New York, July 2, 1966, sixth inning.
           Oakland vs. Minnesota, June 22, 1969, first game, third inning.

Most Home Runs, Inning, None on Base

    N. L.— 4— New York vs. Philadelphia, August 13, 1939, first game, fourth inning.
    A. L.— 4— Cleveland vs. Los Angeles, July 31, 1963, second game, sixth inning (consecutive).
           Minnesota vs. Kansas City, May 2, 1964, eleventh inning (consecutive).
            Minnesota vs. Kansas City, June 9, 1966, seventh inning (also 1 home run with 1 on base).
           Boston vs. New York, June 17, 1977, first inning.
           Boston vs. Toronto, July 4, 1977, eighth inning.
           Boston vs. Milwaukee, May 31, 1980, fourth inning.

Most Home Runs, Start of Game

    N. L.— 3— San Diego vs. San Francisco, April 13, 1987 (Wynne, Gwynn, Kruk).
    A. A.— 2— Boston vs. Baltimore, June 25, 1891 (Brown, Joyce).
           Philadelphia vs. Boston, August 21, 1891 (McTamany, Larkin).
    A. L.— 2— Chicago vs. Boston, September 2, 1937, first game (Berger, Kreevich).
           Detroit vs. Philadelphia, June 22, 1939 (McCosky, Averill).
           New York vs. Chicago, April 27, 1955 (Bauer, Carey).
           Kansas City vs. Boston, September 18, 1958 (Tuttle, Maris).
           Minnesota vs. Cleveland, May 10, 1962 (Green, Power).
           Boston vs. Minnesota, May 1, 1971 (Aparicio, Smith).
           Cleveland vs. Detroit, June 19, 1971 (Nettles, Pinson).
           Boston vs. Milwaukee, June 20, 1973 (Miller, Smith).
           Milwaukee vs. Boston, July 29, 1975 (Money, Porter).
           Boston vs. New York, June 17, 1977 (Burleson, Lynn).
           Oakland vs. Toronto, September 9, 1983 (Henderson, Davis).
           Kansas City vs. Milwaukee, May 3, 1984 (Motley, Sheridan).
           Boston vs. Cleveland, September 5, 1985, first game (Evans, Boggs).
           Minnesota vs. Baltimore, July 18, 1986 (Puckett, Gaetti).
           Detroit vs. Cleveland, August 5, 1986, second game (Whitaker, Trammell).

Most Times, Three or More Home Runs, Inning, League

    N. L.— 40— New York-San Francisco, 1883 to date.
    A. L.— 39— New York, 1903 to date.

Most Times, Three Consec. Home Runs, Inning, League

    N. L.— 11— New York-San Francisco, 1932, 1939 (2), 1948, 1949, 1953, 1954, 1956 in New York, 1963, 1969, 1982 in San Francisco.
    A. L.— 7— Cleveland, 1902, 1939, 1950, 1951, 1962, 1963, 1970.

Most Times, Three or More Home Runs, Inning, Season

    N. L.— 5— New York, 1954.
           Chicago, 1955.
    A. L.— 4— Minnesota, 1964.

Most Times Hitting Two or More Consecutive Home Runs, Season

    A. L.— 16— Boston, 161 games, 1977.
                Milwaukee, 163 games, 1982.
    N. L.— 12— Cincinnati, 155 games, 1956.

Grand Slams

Most Grand Slams, Season

    A. L.— 10— Detroit, 1938.
                New York, 1987.
    N. L.— 9— Chicago, 1929.

Most Grand Slams by Pinch-Hitters, Season

    N. L.—3— San Francisco, 1973 (Arnold, Bonds, Goodson), 1978 (Ivie 2, Clark).
            Chicago, 1975 (Summers, LaCock, Hosley).
            Philadelphia, 1978 (Johnson 2, McBride).
    A. L.—3— Baltimore, 1982 (Ayala, Ford, Crowley).

Most Grand Slams, Game

    A. L.—2— Chicago vs. Detroit, May 1, 1901 (Hoy, MacFarland).
           Boston vs. Chicago, May 13, 1934 (Walters, Morgan).
           New York vs. Philadelphia, May 24, 1936 (Lazzeri 2).
           Boston vs. Philadelphia, July 4, 1939, second game (Tabor 2).
           Boston vs. St. Louis, July 27, 1946 (York 2).
           Detroit vs. Philadelphia, June 11, 1954, first game (Boone, Kaline).
           Baltimore vs. New York, April 24, 1960 (Pearson, Klaus).
           Boston vs. Chicago, May 10, 1960 (Wertz, Repulski).
           Baltimore vs. Minnesota, May 9, 1961 (Gentile 2).
           Minnesota vs. Cleveland, July 18, 1962, first inning (Allison, Killebrew).
           Detroit vs. Cleveland, June 24, 1968 (Northrup 2).
           Baltimore vs. Washington, June 26, 1970 (Frank Robinson 2).
           Milwaukee vs. Chicago, June 17, 1973 (Porter, Lahoud).
           Milwaukee vs. Boston, April 12, 1980 (Cooper, Money).
           California vs. Detroit, April 27, 1983 (Lynn, Sconiers).
           Boston vs. Detroit, August 7, 1984, first game (Buckner, Armas).
           California vs. Oakland, July 31, 1986 (Downing, Boone).
           Baltimore vs. Texas, August 6, 1986 (Sheets, Dwyer).
           Boston vs. Baltimore, June 10, 1987 (Burks, Barrett).
           New York vs. Toronto, June 29, 1987 (Mattingly, Winfield).
    N. L.—2— Chicago vs. Pittsburgh, August 16, 1890, (Burns, Kittredge).
           Brooklyn vs. Cincinnati, September 23, 1901 (Kelley, Sheckard).
           Boston vs. Chicago, August 12, 1903, second game (Stanley, Moran).
           Philadelphia vs. Boston, April 28, 1921 (Miller, Meadows).
           New York vs. Philadelphia, September 5, 1924, second game (Kelly, Jackson).
           Pittsburgh vs. St. Louis, June 22, 1925 (Grantham, Traynor).
           St. Louis vs. Philadelphia, July 6, 1929, second game (Bottomley, Hafey).
           Pittsburgh vs. Philadelphia, May 1, 1933 (Vaughan, Grace).
           Boston vs. Philadelphia$ April 30, 1938 (Moore, Maggert).
           New York vs. Brooklyn, July 4, 1938, second game (Bartell, Mancuso).
           New York vs. St. Louis, July 13, 1951 (Westrum, Williams).
           Cincinnati vs. Pittsburgh, July 29, 1955 (Thurman, Burgess).
           Atlanta vs. San Francisco, July 3, 1966 (Cloninger 2).
           Houston vs. New York, July 30, 1969, first game (Menke, Wynn).
           San Francisco vs. Montreal, April 26, 1970, first game (McCovey, Dietz).
           Pittsburgh vs. Chicago, September 14, 1982 (Hebner, Madlock).
           Los Angeles vs. Montreal, August 23, 1985 (Guerrero, Duncan).
           Atlanta vs. Houston, May 2, 1987 (Nettles, James).
           Chicago vs. Houston, June 3, 1987 (Dayett, Moreland).

Most Grand Slams, Game, Both Clubs (Each Club Connecting)

    A. L.—3— Baltimore 2 (Sheets, Dwyer), Texas 1 (Harrah), August 6, 1986.
    N. L.—3— Chicago 2 (Dayett, Moreland), Houston 1 (Hatcher), June 3, 1987.

Most Grand Slams by Pinch-Hitters, Game, Both Clubs

    N. L.—2— New York, 1 (Crawford), Boston 1 (Bell), May 26, 1929.
    A. L.— 1— Held by many clubs.

Most Grand Slams, Doubleheader

    N. L.-A. L.—2— Made in many doubleheaders.
    N. L.—Last time—Cincinnati vs. Atlanta, September 12, 1974.
    A. L.—Last time—Baltimore vs. Chicago, August 14, 1976.

Most Grand Slams, Doubleheader, Both Clubs

    N. L.—3— Cincinnati 2, Atlanta 1, September 12, 1974.
    A. L.—2— Last time—Baltimore 2, Chicago 0, August 14, 1976.

Most Grand Slams, Two Consec. Games (Connecting Each Game)

    N. L.—3— Brooklyn, September 23 (2), September 24 (1), 1901.
           Pittsburgh, June 20 (1), June 22 (2), 1925.
    A. L.—3— Milwaukee, April 10 (1), April 12 (2), 1980.

Most Consecutive Games, One or More Grand Slams

    A. L.—3— Milwaukee, April 7, 8, 9, 1978. (First three games of season.)
    N. L.—2— Held by many clubs.

Most Grand Slams, Inning

    A. L.—2— Minnesota vs. Cleveland, July 18, 1962, first inning (Allison, Killebrew).
           Milwaukee vs. Boston, April 12, 1980, second inning (Cooper, Money).
           Baltimore vs. Texas, August 6, 1986, fourth inning (Sheets, Dwyer).
    N. L.—2— Chicago vs. Pittsburgh, August 16, 1890, fifth inning (Burns, Kittredge).
           Houston vs. New York, July 30, 1969, first game, ninth inning (Menke, Wynn).

Most Grand Slams, Inning, Both Clubs

    N. L.—2— Chicago 2, (Burns, Kittredge), Pittsburgh 0, August 16, 1890, fifth inning.
           New York 1, (Irvin), Chicago 1 (Walker), May 18, 1950, sixth inning.
           Houston 2 (Menke, Wynn), New York 0, July 30, 1969, first game, ninth inning.
           Atlanta 1, (Evans), Cincinnati 1, (Geronimo), September 12, 1974, first game, second inning.
    A. L.—2— Washington 1 (Tasby), Boston 1 (Pagliaroni), June 18, 1961, first game, ninth inning.
           Minnesota 2 (Allison, Killebrew), Cleveland 0, July 18, 1962, first inning.
           Milwaukee 2 (Cooper, Money), Boston 0, April 12, 1980, second inning.
           Cleveland 1 (Orta), Texas 1 (Sundberg), April 14, 1980, first inning.
           Baltimore 2 (Sheets, Dwyer), Texas 0, August 6, 1986, fourth inning.

Total Bases

Most Total Bases, Season

    A. L.— 2703— New York, 155 games, 1936.
    N. L.— 2684— Chicago, 156 games, 1930.

Fewest Total Bases, Season

    A. L.— 1310— Chicago, 156 games, 1910.
    N. L.— 1358— Brooklyn, 154 games, 1908.

Most Total Bases, Game

    A. L.— 60— Boston vs. St. Louis, June 8, 1950.
    N. L.— 58— Montreal vs. Atlanta, July 30, 1978.

Most Total Bases, Nine-Inning Game, Both Clubs

    N. L.— 79— St. Louis 41, Philadelphia 38, May 11, 1923.
    A. L.— 77— New York 50, Philadelphia 27, June 3, 1932.

Most Total Bases, Extra-Inning Game, Both Clubs

    N. L.— 97— Chicago 49, Philadelphia 48, May 17, 1979, 10 innings.
    A. L.— 85— Cleveland 45, Philadelphia 40, July 10, 1932, 18 innings.

Most Total Bases, Doubleheader

    A. L.— 87— New York vs. Philadelphia, June 28, 1939.
    N. L.— 73— Milwaukee vs. Pittsburgh, August 30, 1953.

Most Total Bases, Doubleheader, Both Clubs

    A. L.— 114— New York 73, Philadelphia 41, May 22, 1930.
    N. L.— 108— St. Louis 62, Philadelphia 46, July 6, 1929.

Most Total Bases, Two Consecutive Games

A. L.— 102— Boston vs. St. Louis, June 7 (42), June 8 (60), 1950.
N. L.— 89— Pittsburgh, June 20 (46), June 22 (43), 1925.

Most Total Bases, Inning

N. L.— 29— Chicago vs. Detroit, September 6, 1883, seventh inning.
N. L. since 1900— 27— San Francisco vs. Cincinnati, August 23, 1961, ninth inning.
A. L.— 25— Boston vs. Philadelphia, September 24, 1940, first game, sixth inning.

Long Hits

Most Long Hits, Season

A. L.— 580— New York, 155 games, 1936; 315 doubles, 83 triples, 182 home runs.
N. L.— 566— St. Louis, 154 games, 1930; 373 doubles, 89 triples, 104 home runs.

Fewest Long Hits, Season

A. L.— 179— Chicago, 156 games, 1910; 116 doubles, 56 triples, 7 home runs.
N. L.— 182— Boston, 155 games, 1909; 124 doubles, 43 triples, 15 home runs.

Most Long Hits, Game

A. L.— 17— Boston vs. St. Louis, June 8, 1950.
N. L.— 16— Chicago vs. Buffalo, July 3, 1883.
N. L. since 1900— 15— Philadelphia vs. Chicago, June 23, 1986.

Most Long Hits, Game, Both Clubs

N. L.— 24— St. Louis 13, Chicago 11, July 12, 1931, second game.
A. L.— 19— Minnesota 12, Toronto 7, May 8, 1979.

Longest Game Without a Long Hit

N. L.— 26 innings— Brooklyn vs. Boston, May 1, 1920.
A. L.— 19 innings— Detroit vs. New York, August 23, 1968, second game.

Longest Game Without a Long Hit, Both Clubs

A. L.— 18 innings— Chicago 0, New York 0, August 21, 1933.
N. L.— 17 innings— Boston 0, Chicago 0, September 21, 1901.

Most Long Hits, Doubleheader

N. L.— 21— Baltimore vs. Cleveland, September 3, 1894.
N. L. since 1900— 18— Chicago vs. St. Louis, July 12, 1931.
A. L.— 18— New York vs. Washington, July 4, 1927.
New York vs. Philadelphia, June 28, 1939.

Most Long Hits, Doubleheader, Both Clubs

N. L.— 35— Chicago 18, St. Louis 17, July 12, 1931.
A. L.— 28— Boston 16, Detroit 12, May 14, 1967.

Longest Doubleheader Without a Long Hit

A. L.— 26 innings— Cleveland vs. Detroit, August 6, 1968.

Most Long Hits, Inning

N. L.— 8— Chicago vs. Detroit, September 6, 1883, seventh inning.
N. L. since 1900— 7— Boston vs. St. Louis, August 25, 1936, first game, first inning.
Philadelphia vs. Cincinnati, June 2, 1949, eighth inning.
Philadelphia vs. Cincinnati, July 6, 1986, third inning.
A. L.— 7— St. Louis vs. Washington, August 7, 1922, sixth inning.
Boston vs. Philadelphia, September 24, 1940, first game, sixth inning.
New York vs. St. Louis, May 3, 1951, ninth inning.

Extra Bases On Long Hits

Most Extra Bases on Long Hits, Season

A. L.— 1027— New York, 155 games, 1936.
N. L.— 1016— Brooklyn, 155 games, 1953.

Fewest Extra Bases on Long Hits, Season

A. L.— 249— Chicago, 156 games, 1910.
N. L.— 255— Boston, 155 games, 1909.

Most Extra Bases on Long Hits, Game

A. L.— 32— Boston vs. St. Louis, June 8, 1950.
N. L.— 30— Montreal vs. Atlanta, July 30, 1978.

Most Extra Bases on Long Hits, Game, Both Clubs

N. L.— 47— Philadelphia 24, Chicago 23, May 17, 1979, 10 innings.
N. L.— 40— Milwaukee 27, Brooklyn 13, July 31, 1954, nine innings.
Chicago 26, New York 14, June 11, 1967, second game, nine innings.

A. L.— 41— New York 27, Philadelphia 14, June 3, 1932.

Most Extra Bases on Long Hits, Doubleheader

A. L.— 44— New York vs. Philadelphia, June 28, 1939.
N. L.— 41— Milwaukee vs. Pittsburgh, August 30, 1953.

Most Extra Bases on Long Hits, Two Consecutive Games

A. L.— 51— Boston vs. St. Louis, June 7 (19), 8 (32), 1950.
N. L.— 44— Milwaukee vs. Brooklyn, July 31 (27), August 1 (17), 1954.

Most Extra Bases on Long Hits, Inning

N. L.— 18— Philadelphia vs. Cincinnati, June 2, 1949, eighth inning.
A. L.— 17— Boston vs. Philadelphia, September 24, 1940, first game, sixth inning.

Runs Batted In

Most Runs Batted In, Season

A. L.— 995— New York, 155 games, 1936.
N. L.— 942— St. Louis, 154 games, 1930.

Fewest Runs Batted In, Season, Since 1920

N. L.— 354— Philadelphia, 151 games, 1942.
A. L.— 424— Texas, 154 games, 1972.

Most Players, 100 or More Runs Batted In, Season

A. L.— 5— New York, 1936.
N. L.— 4— Pittsburgh, 1925; Chicago, 1929; Philadelphia, 1929.

Most Runs Batted In, Game

A. L.— 29— Boston vs. St. Louis, June 8, 1950.
N. L.— 26— New York vs. Brooklyn, April 30, 1944, first game.

Most Runs Batted In, Game, Both Clubs

N. L.— 45— Philadelphia 23, Chicago 22, May 17, 1979, 10 innings.
N. L.— 43— Chicago 24, Philadelphia 19, August 25, 1922.
A. L.— 35— Boston 21, Philadelphia 14, June 29, 1950.

Longest Game Without a Run Batted In, Both Clubs

N. L.— 19 innings— 0— Cincinnati 0, Brooklyn 0, September 11, 1946.
A. L.— 18 innings— 0— Washington 0, Detroit 0, July 16, 1909.
Washington 0, Chicago 0, May 15, 1918.

Most Runs Batted In, Doubleheader

A. L.— 34— Boston vs. Philadelphia, July 4, 1939.
N. L.— 31— St. Louis vs. Philadelphia, July 6, 1929.

Most Runs Batted In, Doubleheader, Both Clubs

A. L.— 49— Boston 34, Philadelphia 15, July 4, 1939.
N. L.— 45— St. Louis 31, Philadelphia 14, July 6, 1929.

Most Runs Batted In, Two Consecutive Games

A. L.— 49— Boston vs. St. Louis, June 7 (20), 8 (29), 1950.
N. L.— 39— Pittsburgh, June 20 (19), June 22 (20), 1925.

Most Runs Batted In, Inning

A. L.— 17— Boston vs. Detroit, June 18, 1953, seventh inning.
N. L.— 15— Chicago vs. Detroit, September 6, 1883, seventh inning.
Brooklyn vs. Cincinnati, May 21, 1952, first inning.

Game-Winning RBIs

Most Game-Winning RBIs, Season (Since 1980)

N. L.— 102— New York, 1986, 108 games won.
A. L.— 97— Detroit, 1984, 104 games won.

Fewest Game-Winning RBIs, Season (Since 1980)

N. L.— 53— Cincinnati, 1982, 61 games won.
A. L.— 55— Seattle, 1980, 59 games won.

Most Games Won With No G-W RBI, Season (Since 1980)

A. L.— 12— Detroit, 1980, 84 games won.
N. L.— 12— Houston, 1980, 93 games won.

Fewest Games Won With No G-W RBI, Season (Since 1980)

A. L.— 0— New York, 1982, 79 games won.
N. L.— 1— Pittsburgh, 1985, 57 games won.
Chicago, 1987, 76 games won.

Bases On Balls

Most Bases on Balls, Season

A. L.— 835— Boston, 155 games, 1949.
N. L.— 732— Brooklyn, 155 games, 1947.

Fewest Bases on Balls, Season
N. L.— 283— Philadelphia, 153 games, 1920.
A. L.— 356— Philadelphia, 156 games, 1920.

Most Bases on Balls, Game, Nine Innings
A. A.— 19— Louisville vs. Cleveland, September 21, 1887.
A. L.— 18— Detroit vs. Philadelphia, May 9, 1916.
   Cleveland vs. Boston, May 20, 1948.
N. L.— 17— Chicago vs. New York, May 30, 1887, a.m. game.
   Brooklyn vs. Philadelphia, August 27, 1903.
   New York vs. Brooklyn, April 30, 1944, first game.

Most Bases on Balls, Game, Nine Innings, Both Clubs
A. L.— 30— Detroit 18, Philadelphia 12, May 9, 1916.
N. L.— 26— Houston 13, San Francisco 13, May 4, 1975, second game.

Most Bases on Balls, Extra-Inning Game
A. L.— 20— Boston vs. Detroit, September 17, 1920, 12 innings.
N. L.— 16— Cincinnati vs. Atlanta, October 1, 1978, 14 innings.

Most Bases on Balls, Extra-Inning Game, Both Clubs
A. L.— 28— Boston 20, Detroit 8, September 17, 1920, 12 innings.
N. L.— 25— Chicago 15, Cincinnati 10, August 9, 1942, first game, 18 innings.
   San Diego 13, Chicago 12, June 17, 1974, 13 innings.

Most Bases on Balls, Game, Nine Innings, No Runs
A. L.— 11— St. Louis vs. New York, August 1, 1941.
N. L.— 10— Chicago vs. Cincinnati, August 19, 1965, first game, 10 innings.
   9— Cincinnati vs. St. Louis, September 1, 1958, first game.

Longest Game Without a Base on Balls
N. L.— 21 innings— New York vs. Pittsburgh, July 17, 1914.
A. L.— 20 innings— Philadelphia vs. Boston, July 4, 1905, p.m. game.

Longest Game Without a Base on Balls, Both Clubs
A. L.— 13 innings— Washington 0, Detroit 0, July 22, 1904.
   Boston 0, Philadelphia 0, September 9, 1907.
N. L.— 12 innings— Chicago 0, Los Angeles 0, July 27, 1980.

Most Bases on Balls, Doubleheader
N. L.— 25— New York vs. Brooklyn, April 30, 1944.
A. L.— 23— Cleveland vs. Philadelphia, June 18, 1950.

Most Bases on Balls, Doubleheader, Both Clubs
N. L.— 42— Houston 21, San Francisco 21, May 4, 1975.
A. L.— 32— Baltimore 18, Chicago 14, May 28, 1954.
   Detroit 20, Kansas City 12, August 1, 1962.

Fewest Bases on Balls, Doubleheader, Both Clubs
N. L.— 1— Cincinnati 1, Brooklyn 0, August 6, 1905.
   Cincinnati 1, Pittsburgh 0, September 7, 1924.
   Brooklyn 1, St. Louis 0, September 22, 1929.
A. L.— 2— Philadelphia 2, Detroit 0, August 28, 1908, 20 innings.
   Philadelphia 1, Chicago 1, July 12, 1912.
   Cleveland 2, Chicago 0, September 6, 1930.

Longest Doubleheader Without a Base on Balls
N. L.— 27 innings— St. Louis vs. New York, July 2, 1933.
A. L.— 20 innings— Detroit vs. Philadelphia, August 28, 1908.

Most Bases on Balls, Two Consecutive Games
A. L.— 29— Detroit vs. Philadelphia, May 9, 10, 1916.
N. L.— 25— New York vs. Brooklyn, April 30, 30, 1944.

Most Bases on Balls, Two Consecutive Games, Both Clubs
A. L.— 48— Detroit 29, Philadelphia 19, May 9, 10, 1916.

Most Bases on Balls, Inning
A. L.— 11— New York vs. Washington, September 11, 1949, first game, third inning.
N. L.— 9— Cincinnati vs. Chicago, April 24, 1957, fifth inning.

Most Consecutive Bases on Balls, Inning
A. L.— 7— Chicago vs. Washington, August 28, 1909, first game, second inning.
N. L.— 7— Atlanta vs. Pittsburgh, May 25, 1983, third inning.

Most Bases on Balls by Pinch-Hitters, Inning
N. L.— 3— Pittsburgh vs. Philadelphia, June 3, 1911, ninth inning.
   Brooklyn vs. New York, April 22, 1922, seventh inning.
   Boston vs. Brooklyn, June 2, 1932, first game, ninth inning.
   Chicago vs. Philadelphia, July 29, 1947, seventh inning.
A. L.— 3— Baltimore vs. Washington, April 22, 1955, seventh inning.
   Washington vs. Boston, May 14, 1961, second game, ninth inning, consecutive.

Most Consecutive Bases on Balls by Pinch-Hitters, Inning
N. L.— 3— Brooklyn vs. New York, April 22, 1922, seventh inning.
   Boston vs. Brooklyn, June 2, 1932, first game, ninth inning.
A. L.— 3— Washington vs. Boston, May 14, 1961, second game, ninth inning.

Most Players, Two Bases on Balls, Inning, Game
A. L.— 4— New York vs. Washington, September 11, 1949, first game, third inning.
N. L.— 2— Made in many innings.

Most Consecutive Bases on Balls, Start of Game
N. L.— 5— New York vs. Cincinnati, June 16, 1941.
A. L.— 3— Made in many games.

Intentional

Most Intentional Bases on Balls, Season, Since 1955
N. L. (162-game season) — 102— Pittsburgh, 163 games, 1979.
N. L. (154-game season) — 91— Brooklyn, 154 games, 1956.
A. L. (162-game season) — 79— Minnesota, 162 games, 1965.
A. L. (154-game season) — 66— New York, 154 games, 1957.

Fewest Intentional Bases on Balls, Season, Since 1955
A. L. (162-game season) — 10— Kansas City, 162 games, 1961.
A. L. (154-game season) — 20— Washington, 154 games, 1959.
N. L. (154-game season) — 22— Los Angeles, 154 games, 1958.
N. L. (162-game season) — 34— New York, 163 games, 1964.

Most Intentional Bases on Balls, Game, Nine Innings
N. L.— 6— San Francisco vs. St. Louis, July 19, 1975.
A. L.— 5— California vs. New York, May 10, 1967.
   Washington vs. Cleveland, September 2, 1970.

Most Intentional Bases on Balls, Extra-Inning Game
N. L.— 7— Houston vs. Philadelphia, July 15, 1984, 16 innings.
A. L.— 5— Chicago vs. Washington, June 29, 1958, second game, 11 innings.
   Minnesota vs. Milwaukee, May 12, 1972, 22-inning suspended game; completed May 13.
   New York vs. California, August 29, 1978.

Most Intentional Bases on Balls, Game, Nine Innings, Both Clubs
A. L.— 6— California 5, New York 1, May 10, 1967.
N. L.— 6— San Francisco 6, St. Louis 0, July 19, 1975.

Most Intentional Bases on Balls, Extra-Inning Game, Both Clubs
N. L.— 10— New York 6, San Diego 4, August 26, 1980, 18 innings.
A. L.— 7— Minnesota 5, Milwaukee 2, May 12, 1972, 22-inning suspended game; completed May 13.

Most Intentional Bases on Balls, Inning
N. L.-A. L.— 3— Made in many innings.

Strikeouts

Most Strikeouts, Season
N.L.— 1203— New York, 163 games, 1968.
A.L.— 1148— Seattle, 162 games, 1986.

Fewest Strikeouts, Season
N. L.— 308— Cincinnati, 153 games, 1921.
A. L.— 326— Philadelphia, 155 games, 1927.

Most Strikeouts, Game, Nine Innings
A. L.— 20— Seattle vs. Boston, April 29, 1986.
N. L.— 19— Boston vs. Providence, June 7, 1884.
   New York vs. St. Louis, September 15, 1969.
   San Diego vs. New York, April 22, 1970.
U. A.— 19— Boston vs. Chicago, July 7, 1884.

Most Strikeouts, Game, Nine Innings, Both Clubs
A. L.— 30— Seattle 18, Oakland 12, April 19, 1986.
U. A.— 29— Boston 19, Chicago 10, July 7, 1884.
   St. Louis 18, Boston 11, July 19, 1884.
N. L.— 29— Boston 19, Providence 10, June 7, 1884.
N. L. since 1900— 28— Cincinnati 15, San Diego 13, September 15, 1972.

Most Strikeouts, Extra-Inning Game
A. L.— 26— California vs. Oakland July 9, 1971, 20 innings.
N. L.— 22— New York vs. San Francisco, May 31, 1964, second game, 23 innings.
   Cincinnati vs. Los Angeles, August 8, 1972, 19 innings.

A. L.—21—Baltimore vs. Washington, September 12, 1962, 16 innings.
  Detroit vs. Cleveland, September 18, 1966, 10 innings.
  Washington vs. Baltimore, June 4, 1967, 19 innings.

Most Strikeouts, Extra-Inning Game, Both Clubs
A. L.—43—California 26, Oakland 17, July 9, 1971, 20 innings.
N. L.—36—New York 22, San Francisco 14, May 31, 1964, second game, 23 innings.
  Pittsburgh 19, Cincinnati 17, September 30, 1964, 16 innings.

Most Strikeouts by Pinch-Hitters, Game, Nine Innings
A. L.—5—Detroit vs. New York, September 8, 1979.
N. L.—4—Brooklyn vs. Philadelphia, April 27, 1950.
  Philadelphia vs. Milwaukee, September 16, 1960.
  Chicago vs. New York, September 21, 1962.
  Chicago vs. New York, May 3, 1969.
  Cincinnati vs. Houston, September 27, 1969.
  Montreal vs. Philadelphia, June 24, 1972.

Most Strikeouts by Pinch-Hitters, Game, Nine Innings, Both Clubs
A. L.—5—New York 4, Boston 1, July 4, 1955, first game.
  Washington 4, Cleveland 1, May 1, 1957.
  Detroit 4, Cleveland 1, August 4, 1967.
N. L.—4—Made in many games. Last time—Montreal 4, Philadelphia 0, June 24, 1972.

Most Consecutive Strikeouts, Game
N. L.—10—San Diego vs. New York, April 22, 1970; 1 in sixth inning, 3 in seventh, eighth and ninth innings.
A. L.— 8—Boston vs. California, July 9, 1972; 2 in first inning, 3 in second and third innings.
  Milwaukee vs. California, August 7, 1973; 1 in first inning, 3 in second and third innings, 1 in fourth inning.
  Seattle vs. Boston, April 29, 1986; 3 in fourth and fifth innings, 2 in sixth inning.

Most Consecutive Strikeouts, Start of Game
N. L.—9—Cleveland vs. New York, August 28, 1884.
N. L. since 1900—8—Los Angeles vs. Houston, September 23, 1986.
A. L.—7—Texas vs. Chicago, May 28, 1986.

Longest Extra-Inning Game Without a Strikeout
N. L.—17 innings—New York vs. Cincinnati, June 26, 1893.
  Cincinnati vs. New York, August 27, 1920, first game.
A. L.—16 innings—Cleveland vs. New York, June 7, 1936.

Longest Extra-Inning Game Without a Strikeout, Both Clubs
A. L.—12 innings—Chicago 0, St. Louis 0, July 7, 1931.
N. L.—10 innings—Boston 0, New York 0, April 19, 1928.

Most Strikeouts, Inning (*Consecutive)
A. A.—4—Pittsburgh vs. Philadelphia, September 30, 1885, seventh inning.
N. L.—4—Chicago vs. New York, October 4, 1888, fifth inning*.
  Cincinnati vs. New York, May 15, 1906, fifth inning*.
  St. Louis vs. Chicago, May 27, 1956, first game, sixth inning*.
  Milwaukee vs. Cincinnati, August 11, 1959, first game, sixth inning.
  Cincinnati vs. Los Angeles, April 12, 1962, third inning*.
  Philadelphia vs. Los Angeles, April 17, 1965, second inning*.
  Pittsburgh vs. St. Louis, June 7, 1966, fourth inning.
  Montreal vs. Chicago, July 31, 1974, first game, second inning*.
  Pittsburgh vs. Atlanta, July 29, 1977, sixth inning.
  Chicago vs. Cincinnati, May 17, 1984, third inning*.
  Chicago vs. Houston, September 3, 1986, fifth inning.
A. L.—4—Boston vs. Washington, April 15, 1911, fifth inning.
  Philadelphia vs. Cleveland, June 11, 1916, sixth inning*.
  Chicago vs. Los Angeles, May 18, 1961, seventh inning.
  Washington vs. Cleveland, September 2, 1964, seventh inning.
  California vs. Baltimore, May 29, 1970, fourth inning*.
  Seattle vs. Cleveland, July 21, 1978, fifth inning*.
  Baltimore vs. Texas, August 2, 1987, second inning*.

Most Strikeouts by Pinch-Hitters, Inning (*Consecutive)
A. L.—3—Philadelphia vs. Washington, September 3, 1910, eighth inning*.
  Chicago vs. Boston, June 5, 1911, ninth inning*.
  Detroit vs. Cleveland, September 19, 1945, eighth inning*.

Philadelphia vs. Cleveland, September 9, 1952, ninth inning.
  Cleveland vs. New York, May 12, 1953, eighth inning*.
  New York vs. Philadelphia, September 24, 1954, ninth inning*.
  Detroit vs. Cleveland, August 4, 1967, eighth inning.
  California vs. Minnesota, May 17, 1971, ninth inning*.
N. L.—3—Pittsburgh vs. Cincinnati, June 5, 1953, ninth inning*.
  Cincinnati vs. Brooklyn, August 8, 1953, ninth inning.
  St. Louis vs. Cincinnati, May 10, 1961, ninth inning.
  Cincinnati vs. Houston, June 2, 1966, eighth inning*.
  Atlanta vs. Houston, June 18, 1967, eighth inning*.
  Cincinnati vs. Houston, September 27, 1969, eighth inning.
  St. Louis vs. Montreal, July 4, 1970, eighth inning.
  Philadelphia vs. Pittsburgh, July 6, 1970, ninth inning.

Most Strikeouts, Doubleheader, 18 Innings
N. L.—26—Philadelphia vs. New York, September 9, 1970.
  San Diego vs. New York, May 29, 1971.
  San Francisco vs. Houston, September 5, 1971.
A. L.—25—Los Angeles vs. Cleveland, July 31, 1963.

Most Strikeouts, Doubleheader, More Than 18 Innings
N. L.—31—Pittsburgh vs. Philadelphia, September 22, 1958, 23 innings.
  New York vs. Philadelphia, October 2, 1965, 27 innings.
A. L.—27—Cleveland vs. Boston, August 25, 1963, 24 innings.

Most Strikeouts, Doubleheader, Both Clubs, 18 Innings
N. L.—41—Philadelphia 26, New York 15, September 9, 1970.
  San Diego 26, New York 15, May 29, 1971.
  Chicago 21, New York 20, September 15, 1971.
A. L.—40—Cleveland 23, Los Angeles 17, September 29, 1962.

Most Strikeouts, Doubleheader, Both Clubs, Over 18 Innings
N. L.—51—New York 30, Philadelphia 21, September 26, 1975, 24 innings.
A. L.—44—Cleveland 27, Boston 17, August 25, 1963, 24 innings.

Longest Doubleheader Without a Strikeout
N. L.—21 innings— Pittsburgh vs. Philadelphia, July 12, 1924.
A. L.—20 innings— Boston vs. St. Louis, July 28, 1917.

Fewest Strikeouts, Doubleheader, Both Clubs
A. L.—1—Cleveland 1, Boston 0, August 28, 1926.
N. L.—2—Brooklyn 2, New York 0, August 13, 1932.
  Pittsburgh 2, St. Louis 0, September 6, 1948.

Most Strikeouts, Two Consecutive Nine-Inning Games
A. L.—36—Seattle vs. Boston, April 29 (20), April 30 (16), 1986.
N. L.—29—San Diego vs. New York, April 21 (10), April 22 (19), 1970.

Most Strikeouts, Two Consecutive Games, Over 18 Innings
N. L.—31—Pittsburgh vs. Philadelphia, September 22, first game, 14 innings (21), September 22, second game, 9 innings (10), 1958, 23 innings.
  New York vs. Philadelphia, October 2, first game, 9 innings (10), October 2, second game, 18 innings (21), 1965, 27 innings.
A. L.—Less than nine-inning record.

Sacrifice Hits

Most Sacrifice Hits, Season, Includes Sacrifice Scoring Flies
A. L.—310—Boston, 157 games, 1917.
N. L.—270—Chicago, 158 games, 1908.

Most Sacrifice Hits, Season, No Sacrifice Flies
N. L.—231—Chicago, 154 games, 1906.
A. L.—207—Chicago, 154 games, 1906.

Fewest Sacrifice Hits, Season, No Sacrifice Flies
A. L.—21—Toronto, 161 games, 1985.
N. L.—32—New York, 154 games, 1957.

Most Sacrifices, Game, Includes Sacrifice Flies
A. L.—8—New York vs. Boston, May 4, 1918, 2 sacrifice scoring flies.
  Chicago vs. Detroit, July 11, 1927.
  St. Louis vs. Cleveland, July 23, 1928.
  Texas vs. Chicago, August 1, 1977.
N. L.—8—Cincinnati vs. Philadelphia, May 6, 1926.

Most Sacrifices, Game, Both Clubs, Includes Sacrifice Flies

A. L.— 11—Washington 7, Boston 4, September 1, 1926.
N. L.— 9— New York 5, Chicago 4, August 29, 1921.
 Cincinnati 8, Philadelphia 1, May 6, 1926.
 San Francisco 6, San Diego 3, May 23, 1970, 15 innings, (no sacrifice flies in game).

Longest Extra-Inning Game Without a Sacrifice

A. L.—24 innings— Detroit vs. Philadelphia, July 21, 1945.
N. L.—23 innings— Brooklyn vs. Boston, June 27, 1939.

Longest Extra-Inning Game Without a Sacrifice, Both Clubs

N. L.—19 innings— Philadelphia 0, Cincinnati 0, September 15, 1950, second game.
A. L.—18 innings— Washington 0, St. Louis 0, June 20, 1952.

Most Sacrifices, Doubleheader, Includes Sacrifice Flies

A. L.— 10—Detroit vs. Chicago, July 7, 1921.
N. L.— 9— Held by many clubs.

Most Sacrifices, Doubleheader, Both Clubs; Includ. Sac. Flies

A. L.— 13— Boston 9, Chicago 4, July 17, 1926.

Fewest Sacrifices, Doubleheader

N. L.-A. L.—0—Made in many doubleheaders.

Longest Doubleheader Without a Sacrifice, Both Clubs

N. L.—28 innings— 0—Cincinnati 0, Philadelphia 0, September 15, 1950.
A. L.—18 innings— 0—Made in many doubleheaders.

Most Sacrifice Hits, Inning, No Sacrifice Flies

A. L.—3—Cleveland vs. St. Louis, July 10, 1949, fifth inning.
 Detroit vs. Baltimore, July 12, 1970, first game, second inning (consecutive).
 Cleveland vs. Chicago, June 8, 1980, sixth inning (consecutive).
N. L.—3—Chicago vs. Milwaukee, August 26, 1962, sixth inning, (consecutive).
 Philadelphia vs. Los Angeles, September 23, 1967, seventh inning, (consecutive).
 Los Angeles vs. San Francisco, May 23, 1972, sixth inning.
 Houston vs. San Diego, April 29, 1975, seventh inning.
 Houston vs. Atlanta, July 6, 1975, ninth inning.

Sacrifice Flies

Most Sacrifice Flies, Season (Run Scoring)

A. L. (162-game season) —77—Oakland, 162 games, 1984.
A. L. (154-game season) —63—Boston, 155 games, 1915.
N. L. (162-game season) —74—Philadelphia, 162 games, 1977.
N. L. (154-game season) —66—New York, 154 games, 1912
 St. Louis, 153 games, 1954.

Fewest Sacrifice Flies, Season

N. L.— 19—San Diego, 161 games, 1971.
A. L.— 23—California, 161 games, 1967.

Most Sacrifice Flies, Game (Run Scoring)

A. L.—4—Boston vs. Detroit, May 13, 1913.
 Cleveland vs. Seattle, June 1, 1980.
 Cleveland vs. Texas, August 13, 1980.
 Cleveland vs. Detroit, September 12, 1981, 12 innings.
 Cleveland vs. New York, September 18, 1985, second game.
 Detroit vs. Baltimore, June 10, 1985, 11 innings.
N. L.—4—New York vs. San Francisco, July 26, 1967.
 New York vs. Philadelphia, September 23, 1972.
 St. Louis vs. Cincinnati, September 2, 1980.
 Cincinnati vs. Houston, May 5, 1982.
 San Francisco vs. New York, August 29, 1987.

Most Sacrifice Flies, Game, Both Clubs (Run Scoring)

A. L.—5—Boston 3, Washington 2, August 31, 1965, second game.
 Cleveland 4, Seattle 1, June 1, 1980.
 Cleveland 4, Texas 1, August 13, 1980.
N. L.—5—St. Louis 4, Cincinnati 1, September 2, 1980.
 Los Angeles 3, San Francisco 2, April 15, 1984, 11 innings.

Most Sacrifice Flies, Inning (Run Scoring)

A. L.—3—Chicago vs. Cleveland, July 1, 1962, second game, fifth inning.
N. L.—2—Made in many innings.

Hit By Pitch

Most Hit by Pitch, Season

N. L.— 148— Baltimore, 154 games, 1898.
A. L.— 80— Washington, 154 games, 1911.
N. L. since 1900—78—St. Louis, 153 games, 1910.
 Montreal, 162 games, 1971.

Fewest Hit by Pitch, Season

A. L.—5—Philadelphia, 154 games, 1937.
N. L.—9—Philadelphia, 152 games, 1939.

Most Hit by Pitch, Game, Nine Innings

A. A.—6—Brooklyn vs. Baltimore, April 25, 1887.
A. L.—6—New York vs. Washington, June 20, 1913, second game.
N. L.—6—Louisville vs. St. Louis, July 31, 1897, first game.
N. L. since 1900—5—Atlanta vs. Cincinnati, July 2, 1969.

Most Hit by Pitch, Extra-Inning Game

N. L.—6—New York vs. Chicago, June 16, 1893, 11 innings.

Most Hit by Pitch, Game, Both Clubs, Nine Innings

N. L.—8—Washington 5, Pittsburgh 3, May 9, 1896.
 Louisville 6, St. Louis 2, July 31, 1897, first game.
N. L. since 1900—7—Brooklyn 4, New York 3, July 17, 1900.
 New York 4, Boston 3, August 1, 1903, second game.
A. L.—7—Detroit 4, Washington 3, August 24, 1914, second game.
 Minnesota 4, Kansas City 3, April 13, 1971.

Most Hit by Pitch, Doubleheader

N. L.—8—New York vs. Boston, August 1, 1903.
A. L.—6—New York vs. Washington, June 20, 1913.

Most Hit by Pitch, Doubleheader, Both Clubs

N. L.— 11—New York 8, Boston 3, August 1, 1903.
A. L.— 8—Detroit 5, Washington 3, August 24, 1914.

Most Hit by Pitch, Inning

N. L.—4—Boston vs. Pittsburgh, August 19, 1893, first game, second inning.
N. L. since 1900—3—New York vs. Pittsburgh, September 25, 1905, first inning.
 Chicago vs. Boston, September 17, 1928, ninth inning.
 Philadelphia vs. Cincinnati, May 15, 1960, first game, eighth inning.
 Atlanta vs. Cincinnati, July 2, 1969, second inning.
 Cincinnati vs. Pittsburgh, May 1, 1974, first inning, consecutive.
A. L.—3—New York vs. Washington, June 20, 1913, second game, first inning.
 Cleveland vs. New York, August 25, 1921, eighth inning.
 Boston vs. New York, June 30, 1954, third inning.
 Baltimore vs. California, August 9, 1968, seventh inning.
 California vs. Chicago, September 10, 1977, first inning, consecutive.

Grounding Into Double Plays

Most Grounding Into Double Plays, Season

A. L.— 171— Boston, 162 games, 1982, 1983.
N. L.— 166— St. Louis, 154 games, 1958.

Fewest Grounding Into Double Plays, Season

N. L.—75—St. Louis, 155 games, 1945.
A. L.—79—Kansas City, 161 games, 1967.

Most Grounding Into Double Plays, Game

N. L.—7—San Francisco vs. Houston, May 4, 1969.
A. L.—6—Washington vs. Cleveland, August 5, 1948.
 Boston vs. California, May 1, 1966, first game.
 Baltimore vs. Kansas City, May 6, 1972.
 Cleveland vs. New York, April 29, 1975.
 Toronto vs. Minnesota, August 29, 1977, first game, 10 innings.
 Milwaukee vs. Chicago, May 8, finished May 9, 1984, 25 innings.

Most Grounding Into Double Plays, Game, Both Clubs

A. L.—9—Boston 6, California 3, May 1, 1966, first game.
N. L.—9—Los Angeles 5, New York 4, May 24, 1973, 19 innings.
 8—Boston 5, Chicago 3, September 18, 1928.

Reaching Base On Errors

Most Times Reaching First Base on Error, Game
N. L.— 10— Chicago vs. Cleveland, July 24, 1882.
A. L.— 8— Detroit vs. Chicago, May 6, 1903.

Most Times Reaching First Base on Error, Game, Both Clubs
N. L.— 16— Chicago 10, Cleveland 6, July 24, 1882.
A. L.— 12— Detroit 8, Chicago 4, May 6, 1903.

Most Times Reaching First Base on Error, Inning
N. L.— 4— St. Louis vs. Pittsburgh, August 5, 1901, eighth inning.
A. L.— 4— St. Louis vs. Boston, June 8, 1911, fourth inning.

League Batting

Service
Players Used

Most Players, Season, Since 1900
A. L.— (14-club league) —537 in 1987.
A. L.— (12-club league) —440 in 1969.
A. L.— (10-club league) —369 in 1962.
A. L.— (8-club league) —323 in 1955.
N. L.— (12-club league) —475 in 1987.
N. L.— (10-club league) —373 in 1967.
N. L.— (8-club league) —333 in 1946.

Most Players in 150 or More Games, Season, Since 1900
N. L.— (12-club league) —40 in 1978, 1979.
N. L.— (10-club league) —34 in 1965.
N. L.— (8-club league) —23 in 1953.
A. L.— (14-club league) —44 in 1985.
A. L.— (12-club league) —32 in 1976.
A. L.— (10-club league) —30 in 1962.
A. L.— (8-club league) — 19 in 1921, 1936.

Fewest Players, Season, Since 1900
A. L.— (12-club league) —412 in 1976.
A. L.— (8-club league) —166 in 1904.
N. L.— (12-club league) —420 in 1979.
N. L.— (8-club league) —188 in 1905.

Most Times Players Used as Pinch-Hitters, Season
N. L.— (12-club league) —3442 in 1986.
N. L.— (10-club league) —2448 in 1965.
N. L.— (8-club league) —1911 in 1960.
A. L.— (12-club league) —2993 in 1970.
A. L.— (10-club league) —2403 in 1967.
A. L.— (8-club league) —1950 in 1960.

Most Times Players Used as Pinch-Hitters, Season, Both Leagues
5804 in 1970— (12-club leagues) —2993 in A. L., 2811 in N. L.
4723 in 1967— (10-club leagues) —2403 in A. L., 2320 in N. L.
3861 in 1960— (8-club leagues) —1950 in A. L., 1911 in N. L.

Most Players Playing All Games, Season, Since 1900
N. L.—10 in 1932.   A. L.—10 in 1933.

Fewest Players Playing All Games, Season
A. L.— 0— 1910, 1963.
N. L.— 0— 1914.

Most Players With Two or More Clubs, Season, Since 1900
A. L.—47 in 1952.   N. L.—31 in 1919.

Fewest Players With Two or More Clubs, Since 1900
A. L.—2 in 1940.   N. L.—5 in 1935.

Most Players With Three or More Clubs, Season, Since 1900
A. L.—4 in 1952.   N. L.—3 in 1919.

Games

Most Games, Season, Since 1900
A. L.— (14-club league) —1135 in 1982, 1983.
A. L.— (12-club league) —973 in 1969, 1970, 1974.
A. L.— (10-club league) —814 in 1964.
A. L.— (8-club league) —631 in 1914.
N. L.— (12-club league) —974 in 1983.
N. L.— (10-club league) —813 in 1965, 1968.
N. L.— (8-club league) —625 in 1914, 1917.

Fewest Games, Season, Since 1900 (Except 1918)
A.L.—608 in 1933.   N. L.—608 in 1934.

Most Times Two Games in One Day, Season
A. L.—153 in 1943.   N. L.—146 in 1943.

Batting Average

Highest Batting Average, Season, Since 1900
N. L.—.303 in 1930.   A. L.—.29244 in 1921.

Lowest Batting Average, Season, Since 1900
A. L.—.23011 in 1968.   N. L.—.23895 in 1908.

Most .400 Batsmen, Season, Qualifiers For Batting Championship
N. L.—3 in 1894.   A. L.—2 in 1911, 1922.
N. L. since 1900—1 in 1922, 1924, 1925, 1930.

Most Clubs Batting .300 or Over, Season, Since 1900
N. L.—6 in 1930.   A. L.—4 in 1921.

Most .300 Batsmen, Season, Qualifiers For Batting Championship
N. L.—33 in 1930.   A. L.—26 in 1924.

Fewest .300 Batsmen, Season, Qualifiers For Batting Title
A L.—1 in 1968.   N. L.—4 in 1907.

Slugging Average

Highest Slugging Average, Season, Since 1900
N. L.—.448 in 1930.   A. L.—.425 in 1987.

Lowest Slugging Average, Season, Since 1900
N. L.—.306 in 1908.   A. L.—.312 in 1910.

At-Bats

Most At-Bats, Season, Since 1900
A. L.— (14-club league) —77,910 in 1984.
A. L.— (12-club league) —66,276 in 1973.
A. L.— (10-club league) —55,239 in 1962.
A. L.— (8-club league) —43,747 in 1930.
N. L.— (12-club league) —66,700 in 1977.
N. L.— (10-club league) —55,449 in 1962.
N. L.— (8-club league) —43,891 in 1936.

Most Players 600 or More At-Bats, Season, Since 1900
A. L.—20 in 1985.   N. L.—19 in 1962.

Runs

Most Runs, Season, Since 1900
N. L.— (12-club league) —8771 in 1970, 1987.
N. L.— (10-club league) —7278 in 1962.
N. L.— (8-club league) —7025 in 1930.
A. L.— (14-club league) —11112 in 1987.
A. L.— (12-club league) —8314 in 1973.
A. L.— (10-club league) —7342 in 1961.
A. L.— (8-club league) —7009 in 1936.

Fewest Runs, Season, Since 1900
N. L.—4136 in 1908.   A. L.—4272 in 1909.

Most Players 100 or More Runs, Season, Since 1900
A. L.—24 in 1936.   N. L.—19 in 1929.

Most Runs, League, One Day, 3 Games
A. L.—62, May 3, 1949.
N. L.—59, August 13, 1959.

Most Runs, League, One Day, 4 Games
N. L.—101, May 17, 1887.
N. L. since 1900—88, April 29, 1901.
A. L.—77, July 9, 1937.

Most Runs, League, Opening Day of Season, 4 Games
N. L.—67, April 19, 1900.   A. L.—65, April 14, 1925.

Fewest Runs, League, Opening Day of Season, 4 Games
A. L.—11, April 16, 1940.   N. L.—13, April 18, 1944.

Most Runs, League, One Day, 5 Games
N. L.—105, May 20, 1897.   A. L.—97, September 9, 1937.

Most Runs, League, One Day, 6 Games
A. L.—112, July 10, 1932.   N. L.—Less than for 5 games.

Most Runs, League, One Day, 7 Games
N. L.—159—August 7, 1894.
N. L. since 1900—118, July 21, 1923.
A. L.—91, July 7, 1923; May 14, 1983.

Most Runs, League, One Day, 8 Games
N. L.—Less than for 7 games.   A. L.—99, July 5, 1937.

Most Runs, Both Leagues, One Day, 15 Games
188 on July 16, 1950; 99 in N. L. (7 games); 89 in A. L. (8 games).

Most Runs, Both Leagues, One Day, 16 Games
191 on May 30, 1950; 104 in N. L. (8 games); 87 in A. L. (8 games).

Most Players Scoring 5 or More Runs, Game, Season, Since 1900
N. L.—7 in 1930.   A. L.—5 in 1939.

Fewest Players Scoring 5 or More Runs, Game, Season, Since 1900
N. L.-A. L.—None in many seasons.

Most Games, 20 or More Runs, League
N. L.—1876 to date—251.
N. L. since 1900 to date—87.
A. L.—1901 to date—83.

Most Games, 20 or More Runs, Season
N. L.—32 in 1894.
N. L. since 1900—5 in 1900, 1925.
A. L.—5 in 1923.

Most Innings, 10 or More Runs, League
N. L.—1876 to date—219.
N. L.—1900 to date—125.
A. L.—1901 to date—158.

Most Innings, 10 or More Runs, Season
N. L.—12 in 1894.
N. L. since 1900—6 in 1922.
A. L.—6 in 1936, 1950, 1979.

Hits

Most Hits, Season, Since 1900
N. L.— (12-club league) —17,465 in 1977.
N. L.— (10-club league) —14,453 in 1962.
N. L.— (8-club league) —13,260 in 1930.
A. L.— (14-club league) —20,958 in 1980.
A. L.— (12-club league) —17,193 in 1973.
A. L.— (10-club league) —14,068 in 1962.
A. L.— (8-club league) —12,657 in 1962.

Fewest Hits, Season, Since 1900
N. L.—9566 in 1907.   A. L.—9719 in 1908.

Most Players 200 or More Hits, Season
N. L.—12 in 1929 and 1930.   A. L.—9 in 1936 and 1937.

Fewest Players 200 or More Hits, Season, Since 1900
N. L.—0— (26 years) 1902, 1904, 1906, 1907, 1909, 1910, 1911, 1913, 1914, 1915, 1916, 1917, 1918, 1919, 1940, 1941, 1942, 1944, 1947, 1950, 1952, 1955, 1960, 1972, 1981, 1983.
A. L.—0— (26 years) 1902, 1903, 1905, 1908, 1913, 1914, 1918, 1919, 1945, 1951, 1952, 1956, 1957, 1958, 1959, 1960, 1961, 1963, 1965, 1966, 1967, 1968, 1969, 1972, 1975, 1981.

Most Players 5 or More Hits, Game, Season, Since 1900
N. L.—27 in 1930.   A. L.—22 in 1936.

Fewest Players 5 or More Hits, Game, Season, Since 1900
N. L.—1 in 1914.   A. L.—2 in 1913, 1914, 1963.

Most Hits, League, One Day, 4 Games
A. L.—119, June 2, 1925.
N. L.—115, July 6, 1934.

Most Hits, League, One Day, 6 Games
A. L.—190, July 10, 1932.

Most Hits, League, One Day, 7 Games
N. L.—175, July 16, 1950.
A. L.—Less than for 6 games.

Most Hits, League, One Day, 8 Games
N. L.—183, July 21, 1963.
A. L.—165, May 30, 1950.

Most Hits, Both Leagues, One Day, 15 Games
337 on July 16, 1950; 175 in N. L. (7 games); 162 in A. L. (8 games).

Most Hits, Both Leagues, One Day, 16 Games
Less than for 15 games.

Singles

Most Singles, Season, Since 1900
A. L.— (14-club league) —15,072 in 1980.
A. L.— (12-club league) —12,729 in 1974.
A. L.— (10-club league) — 9,878 in 1962.
A. L.— (8-club league) — 9,214 in 1921.
N. L.— (12-club league) —12,564 in 1980.
N. L.— (10-club league) —10,476 in 1922.
N. L.— (8-club league) — 9,476 in 1962.

Fewest Singles, Season, Since 1900
N. L.—7466 in 1956.   A. L.—7573 in 1959.

Doubles

Most Doubles, Season, Since 1900
A. L.— (14-club league) —3710 in 1983.
A. L.— (12-club league) —2624 in 1973.
A. L.— (8-club league) —2400 in 1936.
N. L.— (12-club league) —3126 in 1987.
N. L.— (8-club league) —2386 in 1930.

Fewest Doubles, Season, Since 1900
N. L.—1148 in 1907.   A. L.—1348 in 1910.

Most Players With 40 or More Doubles, Season, Since 1900
N. L.—12 in 1920.   A. L.—12 in 1937.

Triples

Most Triples, Season, Since 1900
A. L.— (14-club league) —644 in 1977.
A. L.— (12-club league) —467 in 1976.
A. L.— (8-club league) —694 in 1921.
N. L.— (12-club league) —554 in 1970.
N. L.— (8-club league) —685 in 1912.

Fewest Triples, Season, Since 1900
A. L.—267 in 1959.   N. L.—323 in 1942.

Most Players With 20 or More Triples, Since 1900
A. L.—4 in 1912.   N. L.—3 in 1911, 1912.

Home Runs
Season

Most Home Runs, Season
A. L.— (14-club league) —2634 in 1987.
A. L.— (12-club league) —1746 in 1970.
A. L.— (10-club league) —1552 in 1962.
A. L.— (8-club league) —1091 in 1959.
N. L.— (12-club league) —1824 in 1987.
N. L.— (10-club league) —1449 in 1962.
N. L.— (8-club league) —1263 in 1965.

Most Home Runs, Season, Both Leagues
(14-club A. L., 12-club N. L.) —4458 in 1987 (2634 in A. L., 1824 in N. L.)
(12-club league) —3429 in 1970 (1746 in A. L., 1683 in N. L.)
(10-club league) —3001 in 1962 (1552 in A. L., 1449 in N. L.)

Fewest Home Runs, Season, Since 1900
A. L.—101 in 1907.   N. L.—126 in 1906.

Most Home Runs by Pinch-Hitters, Season
N.L.— (12-club league) —55 in 1983.
N.L.— (10-club league) —45 in 1962.

N.L.— (8-club league) —42 in 1958.
A.L.— (14-club league) —53 in 1980.
A.L.— (12-club league) —49 in 1970.
A.L.— (10-club league) —50 in 1961.
A.L.— (8-club league) —29 in 1953.

Most Home Runs by Pinch-Hitters, Season, Both Leagues
103 in 1987 (14-club A.L., 12-club N.L) —53 in N.L., 50 in A.L.
95 in 1970 (12-club leagues) —49 in A.L., 46 in N.L.
84 in 1962 (10-club leagues) —45 in N.L., 39 in A.L.

Most Clubs 100 or More Home Runs, Season
A. L.— (14-club league) —14 in 1977, 1982, 1985, 1986, 1987.
A. L.— (12-club league) —11 in 1970, 1973.
A. L.— (10-club league) —10 in 1964.
A. L.— (8-club league) — 8 in 1958, 1960.
N. L.— (12-club league) —11 in 1970, 1986, 1987.
N. L.— (10-club league) —10 in 1962.
N. L.— (8-club league) — 8 in 1956, 1958, 1959, 1961.

Most Players, 50 or More Home Runs, Season
A. L.—2 in 1938, 1961.   N. L.—2 in 1947.

Most Players 40 or More Home Runs, Season
N. L.— (12-club league) —4 in 1973.
N. L.— (8-club league) —6 in 1954, 1955.
A. L.— (12-club league) —5 in 1969.
A. L.— (10-club league) —6 in 1961.
A. L.— (8-club league) —3 in 1936.

Most Players 30 or More Home Runs, Season
A. L.— (14-club league) —20 in 1987.
A. L.— (12-club league) —10 in 1969.
A. L.— (10-club league) — 9 in 1964.
N. L.— (12-club league) —12 in 1970.
N. L.— (10-club league) —10 in 1965.

Most Players 20 or More Home Runs, Season
A. L.— (14-club league) —51 in 1987.
A. L.— (12-club league) —25 in 1970.
A. L.— (10-club league) —25 in 1964.
A. L.— (8-club league) — 18 in 1959.
N. L.— (12-club league) —29 in 1970.
N. L.— (10-club league) —25 in 1962.
N. L.— (8-club league) —23 in 1956.

Most Players Hitting Homers, All Parks, 8-Club League, Season
N. L.—11 in 1956 (8 parks, excluding Jersey City; 5 of 11 connected there) .
A. L.— 7 in 1953 (8 parks) .

Most Players Hitting Homers, All Parks, 10-Club League, Season
A. L.—4 in 1962.
N. L.—3 in 1963.

Most Players Hitting Homers, All Parks, 12-Club League, Season
N. L.—3 in 1970.
A. L.—1 in 1975.

One Day

Most Players Two or More Home Runs, Game, Season
A. L.— (14-club league) —156 in 1987.
A. L.— (12-club league) —93 in 1969.
A. L.— (10-club league) —98 in 1964.
A. L.— (8-club league) —62 in 1960.
N. L.— (12-club league) —110 in 1987.
N. L.— (10-club league) —82 in 1966.
N. L.— (8-club league) —84 in 1955.

Fewest Players Two or More Home Runs, Game, Season
N. L.—0 in 1907, 1918.   A. L.—0 in 1908, 1915.

Most Players Two or More Home Runs, Game, One Day
N. L.— (12-club league) —5—May 8, 1970.
N. L.— (10-club league) —5—June 5, 1966.
N. L.— (8-club league) —5—August 16, 1947; April 16, 1955.
A. L.— (14-club league) —6—August 2, 1983; May 8, 1987.
A. L.— (10-club league) —5—June 11, 1961; May 20, 1962.
A. L.— (8-club league) —4—April 30, 1933; May 30, 1956.

Most Players Two Home Runs, Game, One Day, Both Leagues
7 on May 8, 1987; 6 in A. L., 1 in N. L.

Most Players Three or More Home Runs, Game, Season
A. L.—9 in 1987.   N. L.—7 in 1950.

Most Players, Three Homers, Game, Season, Both Leagues
15 in 1987; 9 in A. L., 6 in N. L.

Most Times 5 or More Home Runs, Game, Club, Season
N. L.— (8-club league) —15 in 1954.
N. L.— (12-club league) —10 in 1970.
N. L.— (10-club league) — 8 in 1966.
A. L.— (8-club league) — 8 in 1950.
A. L.— (10-club league) — 7 in 1966.
A. L.— (12-club league) — 8 in 1969.
A. L.— (14-club league) —25 in 1987.

Most Times 3 or More Home Runs, Inning, Club, Season
N. L.— (12-club league) —10 in 1970.
N. L.— (8-club league) —13 in 1954, 1955.
A. L.— (14-club league) —12 in 1987.
A. L.— (12-club league) — 7 in 1966, 1973, 1974.
A. L.— (10-club league) —10 in 1961, 1962.
A. L.— (8-club league) — 5 in 1936, 1947, 1953, 1954, 1956, 1957, 1959.

Most Home Runs, One Day, by Pitchers
A. L.—4—July 31, 1935
N. L.—3—June 3, 1892; May 13, 1942; July 2, 1961; June 23, 1971.

Most Home Runs, One Day, by Pinch-Hitters
N. L.—4—June 2, 1928; July 21, 1930.
A. L.—4—June 28, 1987.

Most Home Runs, League, One Day
N.L.—30— May 8, 1970 (7 games) .
A.L.—30— June 10, 1962 (10 games) .
             June 14, 1964 (10 games) .

Most Home Runs, Both Leagues, One Day
54—June 10, 1962; 30 in A. L. (10 games) , 24 in N. L. (10 games) .

Grand Slams

Most Grand Slams, Season
A. L.— (14-club league) —55 in 1987.
A. L.— (12-club league) —39 in 1970.
A. L.— (10-club league) —48 in 1961.
A. L.— (8-club league) —37 in 1938.
N. L.— (12-club league) —49 in 1970.
N. L.— (10-club league) —37 in 1962.
N. L.— (8-club league) —35 in 1950.

Most Grand Slams, Season, Both Leagues
100 in 1987— (14-club A.L., 12-club N.L.) —55 in A.L.; 45 in N.L.
88 in 1970— (12-club league) —49 in N. L.; 39 in A. L.
77 in 1961— (10-club A. L., 8-club N. L.) —48 in A.L.; 29 in N.L.

Fewest Grand Slams, Season
A. L.—0 in 1918 (Short season due to war) .
N. L.—1 in 1920.
A. L.—1 in 1907, 1909, 1915.

Fewest Grand Slams, Season, Both Leagues
3—1907 (2 in N. L., 1 in A. L.) .

Most Grand Slams by Pinch-Hitters, Season
A. L.— (14-club league) —5 in 1982.
A. L.— (12-club league) —3 in 1970, 1971, 1973.
A. L.— (10-club league) —7 in 1961.
A. L.— (8-club league) —5 in 1953.
N. L.— (12-club league) —9 in 1978.
N. L.— (8-club league) —4 in 1959.

Most Grand Slams by Pinch-Hitters, Season, Both Leagues
(14-club A. L.; 12-club N. L.) —13 in 1978 (9 in N. L.; 4 in A. L.) .
(12-club leagues) —9 in 1973 (6 in N. L.; 3 in A. L.) .
(8-club leagues) —8 in 1953 (5 in A. L.; 3 in N. L.) .

Most Grand Slams, One Day
N. L.—3—Performed many times. Last times—May 2, 1987; June 3, 1987.
A. L.—3—Performed many times. Last times—June 10, 1987; June 29, 1987.

Most Grand Slams, One Day, Both Leagues
4—September 18, 1949 (3 in N. L.; 1 in A. L.) .
   April 24, 1960 (3 in A. L.; 1 in N. L.) .
   August 22, 1963 (2 in A. L.; 2 in N. L.) .
   May 10, 1969 (2 in N. L.; 2 in A. L.) .

August 3, 1969 (3 in A. L.; 1 in N. L.).
June 20, 1971 (3 in N. L.; 1 in A. L.).
June 24, 1974 (3 in A. L.; 1 in N. L.).
September 8, 1974 (2 in A. L.; 2 in N. L.).
August 10, 1986 (3 in A. L.; 1 in N. L.).
June 10, 1987 (3 in A. L.; 1 in N. L.).

Total Bases

Most Total Bases, Season, Since 1900

A. L.— (14-club league) —33,111 in 1987.
A. L.— (12-club league) —25,281 in 1973.
A. L.— (10-club league) —21,762 in 1962.
A. L.— (8-club league) —18,427 in 1936.
N. L.— (12-club league) —26,743 in 1987.
N. L.— (10-club league) —21,781 in 1962.
N. L.— (8-club league) —19,572 in 1930.

Most Players 300 or More Total Bases, Season, Since 1900

N. L.—14 in 1930.　A. L.—12 in 1930, 1937.

Most Players 400 or More Total Bases, Season

N. L.—3 in 1930.　A. L.—2 in 1927, 1936.

Long Hits & Extra Bases On Long Hits

Most Long Hits, Season, Since 1900

A. L.— (14-club league) —6762 in 1987.
A. L.— (12-club league) —4611 in 1970.
A. L.— (10-club league) —4190 in 1962.
A. L.— (8-club league) —3706 in 1936.
N. L.— (12-club league) —5385 in 1987.
N. L.— (10-club league) —3977 in 1962.
N. L.— (8-club league) —3903 in 1930.

Most Extra Bases on Long Hits, Season, Since 1900

A. L.— (14-club league) —12,491 in 1987.
A. L.— (12-club league) —8476 in 1970.
A. L.— (10-club league) —7694 in 1962.
A. L.— (8-club league) —5842 in 1940.
N. L.— (12-club league) —9468 in 1987.
N. L.— (10-club league) —7328 in 1962.
N. L.— (8-club league) —6312 in 1930.

Runs Batted In

Most Runs Batted In, Season

A. L.— (14-club league) —10,480 in 1987.
A. L.— (12-club league) —7769 in 1973.
A. L.— (10-club league) —6842 in 1961.
A. L.— (8-club league) —6520 in 1936.
N. L.— (12-club league) —8233 in 1987.
N. L.— (10-club league) —6760 in 1962.
N. L.— (8-club league) —6582 in 1930.

Most Players 100 or More Runs Batted In, Season

A. L.—18 in 1936.　N. L.—17 in 1930.

Bases On Balls

Most Bases on Balls, Season, Since 1900

A. L.— (14-club league) —7812 in 1987.
A. L.— (12-club league) —7032 in 1969.
A. L.— (10-club league) —5902 in 1961.
A. L.— (8-club league) —5627 in 1949.
N. L.— (12-club league) —6919 in 1970.
N. L.— (10-club league) —5265 in 1962.
N. L.— (8-club league) —4537 in 1950.

Fewest Bases on Balls, Season, Since 1900

A. L.— (12-club league) —6128 in 1976.
A. L.— (8-club league) —3797 in 1922.
N. L.— (12-club league) —5964 in 1982.
N. L.— (8-club league) —2906 in 1921.

Most Players 100 or More Bases on Balls, Season

A. L.— (12-club league) —7 in 1970.
N. L.— (12-club league) —5 in 1970.
A. L.— (8-club league) —8 in 1949.
N. L.— (8-club league) —4 in 1949, 1951.

Intentional

Most Intentional Bases on Balls, Season

N. L.— (12-club league) —862 in 1973.
A. L.— (12-club league) —668 in 1969.

Fewest Intentional Bases on Balls, Season

A. L.— (12-club league) —471 in 1976.
N. L.— (12-club league) —685 in 1976.

Strikeouts

Most Strikeouts, Season, Since 1900

A. L.— (14-club league) —13,442 in 1987.
A. L.— (12-club league) —10,957 in 1970.
A. L.— (10-club league) —9956 in 1964.
A. L.— (8-club league) —6081 in 1959.
N. L.— (12-club league) —11,657 in 1987.
N. L.— (10-club league) —9649 in 1965.
N. L.— (8-club league) —6824 in 1960.

Fewest Strikeouts, Season, Since 1900

A. L.— (8-club league) —3245 in 1924.
N. L.— (8-club league) —3359 in 1926.
A. L.— (12-club league) —9143 in 1976.
N. L.— (12-club league) —9602 in 1976.

Most Players 100 or More Strikeouts, Season

A. L.— (14-club league) —27 in 1986, 1987.
A. L.— (12-club league) —11 in 1970.
A. L.— (10-club league) —15 in 1967.
A. L.— (8-club league) — 3 in 1958, 1959, 1960.
N. L.— (12-club league) —16 in 1970.
N. L.— (10-club league) —17 in 1965.
N. L.— (8-club league) — 4 in 1960.

Sacrifice Hits & Flies

Most Sacrifices, Season, Including Scoring Flies, Since 1900

A. L.—1731 in 1917.　N. L.—1655 in 1908.

Most Sacrifices, Season, No Sacrifice Flies

A. L.—1349 in 1906.　N. L.—1349 in 1907.

Fewest Sacrifices, Season, No Sacrifice Flies

N. L.—510 in 1957.　A. L.—531 in 1958.

Most Sacrifice Flies, Season

A. L.— (14-club league) —765 in 1979.
A. L.— (12-club league) —624 in 1976.
A. L.— (10-club league) —448 in 1961.
A. L.— (8-club league) —370 in 1954.
N. L.— (12-club league) —580 in 1982.
N. L.— (10-club league) —410 in 1962.
N. L.— (8-club league) —425 in 1954.

Fewest Sacrifice Flies, Season

N. L.— (12-club league) —430 in 1969.
N. L.— (10-club league) —363 in 1966.
N. L.— (8-club league) —304 in 1959.
A. L.— (14-club league) —629 in 1987.
A. L.— (12-club league) —484 in 1969.
A. L.— (10-club league) —348 in 1967.
A. L.— (8-club league) —312 in 1959.

Hit By Pitch

Most Hit by Pitch, Season

A. L.— (14-club league) —500 in 1986.
A. L.— (12-club league) —439 in 1969.
A. L.— (8-club league) —464 in 1911.
N. L.— (12-club league) —443 in 1969.
N. L.— (8-club league) —415 in 1903.

Fewest Hit by Pitch, Season

A. L.— (14-club league) —372 in 1982.
N. L.— (12-club league) —249 in 1984.
A. L.— (12-club league) —374 in 1976.
A. L.— (8-club league) —132 in 1947.
N. L.— (8-club league) —157 in 1943.

Grounding Into Double Plays

Most Grounding Into Double Play, Season

A. L.— (14-club league) —1968 in 1980.
A. L.— (12-club league) —1608 in 1973.
A. L.— (10-club league) —1256 in 1961.
A. L.— (8-club league) —1181 in 1950.

N. L.— (12-club league) —1547 in 1971.
N. L.— (10-club league) —1251 in 1962.
N. L.— (8-club league) —1047 in 1958.

Fewest Grounding Into Double Play, Season

N. L.— (8-club league) — 820 in 1945.
N. L.— (12-club league) —1350 in 1982.
A. L.— (12-club league) —1440 in 1976.
A. L.— (8-club league) — 890 in 1945.

Individual Baserunning

Stolen Bases

Most Stolen Bases, League

N. L.— 938— Louis C. Brock, Chicago, St. Louis, 19 years, 1961 through 1979.
A. L.— 892— Tyrus R. Cobb, Detroit, Philadelphia, 24 years, 1905 through 1928.

Highest Stolen Base Percentage, League (min. 300 attempts)

N. L.—.874— Timothy Raines, Montreal, 1979 through 1987.
A. L.—.841— Willie J. Wilson, Kansas City, 1976 through 1987.

Most Stolen Bases, Consecutive, With No Caught Stealing, League

N. L.— 38— David E. Lopes, Los Angeles, June 10 through August 24, 1975.
A. L.— 32— Willie J. Wilson, Kansas City, July 23 through September 23, 1980.
Julio L. Cruz, Seattle, September 22, 1980 through June 11, 1981.

Most Stolen Bases, Season

A. A.— 156— Harry D. Stovey, Philadelphia, 130 games, 1888.
A. L.— 130— Rickey H. Henderson, Oakland, 149 games, 1982 (42 caught stealing).
N. L.— 118— Louis C. Brock, St. Louis, 153 games, 1974 (33 caught stealing).

Most Stolen Bases, Rookie Season

N. L.— 110— Vincent M. Coleman, St. Louis, 151 games, 1985.
A. A.— 98— Michael J. Griffin, Baltimore, 136 games, 1887.
A. L.— 50— John A. Cangelosi, Chicago, 137 games, 1986.

Most Stolen Bases, With No Caught Stealing, Season

A. L.— 16— Jimmy D. Sexton, Oakland, 69 games, 1982.
N. L.— 12— Miguel A. Dilone, Pittsburgh, 29 games, 1977.

Most Years Leading League in Most Stolen Bases

N. L.— 10— Max Carey, Pittsburgh, 1913, 1915, 1916, 1917, 1918, 1920, 1922, 1923, 1924, 1925.
A. L.— 9— Luis E. Aparicio, Chicago, Baltimore, 1956 through 1964.

Most Consecutive Years Leading League in Most Stolen Bases

A. L.— 9— Luis E. Aparicio, Chicago, Baltimore, 1956 through 1964.
N. L.— 6— Maurice M. Wills, Los Angeles, 1960 through 1965.

Most Years, 50 or More Stolen Bases, League

N. L.— 12— Louis C. Brock, St. Louis, 1965, 1966, 1967, 1968, 1969, 1970, 1971, 1972, 1973, 1974, 1975, 1976.
A. L.— 8— Tyrus R. Cobb, Detroit, 1909, 1910, 1911, 1912, 1913, 1915, 1916, 1917.

Most Consecutive Years, 50 or More Stolen Bases, League

N. L.— 12— Louis C. Brock, St. Louis, 1965 through 1976.
A. L.— 7— Rickey H. Henderson, Oakland, New York, 1980 through 1986.

Fewest Stolen Bases, Season, for Leader in Most Stolen Bases

A. L.— 15— Dominic P. DiMaggio, Boston, 141 games, 1950.
N. L.— 16— Stanley C. Hack, Chicago, 152 games, 1938.

Most At-Bats, Season, No Stolen Bases

A. L.— 677— Donald A. Mattingly, New York, 162 games, 1986; 0 caught stealing.
N. L.— 662— Peter E. Rose, Cincinnati, 162 games, 1975; 1 caught stealing.

Most Years, No Stolen Bases, League, 150 or More Games

Both Leagues—4—Deron R. Johnson, Cincinnati N.L., Philadelphia N.L., Chicago A.L., Boston A.L., 1965, 1970, 1971, 1975; 3 in N.L., 1 in A.L.
A. L.— 4— Kenneth W. Singleton, Baltimore, 1977, 1980, 1982, 1983.

N. L.—3—C. Dallan Maxvill, St. Louis, 1967, 1968, 1970.
Deron R. Johnson, Cincinnati, Philadelphia, 1965, 1970, 1971.

Most Stolen Bases, Game

N. L.—7—George F. Gore, Chicago, June 25, 1881.*
William R. Hamilton, Philadelphia, August 31, 1894; second game.
A. L.—6—Edward T. Collins, Philadelphia, September 11, 1912; also September 22, 1912, first game.
N. L. since 1900—5—Dennis L. McGann, New York, May 27, 1904.
David E. Lopes, Los Angeles, August 24, 1974.
Lonnie Smith, St. Louis, September 4, 1982.
Alan A. Wiggins, San Diego, May 17, 1984.
Anthony K. Gwynn, San Diego, September 20, 1986.
*Stolen bases not officially compiled until 1886.

Most Stolen Bases, Two Consecutive Games

N. L.—8—Walter Wilmot, Chicago, August 6 (4), 7 (4), 1894.
A. L.—7—Edward T. Collins, Philadelphia, September 10 (1), 11 (6), 1912.
Amos J. Otis, Kansas City, April 30 (3), May 1 (4), 1975, 13 innings.
Rickey H. Henderson, Oakland, July 3 (4), 15 innings, July 4 (3), 1983.

Most Stolen Bases, Inning

N. L.—3—Held by many players. Last player—Johnnie B. Baker, San Francisco, June 27, 1984, third inning.
A. L.—3—Held by many players. Last player—Paul L. Molitor, Milwaukee, July 26, 1987, first inning.

Most Stolen Bases, Inning, by Pinch-Runner

N. L.—2—William A. O'Hara, New York, September 1, 1909, sixth inning.
William A. O'Hara, New York, September 2, 1909, ninth inning.
Jacob A. Pitler, Pittsburgh, May 24, 1918, ninth inning.
David I. Concepcion, Cincinnati, July 7, 1974, first game, seventh inning.
Ronald LeFlore, Montreal, October 5, 1980, eighth inning.
A. L.—2—Raymond L. Dowd, Philadelphia, July 9, 1919, second game, ninth inning.
Allan S. Lewis, Kansas City, July 15, 1967, seventh inning.
Dagoberto B. Campaneris, Oakland, October 4, 1972, fourth inning.
Donald Hopkins, Oakland, April 20, 1975, second game, seventh inning.

Pinch-Runner and Pinch-Hitter, Same Game (Different Innings)

A. L.—Tharon P. Collins, St. Louis, June 8, 1923; pinch-runner in third inning, pinch-hitter in ninth inning.

Steals Of Home

Most Times Stole Home, League

A. L.—50—Tyrus R. Cobb, Detroit, Philadelphia 24 years, 1905 through 1928.
N. L.—33—Max G. Carey, Pittsburgh, Brooklyn, 20 years, 1910 through 1929.

Most Times Stole Home, Season

N. L.—7—Harold P. Reiser, Brooklyn, 122 games, 1946 (34 stolen bases).
A. L.—7—Rodney C. Carew, Minnesota, 123 games, 1969 (19 stolen bases).

Most Times Stole Way First to Home, Inning, League

A. L.—4—Tyrus R. Cobb, Detroit, 1909, 1911, 1912 (2).
N. L.—3—John P. Wagner, Pittsburgh, 1902, 1907, 1909.

N. L.—Last player—Johnnie B. Baker, San Francisco, June 27, 1984, third inning.
A. L.—Last player—Paul L. Molitor, Milwaukee, July 26, 1987, first inning.

Most Times Stole Home, Game

N. L.—2—John P. Wagner, Pittsburgh, June 20, 1901.
      Edward J. Konetchy, St. Louis, September 30, 1907.
      Joseph B. Tinker, Chicago, June 28, 1910.
      Lawrence J. Doyle, New York, September 18, 1911.
      Sherwood R. Magee, Philadelphia, July 20, 1912.
      Walter P. Gautreau, Boston, September 3, 1927, first game.
A. L.—2—Joseph J. Jackson, Cleveland, August 11, 1912.
      Guy Zinn, New York, August 15, 1912.
      Edward T. Collins, Philadelphia, September 6, 1913.
      Tyrus R. Cobb, Detroit, June 18, 1915.
      William J. Barrett, Chcago, May 1, 1924.
      Victor P. Power, Cleveland, August 14, 1958, 10 innings.

Caught Stealing & Caught Off Base

Most Caught Stealing, League

N. L.— 307— Louis C. Brock, Chicago, St. Louis, 19 years, 1961 through 1979.
A. L.— 199— Dagoberto B. Campaneris, Kansas City, Oakland, Texas, California, New York, 19 years, 1964 through 1983, except 1982.

Most Caught Stealing, Season

A. L.—42— Rickey H. Henderson, Oakland, 149 games, 1982, 130 stolen bases.
N. L.—36— Miller J. Huggins, St. Louis, 148 games, 1914, 32 stolen bases.

Most Caught Stealing, Rookie Season

N. L. (162-game season)—25—Vincent M. Coleman, St. Louis, 151 games, 1985.
N. L. (154-game season)—18—Joseph A. Rapp, New York-Philadelphia, 110 games, 1921.
A. L. (162-game season)—21—Michael L. Edwards, Oakland, 142 games, 1978.
A. L. (154-game season)—17—Luzerne A. Blue, Detroit, 153 games, 1921.

Most Years Leading League in Caught Stealing

N. L.—7—Maurice M. Wills, Los Angeles, Pittsburgh, Montreal, 1961, 1962 (tied), 1963, 1965, 1966, 1968, 1969.
      Louis C. Brock, Chicago, St. Louis, 1964, 1967, 1971, 1973, 1974, 1976, 1977 (tied).

A. L.—6—Orestes A. Minoso, Chicago, Cleveland, 1952, 1953, 1954, 1957, 1958, 1960.

Fewest Caught Stealing, Season, 50 or More Stolen Bases

N. L.—2—Max Carey, Pittsburgh, 155 games, 1922, 51 stolen bases.
A. L.—8—Luis E. Aparicio, Chicago, 153 games, 1960, 51 stolen bases.
      Dagoberto B. Campaneris, Oakland, 135 games, 1969, 62 stolen bases.
      Amos J. Otis, Kansas City, 147 games, 1971, 52 stolen bases.
      Willie J. Wilson, Kansas City, 137 games, 1983, 59 stolen bases.

Fewest Caught Stealing, Season, 150 or More Games

N. L.-A. L.—0—Held by many players.

Fewest Caught Stealing, Season, for Leader in Caught Stealing

A. L.— 9— Walter A. Evers, Detroit, 143 games, 1950.
      Manuel J. Rivera, Chicago, 139 games, 1956.
N. L.— 10— Willie H. Mays, New York, 152 games, 1956.

Most Consec. Games With No Caught Stealing, Major Leagues

1206—Augustus Triandos, New York A. L., Baltimore A. L., Detroit A.L., Philadelphia N. L., Houston N. L., August 3, 1953 through August 15, 1965 (1 stolen base).

Most Consecutive Games With No Caught Stealing, League

A. L.— 1079— August Triandos, New York, Baltimore, Detroit, August 3, 1953, through September 28, 1963 (1 stolen base).
N. L.— 592— Frank J. Torre, Milwaukee, Philadelphia, April 20, 1956 through August 10, 1962 (4 stolen bases).

Most Caught Stealing, Game

N. L.—4—Robert R. Thompson, San Francisco, June 27, 1986, 12 innings.
Nine innings—N. L.-A. L.—3—Held by many players.

Most Caught Off Base, Game

A. A.—3—John Stricker, Philadelphia, August 29, 1883.
N. L.—3—Benjamin M. Kauff, New York, May 26, 1916.

Most Times Out, Hit by Batted Ball, Game

N. L.—2—Walter Wilmot, Chicago, September 30, 1890.
A. L.—2—Ernest G. Shore, Boston, July 28, 1917, second game.

Most Caught Stealing, Inning

A. L.—2—Donald E. Baylor, Baltimore, June 15, 1974, ninth inning.
N. L.—2—James F. Morrison, Pittsburgh, June 15, 1987, eighth inning.

Club Baserunning

Stolen Bases

Most Stolen Bases, Season

A. A.— 638— Philadelphia, 137 games, 1887.
N. L.— 426— New York, 136 games, 1893.
N. L. since 1900—347—New York, 154 games, 1911.
A. L.— 341— Oakland, 161 games, 1976.

Most Players, 50 or More Stolen Bases, Season

A. L.—3—Oakland, 161 games, 1976. William A. North (75), Dagoberto B. Campaneris (54), Don E. Baylor (52).
N. L.—3—San Diego, 163 games, 1980. Eugene Richards (61), Osborne E. Smith (57), Jerry W. Mumphrey (52).

Most Years Leading League, Stolen Bases (Since 1900)

A. L.—30—Chicago.
N. L.—21—Brooklyn-Los Angeles (12-Brooklyn, 9-Los Angeles).
      19—St. Louis.

Fewest Stolen Bases, Season

A. L. (154-game season)—13—Washington, 154 games, 1957.
A. L. (162-game season)—18—Boston, 162 games, 1964.
N. L. (154-game season)—17—St. Louis, 157 games, 1949.
N. L. (162-game season)—22—San Francisco, 162 games, 1967.

Most Stolen Bases, Game

A. A.— 19— Philadelphia vs. Syracuse, April 22, 1890.
N. L.— 17— New York vs. Pittsburgh, May 23, 1890.
A. L.— 15— New York vs. St. Louis, September 28, 1911

N. L. since 1900—11—New York vs. Boston, June 20, 1912.
      St. Louis vs. Pittsburgh, August 13, 1916, second game, 5 innings.

Most Stolen Bases, Game, Both Clubs

A. A.—21—Philadelphia 19, Syracuse 2, April 22, 1890.
N. L.—20—New York 17, Pittsburgh 3, May 23, 1890.
N. L. since 1900—16—New York 11, Boston 5, June 20, 1912.
A. L.—15—New York 15, St. Louis 0, September 28, 1911.
      St. Louis 8, Detroit 7, October 1, 1916.

Most Triple Steals, Game

A. L.—2—Philadelphia vs. Cleveland, July 25, 1930, first and fourth innings.
N. L.—1—Made in many games.

Most Triple Steals, Game, Both Clubs

A. L.—2—Philadelphia 2, Cleveland 0, July 25, 1930.
N. L.—1—Made in many games.

Longest Game Without Stolen Base

N. L.—26 innings— Boston vs. Brooklyn, May 1, 1920.
A. L.—24 innings— Detroit vs. Philadelphia, July 21, 1945.
      Philadelphia vs. Detroit, July 21, 1945.

Longest Game Without Stolen Base, Both Clubs

A. L.—24 innings— Detroit 0, Philadelphia 0, July 21, 1945.
N. L.—23 innings— San Francisco 0, New York 0, May 31, 1964, second game.

Most Stolen Bases, Inning
A. L.—8—Washington vs. Cleveland, July 19, 1915, first inning.
N. L.—8—Philadelphia vs. New York, July 7, 1919, first game, ninth inning.

Steals Of Home

Most Times Stole Home, Season
A. L.—18—New York, 153 games, 1912 (245 stolen bases).
N. L.—17—Chicago, 157 games, 1911 (214 stolen bases).
New York, 154 games, 1912 (319 stolen bases).

Most Times Stole Home, Game
A. L.—3—Chicago vs. St. Louis, July 2, 1909.
New York vs. Philadelphia, April 17, 1915.
N. L.—3—St. Louis vs. Boston, September 30, 1907.
Chicago vs. Boston, August 23, 1909.
New York vs. Pittsburgh, September 18, 1911.

Most Times Stole Home, Game, Both Clubs
A. L.—3—Chicago 3, St. Louis 0, July 2, 1909.
New York 3, Philadelphia 0, April 17, 1915.
Detroit 2, St. Louis 1, April 22, 1924.
N. L.—3—St. Louis 3, Boston 0, September 30, 1907.
Chicago 3, Boston 0, August 23, 1909.
New York 3, Pittsburgh 0, September 18, 1911.

Most Times Stole Home, Inning
N. L.—2—Made in many innings. Last time—St. Louis vs. Brooklyn, September 19, 1925, seventh inning.
A. L.—2—Made in many innings. Last time—Oakland vs. Kansas City, May 28, 1980, first inning.

Caught Stealing & Caught Off Base

Most Caught Stealing, Season, Since 1920
N. L.—149—Chicago, 154 games, 1924.
A. L.—123—Oakland, 161 games, 1976.

Fewest Caught Stealing, Season
N. L.—8—Milwaukee, 154 games, 1958 (26 stolen bases).
A. L.—11—Kansas City, 155 games, 1960 (16 stolen bases).
Cleveland, 161 games, 1961 (34 stolen bases).

Most Caught Stealing, Game
N. L.—8—Baltimore vs. Washington, May 11, 1897.
N. L. since 1900—7—St. Louis vs. Brooklyn, August 23, 1909, second game.
A. L.—6—St. Louis vs. Philadelphia, May 12, 1915.
Chicago vs. Philadelphia, June 18, 1915.

Most Caught Stealing, Inning
A. A.—3—Cincinnati vs. Philadelphia, July 26, 1887, third inning.
A. L.—3—Detroit vs. New York, August 3, 1914, second inning.
N. L.—2—Made in many innings.

Most Men Caught Off Base, Game, One Club
N. L.—5—Chicago vs. Brooklyn, June 24, 1901.
A. A.—3—Philadelphia vs. Louisville, August 29, 1883.
A. L.—3—New York vs. Washington, June 29, 1910.
Toronto vs. Baltimore, August 24, 1983.

Left On Base

Most Left on Base, Season
A. L.—1334—St. Louis, 157 games, 1941.
N. L. (162-game season)—1328—Cincinnati, 162 games, 1976.
N. L. (154-game season)—1278—Brooklyn, 155 games, 1947.

Fewest Left on Base, Season
A. L. (154-game season)—925—Kansas City, 154 games, 1957.
A. L. (162-game season)—995—Kansas City, 160 games, 1966.
N. L. (154-game season)—964—Chicago, 154 games, 1924.
N. L. (162-game season)—1019—San Francisco, 161 games, 1966.

Most Left on Base, Game, Nine Innings
A. L.—20—New York vs. Boston, September 21, 1956.
A. A.—18—Baltimore vs. Cincinnati, July 7, 1891.
N. L.—18—Boston vs. Baltimore, August 5, 1897.
Pittsburgh vs. Cincinnati, September 8, 1905.
Boston vs. St. Louis, July 11, 1923.
St. Louis vs. Philadelphia, September 15, 1928, second game.

New York vs. Philadelphia, August 7, 1943.
St. Louis vs. Cincinnati, June 10, 1944.
St. Louis vs. Philadelphia, September 14, 1950.
Pittsburgh vs. Boston, June 5, 1951.
Atlanta vs. Los Angeles, June 23, 1986.

Most Left on Base, Shutout Defeat
A. L.—15—New York vs. St. Louis, May 22, 1913.
Washington vs. Cleveland, July 29, 1931.
St. Louis vs. New York, August 1, 1941.
Kansas City vs. Detroit, May 12, 1975.
N. L.—14—Pittsburgh vs. Philadelphia, May 10, 1913.
Cincinnati vs. St. Louis, April 20, 1937, 10 innings.
St. Louis vs. Chicago, April 15, 1958.
Los Angeles vs. Chicago, April 23, 1966.
Philadelphia vs. Montreal, September 22, 1971.

Most Left on Base, 10-Inning Game
N. L.—19—San Francisco vs. Los Angeles, September 21, 1969.
A. L.—19—Baltimore vs. Milwaukee, September 13, 1973.
Texas vs. Detroit, August 26, 1975.

Most Left on Base, 11-Inning Game
A. L.—20—Philadelphia vs. Detroit, May 12, 1916.
New York vs. Minnesota, April 24, 1971.
N. L.—20—New York vs. Philadelphia, April 23, 1929.

Most Left on Base, 12-Inning Game
N. L.-A. L.—Less than 11-inning game.

Most Left on Base, 13-Inning Game
A. L.—22—Boston vs. St. Louis, August 22, 1951.
N. L.—20—Pittsburgh vs. Philadelphia September 22, 1931.
Brooklyn vs. Milwaukee, August 2, 1954.
Cincinnati vs. San Diego, May 23, 1974.

Most Left on Base, 14-Inning Game
N. L.—25—Houston vs. San Francisco, July 11, 1970.
A. L.—22—Texas vs. Detroit, August 9, 1974.

Most Left on Base, 15-Inning Game
A. L.—23—Chicago vs. Cleveland, May 27, 1956, first game.
N. L.—22—St. Louis vs. Cincinnati, September 3, 1949.

Most Left on Base, 16-Inning Game
N. L.—20—Philadelphia vs. Brooklyn, September 4, 1922, second game.
A. L.—Less than for 15-inning game.

Most Left on Base, 17-Inning Game
N. L.—24—St. Louis vs. Pittsburgh, August 2, 1982.
A. L.—23—Cleveland vs. Philadelphia, August 14, 1929.

Most Left on Base, 18-Inning Game
A. L.—24—Cleveland vs. Philadelphia, July 10, 1932.
N. L.—23—Chicago vs. Cincinnati, August 9, 1942, first game.

Most Left on Base, 19-Inning Game
N. L.—26—San Diego vs. Pittsburgh, August 25, 1979.
A. L.—Less than for 18-inning game.

Most Left on Base, 20-Inning Game
N. L.—27—Atlanta vs. Philadelphia, May 4, 1973.
A. L.—Less than for 18-inning game.

Most Left on Base, Nine-Inning Game, Both Clubs
N. L.—30—Brooklyn 16, Pittsburgh 14, June 30, 1893.
New York 17, Philadelphia 13, July 18, 1943, first game.
A. L.—30—New York 15, Chicago 15, August 27, 1935, first game.
Los Angeles 15, Washington 15, July 21, 1961.

Most Left on Base, Ten-Inning Game, Both Clubs
N. L.—32—Philadelphia 18, Brooklyn 14, September 8, 1925, second game.
A. L.—Less than for 9-inning game.

Most Left on Base, 11-Inning Game, Both Clubs
A. L.—36—Philadelphia 20, Detroit 16, May 12, 1916.
N. L.—Less than for 10-inning game.

Most Left on Base, 12-Inning Game, Both Clubs
N. L.—33—Pittsburgh 18, New York 15, August 22, 1940, first game.
A. L.—Less than for 11-inning game.

Most Left on Base, 13-Inning Game, Both Clubs
A. L.—37—New York 19, Boston 18, September 29, 1956.
N. L.—37—Cincinnati 20, San Diego 17, May 23, 1974.

Most Left on Base, 14-Inning Game, Both Clubs

N. L.— 37—Houston 20, Cincinnati 17, July 2, 1976, first game.
A. L.—Less than for 13-inning game.

Most Left on Base, 15-Inning Game, Both Clubs

A. L.— 40—Chicago 23, Cleveland 17, May 27, 1956, first game.
N. L.— 40—St. Louis 22, Cincinnati 18, September 3, 1949.

Most Left on Base, 16-Inning Game, Both Clubs

A. L.— 37—Chicago 21, Detroit 16, May 9, 1952.
N. L.—Less than for 15-inning game.

Most Left on Base, 17-Inning Game, Both Clubs

A. L.— 38—Boston 21, Baltimore 17, June 23, 1954.
N. L.— 37—St. Louis 24, Pittsburgh 13, August 2, 1982.

Most Left on Base, 18-Inning Game, Both Clubs

N. L.— 44—Chicago 23, Cincinnati 21, August 9, 1942, first game.
A. L.— 44—Minnesota 23, Seattle 21, July 19, 1969.

Most Left on Base, 19-Inning Game, Both Clubs

A. L.—Less than for 18-inning game.
N. L.—Less than for 18-inning game.

Most Left on Base, 20-Inning Game, Both Clubs

N. L.—Less than for 18-inning game.
A. L.—Less than for 18-inning game.

Most Left on Base, 21-Inning Game, Both Clubs

N. L.—Less than for 18-inning game.
A. L.—Less than for 18-inning game

Most Left on Base, 22-Inning Game, Both Clubs

A. L.— 43—Detroit 23, New York 20, June 24, 1962.
N. L.— 42—Pittsburgh 24, Brooklyn 18, August 22, 1917.

Most Left on Base, 25-Inning Game, Both Clubs

N. L.— 45—New York 25, St. Louis 20, September 11, 1974.
A. L.—Less than for 18-inning game.

Most Left on Base, Extra-Inning Game

N. L.— 27—Atlanta vs. Philadelphia, May 4, 1973, 20 innings.
A. L.— 24—Cleveland vs. Philadelphia, July 10, 1932, 18 innings.
Chicago vs. Milwaukee, May 8, finished May 9, 1984, 25 innings.

Most Left on Base, Extra-Inning Game, Both Clubs

N. L.— 45—New York 25, St. Louis 20, September 11, 1974, 23 innings.
A. L.— 44—Minnesota 23, Seattle 21, July 19, 1969, 18 innings.

Fewest Left on Base, 9-Inning Game

A. L.-N. L.—0—Made in many games.

Fewest Left on Base, Extra-Inning Game

A. L.—0—Philadelphia vs. New York, June 22, 1929, second game, 14 innings.
N. L.—No game over nine-innings with none left on base.

Fewest Left on Base, Extra-Inning Game, Both Clubs

N. L.—3—Chicago 2, Cincinnati 1, May 2, 1917, 10 innings.
A. L.—4—Made in many games.

Fewest Left on Base, Game, Both Clubs

N. L.—1—Los Angeles 1, Chicago 0, September 9, 1965.
A. L.—2—Made in many games. Last time—Cleveland 1, Oakland 1, July 19, 1974.

Fewest Left on Base, Two Consecutive Games

A. L.—2—Washington, May 27 (2), May 29 (0), 1952, (18 innings).
Chicago vs. California, September 18 (1), September 19 (1), 1971, (17 innings).
N. L.—2—San Francisco, May 6 (2), May 7 (0), 1960 (16 innings).
San Francisco, June 13 (1), 10 innings, June 14 (1), 8 innings (18 innings), 1963.

Most Left on Base, Doubleheader, 18 Innings

A. L.— 30—Philadelphia vs. St. Louis, June 12, 1949, 18 innings.
N. L.— 29—St. Louis vs. Philadelphia, September 15, 1928, 18 innings.
Philadelphia vs. Milwaukee, May 15, 1955, 18 innings.

Most Left on Base, Doubleheader, More Than 18 Innings

A. L.— 34—Cleveland vs. New York, August 18, 1943, 21 ⅓ innings.
N. L.— 30—Pittsburgh vs. Brooklyn, June 4, 1946, 20 innings.
Philadelphia vs. Brooklyn, May 30, 1950 19 innings.

Most Left on Base, Doubleheader, Both Clubs, 18 Innings

N. L.— 49—Brooklyn 25, Pittsburgh 24, July 24, 1926.
A. L.— 49—New York 27, Chicago 22, August 27, 1935.

Fewest Left on Base, Doubleheader

A. L.—3—Washington vs. New York, August 6, 1963, 17 innings.
N. L.—3—San Francisco vs. Houston, September 24, 1978, 16 innings.

Fewest Left on Base, Doubleheader, Both Clubs

N. L.— 10—St. Louis 6, Boston 4, July 19, 1924.
A. L.— 13—Chicago 9, Philadelphia 4, July 18, 1918.

League Baserunning

Stolen Bases

Most Stolen Bases, Season, Since 1900

N. L.— (12-club league) —1851 in 1987.
N. L.— (8-club league) —1691 in 1911.
A. L.— (14-club league) —1734 in 1987.
A. L.— (12-club league) —1690 in 1976.
A. L.— (8-club league) —1810 in 1912.

Fewest Stolen Bases, Season, Since 1900

A. L.— (8-club league) —278 in 1950.
A. L.— (12-club league) —863 in 1970.
N. L.— (8-club league) —337 in 1954.
N. L.— (12-club league) —817 in 1969.

Caught Stealing

Most Caught Stealing, Season

A. L.— (14-club league) —936 in 1977.
A. L.— (12-club league) —867 in 1976.
A. L.— (10-club league) —471 in 1968.
A. L.— (8-club league) —707 in 1920.
N. L.— (12-club league) —870 in 1983.
N. L.— (10-club league) —494 in 1966.
N. L.— (8-club league) —517 in 1925.

Fewest Caught Stealing, Season

N. L.— (12-club league) —492 in 1971.
N. L.— (10-club league) —409 in 1962.
N. L.— (8-club league) —218 in 1953.
A. L.— (12-club league) —539 in 1972.
A. L.— (10-club league) —270 in 1963.
A. L.— (8-club league) —231 in 1950.

Left On Base

Most Left on Base, Season, Since 1900

A. L.— (14-club league) —15,991 in 1984.
A. L.— (12-club league) —13,925 in 1973.
A. L.— (10-club league) —11,680 in 1961.
A. L.— (8-club league) — 9,628 in 1936.
N. L.— (12-club league) —14,468 in 1975.
N. L.— (10-club league) —11,416 in 1962.
N. L.— (8-club league) — 9,424 in 1945.

Fewest Left on Base, Season, Since 1900

N. L.— (12-club league) —13,494 in 1976.
A. L.— (10-club league) —10,668 in 1966.
A. L.— (8-club league) — 8,619 in 1958.
N. L.— (12-club league) —13,525 in 1982.
N. L.— (10-club league) —10,994 in 1966.
N. L.— (8-club league) — 8,254 in 1920.

Individual Pitching

Years

Most Years Pitched in Major Leagues

25—James L. Kaat, Washington A.L., Minnesota A.L., Chicago A.L., Philadelphia N.L., New York A.L., St. Louis N.L., 1959 through 1983.

Most Years Pitched, League

A. L.—23—Early Wynn, Washington, Cleveland, Chicago, 1939, 1941 through 1963 (except 1945, in military service), 691 games.

N. L.—22—Steven N. Carlton, St. Louis, Philadelphia, San Francisco, 1965 through 1986, 695 games.

Most Consecutive Years Pitched in Major Leagues

25—James L. Kaat, Washington A. L., Minnesota A. L., Chicago A. L., Philadelphia N. L., New York A. L., St. Louis N. L., 1959 through 1983.

Most Consecutive Years Pitched, League

A. L.—22—Herbert J. Pennock, Philadelphia, Boston, New York, 1912 through 1934 (except 1918, in military service).

Samuel P. Jones, Cleveland, Boston, New York, St. Louis, Washington, Chicago, 1914 through 1935.

Early Wynn, Washington, Cleveland, Chicago, 1941 through 1963 (except 1945, in military service).

Charles H. Ruffing, Boston, New York, Chicago, 1924 through 1947 (except 1943, 1944 in military service).

N. L.—22—Steven N. Carlton, St. Louis, Philadelphia, San Francisco, 1965 through 1986.

Most Years Pitched, One Club

A. L.—21—Walter P. Johnson, Washington, 1907 through 1927, 802 games.

Theodore A. Lyons, Chicago, 1923 through 1946 (except 1943, 1944, 1945, in military service), 594 games.

N. L.—20—Warren E. Spahn, Boston, Milwaukee, 1942 through 1964 (except 1943, 1944, 1945, in military service), 714 games.

Philip H. Niekro, Milwaukee, Atlanta, 1964 through 1983, 739 games.

Most Consecutive Years Pitched, One Club

A. L.—21—Walter P. Johnson, Washington, 1907 through 1927, 802 games.

Theodore A. Lyons, Chicago, 1923 through 1946 (except 1943, 1944, 1945, in military service), 594 games.

N. L.—20—Warren E. Spahn, Boston, Milwaukee, 1942 through 1964 (except 1943, 1944, 1945, in military service), 714 games.

Leagues & Clubs

Most Leagues Pitched In

4—Edward Bakely, A. A., U. A., N. L., P. L.
Edward N. Crane, U. A., N. L., P. L., A. A.
Francis I. Foreman, U. A., A. A., N. L., A. L.
Cornelius B. Murphy, U. A., N. L., P. L., A. A.

Most Clubs Pitched On, Major Leagues

10—Robert Lane Miller, St. Louis N. L., New York N. L., Los Angeles N. L., Minnesota A. L., Cleveland A. L., Chicago A. L., Chicago N. L., San Diego N. L., Pittsburgh N. L., Detroit A. L., 1957, 1959 through 1974, 17 years, 694 games.

Kenneth A. Brett, Boston A. L., Milwaukee A. L., Philadelphia N. L., Pittsburgh N. L., New York A. L., Chicago A. L., California A. L., Minnesota A. L., Los Angeles N. L., Kansas City A. L., 1967, 1969 through 1981, 14 years, 349 games.

Most Clubs Pitched On, League

N. L.—6—Burleigh A. Grimes, Pittsburgh, Brooklyn, New York, Boston, St. Louis, Chicago, 1916 through 1934, 19 years, 605 games.

Robert Lane Miller, St. Louis, New York, Los Angeles, Chicago, San Diego, Pittsburgh, 1957 through 1974 except 1958, 1968, 1969, 15 years, 549 games.

Elias Sosa, San Francisco, St. Louis, Atlanta, Los Angeles, Montreal, San Diego, 1972 through 1983, except 1978, 1982, 10 years, 495 games.

A. L.—(12-club league)—7—Kenneth G. Sanders, Kansas City No. 1, 1964, Boston, Kansas City No. 1, 1966, Oakland, 1968, Milwaukee, 1970, 1971, 1972, Minnesota, 1973, Cleveland, 1973, 1974, California, 1974, Kansas City No. 2, 1976, 9 years, 348 games. (Note: Oakland considered part of Kansas City No. 1 franchise and is not considered as separate club).

Kenneth A. Brett, Boston, Milwaukee, New York, Chicago, California, Minnesota, Kansas City, 1967, 1969 through 1972, 1976 through 1981, 11 years, 238 games.

A. L.—(8-club league)—6—Samuel P. Jones, Cleveland, Boston, New York, St. Louis, Washington, Chicago, 1914 through 1935, 22 years, 647 games.

Peter W. Appleton, Cleveland, Boston, New York, Washington, Chicago, St. Louis, 1930 through 1945 except 1934, 1935, 1943, 1944, 12 years, 304 games.

Louis N. Newsom, St. Louis, Washington, Boston, Detroit, Philadelphia, New York, 1934 through 1947, also Washington, 1952, Philadelphia, 1952, 1953, 16 years, 555 games.

William R. Wight, New York, Chicago, Boston, Detroit, Cleveland, Baltimore, 1946 through 1957, except 1954, 11 years, 312 games.

Most Clubs Pitched On, One Season, in Major Leagues

4—G. Willis Hudlin, Cleveland A. L., Washington A. L., St. Louis A. L., New York N. L., 19 games, 1940.

Theodore G. Gray, Chicago A. L., Cleveland A. L., New York A. L., Baltimore A. L., 14 games, 1955.

Michael D. Kilkenny, Detroit A. L., Oakland A. L., San Diego N. L., Cleveland A. L., 29 games, 1972.

Most Clubs Pitched On, One Season, League

A. L.—4—Theodore G. Gray, Chicago, Cleveland, New York, Baltimore, 14 games, 1955.

N. L.—3—Held by many pitchers. Last pitcher—Robert L. Miller, Chicago, San Diego, Pittsburgh, 56 games, 1971.

Games

Most Games Pitched, Major Leagues

1070—J. Hoyt Wilhelm, New York N. L., St. Louis N. L., Cleveland A. L., Baltimore A. L., Chicago A. L., California A. L., Atlanta N. L., Chicago N. L., Los Angeles N. L., 21 years, 1952 through 1972, 448 games in N. L., 622 in A. L.

Most Games Pitched, League

N. L.—943—Kenton C. Tekulve, Pittsburgh, Philadelphia, 14 years, 1974 through 1987, started 0, relieved 943.

A. L.—807—Albert W. Lyle, Boston, New York, Texas, Chicago, 15 years, 1967 through 1982, except 1981, started 0, relieved 807.

Most Games Pitched, One Club

A. L.—802—Walter P. Johnson, Washington, 21 years, 1907 through 1927, started 666, relieved 136.

N. L.—802—El Roy L. Face, Pittsburgh, 15 years, 1953 through 1968 except 1954, started 27, relieved 775.

Most Doubleheaders Pitched in Major Leagues

5—Joseph J. McGinnity, Baltimore A. L., 1901 (2); New York N. L., 1903 (3); 2 in A.L., 3 in N. L., Won 3 in N. L., split 2 in A. L.

Most Doubleheaders Pitched, League

N. L.—3—Joseph J. McGinnity, New York, 1903.
A. L.—2—Held by many pitchers.

Most Games Pitched, Season

N. L.—106—Michael G. Marshall, Los Angeles, 1974 (208 innings).
A. L.—90—Michael G. Marshall, Minnesota, 1979 (143 innings).

Most Games Pitched, Rookie Season

A. L.—80— Mitchell S. Williams, Texas, 1986 (0 complete, 98 innings).

N. L.—78— Timothy P. Burke, Montreal, 1985 (0 complete, 120 1/3 innings).

Most Years Leading Major Leagues in Most Games

7—Joseph J. McGinnity, Brooklyn N. L., Baltimore A. L., New York N. L., 1900, 1901, 1903, 1904, 1905, 1906, 1907.

Most Years Leading League in Most Games

N. L.—6—Joseph J. McGinnity, Brooklyn, New York, 1900, 1903, 1904, 1905, 1906, 1907.

A. L.—6—Fred Marberry, Washington, 1924, 1925, 1926, 1928, 1929, 1932.

Fewest Games Pitched, Season, for Leader in Most Games

A. L.—40—Joseph W. Haynes, Chicago, 1942 (103 innings).

N. L.—41—Remy Kremer, Pittsburgh, 1924 (259 innings).
John D. Morrison, Pittsburgh, 1924 (238 innings).

Most Doubleheaders Pitched, Season

N. L.—3—Joseph J. McGinnity, New York, August 1, 8, 31, 1903. Won 3.

A. L.—2—Joseph J. McGinnity, Baltimore, 1901. Split 2.
John R. Watson, Philadelphia, 1918. Split 1, lost 1 game and tied 1 in other doubleheader.

Most Times Pitched Opening Game of Season

Both Leagues—16—G. Thomas Seaver, New York N.L., Cincinnati N.L., Chicago A.L., 1968 through 1979, 1981, 1983, 1985, 1986; 14 in N.L., 2 in A.L. won 7, lost 2.

N. L.—15—Steven N. Carlton, St. Louis, Philadelphia, 1965, 1972 through 1986, except 1976, 1978 to 1979, 1981. Won 3, lost 9.

A. L.—14—Walter P. Johnson, Washington, 1910 through 1926, except 1911, 1922, 1925. Won 9, lost 5.

Games Started

Most Games Started in Major Leagues

818—Denton T. Young, Cleveland N. L., St. Louis N. L., Boston A. L., Cleveland A. L., Boston N. L., 22 years, 1890 through 1911; 460 in N. L., 358 in A. L.

Most Games Started, League

N. L.—677— Steven N. Carlton, St. Louis, Philadelphia, San Francisco, 22 years, 1965 through 1986.

A. L.—666— Walter P. Johnson, Washington, 21 years, 1907 through 1927.

Most Season Opening Games Started

Both leagues—16—G. Thomas Seaver, New York N. L., Cincinnati N. L., Chicago A. L., 1968 through 1979, 1981, 1983, 1985, 1986; 14 in N. L., 2 in A. L.

A. L.—14—Walter P. Johnson, Washington, 1910 through 1926, except 1911, 1922, 1925.

N. L.—14—G. Thomas Seaver, New York, Cincinnati, 1968 through 1979, 1981, 1983.
Steven N. Carlton, Philadelphia, 1972 through 1986, except 1976.

Most Consecutive Starting Assignments, League, Since 1900

Both Leagues—544—Steven N. Carlton, St. Louis N.L., Philadelphia N.L., San Francisco N.L., Chicago A.L., May 15, 1971 through 1986; 534 in N.L., 10 in A.L.

N. L.—534— Steven N. Carlton, St. Louis, Philadelphia, San Francisco, May 15, 1971 through 1986.

A. L.—272— Melvin L. Stottlemyre, New York, April 10, 1967 through June 11, 1974.

Most Games Started, Season

N. L.—74—William H. White, Cincinnati, 1879 (pitched 75 games).

A. L.—51—John D. Chesbro, New York, 1904 (pitched 55 games).

N. L. since 1900—48—Joseph J. McGinnity, New York, 1903 (pitched 55 games).

Most Years Leading League in Games Started

N. L.—6—Robin E. Roberts, Philadelphia, 1950 (tied), 1951, 1952, 1953, 1954, 1955.

A. L.—5—Robert W. Feller, Cleveland, 1940, 1941, 1946, 1947, 1948.
Early Wynn, Washington, Cleveland, Chicago, 1943 (tied), 1951 (tied), 1954, 1957, 1959 (tied).

All Games Started, Season, None as Reliever (Most), Since 1900

A. L.—49— Wilbur F. Wood, Chicago, 1972 (20 complete).

N. L.—44— Philip H. Niekro, Atlanta, 1979 (23 complete).

Games Started, Season, None Complete (Most)

N. L.—37—Stephen W. Bedrosian, Atlanta, 1985.

A. L.—33—Milton E. Wilcox, Detroit, 1984.

Most Games Taken Out as Starting Pitcher, Season

N. L.—37—Stephen W. Bedrosian, Atlanta, 1985 (started 37).

A. L.—36—Stanley R. Bahnsen, Chicago, 1972 (started 41).

Games Relieved

Most Games in Major Leagues as Relief Pitcher

1018—J. Hoyt Wilhelm, New York N. L., St. Louis N. L., Cleveland A. L., Baltimore A. L., Chicago A. L., California A. L., Atlanta N. L., Chicago N. L., Los Angeles N. L., 21 years, 1952 through 1972; 448 in N. L., 570 in A. L.

Most Games, League, as Relief Pitcher

N. L.— 943— Kenton C. Tekulve, Pittsburgh, Philadelphia, 14 years, 1974 through 1987.

A. L.— 807— Albert W. Lyle, Boston, New York, Texas, Chicago, 15 years, 1967 through 1982, except 1981.

Most Consecutive Appearances as Relief Pitcher, League

N. L.— 943— Kenton C. Tekulve, Pittsburgh, Philadelphia, May 20, 1974 through 1987.

A. L.— 807— Albert W. Lyle, Boston, New York, Texas, Chicago, July 4, 1967 through September 9, 1980; August 23, 1982 through September 27, second game, 1982.

Most Games Pitched League, All in Relief (None Started)

N. L.— 943— Kenton C. Tekulve, Pittsburgh, Philadelphia, May 20, 1974 through 1987.

A. L.— 807— Albert W. Lyle, Boston, New York, Texas, Chicago, July 4, 1967 through September 9, 1980; August 23, 1982 through September 27, second game, 1982.

Most Games, Season, as Relief Pitcher

N. L.— 106— Michael G. Marshall, Los Angeles, 1974, started none, 208 innings.

A. L.— 89— Michael G. Marshall, Minnesota, 1979, 141 innings (also started 1 game—2 innings).
Mark A. Eichhorn, Toronto, 1987, started none, 127 2/3 innings.

All Games Pitched, Season, None Started (Most)

N. L.— 106— Michael G. Marshall, Los Angeles, 1974 (finished 83), 208 innings.

A. L.— 89— Mark A. Eichhorn, Toronto, 1987 (finished 27), 127 2/3 innings.

Most Consecutive Games Pitched as Relief Pitcher

N. L.—13—Michael G. Marshall, Los Angeles, June 18 through July 3, first game, 1974, 26 2/3 innings.

A. L.—13—Dale R. Mohorcic, Texas, August 6 through 20, 1986, 14 innings.

Games Finished

Most Games Finished, Major Leagues

651—J. Hoyt Wilhelm, New York N. L., St. Louis N. L., Cleveland A. L., Baltimore A. L., Chicago A. L., California A. L., Atlanta N. L., Chicago N. L., Los Angeles N. L., 21 years, 1952 through 1972, 245 in N. L., 406 in A. L.

Most Games Finished, League

A. L.— 599— Albert W. Lyle, Boston, New York, Texas, Chicago 15 years, 1967 through 1982, except 1981.

N. L.— 583— Kenton C. Tekulve, Pittsburgh, Philadelphia, 14 years, 1974 through 1987.

Most Games Finished, Season

A. L.—84—Michael G. Marshall, Minnesota, 1979 (90 games).

N. L.—83—Michael G. Marshall, Los Angeles, 1974 (106 games).

Most Years Leading League in Games Finished

Both Leagues—5—Michael G. Marshall, Montreal, Los Angeles, N. L., 1971, 1972, 1973, 1974, Minnesota, A. L., 1979.

A. L.—5—Fred Marberry, Washington, 1924, 1925, 1926, 1928, 1929.

N. L.—4—Ace T. Adams, New York, 1942, 1943, 1944, 1945.
El Roy L. Face, Pittsburgh, 1958, 1960, 1961, 1962.
Michael G. Marshall, Montreal, Los Angeles, 1971, 1972, 1973, 1974.

Complete Games

Most Complete Games Pitched in Major Leagues
751—Denton T. Young, Cleveland N. L., St. Louis N. L., Boston A. L., Cleveland A. L., Boston N. L., 22 years, 1890 through 1911; 428 in N. L., 323 in A. L.

Most Complete Games, League, Righthander
N. L.— 557— James F. Galvin, Buffalo, Pittsburgh, St. Louis, 12 years, 1879 through 1892, except 1886, 1890.
A. L.— 531— Walter P. Johnson, Washington, 21 years, 1907 through 1927.
N. L. since 1900—437—Grover C. Alexander, Philadelphia, Chicago, St. Louis, 20 years, 1911 through 1930.

Most Complete Games, League, Lefthander
A. L.— 387— Edward S. Plank, Philadelphia, St. Louis, 16 years, 1901 through 1917, except 1915.
N. L.— 382— Warren E. Spahn, Boston, Milwaukee, New York, San Francisco, 21 years, 1942 through 1965, except 1943, 1944, 1945 in military service.

Most Complete Games, Season
N. L.— 74— William H. White, Cincinnati, 1879; pitched in 75 games.
A. L.— 48— John D. Chesbro, New York, 1904; pitched in 55 games.
N. L. since 1900—45—Victor G. Willis, Boston, 1902; pitched in 51 games.

Most Consecutive Complete Games Pitched, Season, Since 1900
N. L.— 39— John W. Taylor, St. Louis, April 15 through October 6, first game, 1904 (352 innings, including two games finished in relief).
A. L.— 37— William H. Dinneen, Boston, April 16 through October 10, first game, 1904 (337 innings).

Most Years Leading League in Complete Games
N. L.— 9—Warren E. Spahn, Boston, Milwaukee, 1949, 1951, 1957, 1958, 1959, 1960 (tied), 1961, 1962, 1963.
A. L.— 6—Walter P. Johnson, Washington, 1910, 1911, 1913, 1914, 1915, 1916.

Most Complete Games, Rookie Season
N. L.— 67— James A. Devlin, Louisville, 1876 (67 games).
N. L. since 1900—41—Irving M. Young, Boston, 1905 (43 games).
A. L.— 36— Roscoe C. Miller, Detroit, 1901 (38 games).

Fewest Complete Games, Season, for Leader
N. L.— 12— Ricky E. Reuschel, Pittsburgh, San Francisco, 1987. Fernando Valenzuela, Los Angeles, 1987.
A. L.— 15— Frank S. Lary, Detroit, 1960. W. Dean Chance, Los Angeles, 1964.

All Games Pitched, Season, None Complete (Most)
N. L.— 106— Michael G. Marshall, Los Angeles, 1974, started none (208 innings).
A. L.— 90— Michael G. Marshall, Minnesota, 1979, started one (143 innings).

Innings

Most Innings Pitched in Major Leagues
7377—Denton T. Young, Cleveland N. L., St. Louis N. L., Boston A.L., Cleveland A.L., Boston N.L., 22 years, 1890 through 1911, 4143 in N.L., 3234 in A.L.

Most Innings Pitched, League
A. L.— 5924—Walter P. Johnson, Washington, 21 years, 1907 through 1927.
N. L.— 5246—Warren E. Spahn, Boston, Milwaukee, New York, San Francisco, 21 years, 1942 through 1965 (except 1943, 1944, 1945, in military service).

Most Consecutive Innings, League, Without Relief, Since 1900
N. L.— 1727— John W. Taylor, Chicago, St. Louis, June 20, 1901, second game, through August 9, 1906, 203 games, 188 complete games, 15 finished.

Most Innings, Major Leagues as Relief Pitcher
1870—J. Hoyt Wilhelm, New York N. L., St. Louis N. L., Cleveland A. L., Baltimore A. L., Chicago A. L., California A. L., Atlanta

N. L., Chicago N. L., Los Angeles N. L., 21 years, 1952 through 1972; 916 in N. L., 954 in A. L.

Most Innings, League, as Relief Pitcher
N. L.— 1304 ⅓—Kenton C. Tekulve, Pittsburgh, Philadelphia, 14 years, 1974 through 1987.
A. L.— 1265 — Albert W. Lyle, Boston, New York, Texas, Chicago, 15 years, 1967 through 1982, except 1981.

Most Years Leading League in Innings Pitched
N. L.— 7—Grover C. Alexander, Philadelphia, Chicago, 1911, 1912 (tied), 1914, 1915, 1916, 1917, 1920.
A. L.— 5— Walter P. Johnson, Washington, 1910, 1913, 1914, 1915, 1916.
Robert W. Feller, Cleveland, 1939, 1940, 1941, 1946, 1947.

Most Innings Pitched, Season
N. L.— 683— William H. White, Cincinnati, 75 games, 1879.
A. L.— 464— Edward A. Walsh, Chicago, 66 games, 1908.
N. L. since 1900—434—Joseph J. McGinnity, New York, 55 games, 1903.

Most Innings Pitched, Rookie Season, Since 1900
N. L.— 378— Irving M. Young, Boston, 43 games, 1905.
A. L.— 316— Ewell A. Russell, Chicago, 43 games, 1913.

Most Innings, Season, as Relief Pitcher
N. L.— 208 — Michael G. Marshall, Los Angeles, 1974, pitched 106 games as relief pitcher.
A. L.— 168 ⅓ — Robert W. Stanley, Boston, 1982, pitched 48 games as relief pitcher. (William R. Campbell, Minnesota, hurled 167 ⅔ innings, rounded to 168, as a relief pitcher in 1976.)

Fewest Innings Pitched, Season, for Leader in Most Innings
A. L.— 256 — Early Wynn, Chicago, 37 games, 1959.
N. L.— 261 ⅓ — Joaquin Andujar, St. Louis, 36 games, 1984.

Most Consecutive Innings, Season, Without Relief, Since 1900
N. L.— 352— John Taylor, St. Louis, April 15 through October 6, first game, 1904; complete season, 39 complete games and 2 games finished.
A. L.— 337— William H. Dinneen, Boston, April 16 through October 10, first game, 1904; complete season, 37 complete games.

Most Years, 200 or More Innings, Pitched, Major Leagues
19—Denton T. Young, Cleveland N. L., St. Louis N. L., Boston A. L., Cleveland A.L., 1891 through 1909, consecutive; 10 in N. L., 9 in A. L.
Philip H. Niekro, Milwaukee, N. L., Atlanta N. L., New York A. L., Cleveland A. L., 1967 through 1986, except 1981; 16 in N. L., 3 in A. L.

Most Years, 200 or More Innings, Pitched League
A. L.— 18— Walter P. Johnson, Washington, 1908 through 1926, except 1920.
N. L.— 17— Warren E. Spahn, Boston, Milwaukee, 1947 through 1963, consecutive.

Most Years, 300 or More Innings, Pitched, Major Leagues
16—Denton T. Young, Cleveland N. L., St. Louis N. L., Boston A. L., 1891 through 1907, except 1906. 10 in N.L., 6 in A. L.

Most Years, 300 or More Innings Pitched League
N. L.— 12—Charles A. Nichols, Boston, 1890 through 1899, 1901, 1904.
N. L. since 1900—11—Christopher Mathewson, New York, 1901, 1903, 1904, 1905, 1907, 1908, 1910, 1911, 1912, 1913, 1914.
A. L.— 9— Walter P. Johnson, Washington, 1910 through 1918, consecutive.

Most Consecutive Years, 300 or More Innings, League, Since 1900
N. L.—9—Walter P. Johnson, Washington, 1910 through 1918.
N. L.—7—Grover C. Alexander, Philadelphia, 1911 through 1917.

Most Years, 400 or More Innings Pitched, League, Since 1900
N. L.—2—Joseph J. McGinnity, New York, 1903, (434), 1904 (408).
A. L.—2—Edward A. Walsh, Chicago, 1907 (419), 1908 (464).

Most Innings Pitched, Game
N. L.— 26— Leon J. Cadore, Brooklyn, May 1, 1920, tie 1-1.
Joseph Oeschger, Boston, May 1, 1920, tie 1-1.
A. L.— 24— John W. Coombs, Philadelphia, September 1, 1906, won 4-1.
Joseph Harris, Boston, September 1, 1906, lost 4-1.

Most Innings Pitched, Game, as Relief Pitcher Finishing Game

  N. L.— 18 ⅓ —George W. Zabel, Chicago, June 17, 1915 (Chicago 4, Brooklyn 3, 19 innings).

  A. L.— 17 —Edwin A. Rommel, Philadelphia, July 10, 1932 (Philadelphia 18, Cleveland 17, 18 innings).

Winning Percentage

Highest Percentage Games Won, League, 200 or More Decisions

  A. L.—.690—Edward C. Ford, New York, 16 years, 1950 through 1967 (except 1951, 1952, in military service). Won 236, lost 106.

  N. L.—.665—Christopher Mathewson, New York, Cincinnati, 17 years, 1900 through 1916. Won 373, lost 188.

Highest Percentage Games Won, Season, 70 or More Decisions

  N. L.—.833—Charles Radbourn, Providence, 1884; won 60, lost 12.

Highest Percentage Games Won, Season, 34 or More Decisions

  A. L.—.886—Robert M. Grove, Philadelphia, 1931; won 31, lost 4.

  N. L.—.842—John D. Chesbro, Pittsburgh, 1902; won 28, lost 6.
      Arthur C. Vance, Brooklyn, 1924; won 28, lost 6.

Highest Percentage Games Won, Season, 20 or More Victories

  A. L.—.893—Ronald A. Guidry, New York, 1978; won 25, lost 3.

  N. L.—.880—Fred E. Goldsmith, Chicago, 1880; won 22, lost 3.
      Elwin C. Roe, Brooklyn, 1951; won 22, lost 3.

Highest Percentage Games Won, Season, 16 or More Decisions

  N. L.—.947—El Roy L. Face, Pittsburgh, 1959; won 18, lost 1.

  A. L.—.938—John T. Allen, Cleveland, 1937; won 15, lost 1.

Most Yrs. Leading in Highest Pct. Games Won, 15 or More Victories

  A. L.—5—Robert M. Grove, Philadelphia, Boston, 1929, 1930, 1931, 1933, 1939.

  N. L.—3—Edward M. Reulbach, Chicago, 1906, 1907, 1908.

Games Won
Career

Most Games Won in Major Leagues

  511—Denton T. Young, Cleveland N. L., St. Louis N. L., Boston A.L., Cleveland A. L., Boston N. L., 22 years, 1890 through 1911, (won 289 in N. L., won 222 in A. L.).

Most Games Won, League, Righthanded Pitcher

  A. L.— 416— Walter P. Johnson, Washington, 21 years, 1907 through 1927, (won 416, lost 279—.599).

  N. L.— 373— Christopher Mathewson, New York, Cincinnati, 17 years, 1900 through 1916, (won 373, lost 188—.665).
      Grover C. Alexander, Philadelphia, Chicago, St. Louis, 20 years, 1911 through 1930, (won 373, lost 208—.642).

Most Games Won, League, Lefthanded Pitcher

  N. L.— 363— Warren E. Spahn, Boston, Milwaukee, New York, San Francisco, 21 years, 1942 through 1965 except 1943, 1944, 1945, in military service. (Won 363, lost 245—.597).

  A. L.— 305— Edward S. Plank, Philadelphia, St. Louis 16 years, 1901 through 1917, except 1915 (won 305, lost 181—.628).

Most Games Won in Major Leagues as Relief Pitcher

  124—J. Hoyt Wilhelm, New York N. L., St. Louis N. L., Cleveland A. L., California A. L., Atlanta N. L., Baltimore A. L., Chicago A. L., Chicago N. L., Los Angeles N. L., 21 years, 1952 through 1972, won 73 in A. L., won 51 in N. L.; lost 102 (67 in A. L., 35 in N. L).

Most Games Won, League, as Relief Pitcher

  N. L.— 96— El Roy Face, Pittsburgh, Montreal, 16 years, 1953 through 1969, except 1954 (lost 82).

  A. L.— 87— Albert W. Lyle, Boston, New York, Texas, Chicago, 15 years, 1967 through 1982, except 1981 (lost 67).

Most Games Won, League, From One Club

  N. L.— 70— Grover C. Alexander, Philadelphia, Chicago, St. Louis, vs. Cincinnati, 20 years, 1911 through 1930.

  A. L.— 66— Walter P. Johnson, Washington, vs. Detroit 21 years, 1907 through 1927.

Most Season Opening Games Won, League

  A. L.—9—Walter P. Johnson, Washington, all complete, 1910, 1913, 1914, 1915, 1916, 1917, 1919, 1924, 1926; seven shutouts. Lost in 1912, 1918, 1920, 1921, 1923; no shutouts.

  N. L.—8—Grover C. Alexander, Philadelphia, Chicago, St. Louis, 7 complete, 1914, 1915, 1916, 1917, 1921, 1922, 1925, 1929; one shutout. Lost in 1912, 1918, 1920, 1927; no shutouts.

Season & Month

Most Games Won, Season, Righthanded Pitcher

  N. L.— 60— Charles G. Radbourn, Providence, 1884 (won 60, lost 12—.833).

  A. L.— 41— John D. Chesbro, New York, 1904 (won 41, lost 13—.759).

  N. L. since 1900—37—Christopher Mathewson, New York, 1908 (won 37, lost 11—.771).

Most Games Won, Season, Lefthanded Pitcher

  N. L.— 42— Charles B. Baldwin, Detroit, 1886 (won 42, lost 14—.750).

  A. L.— 31— Robert M. Grove, Philadelphia, 1931 (won 31, lost 4—.886).

  N. L. since 1900—27—Sanford Koufax, Los Angeles, 1966 (won 27, lost 9—.750).
      Steven N. Carlton, Philadelphia, 1972 (won 27, lost 10—.730).

Most Games Won, Season, All as Relief Pitcher

  N. L.— 18— El Roy Face, Pittsburgh, 1959 (won 18, lost 1—.947).

  A. L.— 17— John F. Hiller, Detroit, 1974 (won 17, lost 14—.548).
      William R. Campbell, Minnesota, 1976 (won 17, lost 5—.773).

Fewest Games Won, Season, for Leader in Most Games Won

  A. L.— 18— Edward C. Ford, New York, 1955 (won 18, lost 7).
      Robert G. Lemon, Cleveland, 1955 (won 18, lost 10).
      Franklin L. Sullivan, Boston, 1955 (won 18, lost 13).
      Charles L. Estrada, Baltimore, 1960 (won 18, lost 11).
      James E. Perry, Cleveland, 1960 (won 18, lost 10).

  N. L.— 18— Richard L. Sutcliffe, Chicago, 1987 (won 18, lost 10).

Most Years Leading League in Games Won

  N. L.—8—Warren E. Spahn, Boston, Milwaukee, 1949, 1950, 1953 (tied), 1957, 1958 (tied), 1959 (tied), 1960 (tied), 1961 (tied).

  A. L.—6—Walter P. Johnson, Washington, 1913, 1914, 1915, 1916, 1918, 1924.
      Robert W. Feller, Cleveland, 1939, 1940, 1941, 1946 (tied), 1947, 1951.

Most Games Won, Rookie Season

  N. L.— 47— Albert G. Spalding, Chicago, 1876 (won 47, lost 13—.783).

  N. L. since 1900—28—Grover C. Alexander, Philadelphia, 1911 (won 28, lost 13—.683).

  A. L.— 24— O. Edgar Summers, Detroit, 1908 (won 24, lost 12—.667).

Most Games Won, Season, From One Club

  N. L.— 12— Charles G. Radbourn, Providence vs. Cleveland, 1884.

  N. L. since 1900—9—Edward M. Reulbach, Chicago vs. Brooklyn, 1908 (won 9, lost 0).

  A. L.— 9— Edward A. Walsh, Chicago vs. New York 1908 (won 9, lost 1), and vs. Boston, 1908 (won 9, lost 0).

Most Games Won, One Month

  N. L.— 15— John G. Clarkson, Chicago, June 1885, won 15, lost 1.

  N. L. since 1900—9—Christopher Mathewson, New York, August, 1903; won 9, lost 1.
      Christopher Mathewson, New York, August, 1904; won 9, lost 1.
      Grover C. Alexander, Chicago, May 1920, won 9, lost 0.

  A. L.— 10— George E. Waddell, Philadelphia, July 1902; won 10, lost 1, tied 1.

20 & 30-Win Seasons

Most Years Winning 30 or More Games, League

  N. L.—7—Charles A. Nichols, Boston, 1891, 1892, 1893, 1894, 1896, 1897, 1898.

N. L. since 1900—4—Christopher Mathewson, New York, 1903, 1904, 1905, 1908.
A. L.—2—Denton T. Young, Boston, 1901, 1902.
Walter P. Johnson, Washington, 1912, 1913.

Most Years Winning 20 or More Games in Major Leagues

16—Denton T. Young, Cleveland N. L., 1891, 1892, 1893, 1894, 1895, 1896, 1897, 1898; St. Louis, N. L., 1899, 1900; Boston, A. L., 1901, 1902, 1903, 1904, 1907, 1908; 10 in N. L., 6 in A. L. (14 consecutive).

Most Years Winning 20 or More Games, League, Righthander

N. L.—13—Christopher Mathewson, New York, 1901, 1903, 1904, 1905, 1906, 1907, 1908, 1909, 1910, 1911, 1912, 1913, 1914 (12 consecutive).
A. L.—12—Walter P. Johnson, Washington, 1910, 1911, 1912, 1913, 1914, 1915, 1916, 1917, 1918, 1919, 1924, 1925 (10 consecutive).

Most Years Winning 20 or More Games, League, Lefthander

N. L.—13—Warren E. Spahn, Boston, Milwaukee, 1947, 1949, 1950, 1951, 1953, 1954, 1956, 1957, 1958, 1959, 1960, 1961, 1963.
A. L.—8—Robert M. Grove, Philadelphia, Boston, 1927, 1928, 1929, 1930, 1931, 1932, 1933, 1935.

Most Consec. Years Winning 20 or More Games, Major Leagues

14—Denton T. Young, Cleveland N. L., St. Louis N. L., 1891 through 1900; Boston A. L., 1901 through 1904; 10 in N. L.; 4 in A. L.

Most Consecutive Years Winning 20 or More Games, League

N. L.—12—Christopher Mathewson, New York, 1903 through 1914.
A. L.—10—Walter P. Johnson, Washington, 1910 through 1919.

Most Consec. Years Winning 20 or More Games, Start of Career

N. L.—10—Charles A. Nichols, Boston, 1890 through 1899. (Also won 21 with St. Louis, 1904.)
A. L.—3—Sylveanus A. Gregg, Cleveland, 1911, 1912, 1913.

Doubleheader

Most Doubleheaders Won, League (Complete Games)

N. L.—3—Joseph J. McGinnity, New York, 1903, Lost 0.
A. L.—2—Edward A. Walsh, Chicago, 1905, 1908, Lost 0.

Most Doubleheaders Won, Season (Complete Games)

N. L.—3—Joseph J. McGinnity, New York, 1903.
A. L.—1—Held by many pitchers. Last pitcher, Emil H. Levsen, Cleveland vs. Boston, at Boston, August 28, 1926. Won 6-1, 5-1.

Consecutive

Most Consecutive Games Won, League

N. L.—24—Carl O. Hubbell, New York, July 17, 1936, through May 27, 1937; 16 in 1936, 8 in 1937.
A. L.—17—John T. Allen, Cleveland, September 10, 1936, through September 30, 1937, first game; 2 in 1936, 15 in 1937.
David A. McNally, Baltimore, September 22, 1968 through July 30, 1969; 2 in 1968, 15 in 1969.

Most Consec. Games Won, Start of Career, As Starting Pitcher

N. L.—12—George L. Wiltse, New York, May 29 through September 15, 1904.
A. L.—9—Edward C. Ford, New York, July 17 through September 24, second game, 1950.

Most Consecutive Games Won, Start of Career, As Relief Pitcher

N. L.—12—Clarence E. Metzger, San Francisco, 1974 (1), San Diego, 1975 (1), 1976 (10), September 21, 1974 through August 8, 1976.
A. L.—9—Joseph W. Pate, Philadelphia, April 15 through August 10, 1926.

Most Consecutive Games Won, League, From One Club

N. L.—24—Christopher Mathewson, New York, vs. St. Louis, June 16, 1904 through September 15, 1908.
A. L.—23—Carl W. Mays, Boston, New York, vs. Philadelphia, August 30, 1918, to July 24, 1923.

Most Consecutive Games Won, Season

N. L.—19—Timothy J. Keefe, New York, June 23 through August 10, 1888.
Richard W. Marquard, New York, April 11 through July 3, 1912, first game.

A. L.—16—Walter P. Johnson, Washington, July 3, second game, through August 23, 1912, first game.
Joseph Wood, Boston, July 8 through September 15, 1912, second game.
Robert M. Grove, Philadelphia, June 8 through August 19, 1931.
Lynwood T. Rowe, Detroit, June 15 through August 25, 1934.

Most Consecutive Games Won, Season, Relief Pitcher

N. L.—17—El Roy L. Face, Pittsburgh, April 22, through August 30, second game, 1959.
A. L.—12—Luis E. Arroyo, New York, July 1 through September 9, 1961.

Most Consecutive Games Won, Start of Season

N. L.—19—Richard W. Marquard, New York, April 11 through July 3, 1912, first game.
A. L.—15—John T. Allen, Cleveland, April 23, 1937, through September 30, 1937, first game.
David A. McNally, Baltimore, April 12 through July 30, 1969.

Most Consecutive Games Won, Rookie Season

N. L.—17—John P. Luby, Chicago, August 6, second game, through October 3, 1890.
N. L. since 1900—12—George L. Wiltse, New York, May 29 through September 15, 1904.
A. L.—12—R. Atley Donald, New York, May 9 through July 25, 1939.
Russell W. Ford, New York, August 9 through October 6, 1910.

Most Consecutive Games Won as Starting Pitcher, Rookie Season

N. L.—17—John P. Luby, Chicago, August 6, second game, through October 3, 1890.
N. L. since 1900—12—George L. Wiltse, New York, May 29 through September 15, 1904.
A. L.—12—R. Atley Donald, New York, May 9 through July 25, 1939.

Most Consecutive Games Won as Relief Pitcher, Rookie Season

N. L.—10—John E. Yuhas, St. Louis, June 5, through September 25, 1952; end of season.
Clarence E. Metzger, San Diego, April 20, through August 8, 1976.
A. L.—9—Joseph W. Pate, Philadelphia, April 15 through August 10, 1926.

Most Consecutive Games Won, Reliever, 3 Consecutive Games

A. L.—3—Harold G. White, Detroit, September 26, second game, 27, 28, 1950, 5⅓ innings.
Grant D. Jackson, Baltimore, September 29, 30, October 1, 1974, 5⅓ innings.
Albert W. Lyle, New York, August 29, 30, 31, 1977, 7⅔ innings.
N. L.—3—Michael G. Marshall, Los Angeles, June 21, 22, 23, 1974, 7 innings.
H. Eugene Garber, Philadelphia, May 15 (second game), 16, 17, 1975, 5⅔ innings.
Alan T. Hrabosky, St. Louis, July 12, 13, 17, 1975, 5 innings.
Kenton C. Tekulve, Pittsburgh, May 6, 7, 9, 1980, 5⅓ innings.

Most Consecutive Games Won, End of Season

N. L.—17—John P. Luby, Chicago, August 6, second game, through October 3, 1890.
N. L. since 1900—16—Carl O. Hubbell, New York, July 17 through September 23, 1936.
A. L.—15—Alvin F. Crowder, Washington, August 2 through September 25, 1932.

Saves

Most Saves, Major Leagues (Since 1969)

341—Roland G. Fingers, Oakland A. L., San Diego N. L., Milwaukee A. L.; 17 years, 1968 through 1985, except 1983; saved 233 in A. L., 108 in N. L.

Most Saves, League (Since 1969)

N. L.—286—H. Bruce Sutter, Chicago, St. Louis, Atlanta, 11 years, 1976 through 1986.
A. L.—237—Daniel R. Quisenberry, Kansas City, 9 years, 1979 through 1987.

Most Saves, Season (Since 1969)

A. L.—46—David A. Righetti, New York, 1986; 74 games in relief, finished 68.

N. L.—45—H. Bruce Sutter, St. Louis, 1984; 71 games in relief, finished 63.

Most Saves, Rookie Season (Since 1969)

N. L.—36—Todd R. Worrell, St. Louis, 1986; 74 games in relief, finished 60.

A. L.—23—Douglas M. Corbett, Minnesota, 1980; 73 games in relief, finished 63.

Games Lost

Most Games Lost in Major Leagues

313—Denton T. Young, Cleveland, N. L., St. Louis, N. L., Boston, A. L., Cleveland, A. L., Boston, N. L.; 22 years, 1890-1911; lost 172 in N. L., lost 141 in A. L.

Most Games Lost, League, Righthander

A. L.—279—Walter P. Johnson, Washington, 21 years, 1907 through 1927.

N. L.—268—James F. Galvin, Buffalo, Pittsburg, St. Louis, 12 years, 1879 through 1892, except 1886 and 1890.

N. L. since 1900—230—Philip H. Niekro, Milwaukee, Atlanta, 21 years, 1964 through 1983, 1987.

Most Games Lost, League, Lefthander

N. L.—251—Eppa Rixey, Philadelphia, Cincinnati, 21 years, 1912 through 1933, (except 1918, in military service).

A. L.—191—James L. Kaat, Washington, Minnesota, Chicago, New York, 19 years, 1959 through 1975, 1979 through 1980.

Most Consecutive Games Lost, League

N. L.—23—Clifton G. Curtis, Boston, June 13, 1910, first game, through May 22, 1911; 18 in 1910, 5 in 1911.

A. L.—19—Robert Groom, Washington, June 19, first game through September 25, 1909.

John H. Nabors, Philadelphia, April 28 through September 28, 1916.

Most Consecutive Games Lost, League, to One Club

N. L.—13—Donald H. Sutton, Los Angeles vs. Chicago, April 23, 1966 through July 24, 1969 (start of career).

A. L.—10—David M. Morehead, Boston vs. Los Angeles, July 28, 1963 through September 28, 1965 (start of career).

Most Consecutive Games Lost, Start of Career

A. L.—16—Terry L. Felton, Minnesota, April 18, 1980, second game, through September 12, 1982.

A. A.—10—Charles Stecher, Philadelphia, September 6 through October 9, 1890.

Most Games Lost, Season

N. L.—48—John H. Coleman, Philadelphia, 1883 (won 11, lost 48, .186).

N. L. since 1900—29—Victor G. Willis, Boston, 1905 (won 12, lost 29, .293).

A. L.—26—John Townsend, Washington, 1904 (won 5, lost 26, .161).

Robert B. Groom, Washington, 1909 (won 6, lost 26, .188).

Most Years Leading League in Games Lost

A. L.—4—Louis N. Newsom, St. Louis, Washington, Detroit, Philadelphia 1934, 1935, 1941, 1945.

Pedro Ramos, Washington, Minnesota, 1958, 1959, 1960, 1961.

N. L.—4—Philip H. Niekro, Atlanta, 1977 (tied), 1978, 1979, 1980.

Fewest Games Lost, Season, for Leader in Most Games Lost

A. L.—14—Theodore G. Gray, Detroit, 1951; won 7, lost 14.

Alexander R. Kellner, Philadelphia, 1951; won 11, lost 14.

Robert G. Lemon, Cleveland 1951; won 17 lost 14.

W. William Pierce, Chicago, 1951; won 15, lost 14.

Duane X. Pillette, St. Louis, 1951; won 6, lost 14.

Paul H. Trout, Detroit, 1951; won 9, lost 14.

N. L.—16—Ronald L. Kline, Pittsburgh, 1958; won 13, lost 16.

Most Games Lost, Season, All as Relief Pitcher

N. L.—16—H. Eugene Garber, Atlanta, 1979 (won 6, lost 16—.273).

A. L.—14—Darold D. Knowles, Washington, 1970 (won 2, lost 14—.125).

John F. Hiller, Detroit, 1974 (won 17, lost 14—.548).

Michael G. Marshall, Minnesota, 1979 (won 10, lost 14—.417, also lost 1 game as starter).

Most Games Lost, Rookie Season

N. L.—34—James A. Devlin, Louisville, 1876 (won 30, lost 34, .469).

Robert T. Mathews, New York, 1876 (won 21, lost 34, .382).

A. L.—26—Robert B. Groom, Washington, 1909 (won 6, lost 26, .188).

N. L. since 1900—25—Harry McIntire, Brooklyn, 1906 (won 8, lost 25, .242).

Most Games Lost, Season to One Club, Since 1900

N. L.—7—Held by 7 pitchers.

Last Time—Calvin C. McLish, Cincinnati vs. Pittsburgh, 1960 (won 0, lost 7).

A. L.—7—Held by 4 pitchers.

Last Time—Camilo A. Pascual, Washington vs. New York, 1956 (won 0, lost 7).

Most Consecutive Games Lost, Season

A. L.—19—Robert Groom, Washington, June 19, first game, through September 25, 1909.

John H. Nabors, Philadelphia, April 28 through September 28, 1916.

N. L.—18—Clifton G. Curtis, Boston, June 13, first game, through September 20, first game, 1910.

Roger L. Craig, New York, May 4 through August 4, 1963.

Most Consecutive Games Lost, Rookie Season

A. L.—19—Robert Groom, Washington, June 19, first game, through September 25, 1909.

N. L.—16—Henry Dean, Cincinnati, July 11 through September 12, 1876.

N. L. since 1900—12—Henry Thielman, Cincinnati, June 29 through September 1, a.m., 1902.

Peter J. Schneider, Cincinnati, July 20 through September 26, first game, 1914.

Most Consecutive Games Lost, Start of Season

A. L.—14—Joseph W. Harris, Boston, May 10 through July 25, 1906.

Matthew L. Keough, Oakland, April 15 through August 8, 1979.

N. L.—12—Russell L. Miller, Philadelphia, May 12 through August 12, 1928.

Robert Lane Miller, New York, April 21 through September 10, 1962.

Kenneth L. Reynolds, Philadelphia, May 29, second game, through August 25, 1972.

Most Consecutive Games Lost, End of Season

A. L.—19—John Nabors, Philadelphia, April 28 through September 28, 1916.

N. L.—18—Clifton G. Curtis, Boston, June 13, first game, through September 20, 1910, first game.

At-Bats & Plate Appearances

Most At-Bats, League

A. L.—21,663—Walter P. Johnson, Washington, 21 years, 1907 through 1927.

N. L.—19,778—Warren E. Spahn, Boston, Milwaukee, New York, San Francisco, 21 years, 1942 through 1965, (except 1943, 1944, 1945 in military service).

Most At-Bats, Season

N. L.—2808—William H. White, Cincinnati, 75 games, 1879; 683 innings.

A. L.—1690—Edward A. Walsh, Chicago, 66 games, 1908; 464 innings.

N. L. since 1900—1658—Joseph J. McGinnity, New York, 55 games, 1903; 434 innings.

Most Years Leading League in Most At-Bats

N. L.—6—Grover C. Alexander, Philadelphia, Chicago, 1911, 1914, 1915, 1916, 1917, 1920.

A. L.—4—Edward A. Walsh, Chicago, 1908, 1910, 1911, 1912.

Walter P. Johnson, Washington, 1913, 1914, 1915, 1916.

Robert G. Lemon, Cleveland, 1948, 1950, 1952, 1953.

Most Consecutive Years Leading League in Most At-Bats

A. L.—4—Walter P. Johnson, Washington, 1913, 1914, 1915, 1916.

N. L.—4—Grover C. Alexander, Philadelphia, 1914, 1915, 1916, 1917.
Robin E. Roberts, Philadelphia, 1952, 1953, 1954, 1955.

Fewest Official At-Bats, Season, for Leader in Most At-Bats
A. L.— 942— James P. Bunning, Detroit, 250 innings, 1959.
N. L.— 1009— George B. Koslo, New York, 265 innings, 1946.

Most At-Bats, Game
N. L.—66— George H. Derby, Buffalo, July 3, 1883.
A. L.—53— Roy Patterson, Chicago, May 5, 1901.
N. L. since 1900—49—Harley Parker, Cincinnati, June 21, 1901. William C. Phillips, Cincinnati, June 24, 1901, second game.

Most Men Facing Pitcher, Nine-Inning Game
N. L.—67— George H. Derby, Buffalo, July 3, 1883.
A. L.—57— Roy Patterson, Chicago, May 5, 1901.
N. L. since 1900—53—William C. Phillips, Cincinnati, June 24, 1901, second game.

Most Men Facing Pitcher, Inning
N. L.—22— Anthony J. Mullane, Baltimore, June 18, 1894, a.m. game, first inning.
N. L. since 1900—16—Harold Kelleher, Philadelphia, May 5, 1938, eighth inning.
A. L.—16— Merle T. Adkins, Boston, July 8, 1902, sixth inning.
Frank J. O'Doul, Boston, July 7, 1923, first game, sixth inning.
Howard J. Ehmke, Boston, September 28, 1923, sixth inning.

Runs

Most Runs Allowed, League
A. L.— 2117— Charles H. Ruffing, Boston, New York, Chicago, 1924 through 1947, except 1943, 1944, 22 years.
N. L.— 2037— Burleigh A. Grimes, Pittsburgh, Brooklyn, New York, Boston, St. Louis, Chicago, 1916 through 1934, 19 years.

Most Runs Allowed, Season
N. L.— 544— John Coleman, Philadelphia, 63 games, 538 innings, 1883.
A. L.— 219— Joseph J. McGinnity, Baltimore, 48 games, 378 innings, 1901.
N. L. since 1900—224—William M. Carrick, New York, 45 games, 342 innings, 1900.

Most Years Leading League in Most Runs Allowed
N. L.—3—Burleigh A. Grimes, Brooklyn, Pittsburgh, 1923, 1924, 1928.
Robin E. Roberts, Philadelphia, 1955, 1956, 1957.
Philip H. Niekro, Atlanta, 1977, 1978, 1979.
A. L.—3—Wilbur F. Wood, Chicago, 1972, 1973, 1975.

Fewest Runs, Season, for Leader in Most Runs Allowed
N. L.— 102— George A. Smith, New York, Philadelphia, 196 innings, 1919.
A. L.— 108— James C. Bagby, Cleveland, 280 innings, 1918.

Most Runs Allowed, Game
N. L.—35— David E. Rowe, Cleveland, July 24, 1882.
A. L.—24— Aloysius J. Travers, Detroit, May 18, 1912 (only major league game).
N. L. since 1900—21—Harley Parker, Cincinnati, June 21, 1901.

Fewest Runs Allowed, Doubleheader
N. L.—0— Edward M. Reulbach, Chicago, September 26, 1908.
A. L.—1— Edward A. Walsh, Chicago, September 29, 1908.
Carl W. Mays, Boston, August 30, 1918.

Most Runs Allowed, Inning
N. L.—16— Anthony J. Mullane, Baltimore, June 18, 1894, a.m. game, first inning.
A. L.—13— Frank J. O'Doul, Boston, July 7, 1923, first game, sixth inning.
N. L. since 1900—12—Harold Kelleher, Philadelphia, May 5, 1938, eighth inning.

Earned Runs

Most Earned Runs Allowed, Season, Since 1900
A. L.— 186— Louis N. Newsom, St. Louis, 330 innings, 1938.
N. L.— 155— Guy T. Bush, Chicago, 225 innings, 1930.

Most Years Leading League in Most Earned Runs Allowed
N. L.—3—Burleigh A. Grimes, Brooklyn, 1922, 1924, 1925.
Murry M. Dickson, St. Louis, Pittsburgh, 1948, 1951, 1952 (tied).
Robin E. Roberts, Philadelphia, 1955, 1956, 1957.
John H. Fisher, New York, 1964 (tied), 1965 (tied), 1967.
A. L.—3—Louis N. Newsom, St. Louis, Washington, Philadelphia, 1938, 1942, 1945.
Wilbur F. Wood, Chicago, 1972, 1973, 1975.

Fewest Earned Runs, Season, for Leader in Most Allowed
A. L.— 83— William Adams, Philadelphia, 169 innings, 1918
George Dauss, Detroit, 250 innings, 1918.
N. L.— 85— Peter J. Schneider, Cincinnati, 217 innings, 1918.
Arthur N. Nehf, Boston, 284 innings, 1918.
A. Wilbur Cooper, Pittsburgh, 287 innings, 1919.

Earned-Run Average

Lowest Earned-Run Average, League, 300 or More Games Won
A. L.—2.47— Walter P. Johnson, Washington, 802 games, 21 years, 1907 through 1927, righthander.
3.06—Robert M. Grove, Philadelphia, Boston, 616 games, 17 years, 1925 through 1941, lefthander.
N. L.—2.56— Grover C. Alexander, Philadelphia, Chicago, St. Louis, 696 games, 20 years, 1911 through 1930, righthander.

Lowest Earned-Run Average, League, 200 or More Games Won
A. L.—2.47— Walter P. Johnson, Washington, 802 games, 21 years, 1907 through 1927, righthander.
2.74—Edwin C. Ford, New York, 498 games, 16 years, 1950 through 1967 (except 1951, 1952 in military service), lefthander.
N. L.—2.56— Grover C. Alexander, Philadelphia, Chicago, St. Louis, 696 games, 20 years, 1911 through 1930, righthander.
2.73—G. Thomas Seaver, New York, Cincinnati, 559 games, 17 years, 1967 through 1983, righthander.

Lowest Earned-Run Average, League, 2000 or More Innings
N. L.—2.33— James L. Vaughn, Chicago, 2,217 innings, 305 games, 9 years, 1913 through 1921, lefthander.
A. L.—2.47— Walter P. Johnson, Washington, 5,924 innings, 802 games, 21 years, 1907 through 1927, righthander.
2.74—Edwin C. Ford, New York, 3,171 innings, 498 games, 16 years, 1950 through 1967 (except 1951, 1952 in military service), lefthander.

Lowest Earned-Run Average, Season, 300 or More Innings
N. L.— 1.12— Robert Gibson, St. Louis, 305 innings, 1968.
A. L.— 1.14— Walter P. Johnson, Washington, 346 innings, 1913.

Lowest ERA, Season, 300 or More Innings, Righthander
N. L.— 1.12— Robert Gibson, St. Louis, 305 innings, 1968.
A. L.— 1.14— Walter P. Johnson, Washington, 346 innings, 1913.

Lowest ERA, Season, 300 or More Innings, Lefthander
N. L.— 1.66— Carl O. Hubbell, New York, 309 innings, 1933.
A. L.— 1.75— George H. Ruth, Boston, 324 innings, 1916.

Lowest Earned-Run Average, Season, 200 or More Innings
A. L.— 1.00— Hubert B. Leonard, Boston, 225 innings, 1914.
N. L.— 1.12— Robert Gibson, St. Louis, 305 innings, 1968.

Most Years Leading League in Lowest Earned-Run Average
A. L.—9—Robert M. Grove, Philadelphia, Boston, 1926, 1929, 1930, 1931, 1932, 1935, 1936, 1938, 1939.
N. L.—5—Grover C. Alexander, Philadelphia, Chicago, 1915, 1916, 1917, 1919, 1920.
Sanford Koufax, Los Angeles, 1962, 1963, 1964, 1965, 1966.

Most Consecutive Years Leading League in Lowest ERA
N. L.—5—Sanford Koufax, Los Angeles, 1962, 1963, 1964, 1965, 1966.
A. L.—4—Robert M. Grove, Philadelphia, 1929, 1930, 1931, 1932.

Highest Earned-Run Average, Season, for Leader in ERA
A. L.— 3.20— Early Wynn, Cleveland, 214 innings, 1950.
N. L.— 3.08— William H. Walker, New York, 178 innings, 1929.

Shutouts

Most Shutout Games Won or Tied, League, Righthanded Pitcher

A. L.— 110— Walter P. Johnson, Washington, 21 years, 1907 through 1927.

N. L.— 90— Grover C. Alexander, Philadelphia, Chicago, St. Louis, 20 years, 1911 through 1930.

Most Shutout Games Won or Tied, League, Lefthanded Pitcher

A. L.— 64— Edward S. Plank, Philadelphia, St. Louis, 16 years, 1901 through 1917, except 1915.

N. L.— 63— Warren E. Spahn, Boston, Milwaukee, New York, San Francisco, 21 years, 1942 through 1965 (except 1943, 1944, 1945, in military service).

Most Shutout Games Won, League, From One Club

A. L.— 23— Walter P. Johnson, Washington, vs. Philadelphia, 21 years, 1907 through 1927.

N. L.— 20— Grover C. Alexander, Philadelphia, Chicago, St. Louis, vs. Cincinnati, 20 years, 1911 through 1930.

Most Shutout Games Lost, League

A. L.— 65— Walter P. Johnson, Washington, 21 years, 1907 through 1927. (Won 109, tied 1, lost 65).

N. L.— 40— Christopher Mathewson, New York, Cincinnati, 17 years, 1900 through 1916. (Won 83, lost 40).

Most Shutouts Won or Tied, Opening Games of Season

A. L.— 7— Walter P. Johnson, Washington, 1910 to 1926.

N. L.— 3— Truett B. Sewell, Pittsburgh, 1943, 1947, 1949.
Christopher J. Short, Philadelphia, 1965, 1968, 1970.
Richard K. Mahler, Atlanta, 1982, 1986, 1987.

Most Shutout Games Won or Tied, Season, Righthanded Pitcher

N. L.— 16— George W. Bradley, St. Louis, 1876.
Grover C. Alexander, Philadelphia, 1916.

A. L.— 13— John W. Coombs, Philadelphia, 1910.

Most Shutout Games Won or Tied, Season, Lefthanded Pitcher

A. A.— 12— Edward Morris, Pittsburgh, 1886.

N. L.— 11— Sanford Koufax, Los Angeles, 1963.

A. L.— 9— George H. Ruth, Boston, 1916.
Ronald A. Guidry, New York, 1978.

Most Shutout Games Participated in, Season

N. L.— 20— Grover C. Alexander, Philadelphia, 1916 (won 16, lost 4).

A. L.— 18— Edward A. Walsh, Chicago, 1908 (won 12, lost 6).

Most Shutout Games Lost, Season

N. L.— 14— James A. Devlin, Louisville, 1876 (won 5, lost 14).

N. L. since 1900— 11— Arthur L. Raymond, St. Louis, 1908 (won 5, lost 11).

A. L.— 10— Walter P. Johnson, Washington, 1909 (won 4, lost 10).

Most Years Leading League in Shutout Games Won or Tied

N. L.— 7— Grover C. Alexander, Philadelphia, Chicago, 1911 (tied), 1913, 1915, 1916, 1917, 1919, 1921 (tied).

A. L.— 7— Walter P. Johnson, Washington, 1911 (tied), 1913, 1914, 1915, 1918 (tied), 1919, 1924.

Most Shutout Games Won or Tied, Rookie Season

N. L.— 16— George W. Bradley, St. Louis, 1876.

N. L. since 1900— 8— Fernando Valenzuela, Los Angeles, 1981.

A. L.— 8— Russell W. Ford, New York, 1910.
Ewell A. Russell, Chicago, 1913.

Most Years 10 or More Shutouts, Won or Tied

A. L.— 2— Edward A. Walsh, Chicago, 1906, 1908.
Walter P. Johnson, Washington, 1913, 1914.

N. L.— 2— Grover C. Alexander, Philadelphia, 1915, 1916.

Most Clubs Shut Out (Won or Tied), One Season

N. L.— (10-club league) —8—Robert Gibson, St. Louis, 1968 (all clubs except Los Angeles).

N. L.— (8-club league) —7—James Galvin, Buffalo, 1884.
Christopher Mathewson, New York, 1907.
Grover C. Alexander, Philadelphia, 1913 and 1916; also with Chicago, 1919.

A. L.— (12-club league) —8—L. Nolan Ryan, California, 1972 (all clubs, except Kansas City, New York, Oakland).

A. L.— (8-club league) —7—Denton T. Young, Boston, 1904.
John W. Coombs, Philadelphia, 1910.

Most Shutout Games Won, Season, From One Club

N. L.— (8-club league) —5—Charles B. Baldwin, Detroit vs. Philadelphia, 1886.
Grover C. Alexander, Philadelphia vs. Cincinnati, 1916.

A. A.— (8-club league) —5—Anthony J. Mullane, Cincinnati vs. New York, 1887.

A. L.— (8-club league) —5—Thomas J. Hughes, Washington vs. Cleveland, 1905.

A. L.— (10-club league) —4—William C. Monbouquette, Boston vs. Washington, 1964.

N. L.— (10-club league) —5—Larry E. Jaster, St. Louis vs. Los Angeles, 1966, consecutive.

A. L.— (12-club league) —4—Melvin L. Stottlemyre, New York vs. California, 1972, consecutive.

Most Shutout Games Lost, Season, to One Club

N. L.— 5— James A. Devlin, Louisville vs. Hartford, 1876.

A. L.— 5— Walter P. Johnson, Washington vs. Chicago, 1909.

N. L. since 1900— 4— Irving M. Young, Boston vs. Pittsburgh, 1906.

Most Shutout Games Won or Tied, One Month

A. L.— 6— G. Harris White, Chicago, September, 1904.
Edward A. Walsh, Chicago, August, 1906, September, 1908.

N. L.— 5— George W. Bradley, St. Louis, May, 1876.
Thomas H. Bond, Hartford, June, 1876.
James F. Galvin, Buffalo, August, 1884.
A. Ben Sanders, Philadelphia, September, 1888.
Donald S. Drysdale, Los Angeles, May, 1968.
Robert Gibson, St. Louis, June, 1968.

Most Shutout Games, Lost, One Month

A. L.— 5— Walter P. Johnson, Washington, July, 1909.

N. L.— 4— James A. Devlin, Louisville, June, 1876.
Fred L. Fitzsimmons, New York, September, 1934.
James C. McAndrew, New York, August, 1968.

Fewest Shutout Games Pitched, Season, for Shutout Leader

N. L.— 3— Held by eight pitchers in 1921.

A. L.— 3— Held by three pitchers in 1930.

Shutout, First Major League Game, Nine Innings

N. L.— Held by 35 pitchers; Last pitcher—James C. Jones, San Diego, September 21, 1986.

A. L.— Held by 35 pitchers; Last pitcher—Michael K. Norris, Oakland, April 10, 1975.

Most Shutouts, First Two Major League Games

N. L.— 2— Albert G. Spalding, Chicago, April 25, 27, 1876.
John M. Ward, Providence, July 18, 20, 1878.
James Hughes, Baltimore, April 18, 22, 1898.
Allan F. Worthington, New York, July 6, 11, 1953.
Karl B. Spooner, Brooklyn, September 22, 26, 1954.

A. L.— 2— Joseph Doyle, New York, August 25, first game, August 30, first game, 1906.
John A. Marcum, Philadelphia, September 7, September 11, second game, 1933.
David M. Ferriss, Boston, April 29, first game, May 6, first game, 1945.
Thomas H. Phoebus, Baltimore, September 15, first game, September 20, 1966.

Most Shutouts Won or Tied, Four Consecutive Days

A. L.— 3— James H. Dygert, Philadelphia, October 1, 3, 4, second game, 1907.
Walter P. Johnson, Washington, September 4, 5, 7, first game, 1908.

N. L.— 2— Held by many pitchers.

Most Shutouts Won or Tied, Five Consecutive Days

N. L.— 3— George W. Bradley, St. Louis, July 11, 13, 15, 1876.
John G. Clarkson, Chicago, May 21, 22, 25, 1885.

Most Consecutive Shutout Games Won or Tied, Season

N. L.— 6— Donald S. Drysdale, Los Angeles, May 14, 18, 22, 26, 31, June 4, 1968.

A. L.— 5— G. Harris White, Chicago, September 12, 16, 19, 25, 30, 1904.

Most Consecutive Shutout Games, Lost, Season

N. L.— 4— James C. McAndrew, New York, July 21, first game, August 4, second game, August 10, second game, August 17, 1968, (allowed 6 runs).

A. L.— 2— Held by many pitchers.

Most Doubleheader Shutouts

N. L.— 1—Edward M. Reulbach, Chicago vs. Brooklyn, September 26, 1908. (Won 5-0; 3-0).

A. L.—None.

Pitching Longest Shutout Game

N. L.—18 innings—John M. Ward, Providence, August 17, 1882, won 1-0.

Carl O. Hubbell, New York, July 2, 1933, first game, won 1-0.

A. L.—18 innings—O. Edgar Summers, Detroit, July 16, 1909, tie 0-0.

Walter P. Johnson, Washington, May 15, 1918, won 1-0.

Consecutive Scoreless Innings

Most Consecutive Scoreless Innings, Season, Righthanded Pitcher

N. L.— 58 — Donald S. Drysdale, Los Angeles, from first inning, May 14 through fourth inning, June 8, 1968.

A. L.— 55⅔— Walter P. Johnson, Washington, from second inning, April 10 through third inning, May 14, 1913 (includes 2 relief appearances).

Most Consecutive Scoreless Innings, Season, Lefthanded Pitcher

N. L.— 45⅓ — Carl O. Hubbell, New York, from seventh inning, July 13 through fifth inning, August 1, 1933 (includes 2 relief appearances).

A. L.— 45 — G. Harris White, Chicago, September 12 through September 30, 1904.

Most Consecutive Scoreless Innings, Start of Career

N. L.— 25—George W. McQuillan, Philadelphia, from first inning, May 8, through ninth inning, September 29, first game, 1907.

A. L.— 22—David M. Ferriss, Boston, from first inning, April 29, through fourth inning, May 13, 1945.

Most Consecutive Scoreless Innings, Game

N. L.— 21—Joseph Oeschger, Boston, May 1, 1920; 6th through 26th inning.

A. L.— 20—Joseph Harris, Boston, September 1, 1906; 4th through 23rd inning.

1-0 Games

Most 1-0 Games Won, League

A. L.—38—Walter P. Johnson, Washington, 21 years, 1907 through 1927.

N. L.— 17—Grover C. Alexander, Philadelphia, Chicago, St. Louis, 20 years, 1911 through 1930.

Most 1-0 Complete Games Won, Season

A. L.—5—Ewell A. Russell, Chicago, 1913.

Walter P. Johnson, Washington, 1913, 1919.

Leslie A. Bush, Boston, 1918.

W. Dean Chance, Los Angeles, 1964 (also 1 incomplete).

N. L.—5—Carl O. Hubbell, New York, 1933.

Most Years Leading League in 1-0 Games Won

A. L.—8—Walter P. Johnson, Washington, 1913 (tied), 1914, 1915 (tied), 1919, 1920 (tied), 1922, 1923 (tied), 1926 (tied).

N. L.—4—Grover C. Alexander, Philadelphia, Chicago, 1913 (tied), 1916 (tied), 1917 (tied), 1922 (tied).

William C. Lee, Chicago, Philadelphia, Boston, 1934 (tied), 1936, 1944 (tied), 1945 (tied).

Most 1-0 Games Won, Season, From One Club

A. L.—3—Stanley Coveleski, Cleveland vs. Detroit, 1917.

Walter P. Johnson, Washington vs. Philadelphia, 1919.

James C. Bagby, Jr., Cleveland vs. Detroit, 1943.

N. L.—2—Held by many pitchers.

Most 1-0 Games Lost, League

A. L.—26—Walter P. Johnson, Washington, 21 years, 1907 through 1927. (Won 38, lost 26).

N. L.—13—H. Lee Meadows, St. Louis, Philadelphia, Pittsburgh, 15 years, 1915 through 1929. (Won 7, lost 13).

Most 1-0 Games Lost, Season

A. L.—5—William E. Donovan, Detroit, 1903. (Won 1, lost 5).

John M. Warhop, New York, 1914. (Won 0, lost 5).

N. L.—5—George W. McQuillan, Philadelphia, 1908. (Won 2, lost 5).

Roger L. Craig, New York, 1963. (Won 0, lost 5).

James P. Bunning, Philadelphia, 1967. (Won 1, lost 5).

Ferguson A. Jenkins, Chicago, 1968. (Won 0, lost 5).

Most 1-0 Games Lost, Season, to One Club

A. L.—3—John M. Warhop, New York vs. Washington, 1914.

N. L.—2—Held by many pitchers.

Hits

Most Hits Allowed, Major Leagues

7078—Denton T. Young, Cleveland N. L., St. Louis N. L., Boston A. L., Cleveland A. L., Boston N. L., 22 years, 1890 through 1911. 4282 hits in N. L., 2796 hits in A. L.

Most Hits Allowed, League

N. L.— 5490— James F. Galvin, Buffalo, Pittsburg, St. Louis, 12 years, 1879 through 1892, except 1886, 1890.

A. L.— 4920— Walter P. Johnson, Washington, 21 years, 1907 through 1927.

N. L. since 1900—4868—Grover C. Alexander, Philadelphia, Chicago, St. Louis, 20 years, 1911 through 1930.

Most Hits Allowed, Season

N. L.— 809— John H. Coleman, Philadelphia, 63 games, 548 innings, 1883.

A. L.— 401— Joseph J. McGinnity, Baltimore, 48 games, 378 innings, 1901.

N. L. since 1900—415—William M. Carrick, New York, 45 games, 342 innings, 1900.

Fewest Hits Allowed, Season, for Leader in Most Hits

N. L.— 234— Michael E. Krukow, San Francisco, 199⅓ innings, 1984.

A. L.— 243— Melvin L. Stottlemyre, New York, 279 innings, 1968.

Most Years Leading League in Most Hits Allowed

N. L.—5—Robin E. Roberts, Philadelphia, 1952, 1953, 1954, 1955, 1956.

A. L.—4—James L. Kaat, Minnesota, Chicago, 1965, 1966, 1967, 1975.

Most Consecutive Hitless Innings, Season

A. L.—24—Denton T. Young, Boston, from seventh inning, April 25 through sixth inning, May 11, 1904.

N. L.—21—John S. Vander Meer, Cincinnati, from first inning, June 11 through third inning, June 19, first game, 1938.

Most Consecutive Batsmen Retired, Season

N. L.—41—James L. Barr, San Francisco, August 23 (last 21), August 29 (first 20), 1972.

A. L.—33—Steven L. Busby, Kansas City, June 19 (last 24), June 24 (first 9), 1974.

John E. Montague, Seattle, July 22 (last 13), July 24 (first 20), first game, 1977.

Most Hits Allowed, Game

N. L.—36—John Wadsworth, Louisville, August 17, 1894.

N. L. since 1900—26—Harley Parker, Cincinnati, June 21, 1901.

A. L.—26—Horace O. Lisenbee, Philadelphia, September 11, 1936.

Aloysius J. Travers, Detroit, May 18, 1912 (only major league game).

Most Hits Allowed, Extra-Inning Game

A. L.—29—Edwin A. Rommel, Philadelphia, July 10, 1932, pitched last 17 innings of 18-inning game.

N. L.—23—Edward J. Pfeffer, Brooklyn, June 1, 1919, 18 innings.

Most Hits Allowed, Two Consecutive Games

N. L.—48—James J. Callahan, Chicago, September 6 (25), September 11, first game (23), 1900.

Most Hits Allowed, Shutout Game, Nine Innings

N. L.— 14— Lawrence D. Cheney, Chicago vs. New York, September 14, 1913 (Won 7-0).

A. L.— 14— Milton Gaston, Washington vs. Cleveland, July 10, 1928, second game (Won 9-0).

Fewest Hits Allowed, First Major League Game, Nine Innings

N. L.—0—Charles L. Jones, Cincinnati, October 15, 1892.

A. L.—1—Adrian C. Joss, Cleveland, April 26, 1902, single in seventh inning.

Miguel Fornieles, Washington, September 2, 1952, second game, single in second inning.

William J. Rohr, Boston, April 14, 1967, single, 2 out in ninth inning.

N. L. since 1900——Juan A. Marichal, San Francisco, July 19, 1960, single, 2 out in eighth inning.

James C. Jones, San Diego, September 21, 1986, triple, 2 out in third inning.

Fewest Hits Allowed, Opening Game of Season, Nine Innings

A. L.— 0— Robert W. Feller, Cleveland, April 16, 1940.

N. L.— 1— Held by many pitchers. (Leon Ames, New York, allowed 0 hits in 9 1/3 innings on April 15, 1909, but lost on 7 hits in 13 innings.)

Last time— Lonnie Warneke, Chicago, April 17, 1934.

Fewest Hits Allowed, Doubleheader, 18 Innings

A. A.— 3— Timothy J. Keefe, New York, July 4, 1883.

N. L.— 6— Fred Toney, Cincinnati, July 1, 1917.

Herman S. Bell, St. Louis, July 19, 1924.

A. L.— 7— Frank M. Owen, Chicago, July 1, 1905.

Edward A. Walsh, Chicago, September 29, 1908.

Fewest Hits Allowed, Two Consecutive Games, 18 Innings

N. L.— 0— John S. Vander Meer, Cincinnati, June 11, 15, 1938.

1— James F. Galvin, Buffalo, August 2 (1), 4 (0), 1884.

Alexander B. Sanders, Louisville, August 22 (0), 26 (1), 1892.

Arthur C. Vance, Brooklyn, September 8, first game (1), September 12, first game (0), 1925.

James A. Tobin, Boston, April 23, first game (1), April 27 (0), 1944.

A. L.— 1— Howard J. Ehmke, Boston, September 7 (0), 11 (1), 1923.

U. A.— 1— Edward L. Cushman, Milwaukee, September 28 (0), October 4, 1884 (1).

A. A.— 2— Thomas Ramsey, Louisville, July 29 (1), 31 (1) (12 innings), 1886.

Fewest Hits Allowed, Three Consecutive Games

N. L.— 3— John S. Vander Meer, Cincinnati, June 5 (3), 11 (0), 15 (0), 1938.

A. L.— 5— Held by many pitchers.

Most Hits Allowed, Inning

N. L.— 13— George E. Weidman, Detroit, September 6, 1883, seventh inning.

A. L.— 12— Merle T. Adkins, Boston, July 8, 1902, sixth inning.

N. L. since 1900— 11— Reginald Grabowski, Philadelphia, August 4, 1934, second game, ninth inning.

Most Consecutive Hits Allowed, Start of Game

N. L.— 7— William G. Bonham, Chicago, August 5, 1975, 3 singles, 2 doubles, 2 homers.

A. L.— 5— Frank D. Tanana, California, May 18, 1980, 1 single, 2 doubles, 2 triples.

Luis E. Leal, Toronto, June 2, 1980, 2 singles, 3 doubles.

Ross Baumgarten, Chicago, September 27, 1981, first game, 5 singles.

Most Consecutive Hits Allowed, Inning or Game

A. L.— 10— William Reidy, Milwaukee, June 2, 1901, ninth inning.

N. L.— 9— J. Erskine Mayer, Philadelphia, August 18, 1913, ninth inning.

No-Hit & One-Hit Games

Most No-Hitters Pitched, Major Leagues, Nine or More Innings

5— L. Nolan Ryan, California, A. L., 1973 (2), 1974, 1975; Houston, N. L., 1981.

Most No-Hit Games, League

N. L.— 4— Sanford Koufax, Los Angeles, 1962, 1963, 1964, 1965.

3— Lawrence J. Corcoran, Chicago, 1880, 1882, 1884.

James W. Maloney, Cincinnati, 1965 (2), 1969.

A. L.— 4— L. Nolan Ryan, California, 1973 (2), 1974, 1975.

3— Robert W. Feller, Cleveland, 1940, 1946, 1951.

Most No-Hit Games, Season

N. L.— 2— John S. Vander Meer, Cincinnati, June 11, 15, 1938, consecutive.

James W. Maloney, Cincinnati, June 14 (first 10 innings of 11-inning game), August 19, 1965, first game, 10 innings.

A. L.— 2— Allie P. Reynolds, New York, July 12, September 28, first game, 1951.

Virgil O. Trucks, Detroit, May 15, August 25, 1952.

L. Nolan Ryan, California, May 15, July 15, 1973.

Most Consecutive No-Hit Games

N. L.— 2— John S. Vander Meer, Cincinnati, June 11, 15, 1938.

A. L.— Never accomplished.

Pitching Longest No-Hit Complete Game

A. A.— 10 innings— Samuel J. Kimber, Brooklyn, vs. Toledo, October 4, 1884.

N. L.— 10 innings— George L. Wiltse, New York vs. Philadelphia, July 4, 1908, a.m. game.

Frederick A. Toney, Cincinnati vs. Chicago, May 2, 1917.

James W. Maloney, Cincinnati vs. Chicago, August 19, 1965, first game.

A. L.— 9 innings— Held by many pitchers.

Pitching Longest One-Hit Complete Game

N. L.— 12 2/3 — Harvey Haddix, Pittsburgh vs. Milwaukee, May 26, 1959, one double.

A. L.— 10 — G. Harris White, Chicago vs. Cleveland, September 6, 1903, one double.

Louis N. Newsom, St. Louis vs. Boston, September 18, 1934, one single.

Rikalbert Blyleven, Texas vs. Oakland, June 21, 1976, one single.

Most Low-Hit (No-Hit and One-Hit) Games, League, 9+ Inn.

Both Leagues— 14— L. Nolan Ryan, New York N. L., California A. L., Houston N. L., 1966, 1968 through 1987; 4 no-hit, 6 one-hit in A.L.; 1 no-hit, 3 one-hit in N.L.

A. L.— 14— Robert W. Feller, Cleveland, 1938 through 1955, 3 no-hit; 11 one-hit. (Also lost one 8-inning one-hit game on April 23, 1952.)

N. L.— 8— Charles G. Radbourn, Buffalo, Providence, Boston, Cincinnati, 1880 through 1889, 1891; 1 no-hit, 7 one-hit.

James W. Maloney, Cincinnati, 1960 through 1970; 3 no-hit, 5 one-hit.

Most Low-Hit (No-Hit and One-Hit) Games, Season, 9+ Inn.

U. A.— 4— Hugh Daily, Chicago, 1884.

N. L.— 4— Grover C. Alexander, Philadelphia, 1915.

A. L.— 3— Adrian C. Joss, Cleveland, 1907.

Robert W. Feller, Cleveland, 1946.

Virgil O. Trucks, Detroit, 1952.

L. Nolan Ryan, California, 1973.

Most Consecutive One-Hit Games

U. A.— 2— Hugh Daily, Chicago, July 7, 10, 1884.

N. L.— 2— Charles G. Buffinton, Philadelphia, August 6, 9, 1887.

Richard W. Marquard, New York, August 28, September 1, second game, 1911.

Lonnie Warneke, Chicago, April 17, 22, 1934 (His first two games of season).

Morton C. Cooper, St. Louis, May 31, first game, June 4, 1943.

A. A.— 2— Thomas Ramsey, Louisville, July 29, 31, 12 innings, 1886.

A. L.— 2— Edward C. Ford, New York, September 2, 7, 1955.

Samuel E. McDowell, Cleveland, April 25, May 1, 1966.

Singles, Doubles & Triples

Most Singles Allowed, Game

N. L.— 28— John Wadsworth, Louisville, August 17, 1894.

A. L.— 23— Charles Baker, Cleveland, April 28, 1901.

Most Singles Allowed, Inning

N. L.— 10— Reginald Grabowski, Philadelphia, August 4, 1934, second game, ninth inning.

A. L.— 10— Eldon L. Auker, Detroit, September 29, 1935, second game, second inning.

Most Doubles Allowed, Game

N. L.— 14— George H. Derby, Buffalo, July 3, 1883.

A. L.— 8— Edward F. LaFitte, Detroit, October 8, 1911, first game.

Most Doubles Allowed, Inning

A. L.— 6— Robert M. Grove, Boston, June 9, 1934, eighth inning.

N. L.— 5— Charles Esper, Washington, April 21, 1894, second inning.

Most Triples Allowed, Game

N. L.— 9— Michael J. Sullivan, Cleveland, September 3, 1894, first game.

A. L.— 5— Barney Pelty, St. Louis, April 27, 1907.

Aloysius J. Travers, Detroit, May 18, 1912.

Most Triples Allowed, Inning

    A. L.—4—Fred Marberry, Detroit, May 6, 1934, fourth inning.
           Aloysius J. Travers, Detroit, May 18, 1912, fifth inning.

Home Runs

Most Home Runs Allowed in Major Leagues

    505—Robin E. Roberts, Philadelphia N. L., Baltimore A. L., Houston N. L., Chicago N. L., 19 years, 1948 through 1966; 418 in N. L., 87 in A. L.

Most Home Runs Allowed, League

    N. L.— 434— Warren E. Spahn, Boston, Milwaukee, New York, San Francisco, 21 years, 1942 through 1965 (except 1943, 1944, 1945, in military service).
    A. L.— 374— James A. Hunter, Kansas City, Oakland, New York, 15 years, 1965 through 1979.

Most Grand Slams Allowed in Major Leagues

    9—Milton S. Pappas, Baltimore A. L., Cincinnati N. L., Atlanta N. L., Chicago N. L., 1959, 1961 (3), 1962, 1965, 1966, 1970, 1971; 6 in A. L., 3 in N. L.
        Ned F. Garver, St. Louis A. L., Detroit A. L., Kansas City A. L., 1949, 1950 (2), 1951, 1952, 1954, 1955 (2), 1959.
        Jerry Reuss, St. Louis N. L., Houston N. L., Pittsburgh N. L., Los Angeles N. L., 1971 (2), 1972, 1973, 1974, 1976 (2), 1979, 1980.

Most Grand Slams Allowed, League

    A. L.—9—Ned F. Garver, St. Louis, Detroit, Kansas City, 1949, 1950 (2), 1951, 1952, 1954, 1955 (2), 1959.
    N. L.—9—Jerry Reuss, St. Louis, Houston, Pittsburgh, Los Angeles, 1971 (2), 1972, 1973, 1974, 1976 (2), 1979, 1980.

Most Home Runs Allowed, Season

    A. L.—50—Rikalbert Blyleven, Minnesota, 36 games, 271⅔ innings, 1986.
    N. L.—46—Robin E. Roberts, Philadelphia, 43 games, 297 innings, 1956.

Most Home Runs Allowed, Season, vs. One Club

    A. L.— 15— James E. Perry, Cleveland vs. New York, 1960.
    N. L.— 13— Warren L. Hacker, Chicago vs. Brooklyn, 1956.
        Warren E. Spahn, Milwaukee vs. Chicago, 1958.

Most Grand Slams Allowed, Season

    A. L.—4—Raymond E. Narleski, Detroit, 1959.
    N. L.—4—Frank E. McGraw, Philadelphia, 1979.

Fewest Home Runs Allowed, Season (Most Innings)

    A. L.—0—Allan S. Sothoron, St. Louis, Boston, Cleveland, 29 games, 178 innings, 1921.
    N. L.—1—Eppa Rixey, Cincinnati, 40 games, 301 innings, 1921.

Fewest Homers Allowed, Season, Since 1950, 250 or More Innings

    N. L.—5—Robert A. Veale, Pittsburgh, 39 games, 266 innings, 1965.
        Ronald L. Reed, Atlanta, St. Louis, 34 games, 250 innings, 1975.
    A. L.—6—E. Miguel Garcia, Cleveland, 45 games, 259 innings, 1954.

Most Years Leading League in Most Home Runs Allowed

    N. L.—5—Robin E. Roberts, Philadelphia, 1954, 1955, 1956, 1957, 1960.
        Ferguson A. Jenkins, Chicago, 1967, 1968 (tied), 1971, 1972, 1973 (also led A. L., 1975, 1979).
    A. L.—3—Pedro Ramos, Washington, Minnesota, 1957, 1958, 1961.
        Dennis D. McLain, Detroit, 1966, 1967, 1968.

Most Years Allowing 30 or More Home Runs, League

    N. L.—8—Robin E. Roberts, Philadelphia, 1953, 1954, 1955, 1956, 1957, 1958, 1959, 1960; (Also 1963 Baltimore A. L.)
    A. L.—4—James T. Grant, Cleveland, Minnesota, 1961, 1963, 1964, 1965.
        Dennis D. McLain, Detroit, Washington, 1966, 1967, 1968, 1971.

Most Home Runs Allowed, Game

    N. L.—7—Charles J. Sweeney, St. Louis, June 12, 1886.
    N. L. since 1900—6—Lawrence J. Benton, New York, May 12, 1930.
        Hollis J. Thurston, Brooklyn, August 13, 1932, first game.
        Wayman W. Kerksieck, Philadelphia, August 13, 1939, first game.
    A. L.—6—Alphonse T. Thomas, St. Louis, June 27, 1936.
        George J. Caster, Philadelphia, September 24, 1940, first game.

Most Home Runs Allowed, Inning

    N. L.—4—William Lampe, Boston, June 6, 1894, third inning.
        Lawrence J. Benton, New York, May 12, 1930, seventh inning.
        Wayman W. Kerksieck, Philadelphia, August 13, 1939, first game, fourth inning.
        Charles Bicknell, Philadelphia, June 6, 1948, first game, sixth inning.
        Benjamin S. Wade, Brooklyn, May 28, 1954, eighth inning.
        Mario M. Soto, Cincinnati, April 29, 1986, fourth inning.
    A. L.—4—George J. Caster, Philadelphia, September 24, 1940, first game, sixth inning.
        Calvin C. McLish, Cleveland, May 22, 1957, sixth inning.
        Paul E. Foytack, Los Angeles, July 31, 1963, second game, sixth inning, consecutive.
        James A. Hunter, New York, June 17, 1977, first inning.
        R. Michael Caldwell, Milwaukee, May 31, 1980, fourth inning.

Most Consecutive Home Runs Allowed, Inning

    A. L.—4—Paul E. Foytack, Los Angeles, July 31, 1963, second game, sixth inning.
    N. L.—3—Held by many pitchers. Last pitchers—Roger L. Mason, San Francisco, April 13, 1987, first inning; Doyle L. Alexander, Atlanta, July 26, 1987, eighth inning.

Long Hits & Total Bases

Most Long Hits Allowed, Game

    N. L.— 16— George H. Derby, Buffalo, July 3, 1883.
    A. L.— 10— Dale D. Gear, Washington, August 10, 1901, second game.

Most Total Bases Allowed, Game

    N. L.— 55— William C. Rhodes, Louisville, June 18, 1893.
    A. L.— 41— Dale D. Gear, Washington, August 10, 1901, second game.
    N. L. since 1900—39—Luther H. Taylor, New York, September 23, 1903.

Most Total Bases Allowed, Inning

    N. L.— 23— William C. Rhodes, Louisville, June 18, 1893, first inning.
    A. L.— 22— George J. Caster, Philadelphia, September 24, 1940, first game, sixth inning.
    N. L. since 1900—18—Charles Bicknell, Philadelphia, June 6, 1948, first game, sixth inning.

Bases On Balls

Most Bases on Balls, Major Leagues

    2355—L. Nolan Ryan, New York N.L., California A.L., Houston N.L., 21 years, 1966, 1968 through 1987.

Most Bases on Balls, League

    A. L.— 1775— Early Wynn, Washington, Cleveland, Chicago, 23 years, 1939, 1941 through 1963 (except 1945, in military service).
    N. L.— 1717— Steven N. Carlton, St. Louis, Philadelphia, San Francisco, 22 years, 1965 through 1986.

Most Bases on Balls, Season

    N. L.— 276— Amos W. Rusie, New York, 64 games, 1890.
    A. L.— 208— Robert W. Feller, Cleveland, 278 innings, 1938.
    N. L. since 1900—185—Samuel Jones, Chicago, 242 innings, 1955.

Most Intentional Bases on Balls, Season

    N. L.— 23— Michael D. Garman, St. Louis, 66 games, 79 innings, 1975.
        Dale A. Murray, Cincinnati, New York, 68 games, 119 innings, 1978.
        Kenton C. Tekulve, Pittsburgh, 85 games, 128⅔ innings, 1982.
    A. L.— 19— John F. Hiller, Detroit, 59 games, 150 innings, 1974.

Most Years Leading League in Most Bases on Balls

    A. L.—6—L. Nolan Ryan, California, 1972, 1973, 1974, 1976, 1977, 1978 (also led N. L. in 1980, 1982, for total of 8 seasons).
    N. L.—5—Amos W. Rusie, New York, 1890, 1891, 1892, 1893, 1894.
    N. L. since 1900—4—James J. Ring, Philadelphia, 1922, 1923, 1924, 1925.
        W. Kirby Higbe, Chicago, Philadelphia, Pittsburgh, Brooklyn, 1939, 1940, 1941, 1947.

Samuel Jones, Chicago, St. Louis, San Francisco, 1955, 1956, 1958, 1959.
Robert A. Veale, Pittsburgh, 1964, 1965 (tied), 1967, 1968.

Fewest Bases on Balls, Season, 250 or More Innings
N. L.— 18— Charles B. Adams, Pittsburgh, 263 innings, 1920.
A. L.— 28— Denton T. Young, Boston, 380 innings, 1904.

Most Consecutive Innings With No Bases on Balls, Season
A. L.— 84 ⅓— William C. Fischer, Kansas City, August 3 through September 30, 1962.
N. L.— 68 — Christopher Mathewson, New York, June 19 through July 18, 1913.
Randall L. Jones, San Diego, May 17, eighth inning, through June 22, 1976, seventh inning.

Most Consecutive Innings With No Bases on Balls, Start of Season
N. L.— 52— Grover C. Alexander, Chicago, April 18 through May 17, 1923.

Most Bases on Balls, Game, 9 Innings
N. L.— 16— William George, New York, May 30, 1887, first game.
George H. Van Haltren, Chicago, June 27, 1887.
P. L.— 16— Henry Gruber, Cleveland, April 19, 1890.
A. L.— 16— Bruno P. Haas, Philadelphia, June 23, 1915. (His first major league game).
N. L. since 1900—14—Henry Mathewson, New York, October 5, 1906.

Most Bases on Balls, Extra-Inning Game
A. L.— 16— Thomas J. Byrne, St. Louis, August 22, 1951, 13 innings.
N. L.— 13— J. Bentley Seymour, New York, May 24, 1899, 10 innings.
Clarence A. Podbielan, Cincinnati, May 18, 1953, 10 innings.

Most Bases on Balls, Shutout Game
A. L.— 11— Vernon Gomez, New York, August 1, 1941.
Melvin L. Stottlemyre, New York, May 21, 1970; pitched first 8 ⅓ innings.
N. L.— 9— Wilmer D. Mizell, St. Louis, September 1, 1958, first game.

Most Bases on Balls, Shutout Game Over 9 Innings
N. L.— 10— James W. Maloney, Cincinnati, August 19, 1965, first game, (10 innings).
James R. Richard, Houston, July 6, 1976, (10 innings).
A. L.—Less than 9-inning game.

Longest Game Without Base on Balls
N. L.—21 innings— Charles B. Adams, Pittsburgh, July 17, 1914.
A. L.—20 innings— Denton T. Young, Boston, July 4, 1905, p.m. game.

Fewest Bases on Balls, Doubleheader, Nine-Inning Games
A. A.—0—Guy J. Hecker, Louisville, July 4, 1884.
A. L.—1—Edward A. Walsh, Chicago, September 29, 1908.
N. L.—1—Grover C. Alexander, Philadelphia, September 23, 1916; September 3, 1917.

Most Bases on Balls, Inning
A. L.—8—William D. Gray, Washington, August 28, 1909, first game, second inning.
N. L.—7—Anthony J. Mullane, Baltimore, June 18, 1894, a.m. game, first inning.
Robert Ewing, Cincinnati, April 19, 1902, fourth inning. (His first major league game).

Most Consecutive Bases on Balls, Inning
A. L.—7—William D. Gray, Washington, August 28, 1909, first game, second inning.
N. L.—6—William H. Kennedy, Brooklyn, August 31, 1900, second inning.

Strikeouts
Career

Most Strikeouts, Major Leagues
4547—L. Nolan Ryan, New York N.L., California A.L., Houston N.L., 21 years, 1966, 1968 through 1987.

Most Strikeouts, League
N. L.— 4000— Steven N. Carlton, St. Louis, Philadelphia, San Francisco, 22 years, 1965 through 1986.
A. L.— 3508— Walter P. Johnson, Washington, 21 years, 1907 through 1927.

Most Strikeouts, League, Righthanded Pitcher
A. L.— 3508— Walter P. Johnson, Washington, 21 years, 1907 through 1927.
N. L.— 3272— G. Thomas Seaver, New York, Cincinnati, 17 years, 1967 through 1983.

Most Strikeouts, League, Lefthanded Pitcher
N. L.— 4000— Steven N. Carlton, St. Louis, Philadelphia, San Francisco, 22 years, 1965 through 1986.
A. L.— 2679— Michael S. Lolich, Detroit, 13 years, 1963 through 1975 (also had 153 for New York, San Diego, NL, 1976, 1978, 1979, for major league total of 2832).

Season

Most Strikeouts, Season
A. A.— 505— Matthew A. Kilroy, Baltimore, 65 games, 570 innings, 1886.
N. L.— 411— Charles G. Radbourn, Providence, 72 games, 679 innings, 1884.
A. L.— 383— L. Nolan Ryan, California, 41 games, 326 innings, 1973.
N. L. since 1900—382—Sanford Koufax, Los Angeles, 43 games, 336 innings, 1965.

Most Strikeouts, Season, Righthanded Pitcher
U. A.— 483— Hugh I. Daily, Chicago, Pittsburgh, Washington, 58 games, 501 innings, 1884.
N. L.— 411— Charles G. Radbourn, Providence, 72 games, 679 innings, 1884.
A. L.— 383— L. Nolan Ryan, California, 41 games, 326 innings, 1973.
N. L. since 1900—313—James R. Richard, Houston, 38 games, 292 innings, 1979.

Most Strikeouts, Season, Lefthanded Pitcher
A. A.— 505— Matthew A. Kilroy, Baltimore, 65 games, 570 innings, 1886.
N. L.— 382— Sanford Koufax, Los Angeles, 43 games, 336 innings, 1965.
A. L.— 349— George E. Waddell, Philadelphia, 46 games, 384 innings, 1904.

Most Strikeouts, Season, Relief Pitcher
A. L.— 181— Richard R. Radatz, Boston, 1964, 79 games, 157 innings.
N. L.— 151— Richard M. Gossage, Pittsburgh, 1977, 72 games, 133 innings.

Most Strikeouts, Rookie Season, Since 1900
N. L.— 276— Dwight E. Gooden, New York, 218 innings, 1984.
A. L.— 245— Herbert J. Score, Cleveland, 227 innings, 1955.

Fewest Strikeouts, Season, for Leader in Most Strikeouts
A. L.— 113— Cecil C. Hughson, Boston, 281 innings, 1942.
Louis N. Newsom, Washington, 214 innings, 1942.
N. L.— 133— George E. Waddell, Pittsburgh, 213 innings, 1900.

Most Years Leading League in Most Strikeouts
A. L.— 12— Walter P. Johnson, Washington, 1910, 1912, 1913, 1914, 1915, 1916, 1917, 1918, 1919, 1921, 1923, 1924.
N. L.— 7— Arthur C. Vance, Brooklyn, 1922 through 1928.

Most Consecutive Years Leading League in Strikeouts
A. L.— 8— Walter P. Johnson, Washington, 1912 through 1919.
N. L.— 7— Arthur C. Vance, Brooklyn, 1922 through 1928.

Most Years 100 or More Strikeouts in Major Leagues
21—Donald H. Sutton, Los Angeles N. L., Houston N. L., Milwaukee A.L., Oakland A.L., California A.L., 1966 through 1986; 17 in N.L.; 4 in A.L.

Most Consecutive Years 100 or More Strikeouts in Major Leagues
21—Donald H. Sutton, Los Angeles N. L., Houston N. L., Milwaukee A.L., Oakland A. L., California A. L., 1966 through 1986; 17 in N. L.; 4 in A. L.

Most Years 100 or More Strikeouts, League
A. L.— 18— Walter P. Johnson, Washington, 1908 through 1926, except 1920.
N. L.— 18— Steven N. Carlton, St. Louis, Philadelphia, 1967 through 1984.

Most Consecutive Years 100 or More Strikeouts, League
N. L.— 18— Steven N. Carlton, St. Louis, Philadelphia, 1967 through 1984.
A. L.— 13— Edward S. Plank, Philadelphia, 1902 through 1914.
Michael S. Lolich, Detroit, 1963 through 1975.

Most Years 200 or More Strikeouts, League

Both Leagues—11—L. Nolan Ryan, California A.L., 1972 through 1979, except 1975; Houston N.L., 1980, 1982, 1985, 1987.

N. L.— 10—G. Thomas Seaver, New York, Cincinnati, 1968 through 1976, 1978.

A. L.— 8—Rikalbert Blyleven, Minnesota, Texas, Cleveland, 1971 through 1976, 1985 through 1986.

Most Consecutive Years 200 or More Strikeouts, League

N. L.—9—G. Thomas Seaver, New York, 1968 through 1976.

A. L.—7—George E. Waddell, Philadelphia, St. Louis, 1902 through 1908.

Walter P. Johnson, Washington, 1910 through 1916.

Most Years, 300 or More Strikeouts, Major Leagues

5—L. Nolan Ryan, California A. L., 1972, 1973, 1974, 1976, 1977.

3—Timothy J. Keefe, New York A. A., 1883, 1884, New York N. L., 1888.

Amos W. Rusie, New York N. L., 1890, 1891, 1892.

Sanford Koufax, Los Angeles N. L., 1963, 1965, 1966.

Most Years, 300 or More Strikeouts, League

A. L.—5—L. Nolan Ryan, California, 1972 (329), 1973 (383), 1974 (367), 1976 (327), 1977 (341).

N. L.—3—Amos W. Rusie, New York, 1890 (345), 1891 (321), 1892 (303).

Sanford Koufax, Los Angeles, 1963 (303), 1965 (382), 1966 (317).

Most Years, 400 or More Strikeouts, League

A. A.—1—505—Matthew A. Kilroy, Baltimore, 1886.

494—Thomas A. Ramsey, Louisville, 1886.

U. A.—1—484—Hugh I. Daily, Chicago, Pittsburgh, Washington, 1884.

U. A., N. L.—455—Fred L. Shaw, Detroit N. L., Boston U. A., 1884.

N. L.—1—411—Charles G. Radbourn, Providence, 1884.

402—Charles G. Buffinton, Boston, 1884.

Game & Inning

Most Strikeouts, Game, 9 Innings

A. L.— 20— W. Roger Clemens, Boston, April 29, 1986.

N. L.— 19— Charles Sweeney, Providence, June 7, 1884.

Steven N. Carlton, St. Louis, September 15, 1969.

G. Thomas Seaver, New York, April 22, 1970.

U. A.— 19— Hugh Daily, Chicago, July 7, 1884.

Most Strikeouts, Extra-Inning Game

A. L.— 21— Thomas E. Cheney, Washington vs. Baltimore, September 12, 1962, 16 innings.

N. L.—Less than nine-inning record.

Most Strikeouts, Game, 9 Innings, Righthanded Pitcher

A. L.— 29— W. Roger Clemens, Boston, April 29, 1986.

N. L.— 19— Charles Sweeney, Providence, June 7, 1884.

G. Thomas Seaver, New York, April 22, 1970.

Most Strikeouts, Game, 9 Innings, Lefthanded Pitcher

N. L.— 19— Steven N. Carlton, St. Louis, September 15, 1969.

A. L.— 18— Ronald A. Guidry, New York, June 17, 1978.

Most Strikeouts, Extra-Inning Game, Righthanded Pitcher

A. L.— 21— Thomas A. Cheney, Washington, September 12, 1962, 16 innings.

N. L.— 18— James W. Maloney, Cincinnati, June 14, 1965, 11 innings.

Most Strikeouts, Extra-Inning Game, Lefthanded Pitcher

N. L.— 18— Warren E. Spahn, Boston, June 14, 1952, 15 innings.

Christopher J. Short, Philadelphia, October 2, 1965, second game, first 15 innings of 18-inning game.

A. L.— 17— George E. Waddell, Philadelphia, September 5, 1905, 13 innings.

George E. Waddell, St. Louis, September 20, 1908, 10 innings.

Vida Blue, Oakland, July 9, 1971, pitched 11 innings of 20-inning game.

Most Strikeouts, Night Game, 9 Innings

A. L.— 20— W. Roger Clemens, Boston, April 29, 1986.

N. L.— 19— Steven N. Carlton, St. Louis, September 15, 1969.

Most Strikeouts, Losing Pitcher, Game, 9 Innings

N. L.— 19— Steven N. Carlton, St. Louis, September 15, 1969, lost 4 to 3.

U. A.— 18— Fred L. Shaw, Boston, July 19, 1884, lost 1 to 0.

Henry Porter, Milwaukee, October 3, 1884, lost 5 to 4.

A. L.— 18— Robert W. Feller, Cleveland, October 2, 1938, first game, lost 4 to 1.

A. A.— 17— Guy J. Hecker, Louisville, August 26, 1884, lost 4 to 3.

Most Strikeouts, Losing Pitcher, Extra-Inning Game

A. L.— 19— L. Nolan Ryan, California, August 20, 1974, 11 innings, lost 1-0.

N. L.— 18— Warren E. Spahn, Boston, June 14, 1952, 15 innings, lost 3-1.

James W. Maloney, Cincinnati, June 14, 1965, 11 innings. lost 1-0.

Most Strikeouts, First Major League Game, Since 1900

N. L.— 15— Karl B. Spooner, Brooklyn, September 22, 1954.

James R. Richard, Houston, September 5, 1971, second game.

A. L.— 12— Elmer G. Myers, Philadelphia, October 6, 1915, second game.

Most Strikeouts, Game, by Relief Pitcher

N. L.— 14— Richard W. Marquard, New York, May 13, 1911 (last 6 innings of nine-inning game).

A. L.— 15— Walter P. Johnson, Washington, July 25, 1913 (last 11 1/3 innings of 15-inning game).

14— Dennis D. McLain, Detroit, June 15, 1965, (6 2/3 innings of nine-inning game.)

Most Times, Fifteen or More Strikeouts, Game, Major Leagues

22—L. Nolan Ryan, 3 in National League, New York, Houston, 13 years, 1966, 1968 through 1971, 1980 through 1987; 19 in American League, California, 8 years, 1972 through 1979.

Most Times, Fifteen or More Strikeouts, Game, League

A. L.— 19— L. Nolan Ryan, California, 1972 (4), 1973 (2), 1974 (6), 1976 (3), 1977 (2), 1978 (1); 1979 (1).

N. L.— 8— Sanford Koufax, Brooklyn, Los Angeles, 1959 (2), 1960 (2), 1961 (1), 1962 (2), 1966 (1).

Most Times, Ten or More Strikeouts, Game, Major Leagues

174—L. Nolan Ryan, 60 in National League, New York, Houston, 13 years, 1966, 1968 through 1971, 1980 through 1987; 114 in American League, California, 8 years, 1972 through 1979.

Most Times, Ten or More Strikeouts, Game, League

A. L.— 114— L. Nolan Ryan, California, 8 years, 1972 through 1979.

N. L.— 97— Sanford Koufax, Brooklyn, Los Angeles, 12 years, 1955 through 1966.

Most Times, Ten or More Strikeouts, Game, Season

A. L.— 23— L. Nolan Ryan, California, 1973.

N. L.— 21— Sanford Koufax, Los Angeles, 1965.

Most Strikeouts, Inning (*Consecutive)

A. A.— 4— Robert T. Mathews, Philadelphia, September 30, 1885, 7th.

N. L.— 4— Edward N. Crane, New York, October 4, 1888, *5th.

George L. Wiltse, New York, May 15, 1906, *5th.

James B. Davis, Chicago, May 27, 1956, first game, *6th.

Joseph H. Nuxhall, Cincinnati, August 11, 1959, first game, 6th.

Peter G. Richert, Los Angeles, April 12, 1962, *3rd.

Donald S. Drysdale, Los Angeles, April 17, 1965, *2nd.

Robert Gibson, St. Louis, June 7, 1966, 4th.

William G. Bonham, Chicago, July 31, 1974, first game, *2nd.

Philip H. Niekro, Atlanta, July 29, 1977, 6th.

Mario M. Soto, Cincinnati, May 17, 1984, *3rd.

Michael W. Scott, Houston, September 3, 1986, 5th.

A. L.— 4— Walter P. Johnson, Washington, April 15, 1911, 5th.

Guy Morton, Cleveland, June 11, 1916, *6th.

Rinold G. Duren, Los Angeles, May 18, 1961, 7th.

A. Lee Stange, Cleveland, September 2, 1964, 7th.

Miguel Cuellar, Baltimore, May 29, 1970, *4th.

Michael D. Paxton, Cleveland, July 21, 1978, *5th.

Robert A. Witt, Texas, August 2, 1987, *2nd.

Three Strikeouts, Inning, on 9 Pitched Balls

A. L.—George E. Waddell, Philadelphia, July 1, 1902, 3rd.

Hollis O. Thurston, Chicago, August 22, 1923, 12th.

Robert M. Grove, Philadelphia, August 23, 1928, 2nd.

Robert M. Grove, Philadelphia, September 27, 1928, 7th.

James P. Bunning, Detroit, August 2, 1959, 9th.

Alphonso E. Downing, New York, August 11, 1967, first game, 2nd.

L. Nolan Ryan, California, July 9, 1972, 2nd.
Ronald A. Guidry, New York, August 7, 1984, second game, 9th.
N. L.—D. Patrick Ragan, Brooklyn, October 5, 1914, second game, 8th.
Horace O. Eller, Cincinnati, August 21, 1917, 9th.
Joseph Oeschger, Boston, September 8, 1921, first game, 4th.
Arthur C. Vance, Brooklyn, September 14, 1924, 3rd.
Sanford Koufax, Los Angeles, June 30, 1962, 1st.
Sanford Koufax, Los Angeles, April 18, 1964, 3rd.
Robert J. Bruce, Houston, April 19, 1964, 8th.
L. Nolan Ryan, New York, April 19, 1968, 3rd.
Robert Gibson, St. Louis, May 12, 1969, 7th.
Lynn E. McGlothen, St. Louis, August 19, 1975, 2nd.
H. Bruce Sutter, Chicago, September 8, 1977, 9th.

Consecutive & In Consecutive Games

Most Consecutive Strikeouts, Game

N. L.—10—G. Thomas Seaver, New York, April 22, 1970, 1 in sixth inning, 3 in seventh inning, 3 in eighth inning, 3 in ninth inning.
A. L.— 8—L. Nolan Ryan, California, July 9, 1972, 2 in first inning, 3 in second inning, 3 in third inning.
L. Nolan Ryan, California, July 15, 1973, 1 in first inning, 3 in second inning, 3 in third inning, 1 in fourth inning.
Ronald G. Davis, New York, May 4, 1981, 2 in seventh inning, 3 in eighth inning, 3 in ninth inning.
W. Roger Clemens, Boston, April 29, 1986, 3 in fourth inning, 3 in fifth inning, 2 in sixth inning.

Most Consecutive Strikeouts, First Major League Game

A. L.—7—Samuel L. Stewart, Baltimore, September 1, 1978, second game, 3 in second inning, 3 in third inning, 1 in fourth inning.
N. L.—6—Karl B. Spooner, Brooklyn, September 22, 1954, 3 in seventh inning, 3 in eighth inning.
Peter G. Richert, Los Angeles, April 12, 1962, 1 in second inning, 4 in third inning, 1 in fourth inning (first six batters he faced in majors).

Most Consecutive Strikeouts, Game, by Relief Pitcher

A. L.—8—Ronald G. Davis, New York, May 4, 1981, 2 in seventh inning, 3 in eighth inning, 3 in ninth inning.
N. L.—6—John R. Meyer, Philadelphia, September 22, 1958, first game, 3 in twelfth inning, 3 in thirteenth inning, (first 6 batters he faced).
Peter G. Richert, Los Angeles, April 12, 1962, 1 in second inning, 4 in third inning, 1 in fourth inning (first 6 batters he faced in majors).
Ronald P. Perranoski, Los Angeles, September 12, 1966, 3 in fifth inning, 3 in sixth inning, (first 6 batters he faced).
Richard A. Kelley, Atlanta, September 8, 1967, 2 in sixth inning, 3 in seventh inning, 1 in eighth inning.
Joseph W. Hoerner, St. Louis, June 1, 1968, 3 in ninth inning, 3 in tenth inning.
Donald E. Gullett, Cincinnati, August 23, 1970, second game, 3 in sixth inning, 3 in seventh inning, (first 6 batters he faced).
H. Bruce Sutter, Chicago, September 8, 1977, 3 in eighth inning, 3 in ninth inning, (first 6 batters he faced).
Guillermo Hernandez, Philadelphia, July 3, 1983, 3 in eighth inning, 3 in ninth inning (all 6 batters he faced).
Joseph W. Price, Cincinnati, May 8, 1985, 3 in eighth inning, 3 in ninth inning.

Most Consecutive Strikeouts, Start of Game

N. L.—9—Michael Welch, New York, August 28, 1884.
N. L. since 1900—8—James J. Deshaies, Houston, September 23, 1986.
A. L.—7—Joseph A. Cowley, Chicago, May 28, 1986.

Most Strikeouts, Two Consecutive Games

U. A.—34—Fred L. Shaw, Boston, July 19 (18), July 21 (16), 1884, 19 innings.
A. L.—32—Luis C. Tiant, Cleveland, June 29, first game (13), July 3 (19) 1968, 19 innings.
L. Nolan Ryan, California, August 7 (13), August 12 (19), 1974, 17 innings.
N. L.—32—Dwight E. Gooden, New York, September 12 (16), September 17 (16), 1984, 17 innings.

Most Strikeouts, Three Consecutive Games

U. A.—48—Fred L. Shaw, Boston, July 16, 19, 21, 1884, 28 innings.

A. L.—47—L. Nolan Ryan, California, August 12 (19), 16 (9), 20 (19), 1974, 27 ⅓ innings.
41—Luis C. Tiant, Cleveland, June 23, first game (9), 29, first game (13), July 3, (19), 1968, 28 innings.
L. Nolan Ryan, California, July 11 (11), 15 (17), 19 (13), 1973, 25 ⅓ innings.
L. Nolan Ryan, California, August 7 (13), 12 (19), 16 (9), 1974, 24 ⅓ innings.
W. Roger Clemens, Boston, April 29 (20), May 4 (10), 9 (11), 1986, 25 ⅓ innings.
N. L.—43—Dwight E. Gooden, New York, September 7 (11), 12 (16), 17 (16), 1984, 26 innings.

Hit Batsmen

Most Hit Batsmen, League

A. L.— 206— Walter P. Johnson, Washington, 21 years, 1907 through 1927.
N. L.— 195— Emerson P. Hawley, St. Louis, Pittsburgh, Cincinnati, New York, 9 years, 1892 through 1900.
N. L.—Since 1900—154—Donald S. Drysdale, Brooklyn, Los Angeles, 14 years, 1956 through 1969.

Most Hit Batsmen, Season

A. A.— 54— Phillip H. Knell, Columbus, 58 games, 1891.
N. L.— 41— Joseph J. McGinnity, Brooklyn, 45 games, 1900.
A. L.— 31— Charles C. Fraser, Philadelphia, 39 games, 1901.

Fewest Hit Batsmen, Season, for Leader in Most Hit Batsmen

A. L.—6—Held by five pitchers. Last two pitchers—Spurgeon F. Chandler, New York, 1940. Alfred J. Smith, Cleveland, 1940.
N. L.—6—Held by five pitchers. Last three pitchers—Rex E. Barney, Brooklyn, 1948. Sheldon L. Jones, New York, 1948. Kent F. Peterson, Cincinnati, 1948.

Most Years Leading League in Most Hit Batsmen

A. L.—6—Howard J. Ehmke, Detroit, Boston, Philadelphia, 1920, 1921, (tied), 1922, 1923 (tied), 1925, 1927.
N. L.—5—Donald S. Drysdale, Los Angeles, 1958, 1959, 1960, 1961, 1965 (tied).

Fewest Hit Batsmen, Season, Most Innings

A. L.—0—Alvin F. Crowder, Washington, 50 games, 327 innings, 1932.
N. L.—0—Sanford Koufax, Los Angeles, 41 games, 323 innings, 1966.

Fewest Hit Batsmen, Three Consecutive Seasons, Most Innings

N. L.—0—Lawrence J. Benton, New York, Cincinnati, 1928, 1929, 1930 (755 innings).
William A. Hallahan, St. Louis, 1932, 1933, 1934 (583 innings).
A. L.—0—William R. Wight, Chicago, Boston, 1949, 1950, 1951 (569 innings).

Most Hit Batsmen, Game, 9 Innings

A. A.—6—Edward Knouff, Baltimore, April 25, 1887.
N. L.—6—John T. Grimes, St. Louis, July 31, 1897, first game.
N. L. since 1900—4—Held by five pitchers. Last time—Myron W. Drabowsky, Chicago, June 2, 1957, first game.
A. L.—4—Held by nine pitchers. Last time—Thomas E. John, Chicago, June 15, 1968.

Most Hit Batsmen, Two Consecutive Games

N. L.—9—Samuel E. Shaw, Chicago, June 13 (5), June 16 (4), 1893.

Longest Game Without Hit Batsman

N. L.—26 innings— Leon Cadore, Brooklyn, May 1, 1920.
Joseph Oeschger, Boston, May 1, 1920.
A. L.—21 innings— Theodore A. Lyons, Chicago, May 24, 1929.

Most Hit Batsmen, Inning (*Consecutive)

N. L.—3—John P. Luby, Chicago, September 5, 1890, 6th.
Emerson P. Hawley, St. Louis, July 4, 1894, first game, *1st.
Emerson P. Hawley, Pittsburgh, May 9, 1896, 7th.
Walter M. Thornton, Chicago, May 18, 1898, *4th.
Charles L. Phillippe, Pittsburgh, September 25, 1905, 1st.
Raymond J. Boggs, Boston, September 17, 1928, 9th.
Raul R. Sanchez, Cincinnati, May 15, 1960, first game, 8th.
Dock P. Ellis, Pittsburgh, May 1, 1974, *1st.

A. L.—3—Melvin A. Gallia, Washington, June 20, 1913, second game, 1st.
    Harry C. Harper, New York, August 25, 1921, 8th.
    Thomas S. Morgan, New York, June 30, 1954, 3rd.
    Wilbur F. Wood, Chicago, September 10, 1977, * 1st.

A. L.—4—Walter P. Johnson, Washington, September 21, 1914, fourth inning.
N. L.—4—Philip N. Niekro, Atlanta, August 4, 1979, second game, fifth inning.

Wild Pitches

Most Wild Pitches, Major Leagues

226—Philip H. Niekro, Milwaukee N.L., Atlanta N.L., New York A.L., Cleveland A.L., Toronto A.L., 24 years, 1964 through 1987.

Most Wild Pitches, League

N. L.—200—Philip H. Niekro, Milwaukee, Atlanta, 21 years, 1964 through 1983, 1987.
A. L.—156—Walter P. Johnson, Washington, 21 years, 1907 through 1927.

Most Wild Pitches, Season

N. L.—64—William Stemmeyer, Boston, 41 games, 1886.
N. L. since 1900—30—Leon K. Ames, New York, 263 innings, 1905.
A. L.—24—John S. Morris, Detroit, 266 innings, 1987.

Fewest Wild Pitches, Season, for Leader in Most Wild Pitches

N. L.—6—W. Kirby Higbe, Brooklyn, 211 innings, 1946.
    Charles M. Schanz, Philadelphia, 116 innings, 1946.
A. L.—7—Held by eight pitchers. Last two pitchers—George L. Earnshaw, Philadelphia, 1928. Joseph B. Shaute, Cleveland, 1928.

Most Years Leading League in Wild Pitches

N. L.—6—Lawrence R. Cheney, Chicago, Brooklyn, 1912, 1913, 1914, 1916, 1917 (tied), 1918.
A. L.—4—John S. Morris, Detroit, 1983, 1984, 1985, 1987.

Fewest Wild Pitches, Season, Most Innings

N. L.—0—Joseph J. McGinnity, New York, 340 innings, 1906.
A. L.—0—Alvin F. Crowder, Washington, 327 innings, 1932.

Fewest Wild Pitches and Hit Batsmen, Season, Most Innings

A. L.—0—Alvin F. Crowder, Washington, 327 innings, 1932.
N. L.—0—Jesse L. Barnes, Boston, 268 innings, 1924.

Most Wild Pitches, Game

N. L.—10—John J. Ryan, Louisville, July 22, 1876.
N. L. since 1900—6—James R. Richard, Houston, April 10, 1979.
    Philip H. Niekro, Atlanta, August 14, 1979, second game.
    William L. Gullickson, Montreal, April 10, 1982.
A. L.—5—Charles Wheatley, Detroit, September 27, 1912.
    John S. Morris, Detroit, August 3, 1987, 10 innings.

Most Wild Pitches, First Major League Game

A. A.—5—Thomas Seymour, Pittsburgh, September 23, 1882 (his only game in majors).
N. L.—5—Michael Corcoran, Chicago, July 15, 1884 (his only game in majors).
    George E. Winkelman, Washington, August 2, 1886.

Most Wild Pitches, Opening Game of Season

N. L.—4—Lawrence R. Cheney, Chicago, April 14, 1914.

Longest Game Without Wild Pitch

N. L.—26 innings—Leon Cadore, Brooklyn, May 1, 1920.
A. L.—24 innings—John W. Coombs, Philadelphia, September 1, 1906.
    Joseph Harris, Boston, September 1, 1906.

Most Wild Pitches, Inning

P. L.—5—Ellsworth Cunningham, Buffalo, September 15, 1890, second game, first inning.

Sacrifice Hits

Most Sacrifices Allowed, Season (Sacrifice Hits and SFs)

A. L.—54—Stanley Coveleski, Cleveland, 316 innings, 1921.
    Edwin A. Rommel, Philadelphia, 298 innings, 1923.
N. L.—49—Eppa Rixey, Philadelphia, 284 innings, 1920.
    John W. Scott, Philadelphia, 233 innings, 1927.

Most Sacrifice Hits Allowed, Season, No Sacrifice Flies

N. L.—35—Edward A. Brandt, Boston, 283 innings, 1933.
A. L.—28—Earl O. Whitehill, Detroit, 272 innings, 1931.

Fewest SHs, Season, for Leader in SHs Allowed, No SFs

N. L.—13—John A. Antonelli, San Francisco, 242 innings, 1958.
    Richard J. Farrell, Philadelphia, 94 innings, 1958.
    Ronald L. Kline, Pittsburgh, 237 innings, 1958.
A. L.—11—Gaylord J. Perry, Seattle, Kansas City, 186 ⅓ innings, 1983.
    Robert W. Stanley, Boston, 145 ⅓ innings, 1983.

Fewest Sacrifice Hits Allowed, Season, Most Innings

N. L.—0—Carlton F. Willey, New York, 30 games, 183 innings, 1963.

Most Years Leading League in Most Sacrifices Allowed

N. L.—3—Eppa Rixey, Philadelphia, Cincinnati, 1920, 1921, 1928.
A. L.—3—Earl O. Whitehill, Detroit, Washington, 1931, 1934, 1935.

Sacrifice Flies

Most Sacrifice Flies Allowed in Major Leagues

141—James L. Kaat, Washington A. L., Minnesota A. L., Chicago A.L., Philadelphia N. L., New York A. L., St. Louis N. L., 25 years, 1959 through 1983, 108 in A. L., 33 in N. L.

Most Sacrifice Flies Allowed, League

A. L.—108—James L. Kaat, Washington, Minnesota, Chicago, New York, 19 years, 1959 through 1975, 1979 through 1980.
N. L.—95—Robert Gibson, St. Louis, 17 years, 1959 through 1975.

Most Sacrifice Flies Allowed, Season

A. L.—17—Lawrence C. Gura, Kansas City, 200 ⅓ innings, 1983.
N. L.—15—Randy L. Lerch, Philadelphia, 214 innings, 1979.

Fewest Sacrifice Flies Allowed, Season, Most Innings

N. L.—0—Philip H. Niekro, Atlanta, 40 games, 284 innings, 1969.

Balks

Most Balks, Season

N. L.—11—Steven N. Carlton, Philadelphia, 251 innings, 1979.
A. L.—9—Charles O. Hough, Texas, 285 ⅓ innings, 1987.

Most Balks, Game

N. L.—5—Robert J. Shaw, Milwaukee, May 4, 1963.
A. L.—4—Victor J. Raschi, New York, May 3, 1950.

Most Balks, Inning

A. L.—3—Milburn J. Shoffner, Cleveland, May 12, 1930, third inning.
N. L.—3—James P. Owens, Cincinnati, April 24, 1963, second inning.
    Robert J. Shaw, Milwaukee, May 4, 1963, third inning.

Club Pitching

Number Of Pitchers Used

Most Players Used as Pitchers, Season

A. L. (162-game season)—25—Seattle, 1969.
A. L. (154-game season)—27—Philadelphia, 1915.
    Kansas City, 1955.
N. L. (162-game season)—27—New York, 1967.
N. L. (154-game season)—24—Cincinnati, 1912.
    Philadelphia, 1946.

Fewest Players Used As Pitchers, Season

A. L. (162-game season)—11—Baltimore, 1972, 1974; Oakland, 1974; Boston, 1976.
A. L. (154-game season)—5—Boston, 1904.
N. L. (162-game season)—11—Philadelphia, 1976; Atlanta, 1980.
N. L. (154-game season)—5—Boston, 1901.

Most Relief Appearances, Season

N. L.—392—Cincinnati, 1987.
A. L.—378—Kansas City, 1965.

Most Consecutive Games, None Complete
N. L.—74—San Diego, May 5 through July 25, 1977.
A. L.—50—Milwaukee, June 9 through September 27, 1981.
   For records on most pitchers used in game, doubleheader and inning, see Club Fielding section, "Number of Players at Positions."

Complete Games

Most Complete Games, Season
A. L. (154-game season)—148—Boston, 157 games, 1904.
A. L. (162-game season)— 94—Oakland, 162 games, 1980.
N. L. (154-game season)—146—St. Louis, 155 games, 1904.
N. L. (162-game season)— 77—San Francisco, 163 games, 1968.

Fewest Complete Games, Season
N. L.— 6—San Diego, 162 games, 1977.
A. L.—10—Oakland, 162 games, 1985.

Innings

Most Innings, Season
A. L. (162-game season)—1507—New York, 164 games, 1964.
A. L. (154-game season)—1465—Cleveland, 161 games, 1910.
N. L. (162-game season)—1493—Pittsburgh, 163 games, 1979.
N. L. (154-game season)—1453—Philadelphia, 159 games, 1913.

Most Pitchers, 300 or More Innings, Season
N. L. (154-game season)—3—Boston, 1905, 1906.
A. L. (154-game season)—3—Detroit, 1904.

Games Won

Most Games Won by Two Pitchers, Season, Club
N. L.—77—Providence 1884; Charles G. Radbourn, 60, Charles J. Sweeney, 17.
   76—New York, 1885; Michael F. Welch, 44, Timothy J. Keefe, 32.
N. L. since 1900—68—New York, 1904; Joseph J. McGinnity, 35, Christopher Mathewson, 33.
A. L.—64—New York, 1904; John D. Chesbro, 41, John Powell, 23.

Most Pitchers Winning 20 or More Games, Season, Since 1900
A. L.—4—Chicago, 1920.
         Baltimore, 1971.
N. L.—3—Pittsburgh, 1902.
         Chicago, 1903.
         New York, 1904, 1905, 1913, 1920.
         Cincinnati, 1923.

Most Consecutive Years With Pitchers Winning 20 or More Games
A. L.—13—Baltimore, 1968 through 1980.
N. L.—12—New York, 1903 through 1914.

Most Consec. Years Without Pitchers Winning 20 or More Games
N. L.—32—Philadelphia, 1918 through 1949.
A. L.—15—Philadelphia, 1934 through 1948.
         St. Louis, 1904 through 1918.

Saves

Most Saves, Season
N. L.—60—Cincinnati, 162 games, 1970.
         Cincinnati, 154 games, 1972.
A. L.—58—Minnesota, 162 games, 1970.
         New York, 162 games, 1986.

Fewest Saves, Season
A. L.—11—Toronto, 162 games, 1979.
N. L.—13—Chicago, 162 games, 1971.
         St. Louis, 156 games, 1972.

Games Lost

Most Pitchers Losing 20 or More Games, Season, Since 1900
N. L.—4—Boston, 1905, 1906.
A. L.—3—Washington, 1904.
         St. Louis, 1905.
         Philadelphia, 1916.

At-Bats & Plate Appearances

Most Opponents' Official At-Bats, Season
N. L.— 5763—Philadelphia, 156 games, 1930.
A. L.— 5671—Boston, 163 games, 1978.

Fewest Opponents' Official At-Bats, Season
A. L.— 4933—Cleveland, 147 games, 1945.
N. L.— 5062—Philadelphia, 155 games, 1947.

Most Opponents' Men Facing Pitcher, Season
N. L.— 6549—Philadelphia, 156 games, 1930.
A. L.— 6439—Cleveland, 163 games, 1986.

Fewest Opponents' Men Facing Pitcher, Season
A. L.— 5653—St. Louis, 155 games, 1936.
N. L.— 5684—Brooklyn, 154 games, 1956.

Runs, Earned Runs & ERA

Most Opponents' Runs, Season
N. L. (154-game season)—1199—Philadelphia, 156 games, 1930.
N. L. (162-game season)— 948—New York, 161 games, 1962.
A. L. (154-game season)—1064—St. Louis, 155 games, 1936.
A. L. (162-game season)— 957—Cleveland, 162 games, 1987.

Fewest Opponents' Runs, Season
A. L. (154-game season)—408—Philadelphia, 153 games, 1909.
A. L. (162-game season)—491—Chicago, 162 games, 1967.
N. L. (154-game season)—379—Chicago, 154 games, 1906.
N. L. (162-game season)—472—St. Louis, 162 games, 1968.

Most Opponents' Earned Runs, Season
N. L.— 1024— Philadelphia, 156 games, 1930.
A. L.— 935— St. Louis, 155 games, 1936.

Fewest Opponents' Earned Runs, Season
N. L.— 332— Philadelphia, 153 games, 1915.
A. L.— 343— Chicago, 156 games, 1917.

Lowest Earned-Run Average, Season
A. L.—2.16—Chicago, 156 games, 1917.
N. L.—2.18—Philadelphia, 153 games, 1915.

Highest Earned-Run Average, Season
N. L.—6.70—Philadelphia, 156 games, 1930.
A. L.—6.24—St. Louis, 155 games, 1936.

Shutouts

Most Shutout Games Won or Tied, Season
N. L. (162-game season)—30—St. Louis, 1968.
N. L. (154-game season)—32—Chicago, 1907, 1909.
A. L. (162-game season)—28—California, 1964.
A. L. (154-game season)—32—Chicago, 1906 (including 2 ties).

Fewest Shutout Games Won or Tied, Season, 150 or More Games
N. L.—0—Brooklyn, 1898.
         Washington, 1898.
         St. Louis, 1898.
         Cleveland, 1899.
A. L.—1—Chicago, 1924.
         Washington, 1956.
         Seattle, 1977.
N. L. since 1900—1—Boston, 1928.

Most Shutout Games Participated, Season
A. L. (154-game season)—47—Chicago, won 22, lost 24 (1 tie), 1910.
A. L. (162-game season)—44—California, won 28, lost 16, 1964.
N. L. (154-game season)—46—St. Louis, won 13, lost 33, 1908.
N. L. (162-game season)—47—New York, won 25, lost 22, 1968.

Fewest Shutout Games Participated, Season
A. L.—5—Chicago, won 3, lost 2, 1977.
N. L.—6—Philadelphia, won 3, lost 3, 1930.

Most Shutouts Won From One Club, Season
N. L. (162-game season)— 7—New York vs. Philadelphia, 1969, (lost 1).
N. L. (154-game season)—10—Pittsburgh vs. Boston, 1906, (lost 1).
A. L. (162-game season)— 8—Oakland vs. Cleveland 1968 (lost 1).

A. L. (154-game season) — 8—Chicago vs. Boston, 1906, (lost 1).
Cleveland vs. Washington, 1956, (lost 0).

Most Consecutive Shutout Games Won, Season
N. L.—6—Pittsburgh, June 2 through June 6, 1903, (51 innings).
A. L.—5—Baltimore, September 2, 2, 4, 6, 6, 1974 (45 innings).

Largest Score, Shutout Day Game
N. L.—28-0—Providence vs. Philadelphia, August 21, 1883.
N. L. since 1900—22-0—Pittsburgh vs. Chicago, September 16, 1975.
A. L.—21-0—Detroit vs. Cleveland, September 15, 1901, 8 innings.
New York vs. Philadelphia, August 13, 1939, second game, 8 innings.

Largest Score, Shutout Night Game
N. L.—19-0—Pittsburgh vs. St. Louis, August 3, 1961, at St. Louis.
Los Angeles vs. San Diego, June 28, 1969, at San Diego.
A. L.—17-0—Los Angeles vs. Washington, August 23, 1963, at Washington.

Most Runs, Shutout Doubleheader
A. L.—26—Detroit vs. St. Louis, September 22, 1936, 12-0; 14-0.
N. L.—19—New York vs. Cincinnati, July 31, 1949, 10-0; 9-0.

Doubleheader Shutouts Since 1900; 101 in N.L., 88 in A.L.
N. L.—Last—September 29, 1987, St. Louis vs. Montreal, 1-0, 3-0, St. Louis winner.
A. L.—Last—April 19, 1987, New York vs. Kansas City, 5-0, 2-0, New York winner.

Most Consecutive Innings Shut Out Opponent, Season
N. L.—56—Pittsburgh, June 1 (last 2 innings) through June 9 (first 3 innings), 1903.
A. L.—54—Baltimore, September 1, (last inning) through September 7, 1974, (first 8 innings).

1-0 Games

Most 1-0 Games Won, Season
A. L.—11—Washington, 1914, (lost 4).
N. L.—10—Pittsburgh, 1908, (lost 1).

Fewest 1-0 Games Won, Season
N. L.-A. L.—0—Held by many clubs.
N. L.—Last club—Cincinnati, 1987.
A. L.—Last clubs—Baltimore, Minnesota, Oakland, Toronto, 1987.

Most 1-0 Games Lost, Season
N. L.—10—Pittsburgh, 1914; Chicago, 1916; Philadelphia, 1967.
A. L.—9—New York, 1914; Chicago, 1968.

Fewest 1-0 Games Lost, Season
N. L.-A. L.—0—Held by many clubs.
N. L.—Last clubs—Atlanta, Chicago, 1987.
A. L.—Last clubs—Baltimore, Boston, Detroit, Milwaukee, Oakland, Seattle, Texas, 1987.

Most Consecutive 1-0 Games Won, Season
A. L.—3—Chicago, April 25, 26, 27, 1909.
N. L.—3—St. Louis, August 31, second game (5 innings), September 1, 1, 1917.

Most Consecutive 1-0 Games Lost, Season
A. L.—3—St. Louis, April 25, 26, 27, 1909.
Washington, May 7, 8, 10 (11 innings), 1909.
N. L.—3—Brooklyn, September 7, 7, 8 (11 innings), 1908.
Pittsburgh, August 31, second game (5 innings), September 1, 1, 1917.
Philadelphia, May 11, 12, 13, 1960.

Most 1-0 Games Won, Season, From One Club
N. L.—4—Held by four clubs. Last club—Cincinnati vs. Brooklyn, 1910.
A. L.—4—Held by four clubs. Last club—Detroit vs. Boston, 1917.

Winning Two 1-0 Games, One Day
N. L.—12 times. Last time—Pittsburgh vs. St. Louis, October 3, 1976.
A. L.—1 time—Baltimore vs. Boston, September 2, 1974.

Hits & Home Runs

Most Opponents' Hits, Season
N. L.—1993—Philadelphia, 156 games, 1930.

A. L.—1776—St. Louis, 155 games, 1936.

Fewest Opponents' Hits, Season
A. L.—1087—Cleveland, 162 games, 1968.
N. L.—1174—Pittsburgh, 153 games, 1909.

Most Home Runs Allowed, Season
A. L. (162-game season)—226—Baltimore, 162 games, 1987.
A. L. (154-game season)—187—Kansas City, 154 games, 1956.
N. L. (162-game season)—192—New York, 161 games, 1962.
N. L. (154-game season)—185—St. Louis, 154 games, 1955.

Most Home Runs Allowed at Home, Season
A. L.—132—at Kansas City, 1964, 81 games.
N. L.—120—at New York, 1962, 80 games.

Most Grand Slams Allowed, Season
A. L.—9—Chicago, 153 games, 1934.
St. Louis, 156 games, 1938.
St. Louis, 154 games, 1950.
N. L.—9—Houston, 162 games, 1987.

Fewest Grand Slams Allowed, Season
N. L.-A. L.—0—Held by many clubs.
N. L.—Last clubs, Houston, New York, 1986.
A. L.—Last club, Seattle, 1987.

No-Hit & One-Hit Games

Most No-Hit Games, Season
A. A.—2—Louisville 1882; Columbus 1884; Philadelphia 1888.
A. L.—2—Boston 1904; Cleveland 1908; Chicago 1914; Boston 1916; St. Louis 1917; New York 1951; Detroit 1952; Boston 1962; California 1973.
N. L.—2—Brooklyn 1906; Cincinnati 1938; Brooklyn 1956; Milwaukee 1960; Cincinnati 1965; Chicago 1972.

Most Consecutive Years With No-Hit Games by Pitchers
N. L.—4—Los Angeles, 1962, 1963, 1964, 1965.
A. L.—3—Boston, 1916, 1917, 1918.
Cleveland, 1946, 1947, 1948.
Baltimore, 1967, 1968, 1969.
California, 1973, 1974, 1975.

Most Consecutive Years Without No-Hit Games by Pitchers
N. L.—57—Philadelphia, 1907 through 1963.
A. L.—39—Detroit, 1913 through 1951.

Most One-Hit Games, Season
A. L. (162-game season)—5—Baltimore, 1964.
A. L. (154-game season)—4—Cleveland, 1907.
New York, 1934.
N. L. (162-game season)—4—Philadelphia, 1979
N. L. (154-game season)—4—Chicago, 1906, 1909.
Philadelphia, 1907, 1911, 1915.

Most Consecutive One-Hit Nine-Inning Games
N. L.—2—Providence vs. New York, June 17, 18, 1884.
Brooklyn vs. Cincinnati, July 5, 6, 1900.
New York vs. Boston, September 28, second game, 30, first game, 1916.
Milwaukee vs. New York, September 10, 11, 1965.
New York vs. Chicago, Philadelphia, May 13, 15, 1970.
Houston vs. Philadelphia, New York, June 18, 19, 1972.
A. L.—2—Cleveland vs. New York, September 25, 26, 1907.
Washington vs. Chicago, August 10, 11, 1917.

Bases On Balls

Most Bases on Balls, Season
A. L. (162-game season)—770—Cleveland, 162 games, 1971.
A. L. (154-game season)—827—Philadelphia, 154 games, 1915.
N. L. (162-game season)—716—Montreal, 162 games, 1970.
N. L. (154-game season)—671—Brooklyn, 157 games, 1946.

Fewest Bases on Balls, Season
N. L.—295—New York, 153 games, 1921.
A. L.—359—Detroit, 158 games, 1909.

Most Intentional Bases on Balls, Season
N. L.—116—San Diego, 162 games, 1974.
A. L.—94—Seattle, 163 games, 1980.

Fewest Intentional Bases on Balls, Season
N. L.—9—Los Angeles, 162 games, 1974.
A. L.—16—Minnesota, 162 games, 1973.
New York, 159 games, 1976.

Strikeouts

Most Strikeouts, Season

    N. L. (162-game season) —1221—Houston, 162 games, 1969.
    N. L. (154-game season) —1122—Los Angeles, 154 games, 1960.
    A. L. (162-game season) —1189—Cleveland, 162 games, 1967.
    A. L. (154-game season) — 896—Detroit, 155 games, 1946.

Fewest Strikeouts, Season

    A. L.— 356— Boston, 154 games, 1930.
    N. L.— 357— New York, 153 games, 1921.

Hit Batsmen & Wild Pitches

Most Hit Batsmen, Season

    N. L.—85—Pittsburgh, 134 games, 1895.
    A. L.—81—Philadelphia, 152 games, 1911.
    N. L. since 1900—68—Brooklyn, 139 games, 1903.

Fewest Hit Batsmen, Season

    A. L. (154-game season) — 5—St. Louis, 154 games, 1945.
    A. L. (162-game season) —10—Baltimore, 162 games, 1983.
    N. L. (154-game season) —10—St. Louis, 155 games, 1948.
    N. L. (162-game season) —11—Pittsburgh, 162 games, 1984.

Most Wild Pitches, Season

    A. L. (162-game season) —94—Texas, 162 games, 1986.
    A. L. (154-game season) —67—Philadelphia, 154 games, 1936.
    N. L. (162-game season) —91—Houston, 162 games, 1970.
    N. L. (154-game season) —70—Los Angeles, 154 games, 1958.

Fewest Wild Pitches, Season

    N. L.— 9—Cincinnati, 155 games, 1944.
    A. L.—10—St. Louis, 154 games, 1930.
             Cleveland, 153 games, 1943.

Sacrifice Hits & Flies

Most Sacrifice Hits Allowed, Season

    N. L. (162-game season) —112—San Diego, 162 games, 1975.
    N. L. (154-game season) —106—New York, 154 games, 1956.
    A. L. (162-game season) —106—Chicago, 163 games, 1961.
    A. L. (154-game season) —110—Kansas City, 158 games, 1960.

Fewest Sacrifice Hits Allowed, Season

    A. L.—31—Minnesota, 162 games, 1984.
    N. L.—44—Montreal, 156 games, 1972.

Most Sacrifice Flies Allowed, Season

    N. L.—79—Pittsburgh, 154 games, 1954.
    A. L.—73—Cleveland, 163 games, 1984.

Fewest Sacrifice Flies Allowed, Season

    N. L.— 17— San Francisco, 162 games, 1963.
    A. L.— 17— Detroit, 164 games, 1968.

Balks

Most Balks, Season

    N. L.—27—Philadelphia, 162 games, 1984.
    A. L.—26—Texas, 162 games, 1987.

Fewest Balks, Season

    A. L.-N. L.—0—Held by many clubs.

Most Balks, Game, Nine Innings

    N. L.—6—Milwaukee vs. Chicago, May 4, 1963.
    A. L.—4—New York vs. Chicago, May 3, 1950.

Most Balks, Game, Nine Innings, Both Clubs

    N. L.—7—Pittsburgh 4, Cincinnati 3, April 13, 1963.
             Milwaukee 6, Chicago 1, May 4, 1963.
    A. L.—5—Cleveland 3, Philadelphia 2, May 12, 1930.

League Pitching

Number Of Pitchers Used

Most Pitchers, League, Season

    A. L.— (14-club league) —236 in 1987.
    A. L.— (12-club league) —189 in 1970.
    A. L.— (10-club league) —170 in 1962.
    A. L.— (8-club league) —141 in 1946, 1955.
    N. L.— (12-club league) —210 in 1987.
    N. L.— (10-club league) —167 in 1967.
    N. L.— (8-club league) —152 in 1946.

Most Pitchers, League, One Day, 1 Game

    N. L.— 13—October 2, 1962.
    A. L.— 8—June 11, 1973.

Most Pitchers, League, One Day, 2 Games

    N. L.—19—May 4, 1954.   A. L.—18—August 10, 1959.

Most Pitchers, League, One Day, 3 Games

    N. L.—32—May 2, 1956.   A. L.—26—May 11, 1970.

Most Pitchers, League, One Day, 4 Games

    N. L.—39—May 6, 1950.   A. L.—33—September 10, 1955.

Most Pitchers, League, One Day, 5 Games

    A. L.—41— August 22, 1962.
              August 17, 1968.
              May 25, 1971.
    N. L.—39— May 13, 1969.

Most Pitchers, League, One Day, 6 Games

    A. L.—52—June 11, 1969.   N. L.—43—September 17, 1972.

Most Pitchers, League, One Day, 7 Games

    N. L.—51—September 23, 1973.   A. L.—49—September 7, 1959.

Most Pitchers, League, One Day, 8 Games

    N. L.—59—May 30, 1956.   A. L.—56—April 16, 1967.

Most Pitchers, League, One Day, 9 Games

    A. L.—66—May 30, 1969, July 20, 1969.   N. L.—50—July 29, 1973.

Most Pitchers, League, One Day, 10 Games

    N. L.—72—September 7, 1964.   A. L.—62—August 9, 1970.

Most Pitchers, Both Leagues, One Day, 8 Games

    60—April 22, 1960, 31 in N. L. (4 games) , 29 in A. L. (4 games) .

Most Pitchers, Both Leagues, One Day, 9 Games

    64—May 6, 1950, 39 in N. L. (4 games) , 25 in A. L. (5 games) .

Most Pitchers, Both Leagues, One Day, 10 Games

    71—August 22, 1962, 41 in A. L. (5 games) , 30 in N. L. (5 games) .

Most Pitchers, Both Leagues, One Day, 11 Games

    73—May 13, 1969, 39 in N. L. (5 games) , 34 in A. L. (6 games) .

Most Pitchers, Both Leagues, One Day, 12 Games

    87—June 11, 1969, 52 in A.L. (6 games) , 35 in N. L. (6 games) .

Most Pitchers, Both Leagues, One Day, 13 Games

    87—May 31, 1970, 45 in N. L. (7 games) , 42 in A. L. (6 games) .

Most Pitchers, Both Leagues, One Day, 14 Games

    88—April 16, 1967, 56 in A. L. (8 games) , 32 in N. L. (6 games) .

Most Pitchers, Both Leagues, One Day, 15 Games

    96—July 8, 1962, 54 in N. L. (8 games) , 42 in A. L. (7 games) .

Most Pitchers, Both Leagues, One Day, 16 Games

    108—May 30, 1969, 66 in A. L. (9 games) , 42 in N. L. (7 games) .

Most Pitchers, Both Leagues, One Day, 17 Games

    Less than for 16 games.

Most Pitchers, Both Leagues, One Day, 18 Games

    121—September 7, 1964, 72 in N. L. (10 games) , 49 in A. L. (8 games) .

Most Pitchers, Both Leagues, One Day, 19 Games

    Less than for 18 games.

Most Pitchers, Both Leagues, One Day, 20 Games

    104—June 10, 1962, 52 in N. L. (10 games) , 52 in A. L. (10 games) .

Complete Games & Innings

Most Complete Games, Season

    A. L.— (8-club league) —1100 in 1904.

A. L.— (10-club league) — 426 in 1968.
A. L.— (12-club league) — 650 in 1975.
A. L.— (14-club league) — 645 in 1978.
N. L.— (8-club league) —1089 in 1904.
N. L.— (10-club league) — 471 in 1968.
N. L.— (12-club league) — 546 in 1971.

Fewest Complete Games, Season

A. L.—312 in 1960.   N. L.—189 in 1987.

Most Pitchers, 300 or More Innings, Season

A. L.— (8-club league) —12 in 1904.
A. L.— (12-club league) —7 in 1973, 1974.
N. L.— (8-club league) —10 in 1905.
N. L.— (12-club league) —8 in 1969.

Games Won & Lost

Most Pitchers Winning 20 or More Games, Season, Since 1900

A. L.— (12-club league) —12 in 1973.
A. L.— (8-club league) —10 in 1907, 1920.
N. L.— (12-club league) —9 in 1969.
N. L.— (8-club league) —9 in 1903.

Fewest Pitchers Winning 20 or More Games, Season, Since 1900

N. L.—0 in 1931, 1983, 1987.   A. L.—0 in 1955, 1960, 1982.

Most Pitchers Losing 20 or More Games, Season

N. L.—8 in 1905.   A. L.—7 in 1904.

Fewest Pitchers Losing 20 or More Games, Season

A. L.—0 in 1911, 1914, 1917, 1918, 1923, 1924, 1926, 1935, 1940, 1944, 1946, 1947, 1949, 1951, 1955, 1958, 1959, 1960, 1962, 1964, 1965, 1967, 1968, 1970, 1972, 1976, 1977, 1978, 1979, 1981, 1982, 1983, 1984, 1985, 1986, 1987 (36 years).

N. L.—0 in 1911, 1915, 1918, 1923, 1925, 1926, 1929, 1930, 1931, 1932, 1937, 1939, 1941, 1946, 1947, 1948, 1949, 1951, 1953, 1956, 1958, 1959, 1961, 1967, 1968, 1970, 1971, 1975, 1976, 1978, 1980, 1981, 1982, 1983, 1984, 1985, 1986, 1987 (38 years).

Runs, Earned Runs & ERA

Most Runs, Season

A. L.— (14-club league) —11,112 in 1987.
A. L.— (12-club league) —8314 in 1973.
A. L.— (10-club league) —7342 in 1961.
A. L.— (8-club league) —7009 in 1936.
N. L.— (12-club league) —8771 in 1970, 1987.
N. L.— (10-club league) —7278 in 1962.
N. L.— (8-club league) —7025 in 1930.

Fewest Runs, Season

N. L.—4136 in 1908.   A. L.—4272 in 1909.

Most Earned Runs, Season

A. L.— (14-club league) —9999 in 1987.
A. L.— (12-club league) —7376 in 1973.
A. L.— (10-club league) —6451 in 1961.
A. L.— (8-club league) —6120 in 1936.
N. L.— (12-club league) —7878 in 1987.
N. L.— (10-club league) —6345 in 1962.
N. L.— (8-club league) —6046 in 1930.

Fewest Earned Runs, Season

N. L.—3258 in 1916.   A. L.—3414 in 1914.

Lowest Earned-Run Average, Season

N. L.—2.62 in 1916.   A. L.—2.73 in 1914.

Highest Earned-Run Average, Season

A. L.—5.04 in 1936.   N. L.—4.97 in 1930.

Shutouts

Most Shutouts, Season

A. L.— (12-club league) —193 in 1972.
A. L.— (10-club league) —154 in 1968.
A. L.— (8-club league) —146 in 1909.
N. L.— (12-club league) —166 in 1969.
N. L.— (10-club league) —185 in 1968.
N. L.— (8-club league) —164 in 1908.

Most Extra-Inning Shutouts, Season

A. L.— (12-club league) —12 in 1976.
A. L.— (10-club league) —10 in 1968.
A. L.— (8-club league) —12 in 1918.
N. L.— (12-club league) —12 in 1976.
N. L.— (10-club league) —11 in 1965.
N. L.— (8-club league) —8 in 1908, 1909, 1910.

Fewest Shutouts, Season

A. L.— (8-club league) —41 in 1930.
A. L.— (10-club league) —100 in 1961.
A. L.— (12-club league) —110 in 1970.
A. L.— (14-club league) —109 in 1985.
N. L.— (8-club league) —48 in 1925.
N. L.— (10-club league) —95 in 1962.
N. L.— (12-club league) —98 in 1987.

Most Shutouts, One Day

N. L.—5—July 13, 1888 (6 games).
June 24, 1892 (8 games).
July 21, 1896 (7 games).
July 8, 1907 (5 games).
September 7, 1908 (8 games).
September 9, 1916 (7 games).
May 31, 1943 (8 games).
June 17, 1969 (9 games).
August 9, 1984 (6 games).
A. L.—5—September 7, 1903 (8 games).
August 5, 1909 (6 games).
May 6, 1945 (8 games).
June 4, 1972 (9 games).

Most Shutouts, One Day, Both Leagues

8—June 4, 1972, 5 in A. L. (9 games), 3 in N. L. (7 games).
7—September 7, 1908, 5 in N. L. (8 games), 2 in A. L. (8 games).
August 23, 1942, 4 in A. L. (8 games), 3 in N. L. (8 games).
May 14, 1944, 4 in N. L. (8 games), 3 in A. L. (8 games).
May 24, 1964, 4 in N. L. (8 games, 3 in A. L. (9 games).
August 26, 1968, 4 in N. L. (8 games), 3 in A. L. (5 games).

1-0 Games

Most 1-0 Games, Season

N. L.— (12-club league) —38 in 1976.
N. L.— (10-club league) —44 in 1968.
N. L.— (8-club league) —43 in 1907.
A. L.— (12-club league) —42 in 1971.
A. L.— (10-club league) —38 in 1968.
A. L.— (8-club league) —41 in 1908.

Fewest 1-0 Games, Season

A. L.— (8-club league) —4 in 1930, 1936.
A. L.— (10-club league) —16 in 1961.
A. L.— (12-club league) —15 in 1970.
A. L.— (14-club league) —11 in 1985.
N. L.— (8-club league) —5 in 1932, 1956.
N. L.— (10-club league) —13 in 1962.
N. L.— (12-club league) —13 in 1983.

Most 1-0 Games, One Day

A. L.—3—May 14, 1914; July 17, 1962.
N. L.—3—July 4, 1918; September 12, 1969; September 1, 1976.

No-Hit & One-Hit Games

Most No-Hit Games (9 or More Innings), Season, Major Leagues

8 in 1884, 4 in A. A., 2 in N. L., 2 in U. A.
Since 1900—7 in 1917, 5 in A. L., 2 in N. L.

Most No-Hit Games (9 or More Innings), Season

A. L.— (12-club league) —4 in 1973.
A. L.— (10-club league) —3 in 1967.
A. L.— (8-club league) —5 in 1917.
N. L.— (12-club league) —5 in 1969.
N. L.— (10-club league) —3 in 1965, 1968.
N. L.— (8-club league) —4 in 1880.

Fewest No-Hit Games, Season

N. L.—0—Made in many seasons—Last season—1987.
A. L.—0—Made in many seasons—Last season—1985.

Most No-Hit Games, One Day

N. L.—2 on April 22, 1898.   A. L.—1 made on many days.

Most One-Hit Games, Season, Nine or More Innings

A. L.— (14-club league) —13 in 1979.
A. L.— (12-club league) —11 in 1973.
A. L.— (10-club league) —11 in 1968.
A. L.— (8-club league) —12 in 1910, 1915.
N. L.— (12-club league) —12 in 1971.
N. L.— (10-club league) —13 in 1965.
N. L.— (8-club league) —12 in 1906, 1910.

Fewest One-Hit Games, Season, Nine or More Innings

A. L.— (12-club league) —4— 1971.
A. L.— (8-club league) —0— 1922, 1926, 1927, 1930.
N. L.— (12-club league) —4— 1980, 1987.
N. L.— (8-club league) —0— 1924, 1929, 1932, 1952.

Home Runs

Most Pitchers Allowing 30 or More Home Runs, Season

A. L.— (14-club league) —18 in 1987.
N. L.— (12-club league) —5 in 1970.

Bases On Balls

Most Bases on Balls, Season

A. L.— (14-club league) —7812 in 1987.
A. L.— (12-club league) —7032 in 1969.
A. L.— (10-club league) —5902 in 1961.
A. L.— (8-club league) —5627 in 1949.
N. L.— (12-club league) —6919 in 1970.
N. L.— (10-club league) —5265 in 1962.
N. L.— (8-club league) —4537 in 1950.

Most Intentional Bases on Balls, Season

N. L.— (12-club league) —862 in 1973.
N. L.— (10-club league) —804 in 1967.
N. L.— (8-club league) —504 in 1956.
A. L.— (14-club league) —646 in 1980.
A. L.— (12-club league) —668 in 1969.
A. L.— (10-club league) —534 in 1965.
A. L.— (8-club league) —353 in 1957.

Fewest Bases on Balls, Season

N. L.—2906 in 1921.   A. L.—3797 in 1922.

Strikeouts

Most Strikeouts, Season

A. L.— (14-club league) —13,442 in 1987.
A. L.— (12-club league) —10,957 in 1970.
A. L.— (10-club league) —9956 in 1964.
A. L.— (8-club league) —6081 in 1959.
N. L.— (12-club league) —11,657 in 1987.
N. L.— (10-club league) —9649 in 1965.
N. L.— (8-club league) —6824 in 1960.

Most Pitchers, 300 or More Strikeouts, Season

A. A.—6 in 1884.
N. L.—4 in 1884.
U. A.—3 in 1884.
A. L.—2 in 1971.
N. L.—since 1900—1 in 1963, 1965, 1966, 1972, 1978, 1979.

Most Pitchers, 200 or More Strikeouts, Season

N. L.—12 in 1969.
A. L.— 7 in 1967, 1973, 1986.

Most Pitchers, 100 or More Strikeouts, Season

N. L.—45 in 1970.
A. L.—41 in 1986, 1987.

Fewest Strikeouts, Season

A. L.—3245 in 1924.   N. L.—3359 in 1926.

Hit Batsmen

Most Hit Batsmen, Season

N. L.— (12-club league) —443 in 1969.
N. L.— (8-club league) —415 in 1903.
A. L.— (14-club league) —500 in 1986.
A. L.— (12-club league) —439 in 1969.
A. L.— (8-club league) —435 in 1909.

Fewest Hit Batsmen, Season

A. L.—132 in 1947.   N. L.—157 in 1943.

Wild Pitches & Balks

Most Wild Pitches, Season

A. L.— (14-club league) —762 in 1987.
A. L.— (12-club league) —636 in 1969.
A. L.— (10-club league) —513 in 1966.
A. L.— (8-club league) —325 in 1936.
N. L.— (12-club league) —648 in 1969.
N. L.— (10-club league) —550 in 1965.
N. L.— (8-club league) —356 in 1961.

Fewest Wild Pitches, Season

A. L.—166 in 1931.   N. L.—174 in 1943.

Most Balks, Season

N. L.— (12-club league) —219 in 1987.
N. L.— (10-club league) —147 in 1963.
A. L.— (14-club league) —137 in 1987.
A. L.— (12-club league) — 60 in 1976.
A. L.— (10-club league) — 51 in 1966.

Fewest Balks, Season

N. L.—13 in 1936, 1946, 1956.   A. L.—18 in 1933, 1941.

Individual Fielding

First Basemen
Years, Games & Innings

Most Years, League

N. L.—22—Willie L. McCovey, San Francisco, San Diego, 1959 through 1980, 2,045 games.
A. L.—20—Joseph I. Judge, Washington, Boston, 1915 through 1934, (consecutive), 2,084 games.

Most Games in Majors

2,368—Jacob P. Beckley, Pittsburgh, N. L., Pittsburgh, P. L., New York, N. L., Cincinnati, N. L., St. Louis, N. L., 1888 through 1907, 20 years.
Since 1900—2,237—James B. Vernon, Washington, A. L., Cleveland, A. L., Boston, A. L., Milwaukee, N. L., 1939 through 1959, except 1944, 1945 (in military service), 19 years.

Most Games, League

N. L.—2,247—Jacob P. Beckley, Pittsburgh, New York, Cincinnati, St. Louis, 1888 through 1907, except 1890; 19 years.

A. L.—2,227—James B. Vernon, Washington, Cleveland, Boston, 1939 through 1958, except 1944, 1945 (in military service); 18 consecutive years.
N. L. since 1900—2,132—Charles J. Grimm, St. Louis, Pittsburgh, Chicago, 1918 through 1936; 19 consecutive years.

Most Consecutive Games, League

A. L.— 885— H. Louis Gehrig, New York, June 2, 1925, through September 27, 1930.
N. L.— 652— Frank A. McCormick, Cincinnati, April 19, 1938, through May 24, 1942, second game.

Most Games, Season

A. L. (162-game season) —162—Norman L. Siebern, Kansas City, 1962.
William J. Buckner, Boston, 1985.
A. L. (154-game season) —157—George LaChance, Boston, 1904.
John A. Donahue, Chicago, 1907.
H. Louis Gehrig, New York, 1937, 1938.

N. L. (162-game season) —162—William D. White, St. Louis, 1963.
Ernest Banks, Chicago, 1965.
Steven P. Garvey, Los Angeles, 1976, 1979, 1980; San Diego, 1985.
Peter E. Rose, Philadelphia, 1980, 1982.
N. L. (154-game season) —158—Edward J. Konetchy, St. Louis, 1911; Boston, 1916.
Richard C. Hoblitzel, Cincinnati, 1911.
Ellsworth T. Dahlgren, Pittsburgh, 1944.
Gilbert R. Hodges, Brooklyn, 1951.

Most Years Leading League in Most Games
N. L.—9—Steven P. Garvey, Los Angeles, 1975, 1976, 1977, 1978, 1979, 1980 (tied), 1981; San Diego, 1984, 1985.
A. L.—7—H. Louis Gehrig, New York, 1926, 1927, 1928 (tied), 1932, 1936, 1937, 1938.

Fewest Games for Leader in Most Games
A. L.— 121—Victor P. Power, Cleveland, 1959.
N. L.— 134—Edward F. Bouchee, Philadelphia, 1959.

Most Innings Played, Game
N. L.—26—Walter L. Holke, Boston, May 1, 1920.
Edward J. Konetchy, Brooklyn, May 1, 1920.
A. L.—25—Ted L. Simmons, Milwaukee, May 8, finished May 9, 1984 (fielded 24 ⅓ innings).

Average

Highest Fielding Average, League, 1000 or More Games
N. L.—.996—Steven P. Garvey, Los Angeles, San Diego, 1972 through 1987, 16 years, 2059 games.
A. L.—.995—James L. Spencer, California, Texas, Chicago, New York, Oakland, 1968 through 1982, 15 years, 1221 games.

Highest Fielding Average, Season, 150 or More Games
N. L.—1.000—Steven P. Garvey, San Diego, 159 games, 1984.
A. L.— .999—John P. McInnis, Boston, 152 games, 1921.

Highest Fielding Average, Season, 100 or More Games
N. L.—1.000—Steven P. Garvey, San Diego, 159 games, 1984.
A. L.— .999—John P. McInnis, Boston, 152, games, 1921.
James L. Spencer, California, Texas, 125 games, 1973.

Most Years Leading League, Fielding, 100 or More Games
N. L.—9—Charles J. Grimm, Pittsburgh, Chicago, 1920, 1922 (tied), 1923, 1924, 1928 (tied), 1930, 1931, 1932 (tied), 1933.
A. L.—6—Joseph I. Judge, Washington, 1923, 1924 (tied), 1925, 1927, 1929, 1930.

Most Consec. Years Leading League, Fielding, 100 or More Games
N. L.—5—Theodore B. Kluszewski, Cincinnati, 1951, 1952, 1953, 1954, 1955.
A. L.—4—Charles A. Gandil, Cleveland, Chicago, 1916, 1917, 1918, 1919.

Lowest Fielding Average, Season, for Leader, 100 or More Games
N. L.—.978—Alex McKinnon, St. Louis, 100 games, 1885.
A. L.—.981—John J. Anderson, Milwaukee, 125 games, 1901.
N. L. since 1900—.986—Dennis L. McGann, St. Louis, 113 games, 1901.
William E. Bransfield, Pittsburgh, 100 games, 1902.

Lowest Fielding Average, Season, 100 or More Games
N. L.—.954—Alex McKinnon, New York, 112 games, 1884.
N. L. since 1900—.970—John J. Doyle, New York, 130 games, 1900.
A. L.—.972—Harry H. Davis, Philadelphia, 100 games, 1903.
Patrick H. Newnam, St. Louis, 103 games, 1910.

Putouts

Most Putouts in Majors
23,696—Jacob P. Beckley, Pittsburgh, N. L., Pittsburgh, P. L., New York, N. L., Cincinnati, N. L., St. Louis, N. L., 1888 through 1907, 20 years.

Most Putouts, League
N. L.—22,438—Jacob P. Beckley, New York, Pittsburgh, Cincinnati, St. Louis, 1888 through 1907, except 1890; 19 years.
N. L. since 1900—20,700—Charles J. Grimm, St. Louis, Pittsburgh, Chicago, 1918 through 1936; 19 consecutive years.
A. L.—19,754—James B. Vernon, Washington, Cleveland, Boston, 1939 through 1958, except 1944, 1945 (in military service); 18 consecutive years.

Most Putouts, Season
A. L.— 1846— John A. Donahue, Chicago, 157 games, 1907.
N. L.— 1759— George L. Kelly, New York, 155 games, 1920.

Most Years Leading League in Putouts
N. L.—6—Jacob P. Beckley, Pittsburgh, Cincinnati, St. Louis, 1892, 1894, 1895, 1900, 1902, 1904.
Frank A. McCormick, Cincinnati, 1939, 1940, 1941, 1942, 1944, 1945.
A. L.—4—Walter C. Pipp, New York, 1915, 1919, 1920, 1922.

Fewest Putouts, Season, 150 or More Games
A. L.—1159— Richard L. Stuart, Boston, 155 games, 1964.
N. L.—1162— Gordon C. Coleman, Cincinnati, 150 games, 1961.

Fewest Putouts, Season, for Leader in Most Putouts
A. L.— 971— Victor W. Wertz, Cleveland, 133 games, 1956.
N. L.— 1127— Edward F. Bouchee, Philadelphia, 134 games, 1959.

Most Putouts, Game, Nine Innings
A. L.—22— Thomas Jones, St. Louis, May 11, 1906.
Harold H. Chase, New York, September 21, 1906, first game.
Donald A. Mattingly, New York, July 20, 1987.
N. L.—22— Ernest Banks, Chicago, May 9, 1963.

Most Putouts, Extra-Inning Game
N. L.—42— Walter L. Holke, Boston, May 1, 1920, 26 innings.
A. L.—32— Michael P. Epstein, Washington, June 12, 1967, 22 innings.
Rodney C. Carew, California, April 13, finished April 14, 1982, 20 innings.

Fewest Putouts, Game, Nine Innings
A. A.—0— Allen B. McCauley, Washington, August 6, 1891.
A. L.—0— John W. Clancy, Chicago, April 27, 1930.
Rudolph P. York, Detroit, June 18, 1943.
Frank Robinson, Baltimore, July 1, 1971.
F. Gene Tenace, Oakland, September 1, 1974.
N. L.—0— James A. Collins, St. Louis, August 21, 1935; also Chicago, June 29, 1937.
Adolph Camilli, Philadelphia, July 30, 1937.
C. Earl Torgeson, Boston, May 30, 1947, first game.
Gary L. Thomasson, San Francisco, July 31, 1977.
Leonard J. Matuszek, Philadelphia, June 1, 1984.

Assists

Most Assists, League
N. L.— 1554— Keith Hernandez, St. Louis, New York, 1974 through 1987, 14 years.
A. L.— 1444— James B. Vernon, Washington, Cleveland, Washington, Boston, 1939 through 1958, except 1944, 1945, (in military service), 18 consecutive years.

Most Assists, Season
A. L.— 184— William J. Buckner, Boston, 162 games, 1985.
N. L.— 166— Sidney E. Bream, Pittsburgh, 153 games, 1986.

Most Years Leading League in Assists
N. L.—8—Fred C. Tenney, Boston, 1899, 1901, 1902, 1903, 1904, 1905, 1906, 1907.
A. L.—6—George H. Sisler, St. Louis, 1919, 1920, 1922, 1924, 1925, 1927.
Victor P. Power, Kansas City, Cleveland, Minnesota, 1955, 1957, 1959, 1960, 1961, 1962.

Fewest Assists, Season, 150 or More Games
N. L.— 54— James L. Bottomley, St. Louis, 154 games, 1926.
A. L.— 58— H. Louis Gehrig, New York, 154 games, 1931.

Fewest Assists, Season, for Leader in Most Assists
N. L.— 83— Herman Reich, Chicago, 85 games, 1949.
A. L.— 85— Walter C. Pipp, New York, 134 games, 1915.

Most Assists, Game, Nine Innings

N. L.—8—Robert E. Robertson, Pittsburgh, June 21, 1971.
A. L.—7—George T. Stovall, St. Louis, August 7, 1912.

Most Assists, Extra-Inning Game

N. L.—8—Robert R. Skinner, Pittsburgh, July 22, 1954, 14 innings.
A. L.—7—Ferris R. Fain, Philadelphia, June 9, 1949, 12 innings.

Most Assists, Doubleheader

A. L.—8—Charles C. Carr, Detroit, June 26, 1904.
George H. Sisler, St. Louis, September 12, 1926.
Rudolph P. York, Chicago, September 27, 1947.
James L. Spencer, California, August 25, 1970, 21 innings.
N. L.—8—Gilbert R. Hodges, Brooklyn, July 24, 1952, 20 innings.
R. Dale Long, Pittsburgh, May 1, 1955.

Most Consecutive Games With One or More Assists, Season

A. L.—16—Victor P. Power, Cleveland, June 9 through June 25, 1960, 29 assists.
N. L.—14—William H. Terry, New York, May 13 through May 27, 1930; 16 assists.

Most Assists, Inning

A. L.—3—Richard L. Stuart, Boston, June 28, 1963, first inning.
James M. Maler, Seattle, April 29, 1982, third inning.
N. L.—3—Andre Thornton, Chicago, August 22, 1975, fifth inning.

Chances Accepted & Offered

Most Chances Accepted, in Majors

25,000—Jacob P. Beckley, Pittsburgh, N. L., Pittsburgh, P. L., New York N. L., Cincinnati, N. L., St. Louis, N. L., 1888-1907, 20 years.

Most Chances Accepted, League

N. L.—23,687—Jacob P. Beckley, Pittsburgh, New York, Cincinnati, St. Louis, 1888 through 1907, except 1890; 19 years.
N. L. since 1900—21,914—Charles J. Grimm, St. Louis, Pittsburgh, Chicago, 1918-1936; 19 years.
A. L.—21,198—James B. Vernon, Washington, Cleveland, Boston, 1939 through 1958, except 1944, 1945 (in military service) 18 years.

Most Chances Accepted, Season

A. L.—1986—John A. Donahue, Chicago, 157 games, 1907.
N. L.—1862—George L. Kelly, New York, 155 games, 1920.

Most Years Leading League in Chances Accepted

N. L.—6—Jacob P. Beckley, Pittsburgh, Cincinnati, St. Louis, 1892, 1894, 1895, 1900, 1902, 1904.
William H. Terry, New York, 1927 (tied), 1928, 1929, 1930, 1932, 1934.
A. L.—4—Walter C. Pipp, New York, 1915, 1919, 1920, 1922.

Fewest Chances Accepted, Season, 150 or More Games

N. L.—1251—Deron R. Johnson, Philadelphia, 154 games, 1970.
A. L.—1263—Richard L. Stuart, Boston, 155 games, 1964.

Fewest Chances Accepted, Season, Leader in Chances Accepted

A. L.—1048—William J. Skowron, New York, 120 games, 1956.
Victor W. Wertz, Cleveland, 133 games, 1956.
N. L.—1222—Edward F. Bouchee, Philadelphia, 134 games, 1959.

Most Chances Accepted, Game, Nine Innings

22—Held by many first basemen in both leagues.
A. L.—Last first baseman—Donald A. Mattingly, New York, July 20, 1987, 22 putouts.
N. L.—Last first baseman—Ernest Banks, Chicago, May 9, 1963, 22 putouts.

Most Chances Accepted, Extra-Inning Game

N. L.—43—Walter L. Holke, Boston, May 1, 1920, 26 innings.
A. L.—34—Rudolph P. York, Detroit, July 21, 1945, 24 innings.
Michael P. Epstein, Washington, June 12, 1967, 22 innings.
Rodney C. Carew, California, April 13, finished April 14, 1982, 20 innings.

Most Chances Accepted, Doubleheader, 18 Innings

A. L.—38—Harold H. Chase, New York, August 5, 1905.
N. L.—35—Harold H. Chase, New York, August 26, 1919.

Most Chances Accepted, Two Consecutive Games

N. L.—39—Harvey L. Cotter, Chicago, July 10, 1924, second game; July 11, 1924.

A. L.—38—Harold H. Chase, New York, August 5, 5, 1905.

Fewest Chances Offered, Game, Nine Innings in Field

A. A.—0—Allen B. McCauley, Washington, August 6, 1891.
A. L.—0—John W. Clancy, Chicago, April 27, 1930.
F. Gene Tenace, Oakland, September 1, 1974.
N. L.—0—James A. Collins, Chicago, June 29, 1937.

Fewest Chances Offered, Game, Eight Innings in Field

A. A.—0—Guy J. Hecker, Louisville, October 9, 1887.
A. L.—0—Norman D. Cash, Detroit, June 27, 1963.
N. L.—1—Held by many first basemen.

Fewest Chances Offered, Doubleheader, 18 Innings

N. L.—7—Adrian C. Anson, Chicago, July 19, 1896.
Frank E. Bowerman, Pittsburgh, August 19, 1899.
N. L. since 1900—8—Edward S. Waitkus, Chicago, May 31, 1948.
George D. Crowe, Cincinnati, June 2, 1957.
A. L.—9—Henry B. Greenberg, Detroit, August 26, 1935.

Fewest Chances Offered, Two Consecutive Games, 18 Innings

A. L.—6—Richard D. Kryhoski, New York, April 29 (3), 30 (3), 1949.
N. L.—7—Adrian C. Anson, Chicago, July 19 (5), 19 (2), 1896.
Frank E. Bowerman, Pittsburgh, August 19 (5), 19 (2), 1899.
Philip J. Cavarretta, Chicago, April 25 (6), 26 (1), 1935.

Fewest Chances Offered, Two Consecutive Games, 17 Innings

A. L.—5—F. Gene Tenace, Oakland, August 31 (5), September 1 (0), 1974.

Errors

Most Errors, League

N. L.—568—Adrian C. Anson, Chicago, 1879 through 1897, 19 years.
A. L.—285—Harold H. Chase, New York, Chicago, 1905 through 1914, 10 years, 1175 games.
N. L. since 1900—252—Fred C. Tenney, Boston, New York, 1900 through 1911, except 1910, 11 years.

Most Errors, Season

U. A.—62—Joseph J. Quinn, St. Louis, 100 games, 1884.
N. L.—58—Adrian C. Anson, Chicago, 108 games, 1884.
N. L. since 1900—43—John J. Doyle, New York, 130 games, 1900.
A. L.—41—Jeremiah Freeman, Washington, 154 games, 1908.

Most Years Leading Major Leagues in Errors

7—Richard L. Stuart, Pittsburgh N. L. 1958 (tied) 1959, 1960 (tied), 1961, 1962 (tied); Boston, A. L., 1963, 1964.

Most Years Leading League in Errors

N. L.—5—Adrian C. Anson, Chicago, 1882, 1884, 1885, 1886, 1892.
Richard L. Stuart, Pittsburgh, 1958 (tied), 1959, 1960 (tied), 1961, 1962 (tied).
Willie L. McCovey, San Francisco, 1967 (tied), 1968, 1970, 1971, 1977.
A. L.—5—Harold H. Chase, New York, Chicago, 1905, 1909, 1911, 1912 (tied), 1913.
George H. Sisler, St. Louis, 1916, 1917, 1924, 1925, 1927.
Ferris R. Fain, Philadelphia, 1947 (tied), 1948, 1949, 1950, 1952.

Fewest Errors, Season, 150 or More Games

N. L.—0—Steven P. Garvey, San Diego, 159 games, 1984.
A. L.—1—John P. McInnis, Boston, 152 games, 1921.

Fewest Errors, Season, for Leader in Most Errors

A. L.—10—Victor P. Power, Kansas City, 144 games, 1955.
Augustus Triandos, Baltimore, 103 games, 1955.
N. L.—13—Stanley F. Musial, St. Louis, 114 games, 1946.
Dee V. Fondy, Chicago, 147 games, 1955.
R. Dale Long, Pittsburgh, 119 games, 1955.
Atanasio R. Perez, Cincinnati, 151 games, 1973.
David A. Kingman, San Francisco, 91 games, 1974.
Willie L. McCovey, San Francisco, 136 games, 1977.
William J. Buckner, Chicago, 144 games, 1983.
Keith Hernandez, St. Louis, New York, 144 games, 1983.
Albert Oliver, Montreal, 153 games, 1983.

Most Consecutive Errorless Games, League

N. L.—193—Steven P. Garvey, San Diego, June 26, second game, 1983 through April 14, 1985 (1623 chances accepted).

A. L.— 178— J. Michael Hegan, Milwaukee, Oakland, September 24, 1970, through May 20, 1973; 8 in 1970; 92 in 1971; 64 in 1972; 14 in 1973 (758 chances accepted) .

A. L.— 163— John P. McInnis, Boston, Cleveland, May 31, 1921, first game, through June 2, 1922; 119 in 1921, 44 in 1922 (1700 chances accepted) .

Most Consecutive Errorless Games, Season

N. L.— 159— Steven P. Garvey, San Diego, April 3 through September 29, 1984 (entire season; 1319 chances accepted) .

A. L.— 119— John P. McInnis, Boston, May 21, first game, through October 2, 1921 (1300 chances accepted) .

Most Chances Accepted, League, No Errors

A. L.— 1700— John P. McInnis, Boston, Cleveland, May 31, 1921, first game, through June 2, 1922, 163 games (1300 in 1921, 400 in 1922) .

N. L.— 1633— Steven P. Garvey, San Diego, June 26, first game, 1983 through April 15, 1985 (255 in 1983, 1319 in 1984, 59 in 1985) .

Most Chances Accepted, Season, No Errors

N. L.— 1319— Steven P. Garvey, San Diego, April 3 through September 29, 1984 (entire season; 159 games) .

A. L.— 1300— John P. McInnis, Boston, May 31, first game, through October 2, 1921, 119 games.

Most Errors, Game, Nine Innings

N. L.— 5— John C. Carbine, Louisville, April 29, 1876.
George Zettlein, Philadelphia, June 22, 1876.
Everett Mills, Hartford, October 7, 1876.
Thomas J. Esterbrook, Buffalo, July 27, 1880.
Roger Connor, Troy City, May 27, 1882.

A. A.— 5— Lewis J. Brown, Louisville, September 10, 1883.

U. A.— 5— John F. Gorman, Kansas City, June 28, 1884.
Joseph J. Quinn, St. Louis, July 4, 1884.

N. L. since 1900— 4— John Menefee, Chicago, October 6, 1901.
John C. Lush, Philadelphia, June 11, 1904, and September 15, 1904, second game.
Fred C. Tenney, Boston, July 12, 1905, first game.

A. L.— 4— Harold H. Chase, Chicago, July 23, 1913.
George H. Sisler, St. Louis, April 14, 1925.
James C. Wasdell, Washington, May 3, 1939.

Most Errors, Two Consecutive Games

A. A.— 8— Lewis J. Brown, Louisville, September 9, 10, 1883.

Longest Errorless Game

N. L.— 26 innings— Walter L. Holke, Boston, May 1, 1920.
Edward J. Konetchy, Brooklyn, May 1, 1920.

A. L.— 25 innings— Ted L. Simmons, Milwaukee, May 8, finished May 9, 1984 (fielded 24 1/3 innings) .

Most Errors, Inning

N. L.— 3— Adolph Camilli, Philadelphia, August 2, 1935, first inning.
Albert Oliver, Pittsburgh, May 23, 1969, fourth inning.
Jack A. Clark, St. Louis, May 25, 1987, second inning.

A. L.— 3— George M. Metkovich, Boston, April 17, 1945, seventh inning.
Tommy L. McCraw, Chicago, May 3, 1968, third inning.
Willie C. Upshaw, Toronto, July 1, 1986, fifth inning.

Double Plays

Most Double Plays in Major Leagues

2044— James B. Vernon, Washington, A. L., Cleveland, A. L., Boston, A. L., Milwaukee, N. L., 1939 through 1959, except 1944, 1945 (in military service) 19 consecutive years, 2237 games; 2041 in A. L., 3 in N. L.

Most Double Plays, League

A. L.— 2041— James B. Vernon, Washington, Cleveland, Boston, 1939 through 1958, except 1944, 1945 (in military service) 18 years, 2227 games.

N. L.— 1708— Charles J. Grimm, St. Louis, Pittsburgh, Chicago, 1918 through 1936, 19 years, 2132 games.

Most Double Plays, Season

A. L.— 194— Ferris R. Fain, Philadelphia, 150 games, 1949.

N. L.— 182— Donn A. Clendenon, Pittsburgh, 152 games, 1966.

Most Unassisted Double Plays, Season

A. L.— 8— James L. Bottomley, St. Louis, 140 games, 1936.

N. L.— 8— William D. White, St. Louis, 151 games, 1961.

Most Years Leading League in Double Plays

N. L.— 6— Keith Hernandez, St. Louis, New York, 1977, 1979, 1980, 1981, 1983, 1984.

A. L.— 4— John P. McInnis, Philadelphia, Boston, 1912, 1914, 1919, 1920 (tied) .
Walter C. Pipp, New York, 1915, 1916, 1917 (tied) , 1920 (tied) .
Cecil C. Cooper, Milwaukee, 1980, 1981, 1982, 1983.

Fewest Double Plays, Season, 150 or More Games

A. L.— 87— H. Louis Gehrig, New York, 155 games, 1926.

N. L.— 89— William J. Buckner, Chicago, 161 games, 1982.
Glenn E. Davis, Houston, 151 games, 1987.

Fewest Double Plays, Season, for Leader in Most Double Plays

A. L.— 98— Victor P. Power, Cleveland, 121 games, 1959.

N. L.— 109— William D. White, St. Louis, 123 games, 1960.

Most Double Plays, Game, Nine Innings

N. L.— 7— Curtis L. Blefary, Houston, May 4, 1969.

A. L.— 6— Ferris R. Fain, Philadelphia, September 1, 1947, second game.
George S. Vico, Detroit, May 19, 1948.
W. Edward Robinson, Cleveland, August 5, 1948.
J. Leroy Thomas, Los Angeles, August 23, 1963.
Robert L. Oliver, Kansas City, May 14, 1971.
John C. Mayberry, Kansas City, May 6, 1972.
Robert L. Oliver, New York, April 29, 1975.

Most Double Plays, Extra-Inning Game

A. L.— 6— James E. Foxx, Philadelphia, August 24, 1935, 15 innings.
Rodney C. Carew, Minnesota, August 29, 1977, first game, 10 innings.

N. L.— 6— Theodore B. Kluszewski, Cincinnati, May 1, 1955, 16 innings.

Most Double Plays Started, Game, Nine Innings

A. L.— 3— Luzerne A. Blue, Detroit, September 8, 1922.
Walter F. Judnich, St. Louis, September 6, 1947.
Victor P. Power, Philadelphia, September 26, 1954.
Peter M. O'Brien, Texas, May 22, 1984.

N. L.— 3— Frank O. Hurst, Philadelphia, September 17, 1930.
Tommie L. Aaron, Milwaukee, May 27, 1962.

Most Unassisted Double Plays, Game

N. L.— 2— Held by 15 first basemen. Last first baseman— David A. Kingman, New York, July 25, 1982.

A. L.— 2— Held by 12 first basemen. Last first baseman— Daniel L. Briggs, California, April 16, 1977.

Most Double Plays, Doubleheader, 18 Innings

N. L.— 8— Raymond E. Sanders, St. Louis, June 11, 1944.

A. L.— 8— Walter F. Judnich, St. Louis, September 16, 1947.
Walter O. Dropo, Boston, June 25, 1950.

Most Double Plays, Doubleheader, More than 18 Innings

A. L.— 10— James B. Vernon, Washington, August 18, 1943, 23 innings.

Second Basemen
Years, Games & Innings

Most Years, Major Leagues

22— Joe L. Morgan, Houston N.L., Cincinnati N.L., San Francisco N.L., Philadelphia N.L., Oakland A.L., 1963 through 1984 (2,527 games) .

Most Years, League

A. L.— 21— Edward T. Collins, Philadelphia, Chicago, 1908 through 1928 (2,651 games) .

N. L.— 21— Joe L. Morgan, Houston, Cincinnati, San Francisco, Philadelphia, 1963 through 1983 (2,427 games) .

Most Games, League

A. L.— 2651— Edward T. Collins, Philadelphia, Chicago, 21 years, 1908 through 1928.

N. L.— 2427— Joe L. Morgan, Houston, Cincinnati, San Francisco, Philadelphia, 1963 through 1983, 21 years.

Most Consecutive Games, League

A. L.— 798— J. Nelson Fox, Chicago, August 7, 1955, through September 3, 1960.

N. L.— 443— David Cash, Pittsburgh, Philadelphia, September 20, 1973 through August 5, 1976.

Most Games, Season

A. L. (162-game season) —162—Jacob Wood, Detroit, 1961.
Robert Grich, Baltimore, 1973.
A. L. (154-game season) —158—Derrill B. Pratt, St. Louis, 1915; also in 1916.
N. L. (162-game season) —163—William S. Mazeroski, Pittsburgh, 1967.
N. L. (154-game season) —156—Claude C. Ritchey, Pittsburgh, 1904.
Miller J. Huggins, Cincinnati, 1907.
Rogers Hornsby, Chicago, 1929.
Williams J. Herman, Chicago, 1939.
Jack R. Robinson, Brooklyn, 1949.

Most Years Leading League in Games

A. L.—8—J. Nelson Fox, Chicago, 1952, 1953, 1954, 1955, 1956, 1957, 1958, 1959.
N. L.—7—William J. Herman, Chicago, Brooklyn, 1932 (tied), 1933, 1935, 1936 (tied), 1938, 1939, 1942.

Fewest Games, Season, for Leader in Most Games

A. L.— 133— Frank LaPorte, St. Louis, 1911.
N. L.— 134— George W. Cutshaw, Pittsburgh, 1917.

Most Innings Played, Game

N. L.— 26—Charles Pick, Boston, May 1, 1920.
Ivan M. Olson, Brooklyn, May 1, 1920.
A. L.— 25—Julio L. Cruz, Chicago, May 8, finished May 9, 1984.
James E. Gantner, Milwaukee, May 8, finished May 9, 1984 (fielded 24 ⅓ innings).

Average

Highest Fielding Average, League, 1000 or More Games

A. L.—.984—J. Nelson Fox, Philadelphia, Chicago, 1947 through 1963, 17 years, 2179 games.
Robert A. Grich, Baltimore, California, 1970 through 1986, except 1977, 16 years, 1,765 games.
N. L.—.984—David Cash, Pittsburgh, Philadelphia, Montreal, San Diego, 1969 through 1980, 12 years, 1,330 games.

Highest Fielding Average, Season, 150 or More Games

A. L.—.99471—Robert Grich, Baltimore, 162 games, 1973.
N. L.—.99380—Ryne D. Sandberg, Chicago, 153 games, 1986.

Highest Fielding Average, Season, 100 or More Games

N. L.—.9956—Kenneth G. Boswell, New York, 101 games, 1970.
A. L.—.9967—Robert A. Grich, California, 116 games, 1985.

Most Years Leading League in Fielding, 100 or More Games

A. L.—9—Edward T. Collins, Philadelphia, Chicago, 1909, 1910, 1914, 1915, 1916, 1920, 1921, 1922, 1924.
N. L.—7—Albert F. Schoendienst, St. Louis, New York, Milwaukee, 1946, 1949, 1953, 1955, 1956, 1957 (tied), 1958.

Most Consec. Years Leading League, Fielding, 100 or More Games

N. L.—6—Claude C. Ritchey, Pittsburgh, 1902, 1903, 1904 (tied), 1905, 1906, 1907.
A. L.—4—Charles L. Gehringer, Detroit, 1934 (tied), 1935, 1936, 1937.

Lowest Fielding Average for Leader, Season, 100 or More Games

N. L.—.928—Charles E. Bassett, Indianapolis, 119 games, 1887.
N. L. since 1900—.953—John B. Miller, Pittsburgh, 150 games, 1909.
A. L.—.960—James T. Williams, New York, 132 games, 1903.

Lowest Fielding Average, Season, 100 or More Games

N. L.—.893—Fred N. Pfeffer, Chicago, 109 games, 1885.
A. L.—.914—Frank H. Truesdale, St. Louis, 122 games, 1910.
N. L. since 1900—.927—John S. Farrell, St. Louis, 118 games, 1903.

Putouts

Most Putouts, League

A. L.— 6526— Edward T. Collins, Philadelphia, Chicago, 1908 through 1928, 21 years.
N. L.— 5541— Joe L. Morgan, Houston, Cincinnati, San Francisco, Philadelphia, 1963 through 1983, 21 years.

Most Putouts, Season

A. A.— 525— John A. McPhee, Cincinnati, 140 games, 1886.
A. L. (162-game season) —484—Robert Grich, Baltimore 160 games, 1974.

A. L. (154-game season) —479—Stanley R. Harris, Washington, 154 games, 1922.
N. L. (154-game season) —466—William J. Herman, Chicago, 153 games, 1933.

Most Years Leading League in Putouts

A. L.— 10— J. Nelson Fox, Chicago, 1952, 1953, 1954, 1955, 1956, 1957, 1958, 1959, 1960, 1961.
N. L.— 7—Fred N. Pfeffer, Chicago, 1884, 1885, 1886, 1887, 1888, 1889, 1891.
William J. Herman, Chicago, Brooklyn, 1933, 1935, 1936, 1938, 1939, 1940 (tied), 1942.

Fewest Putouts, Season, 150 or More Games

N. L.— 260— John B. Miller, Pittsburgh, 150 games, 1909.
A. L.— 287— Daniel F. Murphy, Philadelphia, 150 games, 1905.

Fewest Putouts, Season, for Leader in Most Putouts

N. L.— 292— Lawrence J. Doyle, New York, 144 games, 1909.
A. L.— 304— Charles L. Gehringer, Detroit, 121 games, 1927.

Most Putouts, Game, Nine Innings

A. A.— 12— Louis Bierbauer, Philadelphia, June 22, 1888.
A. L.— 12— Robert F. Knoop, California, August 30, 1966.
N. L.— 11— Samuel W. Wise, Washington, May 9, 1893.
John A. McPhee, Cincinnati, April 21, 1894.
Napoleon Lajoie, Philadelphia, April 25, 1899.
William J. Herman, Chicago, June 28, 1933, first game.
Eugene W. Baker, Chicago, May 27, 1955.
Charles L. Neal, Los Angeles, July 2, 1959.
M. Julian Javier, St. Louis, June 27, 1964.

Most Putouts, Extra-Inning Game

N. L.— 15— Jacob Pitler, Pittsburgh, August 22, 1917, 22 innings.
A. L.— 12— William F. Gardner, Baltimore, May 21, 1957, 16 innings.
Vern G. Fuller, Cleveland, April 11, 1969, 16 innings.

Longest Game, No Putouts

A. L.— 15 innings—Stephen D. Yerkes, Boston, June 11, 1913.
Robert D. Doyle, California, June 14, 1974.
N. L.— 12 innings—Kenneth G. Boswell, New York, August 7, 1972 (none out in 13th inning).

Most Putouts, Two Consecutive Nine-Inning Games

A. A.— 19— William F. Greenwood, Rochester, July 15, 16, 1890.

Most Putouts, Doubleheader, 18 Innings

N. L.— 16— Fred N. Pfeffer, Chicago, May 31, 1897.
William J. Herman, Chicago, June 28, 1933.
A. L.— 15— Casimer E. Michaels, Washington, July 30, 1950.

Fewest Putouts, Longest Doubleheader

A. L.—0—Edward C. Foster, Washington, July 5, 1917, 21 ⅓ innings.
N. L.—0—Claude C. Ritchey, Pittsburgh, September 2, 1901, 18 innings.
Eugene N. DeMontreville, Boston, September 20, 1901, 18 innings.
John J. Evers, Boston, August 3, 1916, 18 innings.
John W. Rawlings, Boston, September 10, 1917, 18 innings.
Lee C. Magee, Cincinnati, August 18, 1918, 18 innings.
Charles L. Herzog, Boston, June 2, 1919, 18 innings.
Milton J. Stock, Brooklyn, August 10, 1925, 18 innings.
Rogers Hornsby, Boston, September 10, 1928, 18 innings.
Carvel W. Rowell, Boston, July 4, 1941, 18 innings.
William J. Rigney, New York, September 1, 1947, 18 innings.
Cornelius J. Ryan, Philadelphia, June 14, 1953, 18 innings.
Antonio Taylor, Philadelphia, August 9, 1960, 18 innings.
Gerald P. Buchek, New York, May 28, 1967, 18 innings.

Assists

Most Assists, League

A. L.— 7630— Edward T. Collins, Philadelphia, Chicago, 21 years, 1908 through 1928.
N. L.— 6738— Joe L. Morgan, Houston, Cincinnati, San Francisco, Philadelphia, 1963 through 1983, 21 years.

Most Assists, Season

N. L.— 641— Frank F. Frisch, St. Louis, 153 games, 1927.
A. L.— 572— Oscar D. Melillo, St. Louis, 148 games, 1930.

Most Years Leading League in Assists

N. L.—9—William S. Mazeroski, Pittsburgh, 1958, 1960, 1961, 1962, 1963, 1964, 1966, 1967, 1968.

A. L.—7—Charles L. Gehringer, Detroit, 1927, 1928, 1933, 1934, 1935, 1936, 1938.

Most Consecutive Years, Leading League in Assists

A. L.—6—Horace M. Clarke, New York, 1967 through 1972.
N. L.—5—William S. Mazeroski, Pittsburgh, 1960 through 1964.

Fewest Assists, Season, 150 or More Games

A. L.— 350—William F. Gardner, Baltimore, 151 games, 1958.
N. L.— 358—Antonio Taylor, Philadelphia, 150 games, 1964.

Fewest Assists, Season, for Leader in Most Assists

N. L.— 381— Emil M. Verban, Philadelphia, 138 games, 1946.
A. L.— 396— J. Nelson Fox, Chicago, 154 games, 1956.

Most Years With 500 or More Assists

A. L.—6—Charles L. Gehringer, Detroit, 1928, 1929, 1930, 1933, 1934, 1936.
N. L.—5—Hugh M. Critz, Cincinnati, New York, 1925, 1926, 1930, 1933, 1934.
    William S. Mazeroski, Pittsburgh, 1961, 1962, 1963, 1964, 1966.

Most Assists, Game, Nine Innings

N. L.— 12— John M. Ward, Brooklyn, June 10, 1892, first game.
    James Gilliam, Jr., Brooklyn, July 21, 1956.
    Ryne D. Sandberg, Chicago, June 12, 1983.
    Glenn D. Hubbard, Atlanta, April 14, 1985.
    Juan M. Samuel, Philadelphia, April 20, 1985.
A. L.— 12— Donald W. Money, Milwaukee, June 24, 1977.
    K. Anthony Phillips, Oakland, July 6, 1986.
    Harold C. Reynolds, Seattle, August 27, 1986.

Most Assists, Extra-Inning Game

N. L.— 15— Lafayette N. Cross, Philadelphia, August 5, 1897, 12 innings.
N. L. since 1900—13—Maurice C. Rath, Cincinnati, August 26, 1919, 15 innings.
A. L.— 13— Roberto Avila, Cleveland, July 1, 1952, 19 innings.
    William L. Randolph, New York, August 25, 1976, 19 innings.

Chances Accepted & Offered

Most Chances Accepted, League

A. L.— 14,156— Edward T. Collins, Philadelphia, Chicago, 1908 through 1928, 21 years.
N. L.— 12,279— Joe L. Morgan, Houston, Cincinnati, San Francisco, Philadelphia, 1963 through 1983, 21 years.

Most Chances Accepted, Season

N. L.— 1037— Frank F. Frisch, St. Louis, 153 games, 1927.
A. L.— 988— Napoleon Lajoie, Cleveland, 156 games, 1908.

Most Years Leading League in Chances Accepted

A. L.—9—J. Nelson Fox, Chicago, 1952, 1953, 1954, 1955, 1956, 1957, 1958, 1959, 1960.
N. L.—8—William S. Mazeroski, Pittsburgh, 1958, 1960, 1961, 1962, 1963, 1964, 1966, 1967.

Fewest Chances Accepted, Season, 150 or More Games

A. L.— 674— Daniel F. Murphy, Philadelphia, 150 games, 1905.
N. L.— 683— Antonio Taylor, Philadelphia, 150 games, 1964.

Fewest Chances Accepted, Season, by Leader

N. L.— 686— John B. Miller, Pittsburgh, 150 games, 1909.
A. L.— 697— Edward T. Collins, Philadelphia, 132 games, 1911.

Most Years With 900 or More Chances Accepted

N. L.—5—William J. Herman, Chicago, 1932, 1933, 1935, 1936, 1938.
A. L.—4—Charles L. Gehringer, Detroit, 1929, 1930, 1933, 1936.

Most Chances Accepted, Game, Nine Innings

A. A.— 18— Clarence L. Childs, Syracuse, June 1, 1890.
N. L.— 18— Terry W. Harmon, Philadelphia, June 12, 1971.
A. L.— 18— Julio L. Cruz, Seattle, June 7, 1981 (first nine innings of 11-inning game; 19 total chances accepted in game) .
    17— James J. Dykes, Philadelphia, August 28, 1921.
    J. Nelson Fox, Chicago, June 12, 1952.

Most Chances Accepted, Extra-Inning Game

N. L.— 21— Eddie Moore, Boston vs. Chicago, May 17, 1927, 22 innings.
A. L.— 20— William L. Randolph, New York, August 25, 1976, 19 innings.

Most Chances Accepted, Doubleheader

N. L.— 26— Frank J. Parkinson, Philadelphia, September 5, 1922.
A. L.— 24— Casimer E. Michaels, Washington, July 30, 1950.
    Alfred M. Martin, New York, September 24, 1952, 19 innings.

Longest Game, No Chances Offered

A. L.— 15— Stephen D. Yerkes, Boston, June 11, 1919.
N. L.— 12— Kenneth G. Boswell, New York, August 7, 1972, (none out in 13th inning) .

Most Chances Accepted, Two Consecutive Games

A. A.— 31— William F. Greenwood, Rochester, July 15, 16, 1890.
N. L.— 28— Fred N. Pfeffer, Chicago, August 13, 14, 1884.
    John N. Ward, New York, July 18, July 19, first game, 1893.
A. L.— 34— Minter C. Hayes, Chicago, July 14, 15, 1932, 22 innings.
    28— Robert P. Doerr, Boston, May 30, second game, June 3, first game, 1946.
N. L. since 1900—26—Frank J. Parkinson, Philadelphia, September 5, 5, 1922.
    Emil Verban, Philadelphia, August 1, 2, 1947.

Fewest Chances Offered, Doubleheader

N. L.—1—Charles L. Herzog, Boston, June 2, 1919.
A. L.—1—Edward C. Foster, Washington, July 5, 1917, 21 ⅓ innings.

Fewest Chances Offered, Two Consecutive Games

N. L.—1—Charles L. Herzog, Boston, April 28, 30, 1919, 19 innings, also June 2, 2, 1919, 18 innings.
    Gerald P. Buchek, New York, May 28, second game, 29, 1967, 17 innings.
A. L.—1—Robert G. Young, St. Louis, April 19, 20, 1951, 17 innings.
    Roberto Avila, Cleveland, April 19, 20, first game, 1952, 18 innings.
    Edward C. Foster, Washington, July 5, 5, 1917, 21 ⅓ innings.

Fewest Chances Offered, Three Consecutive Games

N. L.—3—Edward R. Stanky, Boston, April 25, 26, 27, 1949, 26 innings.
A. L.—4—Held by many second basemen.

Fewest Chances Offered, Four Consecutive Games

N. L.—5—Charles L. Herzog, Boston, June 2, 2, 3, 3, 1919, 37 innings.
A. L.—6—Held by many second basemen.

Errors

Most Errors in Major Leagues

828—Fred N. Pfeffer, Troy, N. L., Chicago, N. L., Chicago, P. L., Louisville, N. L., New York, N. L., 16 years, 1882 through 1897; 654 in N. L., 74 in P. L.

Most Errors, League

N. L.— 754— Fred N. Pfeffer, Troy, Chicago, Louisville, New York, 1882 through 1897, except 1890, 15 years.
A. L.— 435— Edward T. Collins, Philadelphia, Chicago, 1908 through 1928, 21 consecutive years.
N. L. since 1900—443—Lawrence J. Doyle, New York, Chicago, 1907 through 1920, 14 consecutive years.

Most Errors, Season

N. L.— 88— Charles M. Smith, Cincinnati, 80 games, 1880.
    Robert Ferguson, Philadelphia, 85 games, 1883.
A. A.— 87— William Robinson, St. Louis, 129 games, 1886.
    William H. McClellan, Brooklyn, 136 games, 1887.
A. L.— 61— William Gleason, Detroit, 136 games, 1901.
    Hobart Ferris, Boston, 138 games, 1901.
N. L. since 1900—55—George F. Grantham, Chicago, 150 games, 1923.

Most Years Leading League in Errors

N. L.—5—Fred N. Pfeffer, Chicago, 1884, 1885, 1886, 1887, 1888, consecutive.
A. L.—4—William A. Wambsganss, Cleveland, Boston, 1917, 1919, 1920, 1924.
    Joseph L. Gordon, New York, 1938, 1941, 1942, 1943 (tied) .
N. L. since 1900—4—William J. Herman, Chicago, 1932, 1933, 1937, 1939.
    Glenn A. Beckert, Chicago, 1966, 1967, 1969, 1970 (tied) .
Both Leagues—4—Rigoberto Fuentes, San Francisco, N. L., 1971, 1972; San Diego, N. L., 1976; Detroit, A. L., 1977.

Fewest Errors, Season, 150 or More Games

A. L.—5—K. Jerry Adair, Baltimore, 153 games, 1964.
Robert Grich, Baltimore, 162 games, 1973.
N. L.—5—Joe L. Morgan, Cincinnati, 151 games, 1977.
Johnny C. Ray, Pittsburgh, 151 games, 1986.
Ryne D. Sandberg, Chicago, 153 games, 1986.

Fewest Errors, Season, for Leader in Most Errors

A. L.— 14—Hector H. Lopez, Kansas City, 96 games, 1958.
N. L.— 15—Ted C. Sizemore, Chicago, 96 games, 1979.
Glenn D. Hubbard, Atlanta, 91 games, 1979.

Most Consecutive Errorless Games, League

N. L.—91—Joe L. Morgan, Cincinnati, July 6, 1977 through April 22, 1978, 410 chances accepted.
A. L.—89—K. Jerry Adair, Baltimore, July 22, 1964 through May 6, 1965, 458 chances accepted.

Most Consecutive Errorless Games, Season

N. L.—89—J. Manuel Trillo, Philadelphia, April 9 through July 30, 1982, 473 chances accepted.
A. L.—86—Richard F. Dauer, Baltimore, April 10 through September 29, 1978, 418 chances accepted.

Most Consecutive Chances Accepted, Season, No Errors

N. L.— 479— J. Manuel Trillo, Philadelphia, April 8 (part) through July 31 (part), 1982, 91 games.
A. L.— 425— Richard F. Dauer, Baltimore, April 10 through September 30 (part), 1978, 87 games.

Most Errors, Game, Nine Innings

N. L.—9—Andrew J. Leonard, Boston, June 14, 1876.
A. L.—5—Charles Hickman, Washington, September 29, 1905.
Napoleon Lajoie, Philadelphia, April 22, 1915.
N. L. since 1900—4—Held by six second basemen. Last player—Kendall C. Wise, Chicago, May 3, 1957.

Longest Errorless Game

N. L.—25 innings—Felix B. Millan, New York, September 11, 1974.
Ted C. Sizemore, St. Louis, September 11, 1974.
A. L.—25 innings—Julio L. Cruz, Chicago, May 8, finished May 9, 1984.
James E. Gantner, Milwaukee, May 8, finished May 9, 1984 (fielded 24 1/3 innings) .

Most Errors, Two Consecutive Games

N. L.— 11—Andrew J. Leonard, Boston, June 10, 14, 1876.

Most Errors, Three Consecutive Games

N. L.— 13—Andrew J. Leonard, Boston, June 10, 14, 15, 1876.

Most Errors, Inning

N. L.—3—John A. McPhee, Cincinnati, September 23, 1894; first game, second inning.
Claude S. Ritchey, Pittsburgh, September 22, 1900, sixth inning.
Carvel W. Rowell, Boston, September 25, 1941, third inning.
Edward R. Stanky, Chicago, June 20, 1943, first game, eighth inning.
George J. Hausmann, New York, August 13, 1944, second game, fourth inning.
Kermit E. Wahl, Cincinnati, September 18, 1945, first game, eleventh inning.
David E. Lopes, Los Angeles, June 2, 1973, first inning.
Ted C. Sizemore, St. Louis, April 17, 1975, sixth inning.
A. L.—3—Derrill B. Pratt, St. Louis, September 1, 1914, second game, fourth inning.
William A. Wambsganss, Cleveland, May 15, 1923, fourth inning.
Timothy L. Cullen, Washington, August 30, 1969, eighth inning, consecutive.

Double Plays

Most Double Plays, League

N. L.— 1706— William S. Mazeroski, Pittsburgh, 17 years, 1956 through 1972.
A. L.— 1568— J. Nelson Fox, Philadelphia, Chicago, 17 years, 1947 through 1963.

Most Double Plays, Season

N. L.— 161— William S. Mazeroski, Pittsburgh, 162 games, 1966.
A. L.— 150— Gerald E. Priddy, Detroit, 157 games, 1950.

Most Years Leading League in Double Plays

N. L.—8—William S. Mazeroski, Pittsburgh, 1960, 1961, 1962, 1963, 1964, 1965, 1966, 1967.
A. L.—5—Napoleon Lajoie, Cleveland, 1903, 1906, 1907, 1908, 1909 (tied) .
Edward T. Collins, Philadelphia, Chicago, 1909 (tied), 1910, 1912, 1916, 1919.
Stanley R. Harris, Washington, 1921, 1922, 1923, 1924 (tied) , 1925.
Robert P. Doerr, Boston, 1938, 1940, 1943, 1946, 1947.
J. Nelson Fox, Chicago, 1954, 1956, 1957, 1958, 1960.

Fewest Double Plays, Season, 150 or More Games

N. L.— 65— George J. Hausmann, New York, 154 games, 1945.
A. L.— 81— Timothy S. Teufel, Minnesota, 157 games, 1984.

Fewest Double Plays, Season, for Leader in Most Double Plays

N. L.— 81— Rogers Hornsby, St. Louis, 154 games, 1922.
A. L.— 84— Charles L. Gehringer, Detroit, 121 games, 1927.

Most Double Plays, Game, Nine Innings

A. L.—6—Robert F. Knoop, California, May 1, 1966, first game.
N. L.—5—Held by many second basemen. Last player—Teodoro N. Martinez, Los Angeles, August 21, 1977.

Most Double Plays, Extra-Inning Game

A. L.—6—Joseph L. Gordon, Cleveland, August 31, 1949, first game, 14 innings.
N. L.—6—Felix B. Millan, Atlanta, August 5, 1971, 17 innings.

Most Double Plays Started, Game

A. L.—5—Gerald E. Priddy, Detroit, May 20, 1950.
N. L.—4—Fred C. Dunlap, Detroit, June 11, 1887.
Frank W. Gustine, Pittsburgh, August 22, 1940, second game.
Emil Verban, Philadelphia, July 18, 1947.
Albert F. Schoendienst, St. Louis, August 20, 1954.
Felix B. Millan, Atlanta, August 5, 1971, 17 innings.

Most Unassisted Double Plays, Game

N. L.—2—David W. Force, Buffalo, September 15, 1881.
Claude C. Ritchey, Louisville, July 9, 1899, first game.
A. L.—2—Michael L. Edwards, Oakland, August 10, 1978.

Most Double Plays, Doubleheader

A. L.—8—Robert P. Doerr, Boston, June 25, 1950.
Robert F. Knoop, California, May 1, 1966.
N. L.—6—Held by many second basemen.

Third Basemen
Years, Games & Innings

Most Years, League

A. L.— 23— Brooks C. Robinson, Baltimore, 1955 through 1977, 2870 games.
N. L.— 16— Harold J. Traynor, Pittsburgh, 1921 through 1937 except 1936, 1,864 games.
Stanley C. Hack, Chicago, 1932 through 1947, 1,836 games.
Edwin L. Mathews, Boston, Milwaukee, Atlanta, Houston, 1952 through 1967, 2,154 games.
Michael J. Schmidt, Philadelphia, 1972 through 1987, 2,066 games.

Most Games, League

A. L.— 2870— Brooks C. Robinson, Baltimore, 23 years, 1955 through 1977.
N. L.— 2154— Edwin L. Mathews, Boston, Milwaukee, Atlanta, Houston, 16 years, 1952 through 1967.

Most Consecutive Games, League

A. L.— 576— Edward F. Yost, Washington, July 3, 1951, to May 11, 1955.
N. L.— 364— Ronald E. Santo, Chicago, April 19, 1964 through May 31, 1966.

Most Games, Season

A. L. (162-game season) —163—Brooks C. Robinson, Baltimore, 1961, 1964.
A. L. (154-game season) —157—George C. Kell, Detroit, 1950.
Edward F. Yost, Washington, 1952.
N. L. (162-game season) —164—Ronald E. Santo, Chicago, 1965.

N. L. (154-game season) —157—Arthur Devlin, New York, 1908.
J. Carlisle Smith, Boston, 1915.
Willie E. Jones, Philadelphia, 1950.
Edwin L. Mathews, Milwaukee, 1953.
Raymond L. Jablonski, St. Louis, 1953.

Most Years Leading League in Most Games

A. L.— 8—Brooks C. Robinson, Baltimore, 1960, 1961, 1962, 1963, 1964, 1966, (tied), 1968 (tied), 1970.
N. L.— 7—Ronald E. Santo, Chicago, 1961 (tied), 1963, 1965, 1966, 1967, 1968, 1969 (tied).

Fewest Games, Season, for Leader in Most Games

N. L.— 111— Arthur C. Whitney, Boston, 1934.
A. L.— 131— George C. Kell, Philadelphia, Detroit, 1946.

Most Innings Played, Game

N. L.— 26— Norman D. Boeckel, Boston, May 1, 1920.
James H. Johnston, Brooklyn, May 1, 1920.
A. L.— 25— Vance A. Law, Chicago, May 8, finished May 9, 1984.
Randy M. Ready, Milwaukee, May 8, finished May 9, 1984 (fielded 24 ⅓ innings).

Average

Highest Fielding Average, League, 1,000 or More Games

A. L.— .971— Brooks C. Robinson, Baltimore, 23 years, 1955 through 1977, 2870 games.
N. L.— .970— Kenneth J. Reitz, St. Louis, San Francisco, Chicago, Pittsburgh, 11 years, 1972 through 1982, 1,321 games.

Highest Fielding Average, Season, 100 or More Games

A. L.— .989— Donald W. Money, Milwaukee, 157 games, 1974.
N. L.— .983— Henry K. Groh, New York, 145 games, 1924.

Highest Fielding Average, Season, 150 or More Games

A. L.— .989— Donald W. Money, Milwaukee, 157 games, 1974.
N. L.— .980— Kenneth J. Reitz, St. Louis, 157 games, 1977.

Most Years Leading League in Fielding, 100 or More Games

A. L.— 11— Brooks C. Robinson, Baltimore, 1960, 1961, 1962, 1963, 1964, 1966, 1967, 1968, 1969 (tied), 1972, 1975.
N. L.— 6— Henry K. Groh, Cincinnati, New York, 1915 (tied), 1917, 1918, 1922, 1923, 1924.
Kenneth J. Reitz, St. Louis, Chicago, 1973, 1974, 1977, 1978, 1980, 1981.

Most Consec. Years Leading in Fielding, 100 or More Games

A. L.— 6— William E. Kamm, Chicago, 1924 through 1929.
N. L.— 4— Willie E. Jones, Philadelphia, 1953 through 1956.

Lowest Fielding Average for Leader, Season, 100 or More Games

N. L.— .891— Edward N. Williamson, Chicago, 111 games, 1885.
N. L. since 1900—.917—Robert L. Lowe, Boston, 111 games, 1901.
Charles Irwin, Cincinnati, Brooklyn, 131 games, 1901.
A. L.— .936— William J. Bradley, Cleveland, 133 games, 1901.

Lowest Fielding Average, Season, 100 or More Games

N. L.— .836— Charles Hickman, New York, 118 games, 1900.
A. L.— .860— Hunter B. Hill, Washington, 135 games, 1904.

Putouts

Most Putouts, League

A. L.— 2697— Brooks C. Robinson, Baltimore, 23 years, 1955 through 1977.
N. L.— 2288— Harold J. Traynor, Pittsburgh, 16 years, 1921 through 1937, except 1936.

Most Putouts, Season

A. A.— 252— Dennis P. Lyons, Philadelphia, 137 games, 1887.
N. L.— 252— James J. Collins, Boston, 142 games, 1900.
A. L.— 243— William E. Kamm, Chicago, 155 games, 1928.

Most Years Leading League in Putouts

A. L.— 8— Edward F. Yost, Washington, Detroit, 1948, 1950, 1951, 1952, 1953, 1954 (tied), 1956, 1959.
N. L.— 7— Harold J. Traynor, Pittsburgh, 1923, 1925, 1926, 1927, 1931, 1933, 1934.
Willie E. Jones, Philadelphia, 1949, 1950, 1952, 1953, 1954, 1955, 1956.
Ronald E. Santo, Chicago, 1962, 1963, 1964, 1965, 1966, 1967, 1969.

Fewest Putouts, Season, for Leader in Most Putouts

N. L.— 116— Harold J. Traynor, Pittsburgh, 110 games, 1934.
A. L.— 121— Wade A. Boggs, Boston 149 games, 1986.

Fewest Putouts, Season, 150 or More Games

A. L.— 82— James A. Presley, Seattle, 154 games, 1985.
N. L.— 86— Kenneth J. Reitz, St. Louis, 150 games, 1980.

Most Putouts, Game, Nine Innings

N. L.— 10— William J. Kuehne, Pittsburgh, May 24, 1889.
N. L. since 1900—9—Robert L. Dillard, St. Louis, June 18, 1900.
A. L.— 7— William J. Bradley, Cleveland, September 21, 1901, first game; also May 13, 1909.
Harry P. Riconda, Philadelphia, July 5, 1924, second game.
Oswald L. Bluege, Washington, June 18, 1927.
Raymond O. Boone, Detroit, April 24, 1954.

Longest Game With No Putouts

N. L.—20 innings   —Lewis A. Malone, Brooklyn, April 30, 1919.
A. L.—18 ⅓ innings—Vernon D. Stephens, Boston, July 13, 1951.

Most Consecutive Games, No Putouts

A. L.— 10—Felix Torres, Los Angeles, June 14 through June 23, 1963.
N. L.— 8—Kenton L. Boyer, St. Louis, August 4, first game through August 11, 1963.

Assists

Most Assists, League

A. L.— 6205— Brooks C. Robinson, Baltimore, 23 years, 1955 through 1977.
N. L.— 4752— Michael J. Schmidt, Philadelphia, 16 years, 1972 through 1987.

Most Assists, Season

A. L. (154-game season) —405—Harlond B. Clift, St. Louis, 155 games, 1937.
A. L. (162-game season) —412—Graig Nettles, Cleveland, 158 games, 1971.
N. L. (154-game season) —384—William Shindle, Baltimore, 134 games, 1892.
N. L. (162-game season) —404—Michael J. Schmidt, Philadelphia, 162 games, 1974.
N. L. since 1900 (154-game season) —371—Thomas W. Leach, Pittsburgh, 146 games, 1904.

Most Years Leading League in Assists

A. L.—8—Brooks C. Robinson, Baltimore, 1960, 1963, 1964, 1966, 1967, 1968, 1969, 1974.
N. L.—7—Ronald E. Santo, Chicago, 1962, 1963, 1964, 1965, 1966, 1967, 1968.
Michael J. Schmidt, Philadelphia, 1974, 1976, 1977, 1980, 1981, 1982, 1983.

Fewest Assists, Season, 150 or More Games

A. L.— 221— Harry Lord, Chicago, 150 games, 1913.
N. L.— 247— Stanley C. Hack, Chicago, 150 games, 1937.

Fewest Assists, Season, for Leader in Most Assists

N. L.— 227— Arthur C. Whitney, Boston, 111 games, 1934.
A. L.— 258— Oswald L. Bluege, Washington, 134 games, 1930.

Most Assists, Game, Nine Innings

N. L.— 11— James L. White, Buffalo, May 16, 1884.
Jeremiah Denny, New York, May 29, 1890.
Damon R. Phillips, Boston, August 29, 1944.
A. L.— 11— Kenneth L. McMullen, Washington, September 26, 1966, first game.
Michael D. Ferraro, New York, September 14, 1968.

Most Assists, Extra-Inning Game

N. L.— 12— Robert M. Byrne, Pittsburgh, June 8, 1910, second game, 11 innings.
A. L.— 11— J. Franklin Baker, New York, May 24, 1918, 19 innings.
Douglas V. DeCinces, California, May 7, 1983, 12 innings.

Most Innings, No Assists, Extra-Inning Game

A. L.— 17— Colbert D. Harrah, Texas, September 17, 1977.

Chances Accepted & Offered

Most Chances Accepted, League

A. L.— 8902— Brooks C. Robinson, Baltimore, 23 years, 1955 through 1977.

N. L.— 6462— Ronald E. Santo, Chicago, 14 years, 1960 through 1973.

Most Chances Accepted, Season
A. L.— 603— Harlond B. Clift, St. Louis, 155 games, 1937.
N. L.— 601— James J. Collins, Boston, 151 games, 1899.
N. L. since 1900—583—Thomas W. Leach, Pittsburgh, 146 games, 1904.

Most Years Leading League in Chances Accepted
N. L.—9—Ronald E. Santo, Chicago, 1961, 1962, 1963, 1964, 1965, 1966, 1967, 1968, 1969 (tied).
A. L.—8—J. Franklin Baker, Philadelphia, New York, 1909, 1910, 1912, 1913, 1914, 1917, 1918, 1919.
Brooks C. Robinson, Baltimore, 1960, 1963, 1964, 1966, 1967, 1968, 1969, 1974.

Fewest Chances Accepted, Season, 150 or More Games
N. L.— 349— James F. Morrison, Pittsburgh, 151 games, 1986.
A. L.— 364— Harry Lord, Chicago, 150 games, 1913.

Fewest Chances Accepted, Season, by Leader
N. L.— 332— Arthur C. Whitney, Boston, 111 games, 1934.
A. L.— 396— Oswald L. Bluege, Washington, 134 games, 1930.

Most Chances Accepted, Game, Nine Innings
N. L.— 13— William J. Kuehne, Pittsburgh, May 24, 1889.
Jeremiah Denny, New York, May 19, 1890.
William Shindle, Baltimore, September 28, 1893.
William M. Joyce, Washington, May 26, 1894.
Arthur Devlin, New York, May 23, 1908, first game.
Anthony F. Cuccinello, Brooklyn, July 12, 1934, first game.
Roy J. Hughes, Chicago, August 29, 1944, second game.
A. L.— 13— William Conroy, Washington, September 25, 1911.

Most Chances Accepted, Extra-Inning Game
N. L.— 16— Jeremiah Denny, Providence, August 17, 1882, 18 innings.
A. L.— 14— James J. Collins, Boston, June 21, 1902, 15 innings.
Benjamin F. Dyer, Detroit, July 16, 1919, 14 innings.
N. L. since 1900—14—Donald A. Hoak, Cincinnati, May 4, 1958, second game, 14 innings.

Most Chances Accepted, Two Consecutive Games
N. L.— 23— Joseph F. Farrell, Detroit, June 30, 1884.
N. L. since 1900—18—Harry M. Steinfeldt, Cincinnati, June 14, 16, 1902.
Robert M. Byrne, Pittsburgh, June 15, 17, 1910.
Edward D. Zimmerman, Brooklyn, July 4, 4, 1911.
Ralph A. Pinelli, Cincinnati, July 11, second game, July 13, 1925.
Lee Handley, Pittsburgh, June 15, 16, first game, 1946.
A. L.— 18— Hobart Ferris, St. Louis, July 12, 13, 1909, first game.
Terrence L. Turner, Cleveland, May 21, June 1, 1916, first game.
Aaron L. Ward, New York, April 20, 21, 1921.

Most Chances Accepted, Doubleheader
N. L.— 18— Edward D. Zimmerman, Brooklyn, July 4, 1911.
A. L.— 16— William P. Purtell, Chicago, July 14, 1909.

Longest Game With No Chances Offered
N. L.—15 innings—Harry M. Steinfeldt, Chicago, August 22, 1908.
Henry K. Groh, Cincinnati, August 26, 1919, second game.
Norman D. Boeckel, Boston, June 16, 1921; also September 12, 1921, first game.
A. L.—12⅔ innings—James R. Tabor, Boston, July 7, 1943.

Longest Doubleheader With No Chances Offered
A. L.—21⅔ innings—William L. Gardner, Cleveland, August 23, 1920.
N. L.—19 innings—Norman D. Boeckel, Boston, July 26, 1922.

Errors

Most Errors in Major Leagues
780—Walter A. Latham, St. Louis A. A., Chicago P. L., Cincinnati N.L., St. Louis N. L., 14 years, 1883 through 1896.

Most Errors, League
N. L.— 553— Jeremiah Denny, Providence, St. Louis, Indianapolis, New York, Cleveland, Philadelphia, Louisville, 1881 through 1894, except 1892, 13 years.
A. L.— 359— James P. Austin, New York, St. Louis, 1909 through 1922; 1925, 1926, 1929, 17 years, 1,433 games.

N. L. since 1900—324—Harold J. Traynor, Pittsburgh, 1921 through 1935; 1937, 16 years, 1,864 games.

Most Errors, Season
N. L.— 91— Charles Hickman, New York, 118 games, 1900.
A. L.— 64— Samuel N. Strang, Chicago, 137 games, 1902.

Most Years Leading League in Errors
N. L.—5—Harold J. Traynor, Pittsburgh, 1926, 1928 (tied), 1931, 1932, 1933.
A. L.—5—James R. Tabor, Boston, 1939, 1940 (tied), 1941, 1942, 1943 (tied).

Fewest Errors, Season, 150 or More Games
A. L.—5—Donald W. Money, Milwaukee, 157 games, 1974.
N. L.—8—Kenneth J. Reitz, St. Louis, 150 games, 1980.

Fewest Errors, Season, for Leader in Most Errors
N. L.— 16— Edwin L. Mathews, Milwaukee, 147 games, 1957.
Gene L. Freese, Pittsburgh, 74 games, 1957.
A. L.— 17— Cecil T. Travis, Washington, 56 games, 1946.

Most Errors, Game
U. A.—6—James B. Donnelly, Kansas City, July 16, 1884.
A. A.—6—James H. Moffett, Toledo, August 2, 1884.
Joseph Werrick, Louisville, July 28, 1888.
William C. Alvord, Toledo, May 22, 1890.
N. L.—6—Joseph H. Mulvey, Philadelphia, July 30, 1884.
N. L. since 1900—5—David L. Brain, Boston, June 11, 1906.
A. L.—4—Held by 20 third basemen. Last third baseman—Floyd K. Rayford, Baltimore, April 21, 1986.

Most Consecutive Errorless Games, League
N. L.— 97— James H. Davenport, San Francisco, July 29, 1966 through April 28, 1968, 209 chances accepted. (Played other positions during streak.)
A. L.— 88— Donald W. Money, Milwaukee, September 28, 1973, second game, through July 16, 1974, 261 chances accepted.

Most Consecutive Errorless Games, Season
A. L.— 86— Donald W. Money, Milwaukee, April 5 through July 16, 1974, 257 chances accepted.
N. L.— 64— James H. Davenport, San Francisco, May 22 through September 30, 1967, first game, 137 chances accepted. (Played other positions during streak.)
57— Robert T. Aspromonte, Houston, July 14 through September 18, 1962, second game, 145 chances accepted.

Most Consecutive Chances Accepted, League, No Errors
A. L.— 261— Donald W. Money, Milwaukee, September 28, 1973, first game (part) through July 16, 1974, 88 games.

Most Consecutive Chances Accepted, Season, No Errors
A. L.— 257— Donald W. Money, Milwaukee, April 5 through July 16, 1974, 88 games.
N. L.— 163— Donald W. Money, Philadelphia, July 27, first game through September 11, 1972, 48 games.

Longest Errorless Game
N. L.—26 innings— Norman D. Boeckel, Boston, May 1, 1920
James H. Johnston, Brooklyn, May 1, 1920.
A. L.—25 innings— Vance A. Law, Chicago, May 8, finished May 9, 1984.

Most Errors, Doubleheader, Since 1900
N. L.—5—William J. Bradley, Chicago, May 30, 1900.
Thomas W. Leach, Pittsburgh, August 20, 1903.
A. L.—4—Held by many third basemen. Last third baseman—Herbert E. Plews, Washington, June 3, 1958.

Most Errors, Two Consecutive Games
A. A.—9—Thomas J. Esterbrook, New York, July 15, 26, 1883.

Most Errors, Inning
N. L.—4—Lewis Whistler, New York, June 19, 1891, fourth inning.
Robert E. Brenly, San Francisco, September 14, 1986, fourth inning.
A. L.—4—James T. Burke, Milwaukee, May 27, 1901, fourth inning.

Double Plays

Most Double Plays, League
A. L.— 618— Brooks C. Robinson, Baltimore, 23 years, 1955 through 1977.

N. L.— 425— Michael J. Schmidt, Philadelphia, 16 years, 1972 through 1987.

Most Double Plays, Season

A. L. (162-game season) —54—Graig Nettles, Cleveland, 158 games, 1971.

A. L. (154-game season) —50—Harlond B. Clift, St. Louis, 155 games, 1937.

N. L. (162-game season) —45—Darrell W. Evans, Atlanta, 160 games, 1974.

N. L. (154-game season) —43—Henry Thompson, New York, 138 games, 1950.

Most Years Leading League in Double Plays

N. L.—6—Henry K. Groh, Cincinnati, New York, 1915, 1916, 1918, 1919, 1920 (tied) , 1922.
Ronald E. Santo, Chicago, 1961, 1964, 1966, 1967, 1968 (tied) , 1971.
Michael J. Schmidt, Philadelphia, 1978, 1979, 1980, 1982 (tied) , 1983, 1987.

A. L.—5—James P. Austin, New York, St. Louis, 1909, 1911, 1913, 1915, 1917.
Kenneth F. Keltner, Cleveland, 1939, 1941, 1942, 1944, 1947.
Frank J. Malzone, Boston, 1957, 1958, 1959, 1960, 1961.

Fewest Double Plays, Season, 150 or More Games

N. L.— 10—Robert T. Aspromonte, Houston, 155 games, 1964.

A. L.— 17—R. Maxwell Alvis, Cleveland, 156 games, 1965.

Fewest Double Plays, Season, for Leader in Most Double Plays

N. L.— 17—Joseph V. Stripp, Brooklyn, 140 games, 1933.
John L. Vergez, New York, 123 games, 1933.
George J. Kurowski, St. Louis, 138 games, 1946.
James R. Tabor, Philadelphia, 124 games, 1946.

A. L.— 23—Martin J. McManus, Detroit, 130 games, 1930.

Most Unassisted Double Plays, Season

A. L.—4—Joseph A. Dugan, New York, 148 games, 1924.

N. L.—2—Held by many third basemen. Last third baseman—T. Michael Shannon, St. Louis, 156 games, 1968.

Most Double Plays, Game

N. L.—4—Harold J. Traynor, Pittsburgh, July 9, 1925, first game.
John L. Vergez, Philadelphia, August 15, 1935.

A. L.—4—Andrew A. Carey, New York, July 31, 1955, second game.
Felix Torres, Los Angeles, August 23, 1963.
Kenneth L. McMullen, Washington, August 13, 1965.

Most Double Plays Started, Game, Nine Innings

N. L.—4—Harold J. Traynor, Pittsburgh, July 9, 1925, first game.
John L. Vergez, Philadelphia, August 15, 1935.

A. L.—4—Felix Torres, Los Angeles, August 23, 1963.
Kenneth L. McMullen, Washington, August 13, 1965.

Most Unassisted Double Plays, Game

N. L.-A. L.—1—Held by many third basemen.

Most Unassisted Double Plays, Two Consecutive Games

A. L.—2—James Delahanty, Detroit, August 28, 29, 1911.
Marvin J. Owen, Detroit, April 28, 29, 1934.

N. L.—Never accomplished.

Shortstops
Years, Games & Innings

Most Years in Majors

20—William F. Dahlen, Chicago N. L., Brooklyn N. L., New York N. L., Boston N. L., 1891 through 1911, except 1910, 2,139 games.
Roderick J. Wallace, St. Louis N. L., St. Louis A. L., 1899 through 1918, 1,828 games.
Lucius B. Appling, Chicago A. L., 1930 through 1950 (except 1944, in military service) , 2,218 games.

Most Years, League

N. L.—20— William F. Dahlen, Chicago, Brooklyn, New York, Boston, 1891 through 1911, except 1910, 2,139 games.

A. L.—20— Lucius B. Appling, Chicago, 1930 through 1950, except 1944 (in military service) , 2,219 games.

N. L. since 1900—19—Walter J. Maranville, Boston, Pittsburgh, Chicago, Brooklyn, St. Louis, 1912 through 1931, except 1924, 2,153 games.

Most Games, League

A. L.— 2581— Luis E. Aparicio, Chicago, Baltimore, Boston, 18 years, 1956 through 1973.

N. L.— 2222— Lawrence R. Bowa, Philadelphia, Chicago, 16 years, 1970 through 1985.

Most Consecutive Games, League

A. L.— 1307— L. Everett Scott, Boston, New York, June 20, 1916, through May 5, 1925.

N. L.— 584— Roy D. McMillan, Cincinnati, September 16, 1951, first game through August 6, 1955.

Most Games, Season

N. L. (162-game season) —165—Maurice M. Wills, Los Angeles, 1962.

N. L. (154-game season) —157—Joseph B. Tinker, Chicago, 1908.
Granville W. Hamner, Philadelphia, 1950.

A. L. (162-game season) —163—O. Antonio Fernandez, Toronto, 1986.

A. L. (154-game season) —158—Edward E. Lake, Detroit, 1947.

Most Games, Season, Lefthanded Shortstop

N. L.— 73— William B. Hulen, Philadelphia, 1896.

Most Years Leading League in Games

N. L.—6—Michael J. Doolan, Philadelphia, 1906, 1909, 1910, 1911, 1912, 1913.
J. Floyd Vaughan, Pittsburgh, 1933 (tied) , 1934, 1936, 1938, 1939, 1940.
Roy D. McMillan, Cincinnati, Milwaukee, 1952, 1953, 1954 (tied) , 1956, 1957, 1961.

A. L.—5—Luis E. Aparicio, Chicago, 1956, 1957, 1958, 1959, 1960 (tied) .

Fewest Games, Season, for Leader in Most Games

N. L.— 141— Walter J. Maranville, Pittsburgh, 1923.

A. L.— 142— Luis Aparicio, Chicago, 1957.

Most Innings Played, Game

N. L.— 26— Charles W. Ward, Brooklyn, May 1, 1920.
Walter J. Maranville, Boston, May 1, 1920.

A. L.— 25— Robin R. Yount, Milwaukee, May 8, finished May 9, 1984 (fielded 24 ⅓ innings) .

Average

Highest Fielding Average, League, 1000 or More Games

N. L.— .980— Lawrence R. Bowa, Philadelphia, Chicago, 16 years, 1970 through 1985, 2,222 games.

A. L.— .977— Mark H. Belanger, Baltimore, 17 years, 1965 through 1981, 1,898 games.

Highest Fielding Average, Season, 150 or More Games

A. L.— .990— Edwin A. Brinkman, Detroit, 156 games, 1972.

N. L.— .987— Lawrence R. Bowa, Philadelphia, 157 games, 1971.
Lawrence R. Bowa, Philadelphia, 150 games, 1972.
Osborne E. Smith, St. Louis, 158 games, 1987.

Highest Fielding Average, Season, 100 or More Games

N. L.— .991— Lawrence R. Bowa, Philadelphia, 146 games, 1979.

A. L.— .990— Edwin A. Brinkman, Detroit, 156 games, 1972.

Most Years Leading League in Fielding, 100 or More Games

A. L.—8—L. Everett Scott, Boston, New York, 1916, 1917, 1918, 1919, 1920, 1921, 1922, 1923, consecutive.
Louis Boudreau, Cleveland, 1940, 1941, 1942, 1943, 1944, 1946, 1947, 1948.
Luis E. Aparicio, Chicago, Baltimore, 1959, 1960, 1961, 1962, 1963, 1964, 1965, 1966, consecutive.

N. L.—6—Lawrence R. Bowa, Philadelphia, Chicago, 1971, 1972, 1974, 1978, 1979, 1983.
Osborne E. Smith, San Diego, St. Louis, 1981, 1982, 1984, 1985, 1986, 1987.

Most Consec. Yrs. Leading League, Fielding, 100 or More Games

A. L.—8—L. Everett Scott, Boston, New York, 1916 through 1923.
Luis E. Aparicio, Chicago, Baltimore, 1959 through 1966.

N. L.—5—Hugh A. Jennings, Baltimore, 1894 through 1898.

N. L. since 1900—4—Edward R. Miller, Boston, Cincinnati, 1940 through 1943.
Osborne E. Smith, St. Louis, 1984 through 1987.

Lowest Fielding Average, Season, for Leader, 100 or More Games

N. L.— .900— John W. Glasscock, Indianapolis, 109 games, 1888.
Arthur A. Irwin, Philadelphia, 121 games, 1888.

A. L.— .934— Fred N. Parent, Boston, 139 games, 1903
Montford M. Cross, Philadelphia, 138 games, 1903.

N. L. since 1900—.936—Thomas W. Corcoran, Cincinnati, 150 games, 1904.

Lowest Fielding Average, Season, 100 or More Games
A. L.—.861—William H. Keister, Baltimore, 114 games, 1901.
N. L.—.884—Thomas E. Burns, Chicago, 111 games, 1885.
N. L. since 1900—.891—Otto A. Krueger, St. Louis, 107 games, 1902.

Putouts

Most Putouts, League
N. L.— 5133— Walter J. Maranville, Boston, Pittsburgh, Chicago, Brooklyn, St. Louis, 1912 through 1931 except 1924; 19 years.
A. L.— 4548— Luis E. Aparicio, Chicago, Baltimore, Boston, 18 years, 1956 through 1973.

Most Putouts, Season
N. L.— 425— Hugh A. Jennings, Baltimore, 131 games, 1895.
A. L.— 425— Owen Bush, Detroit, 157 games, 1914.
N. L. since 1900—407—Walter J. Maranville, Boston, 156 games, 1914.

Most Years Leading League in Putouts
N. L.—6—Walter J. Maranville, Boston, Pittsburgh, 1914, 1915 (tied), 1916, 1917, 1919, 1923.
A. L.—4—Joseph W. Sewell, Cleveland, 1924, 1925, 1926, 1927.
Louis Boudreau, Cleveland, 1941, 1943, 1944, 1946.
Edwin D. Joost, Philadelphia, 1947, 1948, 1949, 1951.
Luis E. Aparicio, Chicago, Baltimore, 1956, 1958, 1959, 1966.

Fewest Putouts, Season, 150 or More Games
N. L.— 180— Lawrence R. Bowa, Philadelphia, 156 games, 1976.
A. L.— 220— Oswaldo J. Guillen, Chicago, 150 games, 1985.

Fewest Putouts, Season, for Leader in Most Putouts
A. L.— 248— Joseph P. DeMaestri, Kansas City, 134 games, 1957.
N. L.— 251— Rafael E. Ramirez, Atlanta, 145 games, 1984.

Most Putouts, Game, Nine Innings
N. L.— 11— William Fuller, New York, August 20, 1895.
Horace H. Ford, Cincinnati, September 18, 1929.
A. L.— 11— Joseph P. Cassidy, Washington, August 30, 1904, first game.

Most Putouts, Opening Game of Season, Nine Innings
N. L.—9—William F. Dahlen, Brooklyn, April 19, 1900.

Most Putouts, Extra-Inning Game
N. L.— 14— Montford M. Cross, Philadelphia, July 7, 1899, 11 innings.
A. L.—Less than nine-inning game.

Most Putouts, Game, No Assists
N. L.—9—Charles L. Herzog, Cincinnati, May 26, 1916.

Assists

Most Assists, League
A. L.— 8016— Luis E. Aparicio, Chicago, Baltimore, Boston, 18 years, 1956 through 1973.
N. L.— 7414— William F. Dahlen, Chicago, Brooklyn, New York, Boston 1891 through 1911, except 1910; 20 years.
N. L.—since 1900—7338—Walter J. Maranville, Boston, Pittsburgh, Chicago, Brooklyn, St. Louis, 1912 through 1931, except 1924; 19 years.

Most Assists, Season
N. L. (162-game season) —621—Osborne E. Smith, San Diego, 158 games, 1980.
N. L. (154-game season) —601—F. Glenn Wright, Pittsburgh, 153 games, 1924.
A. L. (162-game season) —583—Calvin E. Ripken, Baltimore, 162 games, 1984.
A. L. (154-game season) —570—Terrence L. Turner, Cleveland, 147 games, 1906.

Most Years Leading League in Assists
A. L.—7—Lucius B. Appling, Chicago, 1933, 1935, 1937, 1939, 1941, 1943, 1946.
Luis E. Aparicio, Chicago, 1956, 1957, 1958, 1959, 1960, 1961, 1968.
N. L.—6—Osborne E. Smith, San Diego, 1979, 1980, 1981, St. Louis, 1982, 1985, 1987.

Most Consecutive Years Leading League in Assists
A. L.—6—Luis E. Aparicio, Chicago, 1956 through 1961.
N. L.—4—George J. Smith, Cincinnati, 1891 through 1894.
Osborne E. Smith, San Diego, St. Louis, 1979 through 1982.

Fewest Assists, Season, 150 or More Games
A. L.— 347— Joaquin F. Gutierrez, Boston, 150 games, 1984.
N. L.— 396— Rafael F. Santana, New York, 153 games, 1985.

Most Years With 500 or More Assists
N. L.—7—Osborne E. Smith, San Diego, 1978, 1979, 1980, St. Louis, 1982, 1983, 1985, 1987.
A. L.—6—Owen Bush, Detroit, 1909, 1911, 1912, 1913, 1914, 1915.

Fewest Assists, Season, for Leader in Most Assists
A. L.— 438— Joseph W. Sewell, Cleveland, 137 games, 1928.
N. L.— 440— John Logan, Milwaukee, 129 games, 1957.

Most Assists, Game, Nine Innings
N. L.— 14— Thomas W. Corcoran, Cincinnati, August 7, 1903.
A. L.— 13— Robert E. Reeves, Washington, August 7, 1927.

Most Assists, Extra-Inning Game
A. L.— 15— Richard P. Burleson, California, April 13, 1982, 20 innings (completed April 14).
N. L.— 14— Herman C. Long, Boston, May 6, 1892, 14 innings.
Derrel M. Harrelson, New York, May 24, 1973, 19 innings.

Fewest Assists, Longest Extra-Inning Game
N. L.— 0— John F. Coffey, Boston, July 26, 1909, 17 innings.
A. L.— 0— John P. Gochnauer, Cleveland, July 14, 1903, 12 innings.

Chances Accepted & Offered

Most Chances Accepted, League
A. L.— 12,564—Luis E. Aparicio, Chicago, Baltimore, Boston, 18 years, 1956 through 1973.
N. L.— 12,471—Walter J. Maranville, Boston, Pittsburgh, Chicago, Brooklyn, St. Louis, 1912 through 1931 except 1924, 19 years.

Most Chances Accepted, Season
N. L.— 984— David J. Bancroft, New York, 156 games, 1922.
A. L.— 969— Owen Bush, Detroit, 157 games, 1914.

Most Years Leading League in Chances Accepted
A. L.—7—Luis E. Aparicio, Chicago, 1956, 1957, 1958, 1959, 1960, 1961, 1968.
N. L.—6—Osborne E. Smith, San Diego, St. Louis, 1978, 1980, 1981, 1983, 1985, 1987.

Fewest Chances Accepted, Season, 150 or More Games
A. L.— 575— Joaquin F. Gutierrez, Boston, 150 games, 1984.
N. L.— 616— David I. Concepcion, Cincinnati, 151 games, 1985.

Fewest Chances Accepted, Season, by Leader
N. L.— 694— Rafael E. Ramirez, Atlanta, 145 games, 1984.
A. L.— 695— Luis E. Aparicio, Chicago, 142 games, 1957.

Most Chances Accepted, Game, Nine Innings
N. L.— 19—Daniel Richardson, Washington, June 20, 1892, first game.
Edwin D. Joost, Cincinnati, May 7, 1941.
A. L.— 17— Roderick J. Wallace, St. Louis, June 10, 1902.

Most Chances Accepted, Extra-Inning Game
N. L.— 21— Edward R. Miller, Boston, June 27, 1939, 23 innings.
A. L.— 18— Fred A. Parent, Boston, July 9, 1902, 17 innings.
Alfonso Carrasquel, Chicago, July 13, 1951, 19 innings.
James L. Webb, Detroit, July 21, 1945, 24 innings.
James E. Runnels, Washington, June 3, 1952, 17 innings.
Ronald L. Hansen, Chicago, August 29, 1965, first game, 14 innings.

Most Chances Accepted, Doubleheader
N. L.— 25— Daniel Richardson, Washington, June 20, 1892.
N. L. since 1900—24—John H. Sand, Philadelphia, July 4, 1924.
David J. Bancroft, Boston, July 31, 1926.
A. L.— 24— George F. McBride, Washington, August 19, 1908.
Roger T. Peckinpaugh, New York, September 8, 1919.
Emory E. Rigney, Boston, July 15, 1926.

Most Chances Accepted, Doubleheader, More Than 18 Innings
A. L.— 28— Ronald L. Hansen, Chicago, August 29, 1965, 23 innings.
N. L.— 26— J. Floyd Vaughan, Pittsburgh, August 22, 1940, 21 innings.

Most Chances Accepted, Three Consecutive Games

A. L.—37—Walter Gerber, St. Louis, May 27, 29, 30, first game, 1923.
N. L.—35—George S. Davis, New York, May 23, 24, 25, 1899.
    George S. Davis, New York, July 19, 20, 21, 1900.

Most Chances Accepted, Four Consecutive Games

A. L.—48—Walter Gerber, St. Louis, May 27, 29, 30, 30, 1923.
N. L.—45—George S. Davis, New York, May 23, 24, 25, 26, 1899.
N. L. since 1900—44—George S. Davis, New York, July 18, 19, 20, 21, 1900.

Longest Game With No Chances Offered

N. L.—12 innings—Irving B. Ray, Boston, August 15, 1888.
A. L.—12 innings—John P. Gochnauer, Cleveland, July 14, 1903.
    11⅔ innings—William G. Rogell, Detroit, June 16, 1937.
N. L. since 1900—11⅔ innings—Edward Feinberg, Philadelphia, May 19, 1939.
    11 innings—William F. Jurges, New York, September 22, 1942 (None out in 12th) .

Fewest Chances Offered, Opening Game of Season

A. L.—0—Frank P. J. Crosetti, New York, April 16, 1940, 9⅔ innings.
N. L.—0—John P. Wagner, Pittsburgh, April 14, 1910, 9 innings.

Fewest Chances Offered, Doubleheader

A. L.—0—Colbert D. Harrah, Texas, June 25, 1976, 18 innings.
N. L.—1—Travis C. Jackson, New York, May 30, 1934, 18 innings.

Fewest Chances Offered, Two Consecutive Games

A. L.—0—Thomas M. Tresh, New York, July 31, August 1, 1968, 18 innings.
    Colbert D. Harrah, Texas, June 25, 25, 1976, 18 innings.
N. L.—1—Travis C. Jackson, New York, May 30, 1934, 18 innings.
    Humberto P. Fernandez, Philadelphia, May 7, 8, 1957, 18 innings.
    Michael T. Fischlin, Houston, June 18, 20, 1978, 18 innings.

Fewest Chances Offered, Three Consecutive Games

A. L.—0—Thomas M. Tresh, New York, July 30, 31, August 1, 1968, 26 innings.
N. L.—3—Humberto P. Fernandez, Philadelphia, May 5, second game, 7, 8, 1957, 27 innings.

Errors

Most Errors in Major Leagues

1037—Herman C. Long, Kansas City, A. A., Boston N. L., New York A. L., Detroit A. L., 15 years, 1889 through 1903.

Most Errors, League

N. L.—972—William F. Dahlen, Chicago, Brooklyn, New York, Boston, 1891 through 1911, except 1910, 20 years, 2,139 games.
A. L.—689—Owen J. Bush, Detroit, Washington, 1908 through 1921, 14 years, 1,866 games.
N. L. since 1900—676—John P. Wagner, Pittsburgh, 1901 through 1917, 17 years, 1,887 games.

Most Errors, Season

P. L.—115—William Shindle, Philadelphia, 132 games, 1890.
N. L.—106—Joseph D. Sullivan, Washington, 127 games, 1893.
A. L.—95—John P. Gochnauer, Cleveland, 128 games, 1903.
N. L. since 1900—81—Rudolph E. Hulswitt, Philadelphia, 138 games, 1903.

Fewest Errors, Season, 150 or More Games

A. L.—7—Edwin A. Brinkman, Detroit, 156 games, 1972.
N. L.—9—Lawrence R. Bowa, Philadelphia, 150 games, 1972.

Fewest Errors, Season, for Leader in Most Errors

N. L.—21—Mariano Duncan, Los Angeles, 67 games, 1987.
A. L.—24—Vernon D. Stephens, Boston, 155 games, 1948.

Most Years Leading League in Errors

N. L.—6—Richard M. Groat, Pittsburgh, St. Louis, 1955, 1956, 1959, 1961, 1962, 1964.
A. L.—5—Lucius B. Appling, Chicago, 1933, 1935, 1937, 1939, 1946.

Most Errors, Game, Nine Innings

N. L.—7—James H. Hallinan, New York, July 29, 1876.
A. A.—7—George Smith, Brooklyn, June 17, 1885.
N. L. since 1900—5—Charles Babb, New York, August 24, 1903, first game; also with Brooklyn, June 20, 1904.
    Phil Lewis, Brooklyn, July 20, 1905.
A. L.—5—Owen Bush, Detroit, August 25, 1911, first game.

Most Errors, Extra-Inning Game

A. L.—6—William J. O'Neill, Boston, May 21, 1904, 13 innings.
N. L.—5—Held by many shortstops.

Most Errors, Opening Game of Season, Nine Innings

N. L.—5—John J. Troy, New York, May 1, 1883.
N. L. since 1900—4—Louis B. Stringer, Chicago, April 15, 1941.
A. L.—3—Held by many shortstops.

Most Errors, First Major League Game

N. L.—4—Louis B. Stringer, Chicago, April 15, 1941.
A. L.—3—Held by many shortstops.

Most Errors, Two Consecutive Nine-Inning Games

A. A.—10—George Smith, Brooklyn, June 16, 17, 1885.
N. L.—9—Fred N. Pfeffer, Troy, September 7, 9, 1882.
A. L.—6—Juan J. Beniquez, Boston, July 13, 14, 1972.

Most Errors, Doubleheader, 18 Innings

P. L.—9—Edward J. Delahanty, Cleveland, July 4, 1890.
N. L.—7—William Shindle, Baltimore, April 23, 1892.
N. L. since 1900—6—Samuel N. Strang, Chicago, Ocotber 8, 1900.
A. L.—5—John P. Gochnauer, Cleveland, September 10, 1902.
    Albert Brancato, Philadelphia, September 13, 1940.
    Zoilo Versalles, Minnesota, July 5, 1963.

Longest Errorless Game

N.L.—26 innings—Walter J. Maranville, Boston, May 1, 1920.
A. L.—25 innings—Robin R. Yount, Milwaukee, May 8, finished May 9, 1984 (fielded 24⅓ innings) .

Most Consecutive Errorless Games, League

A. L.—72—Edwin A. Brinkman, Detroit, May 21 through August 4, 1972, 331 chances accepted.
N. L.—68—John J. Kerr, New York, July 28, second game, 1946 through May 24, 1947, 52 in 1946; 16 in 1947, 375 chances accepted.

Most Consecutive Errorless Games, Season

A. L.—72—Edwin A. Brinkman, Detroit, May 21 through August 4, 1972, 331 chances accepted.
N. L.—59—Roger H. Metzger, Houston, June 8 through August 14, 1976, 269 chances accepted.

Most Consecutive Chances Accepted, League, No Errors

N. L.—383—John J. Kerr, New York, July 28, first game (part) , 1946 through May 25, 1947 (part) ; 286 in 1946; 97 in 1947; 70 games.
A. L.—331—Edwin A. Brinkman, Detroit, May 21 through August 4, 1972, 72 games.

Most Consecutive Chances Accepted, Season, No Errors

A. L.—331—Edwin A. Brinkman, Detroit, May 21 through August 4, 1972, 72 games.
N. L.—286—John J. Kerr, New York, July 28, first game (part) , through September 29, 1946, 53 games.

Most Errors, Inning

N. L.—4—William Fuller, Washington, August 17, 1888, second inning.
    Leonard R. Merullo, Chicago, September 13, 1942, second game, second inning.
A. L.—4—Raymond J. Chapman, Cleveland, June 20, 1914, fifth inning.

Double Plays

Most Double Plays, League

A. L.—1553—Luis E. Aparicio, Chicago, Baltimore, Boston, 18 years, 1956 through 1973.
N. L.—1304—Roy D. McMillan, Cincinnati, Milwaukee, New York, 16 years, 1951 through 1966.

Most Double Plays, Season

A. L.—147—Richard P. Burleson, Boston, 155 games, 1980.
N. L.—137—Robert P. Wine, Montreal, 159 games, 1970.

Most Years Leading League in Double Plays

A. L.—6—George F. McBride, Washington, 1908, 1909, 1910, 1911, 1912 (tied) , 1914.
N. L.—5—Michael J. Doolan, Philadelphia, 1907, 1909 (tied) , 1910, 1911, 1913.
    Richard M. Groat, Pittsburgh, St. Louis, 1958, 1959, 1961, 1962, 1964.

Fewest Double Plays, Season, 150 or More Games

A. L.— 60— Joaquin F. Gutierrez, Boston, 150 games, 1984.
N. L.— 64— William E. Russell, Los Angeles, 150 games, 1982.
Ivan DeJesus, Philadelphia, 158 games, 1983.
David I. Concepcion, Cincinnati, 151 games 1985.

Fewest Double Plays, Season, for Leader in Most Double Plays

A. L.— 81— Roger Peckinpaugh, Washington, 155 games, 1924.
N. L.— 81— John J. Kerr, New York, 148 games, 1945.

Most Double Plays, Nine-Inning Game

A. L.—5—29 times. Held by 25 shortstops. Last shortstop—Nelson A. Norman, Texas, April 23, 1979.
N. L.—5—18 times. Held by 18 shortstops. Last shortstop—David E. Concepcion, Cincinnati, June 25, 1975.

Most Double Plays, Extra-Inning Game

A. L.—6—Dagoberto B. Campaneris, Oakland, September 13, 1970, first game, 11 innings.
N. L.—6—Osborne E. Smith, San Diego, August 25, 1979, 19 innings.
Rafael E. Ramirez, Atlanta, June 27, 1982, 14 innings.

Most Double Plays Started, Game

A. L.—5—Charles T. O'Leary, Detroit, July 23, 1905.
John P. Sullivan, Washington, August 13, 1944, second game.
James L. Fregosi, California, May 1, 1966, first game.
N. L.—4—William L. Kopf, Boston, April 28, 1922.
James E. Cooney, Chicago, June 13, 1926.
William H. Myers, Cincinnati, June 4, 1939.
Alvin R. Dark, New York, July 21, 1955.
Donald E. Kessinger, July 21, 1971.

Most Unassisted Double Plays, Game

A. L.—2—Lee Ford Tannehill, Chicago, August 4, 1911, first game.
N. L.—1—Held by many shortstops.

Outfielders
Years, Games & Innings

Most Years, League

A. L.—24—Tyrus R. Cobb, Detroit, Philadelphia, 1905 through 1928, 2938 games.
N. L.—22—Willie H. Mays, original New York club, San Francisco, present New York club, 1951 through 1973 (except 1953 in military service), 2843 games.

Most Games, League

A. L.—2938—Tyrus R. Cobb, Detroit, Philadelphia, 1905 through 1928, 24 years.
N. L.—2843—Willie H. Mays, original New York club, San Francisco, present New York club, 1951 through 1973, 22 years, (except 1953 in military service).

Most Consecutive Games Played, League

N. L.—897—Billy L. Williams, Chicago, September 22, 1963 through June 13, 1969.
A. L.—511—J. Clyde Milan, Washington, August 12, 1910, through October 3, 1913, second game.

Most Games, Season

A. L. (162-game season)—163—Leon L. Wagner, Cleveland, 1964.
A. L. (154-game season)—162—James E. Barrett, Detroit, 1904.
N. L. (162-game season)—164—Billy L. Williams, Chicago, 1965.
N. L. (154-game season)—160—Thomas H. Griffith, Cincinnati, 1915.

Most Years Leading League in Most Games

N. L.—6—George J. Burns, New York, Cincinnati, 1914 (tied), 1916 (tied), 1919, 1920 (tied), 1922, 1923 (tied).
Billy L. Williams, Chicago, 1964 (tied), 1965, 1966, 1967, 1968, 1970 (tied).
A. L.—5—Rocco D. Colavito, Cleveland, Detroit, 1959, 1961, 1962, 1963, 1965.

Fewest Games, Season, for Leader in Most Games

A. L.— 147—Theodore S. Williams, Boston, 1951.
N. L.— 149— Max Carey, Pittsburgh, 1924.
Chester J. Ross, Boston, 1940.

Most Innings Played, Game

N. L.—26—Walton E. Cruise, Boston, May 1, 1920.
Leslie Mann, Boston, May 1, 1920.
Bernard E. Neis, Brooklyn, May 1, 1920.

Raymond R. Powell, Boston, May 1, 1920.
Zachariah D. Wheat, Brooklyn, May 1, 1920.
A. L.— 25— Harold D. Baines, Chicago, May 8, finished May 9, 1984.
Rudy K. Law, Chicago, May 8, finished May 9, 1984.
Benjamin A. Oglivie, Milwaukee, May 8, finished May 9, 1984 (fielded 24 1/3 innings).

Average

Highest Fielding Average, League, 1000 or More Games

N. L.—.9931—Terrance S. Puhl, Houston, 11 years, 1977 through 1987, 1,110 games.
A. L.—.9910—Amos J. Otis, Kansas City, 14 years, 1970 through 1983, 1,845 games.

Highest Fielding Average, Season, 100 or More Games

N. L.— 1.000—Daniel W. Litwhiler, Philadelphia, 151 games, 1942.
Willard W. Marshall, Boston, 136 games, 1951.
A. Antonio Gonzalez, Philadelphia, 114 games, 1962.
Donald L. Demeter, Philadelphia, 119 games, 1963.
Curtis C. Flood, St. Louis, 159 games, 1966.
John W. Callison, Philadelphia, 109 games, 1968.
Terry S. Puhl, Houston, 152 games, 1979.
Gary L. Woods, Chicago, 103 games, 1982.
A. L.— 1.000—Rocco D. Colavito, Cleveland, 162 games, 1965.
Russell H. Snyder, Baltimore, 106 games, 1965.
Kenneth S. Harrelson, Boston, 132 games, 1968.
Mitchell J. Stanley, Detroit, 130 games, 1968.
A. Kent Berry, Chicago, 120 games, 1969.
Mitchell J. Stanley, Detroit, 132 games, 1970.
Roy H. White, New York, 145 games, 1971.
Albert W. Kaline, Detroit, 129 games, 1971.
A. Kent Berry, California, 116 games, 1972.
Carl M. Yastrzemski, Boston, 140 games, 1977.
William A. Sample, Texas, 103 games, 1979.
Gary S. Roenicke, Baltimore, 113 games, 1980.
Robert C. Clark, California, 102 games, 1982.
Brian J. Downing, California, 158 games, 1982.
John L. Lowenstein, Baltimore, 112 games, 1982.
Brian J. Downing, California, 131 games, 1984.

Highest Fielding Average, Season, 150 or More Games

N. L.— 1.000—Daniel W. Litwhiler, Philadelphia, 151 games, 1942.
Curtis C. Flood, St. Louis, 159 games, 1966.
Terry S. Puhl, Houston, 152 games, 1979.
A. L.— 1.000—Rocco D. Colavito, Cleveland, 162 games, 1965.
Brian J. Downing, California, 158 games, 1982.

Most Years Leading in Fielding, 100 or More Games
(162-Game Season, 108 or More Games)

A. L.—5—Amos E. Strunk, Philadelphia, Boston, Chicago, 1912, 1914, 1917, (tied), 1918, 1920.
N. L.—4—Joseph Hornung, Boston, 1881, 1882, 1883, 1887.
Walter S. Brodie, Boston, Pittsburgh, Baltimore, 1890, 1891, 1897, 1899.
N. L. since 1900—3—Stanley F. Musial, St. Louis, 1949, 1954, 1961.
A. Antonio Gonzalez, Philadelphia, 1962, 1964, 1967.
Peter E. Rose, Cincinnati, 1970, 1971 (tied), 1974.

Most Consec. Yrs. Leading League, Fielding, 100 or More Games

N. L.—3—Joseph Hornung, Boston, 1881, 1882, 1883.
A. L.—3—Eugene R. Woodling, New York, 1951 (tied), 1952, 1953 (tied).
N. L. since 1900—2—Held by many outfielders. Last outfielder—Peter E. Rose, Cincinnati, 1970, 1971 (tied).

Lowest Fielding Average, Season, for Leader, 100 or More Games

N. L.—.941—Patrick Gillespie, New York, 102 games, 1885.
A. L.—.959—Charles S. Stahl, Boston, 130 games, 1901.
N. L. since 1900—.968—John J. Murray, New York, 143 games, 1912.
Max Carey, Pittsburgh, 150 games, 1912.
Zachariah D. Wheat, Brooklyn, 120 games, 1912.

Lowest Fielding Average, Season, 100 or More Games

N. L.—.843—John Manning, Philadelphia, 103 games, 1884.
A. L.—.872—William J. O'Neill, Washington, 112 games, 1904.
N. L.—since 1900—.900—Michael J. Donlin, Cincinnati, 118 games, 1903.

Putouts

Most Putouts, League

N. L.— 7095— Willie H. Mays, original New York club, San Francisco, present New York club, 22 years, 1951 through 1973 (except 1953 in military service).

A. L.— 6794— Tristram Speaker, Boston, Cleveland, Washington, Philadelphia, 1907-1928, 22 years.

Most Putouts, Season

N. L.— 547— Taylor L. Douthit, St. Louis, 154 games, 1928.
A. L.— 512— Chester E. Lemon, Chicago, 149 games, 1977.

Most Years Leading League in Putouts

N. L.—9—Max Carey, Pittsburgh, 1912, 1913, 1916, 1917, 1918, 1921, 1922, 1923, 1924.
Richie Ashburn, Philadelphia, 1949, 1950, 1951, 1952, 1953, 1954, 1956, 1957, 1958.
A. L.—7—Tristram Speaker, Boston, Cleveland, 1909, 1910, 1913, 1914, 1915, 1918, 1919.

Fewest Putouts, Season, 150 or More Games

A. L.— 182— Edgar Hahn, Chicago, 156 games, 1907.
N. L.— 210— Samuel L. Thompson, Philadelphia, 151 games, 1892.
N. L. since 1900—221—Frank M. Schulte, Chicago, 150 games, 1910.

Fewest Putouts, Season, for Leader in Most Putouts

A. L.— 319— Tristram Speaker, Boston, 142 games, 1909.
N. L.— 321— Roy Thomas, Philadelphia, 139 games, 1904.

Most Years With 500 or More Putouts

N. L.—4—Richie Ashburn, Philadelphia, 1949, 1951, 1956, 1957.
A. L.—1—Dominic P. DiMaggio, Boston, 1948.
Chester E. Lemon, Chicago, 1977.
Dwayne K. Murphy, Oakland, 1980.

Most Years With 400 or More Putouts

N. L.—9—Richie Ashburn, Philadelphia, 1949, 1950, 1951, 1952, 1953, 1954, 1956, 1957, 1958.
A. L.—5—Chester E. Lemon, Chicago, Detroit, 1977, 1979, 1983, 1984, 1985.

Most Putouts, Game, Nine Innings, Center Field

N. L.— 12— Earl B. Clark, Boston, May 10, 1929.
A. L.— 12— Lyman W. Bostock, Minnesota, May 25, 1977, second game.

Most Putouts, Extra-Inning Game, Center Field

A. L.— 12— Harry D. Bay, Cleveland, July 19, 1904, 12 innings.
Ruppert S. Jones, Seattle, May 16, 1978, 16 innings.
Richard E. Manning, Milwaukee, July 11, 1983, 15 innings.
Gary G. Pettis, California, June 4, 1985, 15 innings.
Oddibe McDowell, Texas, July 20, 1985, 15 innings.
N. L.— 12— Carden E. Gillenwater, Boston, September 11, 1946, 17 innings.
Lloyd Merriman, Cincinnati, September 7, 1951, 18 innings.
Garry L. Maddox, Philadelphia, June 10, 1984, 12 innings.

Most Putouts, Game, Nine Innings, Left Field

N. L.— 11— Richard J. Harley, St. Louis, June 30, 1898.
T. Frederick Hartsel, Chicago, September 10, 1901.
A. L.— 11— Paul E. Lehner, Philadelphia, June 25, 1950, second game.
Willie Horton, Detroit, July 18, 1969.

Most Putouts, Extra-Inning Game, Left Field

A. L.— 12— Thomas McBride, Washington, July 2, 1948, 12 innings.
N. L.—Less than nine-inning game.

Most Putouts, Game, Right Field

A. L.— 11— Antonio R. Armas, Oakland, June 12, 1982.
N. L.— 10— William B. Nicholson, Chicago, September 17, 1945.

Most Putouts, Doubleheader, Center Field, 18 Innings

N. L.— 18— Lloyd J. Waner, Pittsburgh, June 26, 1935.
A. L.— 17— Lyman W. Bostock, Minnesota, May 25, 1977.

Most Consecutive Putouts, Game

A. L.—7—W. Benjamin Chapman, Boston, June 25, 1937, right field.
N. L.—6—Edd J. Roush, Cincinnati, July 4, 1919, a.m. game, center field.

Assists

Most Assists, League

A. L.— 450— Tristram Speaker, Boston, Cleveland, Washington, Philadelphia, 1907 through 1928, 22 years.
N. L.— 356— James E. Ryan, Chicago, 1885 through 1900 except 1890; 15 years.
N. L. since 1900—339— Max Carey, Pittsburgh, Brooklyn, 1910 through 1929; 20 years.

Most Assists, Season

N. L.— 45— A. Harding Richardson, Buffalo, 78 games, 1881.
N. L. since 1900—44—Charles H. Klein, Philadelphia, 156 games, 1930.
A. L.— 35— Samuel Mertes, Chicago, 123 games, 1902.
Tristram Speaker, Boston, 142 games, 1909, also 153 games, 1912.

Most Years Leading League in Assists

A. L.—7—Carl M. Yastrzemski, Boston, 1962, 1963, 1964 (tied), 1966, 1969, 1971, 1977.
N. L.—5—Roberto W. Clemente, Pittsburgh, 1958, 1960, 1961, 1966, 1967.

Fewest Assists, Season, 150 or More Games

A. L.—1—Harmon C. Killebrew, Minnesota, 157 games, 1964.
N. L.—3—Billy L. Williams, Chicago, 162 games, 1967.
Louis C. Brock, St. Louis, 159 games, 1973.

Fewest Assists, Season, for Leader in Most Assists

A. L.— 13— A. Kent Berry, California, 116 games, 1972.
Carlos May, Chicago, 145 games, 1972.
N. L.— 14— William H. Bruton, Milwaukee, 141 games, 1954.
Donald F. Mueller, New York, 153 games, 1954.
Frank J. Thomas, Pittsburgh, 153 games, 1954.

Most Assists, Game, Nine Innings

N. L.—4—Harry C. Schafer, Boston, September 26, 1877.
William W. Crowley, Buffalo, May 24, 1880.
William W. Crowley, Buffalo, August 27, 1880.
Frederick C. Clarke, Pittsburgh, August 23, 1910.
Walter A. Berger, Boston, April 27, 1931.
A. L.—4—William J. Holmes, Chicago, August 21, 1903.
Lee C. Magee, New York, June 28, 1916.
Oscar C. Felsch, Chicago, August 14, 1919.
Robert W. Meusel, New York, September 5, 1921, second game.
Elton Langford, Cleveland, May 1, 1928.

Most Assists, Extra-Inning Game

N. L.—4—Charles B. Miller, May 30, 1895, second game, 11 innings.
A. L.—3—Held by many outfielders.

Most Assists, Game, Outfielder to Catcher

N. L.—3—William E. Hoy, Washington, June 19, 1899.
James T. Jones, New York, June 30, 1902.
John McCarthy, Chicago, April 26, 1905.
A. L.—2—Held by many outfielders.

Most Assists, Inning

A. L.-N. L.—2—Held by many outfielders.

Chances Accepted & Offered

Most Chances Accepted, League

N. L.— 7290— Willie H. Mays, original New York club, San Francisco, present New York club, 22 years, 1951 through 1973 (except 1953 in military service).
A. L.— 7244— Tristram Speaker, Boston, Cleveland, Washington, Philadelphia, 22 years, 1907 through 1928.

Most Chances Accepted, Season

N. L.— 557— Taylor L. Douthit, St. Louis, 154 games, 1928.
A. L.— 524— Chester E. Lemon, Chicago, 149 games, 1977.

Most Years Leading League in Chances Accepted

N. L.—9—Max Carey, Pittsburgh, 1912, 1913, 1916, 1917, 1918, 1921, 1922, 1923, 1924.
Richie Ashburn, Philadelphia, 1949, 1950, 1951, 1952, 1953, 1954, 1956, 1957, 1958.
A. L.—8—Tristram Speaker, Boston, Cleveland, 1909, 1910, 1912, 1913, 1914, 1915, 1918, 1919.

Fewest Chances Accepted, Season, 150 or More Games

A. L.— 206— Edgar Hahn, Chicago, 156 games, 1907.
N. L.— 235— Johnnie B. Baker, Los Angeles, 152 games, 1977.

Fewest Chances Accepted, Season, for Leader

A. L.— 333— Samuel Crawford, Detroit, 144 games, 1907.
N. L.— 342— Roy Thomas, Philadelphia, 139 games, 1904.

Most Chances Accepted, Game, Nine Innings, Center Field

N. L.— 13— Earl B. Clark, Boston, May 10, 1929.
A. L.— 12— Oscar C. Felsch, Chicago, June 23, 1919.
John A. Mostil, Chicago, May 22, 1928.
Lyman W. Bostock, Minnesota, May 25, 1977, second game.

Most Chances Accepted, Extra-Inning Game, Center Field

A. L.— 12— Harry D. Bay, Cleveland, July 19, 1904, 12 innings.
Ruppert S. Jones, Seattle, May 16, 1978, 16 innings.
Richard E. Manning, Milwaukee, July 11, 1983, 15 innings.
Gary G. Pettis, California, June 4, 1985, 15 innings.
Oddibe McDowell, Texas, July 20, 1985, 15 innings.
N. L.— 12— Carden E. Gillenwater, Boston, September 11, 1946, 17 innings.
Lloyd Merriman, Cincinnati, September 7, 1951, 18 innings.
Garry L. Maddox, Philadelphia, June 10, 1984, 12 innings.

Most Chances Accepted, Game, Nine Innings, Left Field

N. L.— 11— Joseph Hornung, Boston, September 23, 1881.
Richard J. Harley, St. Louis, June 30, 1898.
T. Frederick Hartsel, Chicago, September 10, 1901.
A. L.— 11— Paul E. Lehner, Philadelphia, June 25, 1950, second game.
Willie Horton, Detroit July 18, 1969.

Most Chances Accepted, Extra-Inning Game, Left Field

A. L.— 12— Thomas McBride, Washington, July 2, 1948, 12 innings.
N. L.—Less than nine-inning game.

Most Chances Accepted, Game, Nine Innings, Right Field

A. L.— 12— Antonio R. Armas, Oakland, June 12, 1982.
N. L.— 11— Harry C. Schafer, Boston, September 26, 1877.
N. L. since 1900— 10—Alfred E. Neale, Cincinnati, July 13, 1920.
Charles D. Stengel, Philadelphia, July 30, 1920.
William B. Nicholson, Chicago, September 17, 1945.
Arnold R. McBride, Philadelphia, September 8, 1978, second game.

Most Chances Accepted, Doubleheader, Center Field

N. L.— 18— Lloyd J. Waner, Pittsburgh, June 26, 1935.
A. L.— 17— Lyman W. Bostock, Minnesota, May 25, 1977.

Most Chances Accepted, Two Consec. Games, Center Field

A. L.— 21— Oscar C. Felsch, Chicago, June 23, 24, 1919.
N. L.— 20— Earl B. Clark, Boston, May 10, 11, 1929.

Longest Game With No Chances Offered

A. L.—22 innings— William H. Bruton, Detroit, June 24, 1962.
Charles A. Peterson, Washington, June 12, 1967.
N. L.—18 innings— Lance Richbourg, Boston, May 14, 1927.
Arthur L. Shamsky, Cincinnati, July 19, 1966.

Longest Season Opening Game With No Chances Offered

A. L.—14 innings—Charles J. Hemphill, New York, April 14, 1910.
Arthur C. Engle, New York, April 14, 1910.
N. L.—13 innings—Charles L. Herzog, New York, April 15, 1909.
William O'Hara, New York, April 15, 1909.

Longest Game With No Chances Offered, Center Field

A. L.—22 innings— William H. Bruton, Detroit, June 24, 1962.
N. L.—17 ⅓ innings—Earnest R. Orsatti, St. Louis, July 2, 1933, first game.

Longest Game With No Chances Offered, Left Field

N. L.—16 innings—Joseph Delahanty, St. Louis, July 19, 1908.
A. L.—16 innings—Robert L. Johnson, Philadelphia, June 5, 1942.
Patrick J. Mullin, Detroit, May 9, 1952.

Longest Game With No Chances Offered, Right Field

A. L.—22 innings—Charles A. Peterson, Washington, June 12, 1967.
N. L.—18 innings—Lance Richbourg, Boston, May 14, 1927.
Arthur L. Shamsky, Cincinnati, July 19, 1966.

Longest Doubleheader With No Chances Offered

A. L.—24 innings— Roger E. Maris, New York, August 6, 1961.
N. L.—21 innings— Dain E. Clay, Cincinnati, September 21, 1944.

Most Consecutive Games With No Chances Offered

A. L.—7—William C. Jacobson, Boston, June 18, 19, 20, 21, 24, 25, 25, 1926, 64 ⅓ innings, right field.
N. L.—6—Frank M. Schulte, Chicago, June 25, 25, 26, 27, 28, 29, 1912, right field.

Errors

Most Errors, Major Leagues

384—William E. Hoy, Washington N. L., Buffalo P. L., St. Louis, A.A., Cincinnati N. L., Louisville N. L., Chicago A. L., 14 years, 1888 through 1902, except 1900.

Most Errors, League

N. L.— 347— George F. Gore, Chicago, New York, St. Louis, 13 years, 1879 through 1892, except 1890.
A. L.— 271— Tyrus R. Cobb, Detroit, Philadelphia, 24 years, 1905 through 1928.
N. L. since 1900—235—Max Carey, Pittsburgh, Brooklyn, 20 years, 1910 through 1929.

Most Errors, Season

P. L.— 52— Edward Beecher, Buffalo, 125 games, 1890.
N. L.— 47— George H. Van Haltren, Baltimore, Pittsburgh, 143 games, 1892.
N. L. since 1900—36—J. Bentley Seymour, Cincinnati, 135 games, 1903.
A. L.— 31— Roy C. Johnson, Detroit, 146 games, 1929.

Most Years Leading League in Errors

N. L.—7—Louis C. Brock, Chicago, St. Louis, 1964, 1965, 1966, 1967, 1968 (tied), 1972, 1973 (tied).
A. L.—5—Burton E. Shotton, St. Louis, Washington, 1912 (tied), 1914, 1915 (tied), 1916, 1918.
Reginald M. Jackson, Oakland, Baltimore, 1968, 1970, 1972, 1975, 1976 (tied).

Fewest Errors, Season, 150 or More Games

N. L.—0—Daniel W. Litwhiler, Philadelphia, 151 games, 1942.
Curtis C. Flood, St. Louis, 159 games, 1966.
Terry S. Puhl, Houston, 152 games, 1979.
A. L.—0—Rocco D. Colavito, Cleveland, 162 games, 1965.
Brian J. Downing, California, 158 games, 1982.

Fewest Errors, Season, for Leader in Most Errors

A. L.—9—Roger E. Maris, Cleveland-Kansas City, 146 games, 1958.
Reginald M. Jackson, Oakland, 135 games, 1972.
N. L.—9—Vincent M. Coleman, St. Louis, 149 games, 1986.
Charles T. Davis, San Francisco, 148 games, 1986.
Gary N. Matthews, Chicago, 105 games, 1986.
David A. Parker, Cincinnati, 159 games, 1986.
Robert J. Reynolds, Pittsburgh, 112 games, 1986.

Most Errors, Game, Nine Innings

N. L.—5—John E. Manning, Boston, May 1, 1876.
Charles N. Snyder, Louisville, July 29, 1876.
James H. O'Rourke, Boston, June 21, 1877.
Charles W. Bennett, Milwaukee, June 15, 1878.
Michael J. Dorgan, New York, May 24, 1884.
Michael J. Tiernan, New York, May 16, 1887.
Martin C. Sullivan, Chicago, May 18, 1887.
A. A.—5—James S. Clinton, Baltimore, May 3, 1884.
U. A.—5—Frederick C. Tenney, Washington, May 29, 1884.
A. L.—5—Albert C. Selbach, Baltimore, August 19, 1902.
N. L. since 1900—4—Fred Nicholson, Boston, June 16, 1922.

Longest Errorless Game

N. L.—26 innings—Walton E. Cruise, Boston, May 1, 1920.
Leslie Mann, Boston, May 1, 1920.
Bernard E. Neis, Brooklyn, May 1, 1920.
Raymond R. Powell, Boston, May 1, 1920.
Zachariah D. Wheat, Brooklyn, May 1, 1920.
A. L.—25 innings—Harold D. Baines, Chicago, May 8, finished May 9, 1984.
Rudy K. Law, Chicago, May 8, finished May 9, 1984.
Benjamin A. Oglivie, Milwaukee, May 8, finished May 9, 1984 (fielded 24 ⅓ innings).

Most Consecutive Errorless Games, Season

A. L.— 162— Rocco D. Colavito, Cleveland, April 13 through October 3, 1965 (274 chances accepted).
N. L.— 159— Curtis C. Flood, St. Louis, April 13 through October 2, 1966 (396 chances accepted).

Most Consecutive Errorless Games, Major Leagues

266—Donald L. Demeter, Philadelphia, N. L., Detroit A. L., September 3, 1962, first game, through July 6, 1965 (449 chances accepted).

Most Consecutive Errorless Games, League

A. L.— 244— Brian J. Downing, California, May 25, 1981 through July 21, second game 1983 (471 chances accepted).
N. L.— 226— Curtis C. Flood, St. Louis, September 3, 1965 through June 2, 1967 (566 chances accepted) also first two chances on June 4, for total of 568.

Most Consecutive Chances Accepted, League, No Errors

N. L.— 568— Curtis C. Flood, St. Louis, September 3, 1965 through June 4 (part) 1967, 227 games.

A. L.— 510— A. Kent Berry, California, September 16, 1971 through July 27, 1973, 211 games.

Most Errors, Inning

N. L.—3—George Gore, Chicago, August 8, 1883, first inning.
Larry D. Herndon, San Francisco, September 6, 1980, fourth inning.

A. A.—3—James A. Donahue, Kansas City, July 4, 1889, p.m. game, first inning.

A. L.—3—Albert C. Selbach, Washington, June 23, 1904, eighth inning.
Harry D. Bay, Cleveland, June 29, 1905, second game, ninth inning.
Harry E. Heilmann, Detroit, May 22, 1914, first inning.
Herschel E. Bennett, St. Louis, April 14, 1925, eighth inning.

Double Plays

Most Double Plays, League

A. L.— 135— Tristram Speaker, Boston, Cleveland, Washington, Philadelphia, 22 years, 1907 through 1928.

N. L.— 86— Max Carey, Pittsburgh, Brooklyn, 20 years, 1910 through 1929.

Most Unassisted Double Plays, Major Leagues

4—Tristram Speaker, Boston A. L., Cleveland A. L., 1909 (1), 1914 (1), 1918 (2).
Elmer J. Smith, Cleveland A. L., New York A. L., Cincinnati N. L., 1915 (1), 1920 (1), 1923 (1), 1925 (1); (3 in A. L., 1 in N. L.)

Most Unassisted Double Plays, League

A. L.—4—Tristram Speaker, Boston, Cleveland, 1 in 1909, 1 in 1914, 2 in 1918.

N. L.—2—Held by many outfielders.

Most Double Plays, Season

A. L.— 15— Oscar C. Felsch, Chicago, 125 games, 1919.

N. L.— 12— Melvin T. Ott, New York, 149 games, 1929.

Most Unassisted Double Plays, Season

A. L.—2—Ralph O. Seybold, Philadelphia, August 15, September 10, first game, 1907.
Tristram Speaker, Cleveland, April 18, April 29, 1918.
Jose D. Cardenal, Cleveland, June 8, July 16, 1968.

N. L.—2—Adam Comorosky, Pittsburgh, May 31, June 13, 1931.

Most Years Leading League in Double Plays

A. L.—5—Tristram Speaker, Boston, Cleveland, 1909, 1912, 1914, 1915, 1916.

N. L.—4—Willie H. Mays, New York, San Francisco, 1954, 1955, 1956, 1965.

Fewest Double Plays, Season, 150 or More Games

N. L.-A. L.—0—Held by many outfielders.

N. L.—Last outfielders—Andre F. Dawson, Chicago, 152 games, 1987; W. Kevin McReynolds, New York, 150 games, 1987; Mitchell D. Webster, Montreal, 153 games, 1987.

A. L.—Last outfielder—James E. Rice, Boston, 156 games, 1986.

Fewest Double Plays, Season, for Leader in Most Double Plays

N. L.—4—Held by 10 players. Last outfielders—Dale B. Murphy, Atlanta, 161 games, 1985; Timothy Raines, Montreal, 146 games, 1985; Andrew J. Van Slyke, St. Louis, 142 games 1985; Glenn D. Wilson, Philadelphia, 158 games, 1985.

A. L.—4—Held by 19 players. Last outfielders—Antonio R. Armas, Oakland 112 games, 1977; Roy H. White, New York, 135 games, 1977.

Most Double Plays Started, Game

A. A.—3—John Nelson, New York, June 9, 1887.

N. L.—3—John McCarthy, Chicago, April 26, 1905.

A. L.—3—Ira Flagstead, Boston, April 19, 1926, p.m. game.

Most Unassisted Double Plays, Game

N. L.-A. L.—1—Held by many outfielders.

N. L.—Last outfielder—Bobby L. Bonds, San Francisco, May 31, 1972, fourth inning.

A. L.—Last outfielder—William A. North, Oakland, July 28, 1974, second game, fifth inning.

Most Triple Plays Started, Season

A. L.—2—Charles D. Jamieson, Cleveland, May 23, June 9, 1928.

N. L.—1—Held by many outfielders.

Catchers
Years, Games & Innings

Most Years in Majors

25—James T. McGuire, Toledo, Cleveland, Rochester, Washington A. A.; Detroit, Philadelphia, Washington, Brooklyn N. L.; Detroit, New York, Boston, Cleveland A. L., 1884 through 1912, except 1889, 1908, 1909, 1911 4 (part) in A. A.; 14 (part) in N. L.; (9 in A. L.) 1,608 games.

Most Years, League

N. L.— 21— Robert A. O'Farrell, Chicago, St. Louis, New York, Cincinnati, 1915 through 1935, 1,338 games.

A. L.— 20— J. Luther Sewell, Cleveland, Washington, Chicago, St. Louis, 1921 through 1942 except 1940, 1941.

Most Games in Majors

1,935—Robert R. Boone, Philadelphia N. L., California A. L., 1972 through 1987, 16 years; 1,095 in N. L., 840 in A. L.

Most Games, League

N. L.— 1,861— Alfonso R. Lopez, Brooklyn, Boston, Pittsburgh, 1928 through 1946, except 1929, 18 years.

A. L.— 1,806— Richard B. Ferrell, St. Louis, Boston, Washington, 1929 through 1947, except 1946, 18 years.

Most Consecutive Games, League

A. L.— 312— Frank W. Hayes, St. Louis, Philadelphia, Cleveland, October 2, second game, 1943 through April 21, 1946.

N. L.— 233— Ray C. Mueller, Cincinnati, July 31, 1943, through May 5, 1946 (spent entire 1945 season in military service).

Most Games, Season

N. L. (162-game season)—160—C. Randolph Hundley, Chicago, 1968 (147 complete).

A. L. (162-game season)—155—James H. Sundberg, Texas, 1975.

A. L. (154-game season)—155—Frank W. Hayes, Philadelphia, 1944 (135 complete).

N. L. (154-game season)—155—Ray C. Mueller, Cincinnati, 1944 (135 complete).

Most Games, Season, Lefthanded Catcher

N. L.— 105— John T. Clements, Philadelphia, 1891.

A. L.— 23— John A. Donahue, St. Louis, 1902.

Catching All Club's Games, Season (Not Complete)

N. L.— 155— Ray C. Mueller, Cincinnati, 1944 (135 complete).

A. L.— 155— Frank W. Hayes, Philadelphia, 1944 (135 complete), (Hayes also caught the full schedule in 1945, when he played for two clubs—151 games, 32 with Philadelphia, 119 with Cleveland).

150— Michael Tresh, Chicago, 1945 (125 complete).

Most Consecutive Games, Season

A. L.— 155— Frank W. Hayes, Philadelphia, April 18 through October 1, second game, 1944 (135 complete).

N. L.— 155— Ray C. Mueller, Cincinnati, April 18 through October 1, 1944 (135 complete).

Most Games, Rookie Season

N. L.— 154— Johnny L. Bench, Cincinnati, 1968.

A. L.— 150— Robert L. Rodgers, Los Angeles, 1962.

Most Years Leading League in Games

A. L.—8—Lawrence P. Berra, New York, 1950, 1951, 1952, 1953, 1954, 1955, 1956, 1957.

N. L.—6—Gary E. Carter, Montreal, 1977, 1978, 1979, 1980, 1981, 1982.

Most Years With 100 or More Games, League

Both leagues—13—Robert R. Boone, Philadelphia N. L., 1973, 1974, 1976 through 1980; California A. L., 1982 through 1987.

A. L.— 13— William M. Dickey, New York, 1929 through 1941.

N. L.— 13— Johnny L. Bench, Cincinnati, 1968 through 1980.

Most Consecutive Years With 100 or More Games, League

A. L.— 13— William M. Dickey, New York, 1929 through 1941.

N. L.— 13— Johnny L. Bench, Cincinnati, 1968 through 1980.

Fewest Games, Season, for Leader in Most Games

N. L.— 96—Ernest N. Lombardi, New York, 1945.
A. L.— 98—Jacob W. Early, Washington, 1942.

Most Innings Caught, Game

A. L.—25— Carlton E. Fisk, Chicago, May 8, finished May 9, 1984.
N. L.—24— Harold King, Houston, April 15, 1968.
Gerald W. Grote, New York, April 15, 1968, (caught 23 ⅓ innings).

Most Innings Caught, Doubleheader

A. L.—29— Ossee F. Schreckengost, Philadelphia, July 4, 1905.
N. L.—27— William C. Fischer, Chicago, June 28, 1916.
August R. Mancuso, New York, July 2, 1933.

Average

Highest Fielding Average, League, 1,000 or More Games

A. L.—.9933—William A. Freehan, Detroit, 15 years, 1961, 1963 through 1976, 1,483 games.
N. L.— .992—John A. Edwards, Cincinnati, St. Louis, Houston, 14 years, 1961 through 1974, 1,392 games.

Highest Fielding Average, Season, 100 or More Games

A. L.—1.000—Warren V. Rosar, Philadelphia, 117 games, 1946.
N. L.— .999—Wesley N. Westrum, New York, 139 games, 1950.

Highest Fielding Average, Season, 150 or More Games

N. L.—.996—C. Randolph Hundley, Chicago, 152 games, 1967.
A. L.—.995—James H. Sundberg, Texas, 150 games, 1979.

Most Years Leading League in Fielding, 100 or More Games

A. L.—8—Raymond W. Schalk, Chicago, 1913, 1914, 1915, 1916, 1917, 1920, 1921, 1922.
N. L.—7—Charles L. Hartnett, Chicago, 1925, 1928, 1930, 1934, 1935, 1936, 1937.

Most Consec. Years Leading in Fielding, 100 or More Games

A. L.—6—William A. Freehan, Detroit, 1965, 1966, 1967 (tied), 1968, 1969 (tied), 1970.
N. L.—4—John G. Kling, Chicago, 1902 through 1905.
Charles L. Hartnett, Chicago, 1934 through 1937.

Lowest Average, Season, for Leader, 100+ Games, Since 1900

A. L.—.954—Maurice R. Powers, Philadelphia, 111 games, 1901.
N. L.—.958—Charles L. Hartnett, Chicago, 110 games, 1925.

Lowest Fielding Average, Season, 100 or More Games

A. L.—.934—Samuel Agnew, St. Louis, 102 games, 1915.
N. L. since 1900—.947—Charles S. Dooin, Philadelphia, 140 games, 1909.

Putouts

Most Putouts, League

A. L.— 9941— William A. Freehan, Detroit, 15 years, 1961, 1963 through 1976.
N. L.— 9563— Gary E. Carter, Montreal, New York, 14 years, 1974 through 1987.

Most Putouts, Season

N. L. (162-game season) —1135—John A. Edwards, Houston, 151 games, 1969.
N. L. (154-game season) — 877—John Roseboro, Los Angeles, 125 games, 1961.
A. L. (162-game season) — 971—William A. Freehan, Detroit, 138 games, 1968.
A. L. (154-game season) — 785—Ossee F. Schreckengost, Philadelphia, 114 games, 1905.

Fewest Putouts, Season, 150 or More Games

N. L.— 471— Ray C. Mueller, Cincinnati, 155 games, 1944.
A. L.— 575— Michael Tresh, Chicago, 150 games, 1945.

Most Years Leading League in Putouts

A. L.—9—Raymond W. Schalk, Chicago, 1913, 1914, 1915, 1916, 1917, 1918, 1919, 1920, 1922.
N. L.—7—Gary E. Carter, Montreal, 1977, 1978, 1979, 1980, 1981, 1982, New York 1985.

Fewest Putouts, Season, for Leader in Most Putouts

N. L.— 409— Charles L. Hartnett, Chicago, 110 games, 1925.
A. L.— 446— George R. Tebbetts, Detroit, 97 games, 1942.

Most Putouts, Game, Nine Innings

N. L.— 20— Gerald W. Grote, New York April 22, 1970, 19 strikeouts.
A. L.— 20— Richard L. Gedman, Boston, April 29, 1986, 20 strikeouts.

Most Putouts, Extra-Inning Game

N. L.— 22— Robert B. Schmidt, San Francisco, June 22, 1958, first game, 14 innings, 19 strikeouts.
Thomas F. Haller, San Francisco, May 31, 1964, second game, 23 innings, 22 strikeouts.
Stephen W. Yeager, Los Angeles, August 8, 1972, 19 innings, 22 strikeouts.
A. L.— 21— Eliseo C. Rodriguez, California, June 14, 1974, 15 innings, 20 strikeouts.

Longest Game, No Putouts

A. L.— 14 innings— Walter H. Schang, Boston, September 13, 1920.
Eugene A. Desautels, Cleveland, August 11, 1942, first game.
N. L.— 13 innings— James Wilson, Philadelphia, August 31, 1927, first game.
Harold Finney, Pittsburgh, September 22, 1931.

Most Consecutive Putouts, Game

N. L.— 10— Gerald W. Grote, New York, April 22, 1970, 1 in sixth inning; 3 in seventh inning; 3 in eighth inning; 3 in ninth inning; 10 strikeouts.
A. L.— 8— Tony Mike Brumley, Washington, September 4, 1965, 3 in first inning; 3 in second inning; 2 in third inning; 8 strikeouts.
John H. Stephenson, California, July 9, 1972, 2 in first inning; 3 in second inning; 3 in third inning; 8 strikeouts.
Arthur W. Kusnyer, California, July 15, 1973, 1 in first inning; 3 in second inning; 3 in third inning; 1 in fourth inning.

Most Consecutive Putouts, Start of Game

N. L.— 9— Arthur E. Wilson, New York, May 30, 1911, a.m. game 4 strikeouts, 3 fouled out, 1 tagged out, 1 forced out.
John A. Bateman, Houston, July 14, 1968, second game, 9 strikeouts.
A. L.— 8— T. Mike Brumley, Washington, September 4, 1965, 8 strikeouts.

Most Putouts, Two Consecutive Games

A. L.— 36— Richard L. Gedman, Boston, April 29 (20), April 30 (16), 1986; 36 strikeouts.
N. L.— 31— Gerald W. Grote, New York, April 21 (11), April 22 (20), 1970; 29 strikeouts.

Most Putouts, Doubleheader, 18 Innings

N. L.— 25— John A. Bateman, Houston, September 10, 1968, 22 strikeouts.
A. L.— 25— Henry Severeid, St. Louis, July 13, 1920, 21 strikeouts.

Most Fouls Caught, Game

N. L.—6—Wesley N. Westrum, New York, August 24, 1949.
A. L.—6—J. Sherman Lollar, Chicago, April 10, 1962.

Most Fouls Caught, Inning

N. L.—3—Arnold M. Owen, Brooklyn, August 4, 1941, third inning.
Wesley N. Westrum, New York, August 24, 1949, ninth inning.
Wesley N. Westrum, New York, September 23, 1956, fifth inning.
A. L.—3—Matthew D. Batts, Detroit, August 2, 1953, second game, fourth inning.

Assists

Most Assists in Majors

1,835—James T. McGuire, Toledo, Cleveland, Rochester, Washington, A. A., Detroit, Philadelphia, Washington, Brooklyn, N. L., Detroit, New York, Boston, Cleveland, A. L., 1884 through 1912, except 1889, 1908, 1909, 1911; 25 years.

Most Assists, League

A. L.— 1,810—Raymond W. Schalk, Chicago, 1912 through 1928; 17 consecutive years.
N. L.— 1,593—Charles S. Dooin, Philadelphia, Cincinnati, New York, 1902 through 1916; 15 consecutive years.

Most Assists, Season

N. L.— 214— Patrick J. Moran, Boston, 107 games, 1903
A. L.— 212— Oscar H. Stanage, Detroit, 141 games, 1911.

Fewest Assists, Season, 150 or More Games

N. L.— 59— C. Randolph Hundley, Chicago, 152 games, 1967.
A. L.— 73— James E. Hegan, Cleveland, 152 games, 1949.
Robert L. Rodgers, Los Angeles, 150 games, 1962.

Most Years Leading League in Assists

N. L.—6—Charles L. Hartnett, Chicago, 1925, 1927, 1928 (tied), 1930, 1934, 1935.
Delmar W. Crandall, Milwaukee, 1953, 1954, 1957, 1958, 1959, 1960.
A. L.—6—James H. Sundberg, Texas, 1975, 1976, 1977, 1978, 1980, 1981.

Fewest Assists, Season, for Leader in Most Assists

N. L.—52—Philip S. Masi, Boston, 95 games, 1945.
A. L.—58—Terrence E. Kennedy, Baltimore, 142 games, 1987.

Most Assists, Game, Nine Innings

N. L.—9—Michael P. Hines, Boston, May 1, 1883.
A. L.—8—Walter H. Schang, Boston, May 12, 1920.
N. L. since 1900—7—Edward McFarland, Philadelphia, May 7, 1901.
William Bergen, Brooklyn, August 23, 1909, second game.
James P. Archer, Pittsburgh, May 24, 1918.
John B. Adams, Philadelphia, August 21, 1919.

Most Assists, Inning

A. A.—3—John A. Milligan, Philadelphia, July 26, 1887, third inning.
A. L.—3—Leslie G. Nunamaker, New York, August 3, 1914, second inning.
Raymond W. Schalk, Chicago, September 30, 1921, eighth inning.
William M. Dickey, New York, May 13, 1929, sixth inning.
James H. Sundberg, Texas, September 3, 1976, fifth inning.
N. L.—3—C. Bruce Edwards, Brooklyn, August 15, 1946, fourth inning.
James R. Campbell, Houston, June 16, 1963, second game, third inning.

Chances Accepted & Offered

Most Chances Accepted, League

A. L.—10,662—William A. Freehan, Detroit, 15 years, 1961, 1963 through 1976.
N. L.—10,553—Gary E. Carter, Montreal, New York, 14 years, 1974 through 1987.

Most Chances Accepted, Season

N. L. (162-game season)—1214—John A. Edwards, Houston, 151 games, 1969.
N. L. (154-game season)—933—John Roseboro, Los Angeles, 125 games, 1961.
A. L. (162-game season)—1044—William A. Freehan, Detroit, 138 games, 1968.
A. L. (154-game season)—924—Charles E. Street, Washington, 137 games, 1909.

Most Years Leading League in Chances Accepted

A. L.—8—Raymond W. Schalk, Chicago, 1913, 1914, 1915, 1916, 1917, 1919, 1920, 1922.
Lawrence P. Berra, New York, 1950, 1951, 1952, 1954, 1955, 1956, 1957, 1959.
N. L.—7—Gary E. Carter, Montreal, 1977, 1978, 1979, 1980, 1981, 1982, New York, 1985.

Fewest Chances Accepted, Season, 150 or More Games

N. L.—536—Ray C. Mueller, Cincinnati, 155 games, 1944.
A. L.—677—Michael Tresh, Chicago, 150 games, 1945.

Fewest Chances Accepted, Season by Leader

N. L.—474—Ernest N. Lombardi, New York, 96 games, 1945.
A. L.—515—George R. Tebbetts, Detroit, 97 games, 1942.

Most Chances Accepted, Game, Nine Innings

U. A.—23—George Bignall, Milwaukee, October 3, 1884, 18 strikeouts.
N. L.—22—Vincent Nava, Providence, June 7, 1884, 19 strikeouts.
N. L. since 1900—20—Gerald W. Grote, New York, April 22, 1970, 19 strikeouts.
A. L.—20—Eliseo C. Rodriguez, California, August 12, 1974, 19 strikeouts.
Richard L. Gedman, Boston, April 29, 1986, 20 strikeouts.

Most Chances Accepted, Extra-Inning Game

A. L.—26—Maurice R. Powers, Philadelphia, September 1, 1906, 24 innings, 18 strikeouts.
N. L.—24—Stephen W. Yeager, Los Angeles, August 8, 1972, 19 innings, 22 strikeouts.

Most Chances Accepted, Doubleheader, 18 Innings

A. L.—27—Henry Severeid, St. Louis, July 13, 1920, 21 strikeouts.
N. L.—26—John A. Bateman, Houston, September 10, 1968, 22 strikeouts.

Most Chances Accepted, Two Consec. 9-Inning Games

A. L.—37—Richard L. Gedman, Boston, April 29, 30, 1986, 36 strikeouts.
N. L.—31—Gerald W. Grote, New York, April 21, 22, 1970; 29 strikeouts.

Most Chances Accepted, Inning

N. L.—5—Joseph H. Garagiola, St. Louis, June 17, 1949, eighth inning, 3 putouts, 2 assists.
A. L.—4—Held by many catchers. Last catcher—F. Gene Tenace, Oakland, May 24, 1975, fifth inning, 3 putouts, 1 assist.

Longest Game With No Chances Offered

A. L.—14 innings—Eugene A. Desautels, Cleveland, August 11, 1942, first game.
N. L.—13 innings—James Wilson, Philadelphia, August 31, 1927, first game.

Longest Night Game With No Chances Offered

A. L.—11 innings—Alfred H. Evans, Washington, September 6, 1946.
N. L.—10 innings—Ernest N. Lombardi, New York, August 4, 1944.

Fewest Chances Offered, Doubleheader

N. L.—0—Harry H. McCurdy, St. Louis, July 10, 1923.
A. L.—2—Everett Yaryan, Chicago, May 26, 1921.
Henry Severeid, St. Louis, September 5, 1921.
J. Luther Sewell, Cleveland, August 28, 1926.

Fewest Chances Offered, Two Consecutive Games

A. L.—0—Ralph Perkins, Philadelphia, September 16, 17, 1922.
N. L.—0—Harry H. McCurdy, St. Louis, July 10, 1923.
Andrew W. Seminick, Cincinnati, September 15, 16, 1953.

Errors

Most Errors, League, Since 1900

N. L.—234—Ivy B. Wingo, St. Louis, Cincinnati 17 years, 1911 through 1929, except 1927, 1928.
A. L.—218—Walter H. Schang, Philadelphia, Boston, New York, St. Louis, Detroit, 19 years, 1913 through 1931.

Most Years Leading League in Errors

N. L.—7—Ivy B. Wingo, St. Louis, Cincinnati, 1912 (tied), 1913, 1916, 1917, 1918, 1920, 1921.
A. L.—6—George R. Tebbetts, Detroit, Boston, 1939, 1940 (tied), 1942 (tied), 1947, 1948, 1949.

Most Errors, Season

N. L.—94—Nathan W. Hicks, New York, 45 games, 1876.
N. L. since 1900—40—Charles S. Dooin, Philadelphia, 140 games, 1909.
A. A.—85—Edward Whiting, Baltimore, 72 games, 1882.
A. L.—41—Oscar H. Stanage, Detroit, 141 games, 1911.

Fewest Errors, Season, 150 or More Games

N. L.—4—C. Randolph Hundley, Chicago, 152 games, 1967.
A. L.—4—James H. Sundberg, Texas, 150 games, 1979.

Fewest Errors, Season, 100 or More Games

A. L.—0—Warren V. Rosar, Philadelphia, 117 games, 1946.
N. L.—1—R. Earl Grace, Pittsburgh, 114 games, 1932.

Fewest Errors, Season, for Leader in Most Errors

A. L.—7—Richard B. Ferrell, St. Louis, 137 games, 1933.
N. L.—9—Henry L. Foiles, Pittsburgh, 109 games, 1957.

Most Errors, Game, Nine Innings (All Fielding Errors)

N. L.—7—John C. Rowe, Buffalo, May 16, 1883.
Lowe, Detroit, June 26, 1884.
A. A.—7—William H. Taylor, Baltimore, May 29, 1886, a.m. game.
N. L. since 1900—4—Charles E. Street, Boston, June 7, 1905.
A. L.—4—John Peters, Cleveland, May 16, 1918.
William G. Styles, Philadelphia, July 29, 1921.
William H. Moore, Boston, September 26, 1927, second game.

Most Errors, Doubleheader

A. A.—8—James A. Donahue, Kansas City, August 31, 1889.
N. L.—8—Lewis Graulich, Philadelphia, September 19, 1891.
N. L. since 1900—4—Held by many catchers.
A. L.—4—Held by many catchers.

Most Errors, Inning

N. L.—4—George F. Miller, St. Louis, May 24, 1895, second inning.
A. L.—3—Edward Sweeney, New York, July 10, 1912, first inning.
John Peters, Cleveland, May 16, 1918, first inning.
N. L. since 1900—3—Jeffrey S. Reed, Montreal, July 28, 1987, seventh inning.

Longest Errorless Game

A. L.—24 innings— Maurice R. Powers, Philadelphia, September 1, 1906.
Warren V. Rosar, Philadelphia, July 21, 1945.
Robert V. Swift, Detroit, July 21, 1945.
N. L.—24 innings— Harold King, Houston, April 15, 1968.
Gerald W. Grote, New York, April 15, 1968 (caught 23 ⅓ innings) .

Most Consecutive Errorless Games, League

A. L.— 148— Lawrence P. Berra, New York, July 28, 1957, second game, through May 10, 1959, second game, 950 chances accepted.
N. L.— 138— John A. Edwards, Houston, July 11, 1970, through August 20, 1971, 805 chances accepted.

Most Consecutive Errorless Games, Season

A. L.— 117— Warren V. Rosar, Philadelphia, April 16 through September 29, 1946, first game, 605 chances accepted.
N. L.— 110— R. Earl Grace, Pittsburgh, April 12 through September 7, 1932, 400 chances accepted.

Most Consecutive Errorless Games, Start of Career

A. L.— 93— Frank A. Pytlak, Cleveland, April 22, 1932, through May 5, 1934.

Most Consecutive Chances Accepted, League, No Errors

A. L.— 950— Lawrence P. Berra, New York, 148 games, July 28, 1957, second game through May 10, 1959, second game.
N. L.— 805— John A. Edwards, Houston, July 11, 1970 through August 20, 1971, 805 chances accepted.

Most Consecutive Chances Accepted, Season, No Errors

A. L.— 605— Warren V. Rosar, Philadelphia, 117 games, April 16 through September 29, 1946, first game.
N. L.— 476— Arnold M. Owen, Brooklyn, 100 games, April 15 through August 29, 1941.

Passed Balls

Most Passed Balls, Season

N. L.—99—Charles N. Snyder, Boston, 58 games, 1881.
Michael P. Hines, Boston, 56 games, 1883.
N. L. since 1900—29—Frank Bowerman, New York 73, games, 1900.
A. L.—35—Eugene J. Petralli, Texas, 63 games, 1987.

Most Years Leading League in Passed Balls

N. L.— 10—Ernest N. Lombardi, Cincinnati, Boston, New York, 1932, 1935, 1936 (tied) , 1937, 1938, 1939, 1940 (tied) , 1941, 1942, 1945.
A. L.— 5—Richard B. Ferrell, St. Louis, Washington, 1931 (tied) , 1939, 1940, 1944, 1945.

Fewest Passed Balls, Season, 150 or More Games

N. L.—1—Gary E. Carter, Montreal, 152 games, 1978.
A. L.—4—James E. Hegan, Cleveland, 152 games, 1949.
Carlton E. Fisk, Boston, 151 games, 1977.

Fewest Passed Balls, Season, 100 or More Games

N. L.—0—Alfred C. Todd, Pittsburgh, 128 games, 1937.
Alfonso R. Lopez, Pittsburgh, 114 games, 1941.
Johnny L. Bench, Cincinnati, 121 games, 1975.
A. L.—0—William M. Dickey, New York, 125 games, 1931.

Fewest Passed Balls, Season, for Leader in Most Passed Balls

A. L.—6—Gordon S. Cochrane, Philadelphia, 117 games, 1931.
Charles F. Berry, Boston, 102 games, 1931.
Richard B. Ferrell, St. Louis, 108 games, 1931.
N. L.—7—Held by five catchers.

Most Passed Balls, Game

A. A.— 12—Frank Gardner, Washington, May 10, 1884.
N. L.— 10—Patrick E. Dealey, Boston, May 1886.
N. L. since 1900—6—Harry Vickers, Cincinnati, October 4, 1902.
A. L.—6—Eugene J. Petralli, Texas, August 30, 1987.

Most Passed Balls, Two Consecutive Games

N. L.— 13— Peter J. Hotaling, Worcester, September 20, 21, 1881.

Longest Game With No Passed Balls

A. L.—25 innings— Carlton E. Fisk, Chicago, May 8, finished May 9, 1984.
N. L.—24 innings— Harold King, Houston, April 15, 1968.
Gerald W. Grote, New York, April 15, 1968 (caught 23 ⅓ innings) .

Most Passed Balls, Inning

A. A.—5—Daniel C. Sullivan, St. Louis, August 9, 1885, third inning.
N. L.—4—Raymond F. Katt, New York, September 10, 1954, eighth inning.
A. L.—4—Eugene J. Petralli, Texas, August 22, 1987, seventh inning.

Double Plays

Most Double Plays, League

A. L.— 217— Raymond W. Schalk, Chicago, 17 years, 1912 through 1928.
N. L.— 163— Charles L. Hartnett, Chicago, New York, 20 years, 1922 through 1941.

Most Unassisted Double Plays, League

A. L.—2—Charles Schmidt, Detroit, 1906, 1907.
Frank P. Crossin, St. Louis, 1914 (2) .
Clinton D. Courtney, Baltimore, 1954, 1960.
Lawrence P. Berra, New York, 1947, 1962.
Robert L. Rodgers, Los Angeles, 1965; California, 1969.
N. L.—2—Miguel A. Gonzalez, St. Louis, 1915, 1918.
Christopher J. Cannizzaro, New York, 1964, 1965.
L. Edgar Bailey, San Francisco, 1963; Chicago, 1965.
Robert D. Taylor, New York, 1964, 1967.

Most Double Plays, Season

A. L.—29—Frank W. Hayes, Philadelphia, Cleveland, 151 games, 1945.
N. L.—23— Thomas F. Haller, Los Angeles, 139 games, 1968.

Most Unassisted Double Plays, Season

A. L.—2—Frank P. Crossin, St. Louis, 1914.
N. L.—1—Held by many catchers.

Most Years Leading League in Double Plays

N. L.—6—Charles L. Hartnett, Chicago, 1925 (tied) , 1927, 1930 (tied) , 1931, 1934, 1935.
A. L.—6—Lawrence P. Berra, New York, 1949, 1950, 1951, 1952, 1954, 1956.

Fewest Double Plays, Season, for Leader in Most Double Plays

N. L.—8—Philip S. Masi, Boston-Pittsburgh, 81 games, 1949.
Clyde E. McCullough, Pittsburgh, 90 games, 1949.
A. L.—9—Earl J. Battey, Minnesota, 131 games, 1961.
Augustus R. Triandos, Baltimore, 114 games, 1961.

Most Double Plays, Nine-Inning Game

N. L.—3—John J. O'Neill, Chicago, April 26, 1905.
J. Frank Hogan, New York, August 19, 1931.
Edward St. Claire, Boston, August 9, 1951.
A. L.—3—Charles F. Berry, Chicago, May 17, 1932.
Joseph C. Martin, Chicago, June 23, 1963, first game.
Earl J. Battey, Minnesota, August 11, 1966.
Edward M. Herrmann, Chicago, July 4, 1972.
J. Rikard Dempsey, Baltimore, June 1, 1977.

Most Double Plays, Extra-Inning Game

N. L.—3—Robert A. O'Farrell, Chicago, July 9, 1919, second game, 10 ⅓ innings.
Ronald W. Hodges, New York, April 23, 1978, 11 ⅔ innings.
A. L.—3—William J. Sullivan, Chicago, July 25, 1912, 10 innings.

Most Double Plays Started, Game

N. L.—3—J. Frank Hogan, New York, August 19, 1931.
A. L.—2—Held by many catchers.

Most Unassisted Double Plays, Game

A. L.-N. L.—1—Held by many players.

Baserunners Vs. Catchers

Most Stolen Bases Off Catcher, Game

A. A.— 19— Grant Briggs, Syracuse, April 22, 1890.
N. L.— 17— George F. Miller, Pittsburgh, May 23, 1890.
N. L. since 1900—11—William C. Fischer, St. Louis, August 13, 1916, second game, five innings.
A. L.— 13— W. Branch Rickey, New York, June 28, 1907.

Most Stolen Bases Off Catcher, Inning
A. L.—8—Stephen F. O'Neill, Cleveland, July 19, 1915, first inning.
N L.—8—Miguel A. Gonzalez, New York, July 7, 1919, first game, ninth inning.

Most Runners Caught Stealing, Game, Nine Innings
N. L.—8—Charles A. Farrell, Washington, May 11, 1897.
N. L. since 1900—7—William Bergen, Brooklyn, August 23, 1909, second game.
A. L.—6—Walter H. Schang, Philadelphia, May 12, 1915.

Most Runners Caught Stealing, Inning
A. A.—3—John Milligan, Philadelphia, July 26, 1887, third inning.
A. L.—3—Leslie G. Nunamaker, New York, August 3, 1914, second inning.
N. L.—2—Held by many catchers.

No-Hitters Caught

Most No-Hit Games Caught, League (Entire Game)
A. L.—4—Raymond W. Schalk, Chicago, 1914 (2), 1917, 1922.
N. L.—3—Roy Campanella, Brooklyn, 1952, 1956 (2).
Delmar W. Crandall, Milwaukee, 1954, 1960 (2).
Alan D. Ashby, Houston, 1979, 1981, 1986.
Both Leagues—3—Jeffrey A. Torborg, Los Angeles N. L., 1965, 1970; California A.L., 1973.

Most No-Hit, Winning Games Caught, League (Entire Game)
A. L.—3—Raymond W. Schalk, Chicago, 1914, 1917, 1922.
William F. Carrigan, Boston, 1911, 1916 (2).
Valentine J. Picinich, Philadelphia, 1916, Washington, 1920, Boston, 1923.
J. Luther Sewell, Cleveland, 1931, Chicago, 1935, 1937.
James E. Hegan, Cleveland, 1947, 1948, 1951.
N. L.—3—Roy Campanella, Brooklyn, 1952, 1956 (2).
Delmar W. Crandall, Milwaukee, 1954, 1960 (2).
Alan D. Ashby, Houston, 1979, 1981, 1986.
Both Leagues—3—Jeffrey A. Torborg, Los Angeles N. L., 1965, 1970; California A. L. 1973.

Pitchers
Years, Games & Innings

Most Games Pitched in Major Leagues
1070—J. Hoyt Wilhelm, New York N. L., St. Louis N. L., Cleveland A. L., Baltimore A. L., Chicago A. L., California A. L., Atlanta N. L., Chicago N. L., Los Angeles N. L., 21 years, 1952 through 1972, 448 in N. L., 622 in A. L.

Most Games, Pitched League
N. L.— 943— Kenton C. Tekulve, Pittsburgh, Philadelphia, 14 years, 1974 through 1987.
A. L.— 807— Albert W. Lyle, Boston, New York, Texas, Chicago, 15 years, 1967 through 1982, except 1981.

Most Games, Pitched Season
N. L.— 106— Michael G. Marshall, Los Angeles, 208 innings, 1974.
A. L.— 90— Michael G. Marshall, Minnesota, 143 innings, 1979.

Most Years Leading League in Games Pitched in Major Leagues
7—Joseph J. McGinnity, Brooklyn N. L., Baltimore A. L., New York N.L., 1900, 1901, 1903, 1904, 1905, 1906, 1907.

Most Years Leading League in Games Pitched
N. L.—6—Joseph J. McGinnity, Brooklyn, New York, 1900, 1903, 1904, 1905, 1906, 1907.
A. L.—6—Fred Marberry, Washington, 1924, 1925, 1926, 1928, 1929, 1932.

Fewest Games, Season, for Leader in Most Games Pitched
A. L.—40—Joseph W. Haynes, Chicago, 1942 (103 innings).
N. L.—41—Remy Kremer, Pittsburgh, 1924 (259 innings).
John D. Morrison, Pittsburgh, 1924 (238 innings).

Most Innings Pitched, Game
N. L.—26 innings— Leon J. Cadore, Brooklyn, May 1, 1920.
Joseph Oeschger, Boston, May 1, 1920.
A. L.—24 innings—John W. Coombs, Philadelphia, September 1, 1906.
Joseph Harris, Boston, September 1, 1906.

Average

Highest Fielding Average, Most Chances Accepted, Season
N. L.—1.000—Randall L. Jones, San Diego, 1976, 40 games, 31 putouts, 81 assists, 112 chances accepted.
A. L.—1.000—Walter P. Johnson, Washington, 1913, 48 games, 21 putouts, 82 assists, 103 chances accepted.

Most Years, Highest Average, With Most Chances Acc., Season
N. L.—4—Claude W. Passeau, Phiadelphia, Chicago, 1939, 1942, 1943, 1945.
Lawrence C. Jackson, St. Louis, Chicago, Philadelphia, 1957, 1964, 1965, 1968.
A. L.—3—Walter P. Johnson, Washington, 1913, 1917, 1922 (tied).

Putouts

Most Putouts, Major Leagues, Since 1900
386—Philip H. Niekro, Milwaukee N.L., Atlanta N.L., New York A.L., Cleveland A.L., Toronto A.L., 24 years, 1964 through 1987.

Most Putouts, League, Since 1900
N. L.— 340— Philip H. Niekro, Milwaukee, Atlanta, 21 years, 1964 through 1983, 1987.
A. L.— 292— James A. Palmer, Baltimore, 19 years, 1965 through 1984, except 1968.

Most Putouts, Season
N. L.— 52— Albert G. Spalding, Chicago, 60 games, 1876.
A. L.— 49— Nicholas Altrock, Chicago, 38 games, 1904.
Michael J. Boddicker, Baltimore, 34 games, 1984.
N. L. since 1900—39—Victor G. Willis, Boston, 43 games, 1904.

Most Years Leading League in Putouts
A. L.—5—Robert G. Lemon, Cleveland, 1948, 1949, 1952, 1953, 1954.
N. L.—4—Grover C. Alexander, Philadelphia, 1914, 1915, 1916, 1917.
Fred L. Fitzsimmons, New York, 1926, 1928, 1930, 1934.

Fewest Putouts, Season, for Leader in Most Putouts
N. L.— 14— S. Howard Camnitz, Pittsburgh, 38 games, 1910.
Arthur N. Nehf, New York, 37 games, 1922.
Anthony C. Kaufmann, Chicago, 37 games, 1922.
A. L.— 16— Roxie Lawson, Detroit, 27 games, 1937.

Most Putouts, Game, Nine Innings
A. L.—6—Rikalbert Blyleven, Cleveland, June 24, 1984.
Eric S. King, Detroit, July 8, 1986.
N. L.—5—Held by many pitchers. Last pitchers—Richard D. Ruthven, Atlanta, April 19, 1978; Mark Lemongello, Houston, August 9, 1978.

Most Putouts, Extra-Inning Game
A. L.—7—Richard J. Fowler, Philadelphia, June 9, 1949, 12 innings.
N. L.—6—Robert T. Purkey, Pittsburgh, July 22, 1954, pitched 11 innings of 14-inning game.

Most Putouts, Inning
A. L.—3—James C. Bagby, Jr., Boston, September 26, 1940, fourth inning.
Robert F. Heffner, Boston, June 28, 1963, first inning.
James L. Beattie, New York, September 13, 1978, second inning.
N. L.—3—Ricky E. Reuschel, Chicago, April 25, 1975, third inning.

Assists

Most Assists, League, Since 1900
N. L.— 1489— Christopher Mathewson, New York, Cincinnati, 17 years, 1900 through 1916.
A. L.— 1337— Walter P. Johnson, Washington, 21 years, 1907 through 1927.

Most Assists, Season
A. L.— 227— Edward A. Walsh, Chicago, 56 games, 1907.
N. L.— 168— John G. Clarkson, Boston, 72 games, 1889.
N. L. since 1900—141—Christopher Mathewson, New York, 56 games, 1908.

Most Years Leading League in Assists
A. L.—6—Robert G. Lemon, Cleveland, 1948, 1949, 1951, 1952, 1953, 1956.
N. L.—5—Christopher Mathewson, New York, 1901, 1905, 1908, 1910, 1911.

Fewest Assists, Season, for Leader in Most Assists

A. L.—43—Charles L. Leibrandt, Kansas City, 35 games, 1986.
N. L.—47—Ronald M. Darling, New York, 36 games, 1985.
Ronald M. Darling, New York, 34 games, 1986.
Robert W. Knepper, Houston, 40 games, 1986.
Fernando Valenzuela, Los Angeles, 34 games, 1986.

Most Assists, Game, Nine Innings

N. L.—11—Truett B. Sewell, Pittsburgh, June 6, 1941, second game.
A. L.—11—Albert C. Orth, New York, August 12, 1906.
Edward A. Walsh, Chicago, April 19, 1907.
Edward A. Walsh, Chicago, August 12, 1907.
George N. McConnell, New York, September 2, 1912, second game.
Meldon J. Wolfgang, Chicago, August 29, 1914.

Most Assists, Extra-Inning Game

N. L.—12—Leon J. Cadore, Brooklyn, May 1, 1920, 26 innings.
A. L.—12—Nicholas Altrock, Chicago, June 7, 1908, 10 innings.
Edward A. Walsh, Chicago, July 16, 1907, 13 innings.

Most Assists, Inning

N. L.-A. L.—3—Held by many pitchers.

Chances Accepted & Offered

Most Chances Accepted, League, Since 1900

N. L.— 1761— Christopher Mathewson, New York, Cincinnati, 17 years, 1900 through 1916.
A. L.— 1606— Walter P. Johnson, Washington, 21 years, 1907 through 1927.

Most Chances Accepted, Season

A. L.— 262— Edward A. Walsh, Chicago, 56 games, 1907.
N. L.— 206— John G. Clarkson, Boston, 72 games, 1889.
N. L. since 1900—168—Christopher Mathewson, New York, 56 games, 1908.

Most Years Leading League in Chances Accepted

A. L.—8—Robert G. Lemon, Cleveland, 1948, 1949, 1950, 1951, 1952, 1953, 1954, 1956.
N. L.—7—Burleigh A. Grimes, Brooklyn, New York, Pittsburgh, 1921, 1922, 1923, 1924, 1925, 1927, 1928.

Fewest Chances Accepted, Season, for Leader

A. L.—63—Franklin L. Sullivan, Boston, 35 games, 1955.
Raymond E. Herbert, Kansas City, 37 games, 1960.
James E. Perry, Cleveland, 41 games, 1960.
N. L.—67—Paul E. Minner, Chicago, 31 games, 1953.
Robin E. Roberts, Philadelphia, 44 games, 1953.
James T. Hearn, New York, 39 games, 1955.

Most Chances Accepted, Game, Nine Innings

A. L.—13—Nicholas Altrock, Chicago, August 6, 1904, 3 putouts, 10 assists.
Edward A. Walsh, Chicago, April 19, 1907, 2 putouts, 11 assists.
N. L.—12—Truett B. Sewell, Pittsburgh, June 6, 1941, second game, 1 putout, 11 assists.

Most Chances Accepted, Extra-Inning Game

A. L.—15—Edward A. Walsh, Chicago, July 16, 1907, 13 innings.
N. L.—13—Leon J. Cadore, Brooklyn, May 1, 1920, 26 innings.

Most Chances Accepted, Two Consecutive Games

A. L.—20—Edward A. Walsh, Chicago, April 13, 19, 1907, 2 putouts, 18 assists.

Most Chances Accepted, Inning

N. L.—4—Philip R. Regan, Chicago, June 6, 1969, sixth inning, 1 putout, 3 assists.
A. L.—3—Held by many pitchers.

Longest Game, No Chances Offered

N. L.—20 innings— Milton Watson, Philadelphia, July 17, 1918.
A. L.—15 innings— Charles H. Ruffing, New York, July 23, 1932, first game.

Fewest Chances Offered, Two Consec. Games, Over 18 Innings

A. A.—0—John Neagle, Pittsburgh, July 13, 17, 1884, 12 innings each.
N. L.-A. L.—1—Held by many pitchers.

Fewest Chances Offered, Doubleheader

A. A.— 1— Thomas Ramsey, Louisville, July 5, 1886, 1 putout.

N. L.—3—Joseph J. McGinnity, New York, August 1, 1903, 1 putout, 1 assist, 1 error.
Grover C. Alexander, Philadelphia, September 3, 1917, 1 putout, 2 assists.
Herman S. Bell, St. Louis, July 19, 1924, 1 putout, 2 assists.
A. L.—3—Edward A. Walsh, Chicago, September 29, 1908, 0 putouts, 3 assists.

Errors

Most Errors, League, Since 1900

N. L.—64—James L. Vaughn, Chicago, 9 years, 1913 through 1921.
A. L.—55—Edward A. Walsh, Chicago, 13 years, 1904 through 1916.

Most Errors, Season

A. A.—63—Timothy J. Keefe, New York, 68 games, 1883.
N. L.—28—James E. Whitney, Boston, 63 games, 1881.
N. L. since 1900—17—Eustace J. Newton, Cincinnati, Brooklyn, 33 games, 1901.
A. L.—15—John D. Chesbro, New York, 55 games, 1904.
George E. Waddell, Philadelphia, 46 games, 1905.
Edward A. Walsh, Chicago, 62 games, 1912.

Most Years Leading League in Errors

N. L.—5—James L. Vaughn, Chicago, 1914, 1915 (tied), 1917 (tied), 1919, 1920.
Warren E. Spahn, Boston, Milwaukee, 1949 (tied), 1950, 1952 (tied), 1954 (tied), 1964 (tied).
A. L.—4—Allan S. Sothoron, St. Louis, 1917, 1918 (tied), 1919, 1920.
L. Nolan Ryan, California, 1975, 1976, 1977 (tied), 1978.

Fewest Errors, Season, for Leader in Most Errors

N. L.-A. L.—4—Held by many pitchers.

Most Errors, Game

N. L.—5—Edward R. Doheny, New York, August 15, 1899.
N. L. since 1900—4—Eustace J. Newton, Cincinnati, September 13, 1900, first game.
Lafayette S. Winham, Pittsburgh, September 21, 1903, first game.
A. L.—4—Chester Ross, Boston, May 17, 1925.

Most Errors, Inning

N. L.—3—J. Bentley Seymour, New York, May 21, 1898, sixth inning.
A. L.—2—Held by many pitchers.

Longest Errorless Game

N. L.—26 innings— Leon J. Cadore, Brooklyn, May 1, 1920.
Joseph Oeschger, Boston, May 1, 1920.
A. L.—24 innings— John W. Coombs, Philadelphia, September 1, 1906.
Joseph Harris, Boston, September 1, 1906.

Most Consecutive Errorless Games, League

A. L.— 385— Paul A. Lindblad, Kansas City, Oakland, Texas, August 27, 1966, first game, through April 30, 1974, 126 chances accepted.
N. L.— 297— Ronald L. Reed, Philadelphia, August 16, 1978 through September 30, 1983, 95 chances accepted.

Most Consecutive Chances Accepted, League, No Errors

N. L.— 273— Claude W. Passeau, Chicago, September 21, first game, 1941 through May 20, 1946, 145 games.
A. L.— 230— J. Rick Langford, Oakland, April 13, 1977 to October 2, 1980, 142 games.

Most Consecutive Errorless Games, Season

A. L.— 88— Wilbur F. Wood, Chicago, April 10 through September 29, 1968 (32 chances accepted).
N. L.— 84— Theodore W. Abernathy, Chicago, April 12, through October 3, 1965 (52 chances accepted).

Double Plays

Most Double Plays, League

N. L.—82—Warren E. Spahn, Boston, Milwaukee, New York, San Francisco, 21 years, 1942 through 1965 (except 1943, 1944, 1945, in military service).
A. L.—78—Robert G. Lemon, Cleveland, 13 years, 1946 through 1958.

Most Unassisted Double Plays, League

N. L.—2—James O. Carleton, Chicago, Brooklyn, 1935, 1940.
Claude W. Passeau, Philadelphia, Chicago, 1938, 1945.
A. L.—1—Held by many pitchers.

Most Double Plays, Season
  A. L.— 15—Robert G. Lemon, Cleveland, 41 games, 1953.
  N. L.— 12—Arthur N. Nehf, New York, 40 games, 1920.
        Curtis B. Davis, Philadelphia, 51 games, 1934.
        Randall L. Jones, San Diego, 40 games, 1976.

Most Years Leading League in Double Plays
  N. L.—5—William H. Walters, Philadelphia, Cincinnati, 1937, 1939,
      1941 (tied), 1943 (tied), 1944 (tied).
      Warren E. Spahn, Milwaukee, 1953 (tied), 1956, 1960
      (tied), 1961 (tied), 1963.
  A. L.—4—G. Willis Hudlin, Cleveland, 1929, 1930, 1931, 1934.

Fewest Double Plays, Season, For Leader in Most Double Plays
  N. L.-A. L.—5—Held by many pitchers.

Most Double Plays Started, Game
  A. L.—4—Milton Gaston, Chicago, May 17, 1932.
      Harold Newhouser, Detroit, May 19, 1948.
  N. L.—3—Held by 5 pitchers. Last pitcher—D. Eugene Conley, Milwaukee, July 19, 1957.

Most Unassisted Double Plays, Game
  N. L.—1—Held by many pitchers. Last pitcher—James C. McAndrew, New York, August 17, 1968.
  A. L.—1—Held by many pitchers. Last pitcher—James L. Kern, Milwaukee, May 8, 1985.

Most Triple Plays Started, Season
  N. L.—2—A. Wilbur Cooper, Pittsburgh, July 7, August 21, 1920.
  A. L.—1—Held by many pitchers.

Club Fielding

Number Of Players At Positions

Infielders

Most First Basemen, Nine-Inning Game
  A. L.—5—Chicago vs. New York, June 25, 1953.
  N. L.—3—Made in many games.

Most First Basemen, Extra-Inning Game
  N. L.—4—Philadelphia vs. Milwaukee, July 23, 1964, 10 innings.
  A. L.—4—Detroit vs. Philadelphia, September 30, 1907, 17 innings.

Most First Basemen, Nine-Inning Game, Both Clubs
  A. L.—6—Chicago 5, New York 1, June 25, 1953.
  N. L.—5—Los Angeles 3, New York 2, September 12, 1966.
      Cincinnati 3, New York 2, August 24, 1968.

Most First Basemen, Extra-Inning Game, Both Clubs
  N. L.—5—Los Angeles 3, Houston 2, June 8, 1962, 13 innings.
      Philadelphia 3, Houston 2, July 17, 1963, 10 innings.
      Philadelphia 4, Milwaukee 1, July 23, 1964, 10 innings.
  A. L.—5—Detroit 4, Philadelphia 1, September 30, 1907, 17 innings.

Most Second Basemen, Nine-Inning Game
  N. L.—4—Brooklyn vs. New York, April 21, 1948.
      Chicago vs. New York, August 21, 1952, second game.
  A. L.—4—Made in six games—Last time—Oakland vs. California, September 27, 1975.

Most Second Basemen, Extra-Inning Game
  A. L.—6—Oakland vs. Chicago, September 19, 1972, 15 innings.
  N. L.—5—New York vs. Cincinnati, July 20, 1954, 13 innings.

Most Second Basemen, Nine-Inning Game, Both Clubs
  A. L.—6—Oakland 4, Cleveland 2, May 5, 1973.
      Oakland 4, Cleveland 2, May 6, 1973, first game.
      Oakland 4, Cleveland 2, May 6, 1973, second game.
  N. L.—5—Brooklyn 4, New York 1, April 21, 1948.
      Chicago 4, New York 1, August 21, 1952, second game.

Most Second Basemen, Extra-Inning Game, Both Clubs
  A. L.—8—Oakland 6, Chicago 2, September 19, 1972, 15 innings.
  N. L.—7—New York 5, Cincinnati 2, July 20, 1954, 13 innings.

Most Third Basemen, Nine-Inning Game
  N. L.—5—Atlanta vs. Philadelphia, April 21, 1966.
      Philadelphia vs. Pittsburgh, August 6, 1971.
  A. L.—4—Kansas City vs. California, September 10, 1969.
      Minnesota vs. Seattle, September 28, 1969, first game.
      Cleveland vs. Minnesota, August 27, 1970.
      Milwaukee vs. Kansas City, September 6, 1971.
      Oakland vs. Cleveland, July 20, 1974.

Most Third Basemen, Extra-Inning Game
  N. L.—4—Made in many games.
  A. L.—4—Made in many games.

Most Third Basemen, Nine-Inning Game, Both Clubs
  N. L.—7—Philadelphia 5, Pittsburgh 2, August 6, 1971.
  A. L.—6—Minnesota 3, Cleveland 3, July 27, 1969.

Most Third Basemen, Extra-Inning Game, Both Clubs
  A. L.—6—Detroit 3, Cleveland 3, July 10, 1969, 11 innings.
  N. L.—5—Made in many games.

Most Shortstops, Nine-Inning Game
  A. L.—4—New York vs. Washington, September 5, 1954.
      Minnesota vs. Oakland, September 22, 1968.
  N. L.—3—Made in many games.

Most Shortstops, Extra-Inning Game
  N. L.—5—Philadelphia vs. Cincinnati, May 8, 1949, 12 innings.
  A. L.—4—Detroit vs. New York, July 28, 1957, second game, 15 innings.
      Baltimore vs. New York, September 26, 1958, 12 innings.

Most Shortstops, Nine-Inning Game, Both Clubs
  A. L.—6—Detroit 3, Washington 3, September 21, 1968.
  N. L.—5—Cincinnati 3, Houston 2, July 13, 1969.
      Montreal 3, Pittsburgh 2, October 1, 1969.

Outfielders

Most Right Fielders, Nine-Inning Game
  N. L.—4—Philadelphia vs. St. Louis, June 2, 1928.
      Los Angeles vs. Houston, June 10, 1962, first game.
  A. L.—4—Baltimore vs. Washington, September 25, 1955.

Most Right Fielders, Extra-Inning Game
  A. L.—6—Kansas City vs. California, September 8, 1965, 13 innings.
  N. L.—5—New York vs. Cincinnati, July 22, 1986, 14 innings.

Most Right Fielders, Nine-Inning Game, Both Clubs
  N. L.—6—Los Angeles 4, Houston 2, June 10, 1962, first game.
  A. L.—5—Chicago 3, St. Louis 2, May 6, 1917, first game.
      Baltimore 4, Washington 1, September 25, 1955.
      Cleveland 3, Detroit 2, June 2, 1962.
      Cleveland 3, Kansas City 2, June 26, 1966, second game.
      Boston 3, California 2, August 20, 1967, second game.
      California 3, Chicago 2, July 20, 1968.
      California 3, Chicago 2, April 14, 1969.
      Oakland 3, Chicago 2, September 7, 1970, second game.
      Boston 3, Oakland 2, May 20, 1975.

Most Right Fielders, Extra-Inning Game, Both Clubs
  A. L.—7—Kansas City 6, California 1, September 8, 1965, 13 innings.
  N. L.—6—Los Angeles 3, San Francisco 3, June 25, 1964, 13 innings.
      New York vs. Cincinnati, July 22, 1986, 14 innings.

Most Center Fielders, Nine-Inning Game
  A. L.—5—Minnesota vs. Oakland, September 22, 1968.
  N. L.—4—Cincinnati vs. St. Louis, May 30, 1942, second game.

Most Center Fielders, Extra-Inning Game
  N. L.—4—Boston vs. Brooklyn, April 25, 1917, 12 innings.
      Philadelphia vs. St. Louis, September 25, 1966, 13 innings.
      Philadelphia vs. Cincinnati, July 20, 1987, 11 innings.
  A. L.—3—Made in many games.

Most Center Fielders, Nine-Inning Game, Both Clubs
  A. L.—7—Minnesota 5, Oakland 2, September 22, 1968.
  N. L.—6—Cincinnati 4, St. Louis 2, May 30, 1942, second game.

Most Center Fielders, Extra-Inning Game, Both Clubs
  N. L.—5—Made in many games.
  A. L.—5—Made in many games.

Most Left Fielders, Nine-Inning Game
  A. L.—4—Baltimore vs. Detroit, September 14, 1960.
      Minnesota vs. California, July 9, 1970.
      Oakland vs. Cleveland, July 20, 1974.

N. L.—4—Brooklyn vs. Philadelphia, September 26, 1946.
    Los Angeles vs. New York, June 4, 1966.

Most Left Fielders, Extra-Inning Game

N. L.—5—Philadelphia vs. Milwaukee, July 23, 1964, 10 innings.
A. L.—4—Boston vs. Chicago, August 16, 1916, first game, 16 innings.
    New York vs. Boston, September 26, 1953, 11 innings.

Most Left Fielders, Nine-Inning Game, Both Clubs

N. L.—6—New York 3, San Francisco 3, September 22, 1963.
A. L.—6—Oakland 4, Cleveland 2, July 20, 1974.

Most Left Fielders, Extra-Inning Game, Both Clubs

N. L.—7—Los Angeles 4, St. Louis 3, May 12, 1962, 15 innings.
A. L.—6—Minnesota 3, Baltimore 3, April 16, 1961, second game, 11 innings.
    Minnesota 3, Oakland 3, September 6, 1969, 18 innings.

Battery

Most Catchers, Nine-Inning Game

N. L.—4—Boston vs. New York, October 6, 1929.
    Brooklyn vs. St. Louis, May 5, 1940.
    New York vs. St. Louis, September 2, 1962.
A. L.—4—Minnesota vs. California, September 27, 1967.

Most Catchers, Extra-Inning Game

A. L.—4—Kansas City vs. Chicago, September 21, 1973, 12 innings.
N. L.—3—Made in many games.

Most Catchers, Nine-Inning Game, Both Clubs

A. L.—6—Chicago 3, Philadelphia 3, July 10, 1926.
N. L.—6—Boston 4, New York 2, October 6, 1929.
    Brooklyn 4, St. Louis 2, May 5, 1940.
    New York 4, St. Louis 2, September 2, 1962.

Most Catchers, Extra-Inning Game, Both Clubs

A. L.—6—Chicago 3, New York 3, September 10, 1955, 10 innings.
    California 3, Oakland 3, September 28, 1969, 11 innings.
    Kansas City 4, Chicago 2, September 21, 1972, 12 innings.
N. L.—5—Made in many games.

Most Pitchers, Nine-Inning Game

A. L.—9—St. Louis vs. Chicago, October 2, 1949, first game.
N. L.—8—Held by many clubs.

Most Pitchers, Extra-Inning Game

N. L.—10—Chicago vs. Pittsburgh, April 20, finished August 11, 1986, 17 innings.
A. L.— 9—Los Angeles vs. Minnesota, April 16, 1963, 13 innings.
    Minnesota vs. Chicago, July 25, 1964, 13 innings.
    Washington vs. Cleveland, September 14, finished September 20, 1971, 20 innings.
    Cleveland vs. Washington, September 14, finished September 20, 1971, 20 innings.

Most Pitchers, Nine-Inning Game, Both Clubs

N. L.— 14—Chicago 7, New York 7, July 23, 1944, second game.
    Cincinnati 8, Milwaukee 6, April 26, 1959.
    Houston 8, Chicago 6, September 11, 1967.
    Houston 8, Los Angeles 6, September 17, 1972.
    Montreal 8, Chicago 6, September 5, 1978.
A. L.— 14—Kansas City 7, Cleveland 7, April 23, 1961.

Most Pitchers, Extra-Inning Game, Both Clubs

A. L.—18—Washington 9, Cleveland 9, September 14, finished, September 20, 1971, 20 innings.
N. L.—17—Chicago 10, Pittsburgh 7, April 20, finished August 11, 1986, 17 innings.
    Houston 9, Chicago 8, September 2, finished September 3, 1986, 18 innings.

Most Pitchers, Shutout Game, Winning Club

A. L.—7—Kansas City vs. Cleveland, September 15, 1966, 11 innings (won 1-0).
N. L.—6—Los Angeles vs. Milwaukee, October 3, 1965 (won 3-0).

Most Pitchers, No-Hit Game, Winning Club

A. L.—4—Oakland vs. California, September 28, 1975 (won 5-0).

Most Pitchers, Doubleheader

N. L.—13—Milwaukee vs. Philadelphia, May 12, 1963, 23 innings.
    San Diego vs. San Francisco, May 30, 1977.
A. L.—12—Cleveland vs. Detroit, September 7, 1959.
    California vs. Detroit, September 30, 1967.

    Washington vs. Chicago, May 30, 1969, 19 innings.
    New York vs. Baltimore, August 9, 1970, 20 innings.
    Washington vs. Cleveland, September 14, finished September 20, 1971, 29 innings.

Most Pitchers, Doubleheader, 18 Innings, Both Clubs

N. L.—22—Milwaukee 11, New York 11, July 26, 1964.
A. L.—21—Detroit 11, Kansas City 10, July 23, 1961.

Most Pitchers, Doubleheader, Both Clubs, More Than 18 Innings

A. L.—22—Washington 12, Cleveland 10, September 14, finished September 20, 1971, 29 innings.
N. L.—20—St. Louis 12, Cincinnati 8, July 1, 1956, 19 innings.

Most Pitchers, Inning

A. L.—6—Oakland vs. Cleveland, September 3, 1983, ninth inning.
N. L.—5—Made in many innings. Last times—Los Angeles vs. New York, August 26, 1987, eighth inning; Chicago vs. Philadelphia, September 16, 1987, seventh inning.

Most Pitchers, Inning, Both Clubs

N. L.—8—Los Angeles 5, New York 3, August 26, 1987, eighth inning.
A. L.—7—Chicago 4, Baltimore 3, July 16, 1955, ninth inning.

Average

Highest Fielding Average, Season

A. L. (162-game season)—.9849—Baltimore, 162 games, 1980.
A. L. (154-game season)—.983 —Cleveland, 157 games, 1947.
    Cleveland, 154 games, 1949.
N. L. (162-game season)—.9846—Cincinnati, 162 games, 1977.
N. L. (154-game season)—.9831—Cincinnati, 154 games, 1958.

Lowest Fielding Average, Season, Since 1900

N. L. (162-game season)—.967—New York, 161 games, 1962.
    New York, 162 games, 1963.
N. L. (154-game season)—.936—Philadelphia, 155 games, 1904.
A. L. (162-game season)—.970—Oakland, 161 games, 1977.
A. L. (154-game season)—.928—Detroit, 136 games, 1901.

Most Consecutive Years Leading League in Fielding

A. L.—6—Boston, 1916 through 1921.
N. L.—4—Chicago, 1905 through 1908.
    St. Louis, 1984 through 1987.

Putouts

Most Putouts, Season

A. L. (162-game season)—4520—New York, 164 games, 1964.
A. L. (154-game season)—4396—Cleveland, 161 games, 1910.
N. L. (162-game season)—4480—Pittsburgh, 163 games, 1979.
N. L. (154-game season)—4359—Philadelphia, 159 games, 1913.

Fewest Putouts, Season

N. L. (162-game season)—4223—Atlanta, 160 games, 1979.
N. L. (154-game season)—3887—Philadelphia, 149 games, 1907.
A. L. (162-game season)—4188—Detroit, 159 games, 1975.
A. L. (154-game season)—3907—Cleveland, 147 games, 1945.

Most Players One or More Putouts, Game, Nine Innings

A. L.— 14— New York vs. Cleveland, July 17, 1952, first game.
N. L.— 13— St. Louis vs. Los Angeles, April 13, 1960.
    Chicago vs. New York, August 8, 1965, second game.

Most Players One or More Putouts, Game, 9 Innings, Both Clubs

A. L.— 22— New York 14, Cleveland 8, July 17, 1952, first game.
N. L.— 22— Chicago 13, New York 9, August 8, 1965, second game.

Most Putouts, Infield, Game, Nine Innings

A. L.— 25— New York vs. Washington, June 23, 1911.
    Cleveland vs. Boston, August 9, 1922.
    Detroit vs. Chicago, September 26, 1924.
    Boston vs. Cleveland, June 24, 1931.
    Detroit vs. Philadelphia, June 20, 1937, first game.
    Detroit vs. New York, May 6, 1941.
N. L.— 25— Chicago vs. Philadelphia, September 24, 1927.
    Pittsburgh vs. New York, June 6, 1941, second game.
    St. Louis vs. Boston, July 17, 1947.
    Chicago vs. Pittsburgh, May 9, 1963.

Most Putouts, Infield, Game, Nine Innings, Both Clubs

N. L.— 46— Cincinnati 24, New York 22, May 7, 1941.
    St. Louis 25, Boston 21, July 17, 1947.
A. L.— 45— Detroit 24, Washington 21, September 15, 1945, second game.
    Boston, 24, Cleveland 21, July 11, 1977.

Fewest Putouts, Infield, Game, Nine Innings
A. L.—3—St. Louis vs. New York, July 20, 1945, second game.
    Boston vs. Seattle, April 29, 1986.
N. L.—3—New York vs. San Diego, April 22, 1970.

Most Putouts, Outfield, Game, Nine Innings
N. L.—19—Pittsburgh vs. Cincinnati, July 5, 1948, second game.
A. L.—18—Cleveland vs. St. Louis, September 28, 1929.
    New York vs. Boston, October 1, 1933.

Most Putouts, Outfield, Game, Nine Innings, Both Clubs
N. L.—30—Chicago 16, Philadelphia 14, August 7, 1953.
A. L.—29—Washington 17, St. Louis 12, May 3, 1939.

Most Putouts, Outfield, Extra-Inning Game
N. L.—23—Brooklyn vs. Boston, May 1, 1920, 26 innings.
    Chicago vs. Boston, May 17, 1927, 22 innings.
A. L.—22—Chicago vs. Washington, May 15, 1918, 18 innings.

Most Putouts, Outfield, Extra-Inning Game, Both Clubs
N. L.—42—New York 21, Pittsburgh 21, July 17, 1914, 21 innings.
A. L.—38—Washington 20, St. Louis 18, July 19, 1924, 16 innings.

Longest Game, Outfield, With No Putouts
N. L.—13 innings—New York vs. Brooklyn, April 15, 1909.
    St. Louis vs. Philadelphia, August 13, 1987.
A. L.—11 innings—St. Louis vs. Cleveland, April 23, 1905.

Fewest Putouts, Outfield, Game, Nine Innings, Both Clubs
A. A.—1—St. Louis 1, New York 0, June 30, 1886.
N. L.—1—Pittsburgh 1, Brooklyn 0, August 26, 1910.
A. L.—2—New York 2, Detroit 0, May 9, 1930.

Most Putouts, Outfield, Doubleheader, More Than 18 Innings
N. L.—29—Boston vs. New York, September 3, 1933, 23 innings.
A. L.—Less than for 18 innings.

Most Putouts, Outfield, Doubleheader
N. L.—27—Pittsburgh vs. Cincinnati, July 5, 1948.
A. L.—24—Detroit vs. Philadelphia, June 28, 1931.

Most Putouts, Outfield, Doubleheader, Both Clubs
N. L.—47—Pittsburgh 26, Boston 21, June 26, 1935.
A. L.—43—Detroit 24, Philadelphia 19, June 28, 1931.

Assists

Most Assists, Season
N. L. (162-game season)—2104—Chicago, 162 games, 1977.
N. L. (154-game season)—2293—St. Louis, 154 games, 1917.
A. L. (162-game season)—2077—California, 162 games, 1983.
A. L. (154-game season)—2446—Chicago, 157 games, 1907.

Fewest Assists, Season
N. L. (154-game season)—1437—Philadelphia, 156 games, 1957.
A. L. (162-game season)—1443—Detroit, 161 games, 1962.

Most Consecutive Years Leading League in Assists
A. L.—6—Chicago, 1905 through 1910.
N. L.—6—New York, 1933 through 1938.

Most Assists, Game, Nine Innings
N. L.—28—Pittsburgh vs. New York, June 7, 1911.
A. L.—27—St. Louis vs. Philadelphia, August 16, 1919.

Most Assists, Game, Nine Innings, Both Clubs
A. L.—45—New York 23, Chicago 22, August 21, 1905.
N. L.—44—Brooklyn 23, New York 21, April 21, 1903.
    New York 25, Cincinnati 19, May 15, 1909.

Most Assists, Extra-Inning Game
N. L.—41—Boston vs. Brooklyn, May 1, 1920, 26 innings.
A. L.—38—Detroit vs. Philadelphia, July 21, 1945, 24 innings.
    Washington vs. Chicago, June 12, 1967, 22 innings.

Most Assists, Extra-Inning Game, Both Clubs
N. L.—72—Boston 41, Brooklyn 31, May 1, 1920, 26 innings.
A. L.—72—Detroit 38, Philadelphia 34, July 21, 1945, 24 innings.

Most Players One or More Assists, Game, Nine Innings
A. L.—11—Washington vs. Philadelphia, October 3, 1920.
    Boston vs. Philadelphia, May 1, 1929.
    Washington vs. Baltimore, April 29, 1956, first game.
    Chicago vs. Kansas City, September 22, 1970, second game.
N. L.—11—Brooklyn vs. Philadelphia, April 22, 1953.

Most Assists, Two Consecutive Games
N. L.—48—Boston vs. New York, June 24, 25, 1918.
A. L.—43—Washington vs. St. Louis, August 19, 20, 1923.

Fewest Assists, Game, Eight Innings
A. L.—0—St. Louis vs. Cleveland, August 8, 1943, second game.
N. L.—1—Held by many clubs.

Fewest Assists, Game, Nine Innings
A. L.—0—Cleveland vs. New York, July 4, 1945, first game.
N. L.—1—Chicago vs. Philadelphia, August 23, 1932.
    Cincinnati vs. Brooklyn, August 6, 1938.
    Pittsburgh vs. Chicago, August 13, 1950, first game.
    New York vs. Chicago, May 6, 1953.
    Philadelphia vs. Chicago, July 17, 1955, second game.
    Philadelphia vs. Chicago, May 2, 1957.
    Philadelphia vs. Milwaukee, June 16, 1965.
    Philadelphia vs. Cincinnati, June 7, 1966.
    Philadelphia vs. Cincinnati, May 18, 1967.
    Houston vs. Cincinnati, May 1, 1969.
    St. Louis vs. Los Angeles, May 25, 1969.
    New York vs. San Diego, April 22, 1970.
    Atlanta vs. Cincinnati, June 25, 1971, first game.
    Philadelphia vs. Chicago, August 6, 1974.
    Pittsburgh vs. Montreal, September 17, 1977.
    New York vs. Atlanta, September 4, 1981.

Fewest Assists, Game, Nine Innings, Both Clubs
A. L.—5—Baltimore 3, Cleveland 2, August 31, 1955.
N. L.—6—Chicago 5, Philadelphia 1, May 2, 1957.
    San Francisco 3, Philadelphia 3, May 13, 1959.

Fewest Assists, Two Consecutive Nine-Inning Games
N. L.—5—Chicago vs. Philadelphia, Brooklyn, August 23 (1), 24 (4), 1932.
A. L.—7—Chicago vs. Boston, June 11 (2), 11 (5), 1960, 17 innings.
    Kansas City vs. Milwaukee, California, April 16 (3), April 17 (4), 1970, 18 innings.

Most Assists, Doubleheader, Nine-Inning Games
N. L.—42—New York vs. Boston, September 30, 1914.
A. L.—41—Boston vs. Detroit, September 20, 1927.
    Boston vs. Washington, September 26, 1927.

Most Assists, Doubleheader, Nine-Inning Games, Both Clubs
N. L.—70—Brooklyn 36, Philadelphia 34, September 5, 1922.
A. L.—68—Detroit 34, Philadelphia 34, September 5, 1901.
    Cleveland 35, Boston 33, September 7, 1935.
    St. Louis 39, Boston 29, July 23, 1939.

Fewest Assists, Doubleheader, Nine-Inning Games
A. L.—8—Philadelphia vs. New York July 7, 1946.
    Minnesota vs. Los Angeles, July 19, 1961, 17⅔ innings.
    7—Chicago vs. Boston, June 11, 1960, 17 innings.
N. L.—7—New York vs. San Diego, May 29, 1971.

Fewest Assists, Doubleheader, Both Clubs
N. L.—22—Milwaukee 14, Philadelphia 8, September 12, 1954.
A. L.—25—Washington 13, New York 12, July 4, 1931.

Most Assists, Infield, Game, Nine Innings
A. L.—21—Detroit vs. Washington, September 2, 1901, second game.
    Seattle Vs. Kansas City, June 15, 1985
    Seattle vs. California, August 13, 1985.
N. L.—21—New York vs. Pittsburgh, July 13, 1919.
    Philadelphia vs. Boston, May 30, 1931, p.m. game.
    Brooklyn vs. Pittsburgh, August 18, 1935, second game.

Most Assists, Infield, Game, Nine Innings, Both Clubs
N. L.—38—Brooklyn 20, Cincinnati 18, June 10, 1917.
A. L.—35—Detroit 19, Cleveland 16, April 18, 1924.
    Chicago 18, Boston 17, September 17, 1945, second game.

Fewest Assists, Infield, Game, Nine Innings
N. L.—0—Pittsburgh vs. Chicago, July 19, 1902.
    New York vs. Philadelphia, July 29, 1934, first game.
    Chicago vs. Cincinnati, April 26, 1935.
    Cincinnati vs. Brooklyn, August 6, 1938.
    Boston vs. Pittsburgh, June 17, 1940, first game.
    New York vs. Chicago, May 6, 1953.
    Philadelphia vs. Chicago, May 2, 1957.
    Houston vs. Cincinnati, September 10, 1968, first game.
    Pittsburgh vs. Montreal, September 17, 1977.

A. L.—0—Boston, vs. Chicago, August 13, 1924, first game.
Cleveland vs. New York, July 4, 1945, first game.
St. Louis vs. New York, July 20, 1945, second game.
Washington vs. St. Louis, May 20, 1952.

Fewest Assists, Infield, Game, Nine Innings, Both Clubs
A. L.—2—Philadelphia 2, Washington 0, May 5, 1910, Washington fielded only 8 innings.
N. L.—2—Chicago 2, Philadelphia 0, May 2, 1957.

Most Assists, Outfield, Game
N. L.—5—Pittsburgh vs. Philadelphia, August 23, 1910.
A. L.—5—New York vs. Boston, September 5, 1921, second game.
Cleveland vs. St. Louis, May 1, 1928.

Most Assists, Game, Outfield to Catcher With Runner Thrown Out
N. L.—3—Washington vs. Indianapolis, June 19, 1889.
New York vs. Boston, June 30, 1902.
Chicago vs. Pittsburgh, April 26, 1905.
A. L.—2—Made in many games.

Longest Game, Outfield, With No Assists
N. L.—26 innings—Boston vs. Brooklyn, May 1, 1920.
A. L.—24 innings—Boston vs. Philadelphia, September 1, 1906.
Philadelphia vs. Detroit, July 21, 1945.

Longest Game, Outfield, With No Assists, Both Clubs
N. L.—24 innings—Houston 0, New York 0, April 15, 1968.
A. L.—22 innings—Chicago 0, Washington 0, June 12, 1967.

Most Assists, Inning
A. L.—10—Cleveland vs. Philadelphia, August 17, 1921, first inning.
Boston vs. New York, May 10, 1952, fifth inning.
N. L.—8—Boston vs. Philadelphia, May 1, 1911, fourth inning.

Chances Accepted & Offered

Most Chances Accepted, Season
A. L. (162-game season)—6499—California, 162 games, 1983.
A. L. (154-game season)—6655—Chicago, 157 games, 1907.
N. L. (162-game season)—6508—Chicago, 162 games, 1977.
N. L. (154-game season)—6472—New York, 155 games, 1920.

Fewest Chances Accepted, Season
A. L. (154-game season)—5470—Cleveland, 147 games, 1945.
N. L. (154-game season)—5545—Philadelphia, 154 games 1955.

Most Chances Accepted, Nine-Inning Game
N. L.—55—Pittsburgh vs. New York, June 7, 1911.
A. L.—54—St. Louis vs. Philadelphia, August 16, 1919.

Most Chances Accepted, Extra-Inning Game
N. L.—119—Boston vs. Brooklyn, May 1, 1920, 26 innings.
A. L.—110—Detroit vs. Philadelphia, July 21, 1945, 24 innings.

Most Chances Accepted, Nine-Inning Game, Both Clubs
N. L.—98—Brooklyn 50, New York 48, April 21, 1903.
New York 52, Cincinnati 46, May 15, 1909.
A. L.—98—Cleveland 49, St. Louis 49, May 7, 1909.

Most Chances Accepted, Infield, Game, Nine Innings
N. L.—45—New York vs. Pittsburgh, July 13, 1919.
Chicago vs. Philadelphia, September 24, 1927.
Chicago vs. Pittsburgh, May 9, 1963.
A. L.—44—Detroit vs. Washington, September 2, 1901, second game.

Most Chances Accepted, Infield, Game, Nine Innings, Both Clubs
N. L.—78—Cincinnati 41, New York 37, May 7, 1941.
A. L.—76—Boston 43, Cleveland 33, June 24, 1931.

Fewest Chances Offered, Infield, Game, Nine Innings
A. L.—3—St. Louis vs. New York, July 20, 1945, second game.
N. L.—4—New York vs. San Diego, April 22, 1970.

Fewest Chances Offered, Infield, Game, Nine Innings, Both Clubs
A. L.—18—Cleveland 9, Baltimore 9, August 31, 1955.
N. L.—19—Chicago 10, Philadelphia 9, May 2, 1957.

Most Chances Accepted, Outfield, Game
N. L.—20—Pittsburgh vs. Cincinnati, July 5, 1948, second game.
A. L.—18—Cleveland vs. St. Louis, September 28, 1929.
New York vs. Boston, October 1, 1933.
Philadelphia vs. Boston, May 27, 1941, second game.
New York vs. Cleveland, June 26, 1955, second game.

Most Chances Accepted, Outfield, Game, Both Clubs
A. L.—30—Washington 17, St. Louis 13, May 3, 1939.
N. L.—30—Chicago 16, Philadelphia 14, August 7, 1953.

Most Chances Accepted, Outfield, Extra-Inn. Game
N. L.—24—Brooklyn vs. Boston, May 1, 1920, 26 innings.
Chicago vs. Boston, May 17, 1927, 22 innings.
A. L.—22—Chicago vs. Washington, May 15, 1918, 18 innings.

Most Chances Accepted, Outfield, Extra-Inn. Game, Both Clubs
N. L.—43—New York 22, Pittsburgh 21, July 17, 1914, 21 innings.
A. L.—40—Washington 21, St. Louis 19, July 19, 1924, 16 innings.

Fewest Chances Offered, Outfield, Game, Nine Innings
N. L.—0—Made in many games.
A. L.—0—Made in many games.

Longest Game, Outfield, With No Chances Offered
N. L.—13 innings—St. Louis vs. Philadelphia, August 13, 1987.
A. L.—11 innings—St. Louis vs. Cleveland, April 23, 1905.

Fewest Chances Offered, Outfield, Game, Nine Inn., Both Clubs
A. A.—2—St. Louis 2, New York 0, June 30, 1886.
N. L.—2—Pittsburgh 1, Brooklyn 1, August 26, 1910.
Cincinnati 1, New York 1, May 7, 1941.
A. L.—3—St. Louis 2, Chicago 1, April 24, 1908.
New York 2, Boston 1, May 4, 1911.
New York 2, Detroit 1, May 9, 1930.

Fewest Chances Offered, Outfield, Two Consecutive Games
U. A.—0—Milwaukee vs. Boston, October 4, 5, 1884.
A. L.—1—St. Louis, April 16, 10 innings, April 17, 1908.
N. L.—2—Held by many clubs.

Most Chances Accepted, Outfield, Doubleheader
N. L.—28—Pittsburgh vs. Cincinnati, July 5, 1948.
A. L.—24—Detroit vs. Philadelphia, June 28, 1931.
Philadelphia vs. Boston, May 27, 1941.

Most Chances Accepted, Outfield, Doubleheader, Both Clubs
N. L.—48—Pittsburgh 26, Boston 22, June 26, 1935.
A. L.—44—Detroit 24, Philadelphia 20, June 28, 1931.

Errors

Most Errors, Season
N. L.—867—Washington, 122 games, 1886.
A. L.—425—Detroit, 136 games, 1901.
N. L. since 1900—408—Brooklyn, 155 games, 1905.

Fewest Errors, Season
A. L. (162-game season)—95—Baltimore, 163 games, 1964.
Baltimore, 162 games, 1980.
N. L. (162-game season)—95—Cincinnati, 162 games, 1977.

Most Errorless Games, Season
A. L. (162-game season)—96—Toronto, 163 games, 1986.
A. L. (154-game season)—84—Detroit, 156 games, 1972.
N. L. (162-game season)—94—Cincinnati, 162 games, 1977.
N. L. (154-game season)—82—Cincinnati, 154 games, 1958.

Most Consecutive Years Leading League in Errors
N. L.—7—Philadelphia, 1930 through 1936.
A. L.—6—Philadelphia, 1936 through 1941.
St. Louis, 1948 through 1953.

Most Years Leading League, Fewest Errors
N. L. since 1900—19—Cincinnati.

Most Errors, Game
N. L.—24—Boston vs. St. Louis, June 14, 1876.
A. L.—12—Detroit vs. Chicago, May 1, 1901.
Chicago vs. Detroit, May 6, 1903.
N. L. since 1900—11—St. Louis vs. Pittsburgh, April 19, 1902.
Boston vs. St. Louis, June 11, 1906.
St. Louis vs. Cincinnati, July 3, 1909, second game.

Most Errors, Game, Both Clubs
N. L.—40—Boston 24, St. Louis 16, June 14, 1876.
A. L.—18—Chicago 12, Detroit 6, May 6, 1903.
N. L. since 1900—15—St. Louis 11, Pittsburgh 4, April 19, 1902.
Boston 10, Chicago 5, October 3, 1904.

Longest Game With No Errors

A. L.—22 innings—Chicago vs. Washington, June 12, 1967.
Washington vs. Chicago, June 12, 1967.
N. L.—21 innings—Boston vs. Pittsburgh, August 1, 1918.
Chicago vs. Philadelphia, July 17, 1918.
San Francisco vs. Cincinnati, September 1, 1967.
San Diego vs. Montreal, May 21, 1977.

Longest Game With No Errors, Both Clubs

A. L.—22 innings—Chicago 0, Washington 0, June 12, 1967.
N. L.—21 innings—Chicago 0, Philadelphia 0, July 17, 1918, none out for Philadelphia in 21st inning.

Most Consecutive Errorless Games, Season

A. L.—12—Detroit, July 29 through August 7, 1963, 105 ⅔ innings.
N. L.—15—Cincinnati, June 15, second game, through June 30, 1975, 144 innings.

Most Errors, Doubleheader, Since 1900

N. L.—17—Cincinnati vs. Brooklyn, September 13, 1900.
Chicago vs. Cincinnati, October 8, 1900.
St. Louis vs. Cincinnati, July 3, 1909.
A. L.—16—Cleveland vs. Washington, September 21, 1901.

Most Errors, Doubleheader, Both Clubs, Since 1900

N. L.—25—Chicago 17, Cincinnati 8, October 8, 1900.
A. L.—22—Cleveland 16, Washington 6, September 21, 1901.

Longest Doubleheader Without an Error

A. L.—27 innings—Detroit vs. New York, August 23, 1968, (first game, Detroit fielded 8 innings; second game 19 innings).
N. L.—25 innings—Philadelphia vs. Cincinnati, July 8, 1924.

Longest Doubleheader Without an Error, Both Clubs

A. L.—24 innings—New York 0, Philadelphia 0, July 4, 1925.
Washington 0, New York 0, August 14, 1960.
N. L.—20 innings—Boston 0, Chicago 0, September 18, 1924.
New York 0, Chicago 0, August 27, 1951.

Most Errors, Infield, Game, Nine Innings

N. L.—17—Boston vs. St. Louis, June 14, 1876.
A. L.—10—Detroit vs. Chicago, May 1, 1901.

Most Errors, Infield, Game, Nine Innings, Both Clubs

N. L.—22—Boston 17, St. Louis 5, June 14, 1876.
A. L.—13—Chicago 8, Detroit 5, May 6, 1903.

Longest Game, Without An Error, Infield

A. L.—25 innings—Chicago vs. Milwaukee, May 8, finished May 9, 1984.
N. L.—24 innings—Houston vs. New York, April 15, 1968.

Most Errors, Outfield, Game, Nine Innings

N. L.—11—Boston vs. Hartford, May 1, 1876.
A. L.— 5—Baltimore vs. St. Louis, August 19, 1902.
N. L. since 1900—4—Made in many games. Last time—San Francisco vs. Los Angeles, July 4, 1971.

Most Errors, Inning, Since 1900

A. L.—7—Cleveland vs. Chicago, September 20, 1905, eighth inning.
N. L.—6—Pittsburgh vs. New York, August 20, 1903, first game, first inning.

Passed Balls

Most Passed Balls, Season

N. L.— 167— Boston, 98 games, 1883.
A. L. (162-game season) —73—Texas, 162 games, 1987.
A. L. (154-game season) —49—Baltimore, 155 games, 1959.
N. L. (154-game season) —since 1900—42—Boston, 156 games, 1905.
N. L. (162-game season) —42—Atlanta, 162 games, 1967.

Fewest Passed Balls, Season

A. L. (162-game season) —3—Boston, 160 games, 1975.
Kansas City, 162 games, 1984.
Toronto, 161 games, 1985.
A. L. (154-game season) —0—New York, 155 games, 1931.
N. L. (162-game season) —2—New York, 162 games, 1980.
N. L. (154-game season) —2—Boston, 153 games, 1943.

Most Passed Balls, Game

A. A.— 12— Washington vs. New York, May 10, 1884.
N. L.— 10— Boston vs. Washington, May 3, 1886.
N. L. since 1900—6—Cincinnati vs. Pittsburgh, October 4, 1902.
A. L.— 6— Texas vs. Detroit, August 30, 1987.

Most Passed Balls, Game, Both Clubs

A. A.— 14— Washington 12, New York 2, May 10, 1884.
N. L.— 11— Troy 7, Cleveland 4, June 16, 1880.
N. L. since 1900—6—Cincinnati 6, Pittsburgh 0, October 4, 1902.
A. L.— 6— Texas 6, Detroit 0, August 30, 1987.

Longest Game With No Passed Balls

N. L.—26 innings—Boston vs. Brooklyn, May 1, 1920.
Brooklyn vs. Boston, May 1, 1920.
A. L.—25 innings—Chicago vs. Milwaukee, May 8, finished May 9, 1984.
Milwaukee vs. Chicago, May 8, finished May 9, 1984 (fielded 24 ⅓ innings) .

Longest Game With No Passed Balls, Both Clubs

N. L.—26 innings—Boston 0, Brooklyn 0, May 1, 1920.
A. L.—25 innings—Chicago 0, Milwaukee 0, May 8, finished May 9, 1984 (Milwaukee fielded 24 ⅓ innings) .

Double Plays

Most Double Plays, Season

A. L. (154-game season) —217—Philadelphia, 154 games, 1949.
A. L. (162-game season) —206—Boston, 160 games, 1980.
Toronto, 162 games, 1980.
N. L. (162-game season) —215—Pittsburgh, 162 games, 1966.
N. L (154-game season) —198—Los Angeles, 154 games, 1958.

Most Years, 200 or More Double Plays

A. L.—3—Philadelphia, 1949 (217) , 1950 (208) , 1951 (204) .
N. L.—1—Pittsburgh, 1966 (215) .

Fewest DPs, Season (A.L.—Since 1912; N.L.—Since 1919)

A. L. (154-game season) —74—Boston, 151 games, 1913.
N. L. (154-game season) —94—Pittsburgh, 153 games, 1935.

Most Times Five or More Double Plays, Game, Season

N. L.—3—New York, 1950.
A. L.—3—Cleveland, 1970.
Kansas City, 1971.

Most Double Plays, Game

A. L.—7—New York vs. Philadelphia, August 14, 1942.
N. L.—7—Houston vs. San Francisco, May 4, 1969.
Atlanta vs. Cincinnati, June 27, 1982, 14 innings.

Most Double Plays, Game, Nine Innings, Both Clubs

A. L.—9—Detroit 5, Washington 4, May 21, 1925.
Cleveland 6, Detroit 3, September 27, 1952.
New York 6, Kansas City 3, July 31, 1955, second game.
Cleveland 5, Boston 4, May 9, 1965, second game.
California 6, Boston 3, May 1, 1966, first game.
Cleveland 5, Chicago 4, May 5, 1970.
Kansas City 6, Oakland 3, May 14, 1971.
N. L.—9—Chicago 5, Cincinnati 4, July 3, 1929.
Los Angeles 5, Pittsburgh 4, April 15, 1961.

Most Double Plays, Extra-Inning Game, Both Clubs

N. L.—10—Boston 5, Cincinnati 5, June 7, 1925, 12 innings.
Cincinnati 6, New York 4, May 1, 1955, 16 innings.

Most Unassisted Double Plays, Game

N. L.-A. L.—2—Made in many games.

Most Unassisted Double Plays, Game, Both Clubs

N. L.-A. L.—2—Made in many games.

Most Double Plays, Doubleheader

A. L.—10—Washington vs. Chicago, August 18, 1943, 22 ⅓ innings.
N. L.— 9—St. Louis vs. Cincinnati, June 11, 1944, 18 innings.

Most Double Plays, Doubleheader, Both Clubs

N. L.—13—New York 7, Philadelphia 6, September 28, 1939.
Pittsburgh 8, St. Louis 5, September 6, 1948.
A. L.—12—Philadelphia 9, Cleveland 3, September 14, 1931.
Boston 7, Chicago 5, September 15, 1947.
New York 7, Kansas City 5, July 31, 1955.
California 8, Boston 4, May 1, 1966.

Most Consecutive Games Making One or More Double Plays

A. L.— 25— Boston, May 7 through June 4, second game, 1951.
Cleveland, August 21, second game through September 12, 1953.
N. L.— 23— Brooklyn, August 7, second game through August 27, 1952.

Most Consecutive Games, One or More Double or Triple Plays

N. L.— 26— New York, August 21 through September 16, second game, 1951 (44 double plays, 1 triple play) .
A. L.— 25— Boston, May 7 through June 4, second game, 1951 (38 double plays) .
Cleveland, August 21, second game, through September 12, 1953 (38 double plays) .

Most Double Plays, Two Consecutive Nine-Inning Games

N. L.— 10— New York vs. Brooklyn, August 12, August 13, first game, 1932.
A. L.— 10— Detroit vs. Boston, May 18 (4) , 19 (6) , 1948.
Cleveland vs. Kansas City, May 3 (5) ; vs. Chicago, May 5 (5) ; 1970.
Kansas City vs. Baltimore, May 5 (4) , May 6 (6) , 1972.

Most DPs, Three Consecutive Games (Making One Each Game)

N. L.— 13— San Francisco, April 24 through April 26, 1987.
A. L.— 12— Boston, June 25 through June 27, 1950.
New York, April 19 through April 21, 1952.
Chicago, September 2 through September 3, second game, 1973.

Most DPs, Four Consecutive Games (Making One Each Game)

N. L.— 15— San Francisco, April 24 through April 27, 1987.
A. L.— 14— Chicago, July 12 through July 14, 1951.
New York, April 18 through April 21, 1952.

Most DPs, Five Consecutive Games (Making One Each Game)

A. L.— 16— New York, April 19 through April 23, 1952.
N. L.— 16— San Francisco, April 22 through April 27, 1987.

Most DPs, Six Consecutive Games (Making One Each Game)

A. L.— 18— New York, April 18 through April 23, 1952.
N. L.— 17— San Francisco, April 21 through April 27, 1987.

Most DPs, Seven Consecutive Games (Making One Each Game)

A. L.— 19— New York, April 17 through April 23, 1952.
N. L.— 18— New York, September 2 through September 8, 1950.

Most DPs, Eight Consecutive Games (Making One Each Game)

A. L.— 20— New York, April 16 through April 23, 1952.
Los Angeles, August 16 through August 24, 1963.
N. L.— 19— New York, September 2 through September 9, 1950.
Los Angeles, June 24, first game through July 1, 1958.

Most DPs, Nine Consecutive Games (Making One Each Game)

A. L.— 22— Philadelphia, May 8 through May 18, 1951.
Los Angeles, August 16 through August 25, 1963.
N. L.— 21— Los Angeles, June 24, first game, through July 3, first game, 1958.

Most DPs, 10 Consecutive Games (Making One Each Game)

A. L.— 24— Philadelphia, May 8 through May 20, first game, 1951.
N. L.— 22— Los Angeles, June 23 through July 3, first game, 1958.

Most DPs, 11 Consecutive Games (Making One Each Game)

A. L.— 26— Philadelphia, May 8 through May 20, second game, 1951.
N. L.— 23— New York, September 2 through September 13, 1950.
Milwaukee, August 19 through August 28, 1956.
Los Angeles, June 22, second game, through July 3, first game, 1958.

Most DPs, 12 Consecutive Games (Making One Each Game)

A. L.— 26— Washington, September 1 through September 9, first game, 1937.
Los Angeles, August 16 through August 29, 1963.
Chicago, September 4, second game, through September 17, 1963.
N. L.— 25— New York, September 4, first game through September 14, second game, 1950.

Most DPs, 13 Consecutive Games (Making One Each Game)

A. L.— 29— Los Angeles, August 16 through August 30, 1963.
N. L.— 27— New York, September 2 through September 14, second game 1950.

Most DPs, 14 Consecutive Games (Making One Each Game)

A. L.— 31— Los Angeles, August 16 through August 31, 1963.
N. L.— 28— New York, September 2 through September 15, 1950.

Most DPs, 15 Consecutive Games (Making One Each Game)

A. L.— 34— Los Angeles, August 16 through September 1, 1963.
N. L.— 29— Philadelphia, July 11 through July 26, 1953.

Most DPs, 16 Consecutive Games (Making One Each Game)

A. L.— 35— Los Angeles, August 15 through September 1, 1963.
N. L.— 29— Cincinnati, May 11 through May 29, 1954.
Philadelphia, July 15 through July 30, 1961.

Most DPs, 17 Consecutive Games (Making One Each Game)

A. L.— 36— Los Angeles, August 14 through September 1, 1963.
N. L.— 27— Brooklyn, August 7, second game through August 22, second game, 1952.

Most DPs, 18 Consecutive Games (Making One Each Game)

A. L.— 38— Los Angeles, August 13 through September 1, 1963.
N. L.— 29— Brooklyn, August 7, second game, through August 23, 1952.
Montreal, July 19, second game, through August 5, first game, 1970.

Most DPs, 19 Consecutive Games (Making One Each Game)

A. L.— 31— Cleveland, August 22 through September 7, first game, 1953.
N. L.— 30— Brooklyn, August 7, second game, through August 24, 1952.

Most DPs, 20 Consecutive Games (Making One Each Game)

N. L.— 33— Brooklyn, August 7, second game, through August 25, first game, 1952.
A. L.— 32— Boston, May 7 through June 1, 1951.
Cleveland, August 21, second game, through September 7, first game, 1953.

Most DPs, 21 Consecutive Games (Making One Each Game)

N. L.— 34— Brooklyn, August 7, second game, through August 25, second game, 1952.
A. L.— 34— Cleveland, August 23, second game, through September 11, 1953.

Most DPs, 22 Consecutive Games (Making One Each Game)

N. L.— 35— Brooklyn, August 7, second game, through August 26, 1952.
A. L.— 35— Cleveland, August 23, first game, through September 11, 1953.

Most DPs, 23 Consecutive Games (Making One Each Game)

N. L.— 36— Brooklyn, August 7, second game, through August 27, 1952.
A. L.— 36— Cleveland, August 22 through September 11, 1953.

Most DPs, 24 Consecutive Games (Making One Each Game)

A. L.— 37— Boston, May 7 through June 4, first game, 1951.
Cleveland, August 21, second game, through September 11, 1953.
N. L.—No performance.

Most DPs, 25 Consecutive Games (Making One Each Game)

A. L.— 38— Boston, May 7 through June 4, second game, 1951.
Cleveland, August 21, second game, through September 12, 1953.
N. L.—No performance.

Triple Plays

Most Triple Plays, Season

A. A.— 3— Cincinnati, 1882.
Rochester, 1890.
A. L.— 3— Detroit, 1911; Boston, 1924, 1979; Oakland, 1979.
N. L.— 3— Philadelphia, 1964; Chicago 1965.

Most Triple Plays, Game

A. L.- N. L.— 1—Made in many games.

Most Triple Plays, Game, Both Clubs

A. L.- N. L.— 1—Made in many games.

Most Triple Plays, Two Consecutive Games

A. L.— 2—Detroit vs. Boston, June 6, 7, 1908.
N. L.— 1—Held by many clubs.

League Fielding

Games

Most Catchers Catching 100 or More Games, Season

A. L.— (14-club league) —12 in 1985.
A. L.— (12-club league) — 8 in 1972, 1974.
A. L.— (10-club league) — 9 in 1966.
A. L.— (8-club league) — 8 in 1921, 1952.
N. L.— (12-club league) —12 in 1987.
N. L.— (10-club league) — 9 in 1965, 1966.
N. L.— (8-club league) — 8 in 1931, 1941.

Fewest Catchers Catching 100 or More Games, Season, Since 1890

A. L.—0 in 1902, 1903, 1942.
N. L.—0 in 1893, 1896, 1900, 1945.

Average

Highest Fielding Percentage, Season

A. L.— (14-club league) —.97985 in 1982.
A. L.— (12-club league) —.97975 in 1964.
A. L.— (8-club league) —.97881 in 1957, 1958.
N. L.— (12-club league) —.97967 in 1971.
N. L.— (8-club league) —.97728 in 1956.

Lowest Fielding Percentage, Season, Since 1900

A. L.— (14-club league) —.97736 in 1977.
A. L.— (12-club league) —.9754 in 1975.
A. L.— (8-club league) —.937 in 1901.
N. L.— (12-club league) —.9765 in 1969.
N. L.— (8-club league) —.949 in 1903.

Putouts

Most Putouts, Season, Since 1900

A. L.— (14-club league) —61,005 in 1982.
A. L.— (12-club league) —52,510 in 1969.
A. L.— (10-club league) —43,847 in 1964.
A. L.— (8-club league) —33,830 in 1916.
N. L.— (12-club league) —52,630 in 1982.
N. L.— (10-club league) —44,042 in 1968.
N. L.— (8-club league) —33,724 in 1917.

Fewest Putouts, Season, Since 1900

A. L.— (14-club league) —60,155 in 1979.
A. L.— (12-club league) —51,821 in 1975.
A. L.— (8-club league) —32,235 in 1938.
N. L.— (12-club league) —52,000 in 1978.
N. L.— (8-club league) —32,296 in 1906.

Most Outfielders With 400 or More Putouts, Season

A. L.—5 in 1979, 1980, 1984, 1985, 1986.
N. L.—4 in 1954, 1982.

Assists

Most Assists, Season, Since 1900

A. L.— (14-club league) —25,626 in 1980.
A. L.— (12-club league) —21,786 in 1976.
A. L.— (10-club league) —17,269 in 1961.
A. L.— (8-club league) —17,167 in 1910.
N. L.— (12-club league) —22,341 in 1980.
N. L.— (10-club league) —18,205 in 1968.
N. L.— (8-club league) —16,759 in 1920.

Fewest Assists, Season, Since 1900

A. L.— (14-club league) —23,398 in 1986.
A. L.— (12-club league) —21,001 in 1971.
A. L.— (8-club league) —13,219 in 1958.
N. L.— (12-club league) —21,038 in 1970.
N. L.— (8-club league) —13,345 in 1956.

Most First Basemen With 100 or More Assists, Season

A. L.—7 in 1985, 1986.
N. L.—6 in 1982.

Most Second Basemen With 500 or More Assists, Season

N. L.—4 in 1924.
A. L.—3 in 1930.

Most Shortstops With 500 or More Assists, Season

N. L.—5 in 1978.
A. L.—5 in 1979.

Chances Accepted

Most Chances Accepted, Season, Since 1900

A. L.— (14-club league) —86,621 in 1980.
A. L.— (12-club league) —74,191 in 1976.
A. L.— (10-club league) —60,997 in 1964.
A. L.— (8-club league) —50,870 in 1910.
N. L.— (12-club league) —74,930 in 1980.
N. L.— (10-club league) —62,247 in 1968.
N. L.— (8-club league) —50,419 in 1920.

Fewest Chances Accepted, Season, Since 1900

A. L.— (14-club league) —84,008 in 1986.
A. L.— (12-club league) —72,875 in 1971.
A. L.— (8-club league) —40,086 in 1938.
N. L.— (12-club league) —73,273 in 1970.
N. L.— (8-club league) —46,404 in 1955.

Errors

Most Errors, Season, Since 1900

A. L.— (14-club league) —1,989 in 1977.
A. L.— (12-club league) —1,747 in 1974.
A. L.— (8-club league) —2,889 in 1901.
N. L.— (12-club league) —1,859 in 1975.
N. L.— (10-club league) —2,590 in 1904.

Fewest Errors, Season, Since 1900

A. L.— (8-club league) —1,002 in 1958.
A. L.— (12-club league) —1,261 in 1964.
A. L.— (14-club league) —1,731 in 1987.
N. L.— (8-club league) —1,082 in 1956.
N. L.— (12-club league) —1,389 in 1968.

Passed Balls

Most Passed Balls, Season, Since 1900

N. L.— (12-club league) —217 in 1969.
N. L.— (10-club league) —216 in 1962.
N. L.— (8-club league) —202 in 1905.
A. L.— (14-club league) —267 in 1987.
A. L.— (12-club league) —247 in 1969.
A. L.— (10-club league) —211 in 1965.
A. L.— (8-club league) —178 in 1914.

Fewest Passed Balls, Season

A. L.— (8-club league) — 53 in 1949.
A. L.— (10-club league) —147 in 1963, 1966.
A. L.— (12-club league) —127 in 1976.
A. L.— (14-club league) —128 in 1977.
N. L.— (8-club league) — 65 in 1936.
N. L.— (10-club league) —148 in 1968.
N. L.— (12-club league) —122 in 1980.

Double Plays

Most Double Plays, Season

A. L.— (14-club league) —2,368 in 1980.
A. L.— (12-club league) —1,994 in 1973.
A. L.— (10-club league) —1,585 in 1961.
A. L.— (8-club league) —1,487 in 1949.
N. L.— (12-club league) —1,888 in 1971.
N. L.— (10-club league) —1,596 in 1962.
N. L.— (8-club league) —1,337 in 1951.

Fewest DPs, Season (A. L.—Since 1912; N. L.—Since 1920)

A. L.— (8-club league) — 818 in 1912.
A. L.— (12-club league) —1,388 in 1967, 1968.
A. L.— (14-club league) —2,119 in 1987.
N. L.— (8-club league) —1,007 in 1920.
N. L.— (12-club league) —1,431 in 1963.

Most Double Plays, One Day, Four Games, One League

N. L.— 19— May 7, 1941.
A. L.— 21— May 20, 1941.

Most Double Plays, One Day, Five Games, One League
   N. L.— 23— September 28, 1939.
   A. L.— 21— May 13, 1970.

Most Double Plays, One Day, Six Games, One League
   A. L.— 23— June 4, 1970.
   N. L.— 22— April 26, 1972.

Most Double Plays, One Day, Seven Games, One League
   A. L.— 25— August 7, 1974.
   N. L.— 23— August 15, 1937.

Most Double Plays, One Day, Eight Games, One League
   A. L.— 29— July 23, 1972.
   N. L.— 25— June 24, 1975.

Most Double Plays, One Day, Nine Games, One League
   N. L.— 28— July 24, 1976.
   A. L.— 25— July 8, 1973; August 7, 1973.

Most Double Plays, One Day, Ten Games, One League
   A. L.— 27— July 4, 1969; July 26, 1973.
   N. L.— 25— July 1, 1973.

Most Times, Five or More Double Plays, One Club, Season
   A. L.— 9 in 1970.
   N. L.— 7 in 1950, 1962.

Most Unassisted Double Plays, Season, by First Basemen
   A. L.— 38 in 1949.
   N. L.— 32 in 1953.

Most Unassisted Double Plays, Season, by Catchers
   N. L.— 5 in 1965.
   A. L.— 3 in 1914, 1969.

Most Unassisted Double Plays, Season, by Pitchers
   N. L.— 3 in 1935, 1940.
   A. L.— 2 in 1908, 1932.

Triple Plays

Most Triple Plays, Season
   N. L.— (12-club league) —4 in 1969, 1971, 1978.
   N. L.— (8-club league) —7 in 1891, 1905, 1910, 1929.
   A. L.— (14-club league) —10 in 1979.
   A. L.— (12-club league) —3 in 1972.
   A. L.— (8-club league) —7 in 1922, 1936.

Fewest Triple Plays, Season
   N. L.— 0 in 1928, 1938, 1941, 1943, 1945, 1946, 1959, 1961, 1974, 1984.
   A. L.— 0 in 1904, 1933, 1942, 1956, 1961, 1962, 1974, 1975, 1987.

Fewest Triple Plays, Season, Both Leagues
   0 in 1961, 1974 (0 in A. L., 0 in N. L.)

Most Triple Plays, One Day
   N. L.— 2— May 29, 1897; August 30, 1921.
   A. L.— 1— Made on many days.

Individual Miscellaneous

Historic Firsts

First Player Two Clubs, Season
   N. L.—Cornelius M. Phelps, New York, Philadelphia, 1876.
   A. L.—Harry P. Lockhead, Detroit, Philadelphia, 1901.

First Player Three Clubs, Season
   N. L.—August H. Krock, Chicago, Indianapolis, Washington, 1889.
   A. L.—Patrick W. Donahue, Boston, Cleveland, Philadelphia, 1910.
      (See next item: Frank Huelsman played with four clubs in 1904)

First Player Four Clubs, Season
   N. L.—Thomas J. Dowse, Louisville, Cincinnati, Philadelphia, Washington, 63 games, 1892.
   A. L.—Frank Huelsman, Chicago, Detroit, St. Louis, Washington, 112 games, 1904.

First Pitcher Two Clubs, Season
   N. L.—Thomas Healy, Providence, Indianapolis, 1878.
   A. L.—Charles Baker, Cleveland, Philadelphia, 1901.

First Pitcher Three Clubs, Season
   N. L.—August H. Krock, Chicago, Indianapolis, Washington, 1889.
   A. L.—William Henry James, Detroit, Boston, Chicago, 1919.

First Player to Enter Military Service in World War I
   Harry M. Gowdy, Boston N. L., June 27, 1917.

First Player to Enter Military Service in World War II
   Hugh N. Mulcahy, Philadelphia N. L., March 8, 1941.

First Player Facing Pitcher Three Times, Inning
   N. L.—Thomas J. Carey, Hartford, May 13, 1876, fourth inning.
   A. L.—Theodore S. Williams, Boston, July 4, 1948, seventh inning.

First Player Seven At-Bats in Nine-Inning Game
   N. L.—John J. Burdock, Hartford, May 13, 1876.
   A. L.—William O. Gilbert, Milwaukee, May 5, 1901.

First Player Eight At-Bats in Nine-Inning Game
   N. L.—Roscoe C. Barnes, Chicago, July 22, 1876.

First Player Five Runs in Nine-Inning Game
   N. L.—George W. Hall, Philadelphia, June 17, 1876.
   A. L.—Michael J. Donlin, Baltimore, June 24, 1901.

First Player Six Runs in Nine-Inning Game
   N. L.—James E. Whitney, Boston, June 9, 1883.
   A. L.—John Pesky, Boston, May 8, 1946.

First Player Five Hits in Nine-Inning Game
   N. L.—Joseph V. Battin, St. Louis, May 13, 1876.
      John J. Burdock, Hartford, May 13, 1876.
      Thomas J. Carey, Hartford, May 13, 1876.
   A. L.—Irving Waldron, Milwaukee, April 28, 1901.

First Player Six Hits in Nine-Inning Game
   N. L.—David Force, Philadelphia, June 27, 1876 (6 at-bats).
   A. L.—Michael J. Donlin, Baltimore, June 24, 1901 (6 at-bats).

First Player Eight Hits in Doubleheader
   A. A.—Henry Simon, Syracuse, October 11, 1890. (See next item: Fred Carroll had 9 hits in doubleheader in 1886.)
   N. L.—Joseph Quinn, St. Louis, September 30, 1893. (See next item: Wilbert Robinson had 9 hits in doubleheader in 1892.)
   A. L.—Charles Hickman, Washington, September 7, 1905.

First Player Nine Hits in Doubleheader
   A. A.—Fred H. Carroll, Pittsburgh, July 5, 1886.
   N. L.—Wilbert Robinson, Baltimore, June 10, 1892.
   A. L.—Ray Morehart, Chicago, August 31, 1926.

First Player Four Long Hits in Nine-Inning Game
   N. L.—George W. Hall, Philadelphia, June 14, 1876 (3 triples, 1 home run).
   A. L.—Frank Dillon, Detroit, April 25, 1901 (4 doubles).

First Player Five Long Hits in Nine-Inning Game
   A. A.—George A. Strief, Philadelphia, June 25, 1885 (4 triples, 1 double).
   N. L.—George F. Gore, Chicago, July 9, 1885 (2 triples, 3 doubles).
   A. L.—Louis Boudreau, Cleveland, July 14, 1946, first game (4 doubles, 1 home run).

First Player Four Doubles in Nine-Inning Game
   N. L.—John O'Rourke, Boston, September 15, 1880.
   A. L.—Frank Dillon, Detroit, April 25, 1901.

First Player Three Triples in Nine-Inning Game
   N. L.—George W. Hall, Philadelphia, June 14, 1876.
      Ezra B. Sutton, Philadelphia, June 14, 1876.
   A. L.—Elmer H. Flick, Cleveland, July 6, 1902.

First Player Four Triples in Nine-Inning Game
   A. A.—George A. Strief, Philadelphia, June 25, 1885.
   N. L.—William M. Joyce, New York, May 18, 1897.
   A. L.—Never accomplished.

First Player Hitting Home Run
   N. L.—Roscoe C. Barnes, Chicago, May 2, 1876.
      Charles Jones, Cincinnati, May 2, 1876.

A. L.—Erwin T. Beck, Cleveland, April 25, 1901.

First Player Two Homers in Nine-Inning Game

N. L.—George W. Hall, Philadelphia, June 17, 1876.
A. L.—John B. Freeman, Boston, June 1, 1901.

First Player Three Homers in Nine-Inning Game

N. L.—Edward N. Williamson, Chicago, May 30, 1884, p.m. game.
A. L.—Kenneth R. Williams, St. Louis, April 22, 1922.

First Player Four Homers in Nine-Inning Game

N. L.—Robert L. Lowe, Boston, May 30, 1894, p.m. game.
A. L.—H. Louis Gehrig, New York, June 3, 1932.

First Player Two Homers in One Inning

N. L.—Charles Jones, Boston, June 10, 1880, eighth inning.
A. L.—Kenneth R. Williams, St. Louis, August 7, 1922, sixth inning.

First Player Grand Slam

N. L.—Roger Connor, Troy, September 10, 1881.
A. L.—Herman W. McFarland, Chicago, May 1, 1901.

First Player Grand Slam as Pinch-Hitter

N. L.—Michael J. O'Neill, St. Louis, June 3, 1902, ninth inning.
A. L.—Martin J. Kavanagh, Cleveland, September 24, 1916, fifth inning.

First Player Home Run, Night Game

N. L.—Floyd C. Herman, Cincinnati, July 10, 1935.
A. L.—Frank W. Hayes, Philadelphia, May 16, 1939.

First Player Hitting for Cycle

N. L.—Charles J. Foley, Buffalo, May 25, 1882.
A. L.—Harry H. Davis, Philadelphia, July 10, 1901.

First Player Five Bases on Balls in Nine-Inning Game

A. A.—Henry Larkin, Philadelphia, May 2, 1887.
N. L.—Fred H. Carroll, Pittsburgh, July 4, 1889, a.m. game.
A. L.—Samuel N. Strang, Chicago, April 27, 1902.

First Player Six Bases on Balls in Nine-Inning Game

N. L.—Walter Wilmot, Chicago, August 22, 1891.
A. L.—James E. Foxx, Boston, June 16, 1938.

First Player Two Bases on Balls in One Inning

N. L.—Elmer E. Smith, Pittsburgh, April 22, 1892, first inning.
A. L.—Owen Bush, Detroit, August 27, 1909, fourth inning.

First Player Four Strikeouts in Nine-Inning Game

N. L.—George H. Derby, Detroit, August 6, 1881. (See next item: Oscar Walker had 5 strikeouts in game in 1879.)
A. L.—J. Emmet Heidrick, St. Louis, May 16, 1902.

First Player Five Strikeouts in Nine-Inning Game

N. L.—Oscar Walker, Buffalo, June 20, 1879.
A. L.—Robert M. Grove, Philadelphia, June 10, 1933, first game.

First Player Two Strikeouts in One Inning

A. L.—William P. Purtell, Chicago, May 10, 1910, sixth inning.
N. L.—Edd J. Roush, Cincinnati, July 22, 1916, sixth inning.

First Pinch-Hitter

N. L.—Michael F. Welch, New York, August 10, 1889 (struck out).
A. L.—John B. McLean, Boston, April 26, 1901 (doubled).

First Hit by Pinch-Hitter

N. L.—John J. Doyle, Cleveland, June 7, 1892 (singled).
A. L.—John B. McLean, Boston, April 26, 1901 (doubled).

First Pitcher to Lose Doubleheader (Two Complete Games)

N. L.—David S. Anderson, Pittsburgh vs. Brooklyn, September 1, 1890; lost 3-2, 8-4 (pitched 2 games of tripleheader).

First Player to be Intentionally Passed With Bases Filled

A. L.—Napoleon Lajoie, Philadelphia, May 23, 1901, ninth inning.

1st Manager Removed From Two Games in One Day by Umpires

N. L.—Melvin T. Ott, New York vs. Pittsburgh, June 9, 1946, doubleheader.
A. L.—Alfred M. Martin, Texas vs. Milwaukee, July 14, 1974, doubleheader.

First Lefthanded Catcher

William A. Harbidge, Hartford, N. L., May 6, 1876.

First Lefthanded Pitcher

Robert Mitchell, Cincinnati, N. L., 1878.

First Bespectacled Pitcher

William H. White, Boston, N. L., 1877.

First Bespectacled Infielder

George Toporcer, St. Louis, N. L., 1921.

First Bespectacled Catcher

Clinton D. Courtney, New York, A. L., 1951.

Club Miscellaneous

Historic Firsts

First Shutout Game

N. L.—April 25, 1876, Chicago 4, Louisville 0.
A. L.—May 15, 1901, Washington 4, Boston 0.

First 1-0 Game

N. L.—May 5, 1876, St. Louis 1, Chicago 0.
A. L.—July 27, 1901, Detroit 1, Baltimore 0.

First Tie Game

N. L.—May 25, 1876, Philadelphia 2, Louisville 2 (14 innings), darkness.
A. L.—May 31, 1901, Washington 3, Milwaukee 3 (7 innings), darkness.

First Extra-Inning Game

N. L.—April 29, 1876, Hartford 3, Boston 2 (10 innings).
A. L.—April 30, 1901, Boston 8, Philadelphia 6 (10 innings).

First Extra-Inning Shutout

N. L.—May 25, 1876, Boston 4, Cincinnati 0 (10 innings).
A. L.—August 11, 1902, Philadelphia 1, Detroit 0 (13 innings).

First Extra-Inning 1-0 Shutout

N. L.—June 10, 1876, New York Mutuals 1, Cincinnati 0 (10 innings).
A. L.—August 11, 1902, Philadelphia 1, Detroit 0 (13 innings).

First Extra-Inning Tie Game

N. L.—May 25, 1876, Philadelphia 2, Louisville 2 (14 innings), darkness.
A. L.—August 27, 1901, Milwaukee 5, Baltimore 5 (11 innings), darkness.

First Time Two Games in One Day

N. L.—September 9, 1876, Hartford 14, Cincinnati 6; Hartford 8, Cincinnati 3.
A. L.—May 30, 1901, Baltimore 10, Detroit 7; Detroit 4, Baltimore 1.
Chicago 8, Boston 3; Chicago 5, Boston 3.
Milwaukee 5, Washington 2; Milwaukee 14, Washington 3.
Philadelphia 3, Cleveland 1; Philadelphia 8, Cleveland 2 (8 innings).

First Doubleheader

N. L.—September 25, 1882, Worcester 4, Providence 3; Providence 8, Worcester 6.
A. L.—July 15, 1901, Washington 3, Baltimore 2; Baltimore 7, Washington 3.

First Doubleheader Shutout Victory

N. L.—July 13, 1888, Pittsburgh 4, Boston 0; Pittsburgh 6, Boston 0.
A. L.—September 3, 1901, Cleveland 1, Boston 0; Cleveland 4, Boston 0.

First Forfeited Game

N. L.—August 21, 1876, St. Louis 7, Chicago 6; forfeited to St. Louis.
A. L.—May 2, 1901, Detroit 7, Chicago 5; forfeited to Detroit.

Last Forfeited Game

N. L.—July 18, 1954, second game, Philadelphia 8, St. Louis 1, at St. Louis; forfeited to Philadelphia.
A. L.—July 12, 1979, second game, Detroit 9, Chicago 0, at Chicago; forfeited to Detroit.

First Game Played by

Boston, N. L.—April 22, 1876—Boston 6, Philadelphia Athletics 5 (A).

Philadelphia Athletics, N. L.—April 22, 1876—Boston 6, Philadelphia 5 (H).

New York Mutuals, N. L.—April 25, 1876—Boston 7, New York Mutuals 6 (H).

Chicago, N. L.—April 25, 1876—Chicago 4, Louisville 0 (A).

Cincinnati, N. L.—April 25, 1876—Cincinnati 2, St. Louis 1 (H).

St. Louis, N. L.—April 25, 1876—Cincinnati 2, St. Louis 1 (A).

Philadelphia, N. L.—May 1, 1883—Providence 4, Philadelphia 3 (H).

New York, N. L. (Original Club)—May 1, 1883—New York 7, Boston 5 (H).

Pittsburgh, N. L.—April 30, 1887—Pittsburgh 6, Chicago 2 (H).

Brooklyn, N. L.—April 19, 1890—Boston 15, Brooklyn 9 (A).

Chicago, A. L.—April 24, 1901—Chicago 8, Cleveland 2 (H).

Cleveland, A. L.—April 24, 1901—Chicago 8, Cleveland 2 (A).

Detroit, A. L.—April 25, 1901—Detroit 14, Milwaukee 13 (H).

Baltimore, A. L.—April 26, 1901—Baltimore 10, Boston 6 (H).

Boston, A. L.—April 26, 1901—Baltimore 10, Boston 6 (A).

Philadelphia, A. L.—April 26, 1901—Washington 5, Philadelphia 1 (H).

Washington, A. L. (Original Club)—April 26, 1901—Washington 5, Philadelphia 1 (A).

Milwaukee, A. L.—April 25, 1901—Detroit 14, Milwaukee 13 (A).

St. Louis, A. L.—April 23, 1902—St. Louis 5, Cleveland 2 (H).

New York, A. L.—April 22, 1903—Washington 3, New York 1 (A).

Milwaukee, N. L. since 1900—April 13, 1953—Milwaukee 2, Cincinnati 0 (A).

Baltimore, A. L. (Present Club)—April 13, 1954—Detroit 3, Baltimore 0 (A).

Kansas City, A. L.—April 12, 1955—Kansas City 6, Detroit 2 (H).

Los Angeles, N. L.—April 15, 1958—San Francisco 8, Los Angeles 0 (A).

San Francisco, N. L.—April 15, 1958—San Francisco 8, Los Angeles 0 (H).

Los Angeles, A. L.—April 11, 1961—Los Angeles 7, Baltimore 2 (A).

Minnesota, A. L.—April 11, 1961—Minnesota 6, New York 0 (A).

Washington, A. L. (Second Club) —April 10, 1961—Chicago 4, Washington 3 (H).

Houston, N. L.—April 10, 1962—Houston 11, Chicago 2 (H).

New York, N. L. (Present Club)—April 11, 1962—St. Louis 11, New York 4 (A).

Atlanta, N. L.—April 12, 1966—Pittsburgh 3, Atlanta 2, 13 innings (H).

Oakland, A. L.—April 10, 1968—Baltimore 3, Oakland 1 (A).

San Diego, N. L.—April 8, 1969—San Diego 2, Houston 1 (H).

Seattle, A. L. (Original Club) —April 8, 1969—Seattle 4, California 3 (A).

Montreal, N. L.—April 8, 1969—Montreal 11, New York 10 (A).

Kansas City, A. L. (Present Club) —April 8, 1969—Kansas City 4, Minnesota 3, 12 innings (A).

Milwaukee, A. L. (Present Club) —April 7, 1970—California 12, Milwaukee 0 (H).

Texas, A. L.—April 15, 1972—California 1, Texas 0 (A).

Seattle, A. L. (Present Club) —April 6, 1977—California 7, Seattle 0 (H).

Toronto, A. L.—April 7, 1977—Toronto 9, Chicago 5 (H).

First Game Played

At Sportsman's Park (later Busch Stadium), St. Louis—May 5, 1876, St. Louis N. L. 1, Chicago 0.
  By St. Louis A. L.—April 23, 1902—St. Louis A. L. 5, Cleveland 2.
  By St. Louis N. L. since 1900—July 1, 1920—Pittsburgh N. L. 6, St. Louis 2 (10 innings).

At Shibe Park (later Connie Mack Stadium), Philadelphia—April 12, 1909, Philadelphia A. L. 8, Boston 1.

At Shibe Park (later Connie Mack Stadium), Philadelphia—May 16, 1927, St. Louis N. L. 2, Philadelphia N. L. 1.

At Forbes Field, Pittsburgh—June 30, 1909, Chicago N. L. 3, Pittsburgh 2.

At Comiskey Park, Chicago—July 1, 1910, St. Louis A. L. 2, Chicago 0.

At League Park, Cleveland—April 21, 1910, Detroit A. L. 5, Cleveland 0.

At Griffith Stadium, Washington—April 12, 1911, Washington A. L. 8, Boston 5.

At Polo Grounds, New York (first game after fire) —June 28, 1911, New York N. L. 3, Boston 0.
  Formal opening—April 19, 1912, New York N. L. 6, Brooklyn 2.

At Redland Field (later Crosley Field), Cincinnati—April 11, 1912, Cincinnati N. L. 10, Chicago 6.

At Navin Field (later Tiger Stadium), Detroit—April 20, 1912, Detroit A. L. 6, Cleveland 5 (11 innings).

At Fenway Park, Boston—April 20, 1912, Boston 7, New York 6 (11 innings).
  Formal opening—May 17, 1912, Chicago A. L. 5, Boston 2.

At Ebbets Field, Brooklyn—April 9, 1913, Philadelphia N. L. 1, Brooklyn 0.

At Wrigley Field, Chicago—April 23, 1914, Chicago F. L. 9, Kansas City 1.

By Chicago N. L.—April 20, 1916—Chicago 7, Cincinnati 6, (11 innings).

At Braves Field, Boston—August 18, 1915—Boston N. L. 3, St. Louis 1.

At Yankee Stadium, New York—April 18, 1923, New York A. L. 4, Boston 1.

At Municipal Stadium, Cleveland—July 31, 1932, Philadelphia A. L. 1, Cleveland 0.

At Milwaukee County Stadium, Milwaukee—April 14, 1953, Milwaukee N. L. 3, St. Louis 2, (10 innings).

At Memorial Stadium, Baltimore—April 15, 1954, Baltimore A. L. 3, Chicago 1.

At Municipal Stadium, Kansas City—April 12, 1955, Kansas City A. L., 6, Detroit 2.

At Roosevelt Stadium, Jersey City—April 19, 1956, Brooklyn N. L. 5, Philadelphia 4, 10 innings.

At Seals Stadium, San Francisco—April 15, 1958—San Francisco N. L. 8, Los Angeles 0.

At Memorial Coliseum, Los Angeles—April 18, 1958—Los Angeles N. L. 6, San Francisco 5.

At Candlestick Park, San Francisco—April 12, 1960—San Francisco 3, St. Louis 1.

At Metropolitan Stadium, Minnesota—April 21, 1961—Washington A. L. 5, Minnesota 3.

At Wrigley Field, Los Angeles—April 27, 1961—Minnesota A. L. 4, Los Angeles 2.

At Dodger Stadium, Los Angeles—April 10, 1962—Cincinnati 6, Los Angeles 3.

At Colt Stadium, Houston—April 10, 1962, Houston N. L. 11, Chicago 2.

At District of Columbia Stadium, Washington—April 9, 1962, Washington 4, Detroit 1.

At Shea Stadium, New York—April 17, 1964—Pittsburgh 4, New York 3.

At Astrodome, Houston—April 12, 1965—Philadelphia 2, Houston 0.

At Atlanta Stadium, Atlanta—April 12, 1966, Pittsburgh N. L. 3, Atlanta 2, 13 innings.

At Anaheim Stadium, California—April 19, 1966—Chicago 3, California 1.

At Busch Memorial Stadium, St. Louis—May 12, 1966, St. Louis N. L. 4, Atlanta 3, 12 innings.

At Oakland-Alameda County Coliseum—April 17, 1968, Baltimore 4, Oakland 1.

At San Diego Stadium, San Diego—April 8, 1969, San Diego 2, Houston 1.

At Sicks' Stadium, Seattle—April 11, 1969, Seattle 7, Chicago 0.

At Jarry Park, Montreal—April 14, 1969, Montreal 8, St. Louis 7.

At Riverfront Stadium, Cincinnati, June 30, 1970, Atlanta 8, Cincinnati 2.

At Three Rivers Stadium, Pittsburgh, July 16, 1970, Cincinnati 3, Pittsburgh 2.

At Veterans Stadium, Philadelphia—April 10, 1971, Philadelphia 4, Montreal 1.

At Arlington Stadium, Texas—April 21, 1972, Texas 7, California 6.

At Royals Stadium, Kansas City—April 10, 1973, Kansas City 12, Texas 1.

At Kingdome, Seattle—April 6, 1977, California 7, Seattle 0.

At Exhibition Stadium, Toronto—April 7, 1977, Toronto 9, Chicago 5.

At Olympic Stadium, Montreal—April 15, 1977, Philadelphia 7, Montreal 2.

At Metrodome, Minnesota—April 6, 1982, Seattle 11, Minnesota 7.

First Sunday Games

At St. Louis N. L.—April 17, 1892, Cincinnati 5, St. Louis 1.

At Cincinnati—April 24, 1892, Cincinnati 10, St. Louis 2.

At Chicago, N. L.—May 14, 1893, Cincinnati 13, Chicago 12.

At Detroit—April 28, 1901, Detroit 12, Milwaukee 11.

At Chicago, A. L.—April 28, 1901, Chicago 13, Cleveland 1.

At Milwaukee, A. L.—May 5, 1901, Milwaukee 21, Chicago 7.

At St. Louis, A. L.—April 27, 1902, Detroit 6, St. Louis 1.

At Cleveland—May 14, 1911, Cleveland 14, New York 3.

At New York, A. L.—June 17, 1917, St. Louis 2, New York 1.

First legalized Sunday—May 11, 1919, Washington 0, New York 0, 12 innings.

At Brooklyn— (No admission fee) —April 17, 1904, Brooklyn 9, Boston 1. (Five Sundays in 1904 and five in 1905). First Sunday game with admission fee—July 1, 1917, Brooklyn 3, Philadelphia 2.
First legalized Sunday—May 4, 1919, Brooklyn 6, Boston 2.
At New York, N. L.—August 19, 1917, Cincinnati 5, New York 0.
First legalized Sunday—May 4, 1919, Philadelphia 4, New York 3.
At Washington—May 19, 1918, Washington 1, Cleveland 0, 12 innings.
At Philadelphia A. L.—August 22, 1926, Philadelphia 3, Chicago 2.
First legalized Sunday—April 22, 1934, Washington 4, Philadelphia 3.
At Boston, A. L.—April 28, 1929, Philadelphia 7, Boston 3.
At Boston, N. L.—May 5, 1929, Pittsburgh 7, Boston 2.
At Philadelphia, N. L.—April 29, 1934, Brooklyn 8, Philadelphia 7.
At Pittsburgh—April 29, 1934, Pittsburgh 9, Cincinnati 5.
At Milwaukee N. L.—May 10, 1953, first game, Milwaukee 6, Chicago 2.
At Baltimore—April 18, 1954, Detroit 8, Baltimore 3.
At Kansas City—April 24, 1955, Kansas City 5, Chicago 0.
At Los Angeles, N. L.—April 20, 1958, San Francisco 12, Los Angeles 2.
At San Francisco—April 27, 1958, Chicago 5, San Francisco 4.
At Minnesota—April 23, 1961, Minnesota 1, Washington 0.
At Los Angeles, A. L.—April 30, 1961, Los Angeles 6, Kansas City 4.
At Houston, N. L.—April 22, 1962, Philadelphia 4, Houston 3.
At Atlanta, N. L.—April 24, 1966, first game, Atlanta 5, New York 2.
At Oakland—April 21, 1968, Washington 2, Oakland 0.
At Seattle—April 13, 1969, Chicago 12, Seattle 7.
At San Diego—April 13, 1969, San Francisco 5, San Diego 1.
At Montreal—April 20, 1969, first game, Chicago 6, Montreal 3.
At Texas—April 23, 1972, Texas 5, California 2.
At Toronto—April 10, 1977, Toronto 3, Chicago 1.

First Night Game

At Cincinnati—May 24, 1935, Cincinnati 2, Philadelphia 1.
By Pittsburgh—At Cincinnati—May 31, 1935, Pittsburgh 4, Cincinnati 1.
By Chicago, N. L.—At Cincinnati—July 1, 1935, Chicago 8, Cincinnati 4.
By Brooklyn—At Cincinnati—July 10, 1935, Cincinnati 15, Brooklyn 2.
By Boston, N. L.—At Cincinnati—July 24, 1935, Cincinnati 5, Boston 4.
By St. Louis, N. L.—At Cincinnati—July 31, 1935, Cincinnati 4, St. Louis 3, 10 innings.
At Brooklyn—June 15, 1938, Cincinnati 6, Brooklyn 0.
At Philadelphia, A. L.—May 16, 1939, Cleveland 8, Philadelphia 3, 10 innings.
By Chicago, A. L.—At Philadelphia—May 24, 1939, Chicago 4, Philadelphia 1.
At Philadelphia, N. L.—June 1, 1939, Pittsburgh 5, Philadelphia 2.
By St. Louis, A. L.—At Philadelphia—June 14, 1939, St. Louis 6, Philadelphia 0.
By Detroit—At Philadelphia—June 20, 1939, Detroit 5, Philadelphia 0.
By New York, A. L.—At Philadelphia—June 26, 1939, Philadelphia 3, New York 2.
At Cleveland—June 27, 1939, Cleveland 5, Detroit 0.
By Washington—At Philadelphia—July 6, 1939, Philadelphia 9, Washington 3.
At Chicago, A. L.—August 14, 1939, Chicago 5, St. Louis 2.
By Boston, A. L.—At Cleveland—July 13, 1939, Boston 6, Cleveland 5, 10 innings.
At New York, N. L.—May 24, 1940, New York 8, Boston 1.
By New York, N. L.—May 24, 1940, New York 8, Boston 1.
At St. Louis, A. L.—May 24, 1940, Cleveland 3. St. Louis 2.
At Pittsburgh—June 4, 1940, Pittsburgh 14, Boston 2.
At St. Louis, N. L.—June 4, 1940, Brooklyn 10, St. Louis 1.
At Washington—May 28, 1941, New York 6, Washington 5.
At Boston, N. L.—May 11, 1946, New York 5, Boston 1.
At New York, A. L.—May 28, 1946, Washington 2, New York 1.
At Boston, A. L.—June 13, 1947, Boston 5, Chicago 3.
At Detroit, A. L.—June 15, 1948, Detroit 4, Philadelphia 1.
By Milwaukee, N. L.—At St. Louis—April 20, 1953, St. Louis 9, Milwaukee 4.
At Milwaukee, N. L.—May 8, 1953, Milwaukee 2, Chicago 0.
At Baltimore, A. L.—April 21, 1954, Cleveland 2, Baltimore 1.
At Kansas City, A. L.—April 18, 1955, Cleveland 11, Kansas City 9.
At San Francisco, N. L.—April 16, 1958, Los Angeles 13, San Francisco 1.
At Los Angeles, N. L.—April 22, 1958, Los Angeles 4, Chicago 2.
By Minnesota, A. L.—April 14, 1961, Minnesota 3, Baltimore 2.
At Minnesota, A. L.—May 18, 1961, Kansas City 4, Minnesota 3.
At Los Angeles, A. L.—April 28, 1961, Los Angeles 6, Minnesota 5, 12 innings.
At Houston, N. L.—April 11, 1962, Houston 2, Chicago 0.

At Atlanta, N. L.—April 12, 1966, Pittsburgh 3, Atlanta 2, 13 innings.
At Oakland, A. L.—April 17, 1968, Baltimore 4, Oakland 1.
At San Diego N. L.—April 8, 1969, San Diego 2, Houston 1.
By Seattle A. L.—April 8, 1969, Seattle 4, California 3.
By Montreal N. L.—April 8, 1969, Montreal 11, New York 10.
At Seattle, A. L.—April 12, 1969, Seattle 5, Chicago 1.
At Montreal, N. L.—April 30, 1969, New York 2, Montreal 1.
By Milwaukee A. L.—April 13, 1970, Oakland 2, Milwaukee 1.
At Milwaukee A. L.—May 5, 1970, Boston 6, Milwaukee 0.
At Texas, A. L.—April 21, 1972, Texas 7, California 6.
At Toronto, A. L.—May 2, 1977, Milwaukee 3, Toronto 1.

First Night Opening Game

N. L.—At St. Louis—April 18, 1950, St. Louis 4, Pittsburgh 2.
A. L.—At Philadelphia—April 17, 1951, Washington 6, Philadelphia 1.

First Ladies Day

N. L.—At Cincinnati, 1876 season.
N. L.—At Philadelphia, 1876 season.
N. L.—At Providence, 1882 season.
N. L.—At New York, June 16, 1883, New York 5, Cleveland 2.
A. L.—At St. Louis, 1912 season.
N. L.—At St. Louis, 1917 season.

First Ladies Night

N. L.—At New York, June 27, 1941, New York 7, Philadelphia 4.
N. L.—At Brooklyn, July 31, 1950, Chicago 8, Brooklyn 5.
A. L.—At Boston, August 17, 1950, Boston 10, Philadelphia 6.

First Day Games Completed With Lights

N. L.—At Boston, April 23, 1950, second game, Philadelphia 6, Boston 5.
A. L.—At New York, August 29, 1950, New York 6, Cleveland 5.

First Time All Games Played at Night

8 (8-club leagues) on August 9, 1946 (4 in N. L.; 4 in A. L.).
12 (12-club leagues) April 25, 1969 (6 in N. L.; 6 in A. L.).

First Time All Games Twilight-Night Doubleheaders

N. L.—On August 25, 1953.

First Time Uniform Numbered

N. L.—Cincinnati, 1883 season.
A. L.—New York, 1929 season (complete).
(Cleveland vs. Chicago at Cleveland, June 26, 1916 wore numbers on the sleeves of their uniforms.)

Night Games & Postponements

Most Night Games, Season (Includes Twilight Games)

A. L. (162-game season) —135—Texas, 1979 (won 68, lost 67).
N. L. (162-game season) —126—Houston, 1985 (won 60, lost 66).

Most Games Postponed, Start of Season

A. L.—5—Chicago, April 6 through 10, 1982.
New York, April 6 through 10, 1982.
N. L.—4—New York, April 12 through 15, 1933.

Most Consecutive Games Postponed, Season

N. L.—9—Philadelphia, August 10 through August 19, 1903.
A. L.—7—Detroit, May 14 through May 18, 1945.
Philadelphia, May 14 through May 18, 1945.
Washington, April 23 through April 29, 1952.

Ties & One-Run Decisions

Most Tie Games, Season

A. L.— 10— Detroit, 1904.
N. L.— 9— St. Louis, 1911.

Fewest Tie Games, Season

N. L.-A. L.—0—By all clubs in many seasons.
N. L.—Last season, 1987.
A. L.—Last season, 1987.

Most One-Run Decision Games, Season

A. L. (162-game season) —74—Chicago, won 30, lost 44, 1968.
A. L. (154-game season) —60—Philadelphia, won 22, lost 38, 1945.
N. L. (162-game season) —75—Houston, won 32, lost 43, 1971.
N. L. (154-game season) —69—Cincinnati, won 28, lost 41, 1946.

Fewest One-Run Decision Games, Season

A. L. (154-game season) —27—Cleveland, won 9, lost 18, 1948.

A. L. (162-game season) —34—Milwaukee, won 12, lost 22, 1980.
Boston, won 24, lost 10, 1986.
Seattle, won 19, lost 15, 1987.
N. L. (154-game season) —28—Brooklyn, won 16, lost 12, 1949.
N. L. (162-game season) —38—Chicago, won 17, lost 21, 1970.

Length Of Games
By Innings

Longest Game, by Innings
N. L.—26 innings— Brooklyn 1, Boston 1, May 1, 1920 at Boston.
A. L.—25 innings— Chicago 7, Milwaukee 6, May 8, finished May 9, 1984, at Chicago.

Longest Night Game, by Innings
N. L.—25 innings— St. Louis 4, New York 3, September 11, 1974 at New York.
A. L.—25 innings— Chicago 7, Milwaukee 6, May 8, finished May 9, 1984, at Chicago.

Longest Opening Game, by Innings
A. L.—15 innings— Washington 1, Philadelphia 0, April 13, 1926 at Washington.
Detroit 4, Cleveland 2, April 19, 1960 at Cleveland.
N. L.—14 innings— Philadelphia 5, Brooklyn 5, April 17, 1923 at Brooklyn.
New York 1, Brooklyn 1, April 16, 1933 at Brooklyn (opener for New York only).
Pittsburgh 4, Milwaukee 3, April 15, 1958 at Milwaukee.
Pittsburgh 6, St. Louis 2, April 8, 1969 at St. Louis.
Cincinnati 2, Los Angeles 1, April 7, 1975 at Cincinnati.

Longest 0-0 Game
N. L.—19 innings— Brooklyn vs. Cincinnati, September 11, 1946 at Brooklyn.
A. L.—18 innings— Detroit vs. Washington, July 16, 1909 at Detroit.

Longest 0-0 Night Game
N. L.—18 innings— Philadelphia vs. New York, October 2, 1965, second game, at New York.
A. L.—None.

Longest 1-0 Day Game
N. L.—18 innings— Providence 1, Detroit 0, August 17, 1882 at Providence.
New York 1, St. Louis 0, July 2, 1933, first game at New York.
A. L.—18 innings— Washington 1, Chicago 0, May 15, 1918 at Washington.
Washington 1, Chicago 0, June 8, 1947, first game at Chicago.

Longest 1-0 Night Game
N. L.—24 innings— Houston 1, New York 0, April 15, 1968 at Houston.
A. L.—20 innings— Oakland 1, California 0, July 9, 1971 at Oakland.

Longest Shutout Game
N. L.—24 innings— Houston 1, New York 0, April 15, 1968 at Houston.
A. L.—20 innings— Oakland 1, California 0, July 9, 1971 at Oakland.

Longest Tie Game
N. L.—26 innings— Boston 1, Brooklyn 1, May 1, 1920 at Boston.
A. L.—24 innings— Detroit 1, Philadelphia 1, July 21, 1945 at Philadelphia.

Most Innings, One Day
N. L.—32— San Francisco at New York, May 31, 1964.
A. L.—29— Boston at Philadelphia, July 4, 1905.
Boston at New York, August 29, 1967.

Most Extra-Inning Games, Season
A. L.—31— Boston, 1943 (won 15, lost 14, 2 tied).
N. L.—27— Boston, 1943 (won 14, lost 13).
Los Angeles, 1967 (won 10, lost 17).

Most Consecutive Extra-Inning Games, One Club
A. L.—5— Detroit, September 9 through 13, 1908 (54 innings).
N. L.—4— Pittsburgh, August 18 through 22, 1917 (59 innings).
San Francisco, July 7 through 10, 1987 (49 innings).

Most Consecutive Extra-Inning Games, Same Clubs
A. L.—4— Chicago and Detroit, September 9 through September 12, 1908 (43 innings).
Cleveland and St. Louis, May 1, 2, 4, 5, 1910 (46 innings).
Boston and St. Louis, May 31, first game, to June 2, second game, 1943 (45 innings).
N. L.—4— New York and Pittsburgh, May 24, 25, June 23, 24, 1978 (44 innings; both clubs played other teams between these contests).
3— Brooklyn and Pittsburgh, August 20, through August 22, 1917 (45 innings).
Chicago and Pittsburgh, August 18, 19, 20, 1961 (33 innings).
Cincinnati and New York, May 5, 6, 7, 1980 (36 innings).

Most Innings, Two Consecutive Extra-Inning Games
N. L.—45— Boston, May 1, 3, 1920.
A. L.—37— Minnesota vs. Milwaukee, May 12, (22), 13 (15), 1972.
Milwaukee vs. Minnesota, May 12, (22), 13 (15), 1972.

Most Innings, Two Consecutive Extra-Inning Games, Same Clubs
N. L.— 40— Boston and Chicago, May 14 (18), 17 (22), 1927.
A. L.—37— Minnesota and Milwaukee, May 12 (22), 13 (15), 1972.

Most Innings, Three Consecutive Extra-Inning Games
N. L.— 58— Brooklyn, May 1 to May 3, 1920.
A. L.— 41— Cleveland, April 16 to April 21, 1935.
Boston, April 8, 10, 11, 1969.

Most Innings, Three Consec. Extra-Inning Games, Same Clubs
N. L.— 45— Brooklyn and Pittsburgh, August 20 through 22, 1917.
A. L.— 40— Chicago and Washington, August 24 through 26, 1915.
Detroit and Philadelphia, May 12 through 14, 1943.

Most Innings, Four Consecutive Extra-Inning Games
N. L.— 59— Pittsburgh, August 18 through August 22, 1917.
A. L.— 51— Chicago, August 23 through August 26, 1915.
Detroit, May 11, second game, through May 14, 1943.

Most Innings, Four Consecutive Extra-Inning Games, Same Clubs
A. L.— 46— Cleveland and St. Louis, May 1, 2, 4, 5, 1910.
N. L.—No performance.

By Time

Longest Game by Time, Nine Innings
N. L.—4 hours, 18 minutes—Los Angeles 8, San Francisco 7, October 2, 1962.
A. L.—4 hours, 16 minutes—Baltimore 18, New York 9, June 8, 1986.

Longest Extra-Inning Game, by Time
A. L.—8 hours, 6 minutes—Chicago 7, Milwaukee 6, May 8, finished May 9, 1984 (25 innings).
N. L.—7 hours, 23 minutes—San Francisco 8, New York 6, May 31, 1964, second game (23 innings).

Longest 1-0 Game, by Time, Nine Innings
A. L.—3 hours, 2 minutes—Milwaukee 1, Minnesota 0, June 29, 1977.
N. L.—2 hours, 46 minutes—Philadelphia 1, New York 0, June 30, 1966.

Longest Extra-Inning 1-0 Game, by Time
N. L.—6 hours, 6 minutes—Houston 1, New York 0, April 15, 1968, 24 innings.
A. L.—5 hours, 5 minutes—Oakland 1, California 0, July 9, 1971, 20 innings.

Longest Extra-Inning 1-0 Night Game, by Time
N. L.—6 hours, 6 minutes—Houston 1, New York 0, April 15, 1968, 24 innings.
A. L.—5 hours, 5 minutes—Oakland 1, California 0, July 9, 1971, 20 innings.

Longest Night Game, by Time, Nine Innings
N. L.—4 hours, 2 minutes—Milwaukee 11, San Francisco 9, June 22, 1962.
A. L.—3 hours, 56 minutes—Texas 11, Chicago 6, August 1, 1977.

Longest Night Game, by Time, Ten Innings
A. L.—3 hours, 59 minutes—Boston 3, New York 3, July 5, 1958.
N. L.—3 hours, 56 minutes—New York 8, St. Louis 7, July 16, 1952.

Longest Extra-Inning Night Game, by Time
A. L.—8 hours, 6 minutes—Chicago 7, Milwaukee 6, 25 innings at Chicago, May 8, 1984; finished May 9.

N. L.—7 hours, 4 minutes—St. Louis 4, New York 3, 25 innings at New York, September 11, 1974.

Longest Doubleheader, by Time, 18 Innings

A. L.—6 hours, 50 minutes—Detroit at Kansas City, July 23, 1961.

N. L.—6 hours, 46 minutes—Brooklyn at New York, August 7, 1952.

Longest Doubleheader, by Time, More Than 18 Innings

N. L.—9 hours, 52 minutes—San Francisco at New York, May 31, 1964, 32 innings.

A. L.—9 hours, 5 minutes—Kansas City at Detroit, June 17, 1967, 28 innings.

Shortest Game, by Time, Nine Innings

N. L.—51 minutes—New York 6, Philadelphia 1, September 28, 1919, first game.

A. L.—55 minutes—St. Louis 6, New York 2, September 26, 1926; second game.

Shortest Night Game, by Time, Nine Innings

N. L.—1 hour, 15 minutes—Boston 2, Cincinnati 0, August 10, 1944.

A. L.—1 hour, 29 minutes—Chicago 1, Washington 0, May 21, 1943.

Shortest 1-0 Game, by Time

N. L.—57 minutes—New York 1, Brooklyn 0, August 30, 1918.

A. L.—1 hour, 13 minutes—Detroit 1, New York 0, August 8, 1920.

Shortest Doubleheader, by Time, 18 Innings

A. L.—2 hours, 7 minutes—New York at St. Louis, September 26, 1926.

N. L.—2 hours, 20 minutes—Chicago at Brooklyn, August 14, 1919.

Games Won

Most Games Won, League

N. L.—8,450—Chicago, 112 years, 1876 to date.

A. L.—7,482—New York, 85 years, 1903 to date.

Most Games Won, Season

N. L. (162-game season) —108—Cincinnati, 1975 (won 108, lost 54).
New York, 1986 (won 108, lost 54).

N. L. (154-game season) —116—Chicago, 1906 (won 116, lost 36).

A. L. (162-game season) —109—New York, 1961 (won 109, lost 53).
Baltimore, 1969 (won 109, lost 53).

A. L. (154-game season) —111—Cleveland, 1954 (won 111, lost 43).

Fewest Games Won, Season

N. L. (154-game season) —20—Cleveland, 1899 (won 20, lost 134).

A. L. (154-game season) —36—Philadelphia, 1916 (won 36, lost 117).

N. L. since 1900 (154-game season) —38—Boston, 1935 (won 38, lost 115).

N. L. since 1900 (162-game season) —40—New York, 1962 (won 40, lost 120).

A. L. (162-game season) —53—Toronto, 1979 (won 53, lost 109).

Most Games Won, Two Consecutive Seasons

N. L. (154-game season) —223—Chicago, 1906, 1907 (lost 81).

N. L. (162-game season) —210—Cincinnati, 1975, 1976 (lost 114).

A. L. (162-game season) —217—Baltimore, 1969, 1970 (lost 107).

A. L. (154-game season) —211—New York, 1927, 1928 (lost 97).

Most Games Won, Three Consecutive Seasons

N. L. (154-game season) —322—Chicago, 1906, 1907, 1908 (lost 130).

N. L. (162-game season) —308—Cincinnati, 1974, 1975, 1976 (lost 178).

A. L. (162-game season) —318—Baltimore, 1969, 1970, 1971 (lost 164).

A. L. (154-game season) —313—Philadelphia, 1929, 1930, 1931 (lost 143).

Most Years Winning 100 or More Games

A. L.—14—New York, 1927, 1928, 1932, 1936, 1937, 1939, 1941, 1942, 1954, 1961, 1963, 1977, 1978, 1980.

N. L.—6—St. Louis, 1931, 1942, 1943, 1944, 1967, 1985.

Most Consecutive Years Winning 100 or More Games

A. L. (162-game season) —3—Baltimore, 1969, 1970, 1971.

A. L. (154-game season) —3—Philadelphia, 1929, 1930, 1931.

N. L. (154-game season) —3—St. Louis, 1942, 1943, 1944.

N. L. (162-game season) —2—Cincinnati, 1975, 1976.
Philadelphia, 1976, 1977.

Most Games Won at Home, Season

A. L. (162-game season) —65—New York, won 65, lost 16, 1961.

A. L. (154-game season) —62—New York, won 62, lost 15, 1932.

N. L. (154-game season) —61—Boston, won 61, lost 15, 1898.

N. L. (162-game season) —64—Cincinnati, won 64, lost 17, 1975.

N. L. (154-game season) —since 1900—60—St. Louis, won 60, lost 17, 1942.
Brooklyn, won 60, lost 17, 1953.

Most Games Won on Road, Season

N. L. (162-game season) —53—Cincinnati, won 53, lost 25, 1972.
New York, won 53, lost 28, 1986.

N. L. (154-game season) —60—Chicago, won 60, lost 15, 1906.

A. L. (162-game season) —55—Oakland, won 55, lost 25, 1971.

A. L. (154-game season) —54—New York, won 54, lost 20, 1939.

Most Games Won From One Club, Season

N. L.— (8-club league) —21—Chicago vs. Boston, 1909 (won 21, lost 1).
Pittsburgh vs. Cincinnati, 1937 (won 21, lost 1).
Chicago vs. Cincinnati, 1945 (won 21, lost 1).

N. L.— (12-club league) —17—Atlanta vs. San Diego, 1974 (won 17, lost 1).
New York vs. Pittsburgh, 1986 (won 17, lost 1).

A. L.— (8-club league) —21—New York vs. St. Louis, 1927 (won 21, lost 1).

A. L.— (12-club league) —15—Baltimore vs. Milwaukee, 1973 (won 15, lost 3).

Most Games Won From One Club, Season, at Home

N. L.—16—Brooklyn vs. Pittsburgh, won 16, lost 2, 1890.
Philadelphia vs. Pittsburgh, won 16, lost 1, 1890.

N. L. since 1900—13—New York vs. Philadelphia, won 13, lost 2, 1904.

A. L.—12—Chicago vs. St. Louis, won 12, lost 0, 1915.

Most Games Won From One Club, Season, on Road

N. L.— (8-club league) —11—Pittsburgh vs. St. Louis, won 11, lost 0, 1908.
Chicago vs. Boston, won 11, lost 0, 1909.
Brooklyn vs. Philadelphia, won 11, lost 0, 1945.

A. L.— (8-club league) —11—Chicago vs. Philadelphia, won 11, lost 0, 1915.
New York vs. St. Louis, won 11, lost 0, 1927.
New York vs. St. Louis, won 11, lost 0, 1939.
Cleveland vs. Boston, won 11, lost 0, 1954.

Most Games Won, Season, by One Run

N. L. (162-game season) —42—San Francisco, won 42, lost 26, 1978.

N. L. (154-game season) —41—Cincinnati, won 41, lost 17, 1940.

A. L. (162-game season) —40—Baltimore, won 40, lost 15, 1970.
Baltimore, won 40, lost 21, 1974.

A. L. (154-game season) —38—New York, won 38, lost 23, 1943.

Fewest Games Won, Season, by One Run

A. L. (154-game season) — 9—Cleveland, won 9, lost 18, 1948.

A. L. (162-game season) —11—Texas, won 11, lost 27, 1985.

N. L. (154-game season) — 9—New York, won 9, lost 24, 1953.

N. L. (162-game season) —16—Montreal, won 16, lost 29, 1969.
Atlanta, won 16, lost 30, 1973.
St. Louis, won 16, lost 32, 1978.
Pittsburgh, won 16, lost 37, 1986.

Most Games Won From League Champions, Season

N. L.—16—St. Louis vs. Chicago, 1945 (won 16, lost 6).

A. L.—14—Philadelphia vs. Detroit, 1909 (won 14, lost 8).
Minnesota vs. Oakland, 1973 (won 14, lost 4).

Most Games Won From One Club, Two Consecutive Seasons

N. L.— (8-club league) —40—Pittsburgh vs. St. Louis, 1907, 1908.

A. L.— (8-club league) —37—Philadelphia vs. St. Louis, 1910, 1911.

Chicago vs. Philadelphia, 1915, 1916.
New York vs. Philadelphia, 1919, 1920.
New York vs. St. Louis, 1926, 1927.

Fewest Games Won From One Club, Season

A. A.— (8-club league) —1—Cleveland vs. St. Louis, won 1, lost 18, 1887.
Louisville vs. Brooklyn, won 1, lost 19, 1889.

N. L.— (8-club league) —1—Kansas City vs. Chicago, won 1, lost 17, 1886.
Washington vs. Chicago, won 1, lost 17, 1886.
Washington vs. Detroit, won 1, lost 17, 1886.
Indianapolis vs. Philadelphia, won 1, lost 17, 1887.
Boston vs. Chicago, won 1 lost 21, 1909.
Boston vs. Pittsburgh, won 1, lost 20, 1909.
Cincinnati vs. Pittsburgh, won 1, lost 21, 1937.
Cincinnati vs. Chicago, won 1, lost 21, 1945.

N. L.— (12-club league) —0—Baltimore vs. Boston, won 0, lost 13, 1892.
Cleveland vs. Brooklyn, won 0, lost 14, 1899.
Cleveland vs. Cincinnati, won 0, lost 14, 1899.

N. L. since 1900— (12-club league) —1—San Diego vs. Atlanta, won 1, lost 17, 1974.
Chicago vs. Cincinnati, won 1, lost 11, 1975.
Atlanta vs. St. Louis, won 1, lost 11, 1977.
Atlanta vs. Montreal, won 1, lost 9, 1979.
Chicago vs. Houston, won 1, lost 11, 1980.
New York vs. San Diego, won 1, lost 11, 1980.
Pittsburgh vs. Atlanta, won 1, lost 11, 1980.
Montreal vs. Los Angeles, won 1, lost 11, 1980.
Philadelphia vs. Los Angeles, won 1, lost 11, 1983.
Pittsburgh vs. New York, won 1, lost 17, 1986.

N. L.— (10-club league) —1—Houston vs. Philadelphia, won 1, lost 17, 1962.

A. L.— (8-club league) —1—St. Louis vs. New York, won 1, lost 21, 1927.

A. L.— (10-club league) —1—Boston vs. Minnesota, won 1, lost 17, 1965.

A. L.— (12-club league) —0—Kansas City vs. Baltimore, won 0, lost 12, 1970.

A. L.— (14-club league) —0—Oakland vs. Baltimore, won 0, lost 11, 1978.

Most Times Winning Two Games in One Day, Season

N. L. (162-game season) —11—New York, won 11, lost 3, 1969.
N. L. (154-game season) —20—Chicago, won 20, lost 3, 1945.
A. L. (162-game season) —15—Chicago, won 15, lost 7, 1961.
A. L. (154-game season) —14—New York, won 14, lost 7, 1943.
Cleveland, won 14, lost 8, 1943.
Washington, won 14, lost 8, 1945.
Boston, won 14, lost 9, 1946.

Most Times Winning 2 Games in 1 Day, From 1 Club, Season

A. L. (154-game season) —7—Chicago vs. Philadelphia, 1943. (Won 7, lost 0) .

N. L. (154-game season) —7—Chicago vs. Cincinnati, 1945. (Won 7, lost 0) .

Fewest Times Winning Two Games in One Day, Season

A. L. (154-game season) —0—Detroit, 1952, lost 13, split 9.
Washington, 1957, lost 7, split 11.

A. L. (162-game season) —0—Held by many clubs.

N. L. (154-game season) —1—Held by many clubs.
N. L. (162-game season) —0—Held by many clubs.

Most Games Won, One Month

N. L.— 29— New York, September, 1916, won 29, lost 5.
A. L.— 28— New York, August, 1938, won 28, lost 8.

Most Games Won, Two Consecutive Days

N. L.— 5— Baltimore, September 7 (3) , 8 (2) , 1896.
A. L.— 4— Made on many days.

Consecutive

Most Consecutive Games Won, Season

N. L.— 26— New York, September 7 through September 30, first game, 1916 (1 tie) .
A. L.— 19— Chicago, August 2 through August 23, 1906 (1 tie) .
New York, June 29, second game, through July 17, second game, 1947.

Most Consecutive Games Won, Season, No Tie Games

N. L.— 21— Chicago, June 2 through July 8, 1880.
Chicago, September 4 through September 27, second game, 1935.
A. L.— 19— New York, June 29, second game, through July 17, second game, 1947.

Most Consecutive Games Won, Start of Season

U. A.— 20— St. Louis, April 20 through May 22, 1884.
N. L.— 13— Atlanta, April 6 through 21, 1982.
A. L.— 13— Milwaukee, April 6 through 20, 1987.

Most Home Games Won Consecutively, Season

N. L.— 26— New York, September 7 through September 30, first game, 1916 (1 tie) .
A. L.— 22— Philadelphia, July 15, first game, through August 31, 1931, not inclusive.

Most Road Games Won Consecutively, Season

N. L.— 17— New York, May 9 through May 29, 1916.
A. L.— 17— Detroit, April 3 through May 24, 1984 (start of season) .

Most Consecutive Games Won From One Club, League

A. L.— (12-club league) —23—Baltimore vs. Kansas City, May 10, 1969 through August 2, 1970, last 11 in 1969, all 12 in 1970.
N. L.— (8-club league) —21—Boston vs. Philadelphia, all 14 in 1883, first 7 in 1884.
A. L.— (8-club league) —21—New York vs. St. Louis, first 21 in 1927.
N.L. since 1900— (8-club league) —20—Pittsburgh vs. Cincinnati, last 17 in 1937, first 3 in 1938.

Most Consecutive Games Won From One Club, League, at Home

A. L.— 22— Boston vs. Philadelphia, all 11 in 1949; all 11 in 1950; April 27, 1949 to September 10, 1950, inclusive.
N. L.— 18— Milwaukee-Atlanta vs. New York, last 6 in 1964, all 9 in 1965, first 3 in 1966; June 27, 1964 through April 24, 1966, first game.

Most Consecutive Games Won From One Club, League, on Road

N. L.— 18— Brooklyn vs. Philadelphia, all 11 in 1945; first 7 in 1946; May 5, first game, 1945 through August 10, 1946.
St. Louis vs. Pittsburgh, last 8 in 1964, all 9 in 1965, first 1 in 1966; May 7, 1964 through April 15, 1966.
A. L.— 13— New York vs. St. Louis, all 11 in 1939, first 2 in 1940; May 10, 1939 through June 15, 1940.
Cleveland vs. California, last 1 in 1973; all 6 in 1974 and 1975, July 18, 1973 through July 13, 1975.

Most Consec. DHs Won, Season (No Other Games Between)

A. L.— 5— New York, August 30 through September 4, 1906.
N. L.— 4— Brooklyn, September 1 through September 4, 1924.
New York, September 10 through September 14, 1928.

Games Lost

Most Games Lost, League

N. L.— 8,385— Philadelphia, 105 years, 1883 to date.
A. L.— 6,658— Chicago, 87 years, 1901 to date.

Most Games Lost, Season

N. L. (154-game season) —134—Cleveland, won 20, lost 134, 1899.
A. L. (154-game season) —117—Philadelphia, won 36, lost 117, 1916.

N. L. since 1900 (162-game season) —120—New York, won 40, lost 120, 1962.

N. L. since 1900 (154-game season) —115—Boston, won 38, lost 115, 1935.

A. L. (162-game season) —109—Toronto, won 53, lost 109, 1979.

Most Games Lost, Two Consecutive Seasons

N. L. (162-game season) —231—New York, 1962-63 (won 91).

A. L. (154-game season) —226—Philadelphia, 1915-16 (won 79).

A. L. (162-game season) —211—Toronto, 1978-79 (won 112).

Most Games Lost, Three Consecutive Seasons

N. L. (162-game season) —340—New York, 1962 through 1964 (won 144).

A. L. (154-game season) —324—Philadelphia, 1915 through 1917 (won 134).

Most Years Losing 100 or More Games

A. L.— 15—Philadelphia-Kansas City, 1915, 1916, 1919, 1920, 1921, 1936, 1940, 1943, 1946, 1950, 1954 in Philadelphia, 1956, 1961, 1964, 1965 in Kansas City.

N. L.— 14—Philadelphia, 1904, 1921, 1923, 1927, 1928, 1930, 1936, 1938, 1939, 1940, 1941, 1942, 1945, 1961.

Most Consecutive Years Losing 100 or More Games

N. L.—5—Philadelphia, 1938 through 1942.

A. L.—4—Washington, 1961 through 1964.

Most Night Games Lost, Season

N. L. (154-game season) —67—Philadelphia, 1961, won 23.

N. L. (162-game season) —82—Atlanta, 1977, won 43.

A. L. (154-game season) —48—Kansas City, 1956, won 20.

A. L. (162-game season) —83—Seattle, 1980, won 44.

Most Games Lost at Home, Season

A. L. (154-game season) —59—St. Louis, won 18, lost 59, 1939.

A. L. (162-game season) —55—Kansas City, won 26, lost 55, 1964.
Toronto, won 25, lost 55, 1977.

N. L. (162-game season) —58—New York, won 22, lost 58, 1962.

N. L. (154-game season) —55—Philadelphia, won 20, lost 55, 1923.
Boston, won 22, lost 55, 1923.
Philadelphia, won 22, lost 55, 1945.

Most Games Lost on Road, Season

N. L. (162-game season) — 64—New York, won 17, lost 64, 1963.

N. L. (154-game season) —102—Cleveland, won 11, lost 102, 1899.

N. L. since 1900 (154-game season) —65—Boston, won 13, lost 65, 1935.

A. L. (154-game season) — 64—Philadelphia, won 13, lost 64, 1916.

A. L. (162-game season) — 60—Toronto, won 21, lost 60, 1979.

Most Games Lost, Season, by One Run

A. L. (162-game season) —44—Chicago, won 30, lost 44, 1968.

N. L. (162-game season) —43—Houston, won 32, lost 43, 1971.

N. L. (154-game season) —41—Cincinnati, won 28, lost 41, 1946.

Fewest Games Lost, Season, by One Run

A. L. (154-game season) —11—Boston, won 21, lost 11, 1950.

A. L. (162-game season) —10—Boston, won 24, lost 10, 1986.

N. L. (154-game season) —12—Brooklyn, won 16, lost 12, 1949.

N. L. (162-game season) —14—Philadelphia, won 26, lost 14, 1962.
St. Louis, won 29, lost 14, 1975.
Montreal, won 28, lost 14, 1987.

Most Times Losing Two Games in One Day, Season

A. L. (162-game season) —13—Chicago, 1970 (won 1).

A. L. (154-game season) —18—Philadelphia, 1943 (won 4).

N. L. (162-game season) —17—New York, 1962 (won 3).

N. L. (154-game season) —19—Chicago, 1950 (won 4).

Fewest Times Losing Two Games in One Day, Season

N. L.-A. L.—0—Held by many clubs.

Most Games Lost, One Month

A. L.— 29—Washington, July, 1909, won 5, lost 29.

N. L.— 27—Pittsburgh, August, 1890, won 1, lost 27.
Cleveland, September, 1899, won 1, lost 27.
St. Louis, September, 1908, won 7, lost 27.
Brooklyn, September, 1908, won 6, lost 27.
Philadelphia, September, 1939, won 6, lost 27.

Most Games Lost, Two Consecutive Days

N. L.—5—Louisville, September 7 (3), 8 (2), 1896.

A. L.—4—Made on many days.

Consecutive

Most Consecutive Games Lost, Season

A. A.— 26—Louisville, May 22 through June 22, 1889, second game.

N. L.— 24—Cleveland, August 26 through September 16, 1899.

A. L.— 20—Boston, May 1 through May 24, 1906.
Philadelphia, July 21 through August 8, 1916.
Philadelphia, August 7 through August 24, first game, 1943.

N. L. since 1900—23—Philadelphia, July 29 through August 20, 1961, first game.

Most Consecutive Games Lost, Start of Season

A. L.— 13—Washington, April 14 through May 4, 1904 (1 tie).
Detroit, April 14 through May 2, 1920.

N. L.— 11—Detroit, May 1 through May 15, 1884.

N. L. since 1900—9—Brooklyn, April 16 through April 26, 1918.
Boston, April 19, morning game, through May 6, 1919.
New York, April 11 through April 22, 1962.
Houston, April 5 through April 13, 1983.

Most Home Games Lost Consecutively, Season

A. L.— 20—St. Louis, June 3 through July 7, 1953.

A. L.— 19—Boston, May 2 through May 24, 1906.

N. L.— 14—Boston, May 8 through May 24, 1911.

Most Road Games Lost Consecutively, Season

N. L.— 22—Pittsburgh, August 13 through September 2, 1890.
New York, June 16, first game through July 28, 1963.

A. L.— 19—Philadelphia, July 25 through August 8, 1916.

Most Consecutive Games Lost to One Club, League

A. L.— (12-club league) —23—Kansas City vs. Baltimore, May 9, 1969 through August 2, 1970, last 11 in 1969, all 12 in 1970.

A. L.— (8-club league) —21—St. Louis vs. New York, first 21 in 1927.

N. L.— (8-club league) —21—Philadelphia vs. Boston, all 14 in 1883, first 7 in 1884.

N. L. since 1900— (8-club league) —20—Cincinnati vs. Pittsburgh, last 17 in 1937, first 3 in 1938.

Most Consec. DHs Lost, Season (No Other Games Between)

N. L.—5—Boston, September 8 through September 14, 1928.

A. L.—4—Boston, June 29 through July 5, 1921.

Winning Percentage
Highest

Highest Percentage Games Won, Season

U. A.—.850—St. Louis, won 91, lost 16, 1884.

N. L.—.798—Chicago, won 67, lost 17, 1880.

N. L. since 1900—.763—Chicago, won 116, lost 36, 1906.

A. L.—.721—Cleveland, won 111, lost 43, 1954.

Highest Pct. Games Won, Season, for League Champions Since 1969

A. L.—.673—Baltimore, won 109, lost 53, 1969.

N. L.—.667—Cincinnati, won 108, lost 54, 1975.
New York, won 108, lost 54, 1986.

Highest Percentage Games Won, Season, for Second-Place Team

N. L.—.759—New York, won 85, lost 27, 1885.

N. L. since 1900—.680—Chicago, won 104, lost 49, 1909.

A. L.—.669—New York, won 103, lost 51, 1954.

Highest Percentage Games Won, Season, for Third-Place Team

N. L.—.691—Hartford, won 47, lost 21, 1876.

A. L.—.617—New York, won 95, lost 59, 1920.

N. L. since 1900—.608—Pittsburgh, won 93, lost 60, 1906.

Highest Percentage Games Won, Season, for Fourth-Place Team

N. L.—.623—Philadelphia, won 71, lost 43, 1886.

N. L.— (10-club league) —.578—Pittsburgh, won 93, lost 68, 1962.

N. L. since 1900 (8-club league) —.569—Pittsburgh, won 87, lost 66, 1904.

A. L.—.597—Cleveland, won 92, lost 62, 1950.

Highest Percentage Games Won, Season, for Fifth-Place Team

A. L.— (10-club league) —.537—Cleveland, won 87, lost 75, 1965.

A. L.— (8-club league) —.536—Philadelphia, won 81, lost 70, 1904.

N. L.—.571—Boston, won 76, lost 57, 1882.

N. L.— (10-club league) —.543—Milwaukee, won 88, lost 74, 1964.

N. L. since 1900 (8-club league) —.529—Chicago, won 81, lost 72, 1924.

Highest Percentage Games Won, Season, for Sixth-Place Team

N. L.— (10-club league) —.528—Philadelphia, won 85, lost 76, 1965.
N. L.—.506—Detroit, won 42, lost 41, 1882.
N. L. since 1900 (8-club league) —.503—Brooklyn, won 77, lost 76, 1928.
A. L.—.513—Detroit, won 79, lost 75, 1962.

Highest Percentage Games Won, Season, for Seventh-Place Team

A. L.—.497—Washington, won 76, lost 77, 1916.
N. L.— (10-club league) —.506—Chicago, won 82, lost 80, 1963.
N. L.— (8-club league) —.464—Brooklyn, won 70, lost 81, 1917.

Highest Percentage Games Won, Season, for Eighth-Place Team

A. L.— (10-club league) —.475—Boston, won 76, lost 84, 1962.
N. L.— (10-club league) —.469—Chicago, won 76, lost 86, 1964.
Los Angeles, won 76, lost 86, 1968 (tied for seventh).

Highest Percentage Games Won, Season, for Ninth-Place Team

N. L.— (10-club league) —.451—New York, won 73, lost 89, 1968.
A. L.— (10-club league) —.444—Kansas City, won 72, lost 90, 1962.
Boston, won 72, lost 90, 1966.
New York, won 72, lost 90, 1967.

Highest Percentage Games Won, Season, for Last-Place Team

N. L.— (8-club league) —.454—New York, won 69, lost 83, 1915.
A. L.— (8-club league) —.431—Chicago, won 66, lost 87, 1924.
A. L.— (10-club league) —.440—New York, won 70, lost 89, 1966.

Highest Percentage Games Won, One Month

U. A.—.947—St. Louis, May, 1884, won 18, lost 1.
N. L.—.944—Providence, August 1884, won 17, lost 1.
N. L. (since 1900) —.897—Chicago, August 1906, won 26, lost 3.
A. L.—.900—Detroit, April 1984, won 18, lost 2.

Lowest

Lowest Percentage Games Won, Season

N. L.—.130—Cleveland, won 20, lost 134, 1899.
A. L.—.235—Philadelphia, won 36, lost 117, 1916.
N. L. since 1900—.248—Boston, won 38, lost 115, 1935.

Lowest Pct. Games Won, Pennant Winner Through 1968

N. L.—.564—Los Angeles, won 88, lost 68, 1959.
A. L. (154-game season) —.575—Detroit won 88, lost 65, 1945.
A. L. (162-game season) —.568—Boston won 92, lost 70, 1967.

Lowest Pct. Games Won, League Champion Since 1969

N. L.—.509—New York, won 82, lost 79, 1973.
A. L.—.525—Minnesota, won 85, lost 77, 1987.

Lowest Pct. Games Won, Second-Place Team Through 1968

A. L.—.532—Chicago, won 82, lost 72, 1958.
N. L.— (8-club league) —.543—Brooklyn, won 75, lost 63, 1902.
N. L.— (10-club league) —.543—San Francisco, won 88, lost 74, 1968.

Lowest Pct. Games Won, Third-Place Team Through 1968

A. L.—.500—Chicago, won 77, lost 77, 1941.
N. L.— (8-club league) —.508—Chicago, won 67, lost 65, 1889.
N. L.— (8-club league) —Since 1900—.519—New York, won 80, lost 74, 1955.
San Francisco won 80, lost 74, 1958.
N. L.— (10-club league) —.519—Chicago, won 84, lost 78, 1968.

Lowest Pct. Games Won, Fourth-Place Team Through 1968

A. L.—.448—Boston, won 69, lost 85, 1954.
N. L.—.464—Philadelphia, won 71, lost 82, 1906.

Lowest Pct. Games Won, Fifth-Place Team Through 1968

A. L.—.409—St. Louis, won 63, lost 91, 1931.
N. L.—.411—Boston, won 46, lost 66, 1885.
N. L. since 1900—.434—Brooklyn, won 66, lost 86, 1906.

Lowest Pct. Games Won, Sixth-Place Team Through 1968

N. L.—.250—Milwaukee, won 15, lost 45, 1878 (six-club league).
N. L. since 1900—.359—Brooklyn, won 55, lost 98, 1909.
A. L.—.386—St. Louis, won 59, lost 94, 1948.

Lowest Pct. Games Won, Seventh-Place Team Through 1968

N. L.—.237—Philadelphia, won 14, lost 45, 1876.
N. L. since 1900—.327—Boston, won 50, lost 103, 1928.
A. L.—.325—Chicago, won 49, lost 102, 1932.

Lowest Pct. Games Won, Eighth-Place Team Through 1968

N. L.—.130—Cleveland, won 20, lost 134, 1899, last in 12-club league.

A. L.— (8-club league) —.235—Philadelphia, won 36, lost 117, 1916.
N. L.— (8-club league) —since 1900—.248—Boston, won 38, lost 115, 1935.
N. L.— (10-club league) —.400—Houston, won 64, lost 96, 1962.
A. L.— (10-club league) —.414—California, won 67, lost 95, 1968.
Chicago, won 67, lost 95, 1968.

Lowest Pct. Games Won, Ninth-Place Team Through 1968

N. L.— (10-club league) —.364—Chicago, won 59, lost 103, 1962.
A. L.— (10-club league) —.379—Kansas City, won 61, lost 100, 1961.
Washington, won 61, lost 100, 1961.

Lowest Percentage Games Won, One Month

N. L.—.036—Pittsburgh, August, 1890, won 1, lost 27.
Cleveland, September, 1899, won 1, lost 27.
A. L.—.067—Philadelphia, July, 1916, won 2, lost 28.
N. L. since 1900—.120—Philadelphia, May, 1928, won 3, lost 22.

Championships & First Division Finishes

Most Championships Won, Club

A. L.—33—New York, 1921, 1922, 1923, 1926, 1927, 1928, 1932, 1936, 1937, 1938, 1939, 1941, 1942, 1943, 1947, 1949, 1950, 1951, 1952, 1953, 1955, 1956, 1957, 1958, 1960, 1961, 1962, 1963, 1964, 1976, 1977, 1978.
N. L.—20—Brooklyn-Los Angeles, 1890, 1899, 1900, 1916, 1920, 1941, 1947, 1949, 1952, 1953, 1955, 1956, in Brooklyn, 1959, 1963, 1965, 1966, 1974, 1977, 1978, 1981 in Los Angeles.
N. L. since 1900—18—Brooklyn-Los Angeles, 1900, 1916, 1920, 1941, 1947, 1949, 1952, 1953, 1955, 1956, in Brooklyn, 1959, 1963, 1965, 1966, 1974, 1977, 1978, 1981 in Los Angeles.

Most Consecutive Championships Won, Club

A. L.—5—New York, 1949, 1950, 1951, 1952, 1953 (Charles D. Stengel, Manager).
New York, 1960, 1961, 1962, 1963, 1964 (Charles D. Stengel, Ralph G. Houk, Lawrence P. Berra, Managers).
A. A.—4—St. Louis, 1885, 1886, 1887, 1888 (Charles A. Comiskey, Manager).
N. L.—4—New York, 1921, 1922, 1923, 1924 (John J. McGraw, Manager).

Most Consecutive Years Without Winning Championship, League

A. L.—42—St. Louis, 1902 through 1943.
N. L.—42—Chicago, 1946 through 1987.

Most Consecutive Years, First Division Finish

A. L.—39—New York, 1926 through 1964.
N. L.—14—Chicago, 1878 through 1891.
Pittsburgh, 1900 through 1913.
Chicago, 1926 though 1939.

Last Place & Second Division Finishes

Most Times Finished in Last Place, League

A. L.—24—Philadelphia-Kansas City-Oakland, 1915, 1916, 1917, 1918, 1919, 1920, 1921, 1935, 1936, 1938, 1940, 1941, 1942, 1943, 1945, 1946, 1950, 1954 in Philadelphia, 1956, 1960, 1961 (tied), 1964, 1965, 1967 in Kansas City.
N. L.—24—Philadelphia, 1883, 1904, 1919, 1920, 1921, 1923, 1926, 1927, 1928, 1930, 1936, 1938, 1939, 1940, 1941, 1942, 1944, 1945, 1947 (tied), 1958, 1959, 1960, 1961, 1972 (E).

Most Consecutive Times Finished in Last Place

A. L.—7—Philadelphia, 1915 through 1921.
N. L.—5—Philadelphia, 1938 through 1942.

Most Consecutive Times Lowest Percentage Games Won, Season

A. L.—7—Philadelphia, 1915 through 1921.
N. L.—5—Philadelphia, 1938 through 1942.

Most Consecutive Years, Second Division Finish, Through 1968

N. L.— 20—Chicago, 1947 through 1966.
A. L.— 16— Philadelphia-Kansas City-Oakland, 1953 through 1968.

Most Consecutive Years Without Lowest Percentage Games Won

N. L.— 82—Brooklyn-Los Angeles, 1906 through 1987.
A. L.— 54—Cleveland, 1915 through 1968.

Games Finished Ahead & Behind

Best Gain in Games by Pennant Winner, One Season

A. A.—64 games—Louisville, won 88, lost 44, .667—1890. (In 1889, won 27, lost 111, .196; in eighth place, last.)
N. L.—41½ games—Brooklyn, won 88, lost 42, .677—1899. (In 1898, won 54, lost 91, .372; in tenth place.)
A. L.— (8-club league) —33 games—Boston, won 104, lost 50, .675 —1946. (In 1945, won 71, lost 83, .461; in seventh place.)
N. L. since 1900— (8-club league) —27 games—New York won 97, lost 57, .630—1954. (In 1953, won 70, lost 84, .455; in fifth place.)
N. L. (12-club league) —27 games—New York, won 100, lost 62, .617, 1969. (In 1968, won 73, lost 89, .451; in ninth place.)

Best Gain in Pos. From Previous Yr., Pennant Winner Through 1968

N. L.—Tenth to first—Brooklyn, 1899—won 88, lost 42, .677. (In 1898 finished tenth in 12-club league, won 54 lost 91, .372.) (41½ games.)
A. A.—Eighth (last) to first—Louisville, 1890—won 88, lost 44, .667. (In 1889 finished eighth, won 27, lost 111, .196.) (64 games.)
A. L. (8-club league) —Seventh to first—New York, 1926—won 91, lost 63, .591. (In 1925 finished seventh, won 69, lost 85, .448.) (22 games.)
Seventh to first—Boston, 1946—won 104, lost 50, .675. (In 1945 finished seventh, won 71, lost 83, .461.) (33 games.)
A. L. (10-club league) —Ninth to first—Boston, 1967—won 92, lost 70, .568. (In 1966 finished ninth in 10-club league, won 72, lost 90, .444.) (20 games.)
N. L. since 1900— (8-club league) —Seventh to first—Los Angeles, 1959—won 88, lost 68, .564. (In 1958 finished seventh, won 71, lost 83, .461.) (16 games.)
N. L. (12-club league) —Ninth to first—New York, 1969—won 100, lost 62, .617. (In 1968, finished ninth in 10-club league, won 73, lost 89, .451.) (27 games.)

Best Gain in Games by Club From Previous Season

A. A.— 64— Louisville, won 88, lost 44, .667-1890, first place. (In 1889 won 27, lost 111, .196; in eighth place, last.)
N. L.— 41½—Brooklyn, won 88, lost 42, .677-1899, first place. (In 1898 won 54, lost 91, .372; in tenth place.)
A. L.— 33—Boston, won 104, lost 50, .675-1946, first place. (In 1945, won 71, lost 83, .461; in seventh place.)
N. L.— (8-club league) since 1900—32½—Boston, won 71, lost 83, .461-1936, in sixth place. (In 1935, won 38, lost 115, .248; in eighth place.)
N. L.— (12-club league) —27 games—New York, won 100, lost 62, .617-1969, in first place. (In 1968, won 73, lost 89, .451, in ninth place.)

Most Games Leading League or Division, Season

N. L.— (8-club league) —27½—Pittsburgh, 1902.
A. L.— (8-club league) —19½—New York, 1936.
A. L.— (14-club league) —20—Chicago, 1983.

Fewest Games Leading League or Division, Season

N. L.— (8-club league) —0—St. Louis and Brooklyn, 1946 (before playoff) ; New York and Brooklyn, 1951 (before playoff) ; Los Angeles and Milwaukee, 1959 (before play-off) .
(12-club league) —0—San Francisco and Los Angeles, 1962 (before playoff) ; Houston and Los Angeles, 1980 (before playoff) .
A. L.— (8-club league) —0—Cleveland and Boston, 1948 (before playoff)
(14-club league) —0—New York and Boston, 1978 (before playoff) .

Most Games Behind Pennant Winner, Season Through 1968

N. L.— (12-club league) —80—Cleveland, 1899.
N. L.— (8-club league) since 1900—66½—Boston, 1906.
A. L.— (8-club league) —64½—St. Louis, 1939.

Fewest G.B. Pennant Winner for Last-Place Club Through 1968

N. L.— (8-club league) —21—New York, 1915.
A. L.— (8-club league) —25—Washington, 1944. (In shortened season of 1918, Philadelphia was 24 games behind.)

Fewest G.B. Western Division Leader, Last-Place Club, Since 1969

A. L.— 10— California, 1987.
Texas, 1987.
N. L.— 19½ — San Diego, 1980.

Fewest G.B. Eastern Division Leader, Last-Place Club, Since 1969

N. L.— 11½ — Philadelphia, 1973.
A. L.— 17—Toronto, 1982.
Cleveland, 1982.

Most G.B. Western Division Leader, Last-Place Club, Since 1969

N. L.— 43½ —Houston, 1975.
A. L.— 42—Chicago, 1970.

Most G.B. Eastern Division Leader, Last-Place Club, Since 1969

A. L.— 50½ — Toronto, 1979.
N. L.— 48—Montreal, 1969.

Largest Lead for Pennant Winner on July 4, P. M. Through 1968

N. L.—14½ games—New York, 1912.
A. L.—12 games—New York, 1928.

Most G.B. for Pennant Winner on July 4, P. M. Through 1968

N. L.—15 games—Boston, 1914 (8th place) .
A. L.—6½ games—Detroit, 1907 (4th place) .

Pennant Clinching Dates

Fewest Games Played for Pennant Clinching (154-Games)

A. L.— 136— New York, September 4, 1941 (won 91, lost 45, .669) .
N. L.— 137— New York, September 22, 1904 (won 100, lost 37, .730) .

Earliest Date for Clinching (154-Games) Through 1968

A. L.—September 4, 1941—New York (won 91, lost 45, .669, 136th game) .
N. L.—September 8, 1955—Brooklyn (won 92, lost 46, .667, 138th game) .

Earliest Date for Western Division Clinching, Since 1969

A. L.—September 15, 1971, first game. Oakland (won 94, lost 55, .631, 148th game) .
N. L.—September 7, 1975, Cincinnati (won 95, lost 47, .669, 142nd game) .

Earliest Date for Eastern Division Clinching, Since 1969

A. L.—September 13, 1969, Baltimore (won 101, lost 45, .690, 146th game) .
N. L.—September 17, 1986, New York (won 95, lost 50, .655, 145th game) .

Days In First Place

Most Days in First Place, Season

A. L. (162-game season) —181—Detroit, entire season, April 3 through September 30, 1984 (5 days tied, 176 days alone) .
A. L. (154-game season) —174—New York, A. L., 1927, entire season, April 12 through October 2, 1927 (8 days tied, 166 days alone) .
N. L. (162-game season) —178—Cincinnati, April 6 through October 1, 1970, except April 11 (sixth day of season) .
N. L. (154-game season) —174—New York, entire season, April 17 through October 7, 1923 (1 day tied, April 17, 173 days alone) .

Fewest Days in 1st Place, Season, for Pennant Winner Through 1968

N. L.— 3— New York, 1951. (Before playoff) .
A. L.— 20—Boston, 1967 (6 days alone) .

Attendance

Highest Home Attendance, Season

N. L.—3,608,881—Los Angeles, 1982.
A. L.—2,807,360—California, 1982.

117

Highest Road Attendance, Season
  A. L.—2,460,645—New York, 1980.
  N. L.—2,323,808—New York, 1987.

Largest Crowd, Day Game
  N. L.—78,672—San Francisco at Los Angeles, April 18, 1958 (home opener).
  A. L.—74,420—Detroit at Cleveland, April 7, 1973 (home opener).

Largest Crowd, Night Game
  A. L.—78,382—Chicago at Cleveland, August 20, 1948.

  N. L.—67,550—Chicago at Los Angeles, April 12, 1960 (home opener).

Largest Crowd, Doubleheader
  A. L.—84,587—New York at Cleveland, September 12, 1954.
  N. L.—72,140—Cincinnati at Los Angeles, August 16, 1961.

Largest Crowd, Opening Day
  N. L.—78,672—San Francisco at Los Angeles, April 18, 1958.
  A. L.—74,420—Detroit at Cleveland, April 7, 1973.

League Miscellaneous

Night Games

Most Night Games, Season
  A.L.— (14-club league) —822 in 1982.
  A.L.— (12-club league) —661 in 1976.
  A.L.— (10-club league) —472 in 1965.
  N.L.— (12-club league) —799 in 1983.
  N.L.— (10-club league) —487 in 1968.

Most Night Games, Season, Both Leagues
  1432 in 1983 (14-club, A.L.; 12-club, N.L.) —633 in A.L., 799 in N.L.
  1274 in 1975 (12-club leagues) —651 in A.L., 623 in N.L.
  960 in 1968 (10-club leagues) —487 in N.L., 473 in A.L.

Canceled & Postponed Games

Most Unplayed Games, Season, Since 1900 (Except 1918)
  A.L.—19 in 1901. N.L.—14 in 1938.

Fewest Unplayed Scheduled Games, Season, Since 1900
  N.L.-A.L.—0—Made in many years.

Fewest Unplayed Games, Season, Both Leagues
  0 in 1930, 1947, 1949, 1951, 1954, 1956, 1959, 1960, 1964, 1972, 1982, 1983 (12 years).

Most Postponed Games, Season
  A.L.— (8-club league) —97 in 1935.
  A.L.— (12-club league) —53 in 1975.
  N.L.— (8-club league) —49 in 1956.
  N.L.— (10-club league) —49 in 1967.
  N.L.— (12-club league) —41 in 1974.

Fewest Postponed Dates, Season
  A.L.—15 in 1987. N.L.—12 in 1987.

Most Postponed Doubleheaders, Season
  A.L.—14 in 1945. N.L.—5 in 1959.

Fewest Postponed Doubleheaders, Season
  A.L.—0 in 1914, 1957. N.L.—0 in 1961, 1966, 1970.

Tie Games

Most Tie Games, Season
  A. L.—19 in 1910. N. L.—16 in 1913.

Most Tie Games, One Day
  N. L.—3, April 26, 1897. A. L.—2, made on many days.

Fewest Tie Games, Season
  N. L.—0 in 1925, 1954, 1958, 1970, 1976, 1977, 1978, 1982, 1984, 1986, 1987.
  A. L.—0 in 1930, 1963, 1965, 1971, 1972, 1973, 1975, 1976, 1977, 1978, 1979, 1987.

Most 0-0 Games, Season
  A. L.—6 in 1904.   N. L.—3 in 1917.

Extra-Inning Games

Most Extra-Inning Games, Season
  A. L.— (14-club league) —107 in 1977, 1980.
  A. L.— (12-club league) —116 in 1976.
  A. L.— (10-club league) — 91 in 1965.
  A. L.— (8-club league) — 91 in 1943.
  N. L.— (12-club league) —116 in 1986.
  N. L.— (10-club league) — 93 in 1967.
  N. L.— (8-club league) — 86 in 1916.

Most Extra-Inning Games, One Day
  N. L.—5—May 30, 1892.
  N. L. since 1900—4—May 12, 1963; May 29, 1966.
  A. L.—4—June 11, 1969; June 4, 1976.

Most Extra-Inning Games, One Day, Both Leagues
  6 on August 22, 1951; 3 in N. L. (5 games), 3 in A. L. (5 games).
  6 on May 12, 1963; 4 in N. L. (8 games), 2 in A. L. (7 games).

100 & 90-Win & Loss Seasons

Most Clubs Winning 100 or More Games, Season
  A. L.— (14-club league) —2 in 1977, 1980, 1987.
  A. L.— (12-club league) —2 in 1971.
  A. L.— (10-club league) —2 in 1961.
  A. L.— (8-club league) —2 in 1915, 1954.
  N. L.— (12-club league) —2 in 1976.
  N. L.— (10-club league) —2 in 1962.
  N. L.— (8-club league) —2 in 1909, 1942.

Most Clubs Winning 90 or More Games, Season
  N. L.— (12-club league) —4 in 1969, 1976, 1980, 1987.
  N. L.— (10-club league) —4 in 1962, 1964.
  N. L.— (8-club league) —3 in many seasons.
  A. L.— (14-club league) —6 in 1977.
  A. L.— (12-club league) —4 in 1975.
  A. L.— (10-club league) —3 in 1961, 1963, 1964, 1965, 1967.
  A. L.— (8-club league) —4 in 1950.

Most Clubs Losing 100 or More Games, Season
  N. L.— (12-club league) —2 in 1969, 1985.
  N. L.— (10-club league) —2 in 1962.
  N. L.— (8-club league) —2 in 1898, 1905, 1908, 1923, 1938.
  A. L.— (14-club league) —2 in 1978, 1979.
  A. L.— (12-club league) —1 in 1970, 1971 1972, 1973, 1975.
  A. L.— (10-club league) —2 in 1961, 1964, 1965.
  A. L.— (8-club league) —2 in 1912, 1932, 1949, 1954.

Home & Road Victories

Most Games Won by Home Clubs, Season
  A. L.— (14-club league) —649 in 1978 (lost 482).
  A. L.— (12-club league) —540 in 1969 (lost 431).
  A. L.— (10-club league) —454 in 1961 (lost 353).
  A. L.— (8-club league) —360 in 1945 (lost 244) and 1949 (lost 256).
  N. L.— (12-club league) —556 in 1978 (lost 415) and 1980 (lost 416).
  N. L.— (10-club league) —464 in 1967 (lost 345).
  N. L.— (8-club league) —358 in 1931 (lost 256) and 1955 (lost 257).

Most Games Won by Home Clubs, One Day, League
  N. L.- A. L.— (8-club leagues) —8—on many days.

Most Games Won by Home Clubs, One Day, Both Leagues
  14 on May 30, 1903 (A. L. won 8, lost 0; N. L. won 6, lost 2).

Most Games Won by Visiting Clubs, Season
  N. L.— (12-club league) —473 in 1982 (lost 499).
  N. L.— (10-club league) —400 in 1968 (lost 410).
  N. L.— (8-club league) —307 in 1948 (lost 308).
  A. L.— (14-club league) —547 in 1980 (lost 582).
  A. L.— (12-club league) —469 in 1971 (lost 497).
  A. L.— (10-club league) —391 in 1968 (lost 418).
  A. L.— (8-club league) —312 in 1953 (lost 301).

Most Games Won by Visiting Clubs, One Day, League

N. L.-A. L.— (8-club leagues) —8—on many days.

Most Games Won by Visiting Clubs, One Day, Both Leagues

(8-club leagues)
12 on July 4, 1935 (N. L. won 7, lost 1; A. L. won 5, lost 3).
12 on August 5, 1951 (N. L. won 7, lost 0; A. L. won 5, lost 2).
12 on June 15, 1958 (A. L. won 8, lost 0; N. L. won 4, lost 1).

One-Run Decisions

Most Games Won by One Run, Season

A. L.— (14-club league) —368 in 1978.
A. L.— (12-club league) —332 in 1969.
A. L.— (10-club league) —281 in 1967, 1968.
A. L.— (8-club league) —217 in 1943.
N. L.— (12-club league) —346 in 1980.
N. L.— (10-club league) —294 in 1968.
N. L.— (8-club league) —223 in 1946.

Fewest Games Won by One Run, Season

A. L.— (14-club league) —302 in 1987.

A. L.— (12-club league) —279 in 1973.
A. L.— (8-club league) —157 in 1938.
N. L.— (12-club league) —294 in 1970.
N. L.— (8-club league) —170 in 1949.

Most Games Won by One Run, One Day

A. L.—6—May 30, 1967, (10 games); August 22, 1967, (9 games).
N. L.—6—June 6, 1967 (7 games); June 8, 1969 (6 games).

Most Games Won by One Run, One Day, Both Leagues

10 on May 30, 1967. A. L. 6 (10 games), N. L. 4 (7 games).

Attendance

Highest Attendance, Season

A. L.— (14-club league) —27,277,351 in 1987.
(12-club league) —14,657,802 in 1976.
(10-club league) —11,336,923 in 1967.
(8-club league) —11,150,099 in 1948.
N. L.— (12-club league) —24,734,155 in 1987.
(10-club league) —15,015,471 in 1966.
(8-club league) —10,684,963 in 1960.

Non-Playing Personnel

Managers

Individual

Most Years as Manager, Major Leagues

53—Connie Mack, Pittsburgh N. L. (1894 through 1896), Philadelphia A. L. (1901 through 1950).

Most Years as Manager, League

A. L.— 50— Connie Mack, Philadelphia, 1901 through 1950.
N. L.— 32— John J. McGraw, Baltimore, 1899; New York, 1902 through 1932.

Most Clubs Managed, Major Leagues

7—Frank C. Bancroft, Worcester N. L., Detroit N. L., Cleveland N.L., Providence N. L., Philadelphia A. A., Indianapolis N. L., Cincinnati N. L.

Most Clubs Managed, Major Leagues Since 1900

6—James Dykes, Chicago A. L., Philadelphia A. L., Baltimore A.L., Cincinnati N. L., Detroit A. L., Cleveland A. L.
Richard H. Williams, Boston A. L., Oakland A. L., California A. L., Montreal N. L., San Diego N.L., Seattle A. L.

Most Clubs Managed, League, Season

U. A.—2—Theodore P. Sullivan, St. Louis, Kansas City, 1884.
A. A.—2—William S. Barnie, Baltimore, Philadelphia, 1891.
N. L.—2—Leo E. Durocher, Brooklyn, New York, 1948.
Leo E. Durocher, Chicago, Houston, 1972.
A. L.—2—James J. Dykes, Detroit, Cleveland, 1960.
Joseph L. Gordon, Cleveland, Detroit, 1960.
Alfred M. Martin, Detroit, Texas, 1973.
Alfred M. Martin, Texas, New York, 1975.
Robert G. Lemon, Chicago, New York, 1978.
Anthony LaRussa, Chicago, Oakland, 1986.

Most Clubs Managed, Different Major Leagues, Season

2—Joseph V. Battin, 1884 (Pittsburgh A. A. and Pittsburgh U.A.).
William H. Watkins, 1888 (Detroit N. L., Kansas City A.A.).
Gustavus H. Schmelz, 1890 (Cleveland N. L., Columbus A.A.).
John J. McGraw, 1902 (Baltimore A. L., New York N.L.).
Rogers Hornsby, 1952 (St. Louis A. L., Cincinnati N. L.).
William C. Virdon, 1975 (New York A. L., Houston N.L.).
Patrick Corrales, 1983 (Philadelphia N.L., Cleveland A.L.).

Most Different Times as Manager, One Major League Club

N. L.—4—Daniel E. Murtaugh, Pittsburgh, 1957 (part) through 1964; 1967 (part), 1970 through 1971, 1973 (part) through 1976, 15 years.
A. L.—4—Alfred M. Martin, New York, 1975 (part) through 1978 (part), 1979 (part), 1983 (complete), 1985 (part).

Most Clubs as Manager, League

N. L.—6—Frank C. Bancroft, Worcester, Detroit, Cleveland, Providence, Indianapolis, Cincinnati.
N. L. since 1900—4—William B. McKechnie, Pittsburgh, St. Louis, Boston, Cincinnati.
Rogers Hornsby, St. Louis, Chicago, Boston, Cincinnati.
Leo E. Durocher, Brooklyn, New York, Chicago, Houston.
A. L.—5—James Dykes, Chicago, Philadelphia, Baltimore, Detroit, Cleveland.
Alfred M. Martin, Minnesota, Detroit, Texas, New York, Oakland.

Most Years Championship Manager, League

N. L.— 10— John J. McGraw, New York, 1904, 1905, 1911, 1912, 1913, 1917, 1921, 1922, 1923, 1924.
A. L.— 10— Charles D. Stengel, New York, 1949, 1950, 1951, 1952, 1953, 1955, 1956, 1957, 1958, 1960.

Most Consecutive Years Championship Manager

A. L.—5—Charles D. Stengel, New York, 1949 through 1953 (first 5 years as New York manager).
A. A.—4—Charles A. Comiskey, St. Louis, 1885 through 1888.
N. L.—4—John J. McGraw, New York, 1921 through 1924.

Most Years Managed, Major Leagues, No Championships Won

26—Eugene W. Mauch, Philadelphia N. L., 1960 into 1968; Montreal N. L., 1969 through 1975; Minnesota A. L., 1976 into 1980; California A.L., 1981 through 1982, 1985 through 1987.

Most Years Managed, League, No Championships Won

A. L.— 20— James J. Dykes, Chicago, 1934 through 1946, Philadelphia, 1951 through 1953, Baltimore, 1954, Detroit, 1959, 1960, Cleveland, 1960, 1961.
N. L.— 16— Eugene W. Mauch, Philadelphia, 1960 into 1968; Montreal, 1969 through 1975.

Most Consec. Years Managed, League, No Championships Won

Both Leagues—23—Eugene W. Mauch, Philadelphia N. L., 1960 into 1968; Montreal N. L., 1969 through 1975; Minnesota A. L., 1976 into 1980; California A.L., 1981 through 1982.
A. L.— 19— Connie Mack, Philadelphia, 1932 through 1950.
N. L.— 16— Eugene W. Mauch, Philadelphia, 1960 into 1968; Montreal, 1969 through 1975.

Youngest Manager to Start Season

Louis Boudreau, Cleveland, A. L., appointed November 25, 1941; 24 years, 4 months, 8 days when appointed. Born, July 17, 1917.

Youngest Manager to Finish Season

Roger T. Peckinpaugh, New York, A. L., appointed September 16, 1914; 23 years, 7 months, 11 days. Born, February 5, 1891.

Oldest to Make Debut as Manager

Thomas C. Sheehan, San Francisco, N. L., appointed June 18, 1960; 66 years, 2 months, 18 days. Born, March 31, 1894.

Club

Most Managers, One Club, Season

A. A.—7—Louisville, 1889.
N. L.—4—Washington, 1892, 1898.
      St. Louis, 1895, 1896, 1897.
N. L.—since 1900—3—Cincinnati, 1902.
      New York, 1902.
      St. Louis, 1905, 1940, 1980.
      Pittsburgh, 1917.
      Chicago, 1925.
      Philadelphia, 1948.
A. L.—4—Texas, 1977.
     3—Boston, 1907.
      St. Louis, 1918, 1933.
      New York, 1946, 1982.
      Detroit, 1966.

League

Most Managers, Season, Since 1900

A. L.—(14-club league)—19 in 1977, 1981, 1986 (Anthony La-Russa, Chicago, Oakland, counted as one).
A. L.—(12-club league)—16 in 1969, 1975.
A. L.—(10-club league)—15 in 1966.
A. L.—(8-club league)—12 in 1933, 1946.

N. L.—(12-club league)—16 in 1972 (Leo E. Durocher, Chicago, Houston, counted as one).
N. L.—(10-club league)—12 in 1965, 1966, 1967, 1968.
N. L.—(8-club league)—12 in 1902, 1948 (Leo E. Durocher, Brooklyn, New York, counted as one in 1948).

Most Playing Managers, Season, Both Leagues

10 in 1934 (8-club leagues)—6 in N. L., 4 in A. L.

Most Managerial Changes, Start of Season

A. L.—(8-club league)—6 in 1955.
N. L.—(8-club league)—4 in 1909, 1913.

Umpires

Most Years Umpired

N. L.—37—William J. Klem, 1905 through 1941.
A. L.—31—Thomas H. Connolly, 1901 through 1931 (also umpired 3 years in the National League, 1898-1899-1900).

Longest Game, Plate Umpire by Time

A. L.—8 hours, 6 minutes—James Evans, Milwaukee at Chicago, May 8, 1984, finished May 9. Chicago won 7-6.
N. L.—7 hours, 23 minutes—Edward L. Sudol, San Francisco at New York, May 31, 1964, second game, 23 innings. San Francisco won 8-6.

Yearly Leaders

American League Pennant Winners

Year	Club	Manager	W.	L.	Pct.	*G.A.
1901—Chicago		Clark Griffith	83	53	.610	4
1902—Philadelphia		Connie Mack	83	53	.610	5
1903—Boston		Jimmy Collins	91	47	.659	14½
1904—Boston		Jimmy Collins	95	59	.617	1½
1905—Philadelphia		Connie Mack	92	56	.622	2
1906—Chicago		Fielder Jones	93	58	.616	3
1907—Detroit		Hugh Jennings	92	58	.613	1½
1908—Detroit		Hugh Jennings	90	63	.588	½
1909—Detroit		Hugh Jennings	98	54	.645	3½
1910—Philadelphia		Connie Mack	102	48	.680	14½
1911—Philadelphia		Connie Mack	101	50	.669	13½
1912—Boston		Jake Stahl	105	47	.691	14
1913—Philadelphia		Connie Mack	96	57	.627	6½
1914—Philadelphia		Connie Mack	99	53	.651	8½
1915—Boston		Bill Carrigan	101	50	.669	2½
1916—Boston		Bill Carrigan	91	63	.591	2
1917—Chicago		Pants Rowland	100	54	.649	9
1918—Boston		Ed Barrow	75	51	.595	2½
1919—Chicago		Kid Gleason	88	52	.629	3½
1920—Cleveland		Tris Speaker	98	56	.636	2
1921—New York		Miller Huggins	98	55	.641	4½
1922—New York		Miller Huggins	94	60	.610	1
1923—New York		Miller Huggins	98	54	.645	16
1924—Washington		Bucky Harris	92	62	.597	2
1925—Washington		Bucky Harris	96	55	.636	8½
1926—New York		Miller Huggins	91	63	.591	3
1927—New York		Miller Huggins	110	44	.714	19
1928—New York		Miller Huggins	101	53	.656	2½
1929—Philadelphia		Connie Mack	104	46	.693	18
1930—Philadelphia		Connie Mack	102	52	.662	8
1931—Philadelphia		Connie Mack	107	45	.704	13½
1932—New York		Joe McCarthy	107	47	.695	13
1933—Washington		Joe Cronin	99	53	.651	7
1934—Detroit		Mickey Cochrane	101	53	.656	7
1935—Detroit		Mickey Cochrane	93	58	.616	3
1936—New York		Joe McCarthy	102	51	.667	19½
1937—New York		Joe McCarthy	102	52	.662	13
1938—New York		Joe McCarthy	99	53	.651	9½
1939—New York		Joe McCarthy	106	45	.702	17
1940—Detroit		Del Baker	90	64	.584	1
1941—New York		Joe McCarthy	101	53	.656	17
1942—New York		Joe McCarthy	103	51	.669	9
1943—New York		Joe McCarthy	98	56	.636	13½
1944—St. Louis		Luke Sewell	89	65	.578	1
1945—Detroit		Steve O'Neill	88	65	.575	1½
1946—Boston		Joe Cronin	104	50	.675	12
1947—New York		Bucky Harris	97	57	.630	12
1948—Cleveland†		Lou Boudreau	97	58	.626	1
1949—New York		Casey Stengel	97	57	.630	1
1950—New York		Casey Stengel	98	56	.636	3
1951—New York		Casey Stengel	98	56	.636	5
1952—New York		Casey Stengel	95	59	.617	2
1953—New York		Casey Stengel	99	52	.656	8½
1954—Cleveland		Al Lopez	111	43	.721	8
1955—New York		Casey Stengel	96	58	.623	3
1956—New York		Casey Stengel	97	57	.630	9
1957—New York		Casey Stengel	98	56	.636	8
1958—New York		Casey Stengel	92	62	.597	10
1959—Chicago		Al Lopez	94	60	.610	5
1960—New York		Casey Stengel	97	57	.630	8
1961—New York		Ralph Houk	109	53	.673	8
1962—New York		Ralph Houk	96	66	.593	5
1963—New York		Ralph Houk	104	57	.646	10½
1964—New York		Yogi Berra	99	63	.611	1
1965—Minnesota		Sam Mele	102	60	.630	7
1966—Baltimore		Hank Bauer	97	63	.606	9
1967—Boston		Dick Williams	92	70	.568	1
1968—Detroit		Mayo Smith	103	59	.636	12
1969—Baltimore (E)		Earl Weaver	109	53	.673	19
1970—Baltimore (E)		Earl Weaver	108	54	.667	15
1971—Baltimore (E)		Earl Weaver	101	57	.639	12
1972—Oakland (W)		Dick Williams	93	62	.600	5½
1973—Oakland (W)		Dick Williams	94	68	.580	6
1974—Oakland (W)		Al Dark	90	72	.556	5
1975—Boston (E)		Darrell Johnson	95	65	.594	4½
1976—New York (E)		Billy Martin	97	62	.610	10½
1977—New York (E)		Billy Martin	100	62	.617	2½
1978—New York (E)‡		B. Martin, B. Lemon	100	63	.613	1
1979—Baltimore (E)		Earl Weaver	102	57	.642	8
1980—Kansas City (W)		Jim Frey	97	65	.599	14
1981—New York (E)		G. Michael, B. Lemon	59	48	.551	§
1982—Milwaukee (E)		B. Rodgers, H. Kuenn	95	67	.586	1
1983—Baltimore (E)		Joe Altobelli	98	64	.605	6
1984—Detroit (E)		Sparky Anderson	104	58	.642	15
1985—Kansas City (W)		Dick Howser	91	71	.562	1
1986—Boston (E)		John McNamara	95	66	.590	5½
1987—Minnesota (W)		Tom Kelly	85	77	.525	2

*Games ahead of second-place club. †Defeated Boston in one-game playoff. ‡Defeated Boston in one-game playoff to win division. §First half 34-22; second 25-26.

National League Pennant Winners

Year	Club	Manager	W.	L.	Pct.	*G.A.
1876—Chicago		Albert Spalding	52	14	.788	6
1877—Boston		Harry Wright	31	17	.646	3
1878—Boston		Harry Wright	41	19	.683	4
1879—Providence		George Wright	55	23	.705	6
1880—Chicago		Adrian Anson	67	17	.798	15
1881—Chicago		Adrian Anson	56	28	.667	9
1882—Chicago		Adrian Anson	55	29	.655	3
1883—Boston		John Morrill	63	35	.643	4
1884—Providence		Frank Bancroft	84	28	.750	10½
1885—Chicago		Adrian Anson	87	25	.777	2
1886—Chicago		Adrian Anson	90	34	.726	2½
1887—Detroit		Wm. Watkins	79	45	.637	3½
1888—New York		James Mutrie	84	47	.641	9
1889—New York		James Mutrie	83	43	.659	1
1890—Brooklyn		Wm. McGunnigle	86	43	.667	6½
1891—Boston		Frank Selee	87	51	.630	3½
1892—Boston		Frank Selee	102	48	.680	8½
1893—Boston		Frank Selee	86	44	.662	4½
1894—Baltimore		Edward Hanlon	89	39	.695	3

Year	Club	Manager	W.	L.	Pct.	*G.A.
1895	Baltimore	Edward Hanlon	87	43	.669	3
1896	Baltimore	Edward Hanlon	90	39	.698	9½
1897	Boston	Frank Selee	93	39	.705	2
1898	Boston	Frank Selee	102	47	.685	6
1899	Brooklyn	Edward Hanlon	88	42	.677	4
1900	Brooklyn	Edward Hanlon	82	54	.603	4½
1901	Pittsburgh	Fred Clarke	90	49	.647	7½
1902	Pittsburgh	Fred Clarke	103	36	.741	27½
1903	Pittsburgh	Fred Clarke	91	49	.650	6½
1904	New York	John McGraw	106	47	.693	13
1905	New York	John McGraw	105	48	.686	9
1906	Chicago	Frank Chance	116	36	.763	20
1907	Chicago	Frank Chance	107	45	.704	17
1908	Chicago	Frank Chance	99	55	.643	1
1909	Pittsburgh	Fred Clarke	110	42	.724	6½
1910	Chicago	Frank Chance	104	50	.675	13
1911	New York	John McGraw	99	54	.647	7½
1912	New York	John McGraw	103	48	.682	10
1913	New York	John McGraw	101	51	.664	12½
1914	Boston	George Stallings	94	59	.614	10½
1915	Philadelphia	Pat Moran	90	62	.592	7
1916	Brooklyn	Wilbert Robinson	94	60	.610	2½
1917	New York	John McGraw	98	56	.636	10
1918	Chicago	Fred Mitchell	84	45	.651	10½
1919	Cincinnati	Pat Moran	96	44	.686	9
1920	Brooklyn	Wilbert Robinson	93	61	.604	7
1921	New York	John McGraw	94	59	.614	4
1922	New York	John McGraw	93	61	.604	7
1923	New York	John McGraw	95	58	.621	4½
1924	New York	John McGraw	93	60	.608	1½
1925	Pittsburgh	Bill McKechnie	95	58	.621	8½
1926	St. Louis	Rogers Hornsby	89	65	.578	2
1927	Pittsburgh	Donie Bush	94	60	.610	1½
1928	St. Louis	Bill McKechnie	95	59	.617	2
1929	Chicago	Joe McCarthy	98	54	.645	10½
1930	St. Louis	Gabby Street	92	62	.597	2
1931	St. Louis	Gabby Street	101	53	.656	13
1932	Chicago	Charlie Grimm	90	64	.584	4
1933	New York	Bill Terry	91	61	.599	5
1934	St. Louis	Frank Frisch	95	58	.621	2
1935	Chicago	Charlie Grimm	100	54	.649	4
1936	New York	Bill Terry	92	62	.597	5
1937	New York	Bill Terry	95	57	.625	3
1938	Chicago	Gabby Hartnett	89	63	.586	2
1939	Cincinnati	Bill McKechnie	97	57	.630	4½
1940	Cincinnati	Bill McKechnie	100	53	.654	12
1941	Brooklyn	Leo Durocher	100	54	.649	2½
1942	St. Louis	Billy Southworth	106	48	.688	2
1943	St. Louis	Billy Southworth	105	49	.682	18
1944	St. Louis	Billy Southworth	105	49	.682	14½
1945	Chicago	Charlie Grimm	98	56	.636	3
1946	St. Louis†	Eddie Dyer	98	58	.628	2
1947	Brooklyn	Burt Shotton	94	60	.610	5
1948	Boston	Billy Southworth	91	62	.595	6½
1949	Brooklyn	Burt Shotton	97	57	.630	1
1950	Philadelphia	Eddie Sawyer	91	63	.591	2
1951	New York‡	Leo Durocher	98	59	.624	1
1952	Brooklyn	Charlie Dressen	96	57	.627	4½
1953	Brooklyn	Charlie Dressen	105	49	.682	13
1954	New York	Leo Durocher	97	57	.630	5
1955	Brooklyn	Walter Alston	98	55	.641	13½
1956	Brooklyn	Walter Alston	93	61	.604	1
1957	Milwaukee	Fred Haney	95	59	.617	8
1958	Milwaukee	Fred Haney	92	62	.597	8
1959	Los Angeles§	Walter Alston	88	68	.564	2
1960	Pittsburgh	Danny Murtaugh	95	59	.617	7
1961	Cincinnati	Fred Hutchinson	93	61	.604	4
1962	San Francisco x	Al Dark	103	62	.624	1
1963	Los Angeles	Walter Alston	99	63	.611	6
1964	St. Louis	Johnny Keane	93	69	.574	1
1965	Los Angeles	Walter Alston	97	65	.599	2
1966	Los Angeles	Walter Alston	95	67	.586	1½
1967	St. Louis	Red Schoendienst	101	60	.627	10½
1968	St. Louis	Red Schoendienst	97	65	.599	9
1969	New York (E)	Gil Hodges	100	62	.617	8
1970	Cincinnati (W)	Sparky Anderson	102	60	.630	14½
1971	Pittsburgh (E)	Danny Murtaugh	97	65	.599	7
1972	Cincinnati (W)	Sparky Anderson	95	59	.617	10½
1973	New York (E)	Yogi Berra	82	79	.509	1½
1974	Los Angeles (W)	Walter Alston	102	60	.630	4
1975	Cincinnati (W)	Sparky Anderson	108	54	.667	20
1976	Cincinnati (W)	Sparky Anderson	102	60	.630	10
1977	Los Angeles (W)	Tommy Lasorda	98	64	.605	10
1978	Los Angeles (W)	Tommy Lasorda	95	67	.586	2½
1979	Pittsburgh (E)	Chuck Tanner	98	64	.605	2
1980	Philadelphia (E)	Dallas Green	91	71	.562	1
1981	Los Angeles (W)	Tommy Lasorda	63	47	.573	y
1982	St. Louis (E)	Whitey Herzog	92	70	.568	3
1983	Philadelphia (E)	P. Corrales, P. Owens	90	72	.556	6
1984	San Diego (W)	Dick Williams	92	70	.568	12
1985	St. Louis (E)	Whitey Herzog	101	61	.623	3
1986	New York (E)	Dave Johnson	108	54	.667	21½
1987	St. Louis (E)	Whitey Herzog	95	67	.586	3

*Games ahead of second-place club. †Defeated Brooklyn, two games to none, in playoff for pennant. ‡Defeated Brooklyn, two games to one, in playoff for pennant. §Defeated Milwaukee, two games to none, in playoff for pennant. xDefeated Los Angeles, two games to one, in playoff for pennant. yFirst half 36-21; second half 27-26.

Batting
Batting Average
American League

Year	Player and Club	B.A.
1901	Napoleon Lajoie, Philadelphia	.422
1902	Edward Delahanty, Washington	.376
1903	Napoleon Lajoie, Cleveland	.355
1904	Napoleon Lajoie, Cleveland	.381
1905	Elmer Flick, Cleveland	.308
1906	George Stone, St. Louis	.358
1907	Tyrus Cobb, Detroit	.350
1908	Tyrus Cobb, Detroit	.324
1909	Tyrus Cobb, Detroit	.377
1910	Tyrus Cobb, Detroit	.385
1911	Tyrus Cobb, Detroit	.420
1912	Tyrus Cobb, Detroit	.410
1913	Tyrus Cobb, Detroit	.390
1914	Tyrus Cobb, Detroit	.368
1915	Tyrus Cobb, Detroit	.369
1916	Tristram Speaker, Cleveland	.386
1917	Tyrus Cobb, Detroit	.383
1918	Tyrus Cobb, Detroit	.382
1919	Tyrus Cobb, Detroit	.384
1920	George Sisler, St. Louis	.407
1921	Harry Heilmann, Detroit	.394
1922	George Sisler, St. Louis	.420
1923	Harry Heilmann, Detroit	.403
1924	George (Babe) Ruth, New York	.378
1925	Harry Heilmann, Detroit	.393
1926	Henry Manush, Detroit	.378
1927	Harry Heilmann, Detroit	.398
1928	Leon (Goose) Goslin, Washington	.379
1929	Lew Fonseca, Cleveland	.369
1930	Aloysius Simmons, Philadelphia	.381
1931	Aloysius Simmons, Philadelphia	.390
1932	Dale Alexander, Detroit-Boston	.367
1933	James Foxx, Philadelphia	.356
1934	H. Louis Gehrig, New York	.363
1935	Charles (Buddy) Myer, Washington	.349
1936	Lucius Appling, Chicago	.388
1937	Charles Gehringer, Detroit	.371
1938	James Foxx, Boston	.349
1939	Joseph DiMaggio, New York	.381
1940	Joseph DiMaggio, New York	.352
1941	Theodore Williams, Boston	.406
1942	Theodore Williams, Boston	.356
1943	Lucius Appling, Chicago	.328
1944	Louis Boudreau, Cleveland	.327
1945	George Stirnweiss, New York	.309
1946	James (Mickey) Vernon, Washington	.353
1947	Theodore Williams, Boston	.343
1948	Theodore Williams, Boston	.369
1949	George Kell, Detroit	.343
1950	William Goodman, Boston	.354
1951	Ferris Fain, Philadelphia	.344
1952	Ferris Fain, Philadelphia	.327
1953	James (Mickey) Vernon, Washington	.337
1954	Roberto Avila, Cleveland	.341
1955	Albert Kaline, Detroit	.340
1956	Mickey Mantle, New York	.353
1957	Theodore Williams, Boston	.388
1958	Theodore Williams, Boston	.328
1959	Harvey Kuenn, Detroit	.353
1960	James (Pete) Runnels, Boston	.320
1961	Norman Cash, Detroit	.361
1962	James (Pete) Runnels, Boston	.326
1963	Carl Yastrzemski, Boston	.321
1964	Pedro (Tony) Oliva, Minnesota	.323
1965	Pedro (Tony) Oliva, Minnesota	.321
1966	Frank Robinson, Baltimore	.316
1967	Carl Yastrzemski, Boston	.326
1968	Carl Yastrzemski, Boston	.301
1969	Rodney Carew, Minnesota	.332
1970	Alexander Johnson, California	.329
1971	Pedro (Tony) Oliva, Minnesota	.337
1972	Rodney Carew, Minnesota	.318
1973	Rodney Carew, Minnesota	.350
1974	Rodney Carew, Minnesota	.364
1975	Rodney Carew, Minnesota	.359
1976	George Brett, Kansas City	.333
1977	Rodney Carew, Minnesota	.388
1978	Rodney Carew, Minnesota	.333
1979	Fredric Lynn, Boston	.333
1980	George Brett, Kansas City	.390
1981	Carney Lansford, Boston	.336
1982	Willie Wilson, Kansas City	.332
1983	Wade Boggs, Boston	.361
1984	Donald Mattingly, New York	.343
1985	Wade Boggs, Boston	.368
1986	Wade Boggs, Boston	.357
1987	Wade Boggs, Boston	.363

National League

Year	Player and Club	B.A.
1876	Roscoe C. Barnes, Chicago	.404
1877	James L. (Deacon) White, Boston	.385
1878	Abner F. Dalrymple, Milwaukee	.356
1879	Adrian (Cap) Anson, Chicago	.407
1880	George F. Gore, Chicago	.365
1881	Adrian (Cap) Anson, Chicago	.399
1882	Dennis (Dan) Brouthers, Buffalo	.367
1883	Dennis (Dan) Brouthers, Buffalo	.371
1884	James H. O'Rourke, Buffalo	.350
1885	Roger Connor, New York	.371
1886	Michael (King) Kelly, Chicago	.388
1887	Adrian (Cap) Anson, Chicago	.421
1888	Adrian (Cap) Anson, Chicago	.343
1889	Dennis (Dan) Brouthers, Boston	.373
1890	John W. Glasscock, New York	.336
1891	William R. Hamilton, Philadelphia	.338
1892	Dennis (Dan) Brouthers, Brooklyn	.335
	Clarence A. (Cupid) Childs, Cleveland	.335
1893	Hugh Duffy, Boston	.378
1894	Hugh Duffy, Boston	.438
1895	Jesse C. Burkett, Cleveland	.423
1896	Jesse C. Burkett, Cleveland	.410
1897	William H. Keeler, Baltimore	.432
1898	William H. Keeler, Baltimore	.379
1899	Edward J. Delahanty, Philadelphia	.408
1900	John (Honus) Wagner, Pittsburgh	.381
1901	Jesse C. Burkett, St. Louis	.382
1902	Clarence Beaumont, Pittsburgh	.357
1903	John (Honus) Wagner, Pittsburgh	.355
1904	John (Honus) Wagner, Pittsburgh	.349
1905	James Bentley Seymour, Cincinnati	.377
1906	John (Honus) Wagner, Pittsburgh	.339
1907	John (Honus) Wagner, Pittsburgh	.350
1908	John (Honus) Wagner, Pittsburgh	.354
1909	John (Honus) Wagner, Pittsburgh	.339
1910	Sherwood Magee, Philadelphia	.331
1911	John (Honus) Wagner, Pittsburgh	.334
1912	Henry Zimmerman, Chicago	.372
1913	Jacob Daubert, Brooklyn	.350
1914	Jacob Daubert, Brooklyn	.329
1915	Lawrence Doyle, New York	.320
1916	Harold Chase, Cincinnati	.339
1917	Edd Roush, Cincinnati	.341
1918	Zachariah Wheat, Brooklyn	.335
1919	Edd Roush, Cincinnati	.321
1920	Rogers Hornsby, St. Louis	.370
1921	Rogers Hornsby, St. Louis	.397
1922	Rogers Hornsby, St. Louis	.401
1923	Rogers Hornsby, St. Louis	.384
1924	Rogers Hornsby, St. Louis	.424
1925	Rogers Hornsby, St. Louis	.403
1926	Eugene Hargrave, Cincinnati	.353
1927	Paul Waner, Pittsburgh	.380
1928	Rogers Hornsby, Boston	.387
1929	Frank O'Doul, Philadelphia	.398
1930	William Terry, New York	.401
1931	Charles (Chick) Hafey, St. Louis	.349
1932	Frank O'Doul, Brooklyn	.368
1933	Charles Klein, Philadelphia	.368
1934	Paul Waner, Pittsburgh	.362
1935	J. Floyd (Arky) Vaughan, Pittsburgh	.385
1936	Paul Waner, Pittsburgh	.373
1937	Joseph Medwick, St. Louis	.374
1938	Ernest Lombardi, Cincinnati	.342
1939	John Mize, St. Louis	.349
1940	Debs Garms, Pittsburgh	.355
1941	Harold (Pete) Reiser, Brooklyn	.343
1942	Ernest Lombardi, Boston	.330
1943	Stanley Musial, St. Louis	.357
1944	Fred (Dixie) Walker, Brooklyn	.357
1945	Philip Cavarretta, Chicago	.355
1946	Stanley Musial, St. Louis	.365
1947	Harry Walker, St. Louis-Philadelphia	.363
1948	Stanley Musial, St. Louis	.376
1949	Jack Robinson, Brooklyn	.342
1950	Stanley Musial, St. Louis	.346
1951	Stanley Musial, St. Louis	.355
1952	Stanley Musial, St. Louis	.336
1953	Carl Furillo, Brooklyn	.344
1954	Willie Mays, New York	.345
1955	Richie Ashburn, Philadelphia	.338
1956	Henry Aaron, Milwaukee	.328
1957	Stanley Musial, St. Louis	.351
1958	Richie Ashburn, Philadelphia	.350
1959	Henry Aaron, Milwaukee	.355
1960	Richard Groat, Pittsburgh	.325
1961	Roberto Clemente, Pittsburgh	.351
1962	H. Thomas Davis, Los Angeles	.346
1963	H. Thomas Davis, Los Angeles	.326
1964	Roberto Clemente, Pittsburgh	.339
1965	Roberto Clemente, Pittsburgh	.329
1966	Mateo Alou, Pittsburgh	.342
1967	Roberto Clemente, Pittsburgh	.357
1968	Peter Rose, Cincinnati	.335
1969	Peter Rose, Cincinnati	.348
1970	Ricardo Carty, Atlanta	.366
1971	Joseph Torre, St. Louis	.363
1972	Billy Williams, Chicago	.333
1973	Peter Rose, Cincinnati	.338
1974	Ralph Garr, Atlanta	.353
1975	Bill Madlock, Chicago	.354
1976	Bill Madlock, Chicago	.339
1977	David Parker, Pittsburgh	.338
1978	David Parker, Pittsburgh	.334
1979	Keith Hernandez, St. Louis	.344
1980	William Buckner, Chicago	.324
1981	Bill Madlock, Pittsburgh	.341
1982	Albert Oliver, Montreal	.331
1983	Bill Madlock, Pittsburgh	.323
1984	Anthony Gwynn, San Diego	.351
1985	Willie McGee, St. Louis	.353
1986	Timothy Raines, Montreal	.334
1987	Anthony Gwynn, San Diego	.370

Note—Bases on balls counted as hits in 1887.

Slugging Average
American League

Year	Player and Club	Slug. Avg.
1901	Napoleon Lajoie, Philadelphia	.635
1902	Edward Delahanty, Washington	.589
1903	Napoleon Lajoie, Cleveland	.533
1904	Napoleon Lajoie, Cleveland	.549
1905	Elmer Flick, Cleveland	.466
1906	George Stone, St. Louis	.496
1907	Tyrus Cobb, Detroit	.473
1908	Tyrus Cobb, Detroit	.475
1909	Tyrus Cobb, Detroit	.517
1910	Tyrus Cobb, Detroit	.554
1911	Tyrus Cobb, Detroit	.621
1912	Tyrus Cobb, Detroit	.586
1913	Joseph Jackson, Cleveland	.551
1914	Tyrus Cobb, Detroit	.513
1915	Jacques F. Fournier, Chicago	.491
1916	Tristram Speaker, Cleveland	.502
1917	Tyrus Cobb, Detroit	.571
1918	George (Babe) Ruth, Boston	.555
1919	George (Babe) Ruth, Boston	.657
1920	George (Babe) Ruth, New York	.847
1921	George (Babe) Ruth, New York	.846
1922	George (Babe) Ruth, New York	.672
1923	George (Babe) Ruth, New York	.764
1924	George (Babe) Ruth, New York	.739
1925	Kenneth Williams, St. Louis	.613
1926	George (Babe) Ruth, New York	.737
1927	George (Babe) Ruth, New York	.772
1928	George (Babe) Ruth, New York	.709
1929	George (Babe) Ruth, New York	.697
1930	George (Babe) Ruth, New York	.732
1931	George (Babe) Ruth, New York	.700
1932	James Foxx, Philadelphia	.749
1933	James Foxx, Philadelphia	.703
1934	H. Louis Gehrig, New York	.706
1935	James Foxx, Philadelphia	.636
1936	H. Louis Gehrig, New York	.696
1937	Joseph DiMaggio, New York	.673
1938	James Foxx, Boston	.704
1939	James Foxx, Boston	.694
1940	Henry Greenberg, Detroit	.670
1941	Theodore Williams, Boston	.735
1942	Theodore Williams, Boston	.648
1943	Rudolph York, Detroit	.527
1944	Robert Doerr, Boston	.528
1945	George Stirnweiss, New York	.476
1946	Theodore Williams, Boston	.667
1947	Theodore Williams, Boston	.634
1948	Theodore Williams, Boston	.615
1949	Theodore Williams, Boston	.650
1950	Joseph DiMaggio, New York	.585
1951	Theodore Williams, Boston	.556
1952	Lawrence Doby, Cleveland	.541
1953	Albert Rosen, Cleveland	.613
1954	Theodore Williams, Boston	.635
1955	Mickey Mantle, New York	.611
1956	Mickey Mantle, New York	.705
1957	Theodore Williams, Boston	.731
1958	Rocco Colavito, Cleveland	.620
1959	Albert Kaline, Detroit	.530
1960	Roger Maris, New York	.581
1961	Mickey Mantle, New York	.687
1962	Mickey Mantle, New York	.605
1963	Harmon Killebrew, Minnesota	.555
1964	John (Boog) Powell, Baltimore	.606
1965	Carl Yastrzemski, Boston	.536
1966	Frank Robinson, Baltimore	.637
1967	Carl Yastrzemski, Boston	.622
1968	Frank Howard, Washington	.552
1969	Reginald Jackson, Oakland	.608
1970	Carl Yastrzemski, Boston	.592
1971	Pedro (Tony) Oliva, Minnesota	.546
1972	Richard Allen, Chicago	.603
1973	Reginald Jackson, Oakland	.531
1974	Richard Allen, Chicago	.563
1975	Fredric Lynn, Boston	.566
1976	Reginald Jackson, Baltimore	.502
1977	James Rice, Boston	.593
1978	James Rice, Boston	.600
1979	Fredric Lynn, Boston	.637
1980	George Brett, Kansas City	.664

Year	Player and Club	Slug. Avg.
1981—	Robert Grich, California	.543
1982—	Robin Yount, Milwaukee	.578
1983—	George Brett, Kansas City	.563
1984—	Harold Baines, Chicago	.541
1985—	George Brett, Kansas City	.585
1986—	Donald Mattingly, New York	.573
1987—	Mark McGwire, Oakland	.618

National League

Year	Player and Club	Slug. Avg.
1900—	John (Honus) Wagner, Pittsburgh	.572
1901—	James Sheckard, Brooklyn	.541
1902—	John (Honus) Wagner, Pittsburgh	.467
1903—	Fred Clarke, Pittsburgh	.532
1904—	John (Honus) Wagner, Pittsburgh	.520
1905—	J. Bentley Seymour, Cincinnati	.559
1906—	Harry Lumley, Brooklyn	.477
1907—	John (Honus) Wagner, Pittsburgh	.513
1908—	John (Honus) Wagner, Pittsburgh	.542
1909—	John (Honus) Wagner, Pittsburgh	.489
1910—	Sherwood Magee, Philadelphia	.507
1911—	Frank Schulte, Chicago	.534
1912—	Henry Zimmerman, Chicago	.571
1913—	Clifford (Gavvy) Cravath, Philadelphia	.568
1914—	Sherwood Magee, Philadelphia	.509
1915—	Clifford (Gavvy) Cravath, Philadelphia	.510
1916—	Zachariah Wheat, Brooklyn	.461
1917—	Rogers Hornsby, St. Louis	.484
1918—	Edd Roush, Cincinnati	.455
1919—	Henry (Hi) Myers, Brooklyn	.436
1920—	Rogers Hornsby, St. Louis	.559
1921—	Rogers Hornsby, St. Louis	.659
1922—	Rogers Hornsby, St. Louis	.722
1923—	Rogers Hornsby, St. Louis	.627
1924—	Rogers Hornsby, St. Louis	.696
1925—	Rogers Hornsby, St. Louis	.756
1926—	Fred Williams, Philadelphia	.569
1927—	Charles Hafey, St. Louis	.590
1928—	Rogers Hornsby, Boston	.632
1929—	Rogers Hornsby, Chicago	.679
1930—	Lewis (Hack) Wilson, Chicago	.723
1931—	Charles Klein, Philadelphia	.584
1932—	Charles Klein, Philadelphia	.646
1933—	Charles Klein, Philadelphia	.602
1934—	James (Rip) Collins, St. Louis	.615
1935—	J. Floyd (Arky) Vaughan, Pittsburgh	.607
1936—	Melvin Ott, New York	.588
1937—	Joseph Medwick, St. Louis	.641
1938—	John Mize, St. Louis	.614
1939—	John Mize, St. Louis	.626
1940—	John Mize, St. Louis	.636
1941—	Harold (Pete) Reiser, Brooklyn	.558
1942—	John Mize, New York	.521
1943—	Stanley Musial, St. Louis	.562
1944—	Stanley Musial, St. Louis	.549
1945—	Tommy Holmes, Boston	.577
1946—	Stanley Musial, St. Louis	.587
1947—	Ralph Kiner, Pittsburgh	.639
1948—	Stanley Musial, St. Louis	.702
1949—	Ralph Kiner, Pittsburgh	.658
1950—	Stanley Musial, St. Louis	.596
1951—	Ralph Kiner, Pittsburgh	.627
1952—	Stanley Musial, St. Louis	.538
1953—	Edwin (Duke) Snider, Brooklyn	.627
1954—	Willie Mays, New York	.667
1955—	Willie Mays, New York	.659
1956—	Edwin (Duke) Snider, Brooklyn	.598
1957—	Willie Mays, New York	.626
1958—	Ernest Banks, Chicago	.614
1959—	Henry Aaron, Milwaukee	.636
1960—	Frank Robinson, Cincinnati	.595
1961—	Frank Robinson, Cincinnati	.611
1962—	Frank Robinson, Cincinnati	.624
1963—	Henry Aaron, Milwaukee	.586
1964—	Willie Mays, San Francisco	.607
1965—	Willie Mays, San Francisco	.645
1966—	Richard Allen, Philadelphia	.632
1967—	Henry Aaron, Atlanta	.573
1968—	Willie McCovey, San Francisco	.545
1969—	Willie McCovey, San Francisco	.656
1970—	Willie McCovey, San Francisco	.612
1971—	Henry Aaron, Atlanta	.669
1972—	Billy Williams, Chicago	.606
1973—	Wilver Stargell, Pittsburgh	.646
1974—	Michael Schmidt, Philadelphia	.546
1975—	David Parker, Pittsburgh	.541
1976—	Joe Morgan, Cincinnati	.576
1977—	George Foster, Cincinnati	.631
1978—	David Parker, Pittsburgh	.585
1979—	David Kingman, Chicago	.613
1980—	Michael Schmidt, Philadelphia	.624
1981—	Michael Schmidt, Philadelphia	.644
1982—	Michael Schmidt, Philadelphia	.547
1983—	Dale Murphy, Atlanta	.540
1984—	Dale Murphy, Atlanta	.547
1985—	Pedro Guerrero, Los Angeles	.577
1986—	Michael Schmidt, Philadelphia	.547
1987—	Jack Clark, St. Louis	.597

Runs
American League

Year	Player and Club	Runs
1901—	Napoleon Lajoie, Philadelphia	145
1902—	David Fultz, Philadelphia	110
1903—	Patrick Dougherty, Boston	108
1904—	Patrick Dougherty, Boston-New York	113
1905—	Harry Davis, Philadelphia	92
1906—	Elmer Flick, Cleveland	98
1907—	Samuel Crawford, Detroit	102
1908—	Matthew McIntyre, Detroit	105
1909—	Tyrus Cobb, Detroit	116
1910—	Tyrus Cobb, Detroit	106
1911—	Tyrus Cobb, Detroit	147
1912—	Edward Collins, Philadelphia	137
1913—	Edward Collins, Philadelphia	125
1914—	Edward Collins, Philadelphia	122
1915—	Tyrus Cobb, Detroit	144
1916—	Tyrus Cobb, Detroit	113
1917—	Owen (Donie) Bush, Detroit	112
1918—	Raymond Chapman, Cleveland	84
1919—	George (Babe) Ruth, Boston	103
1920—	George (Babe) Ruth, New York	158
1921—	George (Babe) Ruth, New York	177
1922—	George Sisler, St. Louis	134
1923—	George (Babe) Ruth, New York	151
1924—	George (Babe) Ruth, New York	143
1925—	John Mostil, Chicago	135
1926—	George (Babe) Ruth, New York	139
1927—	George (Babe) Ruth, New York	158
1928—	George (Babe) Ruth, New York	163
1929—	Charles Gehringer, Detroit	131
1930—	Aloysius Simmons, Philadelphia	152
1931—	H. Louis Gehrig, New York	163
1932—	James Foxx, Philadelphia	151
1933—	H. Louis Gehrig, New York	138
1934—	Charles Gehringer, Detroit	134
1935—	H. Louis Gehrig, New York	125
1936—	H. Louis Gehrig, New York	167
1937—	Joseph DiMaggio, New York	151
1938—	Henry Greenberg, Detroit	144
1939—	Robert (Red) Rolfe, New York	139
1940—	Theodore Williams, Boston	134
1941—	Theodore Williams, Boston	135
1942—	Theodore Williams, Boston	141
1943—	George Case, Washington	102
1944—	George Stirnweiss, New York	125
1945—	George Stirnweiss, New York	107
1946—	Theodore Williams, Boston	142
1947—	Theodore Williams, Boston	125
1948—	Thomas Henrich, New York	138
1949—	Theodore Williams, Boston	150
1950—	Dominic DiMaggio, Boston	131
1951—	Dominic DiMaggio, Boston	113
1952—	Lawrence Doby, Cleveland	104
1953—	Albert Rosen, Cleveland	115
1954—	Mickey Mantle, New York	129
1955—	Alphonse Smith, Cleveland	123
1956—	Mickey Mantle, New York	132
1957—	Mickey Mantle, New York	121
1958—	Mickey Mantle, New York	127
1959—	Edward Yost, Detroit	115
1960—	Mickey Mantle, New York	119
1961—	Mickey Mantle, New York	132
	Roger Maris, New York	132
1962—	Albert G. Pearson, Los Angeles	115
1963—	W. Robert Allison, Minnesota	99
1964—	Pedro (Tony) Oliva, Minnesota	109
1965—	Zoilo Versalles, Minnesota	126
1966—	Frank Robinson, Baltimore	122
1967—	Carl Yastrzemski, Boston	112
1968—	Richard McAuliffe, Detroit	95
1969—	Reginald Jackson, Oakland	123
1970—	Carl Yastrzemski, Boston	125
1971—	Donald Buford, Baltimore	99
1972—	Bobby Murcer, New York	102
1973—	Reginald Jackson, Oakland	99
1974—	Carl Yastrzemski, Boston	93
1975—	Fredric Lynn, Boston	103
1976—	Roy White, New York	104
1977—	Rodney Carew, Minnesota	128
1978—	Ronald LeFlore, Detroit	126
1979—	Donald Baylor, California	120
1980—	Willie Wilson, Kansas City	133
1981—	Rickey Henderson, Oakland	89
1982—	Paul Molitor, Milwaukee	136
1983—	Calvin Ripken, Baltimore	121
1984—	Dwight Evans, Boston	121
1985—	Rickey Henderson, New York	146
1986—	Rickey Henderson, New York	130
1987—	Paul Molitor, Milwaukee	114

National League

Year	Player and Club	Runs
1900—	Roy Thomas, Philadelphia	131
1901—	Jesse Burkett, St. Louis	139
1902—	John (Honus) Wagner, Pittsburgh	105
1903—	Clarence Beaumont, Pittsburgh	137
1904—	George Browne, New York	99
1905—	Michael Donlin, New York	124
1906—	John (Honus) Wagner, Pittsburgh	103
	Frank Chance, Chicago	103
1907—	W. Porter Shannon, New York	104
1908—	Frederick Tenney, New York	101
1909—	Thomas Leach, Pittsburgh	126
1910—	Sherwood Magee, Philadelphia	110
1911—	James Sheckard, Chicago	121
1912—	Robert Bescher, Cincinnati	120
1913—	Thomas Leach, Chicago	99
	Max Carey, Pittsburgh	99
1914—	George Burns, New York	100
1915—	Clifford (Gavvy) Cravath, Philadelphia	89
1916—	George Burns, New York	105
1917—	George Burns, New York	103
1918—	Henry Groh, Cincinnati	88
1919—	George Burns, New York	86
1920—	George Burns, New York	115
1921—	Rogers Hornsby, St. Louis	131
1922—	Rogers Hornsby, St. Louis	141
1923—	Ross Youngs, New York	121
1924—	Frank Frisch, New York	121
	Rogers Hornsby, St. Louis	121
1925—	Hazen (Kiki) Cuyler, Pittsburgh	144
1926—	Hazen (Kiki) Cuyler, Pittsburgh	113
1927—	Lloyd Waner, Pittsburgh	133
	Rogers Hornsby, New York	133
1928—	Paul Waner, Pittsburgh	142
1929—	Rogers Hornsby, Chicago	156
1930—	Charles (Chuck) Klein, Philadelphia	158
1931—	William Terry, New York	121
	Charles (Chuck) Klein, Philadelphia	121
1932—	Charles (Chuck) Klein, Philadelphia	152
1933—	John (Pepper) Martin, St. Louis	122
1934—	Paul Waner, Pittsburgh	122
1935—	August Galan, Chicago	133
1936—	J. Floyd (Arky) Vaughan, Pittsburgh	122
1937—	Joseph Medwick, St. Louis	111
1938—	Melvin Ott, New York	116
1939—	William Werber, Cincinnati	115
1940—	J. Floyd (Arky) Vaughan, Pittsburgh	113
1941—	Harold (Pete) Reiser, Brooklyn	117
1942—	Melvin Ott, New York	118
1943—	J. Floyd (Arky) Vaughan, Brooklyn	112
1944—	William Nicholson, Chicago	116
1945—	Edward Stanky, Brooklyn	128
1946—	Stanley Musial, St. Louis	124
1947—	John Mize, New York	137
1948—	Stanley Musial, St. Louis	135
1949—	Harold (Pee Wee) Reese, Brooklyn	132
1950—	C. Earl Torgeson, Boston	120
1951—	Stanley Musial, St. Louis	124
	Ralph Kiner, Pittsburgh	124
1952—	Stanley Musial, St. Louis	105
	Solomon Hemus, St. Louis	105
1953—	Edwin (Duke) Snider, Brooklyn	132
1954—	Stanley Musial, St. Louis	120
	Edwin (Duke) Snider, Brooklyn	120
1955—	Edwin (Duke) Snider, Brooklyn	126
1956—	Frank Robinson, Cincinnati	122
1957—	Henry Aaron, Milwaukee	118
1958—	Willie Mays, San Francisco	121
1959—	Vada Pinson, Cincinnati	131
1960—	William Bruton, Milwaukee	112
1961—	Willie Mays, San Francisco	129
1962—	Frank Robinson, Cincinnati	134
1963—	Henry Aaron, Milwaukee	121
1964—	Richard Allen, Philadelphia	125
1965—	Tommy Harper, Cincinnati	126
1966—	Felipe Alou, Atlanta	122
1967—	Henry Aaron, Atlanta	113
	Louis Brock, St. Louis	113
1968—	Glenn Beckert, Chicago	98
1969—	Bobby Bonds, San Francisco	120
	Peter Rose, Cincinnati	120
1970—	Billy Williams, Chicago	137
1971—	Louis Brock, St. Louis	126
1972—	Joe Morgan, Cincinnati	122
1973—	Bobby Bonds, San Francisco	131
1974—	Peter Rose, Cincinnati	110
1975—	Peter Rose, Cincinnati	112
1976—	Peter Rose, Cincinnati	130
1977—	George Foster, Cincinnati	124
1978—	Ivan DeJesus, Chicago	104
1979—	Keith Hernandez, St. Louis	116
1980—	Keith Hernandez, St. Louis	111
1981—	Michael Schmidt, Philadelphia	78
1982—	Lonnie Smith, St. Louis	120
1983—	Timothy Raines, Montreal	133
1984—	Ryne Sandberg, Chicago	114
1985—	Dale Murphy, Atlanta	118
1986—	Anthony Gwynn, San Diego	107
	Von Hayes, Philadelphia	107
1987—	Timothy Raines, Montreal	123

Hits

American League

Year	Player and Club	Hits
1901	Napoleon Lajoie, Philadelphia	229
1902	Charles Hickman, Bos.-Clev.	194
1903	Patrick Dougherty, Boston	195
1904	Napoleon Lajoie, Cleveland	211
1905	George Stone, St. Louis	187
1906	Napoleon Lajoie, Cleveland	214
1907	Tyrus Cobb, Detroit	212
1908	Tyrus Cobb, Detroit	188
1909	Tyrus Cobb, Detroit	216
1910	Napoleon Lajoie, Cleveland	227
1911	Tyrus Cobb, Detroit	248
1912	Tyrus Cobb, Detroit	227
1913	Joseph Jackson, Cleveland	197
1914	Tristram Speaker, Boston	193
1915	Tyrus Cobb, Detroit	208
1916	Tristram Speaker, Cleveland	211
1917	Tyrus Cobb, Detroit	225
1918	George Burns, Philadelphia	178
1919	Tyrus Cobb, Detroit	191
	Robert Veach, Detroit	191
1920	George Sisler, St. Louis	257
1921	Harry Heilmann, Detroit	237
1922	George Sisler, St. Louis	246
1923	Charles Jamieson, Cleveland	222
1924	Edgar (Sam) Rice, Washington	216
1925	Aloysius Simmons, Philadelphia	253
1926	George Burns, Cleveland	216
	Edgar (Sam) Rice, Washington	216
1927	Earle Combs, New York	231
1928	Henry Manush, St. Louis	241
1929	Dale Alexander, Detroit	215
	Charles Gehringer, Detroit	215
1930	U. John Hodapp, Cleveland	225
1931	H. Louis Gehrig, New York	211
1932	Aloysius Simmons, Philadelphia	216
1933	Henry Manush, Washington	221
1934	Charles Gehringer, Detroit	214
1935	Joseph Vosmik, Cleveland	216
1936	H. Earl Averill, Cleveland	232
1937	Roy (Beau) Bell, St. Louis	218
1938	Joseph Vosmik, Boston	201
1939	Robert (Red) Rolfe, New York	213
1940	Raymond (Rip) Radcliff, St. Louis	200
	W. Barney McCosky, Detroit	200
	Roger (Doc) Cramer, Boston	200
1941	Cecil Travis, Washington	218
1942	John Pesky, Boston	205
1943	Richard Wakefield, Detroit	200
1944	George Stirnweiss, New York	205
1945	George Stirnweiss, New York	195
1946	John Pesky, Boston	208
1947	John Pesky, Boston	207
1948	Robert Dillinger, St. Louis	207
1949	L. Dale Mitchell, Cleveland	203
1950	George Kell, Detroit	218
1951	George Kell, Detroit	191
1952	J. Nelson Fox, Chicago	192
1953	Harvey Kuenn, Detroit	209
1954	J. Nelson Fox, Chicago	201
	Harvey Kuenn, Detroit	201
1955	Albert Kaline, Detroit	200
1956	Harvey Kuenn, Detroit	196
1957	J. Nelson Fox, Chicago	196
1958	J. Nelson Fox, Chicago	187
1959	Harvey Kuenn, Detroit	198
1960	Orestes (Minnie) Minoso, Chicago	184
1961	Norman Cash, Detroit	193
1962	Robert Richardson, New York	209
1963	Carl Yastrzemski, Boston	183
1964	Pedro (Tony) Oliva, Minnesota	217
1965	Pedro (Tony) Oliva, Minnesota	185
1966	Pedro (Tony) Oliva, Minnesota	191
1967	Carl Yastrzemski, Boston	189
1968	Dagoberto Campaneris, Oakland	177
1969	Pedro (Tony) Oliva, Minnesota	197
1970	Pedro (Tony) Oliva, Minnesota	204
1971	Cesar Tovar, Minnesota	204
1972	Joseph Rudi, Oakland	181
1973	Rodney Carew, Minnesota	203
1974	Rodney Carew, Minnesota	218
1975	George Brett, Kansas City	195
1976	George Brett, Kansas City	215
1977	Rodney Carew, Minnesota	239
1978	James Rice, Boston	213
1979	George Brett, Kansas City	212
1980	Willie Wilson, Kansas City	230
1981	Rickey Henderson, Oakland	135
1982	Robin Yount, Milwaukee	210
1983	Calvin Ripken, Baltimore	211
1984	Donald Mattingly, New York	207
1985	Wade Boggs, Boston	240
1986	Donald Mattingly, New York	238
1987	Kirby Puckett, Minnesota	207
	Kevin Seitzer, Kansas City	207

National League

Year	Player and Club	Hits
1900	William Keeler, Brooklyn	208
1901	Jesse Burkett, St. Louis	228
1902	Clarence Beaumont, Pittsburgh	194
1903	Clarence Beaumont, Pittsburgh	209
1904	Clarence Beaumont, Pittsburgh	185
1905	J. Bentley Seymour, Cincinnati	219
1906	Harry Steinfeldt, Chicago	176
1907	Clarence Beaumont, Boston	187
1908	John (Honus) Wagner, Pittsburgh	201
1909	Lawrence Doyle, New York	172
1910	John (Honus) Wagner, Pittsburgh	178
	Robert Byrne, Pittsburgh	178
1911	Roy Miller, Boston	192
1912	Henry Zimmerman, Chicago	207
1913	Clifford (Gavvy) Cravath, Philadelphia	179
1914	Sherwood Magee, Philadelphia	171
1915	Lawrence Doyle, New York	189
1916	Harold Chase, Cincinnati	184
1917	Henry Groh, Cincinnati	182
1918	Charles Hollocher, Chicago	161
1919	Ivy Olson, Brooklyn	164
1920	Rogers Hornsby, St. Louis	218
1921	Rogers Hornsby, St. Louis	235
1922	Rogers Hornsby, St. Louis	250
1923	Frank Frisch, New York	223
1924	Rogers Hornsby, St. Louis	227
1925	James Bottomley, St. Louis	227
1926	Edward Brown, Boston	201
1927	Paul Waner, Pittsburgh	237
1928	Fred Lindstrom, New York	231
1929	Frank O'Doul, Philadelphia	254
1930	William Terry, New York	254
1931	Lloyd Waner, Pittsburgh	214
1932	Charles Klein, Philadelphia	226
1933	Charles Klein, Philadelphia	223
1934	Paul Waner, Pittsburgh	217
1935	William Herman, Chicago	227
1936	Joseph Medwick, St. Louis	223
1937	Joseph Medwick, St. Louis	237
1938	Frank McCormick, Cincinnati	209
1939	Frank McCormick, Cincinnati	209
1940	Stanley Hack, Chicago	191
	Frank McCormick, Cincinnati	191
1941	Stanley Hack, Chicago	186
1942	Enos Slaughter, St. Louis	188
1943	Stanley Musial, St. Louis	220
1944	Stanley Musial, St. Louis	197
	Philip Cavarretta, Chicago	197
1945	Thomas Holmes, Boston	224
1946	Stanley Musial, St. Louis	228
1947	Thomas Holmes, Boston	191
1948	Stanley Musial, St. Louis	230
1949	Stanley Musial, St. Louis	207
1950	Edwin (Duke) Snider, Brooklyn	199
1951	Richie Ashburn, Philadelphia	221
1952	Stanley Musial, St. Louis	194
1953	Richie Ashburn, Philadelphia	205
1954	Donald Mueller, New York	212
1955	Theodore Kluszewski, Cincinnati	192
1956	Henry Aaron, Milwaukee	200
1957	Al (Red) Schoendienst, N.Y.-Milw.	200
1958	Richie Ashburn, Philadelphia	215
1959	Henry Aaron, Milwaukee	223
1960	Willie Mays, San Francisco	190
1961	Vada Pinson, Cincinnati	208
1962	H. Thomas Davis, Los Angeles	230
1963	Vada Pinson, Cincinnati	204
1964	Roberto Clemente, Pittsburgh	211
	Curtis Flood, St. Louis	211
1965	Peter Rose, Cincinnati	209
1966	Felipe Alou, Atlanta	218
1967	Roberto Clemente, Pittsburgh	209
1968	Felipe Alou, Atlanta	210
	Peter Rose, Cincinnati	210
1969	Mateo Alou, Pittsburgh	231
1970	Peter Rose, Cincinnati	205
	Billy Williams, Chicago	205
1971	Joseph Torre, St. Louis	230
1972	Peter Rose, Cincinnati	198
1973	Peter Rose, Cincinnati	230
1974	Ralph Garr, Atlanta	214
1975	David Cash, Philadelphia	213
1976	Peter Rose, Cincinnati	215
1977	David Parker, Pittsburgh	215
1978	Steven Garvey, Los Angeles	202
1979	Garry Templeton, St. Louis	211
1980	Steven Garvey, Los Angeles	200
1981	Peter Rose, Philadelphia	140
1982	Albert Oliver, Montreal	204
1983	Jose Cruz, Houston	189
	Andre Dawson, Montreal	189
1984	Anthony Gwynn, San Diego	213
1985	Willie McGee, St. Louis	216
1986	Anthony Gwynn, San Diego	211
1987	Anthony Gwynn, San Diego	218

Singles

American League

Year	Player and Club	1B.
1901	Napoleon Lajoie, Philadelphia	154
1902	Fielder Jones, Chicago	148
1903	Patrick Dougherty, Boston	161
1904	William Keeler, New York	164
1905	William Keeler, New York	147
1906	William Keeler, New York	166
1907	Tyrus Cobb, Detroit	163
1908	Matthew McIntyre, Detroit	131
	George Stone, St. Louis	131
1909	Tyrus Cobb, Detroit	164
1910	Napoleon Lajoie, Cleveland	165
1911	Tyrus Cobb, Detroit	169
1912	Tyrus Cobb, Detroit	167
1913	Edward Collins, Philadelphia	145
1914	John McInnis, Philadelphia	160
1915	Tyrus Cobb, Detroit	161
1916	Tristram Speaker, Cleveland	160
1917	Tyrus Cobb, Detroit	151
	J. Clyde Milan, Washington	151
1918	George Burns, Philadelphia	141
1919	Edgar Rice, Washington	144
1920	George Sisler, St. Louis	171
1921	John Tobin, St. Louis	179
1922	George Sisler, St. Louis	178
1923	Charles Jamieson, Cleveland	172
1924	Charles Jamieson, Cleveland	168
1925	Edgar Rice, Washington	182
1926	Edgar Rice, Washington	167
1927	Earle Combs, New York	166
1928	Henry Manush, St. Louis	161
1929	Earle Combs, New York	151
1930	Edgar Rice, Washington	158
1931	Oscar Melillo, St. Louis	142
	Jonathan Stone, Detroit	142
1932	Henry Manush, Washington	145
1933	Henry Manush, Washington	167
1934	Roger Cramer, Philadelphia	158
1935	Roger Cramer, Philadelphia	170
1936	Raymond Radcliff, Chicago	161
1937	John Lewis, Washington	162
1938	Melo Almada, Wash.-St. Louis	158
1939	Roger Cramer, Boston	147
1940	Roger Cramer, Boston	160
1941	Cecil Travis, Washington	153
1942	John Pesky, Boston	165
1943	Roger Cramer, Detroit	159
1944	George Stirnweiss, New York	146
1945	Irvin Hall, Philadelphia	139
1946	John Pesky, Boston	159
1947	John Pesky, Boston	172
1948	L. Dale Mitchell, Cleveland	162
1949	L. Dale Mitchell, Cleveland	161
1950	Philip Rizzuto, New York	150
1951	George Kell, Detroit	150
1952	J. Nelson Fox, Chicago	157
1953	Harvey Kuenn, Detroit	167
1954	J. Nelson Fox, Chicago	167
1955	J. Nelson Fox, Chicago	157
1956	J. Nelson Fox, Chicago	158
1957	J. Nelson Fox, Chicago	155
1958	J. Nelson Fox, Chicago	160
1959	J. Nelson Fox, Chicago	149
1960	J. Nelson Fox, Chicago	139
1961	Robert Richardson, New York	148
1962	Robert Richardson, New York	158
1963	Albert Pearson, Los Angeles	139
1964	Robert Richardson, New York	148
1965	Donald Buford, Chicago	129
1966	Luis Aparicio, Baltimore	143
1967	Horace Clarke, New York	140
1968	Dagoberto Campaneris, Oakland	139
1969	Horace Clarke, New York	146
1970	Alexander Johnson, California	156
1971	Cesar Tovar, Minnesota	171
1972	Rodney Carew, Minnesota	143
1973	Rodney Carew, Minnesota	156
1974	Rodney Carew, Minnesota	180
1975	Thurman Munson, New York	151
1976	George Brett, Kansas City	160
1977	Rodney Carew, Minnesota	171
1978	Ronald LeFlore, Detroit	153
1979	Willie Wilson, Kansas City	148
1980	Willie Wilson, Kansas City	184
1981	Willie Wilson, Kansas City	115
1982	Willie Wilson, Kansas City	157
1983	Wade Boggs, Boston	154
1984	Wade Boggs, Boston	162
1985	Wade Boggs, Boston	187
1986	O. Antonio Fernandez, Toronto	161
1987	Kevin Seitzer, Kansas City	151

National League

Year	Player and Club	1B.
1900	William Keeler, Brooklyn	179
1901	Jesse Burkett, St. Louis	180

Year	Player and Club	1B.
1902—	Clarence Beaumont, Pittsburgh	167
1903—	Clarence Beaumont, Pittsburgh	166
1904—	Clarence Beaumont, Pittsburgh	158
1905—	Michael Donlin, New York	162
1906—	Miller Huggins, Cincinnati	141
	William Shannon, St. Louis-New York	141
1907—	Clarence Beaumont, Pittsburgh	150
1908—	Michael Donlin, New York	153
1909—	Edward Grant, Philadelphia	147
1910—	Edward Grant, Philadelphia	134
1911—	Jacob Daubert, Brooklyn	146
	Roy Miller, Boston	146
1912—	William Sweeney, Boston	159
1913—	Jacob Daubert, Brooklyn	152
1914—	Beals Becker, Philadelphia	128
1915—	Lawrence Doyle, New York	135
1916—	David Robertson, New York	142
1917—	Benjamin Kauff, New York	141
	Edd Roush, Cincinnati	141
1918—	Charles Hollocher, Chicago	130
1919—	Ivan Olson, Brooklyn	140
1920—	Milton Stock, St. Louis	170
1921—	Carson Bigbee, Pittsburgh	161
1922—	Carson Bigbee, Pittsburgh	166
1923—	Frank Frisch, New York	169
1924—	Zachariah Wheat, Brooklyn	149
1925—	Milton Stock, Brooklyn	164
1926—	Edward Brown, Boston	160
1927—	Lloyd Waner, Pittsburgh	198
1928—	Lloyd Waner, Pittsburgh	180
1929—	Frank O'Doul, Philadelphia	181
	Lloyd Waner, Pittsburgh	181
1930—	William Terry, New York	177
1931—	Lloyd Waner, Pittsburgh	172
1932—	Frank O'Doul, Brooklyn	158
1933—	Charles Fullis, Philadelphia	162
1934—	William Terry, New York	169
1935—	Forrest Jensen, Pittsburgh	160
1936—	Joseph Moore, New York	160
1937—	Paul Waner, Pittsburgh	178
1938—	Frank McCormick, Cincinnati	160
1939—	John Hassett, Boston	162
1940—	Burgess Whitehead, New York	141
1941—	Stanley Hack, Chicago	141
1942—	Enos Slaughter, St. Louis	127
1943—	Nicholas Witek, New York	172
1944—	Philip Cavarretta, Chicago	142
1945—	Stanley Hack, Chicago	155
1946—	Stanley Musial, St. Louis	142
1947—	Thomas Holmes, Boston	146
1948—	Stanley Rojek, Pittsburgh	150
1949—	Al (Red) Schoendienst, St. Louis	160
1950—	Edward Waitkus, Philadelphia	143
1951—	Richie Ashburn, Philadelphia	181
1952—	Robert Adams, Cincinnati	145
1953—	Richie Ashburn, Philadelphia	169
1954—	Donald Mueller, New York	165
1955—	Donald Mueller, New York	152
1956—	John Temple, Cincinnati	157
1957—	Richie Ashburn, Philadelphia	152
1958—	Richie Ashburn, Philadelphia	176
1959—	Don Blasingame, St. Louis	144
1960—	Richard Groat, Pittsburgh	154
1961—	Vada Pinson, Cincinnati	150
	Maurice Wills, Los Angeles	150
1962—	Maurice Wills, Los Angeles	179
1963—	Curtis Flood, St. Louis	152
1964—	Curtis Flood, St. Louis	178
1965—	Maurice Wills, Los Angeles	165
1966—	Roland Jackson, Houston	160
1967—	Maurice Wills, Pittsburgh	162
1968—	Curtis Flood, St. Louis	160
1969—	Mateo Alou, Pittsburgh	183
1970—	Mateo Alou, Pittsburgh	171
1971—	Ralph Garr, Atlanta	180
1972—	Louis Brock, St. Louis	156
1973—	Peter Rose, Cincinnati	181
1974—	David Cash, Philadelphia	167
1975—	David Cash, Philadelphia	166
1976—	Guillermo Montanez, San Fran.-Atl.	164
1977—	Garry Templeton, St. Louis	155
1978—	Lawrence Bowa, Philadelphia	153
1979—	Peter Rose, Philadelphia	159
1980—	Eugene Richards, San Diego	155
1981—	Peter Rose, Philadelphia	117
1982—	William Buckner, Chicago	147
1983—	Rafael Ramirez, Atlanta	160
1984—	Anthony Gwynn, San Diego	177
1985—	Willie McGee, St. Louis	162
1986—	Anthony Gwynn, San Diego	157
	Stephen Sax, Los Angeles	157
1987—	Anthony Gwynn, San Diego	162

Doubles

American League

Year	Player and Club	2B.
1901—	Napoleon Lajoie, Philadelphia	48
1902—	Harry Davis, Philadelphia	43
1903—	Ralph Seybold, Philadelphia	43
1904—	Napoleon Lajoie, Cleveland	50
1905—	Harry Davis, Philadelphia	47
1906—	Napoleon Lajoie, Cleveland	49
1907—	Harry Davis, Philadelphia	37
1908—	Tyrus Cobb, Detroit	36
1909—	Samuel Crawford, Detroit	35
1910—	Napoleon Lajoie, Cleveland	53
1911—	Tyrus Cobb, Detroit	47
1912—	Tristram Speaker, Boston	53
1913—	Joseph Jackson, Cleveland	39
1914—	Tristram Speaker, Boston	46
1915—	Robert Veach, Detroit	40
1916—	John Graney, Cleveland	41
	Tristram Speaker, Cleveland	41
1917—	Tyrus Cobb, Detroit	44
1918—	Tristram Speaker, Cleveland	33
1919—	Robert Veach, Detroit	45
1920—	Tristram Speaker, Cleveland	50
1921—	Tristram Speaker, Cleveland	52
1922—	Tristram Speaker, Cleveland	48
1923—	Tristram Speaker, Cleveland	59
1924—	Joseph Sewell, Cleveland	45
	Harry Heilmann, Detroit	45
1925—	Martin McManus, St. Louis	44
1926—	George Burns, Cleveland	64
1927—	H. Louis Gehrig, New York	52
1928—	Henry Manush, St. Louis	47
	H. Louis Gehrig, New York	47
1929—	Henry Manush, St. Louis	45
	Roy Johnson, Detroit	45
	Charles Gehringer, Detroit	45
1930—	U. John Hodapp, Cleveland	51
1931—	Earl Webb, Boston	67
1932—	Eric McNair, Philadelphia	47
1933—	Joseph Cronin, Washington	45
1934—	Henry Greenberg, Detroit	63
1935—	Joseph Vosmik, Cleveland	47
1936—	Charles Gehringer, Detroit	60
1937—	Roy (Beau) Bell, St. Louis	51
1938—	Joseph Cronin, Boston	51
1939—	Robert (Red) Rolfe, New York	46
1940—	Henry Greenberg, Detroit	50
1941—	Louis Boudreau, Cleveland	45
1942—	Donald Kolloway, Chicago	40
1943—	Richard Wakefield, Detroit	38
1944—	Louis Boudreau, Cleveland	45
1945—	Wallace Moses, Chicago	35
1946—	James (Mickey) Vernon, Wash.	51
1947—	Louis Boudreau, Cleveland	45
1948—	Theodore Williams, Boston	44
1949—	Theodore Williams, Boston	39
1950—	George Kell, Detroit	56
1951—	George Kell, Detroit	36
	Edward Yost, Washington	36
	Sabath (Sam) Mele, Washington	36
1952—	Ferris Fain, Philadelphia	43
1953—	James (Mickey) Vernon, Washington	43
1954—	James (Mickey) Vernon, Washington	33
1955—	Harvey Kuenn, Detroit	38
1956—	James Piersall, Boston	40
1957—	Orestes (Minnie) Minoso, Chicago	36
	William Gardner, Baltimore	36
1958—	Harvey Kuenn, Detroit	39
1959—	Harvey Kuenn, Detroit	42
1960—	John (Tito) Francona, Cleveland	36
1961—	Albert Kaline, Detroit	41
1962—	Floyd Robinson, Chicago	45
1963—	Carl Yastrzemski, Boston	40
1964—	Pedro (Tony) Oliva, Minnesota	43
1965—	Zoilo Versalles, Minnesota	45
	Carl Yastrzemski, Boston	45
1966—	Carl Yastrzemski, Boston	39
1967—	Pedro (Tony) Oliva, Minnesota	34
1968—	C. Reginald Smith, Boston	37
1969—	Pedro (Tony) Oliva, Minnesota	39
1970—	Pedro (Tony) Oliva, Minnesota	36
	Amos Otis, Kansas City	36
	Cesar Tovar, Minnesota	36
1971—	C. Reginald Smith, Boston	33
1972—	Louis Piniella, Kansas City	33
1973—	Salvatore Bando, Oakland	32
	Pedro Garcia, Milwaukee	32
1974—	Joseph Rudi, Oakland	39
1975—	Fredric Lynn, Boston	47
1976—	Amos Otis, Kansas City	40
1977—	Harold McRae, Kansas City	54
1978—	George Brett, Kansas City	45
1979—	Chester Lemon, Chicago	44
	Cecil Cooper, Milwaukee	44
1980—	Robin Yount, Milwaukee	49
1981—	Cecil Cooper, Milwaukee	35
1982—	Harold McRae, Kansas City	46
	Robin Yount, Milwaukee	46
1983—	Calvin Ripken, Baltimore	47
1984—	Donald Mattingly, New York	44
1985—	Donald Mattingly, New York	48
1986—	Donald Mattingly, New York	53
1987—	Paul Molitor, Milwaukee	41

National League

Year	Player and Club	2B.
1876—	Roscoe Barnes, Chicago	23
1877—	Adrian (Cap) Anson, Chicago	20
1878—	Lewis Brown, Providence	18
1879—	Charles Eden, Cleveland	31
1880—	Fred Dunlap, Cleveland	27
1881—	Michael (King) Kelly, Chicago	28
1882—	Michael (King) Kelly, Chicago	36
1883—	Edward Williamson, Chicago	50
1884—	Paul Hines, Providence	34
1885—	Adrian (Cap) Anson, Chicago	35
1886—	Dennis (Dan) Brouthers, Detroit	41
1887—	Dennis (Dan) Brouthers, Detroit	35
1888—	James Ryan, Chicago	37
1889—	John Glasscock, Indianapolis	39
1890—	Samuel Thompson, Philadelphia	38
1891—	Michael Griffin, Brooklyn	36
1892—	Dennis (Dan) Brouthers, Brooklyn	33
	Edward Delehanty, Philadelphia	33
1893—	Oliver (Pat) Tebeau, Cleveland	35
1894—	Hugh Duffy, Boston	50
1895—	Edward Delahanty, Philadelphia	47
1896—	Edward Delahanty, Philadelphia	42
1897—	Jacob Stenzel, Baltimore	40
1898—	Napoleon Lajoie, Philadelphia	40
1899—	Edward Delahanty, Philadelphia	56
1900—	John (Honus) Wagner, Pittsburgh	45
1901—	John (Honus) Wagner, Pittsburgh	39
	Jacob Beckley, Cincinnati	39
1902—	John (Honus) Wagner, Pittsburgh	33
1903—	Fred Clarke, Pittsburgh	32
	Samuel Mertes, New York	32
	Harry Steinfeldt, Cincinnati	32
1904—	John (Honus) Wagner, Pittsburgh	44
1905—	J. Bentley Seymour, Cincinnati	40
1906—	John (Honus) Wagner, Pittsburgh	38
1907—	John (Honus) Wagner, Pittsburgh	38
1908—	John (Honus) Wagner, Pittsburgh	39
1909—	John (Honus) Wagner, Pittsburgh	39
1910—	Robert Byrne, Pittsburgh	43
1911—	Edward Konetchy, St. Louis	38
1912—	Henry Zimmerman, Chicago	41
1913—	J. Carlisle Smith, Brooklyn	40
1914—	Sherwood Magee, Philadelphia	39
1915—	Lawrence Doyle, New York	40
1916—	O. Albert Niehoff, Philadelphia	42
1917—	Henry Groh, Cincinnati	39
1918—	Henry Groh, Cincinnati	28
1919—	Ross Youngs, New York	31
1920—	Rogers Hornsby, St. Louis	44
1921—	Rogers Hornsby, St. Louis	44
1922—	Rogers Hornsby, St. Louis	46
1923—	Edd Roush, Cincinnati	41
1924—	Rogers Hornsby, St. Louis	43
1925—	James Bottomley, St. Louis	44
1926—	James Bottomley, St. Louis	40
1927—	J. Riggs Stephenson, Chicago	46
1928—	Paul Waner, Pittsburgh	50
1929—	John Frederick, Brooklyn	52
1930—	Charles Klein, Philadelphia	59
1931—	Earl (Sparky) Adams, St. Louis	46
1932—	Paul Waner, Pittsburgh	62
1933—	Charles Klein, Philadelphia	44
1934—	Hazen (Kiki) Cuyler, Chicago	42
	Ethan Allen, Philadelphia	42
1935—	William Herman, Chicago	57
1936—	Joseph Medwick, St. Louis	64
1937—	Joseph Medwick, St. Louis	56
1938—	Joseph Medwick, St. Louis	47
1939—	Enos Slaughter, St. Louis	52
1940—	Frank McCormick, Cincinnati	44
1941—	Harold (Pete) Reiser, Brooklyn	39
	John Mize, St. Louis	39
1942—	Martin Marion, St. Louis	38
1943—	Stanley Musial, St. Louis	48
1944—	Stanley Musial, St. Louis	51
1945—	Thomas Holmes, Boston	47
1946—	Stanley Musial, St. Louis	50
1947—	Edward Miller, Cincinnati	38
1948—	Stanley Musial, St. Louis	46
1949—	Stanley Musial, St. Louis	41
1950—	Al (Red) Schoendienst, St. Louis	43
1951—	Alvin Dark, New York	41
1952—	Stanley Musial, St. Louis	42
1953—	Stanley Musial, St. Louis	53
1954—	Stanley Musial, St. Louis	41
1955—	John Logan, Milwaukee	37
	Henry Aaron, Milwaukee	37
1956—	Henry Aaron, Milwaukee	34
1957—	Donald Hoak, Cincinnati	39
1958—	Orlando Cepeda, San Francisco	38
1959—	Vada Pinson, Cincinnati	47
1960—	Vada Pinson, Cincinnati	37
1961—	Henry Aaron, Milwaukee	39
1962—	Frank Robinson, Cincinnati	51
1963—	Richard Groat, St. Louis	43
1964—	A. Lee Maye, Milwaukee	44
1965—	Henry Aaron, Milwaukee	40

Year	Player and Club	2B.
1966	John Callison, Philadelphia	40
1967	Daniel Staub, Houston	44
1968	Louis Brock, St. Louis	46
1969	Mateo Alou, Pittsburgh	41
1970	M. Wesley Parker, Los Angeles	47
1971	Cesar Cedeno, Houston	40
1972	Cesar Cedeno, Houston	39
	Guillermo Montanez, Philadelphia	39
1973	Wilver Stargell, Pittsburgh	43
1974	Peter Rose, Cincinnati	45
1975	Peter Rose, Cincinnati	47
1976	Peter Rose, Cincinnati	42
1977	David Parker, Pittsburgh	44
1978	Peter Rose, Cincinnati	51
1979	Keith Hernandez, St. Louis	48
1980	Peter Rose, Philadelphia	42
1981	William Buckner, Chicago	35
1982	Albert Oliver, Montreal	43
1983	William Buckner, Chicago	38
	Albert Oliver, Montreal	38
	Johnny Ray, Pittsburgh	38
1984	Timothy Raines, Montreal	38
	Johnny Ray, Pittsburgh	38
1985	David Parker, Cincinnati	42
1986	Von Hayes, Philadelphia	46
1987	Timothy Wallach, Montreal	42

Triples
American League

Year	Player and Club	3B.
1901	James Williams, Baltimore	22
1902	James Williams, Baltimore	23
1903	Samuel Crawford, Detroit	25
1904	Charles (Chick) Stahl, Boston	22
1905	Elmer Flick, Cleveland	19
1906	Elmer Flick, Cleveland	22
1907	Elmer Flick, Cleveland	18
1908	Tyrus Cobb, Detroit	20
1909	J. Franklin Baker, Philadelphia	19
1910	Samuel Crawford, Detroit	19
1911	Tyrus Cobb, Detroit	24
1912	Joseph Jackson, Cleveland	26
1913	Samuel Crawford, Detroit	23
1914	Samuel Crawford, Detroit	26
1915	Samuel Crawford, Detroit	19
1916	Joseph Jackson, Chicago	21
1917	Tyrus Cobb, Detroit	24
1918	Tyrus Cobb, Detroit	14
1919	Robert Veach, Detroit	17
1920	Joseph Jackson, Chicago	20
1921	Howard Shanks, Washington	19
1922	George Sisler, St. Louis	18
1923	Sam Rice, Washington	18
	Leon (Goose) Goslin, Washington	18
1924	Walter Pipp, New York	19
1925	Leon (Goose) Goslin, Washington	20
1926	H. Louis Gehrig, New York	20
1927	Earle Combs, New York	23
1928	Earle Combs, New York	21
1929	Charles Gehringer, Detroit	19
1930	Earle Combs, New York	22
1931	Roy Johnson, Detroit	19
1932	Joseph Cronin, Washington	18
1933	Henry Manush, Washington	17
1934	W. Benjamin Chapman, New York	13
1935	Joseph Vosmik, Cleveland	20
1936	Earl Averill, Cleveland	15
	Joe DiMaggio, New York	15
	Robert (Red) Rolfe, New York	15
1937	Fred (Dixie) Walker, Chicago	16
	Mike Kreevich, Chicago	16
1938	J. Geoffrey Heath, Cleveland	18
1939	John (Buddy) Lewis, Washington	16
1940	Barney McCosky, Detroit	19
1941	J. Geoffrey Heath, Cleveland	20
1942	Stanley Spence, Washington	15
1943	John Lindell, New York	12
	Wallace Moses, Chicago	12
1944	John Lindell, New York	16
	George Stirnweiss, New York	16
1945	George Stirnweiss, New York	22
1946	Henry Edwards, Cleveland	16
1947	Thomas Henrich, New York	13
1948	Thomas Henrich, New York	14
1949	L. Dale Mitchell, Cleveland	23
1950	Dom DiMaggio, Boston	11
	Robert Doerr, Boston	11
	Walter (Hoot) Evers, Detroit	11
1951	Orestes (Minnie) Minoso, Clev.-Chicago	14
1952	Roberto Avila, Chicago	11
1953	Manuel (Jim) Rivera, Chicago	16
1954	Orestes (Minnie) Minoso, Chicago	18
1955	Mickey Mantle, New York	11
	Andrew Carey, New York	11
1956	Orestes (Minnie) Minoso, Chicago	11
	Jack Jensen, Boston	11
	Harry Simpson, Kansas City	11
	James Lemon, Washington	11

Year	Player and Club	3B.
1957	Gilbert McDougald, New York	9
	Henry Bauer, New York	9
	Harry Simpson, New York	9
1958	Victor Power, Kansas City-Cleveland	10
1959	W. Robert Allison, Washington	9
1960	J. Nelson Fox, Chicago	10
1961	Jacob Wood, Detroit	14
1962	Gino Cimoli, Kansas City	15
1963	Zoilo Versalles, Minnesota	13
1964	Richard Rollins, Minnesota	10
	Zoilo Versalles, Minnesota	10
1965	Dagoberto Campaneris, Kansas City	12
	Zoilo Versalles, Minnesota	12
1966	Robert Knoop, California	11
1967	Paul L. Blair, Baltimore	12
1968	James Fregosi, California	13
1969	Delbert Unser, Washington	8
1970	Cesar Tovar, Minnesota	13
1971	Freddie Patek, Kansas City	11
1972	Carlton Fisk, Boston	9
	Joseph Rudi, Oakland	9
1973	Alonza Bumbry, Baltimore	11
	Rodney Carew, Minnesota	11
1974	John (Mickey) Rivers, California	11
1975	George Brett, Kansas City	13
	John (Mickey) Rivers, California	13
1976	George Brett, Kansas City	14
1977	Rodney Carew, Minnesota	16
1978	James Rice, Boston	15
1979	George Brett, Kansas City	20
1980	Alfredo Griffin, Toronto	15
	Willie Wilson, Kansas City	15
1981	John Castino, Minnesota	9
1982	Willie Wilson, Kansas City	15
1983	Robin Yount, Milwaukee	10
1984	Dave Collins, Toronto	15
	Lloyd Moseby, Toronto	15
1985	Willie Wilson, Kansas City	21
1986	Brett Butler, Cleveland	14
1987	Willie Wilson, Kansas City	15

National League

Year	Player and Club	3B.
1876	George Hall, Athletics	12
1877	Lewis Brown, Boston	9
	Calvin McVey, Chicago	9
	James (Deacon) White, Boston	9
1878	Thomas York, Providence	9
1879	Lewis Dickerson, Cincinnati	14
	Michael (King) Kelly, Cincinnati	14
1880	Harry Stovey, Worcester	14
1881	John Rowe, Buffalo	11
1882	Roger Connor, Troy	17
1883	Dennis (Dan) Brouthers, Buffalo	17
1884	William (Buck) Ewing, New York	18
1885	Roger Connor, New York	15
	James O'Rourke, New York	15
1886	Roger Connor, New York	19
1887	Samuel Thompson, Detroit	23
1888	Roger Connor, New York	17
	Richard Johnston, Boston	17
1889	Roger Connor, New York	17
	James Fogarty, Philadelphia	17
	Walter Wilmot, Washington	17
1890	John McPhee, Cincinnati	25
1891	Jacob Beckley, Pittsburgh	20
1892	Dennis (Dan) Brouthers, Brooklyn	20
1893	Perry Werden, St. Louis	33
1894	Henry Reitz, Baltimore	29
1895	Albert Selbach, Washington	22
	Samuel Thompson, Philadelphia	22
1896	Thomas McCreery, Louisville	21
	George Van Haltren, New York	21
1897	Harry Davis, Pittsburgh	28
1898	John Anderson, Brooklyn-Washington	19
1899	James Williams, Pittsburgh	27
1900	John (Honus) Wagner, Pittsburgh	22
1901	James Sheckard, Brooklyn	21
1902	Samuel Crawford, Cincinnati	23
1903	John (Honus) Wagner, Pittsburgh	19
1904	Harry Lumley, Brooklyn	18
1905	J. Bentley Seymour, Cincinnati	21
1906	Fred Clarke, Pittsburgh	13
	Frank Schulte, Chicago	13
1907	John Ganzel, Cincinnati	16
	Charles Alperman, Brooklyn	16
1908	John (Honus) Wagner, Pittsburgh	19
1909	Michael Mitchell, Cincinnati	17
1910	Michael Mitchell, Cincinnati	18
1911	Lawrence Doyle, New York	25
1912	John (Chief) Wilson, Pittsburgh	36
1913	Victor Saier, Chicago	21
1914	Max Carey, Pittsburgh	17
1915	Thomas Long, St. Louis	25
1916	William Hinchman, Pittsburgh	16
1917	Rogers Hornsby, St. Louis	17
1918	Jacob Daubert, Brooklyn	15
1919	Henry (Hi) Myers, Brooklyn	14
	William Southworth, Pittsburgh	14

Year	Player and Club	3B.
1920	Henry (Hi) Myers, Brooklyn	22
1921	Rogers Hornsby, St. Louis	18
	Raymond Powell, Boston	18
1922	Jacob Daubert, Cincinnati	22
1923	Max Carey, Pittsburgh	19
	Harold (Pie) Traynor, Pittsburgh	19
1924	Edd Roush, Cincinnati	21
1925	Hazen (Kiki) Cuyler, Pittsburgh	26
1926	Paul Waner, Pittsburgh	22
1927	Paul Waner, Pittsburgh	18
1928	James Bottomley, St. Louis	20
1929	Lloyd Waner, Pittsburgh	20
1930	Adam Comorosky, Pittsburgh	23
1931	William Terry, New York	20
1932	Floyd (Babe) Herman, Cincinnati	19
1933	J. Floyd (Arky) Vaughan, Pittsburgh	19
1934	Joseph Medwick, St. Louis	18
1935	Ival Goodman, Cincinnati	18
1936	Ival Goodman, Cincinnati	14
1937	J. Floyd (Arky) Vaughan, Pittsburgh	17
1938	John Mize, St. Louis	16
1939	William Herman, Chicago	18
1940	J. Floyd (Arky) Vaughan, Pittsburgh	15
1941	Harold (Pete) Reiser, Brooklyn	17
1942	Enos Slaughter, St. Louis	17
1943	Stanley Musial, St. Louis	20
1944	John Barrett, Pittsburgh	19
1945	Luis Olmo, Brooklyn	13
1946	Stanley Musial, St. Louis	20
1947	Harry Walker, St. Louis-Philadelphia	16
1948	Stanley Musial, St. Louis	18
1949	Stanley Musial, St. Louis	13
	Enos Slaughter, St. Louis	13
1950	Richie Ashburn, Philadelphia	14
1951	Stanley Musial, St. Louis	12
	David (Gus) Bell, Pittsburgh	12
1952	Robert Thomson, New York	14
1953	James Gilliam, Brooklyn	17
1954	Willie Mays, New York	13
1955	Willie Mays, New York	13
	R. Dale Long, Pittsburgh	13
1956	William Bruton, Milwaukee	15
1957	Willie Mays, New York	20
1958	Richie Ashburn, Philadelphia	13
1959	Wallace Moon, Los Angeles	11
	Charles Neal, Los Angeles	11
1960	William Bruton, Milwaukee	13
1961	George Altman, Chicago	12
1962	John Callison, Philadelphia	10
	William Virdon, Pittsburgh	10
	Willie Davis, Los Angeles	10
	Maurice Wills, Los Angeles	10
1963	Vada Pinson, Cincinnati	14
1964	Richard Allen, Philadelphia	13
	Ronald Santo, Chicago	13
1965	John Callison, Philadelphia	16
1966	J. Timothy McCarver, St. Louis	13
1967	Vada Pinson, Cincinnati	13
1968	Louis Brock, St. Louis	14
1969	Roberto Clemente, Pittsburgh	12
1970	William Davis, Los Angeles	16
1971	Joe Morgan, Houston	11
	Roger Metzger, Houston	11
1972	Lawrence Bowa, Philadelphia	13
1973	Roger Metzger, Houston	14
1974	Ralph Garr, Atlanta	17
1975	Ralph Garr, Atlanta	11
1976	David Cash, Philadelphia	12
1977	Garry Templeton, St. Louis	18
1978	Garry Templeton, St. Louis	13
1979	Garry Templeton, St. Louis	19
1980	Omar Moreno, Pittsburgh	13
	Rodney Scott, Montreal	13
1981	G. Craig Reynolds, Houston	12
	Eugene Richards, San Diego	12
1982	Richard Thon, Houston	10
1983	Brett Butler, Atlanta	13
1984	Juan Samuel, Philadelphia	19
	Ryne Sandberg, Chicago	19
1985	Willie McGee, St. Louis	18
1986	Mitchell Webster, Montreal	13
1987	Juan Samuel, Philadelphia	15

Home Runs
American League

Year	Player and Club	HR.
1901	Napoleon Lajoie, Philadelphia	14
1902	Ralph (Socks) Seybold, Philadelphia	16
1903	John (Buck) Freeman, Boston	13
1904	Harry Davis, Philadelphia	10
1905	Harry Davis, Philadelphia	8
1906	Harry Davis, Philadelphia	12
1907	Harry Davis, Philadelphia	8
1908	Samuel Crawford, Detroit	7
1909	Tyrus Cobb, Detroit	9
1910	J. Garland (Jake) Stahl, Boston	10
1911	J. Franklin Baker, Philadelphia	11

Year	Player and Club	HR.
1912—	J. Franklin Baker, Philadelphia	10
	Tristram Speaker, Boston	10
1913—	J. Franklin Baker, Philadelphia	12
1914—	J. Franklin Baker, Philadelphia	9
1915—	Robert Roth, Chicago-Cleveland	7
1916—	Walter Pipp, New York	12
1917—	Walter Pipp, New York	9
1918—	George (Babe) Ruth, Boston	11
	Tilly Walker, Philadelphia	11
1919—	George (Babe) Ruth, Boston	29
1920—	George (Babe) Ruth, New York	54
1921—	George (Babe) Ruth, New York	59
1922—	Kenneth Williams, St. Louis	39
1923—	George (Babe) Ruth, New York	41
1924—	George (Babe) Ruth, New York	46
1925—	Robert Meusel, New York	33
1926—	George (Babe) Ruth, New York	47
1927—	George (Babe) Ruth, New York	60
1928—	George (Babe) Ruth, New York	54
1929—	George (Babe) Ruth, New York	46
1930—	George (Babe) Ruth, New York	49
1931—	George (Babe) Ruth, New York	46
	H. Louis Gehrig, New York	46
1932—	James Foxx, Philadelphia	58
1933—	James Foxx, Philadelphia	48
1934—	H. Louis Gehrig, New York	49
1935—	James Foxx, Philadelphia	36
	Henry Greenberg, Detroit	36
1936—	H. Louis Gehrig, New York	49
1937—	Joseph DiMaggio, New York	46
1938—	Henry Greenberg, Detroit	58
1939—	James Foxx, Boston	35
1940—	Henry Greenberg, Detroit	41
1941—	Theodore Williams, Boston	37
1942—	Theodore Williams, Boston	36
1943—	Rudolph York, Detroit	34
1944—	Nicholas Etten, New York	22
1945—	Vernon Stephens, St. Louis	24
1946—	Henry Greenberg, Detroit	44
1947—	Theodore Williams, Boston	32
1948—	Joseph DiMaggio, New York	39
1949—	Theodore Williams, Boston	43
1950—	Albert Rosen, Cleveland	37
1951—	Gus Zernial, Chicago-Philadelphia	33
1952—	Lawrence Doby, Cleveland	32
1953—	Albert Rosen, Cleveland	43
1954—	Lawrence Doby, Cleveland	32
1955—	Mickey Mantle, New York	37
1956—	Mickey Mantle, New York	52
1957—	Roy Sievers, Washington	42
1958—	Mickey Mantle, New York	42
1959—	Rocco Colavito, Cleveland	42
	Harmon Killebrew, Washington	42
1960—	Mickey Mantle, New York	40
1961—	Roger Maris, New York	61
1962—	Harmon Killebrew, Minnesota	48
1963—	Harmon Killebrew, Minnesota	45
1964—	Harmon Killebrew, Minnesota	49
1965—	Anthony Conigilaro, Boston	32
1966—	Frank Robinson, Baltimore	49
1967—	Harmon Killebrew, Minnesota	44
	Carl Yastrzemski, Boston	44
1968—	Frank Howard, Washington	44
1969—	Harmon Killebrew, Minnesota	49
1970—	Frank Howard, Washington	44
1971—	William E. Melton, Chicago	33
1972—	Richard Allen, Chicago	37
1973—	Reginald Jackson, Oakland	32
1974—	Richard Allen, Chicago	32
1975—	Reginald Jackson, Oakland	36
	George Scott, Milwaukee	36
1976—	Graig Nettles, New York	32
1977—	James Rice, Boston	39
1978—	James Rice, Boston	46
1979—	J. Gorman Thomas, Milwaukee	45
1980—	Reginald Jackson, New York	41
	Benjamin Oglivie, Milwaukee	41
1981—	Antonio Armas, Oakland	22
	Dwight Evans, Boston	22
	Robert Grich, California	22
	Eddie Murray, Baltimore	22
1982—	Reginald Jackson, California	39
	J. Gorman Thomas, Milwaukee	39
1983—	James Rice, Boston	39
1984—	Antonio Armas, Boston	43
1985—	Darrell Evans, Detroit	40
1986—	Jesse Barfield, Toronto	40
1987—	Mark McGwire, Oakland	49

National League

Year	Player and Club	HR.
1876—	George Hall, Philadelphia	5
1877—	George Shaffer, Louisville	3
1878—	Paul Hines, Providence	4
1879—	Charles Jones, Boston	9
1880—	James O'Rourke, Boston	6
	Harry Stovey, Worcester	6
1881—	Dennis (Dan) Brouthers, Buffalo	8
1882—	George Wood, Detroit	7
1883—	William (Buck) Ewing, New York	10
1884—	Edward Williamson, Chicago	27
1885—	Abner Dalrymple, Chicago	11
1886—	Harding Richardson, Detroit	11
1887—	Roger Connor, New York	17
	William O'Brien, Washington	17
1888—	Roger Connor, New York	14
1889—	Samuel Thompson, Philadelphia	20
1890—	Thomas Burns, Brooklyn	13
	Michael Tiernan, New York	13
1891—	Harry Stovey, Boston	16
	Michael Tiernan, New York	16
1892—	James Holliday, Cincinnati	13
1893—	Edward Delahanty, Philadelphia	19
1894—	Hugh Duffy, Boston	18
	Robert Lowe, Boston	18
1895—	William Joyce, Washington	17
1896—	Edward Delahanty, Philadelphia	13
	Samuel Thompson, Philadelphia	13
1897—	Napoleon Lajoie, Philadelphia	10
1898—	James Collins, Boston	14
1899—	John (Buck) Freeman, Washington	25
1900—	Herman Long, Boston	12
1901—	Samuel Crawford, Cincinnati	16
1902—	Thomas Leach, Pittsburgh	6
1903—	James Sheckard, Brooklyn	9
1904—	Harry Lumley, Brooklyn	9
1905—	Fred Odwell, Cincinnati	9
1906—	Timothy Jordan, Brooklyn	12
1907—	David Brain, Boston	10
1908—	Timothy Jordan, Brooklyn	12
1909—	John (Red) Murray, New York	7
1910—	Fred Beck, Boston	10
	Frank Schulte, Chicago	10
1911—	Frank Schulte, Chicago	21
1912—	Henry Zimmerman, Chicago	14
1913—	Clifford (Gavvy) Cravath, Philadelphia	19
1914—	Clifford (Gavvy) Cravath, Philadelphia	19
1915—	Clifford (Gavvy) Cravath, Philadelphia	24
1916—	Dave Robertson, New York	12
	Fred (Cy) Williams, Chicago	12
1917—	Dave Robertson, New York	12
	Clifford (Gavvy) Cravath, Philadelphia	12
1918—	Clifford (Gavvy) Cravath, Philadelphia	8
1919—	Clifford (Gavvy) Cravath, Philadelphia	12
1920—	Fred (Cy) Williams, Philadelphia	15
1921—	George Kelly, New York	23
1922—	Rogers Hornsby, St. Louis	42
1923—	Fred (Cy) Williams, Philadelphia	41
1924—	Jacques Fournier, Brooklyn	27
1925—	Rogers Hornsby, St. Louis	39
1926—	Lewis (Hack) Wilson, Chicago	21
1927—	Lewis (Hack) Wilson, Chicago	30
	Fred (Cy) Williams, Philadelphia	30
1928—	Lewis (Hack) Wilson, Chicago	31
	James Bottomley, St. Louis	31
1929—	Charles Klein, Philadelphia	43
1930—	Lewis (Hack) Wilson, Chicago	56
1931—	Charles Klein, Philadelphia	31
1932—	Charles Klein, Philadelphia	38
	Melvin Ott, New York	38
1933—	Charles Klein, Philadelphia	28
1934—	James (Rip) Collins, St. Louis	35
	Melvin Ott, New York	35
1935—	Walter Berger, Boston	34
1936—	Melvin Ott, New York	33
1937—	Melvin Ott, New York	31
	Joseph Medwick, St. Louis	31
1938—	Melvin Ott, New York	36
1939—	John Mize, St. Louis	28
1940—	John Mize, St. Louis	43
1941—	Adolph Camilli, Brooklyn	34
1942—	Melvin Ott, New York	30
1943—	William Nicholson, Chicago	29
1944—	William Nicholson, Chicago	33
1945—	Thomas Holmes, Boston	28
1946—	Ralph Kiner, Pittsburgh	23
1947—	Ralph Kiner, Pittsburgh	51
	John Mize, New York	51
1948—	Ralph Kiner, Pittsburgh	40
	John Mize, New York	40
1949—	Ralph Kiner, Pittsburgh	54
1950—	Ralph Kiner, Pittsburgh	47
1951—	Ralph Kiner, Pittsburgh	42
1952—	Ralph Kiner, Pittsburgh	37
	Hank Sauer, Chicago	37
1953—	Edwin Mathews, Milwaukee	47
1954—	Theodore Kluszewski, Cincinnati	49
1955—	Willie Mays, New York	51
1956—	Edwin (Duke) Snider, Brooklyn	43
1957—	Henry Aaron, Milwaukee	44
1958—	Ernest Banks, Chicago	47
1959—	Edwin Mathews, Milwaukee	46
1960—	Ernest Banks, Chicago	41
1961—	Orlando Cepeda, San Francisco	46
1962—	Willie Mays, San Francisco	49
1963—	Henry Aaron, Milwaukee	44
	Willie McCovey, San Francisco	44
1964—	Willie Mays, San Francisco	47
1965—	Willie Mays, San Francisco	52
1966—	Henry Aaron, Atlanta	44
1967—	Henry Aaron, Atlanta	39
1968—	Willie McCovey, San Francisco	36
1969—	Willie McCovey, San Francisco	45
1970—	Johnny Bench, Cincinnati	45
1971—	Wilver Stargell, Pittsburgh	48
1972—	Johnny Bench, Cincinnati	40
1973—	Wilver Stargell, Pittsburgh	44
1974—	Michael Schmidt, Philadelphia	36
1975—	Michael Schmidt, Philadelphia	38
1976—	Michael Schmidt, Philadelphia	38
1977—	George Foster, Cincinnati	52
1978—	George Foster, Cincinnati	40
1979—	David Kingman, Chicago	48
1980—	Michael Schmidt, Philadelphia	48
1981—	Michael Schmidt, Philadelphia	31
1982—	David Kingman, New York	37
1983—	Michael Schmidt, Philadelphia	40
1984—	Dale Murphy, Atlanta	36
	Michael Schmidt, Philadelphia	36
1985—	Dale Murphy, Atlanta	37
1986—	Michael Schmidt, Philadelphia	37
1987—	Andre Dawson, Chicago	49

Total Bases
American League

Year	Player and Club	T.B.
1901—	Napoleon Lajoie, Philadelphia	345
1902—	John (Buck) Freeman, Boston	287
1903—	John (Buck) Freeman, Boston	281
1904—	Napoleon Lajoie, Cleveland	304
1905—	George Stone, St. Louis	260
1906—	George Stone, St. Louis	288
1907—	Tyrus Cobb, Detroit	286
1908—	Tyrus Cobb, Detroit	276
1909—	Tyrus Cobb, Detroit	296
1910—	Napoleon Lajoie, Cleveland	304
1911—	Tyrus Cobb, Detroit	367
1912—	Joseph Jackson, Cleveland	331
1913—	Samuel Crawford, Detroit	298
1914—	Tristram Speaker, Boston	287
1915—	Tyrus Cobb, Detroit	274
1916—	Joseph Jackson, Chicago	293
1917—	Tyrus Cobb, Detroit	336
1918—	George Burns, Philadelphia	236
1919—	George (Babe) Ruth, Boston	284
1920—	George Sisler, St. Louis	399
1921—	George (Babe) Ruth, New York	457
1922—	Kenneth Williams, St. Louis	367
1923—	George (Babe) Ruth, New York	399
1924—	George (Babe) Ruth, New York	391
1925—	Aloysius Simmons, Philadelphia	392
1926—	George (Babe) Ruth, New York	365
1927—	H. Louis Gehrig, New York	447
1928—	George (Babe) Ruth, New York	380
1929—	Aloysius Simmons, Philadelphia	373
1930—	H. Louis Gehrig, New York	419
1931—	H. Louis Gehrig, New York	410
1932—	James Foxx, Philadelphia	438
1933—	James Foxx, Philadelphia	403
1934—	H. Louis Gehrig, New York	409
1935—	Henry Greenberg, Detroit	389
1936—	Harold Trosky, Cleveland	405
1937—	Joseph DiMaggio, New York	418
1938—	James Foxx, Boston	398
1939—	Theodore Williams, Boston	344
1940—	Henry Greenberg, Detroit	384
1941—	Joseph DiMaggio, New York	348
1942—	Theodore Williams, Boston	338
1943—	Rudolph York, Detroit	301
1944—	John Lindell, New York	297
1945—	George Stirnweiss, New York	301
1946—	Theodore Williams, Boston	343
1947—	Theodore Williams, Boston	335
1948—	Joseph DiMaggio, New York	355
1949—	Theodore Williams, Boston	368
1950—	Walter Dropo, Boston	326
1951—	Theodore Williams, Boston	295
1952—	Albert Rosen, Cleveland	297
1953—	Albert Rosen, Cleveland	367
1954—	Orestes (Minnie) Minoso, Chicago	304
1955—	Albert Kaline, Detroit	321
1956—	Mickey Mantle, New York	376
1957—	Roy Sievers, Washington	331
1958—	Mickey Mantle, New York	307
1959—	Rocco Colavito, Cleveland	301
1960—	Mickey Mantle, New York	294
1961—	Roger Maris, New York	366
1962—	Rocco Colavito, Detroit	309
1963—	Richard Stuart, Boston	319
1964—	Pedro (Tony) Oliva, Minnesota	374
1965—	Zoilo Versalles, Minnesota	308
1966—	Frank Robinson, Baltimore	367
1967—	Carl Yastrzemski, Boston	360
1968—	Frank Howard, Washington	330

Year	Player and Club	T.B.
1969	Frank Howard, Washington	340
1970	Carl Yastrzemski, Boston	335
1971	C. Reginald Smith, Boston	302
1972	Bobby Murcer, New York	314
1973	David L. May, Milwaukee	295
	George Scott, Milwaukee	295
	Salvatore L. Bando, Oakland	295
1974	Joseph Rudi, Oakland	287
1975	George Scott, Milwaukee	318
1976	George Brett, Kansas City	298
1977	James Rice, Boston	382
1978	James Rice, Boston	406
1979	James Rice, Boston	369
1980	Cecil Cooper, Milwaukee	335
1981	Dwight Evans, Boston	215
1982	Robin Yount, Milwaukee	367
1983	James Rice, Boston	344
1984	Antonio Armas, Boston	339
1985	Donald Mattingly, New York	370
1986	Donald Mattingly, New York	388
1987	George Bell, Toronto	369

National League

Year	Player and Club	T.B.
1900	Elmer Flick, Philadelphia	305
1901	Jesse Burkett, St. Louis	313
1902	Samuel Crawford, Cincinnati	256
1903	Clarence Beaumont, Pittsburgh	272
1904	John (Honus) Wagner, Pittsburgh	255
1905	J. Bentley Seymour, Cincinnati	325
1906	John (Honus) Wagner, Pittsburgh	237
1907	John (Honus) Wagner, Pittsburgh	264
1908	John (Honus) Wagner, Pittsburgh	308
1909	John (Honus) Wagner, Pittsburgh	242
1910	Sherwood Magee, Philadelphia	263
1911	Frank Schulte, Chicago	308
1912	Henry Zimmerman, Chicago	318
1913	Cliff (Gavvy) Cravath, Philadelphia	298
1914	Sherwood Magee, Philadelphia	277
1915	Cliff (Gavvy) Cravath, Philadelphia	266
1916	Zachariah Wheat, Brooklyn	262
1917	Rogers Hornsby, St. Louis	253
1918	Charles Hollocher, Chicago	202
1919	Henry (Hi) Myers, Brooklyn	223
1920	Rogers Hornsby, St. Louis	329
1921	Rogers Hornsby, St. Louis	378
1922	Rogers Hornsby, St. Louis	450
1923	Frank Frisch, New York	311
1924	Rogers Hornsby, St. Louis	373
1925	Rogers Hornsby, St. Louis	381
1926	James Bottomley, St. Louis	305
1927	Paul Waner, Pittsburgh	342
1928	James Bottomley, St. Louis	362
1929	Rogers Hornsby, Chicago	409
1930	Charles Klein, Philadelphia	445
1931	Charles Klein, Philadelphia	347
1932	Charles Klein, Philadelphia	420
1933	Charles Klein, Philadelphia	365
1934	James (Rip) Collins, St. Louis	369
1935	Joseph Medwick, St. Louis	365
1936	Joseph Medwick, St. Louis	367
1937	Joseph Medwick, St. Louis	406
1938	John Mize, St. Louis	326
1939	John Mize, St. Louis	353
1940	John Mize, St. Louis	368
1941	Harold (Pete) Reiser, Brooklyn	299
1942	Enos Slaughter, St. Louis	292
1943	Stanley Musial, St. Louis	347
1944	William Nicholson, Chicago	317
1945	Thomas Holmes, Boston	367
1946	Stanley Musial, St. Louis	366
1947	Ralph Kiner, Pittsburgh	361
1948	Stanley Musial, St. Louis	429
1949	Stanley Musial, St. Louis	382
1950	Edwin (Duke) Snider, Brooklyn	343
1951	Stanley Musial, St. Louis	355
1952	Stanley Musial, St. Louis	311
1953	Edwin (Duke) Snider, Brooklyn	370
1954	Edwin (Duke) Snider, Brooklyn	378
1955	Willie Mays, New York	382
1956	Henry Aaron, Milwaukee	340
1957	Henry Aaron, Milwaukee	369
1958	Ernest Banks, Chicago	379
1959	Henry Aaron, Milwaukee	400
1960	Henry Aaron, Milwaukee	334
1961	Henry Aaron, Milwaukee	358
1962	Willie Mays, San Francisco	382
1963	Henry Aaron, Milwaukee	370
1964	Richard Allen, Philadelphia	352
1965	Willie Mays, San Francisco	360
1966	Felipe Alou, Atlanta	355
1967	Henry Aaron, Atlanta	344
1968	Billy Williams, Chicago	321
1969	Henry Aaron, Atlanta	332
1970	Billy Williams, Chicago	373
1971	Joseph Torre, St. Louis	352
1972	Billy Williams, Chicago	348
1973	Bobby Bonds, San Francisco	341
1974	Johnny Bench, Cincinnati	315
1975	Gregory Luzinski, Philadelphia	322
1976	Michael Schmidt, Philadelphia	306
1977	George Foster, Cincinnati	388
1978	David Parker, Pittsburgh	340
1979	David Winfield, San Diego	333
1980	Michael Schmidt, Philadelphia	342
1981	Michael Schmidt, Philadelphia	228
1982	Albert Oliver, Montreal	317
1983	Andre Dawson, Montreal	341
1984	Dale Murphy, Atlanta	332
1985	David Parker, Cincinnati	350
1986	David Parker, Cincinnati	304
1987	Andre Dawson, Chicago	353

Runs Batted In

American League

Year	Player and Club	RBI
1907	Tyrus Cobb, Detroit	116
1908	Tyrus Cobb, Detroit	101
1909	Tyrus Cobb, Detroit	115
1910	Samuel Crawford, Detroit	115
1911	Tyrus Cobb, Detroit	144
1912	J. Franklin Baker, Philadelphia	133
1913	J. Franklin Baker, Philadelphia	126
1914	Samuel Crawford, Detroit	112
1915	Samuel Crawford, Detroit	116
1916	Walter Pipp, New York	99
1917	Robert Veach, Detroit	115
1918	George Burns, Philadelphia	74
	Robert Veach, Detroit	74
1919	George (Babe) Ruth, Boston	112
1920	George (Babe) Ruth, New York	137
1921	George (Babe) Ruth, New York	171
1922	Kenneth Williams, St. Louis	155
1923	George (Babe) Ruth, New York	131
1924	Leon (Goose) Goslin, Washington	129
1925	Robert Meusel, New York	138
1926	George (Babe) Ruth, New York	145
1927	H. Louis Gehrig, New York	175
1928	George (Babe) Ruth, New York	142
	H. Louis Gehrig, New York	142
1929	Aloysius Simmons, Philadelphia	157
1930	H. Louis Gehrig, New York	174
1931	H. Louis Gehrig, New York	184
1932	James Foxx, Philadelphia	169
1933	James Foxx, Philadelphia	163
1934	H. Louis Gehrig, New York	165
1935	Henry Greenberg, Detroit	170
1936	Harold Trosky, Cleveland	162
1937	Henry Greenberg, Detroit	183
1938	James Foxx, Boston	175
1939	Theodore Williams, Boston	145
1940	Henry Greenberg, Detroit	150
1941	Joseph DiMaggio, New York	125
1942	Theodore Williams, Boston	137
1943	Rudolph York, Detroit	118
1944	Vernon Stephens, St. Louis	109
1945	Nicholas Etten, New York	111
1946	Henry Greenberg, Detroit	127
1947	Theodore Williams, Boston	114
1948	Joseph DiMaggio, New York	155
1949	Theodore Williams, Boston	159
	Vernon Stephens, Boston	159
1950	Walter Dropo, Boston	144
	Vernon Stephens, Boston	144
1951	Gus Zernial, Chicago-Philadelphia	129
1952	Albert Rosen, Cleveland	105
1953	Albert Rosen, Cleveland	145
1954	Lawrence Doby, Cleveland	126
1955	Raymond Boone, Detroit	116
	Jack Jensen, Boston	116
1956	Mickey Mantle, New York	130
1957	Roy Sievers, Washington	114
1958	Jack Jensen, Boston	122
1959	Jack Jensen, Boston	112
1960	Roger Maris, New York	112
1961	Roger Maris, New York	142
1962	Harmon Killebrew, Minnesota	126
1963	Richard Stuart, Boston	118
1964	Brooks Robinson, Baltimore	118
1965	Rocco Colavito, Cleveland	108
1966	Frank Robinson, Baltimore	122
1967	Carl Yastrzemski, Boston	121
1968	Kenneth Harrelson, Boston	109
1969	Harmon Killebrew, Minnesota	140
1970	Frank Howard, Washington	126
1971	Harmon Killebrew, Minnesota	119
1972	Richard Allen, Chicago	113
1973	Reginald Jackson, Oakland	117
1974	Jeffrey Burroughs, Texas	118
1975	George Scott, Milwaukee	109
1976	Lee May, Baltimore	109
1977	Larry Hisle, Minnesota	119
1978	James Rice, Boston	139
1979	Donald Baylor, California	139
1980	Cecil Cooper, Milwaukee	122
1981	Eddie Murray, Baltimore	78
1982	Harold McRae, Kansas City	133
1983	Cecil Cooper, Milwaukee	126
	James Rice, Boston	126
1984	Antonio Armas, Boston	123
1985	Donald Mattingly, New York	145
1986	Joseph Carter, Cleveland	121
1987	George Bell, Toronto	134

National League

Year	Player and Club	RBI
1907	John (Honus) Wagner, Pittsburgh	91
1908	John (Honus) Wagner, Pittsburgh	106
1909	John (Honus) Wagner, Pittsburgh	102
1910	Sherwood Magee, Philadelphia	116
1911	Frank Schulte, Chicago	121
1912	Henry Zimmerman, Chicago	98
1913	Cliff (Gavvy) Cravath, Philadelphia	118
1914	Sherwood Magee, Philadelphia	101
1915	Cliff (Gavvy) Cravath, Philadelphia	118
1916	Harold Chase, Cincinnati	84
1917	Henry Zimmerman, New York	100
1918	Frederick Merkle, Chicago	71
1919	Henry (Hi) Myers, Brooklyn	72
1920	George Kelly, New York	94
	Rogers Hornsby, St. Louis	94
1921	Rogers Hornsby, St. Louis	126
1922	Rogers Hornsby, St. Louis	152
1923	Emil Meusel, New York	125
1924	George Kelly, New York	136
1925	Rogers Hornsby, St. Louis	143
1926	James Bottomley, St. Louis	120
1927	Paul Waner, Pittsburgh	131
1928	James Bottomley, St. Louis	136
1929	Lewis (Hack) Wilson, Chicago	159
1930	Lewis (Hack) Wilson, Chicago	190
1931	Charles Klein, Philadelphia	121
1932	Frank (Don) Hurst, Philadelphia	143
1933	Charles Klein, Philadelphia	120
1934	Melvin Ott, New York	135
1935	Walter Berger, Boston	130
1936	Joseph Medwick, St. Louis	138
1937	Joseph Medwick, St. Louis	154
1938	Joseph Medwick, St. Louis	122
1939	Frank McCormick, Cincinnati	128
1940	John Mize, St. Louis	137
1941	Adolph Camilli, Brooklyn	120
1942	John Mize, New York	110
1943	William Nicholson, Chicago	128
1944	William Nicholson, Chicago	122
1945	Fred (Dixie) Walker, Brooklyn	124
1946	Enos Slaughter, St. Louis	130
1947	John Mize, New York	138
1948	Stanley Musial, St. Louis	131
1949	Ralph Kiner, Pittsburgh	127
1950	Delmer Ennis, Philadelphia	126
1951	Monford Irvin, New York	121
1952	Henry Sauer, Chicago	121
1953	Roy Campanella, Brooklyn	142
1954	Theodore Kluszewski, Cincinnati	141
1955	Edwin (Duke) Snider, Brooklyn	136
1956	Stanley Musial, St. Louis	109
1957	Henry Aaron, Milwaukee	132
1958	Ernest Banks, Chicago	129
1959	Ernest Banks, Chicago	143
1960	Henry Aaron, Milwaukee	126
1961	Orlando Cepeda, San Francisco	142
1962	H. Thomas Davis, Los Angeles	153
1963	Henry Aaron, Milwaukee	130
1964	Kenton Boyer, St. Louis	119
1965	Deron Johnson, Cincinnati	130
1966	Henry Aaron, Atlanta	127
1967	Orlando Cepeda, St. Louis	111
1968	Willie McCovey, San Francisco	105
1969	Willie McCovey, San Francisco	126
1970	Johnny Bench, Cincinnati	148
1971	Joseph Torre, St. Louis	137
1972	Johnny Bench, Cincinnati	125
1973	Wilver Stargell, Pittsburgh	119
1974	Johnny Bench, Cincinnati	129
1975	Gregory Luzinski, Philadelphia	120
1976	George Foster, Cincinnati	121
1977	George Foster, Cincinnati	149
1978	George Foster, Cincinnati	120
1979	David Winfield, San Diego	118
1980	Michael Schmidt, Philadelphia	121
1981	Michael Schmidt, Philadelphia	91
1982	Dale Murphy, Atlanta	109
	Albert Oliver, Montreal	109
1983	Dale Murphy, Atlanta	121
1984	Gary Carter, Montreal	106
	Michael Schmidt, Philadelphia	106
1985	David Parker, Cincinnati	125
1986	Michael Schmidt, Philadelphia	119
1987	Andre Dawson, Chicago	137

Note—Not compiled prior to 1907; officially adopted in 1920.

Bases On Balls

American League

Year	Player and Club	BB.
1913—	Burton Shotton, St. Louis	102
1914—	Owen (Donie) Bush, Detroit	112
1915—	Edward Collins, Chicago	119
1916—	Burton Shotton, St. Louis	111
1917—	John Graney, Cleveland	94
1918—	Raymond Chapman, Cleveland	84
1919—	John Graney, Cleveland	105
1920—	George (Babe) Ruth, New York	148
1921—	George (Babe) Ruth, New York	144
1922—	L. W. (Whitey) Witt, New York	89
1923—	George (Babe) Ruth, New York	170
1924—	George (Babe) Ruth, New York	142
1925—	William Kamm, Chicago	90
	John Mostil, Chicago	90
1926—	George (Babe) Ruth, New York	144
1927—	George (Babe) Ruth, New York	138
1928—	George (Babe) Ruth, New York	135
1929—	Max Bishop, Philadelphia	128
1930—	George (Babe) Ruth, New York	136
1931—	George (Babe) Ruth, New York	128
1932—	George (Babe) Ruth, New York	130
1933—	George (Babe) Ruth, New York	114
1934—	James Foxx, Philadelphia	111
1935—	H. Louis Gehrig, New York	132
1936—	H. Louis Gehrig, New York	130
1937—	H. Louis Gehrig, New York	127
1938—	James Foxx, Boston	119
	Henry Greenberg, Detroit	119
1939—	Harlond Clift, St. Louis	111
1940—	Charles Keller, New York	106
1941—	Theodore Williams, Boston	145
1942—	Theodore Williams, Boston	145
1943—	Charles Keller, New York	106
1944—	Nicholas Etten, New York	97
1945—	Roy Cullenbine, Cleveland-Detroit	112
1946—	Theodore Williams, Boston	156
1947—	Theodore Williams, Boston	162
1948—	Theodore Williams, Boston	126
1949—	Theodore Williams, Boston	162
1950—	Edward Yost, Washington	141
1951—	Theodore Williams, Boston	144
1952—	Edward Yost, Washington	129
1953—	Edward Yost, Washington	123
1954—	Theodore Williams, Boston	136
1955—	Mickey Mantle, New York	113
1956—	Edward Yost, Washington	151
1957—	Mickey Mantle, New York	146
1958—	Mickey Mantle, New York	129
1959—	Edward Yost, Detroit	135
1960—	Edward Yost, Detroit	125
1961—	Mickey Mantle, New York	126
1962—	Mickey Mantle, New York	122
1963—	Carl Yastrzemski, Boston	95
1964—	Norman Siebern, Baltimore	106
1965—	Rocco Colavito, Cleveland	93
1966—	Harmon Killebrew, Minnesota	103
1967—	Harmon Killebrew, Minnesota	131
1968—	Carl Yastrzemski, Boston	119
1969—	Harmon Killebrew, Minnesota	145
1970—	Frank Howard, Washington	132
1971—	Harmon Killebrew, Minnesota	114
1972—	Richard Allen, Chicago	99
	Roy White, New York	99
1973—	John Mayberry, Kansas City	122
1974—	F. Gene Tenace, Oakland	110
1975—	John Mayberry, Kansas City	119
1976—	D. Michael Hargrove, Texas	97
1977—	Colbert (Toby) Harrah, Texas	109
1978—	D. Michael Hargrove, Texas	107
1979—	Darrell Porter, Kansas City	121
1980—	Willie Randolph, New York	119
1981—	Dwight Evans, Boston	85
1982—	Rickey Henderson, Oakland	116
1983—	Rickey Henderson, Oakland	103
1984—	Eddie Murray, Baltimore	107
1985—	Dwight Evans, Boston	114
1986—	Wade Boggs, Boston	105
1987—	Brian Downing, California	106
	Dwight Evans, Boston	106

National League

Year	Player and Club	BB.
1910—	Miller Huggins, St. Louis	116
1911—	James Sheckard, Chicago	147
1912—	James Sheckard, Chicago	122
1913—	Robert Bescher, Cincinnati	94
1914—	Miller Huggins, St. Louis	105
1915—	Clifford (Gavvy) Cravath, Philadelphia	86
1916—	Henry Groh, Cincinnati	84
1917—	George Burns, New York	75
1918—	Max Carey, Pittsburgh	62
1919—	George Burns, New York	82
1920—	George Burns, New York	76
1921—	George Burns, New York	80
1922—	Max Carey, Pittsburgh	80
1923—	George Burns, New York	101
1924—	Rogers Hornsby, St. Louis	89
1925—	Jacques Fournier, Brooklyn	86
1926—	Lewis (Hack) Wilson, Chicago	69
1927—	Rogers Hornsby, New York	86
1928—	Rogers Hornsby, Boston	107
1929—	Melvin Ott, New York	113
1930—	Lewis (Hack) Wilson, Chicago	105
1931—	Melvin Ott, New York	80
1932—	Melvin Ott, New York	100
1933—	Melvin Ott, New York	75
1934—	J. Floyd (Arky) Vaughan, Pittsburgh	94
1935—	J. Floyd (Arky) Vaughan, Pittsburgh	97
1936—	J. Floyd (Arky) Vaughan, Pittsburgh	118
1937—	Melvin Ott, New York	102
1938—	Adolph Camilli, Brooklyn	119
1939—	Adolph Camilli, Brooklyn	110
1940—	Elburt Fletcher, Pittsburgh	119
1941—	Elburt Fletcher, Pittsburgh	118
1942—	Melvin Ott, New York	109
1943—	August Galan, Brooklyn	103
1944—	August Galan, Brooklyn	101
1945—	Edward Stanky, Brooklyn	148
1946—	Edward Stanky, Brooklyn	137
1947—	Henry Greenberg, Pittsburgh	104
	Harold (Pee Wee) Reese, Brooklyn	104
1948—	Robert Elliott, Boston	131
1949—	Ralph Kiner, Pittsburgh	117
1950—	Edward Stanky, New York	144
1951—	Ralph Kiner, Pittsburgh	137
1952—	Ralph Kiner, Pittsburgh	110
1953—	Stanley Musial, St. Louis	105
1954—	Richie Ashburn, Philadelphia	125
1955—	Edwin Mathews, Milwaukee	109
1956—	Edwin (Duke) Snider, Brooklyn	99
1957—	Richie Ashburn, Philadelphia	94
	John Temple, Cincinnati	94
1958—	Richie Ashburn, Philadelphia	97
1959—	James Gilliam, Los Angeles	96
1960—	Richie Ashburn, Chicago	116
1961—	Edwin Mathews, Milwaukee	93
1962—	Edwin Mathews, Milwaukee	101
1963—	Edwin Mathews, Milwaukee	124
1964—	Ronald Santo, Chicago	86
1965—	Joe Morgan, Houston	97
1966—	Ronald Santo, Chicago	95
1967—	Ronald Santo, Chicago	96
1968—	Ronald Santo, Chicago	96
1969—	James Wynn, Houston	148
1970—	Willie McCovey, San Francisco	137
1971—	Willie Mays, San Francisco	112
1972—	Joe Morgan, Cincinnati	115
1973—	Darrell Evans, Atlanta	124
1974—	Darrell Evans, Atlanta	126
1975—	Joe Morgan, Cincinnati	132
1976—	James Wynn, Atlanta	127
1977—	F. Gene Tenace, San Diego	125
1978—	Jeffrey Burroughs, Atlanta	117
1979—	Michael Schmidt, Philadelphia	120
1980—	Daniel Driessen, Cincinnati	93
	Joe Morgan, Houston	93
1981—	Michael Schmidt, Philadelphia	73
1982—	Michael Schmidt, Philadelphia	107
1983—	Michael Schmidt, Philadelphia	128
1984—	Gary Matthews, Chicago	103
1985—	Dale Murphy, Atlanta	90
1986—	Keith Hernandez, New York	94
1987—	Jack Clark, St. Louis	136

Note—Not included in batting records in A.L. prior to 1913 and N.L. prior to 1910.

Strikeouts

American League

Year	Player and Club	SO.
1913—	Daniel Moeller, Washington	106
1914—	August Williams, St. Louis	120
1915—	John Lavan, St. Louis	83
1916—	Walter Pipp, New York	82
1917—	Robert Roth, Cleveland	73
1918—	George (Babe) Ruth, Boston	58
1919—	Maurice Shannon, Phila.-Boston	70
1920—	Aaron Ward, New York	84
1921—	Robert Meusel, New York	88
1922—	James Dykes, Philadelphia	98
1923—	George (Babe) Ruth, New York	93
1924—	George (Babe) Ruth, New York	81
1925—	Martin McManus, St. Louis	69
1926—	Anthony Lazzeri, New York	96
1927—	George (Babe) Ruth, New York	89
1928—	George (Babe) Ruth, New York	87
1929—	James Foxx, Philadelphia	70
1930—	James Foxx, Philadelphia	66
	Edward Morgan, Cleveland	66
1931—	James Foxx, Philadelphia	84
1932—	Bruce Campbell, Chicago-St. Louis	104
1933—	James Foxx, Philadelphia	93
1934—	Harlond Cliff, St. Louis	100
1935—	James Foxx, Philadelphia	99
1936—	James Foxx, Boston	119
1937—	Frank Crosetti, New York	105
1938—	Frank Crosetti, New York	97
1939—	Hank Greenberg, Detroit	95
1940—	Samuel Chapman, Philadelphia	96
1941—	James Foxx, Boston	103
1942—	Joseph Gordon, New York	95
1943—	Chester Laabs, St. Louis	105
1944—	J. Patrick Seerey, Cleveland	99
1945—	J. Patrick Seerey, Cleveland	97
1946—	Charles Keller, New York	101
	J. Patrick Seerey, Cleveland	101
1947—	Edwin Joost, Philadelphia	110
1948—	J. Patrick Seerey, Cleve.-Chicago	102
1949—	Richard Kokos, St. Louis	91
1950—	Gus Zernial, Chicago	110
1951—	Gus Zernial, Chicago-Philadelphia	101
1952—	Lawrence Doby, Cleveland	111
	Mickey Mantle, New York	111
1953—	Lawrence Doby, Cleveland	121
1954—	Mickey Mantle, New York	107
1955—	Norbert Zauchin, Boston	105
1956—	James Lemon, Washington	138
1957—	James Lemon, Washington	94
1958—	James Lemon, Washington	120
	Mickey Mantle, New York	120
1959—	Mickey Mantle, New York	126
1960—	Mickey Mantle, New York	125
1961—	Jacob Wood, Detroit	141
1962—	Harmon Killebrew, Minnesota	142
1963—	David Nicholson, Chicago	175
1964—	Nelson Mathews, Kansas City	143
1965—	Zoilo Versalles, Minnesota	122
1966—	George Scott, Boston	152
1967—	Frank Howard, Washington	155
1968—	Reginald Jackson, Oakland	171
1969—	Reginald Jackson, Oakland	142
1970—	Reginald Jackson, Oakland	135
1971—	Reginald Jackson, Oakland	161
1972—	A. Bobby Darwin, Minnesota	145
1973—	A. Bobby Darwin, Minnesota	137
1974—	A. Bobby Darwin, Minnesota	127
1975—	Jeffrey Burroughs, Texas	155
1976—	James Rice, Boston	123
1977—	Clell (Butch) Hobson, Boston	162
1978—	Gary Alexander, Oakland-Cleveland	166
1979—	J. Gorman Thomas, Milwaukee	175
1980—	J. Gorman Thomas, Milwaukee	170
1981—	Antonio Armas, Oakland	115
1982—	Reginald Jackson, California	156
1983—	Ronald Kittle, Chicago	150
1984—	Antonio Armas, Boston	156
1985—	Stephen Balboni, Kansas City	166
1986—	Peter Incaviglia, Texas	185
1987—	Robert Deer, Milwaukee	186

National League

Year	Player and Club	SO.
1910—	John Hummell, Brooklyn	81
1911—	Robert Coulson, Brooklyn	78
	Robert Bescher, Cincinnati	78
1912—	Edward McDonald, Boston	91
1913—	George Burns, New York	74
1914—	Frederick Merkle, New York	80
1915—	H. Douglas Baird, Pittsburgh	88
1916—	Clifford (Gavvy) Cravath, Philadelphia	89
1917—	Fred Williams, Chicago	78
1918—	Ross Youngs, New York	49
	George Paskert, Chicago	49
1919—	Raymond Powell, Boston	79
1920—	George Kelly, New York	92
1921—	Raymond Powell, Boston	85
1922—	Frank Parkinson, Philadelphia	93
1923—	George Grantham, Chicago	92
1924—	George Grantham, Chicago	63
1925—	Chas. (Gabby) Hartnett, Chicago	77
1926—	Bernard Friberg, Philadelphia	77
1927—	Lewis (Hack) Wilson, Chicago	70
1928—	Lewis (Hack) Wilson, Chicago	94
1929—	Lewis (Hack) Wilson, Chicago	83
1930—	Lewis (Hack) Wilson, Chicago	84
1931—	H. Nicholas Cullop, Cincinnati	86
1932—	Lewis (Hack) Wilson, Brooklyn	85
1933—	Walter Berger, Boston	77
1934—	Adolph Camilli, Chicago-Philadelphia	94
1935—	Adolph Camilli, Philadelphia	113
1936—	Wilbur Brubaker, Pittsburgh	96
1937—	Vincent DiMaggio, Boston	111
1938—	Vincent DiMaggio, Boston	134
1939—	Adolph Camilli, Brooklyn	107
1940—	Chester Ross, Boston	128
1941—	Adolph Camilli, Brooklyn	115
1942—	Vincent DiMaggio, Pittsburgh	87
1943—	Vincent DiMaggio, Pittsburgh	126
1944—	Vincent DiMaggio, Pittsburgh	83
1945—	Vincent DiMaggio, Philadelphia	91
1946—	Ralph Kiner, Pittsburgh	109

Year	Player and Club	SO.
1947—	William Nicholson, Chicago	83
1948—	Henry Sauer, Cincinnati	85
1949—	Edwin (Duke) Snider, Brooklyn	92
1950—	Roy Smalley, Chicago	114
1951—	Gilbert Hodges, Brooklyn	99
1952—	Edwin Mathews, Boston	115
1953—	Stephen Bilko, St. Louis	125
1954—	Edwin (Duke) Snider, Brooklyn	96
1955—	Walter Post, Cincinnati	102
1956—	Walter Post, Cincinnati	124
1957—	Edwin (Duke) Snider, Brooklyn	104
1958—	Harry Anderson, Philadelphia	95
1959—	Walter Post, Philadelphia	101
1960—	J. Francisco Herrera, Philadelphia	136
1961—	Richard Stuart, Pittsburgh	121
1962—	Kenneth Hubbs, Chicago	129
1963—	Donn Clendenon, Pittsburgh	136
1964—	Richard Allen, Philadelphia	138
1965—	Richard Allen, Philadelphia	150
1966—	Byron Browne, Chicago	143
1967—	James Wynn, Houston	137
1968—	Donn Clendenon, Pittsburgh	163
1969—	Bobby Bonds, San Francisco	187
1970—	Bobby Bonds, San Francisco	189
1971—	Wilver Stargell, Pittsburgh	154
1972—	Lee May, Houston	145
1973—	Bobby Bonds, San Francisco	148
1974—	Michael Schmidt, Philadelphia	138
1975—	Michael Schmidt, Philadelphia	180
1976—	Michael Schmidt, Philadelphia	149
1977—	Gregory Luzinski, Philadelphia	140
1978—	Dale Murphy, Atlanta	145
1979—	David Kingman, Chicago	131
1980—	Dale Murphy, Atlanta	133
1981—	David Kingman, New York	105
1982—	David Kingman, New York	156
1983—	Michael Schmidt, Philadelphia	148
1984—	Juan Samuel, Philadelphia	168
1985—	Dale Murphy, Atlanta	141
	Juan Samuel, Philadelphia	141
1986—	Juan Samuel, Philadelphia	142
1987—	Juan Samuel, Philadelphia	162

Note—Not included in batting records in A.L. prior to 1913 and N.L. prior to 1910.

Baserunning

Stolen Bases

American League

Year	Player and Club	SB.
1901—	Frank Isbell, Chicago	48
1902—	Fred (Topsy) Hartsel, Philadelphia	54
1903—	Harry Bay, Cleveland	46
1904—	Elmer Flick, Cleveland	42
	Harry Bay, Cleveland	42
1905—	Daniel Hoffman, Philadelphia	46
1906—	Elmer Flick, Cleveland	39
	John Anderson, Washington	39
1907—	Tyrus Cobb, Detroit	49
1908—	Patrick Dougherty, Chicago	47
1909—	Tyrus Cobb, Detroit	76
1910—	Edward Collins, Philadelphia	81
1911—	Tyrus Cobb, Detroit	83
1912—	J. Clyde Milan, Washington	88
1913—	J. Clyde Milan, Washington	75
1914—	Frederick Maisel, New York	74
1915—	Tyrus Cobb, Detroit	96
1916—	Tyrus Cobb, Detroit	68
1917—	Tyrus Cobb, Detroit	55
1918—	George Sisler, St. Louis	45
1919—	Edward Collins, Chicago	33
1920—	Edgar (Sam) Rice, Washington	63
1921—	George Sisler, St. Louis	35
1922—	George Sisler, St. Louis	51
1923—	Edward Collins, Chicago	49
1924—	Edward Collins, Chicago	42
1925—	John Mostil, Chicago	43
1926—	John Mostil, Chicago	35
1927—	George Sisler, St. Louis	27
1928—	Charles (Buddy) Myer, Boston	30
1929—	Charles Gehringer, Detroit	27
1930—	Martin McManus, Detroit	23
1931—	W. Benjamin Chapman, New York	61
1932—	W. Benjamin Chapman, New York	38
1933—	W. Benjamin Chapman, New York	27
1934—	William Werber, Boston	40
1935—	William Werber, Boston	29
1936—	Lynford Lary, St. Louis	37
1937—	William Werber, Philadelphia	35
	W. Benjamin Chapman, Wash.-Bos.	35
1938—	Frank Crosetti, New York	27
1939—	George Case, Washington	51
1940—	George Case, Washington	35
1941—	George Case, Washington	33
1942—	George Case, Washington	44
1943—	George Case, Washington	61
1944—	George Stirnweiss, New York	55
1945—	George Stirnweiss, New York	33
1946—	George Case, Cleveland	28
1947—	Robert Dillinger, St. Louis	34
1948—	Robert Dillinger, St. Louis	28
1949—	Robert Dillinger, St. Louis	20
1950—	Dominic DiMaggio, Boston	15
1951—	Orestes (Minnie) Minoso, Clev.-Chicago	31
1952—	Orestes (Minnie) Minoso, Chicago	22
1953—	Orestes (Minnie) Minoso, Chicago	25
1954—	Jack Jensen, Boston	22
1955—	Manuel (Jim) Rivera, Chicago	25
1956—	Luis Aparicio, Chicago	21
1957—	Luis Aparicio, Chicago	28
1958—	Luis Aparicio, Chicago	29
1959—	Luis Aparicio, Chicago	56
1960—	Luis Aparicio, Chicago	51
1961—	Luis Aparicio, Chicago	53
1962—	Luis Aparicio, Chicago	31
1963—	Luis Aparicio, Baltimore	40
1964—	Luis Aparicio, Baltimore	57
1965—	Dagoberto Campaneris, Kansas City	51
1966—	Dagoberto Campaneris, Kansas City	52
1967—	Dagoberto Campaneris, Kansas City	55
1968—	Dagoberto Campaneris, Oakland	62
1969—	Tommy Harper, Seattle	73
1970—	Dagoberto Campaneris, Oakland	42
1971—	Amos Otis, Kansas City	52
1972—	Dagoberto Campaneris, Oakland	52
1973—	Tommy Harper, Boston	54
1974—	William North, Oakland	54
1975—	John (Mickey) Rivers, California	70
1976—	William North, Oakland	75
1977—	Freddie Patek, Kansas City	53
1978—	Ronald LeFlore, Detroit	68
1979—	Willie Wilson, Kansas City	83
1980—	Rickey Henderson, Oakland	100
1981—	Rickey Henderson, Oakland	56
1982—	Rickey Henderson, Oakland	130
1983—	Rickey Henderson, Oakland	108
1984—	Rickey Henderson, Oakland	66
1985—	Rickey Henderson, New York	80
1986—	Rickey Henderson, New York	87
1987—	Harold Reynolds, Seattle	60

National League

Year	Player and Club	SB.
1886—	George Andrews, Philadelphia	56
1887—	John M. Ward, New York	111
1888—	William (Dummy) Hoy, Washington	82
1889—	James Fogarty, Philadelphia	99
1890—	William Hamilton, Philadelphia	102
1891—	William Hamilton, Philadelphia	115
1892—	John M. Ward, Brooklyn	94
1893—	John M. Ward, New York	72
1894—	William Hamilton, Philadelphia	99
1895—	William Hamilton, Philadelphia	95
1896—	William Lange, Chicago	100
1897—	William Lange, Chicago	83
1898—	Frederick Clarke, Louisville	66
1899—	James Sheckard, Baltimore	78
1900—	James Barrett, Cincinnati	46
1901—	John (Honus) Wagner, Pittsburgh	48
1902—	John (Honus) Wagner, Pittsburgh	43
1903—	S. James Sheckard, Brooklyn	67
	Frank Chance, Chicago	67
1904—	John (Honus) Wagner, Pittsburgh	53
1905—	William Maloney, Chicago	59
	Arthur Devlin, New York	59
1906—	Frank Chance, Chicago	57
1907—	John (Honus) Wagner, Pittsburgh	61
1908—	John (Honus) Wagner, Pittsburgh	53
1909—	Robert Bescher, Cincinnati	54
1910—	Robert Bescher, Cincinnati	70
1911—	Robert Bescher, Cincinnati	81
1912—	Robert Bescher, Cincinnati	67
1913—	Max Carey, Pittsburgh	61
1914—	George Burns, New York	62
1915—	Max Carey, Pittsburgh	36
1916—	Max Carey, Pittsburgh	63
1917—	Max Carey, Pittsburgh	46
1918—	Max Carey, Pittsburgh	58
1919—	George Burns, New York	40
1920—	Max Carey, Pittsburgh	52
1921—	Frank Frisch, New York	49
1922—	Max Carey, Pittsburgh	51
1923—	Max Carey, Pittsburgh	51
1924—	Max Carey, Pittsburgh	49
1925—	Max Carey, Pittsburgh	46
1926—	Hazen (Kiki) Cuyler, Pittsburgh	35
1927—	Frank Frisch, St. Louis	48
1928—	Hazen (Kiki) Cuyler, Chicago	37
1929—	Hazen (Kiki) Cuyler, Chicago	43
1930—	Hazen (Kiki) Cuyler, Chicago	37
1931—	Frank Frisch, St. Louis	28
1932—	Charles Klein, Philadelphia	20
1933—	John (Pepper) Martin, St. Louis	26
1934—	John (Pepper) Martin, St. Louis	23
1935—	August Galan, Chicago	22
1936—	John (Pepper) Martin, St. Louis	23
1937—	August Galan, Chicago	23
1938—	Stanley Hack, Chicago	16
1939—	Stanley Hack, Chicago	17
	Lee Handley, Pittsburgh	17
1940—	Linus Frey, Cincinnati	22
1941—	Daniel Murtaugh, Philadelphia	18
1942—	Harold (Pete) Reiser, Brooklyn	20
1943—	J. Floyd (Arky) Vaughan, Brooklyn	20
1944—	John Barrett, Pittsburgh	28
1945—	Al. (Red) Schoendienst, St. Louis	26
1946—	Harold (Pete) Reiser, Brooklyn	34
1947—	Jack Robinson, Brooklyn	29
1948—	Richie Ashburn, Philadelphia	32
1949—	Jack Robinson, Brooklyn	37
1950—	Samuel Jethroe, Boston	35
1951—	Samuel Jethroe, Boston	35
1952—	Harold (Pee Wee) Reese, Brooklyn	30
1953—	William Bruton, Milwaukee	26
1954—	William Bruton, Milwaukee	34
1955—	William Bruton, Milwaukee	35
1956—	Willie Mays, New York	40
1957—	Willie Mays, New York	38
1958—	Willie Mays, San Francisco	31
1959—	Willie Mays, San Francisco	27
1960—	Maurice Wills, Los Angeles	50
1961—	Maurice Wills, Los Angeles	35
1962—	Maurice Wills, Los Angeles	104
1963—	Maurice Wills, Los Angeles	40
1964—	Maurice Wills, Los Angeles	53
1965—	Maurice Wills, Los Angeles	94
1966—	Louis Brock, St. Louis	74
1967—	Louis Brock, St. Louis	52
1968—	Louis Brock, St. Louis	62
1969—	Louis Brock, St. Louis	53
1970—	Robert Tolan, Cincinnati	57
1971—	Louis Brock, St. Louis	64
1972—	Louis Brock, St. Louis	63
1973—	Louis Brock, St. Louis	70
1974—	Louis Brock, St. Louis	118
1975—	David Lopes, Los Angeles	77
1976—	David Lopes, Los Angeles	63
1977—	Franklin Taveras, Pittsburgh	70
1978—	Omar Moreno, Pittsburgh	71
1979—	Omar Moreno, Pittsburgh	77
1980—	Ronald LeFlore, Montreal	97
1981—	Timothy Raines, Montreal	71
1982—	Timothy Raines, Montreal	78
1983—	Timothy Raines, Montreal	90
1984—	Timothy Raines, Montreal	75
1985—	Vincent Coleman, St. Louis	110
1986—	Vincent Coleman, St. Louis	107
1987—	Vincent Coleman, St. Louis	109

Pitching

Winning Percentage

American League

Year	Pitcher and Club	W.	L.	Pct.
1901—	Griffith, Chicago	24	7	.774
1902—	Bernhard, Phil.-Clev.	18	5	.783
1903—	Moore, Cleveland	22	7	.759
1904—	Chesbro, New York	41	13	.759
1905—	Tannehill, Boston	22	9	.710
1906—	Plank, Philadelphia	19	6	.760
1907—	Donovan, Detroit	25	4	.862
1908—	Walsh, Chicago	40	15	.727
1909—	Mullin, Detroit	29	8	.784
1910—	Bender, Philadelphia	23	5	.821
1911—	Bender, Philadelphia	17	5	.773
1912—	Wood, Boston	34	5	.872
1913—	Johnson, Washington	36	7	.837
1914—	Bender, Philadelphia	17	3	.850
1915—	Wood, Boston	15	5	.750
1916—	Cicotte, Chicago	15	7	.682
1917—	Russell, Chicago	15	5	.750
1918—	Jones, Boston	16	5	.762
1919—	Cicotte, Chicago	29	7	.806
1920—	Bagby, Cleveland	31	12	.721
1921—	Mays, New York	27	9	.750
1922—	Bush, New York	26	7	.788
1923—	Pennock, New York	19	6	.760
1924—	Johnson, Washington	23	7	.767
1925—	Coveleski, Washington	20	5	.800
1926—	Uhle, Cleveland	27	11	.711
1927—	Hoyt, New York	22	7	.759
1928—	Crowder, St. Louis	21	5	.808
1929—	Grove, Philadelphia	20	6	.769
1930—	Grove, Philadelphia	28	5	.848
1931—	Grove, Philadelphia	31	4	.886
1932—	Allen, New York	17	4	.810
1933—	Grove, Philadelphia	24	8	.750
1934—	Gomez, New York	26	5	.839
1935—	Auker, Detroit	18	7	.720
1936—	Pearson, New York	19	7	.731

Year	Pitcher and Club	W.	L.	Pct.
1937—	Allen, Cleveland	15	1	.938
1938—	Ruffing, New York	21	7	.750
1939—	Grove, Boston	15	4	.789
1940—	Rowe, Detroit	16	3	.842
1941—	Gomez, New York	15	5	.750
1942—	Bonham, New York	21	5	.808
1943—	Chandler, New York	20	4	.833
1944—	Hughson, Boston	18	5	.783
1945—	Newhouser, Detroit	25	9	.735
1946—	Ferriss, Boston	25	6	.806
1947—	Reynolds, New York	19	8	.704
1948—	Kramer, Boston	18	5	.783
1949—	Kinder, Boston	23	6	.793
1950—	Raschi, New York	21	8	.724
1951—	Feller, Cleveland	22	8	.733
1952—	Shantz, Philadelphia	24	7	.774
1953—	Lopat, New York	16	4	.800
1954—	Consuegra, Chicago	16	3	.842
1955—	Byrne, New York	16	5	.762
1956—	Ford, New York	19	6	.760
1957—	Donovan, Chicago	16	6	.727
—	Sturdivant, New York	16	6	.727
1958—	Turley, New York	21	7	.750
1959—	Shaw, Chicago	18	6	.750
1960—	Perry, Cleveland	18	10	.643
1961—	Ford, New York	25	4	.862
1962—	Herbert, Chicago	20	9	.690
1963—	Ford, New York	24	7	.774
1964—	Bunker, Baltimore	19	5	.792
1965—	Grant, Minnesota	21	7	.750
1966—	Siebert, Cleveland	16	8	.667
1967—	Horlen, Chicago	19	7	.731
1968—	McLain, Detroit	31	6	.838
1969—	Palmer, Baltimore	16	4	.800
1970—	Cuellar, Baltimore	24	8	.750
1971—	McNally, Baltimore	21	5	.808
1972—	Hunter, Oakland	21	7	.750
1973—	Hunter, Oakland	21	5	.808
1974—	Cuellar, Baltimore	22	10	.688
1975—	Torrez, Baltimore	20	9	.690
1976—	Campbell, Minnesota	17	5	.773
1977—	Splittorff, Kansas City	16	6	.727
1978—	Guidry, New York	25	3	.893
1979—	Caldwell, Milwaukee	16	6	.727
1980—	Stone, Baltimore	25	7	.781
1981—	Vuckovich, Milwaukee	14	4	.778
1982—	Vuckovich, Milwaukee	18	6	.750
1983—	Dotson, Chicago	22	7	.759
1984—	Alexander, Toronto	17	6	.739
1985—	Guidry, New York	22	6	.786
1986—	Clemens, Boston	24	4	.857
1987—	Clemens, Boston	20	9	.690

National League

Year	Pitcher and Club	W.	L.	Pct.
1876—	Spalding, Chicago	47	13	.783
1877—	Bond, Boston	31	17	.646
1878—	Bond, Boston	40	19	.678
1879—	Ward, Providence	44	18	.710
1880—	Goldsmith, Chicago	22	3	.880
1881—	Radbourn, Providence	25	11	.694
1882—	Corcoran, Chicago	27	13	.675
1883—	McCormick, Cleveland	27	13	.675
1884—	Radbourn, Providence	60	12	.833
1885—	Welch, New York	44	11	.800
1886—	Flynn, Chicago	24	6	.800
1887—	Getzein, Detroit	29	13	.690
1888—	Keefe, New York	35	12	.745
1889—	Clarkson, Boston	49	19	.721
1890—	Lovett, Brooklyn	32	11	.744
1891—	Ewing, New York	22	8	.733
1892—	Young, Cleveland	36	11	.766
1893—	Killen, Pittsburgh	34	10	.773
1894—	Meekin, New York	34	9	.791
1895—	Hoffer, Baltimore	30	7	.811
1896—	Hoffer, Baltimore	26	7	.788
1897—	Rusie, New York	29	8	.784
1898—	Lewis, Boston	25	8	.758
1899—	Hughes, Brooklyn	28	6	.824
1900—	McGinnity, Brooklyn	29	9	.763
1901—	Chesbro, Pittsburgh	21	9	.700
1902—	Chesbro, Pittsburgh	28	6	.824
1903—	Leever, Pittsburgh	25	7	.781
1904—	McGinnity, New York	35	8	.814
1905—	Leever, Pittsburgh	20	5	.800
1906—	Reulbach, Chicago	19	4	.826
1907—	Reulbach, Chicago	17	4	.810
1908—	Reulbach, Chicago	24	7	.774
1909—	Mathewson, New York	25	6	.806
	Camnitz, Pittsburgh	25	6	.806
1910—	Cole, Chicago	20	4	.833
1911—	Marquard, New York	24	7	.774
1912—	Hendrix, Pittsburgh	24	9	.727
1913—	Humphries, Chicago	16	4	.800
1914—	James, Boston	26	7	.788
1915—	Alexander, Philadelphia	31	10	.756
1916—	Hughes, Boston	16	3	.842
1917—	Schupp, New York	21	7	.750
1918—	Hendrix, Chicago	20	7	.741
1919—	Ruether, Cincinnati	19	6	.760
1920—	Grimes, Brooklyn	23	11	.676
1921—	Doak, St. Louis	15	6	.714
1922—	Donohue, Cincinnati	18	9	.667
1923—	Luque, Cincinnati	27	8	.771
1924—	Yde, Pittsburgh	16	3	.842
1925—	Sherdel, St. Louis	15	6	.714
1926—	Kremer, Pittsburgh	20	6	.769
1927—	Benton, Boston-N.Y.	17	7	.708
1928—	Benton, New York	25	9	.735
1929—	Root, Chicago	19	6	.760
1930—	Fitzsimmons, New York	19	7	.731
1931—	Derringer, St. Louis	18	8	.692
1932—	Warneke, Chicago	22	6	.786
1933—	Cantwell, Boston	20	10	.667
1934—	J. Dean, St. Louis	30	7	.811
1935—	Lee, Chicago	20	6	.769
1936—	Hubbell, New York	26	6	.813
1937—	Hubbell, New York	22	8	.733
1938—	Lee, Chicago	22	9	.710
1939—	Derringer, Cincinnati	25	7	.781
1940—	Fitzsimmons, Brooklyn	16	2	.889
1941—	Riddle, Cincinnati	19	4	.826
1942—	French, Brooklyn	15	4	.789
1943—	Cooper, St. Louis	21	8	.724
1944—	Wilks, St. Louis	17	4	.810
1945—	Brecheen, St. Louis	15	4	.789
1946—	Dickson, St. Louis	15	6	.714
1947—	Jansen, New York	21	5	.808
1948—	Brecheen, St. Louis	20	7	.741
1949—	Roe, Brooklyn	15	6	.714
1950—	Maglie, New York	18	4	.818
1951—	Roe, Brooklyn	22	3	.880
1952—	Wilhelm, New York	15	3	.833
1953—	Erskine, Brooklyn	20	6	.769
1954—	Antonelli, New York	21	7	.750
1955—	Newcombe, Brooklyn	20	5	.800
1956—	Newcombe, Brooklyn	27	7	.794
1957—	Buhl, Milwaukee	18	7	.720
1958—	Spahn, Milwaukee	22	11	.667
	Burdette, Milwaukee	20	10	.667
1959—	Face, Pittsburgh	18	1	.947
1960—	Broglio, St. Louis	21	9	.700
1961—	Podres, Los Angeles	18	5	.783
1962—	Purkey, Cincinnati	23	5	.821
1963—	Perranoski, Los Angeles	16	3	.842
1964—	Koufax, Los Angeles	19	5	.792
1965—	Koufax, Los Angeles	26	8	.765
1966—	Marichal, San Francisco	25	6	.806
1967—	Hughes, St. Louis	16	6	.727
1968—	Blass, Pittsburgh	18	6	.750
1969—	Seaver, New York	25	7	.781
1970—	Gibson, St. Louis	23	7	.767
1971—	Gullett, Cincinnati	16	6	.727
1972—	Nolan, Cincinnati	15	5	.750
1973—	John, Los Angeles	16	7	.696
1974—	Messersmith, Los Angeles	20	6	.769
1975—	Gullett, Cincinnati	15	4	.789
1976—	Carlton, Philadelphia	20	7	.741
1977—	Candelaria, Pittsburgh	20	5	.800
1978—	Perry, San Diego	21	6	.778
1979—	Seaver, Cincinnati	16	6	.727
1980—	Bibby, Pittsburgh	19	6	.760
1981—	Seaver, Cincinnati	14	2	.875
1982—	Niekro, Atlanta	17	4	.810
1983—	Denny, Philadelphia	19	6	.760
1984—	Sutcliffe, Chicago	16	1	.941
1985—	Hershiser, Los Angeles	19	3	.864
1986—	Ojeda, New York	18	5	.783
1987—	Gooden, New York	15	7	.682

Note—Based on 15 or more victories.

Note—1981 percentages based on 10 or more victories.

Earned-Run Average

American League

Year	Pitcher and Club	G.	IP.	ERA.
1913—	Johnson, Washington	48	346	1.14
1914—	Leonard, Boston	35	225	1.00
1915—	Wood, Boston	25	157	1.49
1916—	Ruth, Boston	44	324	1.75
1917—	Cicotte, Chicago	49	346	1.53
1918—	Johnson, Washington	39	325	1.27
1919—	Johnson, Washington	39	290	1.49
1920—	Shawkey, New York	38	267	2.45
1921—	Faber, Chicago	43	331	2.47
1922—	Faber, Chicago	43	353	2.80
1923—	S. Coveleski, Cleveland	33	228	2.76
1924—	Johnson, Washington	38	278	2.72
1925—	S. Coveleski, Washington	32	241	2.84
1926—	Grove, Philadelphia	45	258	2.51
1927—	Moore, New York	50	213	2.28
1928—	Braxton, Washington	38	218	2.52
1929—	Grove, Philadelphia	42	275	2.81
1930—	Grove, Philadelphia	50	291	2.54
1931—	Grove, Philadelphia	41	289	2.06
1932—	Grove, Philadelphia	44	292	2.84
1933—	Pearson, Cleveland	19	135	2.33
1934—	Gomez, New York	38	282	2.33
1935—	Grove, Boston	35	273	2.70
1936—	Grove, Boston	35	253	2.81
1937—	Gomez, New York	34	278	2.33
1938—	Grove, Boston	24	164	3.07
1939—	Grove, Boston	23	191	2.54
1940—	Feller, Cleveland	43	320	2.62
1941—	T. Lee, Chicago	35	300	2.37
1942—	Lyons, Chicago	20	180	2.10
1943—	Chandler, New York	30	253	1.64
1944—	Trout, Detroit	49	352	2.12
1945—	Newhouser, Detroit	40	313	1.81
1946—	Newhouser, Detroit	37	293	1.94
1947—	Chandler, New York	17	128	2.46
1948—	Bearden, Cleveland	37	230	2.43
1949—	Parnell, Boston	39	295	2.78
1950—	Wynn, Cleveland	32	214	3.20
1951—	Rogovin, Detroit-Chicago	27	217	2.78
1952—	Reynolds, New York	35	244	2.07
1953—	Lopat, New York	25	178	2.43
1954—	Garcia, Cleveland	45	259	2.64
1955—	Pierce, Chicago	33	206	1.97
1956—	Ford, New York	31	226	2.47
1957—	Shantz, New York	30	173	2.45
1958—	Ford, New York	30	219	2.01
1959—	Wilhelm, Baltimore	32	226	2.19
1960—	Baumann, Chicago	47	185	2.68
1961—	Donovan, Washington	23	169	2.40
1962—	Aguirre, Detroit	42	216	2.21
1963—	Peters, Chicago	41	243	2.33
1964—	Chance, Los Angeles	46	278	1.65
1965—	McDowell, Cleveland	42	273	2.18
1966—	Peters, Chicago	30	205	1.98
1967—	Horlen, Chicago	35	258	2.06
1968—	Tiant, Cleveland	34	258	1.60
1969—	Bosman, Washington	31	193	2.19
1970—	Segui, Oakland	47	162	2.56
1971—	Blue, Oakland	39	312	1.82
1972—	Tiant, Boston	43	179	1.91
1973—	Palmer, Baltimore	38	296	2.40
1974—	Hunter, Oakland	41	318	2.49
1975—	Palmer, Baltimore	39	323	2.09
1976—	Fidrych, Detroit	31	250	2.34
1977—	Tanana, California	31	241	2.54
1978—	Guidry, New York	35	274	1.74
1979—	Guidry, New York	33	236	2.78
1980—	May, New York	41	175	2.47
1981—	McCatty, Oakland	22	186	2.32
1982—	Sutcliffe, Cleveland	34	216	2.96
1983—	Honeycutt, Texas	25	174.2	2.42
1984—	Boddicker, Baltimore	34	261.1	2.79
1985—	Stieb, Toronto	36	265	2.48
1986—	Clemens, Boston	33	254	2.48
1987—	Key, Toronto	36	261	2.76

National League

Year	Pitcher and Club	G.	IP.	ERA.
1912—	Tesreau, New York	36	243	1.96
1913—	Mathewson, New York	40	306	2.06
1914—	Doak, St. Louis	36	256	1.72
1915—	Alexander, Philadelphia	49	376	1.22
1916—	Alexander, Philadelphia	48	390	1.55
1917—	Alexander, Philadelphia	45	388	1.83
1918—	Vaughn, Chicago	35	290	1.74
1919—	Alexander, Chicago	30	235	1.72
1920—	Alexander, Chicago	46	363	1.91
1921—	Doak, St. Louis	32	209	2.58
1922—	Ryan, New York	46	192	3.00
1923—	Luque, Cincinnati	41	322	1.93
1924—	Vance, Brooklyn	35	309	2.16
1925—	Luque, Cincinnati	36	291	2.63
1926—	Kremer, Pittsburgh	37	231	2.61
1927—	Kremer, Pittsburgh	35	226	2.47
1928—	Vance, Brooklyn	38	280	2.09
1929—	Walker, New York	29	178	3.08
1930—	Vance, Brooklyn	35	259	2.61
1931—	Walker, New York	37	239	2.26
1932—	Warneke, Chicago	35	277	2.37
1933—	Hubbell, New York	45	309	1.66
1934—	Hubbell, New York	49	313	2.30
1935—	Blanton, Pittsburgh	35	254	2.59
1936—	Hubbell, New York	42	304	2.31
1937—	Turner, Boston	33	257	2.38
1938—	W. Lee, Chicago	44	291	2.66
1939—	Walters, Cincinnati	39	319	2.29
1940—	Walters, Cincinnati	36	305	2.48
1941—	E. Riddle, Cincinnati	33	217	2.24
1942—	M. Cooper, St. Louis	37	279	1.77
1943—	Pollet, St. Louis	16	118	1.75
1944—	Heusser, Cincinnati	30	193	2.38
1945—	Borowy, Chicago	15	122	2.14
1946—	Pollet, St. Louis	40	266	2.10
1947—	Spahn, Boston	40	290	2.33
1948—	Brecheen, St. Louis	33	233	2.24
1949—	Koslo, New York	38	212	2.50
1950—	Hearn, St.Louis-N.Y.	22	134	2.49

Year	Pitcher and Club	G.	IP.	ERA.
1951—Nichols, Boston		33	156	2.88
1952—Wilhelm, New York		71	159	2.43
1953—Spahn, Milwaukee		35	266	2.10
1954—Antonelli, New York		39	259	2.29
1955—Friend, Pittsburgh		44	200	2.84
1956—Burdette, Milwaukee		39	256	2.71
1957—Podres, Brooklyn		31	196	2.66
1958—Miller, San Francisco		32	182	2.47
1959—S. Jones, San Francisco		50	271	2.82
1960—McCormick, San Fran.		40	253	2.70
1961—Spahn, Milwaukee		38	263	3.01
1962—Koufax, Los Angeles		28	184	2.54
1963—Koufax, Los Angeles		40	311	1.88
1964—Koufax, Los Angeles		29	223	1.74
1965—Koufax, Los Angeles		43	336	2.04
1966—Koufax, Los Angeles		41	323	1.73
1967—P. Niekro, Atlanta		46	207	1.87
1968—Gibson, St. Louis		34	305	1.12
1969—Marichal, San Francisco		37	300	2.10
1970—Seaver, New York		37	291	2.81
1971—Seaver, New York		36	286	1.76
1972—Carlton, Philadelphia		41	346	1.98
1973—Seaver, New York		36	290	2.08
1974—Capra, Atlanta		39	217	2.28
1975—Jones, San Diego		37	285	2.24
1976—Denny, St. Louis		30	207	2.52
1977—Candelaria, Pittsburgh		33	231	2.34
1978—Swan, New York		29	207	2.43
1979—Richard, Houston		38	292	2.71
1980—Sutton, Los Angeles		32	212	2.21
1981—Ryan, Houston		21	149	1.69
1982—Rogers, Montreal		35	277	2.40
1983—Hammaker, San Fran.		23	172.1	2.25
1984—Pena, Los Angeles		28	199.1	2.48
1985—Gooden, New York		35	276.2	1.53
1986—Scott, Houston		37	275.1	2.22
1987—Ryan, Houston		34	211.2	2.76

Note—Based on 10 complete games through 1950, then 154 innings until 1961 in A.L. and 1962 in N.L., when it became 162 innings.

Note—Earned-run records not tabulated in N.L. prior to 1912 and A.L. prior to 1913.

Note—1981 earned-run champion determined by taking leader who pitched as many innings as his team's total number of games played.

Note—Wilcy Moore pitched only six complete games—he started 12—in 1927, but was recognized as A.L. leader because of 213 innings pitched; Ernie Bonham, New York, had 1.91 ERA and ten complete games in 1940, but appeared in only 12 games and 99 innings, and Bob Feller was recognized as leader.

Shutouts
American League

Year	Pitcher and Club	ShO.
1901—Clark Griffith, Chicago		5
Denton (Cy) Young, Boston		5
1902—Adrian Joss, Cleveland		5
1903—Denton (Cy) Young, Boston		7
1904—Denton (Cy) Young, Boston		10
1905—Edward Killian, Detroit		8
1906—Edward Walsh, Chicago		10
1907—Edward Plank, Philadelphia		8
1908—Edward Walsh, Chicago		12
1909—Edward Walsh, Chicago		8
1910—John Coombs, Philadelphia		13
1911—Walter Johnson, Washington		6
Edward Plank, Philadelphia		6
1912—Joseph Wood, Boston		10
1913—Walter Johnson, Washington		11
1914—Walter Johnson, Washington		9
1915—Walter Johnson, Washington		7
1916—George (Babe) Ruth, Boston		9
1917—Stanley Coveleski, Cleveland		9
1918—Walter Johnson, Washington		8
Carl Mays, Boston		8
1919—Walter Johnson, Washington		7
1920—Carl Mays, New York		6
1921—Samuel Jones, Boston		5
1922—George Uhle, Cleveland		5
1923—Stanley Coveleski, Cleveland		5
1924—Walter Johnson, Washington		6
1925—Theodore Lyons, Chicago		5
1926—Edwin Wells, Detroit		4
1927—Horace Lisenbee, Washington		4
1928—Herbert Pennock, New York		5
1929—George Blaeholder, St. Louis		4
Alvin Crowder, St. Louis		4
Samuel Gray, St. Louis		4
Daniel MacFayden, Boston		4
1930—Clinton Brown, Cleveland		3
George Earnshaw, Philadelphia		3
George Pipgras, New York		3
1931—Robert Grove, Philadelphia		4
Victor Sorrell, Detroit		4
1932—Thomas Bridges, Detroit		4
Robert Grove, Philadelphia		4
1933—Oral Hildebrand, Cleveland		6
1934—Vernon Gomez, New York		6
Melvin Harder, Cleveland		6
1935—Lynwood Rowe, Detroit		6
1936—Robert Grove, Boston		6
1937—Vernon Gomez, New York		6
1938—Vernon Gomez, New York		4
1939—Charles Ruffing, New York		5
1940—Robert Feller, Cleveland		4
Theodore Lyons, Chicago		4
Albert Milnar, Cleveland		4
1941—Robert Feller, Cleveland		6
1942—Ernest Bonham, New York		6
1943—Spurgeon F. Chandler, New York		5
Paul Trout, Detroit		5
1944—Paul Trout, Detroit		7
1945—Harold Newhouser, Detroit		8
1946—Robert Feller, Cleveland		10
1947—Robert Feller, Cleveland		5
1948—Robert Lemon, Cleveland		10
1949—Edward Garcia, Cleveland		6
Ellis Kinder, Boston		6
Virgil Trucks, Detroit		6
1950—Arthur Houtteman, Detroit		4
1951—Allie Reynolds, New York		7
1952—Edward Garcia, Cleveland		6
Allie Reynolds, New York		6
1953—Erwin Porterfield, Washington		9
1954—Edward Garcia, Cleveland		5
Virgil Trucks, Chicago		5
1955—William Hoeft, Detroit		7
1956—Herbert Score, Cleveland		5
1957—James Wilson, Chicago		5
1958—Edward Ford, New York		7
1959—Camilo Pascual, Washington		6
1960—Edward Ford, New York		4
James Perry, Cleveland		4
Early Wynn, Chicago		4
1961—Stephen Barber, Baltimore		8
Camilo Pascual, Minnesota		8
1962—Richard Donovan, Cleveland		5
James Kaat, Minnesota		5
Camilo Pascual, Minnesota		5
1963—Raymond Herbert, Chicago		7
1964—W. Dean Chance, Los Angeles		11
1965—James Grant, Minnesota		6
1966—Thomas John, Chicago		5
Samuel McDowell, Cleveland		5
Luis Tiant, Cleveland		5
1967—Steven Hargan, Cleveland		6
Joel Horlen, Chicago		6
Thomas John, Chicago		6
Michael Lolich, Detroit		6
James McGlothlin, California		6
1968—Luis Tiant, Cleveland		9
1969—Dennis McLain, Detroit		9
1970—Charles Dobson, Oakland		5
James Palmer, Baltimore		5
1971—Vida Blue, Oakland		8
1972—L. Nolan Ryan, California		9
1973—Rikalbert Blyleven, Minnesota		9
1974—Luis Tiant, Boston		7
1975—James Palmer, Baltimore		10
1976—L. Nolan Ryan, California		7
1977—Frank Tanana, California		7
1978—Ronald Guidry, New York		9
1979—L. Nolan Ryan, California		5
Michael Flanagan, Baltimore		5
Dennis Leonard, Kansas City		5
1980—Thomas John, New York		6
1981—Richard Dotson, Chicago		4
Kenneth Forsch, California		4
Steven McCatty, Oakland		4
George Medich, Texas		4
1982—David Stieb, Toronto		5
1983—Michael Boddicker, Baltimore		5
1984—Robert Ojeda, Boston		5
Geoffrey Zahn, California		5
1985—Rikalbert Blyleven, Cleveland-Minn.		5
1986—John Morris, Detroit		6
1987—W. Roger Clemens, Boston		7

National League

Year	Pitcher and Club	ShO.
1900—Clark Griffith, Chicago		4
Frank Hahn, Cincinnati		4
Charles Nichols, Boston		4
Denton (Cy) Young, St. Louis		4
1901—John Chesbro, Pittsburgh		6
Albert Orth, Philadelphia		6
Victor Willis, Boston		6
1902—John Chesbro, Pittsburgh		8
Christopher Mathewson, New York		8
1903—Samuel Leever, Pittsburgh		7
1904—Joseph McGinnity, New York		9
1905—Christopher Mathewson, New York		9
1906—Mordecai Brown, Chicago		9
1907—Orval Overall, Chicago		9
Christopher Mathewson, New York		9
1908—Christopher Mathewson, New York		12
1909—Orval Overall, Chicago		9
1910—Earl Moore, Philadelphia		7
1911—Grover Alexander, Philadelphia		7
1912—George Rucker, Brooklyn		6
1913—Grover Alexander, Philadelphia		9
1914—Charles Tesreau, New York		8
1915—Grover Alexander, Philadelphia		12
1916—Grover Alexander, Philadelphia		16
1917—Grover Alexander, Philadelphia		8
1918—George Tyler, Chicago		8
James Vaughn, Chicago		8
1919—Grover Alexander, Chicago		9
1920—Charles Adams, Pittsburgh		8
1921—Grover Alexander, Chicago		3
Philip Douglas, New York		3
Dana Filligim, Boston		3
Adolfo Luque, Cincinnati		3
Clarence Mitchell, Brooklyn		3
John Morrison, Pittsburgh		3
Joseph Oeschger, Boston		3
Jesse Haines, St. Louis		3
1922—Arthur Vance, Brooklyn		6
1923—Adolfo Luque, Cincinnati		6
1924—Jesse Barnes, Boston		4
A. Wilbur Cooper, Pittsburgh		4
Remy Kremer, Pittsburgh		4
Eppa Rixey, Cincinnati		4
Allen Sothoron, St. Louis		4
Emil Yde, Pittsburgh		4
1925—Harold Carlson, Philadelphia		4
Adolfo Luque, Cincinnati		4
Arthur Vance, Brooklyn		4
1926—Peter Donohue, Cincinnati		5
1927—Jesse Haines, St. Louis		6
1928—John Blake, Chicago		4
Burleigh Grimes, Pittsburgh		4
Charles Lucas, Cincinnati		4
Douglas McWeeney, Brooklyn		4
Arthur Vance, Brooklyn		4
1929—Perce Malone, Chicago		5
1930—Charles Root, Chicago		4
Arthur Vance, Brooklyn		4
1931—William Walker, New York		6
1932—Lonnie Warneke, Chicago		4
Jerome Dean, St. Louis		4
Stephen Swetonic, Pittsburgh		4
1933—Carl Hubbell, New York		10
1934—Jerome Dean, St. Louis		7
1935—Darrell Blanton, Pittsburgh		4
Freddie Fitzsimmons, New York		4
Lawrence French, Chicago		4
Van Mungo, Brooklyn		4
James Weaver, Pittsburgh		4
1936—Darrell Blanton, Pittsburgh		4
James Carleton, Chicago		4
Lawrence French, Chicago		4
William Lee, Chicago		4
Alfred Smith, New York		4
William Walters, Philadelphia		4
Lonnie Warneke, Chicago		4
1937—Louis Fette, Boston		5
Lee Grissom, Cincinnati		5
James Turner, Boston		5
1938—William Lee, Chicago		9
1939—Louis Fette, Boston		6
1940—William Lohrman, New York		5
Manuel Salvo, Boston		5
J. Whitlow Wyatt, Brooklyn		5
1941—J. Whitlow Wyatt, Brooklyn		7
1942—Morton Cooper, St. Louis		10
1943—Hiram Bithorn, Chicago		7
1944—Morton Cooper, St. Louis		7
1945—Claude Passeau, Chicago		5
1946—Ewell Blackwell, Cincinnati		6
1947—Warren Spahn, Boston		7
1948—Harry Brecheen, St. Louis		7
1949—Kenneth Heintzelman, Phila.		5
Donald Newcombe, Brooklyn		5
Howard Pollet, St. Louis		5
Kenneth Raffensberger, Cin.		5
1950—James Hearn, New York		5
Lawrence Jansen, New York		5
Salvatore Maglie, New York		5
Robin Roberts, Philadelphia		5
1951—Warren Spahn, Boston		7
1952—Ken Raffensberger, Cincinnati		6
Curtis Simmons, Philadelphia		6
1953—Harvey Haddix, St. Louis		6
1954—John Antonelli, New York		6
1955—Joseph Nuxhall, Cincinnati		5
1956—John Antonelli, New York		6
S. Lewis Burdette, Milwaukee		6
1957—John Podres, Brooklyn		6
1958—Carlton Willey, Milwaukee		4
1959—John Antonelli, San Francisco		4
Robert Buhl, Milwaukee		4
S. Lewis Burdette, Milwaukee		4
Roger Craig, Los Angeles		4

Shutouts (continued)

Year	Pitcher and Club	ShO.
	Donald Drysdale, Los Angeles	4
	Sam Jones, San Francisco	4
	Warren Spahn, Milwaukee	4
1960	John Sanford, San Francisco	6
1961	Joseph Jay, Cincinnati	4
	Warren Spahn, Milwaukee	4
1962	Robert Friend, Pittsburgh	5
	Robert Gibson, St. Louis	5
1963	Sanford Koufax, Los Angeles	11
1964	Sanford Koufax, Los Angeles	7
1965	Juan Marichal, San Francisco	10
1966	James Bunning, Philadelphia	5
	Robert Gibson, St. Louis	5
	Lawrence Jackson, Philadelphia	5
	Larry Jaster, St. Louis	5
	Sanford Koufax, Los Angeles	5
	James Maloney, Cincinnati	5
1967	James Bunning, Philadelphia	6
1968	Robert Gibson, St. Louis	13
1969	Juan Marichal, San Francisco	8
1970	Gaylord Perry, San Francisco	5
1971	Stephen Blass, Pittsburgh	5
	Alphonso Downing, Los Angeles	5
	Robert Gibson, St. Louis	5
	Milton Pappas, Chicago	5
1972	Donald Sutton, Los Angeles	9
1973	John Billingham, Cincinnati	7
1974	Jonathan Matlack, New York	7
1975	John Messersmith, Los Angeles	7
1976	Jonathan Matlack, New York	6
	John Montefusco, San Francisco	6
1977	G. Thomas Seaver, N.Y.-Cincinnati	7
1978	Robert Knepper, San Francisco	6
1979	G. Thomas Seaver, Cincinnati	5
	Joseph Niekro, Houston	5
	Stephen Rogers, Montreal	5
1980	Jerry Reuss, Los Angeles	6
1981	Fernando Valenzuela, Los Angeles	8
1982	Steven Carlton, Philadelphia	6
1983	Stephen Rogers, Montreal	5
1984	Joaquin Andujar, St. Louis	4
	Orel Hershiser, Los Angeles	4
	Alejandro Pena, Los Angeles	4
1985	John Tudor, St. Louis	10
1986	Robert Knepper, Houston	5
	Michael Scott, Houston	5
1987	Ricky Reuschel, Pitt.-S.F.	4
	Robert Welch, Los Angeles	4

Strikeouts
American League

Year	Pitcher and Club	SO.
1901	Denton (Cy) Young, Boston	159
1902	George (Rube) Waddell, Philadelphia	210
1903	George (Rube) Waddell, Philadelphia	301
1904	George (Rube) Waddell, Philadelphia	349
1905	George (Rube) Waddell, Philadelphia	286
1906	George (Rube) Waddell, Philadelphia	203
1907	George (Rube) Waddell, Philadelphia	226
1908	Edward Walsh, Chicago	269
1909	Frank Smith, Chicago	177
1910	Walter Johnson, Washington	313
1911	Edward Walsh, Chicago	255
1912	Walter Johnson, Washington	303
1913	Walter Johnson, Washington	243
1914	Walter Johnson, Washington	225
1915	Walter Johnson, Washington	203
1916	Walter Johnson, Washington	228
1917	Walter Johnson, Washington	188
1918	Walter Johnson, Washington	162
1919	Walter Johnson, Washington	147
1920	Stanley Coveleski, Cleveland	133
1921	Walter Johnson, Washington	143
1922	Urban Shocker, St. Louis	149
1923	Walter Johnson, Washington	130
1924	Walter Johnson, Washington	158
1925	Robert Grove, Philadelphia	116
1926	Robert Grove, Philadelphia	194
1927	Robert Grove, Philadelphia	174
1928	Robert Grove, Philadelphia	183
1929	Robert Grove, Philadelphia	170
1930	Robert Grove, Philadelphia	209
1931	Robert Grove, Philadelphia	175
1932	Charles (Red) Ruffing, New York	190
1933	Vernon Gomez, New York	163
1934	Vernon Gomez, New York	158
1935	Thomas Bridges, Detroit	163
1936	Thomas Bridges, Detroit	175
1937	Vernon Gomez, New York	194
1938	Robert Feller, Cleveland	240
1939	Robert Feller, Cleveland	246
1940	Robert Feller, Cleveland	261
1941	Robert Feller, Cleveland	260
1942	Louis (Bobo) Newsom, Washington	113
	Cecil (Tex) Hughson, Boston	113
1943	Allie Reynolds, Cleveland	151
1944	Harold Newhouser, Detroit	187
1945	Harold Newhouser, Detroit	212
1946	Robert Feller, Cleveland	348
1947	Robert Feller, Cleveland	196
1948	Robert Feller, Cleveland	164
1949	Virgil Trucks, Detroit	153
1950	Robert Lemon, Cleveland	170
1951	Victor Raschi, New York	164
1952	Allie Reynolds, New York	160
1953	W. William Pierce, Chicago	186
1954	Robert Turley, Baltimore	185
1955	Herbert Score, Cleveland	245
1956	Herbert Score, Cleveland	263
1957	Early Wynn, Cleveland	184
1958	Early Wynn, Chicago	179
1959	James Bunning, Detroit	201
1960	James Bunning, Detroit	201
1961	Camilo Pascual, Minnesota	221
1962	Camilo Pascual, Minnesota	206
1963	Camilo Pascual, Minnesota	202
1964	Alphonso Downing, New York	217
1965	Samuel McDowell, Cleveland	325
1966	Samuel McDowell, Cleveland	225
1967	James Lonborg, Boston	246
1968	Samuel McDowell, Cleveland	283
1969	Samuel McDowell, Cleveland	279
1970	Samuel McDowell, Cleveland	304
1971	Michael Lolich, Detroit	308
1972	L. Nolan Ryan, California	329
1973	L. Nolan Ryan, California	383
1974	L. Nolan Ryan, California	367
1975	Frank Tanana, California	269
1976	L. Nolan Ryan, California	327
1977	L. Nolan Ryan, California	341
1978	L. Nolan Ryan, California	260
1979	L. Nolan Ryan, California	223
1980	Leonard Barker, Cleveland	187
1981	Leonard Barker, Cleveland	127
1982	Floyd Bannister, Seattle	209
1983	John Morris, Detroit	232
1984	Mark Langston, Seattle	204
1985	Rikalbert Blyleven, Cleveland-Minn.	206
1986	Mark Langston, Seattle	245
1987	Mark Langston, Seattle	262

National League

Year	Pitcher and Club	SO.
1900	George (Rube) Waddell, Pittsburgh	133
1901	Frank (Noodles) Hahn, Cincinnati	233
1902	Victor Willis, Boston	226
1903	Christopher Mathewson, New York	267
1904	Christopher Mathewson, New York	212
1905	Christopher Mathewson, New York	206
1906	Frederick Beebe, Chicago-St. Louis	171
1907	Christopher Mathewson, New York	178
1908	Christopher Mathewson, New York	259
1909	Orval Overall, Chicago	205
1910	Christopher Mathewson, New York	190
1911	Richard (Rube) Marquard, N.Y.	237
1912	Grover Alexander, Philadelphia	195
1913	Thomas Seaton, Philadelphia	168
1914	Grover Alexander, Philadelphia	214
1915	Grover Alexander, Philadelphia	241
1916	Grover Alexander, Philadelphia	167
1917	Grover Alexander, Philadelphia	200
1918	James (Hippo) Vaughn, Chicago	148
1919	James (Hippo) Vaughn, Chicago	141
1920	Grover Alexander, Chicago	173
1921	Burleigh Grimes, Brooklyn	136
1922	Arthur (Dazzy) Vance, Brooklyn	134
1923	Arthur (Dazzy) Vance, Brooklyn	197
1924	Arthur (Dazzy) Vance, Brooklyn	262
1925	Arthur (Dazzy) Vance, Brooklyn	221
1926	Arthur (Dazzy) Vance, Brooklyn	140
1927	Arthur (Dazzy) Vance, Brooklyn	184
1928	Arthur (Dazzy) Vance, Brooklyn	200
1929	Perce (Pat) Malone, Chicago	166
1930	William Hallahan, St. Louis	177
1931	William Hallahan, St. Louis	159
1932	Jerome (Dizzy) Dean, St. Louis	191
1933	Jerome (Dizzy) Dean, St. Louis	199
1934	Jerome (Dizzy) Dean, St. Louis	195
1935	Jerome (Dizzy) Dean, St. Louis	182
1936	Van Lingle Mungo, Brooklyn	238
1937	Carl Hubbell, New York	159
1938	Claiborne Bryant, Chicago	135
1939	Claude Passeau, Phila.-Chi.	137
	William (Bucky) Walters, Cincinnati	137
1940	W. Kirby Higbe, Philadelphia	137
1941	John Vander Meer, Cincinnati	202
1942	John Vander Meer, Cincinnati	186
1943	John Vander Meer, Cincinnati	174
1944	William Voiselle, New York	161
1945	Elwin (Preacher) Roe, Pittsburgh	148
1946	John Schmitz, Chicago	135
1947	Ewell Blackwell, Cincinnati	193
1948	Harry Brecheen, St. Louis	149
1949	Warren Spahn, Boston	151
1950	Warren Spahn, Boston	191
1951	Warren Spahn, Boston	164
	Donald Newcombe, Brooklyn	164
1952	Warren Spahn, Boston	183
1953	Robin Roberts, Philadelphia	198
1954	Robin Roberts, Philadelphia	185
1955	Samuel Jones, Chicago	198
1956	Samuel Jones, Chicago	176
1957	John Sanford, Philadelphia	188
1958	Samuel Jones, St. Louis	225
1959	Donald Drysdale, Los Angeles	242
1960	Donald Drysdale, Los Angeles	246
1961	Sanford Koufax, Los Angeles	269
1962	Donald Drysdale, Los Angeles	232
1963	Sanford Koufax, Los Angeles	306
1964	Robert Veale, Pittsburgh	250
1965	Sanford Koufax, Los Angeles	382
1966	Sanford Koufax, Los Angeles	317
1967	James Bunning, Philadelphia	253
1968	Robert Gibson, St. Louis	268
1969	Ferguson Jenkins, Chicago	273
1970	G. Thomas Seaver, New York	283
1971	G. Thomas Seaver, New York	289
1972	Steven Carlton, Philadelphia	310
1973	G. Thomas Seaver, New York	251
1974	Steven Carlton, Philadelphia	240
1975	G. Thomas Seaver, New York	243
1976	G. Thomas Seaver, New York	235
1977	Philip Niekro, Atlanta	262
1978	James R. Richard, Houston	303
1979	James R. Richard, Houston	313
1980	Steven Carlton, Philadelphia	286
1981	Fernando Valenzuela, Los Angeles	180
1982	Steven Carlton, Philadelphia	286
1983	Steven Carlton, Philadelphia	275
1984	Dwight Gooden, New York	276
1985	Dwight Gooden, New York	268
1986	Michael Scott, Houston	306
1987	L. Nolan Ryan, Houston	270

Career Milestones

Batting
20-Year Players (58)
(Pitchers Listed In Pitching Section)

Player	Yrs.	G.
James T. McGuire	26	1781
Edward T. Collins	25	2826
Roderick J. Wallace	25	2369
Peter E. Rose	24	3562
Tyrus R. Cobb	24	3033
Carl M. Yastrzemski	23	3308
Walter J. V. Maranville	23	2670
Rogers Hornsby	23	2259
Henry L. Aaron	23	3298
Daniel J. Staub	23	2951
Brooks C. Robinson	23	2896
Atanasio R. Perez	23	2777
Stanley F. Musial	22	3026
Willie H. Mays	22	2992
Albert W. Kaline	22	2834
Tristram Speaker	22	2789
Melvin T. Ott	22	2730
Joe L. Morgan	22	2649
Willie L. McCovey	22	2588
George H. Ruth	22	2503
Harmon C. Killebrew	22	2435
William F. Dahlen	22	2431
James J. Dykes	22	2282
Adrian C. Anson	22	2253
Philip J. Cavarretta	22	2030
Harry H. Davis	22	1746
William J. Gleason	22	1942
Reginald M. Jackson	21	2820
Frank Robinson	21	2808
John P. Wagner	21	2785
Napoleon Lajoie	21	2475
Ronald R. Fairly	21	2442
Wilver D. Stargell	21	2360
Lafayette N. Cross	21	2259
Frederick C. Clarke	21	2204
Robert A. O'Farrell	21	1492

Player	Yrs.	G.
J. Timothy McCarver	21	1909
John J. O'Connor	21	1404
Paul G. Waner	20	2549
Max G. Carey	20	2469
Lucius B. Appling	20	2422
Edgar C. Rice	20	2404
Ted L. Simmons	20	2378
Jacob P. Beckley	20	2373
George S. Davis	20	2370
James E. Foxx	20	2317
Roger M. Cramer	20	2239
Aloysius H. Simmons	20	2215
Joseph I. Judge	20	2170
Charles J. Grimm	20	2166
Joseph E. Cronin	20	2124
James B. Vernon	20	2409
Charles L. Hartnett	20	1990
Elmer W. Valo	20	1806
John W. Johnstone	20	1748
J. Luther Sewell	20	1630
Manuel R. Mota	20	1536
John W. Cooney	20	1172

Batting .300 In Season, 10 Times (65)

(50 Or More Games, Season)

Player	Yrs.	Cns.
Henry L. Aaron	14	5
Adrian C. Anson	20	*15
Lucius B. Appling	14	9
Jacob P. Beckley	13	6
Dennis L. Brouthers	15	14
L. Rogers Browning	10	7
Jesse C. Burkett	11	10
Rodney C. Carew	15	15
Frederick C. Clarke	11	5
Roberto W. Clemente	13	8
Tyrus R. Cobb	23	23
Edward T. Collins	17	9
Roger Connor	12	6
Samuel Crawford	10	4
Hazen S. Cuyler	10	4
Jacob E. Daubert	10	6
Virgil L. Davis	10	7
Edward J. Delahanty	12	12
William M. Dickey	11	6
Joseph P. DiMaggio	11	7
Patrick J. Donovan	10	6
Hugh Duffy	11	10
William B. Ewing	10	8
James E. Foxx	12	5
Frank F. Frisch	13	11
H. Louis Gehrig	12	12
Charles L. Gehringer	13	8
Leon A. Goslin	11	7
William R. Hamilton	12	12
Harry E. Heilmann	12	12
Rogers Hornsby	14	12
William H. Keeler	13	13
Joseph J. Kelley	11	11
Napoleon Lajoie	15	10
Ernest N. Lombardi	10	5
Mickey C. Mantle	10	5
Henry E. Manush	11	7
Willie H. Mays	10	7
John P. McInnis	11	5
Joseph M. Medwick	12	*10
Stanley F. Musial	17	*16
Albert Oliver	11	9
James H. O'Rourke	13	5
Melvin T. Ott	10	3
Edgar C. Rice	13	5
Peter E. Rose	15	9
Edd J. Roush	12	11
George H. Ruth	17	8
James E. Ryan	13	7
Aloysius H. Simmons	13	*11
George H. Sisler	13	9
Enos B. Slaughter	10	5
Tristram Speaker	18	10
J. Riggs Stephenson	12	8
William H. Terry	11	10
Harold J. Traynor	10	6
George E. Van Haltren	13	9
J. Floyd Vaughan	12	*10
John P. Wagner	17	*17
Fred R. Walker	10	6
Lloyd J. Waner	10	6
Paul G. Waner	14	*12
Zachariah D. Wheat	13	6
Kenneth R. Williams	10	7
Theodore S. Williams	16	*15

*From start of career.

.300 Lifetime Average (179)

(10 or more years or 1,000 or more hits)

Player	Yrs.	H.	B.A.
Tyrus R. Cobb	24	4191	.367
Rogers Hornsby	23	2930	.358
Joseph J. Jackson	13	1772	.356
L. Rogers Browning	13	1719	.354
Wade A. Boggs	6	1178	.354
David L. Orr	8	1163	.352
Dennis L. Brouthers	19	2349	.349
Frank J. O'Doul	11	1140	.349
Edward J. Delahanty	16	2593	.346
Tristram Speaker	22	3515	.345
William H. Keeler	19	2955	.345
Theodore S. Williams	19	2654	.344
William R. Hamilton	14	2157	.344
Jacob C. Stenzel	9	1028	.344
George H. Ruth	22	2873	.342
Jesse C. Burkett	16	2872	.342
Harry E. Heilmann	17	2660	.342
William H. Terry	14	2193	.341
George H. Sisler	15	2812	.340
H. Louis Gehrig	17	2721	.340
James E. O'Neill	10	1428	.340
Napoleon Lajoie	21	3252	.339
Adrian C. Anson	22	3081	.339
Samuel L. Thompson	15	2016	.336
J. Riggs Stephenson	14	1515	.336
William A. Lange	7	1072	.336
Anthony K. Gwynn	6	988	.335
Aloysius H. Simmons	20	2927	.334
John J. McGraw	16	1307	.334
Michael J. Donlin	12	1287	.334
Edward T. Collins	25	3309	.333
Paul G. Waner	20	3152	.333
Stanley F. Musial	22	3630	.331
Dennis L. Lyons	13	1404	.331
Henry E. Manush	17	2524	.330
Hugh Duffy	17	2307	.330
John P. Wagner	21	3430	.329
Rodney C. Carew	19	3053	.328
Robert R. Fothergill	12	1064	.325
James E. Foxx	20	2646	.325
Roger Connor	18	2535	.325
Joseph P. DiMaggio	13	2214	.325
Edd J. Roush	16	2158	.325
Earle B. Combs	12	1866	.325
Joseph M. Medwick	17	2471	.324
Floyd C. Herman	13	1818	.324
Edgar C. Rice	20	2987	.322
Ross Youngs	10	1491	.322
George E. VanHaltren	17	2573	.321
Hazen S. Cuyler	18	2299	.321
Joseph J. Kelley	17	2245	.321
Harry D. Stovey	14	1925	.321
Charles L. Gehringer	19	2839	.320
Harold J. Traynor	17	2416	.320
Charles H. Klein	17	2076	.320
Gordon S. Cochrane	13	1652	.320
James W. Holliday	10	1152	.320
Kenneth R. Williams	14	1552	.319
J. Floyd Vaughan	14	2103	.318
H. Earl Averill	13	2019	.318
Roberto W. Clemente	18	3000	.317
Zachariah D. Wheat	19	2884	.317
Michael J. Tiernan	13	1875	.317
Charles J. Hafey	13	1466	.317
Joseph Harris	10	963	.317
Lloyd J. Waner	18	2459	.316
Frank F. Frisch	19	2880	.316
Leon A. Goslin	18	2735	.316
Henry E. Larkin	10	1493	.316
Lewis R. Fonseca	12	1075	.316
Frederick C. Clarke	21	2703	.315
Elmer H. Flick	13	1767	.315
John T. Tobin	11	1579	.315
James E. Ryan	18	2577	.314
James H. O'Rourke	19	2314	.314
Cecil H. Travis	12	1544	.314
Hugh A. Jennings	18	1520	.314
Elmer E. Smith	14	1473	.314
Bibb A. Falk	12	1463	.314
William M. Dickey	17	1969	.313
Michael J. Kelly	16	1853	.313
Jacques F. Fournier	15	1631	.313
Henry B. Greenberg	13	1628	.313
Joseph W. Sewell	14	2226	.312
John R. Mize	15	2011	.312
Edmund J. Miller	16	1937	.312
Clarence A. Childs	13	1757	.312
W. Barney McCosky	11	1301	.312
L. Dale Mitchell	11	1244	.312
George H. Brett	15	2219	.312
Clarence H. Beaumont	12	1754	.311
Fred C. Lindstrom	13	1747	.311
William C. Jacobson	11	1714	.311
William Ewing	18	1663	.311
Jack R. Robinson	10	1518	.311

Player	Yrs.	H.	B.A.
Raymond A. Radcliff	10	1267	.311
Taft S. Wright	9	1115	.311
Lucius B. Appling	20	2749	.310
James L. Bottomley	16	2313	.310
Edwin J. McKean	13	2139	.310
Robert H. Veach	14	2064	.310
Emil F. Meusel	11	1521	.310
Thomas P. Burns	11	1451	.310
Jonathan T. Stone	11	1391	.310
Eugene F. Hargrave	12	786	.310
E. Gordon Phelps	11	657	.310
Pedro Guerrero	10	1049	.310
Samuel Crawford	19	2964	.309
Jacob P. Beckley	20	2930	.309
Robert W. Meusel	11	1693	.309
Richie Ashburn	15	2574	.308
John P. McInnis	19	2406	.308
Walter S. Brodie	12	1749	.308
George F. Gore	14	1653	.308
Virgil L. Davis	16	1312	.308
Harvey L. Hendrick	11	896	.308
Eugene N. DeMontreville	11	1106	.308
Timothy Raines	9	1203	.308
George H. Burns	16	2018	.307
J. Franklin Baker	13	1838	.307
Michael J. Griffin	12	1830	.307
Joseph F. Vosmik	13	1682	.307
Charles S. Stahl	10	1552	.307
Lewis R. Wilson	12	1461	.307
John M. Pesky	10	1455	.307
Frederick M. Leach	10	1147	.307
John F. Moore	10	926	.307
Henry J. Bonura	8	1099	.307
Mateo R. Alou	15	1777	.307
Fred R. Walker	18	2064	.306
George C. Kell	15	2054	.306
Ernest N. Lombardi	17	1792	.306
James L. White	15	1612	.306
Charles W. Jones	11	1062	.306
Ralph A. Garr	13	1562	.306
Henry L. Aaron	23	3771	.305
Bill Madlock	15	2008	.305
Melvin T. Ott	22	2876	.304
William J. Herman	15	2345	.304
Patrick J. Donovan	17	2254	.304
Paul A. Hines	16	1884	.304
J. Bentley Seymour	16	1720	.304
A. Harding Richardson	14	1705	.304
W. Curtis Walker	12	1475	.304
Samuel A. Leslie	10	749	.304
Pedro (Tony) Oliva	15	1917	.304
Manuel R. Mota	20	1149	.304
Jacob E. Daubert	15	2326	.303
Charles S. Myer	17	2131	.303
Harvey E. Kuenn	15	2092	.303
Charles D. Jamieson	18	1990	.303
George W. Harper	11	1030	.303
Earl C. Smith	12	686	.303
John E. Stivetts	11	592	.303
Albert Oliver	18	2743	.303
Peter E. Rose	24	4256	.303
Wm. Benjamin Chapman	15	1958	.302
Harold A. Trosky	11	1561	.302
George F. Grantham	13	1508	.302
Thomas F. Holmes	11	1507	.302
Carl N. Reynolds	13	1357	.302
Charles T. Hickman	12	1199	.302
Homer W. Summa	10	905	.302
Samuel D. Hale	10	880	.302
Robert L. Caruthers	10	758	.302
John J. Doyle	17	1814	.302
Willie H. Mays	22	3283	.302
James E. Rice	14	2275	.302
Joseph E. Cronin	20	2285	.301
Stanley C. Hack	16	2193	.301
Raymond B. Bressler	19	1170	.301
John A. Mostil	10	1054	.301
Raymond F. Blades	10	726	.301
Keith Hernandez	14	2010	.301
Enos B. Slaughter	19	2383	.300
William D. Goodman	16	1691	.300
Walter A. Berger	11	1550	.300
Ethan N. Allen	13	1325	.300
Earl H. Sheely	9	1340	.300

2,300 Games (60)

Player	G.	B.A.
Peter E. Rose	3562	.303
Carl M. Yastrzemski	3308	.285
Henry L. Aaron	3298	.305
Tyrus R. Cobb	3033	.367
Stanley F. Musial	3026	.331
Willie H. Mays	2992	.302
Daniel J. Staub	2951	.279
Brooks C. Robinson	2896	.267
Albert W. Kaline	2834	.297
Edward T. Collins	2826	.333

Player	G.	B.A.
Reginald M. Jackson	2820	.262
Frank Robinson	2808	.294
Tristram Speaker	2790	.345
John P. Wagner	2785	.329
Atanasio R. Perez	2777	.279
Melvin T. Ott	2730	.304
Walter J. V. Maranville	2670	.258
Joe L. Morgan	2649	.271
Graig Nettles	2620	.248
Louis C. Brock	2616	.293
Luis E. Aparicio	2599	.262
Willie L. McCovey	2588	.270
Paul G. Waner	2549	.333
Ernest Banks	2528	.274
Samuel Crawford	2505	.309
George H. Ruth	2503	.342
Billy L. Williams	2488	.290
Napoleon Lajoie	2475	.339
Max G. Carey	2469	.285
Vada E. Pinson	2469	.286
Rodney C. Carew	2469	.328
Ronald R. Fairly	2442	.266
Darrell W. Evans	2436	.251
Harmon C. Killebrew	2435	.256
Roberto W. Clemente	2433	.317
William F. Dahlen	2431	.275
William H. Davis	2429	.279
Lucius B. Appling	2422	.310
James B. Vernon	2409	.286
Zachariah D. Wheat	2406	.317
Edgar C. Rice	2404	.322
David I. Concepcion	2404	.268
Mickey C. Mantle	2401	.298
Edwin L. Mathews	2391	.271
Enos B. Slaughter	2380	.300
Ted L. Simmons	2378	.286
Jacob P. Beckley	2373	.309
George S. Davis	2370	.297
Roderick J. Wallace	2369	.267
Albert Oliver	2368	.303
J. Nelson Fox	2367	.288
Wilver D. Stargell	2360	.282
Steven P. Garvey	2332	.294
Dagoberto B. Campaneris	2328	.259
Charles L. Gehringer	2323	.320
James E. Foxx	2317	.325
Jose Cruz	2315	.285
Frank F. Frisch	2311	.316
William J. Buckner	2308	.292
Harry B. Hooper	2308	.281

500 Consecutive Games Played (32)

Player	Games
H. Louis Gehrig	2130
L. Everett Scott	1307
Steven P. Garvey	1207
Billy L. Williams	1117
Joseph W. Sewell	1103
Calvin E. Ripken	927
Stanley F. Musial	895
Edward F. Yost	829
Augustus R. Suhr	822
J. Nelson Fox	798
*Peter E. Rose	745
Dale A. Murphy	740
Richie Ashburn	730
Ernest Banks	717
*Peter E. Rose	678
H. Earl Averill	673
Frank A. McCormick	652
Santos C. Alomar	648
Edward W. Brown	618
Roy D. McMillan	585
George B. Pinckney	577
Walter S. Brodie	574
Aaron L. Ward	565
George J. LaChance	540
John F. Freeman	535
Fred W. Luderus	533
J. Clyde Milan	511
*Charles L. Gehringer	511
Vada E. Pinson	508
Anthony F. Cuccinello	504
*Charles L. Gehringer	504
Omar R. Moreno	503

*Only players with two streaks.

9,000 At-Bats (41)

Player	AB.
Peter E. Rose	14053
Henry L. Aaron	12364
Carl M. Yastrzemski	11988
Tyrus R. Cobb	11429
Stanley F. Musial	10972
Willie H. Mays	10881

Player	AB.
Brooks C. Robinson	10654
John P. Wagner	10427
Louis C. Brock	10332
Luis E. Aparicio	10230
Tristram Speaker	10196
Albert W. Kaline	10116
Walter J. V. Maranville	10078
Frank Robinson	10006
Edward T. Collins	9946
Reginald M. Jackson	9864
Atanasio R. Perez	9778
Daniel J. Staub	9720
Vada E. Pinson	9645
Napoleon Lajoie	9589
Samuel Crawford	9579
Jacob P. Beckley	9476
Paul G. Waner	9459
Melvin T. Ott	9456
Roberto W. Clemente	9454
Ernest Banks	9421
Max G. Carey	9363
Billy L. Williams	9350
Rodney C. Carew	9315
Joe L. Morgan	9277
Edgar C. Rice	9269
J. Nelson Fox	9232
William H. Davis	9174
Roger M. Cramer	9140
Frank F. Frisch	9112
Zachariah D. Wheat	9106
Adrian C. Anson	9084
Lafayette N. Cross	9065
Albert Oliver	9049
George S. Davis	9027
William F. Dahlen	9019

1,500 Runs (45)

Player	Runs
Tyrus R. Cobb	2245
George H. Ruth	2174
Henry L. Aaron	2174
Peter E. Rose	2165
Willie H. Mays	2062
Stanley F. Musial	1949
H. Louis Gehrig	1888
Tristram Speaker	1881
Melvin T. Ott	1859
Frank Robinson	1829
Edward T. Collins	1816
Carl M. Yastrzemski	1816
Theodore S. Williams	1798
Charles L. Gehringer	1774
James E. Foxx	1751
John P. Wagner	1740
William H. Keeler	1720
Adrian C. Anson	1712
Jesse C. Burkett	1708
William R. Hamilton	1690
Mickey C. Mantle	1677
John A. McPhee	1674
George E. Van Haltren	1650
Joe L. Morgan	1650
James E. Ryan	1640
Paul G. Waner	1627
Albert W. Kaline	1622
Frederick C. Clarke	1620
Louis C. Brock	1610
Roger Connor	1607
Jacob P. Beckley	1601
Edward J. Delahanty	1596
William F. Dahlen	1594
Rogers Hornsby	1579
Reginald M. Jackson	1551
George S. Davis	1546
Max G. Carey	1545
Hugh Duffy	1545
Frank F. Frisch	1532
Edgar C. Rice	1514
Edwin L. Mathews	1509
Thomas T. Brown	1507
Dennis L. Brouthers	1507
Aloysius H. Simmons	1507
Napoleon Lajoie	1506

2,500 Hits (62)

Player	Hits
Peter E. Rose	4256
Tyrus R. Cobb	4191
Henry L. Aaron	3771
Stanley F. Musial	3630
Tristram Speaker	3515
John P. Wagner	3430
Carl M. Yastrzemski	3419
Edward T. Collins	3309
Willie H. Mays	3283
Napoleon Lajoie	3252
Paul G. Waner	3152

Player	Hits
Adrian C. Anson	3081
Rodney C. Carew	3053
Louis C. Brock	3023
Albert W. Kaline	3007
Roberto W. Clemente	3000
Edgar C. Rice	2987
Samuel Crawford	2964
William H. Keeler	2955
Frank Robinson	2943
Jacob P. Beckley	2930
Rogers Hornsby	2930
Aloysius H. Simmons	2927
Zachariah D. Wheat	2884
Frank F. Frisch	2880
Melvin T. Ott	2876
George H. Ruth	2873
Jesse C. Burkett	2872
Brooks C. Robinson	2848
Charles L. Gehringer	2839
George H. Sisler	2812
Vada E. Pinson	2757
Lucius B. Appling	2749
Albert Oliver	2743
Leon A. Goslin	2735
Atanasio R. Perez	2732
H. Louis Gehrig	2721
Daniel J. Staub	2716
Billy L. Williams	2711
Roger M. Cramer	2705
Fred C. Clarke	2703
George S. Davis	2683
Luis E. Aparicio	2677
Max Carey	2665
J. Nelson Fox	2663
Harry E. Heilmann	2660
Lafayette N. Cross	2654
Theodore S. Williams	2654
James E. Foxx	2646
Walter J. Maranville	2605
Steven P. Garvey	2599
William J. Buckner	2598
Edward J. Delahanty	2593
Reginald M. Jackson	2584
Ernest Banks	2583
James Ryan	2577
Richie Ashburn	2574
George E. Van Haltren	2573
William H. Davis	2561
Roger Connor	2535
Henry E. Manush	2524
Joe L. Morgan	2517

200 Hits In Season, 4 Times (29)

Player	Yrs.
Peter E. Rose	10
Tyrus R. Cobb	9
H. Louis Gehrig	8
William H. Keeler	8
Paul G. Waner	8
Charles L. Gehringer	7
Rogers Hornsby	7
Jesse C. Burkett	6
Stanley F. Musial	6
Edgar C. Rice	6
Aloysius H. Simmons	6
George H. Sisler	6
William H. Terry	6
Steven P. Garvey	6
Charles H. Klein	5
Napoleon Lajoie	5
Wade A. Boggs	5
Vada E. Pinson	4
Harry E. Heilmann	4
Joseph J. Jackson	4
Henry E. Manush	4
Joseph M. Medwick	4
Tristram Speaker	4
John T. Tobin	4
Lloyd J. Waner	4
Roberto W. Clemente	4
Louis C. Brock	4
Rodney C. Carew	4
James E. Rice	4

2,000 Singles (36)

Player	1B.
Peter E. Rose	3215
Tyrus R. Cobb	3052
Edward T. Collins	2639
William H. Keeler	2534
John P. Wagner	2426
Rodney C. Carew	2404
Tristram Speaker	2383
Napoleon Lajoie	2354
Adrian C. Anson	2330

Player	1B.
Jesse C. Burkett	2301
Henry L. Aaron	2294
Edgar C. Rice	2272
Carl M. Yastrzemski	2262
Stanley F. Musial	2253
Louis C. Brock	2247
Paul G. Waner	2243
Frank F. Frisch	2171
Roger M. Cramer	2163
Lucius B. Appling	2162
J. Nelson Fox	2161
Roberto W. Clemente	2154
Jacob P. Beckley	2142
George H. Sisler	2122
Richie Ashburn	2119
Luis E. Aparicio	2108
Zachariah D. Wheat	2104
Samuel Crawford	2102
Lafayette N. Cross	2077
Fred C. Clarke	2061
Albert W. Kaline	2035
Lloyd J. Waner	2032
Brooks C. Robinson	2030
Walter J. Maranville	2020
Max Carey	2018
George E. Van Haltren	2008
George S. Davis	2007

400 Doubles (83)

Player	2B.
Tristram Speaker	793
Peter E. Rose	746
Stanley F. Musial	725
Tyrus R. Cobb	724
Napoleon Lajoie	652
John P. Wagner	651
Carl M. Yastrzemski	646
Henry L. Aaron	624
Paul G. Waner	605
Charles L. Gehringer	574
Harry E. Heilmann	542
Rogers Hornsby	541
Joseph M. Medwick	540
Aloysius H. Simmons	539
H. Louis Gehrig	534
Adrian C. Anson	530
Albert Oliver	529
Frank Robinson	528
Theodore S. Williams	525
Willie H. Mays	523
Joseph E. Cronin	516
Edward J. Delahanty	508
George H. Ruth	506
Atanasio R. Perez	505
Leon A. Goslin	500
Daniel J. Staub	499
Edgar C. Rice	498
Albert W. Kaline	498
Henry E. Manush	491
James B. Vernon	490
Melvin T. Ott	488
William J. Herman	486
Louis C. Brock	486
Vada E. Pinson	485
Harold A. McRae	484
Brooks C. Robinson	482
William J. Buckner	480
Ted L. Simmons	477
Zachariah D. Wheat	476
Frank F. Frisch	466
James L. Bottomley	465
Reginald M. Jackson	463
James E. Foxx	458
Samuel Crawford	455
Jacob P. Beckley	455
James J. Dykes	453
Joe L. Morgan	449
Dennis L. Brouthers	446
George H. Brett	446
Rodney C. Carew	445
George H. Burns	444
Richard Bartell	442
George S. Davis	442
Lucius B. Appling	440
Roberto W. Clemente	440
Steven P. Garvey	440
James E. Ryan	439
Edward T. Collins	437
Joseph W. Sewell	436
Cesar Cedeno	436
Wallace Moses	435
Billy L. Williams	434
Joseph I. Judge	433
Roger Connor	429
Albert F. Schoendienst	427
Sherwood R. Magee	425
George H. Sisler	425
David G. Parker	425

Player	2B.
Wilver D. Stargell	423
Max G. Carey	419
Orlando M. Cepeda	417
Cecil C. Cooper	415
Enos B. Slaughter	413
Joseph A. Kuhel	412
David G. Bell	411
W. Benjamin Chapman	407
Ernest Banks	407
Robin R. Yount	405
William F. Dahlen	403
H. Earl Averill	401
Martin J. McManus	401
Lafayette N. Cross	401
Keith Hernandez	400

150 Triples (50)

Player	3B.
Samuel Crawford	312
Tyrus R. Cobb	298
John P. Wagner	252
Jacob P. Beckley	246
Roger Connor	227
Tristram Speaker	222
Frederick C. Clarke	219
Dennis L. Brouthers	212
Paul G. Waner	191
Joseph J. Kelley	189
Edward T. Collins	186
Jesse C. Burkett	185
Harry D. Stovey	185
Edgar C. Rice	184
Edward J. Delahanty	182
John A. McPhee	180
William B. Ewing	179
Walter J. Maranville	177
Stanley F. Musial	177
Leon A. Goslin	173
Zachariah D. Wheat	172
Elmer H. Flick	170
Thomas W. Leach	170
Rogers Hornsby	169
Joseph J. Jackson	168
Edd J. Roush	168
George S. Davis	167
William F. Dahlen	166
Sherwood R. Magee	166
Roberto W. Clemente	166
Jacob P. Daubert	165
Napoleon Lajoie	164
George H. Sisler	164
Harold J. Traynor	164
Edward J. Konetchy	163
H. Louis Gehrig	163
Harry B. Hooper	160
Henry E. Manush	160
Max Carey	159
Joseph I. Judge	159
Michael J. Tiernan	159
George E. Van Haltren	159
Hazen S. Cuyler	157
William H. Keeler	155
Earle B. Combs	154
James E. Ryan	153
Edwin J. McKean	152
James L. Bottomley	151
Thomas W. Corcoran	151
Harry E. Heilmann	151

250 Home Runs (87)

Player	HR.
Henry L. Aaron	755
George H. Ruth	714
Willie H. Mays	660
Frank Robinson	586
Harmon C. Killebrew	573
Reginald M. Jackson	563
Mickey C. Mantle	536
James E. Foxx	534
Michael J. Schmidt	530
Theodore S. Williams	521
Willie L. McCovey	521
Edwin L. Mathews	512
Ernest Banks	512
Melvin T. Ott	511
H. Louis Gehrig	493
Stanley F. Musial	475
Wilver D. Stargell	475
Carl M. Yastrzemski	452
David A. Kingman	442
Billy L. Williams	426
Edwin D. Snider	407
Albert W. Kaline	399
Johnny L. Bench	389
Graig Nettles	389
Frank O. Howard	382
Darrell W. Evans	381

Player	HR.
Orlando M. Cepeda	379
Atanasio R. Perez	379
Norman D. Cash	377
Rocco D. Colavito	374
Gilbert R. Hodges	370
Ralph M. Kiner	369
James E. Rice	364
Joseph P. DiMaggio	361
John R. Mize	359
Lawrence P. Berra	358
Lee A. May	354
Richard A. Allen	351
George A. Foster	348
Ronald E. Santo	342
John W. Powell	339
Joseph W. Adcock	336
Bobby L. Bonds	332
David M. Winfield	332
Henry B. Greenberg	331
Donald E. Baylor	331
Willie W. Horton	325
Dwight M. Evans	325
Roy E. Sievers	318
Ronald C. Cey	316
C. Reginald Smith	314
Dale B. Murphy	310
Aloysius H. Simmons	307
Gregory M. Luzinski	307
Eddie C. Murray	305
Carlton E. Fisk	304
Rogers Hornsby	301
Charles H. Klein	300
Daniel J. Staub	292
James S. Wynn	291
Gary E. Carter	291
Robert L. Johnson	288
Henry J. Sauer	288
Delmer Ennis	288
Frank J. Thomas	286
Kenton L. Boyer	282
Theodore B. Kluszewski	279
Rudolph P. York	277
Roger E. Maris	275
Steven P. Garvey	272
George C. Scott	271
Brooks C. Robinson	268
Joe L. Morgan	268
J. Gorman Thomas	268
Victor W. Wertz	266
Robert B. Thomson	264
George A. Hendrick	264
Fredric M. Lynn	264
W. Robert Allison	256
Vada E. Pinson	256
John C. Mayberry	255
Joseph L. Gordon	253
Lawrence E. Doby	253
Andre Thornton	253
Joseph P. Torre	252
Bobby R. Murcer	252
Fred Williams	251

8 Grand Slams (65)

Player	Total
H. Louis Gehrig	23
Willie L. McCovey	18
James E. Foxx	17
Theodore S. Williams	17
George H. Ruth	16
Henry L. Aaron	16
David A. Kingman	16
Gilbert R. Hodges	14
Eddie C. Murray	14
Joseph P. DiMaggio	13
Ralph M. Kiner	13
George A. Foster	13
Rudolph P. York	12
Rogers Hornsby	12
Ernest Banks	12
Joseph O. Rudi	12
Donald E. Baylor	12
Henry B. Greenberg	11
Harmon C. Killebrew	11
Wilver D. Stargell	11
Lee A. May	11
Johnny L. Bench	11
Reginald M. Jackson	11
Gary E. Carter	11
Aloysius H. Simmons	10
Vernon D. Stephens	10
Victor W. Wertz	10
Joseph W. Adcock	10
Roy E. Sievers	10
John D. Milner	10
Jeffrey A. Burroughs	10
Darrell W. Evans	10
Lawrence P. Berra	9
W. Walker Cooper	9

Player	Total
Samuel B. Chapman	9
Mickey C. Mantle	9
Stanley F. Musial	9
Albert L. Rosen	9
Richard L. Stuart	9
Gus E. Zernial	9
Orlando M. Cepeda	9
Americo P. Petrocelli	9
Willie W. Horton	9
Daniel J. Staub	9
Ted L. Simmons	9
Raymond A. Boone	8
William M. Dickey	8
Robert P. Doerr	8
Carl A. Furillo	8
Robert L. Johnson	8
George L. Kelly	8
Jack E. Jensen	8
Anthony M. Lazzeri	8
Edwin L. Mathews	8
William B. Nicholson	8
Ronald J. Northey	8
James T. Northrup	8
Robert B. Thomson	8
Andrew W. Seminick	8
Norman D. Cash	8
Willie H. Mays	8
Richard J. McAuliffe	8
Vada E. Pinson	8
Billy L. Williams	8
Richard A. Allen	8

10 Pinch Home Runs (21)

Player	Total
Clifford Johnson	20
Gerald T. Lynch	18
Forrest H. Burgess	16
William J. Brown	16
Willie L. McCovey	16
George D. Crowe	14
Jose M. Morales	12
Robert H. Cerv	12
Joseph W. Adcock	12
Fred C. Williams	11
Fred D. Whitfield	11
Jeffrey A. Burroughs	11
John W. Johnstone	11
Graig Nettles	11
Gus E. Zernial	10
Walter C. Post	10
Donald R. Mincher	10
Kenneth L. McMullen	10
Michael K. Lum	10
John J. Summers	10
John W. Turner	10

25 Multiple-HR Games (47)

Player	Total
George H. Ruth	72
Willie H. Mays	63
Henry L. Aaron	62
James E. Foxx	55
Frank Robinson	54
Edwin L. Mathews	49
Melvin T. Ott	49
Mickey C. Mantle	46
Harmon C. Killebrew	46
Willie L. McCovey	44
Michael J. Schmidt	44
H. Louis Gehrig	43
David A. Kingman	43
Ernest Banks	42
Reginald M. Jackson	42
Ralph M. Kiner	40
Stanley F. Musial	37
Theodore S. Williams	37
Wilver D. Stargell	36
Joseph P. DiMaggio	35
Henry B. Greenberg	35
Lee A. May	35
Edwin D. Snider	34
James E. Rice	34
Rocco D. Colavito	32
Gus E. Zernial	32
Richard A. Allen	32
Henry J. Sauer	31
Billy L. Williams	31
Gilbert R. Hodges	30
John R. Mize	30
Willie W. Horton	30
Joseph W. Adcock	28
Charles H. Klein	28
Roy E. Sievers	27
Lewis R. Wilson	27
Carl M. Yastrzemski	27
Graig Nettles	27
Gary E. Carter	27

Player	Total
Frank O. Howard	26
Ronald E. Santo	26
J. Robert Horner	26
Andre F. Dawson	26
Dale B. Murphy	26
Roger E. Maris	25
Harold A. Trosky	25
Norman D. Cash	25

4,000 Total Bases (43)

Player	TB
Henry L. Aaron	6856
Stanley F. Musial	6134
Willie H. Mays	6066
Tyrus R. Cobb	5862
George H. Ruth	5793
Peter E. Rose	5752
Carl M. Yastrzemski	5539
Frank Robinson	5373
Tristram Speaker	5103
H. Louis Gehrig	5060
Melvin T. Ott	5041
James E. Foxx	4956
John P. Wagner	4888
Theodore S. Williams	4884
Albert W. Kaline	4852
Reginald M. Jackson	4834
Rogers Hornsby	4712
Ernest Banks	4706
Aloysius H. Simmons	4685
Billy L. Williams	4599
Atanasio R. Perez	4532
Mickey C. Mantle	4511
Roberto W. Clemente	4492
Napoleon Lajoie	4478
Paul G. Waner	4478
Edwin L. Mathews	4349
Samuel E. Crawford	4328
Leon A. Goslin	4325
Brooks C. Robinson	4270
Vada E. Pinson	4264
Edward T. Collins	4259
Charles L. Gehringer	4257
Louis C. Brock	4238
Willie L. McCovey	4219
Michael J. Schmidt	4191
Wilver D. Stargell	4190
Daniel J. Staub	4185
Adrian C. Anson	4145
Harmon C. Killebrew	4143
Jacob P. Beckley	4138
Zachariah D. Wheat	4100
Albert Oliver	4083
Harry E. Heilmann	4053

Slugging Average, Players With 4,000 Total Bases (43)

Player	T.B.	S.A.
George H. Ruth	5793	.690
Theodore S. Williams	4884	.634
H. Louis Gehrig	5060	.632
James E. Foxx	4956	.609
Rogers Hornsby	4712	.577
Stanley F. Musial	6134	.559
Mickey C. Mantle	4511	.557
Willie H. Mays	6066	.557
Henry L. Aaron	6856	.555
Frank Robinson	5373	.537
Michael J. Schmidt	4191	.536
Aloysius H. Simmons	4685	.535
Melvin T. Ott	5041	.533
Wilver D. Stargell	4190	.529
Harry E. Heilmann	4053	.520
Willie L. McCovey	4219	.515
Tyrus R. Cobb	5862	.513
Edwin L. Mathews	4349	.509
Harmon C. Killebrew	4143	.509
Leon A. Goslin	4325	.500
Tristram Speaker	5103	.500
Ernest Banks	4706	.500
Billy L. Williams	4599	.492
Reginald M. Jackson	4834	.490
Charles L. Gehringer	4257	.481
Albert W. Kaline	4852	.480
Roberto W. Clemente	4492	.475
Paul G. Waner	4478	.473
John P. Wagner	4888	.469
Napoleon Lajoie	4478	.467
Atanasio R. Perez	4532	.463
Carl M. Yastrzemski	5539	.462
Adrian C. Anson	4145	.456
Samuel E. Crawford	4328	.452
Albert Oliver	4083	.451
Zachariah D. Wheat	4100	.450
Vada E. Pinson	4264	.442
Jacob P. Beckley	4138	.437

Player	T.B.	S.A.
Daniel J. Staub	4185	.431
Edward T. Collins	4259	.428
Louis C. Brock	4238	.410
Peter E. Rose	5752	.409
Brooks C. Robinson	4270	.401

800 Long Hits (46)
(Doubles, Triples, & Home Runs)

Player	LH.
Henry L. Aaron	1477
Stanley F. Musial	1377
George H. Ruth	1356
Willie H. Mays	1323
H. Louis Gehrig	1190
Frank Robinson	1186
Carl M. Yastrzemski	1157
Tyrus R. Cobb	1139
Tristram Speaker	1132
James E. Foxx	1117
Theodore S. Williams	1117
Reginald M. Jackson	1075
Melvin T. Ott	1071
Peter E. Rose	1041
Rogers Hornsby	1011
Ernest Banks	1009
John P. Wagner	1004
Aloysius H. Simmons	995
Albert W. Kaline	972
Michael J. Schmidt	967
Atanasio R. Perez	963
Wilver D. Stargell	953
Mickey C. Mantle	952
Billy L. Williams	948
Edwin L. Mathews	938
Leon A. Goslin	921
Willie L. McCovey	920
Paul G. Waner	909
Charles L. Gehringer	904
Napoleon Lajoie	898
Harmon C. Killebrew	887
Joseph P. DiMaggio	881
Harry E. Heilmann	876
Vada E. Pinson	868
Samuel E. Crawford	862
Joseph M. Medwick	858
Edwin D. Snider	850
Roberto W. Clemente	846
Daniel J. Staub	838
James L. Bottomley	835
Albert Oliver	825
Orlando M. Cepeda	823
Brooks C. Robinson	818
Joe L. Morgan	813
John R. Mize	809
Joseph E. Cronin	803

1,400 Extra Bases On Long Hits (61)

Player	EBLH.
Henry L. Aaron	3085
George H. Ruth	2920
Willie H. Mays	2783
Stanley F. Musial	2504
Frank Robinson	2430
H. Louis Gehrig	2339
James E. Foxx	2310
Reginald M. Jackson	2250
Theodore S. Williams	2230
Melvin T. Ott	2165
Ernest Banks	2123
Carl M. Yastrzemski	2120
Mickey C. Mantle	2096
Michael J. Schmidt	2084
Harmon C. Killebrew	2057
Edwin L. Mathews	2034
Willie L. McCovey	2008
Wilver D. Stargell	1951
Billy L. Williams	1888
Albert W. Kaline	1845
Atanasio R. Perez	1800
Rogers Hornsby	1782
Aloysius H. Simmons	1758
Edwin D. Snider	1749
Joseph P. DiMaggio	1734
Tyrus R. Cobb	1671
David A. Kingman	1616
John R. Mize	1610
Orlando M. Cepeda	1608
Johnny L. Bench	1596
Leon A. Goslin	1590
Tristram Speaker	1588
James E. Rice	1585
Graig Nettles	1547
Richard A. Allen	1531
Darrell W. Evans	1527

Player	EBLH.
Ronald E. Santo	1525
David M. Winfield	1515
Henry B. Greenberg	1514
Vada E. Pinson	1507
Gilbert R. Hodges	1501
Peter E. Rose	1496
Lawrence P. Berra	1493
Roberto W. Clemente	1492
Daniel J. Staub	1469
Lee A. May	1464
Frank O. Howard	1461
John P. Wagner	1458
Norman D. Cash	1454
Robert L. Johnson	1450
Rocco D. Colavito	1447
Charles L. Klein	1446
Joe L. Morgan	1445
George A. Foster	1445
Bobby L. Bonds	1430
James L. Bottomley	1424
Brooks C. Robinson	1422
C. Reginald Smith	1419
Charles L. Gehringer	1418
Donald E. Baylor	1408
Ralph M. Kiner	1401

1,200 Runs Batted In (67)

Player	RBI.
Henry L. Aaron	2297
George H. Ruth	2204
H. Louis Gehrig	1990
Tyrus R. Cobb	1960
Stanley F. Musial	1951
James E. Foxx	1921
Willie H. Mays	1903
Melvin T. Ott	1861
Carl M. Yastrzemski	1844
Theodore S. Williams	1839
Aloysius H. Simmons	1827
Frank Robinson	1812
Reginald M. Jackson	1702
Atanasio R. Perez	1652
Ernest Banks	1636
Leon A. Goslin	1609
Harmon C. Killebrew	1584
Albert W. Kaline	1583
Rogers Hornsby	1578
Tristram Speaker	1562
Willie L. McCovey	1555
Harry E. Heilmann	1551
Wilver D. Stargell	1540
Joseph P. DiMaggio	1537
Mickey C. Mantle	1509
Michael J. Schmidt	1505
Billy L. Williams	1476
Daniel J. Staub	1466
Edwin L. Mathews	1453
Lawrence P. Berra	1430
Charles L. Gehringer	1427
Joseph E. Cronin	1423
James L. Bottomley	1422
Joseph M. Medwick	1383
Ted L. Simmons	1378
Johnny L. Bench	1376
Orlando M. Cepeda	1365
Brooks C. Robinson	1357
James E. Rice	1351
John R. Mize	1337
Edwin D. Snider	1333
Ronald E. Santo	1331
David M. Winfield	1331
Albert Oliver	1326
Peter E. Rose	1314
James B. Vernon	1311
Paul G. Waner	1309
Steven P. Garvey	1308
Edward T. Collins	1307
Roberto W. Clemente	1305
Enos B. Slaughter	1304
Graig Nettles	1300
Delmer Ennis	1284
Robert L. Johnson	1283
Henry B. Greenberg	1276
Gilbert R. Hodges	1274
Harold J. Traynor	1273
Zachariah D. Wheat	1265
Darrell W. Evans	1251
Robert P. Doerr	1247
Lee A. May	1244
Frank F. Frisch	1242
Donald E. Baylor	1242
George A. Foster	1239
David A. Kingman	1210
William M. Dickey	1209
Charles H. Klein	1202

1,000 Bases On Balls (55)

Player	BB.
George H. Ruth	2056
Theodore S. Williams	2019
Joe L. Morgan	1865
Carl M. Yastrzemski	1845
Mickey C. Mantle	1734
Melvin T. Ott	1708
Edward F. Yost	1614
Stanley F. Musial	1599
Peter E. Rose	1566
Harmon C. Killebrew	1559
H. Louis Gehrig	1508
Darrell W. Evans	1480
Willie H. Mays	1464
James E. Foxx	1452
Edwin L. Mathews	1444
Michael J. Schmidt	1437
Frank Robinson	1420
Henry L. Aaron	1402
Reginald M. Jackson	1376
Willie L. McCovey	1345
Lucius B. Appling	1302
Albert W. Kaline	1277
Kenneth W. Singleton	1262
Daniel J. Staub	1255
James S. Wynn	1224
Edward T. Collins	1213
Harold H. Reese	1210
Richie Ashburn	1198
Charles L. Gehringer	1185
Max F. Bishop	1153
Colbert D. Harrah	1153
Tristram Speaker	1146
Ronald E. Santo	1108
Dwight M. Evans	1095
Luzerne A. Blue	1092
Stanley C. Hack	1092
Paul G. Waner	1091
Robert A. Grich	1087
Graig Nettles	1079
Robert L. Johnson	1073
Harlond B. Clift	1070
Joseph E. Cronin	1059
Ronald R. Fairly	1052
Billy L. Williams	1045
Norman D. Cash	1043
Edwin D. Joost	1041
Max Carey	1040
Rogers Hornsby	1038
James Gilliam	1036
Salvatore L. Bando	1031
Enos B. Slaughter	1018
Rodney C. Carew	1018
Ronald C. Cey	1012
Ralph M. Kiner	1011
John W. Powell	1001

Note—Does not include any seasons in N.L. before 1910 and in A.L. prior to 1913.

1,000 Strikeouts (80)

Player	SO.
Reginald M. Jackson	2597
Wilver D. Stargell	1936
Atanasio R. Perez	1867
Michael J. Schmidt	1824
David A. Kingman	1816
Bobby L. Bonds	1757
Louis C. Brock	1730
Mickey C. Mantle	1710
Harmon C. Killebrew	1699
Lee A. May	1570
Richard A. Allen	1556
Willie L. McCovey	1550
Frank Robinson	1532
Willie H. Mays	1526
Robert J. Monday	1513
Gregory M. Luzinski	1495
Edwin L. Mathews	1487
Frank O. Howard	1460
James S. Wynn	1427
George A. Foster	1419
George C. Scott	1418
Carl M. Yastrzemski	1393
Dwight M. Evans	1387
Henry L. Aaron	1383
Ronald E. Santo	1343
J. Gorman Thomas	1339
George H. Ruth	1330
Deron R. Johnson	1318
Willie M. Horton	1313
James E. Foxx	1311
James E. Rice	1295
Johnny L. Bench	1278
Robert A. Grich	1278
Darrell W. Evans	1275
Larry A. Parrish	1248
Kenneth W. Singleton	1246
Edwin D. Snider	1237
Ernest Banks	1236
Ronald C. Cey	1235
Roberto W. Clemente	1230
Dale B. Murphy	1230
John W. Powell	1226
Vada E. Pinson	1196
Graig Nettles	1190
David A. Parker	1176
Orlando M. Cepeda	1169
David I. Concepcion	1163
Peter E. Rose	1143
Dagoberto B. Campaneris	1142
Donn A. Clendenon	1140
Gilbert R. Hodges	1137
David M. Winfield	1136
Leonardo A. Cardenas	1135
Jeffrey A. Burroughs	1135
Robert S. Bailey	1126
Gary N. Matthews	1125
James L. Fregosi	1097
Joseph P. Torre	1094
Norman D. Cash	1091
Antonio Taylor	1083
Claudell Washington	1083
Tommy Harper	1080
Carlton E. Fisk	1078
Antonio R. Armas	1066
John W. Callison	1064
Joseph W. Adcock	1059
Douglas L. Rader	1057
Billy L. Williams	1046
W. Robert Allison	1033
C. Reginald Smith	1030
Rodney C. Carew	1028
Donald E. Baylor	1025
Darrell R. Porter	1025
Jose Cruz	1023
Albert W. Kaline	1020
Kenton L. Boyer	1017
Joe L. Morgan	1015
Lawrence E. Doby	1011
Amos J. Otis	1008
Steven P. Garvey	1003

Baserunning
400 Stolen Bases (54)

Player	SB.
Louis C. Brock	938
William R. Hamilton	937
Tyrus R. Cobb	892
Walter A. Latham	791
Harry D. Stovey	744
Edward T. Collins	743
Max G. Carey	738
John P. Wagner	720
Rickey H. Henderson	701
Thomas T. Brown	697
Joe L. Morgan	689
Dagoberto B. Campaneris	649
George S. Davis	632
William E. Hoy	605
John M. Ward	605
John A. McPhee	602
Hugh A. Duffy	597
William F. Dahlen	587
Maurice M. Wills	586
John J. Doyle	560
David E. Lopes	557
Herman C. Long	554
Cesar Cedeno	550
Michael J. Griffin	549
George E. Van Haltren	537
Patrick J. Donovan	531
Willie J. Wilson	529
Frederick C. Clarke	527
Curtis B. Welch	526
William H. Keeler	519
Timothy Raines	511
Thomas F. M. McCarthy	506
Luis E. Aparicio	506
J. Clyde Milan	495
Omar R. Moreno	487
Edward J. Delahanty	478
James T. Sheckard	475
Bobby L. Bonds	461
Joseph J. Kelley	458
Ronald LeFlore	455
William A. Lange	453
Michael J. Tiernan	449
John J. McGraw	444
Sherwood R. Magee	441
Charles A. Comiskey	440
James E. Ryan	434
Tristram Speaker	433

Player	SB.
Robert H. Bescher	428
Thomas W. Corcoran	420
Frank F. Frisch	419
Tommy Harper	408
Thomas P. Daly	407
Owen J. Bush	405
Frank L. Chance	405

10 Steals Of Home (37)

Player	SOH.
Tyrus R. Cobb	50
Max G. Carey	33
George J. Burns	28
John P. Wagner	27
Frank Schulte	23
Sherwood R. Magee	23
John J. Evers	21
George H. Sisler	20
Jack R. Robinson	19
Frank F. Frisch	19
Tristram Speaker	18
James T. Sheckard	18
Joseph B. Tinker	18
Edward T. Collins	17
Lawrence J. Doyle	17
Rodney C. Carew	17
Thomas W. Leach	16
Fred C. Clarke	15
H. Louis Gehrig	15
W. Benjamin Chapman	15
Victor S. Saier	14
Robert M. Byrne	14
Frederick C. Maisel	14
Fred C. Merkle	14
Henry Zimmerman	13
Owen J. Bush	12
Edgar C. Rice	12
Harry B. Hooper	11
George J. Moriarty	11
Robert F. Roth	11
John F. Collins	11
Charles L. Herzog	10
George H. Ruth	10
Ross M. Youngs	10
James H. Johnston	10
William M. Werber	10
Walter J. V. Maranville	10

Note—Steals of home are not recorded as official statistics and most are uncovered in newspaper accounts. Researchers are constantly finding additional steals of home for many players, which explains the changes in this list each year.

Pitching

600 Games (75)
Or 20 Years (30)

Pitcher	Yrs.	G.
J. Hoyt Wilhelm	21	1070
Lyndall D. McDaniel	21	987
Roland G. Fingers	17	944
Kenton C. Tekulve	14	943
Denton T. Young	22	906
H. Eugene Garber	18	905
Albert W. Lyle	16	899
James L. Kaat	25	898
Donald J. McMahon	18	874
Philip H. Niekro	24	864
El Roy Face	16	848
Frank E. McGraw	19	824
Walter P. Johnson	21	802
Gaylord J. Perry	22	777
Darold D. Knowles	16	765
Richard M. Gossage	16	765
Donald H. Sutton	22	758
Ronald L. Reed	19	751
Warren E. Spahn	21	750
Thomas H. Burgmeier	17	745
Gary R. Lavelle	13	745
Steven N. Carlton	23	737
Ronald P. Perranoski	13	737
Ronald L. Kline	17	736
Clay P. Carroll	15	731
Michael G. Marshall	14	723
Thomas E. John	24	715
John C. Klippstein	18	711
Stuart L. Miller	16	704
William R. Campbell	15	700
Joseph F. Niekro	21	697
James F. Galvin	14	697
Grover C. Alexander	20	696
Robert L. Miller	17	694
Eppa Rixey	21	692
Grant D. Jackson	18	692
Early Wynn	23	691

Pitcher	Yrs.	G.
Eddie G. Fisher	15	690
Theodore W. Abernathy	14	681
Robin E. Roberts	19	676
Waite C. Hoyt	21	675
Urban C. Faber	20	669
David J. Giusti	15	668
John P. Quinn	21	665
Ferguson A. Jenkins	19	664
G. Thomas Seaver	20	656
Paul A. Lindblad	14	655
Wilbur F. Wood	18	651
Guillermo Hernandez	11	649
Charles O. Hough	18	649
Samuel P. Jones	22	647
David E. LaRoche	14	647
L. Nolan Ryan	21	645
Emil J. Leonard	20	640
Gerald L. Staley	15	640
Diego P. Segui	15	639
Christopher Mathewson	17	635
Charles H. Root	17	632
James E. Perry	17	630
S. Lewis Burdette	18	626
Murry M. Dickson	18	625
Woodrow T. Fryman	18	625
Charles H. Ruffing	22	624
H. Bruce Sutter	11	623
Charles A. Nichols	15	620
Richard W. Tidrow	13	620
Herbert J. Pennock	22	617
Robert M. Grove	17	616
Burleigh A. Grimes	19	615
Terry J. Forster	16	614
Jerry M. Koosman	19	612
Robert B. Friend	16	602
Allan F. Worthington	14	602
Elias Sosa	12	601
Louis N. Newsom	20	600
Theodore A. Lyons	21	594
Melvin L. Harder	20	582
Curtis T. Simmons	20	569
Adolfo Luque	20	550
Clark C. Griffith	20	416

500 Games Started (31)

Pitcher	GS.
Denton T. Young	818
Donald H. Sutton	740
Philip H. Niekro	716
Steven N. Carlton	708
Gaylord J. Perry	690
James F. Galvin	682
Walter P. Johnson	666
Warren E. Spahn	665
Thomas E. John	658
G. Thomas Seaver	647
James L. Kaat	625
Early Wynn	612
L. Nolan Ryan	611
Robin E. Roberts	609
Grover C. Alexander	598
Ferguson A. Jenkins	594
Timothy J. Keefe	593
Rikalbert Blyleven	572
Charles A. Nichols	561
Eppa Rixey	552
Christopher Mathewson	551
Michael F. Welch	549
Charles H. Ruffing	536
Jerry M. Koosman	527
James A. Palmer	521
James P. Bunning	519
John G. Clarkson	518
John J. Powell	517
Anthony J. Mullane	505
August Weyhing	503
Charles Radbourn	503

250 Complete Games (76)

Pitcher	CG.
Denton T. Young	751
James F. Galvin	641
Timothy J. Keefe	554
Walter P. Johnson	531
Charles A. Nichols	531
Michael F. Welch	525
John G. Clarkson	485
Charles G. Radbourn	479
Anthony J. Mullane	464
James McCormick	462
August W. Weyhing	448
Grover C. Alexander	436
Christopher Mathewson	434
John J. Powell	422
William H. White	394
Amos W. Rusie	391
Victor G. Willis	387

Pitcher	CG.
Edward S. Plank	387
Warren E. Spahn	382
James E. Whitney	373
William J. Terry	368
Theodore A. Lyons	356
Charles G. Buffinton	350
Charles C. Fraser	342
George E. Mullin	339
Clark C. Griffith	337
Charles H. Ruffing	335
Charles F. King	327
Albert L. Orth	323
William F. Hutchinson	321
Burleigh A. Grimes	314
Joseph J. McGinnity	314
Frank L. Donahue	312
Guy J. Hecker	310
William H. Dinneen	305
Robin E. Roberts	305
Gaylord J. Perry	303
Theodore P. Breitenstein	300
Robert M. Grove	300
Robert L. Caruthers	299
Emerson P. Hawley	297
William V. Kennedy	297
Edward Morris	297
Marcus E. Baldwin	296
Thomas H. Bond	294
William E. Donovan	290
Eppa Rixey	290
Early Wynn	290
Robert T. Mathews	289
Ellsworth E. Cunningham	286
John C. Stivetts	281
A. Wilbur Cooper	279
Robert W. Feller	279
John W. Taylor	278
John J. McMahon	277
Charles H. Getzein	277
Urban C. Faber	275
John F. Dwyer	270
Jouett Meekin	270
Ferguson A. Jenkins	267
Jesse N. Tannehill	266
Elton P. Chamberlain	264
Matthew A. Kilroy	264
Guy H. White	262
John D. Chesbro	261
George E. Waddell	261
Philip H. Ehret	260
Carl O. Hubbell	258
Lawrence J. Corcoran	256
Robert Gibson	255
Steven N. Carlton	254
Frank B. Killen	253
George B. Mercer	252
Paul M. Derringer	251
Samuel P. Jones	250
Edward A. Walsh	250

3,500 Innings (54)

Pitcher	Innings
Denton T. Young	7377
James F. Galvin	5959
Walter P. Johnson	5923
Philip H. Niekro	5403⅔
Gaylord J. Perry	5352
Warren E. Spahn	5246
Steven N. Carlton	5206⅔
Donald H. Sutton	5194⅓
Grover C. Alexander	5188
Charles A. Nichols	5067
Timothy J. Keefe	5043
Michael F. Welch	4784
G. Thomas Seaver	4782
Christopher Mathewson	4781
Robin E. Roberts	4689
Early Wynn	4566
Charles G. Radbourn	4543
John G. Clarkson	4534
James L. Kaat	4527⅔
Anthony J. Mullane	4506
Ferguson A. Jenkins	4498⅔
Eppa Rixey	4494
Thomas E. John	4467⅓
John J. Powell	4390
Charles H. Ruffing	4342
August P. Weyhing	4335
L. Nolan Ryan	4327
James McCormick	4264
Rikalbert Blyleven	4255
Edward S. Plank	4234
Burleigh A. Grimes	4178
Theodore A. Lyons	4162
Urban C. Faber	4087
Victor G. Willis	3994
James A. Palmer	3947⅓
Robert M. Grove	3940

Pitcher	Innings
Robert Gibson	3885
Samuel P. Jones	3884
Jerry M. Koosman	3839⅓
Robert W. Feller	3828
Waite C. Hoyt	3762
James P. Bunning	3759
Louis N. Newsom	3758
Amos W. Rusie	3750
Paul M. Derringer	3646
Michael S. Lolich	3640
Robert B. Friend	3612
Carl O. Hubbell	3591
Joseph F. Niekro	3573
Herbert J. Pennock	3572
Earl O. Whitehill	3563
William H. White	3543
William J. Terry	3523
Juan A. Marichal	3506

1,500 Runs (65)

Pitcher	Runs
James F. Galvin	3303
Denton T. Young	3168
August P. Weyhing	2770
Michael F. Welch	2555
Anthony J. Mullane	2520
Charles A. Nichols	2477
Timothy J. Keefe	2461
John G. Clarkson	2396
Philip H. Niekro	2337
Charles G. Radbourn	2300
James McCormick	2129
Gaylord J. Perry	2128
Charles H. Ruffing	2117
Steven N. Carlton	2111
James E. Whitney	2060
Donald H. Sutton	2060
Theodore A. Lyons	2056
Burleigh A. Grimes	2048
James L. Kaat	2038
Early Wynn	2037
Earl O. Whitehill	2018
Warren E. Spahn	2016
Samuel P. Jones	2008
Eppa Rixey	1986
Charles C. Fraser	1984
John Powell	1976
Robin E. Roberts	1962
Amos W. Rusie	1908
Louis N. Newsom	1908
Walter P. Johnson	1902
Thomas E. John	1876
Ferguson A. Jenkins	1853
Grover C. Alexander	1851
Charles F. King	1834
Urban C. Faber	1813
John E. Stivetts	1809
Waite C. Hoyt	1780
L. Nolan Ryan	1718
Melvin L. Harder	1714
Albert L. Orth	1711
Herbert J. Pennock	1699
G. Thomas Seaver	1674
Rikalbert Blyleven	1664
Paul M. Derringer	1652
Robert B. Friend	1652
Victor G. Willis	1644
Francis R. Donahue	1640
George E. Uhle	1635
Christopher Mathewson	1613
Irving D. Hadley	1609
Jerry M. Koosman	1608
Joseph F. Niekro	1607
George A. Dauss	1599
Robert M. Grove	1594
John J. McMahon	1580
John P. Quinn	1569
Robert W. Feller	1557
Jesse J. Haines	1556
Jonathan T. Zachary	1552
Curtis T. Simmons	1551
Michael S. Lolich	1537
Jerry Reuss	1530
James P. Bunning	1527
George E. Mullin	1507
Fred L. Fitzsimmons	1505

3.50 Or Under ERA (46)

(Pitchers with 3,000 or More Innings; does not include any seasons in N.L. before 1912 and in A.L. prior to 1913.)

Pitcher	IP.	ERA.
(a) Walter P. Johnson	4195	2.37
(b) Grover C. Alexander	4822	2.56
Edward C. Ford	3171	2.74
G. Thomas Seaver	4782	2.86
James A. Palmer	3947⅓	2.86
Stanley Coveleski	3071	2.88
Juan A. Marichal	3506	2.89
A. Wilbur Cooper	3482	2.89
Robert Gibson	3885	2.91
Carl W. Mays	3022	2.92
Donald S. Drysdale	3432	2.95
Carl O. Hubbell	3591	2.98
Robert M. Grove	3940	3.06
Warren E. Spahn	5246	3.08
Gaylord J. Perry	5352	3.10
L. Nolan Ryan	4327	3.13
Rikalbert Blyleven	4255	3.14
Eppa Rixey	4494	3.15
Urban C. Faber	4087	3.15
Steven N. Carlton	5206⅔	3.19
Adolfo Luque	3221	3.24
Robert W. Feller	3828	3.25
Donald H. Sutton	5194⅓	3.25
Emil J. Leonard	3220	3.25
Thomas E. John	4467⅓	3.26
James A. Hunter	3449	3.26
Vida R. Blue	3344	3.26
James P. Bunning	3759	3.27
W. William Pierce	3305	3.27
Luis C. Tiant	3485⅔	3.30
William H. Walters	3104	3.30
Claude W. Osteen	3459	3.30
George Dauss	3374	3.32
Ferguson A. Jenkins	4498⅔	3.34
Philip H. Niekro	5403⅔	3.35
Jerry M. Koosman	3839⅓	3.36
H. Lee Meadows	3151	3.38
Robin E. Roberts	4689	3.40
Lawrence C. Jackson	3262	3.40
Milton S. Pappas	3186	3.40
Michael S. Lolich	3640	3.44
Lawrence H. French	3152	3.44
James E. Perry	3287	3.44
James L. Kaat	4527⅔	3.46
Paul M. Derringer	3646	3.46
Leslie A. Bush	3088	3.49

(a) Does not include 1729 innings pitched 1907 through 1912; allowed 520 total runs in that period; earned-run total not available and if all the 520 runs were included in Johnson's earned-run total, his career earned-run average would be 2.47.

(b) Does not include 367 innings pitched in 1911; allowed 133 total runs in that year; earned-run total not available. If all the 133 runs were included in Alexander's earned-run total, his career ERA would be 2.61.

4,000 Hits (31)

Pitcher	Hits
Denton T. Young	7078
James F. Galvin	*6334
Philip H. Niekro	5044
Gaylord J. Perry	4938
Walter P. Johnson	4920
Grover C. Alexander	4868
Charles A. Nichols	4854
Warren E. Spahn	4830
August P. Weyhing	*4669
Steven N. Carlton	4652
Michael F. Welch	4646
Eppa Rixey	4633
James L. Kaat	4620
Donald H. Sutton	4601
Robin E. Roberts	4582
Timothy J. Keefe	*4524
Charles Radbourn	*4500
Theodore A. Lyons	4489
Thomas E. John	4475
Burleigh A. Grimes	4406
John G. Clarkson	*4376
John J. Powell	4323
Charles H. Ruffing	4294
Early Wynn	4291
Anthony J. Mullane	*4238
Christopher Mathewson	4203
James McCormick	*4166
Ferguson A. Jenkins	4142
Urban C. Faber	4104
Samuel P. Jones	4084
Waite C. Hoyt	4037

*Includes 1887 bases on balls, scored as hits under rules in effect for that year.

7 Grand Slams (22)

Pitcher	Total
Ned F. Garver	9
Milton S. Pappas	9
Jerry Reuss	9
James L. Kaat	8
Lyndall D. McDaniel	8
El Roy L. Face	8
Robert W. Feller	8
Early Wynn	8
John C. Klippstein	8
James T. Brewer	8
Frank E. McGraw	8
Lawrence H. French	7
James T. Hearn	7
John S. Sanford	7
Lonnie Warneke	7
Raymond M. Sadecki	7
Gaylord J. Perry	7
Michael A. Torrez	7
William H. Sherdel	7
Philip H. Niekro	7
Rikalbert Blyleven	7
C. Douglas Bair	7

200 Victories (85)

Pitcher	W.	L.	Pct.
Denton T. Young	511	313	.620
Walter P. Johnson	416	279	.599
Christopher Mathewson	373	188	.665
Grover C. Alexander	373	208	.642
Warren E. Spahn	363	245	.597
Charles A. Nichols	361	208	.634
James F. Galvin	361	309	.539
Timothy J. Keefe	342	224	.604
Steven N. Carlton	329	243	.575
John G. Clarkson	327	176	.650
Donald H. Sutton	321	250	.562
Philip H. Niekro	318	274	.537
Gaylord J. Perry	314	265	.542
G. Thomas Seaver	311	205	.603
Charles G. Radbourn	308	191	.617
Michael F. Welch	307	209	.595
Edward S. Plank	305	181	.628
Robert M. Grove	300	141	.680
Early Wynn	300	244	.551
Robin E. Roberts	286	245	.539
Anthony J. Mullane	285	213	.572
Ferguson A. Jenkins	284	226	.557
James L. Kaat	283	237	.544
Thomas E. John	277	216	.562
Charles H. Ruffing	273	225	.548
Burleigh A. Grimes	270	212	.560
James A. Palmer	268	152	.638
Robert W. Feller	266	162	.621
Eppa Rixey	266	251	.515
James McCormick	265	215	.552
August P. Weyhing	262	224	.539
L. Nolan Ryan	261	242	.519
Theodore A. Lyons	260	230	.531
Urban C. Faber	254	212	.545
Carl O. Hubbell	253	154	.622
Robert Gibson	251	174	.591
Joseph J. McGinnity	247	145	.630
John Powell	247	254	.493
Victor G. Willis	244	204	.545
Rikalbert Blyleven	244	209	.539
Juan A. Marichal	243	142	.631
Amos W. Rusie	241	158	.604
Clark C. Griffith	240	140	.632
Herbert J. Pennock	240	162	.597
Waite C. Hoyt	237	182	.566
Edward C. Ford	236	106	.690
Charles G. Buffinton	230	151	.604
Luis C. Tiant	229	172	.571
Samuel P. Jones	229	217	.513
William H. White	227	167	.576
James A. Hunter	224	166	.574
James P. Bunning	224	184	.549
Melvin L. Harder	223	186	.545
Paul Derringer	223	212	.513
George Dauss	222	182	.550
Jerry M. Koosman	222	209	.515
Joseph F. Niekro	220	203	.520
Earl O. Whitehill	218	186	.540
Robert L. Caruthers	217	101	.682
Fred L. Fitzsimmons	217	146	.598
Michael S. Lolich	217	191	.532
A. Wilbur Cooper	216	178	.548
Stanley Coveleski	215	141	.604
James E. Perry	215	174	.553
John P. Quinn	212	181	.539
George Mullin	212	181	.539
W. William Pierce	211	169	.555
Louis N. Newsom	211	222	.487
Edward V. Cicotte	210	149	.585
Jesse J. Haines	210	158	.571
Vida R. Blue	209	161	.565
Milton S. Pappas	209	164	.560
Donald S. Drysdale	209	166	.557
Mordecai P. Brown	208	111	.652
Charles A. Bender	208	112	.650
Carl W. Mays	208	126	.623
Robert G. Lemon	207	128	.618
Harold Newhouser	207	150	.580
Charles F. King	206	152	.575
John E. Stivetts	205	128	.616

Pitcher	W.	L.	Pct.
William J. Terry	205	197	.510
S. Lewis Burdette	203	144	.585
Charles H. Root	201	160	.557
Richard W. Marquard	201	177	.532
George E. Uhle	200	166	.546

20 Victories, 5 Times (52)

Pitcher	Years
Denton T. Young	16
Christopher Mathewson	13
Warren E. Spahn	13
Walter P. Johnson	12
Charles A. Nichols	11
James F. Galvin	10
Grover C. Alexander	9
Charles Radbourn	9
Michael F. Welch	9
John G. Clarkson	8
Robert M. Grove	8
James McCormick	8
Joseph J. McGinnity	8
Anthony J. Mullane	8
Amos W. Rusie	8
James A. Palmer	8
Charles G. Buffinton	7
Clark C. Griffith	7
Timothy J. Keefe	7
Robert G. Lemon	7
Edward S. Plank	7
August Weyhing	7
Victor G. Willis	7
Ferguson A. Jenkins	7
Mordecai P. Brown	6
Robert L. Caruthers	6
Robert W. Feller	6
Wesley C. Ferrell	6
Juan A. Marichal	6
Robin E. Roberts	6
Jesse N. Tannehill	6
Steven N. Carlton	6
Thomas H. Bond	5
John D. Chesbro	5
Lawrence J. Corcoran	5
Stanley Coveleski	5
Robert Gibson	5
Burleigh A. Grimes	5
Carl O. Hubbell	5
Charles F. King	5
John J. McMahon	5
Carl W. Mays	5
George E. Mullin	5
Charles L. Phillippe	5
John C. Stivetts	5
James L. Vaughn	5
William H. White	5
James E. Whitney	5
Early Wynn	5
James A. Hunter	5
G. Thomas Seaver	5
Gaylord J. Perry	5

30 Victories, 2 Times (32)

Pitcher	Years
Charles A. Nichols	7
John G. Clarkson	6
Timothy J. Keefe	6
Anthony J. Mullane	5
Denton T. Young	5
Thomas H. Bond	4
Lawrence J. Corcoran	4
James McCormick	4
Christopher Mathewson	4
Charles F. King	4
William H. White	4
Michael F. Welch	4
James F. Galvin	3
William F. Hutchison	3
Robert L. Caruthers	3
Robert T. Mathews	3
Grover C. Alexander	3
Edward Morris	3
Charles Radbourn	3
Amos W. Rusie	3
George S. Haddock	2
Walter P. Johnson	2
Guy J. Hecker	2
David L. Foutz	2
Frank B. Killen	2
Joseph J. McGinnity	2
John J. McMahon	2
John M. Ward	2
John C. Stivetts	2
Thomas A. Ramsey	2
August Weyhing	2
James E. Whitney	2

100 Saves (32)
(Since 1969)

Pitcher	Saves
Roland G. Fingers	341
Richard M. Gossage	289
H. Bruce Sutter	286
Daniel R. Quisenberry	237
Albert W. Lyle	222
H. Eugene Garber	212
Jeffrey J. Reardon	193
Lee A. Smith	180
Frank E. McGraw	179
Kenton C. Tekulve	179
Michael G. Marshall	178
J. David Giusti	140
David A. Righetti	138
Gary R. Lavelle	135
Gregory B. Minton	135
Ronald G. Davis	130
Terry J. Forster	127
David E. LaRoche	126
William R. Campbell	126
David S. Smith	124
Robert W. Stanley	123
Guillermo Hernandez	122
John F. Hiller	119
Felix A. Martinez	115
Clay P. Carroll	113
James T. Brewer	112
Darold D. Knowles	112
Stephen W. Bedrosian	110
Jesse Orosco	107
William H. Caudill	106
Wayne A. Granger	104
Ronald L. Reed	103

40 Shutouts (48)

Pitcher	Games
Walter P. Johnson	110
Grover C. Alexander	90
Christopher Mathewson	83
Denton T. Young	77
Edward S. Plank	64
Warren E. Spahn	63
G. Thomas Seaver	61
Edward A. Walsh	58
Donald H. Sutton	58
James F. Galvin	57
Robert Gibson	56
Steven N. Carlton	55
Rikalbert Blyleven	55
L. Nolan Ryan	54
James A. Palmer	53
Gaylord J. Perry	53
Juan A. Marichal	52
Mordecai P. Brown	50
George E. Waddell	50
Victor G. Willis	50
Early Wynn	49
Donald S. Drysdale	49
Luis C. Tiant	49
Ferguson A. Jenkins	49
Charles A. Nichols	48
John J. Powell	46
Guy H. White	46
Thomas E. John	46
Charles B. Adams	45
Adrian C. Joss	45
Charles H. Ruffing	45
Robin E. Roberts	45
Edward C. Ford	45
Philip H. Niekro	45
Robert W. Feller	44
Milton S. Pappas	43
William H. Walters	42
James A. Hunter	42
Charles A. Bender	41
Michael S. Lolich	41
James L. Vaughn	41
Michael Welch	41
Lawrence H. French	40
Sanford Koufax	40
James P. Bunning	40
Melvin L. Stottlemyre	40
Claude W. Osteen	40
Timothy J. Keefe	40

10 Complete-Game 1-0 Victories (25)

Pitcher	Games
Walter P. Johnson	38
Grover C. Alexander	17
Christopher Mathewson	14
Rikalbert Blyleven	14
Edward S. Plank	13
Edward A. Walsh	13
Guy Harris White	13

Pitcher	Games
Denton T. Young	13
W. Dean Chance	13
Stanley Coveleski	12
Gaylord J. Perry	12
Steven N. Carlton	12
George N. Rucker	11
Charles A. Nichols	11
Ferguson A. Jenkins	11
Leslie A. Bush	10
Paul Derringer	10
William L. Doak	10
Adrian C. Joss	10
Richard Rudolph	10
James L. Vaughn	10
George A. Tyler	10
Warren E. Spahn	10
Sanford Koufax	10
L. Nolan Ryan	10

1,200 Bases On Balls (36)

Pitcher	BB.
L. Nolan Ryan	2355
Steven N. Carlton	1828
Philip H. Niekro	1809
Early Wynn	1775
Robert W. Feller	1764
Louis N. Newsom	1732
Amos W. Rusie	1637
August P. Weyhing	1569
Charles H. Ruffing	1541
Irving G. Hadley	1442
Warren E. Spahn	1434
Earl O. Whitehill	1431
Samuel P. Jones	1396
G. Thomas Seaver	1390
Anthony J. Mullane	1379
Gaylord J. Perry	1379
Michael A. Torrez	1371
Walter P. Johnson	1353
Robert Gibson	1336
Charles C. Fraser	1332
Donald H. Sutton	1313
Samuel E. McDowell	1312
James A. Palmer	1311
Michael F. Welch	1305
Burleigh A. Grimes	1295
Mark E. Baldwin	1285
Allie P. Reynolds	1261
Leslie A. Bush	1260
Joseph H. Niekro	1253
Robert G. Lemon	1251
Harold Newhouser	1249
Charles A. Nichols	1245
William J. Terry	1244
Timothy J. Keefe	1225
Urban C. Faber	1213
Denton T. Young	1209

2,000 Strikeouts (38)

Pitcher	SO.
L. Nolan Ryan	4547
Steven N. Carlton	4131
G. Thomas Seaver	3640
Gaylord J. Perry	3534
Donald H. Sutton	3530
Walter P. Johnson	3508
Philip H. Niekro	3342
Rikalbert Blyleven	3286
Ferguson A. Jenkins	3192
Robert Gibson	3117
James P. Bunning	2855
Michael S. Lolich	2832
Denton T. Young	2819
Warren E. Spahn	2583
Jerry M. Koosman	2556
Robert W. Feller	2581
Timothy J. Keefe	2538
Christopher Mathewson	2505
Donald S. Drysdale	2486
James L. Kaat	2461
Samuel E. McDowell	2453
Luis C. Tiant	2416
Sanford Koufax	2396
Robin E. Roberts	2357
Early Wynn	2334
George E. Waddell	2310
Juan A. Marichal	2303
Robert M. Grove	2266
James A. Palmer	2212
Grover C. Alexander	2198
Vida R. Blue	2175
Camilo A. Pascual	2167
Thomas E. John	2146
Edward S. Plank	2112
Louis N. Newsom	2082
Frank D. Tanana	2071
Arthur C. Vance	2045
James A. Hunter	2012

General Reference Data

Batting

Triple Crown Hitters

American League (8)

Year—Player, Club	B.A.	HR.	RBI.
1909—Tyrus R. Cobb, Detroit	.377	9	*115
1933—James E. Foxx, Phila.	.356	48	163
1934—H. Louis Gehrig, N.Y.	.363	49	165
1942—Theodore S. Williams, Bos.	.356	36	137
1947—Theodore S. Williams, Bos.	.343	32	114
1956—Mickey C. Mantle, N.Y.	.353	52	130
1966—Frank Robinson, Balt.	.316	49	122
1967—Carl M. Yastrzemski, Bos.	.326	44	121

National League (5)

Year—Player, Club	B.A.	HR.	RBI.
1912—Henry Zimmerman, Chi.	.372	14	*98
1922—Rogers Hornsby, St. L.	.401	42	152
1925—Rogers Hornsby, St. L.	.403	39	143
1933—Charles H. Klein, Phila.	.368	28	120
1937—Joseph M. Medwick, St. L.	.374	31	154

*RBIs not officially adopted until 1920.

40 Home Runs In Season

National League (71)

HR.	Player and Club	Year
56	Lewis R. Wilson, Chicago	1930
54	Ralph M. Kiner, Pittsburgh	1949
52	Willie H. Mays, San Francisco	1965
52	George A. Foster, Cincinnati	1977
51	Ralph M. Kiner, Pittsburgh	1947
51	John R. Mize, New York	1947
51	Willie H. Mays, New York	1955
49	Theodore B. Kluszewski, Cin	1954
49	Willie H. Mays, San Francisco	1962
49	Andre F. Dawson, Chicago	1987
48	Wilver D. Stargell, Pittsburgh	1971
48	David A. Kingman, Chicago	1979
48	Michael J. Schmidt, Phila.	1980
47	Ralph M. Kiner, Pittsburgh	1950
47	Edwin L. Mathews, Milwaukee	1953
47	Theodore B. Kluszewski, Cin	1955
47	Ernest Banks, Chicago	1958
47	Willie H. Mays, San Francisco	1964
47	Henry L. Aaron, Atlanta	1971
46	Edwin L. Mathews, Milwaukee	1959
46	Orlando M. Cepeda, S. Fran	1961
45	Ernest Banks, Chicago	1959
45	Henry L. Aaron, Milwaukee	1962
45	Willie L. McCovey, S. Fran	1969
45	Johnny L. Bench, Cincinnati	1970
45	Michael J. Schmidt, Phila.	1979
44	Ernest Banks, Chicago	1955
44	Henry L. Aaron, Milwaukee	1957
44	Henry L. Aaron, Milwaukee	1963
44	Willie L. McCovey, S. Fran	1963
44	Henry L. Aaron, Atlanta	1966
44	Henry L. Aaron, Atlanta	1969
44	Wilver D. Stargell, Pittsburgh	1973
44	Dale B. Murphy, Atlanta	1987
43	Charles H. Klein, Philadelphia	1929
43	John R. Mize, St. Louis	1940
43	Edwin D. Snider, Brooklyn	1956
43	Ernest Banks, Chicago	1957
43	David A. Johnson, Atlanta	1973
42	Rogers Hornsby, St. Louis	1922
42	Melvin T. Ott, New York	1929
42	Ralph M. Kiner, Pittsburgh	1951
42	Edwin D. Snider, Brooklyn	1953
42	Gilbert R. Hodges, Brooklyn	1954
42	Edwin D. Snider, Brooklyn	1955
42	Billy L. Williams, Chicago	1970
41	Fred Williams, Philadelphia	1923
41	Roy Campanella, Brooklyn	1953
41	Henry J. Sauer, Chicago	1954
41	Willie H. Mays, New York	1954
41	Edwin L. Mathews, Milwaukee	1955
41	Ernest Banks, Chicago	1960
41	Darrell W. Evans, Atlanta	1973
41	Jeffrey A. Burroughs, Atlanta	1977
40	Charles H. Klein, Philadelphia	1930
40	Ralph M. Kiner, Pittsburgh	1948
40	John R. Mize, New York	1948
40	Gilbert R. Hodges, Brooklyn	1951
40	Theodore B. Kluszewski, Cin	1953
40	Edwin D. Snider, Brooklyn	1954
40	Edwin L. Mathews, Milwaukee	1954
40	Walter C. Post, Cincinnati	1955
40	Edwin D. Snider, Brooklyn	1957
40	Henry L. Aaron, Milwaukee	1960
40	Willie H. Mays, San Francisco	1961
40	Richard A. Allen, Philadelphia	1966
40	Atanasio R. Perez, Cincinnati	1970
40	Johnny L. Bench, Cincinnati	1972
40	Henry L. Aaron, Atlanta	1973
40	George A. Foster, Cincinnati	1978
40	Michael J. Schmidt, Phila.	1983

Home Runs By Clubs, Each Year

American League (1901-1987)

*Denotes leader or tie.

Year	Balt.	Bos.	Calif.	Chi.	Cleve.	K.C.	Det.	Minn.	N.Y.	Oak.	Mil.	Tex.	Lg.
1901	..	*36	..	31	11	..	29	34	..	34	..	..	226
1902	29	43	..	14	32	..	21	*47	..	38	..	..	256
1903	11	*48	..	14	30	..	12	17	18	32	..	..	182
1904	10	26	..	14	22	..	14	9	27	*31	..	..	153
1905	16	*29	..	11	22	..	10	25	17	23	..	..	153
1906	20	13	..	7	12	..	9	26	17	*31	..	..	135
1907	19	14	..	7	11	..	11	11	15	*22	..	..	101
1908	*21	13	..	3	18	..	19	8	12	20	..	..	114
1909	10	*21	..	4	10	..	20	8	16	20	..	..	109
1910	12	*44	..	7	8	..	28	8	19	18	..	..	144
1911	16	*35	..	20	19	..	28	15	25	*35	..	..	193
1912	19	*28	..	17	10	..	18	17	18	22	..	..	149
1913	18	17	..	23	16	..	24	19	8	*33	..	..	158
1914	17	18	..	19	11	..	25	18	12	*28	..	..	148
1915	19	13	..	25	20	..	23	12	*31	16	..	..	159
1916	14	14	..	17	16	..	17	12	*35	19	..	..	144
1917	15	14	..	19	13	..	25	4	*27	16	..	..	133
1918	5	16	..	8	9	..	13	4	20	*22	..	..	97
1919	32	33	..	25	24	..	23	24	*45	35	..	..	241
1920	50	22	..	36	35	..	30	36	*115	46	..	..	370
1921	66	17	..	35	42	..	58	42	*134	83	..	..	477
1922	97	45	..	45	32	..	54	45	95	*111	..	..	524
1923	82	34	..	42	59	..	41	26	*105	52	..	..	441
1924	67	30	..	41	40	..	35	22	*98	63	..	..	396
1925	*110	41	..	38	52	..	50	56	*110	76	..	..	533
1926	72	32	..	32	27	..	36	43	*121	61	..	..	424
1927	55	28	..	36	26	..	51	29	*158	56	..	..	439
1928	63	38	..	24	34	..	62	40	*133	89	..	..	483
1929	47	28	..	37	62	..	110	48	*142	122	..	..	596
1930	75	47	..	63	72	..	82	57	*152	125	..	..	673
1931	76	37	..	27	71	..	43	49	*155	118	..	..	576
1932	67	53	..	36	78	..	80	61	160	*173	..	..	708
1933	64	50	..	43	50	..	57	60	*144	140	..	..	608
1934	62	51	..	71	100	..	74	51	135	*144	..	..	688
1935	73	69	..	74	93	..	106	32	104	*112	..	..	663
1936	79	86	..	60	123	..	94	62	*182	72	..	..	758
1937	71	100	..	67	103	..	150	47	*174	94	..	..	806
1938	92	98	..	67	113	..	137	85	*174	98	..	..	864
1939	91	124	..	64	85	..	124	44	*166	98	..	..	796
1940	118	145	..	73	101	..	134	52	*155	105	..	..	883
1941	91	124	..	47	103	..	81	52	*151	85	..	..	734
1942	98	103	..	25	50	..	76	40	*108	33	..	..	533
1943	78	57	..	33	55	..	77	47	*100	26	..	..	473
1944	72	69	..	23	70	..	60	33	*96	36	..	..	459
1945	63	50	..	22	65	..	77	27	*93	33	..	..	430
1946	84	109	..	37	79	..	108	60	*136	40	..	..	653
1947	90	103	..	53	112	..	103	42	*115	61	..	..	679
1948	63	121	..	55	*155	..	78	31	139	68	..	..	710
1949	117	*131	..	43	112	..	88	81	115	82	..	..	769
1950	106	161	..	93	*164	..	114	76	159	100	..	..	973
1951	86	127	..	86	*140	..	104	54	*140	102	..	..	839
1952	82	113	..	80	*148	..	103	50	129	89	..	..	794
1953	112	101	..	74	*160	..	108	69	139	116	..	..	879
1954	52	132	..	94	*156	..	90	81	133	94	..	..	823
1955	54	137	..	116	148	..	130	80	*175	121	..	..	961
1956	91	139	..	128	153	..	150	112	*190	112	..	..	1075
1957	87	153	..	106	140	..	116	111	145	*166	..	..	1024
1958	108	155	..	101	161	..	109	121	*164	138	..	..	1057
1959	109	125	..	97	*167	..	160	163	153	117	..	..	1091
1960	123	124	..	112	127	..	150	147	*193	110	..	..	1086
1961	149	112	189	138	150	..	180	167	*240	90	..	119	1534
1962	156	146	137	92	180	..	*209	185	199	116	..	132	1552
1963	146	171	95	114	169	..	148	*225	188	95	..	138	1489
1964	162	186	102	106	164	..	157	*221	162	166	..	125	1551
1965	125	*165	92	125	156	..	162	150	149	110	..	136	1370
1966	175	145	122	87	155	..	*179	144	162	70	..	126	1365
1967	138	*158	114	89	131	..	152	131	100	69	..	115	1197
1968	133	125	83	71	75	..	*185	105	109	94	..	124	1104
1969	175	*197	88	112	119	98	182	163	94	148	y125	148	1649
1970	179	*203	114	123	183	97	148	153	111	171	126	138	*1746
1971	158	161	96	138	109	80	*179	116	97	160	104	86	1484
1972	100	124	78	108	91	78	122	93	103	*134	88	56	1175
1973	119	147	93	111	*158	114	157	120	131	147	145	110	1552
1974	116	109	95	*135	131	89	131	111	101	132	120	99	1369
1975	124	134	55	94	*153	118	125	121	110	151	146	134	1465
1976	119	*134	63	73	85	65	101	81	120	113	88	80	1122
Totals	5910	6393	1616	4437	6386	739	6576	5068	8223	6228	942	1866	54,467

Year	Balt.	Bos.	Calif.	Chi.	Clev.	K.C.	Det.	Minn.	N.Y.	Oak.	Mil.	Tex.	Sea.	Tor.	Lg.
1977	148	*213	131	192	100	146	166	123	184	117	125	135	133	100	2013
1978	154	172	108	106	106	98	129	82	125	100	*173	132	97	98	1680
1979	181	*194	164	127	138	116	164	112	150	108	185	140	132	95	2006
1980	156	162	106	91	89	115	143	99	189	137	*203	124	104	126	1844
1981	88	90	97	76	39	61	65	47	100	*104	96	49	89	61	1062
1982	179	136	186	136	109	132	177	148	161	149	*216	115	130	106	2080
1983	*168	142	154	157	86	109	156	141	153	121	132	106	111	167	1903
1984	160	181	150	172	123	117	*187	114	130	158	96	120	129	143	1980
1985	*214	162	153	146	116	154	202	141	176	155	101	129	171	158	2178
1986	169	144	167	121	157	137	*198	196	188	163	127	184	158	181	2290
1987	211	174	172	173	187	168	*225	196	196	199	163	194	161	215	2634
Totals	7738	8163	3204	5934	7636	2092	8388	6467	9975	7739	2559	3294	1415	1450	76,137

Note: Figures in Baltimore column 1902-1953 are for St. Louis (3012); in Oakland column 1901-54 are for Philadelphia (3498), Kansas City 1955-67 (1480); Minnesota column 1901-1960 are for old Washington

club (2782). Texas column represents second Washington club, 1961 through 1971. Figures in Totals column are all inclusive. (Baltimore had 24 in 1901 and 32 in 1902 and Milwaukee had 27 in 1901); these are included in League Totals but not in Club Totals. yPredecessor Seattle club. California column represents the Los Angeles Angels for 1961 through September 1, 1965.

National League (1900-1987)

*Denotes leaders or tie.

Year	Atl.	Chi.	Cinn.	Hous.	L.A.	Mont.	N.Y.	Phila.	Pitts.	St.L.	S.D.	S.F.	Lg.
1900	*47	33	30	..	27	..	..	28	26	37	..	23	251
1901	28	18	38	..	32	..	..	23	28	*39	..	19	225
1902	13	7	18	..	*19	..	..	5	18	10	..	6	96
1903	25	10	28	..	14	..	..	12	*33	5	..	20	147
1904	24	22	21	..	15	..	..	23	15	24	..	*31	175
1905	17	12	27	..	29	..	..	16	22	20	..	*39	182
1906	16	20	16	..	*25	..	..	12	12	10	..	15	126
1907	22	13	15	..	18	..	..	12	19	10	..	*23	141
1908	17	19	14	..	*28	..	..	11	25	17	..	20	151
1909	15	20	22	..	16	..	..	12	25	15	..	*26	151
1910	31	*34	23	..	25	..	..	22	33	15	..	31	214
1911	37	54	21	..	28	..	..	*60	48	27	..	39	314
1912	35	42	19	..	32	..	..	42	39	27	..	*48	284
1913	32	59	27	..	39	..	..	*73	35	15	..	31	311
1914	35	41	16	..	31	..	..	*62	18	33	..	30	266
1915	17	53	15	..	14	..	..	*58	24	20	..	*24	225
1916	22	*46	14	..	28	..	..	42	20	25	..	42	239
1917	22	17	26	..	25	..	..	38	9	26	..	*39	202
1918	13	20	15	..	10	..	..	25	15	*27	..	13	138
1919	24	21	19	..	25	..	..	*42	17	18	..	40	206
1920	23	34	18	..	28	..	..	*64	16	32	..	46	261
1921	61	37	20	..	59	..	..	*88	37	83	..	75	460
1922	32	42	45	..	56	..	..	*116	52	107	..	80	530
1923	32	90	45	..	62	..	..	*112	49	63	..	85	538
1924	25	66	36	..	72	..	..	94	43	67	..	*95	498
1925	41	85	44	..	64	..	..	100	77	109	..	*114	634
1926	16	66	35	..	40	..	..	75	44	*90	..	73	439
1927	37	74	29	..	39	..	..	57	54	84	..	*109	483
1928	52	92	32	..	66	..	..	85	52	113	..	*118	610
1929	32	139	34	..	99	..	..	*153	60	100	..	136	753
1930	66	*171	74	..	122	..	..	126	86	104	..	143	892
1931	34	83	21	..	71	..	..	81	41	60	..	*101	492
1932	63	69	47	..	109	..	..	*122	47	76	..	116	549
1933	54	72	34	..	62	..	..	60	39	57	..	*82	460
1934	83	101	55	..	79	..	..	56	52	104	..	*126	656
1935	75	88	73	..	59	..	..	92	66	86	..	*123	662
1936	68	76	82	..	33	..	..	*103	60	88	..	97	607
1937	63	96	73	..	37	..	..	103	47	94	..	*111	624
1938	54	65	110	..	61	..	..	40	65	91	..	*125	611
1939	56	91	98	..	78	..	..	49	63	98	..	*116	649
1940	59	86	89	..	93	..	..	75	76	*119	..	91	688
1941	48	99	64	..	*101	..	..	64	56	70	..	95	597
1942	68	75	66	..	62	..	..	44	54	60	..	*109	538
1943	39	52	43	..	39	..	..	66	42	70	..	*81	432
1944	79	71	51	..	56	..	..	55	70	*100	..	93	575
1945	101	57	56	..	57	..	..	56	72	64	..	*114	577
1946	44	56	65	..	55	..	..	80	60	81	..	*121	562
1947	85	71	95	..	83	..	..	60	156	115	..	*221	886
1948	95	87	104	..	91	..	..	91	108	105	..	*164	845
1949	103	97	86	..	*152	..	..	122	126	102	..	147	935
1950	148	161	99	..	*194	..	..	125	138	102	..	133	1100
1951	130	103	88	..	*184	..	..	108	137	95	..	179	1024
1952	110	107	104	..	*153	..	..	93	92	97	..	151	907
1953	156	137	166	..	*208	..	..	115	99	140	..	176	1197
1954	139	159	147	..	*186	..	..	102	76	119	..	*186	1114
1955	182	164	181	..	*201	..	..	132	91	143	..	169	1263
1956	177	142	*221	..	179	..	..	121	110	124	..	145	1219
1957	*199	147	187	..	147	..	..	117	92	132	..	157	1178
1958	167	*182	123	..	172	..	..	124	134	111	..	170	1183
1959	*177	163	161	..	148	..	..	113	112	118	..	167	1159
1960	*170	119	140	..	126	..	..	99	120	138	..	130	1042
1961	*188	176	158	..	157	..	..	103	128	103	..	183	1196
1962	181	126	167	105	140	..	139	142	108	137	..	*204	1449
1963	139	127	122	62	110	..	96	126	108	128	..	*197	1215
1964	159	145	130	70	79	..	103	130	121	109	..	*165	1211
1965	*196	134	183	97	78	..	107	144	111	109	..	159	1318
1966	*207	140	149	112	108	..	98	117	158	108	..	181	1378
1967	*158	128	109	93	82	..	83	103	91	115	..	140	1102
1968	80	*130	106	66	67	..	81	100	80	73	..	108	891
1969	141	142	*171	104	97	125	109	137	119	90	99	136	1470
1970	160	179	*191	129	87	136	120	101	130	113	172	165	*1683
1971	153	128	138	71	95	88	98	123	*154	95	96	140	1379
1972	144	133	124	134	98	91	105	98	110	70	102	*150	1359
1973	*206	117	137	134	110	125	85	134	154	75	112	161	1550
1974	120	110	135	110	*139	86	96	95	114	83	99	93	1280
1975	107	95	124	84	118	98	101	125	*138	81	78	84	1233
1976	82	105	*141	66	91	94	102	110	110	63	64	85	1113
1977	139	111	181	114	*191	138	88	186	133	96	120	134	1631
1978	123	72	136	70	*149	121	86	133	115	79	75	117	1276
1979	126	135	132	49	*183	143	74	119	148	100	93	125	1427
1980	144	107	113	75	*148	114	61	117	116	101	67	80	1243
1981	64	57	64	45	*82	81	57	69	55	50	32	63	719
1982	*146	102	82	74	138	133	97	112	134	67	81	133	1299
1983	130	140	107	97	*146	102	112	125	121	83	93	142	1398
1984	111	136	106	79	102	96	107	*147	98	75	109	112	1278
1985	126	*150	114	121	129	118	134	141	80	87	109	115	1424
1986	138	*155	144	125	130	110	148	154	111	58	136	114	1523
1987	152	*209	192	122	125	120	192	169	131	94	113	205	1824
Totals	7755	8022	7421	2408	7642	2119	2679	7716	6728	6782	1850	9320	70,442

Note: Figures in Atlanta column 1900-1952 are for Boston (2588) and 1953-65 for Milwaukee (2230); in Los Angeles column 1900-1957 are for Brooklyn (4017); San Francisco column 1900-1957 are for New York Giants (5162); New York column represents the present Met franchise. Figures in Totals columns are all inclusive.

40 Homers In Season (Cont.)

American League (68)

HR.	Player and Club	Year
61	Roger E. Maris, New York	1961
60	George H. Ruth, New York	1927
59	George H. Ruth, New York	1921
58	James E. Foxx, Philadelphia	1932
58	Henry B. Greenberg, Detroit	1938
54	George H. Ruth, New York	1920
54	George H. Ruth, New York	1928
54	Mickey C. Mantle, New York	1961
52	Mickey C. Mantle, New York	1956
50	James E. Foxx, Boston	1938
49	George H. Ruth, New York	1930
49	H. Louis Gehrig, New York	1934
49	H. Louis Gehrig, New York	1936
49	Harmon C. Killebrew, Minn	1964
49	Frank Robinson, Baltimore	1966
49	Harmon C. Killebrew, Minn	1969
49	Mark D. McGwire, Oakland	1987
48	James E. Foxx, Philadelphia	1933
48	Harmon C. Killebrew, Minn	1962
48	Frank O. Howard, Washington	1969
47	George H. Ruth, New York	1926
47	H. Louis Gehrig, New York	1927
47	Reginald M. Jackson, Oakland	1969
47	George A. Bell, Toronto	1987
46	George H. Ruth, New York	1924
46	George H. Ruth, New York	1929
46	H. Louis Gehrig, New York	1931
46	George H. Ruth, New York	1931
46	Joseph P. DiMaggio, New York	1937
46	James E. Gentile, Baltimore	1961
46	Harmon C. Killebrew, Minn	1961
46	James E. Rice, Boston	1978
45	Rocco D. Colavito, Detroit	1961
45	Harmon C. Killebrew, Minn	1963
45	J. Gorman Thomas, Milwaukee	1979
44	James E. Foxx, Philadelphia	1934
44	Henry B. Greenberg, Detroit	1946
44	Harmon C. Killebrew, Minn	1967
44	Carl M. Yastrzemski, Boston	1967
44	Frank O. Howard, Washington	1968
44	Frank O. Howard, Washington	1970
43	Theodore S. Williams, Boston	1949
43	Albert L. Rosen, Cleveland	1953
43	Antonio R. Armas, Boston	1984
42	Harold A. Trosky, Cleveland	1936
42	Gus E. Zernial, Philadelphia	1953
42	Roy E. Sievers, Washington	1957
42	Mickey C. Mantle, New York	1958
42	Rocco D. Colavito, Cleveland	1959
42	Harmon C. Killebrew, Wash.	1959
42	Richard L. Stuart, Boston	1963
41	George H. Ruth, New York	1923
41	Henry L. Gehrig, New York	1930
41	George H. Ruth, New York	1932
41	James E. Foxx, Boston	1936
41	Henry B. Greenberg, Detroit	1940
41	Rocco D. Colavito, Cleveland	1958
41	Norman D. Cash, Detroit	1961
41	Harmon C. Killebrew, Minn	1970
41	Reginald M. Jackson, New York	1980
41	Benjamin A. Oglivie, Milwaukee	1980
40	Henry B. Greenberg, Detroit	1937
40	Mickey C. Mantle, New York	1960
40	Americo Petrocelli, Boston	1969
40	Carl M. Yastrzemski, Boston	1969
40	Carl M. Yastrzemski, Boston	1970
40	Darrell W. Evans, Detroit	1985
40	Jesse L. Barfield, Toronto	1986

400 Total Bases In Season

National League (10)

T.B.	Player and Club	Year
450	Rogers Hornsby, St. Louis	1922
445	Charles H. Klein, Philadelphia	1930
429	Stanley F. Musial, St. Louis	1948
423	Lewis R. Wilson, Chicago	1930
420	Charles H. Klein, Philadelphia	1932
416	Floyd C. Herman, Brooklyn	1930
409	Rogers Hornsby, Chicago	1929
406	Joseph M. Medwick, St. Louis	1937
405	Charles H. Klein, Philadelphia	1929
400	Henry L. Aaron, Milwaukee	1959

American League (12)

T.B.	Player and Club	Year
457	George H. Ruth, New York	1921
447	H. Louis Gehrig, New York	1927
438	James E. Foxx, Philadelphia	1932
419	H. Louis Gehrig, New York	1930
418	Joseph P. DiMaggio, New York	1937
417	George H. Ruth, New York	1927
410	H. Louis Gehrig, New York	1931
409	H. Louis Gehrig, New York	1934
406	James E. Rice, Boston	1978
405	Harold A. Trosky, Cleveland	1936
403	H. Louis Gehrig, New York	1936
403	James E. Foxx, Philadelphia	1933

Players With Four Homers In Game
National League (8)
ROBERT L. LOWE, Boston, May 30, 1894†, (H).
Edward J. Delahanty, Philadelphia, July 13, 1896, (A), (3 consec.).
Charles H. Klein, Phila., July 10, 1936, 10 inn., (A), (3 consec.).
Gilbert R. Hodges, Brooklyn, August 31, 1950, (H).
Joseph W. Adcock, Milwaukee, July 31, 1954, (A), (3 consec.).
Willie H. Mays, San Francisco, April 30, 1961, (A).
MICHAEL J. SCHMIDT, Philadelphia, April 17, 1976, 10 inn., (A).
J. Robert Horner, Atlanta, July 6, 1986 (H).

American League (3)
H. LOUIS GEHRIG, New York, June 3, 1932, (A).
J. Patrick Seerey, Chicago, July 18, 1948*, (A), (11 inn.—3 consec.).
ROCCO D. COLAVITO, Cleveland, June 10, 1959, (A).

Note—Capitalized name denotes consecutive homers (bases on balls excluded).
*First game. †Second game.

Players With Three Homers In Game
National League (144)
Edward N. Williamson, Chicago, May 30, 1884†, (H).
ADRIAN C. ANSON, Chicago, August 6, 1884, (H).
JOHN E. MANNING, Philadelphia, October 9, 1884, (A).
Dennis L. Brouthers, Detroit, September 10, 1886, (A).
Roger Connor, New York, May 9, 1888, (H).
W. Frank Shugart, St. Louis, May 10, 1894, (A).
WILLIAM JOYCE, Washington, August 20, 1894, (H).
Thomas L. McCreery, Louisville, July 12, 1897, (A).
Jacob P. Beckley, Cincinnati, September 26, 1897*, (A).
Walter J. Henline, Philadelphia, September 15, 1922, (H).
Fred C. Williams, Philadelphia, May 11, 1923, (H).
GEORGE L. KELLY, New York, September 17, 1923, (A).
George L. Kelly, New York, June 14, 1924, (H).
Jacques F. Fournier, Brooklyn, July 13, 1926, (A).
Lester R. Bell, Boston, June 2, 1928, (H).
GEORGE W. HARPER, St. Louis, September 20, 1928*, (A).
Lewis R. Wilson, Chicago, July 26, 1930, (A).
MELVIN T. OTT, New York, August 31, 1930†, (H).
ROGERS HORNSBY, Chicago, April 24, 1931, (A).
GEORGE A. WATKINS, St. Louis, June 24, 1931†, (A).
William H. Terry, New York, August 13, 1932*, (H).
Floyd C. Herman, Chicago, July 20, 1933, (H).
Harold B. Lee, Boston, July 6, 1934, (A).
George H. Ruth, Boston, May 25, 1935, (A).
JOHN F. MOORE, Philadelphia, July 22, 1936, (H).
Alexander Kampouris, Cincinnati, May 9, 1937, (H).
JOHN R. MIZE, St. Louis, July 13, 1938, (H).
John R. Mize, St. Louis, July 20, 1938†, (H).
HENRY C. LEIBER, Chicago, July 4, 1939*, (H).
John R. Mize, St. Louis, May 13, 1940, 14 inn., (A).
JOHN R. MIZE, St. Louis, September 8, 1940*, (H).
JAMES A. TOBIN, Boston, May 13, 1942, (H).
CLYDE E. McCULLOUGH, Chicago, July 26, 1942*, (A).
WILLIAM B. NICHOLSON, Chicago, July 23, 1944*, (A).
JOHN R. MIZE, New York, April 24, 1947, (A).
WILLARD MARSHALL, New York, July 18, 1947, (A).
RALPH M. KINER, Pittsburgh, August 16, 1947, (H).
RALPH M. KINER, Pittsburgh, September 11, 1947†, (H).
Ralph M. Kiner, Pittsburgh, July 5, 1948*, (H).
EUGENE V. HERMANSKI, Brooklyn, August 5, 1948, (H).
Andrew W. Seminick, Philadelphia, June 2, 1949, (H).
W. Walker Cooper, Cincinnati, July 6, 1949, (H).
ROBERT I. ELLIOTT, Boston, September 24, 1949, (A).
EDWIN D. SNIDER, Brooklyn, May 30, 1950†, (H).
Wesley N. Westrum, New York, June 24, 1950, (H).
ANDREW W. PAFKO, Chicago, August 2, 1950†, (A).
ROY CAMPANELLA, Brooklyn, August 26, 1950, (A).
HENRY J. SAUER, Chicago, August 28, 1950*, (H).
THOMAS M. BROWN, Brooklyn, September 18, 1950, (H).
Ralph M. Kiner, Pittsburgh, July 18, 1951, (H).
DELBERT Q. WILBER, Philadelphia, August 27, 1951†, (H).
Donald F. Mueller, New York, September 1, 1951, (H).
Henry J. Sauer, Chicago, June 11, 1952, (H).
EDWIN L. MATHEWS, Boston, September 27, 1952, (A).
JAMES L. RHODES, New York, August 26, 1953, (H).
James T. Pendleton, Milwaukee, August 30, 1953*, (A).
Stanley F. Musial, St. Louis, May 2, 1954*, (H).
HENRY C. THOMPSON, New York, June 3, 1954, (A).
JAMES L. RHODES, New York, July 28, 1954, (H).
Edwin D. Snider, Brooklyn, June 1, 1955, (H).
DAVID R. BELL, Cincinnati, July 21, 1955, (H).
Delmer Ennis, Philadelphia, July 23, 1955, (H).
Forrest H. Burgess, Cincinnati, July 29, 1955, (H).
Ernest Banks, Chicago, August 4, 1955, (H).
DAVID R. BELL, Cincinnati, May 29, 1956, (H).
L. Benjamin Bailey, Cincinnati, June 24, 1956*, (A).
Theodore J. Kluszewski, Cincinnati, July 1, 1956*, 10 inn., (A).
ROBERT B. THURMAN, Cincinnati, August 18, 1956, (H).
ERNEST BANKS, Chicago, September 14, 1957†, (H).
R. Lee Walls, Chicago, April 24, 1958, (A).
Roman G. Mejias, Pittsburgh, May 4, 1958*, (A).
Walter J. Moryn, Chicago, May 30, 1958†, (H).
FRANK J. THOMAS, Pittsburgh, August 16, 1958, (A).
Donald L. Demeter, Los Angeles, April 21, 1959, 11 inn., (H).
Henry L. Aaron, Milwaukee, June 21, 1959, (A).

FRANK ROBINSON, Cincinnati, August 22, 1959, (H).
RICHARD L. STUART, Pittsburgh, June 30, 1960†, (H).
Willie H. Mays, San Francisco, June 29, 1961, 10 inn., (A).
WILLIAM D. WHITE, St. Louis, July 5, 1961, (A).
Donald L. Demeter, Philadelphia, September 12, 1961, (A).
ERNEST BANKS, Chicago, May 29, 1962, (H).
STANLEY F. MUSIAL, St. Louis, July 8, 1962, (A).
Willie H. Mays, San Francisco, June 2, 1963, (A).
Ernest Banks, Chicago, June 9, 1963, (H).
WILLIE L. McCOVEY, San Francisco, September 22, 1963, (H).
WILLIE L. McCOVEY, San Francisco, April 22, 1964, (A).
JOHN W. CALLISON, Philadelphia, September 27, 1964, (H).
John W. Callison, Philadelphia, June 6, 1965†, (A).
Wilver D. Stargell, Pittsburgh, June 24, 1965, (A).
JAMES L. HICKMAN, New York, September 3, 1965, (A).
Eugene G. Oliver, Atlanta, July 30, 1966†, (H).
ARTHUR L. SHAMSKY, Cincinnati, August 12, 1966, 13 inn., (H).
Willie L. McCovey, San Francisco, September 17, 1966, 10 inn. (H).
Roberto W. Clemente, Pittsburgh, May 15, 1967, 10 inn. (A).
ADOLFO E. PHILLIPS, Chicago, June 11, 1967†, (H).
JAMES S. WYNN, Houston, June 15, 1967, (A).
Wilver D. Stargell, Pittsburgh, May 22, 1968, (A).
Billy L. Williams, Chicago, September 10, 1968, (H).
RICHARD A. ALLEN, Philadelphia, September 29, 1968, (A).
J. ROBERT TILLMAN, Atlanta, July 30, 1969*, (H).
ROBERTO W. CLEMENTE, Pittsburgh, August 13, 1969, (A).
Ricardo A. Carty, Atlanta, May 31, 1970, (H).
Michael K. Lum, Atlanta, July 3, 1970*, (H).
JOHNNY L. BENCH, Cincinnati, July 26, 1970, (H).
ORLANDO M. CEPEDA, Atlanta, July 26, 1970*, (A).
Wilver D. Stargell, Pittsburgh, April 10, 1971, 12 inn., (A).
WILVER D. STARGELL, Pittsburgh, April 21, 1971, (H).
DERON R. JOHNSON, Philadelphia, July 11, 1971, (H).
ROBERT J. MONDAY, Chicago, May 16, 1972, (H).
Nathan Colbert, San Diego, August 1, 1972†, (A).
Johnny L. Bench, Cincinnati, May 9, 1973, (A).
Lee A. May, Houston, June 21, 1973, (A).
George E. Mitterwald, Chicago, April 17, 1974, (H).
James S. Wynn, Los Angeles, May 11, 1974, (A).
David E. Lopes, Los Angeles, August 20, 1974, (A).
C. Reginald Smith, St. Louis, May 22, 1976, (A).
David A. Kingman, New York, June 4, 1976, (A).
William H. Robinson, Pittsburgh, June 5, 1976, 15 inn., (H).
Gary N. Matthews, San Francisco, September 25, 1976, (H).
GARY E. CARTER, Montreal, April 20, 1977, (H).
LARRY A. PARRISH, Montreal, May 29, 1977, (A).
GEORGE A. FOSTER, Cincinnati, July 14, 1977, (H).
Peter E. Rose, Cincinnati, April 29, 1978, (A).
David A. Kingman, Chicago, May 14, 1978, (A).
LARRY A. PARRISH, Montreal, July 30, 1978, (A).
David A. Kingman, Chicago, May 17, 1979 (H).
Dale B. Murphy, Atlanta, May 18, 1979, (H).
MICHAEL J. SCHMIDT, Philadelphia, July 7, 1979, (H).
DAVID A. KINGMAN, Chicago, July 28, 1979 (H).
Larry A. Parrish, Montreal, April 25, 1980, (A).
Johnny L. Bench, Cincinnati, May 29, 1980, (A).
Claudell Washington, New York, June 22, 1980, (A).
Darrell W. Evans, San Francisco, June 15, 1983, (A).
DARRYL E. STRAWBERRY, New York, August 5, 1985, (A).
GARY E. CARTER, New York, September 3, 1985, (A).
Andre F. Dawson, Montreal, September 24, 1985, (A).
G. Kenneth Griffey, Atlanta, July 22, 1986, 11 inn., (H).
Eric K. Davis, Cincinnati, September 10, 1986, (A).
ERIC K. DAVIS, Cincinnati, May 3, 1987, (A).
Timothy C. Wallach, Montreal, May 4, 1987, (A).
MICHAEL J. SCHMIDT, Philadelphia, June 14, 1987, (A).
Andre F. Dawson, Chicago, August 1, 1987, (H).
GLENN E. DAVIS, Houston, September 10, 1987, (H).
Darnell Coles, Pittsburgh, September 30, 1987†, (H).

American Association (1)
Guy J. Hecker, Louisville, August 15, 1886†, (H).

American League (137)
Kenneth R. Williams, St. Louis, April 22, 1922, (H).
Joseph H. Hauser, Philadelphia, August 2, 1924, (A).
Leon A. Goslin, Washington, June 19, 1925, 12 inn., (A).
Tyrus R. Cobb, Detroit, May 5, 1925 (A).
Gordon S. Cochrane, Philadelphia, May 21, 1925, (A).
Anthony M. Lazzeri, New York, June 8, 1927, (H).
H. Louis Gehrig, New York, June 23, 1927, (H).
H. Louis Gehrig, New York, May 4, 1929, (A).
George H. Ruth, New York, May 21, 1930*, (A).
H. Louis Gehrig, New York, May 22, 1930†, (A).
CARL N. REYNOLDS, Chicago, July 2, 1930†, (A).
LEON A. GOSLIN, St. Louis, August 19, 1930, (A).
H. EARL AVERILL, Cleveland, September 17, 1930*, (H).
Leon A. Goslin, St. Louis, June 23, 1932, (H).
W. Benjamin Chapman, New York, July 9, 1932†, (H).
James E. Foxx, Philadelphia, July 10, 1932, 18 inn., (A).
Aloysius H. Simmons, Philadelphia, July 15, 1932, (H).
JAMES E. FOXX, Philadelphia, June 8, 1933 (H).
HAROLD A. TROSKY, Cleveland, May 30, 1934†, (H).
PARKE E. COLEMAN, Philadelphia, August 17, 1934*, (H).
M. FRANK HIGGINS, Philadelphia, June 27, 1935, (A).
JULIUS J. SOLTERS, St. Louis, July 7, 1935, (A).
Anthony M. Lazzeri, New York, May 24, 1936, (A).
JOSEPH P. DiMAGGIO, New York, June 13, 1937†, 11 inn., (A).

Harold A. Trosky, Cleveland, July 5, 1937*, (A).
MERVYN J. CONNORS, Chicago, September 17, 1938†, (H).
KENNETH F. KELTNER, Cleveland, May 25, 1939 (A).
James R. Tabor, Boston, July 4, 1939†, (A).
WILLIAM M. DICKEY, New York, July 26, 1939, (H).
M. FRANK HIGGINS, Detroit, May 20, 1940, (H):
Charles E. Keller, New York, July 28, 1940*, (A).
Rudolph B. York, Detroit, September 1, 1941*, (H).
J. Patrick Seerey, Cleveland, July 13, 1945, (A).
Theodore S. Williams, Boston, July 14, 1946*, (H).
JOSEPH P. DiMAGGIO, New York, May 23, 1948*, (A).
Patrick J. Mullin, Detroit, June 26, 1949†, (A).
Robert P. Doerr, Boston, June 8, 1950, (H).
LAWRENCE E. DOBY, Cleveland, August 2, 1950, (H).
Joseph P. DiMaggio, New York, September 10, 1950, (A).
JOHN R. MIZE, New York, September 15, 1950, (A).
Gus E. Zernial, Chicago, October 1, 1950†, (H).
Robert F. Avila, Cleveland, June 20, 1951, (A).
Clyde F. Vollmer, Boston, July 26, 1951, (H).
Albert L. Rosen, Cleveland, April 29, 1952, (A).
WILLIAM V. GLYNN, Cleveland, July 5, 1954*, (H).
Albert W. Kaline, Detroit, April 17, 1955, (H).
Mickey C. Mantle, New York, May 13, 1955, (H).
Norbert H. Zauchin, Boston, May 27, 1955, (A).
JAMES R. LEMON, Washington, August 31, 1956, (H).
Theodore S. Williams, Boston, May 8, 1957, (H).
Theodore S. Williams, Boston, June 13, 1957, (A).
Hector H. Lopez, Kansas City, June 26, 1958, (H).
PRESTON M. WARD, Kansas City, September 9, 1958, (A).
CHARLES R. MAXWELL, Detroit, May 3, 1959†, (H).
Robert H. Cerv, Kansas City, August 20, 1959, (A).
WILLIE C. KIRKLAND, Cleveland, July 9, 1961†, (H).
Rocco D. Colavito, Detroit, August 27, 1961†, (A).
J. Leroy Thomas, Los Angeles, Sept. 5, 1961†, (A).
ROCCO D. COLAVITO, Detroit, July 5, 1962, (A).
Stephen Boros, Detroit, August 6, 1962, (A).
DONALD G. LEPPERT, Washington, April 11, 1963, (H).
W. ROBERT ALLISON, Minnesota, May 17, 1963, (A).
JOHN W. POWELL, Baltimore, August 10, 1963, (A).
Harmon C. Killebrew, Minnesota, September 21, 1963*, (A).
James H. King, Washington, June 8, 1964, (H).
John W. Powell, Baltimore, June 27, 1964 (A).
MANUEL E. JIMENEZ, Kansas City, July 4, 1964, (A).
THOMAS M. TRESH, New York, June 6, 1965†, (H).
John W. Powell, Baltimore, August 15, 1966, (A).
Tommy L. McCraw, Chicago, May 24, 1967 (A).
Curtis L. Blefary, Baltimore, June 6, 1967*, (A).
KENNETH S. HARRELSON, Boston, June 14, 1968, (A).
Michael P. Epstein, Washington, May 16, 1969, (A).
Joseph M. Lahoud, Boston, June 11, 1969, (A).
WILLIAM E. MELTON, Chicago, June 24, 1969†, (A).
Reginald M. Jackson, Oakland, July 2, 1969, (H).
Paul L. Blair, Baltimore, April 29, 1970, (A).
Anthony Horton, Cleveland, May 24, 1970†, (H).
Willie Horton, Detroit, June 9, 1970, (H).
BOBBY R. MURCER, New York, June 24, 1970†, (H).
William A. Freehan, Detroit, August 9, 1971 (A).
GEORGE A. HENDRICK, Cleveland, June 19, 1973, (H).
Antonio L. (Pedro) Oliva, Minnesota, July 3, 1973, (A).
Leroy B. Stanton, California, July 10, 1973, 10 inn., (A).
Bobby R. Murcer, New York, July 13, 1973, (H).
ROBERT GRICH, Baltimore, June 18, 1974, (A).
Fredric M. Lynn, Boston, June 18, 1975, (A).
John C. Mayberry, Kansas City, July 1, 1975, (A).
DONALD E. BAYLOR, Baltimore, July 2, 1975, (A).
TOLIA SOLAITA, Kansas City, September 7, 1975, 11 inn., (A).
Carl M. Yastrzemski, Boston, May 19, 1976, (A).
Willie W. Horton, Texas, May 15, 1977, (A).
JOHN C. MAYBERRY, Kansas City, June 1, 1977, (A).
CLIFFORD JOHNSON, New York, June 30, 1977, (A).
JAMES E. RICE, Boston, August 29, 1977, (H).
Albert Oliver, Texas, May 23, 1979, (A).
Benjamin A. Oglivie, Milwaukee, July 8, 1979*, (H).
CARNEY R. LANSFORD, California, September 1, 1979, (A).
Otoniel Velez, Toronto, May 4, 1980*, 10 inn., (H).
Freddie J. Patek, California, June 20, 1980, (A).
ALBERT OLIVER, Texas, August 17, 1980†, (A).
Eddie C. Murray, Baltimore, September 14, 1980, 13 inn., (A).
Jeffrey A. Burroughs, Seattle, August 14, 1981†, (A).
Paul L. Molitor, Milwaukee, May 12, 1982, (A).
LARRY D. HERNDON, Detroit, May 18, 1982, (H).
BENJAMIN A. OGLIVIE, Milwaukee, June 20, 1982, (A).
HAROLD D. BAINES, Chicago, July 7, 1982, (H).
DOUGLAS V. DeCINCES, California, August 3, 1982, (H).
Douglas V. DeCinces, California, August 8, 1982, (A).
George H. Brett, Kansas City, April 20, 1983, (H).
Benjamin A. Oglivie, Milwaukee, May 14, 1983, (H).
Darnell G. Ford, Baltimore, July 20, 1983, (A).
James E. Rice, Boston, August 29, 1983†, (A).
DAVID A. KINGMAN, Oakland, April 16, 1984, (A).
Harold D. Baines, Chicago, September 17, 1984, (A).
J. GORMAN THOMAS, Seattle, April 11, 1985, (H).
LARRY A. PARRISH, Texas, April 29, 1985, (H).
Eddie C. Murray, Baltimore, August 26, 1985, (A).
Leondaus Lacy, Baltimore, June 8, 1986, (A).

JUAN J. BENIQUEZ, Baltimore, June 12, 1986, (H).
Joseph C. Carter, Cleveland, August 29, 1986, (A).
James A. Presley, Seattle, September 1, 1986, (H).
Reginald M. Jackson, California, September 18, 1986, (H).
J. Cory Snyder, Cleveland, May 21, 1987, (H).
Joseph C. Carter, Cleveland, May 28, 1987, (A).
Mark D. McGwire, Oakland, June 27, 1987, (A).
Bill Madlock, Detroit, June 28, 1987, 11 inn., (A).
BROOK W. JACOBY, Cleveland, July 3, 1987, (H).
Dale C. Sveum, Milwaukee, July 17, 1987, (H).
Michael C. Brantley, Seattle, September 14, 1987, (H).
L. Ernest Whitt, Toronto, September 14, 1987, (H).
Wallace K. Joyner, California, October 3, 1987, (H).

Note—Capitalized name denotes consecutive homers (bases on balls excluded).
*First game. †Second game.

Clubs With Five Homers In Inning
National League (3)

Date		Inn.	Club and Players
June	6, 1939	4	New York (Danning, Demaree, WHITEHEAD, SALVO, MOORE).
June	2, 1949	8	Philadelphia (Ennis, Seminick, Jones, Rowe, Seminick).
Aug.	23, 1961	9	San Francisco (Cepeda, F. Alou, Davenport, Mays, Orsino).

American League (1)

Date		Inn.	Club and Players
June	9, 1966	7	Minnesota (Rollins, Versalles, OLIVA, MINCHER, KILLEBREW).

Note—Capitalized letters denote three or more homers were consecutive.
*First Game. †Second Game.

Clubs With Four Homers In Inning
National League (13)

Date		Inn.	Club and Players
June	6, 1894	3	Pittsburgh (Stenzel, Lyons, Bierbauer, Stenzel).
May	12, 1930	7	Chicago (Heathcote, Wilson, Grimm, Beck).
Aug.	13, 1939*	4	New York (Bonura, KAMPOURIS, LOHRMAN, MOORE).
June	6, 1948*	6	St. Louis (Dusak, Schoendienst, Slaughter, Jones).
May	28, 1954	8	New York (Williams, Dark, Irvin, Gardner).
July	8, 1956*	4	New York (Mays, THOMPSON, SPENCER, WESTRUM).
June	8, 1961	7	Milwaukee (MATHEWS, AARON, ADCOCK, THOMAS).
June	8, 1965	10	Milwaukee (Torre, Mathews, Aaron, Oliver).
July	10, 1970	9	San Diego (Murrell, Spiezio, Campbell, Gaston).
June	21, 1971*	8	Atlanta (Lum, King, H. Aaron, Evans).
July	30, 1978	3	Montreal (Dawson, Parrish, Cash, Dawson).
Aug.	17, 1985	7	Philadelphia (SAMUEL, WILSON, SCHMIDT, Daulton).
Apr.	29, 1986	4	Montreal (Dawson, Brooks, Wallach, Fitzgerald).

American League (13)

Date		Inn.	Club and Players
Sept.	24, 1940*	6	Boston (WILLIAMS, FOXX, CRONIN, Tabor).
June	23, 1950	4	Detroit (Trout, Priddy, Wertz, Evers).
May	22, 1957	6	Boston (Mauch, Williams, Gernert, Malzone).
Aug.	26, 1957	7	Boston (Zauchin, Lepcio, Piersall, Malzone).
July	31, 1963†	6	Cleveland (HELD, RAMOS, FRANCONA, BROWN).
May	2, 1964	11	Minnesota (OLIVA, ALLISON, HALL, KILLEBREW).
May	17, 1967	7	Baltimore (Etchebarren, Bowens, Powell, D. Johnson).
July	29, 1974	1	Detroit (KALINE, FREEHAN, STANLEY, Brinkman).
June	17, 1977	1	Boston (Burleson, Lynn, Fisk, Scott).
July	4, 1977	8	Boston (LYNN, RICE, YASTRZEMSKI, Scott).
May	31, 1980	4	Boston (Stapleton, PEREZ, FISK, HOBSON).
May	16, 1983	9	Minnesota (Engle, Mitchell, Gaetti, Hatcher).
Sept.	10, 1986	4	Detroit (Lemon, Heath, Gibson, Coles).

Note—Capitalized letters denote three or more homers were consecutive.
*First game. †Second game.

Clubs With Three Consecutive Homers In Inning
National League (49)

Date		Inn.	Club and Players
May	10, 1894	7	St. Louis (SHUGART, MILLER, PEITZ).
Aug.	13, 1932*	4	New York (TERRY, OTT, LINDSTROM).
June	10, 1935	8	Pittsburgh (P. WANER, VAUGHAN, YOUNG).
July	9, 1938	3	Boston (CUCCINELLO, WEST, FLETCHER).
June	6, 1939‡	4	New York (WHITEHEAD, SALVO, MOORE).
Aug.	13, 1939*‡	4	New York (KAMPOURIS, LOHRMAN, MOORE).
Aug.	11, 1941	5	Chicago (CAVARRETTA, HACK, NICHOLSON).
June	11, 1944†	8	St. Louis (W. COOPER, KUROWSKI, LITWHILER).
Aug.	11, 1946*	8	Cincinnati (HATTON, WEST, MUELLER).
June	20, 1948†	8	New York (MIZE, MARSHALL, GORDON).
June	4, 1949	6	New York (LOCKMAN, GORDON, MARSHALL).
April	19, 1952	7	Brooklyn (CAMPANELLA, PAFKO, SNIDER).
Sept.	27, 1952	7	Pittsburgh (KINER, GARAGIOLA, BELL).
Sept.	4, 1953	4	New York (WESTRUM, CORWIN, LOCKMAN).
June	20, 1954	6	New York (HOFMAN, WESTRUM, RHODES).
Aug.	15, 1954	9	Cincinnati (BELL, KLUSZEWSKI, GREENGRASS).
April	16, 1955	2	Chicago (JACKSON, BANKS, FONDY).
July	6, 1955*	6	Pittsburgh (LYNCH, THOMAS, LONG).

145

Date	Inn.	Club and Players
May 30, 1956*	1	Milwaukee (MATHEWS, AARON, THOMSON).
May 31, 1956	9	Cincinnati (BELL, KLUSZEWSKI, ROBINSON).
June 29, 1956	9	Brooklyn (SNIDER, JACKSON, HODGES).
July 8, 1956*‡	4	New York (THOMPSON, SPENCER, WESTRUM).
April 21, 1957*	3	Pittsburgh (THOMAS, SMITH, GROAT).
June 26, 1957	5	Milwaukee (AARON, MATHEWS, COVINGTON).
May 7, 1958	5	Pittsburgh (SKINNER, KLUSZEWSKI, THOMAS).
May 31, 1958	1	Milwaukee (AARON, MATHEWS, COVINGTON).
June 8, 1961‡	7	Milw. (MATHEWS, AARON, ADCOCK, THOMAS).
June 18, 1961	3	Milwaukee (AARON, ADCOCK, THOMAS).
April 28, 1962	6	New York (THOMAS, NEAL, HODGES).
Aug. 27, 1963	3	San Francisco (MAYS, CEPEDA, F. ALOU).
July 18, 1964	8	St. Louis (BOYER, WHITE, McCARVER).
Aug. 5, 1969*	5	San Francisco (MARSHALL, HUNT, BONDS).
May 18, 1970	8	New York (MARSHALL, FOY, GROTE).
Aug. 1, 1970	7	Pittsburgh (ROBERTSON, STARGELL, PAGAN).
July 16, 1974	9	San Diego (COLBERT, McCOVEY, WINFIELD).
July 20, 1974	5	New York (THEODORE, STAUB, JONES).
May 17, 1977	5	Chicago (BIITTNER, MURCER, MORALES).
Sept. 30, 1977	2	Philadelphia (LUZINSKI, HEBNER, MADDOX).
Aug. 14, 1978	3	Atlanta (MATTHEWS, BURROUGHS, HORNER).
June 17, 1979	4	Montreal (PEREZ, CARTER, VALENTINE).
July 11, 1979	1	San Diego (TURNER, WINFIELD, TENACE).
May 27, 1980	3	Cincinnati (GRIFFEY, FOSTER, DRIESSEN).
Aug. 31, 1980†	2	Los Angeles (CEY, MONDAY, FERGUSON).
July 11, 1982	2	San Francisco (SMITH, MAY, SUMMERS).
June 24, 1984	5	Houston (CABELL, GARNER, CRUZ).
Aug. 17, 1985‡	7	Philadelphia (SAMUEL, WILSON, SCHMIDT).
July 27, 1986	3	New York (CARTER, STRAWBERRY, MITCHELL).
April 13, 1987	1	San Diego (WYNNE, GWYNN, KRUK).
July 26, 1987	8	Philadelphia (THOMPSON, HAYES, SCHMIDT).

American League (63)

Date	Inn.	Club and Players
June 30, 1902*	6	Cleveland (LAJOIE, HICKMAN, BRADLEY).
May 2, 1922	4	Philadelphia (WALKER, PERKINS, MILLER).
Sept. 10, 1925*	4	New York (MEUSEL, RUTH, GEHRIG).
May 4, 1929	7	New York (RUTH, GEHRIG, MEUSEL).
June 18, 1930	5	Philadelphia (SIMMONS, FOXX, MILLER).
July 17, 1934	4	Philadelphia (JOHNSON, FOXX, HIGGINS).
June 25, 1939*	7	Cleveland (CHAPMAN, TROSKY, HEATH).
Sept. 24, 1940*‡	6	Boston (WILLIAMS, FOXX, CRONIN).
May 23, 1946	5	New York (DiMAGGIO, ETTEN, GORDON).
April 23, 1947	8	Detroit (CULLENBINE, WAKEFIELD, EVERS).
May 13, 1947	6	New York (KELLER, DiMAGGIO, LINDELL).
April 19, 1948*	2	Boston (SPENCE, STEPHENS, DOERR).
June 6, 1948†	6	Boston (WILLIAMS, SPENCE, STEPHENS).
July 28, 1950	3	Cleveland (DOBY, ROSEN, EASTER).
Sept. 2, 1951	1	Cleveland (SIMPSON, ROSEN, EASTER).
July 16, 1953†	5	St. Louis (COURTNEY, KRYHOSKI, DYCK).
July 7, 1956	7	Detroit (KUENN, TORGESON, MAXWELL).
Sept. 7, 1959	2	Boston (BUDDIN, CASALE$ GREEN).
April 30, 1961†	7	Baltimore (GENTILE, TRIANDOS, HANSEN).
May 23, 1961	9	Detroit (CASH, BOROS, BROWN).
June 27, 1961	1	Washington (GREEN, TASBY, LONG).
June 17, 1962*	2	Cleveland (KINDALL, PHILLIPS, MAHONEY).
Aug. 19, 1962	7	Kansas City (CIMOLI, CAUSEY, BRYAN).
Aug. 28, 1962	4	Los Angeles (J. L. THOMAS, WAGNER, RODGERS).
July 31, 1963†‡	6	Cleveland (HELD, RAMOS, FRANCONA, BROWN).
May 2, 1964‡	11	Minnesota (OLIVA, ALLISON, HALL, KILLEBREW).
Sept. 10, 1965	8	Baltimore (ROBINSON, BLEFARY, ADAIR).
June 9, 1966‡	7	Minnesota (OLIVA, MINCHER, KILLEBREW).
June 29, 1966	3	New York (RICHARDSON, MANTLE, PEPITONE).
July 2, 1966	6	Washington (HOWARD, LOCK, McMULLEN).
June 22, 1969*	3	Oakland (KUBIAK, JACKSON, BANDO).
Aug. 10, 1969	6	New York (MURCER, MUNSON, MICHAEL).
Sept. 4, 1969	9	Baltimore (F. ROBINSON, POWELL, B. C. ROBINSON).
Aug. 22, 1970	6	Cleveland (SIMS, NETTLES, LEON).
April 17, 1971	7	Detroit (NORTHRUP, CASH, HORTON).
June 27, 1972	1	Detroit (RODRIGUEZ, KALINE, HORTON).
July 15, 1973	8	Minnesota (MITTERWALD, LIS, HOLT).
July 29, 1974‡	1	Detroit (KALINE, FREEHAN, STANLEY).
May 11, 1977	2	California (BONDS, BAYLOR, JACKSON).
July 4, 1977	8	Boston (LYNN, RICE, YASTRZEMSKI).
Aug. 13, 1977	6	Boston (SCOTT, HOBSON, EVANS).
May 8, 1979	6	Baltimore (MURRAY, MAY, ROENICKE).
May 31, 1980‡	4	Boston (PEREZ, FISK, HOBSON).
June 3, 1980	3	Oakland (REVERING, PAGE, ARMAS).
May 28, 1982	6	Milwaukee (COOPER, MONEY, THOMAS).
June 5, 1982	7	Milwaukee (YOUNT, COOPER, OGLIVIE).
June 7, 1982	8	Minnesota (WASHINGTON, BRUNANSKY, HRBEK).
Sept. 12, 1982	3	Milwaukee (COOPER, SIMMONS, OGLIVIE).
Aug. 2, 1983	3	Seattle (S. HENDERSON, D. HENDERSON, RAMOS).
Sept. 9, 1983	1	Chicago (FISK, PACIOREK, LUZINSKI).
April 24, 1984	4	California (R.M. JACKSON, DOWNING, GRICH).
April 26, 1984	6	Toronto (UPSHAW, BELL, BARFIELD).
May 29, 1984	6	New York (MATTINGLY, BAYLOR, WINFIELD).
June 3, 1984	4	New York (GAMBLE, KEMP, HARRAH).
June 29, 1984	5	Cleveland (THORNTON, HALL, WILLARD).
Aug. 19, 1984	7	Kansas City (MOTLEY, WHITE, BALBONI).
Aug. 24 1985	9	Chicago (LAW, LITTLE, BAINES).
Sept. 16 1985	8	Baltimore (RIPKEN, MURRAY, LYNN).
July 8, 1986	4	Detroit (GIBSON, PARRISH, EVANS).
July 31, 1986	5	Detroit (TRAMMELL, GIBSON, GRUBB).
Sept. 28, 1986	4	Kansas City (BRETT, WHITE, QUIRK).
June 28, 1987	9	Detroit (GRUBB, NOKES, MADLOCK).
Sept. 12, 1987	8	Toronto (WHITT, BARFIELD, GRUBER).

Players League (1)

Date	Inn.	Club and Players
May 31, 1890	8	New York (GORE, EWING, CONNOR).

Note—Capitalized letters denote three homers were consecutive.
*First game. †Second game. ‡Club had more than three homers in inning.

Six Hits In One Game

National League (68)

*First game. †Second game. H—At Home. A—On Road.

Player Club Date	Place	AB	R	H	2B	3B	HR
David Force, Philadelphia, June 27, 1876	H	6	3	6	1	0	0
Calvin A. McVey, Chicago, July 22, 1876	H	7	4	6	1	0	0
Calvin A. McVey, Chicago, July 25, 1876	H	7	4	6	1	0	0
Roscoe C. Barnes, Chicago, July 27, 1876	H	6	3	6	1	1	0
Paul A. Hines, Prov., Aug. 26, 1879 (10 inn.)	H	6	1	6	0	0	0
George Gore, Chicago, May 7, 1880	H	6	5	6	0	0	0
Lew P. Dickerson, Wor., June 16, 1881	H	6	3	6	0	1	0
Samuel W. Wise, Boston, June 20, 1883	H	7	5	6	1	1	0
Dennis L. Brouthers, Buff., July 19, 1883	H	6	3	6	2	0	0
Daniel Richardson, N.Y., June 11, 1887	H	7	2	6	0	0	0
Michael J. Kelly, Boston, August 27, 1887	H	7	6	6	1	0	1
Jeremiah Denny, Ind., May 4, 1889	H	6	3	6	1	0	1
Lawrence Twitchell, Cleve., Aug. 15, 1889	H	6	5	6	1	3	1
John W. Glasscock, N.Y., Sept. 27, 1890	A	6	2	6	0	0	0
Robert L. Lowe, Boston, June 11, 1891	H	6	4	6	1	0	1
Henry Larkin, Washington, June 7, 1892	H	7	3	6	0	1	0
Wilbert Robinson, Balt., June 10, 1892*	H	7	1	7	1	0	0
John J. Boyle, Phila., July 6, 1893 (11 inn.)	A	6	1	6	1	0	0
Richard Cooley, St. Louis, Sept. 30, 1893†	A	6	1	6	1	1	0
Edward J. Delahanty, Phila., June 16, 1894	H	6	4	6	1	0	0
Walter S. Brodie, Baltimore, July 9, 1894	H	6	2	6	2	1	0
Charles L. Zimmer, Cleve., July 11, 1894 (10 inn.)	H	6	3	6	2	0	0
Samuel L. Thompson, Phila., Aug. 17, 1894	H	7	4	6	1	1	1
Roger Connor, St. Louis, June 1, 1895	A	6	4	6	2	1	0
George S. Davis, N.Y., Aug. 15, 1895	A	6	3	6	2	1	0
Jacob C. Stenzel, Pitts., May 14, 1896	H	6	3	6	0	0	0
Fred C. Tenney, Boston, May 31, 1897	H	8	3	6	1	0	0
Richard Harley, St.L., June 24, 1897 (12 inn.)	A	6	2	6	1	0	0
William J. McCormick, Chi., June 29, 1897	H	8	5	6	0	1	1
Thomas J. Tucker, Washington, July 15, 1897	A	6	1	6	1	0	0
William H. Keeler, Baltimore, Sept. 3, 1897	H	6	5	6	0	1	0
John J. Doyle, Baltimore, Sept. 3, 1897	H	6	2	6	2	0	0
Charles S. Stahl, Boston, May 31, 1899	H	6	4	6	0	0	0
Clarence H. Beaumont, Pitts., July 22, 1899	H	6	6	6	0	0	0
Albert K. Selbach, N.Y., June 9, 1901	A	7	4	6	2	0	0
George W. Cutshaw, Bkn., August 9, 1915	A	6	2	6	0	0	0
Carson L. Bigbee, Pitts., Aug. 22, 1917 (22 inn.)	A	11	0	6	0	0	0
David J. Bancroft, N.Y., June 28, 1920	A	6	2	6	0	0	0
John B. Gooch, Pittsburgh, July 7, 1922 (18 inn.)	H	8	1	6	1	0	0
Max Carey, Pittsburgh, July 7, 1922 (18 inn.)	H	6	3	6	1	0	0
Jacques F. Fournier, Brooklyn, June 29, 1923	A	6	1	6	2	0	1
Hazen S. Cuyler, Pittsburgh, Aug. 9, 1924*	A	6	3	6	3	1	0
Frank F. Frisch, New York, Sept. 10, 1924*	H	7	3	6	0	0	1
James L. Bottomley, St.L., Sept. 16, 1924	A	6	3	6	1	0	2
Paul G. Waner, Pittsburgh, August 26, 1926	H	6	1	6	2	1	0
Lloyd J. Waner, Pitts., June 15, 1929 (14 inn.)	H	8	2	6	1	1	0
John H. DeBerry, Bkn., June 23, 1929 (14 inn.)	H	7	0	6	0	0	0
Walter J. Gilbert, Brooklyn, May 30, 1931†	A	7	3	6	1	0	0
James L. Bottomley, St.L., Aug. 5, 1931†	A	6	2	6	1	0	0
Anthony Cuccinello, Cin., Aug. 13, 1931*	A	6	4	6	2	1	0
Terry B. Moore, St. Louis, September 5, 1935	H	6	2	6	1	0	0
Ernest N. Lombardi, Cincinnati, May 9, 1937	A	6	3	6	1	0	0
Frank Demaree, Chi., July 5, 1937* (14 inn.)	H	7	2	6	3	0	0
Harry A. Lavagetto, Bkn., Sept. 23, 1939*	A	6	4	6	1	1	0
W. Walker Cooper, Cin., July 6, 1949	H	7	5	6	0	0	3
John L. Hopp, Pitts., May 14, 1950†	A	6	3	6	0	0	2
Cornelius J. Ryan, Phila., April 16, 1953	A	6	3	6	2	0	0
Richard M. Groat, Pitts., May 13, 1960	A	6	2	6	3	0	0
Jesus M. Alou, S.F., July 10, 1964	A	6	1	6	0	0	1
Joe L. Morgan, Hous., July 8, 1965 (12 inn.)	A	6	4	6	0	1	2
Felix B. Millan, Atlanta, July 6, 1970	H	6	2	6	1	1	0
Donald E. Kessinger, Chi., July 17, 1971 (10 inn.)	H	6	3	6	1	0	0
Willie H. Davis, L.A., May 24, 1973 (19 inn.)	H	9	1	6	0	0	0
Bill Madlock, Chicago, July 26, 1975 (10 inn.)	H	6	1	6	0	1	0
Renaldo A. Stennett, Pitts., Sept. 16, 1975	A	7	5	7	2	1	0
Jose D. Cardenal, Chicago, May 2, 1976* (14 inn.)	A	7	2	6	1	0	1
Eugene Richards, S.D., July 26, 1977† (15 inns.)	H	7	1	6	1	0	0
Joseph H. Lefebvre, S.D., Sept. 13, 1982 (16 inn.)	A	8	1	6	1	0	1

American League (38)

Player Club Date	Place	AB	R	H	2B	3B	HR
Michael J. Donlin, Balt., June 24, 1901	H	6	5	6	2	2	0
William G. Nance, Detroit, July 13, 1901	H	6	3	6	1	0	0
Erwin K. Harvey, Cleve., April 25, 1902	A	6	3	6	0	0	0
Daniel F. Murphy, Phila., July 8, 1902	A	6	3	6	0	0	1
James T. Williams, Baltimore, Aug. 25, 1902	H	6	1	6	1	1	0
Robert H. Veach, Det., Sept. 17, 1920 (12 inn.)	H	6	2	6	1	1	1
George H. Sisler, St.L., Aug. 9, 1921 (19 inn.)	A	9	2	6	0	1	0
Frank W. Brower, Cleveland, August 7, 1923	A	6	3	6	1	0	0
George H. Burns, Cleve., June 19, 1924*	A	6	2	6	3	1	0
Tyrus R. Cobb, Detroit, May 5, 1925	A	6	4	6	1	0	3
James E. Foxx, Phila., May 30, 1930* (13 inn.)	H	7	0	6	2	1	0
Roger M. Cramer, Philadelphia, June 20, 1932	A	6	3	6	0	0	0
Jas. E. Foxx, Phil., July 10, 1932, (18 inn.)	A	9	4	6	1	0	3
John H. Burnett, Cleve., July 10, 1932, (18 inn.)	H	11	4	9	2	0	0
Samuel West, St.L., April 13, 1933, (11 inn.)	H	6	2	6	1	0	0
Myril O. Hoag, New York, June 6, 1934*	A	6	3	6	0	0	0

Player Club Date	Place	AB	R	H	2B	3B	HR
Rob. Johnson, Phil., June 16, 1934† (11 inn.)	H	6	3	6	1	0	2
Roger M. Cramer, Phila., July 13, 1935*	H	6	3	6	1	0	0
Bruce D. Campbell, Cleve., July 2, 1936*	A	6	1	6	1	0	0
Raymond A. Radcliff, Chi., July 18, 1936†	A	7	4	6	2	0	0
Henry Steinbacher, Chi., June 22, 1938	H	6	3	6	1	0	0
George Myatt, Wash., May 1, 1944	A	6	3	6	1	0	0
Stanley O. Spence, Wash., June 1, 1944	A	6	2	6	0	0	1
George C. Kell, Detroit, Sept. 20, 1946	A	7	4	6	0	0	0
James R. Fridley, Cleve., April 29, 1952*	A	6	4	6	0	0	0
James A. Piersall, Bos., June 10, 1953*	A	6	2	6	1	0	0
Jos. DeMaestri, K.C., July 8, 1955 (11 inn.)	A	6	2	6	1	0	0
Jas. Runnels, Bos., Aug. 30, 1960* (15 inn.)	H	7	1	6	1	0	0
Rocco D. Colavito, Det., June 24, 1962, (22 inn.)	H	10	1	7	0	1	0
Floyd A. Robinson, Chicago, July 22, 1962	A	6	3	6	0	0	0
Robert L. Oliver, Kansas City, May 4, 1969	A	6	2	6	1	0	1
Jas. Northrup, Det., August 28, 1969, (13 inn.)	H	6	2	6	0	0	2
Cesar D. Gutierrez, Det., June 21, 1970† (12 inn.)	A	7	3	7	1	0	0
John E. Briggs, Milwaukee, Aug. 4, 1973	A	6	2	6	2	0	0
Jorge Orta, Cleveland, June 15, 1980	H	6	4	6	1	0	0
Gerald P. Remy, Bos., Sept. 3, 1981, (20 inn.)	H	10	2	6	0	0	0
Kevin L. Seitzer, K.C., August 2, 1987	H	6	4	6	1	0	2
Kirby Puckett, Minnesota, August 30, 1987	A	6	4	6	0	2	0

American Association (15)

Player Club Date	Place	AB	R	H	2B	3B	HR
William W. Carpenter, Cin., Sept. 12, 1883	H	7	5	6	0	0	0
John G. Reilly, Cin., Sept. 12, 1883	H	7	6	6	1	1	0
Oscar Walker, Brooklyn, May 31, 1884	H	6	5	6	1	1	0
Alonzo Knight, Phila., July 30, 1884	H	6	5	6	0	1	0
David L. Orr, New York, June 12, 1885	H	6	4	6	2	1	1
Henry Larkin, Phila., June 16, 1885	H	6	4	6	2	1	1
George B. Pinckney, Bkn., June 25, 1885	H	6	5	6	0	0	0
Walter L. Latham, St.L., April 24, 1886	H	6	5	6	0	1	0
Guy J. Hecker, Lou., Aug. 15, 1886†	H	7	7	6	0	0	3
H. Dennis Lyons, Phila., April 26, 1887	H	6	4	6	2	1	0
Peter J. Hotaling, Cleve., June 6, 1888	H	7	5	6	0	1	0
James J. McTamany, K.C., June 15, 1888	H	6	3	6	0	0	1
William D. O'Brien, Brooklyn, Aug. 8, 1889	A	6	1	6	3	0	0
William B. Weaver, Louisville, Aug. 12, 1890	H	6	3	6	1	2	0
Frank Sheibeck, Toledo, Sept. 27, 1890	H	6	4	6	1	1	0

Players League (2)

Player Club Date	Place	AB	R	H	2B	3B	HR
Edward J. Delahanty, Cleve., June 2, 1890	H	6	4	6	1	1	0
William Shindle, Phila., Aug. 26, 1890	H	6	3	6	2	1	0

Joe DiMaggio's 56-Game Hitting Streak—1941

Date	Opp. Pitcher and Club	AB	R	H	2B	3B	HR	RBI
May 15	Smith, Chicago	4	0	1	0	0	0	1
16	Lee, Chicago	4	2	2	0	1	1	1
17	Rigney, Chicago	3	1	1	0	0	0	0
18	Harris (2), Niggeling (1), St. L.	3	3	3	1	0	0	1
19	Galehouse, St. Louis	3	0	1	0	0	0	0
20	Auker, St. Louis	5	1	1	0	0	0	1
21	Rowe (1), Benton (1), Detroit	5	0	2	0	0	0	1
22	McKain, Detroit	4	0	1	0	0	0	0
23	Newsome, Boston	5	0	1	0	0	0	2
24	Johnson, Boston	4	2	1	0	0	0	2
25	Grove, Boston	4	0	1	0	0	0	0
27	Chase (1), Anderson (2), Carrasquel (1), Washington	5	3	4	0	0	1	3
28	Hudson, Washington (Night)	4	1	1	0	0	1	3
29	Sundra, Washington	3	1	1	0	0	0	0
30	Johnson, Boston	2	1	1	0	0	0	0
30	Harris, Boston	3	0	1	0	0	0	0
June 1	Milnar, Cleveland	4	1	1	0	0	0	0
1	Harder, Cleveland	4	0	1	0	0	0	0
2	Feller, Cleveland	4	2	2	1	0	0	0
3	Trout, Detroit	4	1	1	0	0	1	1
5	Newhouser, Detroit	5	1	1	0	1	0	1
7	Muncrief (1), Allen (1), Caster (1), St. Louis	5	2	3	0	0	0	1
8	Auker, St. Louis	4	3	2	0	0	2	4
8	Caster (1), Kramer (1), St. L.	4	1	2	1	0	2	3
10	Rigney, Chicago	5	1	1	0	0	0	0
12	Lee, Chicago (Night)	4	1	2	0	0	1	1
14	Feller, Cleveland	2	0	1	1	0	0	1
15	Bagby, Cleveland	3	1	1	0	0	1	1
16	Milnar, Cleveland	5	0	1	1	0	0	0
17	Rigney, Chicago	4	1	1	0	0	0	0
18	Lee, Chicago	3	0	1	0	0	0	0
19	Smith (1), Ross (2), Chicago	3	2	3	0	0	1	2
20	Newsom (2), McKain (2), Det.	5	3	4	1	0	0	1
21	Trout, Detroit	4	0	1	0	0	0	1
22	Newhouser (1), Newsom (1), Det.	5	1	2	1	0	1	2
24	Muncrief, St. Louis	4	1	1	0	0	0	0
25	Galehouse, St. Louis	4	1	1	0	0	1	3
26	Auker, St. Louis	4	0	1	0	0	0	1
27	Dean, Philadelphia	3	1	2	0	0	0	2
28	Babich (1), Harris (1), Phil.	5	1	2	1	0	0	0
29	Leonard, Washington	4	1	1	0	0	0	0
29	Anderson, Washington	5	1	1	0	0	0	1
July 1	Harris (1), Ryba (1), Boston	4	0	2	0	0	0	1
1	Wilson, Boston	3	1	1	0	0	0	0
2	Newsome, Boston	5	1	1	0	0	1	3

Date	Opp. Pitcher and Club	AB	R	H	2B	3B	HR	RBI
5	Marchildon, Philadelphia	4	2	1	0	0	1	2
6	Babich (1), Hadley (3), Phil.	5	2	4	1	0	1	2
6	Knott, Philadelphia	4	0	2	0	1	0	2
10	Niggeling, St. Louis (Night)	2	0	1	0	0	0	0
11	Harris (3), Kramer (1), St. L.	5	1	4	0	0	1	2
12	Auker (1), Muncrief (1), St. L.	5	1	2	1	0	0	1
13	Lyons (2), Hallett (1), Chicago	4	2	3	0	0	0	0
13	Lee, Chicago	4	0	1	0	0	0	0
14	Rigney, Chicago	3	0	1	0	0	0	0
15	Smith, Chicago	4	1	2	1	0	0	0
16	Milnar (2), Krakauskas (1), Cle.	4	3	3	1	0	0	0
Totals for 56 games		223	56	91	16	4	15	55

Stopped July 17 at Cleveland, New York won, 4 to 3. First inning, Alfred J. Smith pitching, thrown out by Keltner; fourth inning, Smith pitching, received base on balls; seventh inning, Smith pitching, thrown out by Keltner; eighth inning, James C. Bagby, Jr., pitching, grounded into double play.

Babe Ruth's 60 Home Runs—1927

HR No.	Team game No.	Date	Opposing Pitcher and Club	Place	Inn.	O.B.
1	4	April 15	Ehmke (R), Phila.	H	1	0
2	11	April 23	Walberg (L), Phila.	A	1	0
3	12	April 24	Thurston (R), Wash.	A	6	0
4	14	April 29	Harriss (R), Boston	A	5	0
5	16	May 1	Quinn (R), Phila.	H	1	1
6	16	May 1	Walberg (L), Phila.	H	8	0
7	24	May 10	Gaston (R), St. Louis	A	1	2
8	25	May 11	Nevers (R), St. Louis	A	1	0
9	29	May 17	Collins (R), Detroit	A	8	0
10	33	May 22	Karr (R), Cleveland	A	6	0
11	34	May 23	Thurston (R), Wash.	A	1	0
12	37	May 28*	Thurston (R), Wash.	H	7	0
13	39	May 29	MacFayden (R), Boston	H	8	0
14	41	May 30‡	Walberg (L), Phila.	A	11	0
15	42	May 31*	Quinn (R), Phila.	A	1	1
16	43	May 31†	Ehmke (R), Phila.	A	5	0
17	47	June 5	Whitehill (L), Detroit	H	6	0
18	48	June 7	Thomas (R), Chi.	H	4	0
19	52	June 11	Buckeye (L), Cleve.	H	3	0
20	52	June 11	Buckeye (L), Cleve.	H	5	0
21	53	June 12	Uhle (R), Cleveland	H	7	0
22	55	June 16	Zachary (L), St. L.	H	1	0
23	60	June 22*	Wiltse (L), Boston	A	5	0
24	60	June 22*	Wiltse (L), Boston	A	7	0
25	70	June 30	Harriss (R), Boston	H	4	0
26	73	July 3	Lisenbee (R), Wash.	A	1	0
27	78	July 8†	Hankins (R), Detroit	A	2	1
28	79	July 9*	Holloway (R), Detroit	A	1	2
29	79	July 9*	Holloway (R), Detroit	A	4	2
30	83	July 12	Shaute (L), Cleve.	A	9	0
31	94	July 24	Thomas (R), Chi.	A	3	0
32	95	July 26*	Gaston (R), St. Louis	H	1	0
33	95	July 26*	Gaston (R), St. Louis	H	6	0
34	98	July 28	Stewart (L), St. L.	H	8	0
35	106	Aug. 5	Smith (R), Detroit	H	8	0
36	110	Aug. 10	Zachary (L), Wash.	A	3	2
37	114	Aug. 16	Thomas (R), Chi.	A	5	0
38	115	Aug. 17	Connally (R), Chi.	A	11	0
39	118	Aug. 20	Miller (L), Cleveland	A	1	0
40	120	Aug. 22	Shaute (L), Cleve.	A	6	0
41	124	Aug. 27	Nevers (R), St. Louis	A	8	0
42	125	Aug. 28	Wingard (L), St. Louis	A	1	0
43	127	Aug. 31	Welzer (R), Boston	H	8	0
44	128	Sept. 2	Walberg (L), Phila.	A	1	0
45	132	Sept. 6*	Welzer (R), Boston	A	6	1
46	132	Sept. 6*	Welzer (R), Boston	A	7	0
47	133	Sept. 6†	Russell (R), Boston	A	9	0
48	134	Sept. 7	MacFayden (R), Boston	A	1	0
49	134	Sept. 7	Harriss (R), Boston	A	8	0
50	138	Sept. 11	Gaston (R), St. Louis	H	4	0
51	139	Sept. 13*	Hudlin (R), Cleveland	H	7	0
52	140	Sept. 13†	Shaute (L), Cleveland	H	4	0
53	143	Sept. 16	Blankenship (R), Chicago	H	3	0
54	147	Sept. 18†	Lyons (R), Chicago	H	5	0
55	148	Sept. 21	Gibson (L), Detroit	H	9	0
56	149	Sept. 22	Holloway (R), Detroit	H	9	0
57	152	Sept. 27	Grove (L), Phila.	H	6	3
58	153	Sept. 29	Lisenbee (R), Wash.	H	1	0
59	153	Sept. 29	Hopkins (R), Washington	H	5	3
60	154	Sept. 30	Zachary (L), Wash.	H	8	1

*First game of doubleheader. †Second game of doubleheader. ‡Afternoon game of split doubleheader.

New York A. L. played 155 games in 1927 (one tie on April 14), with Ruth participating in 151 games. (No home run for Ruth in game No. 155 on October 1).

Roger Maris' 61 Home Runs—1961

HR No.	Team game No.	Date	Opposing Pitcher and Club	Place	Inn.	O.B.
1	11	April 26	Foytack (R), Detroit	A	5	0
2	17	May 3	Ramos (R), Minnesota	A	7	2
3	20	May 6	Grba (R), Los Angeles	A	5	0
4	29	May 17	Burnside (L), Washington	H	8	1
5	30	May 19	Perry (R), Cleveland	A	1	1

HR No.	Team game No.	Date	Opposing Pitcher and Club	Place	Inn.	O.B.
6	31	May 20	Bell (R), Cleveland	A	3	0
7	32	May 21	Estrada (R), Baltimore	H	1	0
8	35	May 24	Conley (R), Boston	H	4	1
9	38	May 28	McLish (R), Chicago	H	2	1
10	40	May 30	Conley (R), Boston	A	3	0
11	40	May 30	Fornieles (R), Boston	A	8	2
12	41	May 31	Muffett (L), Boston	A	3	0
13	43	June 2	McLish (R), Chicago	A	3	2
14	44	June 3	Shaw (R), Chicago	A	8	2
15	45	June 4	Kemmerer (R), Chicago	A	3	0
16	48	June 6	Palmquist (R), Minnesota	H	6	2
17	49	June 7	Ramos (R), Minnesota	H	3	2
18	52	June 9	Herbert (R), Kan. City	H	7	1
19	55	June 11†	Grba (R), Los Angeles	H	3	0
20	55	June 11†	James (R), Los Angeles	H	7	0
21	57	June 13	Perry (R), Cleveland	A	6	0
22	58	June 14	Bell (R), Cleveland	A	4	1
23	61	June 17	Mossi (L), Detroit	A	4	0
24	62	June 18	Casale (R), Detroit	A	8	1
25	63	June 19	Archer (L), Kansas City	A	9	0
26	64	June 20	Nuxhall (L), Kansas City	A	1	0
27	66	June 22	Bass (R), Kansas City	A	2	1
28	74	July 1	Sisler (R), Washington	H	9	1
29	75	July 2	Burnside (L), Washington	H	3	2
30	75	July 2	Klippstein (R), Washington	H	7	1
31	77	July 4†	Lary (R), Detroit	H	8	0
32	78	July 5	Funk (R), Cleveland	H	7	0
33	82	July 9*	Monbouquette (R), Bos.	H	7	0
34	84	July 13	Wynn (R), Chicago	A	1	0
35	86	July 15	Herbert (R), Chicago	A	3	0
36	92	July 21	Monbouquette (R), Bos.	A	1	0
37	95	July 25*	Baumann (L), Chicago	H	4	0
38	95	July 25*	Larsen (R), Chicago	H	8	0
39	96	July 25*	Kemmerer (R), Chicago	H	4	0
40	96	July 25†	Hacker (R), Chicago	H	6	2
41	106	Aug. 4	Pascual (R), Minnesota	H	1	2
42	114	Aug. 11	Burnside (L), Washington	A	5	0
43	115	Aug. 12	Donovan (R), Washington	A	4	0
44	116	Aug. 13*	Daniels (R), Washington	A	4	0
45	117	Aug. 13†	Kutyna (R), Washington	A	1	0
46	118	Aug. 15	Pizarro (L), Chicago	H	4	0
47	119	Aug. 16	Pierce (L), Chicago	H	1	1
48	119	Aug. 16	Pierce (L), Chicago	H	3	1
49	124	Aug. 20	Perry (R), Cleveland	A	3	1
50	125	Aug. 22	McBride (R), L. Angeles	A	6	1
51	129	Aug. 26	Walker (R), Kansas City	A	6	0
52	135	Sept. 2	Lary (R), Detroit	H	6	0
53	135	Sept. 2	Aguirre (L), Detroit	H	8	1
54	140	Sept. 6	Cheney (R), Washington	H	4	0
55	141	Sept. 7	Stigman (L), Cleveland	H	3	0
56	143	Sept. 9	Grant (R), Cleveland	H	7	0
57	151	Sept. 16	Lary (R), Detroit	A	3	1
58	152	Sept. 17	Fox (R), Detroit	A	12	1

HR No.	Team game No.	Date	Opposing Pitcher and Club	Place	Inn.	O.B.
59	155	Sept. 20	Pappas (R), Baltimore	A	3	0
60	159	Sept. 26	Fisher (R), Baltimore	H	3	0
61	163	Oct. 1	Stallard (R), Boston	H	4	0

*First game of doubleheader. †Second game of doubleheader.

New York played 163 games in 1961 (one tie on April 22). Maris did not hit homer in this game. Maris played in 161 games.

30 Stolen Bases & 30 Homers In Season
American League (6)

Player	Year	G.	SB.	HR.
Kenneth R. Williams, St. Louis	1922	153	37	39
Tommy Harper, Milwaukee	1970	154	38	31
Bobby L. Bonds, New York	1975	145	30	32
Bobby L. Bonds, California	1977	158	41	37
Bobby L. Bonds, Chicago, Texas	1978	156	43	31
Joseph C. Carter, Cleveland	1987	149	31	32

National League (9)

Player	Year	G.	SB.	HR.
Willie H. Mays, New York	1956	152	40	36
Willie H. Mays, New York	1957	152	38	35
Henry L. Aaron, Milwaukee	1963	161	31	44
Bobby L. Bonds, San Francisco	1969	158	45	32
Bobby L. Bonds, San Francisco	1973	160	43	39
Dale B. Murphy, Atlanta	1983	162	30	36
Eric K. Davis, Cincinnati	1987	129	50	37
Howard M. Johnson, New York	1987	157	32	36
Darryl E. Strawberry, New York	1987	154	36	39

50 Stolen Bases & 20 Homers In Season
American League (2)

Player	Year	G.	SB.	HR.
Rickey H. Henderson, New York	1985	143	80	24
Rickey H. Henderson, New York	1986	153	87	28

National League (10)

Player	Year	G.	SB.	HR.
Louis C. Brock, St. Louis	1967	159	52	21
Cesar Cedeno, Houston	1972	139	55	22
Cesar Cedeno, Houston	1973	139	56	25
Joe L. Morgan, Cincinnati	1973	157	67	26
Cesar Cedeno, Houston	1974	160	57	26
Joe L. Morgan, Cincinnati	1974	149	58	22
Joe L. Morgan, Cincinnati	1976	141	60	27
Ryne D. Sandberg, Chicago	1985	153	54	26
Eric K. Davis, Cincinnati	1986	132	80	27
Eric K. Davis, Cincinnati	1987	129	50	37

.400 Hitters (42)

Year	Player and Club	B.A.
1887	James O'Neill, St. L. AA	*†.492
1887	L. Rogers Browning, Lou. AA	*†.471
1887	Dennis P. Lyons, Phil. AA	†.469
1887	Robert L. Caruthers, St. L. AA	†.459
1894	Hugh Duffy, Bos. NL	.438
1897	William H. Keeler, Balt. NL	*.432
1887	William Robinson, St. L. AA	†.426
1924	Rogers Hornsby, St. L. NL	*.424
1894	George Turner, Phil. NL	.423
1895	Jesse C. Burkett, Clev. NL	.423
1901	Napoleon Lajoie, Phil. AL	*.422
1887	Adrian C. Anson, Chi. NL	.421
1884	Fred Dunlap, St. L. UA	.420
1911	Tyrus R. Cobb, Det. AL	*.420
1922	George H. Sisler, St. L. AL	*.420
1887	Dennis Brouthers, Det. NL	†.419
1887	Joseph Mack, Lou. AA	†.410
1896	Jesse C. Burkett, Clev. NL	*.410
1912	Tyrus R. Cobb, Det. AL	.410
1893	Jacob Stenzel, Pit. NL	.409
1884	Thomas Esterbrook, N.Y. AA	.408
1899	Edward J. Delahanty, Phil. NL	*.408
1911	Joseph J. Jackson, Clev. AL	*.408
1879	Adrian C. Anson, Chi. NL	.407
1920	George H. Sisler, St. L. AL	*.407
1887	Samuel Thompson, Det. NL	.406

Year	Player and Club	B.A.
1897	Fred C. Clarke, Lou. NL	*.406
1941	Theodore S. Williams, Bos. AL	*.406
1876	Roscoe C. Barnes, Chi. NL	.404
1884	Harry D. Stovey, Phil. AA	.404
1887	Paul Radford, N.Y. AA	.404
1894	Samuel Thompson, Phil. NL	*.404
1887	Dave Orr, N.Y. AA	†.403
1923	Harry E. Heilmann, Det. AL	*.403
1925	Rogers Hornsby, St. L. NL	*.403
1887	Harry D. Stovey, Phil. AA	†.402
1899	Jesse C. Burkett, St. L. NL	*.402
1887	Harry D. Stovey, Balt. AA	†.401
1922	Tyrus R. Cobb, Det. AL	*.401
1922	Rogers Hornsby, St. L. NL	*.401
1930	William H. Terry, N.Y. NL	*.401
1894	Edward J. Delahanty, Phil. NL	*.400

*Qualify as .400 hitters under present rule 10.23 of Official Baseball Rules.
†Bases on balls counted as hits in 1887.

30-Game Batting Streaks (30)

Year	Player and Club	G.
1941	Joseph P. DiMaggio, N.Y. AL	56
1897	*William H. Keeler, Balt. NL	44
1978	Peter E. Rose, Cin. NL	44

Year	Player and Club	G.
1894	William F. Dahlen, Chi. NL	42
1922	George H. Sisler, St. L. AL	41
1911	Tyrus R. Cobb, Det. AL	40
1987	Paul L. Molitor, Mil. AL	39
1945	Thomas F. Holmes, Bos. NL	37
1894	William R. Hamilton, Phil. NL	36
1895	Fred C. Clarke, Lou. NL	35
1917	Tyrus R. Cobb, Det. AL	35
1925	*George H. Sisler, St. L. AL	34
1930	Jonathan F. Stone, Det. AL	34
1938	George H. McQuinn, St. L. AL	34
1949	Dominic P. DiMaggio, Bos. AL	34
1987	Benito Santiago, S.D. NL	34
1893	George S. Davis, N.Y. NL	33
1922	Rogers Hornsby, St. L. NL	33
1933	Henry E. Manush, Wash. AL	33
1899	Edward J. Delahanty, Phil. NL	31
1924	Edgar C. Rice, Wash. AL.	31
1969	Willie H. Davis, L.A. NL	31
1970	Ricardo A. J. Carty, Atl. NL	31
1980	Kenneth F. Landreaux, Minn. AL	31
1898	Elmer E. Smith, Cin. NL	30
1912	Tristram E. Speaker, Bos. AL	30
1934	Leon A. Goslin, Det. AL	30
1950	Stanley F. Musial, St. L. NL	30
1976	*Ronald LeFlore, Det. AL	30
1980	George H. Brett, K.C. AL	30

*From start of season.

Pitching
20-Game Winners
National League

(Number in parentheses after club denotes position of team at close of season)

1876 (5)

	W.	L.
Albert Spalding, Chicago (1)	47	13
George Bradley, St. Louis (2)	45	19
Thomas H. Bond, Hartford (3)	32	13
James Devlin, Louisville (5)	30	34
Robert Mathews, New York (6)	21	34

1877 (3)

	W.	L.
Thomas H. Bond, Boston (1)	31	17
James Devlin, Louisville (2)	28	20
Frank Larkin, Hartford (3)	22	21

1878 (4)

	W.	L.
Thomas Bond, Boston (1)	40	19
William White, Cincinnati (2)	29	21
Frank Larkin, Chicago (4)	29	26
John Ward, Providence (3)	22	13

1879 (6)

	W.	L.
John Ward, Providence (1)	44	18
William White, Cincinnati (5)	43	31
Thomas Bond, Boston (2)	42	19
James Galvin, Buffalo (3T)	37	27
Frank Larkin, Chicago (3T)	30	23
James McCormick, Cleve. (6)	20	40

1880 (8)

	W.	L.
James McCormick, Cleve. (3)	45	28
Lawrence Corcoran, Chi. (1)	43	14
John Ward, Providence (2)	40	23
Michael Welch, Troy (4)	34	30
J. Lee Richmond, Worc. (5)	31	33
Thomas Bond, Boston (6)	26	29
Frederick Goldsmith, Chi.(1)	22	3
James Galvin, Buffalo (7)	20	37

1881 (9)

	W.	L.
Lawrence Corcoran, Chi. (1)	31	14
James Whitney, Boston (6)	31	33
James Galvin, Buffalo (3)	29	24
George Derby, Detroit (4)	29	26
James McCormick, Cleve. (7)	26	30
Charles Radbourn, Prov. (2)	25	11
Frederick Goldsmith, Chi. (1)	25	13
J. Lee Richmond, Worcester (8)	25	27
Michael Welch, Troy (5)	21	18

1882 (7)

	W.	L.
James McCormick, Cleve. (5)	36	29
Charles Radbourn, Prov. (2)	31	19
James Galvin, Buffalo (3T)	28	22
Frederick Goldsmith, Chi. (1)	28	16
Lawrence Corcoran, Chi. (1)	27	13
George Weidman, Detroit (6)	26	20
James Whitney, Boston (3T)	24	22

1883 (9)

	W.	L.
Charles Radbourn, Prov. (3)	49	25
James Galvin, Buffalo (5)	46	29
James Whitney, Boston (1)	38	22
Lawrence Corcoran, Chi. (2)	31	21
Frederick Goldsmith, Chi. (2)	28	18
James McCormick, Cleve. (4)	27	13
Michael Welch, New York (4)	25	23
Charles Buffinton, Boston (1)	24	13
Hugh Daly, Cleveland (4)	24	18

1884 (7)

	W.	L.
Charles Radbourn, Prov. (1)	60	12
Charles Buffinton, Boston (2)	47	16
James Galvin, Buffalo (3)	46	22
Michael Welch, New York (4T)	39	21
Lawrence Corcoran, Chi. (4T)	35	23
James Whitney, Boston (2)	24	17
Charles Ferguson, Phila. (6)	21	24

1885 (9)

	W.	L.
John Clarkson, Chicago (1)	53	16
Michael Welch, New York (2)	44	11
Timothy Keefe, New York (2)	32	13
Charles Ferguson, Phila. (3)	26	19
Charles Radbourn, Prov. (4)	26	20
Edward Dailey, Phila. (3)	26	22
Frederick Shaw, Prov. (4)	23	26
Charles Buffinton, Boston (5)	22	27
James McCormick, 1-3 Providence (4) 20-4 Chicago (1)	21	7

1886 (11)

	W.	L.
Charles Baldwin, Detroit (2)	42	13
Timothy Keefe, New York (3)	42	20
John Clarkson, Chicago (1)	35	17
Michael Welch, New York (3)	33	22
Charles Ferguson, Phila. (4)	32	9
Charles Getzein, Detroit (2)	31	11
James McCormick, Chicago (1)	31	11
Charles Radbourn, Boston (5)	27	30
Daniel Casey, Philadelphia (4)	25	19
John Flynn, Chicago (1)	24	6
William Stemmeyer, Boston (5)	22	18

1887 (11)

	W.	L.
John Clarkson, Chicago (3)	38	21
Timothy Keefe, New York (4)	35	19
Charles Getzein, Detroit (2)	29	13
Daniel Casey, Philadelphia (2)	28	13
James Galvin, Pittsburgh (6)	28	21
James Whitney, Wash. (7)	24	21
Charles Radbourn, Boston (5)	24	23
Michael Welch, New York (4)	22	15
Michael Madden, Boston (5)	22	14
Charles Ferguson, Phila. (2)	21	10
Charles Buffinton, Phila. (2)	21	17

1888 (8)

	W.	L.
Timothy Keefe, New York (1)	35	12
John Clarkson, Boston (4)	33	20
Peter Conway, Detroit (5)	30	14
Edward Morris, Pittsburgh (6)	29	23
Charles Buffinton, Phila. (3)	28	17
Michael Welch, New York (1)	26	19
August Krock, Chicago (2)	25	14
James Galvin, Pittsburgh (6)	23	25

1889 (10)

	W.	L.
John Clarkson, Boston (2)	49	19
Timothy Keefe, New York (1)	28	13
Michael Welch, New York (1)	27	12
Charles Buffinton, Phila. (4)	26	17
James Galvin, Pittsburgh (5)	23	16
John O'Brien, Cleveland (6)	22	17
Henry Staley, Pittsburgh (5)	21	26
Charles Radbourn, Boston (2)	20	11
Edward Beatin, Cleveland (6)	20	14
Henry Boyle, Indianapolis (7)	20	23

1890 (13)

	W.	L.
William Hutchinson, Chi. (2)	42	25
William Gleason, Phila. (3)	38	16
Thomas Lovett, Brooklyn (1)	32	11
Amos Rusie, New York (6)	29	30
William Rhines, Cincinnati (4)	28	17
Charles Nichols, Boston (5)	27	19
John Clarkson, Boston (5)	26	18
William Terry, Brooklyn (1)	25	16
Charles Getzen, Boston (5)	24	18
Robert Caruthers, Brooklyn (1)	23	11
Thomas Vickery, Phila. (3)	22	23
Edward Beatin, Cleveland (7)	22	31
John Luby, Chicago (2)	21	9

1891 (12)

	W.	L.
William Hutchinson, Chi. (2)	43	19
John Clarkson, Boston (1)	34	19
Amos Rusie, New York (3)	32	19
Charles Nichols, Boston (1)	30	17
Denton Young, Cleveland (5)	27	20
William Gleason, Phila. (4)	24	19
Anthony Mullane, Cin. (7)	24	25
John Ewing, New York (3)	22	8
Henry Staley, 4-3 Pittsburgh (8) 17-10 Boston (1)	21	13
Thomas Lovett, Brooklyn (6)	21	20
Marcus Baldwin, Pitts. (8)	21	27
Charles Esper, Philadelphia (4)	20	14

1892 (22)

	W.	L.
William Hutchinson, Chi. (7)	37	34
Denton Young, Cleveland (2)	36	11
Charles Nichols, Boston (1)	35	16
John Stivetts, Boston (1)	33	14
George Haddock, Brooklyn (3)	31	13
Amos Rusie, New York (8)	31	28
Frank Killen, Washington (10)	30	23
George Cuppy, Cleveland (2)	28	12
August Weyhing, Phila. (4)	28	18
Marcus Baldwin, Pitts. (6)	27	20
Edward Stein, Brooklyn (3)	26	16
Henry Staley, Boston (1)	24	11
John Clarkson, 8-6 Boston (1) 16-10 Cleveland (2)	24	16
Addison Gumbert, Chicago (7)	23	21
Charles King, New York (8)	22	24
Anthony Mullane, Cin. (5)	21	10
William Terry 2-4, Balt. (12) 19-6 Pittsburgh (6)	21	10
John Dwyer 3-11, St. Louis (11) 18-8 Cincinnati (5)	21	19
Scott Stratton, Louisville (9)	21	19
Elton Chamberlain, Cin. (5)	20	22
William Gleason, St. Louis (11)	20	24
John McMahon, Baltimore (12)	20	25

1893 (7)

	W.	L.
Frank Killen, Pittsburgh (2)	34	10
Charles Nichols, Boston (1)	34	14
Denton Young, Cleveland (3)	32	16
Amos Rusie, New York (5)	29	18
William Kennedy, Brkn. (6T)	26	19
John McMahon, Baltimore (8)	24	16
August Weyhing, Phila. (4)	24	16

1894 (13)

	W.	L.
Amos Rusie, New York (2)	36	13
Jouett Meekin, New York (2)	34	9
Charles Nichols, Boston (3)	32	13
John Stivetts, Boston (3)	28	13
Theo. Breitenstein, St. L. (9)	27	23
John McMahon, Baltimore (1)	25	8
Edward Stein, Brooklyn (5)	25	15
Denton Young, Cleveland (6)	25	23
George Cuppy, Cleveland (6)	23	17
John Taylor, Philadelphia (4)	22	12
William Kennedy, Brkn. (5)	22	20
Clark Griffith, Chicago (8)	21	11
John Dwyer, Cincinnati (10)	20	18

1895 (13)

	W.	L.
Denton Young, Cleveland (2)	35	10
Emerson Hawley, Pitts. (7)	32	13
William Hoffer, Baltimore (1)	30	7
John Taylor, Philadelphia (3)	26	13
Wilfred Carsey, Phila. (3)	26	15
Charles Nichols, Boston (5T)	26	15
Clark Griffith, Chicago (4)	25	13
George Cuppy, Cleveland (2)	25	15
William Terry, Chicago (4)	23	13
Amos Rusie, New York (9)	22	21
George Hemming, Balti. (1)	20	10
William Rhines, Cincinnati (8)	20	10
Theo. Breitenstein, St. L. (11)	20	29

1896 (12)

	W.	L.
Charles Nichols, Boston (4)	30	14
Frank Killen, Pittsburgh (6)	29	15
Denton Young, Cleveland (2)	29	16
William Hoffer, Baltimore (1)	26	7
Jouett Meekin, New York (7)	26	13
John Dwyer, Cincinnati (3)	25	10
George Cuppy, Cleveland (2)	25	15
George Mercer, Wash. (9T)	25	19
Clark Griffith, Chicago (5)	22	13
John Stivetts, Boston (5)	22	13
John Taylor, Philadelphia (8)	21	20
Emerson Hawley, Pitts. (6)	21	21

1897 (13)

	W.	L.
Charles Nichols, Boston (1)	31	11
Amos Rusie, New York (3)	29	8
Frederick Klobedanz, Bos. (1)	25	8
Joseph Corbett, Baltimore (2)	24	8
George Mercer, Wash. (6T)	24	21
Theo. Breitenstein, Cin. (4)	23	12
William Hoffer, Baltimore (2)	22	10
Denton Young, Cleveland (5)	21	18
Clark Griffith, Chicago (9)	21	19
Jeremiah Nops, Baltimore (2)	20	7
Jouett Meekin, New York (3)	20	11
Edward Lewis, Boston (1)	20	12
J. Bentley Seymour, N.Y. (3)	20	14

1898 (17)

	W.	L.
Charles Nichols, Boston (1)	31	12
Ellsw'th Cunningham, Lou. (9)	28	15
James McJames, Baltimore (2)	27	14
Emerson Hawley, Cin. (3)	26	12
Clark Griffith, Chicago (4)	26	10
Edward Lewis, Boston (1)	25	14
Denton Young, Cleveland (5)	25	14
J. Bentley Seymour, N. Y. (7)	25	14
Wiley Piatt, Philadelphia (6)	24	14
Jesse Tannehill, Pitts. (8)	24	14
John Powell, Cleveland (5)	24	15
Victor Willis, Boston (1)	23	12
James Hughes, Baltimore (2)	21	11
Theo. Breitenstein, Cin. (3)	21	14
Albert Maul, Baltimore (2)	20	7
Amos Rusie, New York (7)	20	10
James Callahan, Chicago (4)	20	14

1899 (17)

	W.	L.
James Hughes, Brooklyn (1)	28	6
Joseph McGinnity, Balti. (4)	28	15
Victor Willis, Boston (2)	27	10
Denton Young, St. Louis (5)	26	15
Frank Hahn, Cincinnati (6)	23	7
James Callahan, Chicago (8)	23	12
Jesse Tannehill, Pitts. (7)	23	15
Wiley Piatt, Philadelphia (3)	23	14
John Powell, St. Louis (5)	23	21
Frank Donahue, Phila. (3)	22	7
Clark Griffith, Chicago (8)	22	13
John Dunn, Brooklyn (1)	21	12
Charles Fraser, Phila. (3)	21	13
Charles Nichols, Boston (2)	21	19
Frank Kitson, Baltimore (4)	20	16
Charles Phillippe, Louis. (9)	20	17
Samuel Leever, Pittsburgh (7)	20	23

1900 (5) — W. L.
Joseph McGinnity, Brkn. (1) ... 29 9
William Kennedy, Brkn. (1) ... 22 15
William Dinneen, Boston (4) ... 21 15
Jesse Tannehill, Pitts (2) ... 20 7
Denton Young, St. Louis (5T) ... 20 18

1901 (8) — W. L.
William Donovan, Brkn. (3) ... 25 15
Charles Phillippe, Pitts. (1) ... 22 12
Frank Hahn, Cincinnati (8) ... 22 19
John Chesbro, Pittsburgh (1) ... 21 9
Albert Orth, Philadelphia (2) ... 20 12
Charles Harper, St. Louis (4) ... 20 12
Frank Donahue, Phila. (2) ... 20 13
Christ. Mathewson, N. Y. (7) ... 20 17

1902 (7) — W. L.
John Chesbro, Pittsburgh (1) ... 28 6
Charles Pittinger, Boston (3) ... 27 14
Victor Willis, Boston (3) ... 27 19
John Taylor, Chicago (5) ... 22 10
Frank Hahn, Cincinnati (4) ... 22 12
Jesse Tannehill, Pitts. (1) ... 20 6
Charles Phillippe, Pitts. (1) ... 20 9

1903 (9) — W. L.
Joseph McGinnity, N. Y. (2) ... 31 20
Christ. Mathewson, N. Y. (2) ... 30 13
Samuel Leever, Pitts. (1) ... 25 7
Charles Phillippe, Pitts. (1) ... 25 9
Frank Hahn, Cincinnati (4) ... 22 12
Harry Schmidt, Brooklyn (5) ... 22 13
John Taylor, Chicago (5) ... 21 14
Jacob Weimer, Chicago (3) ... 20 8
Robert Wicker, 0-0, St. Louis (8)
    20-9 Chicago (3) ... 20 9

1904 (7) — W. L.
Joseph McGinnity, N. Y. (1) ... 35 8
Christ. Mathewson, N. Y. (1) ... 33 12
Charles Harper, Cincinnati (3) ... 23 9
Charles Nichols, St. Louis (5) ... 21 13
Luther Taylor, New York (1) ... 21 15
Jacob Weimer, Chicago (2) ... 20 14
John Taylor, St. Louis (5) ... 20 19

1905 (8) — W. L.
Christ. Mathewson, N. Y. (1) ... 31 9
Charles Pittinger, Phila. (4) ... 23 14
Leon Ames, New York (1) ... 22 8
Joseph McGinnity, N. Y. (1) ... 21 15
Samuel Leever, Pittsburgh (2) ... 20 5
Robert Ewing, Cincinnati (5) ... 20 11
Charles Phillippe, Pitts. (2) ... 20 13
Irving Young, Boston (7) ... 20 21

1906 (8) — W. L.
Joseph McGinnity, N. Y. (2) ... 27 12
Mordecai Brown, Chicago (1) ... 26 6
Victor Willis, Pittsburgh (3) ... 23 13
Samuel Leever, Pittsburgh (3) ... 22 7
Christ. Mathewson, N. Y. (2) ... 22 12
John Pfiester, Chicago (1) ... 20 8
John Taylor, 8-9 St. Louis (7)
    12-3 Chicago (1) ... 20 12
Jacob Weimer, Cincinnati (6) ... 20 14

1907 (6) — W. L.
Christ. Mathewson, N. Y. (4) ... 24 12
Orval Overall, Chicago (1) ... 23 8
Frank Sparks, Philadelphia (3) ... 22 8
Victor Willis, Pittsburgh (2) ... 21 11
Mordecai Brown, Chicago (1) ... 20 6
Albert Leifield, Pittsburgh (2) ... 20 16

1908 (7) — W. L.
Christ. Mathewson, N. Y. (2T) ... 37 11
Mordecai Brown, Chicago (1) ... 29 9
Edward Reulbach, Chicago (1) ... 24 7
Nicholas Maddox, Pitts. (2T) ... 23 8
Victor Willis, Pittsburgh (2T) ... 23 11
George Wiltse, New York (2T) ... 23 14
George McQuillan, Phila. (4) ... 23 17

1909 (6) — W. L.
Mordecai Brown, Chicago (2) ... 27 9
S. Howard Camnitz, Pitts. (1) ... 25 6
Christ. Mathewson, N. Y. (3) ... 25 6
Victor Willis, Pittsburgh (1) ... 22 11
George Wiltse, New York (3) ... 20 11
Orval Overall, Chicago (2) ... 20 11

1910 (5) — W. L.
Christ. Mathewson, N. Y. (2) ... 27 9
Mordecai Brown, Chicago (1) ... 25 14
Earl Moore, Philadelphia (4) ... 22 15
Leonard Cole, Chicago (1) ... 20 4
George Suggs, Cincinnati (5) ... 20 12

1911 (8) — W. L.
Grover Alexander, Phila. (4) ... 28 13
Christ. Mathewson, N. Y. (1) ... 26 13
Richard Marquard, N. Y. (1) ... 24 7
Robert Harmon, St. Louis (5) ... 23 16
Charles Adams, Pittsburgh (3) ... 22 12
George Rucker, Brooklyn (7) ... 22 18
Mordecai Brown, Chicago (2) ... 21 11
S. Howard Camnitz, Pitts. (3) ... 20 15

1912 (5) — W. L.
Lawrence Cheney, Chicago (3) ... 26 10
Richard Marquard, N. Y. (1) ... 26 11
Claude Hendrix, Pitts. (2) ... 24 9
Christ. Mathewson, N. Y. (1) ... 23 12
S. Howard Camnitz, Pitts. (2) ... 22 12

1913 (7) — W. L.
Thomas Seaton, Phila. (2) ... 27 12
Christ. Mathewson, N. Y. (1) ... 25 11
Richard Marquard, N. Y. (1) ... 23 10
Grover Alexander, Phila. (2) ... 22 8
Charles Tesreau, New York (2) ... 22 13
Charles Adams, Pittsburgh (4) ... 21 10
Lawrence Cheney, Chicago (3) ... 21 14

1914 (9) — W. L.
Richard Rudolph, Boston (1) ... 27 10
Grover Alexander, Phila. (6) ... 27 15
William James, Boston (1) ... 26 7
Charles Tesreau, New York (2) ... 26 10
Christ. Mathewson, N. Y. (2) ... 24 13
Edward Pfeffer, Brooklyn (5) ... 23 12
James Vaughn, Chicago (4) ... 21 13
J. Erskine Mayer, Phila. (6) ... 21 19
Lawrence Cheney, Chicago (4) ... 20 18

1915 (5) — W. L.
Grover Alexander, Phila. (1) ... 31 10
Richard Rudolph, Boston (2) ... 22 19
Albert Mamaux, Pittsburgh (5) ... 21 8
J. Erskine Mayer, Phila. (1) ... 21 15
James Vaughn, Chicago (4) ... 20 12

1916 (4) — W. L.
Grover Alexander, Phila. (2) ... 33 12
Edward Pfeffer, Brooklyn (1) ... 25 11
Eppa Rixey, Philadelphia (2) ... 22 10
Albert Mamaux, Pittsburgh (6) ... 21 15

1917 (5) — W. L.
Grover Alexander, Phila. (2) ... 30 13
Fred Toney, Cincinnati (4) ... 24 16
James Vaughn, Chicago (5) ... 23 13
Ferdinand Schupp, N. Y. (1) ... 21 7
Peter Schneider, Cin. (4) ... 20 19

1918 (2) — W. L.
James Vaughn, Chicago (1) ... 22 10
Claude Hendrix, Chicago (1) ... 20 7

1919 (3) — W. L.
Jesse Barnes, New York (2) ... 25 9
Harry Sallee, Cincinnati (1) ... 21 7
James Vaughn, Chicago (3) ... 21 14

1920 (7) — W. L.
Grover Alexander, Chi. (5T) ... 27 14
A. Wilbur Cooper, Pitts. (4) ... 24 15
Burleigh Grimes, Brooklyn (1) ... 23 11
Fred Toney, New York (2) ... 21 11
Arthur Nehf, New York (2) ... 21 12
William Doak, St. Louis (5T) ... 20 12
Jesse Barnes, New York (2) ... 20 15

1921 (4) — W. L.
Burleigh Grimes, Brooklyn (5) ... 22 13
A. Wilbur Cooper, Pitts. (2) ... 22 14
Arthur Nehf, New York (1) ... 20 10
Joseph Oeschger, Boston (4) ... 20 14

1922 (3) — W. L.
Eppa Rixey, Cincinnati (2) ... 25 13
A. Wilbur Cooper, Pitts. (3T) ... 23 14
Walter Ruether, Brooklyn (6) ... 21 12

1923 (7) — W. L.
Adolfo Luque, Cincinnati (2) ... 27 8
John Morrison, Pittsburgh (3) ... 25 13
Grover Alexander, Chicago (4) ... 22 12
Peter Donohue, Cincinnati (2) ... 21 15
Burleigh Grimes, Brooklyn (6) ... 21 18
Jesse Haines, St. Louis (5) ... 20 13
Eppa Rixey, Cincinnati (2) ... 20 15

1924 (4) — W. L.
Arthur Vance, Brooklyn (2) ... 28 6
Burleigh Grimes, Brooklyn (2) ... 22 13
Carl Mays, Cincinnati (2) ... 20 9
A. Wilbur Cooper, Pitts. (3) ... 20 14

1925 (3) — W. L.
Arthur Vance, Brooklyn (6T) ... 22 9
Eppa Rixey, Cincinnati (3) ... 21 11
Peter Donohue, Cincinnati (3) ... 21 14

1926 (4) — W. L.
Remy Kremer, Pittsburgh (3) ... 20 6
Charles Rhem, St. Louis (1) ... 20 7
H. Lee Meadows, Pitts. (3) ... 20 9
Peter Donohue, Cincinnati (2) ... 20 14

1927 (4) — W. L.
Charles Root, Chicago (4) ... 26 15
Jesse Haines, St. Louis (2) ... 24 10
Carmen Hill, Pittsburgh (1) ... 22 11
Grover Alexander, St. L. (2) ... 21 10

1928 (6) — W. L.
Lawrence Benton, N. Y. (2) ... 25 9
Burleigh Grimes, Pitts. (4) ... 25 14
Arthur Vance, Brooklyn (6) ... 22 10
William Sherdel, St. Louis (1) ... 21 10
Jesse Haines, St. Louis (1) ... 20 8
Fred Fitzsimmons, N. Y. (2) ... 20 9

1929 (1) — W. L.
Perce Malone, Chicago (1) ... 22 10

1930 (2) — W. L.
Perce Malone, Chicago (2) ... 20 9
Remy Kremer, Pittsburgh (5) ... 20 12

1931 (0)

1932 (2) — W. L.
Lonnie Warneke, Chicago (1) ... 22 6
W. William Clark, Brkn. (3) ... 20 12

1933 (4) — W. L.
Carl Hubbell, New York (1) ... 23 12
Benjamin Cantwell, Boston (4) ... 20 10
Guy Bush, Chicago (3) ... 20 12
Jerome Dean, St. Louis (5) ... 20 18

1934 (4) — W. L.
Jerome Dean, St. Louis (1) ... 30 7
Harold Schumacher, N. Y. (2) ... 23 10
Lonnie Warneke, Chicago (3) ... 22 10
Carl Hubbell, New York (2) ... 21 12

1935 (5) — W. L.
Jerome Dean, St. Louis (2) ... 28 12
Carl Hubbell, New York (3) ... 23 12
Paul Derringer, Cin. (6) ... 22 13
William C. Lee, Chicago (1) ... 20 6
Lonnie Warneke, Chicago (1) ... 20 13

1936 (2) — W. L.
Carl Hubbell, New York (1) ... 26 6
Jerome Dean, St. Louis (2T) ... 24 13

1937 (4) — W. L.
Carl Hubbell, New York (1) ... 22 8
Clifford Melton, New York (1) ... 20 9
Louis Fette, Boston (5) ... 20 10
James Turner, Boston (5) ... 20 11

1938 (2) — W. L.
William C. Lee Chicago (1) ... 22 9
Paul Derringer, Cincinnati (4) ... 21 14

1939 (4) — W. L.
William Walters, Cin. (1) ... 27 11
Paul Derringer, Cincinnati (1) ... 25 7
Curtis Davis, St. Louis (2) ... 22 16
Luke Hamlin, Brooklyn (3) ... 20 13

1940 (3) — W. L.
William Walters, Cin. (1) ... 22 10
Paul Derringer, Cincinnati (1) ... 20 12
Claude Passeau, Chicago (5) ... 20 13

1941 (2) — W. L.
W. Kirby Higbe, Brooklyn (1) ... 22 9
J. Whitlow Wyatt, Brkn. (1) ... 22 10

1942 (2) — W. L.
Morton Cooper, St. Louis (1) ... 22 7
John Beazley, St. Louis (1) ... 21 6

1943 (3) — W. L.
Morton Cooper, St. Louis (1) ... 21 8
Truett Sewell, Pittsburgh (4) ... 21 9
Elmer Riddle, Cincinnati (2) ... 21 11

1944 (4) — W. L.
William Walters, Cin. (3) ... 23 8
Morton Cooper, St. Louis (1) ... 22 7
Truett Sewell, Pittsburgh (2) ... 21 12
William Voiselle, New York (5) ... 21 16

1945 (2) — W. L.
Charles Barrett, 2-3 Boston (6)
    21-9 St. Louis (2) ... 23 12
Henry Wyse, Chicago (1) ... 22 10

1946 (2) — W. L.
Howard Pollet, St. Louis (1) ... 21 10
John Sain, Boston (4) ... 20 14

1947 (5) — W. L.
Ewell Blackwell, Cin. (5) ... 22 8
Lawrence Jansen, N. Y. (4) ... 21 5
Warren Spahn, Boston (3) ... 21 10
Ralph Branca, Brooklyn (1) ... 21 12
John Sain, Boston (3) ... 21 12

1948 (2) — W. L.
John Sain, Boston (1) ... 24 15
Harry Brecheen, St. Louis (2) ... 20 7

1949 (2) — W. L.
Warren Spahn, Boston (4) ... 21 14
Howard Pollet, St. Louis (2) ... 20 9

1950 (2) — W. L.
Warren Spahn, Boston (4) ... 21 17
Robin Roberts, Phila. (1) ... 20 11
John Sain, Boston (4) ... 20 13

1951 (7) — W. L.
Salvatore Maglie, N. Y. (1) ... 23 6
Lawrence Jansen, N. Y. (1) ... 23 11
Elwin Roe, Brooklyn (2) ... 22 3
Warren Spahn, Boston (4) ... 22 14

	W.	L.
Robin Roberts, Phila. (5)	21	15
Donald Newcombe, Brkn. (2)	20	9
Murry Dickson, Pitts. (7)	20	16

1952 (1)

	W.	L.
Robin Roberts, Phila. (4)	28	7

1953 (4)

	W.	L.
Warren Spahn, Milwaukee (2)	23	7
Robin Roberts, Phila. (3T)	23	16
Carl Erskine, Brooklyn (1)	20	6
Harvey Haddix, St. Louis (3T)	20	9

1954 (3)

	W.	L.
Robin Roberts, Phila. (4)	23	15
John Antonelli, New York (1)	21	7
Warren Spahn, Milwaukee (3)	21	12

1955 (2)

	W.	L.
Robin Roberts, Phila. (4)	23	14
Donald Newcombe, Brook. (1)	20	5

1956 (3)

	W.	L.
Donald Newcombe, Brook. (1)	27	7
Warren Spahn, Milwaukee (2)	20	11
John Antonelli, New York (6)	20	13

1957 (1)

	W.	L.
Warren Spahn, Milwaukee (1)	21	11

1958 (3)

	W.	L.
Warren Spahn, Milwaukee (1)	22	11
Robert Friend, Pittsburgh (2)	22	14
S. Lewis Burdette, Milw. (1)	20	10

1959 (3)

	W.	L.
S. Lewis Burdette, Milw. (2)	21	15
Warren Spahn, Milwaukee (2)	21	15
Samuel Jones, San Fran. (3)	21	15

1960 (3)

	W.	L.
Ernest Broglio, St. Louis (3)	21	9
Warren Spahn, Milwaukee (2)	21	10
Vernon Law, Pittsburgh (1)	20	9

1961 (2)

	W.	L.
Joseph Jay, Cincinnati (1)	21	10
Warren Spahn, Milwaukee (4)	21	13

1962 (4)

	W.	L.
Donald Drysdale, L. A. (2)	25	9
John Sanford, S. F. (1)	24	7
Robert Purkey, Cincinnati (3)	23	5
Joseph Jay, Cincinnati (3)	21	14

1963 (5)

	W.	L.
Sanford Koufax, L. A. (1)	25	5
Juan A. Marichal, S. F. (3)	25	8
James W. Maloney, Cinn. (5)	23	7
Warren E. Spahn, Milw. (6)	23	7
Richard C. Ellsworth, Chi. (7)	22	10

1964 (3)

	W.	L.
Lawrence C. Jackson, Chi. (8)	24	11
Juan A. Marichal, San F. (4)	21	8
Raymond M. Sadecki, St.L. (1)	20	11

1965 (7)

	W.	L.
Sanford Koufax, L. A. (1)	26	8
Tony Cloninger, Milw. (5)	24	11
Donald Drysdale, L. A. (2)	23	12
Samuel J. Ellis, Cincinnati (4)	22	10
Juan A. Marichal, S. F. (2)	22	13
James W. Maloney, Cin. (4)	20	9
Robert Gibson, St. Louis (7)	20	12

1966 (5)

	W.	L.
Sanford Koufax, L. A. (1)	27	9
Juan A. Marichal, S. F. (2)	25	6
Gaylord J. Perry, S. F. (2)	21	8
Robert Gibson, St. Louis (6)	21	12
Christopher J. Short, Phila. (4)	20	10

1967 (2)

	W.	L.
Michael F. McCormick, S.F. (2)	22	10
Ferguson A. Jenkins, Chi. (3)	20	13

1968 (3)

	W.	L.
Juan A. Marichal, S. F. (2)	26	9
Robert Gibson, St. Louis (1)	22	9
Ferguson A. Jenkins, Chi. (3)	20	15

1969 (9)

	W.	L.
G. Thomas Seaver, N. Y. (1E)	25	7
Philip H. Niekro, Atl. (1W)	23	13
Juan A. Marichal, S. F. (2W)	21	11
Ferguson A. Jenkins, Chi. (2E)	21	15
William R. Singer, L. A. (4W)	20	12
Lawrence E. Dierker, Hou. (5W)	20	13
Robert Gibson, St. Louis (4E)	20	13
William A. Hands, Chi. (2E)	20	14
Claude W. Osteen, L. A. (4W)	20	15

1970 (4)

	W.	L.
Robert Gibson, St. Louis (4E)	23	7
Gaylord J. Perry, S. F. (3W)	23	13
Ferguson A. Jenkins, Chi. (2E)	22	16
James J. Merritt, Cin. (1W)	20	12

1971 (4)

	W.	L.
Ferguson A. Jenkins, Chi. (3ET)	24	13
Alphonso E. Downing, L. A. (2W)	20	9
Steven N. Carlton, St. L. (2)	20	9
G. Thomas Seaver, N. Y. (3ET)	20	10

1972 (4)

	W.	L.
Steven N. Carlton, Phila. (6E)	27	10
G. Thomas Seaver, N. Y. (3E)	21	12
Claude W. Osteen, L. A. (3W)	20	11
Ferguson A. Jenkins, Chi. (2E)	20	12

1973 (1)

	W.	L.
Ronald R. Bryant, San Fran. (3W)	24	12

1974 (2)

	W.	L.
John A. Messersmith, Los Ang. (1W)	20	6
Philip H. Niekro, Atlanta (3W)	20	13

1975 (2)

	W.	L.
G. Thomas Seaver, N. Y. (3ET)	22	9
Randall L. Jones, San Diego (4W)	20	12

1976 (5)

	W.	L.
Randall L. Jones, S. D. (5W)	22	14
Jerry M. Koosman, N. Y. (3E)	21	10
Donald H. Sutton, L. A. (2W)	21	10
Steven N. Carlton, Phila. (1E)	20	7
James R. Richard, Hou. (3W)	20	15

1977 (6)

	W.	L.
Steven N. Carlton, Phila. (1E)	23	10
G. Thomas Seaver, N.Y.-Cin. (2W)	21	6
John R. Candelaria, Pitts. (2E)	20	5
Robert H. Forsch, St. L. (3E)	20	7
Thomas E. John, L. A. (1W)	20	7
Ricky E. Reuschel, Chi. (4E)	20	10

1978 (2)

	W.	L.
Gaylord J. Perry, S. D. (3W)	21	6
Ross A. Grimsley, Mon. (4E)	20	11

1979 (2)

	W.	L.
Joseph F. Niekro, Hou. (2W)	21	11
Philip H. Niekro, Atl. (6W)	21	20

1980 (2)

	W.	L.
Steven N. Carlton, Phila. (1E)	24	9
Joseph F. Niekro, Hou. (1W)	20	12

1981 (0)

1982 (1)

	W.	L.
Steven N. Carlton, Phila. (2E)	23	11

1983 (0)

1984 (1)

	W.	L.
Joaquin Andujar, St. L. (3E)	20	14

1985 (4)

	W.	L.
Dwight E. Gooden, N.Y. (2E)	24	4
John T. Tudor, St.L. (1E)	21	8
Joaquin Andujar, St.L. (1E)	21	12
Thomas L. Browning, Cin. (2W)	20	9

1986 (2)

	W.	L.
Fernando Valenzuela, L.A. (5W)	21	11
Michael E. Krukow, S.F. (3W)	20	9

1987 (0)

American League

1901 (5)

	W.	L.
Denton Young, Boston (2)	33	10
Joseph McGinnity, Balt. (5)	26	21
Clark Griffith, Chicago (1)	24	7
C. Roscoe Miller, Detroit (3)	23	13
Charles Fraser, Phila. (4)	20	15

1902 (7)

	W.	L.
Denton Young, Boston (3)	32	10
George Waddell, Phila. (1)	23	7
Frank Donahue, St. Louis (2)	22	11
John Powell, St. Louis (2)	22	17
William Dinneen, Boston (3)	21	21
Roy Patterson, Chicago (4)	20	12
Edward Plank, Phila. (1)	20	15

1903 (7)

	W.	L.
Denton Young, Boston (1)	28	10
Edward Plank, Phila. (2)	23	16
Thomas Hughes, Boston (1)	21	7
William Dinneen, Boston (1)	21	11
William Sudhoff, St. Louis (6)	21	15
John Chesbro, New York (4)	21	15
George Waddell, Phila. (2)	21	16

1904 (9)

	W.	L.
John Chesbro, New York (2)	41	13
Denton Young, Boston (1)	26	16
Edward Plank, Phila. (5)	26	17
George Waddell, Phila. (5)	25	19
William Bernhard, Cleve. (4)	23	13
William Dinneen, Boston (1)	23	14
John Powell, New York (2)	23	19
Jesse Tannehill, Boston (1)	21	11
Frank Owen, Chicago (3)	21	15

1905 (9)

	W.	L.
George Waddell, Phila. (1)	26	11
Edward Plank, Phila. (1)	25	12
Nicholas Altrock, Chicago (2)	24	12
Edward Killian, Detroit (3)	23	13
Jesse Tannehill, Boston (4)	22	9
Frank Owen, Chicago (2)	21	13
George Mullin, Detroit (3)	21	20
Adrian Joss, Cleveland (5)	20	11
Frank Smith, Chicago (2)	20	14

1906 (8)

	W.	L.
Albert Orth, New York (2)	27	17
John Chesbro, New York (2)	24	16
Robert Rhoades, Cleveland (3)	22	10
Frank Owen, Chicago (1)	22	13
Adrian Joss, Cleveland (3)	21	9
George Mullin, Detroit (6)	21	18
Nicholas Altrock, Chicago (1)	20	13
Otto Hess, Cleveland (3)	20	17

1907 (10)

	W.	L.
Adrian Joss, Cleveland (4)	27	10
G. Harris White, Chicago (3)	27	13
William Donovan, Detroit (1)	25	4
Edward Killian, Detroit (1)	25	13
Edward Plank, Phila. (2)	24	16
Edward Walsh, Chicago (3)	24	18
Frank Smith, Chicago (2)	22	11
Denton Young, Boston (7)	22	15
James Dygert, Phila. (2)	20	9
George Mullin, Detroit (1)	20	20

1908 (4)

	W.	L.
Edward Walsh, Chicago (3)	40	15
Adrian Joss, Cleveland (2)	24	11
Oren Summers, Detroit (1)	24	12
Denton Young, Boston (5)	21	11

1909 (3)

	W.	L.
George Mullin, Detroit (1)	29	8
Frank Smith, Chicago (4)	25	17
R. Edgar Willett, Detroit (1)	22	10

1910 (5)

	W.	L.
John Coombs, Phila. (1)	31	9
Russell Ford, New York (2)	26	6
Walter Johnson, Wash. (7)	25	17
Charles Bender, Phila. (1)	23	5
George Mullin, Detroit (3)	21	12

1911 (7)

	W.	L.
John Coombs, Phila. (1)	28	12
Edward Walsh, Chicago (4)	27	18
Walter Johnson, Wash. (7)	25	13
Sylveanus Gregg, Cleve. (3)	23	7
Joseph Wood, Boston (5)	23	17
Edward Plank, Phila. (1)	22	8
Russell Ford, New York (6)	22	11

1912 (8)

	W.	L.
Joseph Wood, Boston (1)	34	5
Walter Johnson, Wash. (2)	32	12
Edward Walsh, Chicago (4)	27	17
Edward Plank, Phila. (3)	26	6
Robert Groom, Wash. (2)	24	13
John Coombs, Phila. (3)	21	10
Hugh Bedient, Boston (1)	20	10
Sylveanus Gregg, Cleve. (5)	20	13

1913 (6)

	W.	L.
Walter Johnson, Wash. (2)	36	7
Fred Falkenberg, Cleve. (3)	23	10
Ewell Russell, Chicago (5)	22	16
Charles Bender, Phila. (1)	21	10
Sylveanus Gregg, Cleve. (3)	20	13
James Scott, Chicago (5)	20	20

1914 (3)

	W.	L.
Walter Johnson, Wash. (3)	28	18
Harry Coveleski, Detroit (4)	22	12
Ray Collins, Boston (2)	20	13

1915 (5)

	W.	L.
Walter Johnson, Wash. (4)	27	13
James Scott, Chicago (3)	24	11
George Dauss, Detroit (2)	24	13
Urban Faber, Chicago (3)	24	14
Harry Coveleski, Detroit (2)	22	13

1916 (4)

	W.	L.
Walter Johnson, Wash. (7)	25	20
Robert Shawkey, New York (4)	24	14
George Ruth, Boston (1)	23	12
Harry Coveleski, Detroit (3)	21	11

1917 (5)

	W.	L.
Edward Cicotte, Chicago (1)	28	12
George Ruth, Boston (2)	24	13
James Bagby, Cleveland (3)	23	13
Walter Johnson, Wash. (5)	23	16
Carl Mays, Boston (2)	22	9

1918 (4)

	W.	L.
Walter Johnson, Wash. (3)	23	13
Stanley Coveleski, Cleve. (2)	22	13
Carl Mays, Boston (1)	21	13
Scott Perry, Philadelphia (8)	20	19

1919 (7)

	W.	L.
Edward Cicotte, Chicago (1)	29	7
Claude Williams, Chicago (1)	23	11
Stanley Coveleski, Cleve. (2)	23	12
George Dauss, Detroit (4)	21	9
Allan Sothoron, St. Louis (5)	21	11
Robert Shawkey, New York (3)	20	13
Walter Johnson, Wash. (7)	20	14

1920 (10)	W.	L.
James Bagby, Cleveland (1)	31	12
Carl Mays, New York (3)	26	11
Stanley Coveleski, Cleve. (1)	24	14
Urban Faber, Chicago (2)	23	13
Claude Williams, Chicago (2)	22	14
Richard Kerr, Chicago (2)	21	9
Edward Cicotte, Chicago (2)	21	10
Raymond Caldwell, Cleve. (1)	20	10
Urban Shocker, St. Louis (4)	20	10
Robert Shawkey, New York (3)	20	13

1921 (5)	W.	L.
Carl Mays, New York (1)	27	9
Urban Shocker, St. Louis (3)	27	12
Urban Faber, Chicago (7)	25	15
Stanley Coveleski, Cleve. (2)	23	13
Samuel Jones, Boston (5)	23	16

1922 (6)	W.	L.
Edwin Rommel, Phila. (7)	27	13
Leslie Bush, New York (1)	26	7
Urban Shocker, St. Louis (2)	24	17
George Uhle, Cleveland (4)	22	16
Urban Faber, Chicago (5)	21	17
Robert Shawkey, New York (1)	20	12

1923 (5)	W.	L.
George Uhle, Cleveland (3)	26	16
Samuel Jones, New York (1)	21	8
George Dauss, Detroit (2)	21	13
Urban Shocker, St. Louis (5)	20	12
Howard Ehmke, Boston (8)	20	17

1924 (4)	W.	L.
Walter Johnson, Wash. (1)	23	7
Herbert Pennock, N. Y. (2)	21	9
Hollis Thurston, Chicago (8)	20	14
Joseph Shaute, Cleveland (6)	20	17

1925 (4)	W.	L.
Edwin Rommel, Phila. (2)	21	10
Theodore Lyons, Chicago (5)	21	11
Stanley Coveleski, Wash. (1)	20	5
Walter Johnson, Wash. (1)	20	7

1926 (2)	W.	L.
George Uhle, Cleveland (2)	27	11
Herbert Pennock, N. Y. (1)	23	11

1927 (3)	W.	L.
Waite Hoyt, New York (1)	22	7
Theodore Lyons, Chicago (5)	22	14
Robert Grove, Phila. (2)	20	13

1928 (5)	W.	L.
Robert Grove, Phila. (2)	24	8
George Pipgras, New York (1)	24	13
Waite Hoyt, New York (1)	23	7
Alvin Crowder, St. Louis (3)	21	5
Samuel Gray, St. Louis (3)	20	12

1929 (3)	W.	L.
George Earnshaw, Phila. (1)	24	8
Wesley Ferrell, Cleveland (3)	21	10
Robert Grove, Phila. (1)	20	6

1930 (5)	W.	L.
Robert Grove, Phila. (1)	28	5
Wesley Ferrell, Cleveland (4)	25	13
George Earnshaw, Phila. (1)	22	13
Theodore Lyons, Chicago (7)	22	15
Walter Stewart, St. Louis (6)	20	12

1931 (5)	W.	L.
Robert Grove, Phila. (1)	31	4
Wesley Ferrell, Cleveland (4)	22	12
George Earnshaw, Phila. (1)	21	7
Vernon Gomez, New York (2)	21	9
George Walberg, Phila. (1)	20	12

1932 (5)	W.	L.
Alvin Crowder, Washington (3)	26	13
Robert Grove, Phila. (2)	25	10
Vernon Gomez, New York (1)	24	7
Wesley Ferrell, Cleveland (4)	23	13
Monte Weaver, Washington (3)	22	10

1933 (3)	W.	L.
Robert Grove, Phila. (3)	24	8
Alvin Crowder, Washington (1)	24	15
Earl Whitehill, Washington (1)	22	8

1934 (4)	W.	L.
Vernon Gomez, New York (2)	26	5
Lynwood Rowe, Detroit (1)	24	8
Thomas Bridges, Detroit (1)	22	11
Melvin Harder, Cleveland (3)	20	12

1935 (4)	W.	L.
Wesley Ferrell, Boston (4)	25	14
Melvin Harder, Cleveland (3)	22	11
Thomas Bridges, Detroit (1)	21	10
Robert Grove, Boston (4)	20	12

1936 (5)	W.	L.
Thomas Bridges, Detroit (2)	23	11
L. Vernon Kennedy, Chi. (3)	21	9
John Allen, Cleveland (5)	20	10
Charles Ruffing, New York (1)	20	12
Wesley Ferrell, Boston (6)	20	15

1937 (2)	W.	L.
Vernon Gomez, New York (1)	21	11
Charles Ruffing, New York (1)	20	7

1938 (2)	W.	L.
Charles Ruffing, New York (1)	21	7
Louis Newsom, St. Louis (7)	20	16

1939 (4)	W.	L.
Robert Feller, Cleveland (3)	24	9
Charles Ruffing, New York (1)	21	7
Emil Leonard, Wash. (6)	20	8
Louis Newsom, (3-1) St. L. (8) (17-10) Detroit (5)	20	11

1940 (2)	W.	L.
Robert Feller, Cleveland (2)	27	11
Louis Newsom, Detroit (1)	21	5

1941 (2)	W.	L.
Robert Feller, Cleveland (4T)	25	13
Thornton Lee, Chicago (3)	22	11

1942 (2)	W.	L.
Cecil Hughson, Boston (2)	22	6
Ernest Bonham, New York (1)	21	5

1943 (2)	W.	L.
Spurgeon Chandler, N. Y. (1)	20	4
Paul Trout, Detroit (5)	20	12

1944 (2)	W.	L.
Harold Newhouser, Detroit (2)	29	9
Paul Trout, Detroit, (2)	27	14

1945 (3)	W.	L.
Harold Newhouser, Detroit (1)	25	9
David Ferriss, Boston (7)	21	10
Roger Wolff, Washington (2)	20	10

1946 (5)	W.	L.
Harold Newhouser, Detroit (2)	26	9
Robert Feller, Cleveland (6)	26	15
David Ferriss, Boston (1)	25	6
Spurgeon Chandler, N. Y. (3)	20	8
Cecil Hughson, Boston (1)	20	11

1947 (1)	W.	L.
Robert Feller, Cleveland (4)	20	11

1948 (3)	W.	L.
Harold Newhouser, Detroit (5)	21	12
H. Eugene Bearden, Cleve. (1)	20	7
Robert Lemon, Cleveland (1)	20	14

1949 (5)	W.	L.
Melvin Parnell, Boston (2)	25	7
Ellis Kinder, Boston (2)	23	6
Robert Lemon, Cleveland (3)	22	10
Victor Raschi, New York (1)	21	10
Alexander Kellner, Phila. (5)	20	12

1950 (2)	W.	L.
Robert Lemon, Cleveland (4)	23	11
Victor Raschi, New York (1)	21	8

1951 (6)	W.	L.
Robert Feller, Cleveland (2)	22	8
Edmund Lopat, New York (1)	21	9
Victor Raschi, New York (1)	21	10
Ned Garver, St. Louis (8)	20	12
Edward Garcia, Cleveland (2)	20	13
Early Wynn, Cleveland (2)	20	13

1952 (5)	W.	L.
Robert Shantz, Phila. (4)	24	7
Early Wynn, Cleveland (2)	23	12
Edward Garcia, Cleveland (2)	22	11
Robert Lemon, Cleveland (2)	22	11
Allie Reynolds, New York (1)	20	8

1953 (4)	W.	L.
Ervin Porterfield, Wash. (5)	22	10
Melvin Parnell, Boston (4)	21	8
Robert Lemon, Cleveland (2)	21	15
Virgil Trucks, 5-4 St. Louis (8) 15-6 Chicago (3)	20	10

1954 (3)	W.	L.
Robert Lemon, Cleveland (1)	23	7
Early Wynn, Cleveland (1)	23	11
Robert Grim, New York (2)	20	6

1955 (0)

1956 (6)	W.	L.
Frank Lary, Detroit (5)	21	13
Herbert Score, Cleveland (2)	20	9
Early Wynn, Cleveland (2)	20	9
W. William Pierce, Chicago (3)	20	9
Robert Lemon, Cleveland (2)	20	14
William Hoeft, Detroit (5)	20	14

1957 (2)	W.	L.
James Bunning, Detroit (4)	20	8
W. William Pierce, Chicago (2)	20	12

1958 (1)	W.	L.
Robert Turley, New York (1)	21	7

1959 (1)	W.	L.
Early Wynn, Chicago (1)	22	10

1960 (0)

1961 (2)	W.	L.
Edward Ford, New York (1)	25	4
Frank Lary, Detroit (2)	23	9

1962 (4)	W.	L.
Ralph Terry, New York (1)	23	12
Raymond Herbert, Chicago (5)	20	9
Richard Donovan, Cleve. (6)	20	10
Camilo Pascual, Minnesota (2)	20	11

1963 (5)	W.	L.
Edward C. Ford, New York (1)	24	7
James A. Bouton, N. Y. (1)	21	7
Camilo Pascual, Minnesota (3)	21	9
Wm. C. Monbouquette, Bos. (7)	20	10
Stephen D. Barber, Balt. (4)	20	13

1964 (2)	W.	L.
W. Dean Chance, L. A. (5)	20	9
Gary C. Peters, Chicago (2)	20	8

1965 (2)	W.	L.
James T. Grant, Minn. (1)	21	7
M. L. Stottlemyre, N. Y. (6)	20	9

1966 (2)	W.	L.
James L. Kaat, Minnesota (2)	25	13
Dennis D. McLain, Detroit (3)	20	14

1967 (3)	W.	L.
James R. Lonborg, Boston (1)	22	9
R. Earl Wilson, Detroit (2T)	22	11
W. Dean Chance, Minn. (2T)	20	14

1968 (4)	W.	L.
Dennis D. McLain, Detroit (1)	31	6
David A. McNally, Balt. (2)	22	10
Luis C. Tiant, Cleveland (3)	21	9
M. L. Stottlemyre, N. Y. (5)	21	12

1969 (6)	W.	L.
Dennis D. McLain, Det. (2E)	24	9
Miguel Cuellar, Balt. (1E)	23	11
James E. Perry, Minn. (1W)	20	6
David A. McNally, Balt. (1E)	20	7
David W. Boswell, Minn. (1W)	20	12
M. L. Stottlemyre, N. Y. (5E)	20	14

1970 (7)	W.	L.
Miguel Cuellar, Baltimore (1E)	24	8
David A. McNally, Balt. (1E)	24	9
James E. Perry, Minn. (1W)	24	12
Clyde Wright, Calif. (3W)	22	12
James A. Palmer, Balt. (1E)	20	10
Fred I. Peterson, N. Y. (2E)	20	11
Samuel E. McDowell, Clev. (5E)	20	12

1971 (10)	W.	L.
Michael S. Lolich, Detroit (2E)	25	14
Vida Blue, Oakland (1W)	24	8
Wilbur F. Wood, Chicago (3W)	22	13
David A. McNally, Balt. (1E)	21	5
James A. Hunter, Oak. (1W)	21	11
Patrick E. Dobson, Balt. (1E)	20	8
James A. Palmer, Balt. (1E)	20	9
Miguel Cuellar, Balt. (1E)	20	9
Joseph H. Coleman, Det. (2E)	20	9
John A. Messersmith, Calif. (4W)	20	13

1972 (6)	W.	L.
Gaylord J. Perry, Clev. (5W)	24	16
Wilbur F. Wood, Chicago (2W)	24	17
Michael S. Lolich, Det. (1E)	22	14
James A. Hunter, Oak. (1W)	21	7
James A. Palmer, Balt. (3E)	21	10
Stanley R. Bahnsen, Chi. (2W)	21	16

1973 (12)	W.	L.
Wilbur F. Wood, Chicago (5W)	24	20
Joseph H. Coleman, Det. (3E)	23	15
James A. Palmer, Balt. (1E)	22	9
James A. Hunter, Oak. (1W)	21	5
Kenneth D. Holtzman, Oakland (1W)	21	13
L. Nolan Ryan, Calif. (4W)	21	16
Vida Blue, Oakland (1W)	20	9
Paul W. Splittorff, K. C. (2W)	20	11
James W. Colborn, Mil. (5E)	20	12
Luis C. Tiant, Boston (2E)	20	13
William R. Singer, Calif. (4W)	20	14
Bert R. Blyleven, Minn. (3W)	20	17

1974 (9)	W.	L.
James A. Hunter, Oak. (1W)	25	12
Ferguson, A. Jenkins, Tex. (2W)	25	12
Miguel Cuellar, Balt. (1E)	22	10
Luis C. Tiant, Boston (3E)	22	13
Steven L. Busby, K. C. (5W)	22	14
L. Nolan Ryan, Calif. (6W)	22	16
James L. Kaat, Chicago (4W)	21	13
Gaylord J. Perry, Cleve. (4E)	21	13
Wilbur F. Wood, Chi. (4W)	20	19

1975 (5) — W. L.
- James A. Palmer, Balt. (2E) — 23 / 11
- James A. Hunter, N. Y. (3E) — 23 / 14
- Vida Blue, Oakland (W1) — 22 / 11
- Michael A. Torrez, Balt. (2E) — 20 / 9
- James L. Kaat, Chicago (W5) — 20 / 14

1976 (3) — W. L.
- James A. Palmer, Balt. (2E) — 22 / 13
- Luis C. Tiant, Boston (3E) — 21 / 12
- Marcus W. Garland, Balt. (2E) — 20 / 7

1977 (3) — W. L.
- James A. Palmer, Balt. (2TE) — 20 / 11
- David A. Goltz, Minn. (4W) — 20 / 11
- Dennis P. Leonard, K. C. (1W) — 20 / 12

1978 (6) — W. L.
- Ronald A. Guidry, N. Y. (1E) — 25 / 3
- R. Michael Caldwell, Milw. (3E) — 22 / 9
- James A. Palmer, Balt. (4E) — 21 / 12
- Dennis P. Leonard, K. C. (1W) — 21 / 17
- Dennis L. Eckersley, Bos. (2E) — 20 / 8
- Eduardo Figueroa, N. Y. (1E) — 20 / 9

1979 (3) — W. L.
- Michael K. Flanagan, Balt. (1E) — 23 / 9
- Thomas E. John, N. Y. (4E) — 21 / 9
- Jerry M. Koosman, Minn. (4W) — 20 / 13

1980 (5) — W. L.
- Steven M. Stone, Balt. (2E) — 25 / 7
- Thomas E. John, N. Y. (1E) — 22 / 9
- Michael K. Norris, Oak. (2W) — 22 / 9
- Scott H. McGregor, Balt. (2E) — 20 / 8
- Dennis P. Leonard, K. C. (1W) — 20 / 11

1981 (0)

1982 (0)

1983 (4) — W. L.
- D. LaMarr Hoyt, Chi. (1W) — 24 / 10
- Richard E. Dotson, Chi. (1W) — 22 / 7
- Ronald A. Guidry, N.Y. (3E) — 21 / 9
- John S. Morris, Det. (2E) — 20 / 13

1984 (1) — W. L.
- Michael J. Boddicker, Balt. (5E) — 20 / 11

1985 (2) — W. L.
- Ronald A. Guidry, N.Y. (2E) — 22 / 6
- Bret W. Saberhagen, K.C. (1W) — 20 / 6

1986 (3) — W. L.
- W. Roger Clemens, Boston (1E) — 24 / 4
- John S. Morris, Detroit (3E) — 21 / 8
- Teodoro V. Higuera, Milwaukee (6E) — 20 / 11

1987 (2) — W. L.
- W. Roger Clemens, Boston (5E) — 20 / 9
- David K. Stewart, Oakland (3W) — 20 / 13

American Association

1882 (5) — W. L.
- William White, Cincinnati (1) — 40 / 12
- Anthony Mullane, Louisville (2) — 30 / 24
- Samuel H. Weaver, Phila. (3) — 26 / 15
- George W. McGinnis, St. L. (5) — 25 / 21
- Henry H. Salisbury, Pitts. (5) — 20 / 19

1883 (8) — W. L.
- William H. White, Cin. (3) — 43 / 22
- Timothy J. Keefe, N. Y. (4) — 41 / 27
- Anthony Mullane, St. L. (2) — 35 / 15
- Robert T. Mathews, Phila. (1) — 30 / 14
- George W. McGinnis, St. L. (2) — 29 / 15
- Guy Hecker, Louisville (5) — 28 / 25
- Frank Mountain, Columbus (6) — 26 / 33
- Samuel H. Weaver, Louisville (5) — 24 / 20

1884 (12) — W. L.
- Guy Hecker, Louisville (3) — 52 / 20
- John H. Lynch, New York (1) — 37 / 15
- Edward Morris, Columbus (2) — 35 / 13
- Timothy J. Keefe, N. Y. (1) — 37 / 17
- Anthony Mullane, Toledo (8) — 35 / 25
- William H. White, Cin. (5) — 34 / 18
- Robert D. Emslie, Balt. (6) — 32 / 18
- Robert T. Mathews, Phila. (1) — 30 / 18
- J. Harding Henderson, Balt. (6) — 27 / 22
- George McGinnis, St. Louis (4) — 24 / 16
- Frank Mountain, Columbus (2) — 24 / 17
- William R. Mountjoy, Cin. (5) — 20 / 12

1885 (9) — W. L.
- Robert L. Caruthers, St. L. (1) — 40 / 13
- Edward Morris, Pittsburg (3) — 39 / 24
- David Foutz, St. Louis (1) — 33 / 14
- Henry Porter, Brooklyn (5T) — 33 / 21
- Robert T. Mathews, Phila. (4) — 30 / 17
- Guy Hecker, Louisville (5T) — 30 / 24
- J. Harding Henderson, Balt. (8) — 26 / 35
- John H. Lynch, New York (7) — 23 / 21
- Lawrence J. McKeon, Cin. (2) — 20 / 13

1886 (11) — W. L.
- David Foutz, St. Louis (1) — 41 / 16
- Edward Morris, Pittsburg (2) — 41 / 20

(1886 continued) — W. L.
- Thomas Ramsey, Louisville (4) — 37 / 27
- Anthony Mullane, Cin. (5) — 31 / 27
- Robert Caruthers, St. Louis (1) — 30 / 14
- James Galvin, Pittsburgh (2) — 29 / 21
- Matthew Kilroy, Baltimore (8) — 29 / 34
- Henry Porter, Brooklyn (3) — 28 / 20
- Guy Hecker, Louisville (4) — 27 / 23
- Albert Atkisson, Phila. (6) — 25 / 17
- John H. Lynch, New York (7) — 20 / 20

1887 (10) — W. L.
- Matthew Kilroy, Baltimore (3) — 46 / 20
- Thomas Ramsey, Louisville (4) — 39 / 27
- Charles F. King, St. Louis (1) — 34 / 11
- Elmer E. Smith, Cincinnati (2) — 33 / 18
- Anthony Mullane, Cin. (2) — 31 / 17
- Robert Caruthers, St. L. (1) — 29 / 9
- John F. Smith, Baltimore (3) — 29 / 29
- August Weyhing, Phila. (5) — 26 / 25
- Edward Seward, Phila. (5) — 25 / 24
- David Foutz, St. Louis (1) — 24 / 12

1888 (12) — W. L.
- Charles F. King, St. L. (1) — 45 / 21
- Edward Seward, Phila (3) — 34 / 19
- Robert Caruthers, Brooklyn (2) — 29 / 15
- August Weyhing, Phila. (3) — 29 / 19
- Elton Chamberlain — 25 / 12
  - 9-8 Louisville (7)
  - 16-4 St. Louis (1)
- Leon Viau, Cincinnati (4) — 27 / 14
- Anthony Mullane, Cin. (4) — 26 / 16
- Nathaniel Hudson, St. L. (1) — 25 / 11
- Michael Hughes, Brooklyn (2) — 25 / 13
- Edward Bakely, Cleveland (6) — 25 / 33
- Elmer E. Smith, Cin. (4) — 22 / 17
- Ellsworth Cunningham, Balt. (5) — 22 / 29

1889 (11) — W. L.
- Robert Caruthers, Brooklyn (1) — 40 / 12
- Elton Chamberlain, St. L. (2) — 35 / 15
- Charles F. King, St. L. (2) — 33 / 17
- James W. Duryea, Cin. (4) — 32 / 21
- August Weyhing, Phila. (3) — 28 / 19
- Matthew Kilroy, Baltimore (5) — 28 / 25
- Mark Baldwin, Columbus (6) — 26 / 24
- Francis Foreman, Balt. (5) — 25 / 21
- William Terry, Brooklyn (1) — 21 / 16
- Edward Seward, Phila. (3) — 21 / 16
- Leon Viau, Cincinnati (4) — 21 / 19

1890 (8) — W. L.
- John McMahon — 36 / 21
  - 29-19 Philadelphia (8)
  - 7- 2 Baltimore (6)
- Scott Stratton, Louisville (1) — 34 / 13
- Henry Gastright, Col. (2) — 29 / 13
- John Stivetts, St. Louis (3) — 29 / 20
- Robert M. Barr, Rochester (5) — 28 / 25
- Thomas Ramsey, St. Louis (3) — 26 / 16
- Philip Ehret, Louisville (1) — 25 / 14
- John J. Healy, Toledo (4) — 22 / 23

1891 (8) — W. L.
- George S. Haddock, Boston (1) — 34 / 12
- John McMahon, Baltimore (3) — 34 / 25
- John Stivetts, St. Louis (2) — 33 / 22
- August Weyhing, Phila. (4) — 31 / 20
- Charles Buffinton, Boston (1) — 28 / 9
- Philip H. Knell, Columbus (5) — 27 / 26
- Elton Chamberlain, Phila. (4) — 23 / 23
- William McGill — 22 / 13
  - 8-8 Cincinnati (5)
  - 14-5 St. Louis (2)

Players League

1890 (10) — W. L.
- Charles F. King, Chicago (4) — 32 / 22
- Mark Baldwin, Chicago (4) — 32 / 24
- August Weyhing, Brooklyn (2) — 30 / 14
- Charles Radbourn, Boston (1) — 27 / 12
- Addison Gumbert, Boston (1) — 24 / 11
- Henry O'Day, New York (3) — 22 / 13
- Henry Gruber, Cleve. (7) — 22 / 23
- Philip H. Knell, Phila. (5) — 21 / 10
- Henry Staley, Pittsburgh (6) — 21 / 23
- William Daley, Boston (1) — 20 / 8

Union Association

1884 (9) — W. L.
- William J. Sweeney, Balt. (3) — 40 / 21
- Hugh I. Daily, Chi. 22-25 (6)
  - 1-1 Washington (5)
  - 5-4 Pittsburgh (8) — 28 / 30
- William H. Taylor, St. L. (1) — 25 / 4
- Richard S. Burns, Chi. (5) — 25 / 15
- Charles Sweeney, St. L. (1) — 24 / 8
- William E. Wise, Wash. (5) — 23 / 20
- James McCormick, Cin. (2) — 22 / 4
- Fred L. Shaw, Boston (4) — 22 / 15
- George Bradley, Cincinnati (2) — 21 / 13

Two Leagues In Season
W. L.
- 1884—William H. Taylor — 43 / 16
  - 25- 4 St. Louis U. A. (1)
  - 18-12 Phila. A. A. (7)
- 1884—Charles Sweeney — 41 / 15
  - 17-7 Providence N. L. (1)
  - 24-8 St. Louis U. A. (1)
- 1884—James McCormick — 41 / 26
  - 19-22 Cleveland N. L. (7)
  - 22- 4 Cincinnati U. A. (2)
- 1884—Fred L. Shaw — 30 / 33
  - 8-18 Detroit N. L. (8)
  - 22-15 Boston U. A. (4)
- 1902—Joseph J. McGinnity — 21 / 18
  - 13-10 Baltimore A. L. (8)
  - 8-8 New York N. L. (8)
- 1904—Patrick J. Flaherty — 21 / 11
  - 2-2 Chicago A. L. (3)
  - 19-9 Pittsburgh N. L. (4)
- 1945—Henry L. Borowy — 21 / 7
  - 10-5 New York A. L. (4)
  - 11-2 Chicago N. L. (1)
- 1984—Richard L. Sutcliffe — 20 / 6
  - 4-5 Cleveland A. L. (6E)
  - 16-1 Chicago N. L. (1E)

Pitchers With 12 Straight Victories In Season

National League (36)

Year—Pitcher	Won
1888—Timothy Keefe, New York	19
1912—Richard Marquard, N. Y.	19
1884—Charles Radbourn, Provi.	18
1885—Michael Welch, New York	17
1890—John Luby, Chicago	17
1959—El Roy Face, Pittsburgh	17
1886—James McCormick, Chi.	16
1936—Carl Hubbell, New York	16
1947—Ewell Blackwell, Cinn.	16
1962—John Sanford, San Fran.	16
1924—Arthur Vance, Brooklyn	15
1968—Robert Gibson, St. Louis	15
1972—Steven Carlton, Phila.	15
1885—James McCormick, Chicago	14
1886—John Flynn, Chicago	14
1904—Joseph McGinnity, N. Y.	14
1909—Edward Reulbach, Chicago	14
1984—Richard Sutcliffe, Chicago	14
1985—Dwight Gooden, New York	14
1880—Lawrence Corcoran, Chi.	13
1884—Charles Buffinton, Boston	13
1892—Denton Young, Cleveland	13
1896—Frank Dwyer, Cincinnati	13
1909—Chris. Mathewson, N. Y.	13
1910—Charles Phillippe, Pitts.	13
1927—Burleigh Grimes, New York	13
1956—Brooks Lawrence, Cinn.	13
1966—Philip Regan, Los Angeles	13
1971—Dock Ellis, Pittsburgh	13
1885—John Clarkson, Chicago	12
1886—Charles Ferguson, Phila.	12
1902—John Chesbro, Pittsburgh	12
1904—George Wiltse, New York	12
1906—Edward Reulbach, Chicago	12
1914—Richard Rudolph, Boston	12
1975—Burt Hooton, Los Angeles	12

American League (37)

Year—Pitcher	Won
1912—Walter Johnson, Wash.	16
1912—Joseph Wood, Bos.	16
1931—Robert Grove, Phila.	16
1934—Lynwood Rowe, Det.	16
1932—Alvin Crowder, Wash.	15
1937—John Allen, Cleve.	15
1969—David McNally, Balt.	15
1974—Gaylord Perry, Cleveland	15
1904—John Chesbro, N. Y.	14
1913—Walter Johnson, Wash.	14
1914—Charles Bender, Phila.	14
1928—Robert Grove, Phila.	14
1961—Edward Ford, N. Y.	14
1980—Steven Stone, Balt.	14
1986—W. Roger Clemens, Bos.	14
1924—Walter Johnson, Wash.	13
1925—Stanley Coveleski, Wash.	13
1930—Wesley Ferrell, Cleve.	13
1940—Louis Newsom, Det.	13
1949—Ellis Kinder, Bos.	13
1971—David McNally, Baltimore	13
1973—James Hunter, Oakland	13

Year—Pitcher	Won
1978—Ronald Guidry, N.Y.	13
1983—D. LaMarr Hoyt, Chicago	13
1901—Denton Young, Bos.	12
1910—Russell Ford, N.Y.	12
1914—Hubert Leonard, Boston	12
1929—Jonathan Zachary, N.Y.	12
1931—George Earnshaw, Phila.	12
1938—John Allen, Cleve.	12
1939—Atley Donald, N.Y.	12
1946—David Ferriss, Bos.	12
1961—Luis Arroyo, New York	12
1963—Edward Ford, N.Y.	12
1968—David McNally, Baltimore	12
1971—Patrick Dobson, Baltimore	12
1985—Ronald Guidry, N.Y.	13

American Association (3)

Year—Pitcher	Won
1890—Scott Stratton, St. Louis	15
1884—John Lynch, New York	14
1882—William White, Cinn.	12

Union Association (1)

Year—Pitcher	Won
1884—James McCormick, Cinn.	14

Pitchers With 12 Straight Losses In Season
National League (26)

Year—Pitcher	Lost
1910—Clifton Curtis, Bos	18
1963—Roger Craig, N.Y.	18
1876—Henry Dean, Cinn.	16
1899—James Hughey, Cleve.	16
1962—N. Craig Anderson, N.Y.	16
1887—Frank Gilmore, Wash.	14
1899—Fred Bates, Cleve.	14
1908—James Pastorius, Brook.	14
1911—Charles Brown, Bos.	14
1884—L. R. Moffatt, Cleve.	13
1917—Burleigh Grimes, Pitts.	13
1922—Joseph Oeschger, Bos.	13
1935—Benjamin Cantwell, Bos.	13
1948—Robert McCall, Chi.	13
1880—William Purcell, Cinn.	12
1883—John Coleman, Phila.	12
1902—Henry Thielman, Cinn.	12
1905—Malcolm Eason, Brook.	12
1914—Richard Marquard, N.Y.	12
1914—Peter Schneider, Cinn.	12
1928—Russell Miller, Phila.	12
1933—Silas Johnson, Cinn.	12
1939—A. Butcher, Phila.-Pitts.	12
1940—Hugh Mulcahy, Phila.	12
1962—Robert Miller, N.Y.	12
1972—Kenneth Reynolds, Phila.	12

American League (17)

Year—Pitcher	Lost
1909—Robert Groom, Washington	19
1916—John Nabors, Phila.	19
1980—Michael Parrott, Seattle	16
1906—Joseph Harris, Boston	14
1949—Howard Judson, Chi.	14
1949—L. Paul Calvert, Wash.	14
1979—Matthew Keough, Oakland	14
1914—Guy Morton, Cleve.	13
1920—Roy Moore, Phila.	13
1930—Frank Henry, Chi.	13
1943—Luman Harris, Phila.	13
1982—Terry Felton, Minn.	13
1929—Charles Ruffing, Bos.	12
1940—Walter Masterson, Wash.	12
1945—Louis Newsom, Phila.	12
1945—Stephen Gerkin, Phila.	12
1953—Charles Bishop, Phila.	12

American Association (2)

Year—Pitcher	Lost
1882—Frederick Nichols, Balt.	12
1889—William Crowell, Cleve.	12

No-Hitters

(National League, 113; American League, 91)

Perfect Games—Nine Or More Innings

*First game. †Second game.

Thirteen perfect games have been pitched in major championship play including one in the 1956 World Series by Don Larsen of the New York Yankees and Harvey Haddix' 12-inning effort for Pittsburgh in 1959. The perfect games follow, with the letter in parentheses after the date indicating home or away:

Year	Score
1880—J. Lee Richmond, Wor. vs. Clev., N. L., June 12 (H)	1—0
John Ward, Prov. vs. Buff., N. L., June 17 (H)	5—0
1904—Denton Young, Bos. vs. Phil., A. L., May 5 (H)	3—0
1908—Adrian Joss, Clev. vs. Chi., A. L., Oct. 2 (H)	1—0
1917—Ernest Shore, Bos. vs. Wash., A. L., June 23* (H)	‡4—0
1922—Charles Robertson, Chi. vs. Det., A. L., Apr. 30 (A)	2—0
1956—Don Larsen, N.Y., A. L., vs. Bkn., N. L. (World Series), Oct. 8 (H)	2—0
1959—Harvey Haddix, Pit. vs. Mil., N. L., May 26, (A). (Pitched 12 perfect innings before Mantilla, leading off 13th, reached base on third baseman Hoak's throwing error. After Mathews sacrificed and Aaron was walked intentionally, Adcock doubled to score Mantilla, ending game.)	0—1
1964—James Bunning, Phil. vs. N.Y., N. L., June 21* (A)	6—0
1965—Sanford Koufax, L.A. vs. Chi., N. L., Sept. 9 (H)	1—0
1968—James A. Hunter, Oak. vs. Min., A. L., May 8 (H)	4—0
1981—Leonard H. Barker, Clev. vs. Tor., A.L., May 15 (H)	3—0
1984—Michael A. Witt, Cal. vs. Tex., A.L., Sept. 30 (A)	1—0

‡Shore's performance is classified as a perfect game even though he did not start the game. George (Babe) Ruth, Boston's starting pitcher was removed by Umpire Clarence (Brick) Owens after giving a base on balls to Ray Morgan, the first batter. Shore, without warming up, took Ruth's place. Morgan was retired trying to steal second. From then on, Shore faced 26 batters, with none reaching base.

No-Hit Games—Ten Or More Innings

Year	Score
1884—Samuel Kimber, Bkn. vs. Tol., A. A., Oct. 4 (H). (Game called after 10 innings on account of darkness.)	0—0
1906—Harry McIntire, Bkn. vs. Pit., N. L., Aug. 1 (H). (Pitched 10⅔ hitless innings before Claude Ritchey singled; lost on 4 hits in 13 inn.)	0—1
1908—George Wiltse, N.Y. vs. Phil., N. L., July 4* (H) (10 inn.)	1—0
1917—Frederick Toney, Cin. vs. Chi., N. L., May 2 (A) (10 innings). (James Vaughn, Chi., pitched 9⅓ no-hit inn. in same game.)	1—0
1965—James Maloney, Cin. vs. N.Y., N. L., June 14 (H) (Pitched 10 hitless innings before Johnny Lewis homered to lead off in 11th; lost on 2 hits in 11 inn.)	0—1
James Maloney, Cin. vs. Chi., N. L., Aug 19* (A) (10 inn.)	1—0

No-Hit Games—Nine Innings

Year	Score
1876—George Bradley, St. L. vs. Hart., N. L., July 15 (H)	2—0
1880—Lawrence Corcoran, Chi. vs. Bos., N. L., Aug. 19 (H)	6—0
James Galvin, Buff. vs. Wor., N. L., Aug. 20 (A)	1—0
1882—Anthony Mullane, Lou. vs. Cin., A. A., Sept. 11 (A) (first at 50-foot distance.)	2—0
Guy Hecker, Lou. vs. Pit., A. A., Sept. 19 (A)	3—1
Lawrence Corcoran, Chi. vs. Wor., N. L., Sept. 20 (H)	5—0
1883—Charles Radbourn, Prov. vs. Clev., N. L., July 25 (A)	8—0
Hugh Daily, Clev. vs. Phil., N. L., Sept. 13 (A)	1—0
1884—Albert Atkisson, Phil. vs. Pit., A. A., May 24 (H)	10—1
Edward Morris, Col. vs. Pit., A. A., May 29 (A)	5—0
Frank Mountain, Col. vs. Wash., A. A., June 5 (A)	12—0
Lawrence Corcoran, Chi. vs. Prov., N. L., June 27 (H)	6—0
James Galvin, Buff. vs. Det., N. L., Aug. 4 (A)	18—0
Richard Burns, Cin. vs. K.C., U. A., Aug. 26 (A)	3—1
Edward Cushman, Mil. vs. Wash., U. A., Sept. 28 (H)	5—0
1885—John Clarkson, Chi. vs. Prov., N. L., July 27 (A)	4—0
Charles Ferguson, Phil. vs. Prov., N. L., Aug. 29 (H)	1—0
1886—Albert Atkisson, Phil. vs. N.Y., A. A., May 1 (H)	3—2
William Terry, Bkn. vs. St. L., A. A., July 24 (H)	1—0
Matthew Kilroy, Balt. vs. Pit., A. A., Oct. 6 (A)	6—0
1888—William Terry, Bkn. vs. Lou., A. A., May 27 (H)	4—0
Henry Porter, K.C. vs. Balt., A. A., June 6 (A)	4—0
Edward Seward, Phil. vs. Cin., A. A., July 26 (H)	12—2
August Weyhing, Phil. vs. K.C., A. A., July 31 (H)	4—0
1890—Ledell Titcomb, Roch. vs. Syr., A. A., Sept. 15 (H)	7—0
1891—Thomas Lovett, Bkn. vs. N.Y., N. L., June 22 (H)	4—0
Amos Rusie, N.Y. vs. Bkn., N. L., July 31 (H)	6—0
Theodore Breitenstein, St. L. vs. Lou., A. A., Oct. 4* (H) (first start in majors)	8—0
1892—John Stivetts, Bos. vs. Bkn., N. L., Aug. 6 (H)	11—0
Alex Sanders, Lou. vs. Balt., N. L., Aug. 22 (H)	6—2
Charles Jones, Cin. vs. Pit., N. L., Oct. 15 (H) (first game in majors)	7—1
1893—William Hawke, Balt. vs. Wash., N. L., Aug. 16 (H) (first at 60-foot-6-inch distance.)	5—0
1897—Denton Young, Clev. vs. Cin., N. L., Sept. 18, first game (H)	6—0
1898—Theodore Brietenstein, Cin. vs. Pit., N. L., Apr. 22 (H)	11—0
James Hughes, Balt. vs. Bos., N. L., Apr. 22 (H)	8—0
Frank Donohue, Phil. vs. Bos., N. L., July 8 (H)	5—0
Walter Thornton, Chi. vs. Bkn., N. L., Aug. 21† (H)	2—0
1899—Charles (Deacon) Phillippe, Lou. vs. N.Y., N. L., May 25 (H)	7—0
Victor Willis, Bos. vs. Wash., N. L., Aug. 7 (H)	7—1
1900—Frank Hahn, Cin. vs. Phil., N. L., July 12 (H)	4—0
1901—Earl Moore, Clev. vs. Chi., A. L., May 9 (H). (Pitched 9 hitless inn. before Samuel B. Mertes singled; lost on 2 hits in 10 inn.)	2—4
Christopher Mathewson, N.Y. vs. St. L., N. L., July 15 (A)	5—0
1902—James Callahan, Chi. vs. Det., A. L., Sept. 20* (A)	3—0
1903—Charles (Chic) Fraser, Phil. vs. Chi., N. L., Sept. 18†, (A)	10—0
1904—Robert Wicker, Chi. vs. N.Y., N. L., June 11 (A) (Pitched 9⅓ hitless inn. before Samuel B. Mertes singled; won on 1 hit in 12 inn.)	1—0
Jesse Tannehill, Bos. vs. Chi., A. L., Aug. 17 (A)	6—0
1905—Christopher Mathewson, N.Y. vs. Chi., N. L., June 13 (A)	1—0
Weldon Henley, Phil. vs. St. L., A. L., July 22*, (A)	6—0
Frank Smith, Chi. vs. Det., A. L., Sept. 6† (A)	15—0
William Dinneen, Bos. vs. Chi., A. L., Sept. 27*, (H)	2—0
1906—John Lush, Phil. vs. Bkn., N. L., May 1 (A)	6—0
Malcolm Eason, Bkn. vs. St. L., N. L., July 20 (A)	2—0
1907—Frank Pfeffer, Bos. vs. Cin., N. L., May 8 (H)	6—0
Nicholas Maddox, Pit. vs. Bkn., N. L., Sept. 20 (H)	2—1
1908—Denton Young, Bos. vs. N.Y., A. L., June 30 (A)	8—0
George Rucker, Bkn. vs. Bos., N. L., Sept. 5†, (A)	6—0
Robert (Dusty) Rhoades, Clev. vs. Bos., A. L., Sept. 18 (H)	2—1
Frank Smith, Chi. vs. Phil., A. L., Sept. 20 (H)	1—0
1909—Leon Ames, N.Y. vs. Bkn., N. L., Apr. 15 (H) (Giants' opening game.) Ames pitched 9⅓ hitless inn. before Charles Alperman singled; lost on 7 hits in 13 inn.	0—3

1910—Adrian Joss, Clev. vs. Chi., A. L., Apr. 20 (A)	1—0
Charles A. Bender, Phil. vs. Clev. A. L., May 12 (H)	4—0
Thomas Hughes, N.Y. vs. Clev., A. L., Aug. 30† (H) (Pitched 9⅓ hitless inn. before Harry Niles singled; lost on 7 hits in 11 inn.)	0—5
1911—Joseph Wood, Bos. vs. St. L., A. L., July 29* (H)	5—0
Edward Walsh, Chi. vs. Bos., A. L., Aug. 27 (H)	5—0
1912—George Mullin, Det. vs. St. L., A. L., July 4† (H)	7—0
Earl Hamilton, St. L. vs. Det., A. L., Aug. 30 (A)	5—1
Charles Tesreau, N.Y. vs. Phil., N. L., Sept. 6* (A)	3—0
1914—James Scott, Chi. vs. Wash., A. L., May 14 (A) (Pitched 9 hitless inn. before Chick Gandil singled; lost on 2 hits in 10 inn.)	0—1
Joseph Benz, Chi. vs. Clev., A. L., May 31 (H)	6—1
George Davis, Bos. vs. Phil., N. L., Sept. 9† (H)	7—0
1915—Richard Marquard, N.Y. vs. Bkn., N. L., Apr. 15 (H)	2—0
James Lavender, Chi. vs. N.Y., N. L., Aug. 31* (A)	2—0
1916—Thomas Hughes, Bos. vs. Pit., N. L., June 16 (H)	2—0
George Foster, Bos. vs. N.Y., A. L., June 21 (H)	2—0
Leslie (Joe) Bush, Phil. vs. Clev., A. L., Aug. 26 (H)	5—0
Hubert (Dutch) Leonard, Bos. vs. St. L., A. L., Aug. 30 (H)	4—0
1917—Edward Cicotte, Chi. vs. St. L., A. L., Apr. 14 (A)	11—0
George Mogridge, N.Y. vs. Bos., A. L., Apr. 24 (A)	2—1
James Vaughn, Chi. vs. Cin., N. L., May 2 (H) (Pitched 9⅓ hitless inn. before Larry Kopf singled; lost on 2 hits in 10 inn. Fred Toney, Cin., pitched 10 no-hit inn. in same game.)	0—1
Ernest Koob, St. L. vs. Chi., A. L., May 5 (H)	1—0
Robert Groom, St. L. vs. Chi., A. L., May 6† (H)	3—0
1918—Hubert Leonard, Bos. vs. Det., A. L., June 3 (A)	5—0
1919—Horace Eller, Cin. vs. St. L., N. L., May 11 (H)	6—0
Raymond Caldwell, Clev. vs. N.Y., A. L., Sept. 10* (A)	3—0
1920—Walter P. Johnson, Wash. vs. Bos., A. L., July 1 (A)	1—0
1922—Jesse Barnes, N.Y. vs. Phil., N. L., May 7 (H)	6—0
1923—Samuel Jones, N.Y. vs. Phil., A. L., Sept. 4 (A)	2—0
Howard Ehmke, Bos. vs. Phil., A. L., Sept. 7 (A)	4—0
1924—Jesse Haines, St. L. vs. Bos., N. L., July 17 (H)	5—0
1925—Arthur (Dazzy) Vance, Bkn. vs. Phil., N. L., Sept. 13* (H)	10—1
1926—Theodore Lyons, Chi. vs. Bos., A. L., Aug. 21 (A)	6—0
1929—Carl Hubbell, N.Y. vs. Pit., N. L., May 8 (H)	11—0
1931—Wesley Ferrell, Clev. vs. St. L., A. L., Apr. 29 (H)	9—0
Robert Burke, Wash. vs. Bos., A. L., Aug. 8 (H)	5—0
1934—Louis Newsom, St. L. vs. Bos., A. L., Sept. 18 (H) (Pitched 9⅔ hitless inn. before Roy Johnson singled; lost on 1 hit in 10 inn.)	1—2
Paul Dean, St. L. vs. Bkn. N. L., Sept. 21† (A)	3—0
1935—Vernon Kennedy, Chi. vs. Clev., A. L., Aug. 31 (H)	5—0
1937—William Dietrich, Chi. vs. St. L., A. L., June 1 (H)	8—0
1938—John Vander Meer, Cin. vs. Bos., N. L., June 11 (H)	3—0
John Vander Meer, Cin. vs. Bkn., N. L., June 15 (A) (Vander Meer's 2 no-hitters were successive.)	6—0
Monte Pearson, N.Y.vs. Clev., A. L., Aug. 27† (H)	13—0
1940—Robert Feller, Clev. vs. Chi., A. L., Apr. 16 (A) (opening day)	1—0
James Carleton, Bkn vs. Cin., N. L., Apr. 30 (A)	3—0
1941—Lonnie Warneke, St. L. vs. Cin., N. L., Aug. 30 (A)	2—0
1944—James Tobin, Bos. vs. Bkn., N. L., Apr. 27 (H)	2—0
Clyde Shoun, Cin. vs. Bos., N. L. May 15 (H)	1—0
1945—Richard Fowler, Phil. vs. St. L., A. L., Sept. 9† (H)	1—0
1946—Edward Head, Bkn. vs. Bos., N. L., Apr. 23 (H)	5—0
Robert Feller, Clev. vs. N.Y., A. L., Apr. 30 (A)	1—0
1947—Ewell Blackwell, Cin. vs. Bos., N. L., June 18, (H)	6—0
Donald Black, Clev. vs. Phil., A. L., July 10* (H)	3—0
William McCahan, Phil. vs. Wash., A. L., Sept. 3 (H)	3—0
1948—Robert Lemon, Clev. vs. Det., A. L., June 30, (A)	2—0
Rex Barney, Bkn. vs. N.Y., N. L., Sept. 9, (A)	2—0
1950—Vernon Bickford, Bos. vs. Bkn., N. L., Aug. 11 (H)	7—0
1951—Clifford Chambers, Pit. vs. Bos., N. L., May 6† (A)	3—0
Robert Feller, Clev. vs. Det., A. L., July 1* (H)	2—1
Allie Reynolds, N. Y. vs. Clev., A. L., July 12, (A)	1—0
Allie Reynolds, N. Y. vs. Bos., A. L., Sept. 28* (H)	8—0
1952—Virgil Trucks, Det. vs. Wash., A. L., May 15 (H)	1—0
Carl Erskine, Bkn. vs. Chi., N. L., June 19 (H)	5—0
Virgil Trucks, Det. vs. N. Y., A. L., Aug. 25 (A)	1—0
1953—Alva (Bobo) Holloman, St. L. vs. Phil., A. L., May 6 (H) (first start in major leagues)	6—0
1954—James Wilson, Mil. vs. Phil., N. L., June 12 (H)	2—0
1955—Samuel Jones, Chi. vs. Pit., N. L., May 12 (H)	4—0
1956—Carl Erskine, Bkn. vs. N. Y., N. L., May 12 (H)	3—0
John Klippstein (7 inn.), Hershell Freeman (1 inn.) and Joseph Black (3 inn.), Cin. vs. Mil. , N. L., May 26 (A) Jack Dittmer doubled for first hit with 2 out in 10th inn. and Black lost on 3 hits in 11 inn.)	1—2
Melvin Parnell, Bos. vs. Chi., A. L., July 14 (H)	4—0
Salvatore Maglie, Bkn. vs. Phil., N. L., Sept. 25 (H)	5—0
1957—Robert Keegan, Chi. vs. Wash., A. L., Aug. 20† (H)	6—0
1958—James Bunning, Det. vs. Bos., A. L., July 20* (A)	3—0
J. Hoyt Wilhelm, Balt. vs. N. Y., A. L., Sept. 20 (H)	1—0
1960—Donald Cardwell, Chi. vs. St. L., N. L., May 15† (H)	4—0
S. Lewis Burdette, Mil. vs. Phil., N. L., Aug. 18 (H)	1—0
Warren Spahn, Mil. vs. Phil., N. L., Sept. 16 (H)	4—0
1961—Warren Spahn, Mil. vs. S. F., N. L., Apr. 28 (H)	1—0
1962—Robert (Bo) Belinsky, L. A. vs. Balt., A. L., May 5 (H)	2—0
Earl Wilson, Bos. vs. L. A., A. L., June 26 (H)	2—0
Sanford Koufax, L. A. vs. N. Y., N. L., June 30 (H)	5—0
William Monbouquette, Bos. vs. Chi., A. L., Aug. 1 (A)	1—0
John Kralick, Minn. vs. K. C., A. L., Aug. 26 (H)	1—0
1963—Sanford Koufax, L. A. vs. S. F., N. L., May 11 (H)	8—0
Donald Nottebart, Hous. vs. Phil., N. L., May 17 (H)	4—1
Juan Marichal, S. F. vs. Hous., N. L., June 15 (H)	1—0
1964—Kenneth Johnson, Hous. vs. Cin., N. L., Apr. 23 (H)	0—1
Sanford Koufax, L. A. vs. Phil., N. L., June 4 (A)	3—0
1965—David Morehead, Bos. vs. Clev., A. L., Sept. 16 (H)	2—0
1966—Wilfred (Sonny) Siebert, Clev. vs. Wash., A. L., June 10 (H)	2—0
1967—Stephen D. Barber (8⅔ inn.) and Stuart L. Miller (⅓ inn.), Balt. vs. Det. A. L., Apr. 30* (H)	1—2
Donald E. Wilson, Hous. vs. Atl., N. L., June 18 (H)	2—0
W. Dean Chance, Min. vs. Clev., A. L., Aug. 25† (A)	2—1
Joel E. Horlen, Chi. vs. Det., A. L., Sept. 10* (H)	6—0
1968—Thomas H. Phoebus, Balt. vs. Bos., A. L., Apr. 27 (H)	6—0
George R. Culver, Cin. vs. Phil., N. L., July 29† (A)	6—1
Gaylord J. Perry, S. F. vs. St. L., N. L., Sept. 17 (H)	1—0
Ray C. Washburn, St. L. vs. S. F., N. L., Sept. 18 (A)	2—0
1969—William H. Stoneman, Mon. vs. Phil., N. L., Apr. 17 (A)	7—0
James W. Maloney, Cin. vs. Hous., N. L., Apr. 30 (H)	10—0
Donald E. Wilson, Hous. vs. Cin., N. L., May 1 (A)	4—0
James A. Palmer, Balt. vs. Oak., A. L., Aug. 13 (H)	8—0
Kenneth D. Holtzman, Chi. vs. Atl., N. L., Aug. 19 (H)	3—0
Robert R. Moose, Pit. vs. N. Y., N. L., Sept. 20 (A)	4—0
1970—Dock P. Ellis, Pit. vs. S. D., N. L., June 12* (A)	2—0
Clyde Wright, Cal. vs. Oak., A. L., July 3 (H)	4—0
William R. Singer, L. A. vs. Phil., N. L., July 20, (H)	5—0
Vida Blue, Oak. vs. Min., A. L., Sept. 21 (H)	6—0
1971—Kenneth D. Holtzman, Chi. vs. Cin., N. L., June 3 (A)	1—0
Richard C. Wise, Phil. vs. Cin., N. L., June 23 (A)	4—0
Robert Gibson, St. L. vs. Pit., N. L., Aug. 14 (A)	11—0
1972—Burt C. Hooton, Chi. vs. Phil., N. L., Apr. 16 (H)	4—0
Milton S. Pappas, Chi. vs. S. D., N. L., Sept. 2 (H)	8—0
William H. Stoneman, Mon. vs. N. Y., N. L., Oct. 2* (H)	7—0
1973—Steven L. Busby, K. C. vs. Det., A. L., Apr. 27 (A)	3—0
L. Nolan Ryan, Cal. vs. K. C., A. L., May 15 (A)	3—0
L. Nolan Ryan, Cal. vs. Det., A. L., July 15 (A)	6—0
James B. Bibby, Tex. vs. Oak., A. L., July 30 (A)	6—0
Philip H. Niekro, Atl. vs. S. D., N. L., Aug. 5 (H)	9—0
1974—Steven L. Busby, K. C. vs. Mil., A. L., June 19 (A)	2—0
Richard A. Bosman, Clev. vs. Oak., A. L., July 19 (H)	4—0
L. Nolan Ryan, Cal. vs. Min., A. L., Sept. 28 (H)	4—0
1975—L. Nolan Ryan, Cal. vs. Balt., A. L., June 1 (H)	1—0
Edward L. Halicki, S. F. vs. N. Y., N. L., Aug.24† (H)	6—0
Vida Blue (5 inn.), W. Glenn Abbott (1 inn.), Paul A. Lindblad (1 inn.) and Roland G. Fingers (2 inn.), Oak. vs. Cal., A. L., Sept. 28, 1975, (H).	5—0
1976—Lawrence E. Dierker, Hous. vs. Mon., N. L., July 9 (H)	6—0
Johnny L. Odom (5 inn.) and Francisco J. Barrios (4 inn.), Chi. vs. Oak., A. L., July 28 (A).	2—1
John R. Candelaria, Pit. vs. L. A., N. L., Aug. 9 (H)	2—0
John J. Montefusco, S. F. vs. Atl., N. L., Sept. 29 (A)	9—0
1977—James W. Colborn, K. C. vs. Tex., A. L., May 14 (H)	6—0
Dennis L. Eckersley, Clev. vs. Cal., A. L., May 30 (H)	1—0
Rikalbert Blyleven, Tex. vs. Cal., A. L., Sept. 22 (A)	6—0
1978—Robert H. Forsch, St. L. vs. Phil., N. L., Apr. 16 (H)	5—0
G. Thomas Seaver, Cin. vs. St. L., N. L., June 16 (H)	4—0
1979—Kenneth R. Forsch, Hous. vs. Atl., N. L., Apr. 7 (H)	6—0
1980—Jerry Reuss, L. A. vs. S. F., N. L., June 27 (A)	8—0
1981—Charles W. Lea, Mon. vs. S. F., N. L., May 10† (H)	4—0
L. Nolan Ryan, Hous. vs. L. A., N. L., Sept. 26 (H)	5—0
1983—David A. Righetti, N. Y. vs. Bos., A. L., July 4 (H)	4—0
Robert H. Forsch, St. L. vs. Mon., N. L., Sept. 26 (H)	3—0
Michael B. Warren, Oak. vs. Chi., A. L., Sept. 29 (H)	3—0
1984—John S. Morris, Det. vs. Chi., A.L., Apr. 7 (A)	4—0
1986—Joseph A. Cowley, Chi. vs. Cal., A.L., Sept. 19 (A)	7—1
Michael W. Scott, Hou. vs. S.F., N.L., Sept. 25 (H)	2—0
1987—Juan M. Nieves, Mil. vs. Balt., A.L., Apr. 15 (A)	7—0

Less Than Nine Innings

1884—Lawrence J. McKeon, 6 inn., Ind. vs. Cin., A. A., May 6 (A)	0—0
Charles Gagus, 8 inn., Wash. vs. Wilm., U. A., Aug. 21 (H)	12—1
Charles H. Getzein, 6 inn., Det. vs. Phil., N. L. Oct. 1 (H)	1—0
Charles J. Sweeney (3 inn.) and Henry J. Boyle (2 inn.), 5 inn., St. L. vs. St. P., U. A., Oct. 5 (H).	0—1
1885—Fred L. Shaw, 5 inn., Prov. vs. Buff., N. L., Oct. 7* (A)	4—0
1888—George E. Van Haltren, 6 inn., Chi. vs. Pit., N. L., June 21 (H)	1—0
Edward N. Crane, 7 inn., N. Y. vs. Wash., N. L., Sept. 27 (H)	3—0
1889—Matthew A. Kilroy, 7 inn., Balt. vs. St. L., A. A., July 29† (H)	0—0
1890—Charles K. King, 8 inn., Chi. vs. Bkn., P. L., June 21 (H)	0—1
George E. Nicol, 7 inn., St. L. vs. Phil., A. A., Sept. 23 (H)	21—2
Henry C. Gastright, 8 inn., Col. vs. Tol., A. A., Oct. 12 (H)	6—0
1892—John E. Stivetts, 5 inn., Bos. vs. Wash., N. L., Oct. 15† (A)	6—0
1893—Elton P. Chamberlain, 7 inn., Cin. vs. Bos., N. L., Sept. 23† (H)	6—0
1894—Edward F. Stein, 6 inn., Bkn. vs. Chi., N. L., June 2 (H)	1—0
1903—Leon K. Ames, 5 inn., N. Y. vs. St. L., N. L., Sept. 14† (A) (first game in majors)	5—0
1905—George E. Waddell, 5 inn., Phil. vs. St. L., A. L., Aug. 15 (H)	2—0

1906—John W. Weimer, 7 inn., Cin. vs. Bkn., N. L., Aug. 24† (H).............. 1—0
James H. Dygert (3 inn.) and George E. Waddell (2 inn.), 5 inn., Phil. vs. Chi., A. L., Aug. 29 (H)............. 4—3
Grant McGlynn, 7 inn., St. L. vs. Bkn., N. L., Sept. 24† (A) .... 1—1
Albert P. Leifield, 6 inn., Pit. vs. Phil., N. L., Sept. 26† (A).......... 8—0

1907—Edward A. Walsh, 5 inn., Chi. vs. N.Y., A. L., May 26 (H)......... 8—1
Edwin Karger, 7 perfect inn., St. L. vs. Bos., N. L., August 11† (H)............. 4—0
S. Howard Camnitz, 5 inn., Pit. vs. N. Y., N. L., Aug. 23† (A) ...... 1—0
Harry P. Vickers, 5 perfect inn., Phil. vs. Wash., A. L., Oct. 5† (A) .... 4—0

1908—John C. Lush, 6 inn., St. L. vs. Bkn., N. L., Aug. 6 (A)........... 2—0
1910—Leonard L. Cole, 7 inn., Chi. vs. St. L., N. L., July 31† (A)...... 4—0
1912—J. Carl Cashion, 6 inn., Wash. vs. Clev., A. L., Aug. 20† (H) .... 2—0
1924—Walter P. Johnson, 7 inn., Wash. vs. St. L., A. L., Aug. 25 (H)...... 2—0
1937—Fred M. Frankhouse, 8 inn., Bkn. vs. Cin., N. L., Aug. 27 (H)......... 5—0
1940—John H. Whitehead, 6 inn., St. L. vs. Det., A. L., Aug. 5† (H)...... 4—0
1944—James A. Tobin, 5 inn., Bos. vs. Phil., N. L., June 22† (H) .... 7—0
1959—Michael F. McCormick, 5 inn., S. F. vs. Phil., N. L., June 12 (A)
(Allowed single to Richie Ashburn in sixth inning, but game was halted because of rain before completion of the inning. The hit was erased because, under existing rules, records reverted to the last completed inning.)............... 3—0
Samuel Jones, 7 inn., S. F. vs. St. L., N. L., Sept. 26 (A) ...... 4—0
1967—W. Dean Chance, 5 perfect inn., Min. vs. Bos., A. L., Aug. 6 (H)..... 2—0
1984—David W. Palmer, 5 perfect inn., Mon. vs. St. L., N.L., Apr. 21† (A)............. 4—0

Two Complete-Game Victories In One Day
National League (34)

Date	Pitcher	Scores	
Sept. 9, 1876	William A. Cummings, Hart	14-4	8-4
Aug. 9, 1878	John M. Ward, Prov.	12-6	8-5
July 12, 1879	James F. Galvin, Buff.	4-3	z5-4
July 4, 1881	Michael F. Welch, Troy	8-0	12-3
July 4, 1882	James F. Galvin, Buff.	9-5	18-8
May 30, 1884	Charles M. Radbourn, Prov.	12-9	9-2
Oct. 7, 1885	Fred L. Shaw, Prov.	*4-0	*6-1
Oct. 10, 1885	Fred L. Shaw, Prov.	†3-0	*7-3
Oct. 9, 1886	Charles J. Ferguson, Phil.	5-1	†6-1
Aug. 20, 1887	James E. Whitney, Wash.	3-1	4-3
Sept. 12, 1889	John G. Clarkson, Bos.	3-2	5-0
May 30, 1890	William F. Hutchinson, Chi.	6-4	11-7
Oct. 4, 1890	Denton T. Young, Clev.	5-1	7-3
Sept. 12, 1891	Mark E. Baldwin, Pit.	13-3	8-4
Sept. 28, 1891	Amos W. Rusie, N.Y.	10-4	†13-5
May 30, 1892	Mark E. Baldwin, Pit.	11-1	4-3
Sept. 5, 1892	John E. Stivetts, Bos.	y2-1	5-2
Oct. 4, 1892	Amos W. Rusie, N.Y.	6-4	9-5
May 30, 1893	William P. Kennedy, Bkn.	3-0	6-2
June 3, 1897	J. Bentley Seymour, N.Y.	6-1	‡10-6
Aug. 1, 1903	Joseph J. McGinnity, N.Y.	4-1	5-2
Aug. 8, 1903	Joseph J. McGinnity, N.Y.	6-1	4-3
Aug. 31, 1903	Joseph J. McGinnity, N.Y.	4-1	9-2
Oct. 3, 1905	William D. Scanlon, Bkn.	4-0	3-2
Sept. 26, 1908	Edward M. Reulbach, Chi.	5-0	3-0
Sept. 9, 1916	William D. Perritt, N.Y.	3-1	3-0
Sept. 20, 1916	Albert W. Demaree, Phil.	7-0	3-2
Sept. 23, 1916	Grover C. Alexander, Phil.	7-3	4-0
July 1, 1917	Fred A. Toney, Cin.	4-1	5-1
Sept. 3, 1917	Grover C. Alexander, Phil.	5-0	9-3
Sept. 18, 1917	William L. Doak, St. L.	2-0	12-4
Aug. 13, 1921	John R. Watson, Bos.	4-3	8-0
July 10, 1923	John D. Stuart, St. L.	11-1	6-3
July 19, 1924	Herman S. Bell, St. L.	6-1	2-1

American League (10)

Date	Pitcher	Scores	
July 1, 1905	Frank M. Owen, Chi.	3-2	2-0
Sept. 26, 1905	Edward A. Walsh, Chi.	10-5	§3-1
Sept. 22, 1906	George E. Mullin, Det.	5-3	4-3
Sept. 25, 1908	Oren E. Summers, Det.	7-2	x1-0
Sept. 29, 1908	Edward A. Walsh, Chi.	5-1	2-0
Sept. 22, 1914	Ray W. Collins, Bos.	5-3	§5-0
July 29, 1916	Arthur J. Davenport, St. L.	3-1	3-2
Aug. 30, 1918	Carl W. Mays, Bos.	12-0	4-1
Sept. 6, 1924	Urban J. Shocker, St. L.	6-2	6-2
Aug. 28, 1926	Emil H. Levsen, Clev.	6-1	5-1

American Association (5)

Date	Pitcher	Scores	
July 4, 1883	Timothy J. Keefe, N.Y.	9-1	3-0
July 4, 1884	Guy J. Hecker, Lou.	5-4	8-2
July 26, 1887	Matthew A. Kilroy, Balt.	‡8-0	9-1
Oct. 1, 1887	Matthew A. Kilroy, Balt.	5-2	‡8-1
Sept. 20, 1888	Anthony J. Mullane, Cin.	1-0	2-1

Players League (3)

Date	Pitcher	Scores	
July 26, 1890	Henry Gruber, Clev.	6-1	8-7
Aug. 20, 1890	Ellsworth E. Cunningham, Buff.	6-2	7-0
Sept. 27, 1890	Edward N. Crane, N.Y.	9-8	8-3

*5 innings. †6 innings. ‡7 innings. §8 innings. x10 innings. y11 innings. z12 innings.

Fielding
Unassisted Triple Plays (8)

Neal Ball, shortstop, Cleveland A. L., vs. Boston at Cleveland, July 19, 1909, first game, second inning. Ball caught McConnell's liner, touched second, retiring Wagner, who was on his way to third base, and then tagged Stahl as he came up to second.

William A. Wambsganss, second baseman, Cleveland A. L. vs. Brooklyn N. L., in World Series game at Cleveland, October 10, 1920, fifth inning. Wambsganss caught Mitchell's line drive, stepped on second to retire Kilduff, then tagged Miller coming from first.

George H. Burns, first baseman, Boston A. L., vs. Cleveland at Boston, September 14, 1923, second inning. Burns caught Brower's liner, tagged Lutzke off first and then ran to second and reached that bag before Stephenson could return from third base.

Ernest K. Padgett, shortstop, Boston N. L., vs. Philadelphia at Boston, October 6, 1923, second game, fourth inning. Padgett caught Holke's liner, ran to second to retire Tierney, then tagged Lee before he could return to first.

F. Glenn Wright, shortstop, Pittsburgh N. L., vs. St. Louis at Pittsburgh, May 7, 1925, ninth inning. Wright caught Bottomley's liner, ran to second to retire Cooney and then tagged Hornsby, who was en route to second.

James E. Cooney, shortstop, Chicago N. L., vs. Pittsburgh at Pittsburgh, May 30, 1927, a.m. game, fourth inning. Cooney caught Paul Waner's liner, stepped on second to retire Lloyd Waner, then tagged Barnhart off first.

John H. Neun, first baseman, Detroit A. L., vs. Cleveland at Detroit, May 31, 1927, ninth inning. Neun caught Summa's liner, ran over and tagged Jamieson between first and second and then touched second base before Myatt could return.

Ronald L. Hansen, shortstop, Washington A. L., vs. Cleveland at Cleveland, July 30, 1968, first inning. With the count 3 and 2 on Azcue, Nelson broke for third base. Hansen caught Azcue's liner, stepped on second to double Nelson and then tagged Snyder going into second base.

(All above unassisted triple plays made with runners on first and second bases only.)

Club Miscellaneous
Lifetime Franchise Won-Lost Records
American League—1901 Through 1987

Present Franchise		Total Games	Won	Lost	Tied	Pct.
Baltimore	1954-87	5377	2918	2450	9	.544
Boston	1901-87	13476	6824	6568	84	.510
California*	1961-87	4312	2083	2226	3	.483
Chicago	1901-87	13486	6727	6658	101	.503
Cleveland	1901-87	13492	6832	6569	91	.510
Detroit	1901-87	13516	6986	6436	94	.520
Kansas City	1969-87	3012	1570	1440	2	.522
Milwaukee	1970-87	2853	1374	1477	2	.482
Minnesota	1961-87	4310	2163	2140	7	.503
New York	1903-87	13192	7482	5625	85	.571
Oakland	1968-87	3178	1608	1569	1	.506
Seattle	1977-87	1729	719	1008	2	.416
Texas	1972-87	2526	1181	1341	4	.468
Toronto	1977-87	1725	807	916	2	.468
Present Totals		96184	49274	46423	487	.515

*Known as Los Angeles 1961-65.

American League—1901 Through 1971

Extinct Franchises		Total Games	Won	Lost	Tied	Pct.
Baltimore	1901-02	276	118	153	5	.437
Kansas City	1955-67	2060	829	1224	7	.404
Milwaukee	1901	139	48	89	2	.353
Philadelphia	1901-54	8213	3886	4248	79	.478
St. Louis	1902-53	7974	3414	4465	95	.434
Seattle	1969	163	64	98	1	.396
aWashington	1901-60	9188	4223	4864	101	.465
bWashington	1961-71	1773	740	1032	1	.418
Extinct Totals		29786	13322	16173	291	.452
American League Totals		125970	62596	62596	778	.500

aOriginal Washington club.
bSecond Washington club.

National League—1876 Through 1987

Present Franchise		Total Games	Won	Lost	Tied	Pct.
Atlanta	1966-87	3499	1656	1837	6	.474
Chicago	1876-87	16425	8450	7823	152	.519
Cincinnati	1890-87	15052	7553	7376	123	.506
Houston	1962-87	4153	1999	2150	4	.482
Los Angeles	1958-87	4778	2601	2172	5	.545
Montreal	1969-87	3013	1449	1562	2	.481
New York	1962-87	4151	1886	2257	8	.455
Philadelphia	1883-87	15820	7324	8385	111	.466
Pittsburgh	1887-87	15434	7903	7405	126	.516
St. Louis	1892-87	14779	7406	7248	125	.505
San Diego	1969-87	3017	1309	1706	2	.434
San Francisco	1958-87	4775	2457	2313	5	.515
Present Totals		104896	51993	52234	669	.499

National League—1876 Through 1965

Extinct Franchise		Total Games	Won	Lost	Tied	Pct.
Baltimore	1892-99	1117	644	447	26	.588
Boston	1876-52	10852	5118	5598	136	.478
Brooklyn	1890-57	10253	5214	4926	113	.514
Buffalo	1879-85	656	314	333	9	.486
Cincinnati	1876-80	348	125	217	6	.368
Cleveland	1879-84	549	242	299	8	.448
Cleveland	1889-99	1534	738	764	32	.492
Detroit	1881-88	879	426	437	16	.494
Hartford	1876-77	129	78	48	3	.619
Indianapolis	1878	63	24	36	3	.405
Indianapolis	1887-89	398	146	249	3	.371
Kansas City	1886	126	30	91	5	.258
Louisville	1876-77	130	65	61	4	.515
Louisville	1892-99	1121	419	683	19	.382
Milwaukee	1878	61	15	45	1	.254
Milwaukee	1953-65	2044	1146	890	8	.563
New York	1876	57	21	35	1	.377
New York	1883-57	11116	6067	4898	151	.553
Philadelphia	1876	60	14	45	1	.242
Providence	1878-85	725	438	278	9	.610
St. Louis	1876-77	124	73	51	0	.589
St. Louis	1885-86	236	79	151	6	.347
Syracuse	1879	71	22	48	1	.317
Troy	1879-82	330	134	191	5	.414
Washington	1886-89	514	163	337	14	.331
Washington	1892-99	1125	410	697	18	.372
Worcester	1880-82	252	90	159	3	.363
Extinct Totals		44870	22255	22014	601	.503
National League Totals		149766	74248	74248	1270	.500

American Association—1882 Through 1891

Extinct Franchise		Total Games	Won	Lost	Tied	Pct.
Baltimore	1882-89	944	403	519	22	.439
Baltimore	1890-91	174	87	81	6	.517
Boston	1891	139	93	42	4	.684
Brooklyn	1884-89	783	410	354	19	.536
Brooklyn	1890	101	26	74	1	.262
Cincinnati	1882-89	957	549	396	12	.580
Cincinnati	1891	102	43	57	2	.431
Cleveland	1887-88	268	89	174	5	.341
Columbus	1883-84	207	101	104	2	.493
Columbus	1889-91	418	200	209	9	.489
Indianapolis	1884	110	29	78	3	.277
Kansas City	1888-89	271	98	171	2	.365
Louisville	1882-91	1233	575	638	20	.475
Milwaukee	1891	36	21	15	0	.583
New York	1883-87	592	270	309	13	.467
Philadelphia	1882-91	1223	633	564	26	.528
Pittsburgh	1882-86	538	236	296	6	.444
Richmond	1884	46	12	30	4	.304
Rochester	1890	133	63	63	7	.500
St. Louis	1882-91	1235	782	433	20	.641
Syracuse	1890	128	55	72	1	.434
Toledo	1884	110	46	58	6	.446
Toledo	1890	134	68	64	2	.515
Washington	1884	63	12	51	0	.191
Washington	1891	139	43	92	4	.324
Association Totals		10084	4944	4944	196	.500

Games Of 18 Or More Innings

American League

25 Innings—(1)
Chicago 7, Milwaukee 6, May 8, 1984 (17 innings), finished May 9, 1984 (8 innings), at Chi.

24 Innings—(2)
Philadelphia 4, Boston 1, September 1, 1906 at Boston.
Detroit 1, Philadelphia 1 (tie), July 21, 1945 at Philadelphia.

22 Innings—(3)
New York 9, Detroit 7, June 24, 1962 at Detroit.
Washington 6, Chicago 5, June 12, 1967 at Washington.
Milwaukee 4, Minnesota 3, May 12, 1972 (21 innings), finished May 13, 1972 (1 inning) at Min.

21 Innings—(3)
Detroit 6, Chicago 5, May 24, 1929 at Chicago.
Oakland 5, Washington 3, June 4, 1971 at Washington.
Chicago 6, Cleveland 3, May 26, 1973, finished May 28, 1973 at Chi.

20 Innings—(8)
Philadelphia 4, Boston 2, July 4, 1905, p.m. game at Boston.
Washington 9, Minnesota 7, August 9, 1967 at Minnesota.
New York 4, Boston 3, August 29, 1967, second game, at New York.
Boston 5, Seattle 3, July 27, 1969, at Seattle.
Oakland 1, California 0, July 9, 1971, at Oakland.
Washington 8, Cleveland 6, Sept. 14, 1971, second game (16 innings), finished Sept. 20, 1971 (4 innings), started in Clev., finished at Wash.
Seattle 8, Boston 7, Sept. 3, 1981, finished Sept. 4, 1981 (1 inning) at Bos.
California 4, Seattle 3, April 13, 1982 (17 innings), finished April 14, 1982 (3 innings), at Cal.

19 Innings—(13)
Washington 5, Philadelphia 4, September 27, 1912 at Philadelphia.
Chicago 5, Cleveland 4, June 24, 1915 at Cleveland.
Cleveland 3, New York 2, May 24, 1918 at New York.
St. Louis 8, Washington 6, August 9, 1921 at Washington.
Chicago 5, Boston 4, July 13, 1951 at Chicago.
Cleveland 4, St. Louis 3, July 1, 1952 at Cleveland.
Cleveland 3, Washington 2, June 14, 1963, second game, at Clev.
Baltimore 7, Washington 5, June 4, 1967 at Baltimore.
Kansas City 6, Detroit 5, June 17, 1967, second game, at Detroit.
Detroit 3, New York 3, (tie), August 23, 1968, second game, at N.Y.
Oakland 5, Chicago 3, Aug. 10, 1972 (17 innings), finished Aug. 11, 1972 (2 innings), at Oak.
New York 5, Minnesota 4, August 25, 1976, at New York.
Cleveland 8, Detroit 4, April 27, 1984, at Detroit.

18 Innings—(19)
Chicago 6, New York 6 (tie), June 25, 1903 at Chicago.
Washington 0, Detroit 0 (tie), July 16, 1909 at Detroit.
Washington 1, Chicago 0, May 15, 1918 at Washington.
Detroit 7, Washington 6, August 4, 1918 at Detroit.
Boston 12, New York 11, September 5, 1927, first game, at Boston.
Philadelphia 18, Cleveland 17, July 10, 1932 at Cleveland.
New York 3, Chicago 3 (tie), August 21, 1933 at Chicago.
Washington 1, Chicago 0, June 8, 1947, first game, at Chicago.
Washington 5, St. Louis 5 (tie), June 20, 1952 at St. Louis.
Chicago 2, Baltimore 1 (tie), August 6, 1959 at Baltimore.
New York 7, Boston 6, April 16, 1967 at New York.
Minnesota 3, New York 2, July 26, 1967, second game, at New York.
Baltimore 3, Boston 2, August 25, 1968, at Baltimore.
Minnesota 11, Seattle 7, July 19, 1969 (16 innings), finished July 20, 1969 (2 innings), at Sea.
Oakland 9, Baltimore 8, August 24, 1969, second game at Oakland.
Minnesota 8, Oakland 6, September 6, 1969, at Oakland.
Washington 2, New York 1, April 22, 1970, at Washington.
Texas 4, Kansas City 3, May 17, 1972, at Kansas City.
Detroit 4, Cleveland 3, June 9, 1982 (14 innings), finished September 24, 1982 (4 innings), at Detroit.

National League

26 Innings—(1)
Brooklyn 1, Boston 1 (tie), May 1, 1920 at Boston.

25 Innings—(1)
St. Louis 4, New York 3, September 11, 1974, at New York.

24 Innings—(1)
Houston 1, New York 0, April 15, 1968, at Houston.

23 Innings—(2)
Brooklyn 2, Boston 2 (tie), June 27, 1939 at Boston.
San Francisco 8, New York 6, May 31, 1964, second game, at N.Y.

22 Innings—(2)
Brooklyn 6, Pittsburgh 5, August 22, 1917 at Brooklyn.
Chicago 4, Boston 3, May 17, 1927 at Boston.

21 Innings—(7)
New York 3, Pittsburgh 1, July 17, 1914 at Pittsburgh.
Chicago 2, Philadelphia 1, July 17, 1918 at Chicago.
Pittsburgh 2, Boston 0, August 1, 1918 at Boston.
San Francisco 1, Cincinnati 0, September 1, 1967, at Cincinnati.
Houston 2, San Diego 1, September 24, 1971, first game, at San Diego.
San Diego 11, Montreal 8, May 21, 1977, at Montreal.
Los Angeles 2, Chicago 1, Aug. 17, 1982 (17 innings), finished Aug. 18, 1982 (4 innings), at Chi.

20 Innings—(8)
Chicago 7, Cincinnati 7 (tie), June 30, 1892 at Cincinnati.
Chicago 2, Philadelphia 1, August 24, 1905 at Philadelphia.
Brooklyn 9, Philadelphia 9 (tie), April 30, 1919 at Philadelphia.
St. Louis 8, Chicago 7, August 28, 1930 at Chicago.
Brooklyn 6, Boston 2, July 5, 1940 at Boston.
Philadelphia 5, Atlanta 4, May 4, 1973, at Philadelphia.
Pittsburgh 5, Chicago 4, July 6, 1980, at Pittsburgh.
Houston 3, San Diego 1, August 15, 1980, at San Diego.

19 Innings—(15)
Chicago 3, Pittsburgh 2, June 22, 1902 at Chicago.
Pittsburgh 7, Boston 6, July 31, 1912 at Boston.
Chicago 4, Brooklyn 3, June 17, 1915 at Chicago.
St. Louis 8, Philadelphia 8 (tie), June 13, 1918 at Philadelphia.
Boston 2, Brooklyn 1, May 3, 1920 at Boston.
Brooklyn 9, Chicago 9, May 17, 1939 at Chicago.
Cincinnati 0, Brooklyn 0 (tie), September 11, 1946 at Brooklyn.
Philadelphia 8, Cincinnati 7, Sept. 15, 1950, second game, at Phil.
Pittsburgh 4, Milwaukee 3, July 19, 1955, at Pittsburgh.
Cincinnati 2, Los Angeles 1, August 8, 1972, at Cincinnati.
New York 7, Los Angeles 3, May 24, 1973, at Los Angeles.
Pittsburgh 4, San Diego 2, August 25, 1979, at San Diego.
New York 16, Atlanta 13, July 4, 1985, at Atlanta.
Montreal 6, Houston 3, July 7, 1985, at Houston.

18 Innings—(30)
Providence 1, Detroit 0, August 17, 1882 at Providence.
Brooklyn 7, St. Louis 7 (tie), August 17, 1902 at St. Louis.
Chicago 2, St. Louis 1, June 24, 1905 at St. Louis.
Pittsburgh 3, Chicago 2, June 28, 1916, second game, at Chicago.
Philadelphia 10, Brooklyn 9, June 1, 1919 at Brooklyn.
New York 9, Pittsburgh 8, July 7, 1922 at Pittsburgh.
Chicago 7, Boston 2, May 14, 1927 at Boston.
New York 1, St. Louis 0, July 2, 1933, first game, at New York.
St. Louis 8, Cincinnati 6, July 1, 1934, first game, at Cincinnati.
Chicago 10, Cincinnati 8, August 9, 1942, first game, at Cincinnati.

Philadelphia 4, Pittsburgh 3, June 9, 1949 at Philadelphia.
Cincinnati 7, Chicago 6, September 7, 1951, at Cincinnati.
Philadelphia 0, New York 0 (tie), Oct. 2, 1965, second game, at N.Y.
Cincinnati 3, Chicago 2, July 19, 1966 at Chicago.
Philadelphia 2, Cincinnati 1, May 21, 1967 at Philadelphia.
Pittsburgh 1, San Diego 0, June 7, 1972, second game, at San Diego.
New York 3, Philadelphia 2, August 1, 1972, first game, at New York.
Montreal 5, Chicago 4, June 27, 1973, finished June 28, 1973 at Chicago.
Chicago 8, Montreal 7, June 28, 1974, first game, at Montreal.
New York 4, Montreal 3, September 16, 1975, at New York.
Pittsburgh 2, Chicago 1, August 10, 1977, at Pittsburgh.
Chicago 9, Cincinnati 8, May 10, 1979, finished July 23 at Chicago.
Houston 3, New York 2, June 18, 1979, at Houston.
San Diego 8, New York 6, August 26, 1980, at New York.
St. Louis 3, Houston 1, May 27, 1983, at Houston.
Pittsburgh 4, San Francisco 3, July 13, 1984, second game, at Pit.
Atlanta 3, Los Angeles 2, September 6, 1984, at Los Angeles.
New York 5, Pittsburgh 4, April 28, 1985, at New York.
San Francisco 5, Atlanta 4, June 11, 1985, at Atlanta.
Houston 8, Chicago 7, September 2, 1986 (14 innings), finished September 3, 1986 (4 innings) at Chicago.

Non-Playing Personnel
Commissioners

Kenesaw M. Landis, Jan. 12, 1921 to Nov. 25, 1944.
Albert B. Chandler, April 24, 1945 to July 15, 1951.
Ford C. Frick, Oct. 8, 1951 through Dec. 14, 1965.
William D. Eckert, Dec. 15, 1965 to Feb. 4, 1969.

Bowie K. Kuhn, Feb. 4, 1969 through Sept. 30, 1984.
Peter V. Ueberroth, Oct. 1, 1984 to present.

Presidents
National League

Morgan G. Bulkeley, 1876.
William A. Hulbert, 1876 to 1882.
Arthur H. Soden, 1882.
Col. A. G. Mills, 1882 to 1884.
Nicholas E. Young, 1884 to 1902.
Harry C. Pulliam, 1902 to July 29, 1909.
John A. Heydler, July 30, August 26, 1909.
Thomas J. Lynch, Dec. 15, 1909 to Dec. 9, 1913.
John K. Tener, Dec. 9, 1913 to Aug. 6, 1918.
John A. Heydler, Dec. 10, 1918 to Dec. 11, 1934.
Ford C. Frick, Dec. 11, 1934 to Oct. 8, 1951.
Warren C. Giles, Oct. 8, 1951 through Dec. 31, 1969.
Charles S. Feeney, Jan. 1, 1970 to Dec. 11, 1986.
A. Bartlett Giamatti, Dec. 11, 1986 to present.

American League

Byron Bancroft Johnson, 1901 to Oct. 17, 1927.
Ernest S. Barnard, Oct. 31, 1927 to Mar. 27, 1931.
William Harridge, May 27, 1931 through Jan. 31, 1959.
Joseph E. Cronin, Feb. 1, 1959 through 1973.
Leland S. MacPhail, Jr., Jan. 1, 1974 through 1983.
Robert W. Brown, 1984 to present.

Clubs With 13 Consecutive Victories In Season
American League

Year	Club	G.	Home	Rd.
1906	Chicago (1 tie)	19	11	8
1947	New York	19	6	13
1953	New York	18	3	15
1912	Washington	17	1	16
1931	Philadelphia	17	5	12
1926	New York	16	12	4
1977	Kansas City	16	9	7
1906	New York	15	12	3
1913	Philadelphia	15	13	2
1946	Boston	15	11	4
1960	New York	15	9	6
1909	Detroit	14	14	0
1916	St. Louis	14	13	1
1934	Detroit	14	9	5
1941	New York	14	6	8
1951	Chicago	14	3	11
1973	Baltimore	14	10	4
1908	Chicago	13	12	1
1910	Philadelphia	13	12	1
1927	Detroit (1 tie)	13	13	0
1931	Philadelphia	13	13	0
1933	Washington	13	1	12
1942	Cleveland	13	4	9
1948	Boston	13	12	1
1951	Cleveland	13	7	6
1954	New York	13	8	5
1961	New York	13	12	1
1978	Baltimore	13	3	10
1987	Milwaukee	13	6	7

National League

Year	Club	G.	Home	Rd.
1916	New York (1 tie)	26	26	0
1880	Chicago	21	11	10
1935	Chicago	21	18	3
1884	Providence	20	16	4
1885	Chicago	18	14	4
1894	Baltimore	18	13	5
1904	New York	18	13	5
1897	Boston	17	16	1
1907	New York	17	14	3
1916	New York	17	0	17
1887	Philadelphia	16	5	11
1890	Philadelphia	16	14	2
1892	Philadelphia	16	11	5
1909	Pittsburgh	16	12	4
1912	New York	16	11	5
1951	New York	16	13	3
1886	Detroit	15	12	3
1903	Pittsburgh	15	11	4
1924	Brooklyn	15	3	12
1936	Chicago	15	11	4
1936	New York	15	7	8
1895	Baltimore	14	13	1
1899	Cincinnati	14	10	4
1903	Pittsburgh	14	7	7
1906	Chicago	14	14	0
1909	Pittsburgh	14	12	2
1913	New York	14	6	8
1932	Chicago	14	14	0

Year	Club	G.	Home	Rd.
1935	St. Louis	14	12	2
1965	San Francisco	14	6	8
1890	Cincinnati	13	13	0
1892	Chicago	13	11	2
1905	New York	13	8	5
1911	Pittsburgh	13	9	4
1922	Pittsburgh	13	2	11
1928	Chicago	13	13	0
1938	Pittsburgh	13	5	8
1947	Brooklyn	13	2	11
1953	Brooklyn	13	7	6
1962	Los Angeles	13	8	5
1965	Los Angeles	13	7	6
1977	Philadelphia	13	8	5
1982	Atlanta	13	5	8

Union Association

Year	Club	G.	Home	Rd.
1884	St. Louis	20	16	4

American Association

Year	Club	G.	Home	Rd.
1887	St. Louis	15	15	0

Clubs With 13 Consecutive Losses In Season
American League

Year	Club	G.	Home	Rd.
1906	Boston	20	19	1
1916	Philadelphia	20	1	19
1943	Philadelphia	20	3	17
1975	Detroit	19	9	10
1920	Philadelphia	18	0	18
1948	Washington	18	8	10
1959	Washington	18	3	15
1926	Boston	17	14	3
1907	Boston (2 ties)	16	9	7
1927	Boston	15	10	5
1937	Philadelphia	15	10	5
1972	Texas	15	5	10
1911	St. Louis	14	6	8
1930	Boston	14	3	11
1940	St. Louis	14	0	14
1945	Philadelphia	14	0	14
1953	St. Louis	14	14	0
1954	Baltimore	14	7	7
1961	Washington	14	11	3
1970	Washington	14	4	10
1977	Oakland	14	9	5
1982	Minnesota	14	6	8
1904	Wash. (1 tie)	13	7	6
1913	New York	13	7	6
1920	Detroit	13	5	8
1924	Chicago	13	2	11
1935	Philadelphia	13	10	3
1936	St. Louis	13	2	11
1953	Detroit (2 ties)	13	12	1
1958	Washington	13	4	9
1959	Kansas City	13	4	9
1961	Minnesota	13	0	13
1962	Washington	13	7	6

National League

Year	Club	G.	Home	Rd.
1899	Cleveland	24	3	21
1961	Philadelphia	23	6	17
1890	Pittsburgh	23	1	22
1894	Louisville	20	0	20
1969	Montreal	20	12	8
1906	Boston	19	3	16
1914	Cincinnati	19	6	13
1876	Cincinnati	18	9	9
1894	Louisville	18	0	18
1894	Washington	17	7	10
1962	New York	17	7	10
1977	Atlanta	17	8	9
1882	Troy	16	5	11
1884	Detroit	16	5	11
1899	Cleveland	16	0	16
1907	Boston	16	5	11
1911	Boston	16	8	8
1944	Brooklyn	16	0	16
1909	Boston	15	0	15
1909	St. Louis	15	11	4
1927	Boston	15	0	15
1935	Boston	15	0	15
1963	New York	15	8	7
1982	New York	15	6	9
1878	Milwaukee	14	7	7
1882	Worcester	14	2	12
1883	Philadelphia	14	4	10
1896	St. Louis	14	5	9
1899	Cleveland	14	0	14
1911	Boston	14	14	0
1916	St. Louis	14	0	14
1935	Boston	14	4	10
1936	Philadelphia	14	10	4
1937	Brooklyn	14	0	14
1937	Cincinnati	14	10	4
1885	Providence	13	2	11
1886	Washington	13	13	0
1902	New York	13	5	8
1909	Boston	13	13	0
1910	St. Louis	13	5	8
1919	Philadelphia	13	0	13
1919	Philadelphia	13	7	6
1930	Cincinnati	13	1	12
1942	Philadelphia	13	4	9
1944	Chicago	13	7	6
1944	New York	13	0	13
1945	Cincinnati	13	2	11
1955	Philadelphia	13	9	4
1962	New York	13	9	4
1976	Atlanta	13	6	7
1980	New York	13	3	10
1982	Chicago	13	7	6
1985	Chicago	13	4	9

American Association

Year	Club	G.	Home	Rd.
1889	Louisville	26	5	21
1890	Philadelphia	22	6	16
1882	Baltimore	15	0	15
1884	Washington	15	0	15

American League Team Records
Baltimore Orioles

Yearly Finishes

Year—Position	W.	L.	Pct.	*G.B.	Manager
1954—Seventh ..	54	100	.351	57	James Dykes
1955—Seventh ..	57	97	.370	39	Paul Richards
1956—Sixth	69	85	.448	28	Paul Richards
1957—Fifth	76	76	.500	21	Paul Richards
1958—Sixth	74	79	.484	17½	Paul Richards
1959—Sixth	74	80	.481	20	Paul Richards
1960—Second....	89	65	.578	8	Paul Richards
1961—Third......	95	67	.586	14	P. Richards, C. L. Harris
1962—Seventh....	77	85	.475	19	William Hitchcock
1963—Fourth.....	86	76	.531	18½	William Hitchcock
1964—Third......	97	65	.599	2	Henry Bauer
1965—Third......	94	68	.580	8	Henry Bauer
1966—First	97	63	.606	+ 9	Henry Bauer
1967—Sixth†	76	85	.472	15½	Henry Bauer
1968—Second....	91	71	.562	12	H. Bauer, E. Weaver

East Division

Year—Position	W.	L.	Pct.	*G.B.	Manager
1969—First‡......	109	53	.673	+19	Earl Weaver
1970—First‡......	108	54	.667	+15	Earl Weaver
1971—First‡......	101	57	.639	+12	Earl Weaver
1972—Third......	80	74	.519	5	Earl Weaver
1973—First§......	97	65	.599	+ 8	Earl Weaver
1974—First§......	91	71	.562	+ 2	Earl Weaver
1975—Second....	90	69	.566	4½	Earl Weaver
1976—Second....	88	74	.543	10½	Earl Weaver
1977—Second†...	97	64	.602	2½	Earl Weaver
1978—Fourth....	90	71	.559	9	Earl Weaver
1979—First‡.....	102	57	.642	+ 8	Earl Weaver
1980—Second....	100	62	.617	3	Earl Weaver
1981—2nd/4th.	59	46	.562	x	Earl Weaver
1982—Second...	94	68	.580	1	Earl Weaver
1983—First‡....	98	64	.605	+ 6	Joseph Altobelli
1984—Fifth....	85	77	.525	19	Joseph Altobelli
1985—Fourth....	83	78	.516	16	J. Altobelli, E. Weaver
1986—Seventh...	73	89	.451	22½	Earl Weaver
1987—Sixth......	67	95	.414	31	Calvin Ripken

*Games behind winner. †Tied for position. ‡Won Championship Series. §Lost Championship Series. xFirst half 31-23; second 28-23.

Individual Records (1954 To Date)
Batting

Most years, non-pitcher	23, Brooks C. Robinson
Most games	163, Brooks C. Robinson, 1961
	163, Brooks C. Robinson, 1964
Most games, league	2896, Brooks C. Robinson
Most at-bats	668, Brooks C. Robinson, 163 games, 1961
Most at-bats, league	10,654, Brooks C. Robinson
Most runs	122, Frank Robinson, 155 games, 1966
Most runs, league	1232, Brooks C. Robinson
Most hits	211, Calvin E. Ripken, 162 games, 1983
Most hits, league	2848, Brooks C. Robinson
Most singles	158, Alonza B. Bumbry, 160 games, 1980
Most singles, league	2030, Brooks C. Robinson
Most doubles	47, Calvin E. Ripken, 162 games, 1983
Most doubles, league	482, Brooks C. Robinson
Most triples	12, Paul L. Blair, 151 games, 1967
Most triples, league	68, Brooks C. Robinson
Most homers, lefthander	46, James E. Gentile, 148 games, 1961
Most homers, righthander	49, Frank Robinson, 155 games, 1966
Most homers, switch-hitter	35, Kenneth W. Singleton, 159 games, 1979
Most homers, rookie	28, Calvin E. Ripken, 160 games, 1982
Most homers at home	27, Frank Robinson, 1966
Most homers on road	30, James, E. Gentile, 1961
Most homers, month	15, James E. Gentile, August, 1961
Most homers, league, switch-hitter	305, Eddie C. Murray
Most homers, league, lefthander	303, John W. Powell
Most homers, league, righthander	268, Brooks C. Robinson
Most grand slams	5, James E. Gentile, 148 games, 1961
Most grand slams, league	14, Eddie C. Murray
Most total bases	367, Frank Robinson, 155 games, 1966
Most total bases, league	4270, Brooks C. Robinson
Most long hits	85, Frank Robinson, 155 games, 1966
Most long hits, league	818, Brooks C. Robinson
Most extra bases on long hits	185, Frank Robinson, 155 games, 1966
Most extra bases on long hits, league	1422, Brooks C. Robinson
Most sacrifice hits	23, Mark H. Belanger, 152 games, 1975
Most sacrifice flies	11, Calvin E. Ripken, 162 games, 1987
Most sacrifice flies, league	114, Brooks C. Robinson
Most stolen bases	57, Luis E. Aparicio, 146 games, 1964
Most stolen bases, league	252, Alonza B. Bumbry
Most caught stealing	18, Donald A. Buford, 144 games, 1969
Most bases on balls	118, Kenneth W. Singleton, 155 games, 1975
Most bases on balls, league	889, John W. Powell
Most strikeouts	125, John W. Powell, 140 games, 1966
Most strikeouts, league	1102, John W. Powell
Fewest strikeouts	19, Richard F. Dauer, 152 games, 1980
Most hit by pitch	20, Robert Grich, 160 games, 1974
Most runs batted in	141, James E. Gentile, 148 games, 1961
Most runs batted in, league	1357, Brooks C. Robinson
Most game-winning RBIs	20, Eddie C. Murray, 151 games, 1982
Highest batting average	.328, Kenneth W. Singleton, 152 games, 1977
Highest batting average, league	.303, Robert C. Nieman
Highest slugging average	.646, James E. Gentile, 148 games, 1961
Highest slugging average, league	.543, Frank Robinson
Longest batting streak	22 games, Eddie C. Murray, 1984
Longest batting streak over two seasons—	
	22 games, Douglas V. DeCinces, 1978 (21), 1979 (1)
Most grounded into double play	32, Calvin E. Ripken, 161 games, 1985
Most grounded into double play, league	297, Brooks C. Robinson
Fewest grounded into double play	2, Mark H. Belanger, 152 games, 1975

Pitching

Most years	19, James A. Palmer
Most games	76, Felix A. Martinez, 1982
Most games, league	558, James A. Palmer
Most games started	40, David A. McNally, 1969
	40, Miguel Cuellar, 1970
	40, David A. McNally, 1970
	40, James A. Palmer, 1976
	40, Michael K. Flanagan, 1978
Most games started, league	521, James A. Palmer
Most complete games	25, James A. Palmer, 1975
Most complete games, league	211, James A. Palmer
Most games finished	59, Stuart L. Miller, 1963
Most innings	323, James A. Palmer, 1975
Most innings, league	3947⅓, James A. Palmer
Most games won	25, Steven M. Stone, 1980
Most games won, league	268, James A. Palmer
Most 20-victory seasons	8, James A. Palmer
Most games, lost	21, Don J. Larsen, 1954
Most games lost, league	152, James A. Palmer
Highest winning percentage	.808, David A. McNally (21-5), 1971
Longest winning streak	15 games, David A. McNally, 1969
Longest winning streak over two seasons—	
	17 games, David A. McNally, 1968 (2), 1969 (15)
Longest losing streak	8, Don J. Larsen, 1954 (twice)
	8, Jeffrey S. Ballard, 1987
Most saves	34, Donald W. Aase, 1986
Most bases on balls	181, Robert L. Turley, 1954
Most bases on balls, league	1311, James A. Palmer
Most strikeouts	202, David A. McNally, 1968
Most strikeouts, league	2212, James A. Palmer
Most strikeouts, game	14, Robert L. Turley, April 21, 1954
	14, Clifford Johnson, September 2, 1957, second game
Most shutouts	10, James A. Palmer, 1975
Most shutouts, league	53, James A. Palmer
Most 1-0 shutouts won	3, Miguel Cuellar, 1974
	3, Ross A. Grimsley, 1974
	3, James A. Palmer, 1975, 1978
Most runs	129, J. Dennis Martinez, 1979
Most earned runs	126, Michael K. Flanagan, 1978
Most hits	279, J. Dennis Martinez, 1979
Most wild pitches	14, Milton S. Pappas, 1959
Most hit batsmen	15, Charles L. Estrada, 1960
Most home runs	35, Robin Roberts, 1963
	35, Scott H. McGregor, 1986
Most sacrifice hits	20, Miguel Cuellar, 1975
Most sacrifice flies	14, James A. Palmer, 1976
Lowest ERA	1.95, David A. McNally, 273 innings, 1968

Club Records

Most players	54 in 1955
Fewest players	30 in 1969
Most games	163 in 1961, 1964, 1982
Most at-bats	5585 in 1980 (162 games)
Most runs	818 in 1985 (161 games)
Fewest runs	483 in 1954 (154 games)
Most opponents' runs	880 in 1987 (162 games)
Most hits	1523 in 1980 (162 games)
Fewest hits	1153 in 1972 (154 games)
Most singles	1080 in 1980 (162 games)
Most doubles	283 in 1983 (162 games)
Most triples	49 in 1954 (154 games)
Most homers	214 in 1985 (161 games)
Fewest homers	52 in 1954
Most homers at Memorial Stad., home & opp. ...	235 in 1987
Most grand slams	8 in 1979, 1982, 1983, 1984
Most pinch home runs	11 in 1982
Most long hits	478 in 1983 (162 games)
Most extra bases on long hits	920 in 1985 (161 games)
Most total bases	2371 in 1985 (161 games)
Most sacrifice hits	110 in 1957 (154 games)
Most sacrifice flies	59 in 1969 (162 games)
Most stolen bases	150 in 1976 (162 games)
Most caught stealing	64 in 1973 (162 games)
Most bases on balls	717 in 1970 (162 games)
Most strikeouts	1019 in 1964 (163 games)
	1019 in 1968 (162 games)
Fewest strikeouts	634 in 1954 (154 games)
Most hit by pitch	58 in 1974 (162 games)

Fewest hit by pitch	19 in 1955 (156 games)
	19 in 1985 (161 games)
Most runs batted in	773 in 1985 (161 games)
Most game-winning RBIs	95 in 1980 (162 games)
	95 in 1983 (162 games)
Highest batting average	.273 in 1980 (162 games)
Lowest batting average	.225 in 1968 (162 games)
Highest slugging average	.430 in 1985 (161 games)
Lowest slugging average	.320 in 1975 (156 games)
Most grounded into double play	159 in 1986 (162 games)
Fewest grounded into double play	102 in 1968 (162 games)
Most left on bases	1262 in 1970 (162 games)
Fewest left on bases	1043 in 1972 (154 games)
Most .300 hitters	3 in 1980
Most putouts	4436 in 1970 (162 games)
Fewest putouts	4082 in 1956 (156 games)
Most assists	1974 in 1975 (159 games)
Fewest assists	1516 in 1958 (154 games)
Most chances accepted	6344 in 1974 (162 games)
Fewest chances accepted	5625 in 1958 (154 games)
Most errors	167 in 1955 (156 games)
Fewest errors	95 in 1964 (163 games)
	95 in 1980 (162 games)
Most errorless games	92 in 1980 (162 games)
Most consecutive errorless games	10 in 1962
Most double plays	189 in 1977 (161 games)
Fewest double plays	131 in 1968 (162 games)
Most passed balls	49 in 1959 (155 games)
Fewest passed balls	4 in 1985 (161 games)
Highest fielding average	.985 in 1964 (163 games)
	.985 in 1980 (162 games)
Lowest fielding average	.972 in 1955 (156 games)
Highest home attendance	2,132,387 in 1985
Highest road attendance	1,880,669 in 1987
Most games won	109 in 1969
Most games lost	100 in 1954
Most games won, month	25, June 1966
Most games lost, month	25, August 1954
Highest percentage games won	.673 in 1969 (won 109, lost 53)
Lowest percentage games won	.351 in 1954 (won 54, lost 100)
Games won, league	2918 in 34 years
Games lost, league	2450 in 34 years
Most shutouts won	21 in 1961
Most shutouts lost	22 in 1955
Most 1-0 games won	8 in 1974
Most 1-0 games lost	5 in 1973
Most consecutive games won	14 in 1973
Most consecutive games lost	14 in 1954
Most times league champions	6
Most last place finishes	0
Most runs, game	19 vs. Cleveland, August 28, 1957
Most runs, game, by opponent	24 by Toronto, June 26, 1978
Most runs, shutout game	17 vs. Chicago, July 27, 1969
Most runs, shutout game, by opponent	16 by New York, April 30, 1960
Most runs doubleheader shutout	13 vs. Washington, July 9, 1959
Most runs, inning	10 vs. New York, July 8, 1969, first game, fourth inning
	10 vs. Oakland, April 29, 1979, seventh inning
	10 vs. Seattle, August 21, 1985, third inning
Longest 1-0 game won	17 innings vs. Milwaukee, September 27, 1974
Longest 1-0 game lost	15 innings vs. Cleveland, May 14, 1961, first game
Most hits, game	26 vs. California, August 28, 1980
Most home runs, game	7 vs. Boston, May 17, 1967
	7 vs. California, August 26, 1985
Most consecutive games, one or more homers	14 (21 homers), 1986
	14 (38 homers), 1987
Most total bases, game	39 vs. Chicago, July 27, 1969
Largest crowd, day game	52,292 vs. Cleveland, April 7, 1986
Largest crowd, doubleheader	51,883 vs. Milwaukee, October 1, 1982
Largest crowd, night game	52,159 vs. Boston, June 27, 1986
Largest crowd, home opener	52,292 vs. Cleveland, April 7, 1986

Frank Robinson

Boston Red Sox

Yearly Finishes

Year—Position	W.	L.	Pct.	*G.B.	Manager
1901—Second	79	57	.581	4	James Collins
1902—Third	77	60	.562	6½	James Collins
1903—First	91	47	.659	+14½	James Collins
1904—First	95	59	.617	+ 1½	James Collins
1905—Fourth	78	74	.513	16	James Collins
1906—Eighth	49	105	.318	45½	J. Collins, C. Stahl
1907—Seventh	59	90	.396	32½	G. Huff, R. Unglaub, J. McGuire
1908—Fifth	75	79	.487	15½	J. McGuire, F. Lake
1909—Third	88	63	.583	9½	Fred Lake
1910—Fourth	81	72	.529	22½	Patrick Donovan
1911—Fifth	78	75	.510	24	Patrick Donovan
1912—First	105	47	.691	+14	J. Garland Stahl
1913—Fourth	79	71	.527	15½	J. Stahl, W. Carrigan
1914—Second	91	62	.595	8½	William Carrigan
1915—First	101	50	.669	+ 2½	William Carrigan
1916—First	91	63	.591	+ 2	William Carrigan
1917—Second	90	62	.592	9	John Barry
1918—First	75	51	.595	+ 1½	Edward Barrow
1919—Sixth	66	71	.482	20½	Edward Barrow
1920—Fifth	72	81	.471	25½	Edward Barrow
1921—Fifth	75	79	.487	23½	Hugh Duffy
1922—Eighth	61	93	.396	33	Hugh Duffy

Year—Position	W.	L.	Pct.	*G.B.	Manager
1923—Eighth	61	91	.401	37	Frank Chance
1924—Seventh	67	87	.435	25	Lee Fohl
1925—Eighth	47	105	.309	49½	Lee Fohl
1926—Eighth	46	107	.301	44½	Lee Fohl
1927—Eighth	51	103	.331	59	William Carrigan
1928—Eighth	57	96	.373	43½	William Carrigan
1929—Eighth	58	96	.377	48	William Carrigan
1930—Eighth	52	102	.338	50	Charles (Heinie) Wagner
1931—Sixth	62	90	.408	45	John Collins
1932—Eighth	43	111	.279	64	J. Collins, M. McManus
1933—Seventh	63	86	.423	34½	Martin McManus
1934—Fourth	76	76	.500	24	Stanley (Bucky) Harris
1935—Fourth	78	75	.510	16	Joseph Cronin
1936—Sixth	74	80	.481	28½	Joseph Cronin
1937—Fifth	80	72	.526	21	Joseph Cronin
1938—Second	88	61	.591	9½	Joseph Cronin
1939—Second	89	62	.589	17	Joseph Cronin
1940—Fourth†	82	72	.532	8	Joseph Cronin
1941—Second	84	70	.545	17	Joseph Cronin
1942—Second	93	59	.612	9	Joseph Cronin
1943—Seventh	68	84	.447	29	Joseph Cronin
1944—Fourth	77	77	.500	12	Joseph Cronin
1945—Seventh	71	83	.461	17½	Joseph Cronin
1946—First	104	50	.675	+12	Joseph Cronin

Year—Position	W.	L.	Pct.	*G.B.	Manager
1947—Third......	83	71	.539	14	Joseph Cronin
1948—Second‡.	96	59	.619	1	Joseph McCarthy
1949—Second....	96	58	.623	1	Joseph McCarthy
1950—Third......	94	60	.610	4	J. McCarthy, S. O'Neill
1951—Third......	87	67	.565	11	Stephen O'Neill
1952—Sixth......	76	78	.494	19	Louis Boudreau
1953—Fourth....	84	69	.549	16	Louis Boudreau
1954—Fourth....	69	85	.448	42	Louis Boudreau
1955—Fourth....	84	70	.545	12	Michael Higgins
1956—Fourth....	84	70	.545	13	Michael Higgins
1957—Third......	82	72	.532	16	Michael Higgins
1958—Third......	79	75	.513	13	Michael Higgins
1959—Fifth......	75	79	.487	19	M. Higgins, W. Jurges
1960—Seventh ..	65	89	.422	32	W. Jurges, M. Higgins
1961—Sixth......	76	86	.469	33	Michael Higgins
1962—Eighth.....	76	84	.475	19	Michael Higgins
1963—Seventh ..	76	85	.472	28	John Pesky
1964—Eighth.....	72	90	.444	27	J. Pesky, W. Herman
1965—Ninth......	62	100	.383	40	William Herman
1966—Ninth......	72	90	.444	26	W. Herman, J. Runnels
1967—First......	92	70	.568	+ 1	Richard Williams
1968—Fourth.....	86	76	.531	17	Richard Williams

East Division

Year—Position	W.	L.	Pct.	*G.B.	Manager
1969—Third......	87	75	.537	22	R. Williams, E. Popowski
1970—Third......	87	75	.537	21	Edward Kasko
1971—Third......	85	77	.525	18	Edward Kasko
1972—Second....	85	70	.548	½	Edward Kasko
1973—Second....	89	73	.549	8	Edward Kasko
1974—Third......	84	78	.519	7	Darrell D. Johnson
1975—First§.....	95	65	.594	+ 4½	Darrell D. Johnson
1976—Third......	83	79	.512	15½	D. Johnson, Don Zimmer
1977—Second†.	97	64	.602	2½	Don Zimmer
1978—Second x	99	64	.607	1	Don Zimmer
1979—Third......	91	69	.569	11½	Don Zimmer
1980—Fourth.....	83	77	.519	19	D. Zimmer, J. Pesky
1981—5th/2d†	59	49	.546	y	Ralph Houk
1982—Third......	89	73	.549	6	Ralph Houk
1983—Sixth......	78	84	.481	20	Ralph Houk
1984—Fourth....	86	76	.531	18	Ralph Houk
1985—Fifth......	81	81	.500	18½	John McNamara
1986—First§.....	95	66	.590	+ 5½	John McNamara
1987—Fifth......	78	84	.481	20	John McNamara

*Games behind winner. †Tied for position. ‡Lost pennant playoff. §Won Championship Series. xLost division playoff. yFirst half 30-26; second 29-23.

Individual Records (1901 To Date)

Batting

Most years, non-pitcher	23, Carl M. Yastrzemski
Most games	163, James E. Rice, 1978
Most games, league	3308, Carl M. Yastrzemski
Most at-bats	677, James E. Rice, 163 games, 1978
Most at-bats, league	11988, Carl M. Yastrzemski
Most runs	150, Theodore S. Williams, 155 games, 1949
Most runs, league	1816, Carl M. Yastrzemski
Most hits	240, Wade A. Boggs, 161 games, 1985
Most hits, league	3419, Carl M. Yastrzemski
Most singles	187, Wade A. Boggs, 161 games, 1985
Most singles, league	2262, Carl M. Yastrzemski
Most doubles	67, Earl W. Webb, 151 games, 1931
Most doubles, league	646, Carl M. Yastrzemski
Most triples	22, Charles S. Stahl, 157 games, 1904
	22, Tris Speaker, 141 games, 1913
Most triples, league	130, Harry B. Hooper
Most homers, righthander	50, James E. Foxx, 149 games, 1938
Most homers, lefthander	44, Carl M. Yastrzemski, 161 games, 1967
Most homers, rookie	34, Walter Dropo, 136 games, 1950
Most homers at home	35, James E. Foxx, 1938
Most homers on road	26, Theodore S. Williams, 1957
Most homers, month	14, Jack E. Jensen, June, 1958
Most homers, league, righthander	344, James E. Rice
Most homers, league, lefthander	521, Theodore S. Williams
Most grand slams	4, George H. Ruth, 130 games, 1919
Most grand slams, league	17, Theodore S. Williams
Most total bases	406, James E. Rice, 163 games, 1978
Most total bases, league	5539, Carl M. Yastrzemski
Most long hits	92, James E. Foxx, 149 games, 1938
Most long hits, league	1157, Carl M. Yastrzemski
Most extra bases on long hits	201, James E. Foxx, 149 games, 1938
Most extra bases on long hits, league	2230, Theodore S. Williams
Most sacrifices (S. H. and S. F.)	54, John J. Barry, 116 games, 1917
Most sacrifice hits	35, Fred N. Parent, 153 games, 1905
Most sacrifice flies	12, Jack E. Jensen, 152 games, 1955
	12, James E. Piersall, 155 games, 1956
	12, Jack E. Jensen, 148 games, 1959
Most stolen bases	54, Tommy Harper, 147 games, 1973
Most stolen bases, league	300, Harry B. Hooper
Most caught stealing	19, Michael W. Menosky, 141 games, 1920
Most bases on balls	162, Theodore S. Williams, 156 games, 1947
	162, Theodore S. Williams, 155 games, 1949
Most bases on balls, league	2019, Theodore S. Williams
Most strikeouts	162, Clell L. Hobson Jr., 159 games, 1977
Most strikeouts, league	1393, Carl M. Yastrzemski
Fewest strikeouts	9, John P. McInnis, 152 games, 1921
Most hit by pitch	35, Donald E. Baylor, 1986

Most runs batted in	175, James E. Foxx, 149 games, 1938
Most runs batted in, league	1844, Carl M. Yastrzemski
Most game-winning RBIs	17, James E. Rice, 159 games, 1984
Most consecutive games with RBI	12, Theodore S. Williams, (18 RBIs), 1942
	12, Joseph E. Cronin, (19 RBIs), 1939
Highest batting average	.406, Theodore S. Williams, 143 games, 1941
Highest batting average, league	.354, Wade A. Boggs
Highest slugging average	.735, Theodore S. Williams, 143 games, 1941
Highest slugging average, league	.634, Theodore S. Williams
Longest batting streak	34 games, Dominic P. DiMaggio, 1949
Most grounded into double play	36, James E. Rice, 159 games, 1984
Fewest grounded into double play	3, Ulysses J. Lupien, 154 games, 1943

Pitching

Most years	11, Ivan M. Delock
	11, Robert W. Stanley
Most games	79, Richard R. Radatz, 1964
Most games, league	537, Robert W. Stanley
Most games started	43, Denton T. Young, 1902
Most games started, league	298, Denton T. Young
Most complete games	41, Denton T. Young, 1902
Most complete games, league	275, Denton T. Young
Most games finished	67, Richard R. Radatz, 1964
Most innings	386, Denton T. Young, 1902
Most innings, league	2730, Denton T. Young
Most games won	34, Joseph Wood, 1912
Most games won, league, righthander	193, Denton T. Young
Most games won, league, lefthander	123, Melvin L. Parnell
Most 20-victory seasons	6, Denton T. Young
Most games lost	25, Charles H. Ruffing, 1928
Most games lost, league	112, Denton T. Young
Highest winning percentage	.882, Robert W. Stanley (15-2), 1978
Longest winning streak	16 games, Joseph Wood, 1912
Longest losing streak	14 games, Joseph J. Harris, 1906
Most saves	33, Robert W. Stanley, 1983
Most bases on balls	134, Melvin L. Parnell, 1949
Most bases on balls, league	758, Melvin L. Parnell
Most strikeouts	258, Joseph Wood, 1912
Most strikeouts, league	1363, Denton T. Young
Most strikeouts, game	20, W. Roger Clemens, April 29, 1986
Most shutouts	10, Denton T. Young, 1904
	10, Joseph Wood, 1912
Most shutouts, league	39, Denton T. Young
Most 1-0 shutouts won	5, Leslie A. Bush, 1918
Most runs	162, Charles H. Ruffing, 1929
	162, Jack Russell, 1930
Most earned runs	139, Jack Russell, 1930
Most hits	337, Denton T. Young, 1902
Most hit batsmen	20, Howard J. Ehmke, 1923
Most wild pitches	21, R. Earl Wilson, 1963
Most home runs	37, R. Earl Wilson, 1964
Most sacrifice hits	24, Cecil C. Hughson, 1943
Most sacrifice flies	14, David M. Morehead, 1964
Lowest ERA	1.01, Hubert B. Leonard, 222 innings, 1914

Club Records

Most players	48 in 1952
Fewest players	18 in 1904
Most games	163 in 1961, 1978, 1985
Most at-bats	5720 in 1985 (163 games)
Most runs	1027 in 1950 (154 games)
Fewest runs	462 in 1906 (155 games)
Most opponents' runs	921 in 1925 (152 games)
Most hits	1665 in 1950 (154 games)
Fewest hits	1175 in 1905 (153 games)
Most singles	1156 in 1950 (154 games)
Most doubles	310 in 1979 (160 games)
Most triples	112 in 1903 (141 games)
Most homers	213 in 1977 (161 games)
Fewest homers (154 or 162-game schedule)....	12 in 1906
Most homers at Fenway Park, home & opp........	219 in 1977
Most grand slams	9 in 1941, 1950, 1987
Most pinch home runs	6 in 1953
Most long hits	538 in 1979 (160 games)
Most extra bases on long hits	1009 in 1977 (161 games)
Most total bases	2560 in 1977 (161 games)
Most sacrifices (S. H. and S. F.)	310 in 1917 (157 games)
Most sacrifice hits	142 in 1906 (155 games)
Most sacrifice flies	59 in 1976 (162 games)
	59 in 1977 (161 games)
	59 in 1979 (160 games)
Most stolen bases	215 in 1909 (151 games)
Most caught stealing	111 in 1920 (154 games)
Most bases on balls	835 in 1949 (155 games)
Most strikeouts	1020 in 1966 (162 games)
	1020 in 1967 (162 games)
Fewest strikeouts	329 in 1921 (154 games)
Most hit by pitch	66 in 1986 (161 games)
Fewest hit by pitch	11 in 1934 (153 games)
Most runs batted in	974 in 1950 (154 games)
Most game-winning RBIs	84 in 1982 (162 games)
	84 in 1986 (161 games)
Highest batting average	.302 in 1950 (154 games)
Lowest batting average	.234 in 1905 (153 games)
	.234 in 1907 (155 games)
Highest slugging average	.465 in 1977 (161 games)
Lowest slugging average	.318 in 1916 (156 games)
	.318 in 1917 (157 games)

Ted Williams

Most grounded into double play .... 171 in 1982 (162 games)
                                                      171 in 1983 (162 games)
Fewest grounded into double play .... 94 in 1942 (152 games)
Most left on bases .... 1304 in 1948 (155 games)
Fewest left on bases .... 1015 in 1929 (155 games)
Most .300 hitters .... 9 in 1950
Most putouts .... 4418 in 1978 (163 games)
Fewest putouts .... 3949 in 1938 (150 games)
Most assists .... 2195 in 1907 (155 games)
Fewest assists .... 1555 in 1964 (162 games)
Most chances accepted .... 6425 in 1907 (155 games)
Fewest chances accepted .... 5667 in 1938 (150 games)
Most errors .... 373 in 1901 (137 games)
Fewest errors .... 110 in 1987 (162 games)
Most errorless games .... 86 in 1971 (162 games)
Most consecutive errorless games .... 10 in 1986
Most double plays .... 207 in 1949 (155 games)
Fewest double plays .... 74 in 1913 (151 games)
Most passed balls .... 30 in 1987 (162 games)
Fewest passed balls .... 3 in 1933 (149 games)
                                           3 in 1975 (160 games)
Highest fielding average .... .982 in 1987 (162 games)
Lowest fielding average .... .943 in 1901 (137 games)
Highest home attendance .... 2,353,114 in 1979
Highest road attendance .... 2,266,765 in 1986
Most games won .... 105 in 1912
Most games lost .... 111 in 1932
Most games won, month .... 24, July 1948
                                        24, August 1949
                                        24, August 1950
Most games lost, month .... 24, July 1925
                                        24, June 1927
                                        24, July 1928
Highest percentage games won .... .691 in 1912 (won 105, lost 47)
Lowest percentage games won .... .279 in 1932 (won 43, lost 111)
Games won, league .... 6824 in 87 years
Games lost, league .... 6568 in 87 years
Most shutouts won .... 26 in 1918
Most shutouts lost .... 28 in 1906
Most 1-0 games won .... 8 in 1918
Most 1-0 games lost .... 7 in 1909, 1914
Most consecutive games won .... 15 in 1946
Most consecutive games lost .... 20 in 1906
Most times league champions 10
Most last place finishes 10
Most runs, game .... 29 vs. St. Louis, June 8, 1950
Most runs, game, by opponent .... 27 by Cleveland, July 7, 1923, first game
Most runs, shutout game .... 19 vs. Philadelphia, April 30, 1950, first game
Most runs, shutout game by opponent .... 19 by Cleveland 19, May 18, 1955
Most runs, doubleheader shutout .... 16 vs. Cleveland, August 21, 1920
Most runs, inning .... 17 vs. Detroit, June 18, 1953, seventh inning
Longest 1-0 game won .... 15 innings vs. Detroit, May 11, 1904
Longest 1-0 game lost .... 15 innings vs. Washington, July 3, 1915
Most hits, game .... 28 vs. St. Louis, June 8, 1950
Most home runs, game .... 8 vs. Toronto, July 4, 1977
Most consecutive games, one or more homers .... 14 (23 homers), 1985
Most total bases, game .... 60 vs. St. Louis, June 8, 1950
Largest crowd, day game .... 36,388 vs. Cleveland, April 22, 1978
Largest crowd, doubleheader .... 47,627 vs. New York, September 22, 1935
Largest crowd, night game .... 36,228 vs. New York, June 28, 1949
Largest crowd, home opener .... 35,343 vs. Baltimore April 14, 1969

California Angels

Yearly Finishes

(Known as Los Angeles Angels through September 1, 1965)

Year—Position	W.	L.	Pct.	*G.B.	Manager
1961—Eighth.....	70	91	.435	38½	William Rigney
1962—Third.....	86	76	.531	10	William Rigney
1963—Ninth	70	91	.435	34	William Rigney
1964—Fifth......	82	80	.506	17	William Rigney
1965—Seventh..	75	87	.463	27	William Rigney
1966—Sixth....	80	82	.494	18	William Rigney
1967—Fifth.....	84	77	.522	7½	William Rigney
1968—Eighth.....	67	95	.414	36	William Rigney

West Division

Year—Position	W.	L.	Pct.	*G.B.	Manager
1969—Third	71	91	.438	26	W. Rigney, H. Phillips
1970—Third	86	76	.531	12	Harold (Lefty) Phillips
1971—Fourth....	76	86	.469	25½	Harold (Lefty) Phillips
1972—Fifth......	75	80	.484	18	Del Rice
1973—Fourth....	79	83	.488	15	Bobby B. Winkles
1974—Sixth......	68	94	.420	22	B. Winkles, D. Williams
1975—Sixth......	72	89	.447	25½	Dick Williams
1976—Fourth†	76	86	.469	14	D. Williams, N. Sherry
1977—Fifth.....	74	88	.457	28	N. Sherry, D. Garcia
1978—Second†.	87	75	.537	5	D. Garcia, J. Fregosi
1979—First§.....	88	74	.543	+ 3	James Fregosi
1980—Sixth......	65	95	.406	31	James Fregosi
1981—4th/7th..	51	59	.464	x	J. Fregosi, G. Mauch
1982—First§....	93	69	.574	+ 3	Gene Mauch
1983—Fifth†.....	70	92	.432	29	John McNamara
1984—Second†.	81	81	.500	3	John McNamara
1985—Second...	90	72	.556	1	Gene Mauch

Year—Position	W.	L.	Pct.	*G.B.	Manager
1986—First§....	92	70	.568	+ 5	Gene Mauch
1987—Sixth†	75	87	.463	10	Gene Mauch

*Games behind winner. †Tied for position. §Lost Championship Series. xFirst half 31-29; second 20-30.

Individual Records (1961 To Date)
Batting

Most years, non-pitcher .... 11, James L. Fregosi
Most games .... 162, Robert F. Knoop, 1964
                                        162, James L. Fregosi, 1966
                                        162, Santos C. Alomar, 1970
                                        162, Santos C. Alomar, 1971
                                        162, Donald E. Baylor, 1979
Most games, league .... 1,429, James L. Fregosi
Most at-bats .... 689, Santos C. Alomar, 162 games, 1971
Most at-bats, league .... 5,244, James L. Fregosi
Most runs .... 120, Donald E. Baylor, 162 games, 1979
Most runs, league .... 703, Brian J. Downing
Most hits .... 202, Alexander Johnson, 156 games, 1970
Most hits, league .... 1,408, James L. Fregosi
Most singles .... 156, Alexander Johnson, 156 games, 1970
Most singles, league .... 1,004, James L. Fregosi
Most doubles .... 42, Douglas V. DeCinces, 153 games, 1982
Most doubles, league .... 221, Brian J. Downing
Most triples .... 13, James L. Fregosi, 159 games, 1968
                                    13, John M. Rivers, 155 games, 1975
Most triples, league .... 70, James L. Fregosi
Most homers, righthander .... 37, Bobby L. Bonds, 158 games, 1977
Most homers, lefthander .... 39, Reginald M. Jackson, 153 games, 1982
Most homers at home .... 21, Don E. Baylor, 1978
                                        21, Reginald M. Jackson, 1982

Fireballing righthander Nolan Ryan

Most homers on road	24, Leon L. Wagner, 1962
	24, Leon L. Wagner, 1963
Most homers, month	12, Bobby L. Bonds, August, 1977
Most homers, rookie	24, J. Leroy Thomas, 130 games, 1961
	24, Devon M. White, 159 games, 1987
Most homers, league, lefthander	123, Reginald M. Jackson
Most homers, league, righthander	169, Brian J. Downing
Most grand slams	3, Joseph O. Rudi, 133 games, 1978
	3, Joseph O. Rudi, 90 games, 1979
Most grand slams, league	7, Joseph O. Rudi
Most total bases	333, Donald E. Baylor, 162 games, 1979
Most total bases, league	2,112, James L. Fregosi
Most long hits	77, Douglas V. DeCinces, 153 games, 1982
Most long hits, league	406, Brian J. Downing
Most extra bases on long hits	152, Bobby L. Bonds, 158 games, 1977
Most extra bases on long hits, league	760, Brian J. Downing
Most sacrifice hits	26, Timothy J. Foli, 150 games, 1982
Most sacrifice flies	13, Darnell G. Ford, 142 games, 1979
Most stolen bases	70, John M. Rivers, 155 games, 1975
Most stolen bases, league	162, Gary G. Pettis
Most caught stealing	21, Gerald P. Remy, 147 games, 1975
Most bases on balls	106, Brian J. Downing, 155 games, 1987
Most bases on balls, league	679, Brian J. Downing
Most strikeouts	156, Reginald M. Jackson, 153 games, 1982
Most strikeouts, league	835, James L. Fregosi
Fewest strikeouts	36, Albert G. Pearson, 160 games, 1962
Most hit by pitch	18, Frederic C. Reichardt, 151 games, 1968
	18, Donald E. Baylor, 158 games, 1978
Longest batting streak	25 games, Rodney C. Carew, 1982
Most runs batted in	139, Donald E. Baylor, 162 games, 1979
Most runs batted in, league	672, Brian J. Downing
Most game-winning RBIs	21, Donald E. Baylor, 157 games, 1982
Highest batting average	.339, Rodney C. Carew, 129 games, 1983
Highest batting average, league	.314, Rodney C. Carew
Highest slugging average	.548, Douglas V. DeCinces, 153 games, 1982
Highest slugging average, league	.490, Leon L. Wagner
Most grounded into double play	26, Lyman W. Bostock, 147 games, 1978
Fewest grounded into double play	5, Leon L. Wagner, 160 games, 1962
	5, Albert G. Pearson, 154 games, 1963

Pitching

Most years	9, Andrew E. Hassler
Most games	72, Alejandro M. Rojas, 1967
Most games, league	304, David E. LaRoche
Most games started	41, L. Nolan Ryan, 1974
Most games started, league	288, L. Nolan Ryan
Most complete games	26, L. Nolan Ryan, 1973
	26, L. Nolan Ryan, 1974

Most complete games, league	156, L. Nolan Ryan
Most games finished	57, Donnie R. Moore, 1985
Most innings	333, L. Nolan Ryan, 1974
Most innings, league	2,182, L. Nolan Ryan
Most games won	22, Clyde Wright, 1970
	22, L. Nolan Ryan, 1974
Most games won, league	138, L. Nolan Ryan
Highest winning percentage	.690, W. Dean Chance (20-9), 1964
Longest winning streak	10 games, Kenneth F. McBride, 1962
Longest losing streak	11 games, Andrew E. Hassler, 1975
Most saves	31, Donnie R. Moore, 1985
Most 20-victory seasons	2, L. Nolan Ryan
Most games lost	19, George S. Brunet, 1967
	19, Clyde Wright, 1970
	19, Frank D. Tanana, 1974
Most games lost, league	121, L. Nolan Ryan
Most bases on balls	204, L. Nolan Ryan, 1977
Most bases on balls, league	1,302, L. Nolan Ryan
Most strikeouts	383, L. Nolan Ryan, 1973
Most strikeouts, league	2,416, L. Nolan Ryan
Most strikeouts, game	19, L. Nolan Ryan, August 12, 1974
	19, L. Nolan Ryan, June 14, 1974, pitched first 13 innings of 15-inning game
	19, L. Nolan Ryan, August 20, 1974, 11 innings
	19, L. Nolan Ryan, June 8, 1977, pitched first 10 innings of 13-inning game
Most shutouts	11, W. Dean Chance, 1964
Most shutouts, league	40, L. Nolan Ryan
Most 1-0 shutouts won	5, W. Dean Chance, 1964
Most runs	128, Michael A. Witt, 1987
Most earned runs	113, William R. Singer, 1973
	113, Thomas E. John, 1983
Most hits	280, William R. Singer, 1973
Most hit batsmen	21, Thomas A. Murphy, 1969
Most wild pitches	21, L. Nolan Ryan, 1977
Most home runs	38, Donald H. Sutton, 1987
Most sacrifice hits	22, L. Nolan Ryan, 1977
Most sacrifice flies	14, L. Nolan Ryan, 1978
Lowest ERA	1.65, W. Dean Chance, 278 innings, 1964

Club Records

Most players	48 in 1975 (161 games)
Fewest players	33 in 1963 (161 games)
Most games	163 in 1969
	163 in 1974
Most at-bats	5640 in 1983 (162 games)
Most runs	866 in 1979 (162 games)
Fewest runs	454 in 1972 (155 games)
Most opponents' runs	803 in 1987 (162 games)

Most hits.. 1563 in 1979 (162 games)
Fewest hits....................................... 1209 in 1968 (162 games)
Most singles..................................... 1114 in 1979 (162 games)
Most doubles.................................... 268 in 1982 (162 games)
Most triples..................................... 54 in 1966 (162 games)
Most homers.................................... 189 in 1961 (162 games)
Fewest homers................................ 55 in 1975
Most homers at Wrigley Field, home & opp........ 248 in 1961
Most homers at Chavez Ravine, home & opp...... 102 in 1964
Most homers at Anaheim Stadium, home & opp... 204 in 1987
Most grand slams.............................. 8 in 1979, 1983
Most pinch home runs...................... 9 in 1987
Most total bases............................... 2396 in 1982 (162 games)
Most long hits.................................. 480 in 1982 (162 games)
Most extra bases on long hits......... 878 in 1982 (162 games)
Most sacrifice hits........................... 114 in 1982 (162 games)
Most sacrifice flies.......................... 61 in 1986 (162 games)
Most stolen bases............................ 220 in 1975 (161 games)
Most caught stealing........................ 108 in 1975 (161 games)
Most bases on balls......................... 681 in 1961 (162 games)
Most strikeouts................................ 1080 in 1968 (162 games)
Fewest strikeouts............................ 682 in 1978 (162 games)
Most hit by pitch............................. 67 in 1978 (162 games)
Fewest hit by pitch.......................... 22 in 1965 (162 games)
Most runs batted in......................... 808 in 1979 (162 games)
Most game-winning RBIs................. 85 in 1982 (162 games)
Highest batting average.................. .282 in 1979 (162 games)
Lowest batting average................... .227 in 1968 (162 games)
Highest slugging average................ .433 in 1982 (162 games)
Lowest slugging average................. .318 in 1968 (162 games)
.318 in 1976 (162 games)
Most grounded into double play..... 147 in 1983 (162 games)
Fewest grounded into double play... 98 in 1975 (161 games)
Most left on bases........................... 1182 in 1986 (162 games)
Fewest left on bases........................ 1044 in 1972 (155 games)
Most .300 hitters............................ 2 in 1963, 1964, 1979, 1982
Most putouts.................................... 4443 in 1971 (162 games)
Fewest putouts................................ 4133 in 1972 (155 games)
Most assists..................................... 2077 in 1983 (162 games)
Fewest assists................................. 1576 in 1980 (160 games)
Most chances accepted .... 6499 in 1983 (162 games)
Fewest chances................................ 5740 in 1972 (155 games)
Most errors...................................... 192 in 1961 (162 games)
Fewest errors................................... 107 in 1986 (162 games)
Most errorless games....................... 90 in 1986 (162 games)
Most consecutive errorless games... 8 in 1972
Most double plays............................ 202 in 1985 (162 games)
Fewest double plays......................... 135 in 1967 (161 games)
135 in 1972 (155 games)
135 in 1978 (162 games)

Most passed balls............................ 30 in 1969 (163 games)
Fewest passed balls......................... 4 in 1982 (162 games)
4 in 1984 (162 games)
Highest fielding average .... .983 in 1982 (162 games)
.983 in 1986 (162 games)
Lowest fielding average .... .969 in 1961 (162 games)
Highest home attendance .... 2,807,360 in 1982
Highest road attendance................ 1,897,660 in 1982
Most games won.............................. 93 in 1982
Most games lost............................... 95 in 1968, 1980
Most games won, month................. 20, June 1967
Most games lost, month.................. 22, June 1961
22, May 1964
22, August 1968
Games won, league......................... 2083 in 27 years
Games lost, league.......................... 2226 in 27 years
Highest percentage games won...... .574 in 1982 (won 93, lost 69)
Lowest percentage games won....... .406 in 1980 (won 65, lost 95)
Most shutouts won.......................... 28 in 1964
Most shutouts lost........................... 23 in 1971
Most 1-0 games won........................ 10 in 1964
Most 1-0 games lost........................ 5 in 1968
Most runs, inning.............13 vs. Texas, September 14, 1978, ninth inning
Most runs, game.............................24 vs. Toronto, August 25, 1979
Most runs, game, by opponent......17 by Kansas City, August 31, 1961, first game
17 by Chicago, May 31, 1978
Most hits, game.............................26 vs. Toronto, August 25, 1979
26 vs. Boston, June 20, 1980
Most home runs, game ....6 vs. Boston June 20, 1980
6 vs. Oakland, April 23, 1985
6 vs. Chicago, June 28, 1987
Most runs, shutout game................17 vs. Washington, August 23, 1963
17 vs. Minnesota, April 23, 1980
Most runs, shutout game, by opponent ....14 by Seattle, August 7, 1987
Most runs, doubleheader shutout ....7 vs. Kansas City, June 26, 1964
Longest 1-0 game won.........15 innings vs. Chicago, April 13, 1963
Longest 1-0 game lost ....20 innings vs. Oakland, July 9, 1971
Longest shutout game won....16 innings, 3-0 vs. Chicago, September 22, 1975
Most consecutive games won ....11 in 1964
Most consecutive games lost ....11 in 1974
Most times league champions .... None
Most last place finishes 1
Most consecutive games, one or more homers ....18 (30 homers), 1982
Most total bases, game.........52 vs. Boston, June 20, 1980
Largest crowd, day game........63,132 vs. Kansas City, July 4, 1983
Largest crowd, doubleheader........41,723 vs. Minnesota, August 5, 1978
Largest crowd, night game........63,073 vs. Baltimore, April 23, 1983
Largest crowd, home opener ....38,076 vs. Oakland, April 13, 1981

Chicago White Sox

Yearly Finishes

Year—Position	W.	L.	Pct.	*G.B.	Manager
1901—First	83	53	.610	+ 4	Clark Griffith
1902—Fourth	74	60	.552	8	Clark Griffith
1903—Seventh	60	77	.438	30½	James Callahan
1904—Third	89	65	.578	6	J. Callahan, F. Jones
1905—Second	92	60	.605	2	Fielder Jones
1906—First	93	58	.616	+ 3	Fielder Jones
1907—Third	87	64	.576	5½	Fielder Jones
1908—Third	88	64	.579	1½	Fielder Jones
1909—Fourth	78	74	.513	20	William Sullivan
1910—Sixth	68	85	.444	35½	Hugh Duffy
1911—Fourth	77	74	.510	24	Hugh Duffy
1912—Fourth	78	76	.506	28	James Callahan
1913—Fifth	78	74	.513	17½	James Callahan
1914—Sixth†	70	84	.455	30	James Callahan
1915—Third	93	61	.604	9½	Clarence Rowland
1916—Second	89	65	.578	2	Clarence Rowland
1917—First	100	54	.649	+ 9	Clarence Rowland
1918—Sixth	57	67	.460	17	Clarence Rowland
1919—First	88	52	.629	+ 3½	William Gleason
1920—Second	96	58	.623	2	William Gleason
1921—Seventh	62	92	.403	36½	William Gleason
1922—Fifth	77	77	.500	17	William Gleason
1923—Seventh	69	85	.448	30	William Gleason
1924—Eighth	66	87	.431	25½	F. Chance, J. Evers
1925—Fifth	79	75	.513	18½	Edward Collins
1926—Fifth	81	72	.529	9½	Edward Collins
1927—Fifth	70	83	.458	29½	Ray Schalk
1928—Fifth	72	82	.468	29	R. Schalk, R. Blackburne
1929—Seventh	59	93	.388	46	Russell Blackburne
1930—Seventh	62	92	.403	40	Owen (Donie) Bush
1931—Eighth	56	97	.366	51	Owen (Donie) Bush
1932—Seventh	49	102	.325	56½	Lewis Fonseca
1933—Sixth	67	83	.447	31	Lewis Fonseca
1934—Eighth	53	99	.349	47	L. Fonseca, J. Dykes
1935—Fifth	74	78	.487	19½	James Dykes
1936—Third	81	70	.536	20	James Dykes
1937—Third	86	68	.558	16	James Dykes
1938—Sixth	65	83	.439	32	James Dykes
1939—Fourth	85	69	.552	22½	James Dykes
1940—Fourth†	82	72	.532	8	James Dykes
1941—Third	77	77	.500	24	James Dykes
1942—Sixth	66	82	.446	34	James Dykes

Year—Position	W.	L.	Pct.	*G.B.	Manager
1943—Fourth	82	72	.532	16	James Dykes
1944—Seventh	71	83	.461	18	James Dykes
1945—Sixth	71	78	.477	15	James Dykes
1946—Fifth	74	80	.481	30	J. Dykes, T. Lyons
1947—Sixth	70	84	.455	27	Theodore Lyons
1948—Eighth	51	101	.336	44½	Theodore Lyons
1949—Sixth	63	91	.409	34	Jack Onslow
1950—Sixth	60	94	.390	38	J. Onslow, J. Corriden
1951—Fourth	81	73	.526	17	Paul Richards
1952—Third	81	73	.526	14	Paul Richards
1953—Third	89	65	.578	11½	Paul Richards
1954—Third	94	60	.610	17	P. Richards, M. Marion
1955—Third	91	63	.591	5	Martin Marion
1956—Third	85	69	.552	12	Martin Marion
1957—Second	90	64	.584	8	Alfonso Lopez
1958—Second	82	72	.532	10	Alfonso Lopez
1959—First	94	60	.610	+ 5	Alfonso Lopez
1960—Third	87	67	.565	10	Alfonso Lopez
1961—Fourth	86	76	.531	23	Alfonso Lopez
1962—Fifth	85	77	.525	11	Alfonso Lopez
1963—Second	94	68	.580	10½	Alfonso Lopez
1964—Second	98	64	.605	1	Alfonso Lopez
1965—Second	95	67	.586	7	Alfonso Lopez
1966—Fourth	83	79	.512	15	Edward Stanky
1967—Fourth	89	73	.549	3	Edward Stanky
1968—Eighth†	67	95	.414	36	E. Stanky, A. Lopez

West Division

Year—Position	W.	L.	Pct.	*G.B.	Manager
1969—Fifth	68	94	.420	29	A. Lopez, D. Gutteridge
1970—Sixth	56	106	.346	42	D. Gutteridge, C. Tanner
1971—Third	79	83	.488	22½	Charles Tanner
1972—Second	87	67	.565	5½	Charles Tanner
1973—Fifth	77	85	.475	17	Charles Tanner
1974—Fourth	80	80	.500	9	Charles Tanner
1975—Fifth	75	86	.466	22½	Charles Tanner
1976—Sixth	64	97	.398	25½	Paul Richards
1977—Third	90	72	.556	12	Robert Lemon
1978—Fifth	71	90	.441	20½	R. Lemon, L. Doby
1979—Fifth	73	87	.456	14	D. Kessinger, A. LaRussa
1980—Fifth	70	90	.438	26	Anthony LaRussa
1981—3rd/6th.	54	52	.509	‡	Anthony LaRussa
1982—Third	87	75	.537	6	Anthony LaRussa

Minnie Minoso (left) and Manager Al Lopez

Year—Position	W.	L.	Pct.	*G.B.	Manager
1983—First§.....	99	63	.611	+20	..............................Anthony LaRussa
1984—Fifth†....	74	88	.457	10	..............................Anthony LaRussa
1985—Third	85	77	.525	6	..............................Anthony LaRussa
1986—Fifth.......	72	90	.444	20	....................A. LaRussa, J. Fregosi
1987—Sixth†....	75	87	.463	10	..............................James Fregosi

*Games behind winner. †Tied for position. ‡First half 31-22; second 23-30. §Lost Championship Series.

Individual Records (1901 To Date)
Batting

Most years, non-pitcher ....20, Lucius B. Appling
Most games ....163, Donald A. Buford, 1966
Most games, league ....2422, Lucius B. Appling
Most at-bats..............................649, J. Nelson Fox, 154 games, 1956
Most at-bats, league..8857, Lucius B. Appling
Most runs..............................135, John A. Mostil, 153 games, 1925
Most runs, league ....1319, Lucius B. Appling
Most hits..............................222, Edward T. Collins, 153 games, 1920
Most hits, league ....2749, Lucius B. Appling
Most singles..............................169, Edward T. Collins, 153 games, 1920
Most singles, league..2162, Lucius B. Appling
Most doubles..............................45, Floyd A. Robinson, 156 games, 1962
Most doubles, league ....440, Lucius B. Appling
Most triples..............................21, Joseph J. Jackson, 153 games, 1916
Most triples, league..104, John F. Collins
104, J. Nelson Fox
Most homers, righthander..........................37, Richard A. Allen, 148 games, 1972
Most homers, lefthander..........................31, Oscar C. Gamble, 137 games, 1977
Most homers at home ....27, Richard A. Allen, 1972
Most homers on road ....19, W. Edward Robinson, 1951
Most homers, rookie..............................35, Ronald D. Kittle, 145 games, 1983
Most homers, month..13, Richard A. Allen, July, 1972
Most homers, league, lefthander..........................160, Harold D. Baines
Most homers, league, righthander ....154, William E. Melton
Most grand slams..............................3, Peter T. Ward, 144 games, 1964
Most grand slams, league..5, Harold D. Baines

Most total bases..............................336, Joseph J. Jackson, 146 games, 1920
Most total bases, league..3528, Lucius B. Appling
Most long hits..............................74, Joseph J. Jackson, 146 games, 1920
Most long hits, league..587, Lucius B. Appling
Most extra bases on long hits ....149, Richard A. Allen, 148 games, 1972
Most extra bases on long hits, league ....823, Orestes A. Minoso
Most sacrifices, (S.H. and S.F).............. 44, George D. Weaver, 151 games, 1916
Most sacrifice hits ....40, Lucius B. Appling, 1905
Most sacrifice flies ....12, Orestes A. Minoso, 1961
Most stolen bases ....77, Rudy K. Law, 141 games, 1983
Most stolen bases, league ....368, Edward T. Collins
Most caught stealing..............................29, Edward T. Collins, 145 games, 1923
Most bases on balls..............................127, Luzerne A. Blue, 155 games, 1931
Most bases on balls, league..1302, Lucius B. Appling
Most strikeouts..............................175, David L. Nicholson, 126 games, 1963
Most strikeouts, league..621, Harold D. Baines
Fewest strikeouts ....11, J. Nelson Fox, 155 games, 1958
Most hit by pitch ....23, Orestes A. Minoso, 151 games, 1956
Most runs batted in..............................138, Henry J. Bonura, 148 games, 1936
Most runs batted in, league..1116, Lucius B. Appling
Most game-winning RBIs ....22, Harold D. Baines, 156 games, 1983
Most consecutive games with RBI ....13, Taft S. Wright (22 RBIs), 1941
Highest batting average ....388, Lucius B. Appling, 138 games, 1936
Highest batting average, league ....340, Joseph J. Jackson
Highest slugging average ....603, Richard A. Allen, 148 games, 1972
Highest slugging average, league..518, Henry J. Bonura
Longest batting streak..............................27 games, Lucius B. Appling, 1936
Most grounded into double play..............................27, J. Sherman Lollar, 140 games, 1959
Fewest grounded into double play..............3, Ulysses J. Lupien, 154 games, 1948
3, Donald A. Buford, 163 games, 1966
3, Donald A. Buford, 156 games, 1967

Pitching

Most years..21, Theodore A. Lyons
Most games..88, Wilbur F. Wood, 1968
Most games, league..669, Urban C. Faber
Most games started..............................49, Edward A. Walsh, 1908
49, Wilbur F. Wood, 1972

Most games started, league .... 484, Urban C. Faber
484, Theodore A. Lyons
Most complete games .... 42, Edward A. Walsh, 1908
Most complete games, league .... 356, Theodore A. Lyons
Most games finished .... 62, Wilbur F. Wood, 1970
Most innings .... 465, Edward A. Walsh, 1908
Most innings, league .... 4162, Theodore A. Lyons
Most games won .... 40, Edward A. Walsh, 1908
Most games won, league .... 260, Theodore A. Lyons
Most 20-victory seasons .... 4, Edward A. Walsh
4, Urban C. Faber
4, Wilbur F. Wood
Most games lost .... 25, Patrick J. Flaherty, 1903
Most games lost, league .... 230, Theodore A. Lyons
Highest winning percentage .... .842, Sandalio Consuegra (16-3), 1954
Longest winning streak .... 13 games, D. LaMarr Hoyt, 1983
Longest losing streak .... 14 games, Howard K. Judson, 1949
Most saves .... 32, Robert H. James, 1985
Most bases on balls .... 147, L. Vernon Kennedy, 1936
Most bases on balls, league .... 1213, Urban C. Faber
Most strikeouts .... 269, Edward A. Walsh, 1908
Most strikeouts, league .... 1796, W. William Pierce
Most strikeouts, game .... 16, Jack Harshman, July 25, 1954, first game
Most shutouts .... 12, Edward A. Walsh, 1908
Most shutouts, league .... 58, Edward A. Walsh
Most 1-0 shutouts won .... 5, Ewell A. Russell, 1913
Most runs .... 182, Richard Kerr, 1921
Most earned runs .... 162, Richard Kerr, 1921
Most hits .... 381, Wilbur F. Wood, 1973
Most hit batsmen .... 16, James Scott, 1909
Most wild pitches .... 17, Thomas E. John, 1970
Most home runs .... 33, W. William Pierce, 1958
Most sacrifice hits .... 21, Wilbur F. Wood, 1972
Most sacrifice flies .... 12, Wilbur F. Wood, 1974
12, C. Barth Johnson, 1976
12, Kenneth P. Kravec, 1979
Lowest ERA .... 1.53, Edward V. Cicotte, 346 innings, 1917

Club Records

Most players .... 50 in 1932
Fewest players .... 19 in 1905
Most games .... 163 in 1961, 1966, 1974, 1985
Most at-bats .... 5633 in 1977 (162 games)
Most runs .... 920 in 1936 (153 games)
Most opponents' runs .... 946 in 1934 (153 games)
Fewest runs .... 447 in 1910 (156 games)
Most hits .... 1597 in 1936 (153 games)
Fewest hits .... 1061 in 1910 (156 games)
Most singles .... 1199 in 1936 (153 games)
Most doubles .... 314 in 1926 (155 games)
Most triples .... 102 in 1915 (155 games)
Most homers .... 192 in 1977 (162 games)
Fewest homers (154 or 162-game schedule) .... 3 in 1908
Most homers at Comiskey Park, home & opp. .... 175 in 1970
Most grand slams .... 7 in 1961
Most pinch home runs .... 9 in 1984
Most total bases .... 2502 in 1977 (162 games)
Most long hits .... 498 in 1977 (162 games)
Most extra bases on long hits .... 934 in 1977 (162 games)
Most sacrifices (S. H. and S. F.) .... 270 in 1915 (154 games)
Most sacrifice hits .... 207 in 1906 (154 games)
Most sacrifice flies .... 63 in 1977 (162 games)
Most stolen bases .... 275 in 1901 (138 games)
Most caught stealing .... 119 in 1923 (156 games)
Most bases on balls .... 702 in 1949 (154 games)
Most strikeouts .... 991 in 1972 (154 games)
Fewest strikeouts .... 355 in 1920 (154 games)
Most hit by pitch .... 75 in 1956 (154 games)
Fewest hit by pitch .... 10 in 1940 (155 games)

Highest batting average .... .295 in 1920 (154 games)
Lowest batting average .... .212 in 1910 (156 games)
Most runs batted in .... 862 in 1936 (153 games)
Most game-winning RBIs .... 95 in 1983 (162 games)
Highest slugging average .... .444 in 1977 (162 games)
Lowest slugging average .... .261 in 1910 (156 games)
Most grounded into double play .... 156 in 1950 (156 games)
156 in 1974 (163 games)
Fewest grounded into double play .... 94 in 1966 (163 games)
Most left on bases .... 1279 in 1936 (153 games)
Fewest left on bases .... 1009 in 1985 (163 games)
Most .300 hitters .... 8 in 1924
Most putouts .... 4471 in 1967 (162 games)
Fewest putouts .... 3943 in 1942 (148 games)
Most assists .... 2446 in 1907 (157 games)
Fewest assists .... 1622 in 1977 (162 games)
Most chances accepted .... 6655 in 1907 (157 games)
Fewest chances accepted .... 5670 in 1942 (148 games)
Most errors .... 358 in 1901 (137 games)
Fewest errors .... 107 in 1957 (155 games)
Most errorless games .... 89 in 1962 (162 games)
Most consecutive errorless games .... 9 in 1955, 1964
Most double plays .... 188 in 1974 (163 games)
Fewest double plays .... 94 in 1915 (155 games)
Most passed balls .... 45 in 1965 (162 games)
Fewest passed balls .... 3 in 1922 (155 games)
Highest fielding average .... .982 in 1954 (155 games)
.982 in 1957 (155 games)
.982 in 1960 (154 games)
.982 in 1962 (162 games)
.982 in 1985 (163 games)
Lowest fielding average .... .938 in 1901 (137 games)
Highest home attendance .... 2,136,988 in 1984
Highest road attendance .... 1,860,940 in 1987
Most games won .... 100 in 1917
Most games lost .... 106 in 1970
Most games won, month .... 23, Sept. 1905
Most games lost, month .... 24, June 1934
24, August 1968
Highest percentage games won .... .649 in 1917 (won 100, lost 54)
Lowest percentage games won .... .325 in 1932 (won 49, lost 102)
Games won, league .... 6727 in 87 years
Games lost, league .... 6658 in 87 years
Most shutouts won .... 30 in 1906
Most shutouts lost .... 24 in 1910
Most 1-0 games won .... 9 in 1909
9 in 1967
Most 1-0 games lost .... 9 in 1968
Most consecutive games won .... 19 in 1906
Most consecutive games lost .... 13 in 1924
Most times league champion 5
Most last place finishes 6
Most runs, game .... 29 vs. Kansas City, April 23, 1955
Most runs game, by opponent .... 22 by Chicago, July 26, 1931, second game
Most runs, shutout game .... 17 vs. Washington, September 19, 1925, second game
17 vs. Cleveland, July 5, 1987
Most runs, shutout game, by opponent .... 17 by Baltimore, July 27, 1969
Most runs, doubleheader shutout .... 17 vs. Detroit, September 6, 1905
Most runs, inning .... 13 vs. Washington, Sept. 26, 1943, first game, fourth inning
Most hits, game .... 29 vs. Kansas City, April 23, 1955
Most home runs, game .... 7 vs. Kansas City, April 23, 1955
Longest 1-0 game won .... 17 innings vs. Cleveland, Sept. 13, 1967, night game
Longest 1-0 game lost .... 18 innings vs. Washington, May 15, 1918
18 innings vs. Washington, June 8, 1947, first game
Most consecutive games, one or more homers .... 16 (32 homers), 1987
Most total bases, game .... 55 vs. Kansas City, April 23, 1955
Largest crowd, day game .... 51,560 vs. Milwaukee, April 14, 1981
Largest crowd, doubleheader .... 55,555 vs. Minnesota, May 20, 1973
Largest crowd, night game .... 53,940 vs. New York, June 8, 1951
Largest crowd, home opener .... 51,560 vs. Milwaukee, April 14, 1981

Cleveland Indians

Yearly Finishes

Year—Position	W.	L.	Pct.	*G.B.	Manager
1901—Seventh ..	54	82	.397	29	James McAleer
1902—Fifth	69	67	.507	14	William Armour
1903—Third	77	63	.550	15	William Armour
1904—Fourth	86	65	.570	7½	William Armour
1905—Fifth	76	78	.494	19	Napoleon Lajoie
1906—Third	89	64	.582	5	Napoleon Lajoie
1907—Fourth	85	67	.559	8	Napoleon Lajoie
1908—Second	90	64	.584	½	Napoleon Lajoie
1909—Sixth	71	82	.464	27½	N. Lajoie, J. McGuire
1910—Fifth	71	81	.467	32	James McGuire
1911—Third	80	73	.523	22	J. McGuire, G. Stovall
1912—Fifth	75	78	.490	30½	H. Davis, J. Birmingham
1913—Third	86	66	.566	9½	Joseph Birmingham
1914—Eighth	51	102	.333	48½	Joseph Birmingham
1915—Seventh ..	57	95	.375	44½	J. Birmingham, L. Fohl
1916—Sixth	77	77	.500	14	Lee Fohl
1917—Third	88	66	.571	12	Lee Fohl
1918—Second	73	54	.575	1½	Lee Fohl
1919—Second	84	55	.604	3½	L. Fohl, T. Speaker
1920—First	98	56	.636	+ 2	Tristram Speaker
1921—Second	94	60	.610	4½	Tristram Speaker
1922—Fourth	78	76	.507	16	Tristram Speaker
1923—Third	82	71	.536	16½	Tristram Speaker
1924—Sixth	67	86	.438	24½	Tristram Speaker
1925—Sixth	70	84	.455	27½	Tristram Speaker
1926—Second	88	66	.571	3	Tristram Speaker
1927—Sixth	66	87	.431	43½	Jack McCallister
1928—Seventh ..	62	92	.403	39	Roger Peckinpaugh
1929—Third	81	71	.533	24	Roger Peckinpaugh
1930—Fourth	81	73	.536	21	Roger Peckinpaugh
1931—Fourth	78	76	.506	30	Roger Peckinpaugh
1932—Fourth	87	65	.572	19	Roger Peckinpaugh
1933—Fourth	75	76	.497	23½	R. Peckinpaugh, W. Johnson
1934—Third	85	69	.552	16	Walter Johnson
1935—Third	82	71	.536	12	W. Johnson, S. O'Neill
1936—Fifth	80	74	.519	22½	Stephen O'Neill
1937—Fourth	83	71	.539	19	Stephen O'Neill
1938—Third	86	66	.566	13	Oscar Vitt
1939—Third	87	67	.565	20½	Oscar Vitt
1940—Second	89	65	.578	1	Oscar Vitt
1941—Fourth†	75	79	.487	26	Roger Peckinpaugh
1942—Fourth	75	79	.487	28	Louis Boudreau
1943—Third	82	71	.536	15½	Louis Boudreau
1944—Fifth†	72	82	.468	17	Louis Boudreau

Sweet-swinging Napoleon Lajoie

Year—Position	W.	L.	Pct.	*G.B.	Manager
1945—Fifth........	73	72	.503	11	......................................Louis Boudreau
1946—Sixth	68	86	.442	36	......................................Louis Boudreau
1947—Fourth.....	80	74	.519	17	......................................Louis Boudreau
1948—First‡....	97	58	.626	+ 1	......................................Louis Boudreau
1949—Third	89	65	.578	8	......................................Louis Boudreau
1950—Fourth.....	92	62	.597	6	......................................Louis Boudreau
1951—Second.....	93	61	.604	5	......................................Alfonso Lopez
1952—Second.....	93	61	.604	2	......................................Alfonso Lopez
1953—Second.....	92	62	.597	8½	......................................Alfonso Lopez
1954—First........	111	43	.721	+ 8	......................................Alfonso Lopez
1955—Second.....	93	61	.604	3	......................................Alfonso Lopez
1956—Second.....	88	66	.571	9	......................................Alfonso Lopez
1957—Sixth	76	77	.497	21½	.............................M. Kerby Farrell
1958—Fourth.....	77	76	.503	14½	..................R. Bragan, J. Gordon
1959—Second.....	89	65	.578	5	......................................Joseph Gordon
1960—Fourth.....	76	78	.494	21	.....................J. Gordon, J. Dykes
1961—Fifth.......	78	83	.484	30½	......................................James Dykes
1962—Sixth	80	82	.494	16	..........................F. Melvin McGaha
1963—Fifth†	79	83	.488	25½	................George (Birdie) Tebbetts
1964—Sixth†	79	83	.488	20	................George (Birdie) Tebbetts
1965—Fifth.......	87	75	.537	15	................George (Birdie) Tebbetts
1966—Fifth.......	81	81	.500	17	...........G. Tebbetts, G. Strickland
1967—Eighth	75	87	.463	17	......................................Joseph Adcock
1968—Third	86	75	.534	16½	......................................Alvin Dark

East Division

Year—Position	W.	L.	Pct.	*G.B.	Manager
1969—Sixth	62	99	.385	46½	......................................Alvin Dark
1970—Fifth.......	76	86	.469	32	......................................Alvin Dark
1971—Sixth	60	102	.370	43	.........................A. Dark, J. Lipon
1972—Fifth.......	72	84	.462	14	......................................Ken Aspromonte

Year—Position	W.	L.	Pct.	*G.B.	Manager
1973—Sixth	71	91	.438	26	......................................Ken Aspromonte
1974—Fourth.....	77	85	.475	14	......................................Ken Aspromonte
1975—Fourth.....	79	80	.497	15½	......................................Frank Robinson
1976—Fourth.....	81	78	.509	16	......................................Frank Robinson
1977—Fifth.......	71	90	.441	28½	.............F. Robinson, J. Torborg
1978—Sixth	69	90	.434	29	......................................Jeffrey Torborg
1979—Sixth	81	80	.503	22	.....................J. Torborg, D. Garcia
1980—Sixth	79	81	.494	23	......................................David Garcia
1981—6th/5th....	52	51	.504	§	......................................David Garcia
1982—Sixth†	78	84	.481	17	......................................David Garcia
1983—Seventh..	70	92	.432	28	.................M. Ferraro, P. Corrales
1984—Sixth	75	87	.463	29	......................................Pat Corrales
1985—Seventh..	60	102	.370	39½	......................................Pat Corrales
1986—Fifth.......	84	78	.519	11½	......................................Pat Corrales
1987—Seventh..	61	101	.377	37	.................P. Corrales, H. Edwards

*Games behind winner. †Tied for position. ‡Won pennant playoff. §First half 26-24; second 26-27.

Individual Records (1901 To Date)
Batting

Most years, non-pitcher ....15, Terrence L. Turner
Most games ....163, Leon L. Wagner, 1964
Most games, league...1619, Terrence L. Turner
Most at-bats ....663, Joseph C. Carter, 162 games, 1986
Most at-bats, league ....6037, Napoleon Lajoie
Most runs..140, H. Earl Averill, 155 games, 1931
Most runs, league...1154, H. Earl Averill
Most hits...233, Joseph J. Jackson, 147 games, 1911
Most hits, league ....2051, Napoleon Lajoie
Most singles.....................................172, Charles D. Jamieson, 152 games, 1923

Most singles, league	1516, Napoleon Lajoie
Most doubles	64, George H. Burns, 151 games, 1926
Most doubles, league	486, Tristram Speaker
Most triples	26, Joseph J. Jackson, 152 games, 1912
Most triples, league	121, H. Earl Averill
Most homers, righthander	43, Albert L. Rosen, 155 games, 1953
Most homers, lefthander	42, Harold A. Trosky, 151 games, 1936
Most homers, rookie	37, Albert L. Rosen, 155 games, 1950
Most homers at home	30, Harold A. Trosky, 1936
Most homers on road	22, Rocco D. Colavito, 1959
Most homers, month	13, Harold A. Trosky, July, 1937
	13, Rocco D. Colavito, August 1958
Most homers, league, lefthander	226, H. Earl Averill
Most homers, league, righthander	214, Andre Thornton
Most grand slams	4, Albert L. Rosen, 154 games, 1951
Most grand slams, league	9, Albert L. Rosen
Most total bases	405, Harold A. Trosky, 151 games, 1936
Most total bases, league	3201, H. Earl Averill
Most long hits	96, Harold A. Trosky, 151 games, 1936
Most long hits, league	724, H. Earl Averill
Most extra bases on long hits	189, Harold A. Trosky, 151 games, 1936
Most extra bases on long hits, league	1904, H. Earl Averill
Most sacrifices (S.H. and S.F.)	67, Raymond J. Chapman, 156 games, 1917
Most sacrifice hits	46, William J. Bradley, 139 games, 1907
Most sacrifice flies	12, Victor P. Power, 1961
Most stolen bases	61, Miguel A. Dilone, 132 games, 1980
Most stolen bases, league	254, Terrence L. Turner
Most caught stealing	23, Bobby L. Bonds, 146 games, 1979
Most bases on balls	111, D. Michael Hargrove, 160 games, 1980
Most bases on balls, league	726, H. Earl Averill
Most strikeouts	166, J. Cory Snyder, 157 games, 1987
Most strikeouts league	805, Lawrence E. Doby
Fewest strikeouts	4, Joseph W. Sewell, 155 games, 1925
	4, Joseph W. Sewell, 152 games, 1929
Most hit by pitch	17, Orestes A. Minoso, 148 games, 1959
Most runs batted in	162, Harold A. Trosky, 151 games, 1936
Most runs batted in, league	1085, H. Earl Averill
Most game-winning RBIs	15, Andre Thornton, 161 games, 1982
Most consecutive games with RBI	9, Albert L. Rosen (18 RBI), 1954
Highest batting average	.408, Joseph J. Jackson, 147 games, 1911
Highest batting average, league	.375, Joseph J. Jackson
Highest slugging average	.644, Harold A. Trosky, 151 games, 1936
Highest slugging average, league	.551, Harold A. Trosky
Longest batting streak	29 games, William J. Bradley, 1902
Most grounded into double play	27, Albert L. Rosen, 155 games, 1950
Fewest grounded into double play	3, Jose D. Cardenal, 157 games, 1968
	3, J. Cory Snyder, 157 games, 1987

Pitching

Most years	20, Melvin L. Harder
Most games	76, Isidro P. Monge, 1979
Most games, league	582, Melvin L. Harder
Most games started	44, George E. Uhle 1923
Most games started, league	484, Robert W. Feller
Most complete games	36, Robert W. Feller, 1946
Most complete games, league	279, Robert W. Feller
Most games finished	54, Daniel R. Spillner, 1982
Most innings	371, Robert W. Feller, 1946
Most innings, league	3828, Robert W. Feller
Most games won	31, James C. Bagby, 1920
Most games won, league	266, Robert W. Feller
Most 20-victory seasons	7, Robert G. Lemon
Most games lost	22, H. Peter Dowling, 1901
Most games lost, league	186, Melvin L. Harder
Highest winning percentage	.938, John T. Allen (15-1), 1937
Longest winning streak	15, John T. Allen, 1937
	15, Gaylord J. Perry, 1974
Longest winning streak over two seasons	17, John T. Allen, 1936 (2), 1937 (15)
Longest losing streak	13, Guy Morton, 1914
Most saves, season	23, Ernie C. Camacho, 1984
Most bases on balls	208, Robert W. Feller, 1938
Most bases on balls, league	1764, Robert W. Feller
Most strikeouts	348, Robert W. Feller, 1946
Most strikeouts, game	19, Luis C. Tiant, July 3, 1968, 10 innings
	18, Robert W. Feller, October 2, 1938, first game
Most strikeouts, league	2581, Robert W. Feller
Most shutouts	10, Robert W. Feller, 1946
	10, Robert G. Lemon, 1948
Most shutouts, league	45, Adrian Joss
Most 1-0 shutouts won	3, Adrian C. Joss, 1908
	3, Stanley Coveleski, 1917
	3, James C. Bagby, Jr., 1943
	3, Robert W. Feller, 1946
Most runs	167, George E. Uhle, 1923
Most earned runs	150, George E. Uhle, 1923
Most hits	378, George E. Uhle, 1923
Most hit batsmen	20, Otto Hess, 1906
Most wild pitches	18, Samuel E. McDowell, 1967
Most home runs	37, Luis C. Tiant, 1969
Most sacrifice hits	20, Early Wynn, 1951
Most sacrifice flies	12, Early Wynn, 1956
	12, Gaylord J. Perry, 1974
	12, Kenneth M. Schrom, 1986
Lowest ERA	1.60, Luis C. Tiant, 258 innings, 1968

Club Records

Most players	48 in 1912, 1946

Fewest players	24 in 1904
Most games	164 in 1964
Most at-bats	5702 in 1986 (163 games)
Most runs	925 in 1921 (154 games)
Fewest runs	472 in 1972 (156 games)
Most opponents' runs	957 in 1987 (162 games)
Most hits	1715 in 1936 (157 games)
Fewest hits	1210 in 1915 (154 games)
Most singles	1218 in 1925 (155 games)
Most doubles	358 in 1930 (154 games)
Most triples	95 in 1920 (154 games)
Most homers	187 in 1987 (162 games)
Fewest homers (154 or 162-game schedule)	8 in 1910
Most homers at Municipal Stad., home & opp.	236 in 1970
Most grand slams	8 in 1979
Most pinch home runs	9 in 1965, 1970
Most total bases	2605 in 1936 (157 games)
Most long hits	562 in 1936 (157 games)
Most extra bases on long hits	890 in 1936 (157 games)
Most sacrifices (S. H. and S. F.)	262 in 1917 (156 games)
Most sacrifice hits	195 in 1906 (157 games)
Most sacrifice flies	74 in 1980 (160 games)
Most stolen bases	211 in 1917 (156 games)
Most caught stealing	92 in 1920 (154 games)
Most bases on balls	723 in 1955 (154 games)
Most strikeouts	1063 in 1964 (164 games)
Fewest strikeouts	331 in 1922 (155 games)
	331 in 1926 (154 games)
Most hit by pitch	54 in 1962 (162 games)
Fewest hit by pitch	11 in 1943 (153 games)
	11 in 1976 (162 games)
Most runs batted in	852 in 1936 (157 games)
Most game-winning RBIs	80 in 1986 (163 games)
Highest batting average	.308 in 1921 (154 games)
Lowest batting average	.234 in 1968 (162 games)
	.234 in 1972 (156 games)
Highest slugging average	.461 in 1936 (157 games)
Lowest slugging average	.305 in 1910 (161 games)
Most grounded into double play	165 in 1980 (160 games)
Fewest grounded into double play	94 in 1941 (155 games)
Most left on bases	1258 in 1982 (162 games)
Fewest left on bases	995 in 1959 (154 games)
Most .300 hitters	9 in 1921
Most putouts	4463 in 1964 (164 games)
Fewest putouts	3907 in 1945 (147 games)
Most assists	2206 in 1907 (158 games)
Fewest assists	1468 in 1968 (162 games)
Most chances accepted	6563 in 1910 (161 games)
Fewest chances accepted	5470 in 1945 (147 games)
Most errors	336 in 1901 (138 games)
Fewest errors	103 in 1949 (154 games)
Most errorless games	85 in 1971 (162 games)
Most consecutive errorless games	11 in 1967
Most double plays	197 in 1953 (155 games)
Fewest double plays	77 in 1915 (154 games)
Most passed balls	35 in 1958 (153 games)
Fewest passed balls	3 in 1943 (153 games)
Highest fielding average	.983 in 1947 (157 games)
	.983 in 1949 (154 games)
	.983 in 1980 (160 games)
Lowest fielding average	.941 in 1901 (138 games)
Highest home attendance	2,620,627 in 1948
Highest road attendance	1,779,735 in 1987
Most games won	111 in 1954
Most games lost	102 in 1914
	102 in 1971
	102 in 1985
Most games won, month	26, August 1954
Most games lost, month	24, July 1914
Highest percentage games won	.721 in 1954 (won 111, lost 43)
Lowest percentage games won	.333 in 1914 (won 51, lost 102)
Games won, league	6832 in 87 years
Games lost, league	6569 in 87 years
Most shutouts won, season	27 in 1906
Most shutouts lost, season	24 in 1914
Most 1-0 games won	6 in 1905, 1908, 1968
Most 1-0 games lost	7 in 1918, 1955
Most consecutive games won	13 in 1942, 1951
Most consecutive games lost	12 in 1931
Most times league champions	3
Most last place finishes	5
Most runs, game	27 vs. Boston, July 7, 1923, first game
Most runs, game, by opponent	24 by Boston, August 21, 1986
Most runs, shutout game	19 vs. Boston, May 18, 1955
Most runs, shutout game, by opponent	21 by Det., Sept. 15, 1901, eight inn.
Most runs, doubleheader shutout	23 vs. Boston, June 23, 1931
Longest 1-0 game won	15 innings vs. Baltimore, May 14, 1961, first game
Longest 1-0 game lost	17 innings vs. Chicago, September 13, 1967
Most runs, inning	14 vs. Philadelphia, June 18, 1950, second game, first inning
Most hits, game	29 vs. St. Louis, August 12, 1948, second game
Most home runs, game	7 vs. Detroit, July 17, 1966, second game
Most consecutive games, one or more homers	16 (25 homers), 1963
Most total bases, game	45 vs. Philadelphia, July 10, 1932, 18 innings
	43 vs. Boston, May 25, 1934
	43 vs. Detroit, July 17, 1966, second game
Largest crowd, day game	74,420 vs. Detroit, April 7, 1973
Largest crowd, doubleheader	84,587 vs. New York, September 12, 1954
Largest crowd, night game	78,382 vs. Chicago, August 20, 1948
Largest crowd, home opener	74,420 vs. Detroit, April 7, 1973

Detroit Tigers

Yearly Finishes

Year—Position	W.	L.	Pct.	*G.B.	Manager
1901—Third	74	61	.548	8½	George Stallings
1902—Seventh	52	83	.385	30½	Frank Dwyer
1903—Fifth	65	71	.478	25	Edward Barrow
1904—Seventh	62	90	.408	32	E. Barrow, R. Lowe
1905—Third	79	74	.516	15½	William Armour
1906—Sixth	71	78	.477	21	William Armour
1907—First	92	58	.613	+ 1½	Hugh Jennings
1908—First	90	63	.588	+ ½	Hugh Jennings
1909—First	98	54	.645	+ 3½	Hugh Jennings
1910—Third	86	68	.558	18	Hugh Jennings
1911—Second	89	65	.578	13½	Hugh Jennings
1912—Sixth	69	84	.451	36½	Hugh Jennings
1913—Sixth	66	87	.431	30	Hugh Jennings
1914—Fourth	80	73	.523	19½	Hugh Jennings
1915—Second	100	54	.649	2½	Hugh Jennings
1916—Third	87	67	.565	4	Hugh Jennings
1917—Fourth	78	75	.510	21½	Hugh Jennings
1918—Seventh	55	71	.437	20	Hugh Jennings
1919—Fourth	80	60	.571	8	Hugh Jennings
1920—Seventh	61	93	.396	37	Hugh Jennings
1921—Sixth	71	82	.464	27	Tyrus Cobb
1922—Third	79	75	.513	15	Tyrus Cobb
1923—Second	83	71	.539	16	Tyrus Cobb
1924—Third	86	68	.558	6	Tyrus Cobb
1925—Fourth	81	73	.526	16½	Tyrus Cobb
1926—Sixth	79	75	.513	12	Tyrus Cobb
1927—Fourth	82	71	.536	27½	George Moriarty
1928—Sixth	68	86	.442	33	George Moriarty
1929—Sixth	70	84	.455	36	Stanley (Bucky) Harris
1930—Fifth	75	79	.487	27	Stanley (Bucky) Harris
1931—Seventh	61	93	.396	47	Stanley (Bucky) Harris
1932—Fifth	76	75	.503	29½	Stanley (Bucky) Harris
1933—Fifth	75	79	.487	25	S. Harris, D. Baker
1934—First	101	53	.656	+ 7	Gordon (Mickey) Cochrane
1935—First	93	58	.616	+ 3	Gordon (Mickey) Cochrane
1936—Second	83	71	.539	19½	Gordon (Mickey) Cochrane
1937—Second	89	65	.578	13	Gordon (Mickey) Cochrane
1938—Fourth	84	70	.545	16	G. Cochrane, D. Baker
1939—Fifth	81	73	.526	26½	Delmer Baker
1940—First	90	64	.584	+ 1	Delmer Baker
1941—Fourth†	75	79	.487	26	Delmer Baker
1942—Fifth	73	81	.474	30	Delmer Baker
1943—Fifth	78	76	.506	20	Stephen O'Neill
1944—Second	88	66	.571	1	Stephen O'Neill
1945—First	88	65	.575	+ 1½	Stephen O'Neill
1946—Second	92	62	.597	12	Stephen O'Neill
1947—Second	85	69	.552	12	Stephen O'Neill
1948—Fifth	78	76	.506	18½	Stephen O'Neill
1949—Fourth	87	67	.565	10	Robert (Red) Rolfe
1950—Second	95	59	.617	3	Robert (Red) Rolfe
1951—Fifth	73	81	.474	25	Robert (Red) Rolfe
1952—Eighth	50	104	.325	45	R. Rolfe, F. Hutchinson
1953—Sixth	60	94	.390	40½	Fred Hutchinson
1954—Fifth	68	86	.442	43	Fred Hutchinson
1955—Fifth	79	75	.513	17	Stanley (Bucky) Harris
1956—Fifth	82	72	.532	15	Stanley (Bucky) Harris
1957—Fourth	78	76	.506	20	John Tighe
1958—Fifth	77	77	.500	15	J. Tighe, W. Norman
1959—Fourth	76	78	.494	18	W. Norman, J. Dykes
1960—Sixth	71	83	.461	26	J. Dykes, J. Gordon
1961—Second	101	61	.623	8	Robert Scheffing
1962—Fourth	85	76	.528	10½	Robert Scheffing
1963—Fifth†	79	83	.488	25½	R. Scheffing, C. Dressen
1964—Fourth	85	77	.525	14	Charles (Chuck) Dressen
1965—Fourth	89	73	.549	13	C. Dressen, R. Swift
1966—Third	88	74	.543	10	C. Dressen, R. Swift, F. Skaff
1967—Second†	91	71	.562	1	Mayo Smith
1968—First	103	59	.636	+12	Mayo Smith

East Division

Year—Position	W.	L.	Pct.	*G.B.	Manager
1969—Second	90	72	.556	19	Mayo Smith
1970—Fourth	79	83	.488	29	Mayo Smith
1971—Second	91	71	.562	12	Alfred (Billy) Martin
1972—First‡	86	70	.551	+ ½	Alfred (Billy) Martin
1973—Third	85	77	.525	12	A. Martin, J. Schultz
1974—Sixth	72	90	.444	19	Ralph Houk
1975—Sixth	57	102	.358	37½	Ralph Houk
1976—Fifth	74	87	.460	24	Ralph Houk
1977—Fourth	74	88	.457	26	Ralph Houk
1978—Fifth	86	76	.531	13½	Ralph Houk
1979—Fifth	85	76	.528	18	L. Moss, G. Anderson
1980—Fifth	84	78	.519	19	George Anderson
1981—4th/2d†	60	49	.550	x	George Anderson
1982—Fourth	83	79	.512	12	George Anderson
1983—Second	92	70	.568	6	George Anderson
1984—First y	104	58	.642	+15	George Anderson
1985—Third	84	77	.522	15	George Anderson
1986—Third	87	75	.537	8½	George Anderson
1987—First‡	98	64	.605	+ 2	George Anderson

*Games behind winner. †Tied for position. ‡Lost Championship Series. xFirst half 31-26; second 29-23. yWon Championship Series.

Individual Records (1901 to Date)

Batting

Most years, non-pitcher	22, Tyrus R. Cobb
	22, Albert W. Kaline
Most games	163, Rocco D. Colavito, 1961
Most games, league	2834, Albert W. Kaline
Most at-bats	679, Harvey E. Kuenn, 155 games, 1953
Most at-bats, league	10,586, Tyrus R. Cobb
Most singles	169, Tyrus R. Cobb, 146 games, 1911
Most singles, league	2839, Tyrus R. Cobb
Most runs	147, Tyrus R. Cobb, 146 games, 1911
Most runs, league	2086, Tyrus R. Cobb
Most hits	248, Tyrus R. Cobb, 146 games, 1911
Most hits, league	3902, Tyrus R. Cobb
Most doubles	63, Henry B. Greenberg, 153 games, 1934
Most doubles, league	664, Tyrus R. Cobb
Most triples	26, Samuel Crawford, 157 games, 1914
Most triples, league	287, Tyrus R. Cobb
Most homers, righthander	58, Henry B. Greenberg, 155 games, 1938
Most homers, lefthander	41, Norman D. Cash, 159 games, 1961
Most homers at home	39, Henry B. Greenberg, 1938
Most homers on road	27, Rocco D. Colavito, 1961
Most homers, rookie	35, Rudolph P. York, 104 games, 1937
Most homers, month	18, Rudolph P. York, August, 1937
Most homers, league, righthander	399, Albert W. Kaline
Most homers, league, lefthander	373, Norman D. Cash
Most grand slams	4, Rudolph P. York, 135 games, 1938
	4, James T. Northrup, 155 games, 1968
Most grand slams, league	10, Rudolph P. York
	10, Henry B. Greenberg
Most total bases	397, Henry B. Greenberg, 154 games, 1937
Most total bases, league	5474, Tyrus R. Cobb
Most long hits	103, Henry B. Greenberg, 154 games, 1937
Most long hits, league	1063, Tyrus R. Cobb
Most extra bases on long hits	205, Henry B. Greenberg, 155 games, 1938
Most extra bases on long hits, league	1845, Albert W. Kaline
Most sacrifices (S. H. and S. F.)	52, Owen Bush, 157 games, 1909
Most sacrifice hits	36, William P. Coughlin, 147 games, 1906
Most sacrifice flies	16, Samuel Crawford, 157 games, 1914
Most stolen bases	96, Tyrus R. Cobb, 156 games, 1915
Most stolen bases, league	865, Tyrus R. Cobb
Most caught stealing	38, Tyrus R. Cobb, 156 games, 1915
Most bases on balls	137, Roy J. Cullenbine, 142 games, 1947
Most bases on balls, league	1277, Albert W. Kaline
Most strikeouts	141, Jacob Wood, 162 games, 1961
Most strikeouts, league	1081, Norman D. Cash
Fewest strikeouts	13, Charles L. Gehringer, 154 games, 1936
	13, Harvey E. Kuenn, 155 games, 1954
Most hit by pitch	24, William A. Freehan, 155 games, 1968
Most runs batted in	183, Henry B. Greenberg, 154 games, 1937
Most runs batted in, league	1826, Tyrus R. Cobb
Most game-winning RBIs	17, Kirk H. Gibson, 149 games, 1984
Most consecutive games with RBI	10, William W. Horton (17 RBIs), 1976
Highest batting average	.420, Tyrus R. Cobb, 146 games, 1911
Highest batting average, league	.368, Tyrus R. Cobb
Highest slugging average	.683, Henry B. Greenberg, 155 games, 1938
Highest slugging average, league	.616, Henry B. Greenberg
Longest batting streak	40 games, Tyrus R. Cobb, 1911
Most grounded into double play	29, James H. Bloodworth, 129 games, 1943
Fewest grounded into double play	0, Richard J. McAuliffe, 151 games, 1968

Pitching

Most years	16, Thomas D. Bridges
Most games	80, Guillermo Hernandez, 1984
Most games, league	545, John F. Hiller
Most games started	45, Michael S. Lolich, 1971
Most games started, league	459, Michael S. Lolich
Most complete games	42, George Mullin, 1904
Most complete games, league	336, George Mullin
Most games finished	68, Guillermo Hernandez, 1984
Most innings	382, George Mullin, 1904
Most innings, league	3398, George Mullin
Most games won	31, Dennis D. McLain, 1968
Most games won, league	222, George Dauss
Most games lost, league	183, George Dauss
Most 20-victory seasons	5, George Mullin
Most games lost	23, George Mullin, 1904
Highest winning percentage	.862, William E. Donovan (25-4), 1907
Longest winning streak	16 games, Lynwood T. Rowe, 1934
Longest losing streak	10 games, Michael S. Lolich, 1967
Most saves	38, John F. Hiller, 1973
Most bases on balls	158, Joseph H. Coleman, 1974
Most bases on balls, league	1227, Harold Newhouser
Most strikeouts	308, Michael S. Lolich, 1971
Most strikeouts, league	2679, Michael S. Lolich
Most strikeouts, game	16, Michael S. Lolich, May 23, 1969
	16, Michael S. Lolich, June 9, 1969, first 9 innings of 10-inning game
Most shutouts	9, Dennis D. McLain, 1969
Most shutouts, league	39, Michael S. Lolich
Most 1-0 shutouts won	4, O. Edgar Summers, 1908
Most runs	160, Joseph H. Coleman, 1974
Most earned runs	142, Michael S. Lolich, 1974
Most hits	336, Michael S. Lolich, 1971
Most hit batsmen	23, Howard J. Ehmke, 1922
Most wild pitches	24, John S. Morris, 1987

Most home runs ....42, Dennis D. McLain, 1966
Most sacrifice hits ....28, Earl O. Whitehill, 1931
Most sacrifice flies ....13, John S. Morris, 1980
Lowest ERA ....1.81, Harold Newhouser, 313 innings, 1945

Club Records

Most players	53 in 1912
Fewest players	24 in 1906, 1907
Most games	164 in 1968
Most at-bats	5649 in 1987 (162 games)
Most runs	958 in 1934 (154 games)
Most opponents' runs	928 in 1929 (155 games)
Fewest runs	499 in 1904 (162 games)
Most hits	1724 in 1921 (154 games)
Fewest hits	1204 in 1905 (154 games)
Most singles	1298 in 1921 (154 games)
Most doubles	349 in 1934 (154 games)
Most triples	102 in 1913 (153 games)
Most homers	225 in 1987 (162 games)
Fewest homers (154 or 162-game schedule)....	9 in 1906
Most homers at Tiger Stadium, home & opp......	226 in 1987
Most grand slams	10 in 1938
Most pinch home runs	8 in 1971
Most total bases	2548 in 1987 (162 games)
Most long hits	546 in 1929 (155 games)
Most extra bases on long hits	1013 in 1987 (162 games)
Most sacrifices (S. H. and S. F.)	256 in 1923 (155 games)
Most sacrifice hits	182 in 1906 (151 games)
Most sacrifice flies	59 in 1983 (162 games)
Most stolen bases	281 in 1909 (158 games)
Most caught stealing	92 in 1921 (154 games)
Most bases on balls	762 in 1947 (158 games)
Most strikeouts	994 in 1967 (163 games)
Fewest strikeouts	376 in 1921 (154 games)
Most hit by pitch	61 in 1968 (164 games)
Fewest hit by pitch	9 in 1945 (155 games)
Most runs batted in	873 in 1937 (155 games)
Most game-winning RBIs	97 in 1984 (162 games)
Highest batting average	.316 in 1921 (154 games)
Lowest batting average	.230 in 1904 (162 games)
Highest slugging average	.453 in 1929 (155 games)
Lowest slugging average	.321 in 1918 (128 games)
Most grounded into double play	164 in 1949 (154 games)
Fewest grounded into double play	99 in 1982 (162 games)
	99 in 1986 (162 games)
Most left on base	1266 in 1924 (156 games)
Fewest left on base	1025 in 1972 (156 games)
Most .300 hitters	8 in 1922, 1924, 1934
Most putouts	4469 in 1968 (164 games)
Fewest putouts	4006 in 1906 (151 games)
Most assists	2272 in 1914 (157 games)
Fewest assists, season	1443 in 1962 (161 games)
Most chances accepted	6504 in 1914 (157 games)
Fewest chances accepted	5594 in 1959 (154 games)
Most errors	425 in 1901 (136 games)
Fewest errors	96 in 1956 (156 games)
Most errorless games	84 in 1964 (163 games)
	84 in 1968 (164 games)
	84 in 1972 (154 games)
	84 in 1973 (162 games)
Most consecutive errorless games	12 in 1963
Most double plays	194 in 1950 (157 games)
Fewest double plays	94 in 1912 (152 games)
	94 in 1917 (154 games)
Most passed balls	28 in 1912 (154 games)
Fewest passed balls	4 in 1924 (156 games)
Highest fielding average	.984 in 1972 (156 games)
Lowest fielding average	.922 in 1901 (136 games)
Highest home attendance	2,704,794 in 1984
Highest road attendance	2,160,289 in 1984
Most games won	104 in 1984
Most games lost	104 in 1952
Most games won, month	23, July 1908
	23, August 1915
	23, August 1934
	23, August 1935
Most games lost, month	24, June 1975
Highest percentage games won	.656 in 1934 (won 101, lost 53)
Lowest percentage games won	.325 in 1952 (won 50, lost 104)
Games won, league	6986 in 87 years
Games lost, league	6436 in 87 years
Most shutouts won	20 in 1917, 1944, 1969
Most shutouts lost	22 in 1904
Most 1-0 games won	9 in 1908
Most 1-0 games lost	7 in 1903, 1943
Most consecutive games won	14 in 1909, 1934
Most consecutive games lost	19 in 1975
Most times league champions	9
Most last place finishes	2

Most runs, game ....21 vs. Cleveland, September 15, 1901, eight innings
21 vs. Philadelphia, July 17, 1908
21 vs. St. Louis, July 25, 1920
21 vs. Chicago, July 1, 1936
Most runs, game, by opponent ....24 by Philadelphia, May 18, 1912
Most runs, shutout game ....21 vs. Cleveland, September 15, 1901, eight innings
Most runs, shutout game, by opponent...........16 by St. Louis, September 9, 1922
Most runs, doubleheader shutout ....26 vs. St. Louis, September 22, 1936
Most runs, inning ....13 vs. New York, June 17, 1925, sixth inning

Hank Greenberg

Longest 1-0 game won ....12 innings vs. St. Louis, September 8, 1917
12 innings vs. Cleveland, June 26, 1919
12 innings vs. Chicago, September 10, 1950, first game
Longest 1-0 game lost ....16 innings vs. Chicago, August 14, 1954
Most hits, game ....28 vs. New York, September 29, 1928
Most home runs, game ....6 vs. St. Louis, August 14, 1937, second game
6 vs. Philadelphia, June 11, 1954, first game
6 vs. Kansas City, July 20, 1962
6 vs. California, July 4, 1968
6 vs. Oakland, August 17, 1969
6 vs. Boston, August 9, 1971
6 vs. Milwaukee, September 10, 1986
Most consecutive games, one or more homers ....17 (26 homers), 1940
Most total bases...........................45 vs. St. Louis, August 14, 1937, second game
Largest crowd, day game ....57,888 vs. Cleveland, September 26, 1948
Largest crowd, doubleheader ....58,369 vs. New York, July 20, 1947
Largest crowd, night game ....56,586 vs. Cleveland, August 9, 1948
Largest crowd, home opener ....54,089 vs. Cleveland, April 6, 1971

Kansas City A's

Yearly Finishes

Year—Position	W.	L.	Pct.	*G.B.	Manager
1955—Sixth	63	91	.409	33	...............................Louis Boudreau
1956—Eighth	52	102	.338	45	...............................Louis Boudreau
1957—Seventh ..	59	94	.386	38½	..................L. Boudreau, H. Craft
1958—Seventh ..	73	81	.474	19	...............................Harry Craft
1959—Seventh ..	66	88	.429	28	...............................Harry Craft
1960—Eighth	58	96	.377	39	...............................Robert Elliott
1961—Ninth†	61	100	.379	47½	...............J. Gordon, H. Bauer
1962—Ninth	72	90	.444	24	...............................Henry Bauer
1963—Eighth	73	89	.451	31½	...............................Edmund Lopat
1964—Tenth	57	105	.352	42	..................E. Lopat, M. McGaha
1965—Tenth	59	103	.364	43	..........M. McGaha, H. Sullivan
1966—Seventh ..	74	86	.463	23	...............................Alvin Dark
1967—Tenth	62	99	.385	29½	..................A. Dark, L. Appling

*Games behind winner.   †Tied for position.

Individual Records (1955 To 1967)
Batting

Most years, non-pitcher ....6, Edwin D. Charles
6, William R. Bryan
6, J. Wayne Causey
Most games..............................162, Norman L. Siebern, 1962
Most games, league ....726, Edwin D. Charles
Most at-bats...............................641, Jerry D. Lumpe, 156 games, 1962
Most at-bats, league ....2782, Jerry D. Lumpe
Most runs ....114, Norman L. Siebern, 162 games, 1962
Most runs, league ....361, Jerry D. Lumpe
Most hits ....193, Jerry D. Lumpe, 156 games, 1962
Most hits, league ....775, Jerry D. Lumpe
Most doubles...............36, Norman L. Siebern, 153 games, 1961
Most doubles, league ....119, Jerry D. Lumpe
Most triples...............15, Gino N. Cimoli, 152 games, 1962
Most triples, league ....34, Jerry D. Lumpe
Most homers, righthander...............38, Robert H. Cerv, 141 games, 1958
Most homers, lefthander...............28, James E. Gentile, 136 games, 1964
Most homers, rookie...............20, Woodson G. Held, 92 games, 1957
Most homers at home ....22, Rocco D. Colavito, 1964
Most homers on road ....17, Robert H. Cerv, 1958
Most homers, month ....10, Rocco D. Colavito, May, 1964
Most homers, league ....78, Norman L. Siebern
Most grand slams..............2, Roger E. Maris, 99 games, 1958
2, Marvin E. Throneberry, 104 games, 1960
Most grand slams, league ....3, Roger E. Maris
3, Marvin E. Throneberry
Most pinch homers, league ....4, George Alusik
4, Robert H. Cerv
Most total bases ....305, Robert H. Cerv, 141 games, 1958
Most total bases, league ....1065, Edwin D. Charles
Most long hits.................67, Rocco D. Colavito, 160 games, 1964
Most extra bases on long hits ....148, Robert H. Cerv, 141 games, 1958
Most sacrifice hits...................11, Richard H. Williams, 130 games, 1959
Most sacrifice flies ....12, Leopoldo J. Posada, 116 games, 1961
Most stolen bases...............55, Dagoberto B. Campaneris, 147 games, 1965
Most stolen bases, league ....168, Dagoberto B. Campaneris
Most caught stealing...................19, Dagoberto B. Campaneris, 144 games, 1965
Most bases on balls...............110, Norman L. Siebern, 162 games, 1962
Most bases on balls, league ....343, Norman L. Siebern
Most strikeouts ....143, Nelson E. Mathews, 157 games, 1964
Fewest strikeouts ....38, Richard D. Howser, 158 games, 1961
38, Jerry D. Lumpe, 156 games, 1962
Most strikeouts, league ....379, Edwin D. Charles
Most hit by pitch..................13, Robert G. Del Greco, 132 games, 1962
Most runs batted in ....117, Norman L. Siebern, 162 games, 1962
Most runs batted in, league ....367, Norman L. Siebern
Highest batting average ....319, Victor P. Power, 147 games, 1955
Highest slugging average ....592, Robert H. Cerv, 148 games, 1958
Longest batting streak ....22 games, Hector H. Lopez, 1957
22 games, Victor P. Power, 1958
Most grounded into double play ....23, Hector H. Lopez, 151 games, 1958
Fewest grounded into double play............4, Norman L. Siebern, 153 games, 1961

Pitching

Most years ....6, John T. Wyatt
Most games.............................81, John T. Wyatt, 1964
Most games, league ....292, John T. Wyatt
Most games started........................35, Buddy L. Daley, 1960
35, Edward C. Rakow, 1962
35, Diego P. Segui, 1964
35, James A. Hunter, 1967
Most games started, league ....98, Raymond E. Herbert
Most complete games..................14, Arthur J. Ditmar, 1956
14, Raymond E. Herbert, 1960
Most complete games, league ....32, Raymond E. Herbert
Most games finished..................57, John T. Wyatt, 1964
57, Jack D. Aker, 1966
Most innings...................260, James A. Hunter, 1967
Most innings, league ....784, Raymond E. Herbert
Most games won..................16, Buddy L. Daley, 1959
16, Buddy L. Daley, 1960
Most games won, league ....39, Buddy L. Daley
Most games lost...................22, Arthur J. Ditmar, 1956
Most games lost, league ....48, Raymond E. Herbert
Highest winning percentage ....552, Leavitt L. Daley (16-13), 1959

Vic Power

Longest winning streak...............................9 games, Buddy L. Daley, 1960
Longest losing streak ....11 games, W. Troy Herriage, 1956
Most bases on balls.........................108, Arthur J. Ditmar, 1956
Most bases on balls, league ....280, Diego P. Segui
Most strikeouts............................196, James A. Hunter, 1967
Most strikeouts, game ....12, James E. Nash, July 13, 1967
12, James E. Nash, July 23, 1967, second game
12, James A. Hunter, September 12, 1967
Most strikeouts, league ....513, Diego P. Segui
Most shutouts..............................5, James A. Hunter, 1967
Most shutouts, league ....8, Ned F. Garver
Most 1-0 shutouts won ....2, Alexander R. Kellner, 1955
2, James A. Hunter, 1967
Most runs.........................141, Arthur J. Ditmar, 1956
Most earned runs.........................125, Arthur J. Ditmar, 1956
Most hits.........................256, Raymond E. Herbert, 1960
Most hit batsmen.........................12, John C. Kucks, 1959
Most wild pitches.........................13, John T. Wyatt, 1965
Most home runs.........................40, Orlando Pena, 1964
Lowest ERA.................2.80, James A. Hunter, 260 innings, 1967

Club Records

Most players	52 in 1955 (155 games), 1961 (162 games)
Fewest players	38 in 1957 (154 games)
Most games	163 in 1964
Most at-bats	5576 in 1962 (162 games)
Most runs	745 in 1962 (162 games)
Most opponents' runs	911 in 1955 (155 games)
Most hits	1467 in 1962 (162 games)
Most singles	1073 in 1962 (162 games)
Most doubles	231 in 1959 (154 games)
Most triples	59 in 1965 (162 games)
Most homers	166 in 1957 (154 games)
	166 in 1964 (163 games)
Fewest homers	69 in 1967
Most homers at Municipal Stad., home & opp.	239 in 1964
Most grand slams	4 in 1958, 1959, 1960
Most pinch home runs	7 in 1964
Most total bases	2151 in 1962 (162 games)
Most long hits	411 in 1964 (163 games)
Most extra bases on long hits	773 in 1957 (154 games)
Most sacrifice hits	89 in 1961 (162 games)
Most sacrifice flies	50 in 1962 (162 games)
Fewest sacrifice flies	25 in 1964 (163 games)
Most stolen bases	132 in 1966 (160 games)
	132 in 1967 (161 games)
Most caught stealing	59 in 1967 (161 games)
Fewest caught stealing	11 in 1960 (155 games)
Most bases on balls	580 in 1961 (162 games)
Most strikeouts	1104 in 1964 (163 games)
Most hit by pitch	42 in 1962 (162 games)
	42 in 1964 (163 games)
	42 in 1967 (161 games)
Fewest hit by pitch	12 in 1960 (155 games)
Most runs batted in	691 in 1962 (162 games)
Highest batting average	.263 in 1959 (154 games)
	.263 in 1962 (162 games)
Lowest batting average	.233 in 1967 (161 games)
Highest slugging average	.394 in 1957 (154 games)
Lowest slugging average	.330 in 1967 (161 games)
Most grounded into double play	154 in 1960 (155 games)
Fewest grounded into double play	79 in 1967 (161 games)
Most left on bases	1224 in 1962 (162 games)
Fewest left on bases	925 in 1957 (154 games)
Most .300 hitters	4 in 1955
Most putouts	4374 in 1963 (162 games)
Most assists	1782 in 1956 (154 games)
Fewest assists	1532 in 1961 (161 games)
Most chances accepted	6103 in 1963 (162 games)
Fewest chances accepted	5750 in 1959 (154 games)
Most errors	175 in 1961 (162 games)
Most errorless games	78 in 1963 (162 games)

Fewest errors	125 in 1957 (154 games)
	125 in 1958 (156 games)
Most consecutive errorless games	8 in 1960, 1964
Most double plays	187 in 1956 (154 games)
Most passed balls	34 in 1958 (156 games)
Highest fielding average	.980 in 1963 (162 games)
Lowest fielding average	.972 in 1961 (162 games)
Highest home attendance	1,393,054 in 1955
Highest road attendance	938,214 in 1967
Most games won	74 in 1966
Most games lost	105 in 1964
Most games won, month	19, July 1959
Most games lost, month	26, August 1961
Highest percentage games won	.474 in 1958 (won 73, lost 81)
Lowest percentage games won	.338 in 1963 (won 52, lost 102)
Games won, league	829 in 13 years
Games lost, league	1224 in 13 years
Most shutouts won	11 in 1963
	11 in 1966
Most shutouts lost	19 in 1967
Most 1-0 games won	4 in 1966
Most 1-0 games lost	5 in 1967
Most consecutive games won	11 in 1959
Most consecutive games lost	13 in 1959
Most times league champions	0
Most last place finishes	6 (tied in 1961)
Most runs, game	20 vs. Minnesota, April 25, 1961
Most runs, game, by opponent	29 by Chicago, April 23, 1955
Most runs, shutout game	16 vs. Chicago, May 23, 1959
Most runs, shutout game, by opponent	16 by Detroit April 17, 1955
	16 by Boston, August 26, 1957
Most runs, doubleheader shutout	9 vs. Detroit, July 9, 1959
Most runs, inning	13 vs. Chicago, April 21, 1956, second inning
Longest 1-0 game won	11 innings vs. Cleveland, September 15, 1966
Longest 1-0 game lost	None over nine innings
Most hits, nine-inning game	21 vs. Washington, June 13, 1956
	21 vs. Chicago, May 23, 1959
	21 vs. Cleveland May 5, 1962, first game
Most hits, extra-inning game	26 vs. New York, July 27, 1956, 14 innings
Most home runs, game	5 vs. Cleveland, April 18, 1955
	5 vs. Cleveland, April 24, 1957
	5 vs. Baltimore, September 9, 1958
Most consecutive games, one or more homers	11 (13 homers), 1964
Most total bases, game	36 vs. New York, July 27, 1956, 14 innings
	34 vs. Washington, June 13, 1956
	34 vs. Chicago, May 23, 1959
	34 vs. Cleveland, May 5, 1962, first game
Largest crowd, day game	34.065 vs. New York, August 27, 1961
Largest crowd, doubleheader	35,147 vs. New York, August 18, 1962
Largest crowd, night game	33,471 vs. New York, April 29, 1955
Largest crowd, home opener	32,147 vs. Detroit, April 12, 1955

Kansas City Royals

Yearly Finishes
West Division

Year—Position	W.	L.	Pct.	*G.B.	Manager
1969—Fourth	69	93	.426	28	Joseph Gordon
1970—Fourth†	65	97	.401	33	C. Metro, R. Lemon
1971—Second	85	76	.528	16	Robert Lemon
1972—Fourth	76	78	.494	16½	Robert Lemon
1973—Second	88	74	.543	6	John A. McKeon
1974—Fifth	77	85	.475	13	John A. McKeon
1975—Second	91	71	.562	7	J. McKeon, D. Herzog
1976—First‡	90	72	.556	+ 2½	Dorrel (Whitey) Herzog
1977—First‡	102	60	.630	+ 8	Dorrel (Whitey) Herzog
1978—First‡	92	70	.568	+ 5	Dorrel (Whitey) Herzog
1979—Second	85	77	.525	3	Dorrel (Whitey) Herzog
1980—First§	97	65	.599	+14	James Frey
1981—5th/1st	50	53	.485	x	J. Frey, R. Howser
1982—Second	90	72	.556	3	Richard Howser
1983—Second	79	83	.488	20	Richard Howser
1984—First‡	84	78	.519	+ 3	Richard Howser
1985—First§	91	71	.562	+ 1	Richard Howser
1986—Third†	76	86	.469	16	R. Howser, M. Ferraro
1987—Second	83	79	.512	2	W. Gardner, J. Wathan

*Games behind winner. †Tied for position. ‡Lost Championship Series. §Won Championship Series. xFirst half 20-30; second 30-23.

Individual Records (1969 To Date)
Batting

Most years, non-pitcher	15, George H. Brett
	15, Frank White
	15, Harold A. McRae
Most games	162, Alfred E. Cowens, 1977
	162, Harold A. McRae, 1977
Most games, league	1957, Frank White
Most at-bats	705, Willie J. Wilson, 161 games, 1980
Most at-bats, league	7102, George H. Brett
Most runs	133, Willie J. Wilson, 161 games, 1980
Most runs, league	1143, George H. Brett
Most hits	230, Willie J. Wilson, 161 games, 1980
Most hits, league	2219, George H. Brett

Most singles	184, Willie J. Wilson, 161 games, 1980
Most singles, league	1428, George H. Brett
Most doubles	54, Harold A. McRae, 162 games, 1977
Most doubles, league	449, Harold A. McRae
Most triples	21, Willie J. Wilson, 141 games, 1985
Most triples, league	114, George H. Brett
Most homers, lefthander	34, John C. Mayberry, 156 games, 1975
Most homers, righthander	36, Stephen C. Balboni, 160 games, 1985
Most homers, rookie	22, Vincent E. Jackson, 116 games, 1987
Most homers, month	12, John C. Mayberry, July, 1975
Most homers at home	17, Stephen C. Balboni, 1985
Most homers on road	23, John C. Mayberry, 1975
Most homers, league, lefthander	231, George H. Brett
Most homers, league, righthander	193, Amos J. Otis
Most grand slams	2, Stephen C. Balboni, 1985
Most grand slams, league	6, Frank White
Most total bases	363, George H. Brett, 154 games, 1979
Most total bases, league	3586, George H. Brett
Most long hits	86, Harold A. McRae, 162 games, 1977
Most long hits, league	791, George H. Brett
Most extra bases on long hits	151, George H. Brett, 154 games, 1979
Most extra bases on long hits, league	1367, George H. Brett
Most sacrifice hits	18, Frank White, 152 games, 1976
Most sacrifice flies	13, Darrell R. Porter, 157 games, 1979
Most stolen bases	83, Willie J. Wilson, 154 games, 1979
Most stolen bases, league	529, Willie J. Wilson
Most caught stealing	16, H. Patrick Kelly, 136 games, 1970
	16, Alfred E. Cowens, 152 games, 1976
Most bases on balls	122, John C. Mayberry, 152 games, 1973
Most bases on balls, league	767, George H. Brett
Most strikeouts	166, Stephen C. Balboni, 160 games, 1985
Most strikeouts, league	953, Amos J. Otis
Fewest strikeouts	24, George H. Brett, 139 games, 1977
Most hit by pitch	13, Harold A. McRae, 162 games, 1977
Most runs batted in	133, Harold A. McRae, 159 games, 1982
Most runs batted in, league	1128, George H. Brett
Most game-winning RBIs	21, Danilo Tartabull, 158 games, 1987
Longest batting streak	30 games, George H. Brett, 1980
Highest batting average	.390 George H. Brett, 117 games, 1980
Highest batting average, league	.312, George H. Brett
Highest slugging average	.664 George H. Brett, 117 games, 1980
Highest slugging average, league	.505, George H. Brett
Most grounded into double play	26, John D. Wathan, 121 games, 1982
Fewest grounded into double play	1, Willie J. Wilson, 154 games, 1979

Pitching

Most years	15, Paul W. Splittorff
Most games	84, Daniel R. Quisenberry, 1985
Most games, league	553, Daniel R. Quisenberry
Most games started	40, Dennis P. Leonard, 1978
Most games started, league	392, Paul W. Splittorff
Most complete games	21, Dennis P. Leonard, 1977
Most complete games, league	103, Dennis P. Leonard
Most games finished	76, Daniel R. Quisenberry, 1985
Most innings	295, Dennis P. Leonard, 1978
Most innings, league	2555, Paul W. Splittorff
Most games won	22, Steven L. Busby, 1974
Most games won, league	166, Paul W. Splittorff
Most games lost	19, Paul W. Splittorff, 1974
Most games lost, league	143, Paul W. Splittorff
Most 20 victory seasons	3, Dennis P. Leonard
Highest winning percentage	.800, Lawrence C. Gura (16-4), 1978
Longest winning streak	11 games, Richard B. Gale, 1980
Longest winning streak, two seasons	11 games, Paul W. Splittorff, 1977-78
Longest losing streak	8 games, Richard A. Drago, 1970
	8 games, Wallace E. Bunker, 1970
	8 games, William F. Butler, 1970
Most saves	45, Daniel R. Quisenberry, 1983
Most bases on balls	120, Mark S. Gubicza, 1987
Most bases on balls, league	780, Paul W. Splittorff
Most strikeouts	244, Dennis P. Leonard, 1977
Most strikeouts, league	1323, Dennis P. Leonard
Most strikeouts, game	13, Steven L. Busby, July 10, 1973
	13, Dennis P. Leonard, July 8, 1977
	13, Dennis P. Leonard, September 23, 1977
Most shutouts won	6, Roger E. Nelson, 1972
Most 1-0 shutouts won	2, Richard A. Drago, 1971
	2, Roger E. Nelson, 1972
	2, Alan J. Fitzmorris, 1974
	2, Dennis P. Leonard, 1979
	2, Lawrence C. Gura, 1982
Most shutouts, league	23, Dennis P. Leonard
Most runs	137, Lawrence C. Gura, 1979
	137, Paul W. Splittorff, 1979
Most earned runs	118, Dennis P. Leonard, 1980
Most hits	284, Steven L. Busby, 1974
Most wild pitches	16, J. Bruce Dal Canton, 1974
Most hit batsmen	13, James W. Colborn, 1977
Most home runs	33, Dennis P. Leonard, 1979
Most sacrifice hits	18, Lawrence C. Gura, 1978
Most sacrifice flies	17, Lawrence C. Gura, 1983
Lowest ERA	2.08, Roger E. Nelson, 173 innings, 1972

Club Records

Most players	39 in 1969 (163 games)
	39 in 1973 (162 games)
	39 in 1982 (162 games)
Fewest players	32 in 1975 (162 games)
Most games	163 in 1969, 1983
Most at-bats	5714 in 1980 (162 games)
Most runs	851 in 1979 (162 games)
Fewest runs	580 in 1972 (154 games)
Most opponents runs	816 in 1979 (162 games)
Fewest opponents runs	566 in 1971 (161 games)
Most hits	1633 in 1980 (162 games)
Fewest hits	1311 in 1969 (163 games)
Most singles	1193 in 1980 (162 games)
Most doubles	305 in 1978 (162 games)
Most triples	79 in 1979 (162 games)
Most homers	168 in 1987 (162 games)
Fewest homers	65 in 1976
Most homers at Municipal Stad., home & opp.	102 in 1969
Most homers at Royals Stadium, home & opp.	134 in 1979
Most grand slams	5 in 1984, 1987
Most pinch home runs	4 in 1971
Most total bases	2440 in 1977 (162 games)
Most long hits	522 in 1977 (162 games)
Most extra bases on long hits	891 in 1977 (162 games)
Most sacrifice hits	72 in 1972 (154 games)
Most sacrifice flies	76 in 1977 (162 games)
Most stolen bases	218 in 1976 (162 games)
Most caught stealing	87 in 1977 (162 games)
Most bases on balls	644 in 1973 (162 games)
Most strikeouts	1034 in 1987 (162 games)
Fewest strikeouts	644 in 1978 (162 games)
Most hit by pitch	45 in 1977 (162 games)
Fewest hit by pitch	23 in 1983 (163 games)
Most runs batted in	791 in 1979 (162 games)
Most game-winning RBIs	92 in 1980 (162 games)
Highest batting average	.286 in 1980 (162 games)
Lowest batting average	.240 in 1969 (162 games)
Most .300 hitters	3 in 1980, 1982, 1983
Highest slugging average	.436 in 1977 (162 games)
Lowest slugging average	.338 in 1969 (163 games)
Most grounded into double play	147 in 1980 (162 games)
Fewest grounded into double play	95 in 1978 (162 games)
Most left on bases	1209 in 1980 (162 games)
Fewest left on bases	1057 in 1985 (162 games)
Most putouts	4417 in 1976 (162 games)
Fewest putouts	4144 in 1972 (154 games)
Most assists	1912 in 1973 (162 games)
Fewest assists	1659 in 1969 (163 games)

Amos Otis

Most chances accepted	6290 in 1974 (162 games)
	6290 in 1985 (162 games)
Fewest chances accepted	5906 in 1972 (154 games)
Most errors	167 in 1974 (162 games)
Fewest errors	116 in 1972 (154 games)
Most errorless games	80 in 1986 (162 games)
Most consecutive errorless games	8 in 1971
Most double plays	192 in 1973 (162 games)
Fewest double plays	114 in 1969 (163 games)
Most passed balls	29 in 1974 (162 games)
Fewest passed balls	3 in 1984 (162 games)
Highest fielding average	.981 in 1972 (154 games)
Lowest fielding average	.974 in 1973 (162 games)
	.974 in 1983 (163 games)
Highest home attendance	2,392,471 in 1987
Highest road attendance	2,047,056 in 1987
Most games won	102 in 1977
Most games lost	97 in 1970
Most games won, month	25, Sept. 1977
Most games lost, month	20, Sept. 1974
Highest percentage games won	.630 in 1977 (won 102 lost 60)
Lowest percentage games won	.401 in 1970 (won 65, lost 97)
Games won, league	1570 in 19 years
Games lost, league	1440 in 19 years
Most shutouts won	16 in 1972
Most shutouts lost	18 in 1971
Most 1-0 shutouts won	5 in 1972
Most 1-0 shutouts lost	4 in 1971
Most consecutive games won	16 in 1977
Most consecutive games lost	11 in 1986
Most times league champions	2
Most last place finishes	0
Most runs, inning	11 vs. Toronto, August 6, 1979, seventh inning
	11 vs. Boston, August 2, 1986, seventh inning
Most runs, game	23 vs. Minnesota, April 6, 1974
Most runs, game, by opponent	19 by California, July 28, 1973
Most runs, shutout game	16 vs. Oakland, June 25, 1984
Most runs, shutout game, by opponent	13 by Oakland, September 10, 1973
Most runs, doubleheader shutout	No performance
Longest 1-0 game won	15 innings vs. Minnesota, May 23, 1981
Longest 1-0 game lost	13 innings vs. Milwaukee, August 23, 1974, second game
Most hits, game	24 vs. Detroit, June 15, 1976
Most home runs, game	5 vs. California, September 7, 1975, 11 innings
	5 vs. Seattle, September 8, 1977
	5 vs. Detroit, April 19, 1985
	5 vs. Minnesota, June 24, 1985
	5 vs. Baltimore, May 9, 1986
	5 vs. California, June 20, 1987
Most consecutive games, one or more homers	12 (19 homers) 1985
Most total bases, game	36 vs. Detroit, June 15, 1976
	36 vs. Chicago, May 13, 1979
	36 vs. Milwaukee, May 11, 1982
Largest crowd, day game	41,329 vs. Oakland, September 21, 1980
Largest crowd, doubleheader	42,039 vs. Milwaukee, August 8, 1983
Largest crowd, night game	41,860 vs. New York, July 26, 1980
Largest crowd, home opener	41,086 vs. Toronto, April 8, 1985

Milwaukee Brewers

Yearly Finishes

West Division

Year—Position	W.	L.	Pct.	*G.B.	Manager
1970—Fourth† ..	65	97	.401	33	J. David Bristol
1971—Sixth	69	92	.429	32	J. David Bristol

East Division

Year—Position	W.	L.	Pct.	*G.B.	Manager
1972—Sixth	65	91	.417	21	J.D. Bristol, D. Crandall
1973—Fifth.......	74	88	.457	23	Del Crandall
1974—Fifth.......	76	86	.469	15	Del Crandall
1975—Fifth.......	68	94	.420	28	Del Crandall
1976—Sixth	66	95	.410	32	Alexander Grammas
1977—Sixth	67	95	.414	33	Alexander Grammas
1978—Third	93	69	.574	6½	George Bamberger
1979—Second...	95	66	.590	8	George Bamberger
1980—Third	86	76	.531	17	G. Bamberger, R. Rodgers
1981—3rd/1st .	62	47	.569	‡	Robert Rodgers
1982—First§.....	95	67	.586	+ 1	R. Rodgers, H. Kuenn
1983—Fifth.......	87	75	.537	11	Harvey Kuenn
1984—Seventh..	67	94	.416	36½	Rene Lachemann
1985—Sixth.......	71	90	.441	28	George Bamberger
1986—Sixth.......	77	84	.478	18	G. Bamberger, T. Trebelhorn
1987—Third......	91	71	.562	7	Thomas Trebelhorn

*Games behind winner. †Tied for position. ‡First half 31-25; second 31-22. §Won Championship Series.

Individual Records (1970 To Date)
Batting

Most years, non-pitcher	14, Charles W. Moore
	14, Robin R. Yount
Most games	162, J. Gorman Thomas, 1980
Most games, league	1969, Robin R. Yount
Most at-bats	666, Paul L. Molitor, 160 games, 1982
Most at-bats, league	7672, Robin R. Yount
Most runs	136, Paul L. Molitor, 160 games, 1982
Most runs, league	1142, Robin R. Yount
Most hits	219, Cecil C. Cooper, 153 games, 1980
Most hits, league	2217, Robin R. Yount
Most singles	157, Cecil C. Cooper, 153 games, 1980
Most singles, league	1547, Robin R. Yount
Most doubles	49, Robin R. Yount, 143 games, 1980
Most doubles, league	405, Robin R. Yount
Most triples	16, Paul L. Molitor, 140 games, 1979
Most triples, league	91, Robin R. Yount
Most homers, lefthander	41, Benjamin A. Oglivie, 156 games, 1980
Most homers, righthander	45, J. Gorman Thomas, 156 games, 1979
Most homers at home	22, J. Gorman Thomas, 1979
Most homers on road	26, Benjamin A. Oglivie, 156 games, 1980
Most homers, rookie	16, Darrell R. Porter, 117 games, 1973
Most homers, month	12, J. Gorman Thomas, August, 1979
Most homers, league, righthander	208, J. Gorman Thomas
Most homers, league, lefthander	201, Cecil C. Cooper
Most grand slams	2, David L. May, 156 games, 1973
	2, Sixto Lezcano, 132 games, 1978
	2, Robin R. Yount, 143 games, 1980
	2, Robert G. Deer, 134 games, 1987
Most grand slams, league	5, Cecil C. Cooper
Most total bases	367, Robin R. Yount, 156 games, 1982
Most total bases, league	3326, Robin R. Yount
Most long hits	87, Robin R. Yount, 156 games, 1982
Most long hits, league	670, Robin R. Yount
Most extra bases on long hits	164, J. Gorman Thomas, 156 games, 1979
Most extra bases on long hits, league	1109, Robin R. Yount
Most sacrifice hits	19, Ronald M. Theobald, 126 games, 1971
Most sacrifice flies	10, Robin R. Yount, 156 games, 1982
	10, James E. Gantner, 153 games, 1984
	10, Cecil C. Cooper, 154 games, 1985
	10, Benjamin A. Oglivie, 101 games, 1985
Most stolen bases	45, Paul L. Molitor, 118 games, 1987
Most stolen bases, league	276, Paul L. Molitor
Most caught stealing	16, Tommy Harper, 154 games, 1970
	16, James E. Wohlford, 129 games, 1977
Most bases on balls	98, J. Gorman Thomas, 156 games, 1979
Most bases on balls, league	611, Robin R. Yount
Most strikeouts	186, Robert G. Deer, 134 games, 1987
Most strikeouts, league	983, J. Gorman Thomas
Fewest strikeouts	42, Cecil C. Cooper, 153 games, 1980
Most hit by pitch	10, Eliseo C. Rodriguez, 94 games, 1973
Longest batting streak	39 games, Paul L. Molitor, 1987
Most runs batted in	126, Cecil C. Cooper, 160 games, 1983
Most runs batted in, league	944, Cecil C. Cooper
Most game-winning RBIs	17, Cecil C. Cooper, 160 games, 1983
	17, Ted L. Simmons, 153 games, 1983
	17, Robin R. Yount, 158 games, 1987
Highest batting average	.353, Paul L. Molitor, 118 games, 1987
Highest batting average, league	.302, Cecil C. Cooper
Highest slugging average	.578, Robin R. Yount, 156 games, 1982
Highest slugging average, league	.470, Cecil C. Cooper
Most grounded into double play	26, George C. Scott, 158 games, 1975
Fewest grounded into double play	3, Tommy Harper, 152 games, 1971

Jim Slaton

Pitching

Most years	12, James M. Slaton
Most games	83, Kenneth G. Sanders, 1971
Most games, league	364, James M. Slaton
Most games started	38, James M. Slaton, 1973
	38, James M. Slaton, 1976
Most games started, league	268, James M. Slaton
Most complete games	23, R. Michael Caldwell, 1978
Most complete games, league	81, R. Michael Caldwell
Most games finished	77, Kenneth Sanders, 1971
Most innings	314, James W. Colborn, 1973
Most innings, league	2025, James M. Slaton
Most games won	22, R. Michael Caldwell, 1978
Most games won, league	117, James M. Slaton
Most games lost	20, Clyde Wright, 1974
Most games lost, league	121, James M. Slaton
Highest winning percentage	.750, Peter D. Vuckovich (18-6), 1982
Most 20 victory seasons	1, James W. Colborn
	1, R. Michael Caldwell
	1, Teodoro V. Higuera
Longest winning streak	8 games, R. Michael Caldwell, 1979
	8 games, Peter D. Vuckovich, 1981
	8 games, Peter D. Vuckovich, 1982 (twice)
	8 games, Bryan E. Haas, 1983
Longest losing streak	10 games, Danny W. Darwin, 1985
Most saves, season	31, Kenneth G. Sanders, 1971
Most bases on balls	106, Peter S. Broberg, 1975
Most bases on balls, league	760, James M. Slaton
Most strikeouts	240, Teodoro V. Higuera, 1987
Most strikeouts, league	929, James M. Slaton
Most strikeouts, game	14, Bryan E. Haas, April 12, 1978
Most shutouts won	6, R. Michael Caldwell
Most shutouts, league	19, James M. Slaton
Most 1-0 shutouts won	1, Held by many pitchers
Most runs	133, James W. Colborn, 1973
Most earned runs	115, R. Michael Caldwell, 1983
Most hits	297, James W. Colborn, 1973
Most hit batsmen	16, Peter S. Broberg, 1975
Most wild pitches	14, James M. Slaton, 1974
	14, Christopher L. Bosio, 1987
Most home runs allowed	35, R. Michael Caldwell, 1983
Most sacrifice hits	15, James M. Slaton, 1976
Most sacrifice flies	13, Lary A. Sorensen, 1978
Lowest ERA	2.37, R. Michael Caldwell, 293 innings, 1978

Club Records

Most players	45 in 1970 (163 games)
Fewest players	31 in 1979 (161 games)
Most games	163 in 1970, 1982
Most at-bats	5733 in 1982 (163 games)
Most runs	891 in 1982 (163 games)
Fewest runs	494 in 1972 (156 games)
Most opponents' runs	817 in 1987 (162 games)
Fewest opponents' runs	595 in 1972 (156 games)
Most hits	1599 in 1982 (163 games)
Fewest hits	1188 in 1971 (161 games)
Most singles	1082 in 1984 (161 games)
Most doubles	298 in 1980 (162 games)
Most triples	57 in 1983 (162 games)
Most homers	216 in 1982 (163 games)
Fewest homers	88 in 1972
	88 in 1976
Most homers at County Stadium, home & opp.	172 in 1979
Most grand slams	8 in 1980
Most pinch home runs	5 in 1970
Most long hits	537 in 1980 (162 games)
Most extra bases on long hits	1007 in 1982 (163 games)
Most total bases	2606 in 1982 (163 games)
Most sacrifice hits	115 in 1970 (163 games)
Most sacrifice flies	57 in 1983 (162 games)
Most stolen bases	176 in 1987 (162 games)
Most caught stealing	75 in 1974 (162 games)
Most bases on balls	598 in 1987 (162 games)
Fewest bases on balls	432 in 1984 (161 games)
Most strikeouts	1040 in 1987 (162 games)
Fewest strikeouts	673 in 1984 (161 games)
Most hit by pitch	42 in 1973 (162 games)
Fewest hit by pitch	18 in 1982 (163 games)
Most runs batted in	843 in 1982 (163 games)
Most game-winning RBIs	87 in 1982 (163 games)
Highest batting average	.280 in 1979 (161 games)
Lowest batting average	.229 in 1971 (156 games)
Most .300 batters	3 in 1979, 1980, 1982, 1983
Highest slugging average	.455 in 1982 (163 games)
Lowest slugging average	.328 in 1972 (156 games)
Most grounded into double play	152 in 1984 (161 games)
Fewest grounded into double play	94 in 1978 (162 games)
Most left on bases	1162 in 1970 (163 games)
	1162 in 1978 (162 games)
Fewest left on bases	1031 in 1972 (156 games)
Most putouts	4402 in 1982 (163 games)
Fewest putouts	4175 in 1972 (156 games)
Most assists	1976 in 1978 (162 games)
Most chances accepted	6284 in 1978 (162 games)
Fewest chances accepted	5784 in 1972 (156 games)
Most errors	180 in 1975 (162 games)
Fewest errors	113 in 1983 (162 games)
Most errorless games	78 in 1971 (161 games)
Most consecutive errorless games	10 in 1970, 1979
Most double plays	189 in 1980 (162 games)
Fewest double plays	142 in 1970 (163 games)
Most passed balls	20 in 1975 (162 games)
Fewest passed balls	4 in 1978 (162 games)
Highest fielding average	.982 in 1983 (162 games)
Lowest fielding average	.971 in 1975 (162 games)
Highest home attendance	2,397,131 in 1983
Highest road attendance	1,999,766 in 1987
Most games won	95 in 1979
	95 in 1982
Most games lost	97 in 1970
Most games won, month	21, June 1978
Most games lost, month	23, August 1977
Games won, league	1374 in 18 years
Games lost, league	1477 in 18 years
Highest percentage games won	.590 in 1979 (won 95, lost 66)
Lowest percentage games won	.401 in 1970 (won 65, lost 97)
Most shutouts won	23 in 1971
Most shutouts lost	20 in 1972
Most 1-0 games won	5 in 1971
Most 1-0 games lost	4 in 1974
Most consecutive games won	13 in 1987
Most consecutive games lost	12 in 1987
Most times league champions	1
Most last place finishes	1
Most runs, game	19 vs. Boston, May, 31, 1980
Most runs, game, by opponent	20 by Boston, September 6, 1975
Most runs, shutout game	14 vs. New York, September 17, 1982
	14 vs. Boston, April 18, 1983
Most runs, shutout game, by opponent	14 by Chicago September 4, 1973
Most runs, doubleheader shutout	No performance
Most runs, inning	9 vs. Boston, April 12, 1980, second inning
	9 vs. New York, September 19, 1982, eighth inning
	9 vs. Boston, September 11, 1984, seventh inning
	9 vs. Baltimore, June 21, 1985, sixth inning
Longest 1-0 game won	14 innings vs. California, August 24, 1983
Longest 1-0 game lost	17 innings vs. Baltimore, September 27, 1974
Most hits, game	22 vs. Boston, May 31, 1980
	22 vs. Boston, April 18, 1983
Most home runs, game	7 vs. Cleveland, April 29, 1980
Most consecutive games, one or more homers	15 (35 homers), 1982
Most total bases, game	36 vs. Cleveland, April 29, 1980
	36 vs. Boston, May 31, 1980
Largest crowd, day game	55,120 vs. Baltimore, April 12, 1977
Largest crowd, doubleheader	54,630 vs. Detroit, July 6, 1979
Largest crowd, night game	55,716 vs. Boston, July 3, 1982
Largest crowd, home opener	55,120 vs. Baltimore, April 12, 1977

Minnesota Twins

Yearly Finishes

Year—Position	W.	L.	Pct.	*G.B.	Manager
1961—Seventh	70	90	.438	38	H. Lavagetto, S. Mele
1962—Second	91	71	.562	5	Sabath (Sam) Mele
1963—Third	91	70	.565	13	Sabath (Sam) Mele
1964—Sixth†	79	83	.488	20	Sabath (Sam) Mele
1965—First	102	60	.630	+ 7	Sabath (Sam) Mele
1966—Second	89	73	.549	9	Sabath (Sam) Mele
1967—Second†	91	71	.562	1	S. Mele, C. Ermer
1968—Seventh	79	83	.488	24	Calvin Ermer

West Division

Year—Position	W.	L.	Pct.	*G.B.	Manager
1969—First‡	97	65	.599	+ 9	Alfred (Billy) Martin
1970—First‡	98	64	.605	+ 9	William Rigney
1971—Fifth	74	86	.463	26½	William Rigney
1972—Third	77	77	.500	15½	W. Rigney, F. Quilici
1973—Third	81	81	.500	13	Frank Quilici
1974—Third	82	80	.506	8	Frank Quilici
1975—Fourth	76	83	.478	20½	Frank Quilici
1976—Third	85	77	.525	5	Gene Mauch
1977—Fourth	84	77	.522	17½	Gene Mauch
1978—Fourth	73	89	.451	19	Gene Mauch
1979—Fourth	82	80	.506	6	Gene Mauch
1980—Third	77	84	.478	19½	G. Mauch, J. Goryl
1981—7th/4th.	41	68	.376	§	J. Goryl, W. Gardner
1982—Seventh	60	102	.370	33	William Gardner
1983—Fifth†	70	92	.432	29	William Gardner
1984—Second†	81	81	.500	3	William Gardner
1985—Fourth†	77	85	.475	14	W. Gardner, R. Miller
1986—Sixth	71	91	.438	21	R. Miller, J.T. Kelly
1987—Firstx	85	77	.525	+ 2	J. Thomas Kelly

*Games behind winner. †Tied for position. ‡Lost Championship Series. §First half 17-39; second 24-29. xWon Championship Series.

Individual Records (1961 To Date)
Batting

Most years, non-pitcher	15, Pedro Oliva
Most games	164, Cesar L. Tovar, 1967
Most games, league	1939, Harmon C. Killebrew
Most at-bats	691, Kirby Puckett, 161 games, 1985
Most at-bats, league	6593, Harmon C. Killebrew
Most runs	128, Rodney C. Carew, 155 games, 1977
Most runs, league	1047, Harmon C. Killebrew
Most hits	239, Rodney C. Carew, 155 games, 1977
Most hits, league	2085, Rodney C. Carew
Most singles	180, Rodney C. Carew, 153 games, 1974
Most singles, league	1616, Rodney C. Carew
Most doubles	45, Zoilo Versalles, 160 games, 1965
Most doubles, league	329, Pedro Oliva
Most triples	16, Rodney C. Carew, 155 games, 1977
Most triples, league	90, Rodney C. Carew
Most homers, righthander	49, Harmon C. Killebrew, 158 games, 1964
	49, Harmon C. Killebrew, 162 games, 1969
Most homers, lefthander	34, Kent A. Hrbek, 143 games, 1987
Most homers, league, righthander	475, Harmon C. Killebrew
Most homers, league, lefthander	220, Pedro Oliva
Most homers at home	29, Harmon C. Killebrew, 1961
Most homers on road	28, Harmon C. Killebrew, 1962
Most homers, month	14, Harmon C. Killebrew, June, 1964
Most homers, rookie	33, Jimmie R. Hall, 156 games, 1963
Most grand slams	3, W. Robert Allison, 159 games, 1961
	3, Rodney C. Carew, 156 games, 1976
	3, Kent A. Hrbek, 158 games, 1985
Most grand slams, league	10, Harmon C. Killebrew
Most total bases	374, Pedro Oliva, 161 games, 1964
Most total bases, league	3412, Harmon C. Killebrew
Most long hits	84, Pedro Oliva, 161 games, 1964
Most long hits, league	728, Harmon C. Killebrew
Most extra bases on long hits	172, Harmon C. Killebrew, 150 games, 1961
Most extra bases on long hits, league	1699, Harmon C. Killebrew
Most sacrifice hits	25, Robert D. Wilfong, 140 games, 1979
Most sacrifice flies	13, Gary J. Gaetti, 145 games, 1982
	13, Thomas A. Brunansky, 157 games, 1985
Most stolen bases	49, Rodney C. Carew, 156 games, 1976
Most stolen bases, league	271, Rodney C. Carew
Most caught stealing	22, Rodney C. Carew, 156 games, 1976
Most bases on balls	145, Harmon C. Killebrew, 162 games, 1969
Most bases on balls, league	1321, Harmon C. Killebrew
Most strikeouts	145, A. Bobby Darwin, 145 games, 1972
Fewest strikeouts	24, Victor P. Power, 138 games, 1963
Most strikeouts, league	1314, Harmon C. Killebrew

Most hit by pitch ....17, Cesar L. Tovar, 157 games, 1968
Most runs batted in ....140, Harmon C. Killebrew, 162 games, 1969
Most runs batted in, league ....1325, Harmon C. Killebrew
Most game-winning RBIs ....15, Thomas A. Brunansky, 151 games, 1983
Most consecutive games with RBI ....9, Harmon C. Killebrew (15 RBI), 1961
                                                        9, Garrabrant R. Alyea (17 RBI), 1970
Highest batting average ....388, Rodney C. Carew, 155 games, 1977
Highest batting average, league ....334, Rodney C. Carew
Highest slugging percentage ....606, Harmon C. Killebrew, 150 games, 1961
Highest slugging average, league ....518, Harmon C. Killebrew
Longest batting streak ....31 games, Kenneth F. Landreaux, 1980
Most grounded into double play ....28, Harmon C. Killebrew, 157 games, 1970
Fewest grounded into double play ....2, Cesar L. Tovar, 157 games, 1968

Pitching

Most years ....13, James L. Kaat
Most games ....90, Michael G. Marshall, 1979
Most games, league ....468, James L. Kaat
Most games started ....42, James L. Kaat, 1965
Most games started, league ....422, James L. Kaat
Most complete games ....25, Rikalbert B. Blyleven, 1973
Most complete games, league ....133, James L. Kaat
Most games finished ....84, Michael G. Marshall, 1979
Most innings ....325, Rikalbert B. Blyleven, 1973
Most innings pitched, league ....2958, James L. Kaat
Most games won ....25, James L. Kaat, 1966
Most games won, league ....189, James L. Kaat
Most games lost, season ....20, Pedro Ramos, 1961
Most games lost, league ....152, James L. Kaat
Highest winning percentage ....773, William R. Campbell (17-5), 1976
Longest winning streak ....9 games, Stanley W. Williams, 1970
Longest losing streak ....13 games, Terry L. Felton, 1982
Most saves ....34, Ronald P. Perranoski, 1970
Most 20 victory seasons ....2, Camilo A. Pascual
                                                2, James E. Perry
Most bases on balls ....127, James M. Hughes, 1975
Most bases on balls, league ....694, James L. Kaat
Most strikeouts ....258, Rikalbert B. Blyleven, 1973
Most strikeouts, league ....1890, Rikalbert Blyleven
Most strikeouts, game ....15, Camilo A. Pascual, July 19, 1961, first game
                                                15, George H. Decker, June 26, 1973
                                                15, Jerry M. Koosman, June 23, 1980
                                                15, Rikalbert Blyleven, August 1, 1986
Most shutouts ....9, Rikalbert B. Blyleven, 1973
Most shutouts, league ....29, Rikalbert B. Blyleven
Most 1-0 shutouts won ....3, Rikalbert B. Blyleven, 1971
Most runs ....141, Frank J. Viola, 1983
Most earned runs ....128, Frank J. Viola, 1983
Most hits ....296, Rikalbert B. Blyleven, 1973
Most hit batsmen ....18, James L. Kaat, 1962
Most wild pitches ....15, David A. Goltz, 1976
Most home runs ....50, Rikalbert Blyleven, 1986
Most sacrifice hits ....17, W. Dean Chance, 1968
                                            17, Jerry M. Koosman, 1980
Most sacrifice flies ....13, Rikalbert B. Blyleven, 1973
Lowest ERA ....2.47, Camilo A. Pascual, 248 innings, 1963

Club Records

Most players .... 44 in 1964 (163 games)
Fewest players .... 31 in 1976 (162 games)
Most games .... 164 in 1967
Fewest games .... 154 in 1972
Most at-bats .... 5677 in 1969 (162 games)
Most runs .... 867 in 1977 (161 games)
Most opponents' runs .... 839 in 1986 (162 games)
Fewest opponents' runs .... 535 in 1972 (154 games)
Most hits .... 1588 in 1977 (161 games)
Fewest hits .... 1274 in 1968 (162 games)
Most singles .... 1192 in 1974 (163 games)
Most doubles .... 282 in 1985 (162 games)
Most triples .... 60 in 1977 (161 games)
Most homers .... 225 in 1963 (161 games)
Fewest homers .... 81 in 1976
Most homers at M'tr'p'l't'n Stad., home & opp. .. 211 in 1963
Most homers at Metrodome, home & opp. .... 223 in 1986
Most grand slams .... 8 in 1961
Most pinch home runs .... 7 in 1964, 1967
Most total bases .... 2395 in 1964 (163 games)
Most long hits .... 494 in 1964 (163 games)
Most extra bases on long hits .... 982 in 1964 (163 games)
Most sacrifice hits .... 142 in 1979 (162 games)
Most sacrifice flies .... 59 in 1965 (162 games)
Most stolen bases .... 146 in 1976 (162 games)
Most caught stealing .... 75 in 1976 (162 games)
Most bases on balls .... 649 in 1962 (163 games)
Most strikeouts .... 1019 in 1964 (163 games)
Fewest strikeouts .... 684 in 1978 (162 games)
Most hit by pitch .... 49 in 1968 (162 games)
Fewest hit by pitch .... 21 in 1980 (161 games)
Most runs batted in .... 804 in 1977 (161 games)
Most game-winning RBIs .... 81 in 1987 (162 games)
Highest batting average .... .282 in 1977 (161 games)
Lowest batting average .... .237 in 1968 (162 games)
Highest slugging average .... .430 in 1963 (161 games)
                                                    .430 in 1987 (162 games)
Lowest slugging average .... .344 in 1972 (154 games)
Most grounded into double play .... 159 in 1974 (163 games)
Fewest grounded into double play .... 93 in 1965 (162 games)

Rod Carew

Most left on bases .... 1263 in 1974 (163 games)
Fewest left on bases .... 1041 in 1987 (162 games)
Most .300 hitters .... 3 in 1969, 1970, 1977
Most putouts .... 4493 in 1969 (162 games)
Fewest putouts .... 4198 in 1972 (154 games)
Most assists .... 2007 in 1979 (162 games)
Fewest assists .... 1559 in 1982 (162 games)
Most chances accepted .... 6349 in 1969 (162 games)
Fewest chances accepted .... 5854 in 1971 (160 games)
Most double plays .... 203 in 1979 (162 games)
Fewest double plays .... 117 in 1968 (162 games)
Most errors .... 174 in 1987 (161 games)
Fewest errors .... 98 in 1987 (162 games)
Most errorless games .... 89 in 1987 (162 games)
Most consecutive errorless games .... 10 in 1987
Most passed balls .... 19 in 1973 (162 games)
Fewest passed balls .... 4 in 1979 (162 games)
                                            4 in 1984 (162 games)
Highest fielding average .... .984 in 1987 (162 games)
Lowest fielding average .... .972 in 1961 (161 games)
Highest home attendance .... 2,081,976 in 1987
Highest road attendance .... 1,880,273 in 1987

Most games won .... 102 in 1965
Most games lost .... 102 in 1982
Most games won, month .... 23, July 1969
Most games lost, month .... 26, May 1981
                                                26, May 1982
Highest percentage games won .... .630, in 1965 (won 102, lost 60)
Lowest percentage games won .... .370, in 1982 (won 60, lost 102)
Games won, league .... 2163 in 27 years
Games lost, league .... 2140 in 27 years
Most shutouts won .... 18 in 1967
                                                18 in 1973
Most shutouts lost .... 14 in 1964
                                                14 in 1972
Most 1-0 games won .... 5 in 1966
Most 1-0 games lost .... 5 in 1974
Most consecutive games won .... 12 in 1980
Most consecutive games lost .... 14 in 1982
Most times league champions 2
Most last place finishes 1

Most runs, game .... 20 vs. Oakland, April 27, 1980
Most runs, game, by opponent .... 23 by Kansas City, April 6, 1974
Most runs, shutout game .... 15 vs. Seattle, July 10, 1977
Most runs, shutout game, by opponent ... 17 by California, April 23, 1980
Most runs, doubleheader shutout ... 14 vs. Cleveland, July 24, 1963
Most runs, inning .... 11 vs. Cleveland, July 18, 1962, first inning
                       11 vs. Oakland, June 21, 1969, tenth inning
                       11 vs. Cleveland, August 5, 1977, fourth inning
Longest 1-0 game won .... 11 innings vs. Milwaukee, August 27, 1975
                       11 innings vs. New York, May 10, 1980
Longest 1-0 game lost .... 15 innings vs. Kansas City, May 23, 1981
Most hits, game .... 24 vs. Boston, May 25, 1977
Most home runs, game .... 8 vs. Washington, August 29, 1963, first game
Most consecutive games, one or more homers ... 16 (28 homers), 1979
Most total bases, game ... 47 vs. Washington, August 29, 1963, first game
Largest crowd, day game .... 53,106 vs. Kansas City, September 27, 1987
Largest crowd, doubleheader .... 43,419 vs. California, July 16, 1967
Largest crowd, night game .... 52,704 vs. Kansas City, September 25, 1987
Largest crowd, home opener .... 52,279 vs. Seattle, April 6, 1982

New York Yankees

Yearly Finishes

(Baltimore Orioles, 1901-1902)

Year—Position	W.	L.	Pct.	*G.B.	Manager
1901—Fifth	68	65	.511	13½	John McGraw
1902—Eighth	50	88	.362	34	J. McGraw, W. Robinson
1903—Fourth	72	62	.537	17	Clark Griffith
1904—Second	92	59	.609	1½	Clark Griffith
1905—Sixth	71	78	.477	21½	Clark Griffith
1906—Second	90	61	.596	3	Clark Griffith
1907—Fifth	70	78	.473	21	Clark Griffith
1908—Eighth	51	103	.331	39½	C. Griffith, N. Elberfeld
1909—Fifth	74	77	.490	23½	George Stallings
1910—Second	88	63	.583	14½	G. Stallings, H. Chase
1911—Sixth	76	76	.500	25½	Hal Chase
1912—Eighth	50	102	.329	55	Harry Wolverton
1913—Seventh	57	94	.377	38	Frank Chance
1914—Sixth†	70	84	.455	30	F. Chance, R. Peckinpaugh
1915—Fifth	69	83	.454	32½	William Donovan
1916—Fourth	80	74	.519	11	William Donovan
1917—Sixth	71	82	.464	28½	William Donovan
1918—Fourth	60	63	.488	13½	Miller Huggins
1919—Third	80	59	.576	7½	Miller Huggins
1920—Third	95	59	.617	3	Miller Huggins
1921—First	98	55	.641	+ 4½	Miller Huggins
1922—First	94	60	.610	+ 1	Miller Huggins
1923—First	98	54	.645	+16	Miller Huggins
1924—Second	89	63	.586	2	Miller Huggins
1925—Seventh	69	85	.448	30	Miller Huggins
1926—First	91	63	.591	+ 3	Miller Huggins
1927—First	110	44	.714	+19	Miller Huggins
1928—First	101	53	.656	+ 2½	Miller Huggins
1929—Second	88	66	.571	18	M. Huggins, A. Fletcher
1930—Third	86	68	.558	16	J. Robert Shawkey
1931—Second	94	59	.614	13½	Joseph McCarthy
1932—First	107	47	.695	+13	Joseph McCarthy
1933—Second	91	59	.607	7	Joseph McCarthy
1934—Second	94	60	.610	7	Joseph McCarthy
1935—Second	89	60	.597	3	Joseph McCarthy
1936—First	102	51	.667	+19½	Joseph McCarthy
1937—First	102	52	.662	+13	Joseph McCarthy
1938—First	99	53	.651	+ 9½	Joseph McCarthy
1939—First	106	45	.702	+17	Joseph McCarthy
1940—Third	88	66	.571	2	Joseph McCarthy
1941—First	101	53	.656	+17	Joseph McCarthy
1942—First	103	51	.669	+ 9	Joseph McCarthy
1943—First	98	56	.636	+13½	Joseph McCarthy
1944—Third	83	71	.539	6	Joseph McCarthy
1945—Fourth	81	71	.533	6½	Joseph McCarthy
1946—Third	87	67	.565	17	J. McCarthy, W. Dickey, J. Neun
1947—First	97	57	.630	+12	Stanley (Bucky) Harris
1948—Third	94	60	.610	2½	Stanley (Bucky) Harris
1949—First	97	57	.630	+ 1	Chas. (Casey) Stengel
1950—First	98	56	.636	+ 3	Chas. (Casey) Stengel
1951—First	98	56	.636	+ 5	Chas. (Casey) Stengel
1952—First	95	59	.617	+ 2	Chas. (Casey) Stengel
1953—First	99	52	.656	+ 8½	Chas. (Casey) Stengel
1954—Second	103	51	.669	8	Chas. (Casey) Stengel
1955—First	96	58	.623	+ 3	Chas. (Casey) Stengel
1956—First	97	57	.630	+ 9	Chas. (Casey) Stengel
1957—First	98	56	.636	+ 8	Chas. (Casey) Stengel
1958—First	92	62	.597	+10	Chas. (Casey) Stengel
1959—Third	79	75	.513	15	Chas. (Casey) Stengel
1960—First	97	57	.630	+ 8	Chas. (Casey) Stengel
1961—First	109	53	.673	+ 8	Ralph Houk
1962—First	96	66	.593	+ 5	Ralph Houk
1963—First	104	57	.646	+10½	Ralph Houk
1964—First	99	63	.611	+ 1	Lawrence (Yogi) Berra
1965—Sixth	77	85	.475	25	John Keane
1966—Tenth	70	89	.440	26½	J. Keane, R. Houk
1967—Ninth	72	90	.444	20	Ralph Houk
1968—Fifth	83	79	.512	20	Ralph Houk

East Division

Year—Position	W.	L.	Pct.	*G.B.	Manager
1969—Fifth	80	81	.497	28½	Ralph Houk
1970—Second	93	69	.574	15	Ralph Houk
1971—Fourth	82	80	.506	21	Ralph Houk
1972—Fourth	79	76	.510	6½	Ralph Houk
1973—Fourth	80	82	.494	17	Ralph Houk
1974—Second	89	73	.549	2	William Virdon
1975—Third	83	77	.519	12	W. Virdon, B. Martin
1976—First‡	97	62	.610	+10½	Billy Martin
1977—First‡	100	62	.617	+ 2½	Billy Martin
1978—First§‡	100	63	.613	+ 1	B. Martin, R. Lemon
1979—Fourth	89	71	.556	13½	R. Lemon, B. Martin
1980—First a	103	59	.636	+ 3	Richard Howser
1981—1st/6th	59	48	.551	b	E. Michael, R. Lemon
1982—Fifth	79	83	.488	16	R. Lemon, E. Michael, C. King
1983—Third	91	71	.562	7	Billy Martin
1984—Third	87	75	.537	17	Lawrence (Yogi) Berra
1985—Second	97	64	.602	2	L. Berra, B. Martin
1986—Second	90	72	.556	5½	Louis Piniella
1987—Fourth	89	73	.549	9	Louis Piniella

*Games behind winner. †Tied for position. ‡Won Championship Series. §Won pennant playoff. aLost Championship Series. bFirst half 34-22; second 25-26.

Individual Records (1903 To Date)
Batting

Most years, non-pitcher .... 18, Lawrence P. Berra
                                      18, Mickey C. Mantle
Most games .... 162, Robert C. Richardson, 1961
                                   162, Roy H. White, 1970
                         162, C. Christopher Chambliss, 1978
                           162, Donald A. Mattingly, 1986
Most games, league .... 2401, Mickey C. Mantle
Most at-bats .... 692, Robert C. Richardson, 161 games, 1962
Most at-bats, league .... 8102, Mickey C. Mantle
Most runs .... 177, George H. Ruth, 152 games, 1921
Most runs, league .... 1959, George H. Ruth
Most hits .... 238, Donald A. Mattingly, 162 games, 1986
Most hits, league .... 2721, H. Louis Gehrig
Most singles .... 166, William H. Keeler, 152 games, 1906
                          166, Earle B. Combs, 152 games, 1927
Most singles, league .... 1531, H. Louis Gehrig
Most doubles .... 53, Donald A. Mattingly, 162 games, 1986
Most doubles, league .... 535, H. Louis Gehrig
Most triples .... 23, Earle B. Combs, 152 games, 1927
Most triples, league .... 162, H. Louis Gehrig
Most homers, righthander .... 46, Joseph P. DiMaggio, 151 games, 1937
Most homers, lefthander .... 61, Roger E. Maris, 161 games, 1961
                         60, George H. Ruth, 151 games, 1927
Most homers, rookie .... 29, Joseph P. DiMaggio, 138 games, 1936
Most grand slams .... 6, Donald A. Mattingly, 141 games, 1987
Most grand slams, league .... 23, H. Louis Gehrig
Most homers at home .... 32, George H. Ruth, 1921 (Polo Grounds)
                         30, H. Louis Gehrig, 1934 (Yankee Stadium)
                         30, Roger E. Maris, 1961 (Yankee Stadium)
Most homers on road .... 32, George H. Ruth, 1927
Most homers, month .... 17, George H. Ruth, September, 1927
Most homers, league, lefthander .... 659, George H. Ruth
Most homers, league, righthander .... 361, Joseph P. DiMaggio
Most total bases .... 457, George H. Ruth, 152 games, 1921
Most total bases, league .... 5131, George H. Ruth
Most long hits .... 119, George H. Ruth, 152 games, 1921
Most long hits, league .... 1190, H. Louis Gehrig
Most extra bases on long hits .... 253, George H. Ruth, 152 games, 1921
Most extra bases on long hits, league .... 2613, George H. Ruth
Most sacrifice hits .... 42, William H. Keeler, 149 games, 1905
Most sacrifice flies .... 17, Roy H. White, 147 games, 1971
Most stolen bases .... 87, Rickey H. Henderson, 153 games, 1986
Most stolen bases, league .... 248, Harold H. Chase
Most caught stealing .... 23, W. Benjamin Chapman, 149 games, 1931

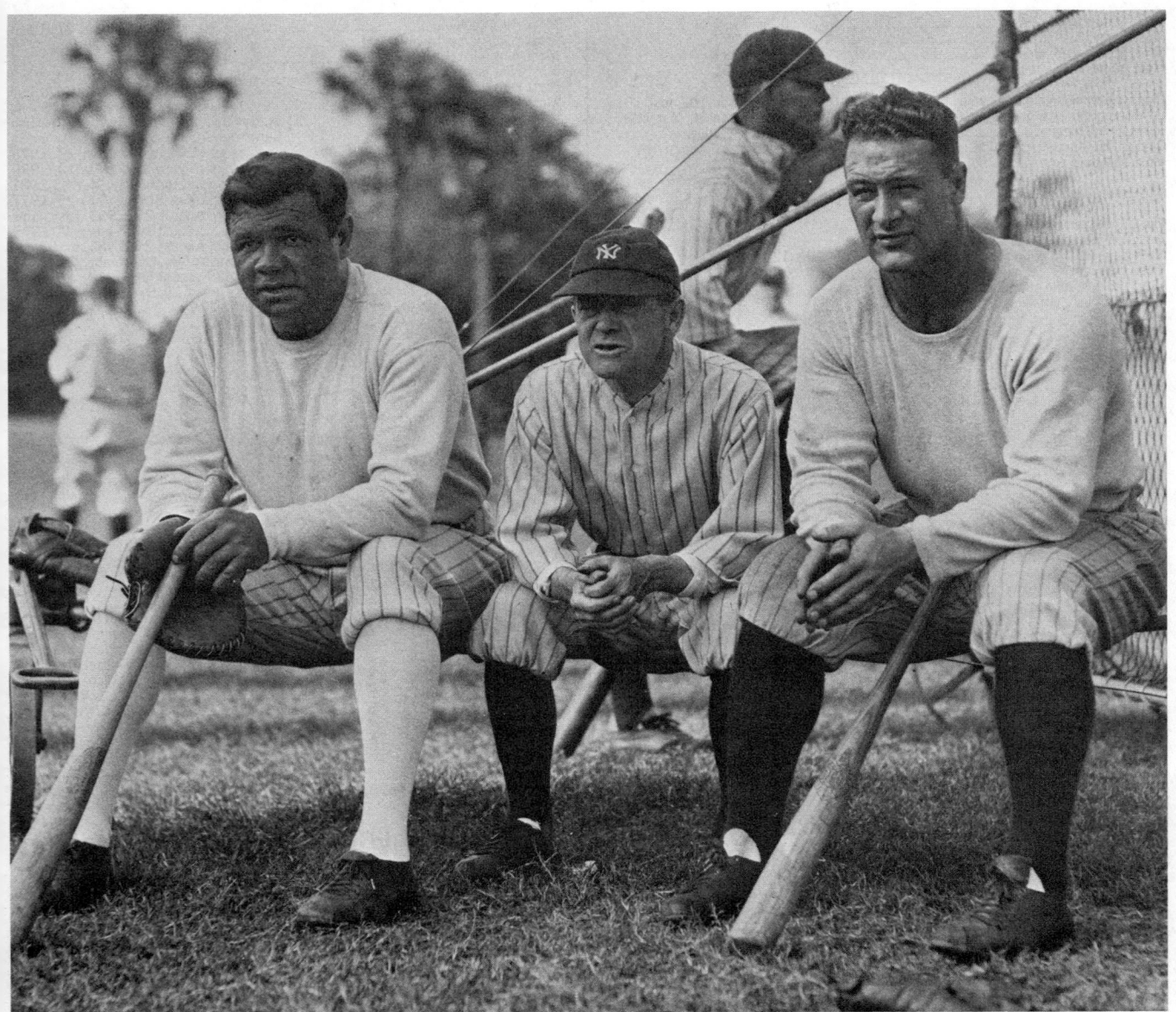

Slugging teammates Babe Ruth (left) and Lou Gehrig (right) with Yankee Manager Miller Huggins

Most bases on balls	170, George H. Ruth, 152 games, 1923
Most bases on balls, league	1847, George H. Ruth
Most strikeouts, season	137, Bobby L. Bonds, 145 games, 1975
Most strikeouts, league	1710, Mickey C. Mantle
Fewest strikeouts	3, Joseph W. Sewell, 124 games, 1932
Most hit by pitch	24, Donald E. Baylor, 142 games, 1985
Most runs batted in	184, H. Louis Gehrig, 155 games, 1931
Most runs batted in, league	1990, H. Louis Gehrig
Most game-winning RBIs	21, David M. Winfield, 152 games, 1983
	21, Donald A. Mattingly, 159 games, 1985
Most consecutive games with RBI	11, George H. Ruth (18 RBIs) 1931
Highest batting average	.393, George H. Ruth, 152 games, 1923
Highest batting average, league	.349, George H. Ruth
Highest slugging average	.847, George H. Ruth, 142 games, 1920
Highest slugging average, league	.711, George H. Ruth
Longest batting streak	56 games, Joseph P. DiMaggio, 1941
Most grounded into double play	30, David M. Winfield, 152 games, 1983
Fewest grounded into double play	2, Mickey C. Mantle, 153 games, 1961

Pitching

Most years	16, Edward C. Ford
Most games	74, David A. Righetti, 1985
	74, David A. Righetti, 1986
Most games, league	498, Edward C. Ford
Most games started	51, John D. Chesbro, 1904
Most games started, league	438, Edward C. Ford
Most complete games	48, John D. Chesbro, 1904
Most complete games, league	262, Charles H. Ruffing
Most games finished	68, David A. Righetti, 1986
Most innings	454, John D. Chesbro, 1904
Most innings, league	3171, Edward C. Ford
Most games won	41, John D. Chesbro, 1904

Most games won, league	236, Edward C. Ford
Most 20 victory seasons	4, J. Robert Shawkey
	4, Vernon Gomez
	4, Charles H. Ruffing
Most games lost	21, Albert C. Orth, 1907
	21, Samuel P. Jones, 1925
	21, Joseph Lake, 1908
	21, Russell Ford, 1912
Most games lost, league	139, Melvin L. Stottlemyre
Highest winning percentage	.893, Ronald A. Guidry (25-3), 1978
Longest winning streak	14 games, John D. Chesbro, 1904
	14 games, Edward C. Ford, 1961
Longest losing streak	9 games, William Hogg, 1908
	9 games, Thaddeus A. Tillotson, 1967
Most saves	46, David A. Righetti, 1986
Most bases on balls	179, Thomas J. Byrne, 1949
Most bases on balls, league	1090, Vernon Gomez
Most strikeouts	248, Ronald A. Guidry, 1978
Most strikeouts, league	1956, Edward C. Ford
Most strikeouts, game	18, Ronald A. Guidry, June 17, 1978
Most shutouts	9, Ronald A. Guidry, 1978
Most shutouts, league	45, Edward C. Ford
Most 1-0 shutouts won	2, Held by many pitchers
Most runs	165, Russell Ford, 1912
Most earned runs	127, Samuel P. Jones, 1925
Most hits	337, John D. Chesbro, 1904
Most hit batsmen	26, John M. Warhop, 1909
Most wild pitches	14, Alphonso E. Downing, 1964
Most home runs	40, Ralph W. Terry, 1962
Most sacrifice hits	22, Vernon Gomez, 1935
Most sacrifice flies	15, George F. Medich, 1975
Lowest ERA	1.64, Spurgeon F. Chandler, 253 innings, 1943

Club Records

Most players	48 in 1987
Fewest players	25 in 1923, 1927
Most games	164 in 1964, 1968
Most at-bats	5705 in 1964 (164 games)
Most runs	1067 in 1931 (155 games)
Fewest runs	459 in 1908 (155 games)
Most opponents' runs	898 in 1930 (154 games)
Most hits	1683 in 1930 (154 games)
Fewest hits	1137 in 1968 (164 games)
Most singles	1157 in 1931 (155 games)
Most doubles	315 in 1936 (155 games)
Most triples	110 in 1930 (154 games)
Most homers	240 in 1961 (163 games)
Fewest homers (154 or 162-game schedule)	8 in 1913
Most homers at Yankee Stadium, home & opp.	189 in 1986
Most pinch home runs	10 in 1961
Most grand slams	10 in 1987
Most long hits	580 in 1936 (155 games)
Most extra bases on long hits	1027 in 1936 (155 games)
Most total bases	2703 in 1936 (155 games)
Most sacrifices (S. H. and S. F.)	218 in 1922 (154 games)
	218 in 1926 (155 games)
Most sacrifice hits	178 in 1906 (155 games)
Most sacrifice flies	72 in 1974 (162 games)
Most stolen bases	289 in 1910 (156 games)
Most caught stealing	82 in 1920 (154 games)
Most bases on balls	766 in 1932 (156 games)
Most strikeouts	1043 in 1967 (163 games)
Fewest strikeouts	420 in 1924 (153 games)
Most hit by pitch	50 in 1985 (161 games)
Fewest hit by pitch	14 in 1969 (162 games)
Most runs batted in	995 in 1936 (155 games)
Most game-winning RBIs	96 in 1980 (162 games)
Highest batting average	.309 in 1930 (154 games)
Lowest batting average	.214 in 1968 (164 games)
Highest slugging average	.489 in 1927 (155 games)
Lowest slugging average	.287 in 1914 (157 games)
Most grounded into double play	152 in 1982 (162 games)
Fewest grounded into double play	91 in 1963 (161 games)
Most left on bases	1239 in 1934 (154 games)
Fewest left on bases	1010 in 1920 (154 games)
Most .300 hitters	9 in 1930
Most putouts	4520 in 1964 (164 games)
Fewest putouts	3993 in 1935 (149 games)
Most assists	2086 in 1904 (155 games)
Fewest assists	1493 in 1948 (154 games)

Most chances accepted	6377 in 1968 (164 games)
Fewest chances accepted	5551 in 1935 (149 games)
Most errors	386 in 1912 (153 games)
Fewest errors	102 in 1987 (162 games)
Most errorless games	91 in 1964 (164 games)
Most consecutive errorless games	10 in 1977
Most double plays	214 in 1956 (154 games)
Fewest double plays	81 in 1912 (153 games)
Most passed balls	32 in 1913 (153 games)
Fewest passed balls	0 in 1931 (155 games)
Highest fielding average	.983 in 1964 (164 games)
	.983 in 1987 (162 games)
Lowest fielding average	.939 in 1912 (153 games)
Highest home attendance	2,627,417 in 1980
Highest road attendance	2,460,645 in 1980
Most games won	110 in 1927
Most games lost	103 in 1908
Most games won, month	28, August 1938
Most games lost, month	24, July 1908
Highest percentage games won	.714 in 1927 (won 110, lost 44)
Lowest percentage games won	.329 in 1912 (won 50, lost 102)
Games won, league	7482 in 85 years
Games lost, league	5625 in 85 years
Most shutouts won	24 in 1951
Most shutouts lost	27 in 1914
Most 1-0 games won	6 in 1908, 1968
Most 1-0 games lost	9 in 1914
Most consecutive games won	19 in 1947
Most consecutive games lost	13 in 1913
Most times league champions	33
Most last place finishes	3
Most runs, game	25 vs. Philadelphia, May 24, 1936
Most runs, game, by opponent	24 by Cleveland, July 29, 1928
Most runs, shutout game	21 vs. Phila., Aug. 13, 1939, second game, eight innings
Most runs, shutout game, by opponent	15 by Chicago, July 15, 1907
	15 by Chicago, May 4, 1950
Most runs, doubleheader shutout	24 vs. Philadelphia, September 4, 1944
Most runs, inning	14 vs. Washington, July 6, 1920, fifth inning
Longest 1-0 game won	15 innings vs. Philadelphia, July 4, 1925, first game
Longest 1-0 game lost	13 innings vs. Chicago, July 25, 1914
Most hits, game	30 vs. Boston, September 28, 1923
Most home runs, game	8 vs. Philadelphia, June 28, 1939, first game
Most consecutive games, one or more homers	25 (40 homers), 1941
Most total bases, game	53 vs. Philadelphia, June 28, 1939, first game
Largest crowd, day game	73,205 vs. Philadelphia, April 19, 1931
Largest crowd, doubleheader	81,841 vs. Boston, May 30, 1938
Largest crowd, night game	74,747 vs. Boston, May 26, 1947
Largest crowd, home opener	55,612 vs. Cleveland, April 13, 1987

Oakland A's

Yearly Finishes

Year—Position	W.	L.	Pct.	*G.B.	Manager
1968—Sixth	82	80	.506	21	Robert Kennedy

West Division

Year—Position	W.	L.	Pct.	*G.B.	Manager
1969—Second	88	74	.543	9	H. Bauer, J. McNamara
1970—Second	89	73	.549	9	John McNamara
1971—First‡	101	60	.627	+16	Richard Williams
1972—First‡‡	93	62	.600	+ 5½	Richard Williams
1973—First‡‡	94	68	.580	+ 6	Richard Williams
1974—First‡‡	90	72	.556	+ 5	Alvin Dark
1975—First‡	98	64	.605	+ 7	Alvin Dark
1976—Second	87	74	.540	2½	Charles Tanner
1977—Seventh	63	98	.391	38½	J. McKeon, B. Winkles
1978—Sixth	69	93	.426	23	B. Winkles, J. McKeon
1979—Seventh	54	108	.333	34	R. James Marshall
1980—Second	83	79	.512	14	Alfred (Billy) Martin
1981—1st/2nd.	64	45	.587	§	Alfred (Billy) Martin
1982—Fifth	68	94	.420	25	Alfred (Billy) Martin
1983—Fourth	74	88	.457	25	Steven Boros
1984—Fourth	77	85	.475	7	S. Boros, J. Moore
1985—Fourth†	77	85	.475	14	Jackie Moore
1986—Third†	76	86	.469	16	J. Moore, A. LaRussa
1987—Third	81	81	.500	4	Anthony LaRussa

*Games behind winner. †Tied for position. ‡Lost Championship Series. ‡‡Won Championship Series. §First half 37-23; second 27-22.

Individual Records (1968 To Date)
Batting

Most years, non-pitcher	10, Joseph O. Rudi
	10, Dwayne K. Murphy
Most games	162, Salvatore L. Bando, 1968
	162, Salvatore L. Bando, 1968
	162, Salvatore L. Bando, 1973
	162, Alfredo C. Griffin, 1985
	162, Alfredo C. Griffin, 1986
Most games, league	1410, Salvatore L. Bando
Most at-bats	642, Dagoberto B. Campaneris, 159 games, 1968
Most at-bats, league	5159, Dagoberto B. Campaneris
Most runs	123, Reginald M. Jackson, 152 games, 1969
Most runs, league	725, Salvatore L. Bando
Most hits	182, Claudell Washington, 148 games, 1975

Most hits, league	1355, Dagoberto B. Campaneris
Most singles	144, Rickey H. Henderson, 158 games, 1980
Most singles, league	1089, Dagoberto B. Campaneris
Most doubles	39, Joseph O. Rudi, 158 games, 1974
	39, Reginald M. Jackson, 157 games, 1975
Most doubles, league	230, Reginald M. Jackson
Most triples	12, Philip M. Garner, 159 games, 1976
Most triples, league	39, Dagoberto B. Campaneris
Most homers league, righthander	192, Salvatore L. Bando
Most homers league, lefthander	268, Reginald M. Jackson
Most homers, righthander	49, Mark D. McGwire, 151 games, 1987
Most homers, lefthander	47, Reginald M. Jackson, 152 games, 1969
Most homers, rookie	49, Mark D. McGwire, 151 games, 1987
Most homers at home	26, Reginald M. Jackson, 1969
Most homers on road	28, Mark D. McGwire, 1987
Most grand slams	3, F. Gene Tenace, 158 games, 1974
	3, David A. Kingman, 158 games, 1984
Most grand slams, league	7, Salvatore L. Bando
Most homers, month	15, Mark D. McGwire, May 1987
Most total bases	344, Mark D. McGwire, 151 games, 1987
Most total bases, league	2287, Reginald M. Jackson
Most long hits	86, Reginald M. Jackson, 152 games, 1969
Most long hits, league	521, Reginald M. Jackson
Most extra bases on long hits	183, Reginald M. Jackson, 152 games, 1969
	183, Mark D. McGwire, 151 games, 1987
Most extra bases on long hits, league	1080, Reginald M. Jackson
Most sacrifice hits	22, Dwayne K. Murphy, 159 games, 1980
Most sacrifice flies	14, David A. Kingman, 147 games, 1984
Most stolen bases	130, Rickey H. Henderson, 149 games, 1982
Most stolen bases, league	493, Rickey H. Henderson
Most caught stealing	42, Rickey H. Henderson, 149 games, 1982
Most bases on balls	118, Salvatore L. Bando, 155 games, 1970
Most bases on balls, league	775, Salvatore L. Bando
Most strikeouts	175, Jose Canseco, 157 games, 1986
Most strikeouts, league	1180, Reginald M. Jackson
Fewest strikeouts	31, Felipe R. Alou, 154 games, 1970
Most hit by pitch	20, Donald E. Baylor, 157 games, 1976.
Most runs batted in	118, Reginald M. Jackson, 152 games, 1969
	118, David A. Kingman, 147 games, 1984
	118, Mark D. McGwire, 151 games, 1987
Most runs batted in, league	789, Salvatore L. Bando
Most game-winning RBIs	17, Jose Canseco, 159 games, 1987
Highest batting average	.319, Rickey H. Henderson, 108 games, 1981
Highest batting average, league	.291, Rickey H. Henderson
Highest slugging average	.618, Mark D. McGwire, 151 games, 1987
Highest slugging average, league	.501, Reginald M. Jackson

Most consecutive games with RBI ....10, Robert J. Monday, (18 RBIs), 1969
Longest batting streak ....24 games, Carney R. Lansford, 1984
Most grounded into double play ....25, Danny A. Cater, 152 games, 1969
Fewest grounded into double play ....3, Reginald M. Jackson, 154 games, 1968

Pitching

Most years	10, Michael K. Norris
	10, J. Rick Langford
Most games, league	502, Roland G. Fingers
Most games	76, Roland G. Fingers, 1974
Most games started	41, James A. Hunter, 1974
Most games started, league	270, James A. Hunter
Most complete games	28, J. Rick Langford, 1980
Most complete games, league	96, James A. Hunter
Most games finished	62, Roland G. Fingers, 1976
	62, William H. Caudill, 1984
Most innings	318, James A. Hunter, 1974
Most innings, league	1946, Vida R. Blue
Most games won, season	25, James A. Hunter, 1974
Most games won, league	131, James A. Hunter
Most 20 victory seasons	4, James A. Hunter
Most games lost	20, Brian P. Kingman, 1980
Most games lost, league	90, J. Rick Langford
Longest winning streak	13 games, James A. Hunter, 1973
Longest losing streak	14 games, Matthew L. Keough, 1979
Highest winning percentage	.808, James A. Hunter (21-5), 1973
Most saves	36, William H. Caudill, 1984
Most bases on balls	112, Johnny L. Odom, 1969
Most bases on balls, league	617, Vida R. Blue
Most strikeouts	301, Vida R. Blue, 1971
Most strikeouts, league	1315, Vida R. Blue

Most strikeouts, game—
    17, Vida Blue, July 9, 1971, first 11 innings of 20-inning game
    16, Jose A. Rijo, April 19, 1986, first eight innings of 9-inning game

Most shutouts won	8, Vida Blue, 1971
Most shutouts won, league	28, Vida R. Blue
Most 1-0 shutouts won	2, Vida Blue, 1971
	2, James A. Hunter, 1971
Most runs	144, Matthew L. Keough, 1982
Most earned runs	133, Matthew L. Keough, 1982
Most hits	284, Vida R. Blue, 1977
Most hit batsmen	10, Steven E. McCatty, 1979
	10, Michael K. Norris, 1981
Most wild pitches	17, Johnny L. Odom, 1968
Most home runs	39, James A. Hunter, 1973
Most sacrifice hits	17, Robert J. Lacey, 1977
Most sacrifice flies	12, Vida Blue, 1974
	12, Roland G. Fingers, 1974
	12, J. Rick Langford, 1980
Lowest ERA	1.82, Vida Blue, 312 innings, 1971

Club Records

Most players	47 in 1972 (155 games)
Fewest players	34 in 1968 (163 games)
	34 in 1980 (162 games)
Most games	163 in 1968
Most at-bats	5614 in 1969 (162 games)
Most runs	806 in 1987 (162 games)
Fewest runs	532 in 1978 (162 games)
Most opponents' runs	860 in 1979 (162 games)
Fewest opponents' runs	457 in 1972 (155 games)
Most hits	1475 in 1985 (162 games)
Fewest hits	1248 in 1972 (155 games)
Most singles	1061 in 1983 (162 games)
Most doubles	263 in 1987 (162 games)
Most triples	40 in 1968 (163 games)
Most homers	199 in 1987 (162 games)
Fewest homers	94 in 1968
Most homers at Oakland Coliseum, home & opp..	163 in 1987
Most grand slams	7 in 1974
Most pinch home runs	8 in 1970
Most long hits	495 in 1987 (162 games)
Most extra bases on long hits	926 in 1987 (162 games)
Most total bases	2358 in 1987 (162 games)
Most sacrifice hits	108 in 1978 (162 games)
Most sacrifice flies	77 in 1984 (162 games)
Most stolen bases	341 in 1976 (161 games)
Most caught stealing	123 in 1976 (161 games)
Most bases on balls	617 in 1969 (162 games)
Most strikeouts	1056 in 1987 (162 games)
Fewest strikeouts	751 in 1979 (162 games)
Most hit by pitch	63 in 1969 (162 games)
Fewest hit by pitch	16 in 1985 (162 games)
Most runs batted in	761 in 1987 (162 games)
Most game-winning RBIs	79 in 1980 (162 games)
Highest batting average	.264 in 1985 (162 games)
Lowest batting average	.236 in 1982 (162 games)
Highest slugging average	.428 in 1987 (162 games)
Lowest slugging average	.343 in 1968 (163 games)
Most grounded into double play	131 in 1979 (162 games)
Fewest grounded into double play	87 in 1968 (163 games)
Most left on bases	1244 in 1969 (162 games)
Fewest left on bases	1030 in 1979 (162 games)
Most putouts	4442 in 1969 (162 games)
Fewest putouts	4288 in 1979 (162 games)
Most assists	1821 in 1976 (161 games)
Fewest assists	1508 in 1984 (162 games)
Most chances accepted	6230 in 1969 (162 games)

Sal Bando

Fewest chances accepted	5798 in 1984 (162 games)
Most errors	190 in 1977 (161 games)
Fewest errors	117 in 1971 (161 games)
Most errorless games	78 in 1969 (162 games)
Most consecutive errorless games	9 in 1975 , 1985
Most double plays	170 in 1973 (162 games)
Fewest double plays	115 in 1980 (162 games)
Most passed balls	26 in 1969 (162 games)
Fewest passed balls	8 in 1982 (162 games)
Highest fielding average	.981 in 1971 (161 games)
Lowest fielding average	.970 in 1977 (161 games)
Highest home attendance	1,735,489 in 1982
Highest road attendance	1,930,731 in 1987
Most games won	101 in 1971
Most games lost	108 in 1979
Most games won, month	23, August 1971
Most games lost, month	24, June 1979
Games won, league	1608 in 20 years
Games lost, league	1569 in 20 years
Highest percentage games won	.627 in 1971 (won 101, lost 60)
Lowest percentage games won	.333 in 1979 (won 54, lost 108)
Most shutouts won	23 in 1972
Most shutouts lost	19 in 1978
Most 1-0 games won	5 in 1971
Most 1-0 games lost	5 in 1971
	5 in 1978
Most consecutive games won	11 in 1981
Most consecutive games lost	14 in 1977
Most times, league champions	3
Most last place finishes	0
Most runs, game	21 vs. Boston, June 14, 1969
Most runs, game, by opponents	20 by Minnesota, April 27, 1980
Most runs, shutout game	13 vs. Kansas City, September 10, 1973
Most runs, shutout game, by opponent	16 by Kansas City, June 25, 1984
Most runs, doubleheader shutout	10 vs. Kansas City, September 9, 1974
Most runs, inning	10 vs. Milwaukee, May 9, 1972, first game, fourth inning
Longest 1-0 game won	20 innings vs. California, July 9, 1971
Longest 1-0 game lost	13 innings vs. Detroit, May 25, 1973
Most hits, nine-inning game	25 vs. Boston, June 14, 1969
Most hits, extra-inning game	29 vs. Texas, July 1, 1979, 15 innings
Most home runs, game	6 vs. Cleveland, July 18, 1980
Most consecutive games, one or more homers	14 (26 homers), 1987
Most total bases, game	38 vs. Boston, June 14, 1969
Largest crowd, day game	48,758 vs. Detroit, June 6, 1970
Largest crowd, doubleheader	48,592 vs. New York, May 3, 1981
Largest crowd, night game	49,300 vs. New York, August 25, 1980
Largest crowd, home opener	48,348 vs. California, April 6, 1982

Philadelphia A's

Yearly Finishes

Year—Position	W.	L.	Pct.	*G.B.	Manager
1901—Fourth....	74	62	.544	9	Connie Mack
1902—First.......	83	53	.610	+ 5	Connie Mack
1903—Second...	75	60	.556	14½	Connie Mack
1904—Fifth.......	81	70	.536	12½	Connie Mack
1905—First.......	92	56	.622	+ 2	Connie Mack
1906—Fourth....	78	67	.538	12	Connie Mack
1907—Second...	88	57	.607	1½	Connie Mack
1908—Sixth......	68	85	.444	22	Connie Mack
1909—Second...	95	58	.621	3½	Connie Mack
1910—First...	102	48	.680	+14½	Connie Mack
1911—First...	101	50	.669	+13½	Connie Mack
1912—Third......	90	62	.592	15	Connie Mack
1913—First.......	96	57	.627	+ 6½	Connie Mack
1914—First.......	99	53	.651	+ 8½	Connie Mack
1915—Eighth.....	43	109	.283	58½	Connie Mack
1916—Eighth.....	36	117	.235	54½	Connie Mack
1917—Eighth.....	55	98	.359	44½	Connie Mack
1918—Eighth.....	52	76	.402	24	Connie Mack
1919—Eighth.....	36	104	.257	52	Connie Mack
1920—Eighth.....	48	106	.312	50	Connie Mack
1921—Eighth.....	53	100	.346	45	Connie Mack
1922—Seventh..	65	89	.422	29	Connie Mack
1923—Sixth......	69	83	.454	29	Connie Mack
1924—Fifth.......	71	81	.467	20	Connie Mack
1925—Second...	88	64	.579	8½	Connie Mack
1926—Third......	83	67	.533	6	Connie Mack
1927—Second...	91	63	.591	19	Connie Mack
1928—Second...	98	55	.641	2½	Connie Mack
1929—First...	104	46	.693	+18	Connie Mack
1930—First...	102	52	.662	+ 8	Connie Mack
1931—First...	107	45	.704	+13½	Connie Mack
1932—Second...	94	60	.610	13	Connie Mack
1933—Third......	79	72	.523	19½	Connie Mack
1934—Fifth.......	68	82	.453	31	Connie Mack
1935—Eighth.....	58	91	.389	34	Connie Mack
1936—Eighth.....	53	100	.346	49	Connie Mack
1937—Seventh..	54	97	.358	46½	Connie Mack
1938—Eighth.....	53	99	.349	46	Connie Mack
1939—Seventh..	55	97	.362	51½	Connie Mack
1940—Eighth.....	54	100	.351	36	Connie Mack
1941—Eighth.....	64	90	.416	37	Connie Mack
1942—Eighth.....	55	99	.357	48	Connie Mack
1943—Eighth.....	49	105	.318	49	Connie Mack
1944—Fifth†	72	82	.468	17	Connie Mack
1945—Eighth.....	52	98	.347	34½	Connie Mack
1946—Eighth.....	49	105	.318	55	Connie Mack
1947—Fifth.......	78	76	.506	19	Connie Mack
1948—Fourth....	84	70	.545	12½	Connie Mack
1949—Fifth.......	81	73	.526	16	Connie Mack
1950—Eighth.....	52	102	.338	46	Connie Mack
1951—Sixth......	70	84	.455	28	James Dykes
1952—Fourth....	79	75	.513	16	James Dykes
1953—Seventh..	59	95	.383	41½	James Dykes
1954—Eighth.....	51	103	.331	60	Edwin Joost

*Games behind winner.   †Tied for position. .

Individual Records (1901 To 1954)

Batting

Most years, non-pitcher..16, Harry H. Davis
Most games.................................157, David E. Philley, 1953
Most games, league...................................1702, James Dykes
Most at-bats ....670, Aloysius H. Simmons, 154 games, 1932
Most at-bats, league ....6023, James Dykes
Most runs...................152, Aloysius H. Simmons, 138 games, 1930
Most runs, league ....997, Robert L. Johnson
Most hits......................253, Aloysius H. Simmons, 153 games, 1925
Most hits, league ....1827, Aloysius H. Simmons
Most singles ....174, Aloysius H. Simmons, 153 games, 1925
Most doubles ....53, Aloysius H. Simmons, 147 games, 1926
Most doubles, league......................................365, James Dykes
Most triples ....21, J. Franklin Baker, 149 games, 1912
Most triples, league..........................104, Daniel F. Murphy
Most homers, righthander ....58, James E. Foxx, 154 games, 1932
Most homers, lefthander ....27, Joseph J. Hauser, 149 games, 1924
Most homers, rookie ....21, Robert L. Johnson, 142 games, 1933
Most homers at home...............31, James E. Foxx, 1932
Most homers on road...............27, James E. Foxx, 1932
Most homers, month...........15, Robert L. Johnson, June, 1934
Most homers, league.....................302, James E. Foxx
Most grand slams ....3, James E. Foxx, 154 games, 1932
........................3, James E. Foxx, 150 games, 1934
........................3, Robert L. Johnson, 152 games, 1933
........................3, Gus E. Zernial, 145 games, 1952
Most grand slams, league..........................9, James E. Foxx
........................9, Samuel B. Chapman
Most total bases............438, James E. Foxx, 154 games, 1932
Most total bases, league ....2998, Aloysius H. Simmons
Most long hits....................100, James E. Foxx, 154 games, 1932
Most extra bases on long hits..........225, James E. Foxx, 154 games, 1932
Most sacrifices (S. H. and S. F.)................43, Roy A. Grover, 141 games, 1917
Most sacrifice hits....................34, Simon Nicholls, 124 games, 1907
Most sacrifice flies...............7, Joseph P. DeMaestri, 146 games, 1954

Most stolen bases.........................81, Edward T. Collins, 153 games, 1910
Most stolen bases, league...........................375, Edward T. Collins
Most caught stealing.........................15, Lawton W. Witt, 154 games, 1921
........................15, Aloysius H. Simmons, 152 games, 1924
........................15, William M. Werber, 134 games, 1938
Most bases on balls.........................149, Edwin D. Joost, 144 games, 1949
Most strikeouts.........................110, Edwin D. Joost, 151 games, 1947
Fewest strikeouts...............17, Richard W. Siebert, 153 games, 1942
Most hit by pitch..................12, Joseph J. Hauser, 146 games, 1923
Most runs batted in.........................169, James E. Foxx, 154 games, 1932
Most runs batted in, league...........................1178, Aloysius H. Simmons
Most consecutive games with RBI ....11, Aloysius H. Simmons, (20 RBIs), 1931
Highest batting average............................422, Napoleon Lajoie, 131 games, 1901
Highest slugging average............................749, James E. Foxx, 154 games, 1932
Longest batting streak..........................29 games, William Lamar, 1925
Most grounded into double play............30, William C. Hitchcock, 115 games, 1950
Fewest grounded into double play.................5, Edwin D. Joost, 151 games, 1947

Pitching

Most years..14, Edward S. Plank
Most games............................58, Morris W. Martin, 1953
Most games, league...524, Edward S. Plank
Most games started..................46, George E. Waddell, 1904
Most complete games.................36, George E. Waddell, 1904
Most games finished.......................47, Jonas A. Berry, 1944
Most innings........................384, George E. Waddell, 1904
Most games won, season..............31, John W. Coombs, 1910
........................31, Robert M. Grove, 1931
Most games won, league............................283, Edward S. Plank
Most 20 victory seasons.......................7, Edward S. Plank
........................7, Robert M. Grove
Most games lost...............................25, Scott Perry, 1920
Most games lost, league...........................158, Edward S. Plank
Highest winning percentage ....886, Robert M. Grove (31-4), 1931
Longest winning streak ....16 games, Robert M. Grove, 1931
Longest losing streak ....19 games, John Nabors, 1916
Most bases on balls ....168, Elmer G. Myers, 1916
Most bases on balls, league............................879, Edward S. Plank
Most strikeouts.....................349, George E. Waddell, 1904
Most strikeouts, league ....1998, Edward S. Plank
Most strikeouts, game ....18, John W. Coombs, September 1, 1906, 24 innings
........................18, John W. Coombs, August 4, 1910, 16 innings
........................14, George E. Waddell, July 14, 1903
........................14, George E. Waddell, September 6, 1904, first game
........................14, George E. Waddell, August 2, 1905
Most shutouts ....13, John W. Coombs, 1910
Most shutouts, league.................................60, Edward S. Plank
Most 1-0 shutouts won ....4, Henry W. Krause, 1909
Most runs........................169, Elmer G. Myers, 1916
Most earned runs ....146, George L. Earnshaw, 1930
Most hits.........................360, John W. Coombs, 1911
Most hit batsmen ....31, Charles C. Fraser, 1901
Most wild pitches ....16, Stuart M. Flythe, 1936
Most home runs ....28, Alexander R. Kellner, 1950
Lowest ERA....................1.98, Scott Perry, 332 innings, 1918

Club Records

Most players	56 in 1915	
Fewest players	19 in 1905	
Most games	158 in 1914	
Most at-bats	5537 in 1932	(154 games)
Most runs	981 in 1932	(154 games)
Fewest runs	447 in 1916	(154 games)
Most hits	1659 in 1925	(153 games)
Fewest hits	1132 in 1908	(157 games)
Most singles	1206 in 1925	(153 games)
Most doubles	323 in 1928	(153 games)
Most triples	108 in 1912	(153 games)
Most homers	173 in 1932	(154 games)
Fewest homers (154 or 162-game schedule)	16 in 1915	
	16 in 1917	
Most homers at Shibe Park, home & opp.	189 in 1932	
Most pinch home runs	6 in 1952	(155 games)
Most grand slams	8 in 1932	
Most long hits	527 in 1932	(154 games)
Most extra bases on long hits	924 in 1932	(154 games)
Most total bases	2530 in 1932	(154 games)
Most sacrifices, (S. H. and S. F.)	239 in 1926	(150 games)
Most sacrifice hits	147 in 1906	(149 games)
Most sacrifice flies	31 in 1954	(156 games)
Most stolen bases	259 in 1912	(153 games)
Most bases on balls	783 in 1949	(154 games)
Most strikeouts	667 in 1954	(156 games)
Fewest strikeouts	326 in 1927	(155 games)
Most hit by pitch	46 in 1920	(156 games)
Fewest hit by pitch	5 in 1937	(154 games)
Most runs batted in	923 in 1932	(154 games)
Highest batting average	.307 in 1925	(153 games)
Lowest batting average	.223 in 1908	(157 games)
Highest slugging average	.457 in 1932	(154 games)
Lowest slugging average	.308 in 1918	(130 games)
Most grounded into double play	170 in 1950	(154 games)
Fewest grounded into double play	105 in 1945	(153 games)
Most left on bases	1235 in 1949	(154 games)
Fewest left on bases	999 in 1924	(152 games)

Hard-hitting Al Simmons

Most .300 hitters	11 in 1927
Most putouts	4231 in 1910 (155 games)
Fewest putouts	3953 in 1906 (149 games)
Most assists	2172 in 1920 (156 games)
Fewest assists	1591 in 1946 (155 games)
Most chances accepted	6297 in 1920 (156 games)
Fewest chances accepted	5610 in 1938 (154 games)
Most errors	317 in 1901 (136 games)
Fewest errors	113 in 1948 (154 games)
Most consecutive errorless games	7 in 1951
Most double plays	217 in 1949 (154 games)
Fewest double plays	102 in 1917 (154 games)
Most passed balls	25 in 1914 (158 games)
Fewest passed balls	5 in 1947 (156 games)
Highest fielding average	.981 in 1948 (154 games)
Lowest fielding average	.936 in 1901 (136 games)
Highest home attendance	945,076 in 1948
Highest road attendance	1,562,360 in 1948
Most games won	107 in 1931
Most games lost	117 in 1916
Most games won, month	26, July 1931
Most games lost, month	28, July 1916
Highest percentage games won	.704 in 1931 (won 107, lost 45)
Lowest percentage games won	.235 in 1916 (won 36, lost 117)
Games won, league	3886 in 54 years
Games lost, league	4248 in 54 years
Most shutouts won	27 in 1909
	also 1 tie, 26 in 1908
Most shutouts lost	24 in 1943

Most 1-0 games won	9 in 1909
Most 1-0 games lost	7 in 1908, 1909
Most consecutive games won	17 in 1931
Most consecutive games lost	20 in 1916, 1943
Most times league champions	9
Most last place finishes	18
Most runs, game	24 vs. Detroit, May 18, 1912
	24 vs. Boston, May 1, 1929
Most runs, game, by opponent	25 by Cleveland, May 11, 1930
	25 by New York, May 24, 1936
Most runs, shutout game	16 vs. Chicago, July 25, 1928, first game
	16 vs. Chicago, August 29, 1937, first game
Most runs, shutout game, by opponent—	
	21 by New York, August 13, 1939, second game, eight innings
Most runs, doubleheader shutout	17 vs. Detroit, August 13, 1902
Most runs, inning	13 vs. Cleveland, June 15, 1925, eighth inning
Most hits, game	29 vs. Boston, May 1, 1929
Longest 1-0 game won	13 innings vs. Detroit, August 11, 1902
	13 innings vs. Boston, September 10, 1904
	13 innings vs. Chicago, May 16, 1909
	13 innings vs. Cleveland, May 14, 1914
Longest 1-0 game, lost	16 innings vs. St. Louis, June 5, 1942
Most home runs, game	7 vs. Detroit, June 3, 1921
Most consecutive games, one or more homers	12 (20 homers), 1951
Most total bases, game	44 vs. Boston, May 1, 1929
Largest crowd, day game	37,534 vs. New York, May 16, 1937
Largest crowd, doubleheader	38,800 vs. New York, July 13, 1931
Largest crowd, night game	37,383 vs. New York, June 27, 1947
Largest crowd, home opener	32,825 vs. New York, April 20, 1927

St. Louis Browns

Yearly Finishes
(Milwaukee Brewers, 1901)

Year—Position	W.	L.	Pct.	*G.B.	Manager
1901—Eighth	48	89	.350	35½	Hugh Duffy
1902—Second	78	58	.574	5	James McAleer
1903—Sixth	65	74	.468	26½	James McAleer
1904—Sixth	65	87	.428	29	James McAleer
1905—Eighth	54	99	.354	40½	James McAleer
1906—Fifth	76	73	.510	16	James McAleer
1907—Sixth	69	83	.454	24	James McAleer
1908—Fourth	83	69	.546	6½	James McAleer
1909—Seventh	61	89	.407	36	James McAleer
1910—Eighth	47	107	.305	57	John O'Connor
1911—Eighth	45	107	.296	56½	Roderick Wallace
1912—Seventh	53	101	.344	53	R. Wallace, G. Stovall
1913—Eighth	57	96	.373	39	G. Stovall, B. Rickey
1914—Fifth	71	82	.464	28½	Branch Rickey
1915—Sixth	63	91	.409	39½	Branch Rickey
1916—Fifth	79	75	.513	12	Fielder Jones
1917—Seventh	57	97	.370	43	Fielder Jones
1918—Fifth	58	64	.475	15	F. Jones, J. Austin, J. Burke
1919—Fifth	67	72	.482	20½	James Burke
1920—Fourth	76	77	.497	21½	James Burke
1921—Third	81	73	.526	17½	Lee Fohl
1922—Second	93	61	.604	1	Lee Fohl
1923—Fifth	74	78	.487	24	Lee Fohl, James Austin
1924—Fourth	74	78	.487	17	George Sisler
1925—Third	82	71	.536	15	George Sisler
1926—Seventh	62	92	.403	29	George Sisler
1927—Seventh	59	94	.336	50½	Dan Howley
1928—Third	82	72	.532	19	Dan Howley
1929—Fourth	79	73	.520	26	Dan Howley
1930—Sixth	64	90	.416	38	William Killefer
1931—Fifth	63	91	.409	45	William Killefer
1932—Sixth	63	91	.409	44	William Killefer
1933—Eighth	55	96	.364	43½	Killefer, Sothoron, Hornsby
1934—Sixth	67	85	.441	33	Rogers Hornsby
1935—Seventh	65	87	.428	28½	Rogers Hornsby
1936—Seventh	57	95	.375	44½	Rogers Hornsby
1937—Eighth	46	108	.299	56	R. Hornsby, J. Bottomley
1938—Seventh	55	97	.362	44	Charles (Gabby) Street
1939—Eighth	43	111	.279	64½	Fred Haney
1940—Sixth	67	87	.435	23	Fred Haney
1941—Sixth†	70	84	.455	31	F. Haney, J. Luther Sewell
1942—Third	82	69	.543	19½	J. Luther (Luke) Sewell
1943—Sixth	72	80	.474	25	J. Luther (Luke) Sewell
1944—First	89	65	.578	+ 1	J. Luther (Luke) Sewell
1945—Third	81	70	.536	6	J. Luther (Luke) Sewell
1946—Seventh	66	88	.429	38	J. L. Sewell, Z. Taylor
1947—Eighth	59	95	.383	38	Herold (Muddy) Ruel
1948—Sixth	59	94	.386	37	James (Zack) Taylor
1949—Seventh	53	101	.344	44	James (Zack) Taylor
1950—Seventh	58	96	.377	40	James (Zack) Taylor
1951—Eighth	52	102	.338	46	James (Zack) Taylor
1952—Seventh	64	90	.416	31	R. Hornsby, M. Marion
1953—Eighth	54	100	.351	46½	Martin Marion

*Games behind winner. †Tied for position.

Individual Records (1902 To 1953)
Batting

Most years, non-pitcher	16, James P. Austin
Most games	159, Derrill B. Pratt, 1915
Most games, league	1,647, George H. Sisler
Most at-bats	671, John T. Tobin, 150 games, 1921
Most at-bats, league	6,667, George H. Sisler
Most runs	145, Harlond B. Clift, 152 games, 1936
Most runs, league	1,091, George H. Sisler
Most hits	257, George H. Sisler, 154 games, 1920
Most hits, league	2,295, George H. Sisler
Most singles	179, John T. Tobin, 150 games, 1921
Most doubles	51, Roy C. Bell, 156 games, 1937
Most doubles, league	343, George H. Sisler
Most triples	20, Henry E. Manush, 154 games, 1928
Most triples, league	145, George H. Sisler
Most homers, righthander	34, Harlond B. Clift, 149 games, 1938
Most homers, lefthander	39, Kenneth R. Williams, 153 games, 1922
Most homers, rookie	24, Walter F. Judnich, 137 games, 1940
Most homers at home	32, Kenneth R. Williams, 1922
Most homers, month	15, Harlond B. Clift, August, 1938
Most homers, league	185, Kenneth R. Williams
Most grand slams	2, Held by many players
Most grand slams, league	5, Kenneth R. Williams.
	5, Harlond B. Clift
	5, Vernon D. Stephens
Most total bases	399, George H. Sisler, 154 games, 1920
Most total bases, league	3,201, George H. Sisler
Most long hits	86, George H. Sisler, 154 games, 1920
Most extra bases on long hits	173, Kenneth R. Williams, 153 games, 1922
Most sacrifices (S.H. and S.F.)	48, Joseph Gedeon, 153 games, 1920
Most sacrifice hits	40, Thomas Jones, 144 games, 1906
Most stolen bases	51, George H. Sisler, 142 games, 1922
Most stolen bases, league	351, George H. Sisler
Most caught stealing	19, George H. Sisler, 142 games, 1922
	19, Kenneth R. Williams, 153 games, 1922

Most bases on balls	126, Luzerne A. Blue, 151 games, 1929
Most strikeouts	120, Gus Williams, 143 games, 1914
Fewest strikeouts	13, John T. Tobin, 151 games, 1921
Most hit by pitch	12, Frank J. O'Rourke, 140 games, 1927
Most runs batted in	155, Kenneth R. Williams, 153 games, 1922
Most runs batted in, league	964, George H. Sisler
Highest batting average	.420, George H. Sisler, 142 games, 1922
Highest batting average, league	.344 George H. Sisler
Highest slugging average	.632, George H. Sisler, 154 games, 1920
Highest slugging average, league	.558, Kenneth R. Williams
Longest batting streak	41 games, George H. Sisler, 1922
Most grounded into double play	21, Glenn R. McQuillen, 100 games, 1942
Fewest grounded into double play	7, Vernon D. Stephens, 150 games, 1947

Pitching

Most years	10, George F. Blaeholder
	10, Barney Pelty
	10, John J. Powell
Most games	60, Marlin H. Stuart, 1953
Most games, league	323, Elam R. VanGilder
Most games started	40, Louis N. Newsom, 1938
Most complete games	36, John Powell, 1902
Most games finished	35, Leroy Paige, 1952
Most innings	348, Urban J. Shocker, 1922
Most games won	27, Urban J. Shocker, 1922
Most games won, league	126, Urban J. Shocker
Most 20 victory seasons	4, Urban J. Shocker
Most games lost	25, Fred Glade, 1905
Most games lost, league	142, John J. Powell
Highest winning percentage	.808, Alvin F. Crowder (21-5), 1928
Longest winning streak	Less than 12
Longest losing streak	Less than 12
Most bases on balls	192, Louis N. Newsom, 1938
Most bases on balls, league	625, Elam R. VanGilder
Most strikeouts	232, George E. Waddell, 1908
Most strikeouts, league	884, John J. Powell
Most strikeouts, game	17, George E. Waddell, September 20, 1908, 10 innings
	16, George E. Waddell, July 29, 1908
Most shutouts	6, Fred Glade, 1904
	6, Harry Howell, 1906
Most shutouts, league	27, John Powell
Most 1-0 shutouts won	3, Fred Glade, 1904
Most runs	205, Louis N. Newsom, 1938
Most earned runs	186, Louis N. Newsom, 1938
Most hits	365, Urban J. Shocker, 1922
Most hit batsmen	19, Barney Pelty, 1907
Most wild pitches	11, Carl Weilman, 1914
	11, Arthur D. Davenport, 1917
	11, John H. Knott, Jr., 1936
Most home runs	21, Urban J. Shocker, 1921
Lowest ERA	2.12, Carl Weilman, 307 innings, 1914

Club Records

Most players	52 in 1951
Fewest players	19 in 1906
Most games	159 in 1914, 1915
Most at-bats	5510 in 1937 (157 games)
Most runs	897 in 1925 (154 games)
Fewest runs	441 in 1909 (154 games)
Most hits	1693 in 1922 (154 games)
Fewest hits	1092 in 1910 (158 games)
Most singles	1239 in 1921 (154 games)
Most doubles	327 in 1937 (156 games)
Most triples	106 in 1921 (154 games)
Most homers	118 in 1940 (154 games)
Fewest homers (154 or 162-game schedule)	9 in 1906
Most homers at Sportsman's Pk., home & opp.	135 in 1940
Most grand slams	5 in 1950
Most home runs by pinch-hitters	4 in 1951
Most total bases	2463 in 1922 (154 games)
Most long hits	482 in 1922 (154 games)
	482 in 1925 (154 games)
Most extra bases on long hits	770 in 1922 (154 games)
	770 in 1925 (154 games)
Most sacrifices, (S. H. and S. F.)	214 in 1928 (154 games)
Most sacrifices hits	163 in 1906 (154 games)
Most stolen bases	234 in 1916 (158 games)
Most bases on balls	775 in 1941 (157 games)
Most strikeouts	863 in 1914 (159 games)
Fewest strikeouts	339 in 1920 (154 games)
Most hit by pitch	43 in 1927 (155 games)
Fewest hit by pitch	12 in 1931 (154 games)
Most runs batted in	761 in 1936 (155 games)
Highest batting average	.313 in 1922 (154 games)
Lowest batting average	.216 in 1910 (158 games)
Highest slugging average	.455 in 1922 (154 games)
Lowest slugging average	.273 in 1910 (158 games)
Most grounded into double play	151 in 1951 (154 games)
Fewest grounded into double play	93 in 1944 (154 games)
Most left on bases	1334 in 1941 (157 games)
Fewest left on bases	1055 in 1951 (154 games)
Most .300 hitters	8 in 1922
Most putouts	4328 in 1916 (158 games)
Fewest putouts	3993 in 1911 (152 games)
Most assists	2189 in 1910 (156 games)

Fewest assists	1584 in 1938 (156 games)
Most chances accepted	6516 in 1916 (158 games)
Fewest chances accepted	5618 in 1938 (156 games)
Most errors	378 in 1910 (158 games)
Fewest errors	134 in 1947 (154 games)
Most consecutive errorless games	8 in 1928
Most double plays	190 in 1948 (155 games)
Fewest double plays	116 in 1914 (159 games)
Most passed balls	30 in 1914 (159 games)
	30 in 1915 (159 games)
Fewest passed balls	4 in 1930 (154 games)
	4 in 1933 (154 games)
Highest fielding average	.977 in 1947 (154 games)
Lowest fielding average	.943 in 1910 (158 games)
Highest home attendance	712,918 in 1922
Highest road attendance	1,170,349 in 1948
Most games won	93 in 1922
Most games lost	111 in 1939
Most games won, month	23, August 1945
Most games lost, month	24, Sept. 1939
	24, July 1952
Highest percentage games won	.604 in 1922 (won 93, lost 61)
Lowest percentage games won	.279 in 1939 (won 43, lost 111)
Games won, league	3416 in 52 years
Games lost, league	4465 in 52 years
Most shutouts won	21 in 1909
Most shutouts lost	25 in 1904
	25 in 1906
	25 in 1910
Most 1-0 games won	6 in 1909
Most 1-0 games lost	7 in 1907
Most consecutive games won	14 in 1916
Most consecutive games lost	14 in 1911, 1953
Most times league champions	1
Most last place finishes	10
Most runs, game	20 vs. Detroit, August 18, 1951
Most runs, game by opponent	29 by Boston, June 8, 1950
Most runs, shutout game	16 vs. Detroit, September 9, 1922
Most runs, shutout game, by opponent	18 by Detroit, April 29, 1935
Most runs, doubleheader shutout	5 vs. Philadelphia, September 23, 1906
Most runs, inning	11 vs. Philadelphia, July 21, 1949, first game, sixth inning
	11 vs. Detroit, August 18, 1951, seventh inning
Longest 1-0 game won	16 innings vs. Philadelphia, June 5, 1942
Longest 1-0 game lost	15 innings vs. Washington, August 14, 1903, first game
	15 innings vs. Washington, July 25, 1918
Most hits, game	24 vs. Philadelphia, September 17, 1920
	24 vs. Washington, June 14, 1932
Most home runs, game	5 vs. New York, September 16, 1940
Most consecutive games, one or more homers	11 (20 homers), 1922
Most total bases, game	40 vs. Chicago, May 31, 1925
Largest crowd, day game	34,625 vs. New York, October 1, 1944
Largest crowd, night game	22,847 vs. Cleveland, May 24, 1940
Largest crowd, home opener	19,561 vs. Detroit, April 18, 1923

Urban Shocker

Seattle Pilots

Yearly Finishes
West Division

Year—Position	W.	L.	Pct.	*G.B.	Manager
1969—Sixth	64	98	.395	33	Joseph Schultz

*Games behind winner.

Individual Records (1969)
Batting

Most games	148, Tommy Harper, 1969
Most at-bats	537, Tommy Harper, 148 games, 1969
Most runs	88, H. Wayne Comer, 147 games, 1969
Most hits	126, Tommy Harper, 148 games, 1969
Most singles	105, Tommy Harper, 148 games, 1969
Most doubles	29, H. Thomas Davis, 123 games, 1969
Most triples	6, J. Michael Hegan, 95 games, 1969
Most homers, lefthander	25, Donald R. Mincher, 140 games, 1969
Most homers, righthander	15, H. Wayne Comer, 147 games, 1969
Most homers, rookie	3, Steven E. Hovley, 91 games, 1969
	3, Daniel Walton, 23 games, 1969
Most homers, month	8, Donald R. Mincher, July, 1969
Most homers at home	13, Donald R. Mincher, 1969
Most homers on road	12, Donald R. Mincher, 1969
Most grand slams	1, Donald R. Mincher, 140 games, 1969
	1, Richard J. Rollins, 58 games, 1969
	1, Frederick L. Talbot, 27 games, 1969
Most total bases	194, Donald R. Mincher, 140 games, 1969
Most long hits	39, Donald R. Mincher, 140 games, 1969
Most extra bases on long hits	89, Donald R. Mincher, 140 games, 1969
Most sacrifice hits	9, Gerald E. McNertney, 128 games, 1969
Most sacrifice flies	5, H. Thomas Davis, 123 games, 1969
Most stolen bases	73, Tommy Harper, 148 games, 1969
Most caught stealing	18, Tommy Harper, 148 games, 1969
Most bases on balls	95, Tommy Harper, 148 games, 1969
Most strikeouts	90, Tommy Harper, 148 games, 1969
Fewest strikeouts	46, H. Thomas Davis, 123 games, 1969
Most hit by pitch	5, Donald R. Mincher, 140 games, 1969
	5, Richard J. Rollins, 58 games, 1969
Most runs batted in	80, H. Thomas Davis, 123 games, 1969
Highest batting average	.271, H. Thomas Davis, 123 games, 1969
Highest slugging average	.454, Donald R. Mincher, 140 games, 1969
Longest batting streak	18 games, H. Thomas Davis, 1969
Most grounded into double play	17, H. Thomas Davis, 123 games, 1969
Fewest grounded into double play	8, Tommy Harper, 148 games, 1969

Pitching

Most games	66, Diego P. Segui, 1969
Most games started	29, Eugene M. Brabender, 1969
Most complete games	7, Eugene M. Brabender, 1969
Most games finished	38, Diego P. Segui, 1969
Most innings	202, Eugene M. Brabender, 1969
Most games won	13, Eugene M. Brabender, 1969
Most games lost	14, Eugene M. Brabender, 1969
Highest winning percentage	.667, Diego P. Segui (12-6), 1969
Longest winning streak	5 games, Diego P. Segui, 1969
Longest losing streak	9 games, John Gelnar, 1969
Most saves	12, Diego P. Segui, 1969
Most bases on balls	103, Eugene M. Brabender, 1969
Most strikeouts	139, Eugene M. Brabender, 1969
Most strikeouts, game	11, Martin W. Pattin, April 29, 1969
Most shutouts won	1, held by 5 pitchers
Most 1-0 shutouts won	1, Eugene M. Brabender
	1, Martin W. Pattin
Most runs	111, Eugene M. Brabender, 1969
Most earned runs	99, Martin W. Pattin, 1969
Most hits	193, Eugene M. Brabender, 1969
Most wild pitches	8, James A. Bouton, 1969
Most hit batsmen	13, Eugene M. Brabender, 1969
Most home runs	29, Martin W. Pattin, 1969
Most sacrifice hits	10, Diego P. Segui, 1969
Most sacrifice flies	6, Eugene M. Brabender, 1969
Lowest ERA	3.36, Diego P. Segui, 142 innings, 1969

Club Records

Most players	53 in 1969 (163 games)
Most games	163 in 1969
Most at-bats	5444 in 1969 (163 games)
Most runs	639 in 1969 (163 games)

Most opponents' runs	799 in 1969	(163 games)
Most hits	1276 in 1969	(163 games)
Most singles	945 in 1969	(163 games)
Most doubles	179 in 1969	(163 games)
Most triples	27 in 1969	(163 games)
Most homers	125 in 1969	(163 games)
Fewest homers	125 in 1969	
Most homers at Sick's Stadium, home & opp.	167 in 1969	
Most grand slams	3 in 1969	
Most pinch home runs	3 in 1969	
Most total bases	1884 in 1969	(163 games)
Most long hits	331 in 1969	(163 games)
Most extra bases on long hits	608 in 1969	(163 games)
Most sacrifice hits	72 in 1969	(163 games)
Most sacrifice flies	29 in 1969	(163 games)
Most stolen bases	167 in 1969	(163 games)
Most caught stealing	59 in 1969	(163 games)
Most bases on balls	626 in 1969	(163 games)
Most strikeouts	1015 in 1969	(163 games)
Most hit by pitch	34 in 1969	(163 games)
Most runs batted in	583 in 1969	(163 games)
Highest batting average	.234 in 1969	(163 games)
Highest slugging average	.346 in 1969	(163 games)
Most grounded into double play	111 in 1969	(163 games)
Most left on bases	1130 in 1969	(163 games)
Most putouts	4391 in 1969	(163 games)
Most assists	1763 in 1969	(163 games)
Most chances accepted	6154 in 1969	(163 games)
Most errors	167 in 1969	(163 games)
Most errorless games	65 in 1969	(163 games)
Most consecutive errorless games	4 in 1969	
Most double plays	149 in 1969	(163 games)
Most passed balls	21 in 1969	(163 games)
Highest fielding average	.974 in 1969	(163 games)
Highest home attendance	677,944 in 1969	
Highest road attendance	889,578 in 1969	
Most games won	64 in 1969	
Most games lost	98 in 1969	
Most games won, month	14, June 1969	
	14, Sept. 1969	
Most games lost, month	22, August 1969	
Highest percentage games won	.395 in 1969 (won 64, lost 98)	
Most consecutive games won	5 in 1969	
Most consecutive games lost	10 in 1969	
Most shutouts won	6 in 1969	
Most shutouts lost	6 in 1969	
Most 1-0 games won	2 in 1969	
Most 1-0 games lost	0 in 1969	
Most times league champions	0	
Most last place finishes	0	

Most runs, inning ....6 vs. Boston, May 16, 1969, eleventh inning
Most runs, game ....16 vs. Washington, May 10, 1969
Most runs, game, by opponent ....15 by Baltimore, August 16, 1969
Most runs shutout game ....8 vs. California, July 9, 1969, first game
Most runs shutout game by opponent ......10 by Baltimore, June 7, 1969
Most runs doubleheader shutout .... No performance
Longest 1-0 game won ....None over 9 innings
Longest 1-0 game lost .... None
Most hits, game ....16 vs. Oakland, September 10, 1969
Most hits, extra-inning game ....20 vs. Minnesota, July 19, 1969, 18 innings
Most home runs, game ....4 vs. Boston, May 16, 1969, 11 innings
Most consecutive games, one or more homers ....5 (8 homers), 1969
Most total bases, game ....31 vs. Boston, May 16, 1969, 11 innings
Largest crowd, day game ....23,657 vs. New York, August 3, 1969
Largest crowd, doubleheader ....18,413 vs. Kansas City, June 20, 1969
Largest crowd, night game ....20,490 vs. Baltimore, May 28, 1969
Largest crowd, home opener ....14,993 vs. Chicago, April 11, 1969

Tommy Harper

Seattle Mariners

Yearly Finishes
West Division

Year—Position	W.	L.	Pct.	*G.B.	Manager
1977—Sixth	64	98	.395	38	Darrell Johnson
1978—Seventh	56	104	.350	35	Darrell Johnson
1979—Sixth	67	95	.414	21	Darrell Johnson
1980—Seventh	59	103	.364	38	D. Johnson, M. Wills
1981—6th/5th	44	65	.404	†	M. Wills, R. Lachemann
1982—Fourth	76	86	.469	17	Rene Lachemann
1983—Seventh	60	102	.370	39	R. Lachemann, D. Crandall
1984—Fifth‡	74	88	.457	10	D. Crandall, C. Cottier
1985—Sixth	74	88	.457	17	Chuck Cottier
1986—Seventh	67	95	.414	25	C. Cottier, R. Williams
1987—Fourth	78	84	.481	7	Richard Williams

*Games behind winner. †First half 21-36; second 23-29. ‡Tied for position.

Individual Records (1977 To Date)
Batting

Most years, non-pitcher	7, Julio L. Cruz
Most games	162, Ruppert S. Jones, 162 games, 1979
	162, Willie W. Horton, 1979
Most games, league	742, Julio L. Cruz
Most at-bats	646, Willie W. Horton, 162 games, 1979

Most at-bats, league	2,667, Julio L. Cruz
Most runs	109, Ruppert S. Jones, 162 games, 1979
Most runs, league	402, Julio L. Cruz
Most hits	192, Philip P. Bradley, 159 games, 1985
Most hits, league	697, Bruce A. Bochte
Most singles	152, John P. Perconte, 155 games, 1984
Most singles, league	530, Julio L. Cruz
Most doubles	39, Alfred E. Cowens, 146 games, 1982
Most doubles, league	134, Bruce A. Bochte
Most triples	10, Philip P. Bradley, 158 games, 1987
Most triples, league	26, Philip P. Bradley
Most homers, righthander	32, J. Gorman Thomas, 136 games, 1985
Most homers, righthander, league	89, James A. Presley
Most homers, lefthander	29, Alvin G. Davis, 157 games, 1987
Most homers, lefthander, league	92, Alvin G. Davis
Most homers, rookie	27, Alvin G. Davis, 152 games, 1984
Most homers at home	18, Alvin G. Davis, 1987
Most homers on road	16, J. Gorman Thomas, 1985
Most homers, month	11, J. Gorman Thomas, July, 1985
Most grand slams	2, Held by many players
Most grand slams, league	4, Alvin G. Davis
Most total bases	319, Philip P. Bradley, 159 games, 1985
Most total bases, league	1040, Alvin G. Davis
Most long hits	68, Alvin G. Davis, 157 games, 1987
Most long hits, league	221, Alvin G. Davis
Most extra bases on long hits	128, Alvin G. Davis, 157 games, 1987
Most extra bases on long hits, league	412, Alvin G. Davis

Most sacrifice hits .... 15, G. Craig Reynolds, 135 games, 1977
15, Lawrence W. Milbourne, 106 games, 1980
Most sacrifice flies .... 10, Bruce A. Bochte, 150 games, 1979
Most stolen bases .... 60, Harold C. Reynolds, 160 games, 1987
Most stolen bases, league .... 290, Julio L. Cruz
Most caught stealing .... 20, Harold C. Reynolds, 160 games, 1987
Most bases on balls .... 97, Alvin G. Davis, 152 games, 1984
Most bases on balls, league .... 335, Alvin G. Davis
Most strikeouts .... 172, James A. Presley, 155 games, 1986
Most strikeouts, league .... 492, James A. Presley
Fewest strikeouts .... 34, Harold C. Reynolds, 160 games, 1987
Most hit by pitch .... 8, Leon K. Roberts, 134 games, 1978
8, Philip P. Bradley, 143 games, 1986
8, Philip P. Bradley, 158 games, 1987
8, Kenneth A. Phelps, 120 games, 1987
Most runs batted in .... 116, Alvin G. Davis, 152 games, 1984
Most runs batted in, league .... 366, Alvin G. Davis
Most game-winning RBIs .... 13, Thomas M. Paciorek, 104 games, 1981
13, Alvin G. Davis, 152 games, 1984
13, James A. Presley, 155 games, 1986
Highest batting average .... .326, Thomas M. Paciorek, 104 games, 1981
Highest batting average, league .... .301, Philip P. Bradley
Highest slugging average .... .516, Alvin G. Davis, 157 games, 1987
Highest slugging average, league .... .472, Alvin G. Davis
Longest batting streak .... 21 games, Daniel T. Meyer, 1979
21 games, Richard W. Zisk, 1982
Most grounded into double play.............. 29, James A. Presley, 155 games, 1985
Fewest grounded into double play................. 5, Spike D. Owen, 152 games, 1984
5, John P. Perconte, 155 games, 1984

Pitching

Most years ....7, James L. Beattie
Most games .... 78, Edward J. Vande Berg, 1982
Most games, league .... 272, Edward J. Vande Berg
Most games started .... 37, Michael W. Moore, 1986
Most games started, league .... 185, Michael W. Moore
Most complete games .... 14, Michael W. Moore, 1985
14, Mark E. Langston, 1987
Most complete games, league .... 47, Michael W. Moore
Most games finished .... 64, William H. Caudill, 1982
Most innings .... 272, Mark E. Langston, 1987
Most innings, league .... 1228⅓, Michael W. Moore
Most games won .... 19, Mark E. Langston, 1987
Most games won, league .... 57, Michael W. Moore
Most games lost .... 19, Matthew J. Young, 1985
19, Michael W. Moore, 1987
Most games lost, league .... 81, Michael W. Moore
Highest winning percentage .... .630, Mark E. Langston (17-10), 1984
.630, Michael W. Moore (17-10), 1985
Longest winning streak .... 7 games, W. Glenn Abbott, 1977
7 games, Mark E. Langston, 1984
Longest losing streak .... 16 games, Michael E. A. Parrott, 1980
Most saves .... 26, William H. Caudill, 1982
26, William H. Caudill, 1983
Most bases on balls .... 123, Mark E. Langston, 1986
Most bases on balls, league .... 472, Michael W. Moore
Most strikeouts .... 262, Mark E. Langston, 1987
Most strikeouts, league .... 783, Mark E. Langston
Most strikeouts, game .... 15, Mark E. Langston, June 25, 1986
Most shutouts won .... 3, Floyd F. Bannister, 1982
3, Mark E. Langston, 1987
Most 1-0 shutouts won .... 1, Held by many pitchers
Most runs .... 145, Michael W. Moore, 1987
Most earned runs .... 129, Mark E. Langston, 1986
Most hits .... 279, Michael W. Moore, 1986
Most hit batsmen .... 12, W. Glenn Abbott, 1977
12, Michael W. Moore, 1986
Most wild pitches .... 13, Gaylord J. Perry, 1982
Most home runs allowed........................... 35, M. Scott Bankhead, 1987
Most sacrifice hits .... 15, Shane W. Rawley, 1980
Most sacrifice flies .... 11, Thomas R. House, 1978
Lowest ERA .... 3.27, Matthew J. Young, 203⅔ innings, 1983

Club Records

Most players.. 43 in 1977 (162 games)
Fewest players... 34 in 1978 (160 games)
34 in 1980 (163 games)
Most games.. 163 in 1980
Fewest games... 160 in 1978
Most at-bats... 5626 in 1982 (162 games)
Fewest at-bats... 5336 in 1983 (162 games)
Most runs.. 760 in 1987 (162 games)
Fewest runs... 558 in 1983 (162 games)
Most opponent's runs.............................. 855 in 1977 (162 games)
Fewest opponent's runs........................... 712 in 1982 (162 games)
Most hits.. 1499 in 1987 (162 games)
Fewest hits... 1280 in 1983 (162 games)
Most singles... 1056 in 1979 (162 games)
Most doubles.. 282 in 1987 (162 games)
Most triples... 52 in 1979 (162 games)
Most homers... 171 in 1985 (162 games)
Fewest homers... 97 in 1978
Most homers at Kingdome, home & opp. .... 218 in 1987
Most grand slams..................................... 7 in 1978 (160 games)
Most pinch home runs............................... 4 in 1978 (160 games)
4 in 1979 (162 games)
4 in 1980 (163 games)
4 in 1986 (162 games)

Glenn Abbott

Most total bases....................................... 2360 in 1987 (162 games)
Most long hits... 491 in 1987 (162 games)
Most extra bases on long hits............................ 866 in 1985 (162 games)
Most sacrifice hits...................................... 106 in 1980 (163 games)
Most sacrifice flies...................................... 54 in 1979 (162 games)
Most stolen bases...................................... 174 in 1987 (162 games)
Most caught stealing..................................... 82 in 1982 (162 games)
Most bases on balls...................................... 572 in 1986 (162 games)
Most strikeouts...................................... 1148 in 1986 (162 games)
Fewest strikeouts.. 702 in 1978 (160 games)
Most hit by pitch... 43 in 1987 (162 games)
Most runs batted in..................................... 717 in 1987 (162 games)
Most game-winning RBIs................................... 73 in 1987 (162 games)
Highest batting average .... .272 in 1987 (162 games)
Lowest batting average .... .240 in 1983 (162 games)
Highest slugging average .... .428 in 1987 (162 games)
Lowest slugging average .... .356 in 1980 (163 games)
Most grounded into double play........................ 158 in 1979 (162 games)
Fewest grounded into double play...................... 101 in 1984 (162 games)
Most left on bases.................................... 1184 in 1984 (162 games)
Fewest left on bases................................... 1034 in 1983 (162 games)
Most .300 hitters .... 1 in many years
Most putouts... 4429 in 1982 (162 games)
Fewest putouts.. 4255 in 1983 (162 games)
Most assists.. 1930 in 1980 (163 games)
Fewest assists.. 1700 in 1984 (162 games)
Most chances accepted................................ 6302 in 1980 (163 games)
Fewest chances accepted.............................. 6026 in 1984 (162 games)
Most errors... 156 in 1986 (162 games)
Most errorless games..................................... 84 in 1987 (162 games)
Most consecutive errorless games .... 10 in 1979
Fewest errors.. 122 in 1985 (162 games)
122 in 1987 (162 games)
Most double plays..................................... 191 in 1986 (162 games)
Fewest double plays................................... 143 in 1984 (162 games)
Most passed balls.. 22 in 1985 (162 games)
Fewest passed balls....................................... 4 in 1987 (162 games)
Highest fielding average .... .980 in 1985 (162 games)
.980 in 1987 (162 games)

Lowest fielding average ... .975 in 1986 (162 games)
Highest home attendance ... 1,338,511 in 1977
Highest road attendance ... 1,795,683 in 1987
Most games won ... 78 in 1987
Most games lost ... 104 in 1978
Most game won, month ... 16, June 1979
16, June 1985
Most games lost, month ... 22, August 1977
Games won, league ... 719 in 11 years
Games lost, league ... 1008 in 11 years
Highest percentage games won ... .481 in 1987 (won 78, lost 84)
Lowest percentage games won ... .350 in 1978 (won 56, lost 104)
Most shutouts won ... 11 in 1982
Most shutouts lost ... 15 in 1978, 1983
Most 1-0 games won ... 3 in 1979
Most 1-0 games lost ... 4 in 1980
Most consecutive games won ... 8 in 1985
Most consecutive games lost ... 12 in 1980
Most times league champions ... 0
Most last place finishes ... 4
Most runs, game ... 16 vs. New York, July 11, 1979
Most runs, game, by opponent ... 19 by Toronto, June 26, 1983
Most runs, shutout game ... 14 vs. California, August 7, 1987
Most runs, shutout game, by opponent ... 15 by Minnesota, July 10, 1977
Most runs, inning ... 9 vs. California, April 6, 1979, second inning
9 vs. New York, July 11, 1979, first inning
9 vs. Chicago, September 15, 1980, third inning
Longest 1-0 game won ... None over nine innings
Longest 1-0 game lost ... 10 innings vs. California, July 25, 1984
Most hits, nine-inning game ... 20 vs. Cleveland, August 30, 1981
20 vs. Texas, June 20, 1985
Most hits, extra-inning game ... 24 vs. Boston, September 3, 1981, 20 innings
Most home runs, game ... 7 vs. Oakland, April 11, 1985
Most consecutive games, one or more homers ... 9 (10 homers), 1986
9 (9 homers), 1986
9 (17 homers), 1987
9 (15 homers), 1987
Most total bases, game ... 36 vs. Oakland, April 11, 1985
Largest crowd, day game ... 47,353 vs. Boston, May 15, 1977
Largest crowd, doubleheader ... 32,597 vs California, August 12, 1985
Largest crowd, night game ... 57,762 vs. California, April 6, 1977
Largest crowd, home opener ... 57,762 vs. California, April 6, 1977

Texas Rangers

Yearly Finishes

West Division

Year—Position	W.	L.	Pct.	*G.B.	Manager
1972—Sixth	54	100	.351	38½	Theodore Williams
1973—Sixth	57	105	.352	37	D. Herzog, B. Martin
1974—Second	84	76	.525	5	Alfred (Billy) Martin
1975—Third	79	83	.488	19	B. Martin, F. Lucchesi
1976—Fourth†	76	86	.469	14	Frank Lucchesi
1977—Second	94	68	.580	8	Lucchesi, Stanky, Ryan, Hunter
1978—Second†	87	75	.537	5	B. Hunter, P. Corrales
1979—Third	83	79	.512	5	Patrick Corrales
1980—Fourth	76	85	.472	20½	Patrick Corrales
1981—2nd/3rd.	57	48	.543	‡	Donald Zimmer
1982—Sixth	64	98	.395	29	D. Zimmer, D. Johnson
1983—Third	77	85	.475	22	Doug Rader
1984—Seventh	69	92	.429	14½	Doug Rader
1985—Seventh	62	99	.385	28½	D. Rader, R. Valentine
1986—Second	87	75	.537	5	Robert Valentine
1987—Sixth†	75	87	.463	10	Robert Valentine

*Games behind winner. †Tied for position. ‡First half 33-22; second 24-26.

Individual Records (1972 To Date)

Batting

Most years, non-pitcher ... 10, James H. Sundberg
Most games ... 163, Albert Oliver, 1980
Most games, league ... 1398, James H. Sundberg
Most at-bats ... 670, David G. Bell, 162 games, 1979
Most at-bats, league ... 4446, James H. Sundberg
Most runs ... 105, Oddibe McDowell, 154 games, 1986
Most runs, league ... 582, Colbert D. Harrah
Most hits ... 210, John M. Rivers, 147 games, 1980
Most hits, league ... 1125, James H. Sundberg
Most singles ... 165, John M. Rivers, 147 games, 1980
Most singles, league ... 856, James H. Sundberg
Most doubles ... 43, Albert Oliver, 163 games, 1980
Most doubles, league ... 193, David G. Bell
Most triples ... 10, Ruben A. Sierra, 113 games, 1986
Most triples, league ... 26, James H. Sundberg
Most homers, righthander ... 32, Larry A. Parrish, 152 games, 1987
Most homers, switch-hitter ... 30, Ruben A. Sierra, 158 games, 1987
Most homers, lefthander ... 23, Peter M. O'Brien, 156 games, 1986
23, Peter M. O'Brien, 159 games, 1987
Most homers, league, righthander ... 142, Larry A. Parrish
Most homers, league, lefthander ... 98, Peter M. O'Brien
Most homers, league, switch-hitter ... 46, Ruben A. Sierra
Most homers, rookie ... 30, Peter J. Incaviglia, 153 games, 1986
Most homers at home ... 17, Peter J. Incaviglia, 1986
Most homers on road ... 20, Jeffrey A. Burroughs, 1973
Most grand slams ... 3, Jeffrey A. Burroughs, 151 games, 1973
3, Larry A. Parrish, 128 games, 1982
Most grand slams, league ... 5, Jeffrey A. Burroughs
Most homers, month ... 10, David A. Hostetler, June, 1982
Most total bases ... 315, Albert Oliver, 163 games, 1980
Most total bases, league ... 1666, Colbert D. Harrah
Most long hits ... 69, Ruben A. Sierra, 158 games, 1987
Most long hits, league ... 317, Colbert D. Harrah
Most extra bases on long hits ... 133, Ruben A. Sierra, 158 games, 1987
Most extra bases on long hits, league ... 581, Larry A. Parrish
Most sacrifice hits ... 40, Dagoberto B. Campaneris, 150 games, 1977
Most sacrifice flies ... 12, Jeffrey A. Burroughs, 152 games, 1974
12, Ruben A. Sierra, 158 games, 1987
Most stolen bases ... 52, Elliott T. Wills, 157 games, 1978
Most stolen bases, league ... 161, Elliott T. Wills
Most caught stealing ... 20, Dagoberto B. Campaneris, 150 games, 1977
20, Bobby L. Bonds, 130 games, 1978
Most bases on balls ... 113, Colbert D. Harrah, 126 games, 1985
Most bases on balls, league ... 668, Colbert D. Harrah
Most strikeouts ... 185, Peter J. Incaviglia, 153 games, 1986
Most strikeouts, league ... 690, James H. Sundberg
Most hit by pitch ... 10, Colbert D. Harrah, 159 games, 1977
Most runs batted in ... 118, Jeffrey A. Burroughs, 152 games, 1974
Most runs batted in, league ... 546, Colbert D. Harrah
Most game-winning RBIs ... 17, Larry A. Parrish, 145 games, 1983
Most consecutive games with RBI ... 10, Jeffrey A. Burroughs, 1974 (20 RBIs)
Highest batting average ... .333, John M. Rivers, 147 games, 1980
Highest batting average, league ... .319, Albert Oliver
Highest slugging average ... .509, Larry A. Parrish, 129 games, 1986
Highest slugging average, league ... .465, Albert Oliver
Longest batting streak ... 24 games, John M. Rivers, 1980
Most grounded into double play ... 24, David G. Bell, 156 games, 1983
Fewest grounded into double play ... 4, John M. Rivers, 147 games, 1980

Pitching

Most years ... 8, Charles O. Hough
Most games ... 85, Mitchell S. Williams, 1987
Most games, league ... 248, Charles O. Hough
Most games started ... 41, James B. Bibby, 1974
41, Ferguson A. Jenkins, 1974
Most complete games ... 29, Ferguson A. Jenkins, 1974
Most games finished ... 63, Greg A. Harris, 1986
Most innings ... 328, Ferguson A. Jenkins, 1974
Most innings, league ... 1655, Charles O. Hough
Most games won ... 25, Ferguson A. Jenkins, 1974
Most games won, league ... 102, Charles O. Hough
Most games lost ... 19, James B. Bibby, 1974
Most games lost, league ... 82, Charles O. Hough
Most 20 victory seasons ... 1, Ferguson A. Jenkins
Highest winning percentage ... .692, Ferguson A. Jenkins (18-8), 1978
Longest winning streak ... 8 games, Danny W. Darwin, 1980
Longest losing streak ... 9 games, David E. Clyde, 1974
Most saves ... 29, James L. Kern, 1979
Most bases on balls ... 143, Robert A. Witt, 1986
Most bases on balls, league ... 625, Charles O. Hough
Most strikeouts ... 225, Ferguson A. Jenkins, 1974
Most strikeouts, league ... 1070, Charles O. Hough
Most strikeouts, game ... 15, James B. Bibby, August 30, 1973, 10⅔ innings
14, Rikalbert Blyleven, July 22, 1977
14, Robert A. Witt, July 6, 1986
Most shutouts ... 6, Ferguson A. Jenkins, 1974
6, Rikalbert Blyleven, 1976
Most shutouts, league ... 17, Ferguson A. Jenkins
Most 1-0 shutouts won ... 4, Ferguson A. Jenkins, 1974
4, Rikalbert Blyleven, 1976
Most runs ... 159, Charles O. Hough, 1987
Most earned runs ... 139, James B. Bibby, 1974
Most hits ... 286, Ferguson A. Jenkins, 1974
Most hit batsmen ... 19, Charles O. Hough, 1987
Most wild pitches ... 22, Robert A. Witt, 1986
Most home runs ... 40, Ferguson A. Jenkins, 1979
Most sacrifice hits ... 16, James H. Umbarger, 1976
Most sacrifice flies ... 14, Charles O. Hough, 1987
Lowest ERA ... 2.17, Michael G. Paul, 162 innings, 1972

Club Records

Most players ... 43 in 1985 (161 games)
Fewest players ... 35 in 1984 (161 games)
Most games ... 163 in 1980, 1983
Most at-bats ... 5690 in 1980 (163 games)
Most runs ... 823 in 1987 (162 games)
Most opponents' runs ... 849 in 1987 (162 games)
Most hits ... 1616 in 1980 (163 games)
Most singles ... 1202 in 1980 (163 games)
Most doubles ... 265 in 1977 (162 games)
Most triples ... 43 in 1986 (162 games)
Most homers ... 194 in 1987 (162 games)
Fewest homers ... 56 in 1972
Most homers at Arlington Stad., home & opp. ... 204 in 1987
Most grand slams ... 5 in 1975, 1980, 1987
Most pinch home runs ... 7 in 1980
Most long hits ... 493 in 1987 (162 games)
Most extra bases on long hits ... 916 in 1987 (162 games)
Most total bases ... 2394 in 1987 (162 games)

Toby Harrah

Most sacrifice hits	116 in 1977 (162 games)
Most sacrifice flies	59 in 1979 (162 games)
Most stolen bases	196 in 1978 (162 games)
Most caught stealing	91 in 1978 (162 games)
Most bases on balls	624 in 1978 (162 games)
Most strikeouts	1088 in 1986 (162 games)
Most hit by pitch	39 in 1977 (162 games)
Most runs batted in	772 in 1977 (162 games)
Most game-winning RBIs	80 in 1986 (162 games)
Highest batting average	.284 in 1980 (163 games)
Highest slugging average	.430 in 1987 (162 games)
Most grounded into double play	156 in 1980 (163 games)
Most left on bases	1215 in 1976 (162 games)
Fewest left on bases	1038 in 1986 (162 games)
Most .300 hitters	3 in 1980
Most putouts	4417 in 1977 (162 games)
Most assists	1980 in 1975 (162 games)
Fewest assists	1655 in 1986 (162 games)
Most chances accepted	6377 in 1975 (162 games)
Most errors	191 in 1975 (162 games)
Fewest errors	113 in 1983 (163 games)
Most errorless games	79 in 1977 (162 games)
	79 in 1986 (162 games)
Most consecutive errorless games	7 in 1977 (162 games)
Most double plays	173 in 1975 (162 games)
Most passed balls	73 in 1987 (162 games)
Fewest passed balls	5 in 1977 (162 games)
Highest fielding average	.982 in 1983 (163 games)
Lowest fielding average	.971 in 1975 (162 games)
Highest home attendance	1,763,053 in 1987
Highest road attendance	1,796,351 in 1987
Most games won	94 in 1977
Most games lost	105 in 1973
Most games won, month	21, Sept. 1978
Most games lost, month	24, August 1973
Highest percentage games won	.580 in 1977 (won 94, lost 68)
Lowest percentage games won	.351 in 1972 (won 54, lost 100)
Games won, league	1181 in 16 years
Games lost, league	1341 in 16 years
Most shutouts won	17 in 1977
Most shutouts lost	27 in 1972
Most 1-0 games won	5 in 1971, 1975, 1976
Most 1-0 games lost	7 in 1976
Most consecutive games won	8 in 1976, 1979
Most consecutive games lost	15 in 1972
Most times league champions	0
Most last place finishes	2
Most runs, game	20 vs. New York, July 19, 1987
Most runs, game by opponent	17 by Oakland, May 10, 1973
Most runs, inning	12 vs. Oakland, July 3, 1983, fifteenth inning
Most runs, shutout game	14 vs. Oakland, July 26, 1977
Most runs, shutout game, by opponent	14 by Chicago, April 18, 1972
	14 by Chicago, September 4, 1973
Most runs, doubleheader shutout	No performance
Longest 1-0 game won	14 innings vs. Boston, April 17, 1983
Longest 1-0 games lost	11 innings vs. Chicago, June 2, 1976
Most hits, game	22 vs. Cleveland, May 12, 1986
	22 vs. Baltimore, May 14, 1983, 11 innings
	22 vs. New York, July 19, 1987
Most home runs, game	7 vs. Minnesota, September 13, 1986
Most consecutive games, one or more homers	13 (18 homers), 1987
Most total bases, game	43 vs. Minnesota, September 13, 1986
Largest crowd, day game	40,078 vs. New York, April 8, 1978
Largest crowd, doubleheader	42,163 vs. Detroit, July 10, 1982
Largest crowd, night game	43,705 vs. Toronto, July 23, 1983
Largest crowd, home opener	42,415 vs. Milwaukee, April 10, 1987

Toronto Blue Jays

Yearly Finishes
East Division

Year—Position	W.	L.	Pct.	*G.B.	Manager
1977—Seventh..	54	107	.335	45½	Roy Hartsfield
1978—Seventh..	59	102	.366	40	Roy Hartsfield
1979—Seventh..	53	109	.327	50½	Roy Hartsfield
1980—Seventh..	67	95	.414	36	Bobby Mattick
1981—7th/7th..	37	69	.349	†	Bobby Mattick
1982—Sixth‡	78	84	.481	17	Robert Cox
1983—Fourth....	89	73	.549	9	Robert Cox
1984—Second...	89	73	.549	15	Robert Cox
1985—First§.....	99	62	.615	+ 2	Robert Cox
1986—Fourth....	86	76	.531	9½	James Williams
1987—Second..	96	66	.593	2	James Williams

*Games behind winner. †First half 16-42; second 21-27. ‡Tied for position. §Lost Championship Series.

Individual Records (1977 To Date)
Batting

Most years, non-pitcher	10, L. Ernest Whitt
Most games	163, O. Antonio Fernandez, 1986
Most games, league	1129, Lloyd A. Moseby
Most at-bats	687, O. Antonio Fernandez, 163 games, 1986
Most at-bats, league	4150, Lloyd A. Moseby
Most runs	111, George A. Bell, 156 games, 1987

Most runs, league	619, Lloyd A. Moseby
Most hits	213, O. Antonio Fernandez, 163 games, 1986
Most hits, league	1095, Lloyd A. Moseby
Most singles	161, O. Antonio Fernandez, 163 games, 1986
Most singles, league	798, Damaso D. Garcia
Most doubles	39, George A. Bell, 159 games, 1982
Most doubles, league	200, Lloyd A. Moseby
Most triples	15, Alfredo C. Griffin, 155 games, 1980
	15, David S. Collins, 128 games, 1984
	15, Lloyd A. Moseby, 158 games, 1984
Most triples, league	50, Alfredo C. Griffin
	50, Lloyd A. Moseby
Most homers, lefthander	30, John C. Mayberry, 149 games, 1980
Most homers, lefthander, league	128, Lloyd A. Moseby
Most homers, righthander	47, George A. Bell, 156 games, 1987
Most homers, righthander, league	156, Jesse L. Barfield
Most homers, rookie	20, Frederick S. McGriff, 107 games, 1987
Most homers, month	11, George A. Bell, May, 1987
	11, George A. Bell, June, 1987
Most homers at home	22, Jesse L. Barfield, 1983
Most homers on road	28, George A. Bell, 1987
Most grand slams	2, Roy L. Howell, 138 games, 1979
	2, George A. Bell, 157 games, 1985
	2, George A. Bell, 156 games, 1987
Most grand slams, league	5, George A. Bell
Most total bases	369, George A. Bell, 156 games, 1987
Most total bases, league	1779, Lloyd A. Moseby
Most long hits	83, George A. Bell, 156 games, 1987

Hard-throwing righthander Jim Clancy

Most long hits, league ....378, Lloyd A. Moseby
Most extra bases on long hits ....181, George A. Bell, 156 games, 1987
Most extra bases on long hits, league ....684, Lloyd A. Moseby
Most sacrifice hits ....19, Luis Gomez, 153 games, 1978
Most sacrifice flies ....9, John A. Martinez, 102 games, 1984
                                 9, George A. Bell, 156 games, 1987
Most stolen bases ....60, David S. Collins, 128 games, 1984
Most stolen bases, league ....200, Lloyd A. Moseby
Most caught stealing ....23, Alfredo C. Griffin, 155 games, 1980
Most bases on balls ....78, Lloyd A. Moseby, 158 games, 1984
                                        78, Willie C. Upshaw, 155 games, 1986
Most bases on balls, league ....421, Lloyd A. Moseby
Most strikeouts ....146, Jesse L. Barfield, 158 games, 1986
Most strikeouts, league ....821, Lloyd A. Moseby
Fewest strikeouts ....21, Robert M. Bailor, 154 games, 1978
Most hit by pitch ....9, David S. Collins, 128 games, 1984
                                        9, Damaso D. Garcia, 152 games, 1984
Most runs batted in.......................134, George A. Bell, 156 games, 1987
Most runs batted in, league ....566, Lloyd A. Moseby
Most game-winning RBIs...............16, Willie C. Upshaw, 160 games, 1983
                                        16, George A. Bell, 156 games, 1987
Highest batting average .... .322, O. Antonio Fernandez, 146 games, 1987
Highest batting average, league............................... .302, O. Antonio Fernandez
Highest slugging average .... .605, George A. Bell, 156 games, 1987
Highest slugging average, league............................ .513, George A. Bell
Longest batting streak ....21 games, Damaso D. Garcia, 1983
                                        21 games, Lloyd A. Moseby, 1983
Most grounded into double play ....21, Ricardo A. J. Carty, 132 games, 1979
Fewest grounded into double play ....5, Alfredo C. Griffin, 162 games, 1983
                                        5, Willie C. Upshaw, 155 games, 1986

Pitching

Most years..11, James Clancy
Most games...............................89, Mark A. Eichhorn, 1987
Most games, league.......................................316, James Clancy
Most games started.......................40, James Clancy, 1982
Most games started, league ....314, James Clancy

Most complete games...................................19, David A. Stieb, 1982
Most complete games, league ....88, David A. Stieb
Most games finished ....62, Thomas A. Henke, 1987
Most innings.................................288⅓, David A. Stieb, 1982
Most innings, league ....2044⅓, David A. Stieb
Most games won...............................17, David A. Stieb, 1982
                                        17, David A. Stieb, 1983
                                        17, Doyle L. Alexander, 1984
                                        17, Doyle L. Alexander, 1985
                                        17, James E. Key, 1987
Most games won, league ....117, James Clancy
Most games lost ....18, Theodore J. Garvin, 1977
                                        18, Phillip L. Huffman, 1979
Most games lost, league ....127, James Clancy
Longest winning streak ....11 games, Dennis P. Lamp, 1985
Longest losing streak ....10 games, Theodore J. Garvin, 1977, 1978
                                        10 games, Paul T. Mirabella, 1980
Highest winning percentage........................ .739, Doyle L. Alexander (17-6), 1984
Most saves...............................34, Thomas A. Henke, 1987
Most bases on balls ....128, James Clancy, 1980
Most bases on balls, league ....767, James Clancy
Most strikeouts ....198, David A. Stieb, 1984
Most strikeouts, league ....1184, David A. Stieb
Most strikeouts, game ....12, Peter D. Vuckovich, June 26, 1977
Most shutouts ....5, David A. Stieb, 1982
Most shutouts, league ....22, David A. Stieb
Most 1-0 shutouts won ....2, James Clancy, 1980
Most runs ....143, David L. Lemanczyk, 1977
Most earned runs ....125, James Clancy, 1984
Most hits..278, David L. Lemanczyk, 1977
Most hit batsmen ....15, David A. Stieb, 1986
Most wild pitches ....20, David L. Lemanczyk, 1977
Most home runs ....33, Theodore J. Garvin, 1977
Most sacrifice hits ....16, Theodore J. Garvin, 1977
Most sacrifice flies ....12, James Clancy, 1983
Lowest ERA ....2.48, David A. Stieb, 265 innings, 1985

Club Records

Most players	40 in 1979 (162 games)
	40 in 1985 (161 games)
Fewest players	33 in 1983 (162 games)
Most games	163 in 1984, 1986
Most at-bats	5716 in 1986 (163 games)
Fewest at-bats	5418 in 1977 (161 games)
Most runs	845 in 1987 (162 games)
Fewest runs	590 in 1978 (161 games)
Most opponent's runs	862 in 1979 (162 games)
Fewest opponent's runs	588 in 1985 (162 games)
Most hits	1555 in 1984 (163 games)
Fewest hits	1358 in 1978 (161 games)
Most singles	1069 in 1984 (163 games)
Most doubles	285 in 1986 (163 games)
Most triples	68 in 1984 (163 games)
Most homers	215 in 1987 (162 games)
Fewest homers	95 in 1979
Most homers at Exhibition Stad., home & opp.	185 in 1983
Most grand slams	3 in 1979 (162 games)
	3 in 1983 (162 games)
	3 in 1985 (161 games)
	3 in 1986 (163 games)
	3 in 1987 (162 games)
Most pinch home runs	6 in 1984 (163 games)
Most total bases	2512 in 1987 (162 games)
Most long hits	530 in 1987 (162 games)
Most extra bases on long hits	998 in 1987 (162 games)
Most sacrifice hits	81 in 1977 (161 games)
Most sacrifice flies	54 in 1983 (162 games)
Most stolen bases	193 in 1984 (163 games)
Most caught stealing	81 in 1982 (162 games)
Most bases on balls	555 in 1987 (162 games)
Fewest bases on balls	415 in 1982 (162 games)
Most strikeouts	970 in 1987 (162 games)
Fewest strikeouts	645 in 1978 (160 games)
Most hit by pitch	52 in 1984 (163 games)
Most runs batted in	790 in 1987 (162 games)
Most game-winning RBIs	90 in 1985 (161 games)
	90 in 1987 (162 games)
Highest batting average	.277 in 1983 (162 games)
Lowest batting average	.250 in 1978 (161 games)
Highest slugging average	.446 in 1987 (162 games)
Lowest slugging average	.359 in 1978 (161 games)
Most grounded into double play	156 in 1977 (161 games)
Fewest grounded into double play	91 in 1984 (163 games)
Most left on bases	1177 in 1984 (163 games)
Fewest left on bases	1064 in 1979 (162 games)
Most .300 hitters	3 in 1983

Most putouts	4428 in 1986 (163 games)
Fewest putouts	4251 in 1979 (162 games)
Most assists	1939 in 1980 (162 games)
Fewest assists	1637 in 1983 (162 games)
Most chances accepted	6337 in 1980 (162 games)
Fewest chances accepted	5973 in 1983 (162 games)
Most errors	164 in 1977 (161 games)
Fewest errors	100 in 1986 (163 games)
Most errorless games	96 in 1986 (163 games)
Most consecutive errorless games	11 in 1986
Most double plays	206 in 1980 (162 games)
Fewest double plays	133 in 1977 (161 games)
Most passed balls	16 in 1978 (161 games)
Fewest passed balls	3 in 1985 (161 games)
Highest fielding average	.984 in 1986 (163 games)
Lowest fielding average	.974 in 1977 (161 games)
Highest home attendance	2,778,429 in 1987
Highest road attendance	1,959,280 in 1987
Most games won	99 in 1985
Most games lost	109 in 1979
Most games won, month	19, May 1984
	19, Sept. 1987
Most games lost, month	23, May 1979
Highest percentage games won	.615 in 1985 (won 99, lost 62)
Lowest percentage games won	.327 in 1979 (won 53, lost 109)
Games won, league	807 in 11 years
Games lost, league	916 in 11 years
Most shutouts won	13 in 1982
Most shutouts lost	20 in 1981
Most 1-0 games won	5 in 1980
Most 1-0 games lost	3 in 1979
Most consecutive games won	11 in 1987
Most consecutive games lost	12 in 1981
Most times league champions	0
Most last place finishes	3
Most runs, game	24 vs. Baltimore, June 26, 1978
Most runs, game, by opponent	24 by California, August 25, 1979
Most runs, shutout game	12 vs. California, May 18, 1987
Most runs, shutout game, by opponent	15 by N.Y., Sept. 25, 1977, first game
Most runs, inning	11 vs. Seattle, July 20, 1984, ninth inning
Longest 1-0 game won	12 innings vs. Boston, September 26, 1986
Longest 1-0 game lost	15 innings vs. Oakland, July 27, 1986
Most hits, game	24 vs. Baltimore, June 26, 1978
Most home runs, game	10 vs. Baltimore, September 14, 1987
Most consecutive games, one or more home runs	13 (17 homers), 1985
Most total bases, game	53 vs. Baltimore, September 14, 1987
Largest crowd, day game	47,828 vs. New York, July 1, 1987
Largest crowd, doubleheader	45,102 vs. New York, August 2, 1983
Largest crowd, night game	47,686 vs. New York, October 4, 1985
Largest crowd, home opener	44,649 vs. Chicago, April 7, 1977

Washington Senators
(Original Club)

Yearly Finishes

Year—Position	W.	L.	Pct.	*G.B.	Manager
1901—Sixth	61	72	.459	20½	James Manning
1902—Sixth	61	75	.449	22	Thomas Loftus
1903—Eighth	43	94	.314	47½	Thomas Loftus
1904—Eighth	38	113	.251	55½	Patrick Donovan
1905—Seventh	64	87	.421	29½	J. Garland Stahl
1906—Seventh	55	95	.367	37½	J. Garland Stahl
1907—Eighth	49	102	.325	43½	Joseph Cantillon
1908—Seventh	67	85	.441	22½	Joseph Cantillon
1909—Eighth	42	110	.276	56	Joseph Cantillon
1910—Seventh	66	85	.437	36½	James McAleer
1911—Seventh	64	90	.416	38½	James McAleer
1912—Second	91	61	.599	14	Clark Griffith
1913—Second	90	64	.584	6½	Clark Griffith
1914—Third	81	73	.526	19	Clark Griffith
1915—Fourth	85	68	.556	17	Clark Griffith
1916—Seventh	76	77	.497	14½	Clark Griffith
1917—Fifth	74	79	.484	25½	Clark Griffith
1918—Third	72	56	.563	4	Clark Griffith
1919—Seventh	56	84	.400	32	Clark Griffith
1920—Sixth	68	84	.447	29	Clark Griffith
1921—Fourth	80	73	.523	18	George McBride
1922—Sixth	69	85	.448	25	Clyde Milan
1923—Fourth	75	78	.490	23½	Owen (Donie) Bush
1924—First	92	62	.597	+ 2	Stanley (Bucky) Harris
1925—First	96	55	.636	+ 8½	Stanley (Bucky) Harris
1926—Fourth	81	69	.540	8	Stanley (Bucky) Harris
1927—Third	85	69	.552	25	Stanley (Bucky) Harris
1928—Fourth	75	79	.487	26	Stanley (Bucky) Harris
1929—Fifth	71	81	.467	34	Walter Johnson
1930—Second	94	60	.610	8	Walter Johnson
1931—Third	92	62	.597	16	Walter Johnson
1932—Third	93	61	.604	14	Walter Johnson
1933—First	99	53	.651	+ 7	Joseph Cronin
1934—Seventh	66	86	.434	34	Joseph Cronin
1935—Sixth	67	86	.438	27	Stanley (Bucky) Harris
1936—Fourth	82	71	.536	20	Stanley (Bucky) Harris
1937—Sixth	73	80	.477	28½	Stanley (Bucky) Harris
1938—Fifth	75	76	.497	23½	Stanley (Bucky) Harris
1939—Sixth	65	87	.428	41½	Stanley (Bucky) Harris
1940—Seventh	64	90	.416	26	Stanley (Bucky) Harris
1941—Sixth†	70	84	.455	31	Stanley (Bucky) Harris
1942—Seventh	62	89	.411	39½	Stanley (Bucky) Harris
1943—Second	84	69	.549	13½	Oswald Bluege
1944—Eighth	64	90	.416	25	Oswald Bluege
1945—Second	87	67	.565	1½	Oswald Bluege
1946—Fourth	76	78	.494	28	Oswald Bluege
1947—Seventh	64	90	.416	33	Oswald Bluege
1948—Seventh	56	97	.366	40	Joseph Kuhel
1949—Eighth	50	104	.325	47	Joseph Kuhel
1950—Fifth	67	87	.435	31	Stanley (Bucky) Harris
1951—Seventh	62	92	.403	36	Stanley (Bucky) Harris
1952—Fifth	78	76	.506	17	Stanley (Bucky) Harris
1953—Fifth	76	76	.500	23½	Stanley (Bucky) Harris
1954—Sixth	66	88	.429	45	Stanley (Bucky) Harris
1955—Eighth	53	101	.344	43	Charles (Chuck) Dressen
1956—Seventh	59	95	.383	38	Charles (Chuck) Dressen
1957—Eighth	55	99	.357	43	C. Dressen, H. Lavagetto
1958—Eighth	61	93	.396	31	Harry (Cookie) Lavagetto
1959—Eighth	63	91	.409	31	Harry (Cookie) Lavagetto
1960—Seventh	73	81	.474	24	Harry (Cookie) Lavagetto

*Games behind winner.   †Tied for position.

Individual Records (1901 To 1960)
Batting

Most years, non-pitcher	19, Edgar C. Rice
Most games	158, Edward C. Foster 1916
Most games, league	2307, Edgar C. Rice
Most at-bats	668, John K. Lewis, 156 games, 1937
Most at-bats, league	8934, Edgar C. Rice
Most runs	127, Joseph E. Cronin, 154 games, 1930
Most runs, league	1467, Edgar C. Rice
Most hits	227, Edgar C. Rice, 152 games, 1925
Most hits, league	2889, Edgar C. Rice
Most singles	182, Edgar C. Rice, 152 games, 1925
Most doubles	51, James B. Vernon, 148 games, 1946
Most doubles, league	478, Edgar C. Rice
Most triples	20, Leon A. Goslin, 150 games, 1925
Most triples, league	183, Edgar C. Rice
Most homers, righthander	42, Roy E. Sievers, 152 games, 1957
	42, Harmon C. Killebrew, 153 games, 1959

190

Most homers, lefthander ....20 James B. Vernon, 151 games, 1954
Most homers, rookie ....30, W. Robert Allison, 150 games, 1959
Most homers, at home..26, Roy E. Sievers, 1957
Most homers, on road..21, Roy E. Sievers, 1958
Most homers, one month..................................15, Harmon C. Killebrew, May, 1959
Most homers, league..180, Roy E. Sievers
Most grand slams ....2, held by many players
                    last player, Roy E. Sievers, 1957
Most grand slams, league..4, Roy E. Sievers
Most total bases ....331, Roy E. Sievers, 152 games, 1957
Most total bases, league ....3832, Edgar C. Rice
Most long hits..........................76, Stanley O. Spence, 152 games, 1946
Most extra bases on long hits..........159, Roy E. Sievers, 152 games, 1957
Most sacrifices (S.H. and S.F.) ....52, Robert S. Ganley, 150 games, 1908
Most sacrifice hits..........................36, Hunter B. Hill, 103 games, 1905
Most sacrifice flies..........................16, Charles A. Gandil, 145 games, 1914
Most stolen bases..........................88, J. Clyde Milan, 154 games, 1912
Most stolen bases, league..................................494, J. Clyde Milan
Most caught stealing..........................30, Edgar C. Rice, 153 games, 1920
Most bases on balls..........................151, Edward F. Yost, 152 games, 1956
Most strikeouts ....138, James R. Lemon, 146 games, 1956
Fewest strikeouts ....9, Edgar C. Rice, 150 games, 1929
Most hit by pitch ....24, Norman A. Elberfeld, 127 games, 1911
Most runs batted in..........................129, Leon A. Goslin, 154 games, 1924
Most runs batted in, league..................................1044, Edgar C. Rice
Highest batting average..................379, Leon A. Goslin, 135 games, 1923
Highest batting average, league ....323, Edgar C. Rice
                     .323, Leon A. Goslin
Highest slugging average............................614, Leon A. Goslin, 135 games, 1928
Longest batting streak....................................33 games, Henry E. Manush, 1933
Most grounded into double play ....25, Samuel J. Dente, 155 games, 1950
Fewest grounded into double play ....5, George W. Case, 154 games, 1940
                   5, George W. Case, 153 games, 1941
                   5, Stanley O. Spence, 153 games, 1944
                   5, Edward F. Yost, 155 games, 1954

Pitching

Most years..21, Walter P. Johnson
Most games..64, Fred Marberry, 1926
Most games, league..802, Walter P. Johnson
Most games started ....42, Walter P. Johnson, 1910
Most games, started, league ....666, Walter P. Johnson
Most complete games..................................38, Walter P. Johnson, 1910
Most complete games, league ....531, Walter P. Johnson
Most games finished..................................47, Fred Marberry, 1926
Most innings..................................374, Walter P. Johnson, 1910
Most innings, league..........................5923, Walter P. Johnson
Most games won..................................36, Walter P. Johnson, 1913
Most games won, league..........................416, Walter P. Johnson
Most 20-victory seasons..........................12, Walter P. Johnson
Highest winning percentage......................837, Walter P. Johnson (36-7), 1913
Longest winning streak....................16 games, Walter P. Johnson, 1912
Longest losing streak ....19 games, Robert Groom, 1909
Most games lost ....26, John Townsend, 1904
                 26, Robert B. Groom, 1909
Most games lost, league..........................279, Walter P. Johnson
Most bases on balls ....146, Louis N. Newsom, 1936
Most bases on balls, league ....1353, Walter P. Johnson
Most strikeouts ....313, Walter P. Johnson, 1910
Most strikeouts, league ....3508, Walter P. Johnson
Most strikeouts, game................................15, Camilo A. Pascual, April 18, 1960
Most shutouts ....12, Walter P. Johnson, 1913
Most 1-0 shutouts won..............5, Walter P. Johnson, 1913 and 1919
Most shutouts, league ....113, Walter P. Johnson
Most runs..................................172, Albert L. Orth, 1903
Most earned runs..................................144, James B. DeShong, 1937
Most hits..................................328, Emil J. Leonard, 1940
Most hit batsmen..................................20, Walter P. Johnson, 1923
Most wild pitches..................................21, Walter P. Johnson, 1910
Most home runs..................................43, Pedro Ramos, 1957
Lowest ERA ....1.14, Walter P. Johnson, 346 innings, 1913

Club Records

Most players.. 44 in 1909
Fewest players.. 25 in 1908, 1917
Most games.. 159 in 1916
Most at-bats.. 5592 in 1935 (154 games)
Most runs.. 892 in 1930 (154 games)
Fewest runs.. 380 in 1909 (156 games)
Most hits.. 1620 in 1930 (154 games)
Fewest hits.. 1112 in 1909 (156 games)
Most singles.. 1209 in 1935 (154 games)
Most doubles.. 308 in 1931 (156 games)
Most triples.. 100 in 1932 (154 games)
Most homers.. 163 in 1959 (154 games)
Fewest homers (154 or 162-game schedule).... 4 in 1917
Most homers at Griffith Stadium, home & opp... 158 in 1956
Most grand slams.. 8 in 1938
Most pinch home runs.. 4 in 1955, 1960
Most total bases.. 2287 in 1930 (154 games)
Most long hits.. 464 in 1932 (154 games)
Most extra bases on long hits .... 732 in 1960 (154 games)
Most sacrifices (S. H. and S. F.)................................ 232 in 1923 (155 games)
                 232 in 1924 (156 games)
Most sacrifice hits.. 135 in 1906 (151 games)
Most sacrifice flies.. 42 in 1954 (155 games)
Most stolen bases.. 291 in 1913 (155 games)
Most bases on balls.. 690 in 1956 (155 games)

Roy Sievers

Most strikeouts.. 883 in 1960 (154 games)
Fewest strikeouts.. 359 in 1927 (157 games)
Most hit by pitch.. 80 in 1911 (154 games)
Fewest hit by pitch.. 8 in 1947 (154 games)
Most runs batted in.. 822 in 1936 (153 games)
Highest batting average .... .303 in 1925 (152 games)
Lowest batting average .... .223 in 1909 (156 games)
Highest slugging average .... .426 in 1930 (154 games)
Lowest slugging average .... .287 in 1910 (157 games)
Most grounded into double play .... 145 in 1951 (154 games)
Fewest grounded into double play .... 94 in 1943 (153 games)
Most left on bases .... 1305 in 1935 (154 games)
Fewest left on bases .... 998 in 1959 (154 games)
Most .300 hitters .... 9 in 1925
Most putouts .... 4291 in 1916 (159 games)
Fewest putouts .... 3944 in 1906 (151 games)
Most assists .... 2232 in 1911 (154 games)
Fewest assists .... 1587 in 1951 (154 games)
Most chances accepted .... 6363 in 1910 (157 games)
Fewest chances accepted .... 5672 in 1953 (152 games)
Most errors .... 325 in 1901 (134 games)
Fewest errors .... 118 in 1958 (156 games)
Most consecutive errorless games .... 9 in 1952
Most double plays .... 186 in 1935 (154 games)
Fewest double plays .... 93 in 1912 (154 games)
Most passed balls .... 40 in 1945 (156 games)
Fewest passed balls .... 3 in 1927 (157 games)
Highest fielding average .... .980 in 1958 (156 games)
Lowest fielding average .... .936 in 1902 (138 games)

Highest home attendance	1,027,216 in 1946
Highest road attendance	1,055,171 in 1948
Most games won	99 in 1933
Most games lost	113 in 1904
Most games won, month	24, August 1945
Most games lost, month	29, July 1909
Highest percentage games won	.651 in 1933 (won 99, lost 53)
Lowest percentage games won	.252 in 1904 (won 38, lost 113)
Games won, league	4223 in 60 years
Games lost, league	4864 in 60 years
Most shutouts won	25 in 1914
Most shutouts lost	29 in 1909
Most 1-0 games won	11 in 1914
Most 1-0 games lost	7 in 1915
Most consecutive games won	17 in 1912
Most consecutive games lost	18 in 1948
	18 in 1959
Most times league champions	3
Most last place finishes	10
Most runs, game	21 vs. Detroit, August 5, 1929
Most runs, game, by opponent	24 by Boston, September 27, 1940

Most runs, shutout game	14 vs. Boston, Sept. 11, 1905, second game, 7 innings
	14 vs. Chicago, September 3, 1942, second game
Most runs, shutout game, by opponent	17 by New York, April 24, 1909
	17 by New York, July 6, 1920
	17 by Chicago, September 19, 1925, second game
Most runs, doubleheader shutout	13 vs. Cleveland, August 20, 1945
Most runs, inning	12 vs. St. Louis, July 10, 1926, eighth inning
Longest 1-0 game won	18 innings vs. Chicago, May 15, 1918
	18 innings vs. Chicago, June 8, 1947, first game
Longest 1-0 game lost	13 innings vs. Boston, August 15, 1916
	13 innings vs. Chicago, July 29, 1918
Most hits, game	24 vs. Detroit, July 9, 1903
	24 vs. Cleveland, July 18, 1925
Most home runs, game	7 vs. Chicago, May 3, 1949, 10 innings
	5, Washington vs. Detroit, May 2, 1959
Most consecutive games, one or more homers	8 (14 homers), 1959
Most total bases, game	41 vs. Detroit, July 9, 1904
Largest crowd, day game	31,728 vs. New York, April 19, 1948
Largest crowd, doubleheader	35,563 vs. New York, July 4, 1936
Largest crowd, night game	30,701 vs. Cleveland, June 17, 1947
Largest crowd, home opener	31,728 vs. New York, April 19, 1948

Washington Senators
(Second Club)

Yearly Finishes

Year—Position	W.	L.	Pct.	*G.B.	Manager
1961—Ninth†	61	100	.379	47½	James (Mickey) Vernon
1962—Tenth	60	101	.373	35½	James (Mickey) Vernon
1963—Tenth	56	106	.346	48½	M. Vernon, G. Hodges
1964—Ninth	62	100	.383	37	Gilbert Hodges
1965—Eighth	70	92	.432	32	Gilbert Hodges
1966—Eighth	71	88	.447	25½	Gilbert Hodges
1967—Sixth†	76	85	.472	15½	Gilbert Hodges
1968—Tenth	65	96	.404	37½	James Lemon

East Division

Year—Position	W.	L.	Pct.	*G.B.	Manager
1969—Fourth	86	76	.531	23	Theodore Williams
1970—Sixth	70	92	.432	38	Theodore Williams
1971—Fifth	63	96	.396	38½	Theodore Williams

*Games behind winner. †Tied for position.

Individual Records (1961 To 1971)

Batting

Most years, non-pitcher	10, Edwin A. Brinkman
Most games	161, Frank O. Howard, 1969
	161, Frank O. Howard, 1970
Most games, league	1142, Edwin A. Brinkman
Most at-bats	635, Delbert B. Unser, 156 games, 1968
Most at-bats, league	3845, Edwin A. Brinkman
Most runs	111, Frank O. Howard, 161 games, 1969
Most runs, league	516, Frank O. Howard
Most hits	175, Frank O. Howard, 161 games, 1969
Most hits, league	1071, Frank O. Howard
Most singles	144, Edwin A. Brinkman, 158 games, 1970
Most singles, league	685, Edwin A. Brinkman
Most doubles	31, Aurelio Rodriguez, 142 games, 1970
Most triples	12, Charles E. Hinton, 150 games, 1963
Most homers, righthander	48, Frank O. Howard, 161 games, 1969
Most homers, lefthander	30, Michael P. Epstein, 131 games, 1969
Most homers, rookie	12, Don W. Lock, 71 games, 1962
Most homers at home	27, Frank O. Howard, 1969
Most homers on road	26, Frank O. Howard, 1968
Most homers, month	15, Frank O. Howard, May, 1968
Most homers, league	237, Frank O. Howard
Most grand slams	2, Donald W. Zimmer, 121 games, 1964
Most grand slams, league	3, Michael P. Epstein
Most total bases	340, Frank O. Howard, 161 games, 1969
Most total bases, league	1968, Frank O. Howard
Most long hits	75, Frank O. Howard, 158 games, 1968
Most long hits, league	403, Frank O. Howard
Most extra bases on long hits	166, Frank O. Howard, 158 games, 1968
Most extra bases on long hits, league	897, Frank O. Howard
Most sacrifice hits	15, Daniel F. O'Connell, 138 games, 1961
Most sacrifice flies	8, Kenneth L. McMullen, 158 games, 1959
Most stolen bases	29, Edwin M. Stroud, 129 games, 1970
Most caught stealing	10, Willie Tasby, 141 games, 1961
	10, Charles E. Hinton, 150 games, 1962
	10, Fred L. Valentine, 146 games, 1966
	10, Delbert B. Unser, 153 games, 1969
Most bases on balls	132, Frank O. Howard, 161 games, 1970
Most strikeouts	155, Frank O. Howard, 149 games, 1967
Fewest strikeouts	41, Edwin A. Brinkman, 158 games, 1968
Most hit by pitch	13, Michael P. Epstein, 123 games, 1968
Most runs batted in	126, Frank O. Howard, 161 games, 1970
Most runs batted in, league	670, Frank O. Howard
Highest batting average	.310 Charles E. Hinton, 151 games, 1962
Highest slugging average	.574, Frank O. Howard, 161 games, 1969
Longest batting streak	19 games, Kenneth L. McMullen, 1967
Most grounded into double play	29, Frank O. Howard, 153 games, 1971
	29, Frank O. Howard, 161 games, 1969
Fewest grounded into double play	4, Delbert B. Unser, 153 games, 1971

Pitching

Most years	9, James Hannan
Most games	74, Ronald L. Kline, 1965
Most games started	36, Claude W. Osteen, 1964
	36, Joseph H. Coleman, 1969
Most complete games	13, Claude W. Osteen, 1964
Most games finished	58, Ronald L. Kline, 1965
Most innings	257, Claude W. Osteen, 1964
Most games won	16, Richard A. Bosman, 1970
Most games won, league	49, Richard A. Bosman
Most games lost	22, Dennis D. McLain, 1971
Most games lost, league	60, Bennie Daniels
Highest winning percentage	737, Richard A. Bosman (14-5), 1969
Longest winning streak	8 games, Richard A. Bosman, 1969
Longest losing streak	10 games, Bennie Daniels, 1962
Most saves	27, Darold D. Knowles, 1970
Most bases on balls	100, Joseph H. Coleman, 1969
Most strikeouts	195, Peter G. Richert, 1966
Most strikeouts, game	21, Thomas E. Cheney, September 12, 1962, 16 innings
	13, James R. Duckworth, September 25, 1965, second game
Most shutouts	4, Thomas E. Cheney, 1963
	4, Frank L. Bertaina, 1967
	4, Camilo A. Pascual, 1968
	4, Joseph H. Coleman, 1969
Most shutouts, league	7, Thomas E. Cheney
Most 1-0 shutouts won	2, Richard E. Donovan, 1961
	2, David R. Stenhouse, 1962
Most runs	115, Dennis D. McLain, 1971
Most earned runs	103, Dennis D. McLain, 1971
Most hits	256, Claude W. Osteen, 1964
Most hit batsmen	12, Joseph H. Coleman, 1968
Most wild pitches	17, Frank L. Bertaina, 1968
Most home runs	36, Peter G. Richert, 1966
Most sacrifice hits	20, Leslie F. Narum, 1965
Most sacrifice flies	12, Held by 4 pitchers
Lowest ERA	2.19, Richard A. Bosman, 193 innings, 1969

Club Records

Most players	43 in 1963 (162 games)
Fewest players	36 in 1969 (162 games)
Most games	162 in 1962, 1963, 1964, 1966, 1969, 1970
Fewest games	159 in 1966, 1971
Most at-bats	5484 in 1962 (162 games)
Most runs	694 in 1969 (162 games)
Fewest runs	524 in 1968 (161 games)
Most opponents' runs	812 in 1963 (162 games)
Most hits	1370 in 1962 (162 games)
Most singles	1006 in 1969 (162 games)
Most doubles	217 in 1961 (161 games)
Most triples	44 in 1961 (161 games)
Most homers	148 in 1969 (162 games)
Fewest homers	86 in 1971
Most homers at Griffith Stadium, home & opp.	87 in 1961
Most homers at RFK Stadium, home & opp.	166 in 1964
Most grand slams	4 in 1961
	4 in 1963
	4 in 1967
Most pinch home runs	8 in 1965, 1966
Most total bases	2060 in 1969 (162 games)
Most long hits	380 in 1961 (161 games)
Most extra bases on long hits	695 in 1969 (162 games)
Most sacrifice hits	84 in 1966 (159 games)
Most sacrifice flies	44 in 1961 (161 games)
Most stolen bases	99 in 1962 (162 games)
Most caught stealing	53 in 1962 (162 games)
Most bases on balls	635 in 1970 (162 games)
Most strikeouts	1125 in 1965 (162 games)
Fewest strikeouts	789 in 1962 (162 games)
Most hit by pitch	46 in 1970 (162 games)
Fewest hit by pitch	15 in 1962 (162 games)

Slugging outfielder-first baseman Frank Howard

Most runs batted in	640 in 1969 (162 games)
Highest batting average	.251 in 1969 (162 games)
Lowest batting average	.223 in 1967 (161 games)
Highest slugging average	.378 in 1969 (162 games)
Lowest slugging average	.326 in 1967 (161 games)
	.326 in 1971 (159 games)
Most grounded into double play	158 in 1969 (162 games)
Fewest grounded into double play	111 in 1963 (162 games)
Most left on bases	1196 in 1970 (162 games)
Fewest left on bases	1054 in 1966 (159 games)
Most .300 hitters	1 in 1961, 1962
Most putouts	4420 in 1967 (161 games)
Fewest putouts	4256 in 1971 (159 games)
Most assists	1946 in 1970 (162 games)
Fewest assists	1647 in 1965 (162 games)
Most chances accepted	6319 in 1970 (162 games)
Fewest chances accepted	5954 in 1965 (162 games)
Most errors	182 in 1963 (162 games)
Fewest errors	116 in 1970 (162 games)
Most errorless games	83 in 1964 (162 games)
Most consecutive errorless games	6 in 1970
Most double plays	173 in 1970 (162 games)
Fewest double plays	139 in 1966 (159 games)
Most passed balls	23 in 1961 (161 games)
	23 in 1971 (159 games)
Fewest passed balls	12 in 1970 (162 games)
Highest fielding average	.982 in 1970 (162 games)
Lowest fielding average	.971 in 1963 (162 games)
Highest home attendance	918,106 in 1969
Highest road attendance	1,042,638 in 1968
Most games won	86 in 1969
Most games lost	106 in 1963
Most games won, month	19, July 1967
Most games lost, month	24, August 1961

Games won, league	740 in 11 years
Games lost, league	1032 in 11 years
Highest percentage games won	.531 in 1969 (won 86, lost 76)
Lowest percentage games won	.346 in 1963 (won 56, lost 106)
Most shutouts won	14 in 1967
Most shutouts lost	22 in 1964
Most 1-0 games won	4 in 1962, 1967, 1968
Most 1-0 games lost	5 in 1963, 1971
Most consecutive games won	8 in 1967
Most consecutive games lost	14 in 1961
	14 in 1970
Most times league champions	0
Most last place finishes	4 (tied in 1961)
Most runs, game	15 vs. Detroit, May 18, 1965
	15 vs. Cleveland, July 5, 1971
Most runs, game, by opponent	18 by Baltimore, April 22, 1965
Most runs, shutout game	13 vs. Los Angeles, June 2, 1965, first game
Most runs, shutout game, by opponent	17 by Los Angeles, August 23, 1963
Most runs, doubleheader shutout	No performance
Most runs, inning	11 vs. Baltimore, May 11, 1962, sixth inning
Longest 1-0 game won	10 innings vs. Chicago, June 9, 1961, first game
	10 innings vs. Chicago, September 19, 1964
Longest 1-0 game lost	10 innings by Washington, September 9, 1966
Most hits, game	20 vs. Boston, July 27, 1962, second game
Most home runs, game	5 vs. Detroit, May 20, 1965
	5 vs. Chicago, May 16, 1969
	5 vs. Chicago, June 13, 1970
Most consecutive games, one or more homers	10 (16 homers), 1970
Most total bases, game	32 vs. Boston, July 27, 1962, second game
	32 vs. Chicago, June 13, 1970
Largest crowd, day game	45,125 vs. New York, April 7, 1969
Largest crowd, doubleheader	40,359 vs. Minnesota, June 14, 1964
Largest crowd, night game	30,421 vs. New York, July 31, 1962
Largest crowd, home opener	45,125 vs. New York, April 7, 1969

National League Team Records

Atlanta Braves

Yearly Finishes

Year—Position	W.	L.	Pct.	*G.B.	Manager
1966—Fifth	85	77	.525	10	R. Bragan, W. Hitchcock
1967—Seventh	77	85	.475	24½	W. Hitchcock, K. Silvestri
1968—Fifth	81	81	.500	16	Luman Harris

West Division

Year—Position	W.	L.	Pct.	*G.B.	Manager
1969—First‡	93	69	.574	+ 3	Luman Harris
1970—Fifth	76	86	.469	26	Luman Harris
1971—Third	82	80	.506	8	Luman Harris
1972—Fourth	70	84	.455	25	L. Harris, E. Mathews
1973—Fifth	76	85	.472	22½	Edwin Mathews
1974—Third	88	74	.543	14	E. Mathews, C. King
1975—Fifth	67	94	.416	40½	C. King, C. Ryan
1976—Sixth	70	92	.432	32	J. David Bristol
1977—Sixth	61	101	.377	37	D. Bristol, T. Turner
1978—Sixth	69	93	.426	26	Robert Cox
1979—Sixth	66	94	.413	23½	Robert Cox
1980—Fourth	81	80	.503	11	Robert Cox
1981—4th/5th.	50	56	.472	§	Robert Cox
1982—First‡	89	73	.549	+ 1	Joseph Torre
1983—Second	88	74	.543	3	Joseph Torre
1984—Second†	80	82	.494	12	Joseph Torre
1985—Fifth	66	96	.407	29	E. Haas, R. Wine
1986—Sixth	72	89	.447	23½	Charles Tanner
1987—Fifth	69	92	.429	20½	Charles Tanner

*Games behind winner. †Tied for postion. ‡Lost Championship Series. §First half 25-29; second 25-27.

Individual Records (1966 To Date)

Batting

Most years, non-pitcher	12, Michael K. Lum
	12, Dale B. Murphy
Most games	162, Felix B. Millan, 1969
	162, Dale B. Murphy, 1982
	162, Dale B. Murphy, 1983
	162, Dale B. Murphy, 1984
	162, Dale B. Murphy, 1985
Most games, league	1519, Dale B. Murphy
Most at-bats	668, Ralph A. Garr, 148 games, 1973
Most at-bats, league	5583, Dale B. Murphy
Most runs	131, Dale B. Murphy, 162 games, 1983
Most runs, league	928, Dale B. Murphy
Most hits	219, Ralph A. Garr, 154 games, 1971
Most hits, league	1555, Dale B. Murphy
Most singles	180, Ralph A. Garr, 154 games, 1971
Most singles, league	971, Dale B. Murphy
Most doubles	37, Henry L. Aaron, 155 games, 1967
	37, Felipe R. Alou, 160 games, 1968
	37, C. Christopher Chambliss, 158 games, 1980
	37, Dion James, 134 games, 1987
Most doubles, league	241, Dale B. Murphy
Most triples	17, Ralph A. Garr, 143 games, 1974
Most triples, league	40, Ralph A. Garr
Most homers, righthander	47, Henry L. Aaron, 139 games, 1971
Most homers, lefthander	41, Darrell W. Evans, 161 games, 1973
Most homers at home	31, Henry L. Aaron, 1971
Most homers on road	23, Henry L. Aaron, 1966
	23, Henry L. Aaron, 1969
Most homers, month	14, J. Robert Horner, July 1980
Most homers, league, righthander	335, Henry L. Aaron
Most homers, league, lefthander	120, Darrell W. Evans
Most homers, rookie	33, Earl C. Williams, 145 games, 1971
Most grand slams	2, held by many players
Most grand slams, league	7, Henry L. Aaron
Most total bases	355, Felipe R. Alou, 154 games, 1966
Most total bases, league	2792, Dale B. Murphy
Most long hits	79, Henry L. Aaron, 155 games, 1967
Most long hits, league	584, Dale B. Murphy
Most extra bases on long hits	169, Henry L. Aaron, 139 games, 1971
Most extra bases on long hits, league	1273, Dale B. Murphy
Most sacrifice hits	20, Rodney C. Gilbreath, 116 games, 1976
	20, Glenn D. Hubbard, 145 games, 1982
Most sacrifice flies	10, J. Robert Horner, 141 games, 1986
Most stolen bases	42, Gerald J. Perry, 142 games, 1987
Most stolen bases, league	174, Jeron K. Royster
Most caught stealing	23, Brett M. Butler, 151 games, 1983
Most bases on balls	127, James S. Wynn, 148 games, 1976
Most bases on balls, league	732, Dale B. Murphy
Most strikeouts	145, Dale B. Murphy, 151 games, 1978
Most strikeouts, league	1230, Dale B. Murphy
Fewest strikeouts	35, Felix B. Millan, 162 games, 1969
Most hit by pitch	12, Felipe R. Alou, 154 games, 1966
Most runs batted in	122, Henry L. Aaron, 158 games, 1966
Most runs batted in, league	927, Dale B. Murphy
Most game-winning RBIs	14, Dale B. Murphy, 162 games, 1982
	14, Claudell Washington, 150 games, 1982
	14, Dale B. Murphy, 162 games, 1983
	14, Dale B. Murphy, 162 games, 1985

Hank Aaron

Highest batting average	.366, Ricardo A. Carty, 136 games, 1970
Highest batting average, league	.317, Ralph A. Garr
Highest slugging average	.669, Henry L. Aaron, 139 games, 1971
Longest batting streak	31 games, Ricardo A. Carty, 1970
Most grounded into double play	22, Joseph P. Torre, 135 games, 1967
Fewest grounded into double play	5, Brett M. Butler, 151 games, 1983

Pitching

Most years	19, Philip H. Niekro
Most games	77, Rick L. Camp, 1980
Most games, league	689, Philip H. Niekro
Most games started	44, Philip H. Niekro, 1979
Most games started, league	594, Philip H. Niekro
Most complete games	23, Philip H. Niekro, 1979
Most complete games, league	226, Philip H. Niekro
Most games finished	56, H. Eugene Garber, 1982
Most innings	342, Philip H. Niekro, 1979
Most innings, league	4532, Philip H. Niekro
Most games won	23, Philip H. Niekro, 1969
Most games won, league	266, Philip H. Niekro
Most 20 victory seasons	3, Philip H. Niekro
Most games lost	20, Philip H. Niekro, 1977, 1979
Most games lost, league	227, Philip H. Niekro
Highest winning percentage	.810, Philip H. Niekro (17-4), 1982
Longest winning streak	9 games, Lee W. Capra, 1974
Longest losing streak	9 games, Thomas W. Boggs, 1981
Longest losing streak over two seasons—	11 games, James J. Acker, 1986 (6), 1987 (5)
Most saves	30, H. Eugene Garber, 1982
Most bases on balls	164, Philip H. Niekro, 1977
Most bases on balls, league	1425, Philip H. Niekro
Most strikeouts	262, Philip H. Niekro, 1977
Most strikeouts, league	2855, Philip H. Niekro
Most strikeouts, game	14, Denver C. Lemaster, August 14, 1966
Most shutouts won	6, Philip H. Niekro, 1974
Most shutouts, league	43, Philip H. Niekro
Most 1-0 shutouts won	2, Philip H. Niekro, 1969
Most runs	166, Philip H. Niekro, 1977
Most earned runs	148, Philip H. Niekro, 1977
Most hits	315, Philip H. Niekro, 1977
Most hit batsmen	13, Philip H. Niekro, 1978
Most wild pitches	27, Tony L. Cloninger, 1966
Most home runs	41, Philip H. Niekro, 1979
Most sacrifice hits	19, Philip H. Niekro, 1969
Most sacrifice flies	12, Tony L. Cloninger, 1966
	12, Carl W. Morton, 1974
Lowest ERA	1.87, Philip H. Niekro, 207 innings, 1967

Club Records

Most players	44 in 1966 (163 games)
Fewest players	32 in 1980 (161 games)
Most games	163 in 1966, 1968, 1974
Most at-bats	5631 in 1973 (162 games)
Most runs	799 in 1973 (162 games)
Fewest runs	514 in 1968 (163 games)
Most opponents' runs	895 in 1977 (162 games)
Most hits	1497 in 1973 (162 games)
Fewest hits	1307 in 1967 (162 games)
Most singles	1109 in 1968 (163 games)
Most doubles	284 in 1987 (161 games)
Most triples	45 in 1983 (162 games)
Most homers	207 in 1966 (163 games)
Fewest homers	80 in 1968
Most homers at Atlanta Stadium, home & opp.	211 in 1970
Most grand slams	7 in 1977
Most pinch home runs	8 in 1977
Most total bases	2402 in 1973 (162 games)
Most long hits	460 in 1987 (161 games)
Most extra bases on long hits	905 in 1966 (163 games)
	905 in 1973 (162 games)
Most sacrifice hits	109 in 1974 (163 games)
Most sacrifice flies	47 in 1976 (162 games)
	47 in 1978 (162 games)
Most stolen bases	151 in 1982 (162 games)
Most caught stealing	88 in 1983 (162 games)
Most bases on balls	641 in 1987 (161 games)
Fewest bases on balls	414 in 1968 (163 games)
Most strikeouts	947 in 1967 (162 games)
Fewest strikeouts	665 in 1969 (162 games)
Most hit by pitch	40 in 1966 (163 games)
Fewest hit by pitch	17 in 1977 (162 games)
	17 in 1983 (162 games)
Most runs batted in	758 in 1973 (162 games)
Most game-winning RBIs	82 in 1982 (162 games)
	82 in 1983 (162 games)
Highest batting average	.272 in 1983 (162 games)
Lowest batting average	.240 in 1967 (162 games)
Highest slugging average	.427 in 1973 (162 games)
Lowest slugging average	.334 in 1976 (162 games)
Most grounded into double play	154 in 1985 (162 games)
Fewest grounded into double play	102 in 1982 (162 games)
Most left on bases	1213 in 1974 (163 games)
Fewest left on bases	1054 in 1980 (161 games)
Most .300 hitters	3 in 1966
	3 in 1970
Most putouts	4424 in 1971 (162 games)

Fewest putouts	4223 in 1979 (160 games)
Most assists	2028 in 1985 (162 games)
Fewest assists	1633 in 1972 (155 games)
Most chances accepted	6400 in 1985 (162 games)
Fewest chances accepted	5764 in 1972 (155 games)
Most errors	183 in 1979 (160 games)
Fewest errors	115 in 1969 (162 games)
Most errorless games	82 in 1987 (161 games)
Most consecutive errorless games	6 in 1967, 1987
Most double plays	197 in 1985 (162 games)
Fewest double plays	114 in 1969 (162 games)
Most passed balls	42 in 1967 (162 games)
Fewest passed balls	6 in 1983 (162 games)
Highest fielding average	.982 in 1987 (161 games)
Lowest fielding average	.970 in 1979 (160 games)
Highest home attendance	2,119,935 in 1983
Highest road attendance	1,985,595 in 1982
Most games won	93 in 1969
Most games lost	101 in 1977
Most games won, month	20, Sept. 1966
Most games lost, month	21, May 1976
Games won, league	1626 in 22 years
Games lost, league	1837 in 22 years
Highest percentage games won	.574 in 1969 (won 93, lost 69)
Lowest percentage games won	.377 in 1977 (won 61, lost 101)
Most shutouts won	21 in 1974
Most shutouts lost	24 in 1978
Most 1-0 shutouts won	7 in 1974
Most 1-0 shutouts lost	3 in 1968
	3 in 1974
Most consecutive games won	13 in 1982
Most consecutive games lost	17 in 1977
Most times league champions	0
Most last place finishes	1
Most runs, game	18 vs. Pittsburgh, June 13, 1973
Most runs, game, by opponent	23 by Cincinnati, April 25, 1977
Most runs, shutout game	14 vs. Houston, July 2, 1980
Most runs, shutout game, by opponent	19 by Montreal, July 30, 1978
Most runs, doubleheader shutout	No performance
Most hits, game	25 vs. Cincinnati, May 1, 1985
Most runs, inning	13 vs. Houston, September 20, 1972, second inning
Longest 1-0 game won	12 innings vs. Los Angeles, Sept. 17, 1976, first game
Longest 1-0 game lost	13 innings vs. Los Angeles, May 18, 1974
Most home runs, game	7 vs. Chicago, August 3, 1967
Most consecutive games, one or more homers	20 (36 homers), 1973
Most total bases, game	39 vs. San Francisco, July 3, 1966
Largest crowd, day game	51,275 vs. Los Angeles, June 26, 1966
Largest crowd, doubleheader	50,597 vs. Chicago, July 4, 1972
Largest crowd, night game	53,775 vs. Los Angeles, April 8, 1974
Largest crowd, home opener	53,775 vs. Los Angeles, April 8, 1974

Boston Braves

Yearly Finishes

Year—Position	W.	L.	Pct.	*G.B.	Manager
1901—Fifth	69	69	.500	20½	Frank Selee
1902—Third	73	64	.533	29	Albert Buckenberger
1903—Sixth	58	80	.420	32	Albert Buckenberger
1904—Seventh	55	98	.359	51	Albert Buckenberger
1905—Seventh	51	103	.331	54½	Fred Tenney
1906—Eighth	49	102	.325	66½	Fred Tenney
1907—Seventh	58	90	.392	47	Fred Tenney
1908—Sixth	63	91	.409	36	Joseph Kelley
1909—Eighth	45	108	.294	65½	F. Bowerman, H. Smith
1910—Eighth	53	100	.346	50½	Fred Lake
1911—Eighth	44	107	.291	54	Fred Tenney
1912—Eighth	52	101	.340	52	John Kling
1913—Fifth	69	82	.457	31½	George Stallings
1914—First	94	59	.614	+10½	George Stallings
1915—Second	83	69	.546	7	George Stallings
1916—Third	89	63	.586	4	George Stallings
1917—Sixth	72	81	.471	25½	George Stallings
1918—Seventh	53	71	.427	28½	George Stallings
1919—Sixth	57	82	.410	38½	George Stallings
1920—Seventh	62	90	.408	30	George Stallings
1921—Fourth	79	74	.516	15	Fred Mitchell
1922—Eighth	53	100	.346	39½	Fred Mitchell
1923—Seventh	54	100	.351	41½	Fred Mitchell
1924—Eighth	53	100	.346	40	David Bancroft
1925—Fifth	70	83	.458	25	David Bancroft
1926—Seventh	66	86	.434	22	David Bancroft
1927—Seventh	60	94	.390	34	David Bancroft
1928—Seventh	50	103	.327	44½	J. Slattery, R. Hornsby
1929—Eighth	56	98	.364	43	E. Fuchs, W. Maranville
1930—Sixth	70	84	.455	22	William McKechnie
1931—Seventh	64	90	.416	37	William McKechnie
1932—Fifth	77	77	.500	13	William McKechnie
1933—Fourth	83	71	.539	9	William McKechnie
1934—Fourth	78	73	.517	16	William McKechnie
1935—Eighth	38	115	.248	61½	William McKechnie
1936—Sixth	71	83	.461	21	William McKechnie
1937—Fifth	79	73	.520	16	William McKechnie
1938—Fifth	77	75	.507	12	Charles (Casey) Stengel
1939—Seventh	63	88	.417	32½	Charles (Casey) Stengel
1940—Seventh	65	87	.428	34½	Charles (Casey) Stengel
1941—Seventh	62	92	.403	38	Charles (Casey) Stengel
1942—Seventh	59	89	.399	44	Charles (Casey) Stengel
1943—Sixth	68	85	.444	36½	Charles (Casey) Stengel
1944—Sixth	65	89	.422	40	Robert Coleman
1945—Sixth	67	85	.441	30	R. Coleman, A. Bissonette
1946—Fourth	81	72	.529	15½	William Southworth
1947—Third	86	68	.558	8	William Southworth
1948—First	91	62	.595	+ 6½	William Southworth
1949—Fourth	75	79	.487	22	William Southworth
1950—Fourth	83	71	.539	8	William Southworth
1951—Fourth	76	78	.494	20½	W. Southworth, T. Holmes
1952—Seventh	64	89	.418	32	T. Holmes, C. Grimm

*Games behind winner.

Individual Records (1876 To 1952)
Batting

Most years, non-pitcher	15, Fred C. Tenney
	15, Walter J. Maranville
	15, John W. Cooney
Most games	158, Edward J. Konetchy, 1916
Most games, league	1795, Walter J. Maranville
Most at-bats	647, Herman A. Long, 151 games, 1892
Most at-bats, league	6764, Herman A. Long
Most at-bats since 1900	637, Eugene Moore, 151 games, 1936
Most at-bats, league, since 1900	6724, Walter J. Maranville
Most runs	160, Hugh Duffy, 124 games, 1894
Most runs since 1900	125, Thomas F. Holmes, 154 games, 1945
Most runs, league	1294, Herman A. Long
Most hits	236, Hugh Duffy, 124 games, 1894
Most hits, league	2002, Fred C. Tenney
Most hits since 1900	224, Thomas F. Holmes, 154 games, 1945
Most singles	166, Lance Richbourg, 148 games, 1928
Most doubles	50, Hugh Duffy, 124 games, 1894
Most doubles since 1900	47, Thomas F. Holmes, 154 games, 1945
Most doubles, league	291, Thomas F. Holmes
Most triples	20, Richard F. Johnston, 124 games, 1887
Most triples since 1900	18, Raymond R. Powell, 149 games, 1921
Most triples, league	103, Walter J. Maranville
Most homers, righthander	38, Walter A. Berger, 151 games, 1930
Most homers, lefthander	28, Thomas F. Holmes, 154 games, 1945
Most homers, rookie	38, Walter A. Berger, 151 games, 1930
Most homers at home	19, Charles T. Workman, 1945
Most homers on road	22, Sidney Gordon, 1950
Most grand slams	4, Sidney Gordon, 134 games, 1950
Most grand slams, league	6, Walter A. Berger

Most home runs, one month ....11, Walter A. Berger, May, 1930
Most homers, league ....199, Walter A. Berger
Most total bases ....372, Hugh Duffy, 124 games, 1894
Most total bases since 1900 ....367, Thomas F. Holmes, 154 games, 1945
Most total bases, league ....2629, Herman A. Long
Most long hits.......................81, Hugh Duffy, 124 games, 1894
.......................81, Thomas F. Holmes, 154 games, 1945
Most extra bases on long hits ....169, Walter A. Berger, 151 games, 1930
Most sacrifices (S.H. and S.F.) .... 37, John P. McInnis, 154 games, 1923
Most sacrifice hits ....31, Frederick E. Maguire, 148 games, 1931
Most stolen bases ....93, William R. Hamilton, 131 games, 1896
Most stolen bases since 1900 .... 57, Ralph Meyers, 140 games, 1913
Most stolen bases, league.........................446, Herman A. Long
Most caught stealing ....20, William H. Southworth, 141 games, 1921
Most bases on balls ....131, Robert I. Elliott, 151 games, 1948
Most strikeouts....................134, Vincent P. DiMaggio, 150 games, 1938
Fewest strikeouts...................9, Thomas F. Holmes, 154 games, 1945
Most hit by pitch ....11, Samuel Jethroe, 148 games, 1951
Most runs batted in...............130, Walter A. Berger, 150 games, 1935
Most runs batted in, league.......................746, Walter A. Berger
Highest batting average ....438, Hugh Duffy, 124 games, 1894
Highest batting average since 1900 .... .387, Rogers Hornsby, 140 games, 1928
Highest batting average, league ....338, William R. Hamilton
Highest batting average, league, since 1900 ....304, Walter A. Berger
Highest slugging average ....632, Rogers Hornsby, 140 games, 1928
Longest batting streak....................37 games, Thomas F. Holmes, 1945
Most grounded into double play.............28, Sidney Gordon, 150 games, 1951
Fewest grounded into double play ....4, Vincent P. DiMaggio, 150 games, 1938

Pitching, Since 1900

Most years ....12, Charles A. Nichols
Most years, league, since 1900 .... 11, Richard Rudolph
Most games.....................................57, John J. Hutchings, 1945
Most games, league.............................517, Charles A. Nichols
Most games started................46, Victor G. Willis, 1902
Most complete games................45, Victor G. Willis, 1902
Most games finished................29, Nelson T. Potter, 1949
Most innings.........................411, Victor G. Willis, 1902
Most games won................27, Charles Pittinger, 1902
27, Victor G. Willis, 1902
27, Richard Rudolph, 1914
Most games won, league..................328, Charles A. Nichols
Most games won, league, since 1900 .... 122, Richard Rudolph
122, Warren E. Spahn
Most 20-victory seasons ....4, John F. Sain
4, Warren E. Spahn
Most games lost ....29, Victor G. Willis, 1905
Highest winning percentage........................ .842, Thomas L. Hughes (16-3), 1916
Longest winning streak.....................12 games, Richard Rudolph, 1914
Longest losing streak..................18 games, Clifton G. Curtis, 1910
Most bases on balls....................149, Charles C. Fraser, 1905
Most bases on balls, league.....................1118, Charles A. Nichols
Most bases on balls, league, since 1900....................... 678, George A. Tyler
Most strikeouts................226, Victor G. Willis, 1902
Most strikeouts, league.....................1649, Charles A. Nichols
Most strikeouts, league, since 1900 .... 1000, Warren E. Spahn
Most strikeouts, game........18, Warren E. Spahn, June 14, 1952, 15 innings
13, Victor G. Willis, May 28, 1902
13, Warren E. Spahn, September 13, 1952
Most shutouts...7, Charles Pittinger, 1902
7, Irving M. Young, 1905
7, Warren E. Spahn, 1947
7, Warren E. Spahn, 1951
Most shutouts, league.........................29, Richard Rudolph
Most 1-0 shutouts won ....4, Richard Rudolph, 1916
4, Joseph Oeschger, 1920
Most runs.......................196, Charles Pittinger, 1903
Most earned runs ....130, John F. Sain, 1949
Most hits......................394, Charles Pittinger, 1903
Most hit batsmen................16, Frank X. Pfeffer, 1906
Most wild pitches................14, Charles Pittinger, 1903
Most home runs..................34, John F. Sain, 1950
Lowest ERA.........................1.90, William L. James, 332 innings, 1914

Club Records

Most players......................................	48 in 1946
Fewest players................................	23 in 1905
Most games...................................	158 in 1914, 1916
Most at-bats....................................	5506 in 1932 (155 games)
Most runs......................................	1221 in 1894 (133 games)
Most runs, since 1900.......................	785 in 1950 (156 games)
Fewest runs...................................	408 in 1906 (152 games)
Most hits.....................................	1567 in 1925 (153 games)
Fewest hits...................................	1115 in 1906 (152 games)
Most singles..................................	196 in 1923 (153 games)
Most doubles..................................	272 in 1948 (154 games)
Most triples..................................	100 in 1921 (153 games)
Most home runs...............................	148 in 1950 (156 games)
Fewest homers (154 or 162-game schedule)....	15 in 1909
Most homers at Braves Field, home & opp.	131 in 1945
Most grand slams.............................	7 in 1950
Most total bases.............................	2173 in 1950 (156 games)
Most long hits...............................	430 in 1950 (156 games)
Most extra bases on long hits	762 in 1950 (156 games)
Most sacrifices, (S. H. and S. F.)...........	221 in 1914 (158 games)
Most sacrifice hits..........................	140 in 1948 (154 games)
Most stolen bases............................	190 in 1909 (155 games)
Most bases on balls..........................	684 in 1949 (157 games)

Warren Spahn

Most strikeouts...............................	711 in 1952 (155 games)
Fewest strikeouts............................	348 in 1926 (153 games)
Most hit by pitch............................	45 in 1917 (157 games)
Fewest hit by pitch..........................	13 in 1941 (156 games)
Most runs batted in..........................	726 in 1950 (156 games)
Highest batting average	.292 in 1925 (153 games)
Lowest batting average	.223 in 1909 (155 games)
Highest slugging average	.405 in 1950 (156 games)
Lowest slugging average	.274 in 1909 (155 games)
Most grounded into double play..............	146 in 1936 (157 games)
Fewest grounded into double play............	93 in 1944 (155 games)
Most left on bases...........................	1255 in 1948 (154 games)
Fewest left on bases.........................	1003 in 1933 (156 games)
Most .300 hitters............................	8 in 1931
Most putouts.................................	4262 in 1948 (158 games)
Fewest putouts...............................	3975 in 1906 (152 games)
Most assists	2225 in 1908 (156 games)
Fewest assists...............................	1665 in 1946 (154 games)
Most chances accepted	6424 in 1914 (158 games)
Fewest chances accepted.....................	5750 in 1935 (153 games)
Most errors..................................	353 in 1904 (155 games)
Fewest errors...............................	138 in 1933 (156 games)
Most consecutive errorless games	5 in 1933 (twice)
Most double plays...........................	178 in 1939 (152 games)
Fewest double plays	101 in 1935 (153 games)
Most passed balls...........................	167 in 1883 (98 games)
Most passed balls since 1900	42 in 1905 (156 games)
Fewest passed balls.........................	2 in 1943 (153 games)
Highest fielding average	.978 in 1933 (156 games)
Lowest fielding average	.945 in 1904 (155 games)
Highest home attendance	1,455,439 in 1948
Highest road attendance	1,308,175 in 1947
Most games won..............................	102 in 1898
Most games won since 1900	94 in 1914

Most games lost	115 in 1935
Most games won, month	26, Sept. 1914
Most games lost, month	25, Sept. 1928
	25, Sept. 1935
Highest percentage games won	.705 in 1897 (won 93, lost 39)
Highest percentage games won since 1900	.614 in 1914 (won 94, lost 59)
Lowest percentage games won	.248 in 1935 (won 38, lost 115)
Games won, league	5118 in 77 years
Games lost, league	5598 in 77 years
Most shutouts won	21 in 1916
Most shutouts lost	28 in 1906
Most 1-0 games won	9 in 1916
Most 1-0 games lost	6 in 1906, 1933
Most consecutive games won	17 in 1897
Most consecutive games won, since 1900	8 in 1948
Most consecutive games lost	19 in 1906
Most times league champions	10
Most last place finishes	9
Most runs, game	30 vs. Detroit, June 9, 1883
Most runs, game, since 1900	20 vs. Philadelphia, June 25, 1900
	20 vs. Philadelphia, October 6, 1910
	20 vs. St. Louis, September 18, 1915, first game
	20 vs. St. Louis, August 25, 1936, first game
Most runs, game, by opponent	27 by Pittsburgh, June 6, 1894
Most runs, game, by opponent, since 1900	26 by Cincinnati, June 4, 1911
Most runs, shutout game	18 vs. Buffalo, October 3, 1885
Most runs, shutout game, since 1900	16 vs. Brooklyn, May 7, 1918
	16 vs. Pittsburgh, September 12, 1952, second game
Most runs, shutout game, by opponent	17 by Chicago, September 16, 1884
Most runs, shutout game, by opp., since 1900	15 by New York, April 15, 1905
	15 by Cincinnati, May 19, 1906
	15 by Philadelphia, July 3, 1928
	15 by New York, May 29, 1936
	15 by New York, July 4, 1934, second game
	15 by St. Louis, August 18, 1934
	15 by St. Louis, May 7, 1950
Most runs, doubleheader shutout	8 vs. Cincinnati, August 7, 1916
	8 vs. Brooklyn, June 30, 1937
	8 vs. Cincinnati, August 3, 1941
Most runs, inning	16 vs. Baltimore, June 18, 1894, a.m. game, first inning
Most runs, inning, since 1900	13 vs. St. Louis, July 25, 1900, first inning
Longest 1-0 game won	13 innings, 5 times; last time vs. Pitts., May 11, 1921
Longest 1-0 game lost	17 innings vs. Chicago, September 21, 1901
Most hits, game	30 vs. St. Louis, September 3, 1896, first game
Most hits, game, since 1900	25 vs. St. Louis, August 25, 1936, first game
Most home runs, game	5 vs. Cincinnati, May 30, 1894, p.m. game
	5 vs. Chicago, May 13, 1942
	5 vs. Cincinnati, May 6, 1950
Most total bases, game	46 vs. Detroit, June 9, 1883
	46 vs. Cleveland, July 5, 1894
Most total bases, game, since 1900	37 vs. Philadelphia, July 6, 1934
	37 vs. Cincinnati, May 6, 1950
Largest crowd, day game	41,527 vs. Chicago, August 8, 1948
Largest crowd, doubleheader	47,123 vs. Philadelphia, May 22, 1932
Largest crowd, night game	39,549 vs. Brooklyn, August 5, 1946
Largest crowd, home opener	25,000 vs. New York, April 16, 1935

Brooklyn Dodgers

Yearly Finishes

Year—Position	W.	L.	Pct.	*G.B.	Manager
1901—Third	79	57	.581	9½	Edward (Ned) Hanlon
1902—Second	75	63	.543	27½	Edward (Ned) Hanlon
1903—Fifth	70	66	.515	19	Edward (Ned) Hanlon
1904—Sixth	56	97	.366	50	Edward (Ned) Hanlon
1905—Eighth	48	104	.316	56½	Edward (Ned) Hanlon
1906—Fifth	66	86	.434	50	Patrick (Patsy) Donovan
1907—Fifth	65	83	.439	40	Patrick (Patsy) Donovan
1908—Seventh	53	101	.344	46	Patrick (Patsy) Donovan
1909—Sixth	55	98	.359	55½	Harry Lumley
1910—Sixth	64	90	.416	40	William Dahlen
1911—Seventh	64	86	.427	33½	William Dahlen
1912—Seventh	58	95	.379	46	William Dahlen
1913—Sixth	65	84	.436	34½	William Dahlen
1914—Fifth	75	79	.487	19½	Wilbert Robinson
1915—Third	80	72	.526	10	Wilbert Robinson
1916—First	94	60	.610	+ 2½	Wilbert Robinson
1917—Seventh	70	81	.464	26½	Wilbert Robinson
1918—Fifth	57	69	.452	25½	Wilbert Robinson
1919—Fifth	69	71	.493	27	Wilbert Robinson
1920—First	93	61	.604	+ 7	Wilbert Robinson
1921—Fifth	77	75	.507	16½	Wilbert Robinson
1922—Sixth	76	78	.494	17	Wilbert Robinson
1923—Sixth	76	78	.494	19½	Wilbert Robinson
1924—Second	92	62	.597	1½	Wilbert Robinson
1925—Sixth†	68	85	.444	27	Wilbert Robinson
1926—Sixth	71	82	.464	17½	Wilbert Robinson
1927—Sixth	65	88	.425	28½	Wilbert Robinson
1928—Sixth	77	76	.503	17½	Wilbert Robinson
1929—Sixth	70	83	.458	28½	Wilbert Robinson
1930—Fourth	86	68	.558	6	Wilbert Robinson
1931—Fourth	79	73	.520	21	Wilbert Robinson
1932—Third	81	73	.526	9	Max Carey
1933—Sixth	65	88	.425	26½	Max Carey
1934—Sixth	71	81	.467	23½	Charles (Casey) Stengel
1935—Fifth	70	83	.458	29½	Charles (Casey) Stengel
1936—Seventh	67	87	.435	25	Charles (Casey) Stengel
1937—Sixth	62	91	.405	33½	Burleigh Grimes
1938—Seventh	69	80	.463	18½	Burleigh Grimes
1939—Third	84	69	.549	12½	Leo Durocher
1940—Second	88	65	.575	12	Leo Durocher
1941—First	100	54	.649	+ 2½	Leo Durocher
1942—Second	104	50	.675	2	Leo Durocher
1943—Third	81	72	.529	23½	Leo Durocher
1944—Seventh	63	91	.409	42	Leo Durocher
1945—Third	87	67	.565	11	Leo Durocher
1946—Second‡	96	60	.615	2	Leo Durocher
1947—First	94	60	.610	+ 5	C. Sukeforth, B. Shotton
1948—Third	84	70	.545	7½	L. Durocher, B. Shotton
1949—First	97	57	.630	+ 1	Burton Shotton
1950—Second	89	65	.578	2	Burton Shotton
1951—Second‡	97	60	.618	1	Charles (Chuck) Dressen
1952—First	96	57	.627	+ 4½	Charles (Chuck) Dressen
1953—First	105	49	.682	+13	Charles (Chuck) Dressen
1954—Second	92	62	.597	5	Walter (Smokey) Alston
1955—First	98	55	.641	+13½	Walter (Smokey) Alston
1956—First	93	61	.604	+ 1	Walter (Smokey) Alston
1957—Third	84	70	.545	11	Walter (Smokey) Alston

*Games behind winner. †Tied for position. ‡Lost pennant playoff.

Individual Records (1890 To 1957)

Batting

Most years, non-pitcher	18, Zachariah D. Wheat
Most games	158, Carl A. Furillo, 1951
	158, Gilbert R. Hodges, 1951
Most games, league	2318, Zachariah D. Wheat
Most at-bats	667, Carl A. Furillo, 158 games, 1951
Most at-bats, league	8859, Zachariah D. Wheat
Most runs	143, Hubert Collins, 129 games, 1890
	143, Floyd C. Herman, 153 games, 1930
Most runs, league	1317, Harold H. Reese
Most hits	241, Floyd C. Herman, 153 games, 1930
Most hits, league	2804, Zachariah D. Wheat
Most singles	179, William H. Keeler, 137 games, 1900
Most singles, league	2038, Zachariah D. Wheat
Most doubles	52, John H. Frederick, 148 games, 1929
Most doubles, league	464, Zachariah D. Wheat
Most triples	27, George Treadway, 122 games, 1894
Most triples, league	171, Zachariah D. Wheat
Most triples since 1900	22, Henry H. Myers, 154 games, 1920
Most homers, righthander	42, Gilbert R. Hodges, 154 games, 1954
Most homers, lefthander	43, Edwin D. Snider, 151 games, 1956
Most homers, rookie	25, Adelphia L. Bissonette, 155 games, 1928
Most homers at home	25 (Incl. 2 at Jersey City), Edwin D. Snider, 1956
	25, Gilbert R. Hodges, 1954
Most homers on road	24, Gilbert R. Hodges, 1951
Most homers, month	15, Edwin D. Snider, August, 1953
Most homers, league, righthander	298, Gilbert R. Hodges
Most homers, league, lefthander	316, Edwin D. Snider
Most grand slams	2, Held by many players
Most grand slams, league	13, Gilbert R. Hodges
Most total bases	416, Floyd C. Herman, 153 games, 1930
Most total bases, league	4003, Zachariah D. Wheat
Most long hits	94, Floyd C. Herman, 153 games, 1930
Most long hits, league	766, Zachariah D. Wheat
Most extra bases on long hits	179, Edwin D. Snider, 149 games, 1954
Most extra bases on long hits, league	1368, Edwin D. Snider
Most sacrifices (S.H. and S.F.)	39, Jacob E. Daubert, 150 games, 1915
Most sacrifice hits	32, James P. Casey, 138 games, 1907
Most sacrifice flies	19, Gilbert R. Hodges, 154 games, 1954
Most stolen bases	94, John M. Ward, 148 games, 1892
Most stolen bases since 1900	67, James T. Sheckard, 139 games, 1903
Most stolen bases, league	231, Harold H. Reese
Most caught stealing	16, James H. Johnston, 152 games, 1921
Most bases on balls	148, Edward R. Stanky, 153 games, 1945
Most strikeouts	115, Adolph Camilli, 149 games, 1941
Fewest strikeouts	15, James H. Johnston, 151 games, 1923
Most hit by pitch	14, Jack R. Robinson, 149 games, 1952
Most runs batted in	142, Roy Campanella, 144 games, 1953
Most runs batted in, league	1227, Zachariah D. Wheat
Highest batting average	.393, Floyd C. Herman, 153 games, 1930
Highest batting average, league	.339, Floyd C. Herman
Highest slugging average	.678, Floyd C. Herman, 153 games, 1930
Highest slugging average, league	.560, Edwin D. Snider
Longest batting streak	29 games, Zachariah D. Wheat, 1916
Most grounded into double play	27, Carl A. Furillo, 149 games, 1956
Fewest grounded into double play	5, Jack R. Robinson, 151 games, 1947
	5, Harold H. Reese, 155 games, 1949
	5, James Gilliam, 153 games, 1956

Pitching, Since 1900

Most years	12, Arthur C. Vance
Most games	62, Clement W. Labine, 1956
Most games, league	378, Arthur C. Vance
Most games started	41, Oscar Jones, 1904
Most complete games	38, Oscar Jones, 1904
Most games finished	47, Clement W. Labine, 1956
Most innings	378, Oscar Jones, 1904
Most games won	29, Joseph J. McGinnity, 1900

Pee Wee Reese

Most games won, league	190, Arthur C. Vance
Most 20 victory seasons	4, Burleigh A. Grimes
Most games lost	27, George G. Bell, 1910
Highest winning percentage	.889, Frederick L. Fitzsimmons (16-2), 1940
Longest winning streak	15 games, Arthur C. Vance, 1924
Longest losing streak	14 games, James W. Pastorius, 1908
Most bases on balls	151, William E. Donovan, 1901
Most bases on balls, league	764, Arthur C. Vance
Most strikeouts	262, Arthur C. Vance, 1924
Most strikeouts, league	1915, Arthur C. Vance
Most strikeouts, game	17, Arthur C. Vance, July 20, 1925, 10 innings
	16, George N. Rucker, July 24, 1909
Most shutouts	7, Burleigh A. Grimes, 1918
	7, J. Whitlow Wyatt, 1941
Most shutouts, league	38, George N. Rucker
Most 1-0 shutouts won	3, George N. Rucker, 1911
Most runs	188, Harry M. McIntire, 1905
Most earned runs	138, Burleigh A. Grimes, 1925
Most hits	364, Joseph J. McGinnity, 1900
Most hit batsmen	41, Joseph J. McGinnity, 1900
Most wild pitches	15, Lawrence D. Cheney, 1916
Most home runs	35, Donald Newcombe, 1955
Lowest ERA	1.58, Richard W. Marquard, 205 innings, 1916

Club Records

Most players	53 in 1944
Fewest players	23 in 1905
Most games	158 in 1951
Most at-bats	5574 in 1936 (156 games)
Most runs	995 in 1953 (155 games)
Fewest runs	375 in 1908 (154 games)
Most hits	1654 in 1930 (154 games)
Fewest hits	1044 in 1908 (154 games)
Most singles	1223 in 1925 (153 games)
Most doubles	303 in 1930 (153 games)
Most triples	99 in 1920 (155 games)
Most homers	208 in 1953 (155 games)
Fewest homers (154 or 162-game schedule)	14 in 1915
Most homers at Ebbets Field, home & opp.	207 in 1950
Most grand slams	8 in 1952
Most pinch home runs	7 in 1932
Most long hits	541 in 1953 (155 games)
Most extra bases on long hits	1016 in 1953 (155 games)
Most total bases	2545 in 1953 (155 games)
Most sacrifices (S. H. and S. F.)	203 in 1916 (156 games)
Most sacrifice hits	197 in 1907 (153 games)
Most sacrifice flies	59 in 1954 (154 games)
Most stolen bases	205 in 1904 (154 games)
Most caught stealing	73 in 1921 (152 games)
Most bases on balls	732 in 1947 (155 games)
Most strikeouts	848 in 1957 (154 games)
Fewest strikeouts	318 in 1922 (155 games)
Most hit by pitch	44 in 1951 (158 games)
Fewest hit by pitch	14 in 1942 (155 games)
	14 in 1944 (155 games)
Most runs batted in	887 in 1953 (155 games)
Fewest runs batted in	499 in 1927 (154 games)
Highest batting average	.304 in 1930 (154 games)
Lowest batting average	.213 in 1908 (154 games)
Highest slugging average	.474 in 1953 (155 games)
Lowest slugging average	.277 in 1908 (154 games)
Most grounded into double play	151 in 1952 (155 games)
Fewest grounded into double play	86 in 1947 (155 games)
Most left on bases	1278 in 1947 (155 games)
Fewest left on bases	1012 in 1921 (152 games)
Most .300 hitters	6 in 1900, 1922, 1925, 1930, 1943, 1953
Most putouts	4295 in 1940 (156 games)
Fewest putouts	3911 in 1909 (155 games)
Most assists	2132 in 1921 (152 games)
Fewest assists	1574 in 1944 (155 games)
Most chances accepted	6334 in 1920 (155 games)
Fewest chances accepted	5672 in 1944 (155 games)
Most errors	408 in 1905 (155 games)
Fewest errors	106 in 1952 (155 games)
Most consecutive errorless games	10 in 1942
Most double plays	192 in 1951 (158 games)
Fewest double plays	95 in 1926 (155 games)
Most passed balls	21 in 1905 (155 games)
Fewest passed balls	4 in 1933 (157 games)
	4 in 1951 (158 games)
	4 in 1953 (155 games)
	4 in 1954 (154 games)
Highest fielding average	.982 in 1952 (155 games)
Lowest fielding average	.937 in 1905 (155 games)
Highest home attendance	1,807,526 in 1947
Highest road attendance	1,863,542 in 1947
Most games won	105 in 1953
Most games lost	104 in 1905
Most games won, month	25, July 1947
	25, August 1953
Most games lost, month	27, Sept. 1908
Highest percentage games won	.682 in 1953 (won 105, lost 49)
Lowest percentage games won	.316 in 1905 (won 48, lost 104)
Games won, league	5214 in 68 years
Games lost, league	4926 in 68 years
Most shutouts won	22 in 1906, 1916
Most shutouts lost	26 in 1907
Most 1-0 games won	7 in 1907
	7 in 1909
Most 1-0 games lost	9 in 1910, 1913
Most consecutive games won	15 in 1924
Most consecutive games lost	16 in 1944
Most times league champions	12
Most last place finishes	1
Most runs, game	25 vs. Pittsburgh, May 20, 1896
	25 vs. Cincinnati, September 23, 1901
Most runs, game, by opponent	28 by Chicago, August 25, 1891
Most runs, game, by opponent, since 1900—	
	26 by New York, April 30, 1944, first game
Most runs, shutout game	15 vs. Philadelphia, August 16, 1952, 6⅓ innings
Most runs, shutout game, by opponent—	
	17 by St. Louis, August 24, 1924, second game
Most runs doubleheader shutout	18 vs. Philadelphia, September 3, 1906
Most runs, inning	15 vs. Cincinnati, May 21, 1952, first inning
Longest 1-0 game won	13 innings vs. St. Louis, August 21, 1909
	13 innings vs. Boston, May 29, 1938
Longest 1-0 game lost	15 innings vs. Cincinnati, June 11, 1915
Most hits, game	28 vs. Pittsburgh, June 23, 1930
Most home runs, game	6 vs. Milwaukee, June 1, 1955
Most consecutive games, one or more homers	24 (39 homers), 1953
Most total bases, game	46 vs. Philadelphia, September 23, 1939, first game
Largest crowd, day game	37,512 vs. New York, August 30, 1947
Largest crowd, doubleheader	41,209 vs. New York, May 30, 1934
Largest crowd, night game	35,583 vs. Philadelphia, September 24, 1949
Largest crowd, home opener	34,530 vs. New York, April 19, 1949

Chicago Cubs

Yearly Finishes

Year—Position	W.	L.	Pct.	*G.B.	Manager
1901—Sixth	53	86	.381	37	Thomas Loftus
1902—Fifth	68	69	.496	34	Frank Selee
1903—Third	82	56	.594	8	Frank Selee
1904—Second	93	60	.608	13	Frank Selee
1905—Third	92	61	.601	13	F. Selee, F. Chance
1906—First	116	36	.763	+20	Frank Chance
1907—First	107	45	.704	+17	Frank Chance
1908—First	99	55	.643	+ 1	Frank Chance
1909—Second	104	49	.680	6½	Frank Chance
1910—First	104	50	.675	+13	Frank Chance
1911—Second	92	62	.597	7½	Frank Chance
1912—Third	91	59	.607	11½	Frank Chance
1913—Third	88	65	.575	13½	John Evers
1914—Fourth	78	76	.506	16½	Henry (Hank) O'Day
1915—Fourth	73	80	.477	17½	Roger Bresnahan
1916—Fifth	67	86	.438	26½	Joseph Tinker
1917—Fifth	74	80	.481	24	Fred Mitchell
1918—First	84	45	.651	+10½	Fred Mitchell
1919—Third	75	65	.536	21	Fred Mitchell
1920—Fifth†	75	79	.487	18	Fred Mitchell
1921—Seventh	64	89	.418	30	J. Evers, W. Killefer
1922—Fifth	80	74	.519	13	William Killefer
1923—Fourth	83	71	.539	12½	William Killefer
1924—Fifth	81	72	.529	12	William Killefer
1925—Eighth	68	86	.442	27½	Killefer, Maranville, Gibson
1926—Fourth	82	72	.532	7	Joseph McCarthy
1927—Fourth	85	68	.556	8½	Joseph McCarthy
1928—Third	91	63	.591	4	Joseph McCarthy
1929—First	98	54	.645	+10½	Joseph McCarthy
1930—Second	90	64	.584	2	J. McCarthy, R. Hornsby
1931—Third	84	70	.545	17	Rogers Hornsby
1932—First	90	64	.584	+ 4	R. Hornsby, C. Grimm
1933—Third	86	68	.558	6	Charles Grimm
1934—Third	86	65	.570	8	Charles Grimm
1935—First	100	54	.649	+ 4	Charles Grimm
1936—Second†	87	67	.565	5	Charles Grimm
1937—Second	93	61	.604	3	Charles Grimm
1938—First	89	63	.586	+ 2	C. Grimm, C. Hartnett
1939—Fourth	84	70	.545	13	Charles (Gabby) Hartnett
1940—Fifth	75	79	.487	25½	Charles (Gabby) Hartnett
1941—Sixth	70	84	.455	30	James Wilson
1942—Sixth	68	86	.442	38	James Wilson
1943—Fifth	74	79	.484	30½	James Wilson
1944—Fourth	75	79	.487	30	J. Wilson, C. Grimm
1945—First	98	56	.636	+ 3	Charles Grimm
1946—Third	82	71	.536	14½	Charles Grimm
1947—Sixth	69	85	.448	25	Charles Grimm
1948—Eighth	64	90	.416	27½	Charles Grimm
1949—Eighth	61	93	.396	36	C. Grimm, F. Frisch
1950—Seventh	64	89	.418	26½	Frank Frisch
1951—Eighth	62	92	.403	34½	F. Frisch, P. Cavarretta
1952—Fifth	77	77	.500	19½	Philip Cavarretta
1953—Seventh	65	89	.422	40	Philip Cavarretta
1954—Seventh	64	90	.416	33	Stanley Hack
1955—Sixth	72	81	.471	26	Stanley Hack
1956—Eighth	60	94	.390	33	Stanley Hack
1957—Seventh†	62	92	.403	33	Robert Scheffing
1958—Fifth†	72	82	.468	20	Robert Scheffing
1959—Fifth†	74	80	.481	13	Robert Scheffing
1960—Seventh	60	94	.390	35	C. Grimm, L. Boudreau
1961—Seventh	64	90	.416	29	Craft, Himsl, Klein, Tappe
1962—Ninth	59	103	.364	42½	Tappe, Klein, Metro
1963—Seventh	82	80	.506	17	Robert Kennedy
1964—Eighth	76	86	.469	17	Robert Kennedy
1965—Eighth	72	90	.444	25	R. Kennedy, L. Klein
1966—Tenth	59	103	.364	36	Leo Durocher
1967—Third	87	74	.540	14	Leo Durocher
1968—Third	84	78	.519	13	Leo Durocher

East Division

Year—Position	W.	L.	Pct.	*G.B.	Manager
1969—Second	92	70	.568	8	Leo Durocher
1970—Second	84	78	.519	5	Leo Durocher
1971—Third†	83	79	.512	14	Leo Durocher
1972—Second	85	70	.548	11	L. Durocher, C. Lockman
1973—Fifth	77	84	.478	5	Carroll (Whitey) Lockman
1974—Sixth	66	96	.407	22	C. Lockman, J. Marshall
1975—Fifth†	75	87	.463	17½	James Marshall
1976—Fourth	75	87	.463	26	James Marshall
1977—Fourth	81	81	.500	20	Herman Franks
1978—Third	79	83	.488	11	Herman Franks
1979—Fifth	80	82	.494	18	H. Franks, J. Amalfitano
1980—Sixth	64	98	.395	27	P. Gomez, J. Amalfitano
1981—6th/5th	38	65	.369	‡	Joe Amalfitano
1982—Fifth	73	89	.451	19	Lee Elia
1983—Fifth	71	91	.438	19	L. Elia, C. Fox
1984—First§	96	65	.596	+6½	James Frey
1985—Fourth	77	84	.478	23½	James Frey
1986—Fifth	70	90	.438	37	J. Frey, G. Michael
1987—Sixth	76	85	.472	18½	G. Michael, F. Lucchesi

*Games behind winner. †Tied for position. ‡First half 15-37; second 23-28. §Lost Championship Series.

Billy Williams

Individual Records (1876 To Date)
Batting

Most years, non-pitcher	22, Adrian C. Anson
Most years, league, since 1900	20, Philip J. Cavarretta
Most games	164, Ronald E. Santo, 1965
	164, Billy L. Williams, 1965
Most games, league	2,528, Ernest Banks
Most at-bats	666, William J. Herman, 154 games, 1935
Most at-bats, league	9,421, Ernest Banks
Most runs	156, Rogers Hornsby, 156 games, 1929
Most runs, league	1,712, Adrian C. Anson
Most runs, league, since 1900	1,306, Billy L. Williams
Most hits	229, Rogers Hornsby, 156 games, 1929
Most hits, league	3,081, Adrian C. Anson
Most hits, league, since 1900	2,583, Ernest Banks
Most singles	165, Earl J. Adams, 146 games, 1927
Most singles, league	2,330, Adrian C. Anson
Most singles, league, since 1900	1,692, Stanley C. Hack
Most doubles	57, William J. Herman, 154 games, 1935
	57, William J. Herman, 153 games, 1936
Most doubles, league	530, Adrian C. Anson
Most doubles, league, since 1900	407, Ernest Banks
Most triples	21, Frank M. Schulte, 154 games, 1911
	21, Victor S. Saier, 149 games, 1913
Most triples, league	137, James E. Ryan
Most triples, league, since 1900	117, Frank Schulte
Most homers, lefthander	42, Billy L. Williams, 161 games, 1970
Most homers, righthander	56, Lewis R. Wilson, 155 games, 1930
Most homers at home	33, Lewis R. Wilson, 1930
Most homers on road	23, Lewis R. Wilson, 1930
	23, Ernest Banks, 1960
	23, David A. Kingman, 1979
Most homers, rookie	25, Billy L. Williams, 146 games, 1961
Most homers, month	15, Andre F. Dawson, August, 1987
Most homers, league, righthander	512, Ernest Banks
Most homers, league, lefthander	392, Billy L. Williams
Most grand slams	5, Ernest Banks, 154 games, 1955
Most grand slams, league	12, Ernest Banks
Most total bases	423, Lewis R. Wilson, 155 games, 1930
Most total bases, league	4,706, Ernest Banks
Most long hits	97, Lewis R. Wilson, 155 games, 1930

Most long hits, league	1,009, Ernest Banks
Most extra bases on long hits	215, Lewis R. Wilson, 155 games, 1930
Most extra bases on long hits, league	2,123, Ernest Banks
Most sacrifices (S.H. and S.F.)	46, James T. Sheckard, 148 games, 1909
Most sacrifice hits	40, James T. Sheckard, 149 games, 1906
Most sacrifice flies	14, Ronald E. Santo, 1969
Most stolen bases	100, William A. Lange, 123 games, 1896
Most stolen bases since 1900	67, Frank L. Chance, 123 games, 1903
Most stolen bases, league	404, Frank L. Chance
Most caught stealing	29, Charles J. Hollocher, 152 games, 1922
Most bases on balls	147, James T. Sheckard, 156 games, 1911
Most bases on balls, league	1,092, Stanley C. Hack
Most strikeouts	143, Byron E. Browne, 120 games, 1966
Most strikeouts, league	1,271, Ronald E. Santo
Fewest strikeouts	5, Charles J. Hollocher, 152 games, 1922
Most hit by pitch	12, Adolfo E. Philips, 116 games, 1966
Most runs batted in	190, Lewis R. Wilson, 155 games, 1930
Most runs batted in, league	1,636, Ernest Banks
Most game-winning RBIs	19, Gary N. Matthews, 147 games, 1984
Most consecutive games with RBI	17, Oscar R. Grimes (22 RBIs), 1922
Highest batting average	.388, Michael J. Kelly, 118 games, 1886
	.388, William A. Lange, 122 games, 1895
Highest batting average since 1900	.380, Rogers Hornsby, 156 games, 1929
Highest batting average, league	.339, Adrian C. Anson
Highest batting average, league, since 1900	.336, J. Riggs Stephenson
Highest slugging average	.723, Lewis R. Wilson, 155 games, 1930
Longest batting streak	42 games, William F. Dahlen, 1894
Longest batting streak since 1900	28 games, Ronald E. Santo, 1966
Most grounded into double play	27, Ronald E. Santo, 149 games, 1973
Fewest grounded into double play	0, August J. Galan, 154 games, 1935

Pitching, Since 1900

Most years	16, Charles H. Root
Most games	84, Theodore W. Abernathy, 1965
	84, Richard W. Tidrow, 1980
Most games, league	605, Charles H. Root
Most games started	42, Ferguson A. Jenkins, 1969
Most games started, league	347, Ferguson A. Jenkins
Most complete games	33, John W. Taylor, 1903
	33, Grover C. Alexander, 1920
Most complete games, league	205, Mordecai P. Brown
Most games finished	62, Theodore W. Abernathy, 1965
Most innings	363, Grover C. Alexander, 1920
Most innings, league	3,138, Charles H. Root
Most games won	29, Mordecai P. Brown, 1908
Most games won, league	201, Charles H. Root
Most 20 victory seasons	6, Mordecai P. Brown
	6, Ferguson A. Jenkins
Most games lost	22, Thomas J. Hughes, 1901
	22, Richard C. Ellsworth, 1966
	22, William G. Bonham, 1974
Most games lost, league	156, Charles H. Root
Highest winning percentage	.941, Richard L. Sutcliffe (16-1), 1984
Longest winning streak	14 games, Edward M. Reulbach, 1909
	14 games, Richard L. Sutcliffe, 1984
Longest winning streak, two seasons	16 games, Richard L. Sutcliffe, 1984-85
Longest losing streak	13 games, Robert L. McCall, 1948
Most saves	37, H. Bruce Sutter, 1979
Most bases on balls	185, Samuel Jones, 1955
Most bases on balls, league	871, Charles H. Root
Most strikeouts	274, Ferguson A. Jenkins, 1970
Most strikeouts, game	17, John T. Pfiester, May 30, 1906, first game, 15 innings
	16, John G. Clarkson, August 18, 1886
	15, Richard Drott, May 26, 1957, first game
	15, Burt C. Hooton, September 15, 1971, second game
	15, Richard L. Sutcliffe, Sept. 3, 1984 (pitched first 8 innings of 12-inning game)
Most strikeouts, league	2,036, Ferguson A. Jenkins
Most shutouts	9, Mordecai P. Brown, 1906, 1908
	9, Orval Overall, 1907, 1909
	9, Grover C. Alexander, 1919
	9, William C. Lee, 1938
Most shutouts, league	48, Mordecai P. Brown
Most 1-0 shutouts won	3, held by many pitchers
Most runs	174, Guy T. Bush, 1930
Most earned runs	155, Guy T. Bush, 1930
Most hits	335, Grover C. Alexander, 1920
Most hit batsmen	20, James J. Callahan, 1900
Most wild pitches	26, Lawrence D. Cheney, 1914
Most home runs	38, Warren L. Hacker, 1955
Most sacrifice hits	23, William G. Bonham, 1974
Most sacrifice flies	14, Ricky E. Reuschel, 1980
Lowest ERA	1.72, Grover Alexander, 235 innings, 1919

Club Records

Most players	49 in 1966
Fewest players	20 in 1905
Most games	164 in 1965
Most at-bats	5619 in 1980 (162 games)
Most runs	998 in 1930 (156 games)
Most opponents' runs	870 in 1930 (156 games)
Fewest runs	530 in 1906 (154 games)
Most hits	1722 in 1930 (156 games)
Fewest hits	1224 in 1907 (155 games)
Most singles	1226 in 1921 (153 games)
Most doubles	340 in 1931 (156 games)
Most triples	101 in 1911 (157 games)
Most homers	209 in 1987 (161 games)
Fewest homers (154 or 162-game schedule)	12 in 1905

Most homers at Wrigley Field, home & opp.	204 in 1987
Most grand slams	9 in 1929
Most pinch home runs	8 in 1958, 1985, 1987
Most total bases	2684 in 1930 (156 games)
Most long hits	548 in 1930 (156 games)
Most extra bases on long hits	962 in 1930 (156 games)
Most sacrifices, (S.H. and S.F.)	270 in 1908 (158 games)
Most sacrifice hits	231 in 1906 (154 games)
Most sacrifice flies	66 in 1975 (162 games)
Most stolen bases	283 in 1906 (154 games)
Most caught stealing	149 in 1924 (154 games)
Most bases on balls	650 in 1975 (162 games)
Most strikeouts	1064 in 1987 (161 games)
Fewest strikeouts	374 in 1921 (153 games)
Most hit by pitch	47 in 1966 (162 games)
Fewest hit by pitch	13 in 1956 (157 games)
Most runs batted in	940 in 1930 (156 games)
Most game-winning RBIs	86 in 1984 (161 games)
Highest batting average	.309 in 1930 (156 games)
Lowest batting average	.238 in 1963 (162 games)
	.238 in 1965 (164 games)
Highest slugging average	.481 in 1930 (156 games)
Lowest slugging average	.311 in 1907 (155 games)
Most grounded into double play	157 in 1938 (154 games)
Fewest grounded into double play	93 in 1945 (155 games)
Most left on bases	1262 in 1975 (162 games)
Fewest left on bases	964 in 1924 (154 games)
Most .300 hitters	8 in 1921
Most putouts	4437 in 1980 (162 games)
Fewest putouts	4024 in 1909 (155 games)
Most assists	2155 in 1916 (156 games)
Fewest assists	1607 in 1956 (157 games)
Most chances accepted	6508 in 1977 (162 games)
Fewest chances accepted	5706 in 1953 (155 games)
Most errors	310 in 1914 (156 games)
Fewest errors	115 in 1983 (162 games)
Most errorless games	83 in 1968 (163 games)
Most consecutive errorless games	8 in 1978, 1984
Most double plays	176 in 1928 (154 games)
Fewest double plays	110 in 1982 (162 games)
Most passed balls	35 in 1961 (156 games)
Fewest passed balls	4 in 1967 (162 games)
Highest fielding average	.982 in 1983 (162 games)
Lowest fielding average	.951 in 1914 (156 games)
Highest home attendance	2,161,534 in 1985
Highest road attendance	2,245,903 in 1985
Most games won	116 in 1906
Most games lost	103 in 1962
	103 in 1966
Most games won, month	26, August 1906
	26, July 1935
	26, July 1945
Most games lost, month	24, July 1957
Highest percentage games won	.798 in 1880 (won 67, lost 17)
Highest percentage games won, since 1900	.763 in 1906 (won 116, lost 36)
Lowest percentage games won	.364 in 1962 (won 59, lost 103)
	.364 in 1966 (won 59, lost 103)
Games won, league	8450 in 112 years
Games lost, league	7823 in 112 years
Most shutouts won	32 in 1907, 1909
Most shutouts lost	22 in 1915
	22 in 1968
Most 1-0 games won	9 in 1906
Most 1-0 games lost	10 in 1916
Most consecutive games won	21 in 1880, 1935
Most consecutive games lost	13 in 1944, 1982, 1985
Most times league champions	16
Most last place finishes	12
Most runs, game	36 vs. Louisville, June 29, 1897
Most runs, game, since 1900	26 vs. Philadelphia, August 25, 1922
Most runs, games, by opponent, since 1900	23 by Philadelphia, August 25, 1922
	23 by Cincinnati, July 6, 1949
	23 by Philadelphia, May 17, 1979, 10 innings
	23 by New York, August 16, 1987
Most runs, shutout game	24 vs. Boston, July 1, 1885
Most runs, shutout game, since 1900	19 vs. New York, June 7, 1906
	19 vs. San Diego, May 13, 1969
Most runs, shutout game, by opponent	22 by Pittsburgh, September 16, 1975
Most runs, doubleheader shutout	12 vs. St. Louis, July 11, 1965
Most runs, inning	18 vs. Detroit, Sept. 6, 1883, seventh inning
Most runs, inning, since 1900	14 vs. Philadelphia, August 25, 1922, fourth inning
Longest 1-0 game won	17 innings vs. Boston, September 21, 1901
Longest 1-0 game lost	17 innings vs. Houston, August 23, 1980
Most hits, game	32 vs. Buffalo, July 3, 1883
	32 vs. Louisville, June 29, 1897
Most hits, game, since 1900	28 vs. Boston, July 3, 1945
Most home runs, game	7 vs. New York, June 11, 1967, second game
	7 vs. San Diego, August 19, 1970
	7 vs. San Diego, May 17, 1977
Most consecutive games, one or more homers*	14 (29 homers), 1884
	14 (27 homers), 1961
	14 (26 homers), 1987
Most total bases, game	54 vs. Brooklyn, August 25, 1891
Most total bases, game, since 1900	49 vs. Phil., May 17, 1979, 10 innings
	45 vs. N.Y., June 11, 1967, second game
Largest crowd, day game	46,572 vs. Brooklyn, May 18, 1947
Largest crowd, doubleheader	46,965 vs. Pittsburgh, May 31, 1948
Largest crowd, home opener	45,777 vs. Pittsburgh, April 14, 1978

*Two-season record is 16; last 2 games of 1953 (3 homers) and first 13 games of 1954 (28 homers).

Cincinnati Reds

Yearly Finishes

Year—Position	W.	L.	Pct.	*G.B.	Manager
1901—Eighth	52	87	.374	38	John McPhee
1902—Fourth	70	70	.500	33½	McPhee, Bancroft, Kelley
1903—Fourth	74	65	.532	16½	Joseph Kelley
1904—Third	88	65	.575	18	Joseph Kelley
1905—Fifth.......	79	74	.516	26	Joseph Kelley
1906—Sixth	64	87	.424	51½	Edward (Ned) Hanlon
1907—Sixth	66	87	.431	41½	Edward (Ned) Hanlon
1908—Fifth.......	73	81	.474	26	John Ganzel
1909—Fourth	77	76	.503	33½	Clark Griffith
1910—Fifth.......	75	79	.487	29	Clark Griffith
1911—Sixth	70	83	.458	29	Clark Griffith
1912—Fourth	75	78	.490	29	Henry (Hank) O'Day
1913—Seventh ..	64	89	.418	37½	Joseph Tinker
1914—Eighth	60	94	.390	34½	Charles (Buck) Herzog
1915—Seventh ..	71	83	.461	20	Charles (Buck) Herzog
1916—Seventh†	60	93	.392	33½	C. Herzog, C. Mathewson
1917—Fourth	78	76	.506	20	Christy Mathewson
1918—Third	68	60	.531	15½	C. Mathewson, H. Groh
1919—First	96	44	.686	+ 9	*............Patrick Moran
1920—Third	82	71	.536	10½	Patrick Moran
1921—Sixth	70	83	.458	24	Patrick Moran
1922—Second....	86	68	.558	7	Patrick Moran
1923—Second....	91	63	.591	4½	Patrick Moran
1924—Fourth	83	70	.542	10	John (Jack) Hendricks
1925—Third	80	73	.523	15	John (Jack) Hendricks
1926—Second....	87	67	.565	2	John (Jack) Hendricks
1927—Fifth.......	75	78	.490	18½	John (Jack) Hendricks
1928—Fifth.......	78	74	.513	16	John (Jack) Hendricks
1929—Seventh ..	66	88	.429	33	John (Jack) Hendricks
1930—Seventh ..	59	95	.383	33	Daniel Howley
1931—Eighth	58	96	.377	43	Daniel Howley
1932—Eighth	60	94	.390	30	Daniel Howley
1933—Eighth	58	94	.382	33	Owen (Donie) Bush
1934—Eighth	52	99	.344	42	R. O'Farrell, C. Dressen
1935—Sixth	68	85	.444	31½	Charles Dressen
1936—Fifth.......	74	80	.481	18	Charles Dressen
1937—Eighth	56	98	.364	40	C. Dressen, R. Wallace
1938—Fourth	82	68	.547	6	William McKechnie
1939—First	97	57	.630	+ 4½	William McKechnie
1940—First	100	53	.654	+12	William McKechnie
1941—Third	88	66	.571	12	William McKechnie
1942—Fourth	76	76	.500	29	William McKechnie
1943—Second....	87	67	.565	18	William McKechnie
1944—Third	89	65	.578	16	William McKechnie
1945—Seventh ..	61	93	.396	37	William McKechnie
1946—Sixth	67	87	.435	30	William McKechnie
1947—Fifth.......	73	81	.474	21	John Neun
1948—Seventh ..	64	89	.418	27	J. Neun, W. Walters
1949—Seventh ..	62	92	.403	35	William (Bucky) Walters
1950—Sixth	66	87	.431	24½	J. Luther Sewell
1951—Sixth	68	86	.442	28½	J. Luther Sewell
1952—Sixth	69	85	.448	27½	L. Sewell, R. Hornsby
1953—Sixth	68	86	.442	37	R. Hornsby, B. Mills
1954—Fifth.......	74	80	.481	23	George (Birdie) Tebbetts
1955—Fifth.......	75	79	.487	23½	George (Birdie) Tebbetts
1956—Third	91	63	.591	2	George (Birdie) Tebbetts
1957—Fourth....	80	74	.519	15	George (Birdie) Tebbetts
1958—Fourth....	76	78	.494	16	B. Tebbetts, J. Dykes
1959—Fifth†	74	80	.481	13	M. Smith, F. Hutchinson
1960—Sixth	67	87	.435	28	Fred Hutchinson
1961—First	93	61	.604	+ 4	Fred Hutchinson
1962—Third	98	64	.605	3½	Fred Hutchinson
1963—Fifth.......	86	76	.531	13	Fred Hutchinson
1964—Second†	92	70	.549	1	F. Hutchinson, R. Sisler
1965—Fourth....	89	73	.549	8	Richard Sisler
1966—Seventh ..	76	84	.475	18	D. Heffner, D. Bristol
1967—Fourth....	87	75	.537	14½	J. David Bristol
1968—Fourth.....	83	79	.512	14	J. David Bristol

West Division

Year—Position	W.	L.	Pct.	*G.B.	Manager
1969—Third	89	73	.549	4	J. David Bristol
1970—First‡......	102	60	.630	+14½	George (Sparky) Anderson
1971—Fourth† ..	79	83	.488	11	George (Sparky) Anderson
1972—First‡......	95	59	.617	+10½	George (Sparky) Anderson
1973—First§......	99	63	.611	+ 3½	George (Sparky) Anderson
1974—Second ..	98	64	.605	4	George (Sparky) Anderson
1975—First‡.....	108	54	.667	+20	George (Sparky) Anderson
1976—First‡.....	102	60	.630	+10	George (Sparky) Anderson
1977—Second...	88	74	.543	10	George (Sparky) Anderson
1978—Second...	92	69	.571	2½	George (Sparky) Anderson
1979—First§......	90	71	.559	+ 1½	John McNamara
1980—Third	89	73	.549	3½	John McNamara
1981—2nd/2nd	66	42	.611	x	John McNamara
1982—Sixth	61	101	.377	28	J. McNamara, R. Nixon
1983—Sixth	74	88	.457	17	Russell Nixon
1984—Fifth.......	70	92	.432	22	V. Rapp, P. Rose
1985—Second...	89	72	.553	5½	Peter Rose
1986—Second...	86	76	.531	10	Peter Rose
1987—Second...	84	78	.519	6	Peter Rose

*Games behind winner. †Tied for position. ‡Won Championship Series.
§Lost Championship Series. xFirst half 35-21; second 31-21.

Pete Rose

Individual Records
(1876 To 1880, 1890 To Date)
Batting

Most years, non-pitcher	19, Peter E. Rose
Most games	163, Leonardo A. Cardenas, 1964
	163, Peter E. Rose, 1974
Most games, league	2722, Peter E. Rose
Most at-bats	680, Peter E. Rose, 160 games, 1973
Most at-bats, league	10934, Peter E. Rose
Most runs	134, Frank Robinson, 162 games, 1962
Most runs, league	1741, Peter E. Rose
Most hits	230, Peter E. Rose, 160 games, 1973
Most hits, league	3358, Peter E. Rose
Most singles	181, Peter E. Rose, 160 games, 1973
Most singles, league	2490, Peter E. Rose
Most doubles	51, Frank Robinson, 162 games, 1962
	51, Peter E. Rose, 159 games, 1978
Most doubles, league	601, Peter E. Rose
Most triples	25, John A. McPhee, 132 games, 1890
Most triples since 1900	23, Samuel Crawford, 140 games, 1902
Most triples, league	153, Edd J. Roush
Most homers, lefthander	49, Theodore B. Kluszewski, 149 games, 1954
Most homers, righthander	52, George A. Foster, 158 games, 1977
Most homers, league, righthander	389, Johnny L. Bench
Most homers, league, lefthander	251, Theodore B. Kluszewski
Most homers, rookie	38, Frank Robinson, 152 games, 1956
Most homers at home	34, Theodore B. Kluszewski, 1954
Most homers on road	31, George A. Foster, 1977
Most homers, month	14, Frank Robinson, August, 1962

Most grand slams ....3, Frank Robinson, 162 games, 1962
3, Lee A. May, 153 games, 1970
3, C. Ray Knight, 162 games, 1980
3, Eric K. Davis, 129 games, 1987
Most grand slams, league ....11, Johnny L. Bench
Most total bases ....388, George A. Foster, 158 games, 1977
Most total bases, league ....4645, Peter E. Rose
Most long hits ....92, Frank Robinson, 162 games, 1962
Most long hits, league ....868, Peter E. Rose
Most extra bases on long hits ....191, George A. Foster, 158 games, 1977
Most extra bases on long hits, league ....1596, Johnny L. Bench
Most sacrifices (S. H. and S. F.) ...... 39, Jacob E. Daubert, 140 games, 1919
Most sacrifice hits ....31, Roy D. McMillan, 154 games, 1954
Most sacrifice flies ....13, John E. Temple, 149 games, 1959
Most stolen bases ....93, W. Arlie Latham, 135 games, 1891
Most stolen bases, since 1900 .... 81, Robert H. Bescher, 153 games, 1911
Most stolen bases, league ....406, Joe L. Morgan
Most caught stealing ....28, Louis B. Duncan, 151 games, 1922
Most bases on balls ....132, Joe L. Morgan, 146 games, 1975
Most bases on balls, league ....1210, Peter E. Rose
Most strikeouts ....142, Lee A. May, 158 games, 1969
Most strikeouts, league ....1306, Atanasio R. Perez
Fewest strikeouts ....13, Frank A. McCormick, 154 games, 1941
Most hit by pitch ....20, Frank Robinson, 152 games, 1956
Most runs batted in ....149, George A. Foster, 158 games, 1977
Most runs batted in, league ....1376, Johnny L. Bench
Most game-winning RBIs ....18, David A. Parker, 160 games, 1985
Highest batting average ....383, John W. Holliday, 122 games, 1894
Highest batting average since 1900 . .377, J. Bentley Seymour, 149 games, 1905
Highest batting average, league ....331, Edd J. Roush
Highest slugging average .....642, Theodore B. Kluszewski, 149 games, 1954
Longest batting streak ....44 games, Peter E. Rose, 1978
Most grounded into double play ....30, Ernest N. Lombardi, 129 games, 1938
Fewest grounded into double play ....3, William H. Myers, 151 games, 1939

Pitching, Since 1900

Most years ....15, Joseph H. Nuxhall
Most games ....90, Wayne A. Granger, 1969
Most games, league ....531, Pedro Borbon
Most games started ....42, Frank Hahn, 1901
Most games started, league ....356, Eppa Rixey
Most complete games ....41, Frank Hahn, 1901
Most complete games, league ....195, William H. Walters
Most games finished ....62, Thomas H. Hume, 1980
Most innings ....375, Frank Hahn, 1901
Most innings, league ....2890, Eppa Rixey
Most games won ....27, Adolfo Luque, 1923
27, William H. Walters, 1939
Most games won, league ....179, Eppa Rixey
Most 20-victory seasons ....4, Paul M. Derringer
Most games lost ....25, Paul M. Derringer, 1933
Most games lost, league ....150, Paul M. Derringer
Highest winning percentage ....826, Elmer R. Riddle (19-4), 1941
Longest winning streak ....16 games, Ewell Blackwell, 1947
Longest losing streak ....12 games, Henry Thielman, 1902
12 games, Peter J. Schneider, 1914
12 games, Silas K. Johnson, 1933
Most saves ....37, Clay P. Carroll, 1972
Most bases on balls ....162, John S. Vander Meer, 1943
Most bases on balls, league ....1072, John S. Vander Meer
Most strikeouts ....274, Mario M. Soto, 1982
Most strikeouts, game ....18, James W. Maloney, June 14, 1965, 11 innings
16, Frank G. Hahn, May 22, 1901
16, James W. Maloney, May 21, 1963
Most strikeouts, league ....1592, James W. Maloney
Most shutouts ....7, Jacob Weimer, 1906
7, Fred A. Toney, 1917
7, Horace O. Eller, 1919
7, John E. Billingham, 1973
Most shutouts, league ....32, William H. Walters
Most 1-0 shutouts won ....4, Jacob Weimer, 1906
Most runs ....158, Frank Hahn, 1901
Most earned runs ....145, Herman R. Wehmeier, 1950
Most hits ....368, Frank Hahn, 1901
Most hit batsmen ....23, Jacob Weimer, 1907
Most wild pitches ....19, James W. Maloney, 1963
19, James W. Maloney, 1965
Most home runs ....35, Samuel, J. Ellis, 1966
Most sacrifice hits ....17, Joseph R. Jay, 1962
17, Bruce M. Berenyi, 1982
Most sacrifice flies ....13, William L. Gullickson, 1986
Lowest ERA ....1.57, Frederick A. Toney, 223 innings, 1915

Club Records

Most players ....45 in 1913
Fewest players ....21 in 1904
Most games ....163 in 1964, 1968, 1969, 1974, 1980
Most at-bats ....5767 in 1968 (163 games)
Most runs ....857 in 1976 (162 games)
Most opponents' runs ....857 in 1930 (154 games)
Fewest opponents' runs ....528 in 1940 (155 games)
Fewest runs ....488 in 1908 (155 games)
Most hits ....1599 in 1976 (162 games)
Fewest hits ....1108 in 1908 (155 games)
Most singles ....1191 in 1922 (156 games)
Most doubles ....281 in 1968 (163 games)
Most triples ....120 in 1926 (157 games)
Most homers ....221 in 1956 (155 games)

Fewest homers (154 or 162-game schedule) .... 14 in 1908
14 in 1916
Most homers at Crosley Field, home & opp. .... 219 in 1957
Most homers at Riverfront Stad., home & opp. .. 191 in 1987
Most grand slams ....7 in 1974, 1980, 1987
Most pinch home runs ....12 in 1957 (154 games)
Most long hits ....512 in 1965 (162 games)
Most extra bases on long hits ....939 in 1965 (162 games)
Most total bases ....2483 in 1965 (162 games)
Most sacrifices (S. H. and S. F.) ....239 in 1926 (157 games)
Most sacrifice hits ....195 in 1907 (156 games)
Most sacrifice flies ....60 in 1976 (162 games)
Most stolen bases ....310 in 1910 (156 games)
Most caught stealing ....136 in 1922 (156 games)
Most bases on balls ....693 in 1974 (163 games)
Most strikeouts ....1042 in 1969 (163 games)
Fewest strikeouts ....308 in 1921 (153 games)
Most hit by pitch ....51 in 1956 (155 games)
Fewest hit by pitch ....11 in 1951 (155 games)
Most runs batted in ....802 in 1976 (162 games)
Most game-winning RBIs ....84 in 1980 (163 games)
84 in 1985 (162 games)
Highest batting average ....296 in 1922 (156 games)
Lowest batting average ....227 in 1908 (155 games)
Highest slugging average ....441 in 1956 (155 games)
Lowest slugging average ....304 in 1906 (155 games)
Most grounded into double play ....143 in 1982 (162 games)
Fewest grounded into double play ....93 in 1935 (154 games)
Most left on bases ....1328 in 1976 (162 games)
Fewest left on bases ....997 in 1921 (153 games)
Most .300 hitters ....8 in 1926
Most putouts ....4471 in 1968 (163 games)
Fewest putouts ....4006 in 1930 (154 games)
Most assists ....2151 in 1905 (155 games)
Fewest assists ....1534 in 1966 (160 games)
Most chances accepted ....6399 in 1915 (160 games)
Fewest chances accepted ....5655 in 1950 (153 games)
Most errors ....314 in 1914 (157 games)
Fewest errors ....95 in 1977 (162 games)
Most errorless games ....94 in 1977 (162 games)
Most consecutive errorless games ....15 in 1975 (162 games)
Most double plays ....194 in 1928 (153 games)
194 in 1931 (154 games)
194 in 1954 (154 games)
Fewest double plays ....116 in 1984 (162 games)
Most passed balls ....39 in 1914 (157 games)
Fewest passed balls ....3 in 1975 (162 games)
Highest fielding average ....984 in 1971 (162 games)
.984 in 1975 (162 games)
.984 in 1976 (162 games)
.984 in 1977 (162 games)
Lowest fielding average ....952 in 1914 (157 games)
Highest home attendance ....2,629,708 in 1976
Highest road attendance ....2,320,693 in 1978
Most games won ....108 in 1975
Most games lost ....101 in 1982
Most games won, month ....24, August 1918
24, July 1973
Most games lost, month ....26, Sept. 1914
Highest percentage games won ....686 in 1919 (won 96, lost 44)
Lowest percentage games won ....138 in 1876 (won 9, lost 56)
Lowest percentage games won, since 1900 .... .344 in 1934 (won 52, lost 99)
Games won, league, 1890 to date ....7553 in 98 years
Games lost, league, 1890 to date ....7376 in 98 years
Most shutouts won ....23 in 1919
Most shutouts lost ....24 in 1908
Most 1-0 games won ....7 in 1910, 1943, 1963
Most 1-0 games lost ....7 in 1907, 1916
Most consecutive games won ....14 in 1899
Most consecutive games won, since 1900 ....12 in 1939, 1957
Most consecutive games lost ....19 in 1914
Most times league champions 8
Most last place finishes ....11 (tied in 1916)
Most runs, game ....30 vs. Louisville, June 18, 1893
Most runs, game, since 1900 ....26 vs. Boston, June 4, 1911
Most runs, game, by opponent ....26 by Philadelphia, July 26, 1892
Most runs, game, by opponent, since 1900 ....25 by New York, June 9, 1901
25 by Brooklyn, September 23, 1901
Most runs, shutout game ....18 vs. Los Angeles, August 8, 1965
Most runs, shutout game, by opponent .....18 by Phil., August 10, 1930, first game
18 by Phil., July 14, 1934, first game
18 by St. Louis, June 10, 1944
Most runs, doubleheader shutout ....14 vs. St. Louis, September 1, 1924
14 vs. Los Angeles, August 16, 1961
Most runs, inning ....14 vs. Louisville, June 18, 1893, first inning
Most runs, inning, since 1900 ....12 vs. New York, May 4, 1942, fourth inning
12 vs. Atlanta, April 25, 1977, fifth inning
Longest 1-0 game won ....15 innings vs. New York, July 16, 1933, first game
15 innings vs. Brooklyn, June 11, 1915
Longest 1-0 game lost ....21 innings vs. San Francisco, September 1, 1967
Most hits, game ....32 vs. Louisville, June 18, 1893
Most hits, game, since 1900 ....28 vs. Philadelphia, May 13, 1902
Most home runs, game ....8 vs. Milwaukee, August 18, 1956
Most consecutive games, one or more homers ....21 (41 homers), 1956
Most total bases, game ....55 vs. Louisville, June 18, 1893
Most total bases, game, since 1900 ....48 vs. Chicago, June 1, 1957
Largest crowd, day game ....55,166 vs. Montreal, April 6, 1987
Largest crowd, doubleheader ....53,328 vs. Pittsburgh, July 9, 1976
Largest crowd, night game ....53,790 vs. Houston, September 17, 1983
Largest crowd, home opener ....55,166 vs. Montreal, April 6, 1987

Houston Astros

Yearly Finishes

(Known as Houston Colts through 1964)

Year—Position	W.	L.	Pct.	*G.B.	Manager
1962—Eighth	64	96	.400	36½	Harry Craft
1963—Ninth	66	96	.407	33	Harry Craft
1964—Ninth	66	96	.407	27	H. Craft, L. Harris
1965—Ninth	65	97	.401	32	C. Luman Harris
1966—Eighth	72	90	.444	23	Grady Hatton
1967—Ninth	69	93	.426	32½	Grady Hatton
1968—Tenth	72	90	.444	25	G. Hatton, H. Walker

West Division

Year—Position	W.	L.	Pct.	*G.B.	Manager
1969—Fifth	81	81	.500	12	Harry Walker
1970—Fourth	79	83	.488	23	Harry Walker
1971—Fourth†	79	83	.488	11	Harry Walker
1972—Second	84	69	.549	10½	H. Walker, L. Durocher
1973—Fourth	82	80	.506	17	L. Durocher, P. Gomez
1974—Fourth	81	81	.500	21	Pedro (Preston) Gomez
1975—Sixth	64	97	.398	43½	P. Gomez, W. Virdon
1976—Third	80	82	.494	22	William Virdon
1977—Third	81	81	.500	17	William Virdon
1978—Fifth	74	88	.457	21	William Virdon
1979—Second	89	73	.549	1½	William Virdon
1980—First‡§	93	70	.571	+1	William Virdon
1981—3rd/1st.	61	49	.555	x	William Virdon
1982—Fifth	77	85	.475	12	W. Virdon, R. Lillis
1983—Third	85	77	.525	6	Robert Lillis
1984—Second†	80	82	.494	12	Robert Lillis
1985—Third†	83	79	.512	12	Robert Lillis
1986—First§	96	66	.593	+10	Harold Lanier
1987—Third	76	86	.469	14	Harold Lanier

*Games behind winner. †Tied for position. ‡Won division playoff. §Lost Championship Series. xFirst half 28-29; second 33-20.

Individual Records (1962 To Date)

Batting

Most years, non-pitcher	14, Robert J. Watson
Most games	162, Enos M. Cabell, 1978
	162, William D. Doran, 1987
Most games, league	1870, Jose D. Cruz
Most at-bats	660, Enos M. Cabell, 162 games, 1978
Most at-bats, league	6629, Jose D. Cruz
Most runs	117, James S. Wynn, 145 games, 1972
Most runs, league	890, Cesar Cedeno
Most hits	195, Enos M. Cabell, 162 games, 1978
Most hits, league	1937, Jose D. Cruz
Most singles	160, Roland T. Jackson, 150 games, 1966
Most singles, league	1384, Jose D. Cruz
Most doubles	44, Daniel J. Staub, 149 games, 1967
Most doubles, league	343, Cesar Cedeno
Most triples	14, Roger T. Metzger, 154 games, 1973
Most triples, league	80, Jose D. Cruz
Most homers, righthander	37, James S. Wynn, 158 games, 1967
Most homers, league, righthander	223, James S. Wynn
Most homers, lefthander	20, Walter J. Bond, 148 games, 1964
Most homers, league, lefthander	138, Jose D. Cruz
Most homers, switch-hitter	20, Kevin C. Bass, 1986
Most homers at home	18, Lee A. May, 1974
Most homers on road	22, James S. Wynn, 1967
Most homers, month	11, James S. Wynn, June, 1967
	11, James S. Wynn, May, 1969
Most homers, rookie	20, Glenn E. Davis, 100 games, 1985
Most grand slams	2, Robert T. Aspromonte, 136 games, 1963
	2, Robert T. Aspromonte, 157 games, 1964
	2, Robert T. Aspromonte, 152 games, 1966
	2, Robert J. Watson, 97 games, 1973
	2, Lee A. May, 148 games, 1973
	2, J. Mark Bailey, 114 games, 1985
Most grand slams, league	6, Robert T. Aspromonte
Most total bases	300, Cesar Cedeno, 139 games, 1972
Most total bases, league	2846, Jose D. Cruz
Most long hits	69, James S. Wynn, 158 games, 1967
	69, Cesar Cedeno, 139 games, 1972
Most long hits, league	561, Cesar Cedeno
Most extra bases on long hits	146, James S. Wynn, 158 games, 1967
Most extra bases on long hits, league	961, James S. Wynn
Most sacrifice hits	34, G. Craig Reynolds, 146 games, 1979
Most sacrifice flies	13, C. Ray Knight, 158 games, 1982
Most stolen bases	61, Cesar Cedeno, 141 games, 1977
Most stolen bases, league	487, Cesar Cedeno
Most caught stealing	23, Jose D. Cruz, 157 games, 1977
Most bases on balls	148, James S. Wynn, 149 games, 1969
Most bases on balls, league	847, James S. Wynn
Most strikeouts	145, Lee A. May, 148 games, 1972
Most strikeouts, league	1088, James S. Wynn
Fewest strikeouts	39, Gregory E. Gross, 156 games, 1974
Most hit by pitch	11, Cesar Cedeno, 141 games, 1977
Most runs batted in	110, Robert J. Watson, 151 games, 1977
Most runs batted in, league	942, Jose D. Cruz
Most game-winning RBIs	18, Richard W. Thon, 154 games, 1983
Highest batting average	.333, Daniel J. Staub, 149 games, 1967
Highest batting average, league	.297, Robert J. Watson
Highest slugging average	.537, Cesar Cedeno, 139 games, 1972
	.537, Cesar Cedeno, 139 games, 1973
Highest slugging average, league	.454, Cesar Cedeno
Longest batting streak	23 games, Arthur H. Howe, 1981
Most grounded into double play	23, Douglas L. Rader, 156 games, 1970
Fewest grounded into double play	4, Joe L. Morgan, 157 games, 1965
	4, Joe L. Morgan, 160 games, 1971
	4, Jose Cruz, 160 games, 1983
	4, Philip M. Garner, 154 games, 1983

Pitching

Most years	13, Lawrence E. Dierker
Most games	70, Kenneth R. Forsch, 1974
Most games, league	421, Kenneth R. Forsch
Most games started	40, Jerry Reuss, 1973
Most games started, league	320, Lawrence E. Dierker
Most complete games	20, Lawrence E. Dierker, 1969
Most complete games, league	106, Lawrence E. Dierker
Most games finished	51, Joseph C. Sambito, 1979
Most innings	305, Lawrence E. Dierker, 1969
Most innings, league	2296, Lawrence E. Dierker
Most games won	21, Joseph F. Niekro, 1979
Most games won, league	144, Joseph F. Niekro
Most 20-victory seasons	2, Joseph F. Niekro
Most games lost, season	20, Richard J. Farrell, 1962
Most games lost, league	117, Lawrence E. Dierker
Highest winning percentage	.750, Vernon G. Ruhle (12-4), 1980
Longest winning streak	9 games, Joseph F. Niekro, 1979
Longest losing streak	11 games, Richard F. Drott, 1963
Most saves	33, David S. Smith, 1986
Most bases on balls	151, James R. Richard, 1976
Most bases on balls, league	818, Joseph F. Niekro
Most strikeouts	313, James R. Richard, 1979
Most strikeouts, league	1638, L. Nolan Ryan
Most strikeouts, game	18, Donald E. Wilson, July 14, 1968, second game
Most shutouts	6, David A. Roberts, 1973
Most shutouts won, league	25, Lawrence E. Dierker
Most 1-0 shutouts won	3, Robert J. Bruce, 1964
	3, Robert W. Knepper, 1981
Most runs	124, Lawrence E. Dierker, 1970
Most earned runs	116, Lawrence E. Dierker, 1970
	116, Jerry Reuss, 1973
Most hits	271, Jerry Reuss, 1973
Most hit batsmen	16, John E. Billingham, 1971
Most wild pitches	21, Joseph F. Niekro, 1985
Most home runs allowed	31, Lawrence E. Dierker, 1970
Most sacrifice hits allowed	22, Robert W. Knepper, 1986
Most sacrifice flies allowed	13, Mark Lemongello, 1978
Lowest ERA	2.22, Miguel A. Cuellar, 227 innings, 1966
	2.22, Michael W. Scott, 275⅓ innings, 1986

Club Records

Most players	48 in 1965 (162 games)
Fewest players	32 in 1972 (153 games)
Most games	163 in 1966, 1980
Most at-bats	5582 in 1985 (162 games)
Most runs	744 in 1970 (162 games)
Fewest runs	464 in 1963 (162 games)
Most opponents' runs	763 in 1970 (162 games)
Most hits	1465 in 1984 (162 games)
Fewest hits	1184 in 1963 (162 games)
Most singles	1097 in 1984 (162 games)
Most doubles	263 in 1977 (162 games)
Most triples	67 in 1980 (163 games)
	67 in 1984 (162 games)
Most homers	134 in 1972 (153 games)
	134 in 1973 (162 games)
Fewest homers	49 in 1979
Most homers at Colt Stadium, home & opp.	85 in 1962
Most homers at Astrodome, home & opp.	115 in 1970
Most grand slams	5 in 1970
	5 in 1973
	5 in 1986
Most pinch home runs	7 in 1974
	7 in 1986
Most total bases	2177 in 1970 (162 games)
Most long hits	437 in 1977 (162 games)
Most extra bases on long hits	731 in 1970 (162 games)
Most sacrifice hits	109 in 1979 (162 games)
Most sacrifice flies	55 in 1984 (162 games)
Most stolen bases	194 in 1980 (163 games)
Most caught stealing	95 in 1979 (162 games)
	95 in 1983 (162 games)
Most bases on balls	699 in 1969 (162 games)
Most strikeouts	988 in 1968 (162 games)
Fewest strikeouts	719 in 1976 (162 games)
Most hit by pitch	49 in 1964 (162 games)
Fewest hit by pitch	13 in 1980 (163 games)
Most runs batted in	694 in 1970 (162 games)
Most game-winning RBIs	90 in 1986 (162 games)
Highest batting average	.264 in 1984 (162 games)
Lowest batting average	.220 in 1963 (162 games)
Most .300 hitters	3 in 1970
Highest slugging average	.393 in 1972 (153 games)

Jim Wynn

Lowest slugging average	.301 in 1963 (162 games)
Most grounded into double play	144 in 1970 (162 games)
Fewest grounded into double play	76 in 1983 (162 games)
Most left on bases	1212 in 1969 (162 games)
Fewest left on bases	1040 in 1964 (162 games)
Most putouts	4448 in 1980 (163 games)
Fewest putouts	4284 in 1964 (162 games)
Most assists	1880 in 1975 (162 games)
Fewest assists	1565 in 1986 (162 games)
Most chances accepted	6255 in 1975 (162 games)
Fewest chances accepted	5827 in 1972 (153 games)
Most errors	174 in 1966 (163 games)
Fewest errors	106 in 1971 (162 games)
Most errorless games	85 in 1973 (162 games)
	85 in 1974 (162 games)
Most consecutive errorless games	11 in 1973
Most double plays	166 in 1975 (162 games)
Fewest double plays	100 in 1963 (162 games)
Most passed balls	38 in 1984 (162 games)
Fewest passed balls	9 in 1986 (162 games)
Highest fielding average	.983 in 1971 (162 games)
Lowest fielding average	.972 in 1966 (163 games)
Highest home attendance	2,278,217 in 1980
Highest road attendance	1,894,294 in 1987
Most games won	96 in 1986
Most games lost	97 in 1965
	97 in 1975
Most games won, month	20, May 1969
	20, July 1976
	20, June 1979
Most games lost, month	24, July 1962
Highest percentage games won	.593 in 1986 (won 96, lost 66)
Lowest percentage games won	.398 in 1975 (won 64, lost 97)
Games won, league	1999 in 26 years
Games lost, league	2150 in 26 years
Most shutouts won	19 in 1979, 1981, 1986
Most shutouts lost	23 in 1963
Most 1-0 games won	9 in 1976
Most 1-0 games lost	6 in 1964, 1969
Most consecutive games won	10 in 1965
	10 in 1969 (twice)
	10 in 1980
Most consecutive games lost	10 in 1963
	10 in 1967 (twice)
	10 in 1974
Most times league champions	0
Most last place finishes	2
Longest 1-0 game won	24 innings vs. New York, April 15, 1968
Longest 1-0 game lost	13 innings vs. Cincinnati, August 6, 1962
Most runs, inning	12 vs. Philadelphia, May 31, 1975, eighth inning
Most runs, game	18 vs. San Francisco, July 7, 1971
	18 vs. Chicago, April 29, 1974
Most runs, game, by opponent	22 by Chicago, June 3, 1987
Most home runs, game	5 vs. Atlanta, April 12, 1970
	5 vs. San Diego, June 26, 1972
	5 vs. San Diego, June 21, 1973
	5 vs. Cincinnati, September 12, 1977
Most consecutive games, one or more homers	10 (15 homers), 1973
Most runs, shutout game	13 vs. Cincinnati, June 4, 1983
Most runs, shutout game, by opponent	16 by Philadelphia, September 10, 1963
Most runs, doubleheader shutout	No performance
Most hits, game	25 vs. Atlanta, May 30, 1976, second game
	25 vs. Cincinnati, July 2, 1976, first game, 14 innings
Most total bases, game	36 vs. Montreal, August 17, 1972
Largest crowd, day game	49,442 vs. Los Angeles, September 5, 1965
Largest crowd, doubleheader	45,115 vs. Atlanta, August 4, 1979
Largest crowd, night game	50,908 vs. Los Angeles, June 22, 1966
Largest crowd, home opener	44,585 vs. Los Angeles, April 6, 1987

Los Angeles Dodgers

Yearly Finishes

Year—Position	W.	L.	Pct.	*G.B.	Manager
1958—Seventh ..	71	83	.461	21	Walter (Smokey) Alston
1959—First§....	88	68	.564	+ 2	Walter (Smokey) Alston
1960—Fourth....	82	72	.532	13	Walter (Smokey) Alston
1961—Second....	89	65	.578	4	Walter (Smokey) Alston
1962—Second‡.	102	63	.618	1	Walter (Smokey) Alston
1963—First.....	99	63	.611	+ 6	Walter (Smokey) Alston
1964—Sixth†	80	82	.494	13	Walter (Smokey) Alston
1965—First.....	97	65	.599	+ 2	Walter (Smokey) Alston
1966—First.....	95	67	.586	+ 1½	Walter (Smokey) Alston
1967—Eighth	73	89	.451	28½	Walter (Smokey) Alston
1968—Seventh ..	76	86	.469	21	Walter (Smokey) Alston

West Division

Year—Position	W.	L.	Pct.	*G.B.	Manager
1969—Fourth.....	85	77	.525	8	Walter (Smokey) Alston
1970—Second....	87	74	.540	14½	Walter (Smokey) Alston
1971—Second....	89	73	.549	1	Walter (Smokey) Alston
1972—Third.....	85	70	.548	10½	Walter (Smokey) Alston
1973—Second....	95	66	.590	3½	Walter (Smokey) Alston
1974—Firstx	102	60	.630	+ 4	Walter (Smokey) Alston
1975—Second....	88	74	.543	20	Walter (Smokey) Alston
1976—Second....	92	70	.568	10	W. Alston, T. Lasorda
1977—Firstx	98	64	.605	+10	Thomas Lasorda
1978—First†x ...	95	67	.586	+ 2½	Thomas Lasorda

Year—Position	W.	L.	Pct.	*G.B.	Manager
1979—Third	79	83	.488	11½	Thomas Lasorda
1980—Second y	92	71	.564	1	Thomas Lasorda
1981—1st/4th..	63	47	.573	z	Thomas Lasorda
1982—Second...	88	74	.543	1	Thomas Lasorda
1983—First a....	91	71	.652	+ 3	Thomas Lasorda
1984—Fourth....	79	83	.488	13	Thomas Lasorda
1985—First a....	95	67	.586	+ 5½	Thomas Lasorda
1986—Fifth.....	73	89	.451	23	Thomas Lasorda
1987—Fourth....	73	89	.451	17	Thomas Lasorda

*Games behind winner. †Tied for position. ‡Lost Pennant playoff. §Won pennant playoff. xWon Championship Series. yLost division playoff. zFirst half 36-21; second 27-26. aLost Championship Series.

Individual Records (1958 To Date)
Batting

Most years, non-pitcher	18, William E. Russell
Most games	165, Maurice M. Wills, 1962
Most games, league	2181, William E. Russell
Most at-bats	695, Maurice M. Wills, 165 games, 1962
Most at-bats, league	7495, William H. Davis
Most runs	130, Maurice M. Wills, 165 games, 1962
Most runs, league	1004, William H. Davis
Most hits	230, H. Thomas Davis, 163 games, 1962
Most hits, league	2091, William H. Davis

Dodger speedster Maury Wills

Most singles ....179, Maurice M. Wills, 165 games, 1962
Most singles, league ....1530, William E. Russell
Most doubles..............................47, M. Wesley Parker, 161 games, 1970
Most doubles, league ....333, Steven P. Garvey
Most triples ....16, William H. Davis, 146 games, 1970
Most triples, league ....110, William H. Davis
Most homers, righthander ....33, Steven P. Garvey, 162 games, 1977
                                              33, Pedro Guerrero, 137 games, 1985
Most homers, lefthander ....27, C. Reginald Smith, 148 games, 1977
Most homers switch-hitter ....32, C. Reginald Smith, 148 games, 1977
Most homers, month ....15, Pedro Guerrero, June, 1985
Most homers, rookie ....23, Frank O. Howard, 117 games, 1960
Most homers, league, righthander ....228, Ronald C. Cey
Most homers, league, lefthander ....154, William H. Davis
Most homers at home ....20, Steven P. Garvey, 1979
Most homers on road ....20, Pedro Guerrero, 1985
Most grand slams ....2, Frank O. Howard, 117 games, 1960
                                              2, Ronald C. Cey, 153 games, 1977
                                              2, Steven P. Garvey, 162 games, 1977
                                              2, Michael A. Marshall, 135 games, 1985
                                              2, Gregory A. Brock, 129 games, 1985
Most grand slams, league ....5, Ronald C. Cey
                                              5, Michael A. Marshall
Most total bases....................356, H. Thomas Davis, 163 games, 1962
Most total bases, league ....3094, William H. Davis
Most long hits.........................66, Steven P. Garvey, 162 games, 1978
                                              66, Pedro Guerrero, 160 games, 1983
Most long hits, league................................585, William H. Davis
Most extra bases on long hits ....136, Pedro Guerrero, 160 games, 1983
Most extra bases on long hits, league.....................1036, Steven P. Garvey
Most sacrifice hits.....................21, Charles L. Neal, 151 games, 1959
Most sacrifice flies ....13, C. Reginald Smith, 128 games, 1978
Most stolen bases....................104, Maurice M. Wills, 165 games, 1962
Most stolen bases, league ....490, Maurice M. Wills
Most caught stealing ....31, Maurice M. Wills, 158 games, 1965
Most bases on balls ....110, James S. Wynn, 130 games, 1975
Most bases on balls, league ....765, Ronald C. Cey
Most strikeouts.................149, Billy Grabarkewitz, 156 games, 1970
Most strikeouts, league ....838, Ronald C. Cey
Fewest strikeouts....................28, James Gilliam, 151 games, 1960
Most hit by pitch......................16, Louis B. Johnson, 131 games, 1965
Most runs batted in.................153, H. Thomas Davis, 163 games, 1962
Most runs batted in, league ....992, Steven P. Garvey
Most game-winning RBIs.................18, Pedro Guerrero, 150 games, 1982
Highest batting average.................. .346, H. Thomas Davis, 163 games, 1962
Longest batting streak ....31 games, William H. Davis, 1969

Highest slugging average ....577, Pedro Guerrero, 137 games, 1985
Most grounded into double play..............25, Steven P. Garvey, 162 games, 1979
Fewest grounded into double play................3, William H. Davis, 160 games, 1968
                                              3, David E. Lopes, 134 games, 1977

Pitching

Most years...15, Donald H. Sutton
Most games.................................106, Michael G. Marshall, 1974
Most games, league.................................534, Donald H. Sutton
Most games started ....42, Donald S. Drysdale, 1963
                                              42, Donald S. Drysdale, 1965
Most games started, league ....517, Donald H. Sutton
Most complete games...............................27, Sanford Koufax, 1965
                                              27, Sanford Koufax, 1966
Most complete games, league ....156, Donald S. Drysdale,
                                              156, Donald H. Sutton
Most games finished ....83, Michael G. Marshall, 1974
Most innings.................................336, Sanford Koufax, 1965
Most innings, league.................................3728, Donald H. Sutton
Most games won.................................27, Sandy Koufax, 1966
Most games won, league.................................230, Donald H. Sutton
Most 20-victory seasons...3, Sanford Koufax
Most games lost.................................18, Claude W. Osteen, 1968
Most games lost, league.................................175, Donald H. Sutton
Highest winning percentage ....864, Orel L. Hershiser (19-3), 1985
Longest winning streak ....13 games, Philip R. Regan, 1966
Longest losing streak...............................11 games, Frederick W. Honeycutt, 1987
Most saves ....24, James T. Brewer, 1970
Most bases on balls.................................124, Fernando Valenzuela, 1987
Most bases on balls, league.................................966, Donald H. Sutton
Most strikeouts.................................382, Sanford Koufax, 1965
Most strikeouts, game.................................18, Sanford Koufax, August 31, 1959
                                              18, Sanford Koufax, April 24, 1962
Most strikeouts, league ....2652, Donald H. Sutton
Most shutouts.................................11, Sanford Koufax, 1963
Most shutouts, league.................................52, Donald H. Sutton
Most 1-0 shutouts won ....4, Donald S. Drysdale, 1968
Most hits.................................298, Claude W. Osteen, 1967
Most runs.................................127, Donald H. Sutton, 1970
Most earned runs.................................118, Donald H. Sutton, 1970
Most home runs.................................38, Donald H. Sutton, 1970
Most hit batsmen.................................20, Donald S. Drysdale, 1961
Most wild pitches.................................17, Sanford Koufax, 1958
Most sacrifice hits.................................27, Fernando Valenzuela, 1983
Most sacrifice flies ....11, Burt C. Hooton, 1979
Lowest ERA ....1.73, Sanford Koufax, 323 innings, 1966

Club Records

Most players	48 in 1987
Fewest players	30 in 1962
Most games	165 in 1962
Most at-bats	5642 in 1982 (162 games)
Most runs	842 in 1962 (165 games)
Fewest runs	470 in 1968 (162 games)
Most opponents' runs	761 in 1958 (154 games)
Fewest opponents' runs	490 in 1966 (162 games)
Most hits	1515 in 1970 (161 games)
Fewest hits	1234 in 1968 (162 games)
Most singles	1128 in 1970 (161 games)
Most doubles	251 in 1978 (162 games)
Most triples	67 in 1970 (161 games)
Most homers	191 in 1977 (162 games)
Fewest homers	67 in 1968
Most homers at L.A. Coliseum, home & opp.	193 in 1958
Most homers at Dodger Stadium, home & opp.	161 in 1977
	161 in 1979
Most grand slams	6 in 1960, 1977, 1979
Most pinch home runs	8 in 1983
Most long hits	442 in 1977 (162 games)
Most extra bases on long hits	852 in 1977 (162 games)
Most total bases	2336 in 1977 (162 games)
Most sacrifice hits	120 in 1964 (164 games)
Most sacrifice flies	64 in 1974 (162 games)
Most stolen bases	198 in 1962 (165 games)
Most caught stealing	77 in 1965 (162 games)
Most bases on balls	611 in 1975 (162 games)
Most strikeouts	980 in 1968 (162 games)
Fewest strikeouts	744 in 1976 (162 games)
Most hit by pitch	52 in 1965 (162 games)
Fewest hit by pitch	14 in 1984 (162 games)
Most runs batted in	781 in 1962 (165 games)
Most game-winning RBIs	87 in 1985 (162 games)
Highest batting average	.272 in 1974 (162 games)
Lowest batting average	.230 in 1968 (162 games)
Highest slugging average	.418 in 1977 (162 games)
Lowest slugging average	.319 in 1968 (162 games)
Most left on bases	1223 in 1982 (162 games)
Fewest left on bases	1012 in 1958 (154 games)
Most grounded into double play	145 in 1979 (162 games)
Fewest grounded into double play	79 in 1965 (162 games)
Most .300 hitters	4 in 1970
Most putouts	4473 in 1973 (162 games)
Fewest putouts	4105 in 1958 (154 games)
Most assists	1946 in 1982 (162 games)
Fewest assists	1573 in 1961 (154 games)
Most errors	193 in 1962 (165 games)
Fewest errors	114 in 1956 (156 games)
Most errorless games	90 in 1979 (162 games)
Most consecutive errorless games	11 in 1979
Most chances accepted	6411 in 1982 (162 games)
Fewest chances accepted	5708 in 1961 (154 games)
Most double plays	198 in 1959 (156 games)
Fewest double plays	106 in 1975 (162 games)

Most passed balls	24 in 1973 (162 games)
Fewest passed balls	6 in 1958 (154 games)
Highest fielding average	.981 in 1959 (156 games)
	.981 in 1973 (162 games)
	.981 in 1977 (162 games)
	.981 in 1979 (162 games)
	.981 in 1980 (163 games)
Lowest fielding average	.970 in 1962 (165 games)
Highest home attendance	3,608,881 in 1982
Highest road attendance	2,250,191 in 1982
Most games won	102 in 1962
	102 in 1974
Most games lost	89 in 1967
	89 in 1986
	89 in 1987
Most games won, month	21, May 1962
	21, July 1963
	21, June 1973
Most games lost, month	20, July 1968
	20, June 1979
Highest percentage games won	.630 in 1974 (won 102, lost 60)
Lowest percentage games won	.451 in 1967 (won 73, lost 89)
	.451 in 1986 (won 73, lost 89)
	.451 in 1987 (won 73, lost 89)
Games won, league	2601 in 30 years
Games lost, league	2172 in 30 years
Most shutouts won	24 in 1963
Most shutouts lost	23 in 1968
Most 1-0 games won	7 in 1963, 1984
Most 1-0 games lost	6 in 1964
	6 in 1968
Most consecutive games won	13 in 1962
	13 in 1965
Most consecutive games lost	10 in 1961
Most times league champions	8
Most last place finishes	0
Most runs, game	19 vs. San Diego, June 28, 1969
	19 vs. San Francisco, May 26, 1970
Most runs game, by opponent	20 by Chicago, May 20, 1967
Most runs, shutout game	19 vs. San Diego, June 28, 1969
Most runs shutout game by opponent	18 by Cincinnati, August 8, 1965
Most runs doubleheader shutout	16 vs. Atlanta, September 19, 1971
Most runs inning	10 vs. San Diego, June 28, 1969, third inning
	10 vs. San Francisco, July 4, 1971, eighth inning
	10 vs. San Diego, September 13, 1977, second inning
Longest 1-0 game won	15 innings vs. New York, April 24, 1970
Longest 1-0 game lost	16 innings vs. Houston, April 21, 1976
Most hits, game	24 vs. Chicago, August 20, 1974
Most home runs, game	7 vs. Chicago, May 5, 1976
	7 vs. Cincinnati, May 25, 1979
Most consecutive games, one or more homers	15 (23 homers), 1977
Most total bases, game	48 vs. Chicago, August 20, 1974
Largest crowd, day game	78,672 vs. San Francisco, April 18, 1958
Largest crowd, doubleheader	72,140 vs. Cincinnati, August 16, 1961
Largest crowd, night game	67,550 vs. Chicago, April 12, 1960
Largest crowd, home opener	78,672 vs. San Francisco, April 18, 1958

Milwaukee Braves

Yearly Finishes

Year—Position	W.	L.	Pct.	*G.B.	Manager
1953—Second	92	62	.597	13	Charles Grimm
1954—Third	89	65	.578	8	Charles Grimm
1955—Second	85	69	.552	13½	Charles Grimm
1956—Second	92	62	.597	1	C. Grimm, F. Haney
1957—First	95	59	.617	+ 8	Fred Haney
1958—First	92	62	.597	+ 8	Fred Haney
1959—Second†	86	70	.551	2	Fred Haney
1960—Second	88	66	.571	7	Charles Dressen
1961—Fourth	83	71	.539	10	C. Dressen, B. Tebbetts
1962—Fifth	86	76	.531	15½	George (Birdie) Tebbetts
1963—Sixth	84	78	.519	15	Robert Bragan
1964—Fifth	88	74	.543	5	Robert Bragan
1965—Fifth	86	76	.531	11	Robert Bragan

*Games behind winner. †Lost to Los Angeles in pennant playoff.

Individual Records (1953 To 1965)
Batting

Most years, non-pitcher	13, Edwin L. Mathews
Most games	161, Henry L. Aaron, 1963
Most games, league	1944, Edwin L. Mathews
Most at-bats	636, William H. Bruton, 149 games, 1955
Most at-bats, league	7080, Henry L. Aaron
Most runs	127, Henry L. Aaron, 156 games, 1962
Most runs, league	1300, Edwin L. Mathews
Most hits	223, Henry L. Aaron, 154 games, 1959
Most hits, league	2266, Henry L. Aaron
Most singles	132, Joseph P. Torre, 154 games, 1964
Most doubles	46, Henry L. Aaron, 154 games, 1959
Most doubles, league	391, Henry L. Aaron
Most triples	15, William H. Bruton, 147 games, 1956
Most triples, league	80, Henry L. Aaron
Most homers, lefthander	47, Edwin L. Mathews, 157 games, 1953
Most homers, righthander	45, Henry L. Aaron, 156 games, 1962

Most homers, month	15, Joseph W. Adcock, July, 1956
Most homers, rookie	22, Ricardo A. Carty, 133 games, 1964
Most homers at home	23, Joseph W. Adcock, 1956
	23, Edwin L. Mathews, 1960
Most homers on road	30, Edwin L. Mathews, 1953
Most homers, league	452, Edwin L. Mathews
Most grand slams	3, Delmar W. Crandall, 133 games, 1955
	3, Henry L. Aaron, 156 games, 1962
Most grand slams, league	9, Henry L. Aaron
Most total bases	400, Henry L. Aaron, 154 games, 1959
Most total bases, league	4011, Henry L. Aaron
Most long hits	92, Henry L. Aaron, 154 games, 1959
Most extra bases on long hits	188, Edwin L. Mathews, 157 games, 1953
Most sacrifice hits	31, John Logan, 148 games, 1956
Most sacrifice flies	12, Henry L. Aaron, 153 games, 1960
	12, Delmar W. Crandall, 142 games, 1960
Most stolen bases	34, William H. Bruton, 142 games, 1954
Most caught stealing	13, William H. Bruton, 142 games, 1954
Most bases on balls	124, Edwin L. Mathews, 158 games, 1963
Most strikeouts	122, Mack Jones, 122 games, 1965
Fewest strikeouts	33, John Logan, 150 games, 1953
Most hit by pitch	9, Frank J. Torre, 129 games, 1957
	9, Mack Jones, 122 games, 1965
Most runs batted in	135, Edwin L. Mathews, 157 games, 1953
Most runs batted in, league	1305, Henry L. Aaron
Highest batting average	.355, Henry L. Aaron, 154 games, 1959
Highest batting average, league	.320, Henry L. Aaron
Highest slugging average	.636, Henry L. Aaron, 154 games, 1959
Longest batting streak	25 games, Henry L. Aaron, 1956
	25 games, Henry L. Aaron, 1962
Most grounded into double play	26, Joseph P. Torre, 154 games, 1964
Fewest grounded into double play	4, Edwin L. Mathews, 151 games, 1956
	4, William H. Bruton, 151 games, 1960

Pitching

Most years	12, Warren E. Spahn
Most games	62, William O. O'Dell, 1965
Most games, started	39, S. Lewis Burdette, 1959

Most complete games .... 24, Warren E. Spahn, 1953
Most games finished .... 49, Donald J. McMahon, 1959
Most innings .... 292, Warren E. Spahn, 1959
Most games won .... 24, Tony L. Cloninger, 1965
Most games won, league .... 234, Warren E. Spahn
Most 20 victory seasons .... 9, Warren E. Spahn
Most games lost .... 15, S. Lewis Burdette, 1959
.... 15, Warren E. Spahn, 1959
Most games lost, league .... 138, Warren E. Spahn
Highest winning percentage .... .767, Warren E. Spahn (23-7), 1953
.... .767, Warren E. Spahn (23-7), 1963
Longest winning streak .... 11 games, Warren E. Spahn, 1954
Most bases on balls .... 121, Robert R. Buhl, 1957
Most strikeouts .... 211, Tony L. Cloninger, 1965
Most strikeouts, game .... 15, Warren E. Spahn, September 16, 1960
Most shutouts .... 7, Warren E. Spahn, 1963
Most shutouts, league .... 36, Warren E. Spahn
Most runs .... 144, S. Lewis Burdette, 1959
Most earned runs .... 131, S. Lewis Burdette, 1959
Most hits .... 312, S. Lewis Burdette, 1959
Most hit batsmen .... 12, Robert J. Shaw, 1962
Most wild pitches .... 22, Tony L. Cloninger, 1965
Most home runs .... 38, S. Lewis Burdette, 1959
Lowest ERA .... 2.10, Warren E. Spahn, 266 innings, 1953

Club Records

Most players	42 in 1964 (162 games)
Fewest players	31 in 1953 (157 games)
	31 in 1954 (154 games)
Most games	163 in 1963
Most at-bats	5591 in 1964 (162 games)
Most runs	803 in 1964 (162 games)
Fewest runs	670 in 1954 (154 games)
Most opponents' runs	744 in 1964 (162 games)
Fewest opponents' runs	541 in 1968 (154 games)
Most hits	1522 in 1964 (162 games)
Most singles	1057 in 1964 (162 games)
Most doubles	274 in 1964 (162 games)
Most triples	62 in 1957 (155 games)
Most homers	199 in 1957 (155 games)
Fewest homers	139 in 1954
Most homers at County Stadium, home & opp.	173 in 1965
Most grand slams	8 in 1962
Most pinch home runs	7 in 1965
Most total bases	2411 in 1957 (155 games)
Most long hits	482 in 1957 (155 games)
Most extra bases on long hits	942 in 1957 (155 games)
Most sacrifice hits	142 in 1956 (155 games)
Most sacrifice flies	60 in 1960 (154 games)
Most stolen bases	75 in 1963 (163 games)
Most caught stealing	52 in 1963 (163 games)
Most bases on balls	581 in 1962 (162 games)
Most strikeouts	976 in 1965 (162 games)
Fewest strikeouts	619 in 1954 (154 games)
Most hit by pitcher	38 in 1964 (162 games)
Most runs batted in	755 in 1964 (162 games)
Highest batting average	.272 in 1964 (162 games)
Highest slugging average	.442 in 1957 (155 games)
Most grounded into double play	134 in 1964 (162 games)
Fewest grounded into double play	99 in 1956 (155 games)
Most left on bases	1138 in 1962 (162 games)
	1138 in 1963 (163 games)
Most .300 hitters	5 in 1964
Most putouts	4416 in 1963 (163 games)
Most assists	1848 in 1961 (155 games)
	1848 in 1963 (163 games)
Most chances accepted	6264 in 1963 (163 games)
Most errors	152 in 1955 (154 games)
Fewest errors	111 in 1961 (155 games)
Most consecutive errorless games	7 in 1954, 1956, 1964
Most double plays	173 in 1957 (155 games)
Most passed balls	28 in 1965 (162 games)
Fewest passed balls	5 in 1956 (155 games, 1959 (157 games)
Highest fielding average	.982 in 1961 (155 games)
Highest home attendance	2,215,404 in 1957
Highest road attendance	1,633,569 in 1959
Most games won	95 in 1957
Most games lost	78 in 1963
Most game won, month	23, August 1953
	23, August 1958
Most games lost, month	18, June 1954
Highest percentage games won	.617 in 1957 (won 95, lost 59)
Lowest percentage games won	.519 in 1963 (won 84, lost 78)
Games won, league	1146 in 13 years
Games lost, league	890 in 13 years
Most shutouts won	18 in 1959, 1963
Most shutouts lost	13 in 1963
Most 1-0 games won	4 in 1963
Most consecutive games won	11 in 1956
Most consecutive games lost	8 in 1961
Most times league champions	2
Most last place finishes	0

Most runs, game .... 23 vs. Chicago, September 2, 1957, first game
Most runs, shutout game .... 15 vs. Cincinnati, May 13, 1956, first game
Most runs, shutout game, by opponent .... 10 by Phila., July 21, 1953, first game
Most runs, doubleheader shutout .... No performance
Most runs, inning .... 10 vs. Pittsburgh, June 12, 1953, second game, first inning
Longest 1-0 game won .... 13 innings vs. Pittsburgh, May 26, 1959

Eddie Mathews

Longest 1-0 game lost .... 16 innings vs. San Francisco, July 2, 1963
Most hits, game .... 26 vs. Chicago, September 2, 1957, first game
Most home runs, game .... 8 vs. Pittsburgh, August 30, 1953, first game
Most consecutive games, one or more homers .... 22 (39 homers), 1956
Most total bases, game .... 47 vs. Pittsburgh, August 30, 1953, first game
Largest crowd, day game .... 48,642 vs. Philadelphia, September 27, 1959
Largest crowd, doubleheader .... 47,604 vs. Cincinnati, September 3, 1956
Largest crowd, night game .... 46,944 vs. New York, August 27, 1954
Largest crowd, home opener .... 43,640 vs. Cincinnati, April 12, 1955

Montreal Expos

Yearly Finishes
East Division

Year—Position	W.	L.	Pct.	*G.B.	Manager
1969—Sixth	52	110	.321	48	Gene Mauch
1970—Sixth	73	89	.451	16	Gene Mauch
1971—Fifth	71	90	.441	25½	Gene Mauch
1972—Fifth	70	86	.449	26½	Gene Mauch
1973—Fourth	79	83	.488	3½	Gene Mauch
1974—Fourth	79	82	.491	8½	Gene Mauch
1975—Fifth†	75	87	.463	17½	Gene Mauch
1976—Sixth	55	107	.340	46	K. Kuehl, C. Fox
1977—Fifth	75	87	.463	26	Richard Williams
1978—Fourth	76	86	.469	14	Richard Williams
1979—Second	95	65	.594	2	Richard Williams
1980—Second	90	72	.556	1	Richard Williams
1981—3rd/1st	60	48	.556	‡	R. Williams, J. Fanning
1982—Third	86	76	.531	6	James Fanning
1983—Third	82	80	.506	8	William Virdon
1984—Fifth	78	83	.484	18	W. Virdon, J. Fanning
1985—Third	84	77	.522	16½	Robert Rodgers
1986—Fourth	78	83	.484	29½	Robert Rodgers
1987—Third	91	71	.562	4	Robert Rodgers

*Games behind winner. †Tied for position. ‡First half 30-25; second 30-23.

Individual Records (1969 To Date)
Batting

Most years, non-pitcher .... 11, Gary E. Carter
11, Andre F. Dawson
Most games .... 162, Daniel J. Staub, 1971
162, Kenneth W. Singleton, 1973
162, Warren L. Cromartie, 1980
Most games, league .... 1443, Andre F. Dawson
Most at-bats .... 659, Warren L. Cromartie, 158 games, 1979
Most at-bats, league .... 5628, Andre F. Dawson
Most runs .... 133, Timothy Raines, 156 games, 1983
Most runs, league .... 828, Andre F. Dawson
Most hits .... 204, Albert Oliver, 160 games, 1982
Most hits, league .... 1575, Andre F. Dawson
Most singles .... 140, Timothy Raines, 151 games, 1986
Most singles, league .... 988, Andre F. Dawson
Most doubles .... 46, Warren L. Cromartie, 158 games, 1979
Most doubles, league .... 295, Andre F. Dawson
Most triples .... 13, Rodney D. Scott, 154 games, 1980
13, Timothy Raines, 150 games, 1985
13, Mitchell D. Webster, 151 games, 1986
Most triples, league .... 67, Andre F. Dawson
Most homers, lefthander .... 30, Daniel J. Staub, 160 games, 1970
Most homers, righthander .... 32, Andre F. Dawson, 159 games, 1983
Most homers, league, righthander .... 225, Andre F. Dawson
Most homers, league, lefthander .... 86, Ronald R. Fairly
Most homers, rookie .... 19, Andre F. Dawson, 139 games, 1977
Most homers, month .... 12, Daniel J. Staub, August, 1970
Most homers at home .... 22, Gary E. Carter, 1977
Most homers on road .... 22, Andre F. Dawson, 1983
Most grand slams .... 2, Held by many players
Most grand slams, league .... 7, Gary E. Carter
Most total bases .... 341, Andre F. Dawson, 159 games, 1983
Most total bases, league .... 2679, Andre F. Dawson
Most long hits .... 78, Andre F. Dawson, 159 games, 1983
Most long hits, league .... 587, Andre F. Dawson
Most extra bases on long hits .... 152, Andre F. Dawson, 159 games, 1983
Most extra bases on long hits, league .... 1104, Andre F. Dawson
Most sacrifice hits .... 23, Larry Lintz, 113 games, 1974
Most sacrifice flies .... 18, Andre F. Dawson, 159 games, 1983
Most stolen bases .... 97, Ronald LeFlore, 139 games, 1980
Most stolen bases, league .... 511, Timothy Raines
Most caught stealing .... 19, Ronald LeFlore, 139 games, 1980
Most bases on balls .... 123, Kenneth W. Singleton, 162 games, 1973
Most bases on balls, league .... 559, Timothy Raines
Most strikeouts .... 128, Andre F. Dawson, 157 games, 1978
Most strikeouts, league .... 896, Andre F. Dawson
Fewest strikeouts .... 29, David Cash, 159 games, 1978
Most hit by pitch .... 50, Ronald K. Hunt, 152 games, 1971
Most runs batted in .... 123, Timothy C. Wallach, 153 games, 1987
Most runs batted in, league .... 838, Andre F. Dawson
Most game-winning RBIs .... 17, Andre F. Dawson, 151 games, 1980
Highest batting average .... .334, Timothy Raines, 151 games, 1986
Highest batting average, league .... .308, Timothy Raines
Highest slugging average .... .551, Larry A. Parrish, 153 games, 1979
Longest batting streak .... 19 games, Warren L. Cromartie, 1979
19 games, Andre F. Dawson, 1980
Most grounded into double play .... 27, John A. Bateman, 139 games, 1971
27, Kenneth W. Singleton, 162 games, 1973
Fewest grounded into double play .... 1, Ronald K. Hunt, 152 games, 1971

Pitching

Most years .... 13, Stephen D. Rogers
Most games .... 92, Michael G. Marshall, 1973
Most games, league .... 399, Stephen D. Rogers
Most games started .... 40, Stephen D. Rogers, 1977
Most games started, league .... 393, Stephen D. Rogers

Andre Dawson

Most complete games .... 20, William H. Stoneman, 1971
Most complete games, league .... 129, Stephen D. Rogers
Most games finished .... 73, Michael G. Marshall, 1973
Most innings .... 302, Stephen D. Rogers, 1977
Most innings, league .... 2839⅓, Stephen D. Rogers
Most games won .... 20, Ross A. Grimsley, 1978
Most games won, league .... 158, Stephen D. Rogers
Most 20 victory seasons .... 1, Ross A. Grimsley
Most games lost .... 22, Stephen D. Rogers, 1974
Most games lost, league .... 152, Stephen D. Rogers
Highest winning percentage .... .783, Bryn N. Smith (18-5), 1985
Longest winning streak .... 8 games, David W. Palmer, 1979
8 games, Charles W. Lea, 1983
Longest losing streak .... 10 games, Steven Renko, 1972
Most saves .... 41, Jeffrey J. Reardon, 1985
Most bases on balls .... 146, William H. Stoneman, 1971
Most bases on balls, league .... 876, Stephen D. Rogers
Most strikeouts .... 251, William H. Stoneman, 1971
Most strikeouts, league .... 1621, Stephen D. Rogers
Most strikeouts, game .... 18, William L. Gullickson, September 10, 1980
Most shutouts won .... 5, William H. Stoneman, 1969
5, Stephen D. Rogers, 1979, 1983
Most shutouts won, league .... 37, Stephen D. Rogers
Most 1-0 shutouts won .... 2, Carl W. Morton, 1970
2, William H. Stoneman, 1972
2, Scott D. Sanderson, 1980
Most runs .... 139, Stephen D. Rogers, 1974
Most earned runs .... 126, Stephen D. Rogers, 1974
Most hits .... 281, Carl W. Morton, 1970
Most wild pitches .... 19, Steven Renko, 1974
Most hit batsmen .... 14, William H. Stoneman, 1970
Most home runs .... 27, Carl W. Morton, 1970
27, Steven Renko, 1970
27, William L. Gullickson, 1984
Most sacrifice hits .... 21, Stephen D. Rogers, 1979
Most sacrifice flies .... 11, Woodrow T. Fryman, 1976
Lowest ERA .... 2.40, Stephen D. Rogers, 277 innings, 1982

Club Records

Most players	47 in 1976 (162 games)
Fewest players	30 in 1972 (156 games)
Most games	163 in 1983
Most at-bats	5675 in 1977 (162 games)
Most runs	741 in 1987 (162 games)
Fewest runs	513 in 1972 (156 games)
Most opponents' runs	807 in 1970 (162 games)
Fewest opponents' runs	581 in 1979 (160 games)
Most hits	1482 in 1983 (163 games)
Fewest hits	1205 in 1972 (156 games)
Most singles	1042 in 1983 (163 games)
Most doubles	310 in 1987 (162 games)
Most triples	61 in 1980 (162 games)
Most homers	143 in 1979 (160 games)
Fewest homers	86 in 1974
Most homers at Jarry Park, home & opp.	168 in 1970
Most homers at Olympic Stadium, home & opp.	136 in 1987
Most grand slams	6 in 1987
Most pinch home runs	9 in 1973
Most total bases	2282 in 1977 (162 games)
Most long hits	482 in 1977 (162 games)
Most extra bases on long hits	808 in 1977 (162 games)
Most sacrifice hits	115 in 1973 (162 games)
Most sacrifice flies	57 in 1983 (163 games)
Most stolen bases	237 in 1980 (162 games)
Most caught stealing	95 in 1986 (161 games)
Most bases on balls	695 in 1973 (162 games)
Most strikeouts	1016 in 1986 (161 games)
Fewest strikeouts	733 in 1983 (163 games)
Most hit by pitch	78 in 1971 (162 games)
Fewest hit by pitch	16 in 1976 (162 games)
Most runs batted in	695 in 1987 (162 games)
Most game-winning RBIs	83 in 1980 (162 games)
Highest batting average	.265 in 1987 (162 games)
Lowest batting average	.234 in 1972 (156 games)
Highest slugging average	.408 in 1979 (160 games)
Lowest slugging average	.325 in 1972 (156 games)
Most grounded into double play	144 in 1973 (162 games)
Fewest grounded into double play	96 in 1972 (156 games)
Most left on bases	1232 in 1973 (162 games)
Fewest left on bases	1026 in 1979 (160 games)
Most .300 hitters	2 in 1973, 1982, 1987
Most putouts	4443 in 1977 (162 games)
Fewest putouts	4204 in 1972 (156 games)
Most assists	1956 in 1976 (162 games)
Fewest assists	1630 in 1982 (162 games)
Most chances accepted	6393 in 1975 (162 games)
Fewest chances accepted	5956 in 1984 (161 games)
Most errors	184 in 1969 (162 games)
Fewest errors	116 in 1983 (163 games)
Most errorless games	79 in 1982 (162 games)
Most consecutive errorless games	10 in 1977
Most double plays	193 in 1970 (162 games)
Fewest double plays	117 in 1982 (162 games)
Most passed balls	24 in 1973 (162 games)
Fewest passed balls	3 in 1978 (162 games)
Highest fielding average	.981 in 1983 (163 games)
	.981 in 1985 (162 games)
Lowest fielding average	.971 in 1969 (162 games)
Highest home attendance	2,320,651 in 1983
Highest road attendance	2,008,030 in 1987
Most games won	95 in 1979
Most games lost	110 in 1969
Most games won, month	23, Sept. 1979
Most games lost, month	23, August 1969
	23, Sept. 1976
Highest percentage games won	.594 in 1979 (won 95, lost 65)
Lowest percentage games won	.321 in 1969 (won 52, lost 110)
Games won, league	1449 in 19 years
Games lost, league	1562 in 19 years
Most shutouts won	18 in 1979
Most shutouts lost	20 in 1972
Most 1-0 shutouts won	4 in 1972
Most 1-0 shutouts lost	5 in 1982
Most consecutive games won	10 in 1979
	10 in 1980
Most consecutive games lost	20 in 1969
Most times league champions	0
Most last place finishes	2 (tied in 1969)
Most runs, inning	12 vs. Chicago, September 24, 1985, fifth inning
Most runs, game	19 vs. New York, July 3, 1973
	19 vs. Chicago, July 4, 1977, first game
	19 vs. Cincinnati, May 7, 1978, first game
	19 vs. Atlanta, July 30, 1978
	19 vs. Houston, June 17, 1979
Most runs, game, by opponent	17 by Houston, August 17, 1972
Most runs, shutout game	19 vs. Atlanta, July 30, 1978
Most runs, shutout game, by opponent	16 by St. Louis, August 11, 1980
Most runs, doubleheader shutout	14 vs. New York, August 5, 1975
Longest 1-0 game won	17 innings vs. Phil., September 21, 1981
Longest 1-0 game lost	12 innings vs. Cin., September 1, 1972
Most hits, game	28 vs. Atlanta, July 30, 1978
Most home runs, game	8 vs. Atlanta, July 30, 1978
Most consecutive games, one or more homers	10 (22 homers) 1969
Most total bases, game	58 vs. Atlanta, July 30, 1978
Largest crowd, day game	57,694 vs. Philadelphia, August 15, 1982
Largest crowd, doubleheader	59,282 vs. St. Louis, September 16, 1977
Largest crowd, night game	57,121 vs. Philadelphia, October 3, 1980
Largest crowd, home opener	57,592 vs. Philadelphia, April 15, 1977

New York Giants

Yearly Finishes

Year—Position	W.	L.	Pct.	*G.B.	Manager
1901—Seventh	52	85	.380	37	George S. Davis
1902—Eighth	48	88	.353	53½	H. Fogel, G. Smith, J. McGraw
1903—Second	84	55	.604	6½	John McGraw
1904—First	106	47	.693	+13	John McGraw
1905—First	105	48	.686	+9	John McGraw
1906—Second	96	56	.632	20	John McGraw
1907—Fourth	82	71	.536	25½	John McGraw
1908—Second†	98	56	.636	1	John McGraw
1909—Third	92	61	.601	18½	John McGraw
1910—Second	91	63	.591	13	John McGraw
1911—First	99	54	.647	+ 7½	John McGraw
1912—First	103	48	.682	+10	John McGraw
1913—First	101	51	.664	+12½	John McGraw
1914—Second	84	70	.545	10½	John McGraw
1915—Eighth	69	83	.454	21	John McGraw
1916—Fourth	86	66	.566	7	John McGraw
1917—First	98	56	.636	+10	John McGraw
1918—Second	71	53	.573	10½	John McGraw
1919—Second	87	53	.621	9	John McGraw
1920—Second	86	68	.558	7	John McGraw
1921—First	94	59	.614	+ 4	John McGraw
1922—First	93	61	.604	+ 7	John McGraw
1923—First	95	58	.621	+ 4½	John McGraw
1924—First	93	60	.608	+ 1½	John McGraw
1925—Second	86	66	.566	8½	John McGraw
1926—Fifth	74	77	.490	13½	John McGraw
1927—Third	92	62	.597	2	John McGraw
1928—Second	93	61	.604	2	John McGraw
1929—Third	84	67	.556	13½	John McGraw
1930—Third	87	67	.565	5	John McGraw
1931—Second	87	65	.572	13	John McGraw
1932—Sixth†	72	82	.468	18	J. McGraw, W. Terry
1933—First	91	61	.599	+ 5	William Terry
1934—Second	93	60	.608	2	William Terry
1935—Third	91	62	.595	8½	William Terry
1936—First	92	62	.597	+ 5	William Terry
1937—First	95	57	.625	+ 3	William Terry
1938—Third	83	67	.553	5	William Terry
1939—Fifth	77	74	.510	18½	William Terry
1940—Sixth	72	80	.474	27½	William Terry
1941—Fifth	74	79	.484	25½	William Terry
1942—Third	85	67	.559	20	Melvin Ott
1943—Eighth	55	98	.359	49½	Melvin Ott
1944—Fifth	67	87	.435	38	Melvin Ott
1945—Fifth	78	74	.513	19	Melvin Ott
1946—Eighth	61	93	.396	36	Melvin Ott
1947—Fourth	81	73	.526	13	Melvin Ott
1948—Fifth	78	76	.506	13½	M. Ott, L. Durocher
1949—Fifth	73	81	.474	24	Leo Durocher
1950—Third	86	68	.558	5	Leo Durocher
1951—First‡	98	59	.624	+ 1	Leo Durocher
1952—Second	92	62	.597	4½	Leo Durocher
1953—Fifth	70	84	.455	35	Leo Durocher
1954—First	97	57	.630	+ 5	Leo Durocher
1955—Third	80	74	.519	18½	Leo Durocher
1956—Sixth	67	87	.435	26	William Rigney
1957—Sixth	69	85	.448	26	William Rigney

*Games behind winner. †Tied for position. ‡Won pennant playoff.

Individual Records (1883 To 1957)
Batting

Most years, non-pitcher	22, Melvin T. Ott
Most games	157, Arthur Devlin, 1908
Most games, league	2730, Melvin T. Ott
Most at-bats	681, Joseph G. Moore, 155 games, 1935
Most at-bats, league	9456, Melvin T. Ott
Most runs	146, Michael J. Tiernan, 122 games, 1889
Most runs, league	1859, Melvin T. Ott
Most runs, since 1900	139, William H. Terry, 154 games, 1930
Most hits	254, William H. Terry, 154 games, 1930
Most hits, league	2876, Melvin T. Ott
Most singles	177, William H. Terry, 154 games, 1930
Most singles, league	1805, Melvin T. Ott
Most doubles	43, William H. Terry, 153 games, 1931
Most doubles, league	488, Melvin T. Ott
Most triples	26, George S. Davis, 133 games, 1893
Most triples since 1900	25, Lawrence J. Doyle, 141 games, 1911
Most triples, league	159, Michael J. Tiernan
Most triples, league, since 1900	117, Lawrence J. Doyle
Most homers, lefthander	51, John R. Mize, 154 games, 1947
Most homers, righthander	51, Willie H. Mays, 152 games, 1955

Most homers, month..................................13, W. Walker Cooper, June, 1947
                                                13, John R. Mize, August, 1947
                                                13, Willie H. Mays, July, 1955
Most homers at home.............................29, John R. Mize, 1947
Most homers on road.............................29, Willie H. Mays, 1955
Most homers, rookie.......29, Robert B. Thomson, 138 games, 1947
Most homers, league, lefthander ....511, Melvin T. Ott
Most homers, league, righthander ....187, Willie H. Mays
Most grand slams ....3, George L. Kelly, 149 games, 1921
                                      3, Sidney Gordon, 142 games, 1948
                                      3, Wesley N. Westrum, 124 games, 1951
Most grand slams, league ....7, George L. Kelly
                                                  7, Melvin T. Ott
Most total bases ....392, William H. Terry, 154 games, 1930
Most total bases, league ....5041, Melvin T. Ott
Most long hits ....87, Willie H. Mays, 151 games, 1954
Most long hits, league ....1071, Melvin T. Ott
Most extra bases on long hits .....197, Willie H. Mays, 152 games, 1955
Most extra bases on long hits, league ....2165, Melvin T. Ott
Most sacrifice hits.............36, Arthur Devlin, 143 games, 1907
Most sacrifice flies...........8, Donald F. Mueller, 153 games, 1954
                                8, Henry C. Thompson, 135 games, 1955
Most stolen bases ....111, John M. Ward, 129 games, 1887
Most stolen bases since 1900 ....62, George J. Burns, 154 games, 1914
Most stolen bases, league ....334, George J. Burns
Most caught stealing ....22, George J. Burns, 154 games, 1920
Most bases on balls ....144, Edward R. Stanky, 152 games, 1950
Most strikeouts ....93, Wesley N. Westrum, 124 games, 1951
Fewest strikeouts..............12, Frank F. Frisch, 151 games, 1923
Most hit by pitch...............19, Arthur Fletcher, 151 games, 1917
Most runs batted in ....151, Melvin T. Ott, 150 games, 1929
Most runs batted in, league ....1860, Melvin T. Ott
Most consecutive games with RBI ....11, Melvin T. Ott (27 RBIs), 1929
Highest batting average ....401, William H. Terry, 154 games, 1930
Highest batting average, league....................341, William H. Terry
Highest slugging average ....667, Willie H. Mays, 151 games, 1954
Highest slugging average, league ....593, Willie H. Mays
Longest batting streak...........33 games, George S. Davis, 1893
Longest batting streak since 1900 ....24 games, Fred C. Lindstrom, 1930
                                                  24 games, Donald F. Mueller, 1955
Most grounded into double play................26, William F. Jurges, 138 games, 1939
                                                26, Sidney Gordon, 131 games, 1943
Fewest grounded into double play ....3, Joseph G. Moore, 152 games, 1936

Pitching, Since 1900

Most years.................................17, Christopher Mathewson
Most games...............................71, J. Hoyt Wilhelm, 1952
Most games, league......................634, Christopher Mathewson
Most games started ....48, Joseph J. McGinnity, 1903
Most complete games...........44, Joseph J. McGinnity, 1903
Most games finished ....52, Ace T. Adams, 1943
Most innings ....434, Joseph J. McGinnity, 1903
Most games won ....37, Christopher Mathewson, 1908
Most games won, league ....372, Christopher Mathewson
Most 20-victory seasons.........13, Christopher Mathewson
Most games lost ....27, Luther H. Taylor, 1901
Most games lost, league........188, Christopher Mathewson
Highest winning percentage............833, J. Hoyt Wilhelm (15-3), 1952
Longest winning streak..........19 games, Richard W. Marquard, 1912
Longest winning streak over two seasons—
                    24 games, Carl O. Hubbell, 1936 (16), 1937 (8)
Longest losing streak...........12 games, Richard W. Marquard, 1914
Most bases on balls.................128, Charles M. Tesreau, 1914
Most bases on balls, league..........902, Harold H. Schumacher
Most strikeouts....................267, Christopher Mathewson, 1903
Most strikeouts, game ....16, Christopher Mathewson, October 3, 1904
Most strikeouts, league............2502, Christopher Mathewson
Most shutouts ....12, Christopher Mathewson, 1908
Most shutouts, league...............83, Christopher Mathewson
Most 1-0 shutouts won..............5, Carl O. Hubbell, 1933
Most runs.........................224, William M. Carrick, 1900
Most earned runs.................117, Fred L. Fitzsimmons, 1932
Most hits.........................415, William M. Carrick, 1900
Most hit batsmen ....36, Edward R. Doheny, 1899
Most wild pitches...................30, Leon K. Ames, 1905
Most home runs......................36, Lawrence J. Jansen, 1949
Lowest ERA ....1.66, Carl O. Hubbell, 309 innings, 1933

Club Records

Most players................................49 in 1946
Fewest players.............................21 in 1905
Most games................................158 in 1904, 1909, 1917
Most at-bats..............................5623 in 1935 (156 games)
Most runs.................................959 in 1930 (154 games)
Fewest runs...............................540 in 1956 (154 games)
Most opponents runs.......................814 in 1930 (154 games)
Most hits.................................1769 in 1930 (154 games)
Fewest hits...............................1217 in 1906 (152 games)
Most singles..............................1279 in 1930 (154 games)
Most doubles..............................276 in 1928 (155 games)
Most triples..............................105 in 1911 (154 games)
Most homers...............................221 in 1947 (155 games)
Fewest homers (154 or 162-game schedule)....15 in 1906
Most grand slams...........................7 in 1951, 1954
Most pinch home runs......................10 in 1954
Most total bases..........................2628 in 1930 (154 games)
Most long hits............................490 in 1930 (154 games)
Most extra bases on long hits.............979 in 1947 (155 games)

Mel Ott

Most sacrifices (S. H. and S. F.)........................	250 in 1908 (157 games)
Most sacrifice hits	166 in 1904 (158 games)
Most sacrifice flies	52 in 1954 (154 games)
Most stolen bases	347 in 1911 (154 games)
Most caught stealing	114 in 1921 (153 games)
Most bases on balls	671 in 1951 (157 games)
Most strikeouts........................	672 in 1952 (154 games)
Fewest strikeouts	376 in 1928 (155 games)
Most hit by pitch	52 in 1917 (158 games)
Fewest hit by pitch	15 in 1933 (156 games)
Most runs batted in	880 in 1930 (154 games)
Highest batting average	.319 in 1930 (154 games)
Lowest batting average	.243 in 1909 (158 games)
Highest slugging average	.473 in 1930 (154 games)
Lowest slugging average	.302 in 1906 (152 games)
Most grounded into double play	153 in 1939 (151 games)
Fewest grounded into double play	96 in 1952 (154 games)
Most left on bases	1214 in 1935 (156 games)
Fewest left on bases	975 in 1926 (151 games)
Most .300 hitters	8 in 1921
	8 in 1922
	8 in 1924
	8 in 1930
	8 in 1931
Most putouts........................	4306 in 1909 (158 games)
Fewest putouts	3964 in 1939 (151 games)
Most assists	2240 in 1920 (155 games)
Fewest assists	1660 in 1956 (154 games)
Most chances accepted	6472 in 1920 (155 games)
Fewest chances accepted	5794 in 1956 (154 games)
Most errors	307 in 1909 (158 games)
Fewest errors	137 in 1950 (154 games)
Most consecutive errorless games	8 in 1950
Most double plays	181 in 1950 (154 games)
Fewest double plays	112 in 1945 (154 games)
Most passed balls........................	26 in 1906 (152 games)
Fewest passed balls........................	4 in 1928 (155 games)
Highest fielding average	.977 in 1940 (152 games)
	.977 in 1942 (154 games)
	.977 in 1950 (154 games)

Lowest fielding average .954 in 1909 (158 games)
Highest home attendance 1,600,793 in 1947
Highest road attendance 1,228,330 in 1949
Most games won 106 in 1904
Most games lost 98 in 1943
Most games won, month 29, Sept. 1916
Most games lost, month 25, August 1953
Highest percentage games won .759 in 1885 (won 85, lost 27)
Highest percentage games won, since 1900 .693 in 1904 (won 106, lost 47)
Lowest percentage games won .353 in 1902 (won 48, lost 88)
Games won, league 6067 in 75 years
Games lost, league 4898 in 75 years
Most shutouts won 25 in 1908
Most shutouts lost 20 in 1915
Most 1-0 games won 6 in 1907
6 in 1933
Most 1-0 games lost 8 in 1907
Most consecutive games won 26 in 1916
Most consecutive games lost 13 in 1902, 1944
Most times league champions 17
Most last place finishes 5
Most runs, game 29 vs. Philadelphia, June 15, 1887
Most runs, game, since 1900 26 vs. Brooklyn, April 30, 1944, first game

Most runs, game, by opponent 28 by Hartford, May 13, 1876
Most runs, game, by opponent, since 1900 21 by St. Louis, August 2, 1948
Most runs, shutout game 24 vs. Buffalo, May 27, 1885
Most runs, shutout game, since 1900 16 vs. Brooklyn, July 3, 1949
Most runs, shutout game, by opponent 19 by Chicago, June 7, 1906
Most runs, doubleheader shutout 19 vs. Cincinnati, July 31, 1949
Most runs, inning 13 vs. Philadelphia, September 8, 1883, third inning
13 vs. Cleveland, July 19, 1890, first game, second inning
13 vs. St. Louis, May 13, 1911, first inning
Longest 1-0 game won 18 innings vs. St. Louis, July 2, 1933, first game
Longest 1-0 game lost 15 innings vs. Cincinnati, July 16, 1933, first game
Most hits, game 31 vs. Cincinnati, June 9, 1901
Most home runs, game 7 vs. Indianapolis, May 9, 1888
7 vs. Cincinnati, June 6, 1939
7 vs. Philadelphia, August 13, 1939, first game
7 vs. Cincinnati, June 24, 1950
7 vs. Pittsburgh, July 8, 1956, first game
Most consecutive games, one or more homers 19 (33 homers), 1947
Most total bases, game 47 vs. Philadelphia, July 11, 1931, first game
Largest crowd, day game 54,922 vs. Brooklyn, April 20, 1941
Largest crowd, doubleheader 60,747 vs. Brooklyn, May 31, 1937
Largest crowd, night game 51,790 vs. Brooklyn, May 27, 1947
Largest crowd, home opener 54,392 vs. Brooklyn, April 14, 1936

New York Mets

Yearly Finishes

Year—Position	W.	L.	Pct.	*G.B.	Manager
1962—Tenth	40	120	.250	60½	Charles (Casey) Stengel
1963—Tenth	51	111	.315	48	Charles (Casey) Stengel
1964—Tenth	53	109	.327	40	Charles (Casey) Stengel
1965—Tenth	50	112	.309	47	C. Stengel, W. Westrum
1966—Ninth	66	95	.410	28½	Wesley Westrum
1967—Tenth	61	101	.377	40½	W. Westrum, F. Parker
1968—Ninth	73	89	.451	24	Gilbert Hodges

East Division

Year—Position	W.	L.	Pct.	*G.B.	Manager
1969—First†	100	62	.617	+ 8	Gilbert Hodges
1970—Third	83	79	.512	6	Gilbert Hodges
1971—Third‡	83	79	.512	14	Gilbert Hodges
1972—Third	83	73	.532	13½	Lawrence P. Berra
1973—First†	82	79	.509	+ 1½	Lawrence P. Berra
1974—Fifth	71	91	.438	17	Lawrence P. Berra
1975—Third‡	82	80	.506	10½	L. Berra, R. McMillan
1976—Third	86	76	.531	15	Joe Frazier
1977—Sixth	64	98	.395	37	J. Frazier, J. Torre
1978—Sixth	66	96	.407	24	Joseph Torre
1979—Sixth	63	99	.389	35	Joseph Torre
1980—Fifth	67	95	.414	24	Joseph Torre
1981—5th/4th.	41	62	.398	§	Joseph Torre
1982—Sixth	65	97	.401	27	George Bamberger
1983—Sixth	68	94	.420	22	G. Bamberger, F. Howard
1984—Second	90	72	.556	6½	David Johnson
1985—Second	98	64	.605	3	David Johnson
1986—First†	108	54	.667	+21½	David Johnson
1987—Second	92	70	.568	3	David Johnson

*Games behind winner. †Won Championship Series. ‡Tied for position. §First half 17-34; second 24-28.

Individual Records (1962 To Date)

Batting

Most years, non-pitcher 18, Edward E. Kranepool
Most games 162, Felix B. Millan, 1975
Most games, league 1,853, Edward E. Kranepool
Most at-bats 676, Felix B. Millan, 162 games, 1975
Most at-bats, league 5,436, Edward E. Kranepool
Most runs 107, Tommie L. Agee, 153 games, 1970
Most runs, league 563, Cleon J. Jones
Most hits 191, Felix B. Millan, 162 games, 1975
Most hits, league 1,418, Edward E. Kranepool
Most singles 155, Felix B. Millan, 153 games, 1973
Most singles, league 1,050, Edward E. Kranepool
Most doubles 37, Felix B. Millan, 162 games, 1975
37, Joel R. Youngblood, 158 games, 1979
37, Leonard K. Dykstra, 132 games, 1987
Most doubles, league 225, Edward E. Kranepool
Most triples 10, William H. Wilson, 154 games, 1984
Most triples, league 56, William H. Wilson
Most homers, righthander 37, David A. Kingman, 123 games, 1976
37, David A. Kingman, 149 games, 1982
Most homers, lefthander 39, Darryl E. Strawberry, 154 games, 1987
Most homers, switch-hitter 36, Howard M. Johnson, 157 games, 1987
Most homers at home 20, Darryl E. Strawberry, 1987
Most homers on road 23, Howard M. Johnson, 1987
Most homers, rookie 26, Darryl E. Strawberry, 122 games, 1983
Most homers, league, lefthander 147, Darryl E. Strawberry
Most homers, league, righthander 154, David A. Kingman
Most homers, month 13, David A. Kingman, July, 1975
13, Gary E. Carter, September, 1985
Most grand slams 3, John D. Milner, 127 games, 1976
Most grand slams, league 5, John D. Milner
Most total bases 310, Darryl E. Strawberry, 154 games, 1987
Most total bases, league 2,047, Edward E. Kranepool
Most long hits 76, Darryl E. Strawberry, 154 games, 1987
Most long hits, league 368, Edward E. Kranepool

Most extra bases on long hits 159, Darryl E. Strawberry, 154 games, 1987
Most extra bases on long hits, league 629, Edward E. Kranepool
Most sacrifice hits 24, Felix B. Millan, 136 games, 1974
Most sacrifice flies 15, Gary E. Carter, 132 games, 1986
Most stolen bases 58, William H. Wilson, 159 games, 1982
Most stolen bases, league 259, William H. Wilson
Most caught stealing 21, Leonard S. Randle, 136 games, 1977
Most bases on balls 97, Keith Hernandez, 154 games, 1984
97, Darryl E. Strawberry, 154 games, 1987
Most bases on balls, league 454, Edward E. Kranepool
Most strikeouts 156, Tommie L. Agee, 153 games, 1970
156, David A. Kingman, 149 games, 1982
Fewest strikeouts 14, Felix B. Millan, 136 games, 1974
Most strikeouts, league 697, Cleon J. Jones
Most hit by pitch 13, Ronald K. Hunt, 143 games, 1963
Most runs batted in 105, Daniel J. Staub, 155 games, 1975
105, Gary E. Carter, 132 games, 1986
Most runs batted in, league 614, Edward E. Kranepool
Most game-winning RBIs 24, Keith Hernandez, 158 games, 1985
Most consecutive games with RBI 8, Keith Hernandez (13 RBIs), 1986
Highest batting average .340, Cleon J. Jones, 137 games, 1969
Highest batting average, league .305, Keith Hernandez
Highest slugging average .583, Darryl E. Strawberry, 154 games, 1987
Longest batting streak 24 games, Hubert Brooks, 1984
Most grounded into double play 26, Cleon J. Jones, 134 games, 1970
Fewest grounded into double play 4, Lee L. Mazzilli, 159 games, 1977
4, Darryl E. Strawberry, 154 games, 1987

Pitching

Most years 12, Jerry M. Koosman
12, G. Thomas Seaver
12, Craig S. Swan
Most games 75, Roger A. McDowell, 1986
Most games, league 401, G. Thomas Seaver
Most complete games 21, G. Thomas Seaver, 1971
Most complete games, league 171, G. Thomas Seaver
Most games started 36, John H. Fisher, 1965
36, G. Thomas Seaver, 1970
36, G. Thomas Seaver, 1973
36, G. Thomas Seaver, 1975
Most games started, league 395, G. Thomas Seaver
Most games finished 52, Jesse Orosco, 1984
52, Roger A. McDowell, 1986
Most innings 291, G. Thomas Seaver, 1970
Most innings, league 3,045, G. Thomas Seaver
Most games won 25, G. Thomas Seaver, 1969
Most games, win, league 198, G. Thomas Seaver
Most 20-victory seasons 4, G. Thomas Seaver
Most games lost 24, Roger L. Craig, 1962
24, John H. Fisher, 1965
Most games lost, league 137, Jerry M. Koosman
Highest winning percentage .857, Dwight E. Gooden, (24-4), 1985
Most saves 31, Jesse Orosco, 1984
Longest winning streak 14 games, Dwight E. Gooden, 1985
Longest losing streak 18 games, Roger L. Craig, 1963
Most bases on balls 116, L. Nolan Ryan, 1971
Most bases on balls, league 847, G. Thomas Seaver
Most strikeouts 289, G. Thomas Seaver, 1971
Most strikeouts, league 2,541, G. Thomas Seaver
Most strikeouts, game 19, G. Thomas Seaver, April 22, 1970
Most shutouts 8, Dwight E. Gooden, 1985
Most shutouts, league 44, G. Thomas Seaver
Most 1-0 shutouts won 2, Held by many pitchers
Most runs 137, James W. Hook, 1962
Most earned runs 117, Roger L. Craig, 1962
Most hits 261, Roger L. Craig, 1962
Most hit batsmen 15, L. Nolan Ryan, 1971
Most wild pitches 18, Jack E. Hamilton, 1966
Most home runs 35, Roger L. Craig, 1962
Most sacrifice hits 21, Michael W. Scott, 1982
Most sacrifice flies 12, Jerry M. Koosman, 1974
Lowest ERA 1.53, Dwight E. Gooden, 276⅔ innings, 1985

Club Records

Most players	54 in 1967 (162 games)
Fewest players	34 in 1968 (163 games)
	34 in 1970 (162 games)
	34 in 1971 (162 games)
	34 in 1972 (156 games)
Most games	164 in 1965
Fewest games	156 in 1972
Most at-bats	5601 in 1987 (162 games)
Most runs	823 in 1987 (162 games)
Fewest runs	473 in 1968 (163 games)
Most opponents' runs	948 in 1962 (161 games)
Most hits	1499 in 1987 (162 games)
Fewest hits	1154 in 1972 (156 games)
Most singles	1087 in 1980 (162 games)
Most doubles	287 in 1987 (162 games)
Most triples	47 in 1978 (162 games)
Most homers	192 in 1987 (162 games)
Fewest homers	61 in 1980
Most homers at Polo Grounds, home & opp.	213 in 1962
Most homers at Shea Stadium, home & opp.	156 in 1987
Most grand slams	7 in 1987
Most pinch home runs	12 in 1983
Most total bases	2430 in 1987 (162 games)
Most long hits	513 in 1987 (162 games)
Most extra bases on long hits	931 in 1987 (162 games)
Most sacrifice hits	108 in 1973 (161 games)
Most sacrifice flies	55 in 1978 (162 games)
Most stolen bases	159 in 1987 (162 games)
Most caught stealing	99 in 1980 (162 games)
Most bases on balls	684 in 1970 (162 games)
Most strikeouts	1203 in 1968 (163 games)
Fewest strikeouts	735 in 1974 (162 games)
Most hit by pitch	48 in 1964 (163 games)
Fewest hit by pitch	20 in 1984 (162 games)
	20 in 1985 (162 games)
Most runs batted in	771 in 1987 (162 games)
Most game-winning RBIs	102 in 1986 (162 games)
Highest batting average	.268 in 1987 (162 games)
Lowest batting average	.219 in 1963 (162 games)
Highest slugging average	.434 in 1987 (162 games)
Lowest slugging average	.315 in 1963 (162 games)
	.315 in 1968 (163 games)
Most grounded into double play	148 in 1974 (162 games)
Fewest grounded into double play	94 in 1987 (162 games)
Most left on bases	1228 in 1974 (162 games)
Fewest left on bases	1032 in 1965 (164 games)
Most .300 hitters	3 in 1964
Most putouts	4464 in 1985 (162 games)
Fewest putouts	4244 in 1972 (156 games)
Most assists	1995 in 1966 (161 games)
Fewest assists	1539 in 1972 (156 games)
Most chances accepted	6309 in 1965 (164 games)
Fewest chances accepted	5783 in 1972 (156 games)
Most errors	210 in 1962 (161 games)
	210 in 1963 (162 games)
Fewest errors	114 in 1971 (162 games)
Most errorless games	88 in 1985 (162 games)
Most consecutive errorless games	9 in 1977
Most double plays	171 in 1966 (161 games)
	171 in 1983 (162 games)
Fewest double plays	116 in 1976 (162 games)
Most passed balls	32 in 1964 (163 games)
Fewest passed balls	2 in 1980 (162 games)
Highest fielding average	.982 in 1985 (162 games)
Lowest fielding average	.967 in 1962 (161 games)
	.967 in 1963 (162 games)
Highest home attendance	3,034,129 in 1987
Highest road attendance	2,323,808 in 1987
Most games won	108 in 1986
Most games lost	120 in 1962
Most games won, month	23, Sept. 1969
Most games lost, month	26, August 1962
Games won, league	1886 in 26 years
Games lost, league	2257 in 26 years
Highest percentage games won	.667 in 1986 (won 108, lost 54)
Lowest percentage games won	.250 in 1962 (won 40, lost 120)
Most shutouts won	28 in 1969
Most shutouts lost	30 in 1963
Most 1-0 games won	9 in 1969
Most 1-0 games lost	8 in 1963
Most consecutive games won	11 in 1969
	11 in 1972
	11 in 1986
Most consecutive games lost	17 in 1962
Most times league champions	3
Most last place finishes	8

Most runs, game.....................23 vs. Chicago, August 16, 1987
Most runs, game, by opponent.....................26 by Philadelphia, June 11, 1985
Most runs, shutout game.....................14 vs. Chicago, July 29, 1965, first game
Most runs, shutout game, by opponent...12 vs. Chicago, May 30, 1963, first game
          12 by Pitts., May 30, 1965, second game
          12 by Pittsburgh, July 1, 1966
          12 by Chicago, Sept. 14, 1974
Most runs, doubleheader shutout.................2 vs. Pittsburgh, September 12, 1969
Most runs, inning...............10 vs. Cincinnati, June 12, 1979, sixth inning
Longest 1-0 game won...............15 innings vs. Los Angeles, June 4, 1969
Longest 1-0 game lost ....24 innings vs. Houston, April 15, 1968

Jerry Koosman

Most hits, extra-inning game.....................28 vs. Atlanta, July 4, 1985, 19 innings
Most hits, nine-inning game.....................23 vs. Chicago, May 26, 1964
Most home runs, game ....5 vs. Philadelphia, April 28, 1962
         5 vs. Cincinnati, August 3, 1962
         5 vs. St. Louis, October 3, 1964
         5 vs. Montreal, May 19, 1970
         5 vs. Atlanta, July 20, 1985
         5 vs. Montreal, June 18, 1987
Most consecutive games, one or more homers.....................10 (14 homers), 1970
            10 (15 homers), 1975
Most total bases, extra-inning game..........38 vs. Atlanta, July 4, 1985, 19 innings
Most total bases, nine-inning game ....37 vs. Atlanta, July 20, 1985
Largest crowd, day game ....56,738 vs. Los Angeles, June 23, 1968
Largest crowd, doubleheader...............57,175 vs. Los Angeles, June 13, 1965
Largest crowd, night game ....56,658 vs. San Francisco, May 13, 1966
Largest crowd, home opener...............52,812 vs. Atlanta, April 15, 1966

Philadelphia Phillies

Yearly Finishes

Year—Position	W.	L.	Pct.	*G.B.	Manager
1901—Second....	83	57	.593	7½	William Shettsline
1902—Seventh..	56	81	.409	46	William Shettsline
1903—Seventh..	49	86	.363	39½	Charles (Chief) Zimmer
1904—Eighth	52	100	.342	53½	Hugh Duffy
1905—Fourth.....	83	69	.546	21½	Hugh Duffy
1906—Fourth.....	71	82	.464	45½	Hugh Duffy
1907—Third.....	83	64	.565	21½	William J. Murray
1908—Fourth.....	83	71	.539	16	William J. Murray
1909—Fifth.....	74	79	.484	36½	William J. Murray
1910—Fourth.....	78	75	.510	25½	Charles (Red) Dooin
1911—Fourth.....	79	73	.520	19½	Charles (Red) Dooin
1912—Fifth.....	73	79	.480	30½	Charles (Red) Dooin
1913—Second.....	88	63	.583	12½	Charles (Red) Dooin
1914—Sixth	74	80	.481	20½	Charles (Red) Dooin
1915—First	90	62	.592	+ 7	Patrick Moran
1916—Second.....	91	62	.595	2½	Patrick Moran
1917—Second.....	87	65	.572	10	Patrick Moran
1918—Sixth	55	68	.447	26	Patrick Moran
1919—Eighth	47	90	.343	47½	J. Coombs, C. Cravath
1920—Eighth	62	91	.405	30½	Clifford (Gavvy) Cravath
1921—Eighth	51	103	.331	43½	W. Donovan, I. Wilhelm
1922—Seventh..	57	96	.373	35½	Irvin Wilhelm
1923—Eighth	50	104	.325	45½	Arthur Fletcher
1924—Seventh..	55	96	.364	37	Arthur Fletcher
1925—Sixth†	68	85	.444	27	Arthur Fletcher
1926—Eighth	58	93	.384	29½	Arthur Fletcher
1927—Eighth	51	103	.331	43	John (Stuffy) McInnis
1928—Eighth	43	109	.283	51	Burton Shotton
1929—Fifth.....	71	82	.464	27½	Burton Shotton
1930—Eighth	52	102	.338	40	Burton Shotton
1931—Sixth	66	88	.429	35	Burton Shotton
1932—Fourth.....	78	76	.506	12	Burton Shotton
1933—Seventh..	60	92	.395	31	Burton Shotton
1934—Seventh..	56	93	.376	37	James Wilson
1935—Seventh.	64	89	.418	35½	James Wilson
1936—Eighth	54	100	.351	38	James Wilson
1937—Seventh..	61	92	.399	34½	James Wilson
1938—Eighth	45	105	.300	43	J. Wilson, J. Lobert
1939—Eighth	45	106	.298	50½	James (Doc) Prothro
1940—Eighth	50	103	.327	50	James (Doc) Prothro
1941—Eighth	43	111	.279	57	James (Doc) Prothro
1942—Eighth	42	109	.278	62½	John (Hans) Lobert
1943—Seventh ..	64	90	.416	41	S. Harris, F. Fitzsimmons
1944—Eighth	61	92	.399	43½	Fred Fitzsimmons
1945—Eighth	46	108	.299	52	F. Fitzsimmons, B. Chapman
1946—Fifth.....	69	85	.448	28	W. Benjamin Chapman
1947—Seventh†	62	92	.403	32	W. Benjamin Chapman
1948—Sixth	66	88	.429	25½	Chapman, Cooke, Sawyer
1949—Third.....	81	73	.526	16	Edwin Sawyer
1950—First	91	63	.591	+ 2	Edwin Sawyer
1951—Fifth.....	73	81	.474	23½	Edwin Sawyer
1952—Fourth.....	87	67	.565	9½	E. Sawyer, S. O'Neill
1953—Third† ..	83	71	.539	22	Stephen O'Neill
1954—Fourth.....	75	79	.487	22	S. O'Neill, T. Moore
1955—Fourth.....	77	77	.500	21½	E. Mayo Smith
1956—Fifth.....	71	83	.461	22	E. Mayo Smith
1957—Fifth.....	77	77	.500	19	E. Mayo Smith
1958—Eighth	69	85	.448	23	M. Smith, E. Sawyer
1959—Eighth	64	90	.416	23	Edwin Sawyer
1960—Eighth	59	95	.383	36	Sawyer, Cohen, Mauch
1961—Eighth	47	107	.305	46	Gene Mauch
1962—Seventh..	81	80	.503	20	Gene Mauch
1963—Fourth.....	87	75	.537	12	Gene Mauch
1964—Second†	92	70	.568	1	Gene Mauch
1965—Sixth	85	76	.528	11½	Gene Mauch
1966—Fourth.....	87	75	.537	8	Gene Mauch
1967—Fifth.....	82	80	.506	19½	Gene Mauch
1968—Seventh†	76	86	.469	21	Mauch, Myatt, Skinner

East Division

Year—Position	W.	L.	Pct.	*G.B.	Manager
1969—Fifth.......	63	99	.389	37	R. Skinner, G. Myatt
1970—Fifth.......	73	88	.453	15½	Frank Lucchesi
1971—Sixth	67	95	.414	30	Frank Lucchesi
1972—Sixth	59	97	.378	37½	F. Lucchesi, P. Owens
1973—Sixth	71	91	.438	11½	Daniel L. Ozark
1974—Third	80	82	.494	8	Daniel L. Ozark
1975—Second..	86	76	.531	6½	Daniel L. Ozark
1976—First‡	101	61	.623	+ 9	Daniel L. Ozark
1977—First‡	101	61	.623	+ 5	Daniel L. Ozark
1978—First‡	90	72	.556	+ 1½	Daniel L. Ozark
1979—Fourth.....	84	78	.519	14	D. Ozark, D. Green
1980—First§	91	71	.562	+ 1	G. Dallas Green
1981—1st/3rd .	59	48	.551	x	G. Dallas Green
1982—Second..	89	73	.549	3	Patrick Corrales
1983—First§	90	72	.556	+ 6	P. Corrales, P. Owens
1984—Fourth.....	81	81	.500	15½	Paul Owens
1985—Fifth.......	75	87	.463	26	John Felske
1986—Second..	86	75	.534	21½	John Felske
1987—Fourth† .	80	82	.494	15	J. Felske, L. Elia

*Games behind winner. †Tied for position. ‡Lost Championship Series. §Won Championship Series. xFirst half 34-21; second 25-27.

Individual Records (1883 To Date)

Batting

Most years, non-pitcher	16, Granville W. Hamner
	16, Michael J. Schmidt
Most games	163, Peter E. Rose, 1979
Most games, league	2,254, Michael J. Schmidt
Most at-bats	701, Juan M. Samuel, 160 games, 1984
Most at-bats, league	7,814, Michael J. Schmidt
Most runs	196, William R. Hamilton, 131 games, 1894
Most runs since 1900	158, Charles H. Klein, 156 games, 1930
Most runs, league	1,435, Michael J. Schmidt
Most hits	254, Frank J. O'Doul, 154 games, 1929
Most hits, league	2,217, Richie Ashburn
Most singles	181, Frank J. O'Doul, 154 games, 1929
	181, Richie Ashburn, 154 games, 1951
Most singles, league	1,811, Richie Ashburn
Most doubles	59, Charles H. Klein, 156 games, 1930
Most doubles, league	432, Edward J. Delahanty
Most doubles, league, since 1900	380, Michael J. Schmidt
Most triples	26, Samuel L. Thompson, 102 games, 1894
Most triples since 1900	19, Juan M. Samuel, 160 games, 1984
Most triples, league	151, Edward J. Delahanty
Most triples, league, since 1900	127, Sherwood R. Magee
Most homers, lefthander	43, Charles H. Klein, 149 games, 1929
Most homers, righthander	48, Michael J. Schmidt, 150 games, 1980
Most homers, rookie	30, Guillermo N. Montanez, 158 games, 1971
Most homers at home	29, Charles A. Klein, 1932
Most homers on road	29, Michael J. Schmidt, 1979
Most homers, month	15, Fred Williams, May, 1923
Most homers, league, righthander	530, Michael J. Schmidt
Most homers, league, lefthander	243, Charles H. Klein
Most grand slams	4, Vincent P. DiMaggio, 127 games, 1945
Most grand slams, league	7, Michael J. Schmidt
Most total bases	445, Charles H. Klein, 156 games, 1930
Most total bases, league	4,191, Michael J. Schmidt
Most long hits	107, Charles H. Klein, 156 games, 1930
Most long hits, league	967, Michael J. Schmidt
Most extra bases on long hits	195, Charles H. Klein, 156 games, 1930
Most extra bases on long hits, league	2,084, Michael J. Schmidt
Most sacrifice hits	43, William Gleason, 155 games, 1905
Most sacrifice flies	13, Guillermo N. Montanez, 158 games, 1971
	13, Michael J. Schmidt, 150 games, 1980
Most stolen bases	115, William R. Hamilton, 133 games, 1891
Most stolen bases since 1900	72, Juan M. Samuel, 160 games, 1984
Most stolen bases, league	437, Edward J. Delahanty
Most stolen bases, league, since 1900	387, Sherwood R. Magee
Most caught stealing	19, Juan M. Samuel, 161 games, 1985
Most bases on balls	128, Michael J. Schmidt, 154 games, 1983
Most bases on balls, league	1,437, Michael J. Schmidt
Most strikeouts	180, Michael J. Schmidt, 158 games, 1975
Fewest strikeouts	8, Emil M. Verban, 155 games, 1947
Most strikeouts, league	1,824, Michael J. Schmidt
Most hit by pitch	14, Edward F. Bouchee, 154 games, 1957
Most runs batted in	170, Charles H. Klein, 154 games, 1930
Most runs batted in, league	1,505, Michael J. Schmidt
Most game-winning RBIs	17, Michael J. Schmidt, 150 games, 1980
	17, Gary N. Matthews, 162 games, 1982
Highest batting average	.408, Edward J. Delahanty, 145 games, 1899
Highest batting average since 1900	.398, Frank J. O'Doul, 154 games, 1929
Highest batting average, league	.362, William R. Hamilton
Highest batting average, league, since 1900	.326, Charles H. Klein
Highest slugging average	.687, Charles H. Klein, 156 games, 1930
Longest batting streak	36 games, William R. Hamilton, 1894
Longest batting streak since 1900	26 games, Charles H. Klein, 1930 (twice)
Most grounded into double play	25, Delmer Ennis, 153 games, 1950
	25, Ted C. Sizemore, 152 games, 1977
Fewest grounded into double play	3, Charles H. Klein, 152 games, 1933
	3, Richie Ashburn, 156 games, 1953
	3, Richie Ashburn, 153 games, 1954

Pitching, Since 1900

Most years	15, Steven N. Carlton, 1987
Most games	90, Kenton C. Tekulve, 1987
Most games, league	529, Robin E. Roberts
Most games started	45, Grover C. Alexander, 1916
Most games started, league	499, Steven L. Carlton
Most complete games	38, Grover C. Alexander, 1916
Most complete games, league	272, Robin E. Roberts
Most games finished	62, C. James Konstanty, 1950
Most innings	389, Grover C. Alexander, 1916
Most innings, league	3,740, Robin E. Roberts
Most games won	33, Grover C. Alexander, 1916
Most games won, league	241, Steven N. Carlton
Most 20-victory seasons	6, Grover C. Alexander
	6, Robin E. Roberts
Most games lost	24, Charles C. Fraser, 1904
Most games lost, league	199, Robin E. Roberts
Highest winning percentage	.800, Robin E. Roberts (28-7), 1952
Longest winning streak	15 games, Steven N. Carlton, 1972
Longest losing streak	12 games, Russell L. Miller, 1928
	12 games, Hugh N. Mulcahy, 1940
	12 games, Kenneth L. Reynolds, 1972
Most saves, season	40, Stephen W. Bedrosian, 1987
Most bases on balls	164, Earl L. Moore, 1911
Most bases on balls, league	1,252, Steven N. Carlton

Most strikeouts	310, Steven N. Carlton, 1972

Most strikeouts, game—
18, Christ. J. Short, Oct. 2, 1965, second game, first 15 inn. of 18-inn. game
17, Arthur Mahaffey, Jr., April 23, 1961, second game

Most strikeouts, league	3,031, Steven N. Carlton
Most shutouts	16, Grover C. Alexander, 1916
Most shutouts, league	61, Grover C. Alexander
Most 1-0 shutouts won	4, Grover C. Alexander, 1916
Most runs	178, Raymond A. Benge, 1930
Most earned runs	147, Robin E. Roberts, 1956
Most hits	348, Claude W. Passeau, 1937
Most hit batsmen	19, Frederick F. Mitchell, 1903
	19, James P. Bunning, 1966
Most wild pitches	22, Jack E. Hamilton, 1962
Most home runs	46, Robin E. Roberts, 1956
Most sacrifice hits	21, Curtis T. Simmons, 1954
	21, Dennis J. Bennett, 1964
	21, James P. Bunning, 1965
	21, Wayne L. Twitchell, 1973
Most sacrifice flies	15, Randy L. Lerch, 37 games, 1979
Lowest ERA	1.22, Grover C. Alexander, 376 innings, 1915

Club Records

Most players	49 in 1946
Fewest players	23 in 1915
Most games	163 in 1979, 1983
Most at-bats	5667 in 1930 (156 games)
Most runs	944 in 1930 (156 games)
Fewest runs	394 in 1942 (151 games)
Most opponents' runs	1199 in 1930 (156 games)
Most hits	1783 in 1930 (156 games)
Fewest hits	1113 in 1907 (149 games)
Most singles	1338 in 1894 (132 games)
Most singles since 1900	1268 in 1930 (156 games)
Most doubles	345 in 1930 (156 games)
Most triples	148 in 1894 (132 games)
Most triples since 1900	82 in 1905 (155 games)
Most homers	186 in 1977 (162 games)
Fewest homers (154 or 162-game schedule)	11 in 1908
Most homers at Baker Bowl, home & opp.	160 in 1929
Most homers at Shibe Park, home & opp.	154 in 1955
Most homers at Veterans Stad., home & opp.	164 in 1977
Most pinch home runs	11 in 1958
Most grand slams	7 in 1925, 1929, 1976
Most total bases	2594 in 1930 (156 games)
Most long hits	519 in 1932 (154 games)
Most extra bases on long hits	936 in 1977 (162 games)
Most sacrifices, (S. H. and S. F.)	239 in 1909 (154 games)
Most sacrifice hits	174 in 1905 (155 games)
Most sacrifice flies	74 in 1977 (162 games)
Most stolen bases	200 in 1908 (155 games)
Most caught stealing	80 in 1921 (153 games)
Most bases on balls	652 in 1930 (156 games)
Most strikeouts	1154 in 1986 (161 games)
Fewest strikeouts	452 in 1924 (152 games)
Most hit by pitch	53 in 1962 (161 games)
Fewest hit by pitch	9 in 1939 (152 games)
Most runs batted in	884 in 1930 (156 games)
Most game-winning RBIs	86 in 1980 (162 games)
Highest batting average	.343 in 1894 (132 games)
Highest batting average since 1900	.315 in 1930 (156 games)
Lowest batting average	.232 in 1942 (151 games)
Highest slugging average	.467 in 1929 (154 games)
Lowest slugging average	.305 in 1907 (149 games)
Most grounded into double play	144 in 1950 (157 games)
Fewest grounded into double play	91 in 1935 (156 games)
	91 in 1973 (162 games)
Most left on bases	1272 in 1975 (162 games)
Fewest left on bases	991 in 1920 (153 games)
Most .300 hitters	10 in 1925
Most putouts	4440 in 1980 (162 games)
Fewest putouts	3887 in 1907 (149 games)
Most assists	2176 in 1921 (154 games)
Fewest assists	1437 in 1957 (156 games)
Most chances accepted	6440 in 1913 (159 games)
Fewest chances accepted	5545 in 1955 (154 games)
Most errors	403 in 1904 (155 games)
Fewest errors	104 in 1978 (162 games)
Most errorless games	89 in 1966 (162 games)
Most consecutive errorless games	11 in 1967
Most double plays	179 in 1961 (155 games)
	179 in 1973 (162 games)
Fewest double plays	112 in 1984 (162 games)
Most passed balls	27 in 1947 (155 games)
	27 in 1971 (162 games)
Fewest passed balls	3 in 1952 (154 games)
	3 in 1956 (154 games)
Highest fielding average	.983 in 1978 (162 games)
	.983 in 1963 (163 games)
Lowest fielding average	.936 in 1904 (155 games)
Highest home attendance	2,775,011 in 1979
Highest road attendance	2,061,384 in 1987
Most games won	101 in 1976, 1977
Most games lost	111 in 1941
Most game won, month	22, Sept. 1916
	22, July 1950
	22, July 1952
	22, May 1976
	22, August 1977

Robin Roberts

	22, Sept. 1983
Most games lost, month	27, Sept. 1939
Highest percentage games won	.623 in 1886 (won 71, lost 43)
	.623 in 1976 (won 101, lost 61)
	.623 in 1977 (won 101, lost 61)
Lowest percentage games won	.173 in 1883 (won 17, lost 81)
Lowest percentage games won, since 1900	.279 in 1941 (won 43, lost 111)
Games won, league	7324 in 105 years
Games lost, league	8385 in 105 years
Most shutouts won	24 in 1916
Most shutouts lost	23 in 1908, 1909
Most 1-0 games won	7 in 1913
Most 1-0 games lost	10 in 1967
Most consecutive games won	16 in 1887, 1890, 1892
Most consecutive games won, since 1900	13 in 1977
Most consecutive games lost, season	23 in 1961
Most times league champions	4
Most last place finishes	24 (tied in 1947)
Most runs, game	29 vs. Louisville, August 17, 1894
Most runs, game, since 1900	26 vs. New York, June 11, 1985
Longest 1-0 game won	15 innings vs. Boston, June 22, 1944, first game
	15 innings vs. Boston, August 7, 1951, second game
	15 innings vs. Chicago, June 19, 1955, first game
Longest 1-0 game lost	17 innings vs. Montreal, September 21, 1981
Most runs, game, by opponent	29 by Boston, June 20, 1883
	29 by New York, June 15, 1887
Most runs, game, by opp., since 1900	28 by St. L., July 6, 1929, second game
Most runs, shutout game	24 vs. Indianapolis, June 28, 1887
Most runs, shutout game, since 1900	18 vs. Pittsburgh, July 11, 1910
	18 vs. Cincinnati, August 10, 1930, first game
	18 vs. Cincinnati, July 14, 1934, first game
Most runs, shutout game, by opponent	28 by Providence, August 21, 1883
Most runs, shutout, by opp., since 1900	16 by Chi., May 4, 1929, first game
Most runs doubleheader shutout	18 vs. Brooklyn, September 26, 1912
Most runs, inning	12 vs. N.Y., Oct. 2, 1897, second inning
	12 vs. Chicago, July 21, 1923, first game, sixth inning
Most hits, game	36 vs. Louisville, August 17, 1894

Most hits, game, since 1900 ....27 vs. New York, June 11, 1985
Most home runs, game..6 vs. St. Louis, May 11, 1923
              6 vs. Pittsburgh, August 28, 1948, second game
              6 vs. Cincinnati, June 2, 1949
              6 vs. San Francisco, April 27, 1965
              6 vs. Chicago, October 3, 1972
              6 vs. Chicago, April 17, 1976, 10 innings
              6 vs. Chicago, August 12, 1977
              6 vs. Chicago, August 17, 1985

Most consecutive games, one or more homers ....13 (16 homers), 1964
Most total bases, game..........................49 vs. Louisville, August 17, 1894
         48 vs. Pittsburgh, July 23, 1930, second game, 13 innings
         48 vs. Chicago, May 17, 1979, 10 innings
         47 vs. New York, June 11, 1985
Largest crowd, day game..........................60,120 vs. Atlanta, May 6, 1973
Largest crowd, doubleheader ....63,346 vs. Pittsburgh, August 10, 1979
Largest crowd, night game....................63,816 vs. Cincinnati, July 3, 1984
Largest crowd, home opener ....60,404 vs. Pittsburgh, April 13, 1981

Pittsburgh Pirates

Yearly Finishes

Year—Position	W.	L.	Pct.	*G.B.	Manager
1901—First	90	49	.647	+ 7½	Fred Clarke
1902—First	103	36	.741	+27½	Fred Clarke
1903—First	91	49	.650	+ 6½	Fred Clarke
1904—Fourth	87	66	.569	19	Fred Clarke
1905—Second	96	57	.627	9	Fred Clarke
1906—Third	93	60	.608	23½	Fred Clarke
1907—Second	91	63	.591	17	Fred Clarke
1908—Second†	98	56	.636	1	Fred Clarke
1909—First	110	42	.724	+ 6½	Fred Clarke
1910—Third	86	67	.562	17½	Fred Clarke
1911—Third	85	69	.552	14½	Fred Clarke
1912—Second	93	58	.616	10	Fred Clarke
1913—Fourth	78	71	.523	21½	Fred Clarke
1914—Seventh	69	85	.448	25½	Fred Clarke
1915—Fifth	73	81	.474	18	Fred Clarke
1916—Sixth	65	89	.422	29	James Callahan
1917—Eighth	51	103	.331	47	Callahan, Wagner, Bezdek
1918—Fourth	65	60	.520	17	Hugo Bezdek
1919—Fourth	71	68	.511	24½	Hugo Bezdek
1920—Fourth	79	75	.513	14	George Gibson
1921—Second	90	63	.588	4	George Gibson
1922—Third†	85	69	.552	8	G. Gibson, W. McKechnie
1923—Third	87	67	.565	8½	William McKechnie
1924—Third	90	63	.588	3	William McKechnie
1925—First	95	58	.621	+ 8½	William McKechnie
1926—Third	84	69	.549	4½	William McKechnie
1927—First	94	60	.610	+ 1½	Owen (Donie) Bush
1928—Fourth	85	67	.559	9	Owen (Donie) Bush
1929—Second	88	65	.575	10½	O. Bush, J. Ens
1930—Fifth	80	74	.519	12	Jewel Ens
1931—Fifth	75	79	.487	26	Jewel Ens
1932—Second	86	68	.558	4	George Gibson
1933—Second	87	67	.565	5	George Gibson
1934—Fifth	74	76	.493	19½	G. Gibson, H. Traynor
1935—Fourth	86	67	.562	13½	Harold (Pie) Traynor
1936—Fourth	84	70	.545	8	Harold (Pie) Traynor
1937—Third	86	68	.558	10	Harold (Pie) Traynor
1938—Second	86	64	.573	2	Harold (Pie) Traynor
1939—Sixth	68	85	.444	28½	Harold (Pie) Traynor
1940—Fourth	78	76	.506	22½	Frank Frisch
1941—Fourth	81	73	.526	19	Frank Frisch
1942—Fifth	66	81	.449	36½	Frank Frisch
1943—Fourth	80	74	.519	25	Frank Frisch
1944—Second	90	63	.588	14½	Frank Frisch
1945—Fourth	82	72	.532	16	Frank Frisch
1946—Seventh	63	91	.409	34	Frank Frisch
1947—Seventh†	62	92	.403	32	W. Herman, W. Burwell
1948—Fourth	83	71	.539	8½	William Meyer
1949—Sixth	71	83	.461	26	William Meyer
1950—Eighth	57	96	.373	33½	William Meyer
1951—Seventh	64	90	.416	32½	William Meyer
1952—Eighth	42	112	.273	54½	William Meyer
1953—Eighth	50	104	.325	55	Fred Haney
1954—Eighth	53	101	.344	44	Fred Haney
1955—Eighth	60	94	.390	38½	Fred Haney
1956—Seventh	66	88	.429	27	Robert Bragan
1957—Seventh†	62	92	.403	33	R. Bragan, D. Murtaugh
1958—Second	84	70	.545	8	Daniel Murtaugh
1959—Fourth	78	76	.506	9	Daniel Murtaugh
1960—First	95	59	.617	+ 7	Daniel Murtaugh
1961—Sixth	75	79	.487	18	Daniel Murtaugh
1962—Fourth	93	68	.578	8	Daniel Murtaugh
1963—Eighth	74	88	.457	25	Daniel Murtaugh
1964—Sixth†	80	82	.494	13	Daniel Murtaugh
1965—Third	90	72	.556	7	Harry Walker
1966—Third	92	70	.568	3	Harry Walker
1967—Sixth	81	81	.500	20½	H. Walker, D. Murtaugh
1968—Sixth	80	82	.494	17	Lawrence Shepard

East Division

Year—Position	W.	L.	Pct.	*G.B.	Manager
1969—Third	88	74	.543	12	L. Shepard, A. Grammas
1970—First‡	89	73	.549	+ 5	Daniel Murtaugh
1971—First§	97	65	.599	+ 7	Daniel Murtaugh
1972—First‡	96	59	.619	+11	William Virdon
1973—Third	80	82	.494	2½	W. Virdon, D. Murtaugh
1974—First‡	88	74	.543	+ 1½	Daniel Murtaugh
1975—First‡	92	69	.571	+ 6½	Daniel Murtaugh
1976—Second	92	70	.568	9	Daniel Murtaugh
1977—Second	96	66	.593	5	Charles Tanner
1978—Second	88	73	.547	1½	Charles Tanner
1979—First§	98	64	.605	+2	Charles Tanner

Year—Position	W.	L.	Pct.	*G.B.	Manager
1980—Third	83	79	.512	8	Charles Tanner
1981—4th/6th	46	56	.451	x	Charles Tanner
1982—Fourth	84	78	.519	8	Charles Tanner
1983—Second	84	78	.519	6	Charles Tanner
1984—Sixth	75	87	.463	21½	Charles Tanner
1985—Sixth	57	104	.354	43½	Charles Tanners
1986—Sixth	64	98	.395	44	James Leyland
1987—Fourth†	80	82	.494	15	James Leyland

*Games behind winner. †Tied for position. ‡Lost Championship Series. §Won Championship Series. xFirst half 25-23; second 21-33.

Individual Records (1887 To Date)
Batting

Most years, non-pitcher .... 21, Wilver D. Stargell
Most games .... 163, William S. Mazeroski, 1967
Most games, league .... 2433, Roberto W. Clemente
Most at-bats .... 698, Mateo R. Alou, 162 games, 1969
Most at-bats, league .... 9454, Roberto W. Clemente
Most runs .... 148, Jacob C. Stenzel, 131 games, 1894
Most runs since 1900 .... 144, Hazen S. Cuyler, 153 games, 1925
Most runs, league .... 1,520, John P. Wagner
Most hits .... 237, Paul G. Waner, 155 games, 1927
Most hits, league .... 3000, Roberto W. Clemente
Most singles .... 198, Lloyd J. Waner, 150 games, 1927
Most singles, league .... 2154, Roberto W. Clemente
Most doubles .... 62, Paul G. Waner, 154 games, 1932
Most doubles, league .... 556, John P. Wagner
             556, Paul G. Waner
Most triples .... 36, J. Owen Wilson, 152 games, 1912
Most triples, league .... 231, John P. Wagner
Most homers, righthander .... 54, Ralph M. Kiner, 152 games, 1949
Most home runs, league, righthander .... 301, Ralph M. Kiner
Most homers, lefthander .... 48, Wilver D. Stargell, 141 games, 1971
Most home runs, league, lefthander .... 475, Wilver D. Stargell
Most homers at home .... 31, Ralph M. Kiner, 1948
Most homers on road .... 27, Wilver D. Stargell, 1971
Most homers, rookie .... 23, John C. Rizzo, 143 games, 1938
             23, Ralph M. Kiner, 144 games, 1946
Most homers, month .... 16, Ralph M. Kiner, September, 1949
Most grand slams .... 4, Ralph Kiner, 1949
Most grand slams, league .... 11, Ralph M. Kiner
             11, Wilver D. Stargell
Most total bases .... 366, Hazen S. Cuyler, 153 games, 1925
Most total bases, league .... 4492, Roberto W. Clemente
Most long hits, league .... 953, Wilver D. Stargell
Most long hits .... 90, Wilver D. Stargell, 148 games, 1973
Most extra bases on long hits .... 191, Ralph M. Kiner, 152 games, 1949
Most extra bases on long hits, league .... 1958, Wilver D. Stargell
Most sacrifices (S.H. and S.F.) .... 42, Harold J. Traynor, 144 games, 1928
Most sacrifice hits .... 35, Robert S. Ganley, 134 games, 1906
Most sacrifice flies .... 13, Bill Madlock, 154 games, 1982
Most stolen bases .... 96, Omar R. Moreno, 162 games, 1980
Most caught stealing .... 33, Omar R. Moreno, 162 games, 1980
Most stolen bases, league .... 688, Max G. Carey
Most bases on balls .... 137, Ralph M. Kiner, 151 games, 1951
Most bases on balls, league .... 937, Wilver D. Stargell
Most strikeouts .... 163, Donn A. Clendenon, 158 games, 1968
Most strikeouts, league .... 1936, Wilver D. Stargell
Fewest strikeouts .... 13, Carson L. Bigbee, 150 games, 1922
             13, Lloyd J. Waner, 152 games, 1928
Most hit by pitch .... 14, Albert Oliver, 151 games, 1970
Most runs batted in .... 131, Paul G. Waner, 155 games, 1927
Most runs batted in, league .... 1540, Wilver D. Stargell
Most game-winning RBIs .... 14, Bill Madlock, 154 games, 1982
             14, Bill Madlock, 130 games, 1983
Most consecutive games with RBI .... 12, Paul G. Waner (23 RBIs), 1927
Highest batting average .... .385, J. Floyd Vaughan, 137 games, 1935
Highest batting average, league .... .340, Paul G. Waner
Highest slugging average .... .658, Ralph M. Kiner, 152 games, 1949
Longest batting streak .... 27 games, James T. Williams, 1899
Longest batting streak, since 1900 .... 26 games, Daniel F. O'Connell, 1953
Long. bat. streak, two seasons .... 30 games, Charles Grimm, 1922 (5), 1923 (25)
Most grounded into double play .... 25, Alfred C. Todd, 133 games, 1938
Fewest grounded into double play .... 4, Omar R. Moreno, 150 games, 1977
             4, Franklin Taveras, 157 games, 1978
             4, Barry L. Bonds, 150 games, 1987

Pitching, Since 1900

Most years .... 18, Charles B. Adams
Most games .... 94, Kenton C. Tekulve, 1979
Most games, league .... 802, El Roy L. Face
Most games started .... 42, Robert B. Friend, 1956

Most games started, league	477, Robert B. Friend
Most complete games	32, Victor G. Willis, 1906
Most complete games, league	263, A. Wilbur Cooper
Most games finished	67, Kenton C. Tekulve, 1979
Most innings	331, Burleigh A. Grimes, 1928
Most innings, league	3,481, Robert B. Friend
Most games won	28, John D. Chesbro, 1902
Most games won, league	202, A. Wilbur Cooper
Most 20-victory seasons	4, Charles L. Phillippe
	4, Victor G. Willis
	4, A. Wilbur Cooper
	4, Jesse N. Tannehill
Most games lost	21, Murry Dickson, 1952
Most games lost, league	218, Robert B. Friend
Highest winning percentage	.947, El Roy L. Face (18-1), 1959
Longest winning streak	17 games, El Roy L. Face, 1959
Longest losing streak	13 games, Burleigh A. Grimes, 1917
Most saves, season	31, Kenton C. Tekulve, 1978
	31, Kenton C. Tekulve, 1979
Most bases on balls	159, Martin J. O'Toole, 1912
Most bases on balls, league	869, Robert B. Friend
Most strikeouts	276, Robert A. Veale, 1965
Most strikeouts, game	16, Robert A. Veale, June 1, 1965
Most strikeouts, league	1,682, Robert B. Friend
Most shutouts	8, John D. Chesbro, 1902
	8, Albert P. Leifield, 1906
	8, Albert L. Mamaux, 1915
	8, Charles B. Adams, 1920
Most shutouts, league	45, Charles B. Adams
Most 1-0 shutouts won	3, Victor G. Willis, 1908
	3, Claude R. Hendrix, 1912
	3, A. Wilbur Cooper, 1917
	3, Edward A. Brandt, 1937
Most runs	181, Remy Kremer, 1930
Most earned runs	154, Remy Kremer, 1930
Most hits	366, Remy Kremer, 1930
Most hit batsmen	21, John D. Chesbro, 1902
Most wild pitches	18, Robert A. Veale, 1964
Most home runs	32, Murry M. Dickson, 1951
Most sacrifice hits	20, Matthew C. Surkont, 1954
	20, Jerry Reuss, 1974
Most sacrifice flies	12, Vernon S. Law, 1954
	12, John R. Candelaria, 1974
Lowest ERA	1.87, A. Wilbur Cooper, 246 innings, 1916

Club Records

Most players	49 in 1987
Fewest players	25 in 1938
Most games	163 in 1965, 1967, 1968, 1979
Most at-bats	5724 in 1967 (163 games)
Most runs	912 in 1925 (153 games)
Fewest runs	464 in 1917 (157 games)
Most opponents' runs	928 in 1930 (154 games)
Most hits	1698 in 1922 (155 games)
Fewest hits	1197 in 1914 (158 games)
Most singles	1297 in 1922 (155 games)
Most doubles	316 in 1925 (153 games)
Most triples	129 in 1912 (152 games)
Most homers	158 in 1966 (162 games)
Fewest homers (154 or 162-game schedule)	9 in 1917
Most homers at Forbes Field, home & opp.	182 in 1947
Most homers at Three Rivers St., home & opp.	155 in 1987
Most grand slams	7 in 1978
Most pinch home runs	8 in 1944
Most total bases	2430 in 1966 (162 games)
Most long hits	498 in 1925 (153 games)
Most extra bases on long hits	844 in 1966 (162 games)
Most sacrifices, (S. H. and S. F.)	214 in 1927 (156 games)
Most sacrifice hits	190 in 1906 (154 games)
Most sacrifice flies	67 in 1982 (162 games)
Most stolen bases	264 in 1907 (157 games)
Most caught stealing	120 in 1977 (162 games)
Most bases on balls	607 in 1947 (156 games)
Most strikeouts	1011 in 1966 (162 games)
Fewest strikeouts	326 in 1922 (155 games)
Most hit by pitch	46 in 1917 (157 games)
	46 in 1969 (162 games)
Fewest hit by pitch	11 in 1937 (154 games)
Most runs batted in	844 in 1930 (154 games)
Most game-winning RBIs	80 in 1980 (162 games)
	80 in 1982 (162 games)
Highest batting average	.309 in 1928 (152 games)
Lowest batting average	.231 in 1952 (155 games)
Highest slugging average	.449 in 1930 (154 games)
Lowest slugging average	.298 in 1917 (157 games)
Most grounded into double play	142 in 1950 (154 games)
Fewest grounded into double play	95 in 1978 (161 games)
Most left on bases	1241 in 1936 (156 games)
Fewest left on bases	992 in 1952 (153 games)
Most .300 hitters	9 in 1928
Most putouts	4480 in 1979 (163 games)
Fewest putouts	3983 in 1934 (151 games)
Most assists	2089 in 1905 (155 games)
Fewest assists	1584 in 1934 (151 games)
Most chances accepted	6462 in 1968 (163 games)
Fewest chances accepted	5567 in 1934 (151 games)
Most errors	291 in 1904 (156 games)
Fewest errors	115 in 1983 (162 games)
Most errorless games	86 in 1983 (162 games)

Ralph Kiner

Most consecutive errorless games	9 in 1983
Most double plays	215 in 1966 (162 games)
Fewest double plays	94 in 1935 (153 games)
Most passed balls	32 in 1953 (154 games)
Fewest passed balls	3 in 1941 (156 games)
	3 in 1943 (157 games)
Highest fielding average	.982 in 1983 (162 games)
Lowest fielding average	.955 in 1904 (156 games)
Highest home attendance	1,705,828 in 1960
Highest road attendance	2,197,247 in 1980
Most games won	110 in 1909
Most games lost	113 in 1890
Most games lost since 1900	112 in 1952
Most games won, month	25, Sept. 1901
	25, Sept. 1908
	25, July 1932
Most games lost, month	24, Sept. 1916
Highest percentage games won	.741 in 1902 (won 103, lost 36)
Lowest percentage games won	.169 in 1890 (won 23, lost 113)
Lowest percentage games won since 1900	.273 in 1952 (won 42, lost 112)
Games won, league	7903 in 101 years
Games lost, league	7405 in 101 years
Most shutouts won	26 in 1906
Most shutouts lost	27 in 1916
Most 1-0 games won	10 in 1908
Most 1-0 games lost	10 in 1914
Most consecutive games won	16 in 1909
Most consecutive games lost	23 in 1890
Most consecutive games lost, since 1900	12 in 1939
Most times league champions	9
Most last place finishes	12 (tied in 1947, 1957)
Most runs, game	27 vs. Boston, June 6, 1894
Most runs, game, since 1900	24 vs. St. Louis, June 22, 1925
Most runs, game, by opponent	28 by Boston, August 27, 1887
Most runs, game, by opponent, since 1900	23 by Phila. , July 13, 1900, 8 innings
	23 by Brooklyn, July 10, 1943
Most runs, shutout game	22 vs. Chicago, September 16, 1975
Most runs, shutout game, by opponent	18 by Philadelphia, July 11, 1910
Most runs, doubleheader shutout	15 vs. Philadelphia, August 7, 1915
Most runs, inning	12 vs. St. Louis, April 22, 1892
	12 vs. Boston, June 6, 1894, third inning
Most runs, inning, since 1900—	
	11 vs. St. Louis, September 7, 1942, first game, sixth inning
Longest 1-0 game won	18 innings vs. San Diego, June 7, 1972, second game
Longest 1-0 game lost	14 innings vs. Cincinnati, June 18, 1943
Most hits, game	27 vs. Philadelphia, August 8, 1922, first game
Most home runs, game	7 vs. Boston, June 8, 1894
	7 vs. St. Louis, August 16, 1947
Most consecutive games, one or more homers	12 (26 homers) 1966
Most total bases, game	47 vs. Atlanta, August 1, 1970
Largest crowd, day game	51,726 vs. San Diego, June 6, 1976
Largest crowd, doubleheader	49,886 vs. New York, July 27, 1972
Largest crowd, night game	52,119 vs. St. Louis, April 10, 1987
Largest crowd, home opener	52,119 vs. St. Louis, April 10, 1987

St. Louis Cardinals

Yearly Finishes

Year—Position	W.	L.	Pct.	*G.B.	Manager
1901—Fourth.....	76	64	.543	14½	Patrick Donovan
1902—Sixth	56	78	.418	44½	Patrick Donovan
1903—Eighth	43	94	.314	46½	Patrick Donovan
1904—Fifth	75	79	.487	31½	Charles (Kid) Nichols
1905—Sixth	58	96	.377	47½	Nichols, Burke, Robison
1906—Seventh ..	52	98	.347	63	John McCloskey
1907—Eighth	52	101	.340	55½	John McCloskey
1908—Eighth	49	105	.318	50	John McCloskey
1909—Seventh ..	54	98	.355	56	Roger Bresnahan
1910—Seventh ..	63	90	.412	40½	Roger Bresnahan
1911—Fifth	75	74	.503	22	Roger Bresnahan
1912—Sixth	63	90	.412	41	Roger Bresnahan
1913—Eighth	51	99	.340	49	Miller Huggins
1914—Third	81	72	.529	13	Miller Huggins
1915—Sixth	72	81	.471	18½	Miller Huggins
1916—Seventh†	60	93	.392	33½	Miller Huggins
1917—Third	82	70	.539	15	Miller Huggins
1918—Eighth	51	78	.395	33	John (Jack) Hendricks
1919—Seventh ..	54	83	.394	40½	Branch Rickey
1920—Fifth†	75	79	.487	18	Branch Rickey
1921—Third	87	66	.569	7	Branch Rickey
1922—Third†	85	69	.552	8	Branch Rickey
1923—Fifth	79	74	.516	16	Branch Rickey
1924—Sixth	65	89	.422	28½	Branch Rickey
1925—Fourth	77	76	.503	18	B. Rickey, R. Hornsby
1926—First	89	65	.578	+ 2	Rogers Hornsby
1927—Second....	92	61	.601	1½	Robert O'Farrell
1928—First	95	59	.617	+ 2	William McKechnie
1929—Fourth.....	78	74	.513	20	W. McKechnie, W. Southworth
1930—First	92	62	.597	+ 2	Charles (Gabby) Street
1931—First	101	53	.656	+13	Charles (Gabby) Street
1932—Sixth†	72	82	.468	18	Charles (Gabby) Street
1933—Fifth	82	71	.536	9½	C. Street, F. Frisch
1934—First	95	58	.621	+ 2	Frank Frisch
1935—Second....	96	58	.623	4	Frank Frisch
1936—Second† .	87	67	.565	5	Frank Frisch
1937—Fourth.....	81	73	.526	15	Frank Frisch
1938—Sixth	71	80	.470	17½	F. Frisch, M. Gonzalez
1939—Second....	92	61	.601	4½	Raymond Blades
1940—Third	84	69	.549	16	Blades, Gonzalez, Southworth
1941—Second....	97	56	.634	2½	William Southworth
1942—First	106	48	.688	+ 2	William Southworth
1943—First	105	49	.682	+18	William Southworth
1944—First	105	49	.682	+14½	William Southworth
1945—Second....	95	59	.617	3	William Southworth
1946—First‡......	98	58	.628	+ 2	Edwin Dyer
1947—Second....	89	65	.578	5	Edwin Dyer
1948—Second....	85	69	.552	6½	Edwin Dyer
1949—Second....	96	58	.623	1	Edwin Dyer
1950—Fifth	78	75	.510	12½	Edwin Dyer
1951—Third	81	73	.526	15½	Martin Marion
1952—Third	88	66	.571	8½	Edward Stanky
1953—Third†	83	71	.539	22	Edward Stanky
1954—Sixth	72	82	.468	25	Edward Stanky
1955—Seventh ..	68	86	.442	30½	E. Stanky, H. Walker
1956—Fourth.....	76	78	.494	17	Fred Hutchinson
1957—Second....	87	67	.565	8	Fred Hutchinson
1958—Fifth†	72	82	.468	20	F. Hutchinson, S. Hack
1959—Seventh ..	71	83	.461	16	Solly Hemus
1960—Third	86	68	.558	9	Solly Hemus
1961—Fifth	80	74	.519	13	S. Hemus, J. Keane
1962—Sixth	84	78	.519	17½	John Keane
1963—Second....	93	69	.574	6	John Keane
1964—First	93	69	.574	+ 1	John Keane
1965—Seventh ..	80	81	.497	16½	Albert (Red) Schoendienst
1966—Sixth	83	79	.512	12	Albert (Red) Schoendienst
1967—First	101	60	.627	+10½	Albert (Red) Schoendienst
1968—First	97	65	.599	+ 9	Albert (Red) Schoendienst

East Division

Year—Position	W.	L.	Pct.	*G.B.	Manager
1969—Fourth.....	87	75	.537	13	Albert (Red) Schoendienst
1970—Fourth.....	76	86	.469	13	Albert (Red) Schoendienst
1971—Second....	90	72	.556	7	Albert (Red) Schoendienst
1972—Fourth.....	75	81	.481	21½	Albert (Red) Schoendienst
1973—Second....	81	81	.500	1½	Albert (Red) Schoendienst
1974—Second....	86	75	.534	1½	Albert (Red) Schoendienst
1975—Third†	82	80	.506	10½	Albert (Red) Schoendienst
1976—Fifth	72	90	.444	29	Albert (Red) Schoendienst
1977—Third	83	79	.512	18	Vernon Rapp
1978—Fifth	69	93	.426	21	V. Rapp, K. Boyer
1979—Third	86	76	.531	12	Kenton Boyer
1980—Fourth.....	74	88	.457	17	Boyer, Herzog, Schoendienst
1981—2nd/2nd	59	43	.578	§	Dorrel (Whitey) Herzog
1982—First x	92	70	.568	+ 3	Dorrel (Whitey) Herzog
1983—Fourth.....	79	83	.488	11	Dorrel (Whitey) Herzog
1984—Third	84	78	.519	12½	Dorrel (Whitey) Herzog
1985—First x	101	61	.623	+ 3	Dorrel (Whitey) Herzog
1986—Third	79	82	.491	28½	Dorrel (Whitey) Herzog
1987—Firstx	95	67	.586	+ 3	Dorrel (Whitey) Herzog

*Games behind winner. †Tied for position. ‡Defeated Brooklyn in pennant playoff. §First half 30-20; second 29-23. xWon Championship Series.

Individual Records (1876 To 1877, 1885 To 1886, 1892 To Date)

Batting

Most years, non-pitcher	22, Stanley F. Musial
Most games, season	162, William D. White, 1963
	162, Kenton L. Boyer, 1964
	162, Curtis C. Flood, 1964
Most games, league	3,026, Stanley F. Musial
Most at-bats	689, Louis C. Brock, 159 games, 1967
Most at-bats, league	10,972, Stanley F. Musial
Most runs	141, Rogers Hornsby, 154 games, 1922
Most runs, league	1,949, Stanley F. Musial
Most hits	250, Rogers Hornsby, 154 games, 1922
Most hits, league	3,630, Stanley F. Musial
Most singles	180, Jesse C. Burkett, 142 games, 1901
Most singles, league	2,253, Stanley F. Musial
Most doubles	64, Joseph M. Medwick, 155 games, 1936
Most doubles, league	725, Stanley F. Musial
Most triples	33, Perry W. Werden, 124 games, 1893
Most triples since 1900	25, Thomas A. Long, 140 games, 1915
Most triples, league	177, Stanley F. Musial
Most homers, lefthander	43, John R. Mize, 155 games, 1940
Most homers, righthander	42, Rogers Hornsby, 154 games, 1922
Most homers at home	25, John R. Mize, 1940
Most homers on road	23, Stanley F. Musial, 1948
Most homers, month	12, George J. Kurowski, August, 1947
Most homers, rookie	21, Raymond L. Jablonski, 157 games, 1953
Most homers, league, lefthander	475, Stanley F. Musial
Most homers, league, righthander	255, Kenton L. Boyer
Most grand slams	3, James L. Bottomley, 153 games, 1925
	3, Keith Hernandez, 161 games, 1977
Most grand slams, league	9, Stanley F. Musial
Most total bases	450, Rogers Hornsby, 154 games, 1922
Most total bases, league	6,134, Stanley F. Musial
Most long hits	103, Stanley F. Musial, 155 games, 1948
Most long hits, league	1,377, Stanley F. Musial
Most extra bases on long hits	200, Rogers Hornsby, 154 games, 1922
Most extra bases on long hits, league	2,504, Stanley F. Musial
Most stolen bases	118, Louis C. Brock, 153 games, 1974
Most stolen bases, league	888, Louis C. Brock
Most caught stealing	36, Miller J. Huggins, 148 games, 1914
Most sacrifices (S.H. and S.F.)	37, Taylor L. Douthit, 139 games, 1926
Most sacrifice hits	36, Harry W. Walker, 148 games, 1943
Most sacrifice flies	14, George A. Hendrick, 136 games, 1982
Most bases on balls	136, Jack A. Clark, 131 games, 1987
Most bases on balls, league	1,599, Stanley F. Musial
Most intentional bases on balls	26, Stanley F. Musial, 135 games, 1958
Most strikeouts	139, Jack A. Clark, 131 games, 1987
Most strikeouts, league	1,469, Louis C. Brock
Fewest strikeouts	10, Frank F. Frisch, 153 games, 1927
Most hit by pitch	31, Louis R. Evans, 151 games, 1910
Most runs batted in	154, Joseph M. Medwick, 156 games, 1937
Most runs batted in, league	1,951, Stanley F. Musial
Most game-winning RBIs	21, Keith Hernandez, 160 games, 1982
Most consecutive games with RBI	10, William D. White (15 RBI), 1961
Highest batting average	.424, Rogers Hornsby, 143 games, 1924
Highest batting average, league	.359, Rogers Hornsby
Highest slugging average	.756, Rogers Hornsby, 138 games, 1925
Longest batting streak	33 games, Rogers Hornsby, 1922
Most grounded into double play	29, Ted L. Simmons, 161 games, 1973
Fewest grounded into double play	2, Louis C. Brock, 155 games, 1965

Pitching, Since 1900

Most years	18, Jesse J. Haines
Most games	75, Todd R. Worrell, 1987
Most games, league	554, Jesse J. Haines
Most games started	41, Robert G. Harmon, 1911
Most games started, league	482, Robert Gibson
Most complete games	39, John W. Taylor, 1904
Most complete games, league	255, Robert Gibson
Most games finished	63, H. Bruce Sutter, 1984
Most innings	352, Grant McGlynn, 1907
Most innings, league	3,885, Robert Gibson
Most games won	30, Jerome H. Dean, 1934
Most games won, league	251, Robert Gibson
Most 20-victory seasons	5, Robert Gibson
Most games lost	25, Grant McGlynn, 1907
	25, Arthur L. Raymond, 1908
Most games lost, league	174, Robert Gibson
Highest winning percentage	.811, Jerome H. Dean (30-7), 1934
Longest winning streak	15 games, Robert Gibson, 1968
Longest losing streak	9 games, William H. McGee, 1938
	9 games, Thomas G. Poholsky, 1951
	9 games, Robert H. Forsch, 1978
Most saves	45, H. Bruce Sutter, 1984
Most bases on balls	181, Robert G. Harmon, 1911
Most bases on balls, league	1,336, Robert Gibson
Most strikeouts	274, Robert Gibson, 1970
Most strikeouts, game	19, Steven N. Carlton, September 15, 1969
Most strikeouts, league	3,117, Robert Gibson
Most shutouts	13, Robert Gibson, 1968
Most shutouts, league	56, Robert Gibson
Most 1-0 shutouts won	4, Robert Gibson, 1968
Most runs	162, Grant McGlynn, 1907

Most earned runs	129, William H. Sherdel, 1929
Most hits	337, Denton T. Young, 1900
Most hit batsmen	17, Gerald L. Staley, 1953
Most wild pitches	15, Fred L. Beebe, 1907
	15, Fred L. Beebe, 1909
	15, David J. LaPoint, 1984
Most home runs	39, Murry M. Dickson, 1948
Most sacrifice hits	17, David J. LaPoint, 1983
Most sacrifice flies	13, Robert H. Forsch, 1979
Lowest ERA	1.12, Robert Gibson, 305 innings, 1968

Club Records

Most players	49 in 1959
Fewest players	25 in 1904
Most games	163 in 1962, 1971, 1975, 1979
Most at-bats	5734 in 1979 (163 games)
Most runs	1004 in 1930 (154 games)
Most opponents' runs	806 in 1929 (154 games)
Fewest runs	372 in 1908 (154 games)
Most hits	1732 in 1930 (154 games)
Fewest hits	1105 in 1908 (154 games)
Most singles	1223 in 1920 (155 games)
Most doubles	373 in 1939 (154 games)
Most triples	96 in 1920 (155 games)
Most homers	143 in 1955 (154 games)
Fewest homers (154 or 162-game schedule)	10 in 1906
Most homers at Sportsman's Pk., home & opp.	176 in 1955
Most homers at Busch Mem. St., home & opp.	113 in 1979
Most grand slams	7 in 1961
Most pinch home runs	7 in 1946, 1960
Most total bases	2595 in 1930 (154 games)
Most long hits	566 in 1930 (154 games)
Most extra bases on long hits	863 in 1930 (154 games)
Most sacrifices (S. H. and S. F.)	212 in 1926 (156 games)
Most sacrifice hits	172 in 1943 (147 games)
Most sacrifice flies	66 in 1954 (154 games)
Most stolen bases	314 in 1985 (162 games)
Most caught stealing	112 in 1977 (162 games)
Most bases on balls	655 in 1910 (153 games)
Most strikeouts	977 in 1966 (162 games)
Fewest strikeouts	414 in 1925 (153 games)
Most hit by pitch	78 in 1910 (153 games)
Fewest hit by pitch	15 in 1925 (153 games)
Most runs batted in	942 in 1930 (154 games)
Most game-winning RBIs	94 in 1985 (162 games)
Highest batting average	.314 in 1930 (154 games)
Lowest batting average	.223 in 1908 (154 games)
Highest slugging average	.471 in 1930 (154 games)
Lowest slugging average	.288 in 1908 (154 games)
Most grounded into double play	166 in 1958 (154 games)
Fewest grounded into double play	75 in 1945 (155 games)
Most left on bases	1251 in 1939 (155 games)
Fewest left on bases	968 in 1924 (154 games)
Most .300 hitters	11 in 1930
Most putouts	4460 in 1979 (163 games)
Fewest putouts	3952 in 1906 (154 games)
Most assists	2293 in 1917 (154 games)
Fewest assists	1595 in 1935 (154 games)
Most chances accepted	6459 in 1917 (154 games)
Fewest chances accepted	5752 in 1935 (154 games)
Most errors	348 in 1908 (154 games)
Fewest errors	108 in 1985 (162 games)
Most errorless games	85 in 1985 (162 games)
Most consecutive errorless games	11 in 1980
Most double plays	192 in 1974 (161 games)
Fewest double plays	122 in 1922 (154 games)
Most passed balls	38 in 1906 (154 games)
Fewest passed balls	4 in 1925 (153 games)
Highest fielding average	.983 in 1985 (162 games)
Lowest fielding average	.946 in 1908 (154 games)
Highest home attendance	3,072,122 in 1987
Highest road attendance	2,321,960 in 1987
Most games won	106 in 1942
Most games lost	111 in 1898
Most games lost since 1900	105 in 1908
Most games won, month	26, July 1944
Most games lost, month	27, Sept. 1908
Highest percentage games won	.703 in 1876 (won 45, lost 19)
Highest percentage games won, since 1900	.688 in 1942 (won 106, lost 48)
Lowest percentage games won	.221 in 1897 (won 29, lost 102)

Bob Gibson

Lowest percentage games won, since 1900	.314 in 1903 (won 43, lost 94)
Games won, league	7406 in 96 years
Games lost, league	7248 in 96 years
Most shutouts won	30 in 1968
Most shutouts lost	33 in 1968
Most 1-0 games won	8 in 1907
	8 in 1968
Most 1-0 games lost	8 in 1918
Most consecutive games won	14 in 1935
Most consecutive games lost	15 in 1909
Most times league champions	15
Most last place finishes	10 (tied in 1916)
Most runs, game	28 vs. Phila., July 6, 1929, second game
Most runs, game, by opponent	28 by Boston, Sept. 3, 1896, first game
Most runs, game, by opponent, since 1900	24 by Pitts., June 22, 1925
Most runs, inning	12 vs. Phila., Sept. 16, 1926, first game, third inning
Most runs, shutout game	18 vs. Cincinnati, June 10, 1944
Most runs, shutout game, by opponent	19 by Pittsburgh, August 3, 1961
Most runs, doubleheader shutout	16 vs. Brooklyn, September 21, 1934
Most hits, game	30 vs. New York, June 1, 1895
Longest 1-0 game won	14 innings vs. Boston, June 15, 1939
Longest 1-0 game lost	18 innings vs. New York, July 2, 1933, first game
Most hits, game, since 1900	28 vs. Phila., July 6, 1929, second game
Most home runs, game	7 vs. Brooklyn, May 7, 1940
Most consecutive games, one or more homers	12 (18 homers) 1955
Most total bases, game	49 vs. Brooklyn, May 7, 1940
Largest crowd, day game	50,548 vs. New York, September 14, 1975
Largest crowd, doubleheader	49,743 vs. Atlanta, June 23, 1968
Largest crowd, night game	50,340 vs. Chicago, July 2, 1977
Largest crowd, home opener	48,672 vs. Chicago, April 8, 1986

San Diego Padres

Yearly Finishes
West Division

Year—Position	W.	L.	Pct.	*G.B.	Manager
1969—Sixth	52	110	.321	41	Pedro (Preston) Gomez
1970—Sixth	63	99	.389	39	Pedro (Preston) Gomez
1971—Sixth	61	100	.379	28½	Pedro (Preston) Gomez
1972—Sixth	58	95	.379	36½	P. Gomez, D. Zimmer
1973—Sixth	60	102	.370	39	Donald Zimmer
1974—Sixth	60	102	.370	42	John McNamara
1975—Fourth	71	91	.438	37	John McNamara
1976—Fifth	73	89	.451	29	John McNamara
1977—Fifth	69	93	.426	29	J. McNamara, A. Dark
1978—Fourth	84	78	.519	11	Roger Craig
1979—Fifth	68	93	.422	22	Roger Craig
1980—Sixth	73	89	.451	19½	Gerald Coleman
1981—6th/6th	41	69	.373	†	Frank Howard
1982—Fourth	81	81	.500	8	Richard Williams
1983—Fourth	81	81	.500	10	Richard Williams
1984—First‡	92	70	.568	+12	Richard Williams
1985—Third§	83	79	.512	12	Richard Williams
1986—Fourth	74	88	.457	22	Steve Boros
1987—Sixth	65	97	.401	25	Lawrence Bowa

*Games behind winner. †First half 23-33; second 18-36. ‡Won Championship Series. §Tied for position.

Nate Colbert

Individual Records (1969 To Date)
Batting

Most years, non-pitcher ....10, Fred L. Kendall
Most games ....162, David M. Winfield, 1980
 162, Steven P. Garvey, 1985
Most games, league ....1117, David M. Winfield
Most at-bats ....654, Steven P. Garvey, 162 games, 1985
Most at-bats, league ....3997, David M. Winfield
Most runs ....119, Anthony K. Gwynn, 157 games, 1987
Most runs, league ....599, David M. Winfield
Most hits ....218, Anthony K. Gwynn, 157 games, 1987
Most hits, league ....1134, David, M. Winfield
Most singles ....177, Anthony K. Gwynn, 158 games, 1984
Most singles, league ....762, David M. Winfield
Most doubles ....42, Terrence E. Kennedy, 153 games, 1982
Most doubles, league ....179, David M. Winfield
Most triples ....13, Anthony K. Gwynn, 157 games, 1987
Most triples, league ....63, Eugene Richards
Most homers, righthander ....38, Nathan Colbert, 156 games, 1970
 38, Nathan Colbert, 151 games, 1972
Most homers, lefthander ....23, Willie L. McCovey, 122 games, 1975
Most homers, rookie ....18, Benito Santiago, 146 games, 1987
Most homers, righthander, league ....163, Nathan Colbert
Most homers, lefthander, league ....76, Terrence E. Kennedy
Most homers, month...11, Nathan Colbert, May 1970
 11, Nathan Colbert, July 1972
 11, Nathan Colbert, August 1972
Most homers at home...16, Nathan Colbert, 1970
 16, Nathan Colbert, 1972
 16, David M. Winfield, 1979
Most homers on road ....22, Nathan Colbert, 1970
 22, Nathan Colbert, 1972
Most grand slams ....2, Nathan Colbert, 151 games, 1972
 2, David M. Winfield, 137 games, 1976
 2, David A. Kingman, 56 games, 1977
 2, Kurt A. Bevacqua, 71 games, 1985
Most grand slams, league...5, Nathan Colbert
Most total bases ....333, David M. Winfield, 159 games, 1979
Most total bases, league ....1853, David M. Winfield
Most long hits ....71, David M. Winfield 159 games, 1979
Most long hits, league ....372, David M. Winfield
Most extra bases on long hits ....149, David M. Winfield, 159 games, 1979
Most extra bases on long hits, league..719, David M. Winfield
Most sacrifice hits ....28, Osborne E. Smith, 159 games, 1980
Most sacrifice flies ....10, Steven P. Garvey, 161 games, 1984
 10, Carmelo Martinez, 149 games, 1984
Most stolen bases...70, Alan A. Wiggins, 158 games, 1984

Most stolen bases, league ....242, Eugene Richards
Most caught stealing.................................21, Alan A. Wiggins, 158 games, 1984
Most bases on balls ....125, F. Gene Tenace, 147 games, 1977
Most bases on balls, league ....463, David M. Winfield
Most strikeouts ....150, Nathan Colbert, 156 games, 1970
Most strikeouts, league ....856, Nathan Colbert
Fewest strikeouts....................23, Anthony K. Gwynn, 158 games, 1984
Most hit by pitch ....13, F. Gene Tenace, 147 games, 1977
Most runs batted in ....118, David M. Winfield, 159 games, 1979
Most runs batted in, league ....626, David M. Winfield
Most game-winning RBIs ....15, Terrence E. Kennedy, 153 games, 1982
 15, Steven P. Garvey, 161 games, 1984
Highest batting average ....370, Anthony K. Gwynn, 157 games, 1987
Highest batting average, league ....335, Anthony K. Gwynn
Highest slugging average ....558, David M. Winfield, 159 games, 1979
Longest batting streak ....34 games, Benito Santiago, 1987
Most grounded into double plays ....25, Steven P. Garvey, 161 games, 1984
 25, Steven P. Garvey, 162 games, 1985
Fewest grounded into double play.................2, Alan A. Wiggins, 158 games, 1984

Pitching

Most years ....8, Randall L. Jones
Most games..83, Craig L. Lefferts, 1986
Most games, league ....265, Roland G. Fingers
Most games started ....40, Randall L. Jones, 1976
Most games started, league ....253, Randall L. Jones
Most complete games ....25, Randall L. Jones, 1976
Most complete games, league ....71, Randall L. Jones
Most games finished ....69, Roland G. Fingers, 1977
Most innings ....315, Randall L. Jones, 1976
Most innings, league..1765, Randall L. Jones
Most games won ....22, Randall L. Jones, 1976
Most games won, league ....92, Randall L. Jones
Most 20-victory seasons ....2, Randall L. Jones, 1974
Most games lost ....22, Randall L. Jones, 1974
Most games lost, league ....105, Randall L. Jones
Highest winning percentage ....778, Gaylord J. Perry (21-6), 1978
Most saves.......................................37, Roland G. Fingers, 1978
Longest winning streak ....11 games, M. Andrew Hawkins, 1985
Longest losing streak ....11 games, Gary D. Ross, 1969
Most bases on balls ....122, Stephen R. Arlin, 1972
Most bases on balls, league ....505, Clayton L. Kirby
Most strikeouts ....231, Clayton L. Kirby, 1971
Most strikeouts, league ....802, Clayton L. Kirby
Most strikeouts, game.....................15, Fredie H. Norman, September, 15, 1972
Most shutouts won ....6, Fredie H. Norman, 1972
 6, Randall L. Jones, 1975
Most shutouts won, league ....18, Randall L. Jones
Most 1-0 shutouts won ....2, Joseph F. Niekro, 1969
 2, Randall L. Jones, 1978
Most runs, allowed..............................126, Patrick E. Dobson, 1970
 126, William B. Greif, 1974
Most earned runs ....117, William B. Greif, 1974
Most hits ....274, Randall L. Jones, 1976
Most wild pitches ....15, Stephen R. Arlin, 1972
Most hit batsmen ....14, William B. Greif, 1974
Most homers ....36, Eddie L. Whitson, 1987
Most sacrifice hits ....23, Randall L. Jones, 1979
Most sacrifice flies ....12, David A. Roberts, 1971
 12, M. Andrew Hawkins, 1985
Lowest ERA ....2.10, David A. Roberts, 270 innings, 1971

Club Records

Most players .... 42 in 1969
Fewest players... 31 in 1984
Most games.. 163 in 1980, 1983
Fewest games.. 153 in 1972
Most at-bats.. 5602 in 1977 (162 games)
Most runs.. 692 in 1977 (162 games)
Fewest runs... 468 in 1969 (162 games)
Most opponents' runs..................................... 834 in 1977 (162 games)
Most hits... 1442 in 1986 (162 games)
Fewest hits.. 1181 in 1972 (153 games)
Most singles.. 1105 in 1980 (163 games)
Most doubles.. 245 in 1977 (162 games)
Most triples... 53 in 1979 (161 games)
Most homers .... 172 in 1970 (162 games)
Fewest homers.. 64 in 1976
Most homers at San Diego Stad., home & opp... 158 in 1986
Most grand slams.. 4 in 1969, 1977, 1983, 1985
Most pinch home runs.................................... 8 in 1986
Most total bases... 2149 in 1970 (162 games)
Most long hits... 416 in 1970 (162 games)
Most extra bases on long hits......................... 796 in 1970 (162 games)
Most sacrifice hits .... 133 in 1975 (162 games)
Most sacrifice flies .... 55 in 1984 (162 games)
Most stolen bases... 239 in 1980 (163 games)
Most caught stealing...................................... 91 in 1987 (162 games)
Most bases on balls.. 602 in 1977 (162 games)
Most strikeouts... 1164 in 1970 (162 games)
Fewest strikeouts... 716 in 1976 (162 games)
Most hit by pitch .... 39 in 1970 (162 games)
Fewest hit by pitch .... 15 in 1973 (153 games)
Most runs batted in .... 652 in 1977 (162 games)
Most game-winning RBIs .... 83 in 1984 (162 games)
Most .300 hitters.. 3 in 1987
Highest batting average .... .261 in 1986 (162 games)
Lowest batting average .... .225 in 1969 (162 games)

Highest slugging average	.391 in 1970	(162 games)
Lowest slugging average	.329 in 1969	(162 games)
Most grounded into double play	134 in 1971	(161 games)
Fewest grounded into double play	81 in 1978	(162 games)
Most left on bases	1239 in 1980	(163 games)
Fewest left on bases	1006 in 1972	(153 games)
Most putouts	4428 in 1982	(162 games)
Fewest putouts	4211 in 1972	(153 games)
Most assists	2012 in 1980	(163 games)
Fewest assists	1621 in 1972	(153 games)
Most chances accepted	6411 in 1980	(163 games)
Fewest chances accepted	5832 in 1972	(153 games)
Most errors	189 in 1977	(162 games)
Fewest errors	124 in 1985	(162 games)
Most errorless games	77 in 1985	(162 games)
Most consecutive errorless games	9 in 1979	
Most double plays	171 in 1978	(162 games)
Fewest double plays	126 in 1974	(162 games)
Most passed balls	22 in 1987	(162 games)
Fewest passed balls	3 in 1970	(162 games)
	3 in 1974	(162 games)
Highest fielding average	.980 in 1980	(163 games)
	.980 in 1985	(162 games)
Lowest field average average	.971 in 1975	(162 games)
	.971 in 1977	(162 games)
Highest home attendance	2,210,352 in 1985	
Highest road attendance	1,994,464 in 1985	
Most games won	92 in 1984	
Most games lost	110 in 1969	
Most games won, month	19, June 1984	
	19, July 1984	
Most games lost, month	22, June 1969	
	22, August 1969	
	22, May 1974	
Games won, league	1309 in 19 years	
Games lost, league	1706 in 19 years	
Highest percentage games won	.568 in 1984 (won 92, lost 70)	
Lowest percentage games won	.321 in 1969 (won 52, lost 110)	
Most shutouts won	19 in 1985	

Most shutouts lost	23 in 1969
	23 in 1976
Most 1-0 shutouts won	6 in 1985
Most 1-0 shutouts lost	4 in 1971, 1972, 1976, 1978
Most consecutive games won	11 in 1982
Most consecutive games lost	11 in 1969
Most times league champions	1
Most last place finishes	6 (tied in 1969)
Most runs, inning	9 vs. Cincinnati, May 3, 1969, first inning
Most runs, nine-inning game	16 vs. Philadelphia, July 26, 1970
	16 vs. San Francisco, April 5, 1983
Most runs, extra-inning game	17 vs. San Francisco, May 23, 1970, 15 innings
Most runs, game, by opponent	23 by Chicago, May 17, 1977
Most runs, shutout game	12 vs. San Francisco, October 3, 1980
	12 vs. Los Angeles, July 30, 1984
	12 vs. Cincinnati, June 14, 1986
Most runs, shutout game, by opponent	19 by Chicago, May 13, 1969
	19 by Los Angeles, June 28, 1969
Most runs, doubleheader shutout	No performance
Longest 1-0 game won	14 innings vs. Cincinnati, August 4, 1974, second game
Longest 1-0 game lost	18 innings vs. Pittsburgh, June 7, 1972, second game
Most hits, game	24 vs. San Francisco, April 19, 1982
Most home runs, game	5 vs. San Francisco, May 23, 1970, 15 innings
	4 vs. Philadelphia, May 5, 1970
	4 vs. Atlanta, July 3, 1970, second game
	4 vs. Philadelphia, July 26, 1970
	4 vs. Los Angeles, April 11, 1971
	4 vs. Cincinnati, September 26, 1973
	4 vs. Atlanta, April 18, 1977
	4 vs. Chicago, August 5, 1977
	4 vs. Cincinnati, June 10, 1984
	4 vs. Chicago, May 4, 1985
	4 vs. Cincinnati, April 13, 1986
Most consecutive games, one or more homers	10 (15 homers), 1970
Most total bases, game	39 vs. S. F., May 23, 1970, 15 innings
	33 vs. Pittsburgh, June 2, 1970, 15 innings
Largest crowd, day game	53,375 vs. San Francisco, June 22, 1985
Largest crowd, doubleheader	43,473 vs. Philadelphia, June 13, 1976
Largest crowd, night game	54,732 vs. Atlanta, June 7, 1986
Largest crowd, home opener	54,490 vs. San Francisco, April 15, 1985

San Francisco Giants

Yearly Finishes

Year—Position	W.	L.	Pct.	*G.B.	Manager
1958—Third	80	74	.519	12	William Rigney
1959—Third	83	71	.539	4	William Rigney
1960—Fifth	79	75	.513	16	W. Rigney, T. Sheehan
1961—Third	85	69	.552	8	Alvin Dark
1962—First‡	103	62	.624	+ 1	Alvin Dark
1963—Third	88	74	.543	11	Alvin Dark
1964—Fourth	90	72	.556	3	Alvin Dark
1965—Second	95	67	.586	2	Herman Franks
1966—Second	93	68	.578	1½	Herman Franks
1967—Second	91	71	.562	10½	Herman Franks
1968—Second	88	74	.543	9	Herman Franks

West Division

Year—Position	W.	L.	Pct.	*G.B.	Manager
1969—Second	90	72	.556	3	Clyde King
1970—Third	86	76	.531	16	C. King, C. Fox
1971—First§	90	72	.556	+ 1	Charles Fox
1972—Fifth	69	86	.445	26½	Charles Fox
1973—Third	88	74	.543	11	Charles Fox
1974—Fifth	72	90	.444	30	C. Fox, W. Westrum
1975—Third	80	81	.497	27½	Wesley Westrum
1976—Fourth	74	88	.457	28	William Rigney
1977—Fourth	75	87	.463	23	Joseph Altobelli
1978—Third	89	73	.549	6	Joseph Altobelli
1979—Fourth	71	91	.438	19½	J. Altobelli, D. Bristol
1980—Fifth	75	86	.466	17	J. David Bristol
1981—5th/3rd.	56	55	.505	x	Frank Robinson
1982—Third	87	75	.537	2	Frank Robinson
1983—Third	79	83	.488	12	Frank Robinson
1984—Sixth	66	96	.407	26	F. Robinson, D. Ozark
1985—Sixth	62	100	.383	33	J. Davenport, R. Craig
1986—Third	83	79	.512	13	Roger Craig
1987—First§	90	72	.556	+ 6	Roger Craig

*Games behind winner. †Tied for position. ‡Won pennant playoff. §Lost Championship Series. xFirst half 27-32; second 29-23.

Individual Records (1958 To Date)
Batting

Most years, non-pitcher	19, Willie L. McCovey
Most games	164, Jose A. Pagan, 1962
Most games, league	2256, Willie L. McCovey
Most at-bats	663, Bobby L. Bonds, 157 games, 1970
Most at-bats, league	7578, Willie H. Mays
Most runs	134, Bobby L. Bonds, 157 games, 1970
Most runs, league	1480, Willie H. Mays
Most hits	208, Willie H. Mays, 152 games, 1958
Most hits, league	2284, Willie H. Mays
Most singles	146, Rigoberto P. Fuentes, 160 games, 1973
Most singles, league	1373, Willie H. Mays

Most doubles	46, Jack A. Clark, 156 games, 1978
Most doubles, league	376, Willie H. Mays
Most triples	12, Willie H. Mays, 153 games, 1960
Most triples, league	76, Willie H. Mays
Most homers, righthander	52, Willie H. Mays, 157 games, 1965
Most homers, lefthander	45, Willie L. McCovey, 149 games, 1969
Most homers, month	17, Willie H. Mays, August, 1965
Most homers at home	28, Willie H. Mays, 1962
Most homers on road	28, Willie H. Mays, 1965
Most homers, rookie	31, James R. Hart, 153 games, 1964
Most homers, league, righthander	459, Willie H. Mays
Most homers, league, lefthander	469, Willie L. McCovey
Most grand slams	3, Willie L. McCovey, 135 games, 1967
Most grand slams, league	16, Willie L. McCovey
Most total bases	382, Willie H. Mays, 162 games, 1962
Most total bases, league	4189, Willie H. Mays
Most long hits	90, Willie H. Mays, 162 games, 1962
Most long hits, league	911, Willie H. Mays
Most extra bases on long hits	193, Willie H. Mays, 162 games, 1962
Most extra bases on long hits, league	1905, Willie H. Mays
Most sacrifice hits	18, Robert R. Thompson, 149 games, 1986
Most sacrifice flies	12, Bobby R. Murcer, 147 games, 1975
Most stolen bases	58, William A. North, 142 games, 1979
Most stolen bases, league	263, Bobby L. Bonds
Most caught stealing	24, William A. North, 142 games, 1979
Most bases on balls	137, Willie L. McCovey, 152 games, 1970
Most intentional bases on balls	45, Willie L. McCovey, 149 games, 1969
Most bases on balls, league	1168, Willie L. McCovey
Most strikeouts	189, Bobby L. Bonds, 157 games, 1970
Most strikeouts, league	1351, Willie L. McCovey
Fewest strikeouts	48, Kenneth J. Reitz, 155 games, 1976
Most hit by pitch	26, Ronald K. Hunt, 117 games, 1970
Most runs batted in	142, Orlando M. Cepeda, 152 games, 1961
Most runs batted in, league	1388, Willie L. McCovey
Most game-winning RBIs	21, Jack A. Clark, 157 games, 1982
Highest batting average	.347, Willie H. Mays, 152 games, 1958
Highest slugging average	.656, Willie L. McCovey, 149 games, 1969
Longest batting streak	26 games, Jack A. Clark, 1978
Most grounded into double play, season	25, Bill Madlock, 140 games, 1977
Fewest grounded into double play	2, Jose A. Uribe, 157 games, 1986
	2, William N. Clark, 150 games, 1987

Pitching

Most years	14, Juan A. Marichal
Most games	78, Gregory B. Minton, 1982
Most games, league	647, Gary R. Lavelle
Most games started	42, John S. Sanford, 1963
Most games started, league	446, Juan A. Marichal
Most complete games	30, Juan A. Marichal, 1968
Most complete games, league	244, Juan A. Marichal
Most games finished	66, Gregory B. Minton, 1982
Most innings	329, Gaylord J. Perry, 1970
Most innings, league	3443, Juan A. Marichal
Most games won, season	26, Juan A. Marichal, 1968
Most games won, league	238, Juan A. Marichal

Juan Marichal

Most games lost, league	140, Juan A. Marichal
Most 20 victory seasons	6, Juan A. Marichal
Most games lost, season	18, Raymond M. Sadecki, 1968
Highest winning percentage	.806, Juan A. Marichal (25-6), 1966
Longest winning streak	16, John S. Sanford, 1962
Longest losing streak	9, Mark W. Davis, 1984
Most saves	30, Gregory B. Minton, 1982
Most bases on balls	124, John F. D'Acquisto, 1974
Most bases on balls, league	690, Juan A. Marichal
Most strikeouts	248, Juan A. Marichal 1963
Most strikeouts, league	2281, Juan A. Marichal
Most strikeouts, game	15, Gaylord J. Perry, July 22, 1966
Most shutouts, season	10, Juan A. Marichal 1965
Most 1-0 shutouts won	2, Held by many pitchers
Most shutouts, league	52, Juan A. Marichal
Most runs	143, Vida R. Blue, 1979
Most earned runs	132, Vida R. Blue, 1979
Most hits	295, Juan A. Marichal 1968
Most hit batsmen	11, Gaylord J. Perry, 1969
Most wild pitches	18, Richard P. Robertson, 1970
Most home runs	34, Juan A. Marichal, 1962
Most sacrifice hits	18, Michael F. McCormick, 1959
	18, Ronald R. Bryant, 1974
Most sacrifice flies	13, Gaylord J. Perry, 1971
Lowest ERA	1.98, Bobby D. Bolin, 177 innings, 1968

Club Records

Most players	46 in 1987 (162 games)
Fewest players	31 in 1968 (163 games)
Most games	165 in 1962
Most at-bats	5650 in 1984 (162 games)
Most runs	878 in 1962 (165 games)
Fewest runs	556 in 1985 (162 games)
Most opponents' runs	826 in 1970 (162 games)
Most hits	1552 in 1962 (165 games)
Fewest hits	1263 in 1985 (162 games)
Most singles	1132 in 1984 (162 games)
Most doubles	274 in 1987 (162 games)
Most triples	62 in 1960 (156 games)
Most homers	205 in 1987 (162 games)
Fewest homers	80 in 1980
Most homers at Seals Stadium, home & opp.	173 in 1958
Most homers at Candlestick Park, home & opp.	190 in 1987
Most grand slams	7 in 1970
Most pinch home runs	11 in 1977
Most long hits	511 in 1987 (162 games)
Most extra bases on long hits	953 in 1987 (162 games)
Most total bases	2463 in 1962 (165 games)
Most sacrifice hits	127 in 1978 (162 games)
Most sacrifice flies	54 in 1980 (161 games)
Most stolen bases	148 in 1986 (162 games)
Most caught stealing	97 in 1987 (162 games)
Most bases on balls	729 in 1970 (162 games)
Most strikeouts	1094 in 1987 (162 games)
Fewest strikeouts	764 in 1961 (155 games)
Most hit by pitch	66 in 1969 (162 games)
Fewest hit by pitch	14 in 1980 (161 games)
Most runs batted in	807 in 1962 (165 games)
Most game-winning RBIs	83 in 1987 (162 games)
Highest batting average	.278 in 1962 (165 games)
Lowest batting average	.233 in 1985 (162 games)
Highest slugging average	.441 in 1962 (165 games)
Lowest slugging average	.341 in 1968 (163 games)
Most left on bases	1280 in 1969 (162 games)
Fewest left on bases	983 in 1961 (155 games)
Most grounded into double play	149 in 1965 (163 games)
Fewest grounded into double play	83 in 1986 (162 games)
Most .300 hitters	4 in 1962
Most putouts	4429 in 1966 (161 games)
Fewest putouts	4129 in 1959 (154 games)
Most assists	1940 in 1976 (162 games)
Fewest assists	1513 in 1961 (155 games)
Most errors	186 in 1976 (162 games)
Fewest errors	129 in 1987 (162 games)
Most errorless games	74 in 1965 (163 games)
	74 in 1967 (162 games)
	74 in 1987 (162 games)
Most consecutive errorless games	8 in 1962
Most chances accepted	6349 in 1969 (162 games)
Fewest chances accepted	5677 in 1961 (155 games)
Most double plays	183 in 1987 (162 games)
Fewest double plays	109 in 1983 (162 games)
Most passed balls	30 in 1970 (162 games)
Fewest passed balls	6 in 1978 (162 games)
Highest fielding average	.980 in 1987 (162 games)
Lowest fielding average	.971 in 1976 (162 games)
Highest home attendance	1,917,168 in 1987
Highest road attendance	2,207,530 in 1966
Most games won	103 in 1962
Most games lost	100 in 1985
Most games won, month	21, Sept. 1965
	21, August 1968
Most games lost, month	21, May 1972
Highest percentage games won	.624 in 1962 (won 103, lost 62)
Lowest percentage games won	.383 in 1985 (won 62, lost 100)
Games won, league	2457 in 30 years
Games lost, league	2313 in 30 years
Most shutouts won	20 in 1968
Most shutouts lost	17 in 1968
	17 in 1976
Most 1-0 games won	6 in 1968
Most 1-0 games lost	4 in 1972, 1978, 1985
Most consecutive games won	14 in 1965
Most consecutive games lost	10 in 1985
Most times league champions	1
Most last place finishes	1
Most runs, inning	13 vs. St. Louis, May 7, 1966, third inning
Most runs, game	19 vs. Phila., September 12, 1958, second game
	19 vs. Chicago, July 4, 1961, first game
	19 vs. Los Angeles, May 13, 1962
Most runs, game, by opponent	20 by Chicago, August 13, 1959
Most runs, shutout game	14 vs. Cincinnati, August 23, 1961
Most runs, shutout game, by opponent	15 by Chicago, August 22, 1970
Most runs, doubleheader shutout	13 vs. Chicago, April 29, 1962
Longest 1-0 game won	21 innings vs. Cincinnati, September 1, 1967
Longest 1-0 game lost	14 innings vs. New York, August 19, 1969
Most hits, game	26 vs. Los Angeles, May 13, 1958
Most home runs, game	8 vs. Milwaukee, April 30, 1961
Most consecutive games, one or more homers	16 (22 homers), 1962
	16 (30 homers), 1963
Most total bases, game	50 vs. Los Angeles, May 13, 1958
Largest crowd, day game	56,196 vs. San Diego, April 10, 1979
Largest crowd, doubleheader	53,178 vs. Los Angeles, July 31, 1983
Largest crowd, night game	55,920 vs. Cincinnati, June 20, 1978
Largest crowd, home opener	56,196 vs. San Diego, April 10, 1979

Oakland A's first baseman Mark McGwire enjoyed a phenomenal 1987 rookie season, hitting an American League-leading 49 home runs. McGwire (left) acknowledges the cheers of California Angels fans after hitting his rookie record-breaking 39th home run at Anaheim Stadium on August 14. Bob Nieman (right) of the St. Louis Browns set a different kind of rookie record on September 14, 1951, when he became the only player in baseball history to homer in his first two major league at-bats. St. Louis Cardinals outfielder Vince Coleman (above) was a phenom in 1985 when he stole a rookie-record 110 bases. He followed that up with totals of 107 and 109 in his next two seasons.

The **1961 New York Yankee power combination of Roger Maris (left, left photo) and Mickey Mantle** accounted for 115 home runs, the most ever produced by teammates. St. Louis Browns pitcher **Bobo Holloman**, pictured above with his wife and son, became the first man in modern major league history to throw a no-hitter in his first major league start. Holloman's performance came May 6, 1953, against the Philadelphia A's. One of the more incredible pitching feats in baseball history was turned in by Cincinnati lefthander **Johnny Vander Meer (right)**, who pitched consecutive no-hitters in 1938.

Championship Series

including:

- Batting (Individual, Club)
- Baserunning (Individual, Club)
- Pitching (Individual, Club)
- Fielding (Individual, Club)
- Miscellaneous
- Non-Playing Personnel
- General Reference Data

Individual Batting

Service

Series & Clubs

Most Series Played

A. L.— 11—Jackson, Reginald M., Oakland, 1971, 1972, 1973, 1974, 1975; New York, 1977, 1978, 1980, 1981; California, 1982, 1986.

N. L.— 8—Hebner, Richard J., Pittsburgh, 1970, 1971, 1972, 1974, 1975; Philadelphia, 1977, 1978; Chicago, 1984.

Most Consecutive Series Played

A. L.—5—Bando, Salvatore L.; Blue, Vida R.; Campaneris, Dagoberto B.; Fingers, Roland G.; Jackson, Reginald M.; Rudi, Joseph O.; Tenace, F. Gene; Oakland, 1971 through 1975.

N. L.—3—Held by many players.

Most Series Playing in All Games

A. L.—9—Jackson, Reginald M., Oakland, 1971, 1972, 1973, 1974, 1975; New York, 1977, 1978, 1980; California, 1982; 37 games.

N. L.—7—Rose, Peter E., Cincinnati, 1970, 1972, 1973, 1975, 1976; Philadelphia, 1980, 1983; 28 games.

Most Series Played, One Club

A. L.—7—Palmer, James A., Baltimore, 1969, 1970, 1971, 1973, 1974, 1979, 1983.

N. L.—6—Bench, Johnny L., Cincinnati, 1970, 1972, 1973, 1975, 1976, 1979.
Stargell, Wilver D., Pittsburgh, 1970, 1971, 1972, 1974, 1975, 1979.
Yeager, Stephen W., Los Angeles, 1974, 1977, 1978, 1981, 1983, 1985.

Most Series Appeared as Pinch-Hitter

Both Leagues—4—Davalillo, Victor J., Pittsburgh NL, 1971, 1972; Oakland AL, 1973; Los Angeles NL, 1977; 5 games.

N. L.—4—Monday, Robert J., Los Angeles, 1977, 1978, 1981, 1983; 4 games.
Hebner, Richard J., Pittsburgh, 1971; Philadelphia, 1977, 1978; Chicago, 1984; 5 games.

A. L.—3—Motton, Curtell H., Baltimore, 1969, 1971, 1974; 4 games.
Holt, James W., Minnesota, 1970; Oakland, 1974, 1975; 4 games.
Johnson, Clifford, New York, 1977, 1978; Toronto, 1985.

Most Times on Winning Club, One or More Games Each Series

A. L.—6—Jackson, Reginald M., Oakland, 1972, 1973, 1974; New York, 1977, 1978, 1981.

N. L.—6—Rose, Peter E., Cincinnati, 1970, 1972, 1975, 1976; Philadelphia, 1980, 1983.

Most Times on Losing Club, One or More Games Each Series

N. L.—7—Hebner, Richard J., Pittsburgh, 1970, 1972, 1974, 1975; Philadelphia, 1977, 1978; Chicago, 1984.

A. L.—5—Grich, Robert A., Baltimore, 1973, 1974; California, 1979, 1982, 1986.
Jackson, Reginald M., Oakland, 1971, 1975; New York, 1980; California, 1982, 1986.

Most Clubs, Total Series

A. L.—4—Baylor, Donald E., Baltimore, 1973, 1974; California 1979, 1982; Boston, 1986; Minnesota, 1987.

N. L.—3—Held by many players.

Youngest & Oldest Players

Youngest Championship Series Player (Non-Pitcher)

A. L.—Washington, Claudell, Oakland; 20 years, 1 month, 5 days on October 5, 1974.

N. L.—Speier, Chris E., San Francisco; 21 years, 3 months, 4 days on October 2, 1971.

Oldest Championship Series Player (Non-Pitcher)

N. L.—Rose, Peter E., Philadelphia; 42 years, 5 months, 24 days on October 8, 1983.

A. L.—Jackson, Reginald M., California; 40 years, 4 months, 17 days on October 15, 1986.

Most Years Between First and Second Series

A. L.— 17—Blyleven, Rikalbert, Minnesota, 1970, 1987.*
12—Alexander, Doyle L., Baltimore, 1973; Toronto, 1985.

N. L.— 13—Niekro, Philip H., Atlanta, 1969, 1982.

*Played in 1979 NLCS with Pittsburgh.

Most Years Between First and Last Series

N. L.— 17—Ryan, L. Nolan, New York, 1969; Houston, 1986.

A. L.— 17—Blyleven, Rikalbert, Minnesota, 1970, 1987.

Positions

Most Positions Played, Total Series

N. L.—4—Rose, Peter E., Cincinnati, 1970, 1972, 1973, 1975, 1976; Philadelphia, 1980; 24 games, right field, left field, third base, first base.

A. L.—3—Tovar, Cesar L., Minnesota, 1969, 1970; Oakland, 1975; 8 games, center field, second base, left field.
Rettenmund, Mervin W., Baltimore, 1969, 1970, 1971, 1973; California, 1979; 10 games, left field, center field, right field.
Tenace, F. Gene, Oakland, 1971, 1972, 1973, 1974, 1975; 18 games, catcher, second base, first base.
Blair, Paul L., Baltimore, 1969, 1970, 1971, 1973, 1974; New York, 1977, 1978; 25 games, center field, right field, second base.
Wathan, John D., Kansas City, 1976, 1977, 1978, 1980, 1984; 8 games, catcher, first base, right field.
Hendrick, George A., Oakland, 1972; California, 1986; 4 games, center field, right field, first base.

Most Positions Played, Series

A. L.—3—Tovar, Cesar L., Minnesota, 1970, center field, second base, left field; 3-game Series, 3 games.

N. L.—2—Held by many players.

Games

Most Games, Total Series

A. L.— 45—Jackson, Reginald M., Oakland, 1971, 1972, 1973, 1974, 1975; New York, 1977, 1978, 1980, 1981; California, 1982; 11 Series, 34 consecutive games.

N. L.— 28—Rose, Peter E., Cincinnati, 1970, 1972, 1973, 1975, 1976; Philadelphia, 1980, 1983; 7 Series, 28 consecutive games.

Most Games, Total Series, One Club

A. L.— 27—George H. Brett, Kansas City, 1976, 1977, 1978, 1980, 1984, 1985; 6 Series.

N. L.— 22—Johnny L. Bench, Cincinnati, 1970, 1972, 1973, 1975, 1976, 1979; 6 Series.
Wilver D. Stargell, Pittsburgh, 1970, 1971, 1972, 1974, 1975, 1979; 6 Series.

Most Games, Pinch-Hitter, Total Series

N. L.—6—Mota, Manuel R., Los Angeles, 1974 (3), 1977 (1), 1978 (2); 6 plate appearances, 5 at-bats.

A. L.—6—Iorg, Dane C., Kansas City, 1984 (2), 1985 (4); 6 plate appearances, 4 at-bats.

Most Games, Pinch-Hitter, Series

N. L.—5—Mazzilli, Lee L., New York, 1986.

A. L.—4—Hendrick, George A., Oakland, 1972.
Iorg, Dane C., Kansas City, 1985.

Most Games, Pinch-Runner, Total Series

Both Leagues—3—Bergman, David B., Houston NL, 1980; Detroit AL, 1984; 2 Series, 0 runs.

A. L.—3—Odom, Johnny L., Oakland, 1972, 1974; 2 Series, 0 runs.
Stapleton, David L., Boston, 1986; 1 Series, 1 run.

N. L.—3—Concepcion, David I., Cincinnati, 1970, 1972; 2 Series, 0 runs.

Most Games, Pinch-Runner, Series

A. L.—3—Stapleton, David L., Boston, 1986.

N. L.—2—Gaspar, Rodney E., New York, 1969.
Jeter, Johnny, Pittsburgh, 1970.
Concepcion, David I., Cincinnati, 1972.
Landestoy, Rafael S.C., Houston, 1980.
Smith, Lonnie, Philadelphia, 1980.
Milner, Eddie J., San Francisco, 1987.

Batting Average

Highest Batting Average, Total Series (50 or More At-Bats)

A. L.—.386—Rivers, John M., New York, 1976, 1977, 1978; 3 Series, 14 games, 57 at-bats, 22 hits.

N. L.—.381—Rose, Peter E., Cincinnati, 1970, 1972, 1973, 1975, 1976; Philadelphia, 1980, 1983; 7 Series, 28 games, 118 at-bats, 45 hits.

Highest Batting Avg., Series (Playing All Games and 8 or More ABs)

3-game Series—N. L.—.778—Johnstone, John W., Philadelphia, 1976.

A. L.—.583—Robinson, Brooks C., Baltimore, 1970.

4-game Series—N. L.—.467—Baker, Johnnie B., Los Angeles, 1978.

Schmidt, Michael J., Philadelphia, 1983.

A. L.—.462—Jackson, Reginald M., New York, 1978.

5-game Series—A. L.—.611—Lynn, Fredric M., California, 1982.

N. L.—.526—Puhl, Terry S., Houston, 1980.

6-game Series—N. L.—.435—Smith, Osborne E., St. Louis, 1985.

7-game Series—A. L.—.455—Boone, Robert R., California, 1986.

N. L.—.417—Leonard, Jeffrey N., San Francisco, 1987.

Slugging Average

Highest Slugging Average, Total Series (50 or More At-Bats)

A. L.—.728—Brett, George H., Kansas City, 1976, 1977, 1978, 1980, 1984, 1985; 6 Series, 27 games, 103 at-bats, 35 hits, 5 doubles, 4 triples, 9 home runs, 75 total bases.

N. L.—.678—Garvey, Steven P., Los Angeles, 1974, 1977, 1978, 1981; San Diego, 1984; 5 Series, 22 games, 90 at-bats, 32 hits, 3 doubles, 1 triple, 8 home runs, 61 total bases.

Highest Slugging Average, Series (10 or More At-Bats)

3-game Series—N. L.—1.182—Stargell, Wilver D., Pittsburgh, 1979.

A. L.—.917—Oliva, Antonio, Minnesota, 1970.

Jackson, Reginald M., Oakland, 1971.

Watson, Robert J., New York, 1980.

Nettles, Graig, New York, 1981.

4-game Series—N. L.—1.250—Robertson, Robert E., Pittsburgh, 1971.

A. L.—1.056—Brett, George H., Kansas City, 1978.

5-game Series—A. L.—1.000—Brunansky, Thomas A., Minnesota, 1987.

N. L.—.833—Davis, Jody R., Chicago, 1984.

6-game Series—N. L.—.750—Madlock, Bill, Los Angeles, 1985.

7-game Series—N. L.—.917—Leonard, Jeffrey N., San Francisco, 1987.

A. L.—.826—Brett, George H., Kansas City, 1985.

At-Bats & Plate Appearances

Most At-Bats, Total Series

A. L.—163—Jackson, Reginald M., Oakland, 1971, 1972, 1973, 1974, 1975; New York, 1977, 1978, 1980, 1981; California, 1982, 1986; 11 Series, 45 games.

N. L.—118—Rose, Peter E., Cincinnati, 1970, 1972, 1973, 1975, 1976; Philadelphia, 1980, 1983; 7 Series, 28 games.

Most At-Bats, Pinch-Hitter, Total Series

N. L.—5—Mota, Manuel R., Los Angeles, 1974 (3), 1977 (1), 1978 (1).

Mazzilli, Lee L., New York, 1986 (5).

A. L.—5—Johnson, Clifford, New York, 1977 (1), 1978 (1), Toronto, 1985 (3).

Most Plate Appearances, Pinch-Hitter, Total Series

N. L.—6—Mota, Manuel R., Los Angeles, 1974 (3), 1977 (1), 1978 (2).

Mazzilli, Lee L., New York, 1986 (5).

A. L.—6—Iorg, Dane C., Kansas City, 1984 (2), 1985 (4).

Most Consecutive Hitless Times at Bat, Total Series

Both Leagues—31—North, William A., Oakland AL, 1974 (last 13 times at bat), 1975 (all 10 times at bat); Los Angeles NL, 1978 (all 8 times at bat).

N. L.—30—Geronimo, Cesar F., Cincinnati, 1973 (last 13 times at bat), 1975 (all 10 times at bat), 1976 (first 7 times at bat).

A. L.—24—Campaneris, Dagoberto B., Oakland, 1974 (last 13 times at bat), 1975 (all 11 times at bat); California, 1979 (0 times at bat).

Most At-Bats, Series

3-game Series—A. L.—15—Belanger, Mark H., Baltimore, 1969.

Blair, Paul L., Baltimore, 1969.

N. L.—15—Oberkfell, Kenneth R., St. Louis, 1982.

4-game Series—N. L.—19—Cash, David, Pittsburgh, 1971.

Maddox, Garry L., Philadelphia, 1978.

A. L.—18—Brett, George H., Kansas City, 1978.

Munson, Thurman L., New York, 1978.

Law, Rudy K., Chicago, 1983.

5-game Series—N. L.—24—Schmidt, Michael J., Philadelphia, 1980.

A. L.—24—Puckett, Kirby, Minnesota, 1987.

6-game Series—N. L.—27—Carter, Gary E., New York, 1986.

Doran, William D., Houston, 1986.

7-game Series—A. L.—32—DeCinces, Douglas V., California, 1986.

N. L.—30—Mitchell, Kevin D., San Francisco, 1987.

Most At-Bats, Pinch-Hitter, Series

N. L.—5—Mazzilli, Lee L., New York, 1986.

A. L.—4—Hendrick, George A., Oakland, 1972.

Most At-Bats, Total Series, No Hits

A. L.—15—Brookens, Thomas D., Detroit, 1984 (2), 1987 (13).

N. L.—11—Didier, Robert D., Atlanta, 1969.

Kirkpatrick, Edgar L., Pittsburgh, 1974 (9), 1975 (2).

Most At-Bats, Game, Nine Innings

A. L.—6—Blair, Paul L., Baltimore, October 6, 1969.

Puckett, Kirby, Minnesota, October 12, 1987.

N. L.—5—Held by many players.

Most At-Bats, Extra-Inning Game

N. L.—7—Davis, Glenn E., Houston, October 15, 1986; 16 innings.

Doran, William D., Houston, October 15, 1986; 16 innings.

Hatcher, William A., Houston, October 15, 1986; 16 innings.

Hernandez, Keith, New York, October 15, 1986; 16 innings.

Wilson, William H., New York, October 15, 1986; 16 innings.

A. L.—6—Buford, Donald A., Baltimore, October 4, 1969; 12 innings.

Grich, Robert A., California, October 11, 1986; 11 innings.

Most At-Bats, Game, Nine Innings, No Hits

A. L.-N. L.—5—Held by many players.

Most At-Bats, Extra-Inning Game, No Hits

A. L.—6—Buford, Donald A., Baltimore, October 4, 1969; 12 innings.

N. L.—6—Ashby, Alan D., Houston, October 15, 1986; 16 innings.

Most At-Bats, Inning

N. L.—2—Garrett, R. Wayne, New York, October 7, 1973; ninth inning.

Yeager, Stephen W., Los Angeles, October 17, 1981; ninth inning.

Hernandez, Keith, St. Louis, October 7, 1982; sixth inning.

Matthews, Gary N., Chicago, October 2, 1984; fifth inning.

Clark, Jack A., St. Louis, October 13, 1985; second inning.

Landrum, Terry L., St. Louis, October 13, 1985; second inning.

Pendleton, Terry L., St. Louis, October 13, 1985; second inning.

A. L.—2—Robinson, Frank, Baltimore, October 3, 1970; fourth inning.

McNally, David A., Baltimore, October 4, 1970; ninth inning.

Rettenmund, Mervin W., Baltimore, October 6, 1973; first inning.

Nettles, Graig, New York, October 14, 1981; fourth inning.

Watson, Robert J., New York, October 14, 1981; fourth inning.

Most Times Faced Pitcher, Inning

N. L.—2—Garrett, R. Wayne, New York, October 7, 1973; ninth inning.

Yeager, Stephen W., Los Angeles, October 17, 1981; ninth inning.

Smith, Lonnie, St. Louis, October 7, 1982; sixth inning.

Hernandez, Keith, St. Louis, October 7, 1982; sixth inning.

Dernier, Robert E., Chicago, October 2, 1984; fifth inning.

Sandberg, Ryne D., Chicago, October 2, 1984; fifth inning.

Matthews, Gary N., Chicago, October 2, 1984; fifth inning.

Clark, Jack A., St. Louis, October 13, 1985; second inning.
Cedeno, Cesar, St. Louis, October 13, 1985; second inning.
Landrum, Terry L., St. Louis, October 13, 1985; second inning.
Pendleton, Terry L., St. Louis, October 13, 1985; second inning.
Nieto, Thomas A., St. Louis, October 13, 1985; second inning.
A. L.—2—Robinson, Frank, Baltimore, October 3, 1970; fourth inning.
McNally, David A., Baltimore, October 4, 1970; ninth inning.
Rettenmund, Mervin W., Baltimore, October 6, 1973; first inning.
Nettles, Graig, New York, October 14, 1981; fourth inning.
Watson, Robert J., New York, October 14, 1981; fourth inning.
Cerone, Richard A., New York, October 14, 1981; fourth inning.

Runs

Most Runs, Total Series

A. L.—22—Brett, George H., Kansas City, 1976, 1977, 1978, 1980, 1984, 1985; 6 Series, 27 games.
N. L.—17—Rose, Peter E., Cincinnati, 1970, 1972, 1973, 1975, 1976; Philadelphia, 1980, 1983; 7 Series, 28 games.

Most Runs, Pinch-Hitter, Total Series

N. L.—2—Cline, Tyrone A., Cincinnati, 1970; 1 Series, 2 games.
A. L.—1—Held by many players.

Most Runs, Pinch-Runner, Total Series

N. L.—2—Clines, Eugene A., Pittsburgh, 1972, 1974; 2 Series, 2 games.
Landestoy, Rafael S.C., Houston, 1980; 1 Series, 2 games.
A. L.—2—Edwards, Marshall L., Milwaukee, 1982; 1 Series, 2 games.
White, Devon M., California, 1986; 1 Series, 2 games.

Most Runs, Series

3-game Series—A. L.—5—Belanger, Mark H., Baltimore, 1970.
N. L.—4—Held by many players.
4-game Series—A. L.—7—Brett, George H., Kansas City, 1978.
N. L.—6—Garvey, Steven P., Los Angeles, 1978.
5-game Series—A. L.—6—McRae, Harold A., Kansas City, 1977.
N. L.—6—Gwynn, Anthony K., San Diego, 1984.
6-game Series—N. L.—6—McGee, Willie D., St. Louis, 1985.
7-game Series—A. L.—8—Rice, James E., Boston, 1986.
N. L.—5—Leonard, Jeffrey N., San Francisco, 1987.
Pena, Antonio F., St. Louis, 1987.

Most Runs, Pinch-Hitter, Series

N. L.—2—Cline, Tyrone A., Cincinnati, 1970; 2 games.
A. L.—1—Held by many players.

Most Runs, Pinch-Runner, Series

N. L.—2—Landestoy, Rafael S.C., Houston, 1980; 2 games.
A. L.—2—Edwards, Marshall L., Milwaukee, 1982; 2 games.
White, Devon M., California, 1986; 2 games.

Most Runs, Game

N. L.—4—Robertson, Robert E., Pittsburgh, October 3, 1971.
Garvey, Steven P., Los Angeles, October 9, 1974.
A. L.—4—Brouhard, Mark S., Milwaukee, October 7, 1982.
Murray, Eddie C., Baltimore, October 7, 1983.
Brett, George H., Kansas City, October 11, 1985.

Most Runs, Inning

A. L.-N. L.—1—Held by many players.

Hits
Career & Series

Most Hits, Total Series

N. L.—45—Rose, Peter E., Cincinnati, 1970, 1972, 1973, 1975, 1976; Philadelphia, 1980, 1983; 7 Series, 28 games.
A. L.—37—Jackson, Reginald M., Oakland, 1971, 1972, 1973, 1974, 1975; New York, 1977, 1978, 1980, 1981; California, 1982, 1986; 11 Series, 45 games.

Most Hits, Pinch-Hitter, Total Series

N. L.—3—Popovich, Paul E., Pittsburgh, 1974; 1 Series, 3 games.
Mota, Manuel R., Los Angeles, 1974, 1977, 1978; 3 Series, 6 games.

A. L.—2—Marquez, Gonzalo, Oakland, 1972; 1 Series, 3 games.
Motton, Curtell H., Baltimore, 1969, 1971, 1974; 3 Series, 4 games.
Alou, Jesus M., Oakland, 1973, 1974; 2 Series, 4 games.
Piniella, Louis V., New York, 1976, 1981; 2 Series, 3 games.
McRae, Harold A., Kansas City, 1984; 1 Series, 2 games.
Iorg, Dane C., Kansas City, 1984, 1985; 2 Series, 6 games.
Johnson, Clifford, New York, 1977, 1978, Toronto, 1985; 3 Series, 5 games.
Mulliniks, S. Rance, Toronto, 1985; 1 Series, 2 games.
Grubb, John M., Detroit, 1987; 1 Series, 3 games.

Most Hits, Series

3-game Series—A. L.—7—Robinson, Brooks C., Baltimore, 1969, 1970.
N. L.—7—Shamsky, Arthur L., New York, 1969.
Johnstone, John W., Philadelphia, 1976.
4-game Series—N. L.—8—Cash, David, Pittsburgh, 1971.
A. L.—7—Brett, George H., Kansas City, 1978.
Carew, Rodney C., California, 1979.
Law, Rudy K., Chicago, 1983.
5-game Series—A. L.—11—Chambliss, C. Christopher, New York, 1976.
Lynn, Fredric M., California, 1982.
N. L.—10—Puhl, Terry S., Houston, 1980.
6-game Series—N. L.—10—Smith, Osborne E., St. Louis, 1985.
7-game Series—A. L.—11—Barrett, Martin G., Boston, 1986.
N. L.—10—Leonard, Jeffrey N., San Francisco, 1987.

Most Hits, Pinch-Hitter, Series

N. L.—3—Popovich, Paul E., Pittsburgh, 1974; 3 games.
A. L.—2—Marquez, Gonzalo, Oakland, 1972; 3 games.
Piniella, Louis V., New York, 1981; 2 games.
McRae, Harold A., Kansas City, 1984; 2 games.
Johnson, Clifford, Toronto, 1985; 3 games.
Mulliniks, S. Rance, Toronto, 1985; 2 games.
Grubb, John M., Detroit, 1987; 3 games.

Most Hits, Two Consecutive Series

N. L.—17—Rose, Peter E., Cincinnati, 1972 (9), 1973 (8).
A. L.—15—Lynn, Fredric M., Boston, 1975 (4); California, 1982 (11).
DeCinces, Douglas V., California, 1982 (6), 1986 (9).

Most Series, One or More Hits

A. L.—10—Jackson, Reginald M., Oakland, 1971, 1972, 1973, 1974, 1975; New York, 1977, 1978, 1980; California, 1982, 1986.
N. L.—7—Hebner, Richard J., Pittsburgh, 1970, 1971, 1972, 1974, 1975; Philadelphia, 1977, 1978.
Rose, Peter E., Cincinnati, 1970, 1972, 1973, 1975, 1976; Philadelphia, 1980, 1983.

Most Consecutive Hits, Total Series

N. L.—6—Garvey, Steven P., Los Angeles, October 9, 1974 (4), October 4, 1977 (2).
A. L.—5—Bando, Salvatore L., Oakland, October 5 (4), October 7 (1), 1975.
Rivers, John M., New York, October 13 (1), October 14 (4), 1976.
Chambliss, C. Christopher, New York, October 3 (1), October 4 (4), 1978.
Boone, Robert R., California, October 11 (2), October 12 (3), 1986 (one sacrifice bunt during streak).

Most Consecutive Hits, Pinch-Hitter, Total Series

N. L.—3—Popovich, Paul E., Pittsburgh, October 5, 6, 9, 1974.
A. L.—2—Motton, Curtell H., Baltimore, October 5, 1969; October 3, 1971.
Piniella, Louis V., New York, October 13, 15, 1981.
McRae, Harold A., Kansas City, October 3, 5, 1984.
Mulliniks, S. Rance, Toronto, October 8, 9, 1985.
Johnson, Clifford, Toronto, October 11, 15, 1985.

Most Consecutive Hits, One Series

A. L.—5—Bando, Salvatore L., Oakland, October 5 (4), October 7 (1), 1975.
Rivers, John M., New York, October 13 (1), October 14 (4), 1976.
Chambliss, C. Christopher, New York, October 3 (1), October 4 (4), 1978.
Boone, Robert R., California, October 11 (2), October 12 (3), 1986 (one sacrifice bunt during streak).

N. L.—5—Matthews, Gary N., Philadelphia, October 5 (1), October 7 (3), October 8 (1), 1983; one walk during streak.

Game & Inning

Most Hits, Game

A. L.—5—Blair, Paul L., Baltimore, October 6, 1969.
N. L.—4—Robertson, Robert E., Pittsburgh, October 3, 1971.
Cey, Ronald C., Los Angeles, October 6, 1974.
Garvey, Steven P., Los Angeles, October 9, 1974.
Baker, Johnnie B., Los Angeles, October 7, 1978; 10 innings.
Puhl, Terry S., Houston, October 12, 1980.
Garvey, Steven P., San Diego, October 6, 1984.
Landrum, Terry L., St. Louis, October 13, 1985.

Most Times Reached Base Safely, Game (Batting 1.000)

A. L.—5—Jackson, Reginald M., New York, October 3, 1978; 2 bases on balls, 1 single, 1 double, 1 home run.
Nettles, Graig, New York, October 14, 1981; 1 hit by pitcher, 3 singles, 1 home run.
Baylor, Donald E., Boston, October 8, 1986; 2 singles, 3 bases on balls.
Gedman, Richard L., Boston, October 12, 1986; 2 singles, 1 double, 1 home run, 1 hit by pitcher.
N. L.—5—Millan, Felix B. M., Atlanta, October 5, 1969; 3 bases on balls, 2 singles.

Getting All Club's Hits, Game (Most)

N. L.—2—Clemente, Roberto W., Pittsburgh, October 10, 1972.
Kosco, Andrew J., Cincinnati, October 7, 1973.
A. L.—2—Wilson, Willie J., Kansas City, October 12, 1985.

Most Consecutive Games, One or More Hits, Total Series

N. L.—15—Rose, Peter E., Cincinnati, 1973 (last 3), 1975 (3), 1976 (3); Philadelphia, 1980 (5), 1983 (first 1).
A. L.—12—Baylor, Donald E., California, 1982 (last 3), Boston, 1986 (7), Minnesota, 1987 (2).

Most Hits, Two Consecutive Games, One Series

A. L.—6—Robinson, Brooks C., Baltimore, October 4 (4), October 5 (2), 1969, first game 12 innings, second game 11 innings.
Bando, Salvatore L., Oakland, October 5 (4), October 7 (2), 1975.
Rivers, John M., New York, October 8 (4), October 9 (2), 1977.
Chambliss, C. Christopher, New York, October 3 (2), October 4 (4), 1978.
Gedman, Richard L., Boston, October 12 (4), October 14 (2), 1986, first game 11 innings.
Owen, Spike D., Boston, October 14 (4), October 15 (2), 1986.
N. L.—6—Shamsky, Arthur L., New York, October 4 (3), October 5 (3), 1969.
Robertson, Robert E., Pittsburgh, October 2 (2), October 3 (4), 1971.
Johnstone, John W., Philadelphia, October 10 (3), October 12 (3), 1976.
Lopes, David E., Los Angeles, October 4 (3), October 5 (3), 1978.

Most Hits, Inning

A. L.—2—Nettles, Graig, New York, October 14, 1981; fourth inning.
N. L.—2—Clark, Jack A., St. Louis, October 13, 1985; second inning.
Landrum, Terry L., St. Louis, October 13, 1985; second inning.

Singles

Most Singles, Total Series

N. L.—34—Rose, Peter E., Cincinnati, 1970, 1972, 1973, 1975, 1976; Philadelphia, 1980, 1983; 7 Series, 28 games.
A. L.—24—Jackson, Reginald M., Oakland, 1971, 1972, 1973, 1974, 1975; New York, 1977, 1978, 1980, 1981; California 1982, 1986; 11 Series, 45 games.

Most Singles, Pinch-Hitter, Total Series

N. L.—3—Popovich, Paul E., Pittsburgh, 1974; 1 Series, 3 games.
A. L.—2—Marquez, Gonzalo, Oakland, 1972; 1 Series, 3 games.
Alou, Jesus M., Oakland, 1973, 1974; 2 Series, 4 games.
Piniella, Louis V., New York, 1976, 1981; 2 Series, 3 games.

Mulliniks, S. Rance, Toronto, 1985; 1 Series, 2 games.
Johnson, Clifford, New York, 1977, 1978; Oakland, 1981; Toronto, 1985; 4 Series, 5 games.
Grubb, John M., Detroit, 1987; 1 Series, 3 games.

Most Singles, Series

3-game Series—N. L.—7—Shamsky, Arthur L., New York, 1969.
A. L.—6—Robinson, Brooks C., Baltimore, 1969.
4-game Series—N. L.—7—Russell, William E., Los Angeles, 1974.
A. L.—6—Chambliss, C. Christopher, New York, 1978.
Law, Rudy K., Chicago, 1983.
5-game Series—A. L.—8—Munson, Thurman L., New York, 1976.
Lynn, Fredric M., California, 1982.
N. L.—8—Rose, Peter E., Philadelphia, 1980.
Puhl, Terry S., Houston, 1980.
6-game Series—N. L.—7—Clark, Jack A., St. Louis, 1985.
Smith, Osborne E., St. Louis, 1985.
7-game Series—A. L.—9—Barrett, Martin G., Boston, 1986.
Boone, Robert R., California, 1986.
N. L.—7—Pena, Antonio F., St. Louis, 1987.

Most Singles, Pinch-Hitter, Series

N. L.—3—Popovich, Paul E., Pittsburgh, 1974; 3 games.
A. L.—2—Marquez, Gonzalo, Oakland, 1972; 3 games.
Piniella, Louis V., New York, 1981; 2 games.
Mulliniks, S. Rance, Toronto, 1985; 2 games.
Johnson, Clifford, Toronto, 1985; 3 games.
Grubb, John M., Detroit, 1987; 3 games.

Most Singles, Game

A. L.—4—Robinson, Brooks C., Baltimore, October 4, 1969; 12 innings.
Chambliss, C. Christopher, New York, October 4, 1978.
N. L.—4—Puhl, Terry S., Houston, October 12, 1980; 10 innings.
Landrum, Terry L., St. Louis, October 13, 1985.

Most Singles, Inning

A. L.—2—Nettles, Graig, New York, October 14, 1981; fourth inning.
N. L.—2—Clark, Jack A., St. Louis, October 13, 1985; second inning.
Landrum, Terry L., St. Louis, October 13, 1985; second inning.

Doubles

Most Doubles, Total Series

N. L.—7—Rose, Peter E., Cincinnati, 1970, 1972, 1973, 1975, 1976; Philadelphia, 1980, 1983; 7 Series, 28 games.
Hebner, Richard J., Pittsburgh, 1970, 1971, 1972, 1974, 1975; Philadelphia, 1977, 1978; Chicago, 1984; 8 Series, 27 games.
Schmidt, Michael J., Philadelphia, 1976, 1977, 1978, 1980, 1983; 5 Series, 20 games.
Cey, Ronald C., Los Angeles, 1974, 1977, 1978, 1981; Chicago, 1984; 5 Series, 22 games.
A. L.—7—McRae, Harold A., Kansas City, 1976, 1977, 1978, 1980, 1984, 1985; 6 Series, 25 games.
Jackson, Reginald M., Oakland, 1971, 1972, 1973, 1974, 1975; New York, 1977, 1978, 1980, 1981; California, 1982, 1986; 11 Series, 45 games.

Most Doubles, Pinch-Hitter, Total Series

N. L.—2—Mota, Manuel R., Los Angeles, 1974, 1977, 1978; 3 Series, 6 games.
A. L.—1—Held by many players.

Most Doubles, Series

3-game Series—N. L.—3—Morgan, Joe L., Cincinnati, 1975.
Porter, Darrell R., St. Louis, 1982.
A. L.—3—Watson, Robert J., New York, 1980.
4-game Series—N. L.—3—Cey, Ronald C., Los Angeles, 1974.
A. L.—3—Carew, Rodney C., California, 1979.
5-game Series—A. L.—4—Alou, Mateo R., Oakland, 1972.
Brunansky, Thomas A., Minnesota, 1987.
N. L.—3—Rose, Peter E., Cincinnati, 1972.
6-game Series—N. L.—4—Herr, Thomas M., St. Louis, 1985.
7-game Series—A. L.—4—Garcia, Damaso D., Toronto, 1985.
N. L.—2—Driessen, Daniel, St. Louis, 1987.
Clark, William N., San Francisco, 1987.

Most Doubles, Game

A. L.-N. L.—2—Held by many players.

Most Doubles, Inning

A. L.-N. L.—1—Held by many players.

Triples

Most Triples, Total Series

A. L.—4—Brett, George H., Kansas City, 1976, 1977, 1978, 1980, 1984, 1985; 6 Series, 27 games.

N. L.—3—McGee, Willie D., St. Louis, 1982, 1985, 1987; 3 Series, 16 games.

Most Triples, Pinch-Hitter, Total Series

N. L.—1—Cline, Tyrone A., Cincinnati, 1970; 1 Series, 2 games.
Dykstra, Leonard K., New York, 1986; 1 Series, 2 games.

A. L.—Never accomplished.

Most Triples, Series

A. L.—2—Brett, George H., Kansas City, 1977; 5-game Series.

N. L.—2—McGee, Willie D., St. Louis, 1982; 3-game Series.

Most Triples, Game

A. L.-N. L.—1—Held by many players.

Most Bases-Loaded Triples, Game

A. L.—1—Sundberg, James H., Kansas City, October 16, 1985.

N. L.—Never accomplished.

Home Runs
Career & Series

Most Home Runs, Total Series

A. L.—9—Brett, George H., Kansas City, 1976, 1977, 1978, 1980, 1984, 1985; 6 Series, 27 games.

N. L.—8—Garvey, Steven P., Los Angeles, 1974, 1977, 1978, 1981; San Diego, 1984; 5 Series, 22 games.

Most Home Runs, Series

3-game Series—N. L.—3—Aaron, Henry L., Atlanta, 1969.
           A. L.—2—Held by many players.

4-game Series—N. L.—4—Robertson, Robert E., Pittsburgh, 1971.
                     Garvey, Steven P., Los Angeles, 1978.
           A. L.—3—Brett, George H., Kansas City, 1978.

5-game Series—N. L.—3—Staub, Daniel J., New York, 1973.
           A. L.—2—Held by many players.

6-game Series—N. L.—3—Madlock, Bill, Los Angeles, 1985.

7-game Series—N. L.—4—Leonard, Jeffrey N., San Francisco, 1987.
           A. L.—3—Brett, George H., Kansas City, 1985.

Most Series, One or More Home Runs

N. L.—5—Bench, Johnny L., Cincinnati, 1970 (1), 1972 (1), 1973 (1), 1976 (1), 1979 (1).

A. L.—4—Nettles, Graig, New York, 1976 (2), 1978 (1), 1980 (1), 1981 (1).
Jackson, Reginald M., Oakland, 1971 (2), 1975 (1); New York, 1978 (2); California, 1982 (1).
Brett, George H., Kansas City, 1976 (1), 1978 (3), 1980 (2), 1985 (3).

Most Series, Two or More Home Runs

A. L.—3—Brett, George H., Kansas City, 1978 (3), 1980 (2), 1985 (3).

N. L.—2—Garvey, Steven P., Los Angeles, 1974 (2), 1978 (4).
Stargell, Wilver D., Pittsburgh, 1974 (2), 1979 (2).
Matthews, Gary N., Philadelphia, 1983 (3); Chicago, 1984 (2).

Game & Inning

Most Home Runs, Game

N. L.—3—Robertson, Robert E., Pittsburgh, October 3, 1971.
    2—Staub, Daniel J., New York, October 8, 1973.
       Garvey, Steven P., Los Angeles, October 9, 1974.
       Garvey, Steven P., Los Angeles, October 4, 1978.
       Matthews, Gary N., Chicago, October 2, 1984.

A. L.—3—Brett, George H., Kansas City, October 6, 1978.
    2—Powell, John W., Baltimore, October 4, 1971.
       Jackson, Reginald M., Oakland, October 5, 1971.
       Bando, Salvatore L., Oakland, October 7, 1973.
       Nettles, Graig, New York, October 13, 1976.
       Brett, George H., Kansas City, October 11, 1985.
       Gaetti, Gary J., Minnesota, October 7, 1987.

Most Grand Slams, Game

A. L.—1—Cuellar, Miguel, Baltimore, October 3, 1970; fourth inning.
Baylor, Donald E., California, October 9, 1982; eighth inning.

N. L.—1—Cey, Ronald C., Los Angeles, October 4, 1977; seventh inning.
Baker, Johnnie B., Los Angeles, October 5, 1977; fourth inning.

Inside-the-Park Home Runs

A. L.—Nettles, Graig, New York, October 9, 1980; fifth inning, 0 on base.
Molitor, Paul L., Milwaukee, October 6, 1982; fifth inning, 1 on base.

N. L.—Never accomplished.

Most Home Runs, Pinch-Hitter, Game

N. L.—1—Martin, Jerry L., Philadephia, October 4, 1978; ninth inning.
McBride, Arnold R., Philadelphia, October 7, 1978; seventh inning.
Spilman, W. Harry, San Francisco, October 9, 1987; ninth inning.

A. L.—1—Lowenstein, John L., Baltimore, October 3, 1979; tenth inning.
Sheridan, Patrick A., Kansas City, October 9, 1985; ninth inning.

Hitting Home Run, Leadoff Batter, Start of Game

A. L.—Campaneris, Dagoberto B., Oakland, October 7, 1973; at Baltimore.
Brett, George H., Kansas City, October 6, 1978; at New York.

N. L.—Dernier, Robert E., Chicago, October 2, 1984; at Chicago.

Home Runs Winning 1-0 Games

A. L.—Bando, Salvatore L., Oakland, October 8, 1974; fourth inning.

N. L.—Schmidt, Michael J., Philadelphia, October 4, 1983; first inning.
Davis, Glenn E., Houston, October 8, 1986; second inning.

Most Home Runs, Game, by Pitcher

A. L.—1—Cuellar, Miguel, Baltimore, October 3, 1970; 3 on base.

N. L.—1—Gullett, Donald E., Cincinnati, October 4, 1975; 1 on base.
Carlton, Steven N., Philadelphia, October 6, 1978; 2 on base.
Sutcliffe, Richard L., Chicago, October 2, 1984; 0 on base.

Most Home Runs, Game, by Rookie

N. L.—1—Garrett, R. Wayne, New York, October 6, 1969.
Clines, Eugene A., Pittsburgh, October 3, 1971.
Speier, Chris E., San Francisco, October 6, 1971.
McGee, Willie D., St. Louis, October 10, 1982.
Lindeman, James W., St. Louis, October 9, 1987.

A. L.—1—Joyner, Wallace K., California, October 8, 1986.
Nokes, Matthew D., Detroit, October 12, 1987.

Most Consecutive Games, Series, Hitting One or More Home Runs

N. L.—4—Leonard, Jeffrey N., San Francisco, October 6, 7, 9, 10, 1987.

A. L.—2—Killebrew, Harmon C., Minnesota, October 3, 4, 1970.
Johnson, David A., Baltimore, October 4, 5, 1970.
Campaneris, Dagoberto B., Oakland, October 7, 9, 1973; second game 11 innings.
Bando, Salvatore L., Oakland, October 6, 8, 1974.
Ford, Darnell G., California, October 3, 4, 1979.
Molitor, Paul L., Milwaukee, October 6, 8, 1982.
Gagne, Gregory C., Minnesota, October 10, 11, 1987.

Most Homers, Two Consec. Games, Series, Homering Each Game

N. L.—4—Robertson, Robert E., Pittsburgh, October 3 (3), 5 (1), 1971.

A. L.—2—Killebrew, Harmon C., Minnesota, October 3, 4, 1970.
Johnson, David A., Baltimore, October 4, 5, 1970.
Campaneris, Dagoberto B., Oakland, October 7, 9, 1973; second game 11 innings.
Bando, Salvatore L., Oakland, October 6, 8, 1974.
Ford, Darnell G., California, October 3, 4, 1979.
Molitor, Paul L., Milwaukee, October 6, 8, 1982.
Gagne, Gregory C., Minnesota, October 10, 11, 1987.

Hitting Home Run in First Championship Series At-Bat

A. L.—Robinson, Frank, Baltimore, October 4, 1969; fourth inning (walked in first inning).
Cash, Norman D., Detroit, October 7, 1972; second inning.
Ford, Darnell G., California, October 3, 1979; first inning.
Lowenstein, John L., Baltimore, October 3, 1979; tenth inning (pinch-hit).
Cerone, Richard A., New York, October 8, 1980; first inning.
Thomas, J. Gorman, Milwaukee, October 5, 1982; second inning.
Gaetti, Gary J., Minnesota, October 7, 1987; second inning.

N. L.—Morgan, Joe L., Cincinnati, October 7, 1972; first inning.
  Sutcliffe, Richard L., Chicago, October 2, 1984; third inning.
  Davis, Glenn E., Houston, October 8, 1986; second inning.

Hitting Home Runs in First Two Championship Series At-Bats

A. L.—Gaetti, Gary J., Minnesota, October 7, 1987; second and fifth innings.

N. L.—Never accomplished.

Most Home Runs, Inning

A. L.-N. L.—1—Held by many players.

Most Home Runs, Two Consecutive Innings

N. L.—2—Staub, Daniel J., New York, October 8, 1973, first and second innings.

A. L.—Never accomplished.

Total Bases

Most Total Bases, Total Series

A. L.—75—Brett, George H., Kansas City, 1976, 1977, 1978, 1980, 1984, 1985; 6 Series, 27 games.

N. L.—63—Rose, Peter E., Cincinnati, 1970, 1972, 1973, 1975, 1976; Philadelphia, 1980, 1983; 7 Series, 28 games.

Most Total Bases, Pinch-Hitter, Total Series

N. L.—6—Martin, Jerry L., Philadelphia, 1977, 1978; 2 Series, 3 games.

A. L.—4—Lowenstein, John L., Baltimore, 1979; 1 Series, 2 games.
  Sheridan, Patrick A., Kansas City, 1985; 1 Series, 2 games.

Most Total Bases, Series

3-game Series—N. L.—16—Aaron, Henry L., Atlanta, 1969.
  A. L.—11—Held by many players.
4-game Series—N. L.—22—Garvey, Steven P., Los Angeles, 1978.
  A. L.—19—Brett, George H., Kansas City, 1978.
5-game Series—A. L.—20—Chambliss, C. Christopher, New York, 1976.
  N. L.—15—Rose, Peter E., Cincinnati, 1973.
    Davis, Jody R., Chicago, 1984.
6-game Series—N. L.—18—Madlock, Bill, Los Angeles, 1985.
7-game Series—N. L.—22—Leonard, Jeffrey N., San Francisco, 1987.
  A. L.—19—Brett, George H., Kansas City, 1985.

Most Total Bases, Pinch-Hitter, Series

N. L.—6—Martin, Jerry L., Philadelphia, 1978; 2 games.

A. L.—4—Lowenstein, John L., Baltimore, 1979; 2 games.
  Sheridan, Patrick A., Kansas City, 1985; 2 games.

Most Total Bases, Game

N. L.—14—Robertson, Robert E., Pittsburgh, October 3, 1971; 3 home runs, 1 double.

A. L.—12—Brett, George H., Kansas City, October 6, 1978; 3 home runs.

Most Total Bases, Inning

A. L.-N. L.—4—Held by many players.

Long Hits

Most Long Hits, Total Series

A. L.—18—Brett, George H., Kansas City, 1976, 1977, 1978, 1980, 1984, 1985; 6 Series, 27 games.

N. L.—12—Garvey, Steven P., Los Angeles, 1974, 1977, 1978, 1981; San Diego, 1984; 5 Series, 22 games.

Most Long Hits, Series

3-game Series—N. L.—5—Aaron, Henry L., Atlanta, 1969.
  A. L.—4—Watson, Robert J., New York, 1980.
4-game Series—N. L.—6—Garvey, Steven P., Los Angeles, 1978.
  A. L.—5—Brett, George H., Kansas City, 1978.
5-game Series—A. L.—6—Brunansky, Thomas A., Minnesota, 1987.
  N. L.—4—Rose, Peter E., Cincinnati, 1972.
    Oliver, Albert, Pittsburgh, 1972.
6-game Series—N. L.—5—Herr, Thomas M., St. Louis, 1985.
7-game Series—A. L.—5—Brett, George H., Kansas City, 1985.
  N. L.—4—Leonard, Jeffrey N., San Francisco, 1987.

Most Long Hits, Game

N. L.—4—Robertson, Robert E., Pittsburgh, October 3, 1971; 3 home runs, 1 double.

A. L.—3—Blair, Paul L., Baltimore, October 6, 1969; 2 doubles, 1 home run.

Brett, George H., Kansas City, October 6, 1978; 3 home runs.

Brett, George H., Kansas City, October 11, 1985; 2 home runs, 1 double.

Most Long Hits, Two Consecutive Games, Series

N. L.—5—Robertson, Robert E., Pittsburgh, October 3 (4), 3 home runs, 1 double; October 5 (1), 1 home run, 1971.

A. L.—4—Brett, George H., Kansas City, October 6 (3), 3 home runs; October 7 (1), 1 triple, 1978.

Most Long Hits, Inning

A. L.-N. L.—1—Held by many players.

Runs Batted In

Most Runs Batted In, Total Series

N. L.—21—Garvey, Steven P., Los Angeles, 1974, 1977, 1978, 1981; San Diego, 1984; 5 Series, 22 games.

A. L.—20—Jackson, Reginald M., Oakland, 1971, 1972, 1973, 1974, 1975; New York, 1977, 1978, 1980, 1981; California, 1982, 1986; 11 Series, 45 games.

Most Runs Batted In, Pinch-Hitter, Total Series

A. L.—3—Lowenstein, John L., Baltimore, 1979; 1 Series, 2 games.

N. L.—2—Martin, Joseph C., New York, 1969; 1 Series, 2 games.
  Martin, Jerry L., Philadelphia, 1977, 1978; 2 Series, 3 games.

Most Runs Batted In, Series

3-game Series—A. L.—9—Nettles, Graig, New York, 1981.
  N. L.—7—Aaron, Henry L., Atlanta, 1969.
4-game Series—N. L.—8—Baker, Johnnie B., Los Angeles, 1977.
    Matthews, Gary N., Philadelphia, 1983.
  A. L.—6—Jackson, Reginald M., New York, 1978.
5-game Series—A. L.—10—Baylor, Donald E., California, 1982.
  N. L.—7—Garvey, Steven P., San Diego, 1984.
6-game Series—N. L.—7—Madlock, Bill, Los Angeles, 1985.
7-game Series—A. L.—7—Downing, Brian J., California, 1986.
  N. L.—7—Leonard, Jeffrey N., San Francisco, 1987.

Most Runs Batted In, Pinch-Hitter, Series

A. L.—3—Lowenstein, John L., Baltimore, 1979; 2 games.

N. L.—2—Martin, Joseph C., New York, 1969; 2 games.
  Martin, Jerry L., Philadelphia, 1978; 2 games.

Most Runs Batted In, Game

A. L.—5—Blair, Paul L., Baltimore, October 6, 1969.
  Baylor, Donald E., California, October 5, 1982.

N. L.—5—Robertson, Robert E., Pittsburgh, October 3, 1971.
  Garvey, Steven P., San Diego, October 6, 1984.

Most Runs Batted In, Pinch-Hitter, Game

A. L.—3—Lowenstein, John L., Baltimore, 1979; tenth inning.

N. L.—2—Martin, Joseph C., New York, October 4, 1969; eighth inning.

Most Consecutive Games, One or More Runs Batted In, Total Series

A. L.—4—Patek, Freddie J., Kansas City, 1977 (first 4); 5 runs batted in.
  Roenicke, Gary S., Baltimore, 1979 (last 1), 1983 (first 3); 5 runs batted in.

N. L.—4—Perez, Atanasio R., Cincinnati, 1973 (last 2), 1975 (first 2); 6 runs batted in.
  Lopes, David E., Los Angeles, 1974 (last 1), 1977 (first 3); 4 runs batted in.
  Luzinski, Gregory M., Philadelphia, 1976 (3), 1977 (first 1); 5 runs batted in.
  Maddox, Garry L., Philadelphia, 1976 (last 1), 1977 (2), 1978 (first 1); 5 runs batted in.
  Foster, George A., Cincinnati, 1976 (3), 1979 (first 1); 6 runs batted in.
  Luzinski, Gregory M., Philadelphia, 1978 (last 2), 1980 (first 2); 6 runs batted in.
  Herr, Thomas M., St. Louis, 1985 (last 4); 6 runs batted in.
  Leonard, Jeffrey N., San Francisco, 1987 (first 4); 5 runs batted in.

Batting In All Club's Runs, Game (Most)

A. L.—3—Campaneris, Dagoberto B., Oakland, October 5, 1974.
  Nettles, Graig, New York, October 13, 1981.

N. L.—2—Foster, George A., Cincinnati, October 2, 1979; 11 innings.
  Marshall, Michael A., Los Angeles, October 7, 1983.
  Madlock, Bill, Los Angeles, October 14, 1985.

Most Runs Batted In, Inning

A. L.—4—Cuellar, Miguel, Baltimore, October 3, 1970; grand slam in fourth inning.

Baylor, Donald E., California, October 9, 1982; grand slam in eighth inning.

N. L.—4—Cey, Ronald C., Los Angeles, October 4, 1977; grand slam in seventh inning.

Baker, Johnnie B., Los Angeles, October 5, 1977; grand slam in fourth inning.

Most Game-Winning RBIs, Total Series (Since 1980)

A. L.—3—Brett, George H., Kansas City, 1980, 1985 (2).

N. L.—2—Luzinski, Gregory M., Philadelphia, 1980 (2).

Matthews, Gary N., Philadelphia, 1983; Chicago, 1984.

Smith, Osborne E., St. Louis, 1982, 1985.

Guerrero, Pedro, Los Angeles, 1983, 1985.

Carter, Gary E., Montreal, 1981; New York, 1986.

Most Game-Winning RBIs, Series (Since 1980)

N. L.—2—Luzinski, Gregory M., Philadelphia, 1980.

Carter, Gary E., New York, 1986.

A. L.—2—Cooper, Cecil C., Milwaukee, 1982.

Oliver, Albert, Toronto, 1985.

Brett, George, Kansas City, 1985.

Bases On Balls

Most Bases on Balls, Total Series

N. L.—23—Morgan, Joe L., Cincinnati, 1972, 1973, 1975, 1976, 1979; Houston, 1980; Philadelphia, 1983; 7 Series, 27 games.

A. L.—17—Jackson, Reginald M., Oakland, 1971, 1972, 1973, 1974, 1975; New York, 1977, 1978, 1980, 1981; California, 1982, 1986; 11 Series, 45 games.

Most Bases on Balls, Pinch-Hitter, Total Series

Both Leagues—2—Rettenmund, Mervin W., Baltimore AL, 1969; Cincinnati NL, 1975; California AL, 1979; 3 Series, 4 games.

N. L.—2—Hague, Joe C., Cincinnati, 1972; 1 Series, 3 games.

A. L.—2—Iorg, Dane C., Kansas City, 1984, 1985; 2 Series, 6 games.

Most Bases on Balls, Series

3-game Series—A. L.—6—Killebrew, Harmon C., Minnesota, 1969.

N. L.—6—Morgan, Joe L., Cincinnati, 1976.

4-game Series—N. L.—9—Wynn, James S., Los Angeles, 1974.

A. L.—5—Jackson, Reginald M., Oakland, 1974.

Murray, Eddie C., Baltimore, 1979.

Roenicke, Gary S., Baltimore 1983.

5-game Series—N. L.—8—Cruz, Jose, Houston, 1980.

A. L.—7—Whitaker, Louis R., Detroit, 1987.

6-game Series—N. L.—5—Guerrero, Pedro, Los Angeles, 1985.

Clark, Jack A., St. Louis, 1985.

Herr, Thomas M., St. Louis, 1985.

Porter, Darrell R., St. Louis, 1985.

7-game Series—A. L.—7—Brett, George H., Kansas City, 1985.

N. L.—5—Thompson, Robert R., San Francisco, 1987.

Most Consecutive Bases on Balls, One Series

A. L.—4—Killebrew, Harmon C., Minnesota, October 4 (3), October 5 (1), 1969.

Roenicke, Gary S., Baltimore, October 6 (1), 7 (1), 8 (2), 1983.

N. L.—3—Foster, George A., Cincinnati, October 2 (1), October 3 (2), 1979.

Cruz, Jose, Houston, October 10 (3), 1980.

Matthews, Gary N., Chicago, October 6 (1), October 7 (2), 1984.

Most Bases on Balls, Game

A. L.—4—Jones, Ruppert S., California, October 11, 1986; 11 innings.

Nine-inning record—A. L.-N. L.—3—Held by many players.

Most Bases on Balls with Bases Filled, Game

A. L.-N. L.—1—Held by many players.

Bases on Balls with Bases Filled by Pinch-Hitters, Game

N. L.—Dyer, Don R., Pittsburgh, October 7, 1975; ninth inning.

A. L.—Never accomplished.

Most Bases on Balls, Two Consecutive Games

A. L.—5—Killebrew, Harmon C., Minnesota, October 4 (3), October 5 (2), 1969; first game 12 innings, second game 11 innings.

N. L.—5—Wynn, James S., Los Angeles, October 5 (2), October 6 (3), 1974.

Most Bases on Balls, Inning

A. L.-N. L.—1—Held by many players.

Strikeouts

Most Strikeouts, Total Series

A. L.—41—Jackson, Reginald M., Oakland, 1971, 1972, 1973, 1974, 1975; New York, 1977, 1978, 1980, 1981; California, 1982, 1986; 11 Series, 45 games.

N. L.—24—Geronimo, Cesar F., Cincinnati, 1972, 1973, 1975, 1976, 1979; 5 Series, 17 games.

Most Strikeouts, Pinch-Hitter, Total Series

N. L.—3—Monday, Robert J., Los Angeles, 1977, 1978, 1981; 3 Series, 3 games.

Mazzilli, Lee L., New York, 1986; 1 Series, 5 games.

A. L.—2—Nokes, Matthew D., Detroit, 1987; 1 Series, 2 games.

Most Strikeouts, Series

3-game Series—A. L.—7—Cardenas, Leonardo A., Minnesota, 1969.

N. L.—7—Geronimo, Cesar F., Cincinnati, 1975.

4-game Series—N. L.—6—Clemente, Roberto W., Pittsburgh, 1971.

Stargell, Wilver D., Pittsburgh, 1971.

Marshall, Michael A., Los Angeles, 1983.

A. L.—5—Otis, Amos J., Kansas City, 1978.

Cruz, Todd R., Baltimore, 1983.

Luzinski, Gregory M., Chicago, 1983.

5-game Series—A. L.—8—Gibson, Kirk H., Detroit, 1987.

N. L.—7—Perez, Atanasio R., Cincinnati, 1972.

Geronimo, Cesar F., Cincinnati, 1973.

6-game Series—N. L.—12—Strawberry, Darryl, E., New York, 1986.

7-game Series—A. L.—8—Balboni, Stephen C., Kansas City, 1985.

Grich, Robert A., California, 1986.

Rice, James E., Boston, 1986.

N. L.—7—Thompson, Robert R., San Francisco, 1987.

Brenly, Robert E., San Francisco, 1987.

Most Strikeouts, Pinch-Hitter, Series

N. L.—3—Mazzilli, Lee L., New York, 1986; 5 games.

A. L.—2—Nokes, Matthew D., Detroit, 1987; 2 games.

Most Consecutive Strikeouts, One Series (Consecutive at-bats)

N. L.—7—Geronimo, Cesar F., Cincinnati, October 4 (1), October 5 (3), October 7 (3), 1975, third game 10 innings, one base on balls during streak.

A. L.—4—Cardenas, Leonardo A., Minnesota, October 4 (2), October 5 (2), 1969; first game 12 innings, second game 11 innings.

Boswell, David W., Minnesota, October 5, 1969; 11 innings.

Bando, Salvatore L., Oakland, October 9 (2), October 10 (2), 1973; first game 11 innings, one base on balls during streak.

Grich, Robert A., California, October 6 (1), October 8 (3), 1982.

Most Consec. Strikeouts, One Series (Consec. Plate Appearances)

N. L.—5—Geronimo, Cesar F., Cincinnati, October 6 (1), October 7 (3), October 9 (1), 1973; third game 12 innings.

A. L.—4—Cardenas, Leonardo A., Minnesota, October 4 (2), October 5 (2), 1969; first game 12 innings, second game 11 innings.

Boswell, David W., Minnesota, October 5, 1969; 11 innings.

Grich, Robert A., California, October 6 (1), October 8 (3), 1982.

Most Strikeouts, Game

A. L.—4—Boswell, David W., Minnesota, October 5, 1969; consecutive, 11 innings.

Nine-inning record—A. L.-N. L.—3—Held by many players.

Most Strikeouts, Inning

A. L.-N. L.—1—Held by many players.

Sacrifice Hits

Most Sacrifice Hits, Total Series

Both Leagues—5—Boone, Robert R., Philadelphia NL, 1976, 1977, 1978, 1980; California AL, 1982, 1986; 6 Series, 27 games.

A. L.—3—Green, Richard L., Oakland, 1971, 1972, 1973, 1974; 4 Series, 17 games.

Boone, Robert R., California, 1982, 1986; 2 Series, 12 games.

N. L.—3—Cabell, Enos M., Houston, 1980, Los Angeles, 1985; 2 Series, 10 games.

Russell, William E., Los Angeles, 1974, 1977, 1978, 1981, 1983; 5 Series, 21 games.

Most Sacrifice Hits, Series

3-game Series—N. L.—2—Ellis, Dock P., Pittsburgh, 1970.
Bibby, James B., Pittsburgh, 1979.
Andujar, Joaquin, St. Louis, 1982.
A. L.—1—Held by many players.
4-game Series—N. L.—2—Perry, Gaylord J. San Francisco, 1971.
A. L.—2—Belanger, Mark H., Baltimore, 1974.
5-game Series—N. L.—3—Cabell, Enos M., Houston, 1980.
A. L.—2—Bando, Salvatore L., Oakland, 1972.
Patek, Freddie J., Kansas City, 1977.
Boone, Robert R., California, 1982.
Moore, Charles W., Milwaukee, 1982.
6-game Series—N. L.—2—Hatcher, William A., Houston, 1986.
7-game Series—A. L.—2—Pettis, Gary G., California, 1986.
N. L.—2—Mathews, Gregory I., St. Louis, 1987.

Most Sacrifice Hits, Game

A. L.-N. L.—2—Held by many players.

Sacrifice Flies

Most Sacrifice Flies, Total Series

A. L.-N. L.—2—Held by many players.

Most Sacrifice Flies, Series

N. L.—2—Perez, Atanasio R., Cincinnati, 1976; 3-game Series.
Foli, Timothy J., Pittsburgh, 1979; 3-game Series.
A. L.—2—DeCinces, Douglas V., Baltimore, 1979; 4-game Series.

Most Sacrifice Flies, Game

A. L.-N. L.—1—Held by many players.

Hit By Pitch

Most Hit by Pitch, Total Series

N. L.—4—Hebner, Richard J., Pittsburgh, 1971 (1), 1972 (1), 1974 (1); Chicago, 1984 (1).

A. L.—3—McRae, Harold A., Kansas City, 1976 (1), 1980 (1), 1985 (1).
Grich, Robert A., California, 1982 (1), 1986 (2).
Baylor, Donald E., Boston, 1986 (2); Minnesota, 1987 (1).

Most Hit by Pitch, Series

A. L.—2—Baylor, Donald E., California, 1986.
Grich, Robert A., California, 1986.
Gladden, C. Daniel, Minnesota, 1987.
Sheridan, Patrick A., Detroit, 1987.
N. L.—1—Held by many players.

Most Hit by Pitch, Game

A. L.—2—Gladden, C. Daniel, Minnesota, October 11, 1987.
Sheridan, Patrick A., Detroit, October 12, 1987.
N. L.—1—Held by many players.

Grounding Into Double Plays

Most Grounding Into Double Play, Total Series

N. L.—5—Guerrero, Pedro, Los Angeles, 1981, 1983, 1985; 3 Series, 15 games.

A. L.—4—Randolph, William L., New York, 1976, 1977, 1980, 1981; 4 Series, 16 games.
DeCinces, Douglas V., Baltimore, 1979; California, 1982, 1986; 3 Series, 16 games.

Most Grounding Into Double Play, Series

N. L.—4—Guerrero, Pedro, Los Angeles, 1981; 19 at-bats in 5 games of 5-game Series.
A. L.—3—Taylor, Antonio, Detroit, 1972; 15 at-bats in 4 games of 5-game Series.
DeCinces, Douglas V., California, 1986; 32 at-bats in 7 games of 7-game Series.

Most Grounding Into Double Play, Game

A. L.—3—Taylor, Antonio, Detroit, October 10, 1972.
N. L.—2—Jones, Cleon J., New York, October 4, 1969.
Guerrero, Pedro, Los Angeles, October 16, 1981.
Royster, Jeron K., Atlanta, October 10, 1982.

Reaching Base On Interference

Most Times Awarded First Base on Catcher's Interference, Game

N. L.—1—Hebner, Richard J., Pittsburgh, October 8, 1974, fifth inning.
Scioscia, Michael L., Los Angeles, October 14, 1985; fourth inning.
A. L.—Never accomplished.

Club Batting

Service
Players Used

Most Players, Series

3-game Series—A. L.—24—Minnesota vs. Baltimore, 1970.
Oakland vs. New York, 1981.
N. L.—24—Pittsburgh vs. Cincinnati, 1975.
4-game Series—N. L.—23—Los Angeles vs. Philadelphia, 1977.
A. L.—23—California vs. Baltimore, 1979.
Chicago vs. Baltimore, 1983.
5-game Series—A. L.—25—Oakland vs. Detroit, 1972.
N. L.—24—Cincinnati vs. New York, 1973.
Houston vs. Philadelphia, 1980.
San Diego vs. Chicago, 1984.
6-game Series—N. L.—25—Los Angeles vs. St. Louis, 1985.
7-game Series—A. L.—24—Toronto vs. Kansas City, 1985.
California vs. Boston, 1986.
N. L.—23—St. Louis vs. San Francisco, 1987.
San Francisco vs. St. Louis, 1987.

Most Players, Series, Both Clubs

3-game Series—A. L.—46—Oakland 24, New York 22, 1981.
N. L.—42—Pittsburgh 24, Cincinnati 18, 1975.

4-game Series—A. L.—45—Chicago 23, Baltimore 22, 1983.
N. L.—44—Los Angeles 22, Pittsburgh 22, 1974.
Los Angeles 23, Philadelphia 21, 1977.
Los Angeles 22, Philadelphia 22, 1978.
5-game Series—A. L.—49—Oakland 25, Detroit 24, 1972.
N. L.—47—Houston 24, Philadelphia 23, 1980.
San Diego 24, Chicago 23, 1984.
6-game Series—N. L.—48—Los Angeles 25, St. Louis 23, 1985.
7-game Series—A. L.—46—Toronto 24, Kansas City 22, 1985.
N. L.—46—St. Louis 23, San Francisco 23, 1987.

Fewest Players, Series

3-game Series—A. L.—14—Baltimore vs. Minnesota, 1970.
Boston vs. Oakland, 1975.
N. L.—15—St. Louis vs. Atlanta, 1982.
4-game Series—A. L.—20—Oakland vs. Baltimore, 1974.
Kansas City vs. New York, 1978.
Baltimore vs. California, 1979.
N. L.—20—Philadelphia vs. Los Angeles, 1983.
5-game Series—N. L.—17—New York vs. Cincinnati, 1973.
A. L.—18—New York vs. Kansas City, 1977.
6-game Series—N. L.—21—Houston vs. New York, 1986.
7-game Series—A. L.—20—Boston vs. California, 1986.
N. L.—23—St. Louis vs. San Francisco, 1987.
San Francisco vs. St. Louis, 1987.

Fewest Players, Series, Both Clubs

3-game Series—A. L.—35—Oakland 20, Baltimore 15, 1971.
New York 20, Kansas City 15, 1980.
N. L.—35—Atlanta 20, St. Louis 15, 1982.
4-game Series—A. L.—41—New York 21, Kansas City 20, 1978.
N. L.—42—Los Angeles 22, Philadelphia 20, 1983.
5-game Series—A. L.—40—Kansas City 22, New York 18, 1977.
Milwaukee 20, California 20, 1982.
N. L.—41—Cincinnati 24, New York 17, 1973.
6-game Series—N. L.—43—New York 22, Houston 21, 1986.
7-game Series—A. L.—44—California 24, Boston 20, 1986.
N. L.—46—St. Louis 23, San Francisco 23, 1987.

Most Times, One Club Using Only Nine Players in Game, Series

3-game Series—A. L.—2—Baltimore vs. Minnesota, 1970.
N. L.—1—Cincinnati vs. Pittsburgh, 1975.
4-game Series—N. L.—1—Los Angeles vs. Pittsburgh, 1974.
Los Angeles vs. Philadelphia, 1977.
A. L.—0—Never accomplished.
5-game Series—N. L.—3—New York vs. Cincinnati, 1973.
A. L.—0—Never accomplished.
6-game Series—N. L.—0—Never accomplished.
7-game Series—A. L.—1—New York vs. Houston, 1986.
N. L.—1—St. Louis vs. San Francisco, 1987.
San Francisco vs. St. Louis, 1987.

Most Players, Game

A. L.—20—Oakland vs. Detroit, October 10, 1972.
Oakland vs. Detroit, October 11, 1972; 10 innings.
N. L.—20—Philadelphia vs. Houston, October 12, 1980; 10 innings.
N. L.—Nine-inning record—19—Los Angeles vs. Philadelphia, October 7, 1977.

Most Players, Nine-Inning Game, Both Clubs

A. L.—35—Oakland 18, New York 17, October 14, 1981.
N. L.—34—Los Angeles, 19, Philadelphia 15, October 7, 1977.

Most Players, Extra-Inning Game, Both Clubs

N. L.—37—Philadelphia 20, Houston 17, October 12, 1980; 10 innings.
A. L.—Less than nine-inning record.

Pinch-Hitters

Most Times Pinch-Hitter Used, Series

3-game Series—A. L.—10—Minnesota vs. Baltimore, 1970.
N. L.—9—Pittsburgh vs. Cincinnati, 1975.
4-game Series—N. L.—8—Los Angeles vs. Pittsburgh, 1974.
Philadelphia vs. Los Angeles, 1977, 1978.
Los Angeles vs. Philadelphia, 1983.
A. L.—8—Baltimore vs. Chicago, 1983.
5-game Series—N. L.—15—Cincinnati vs. New York, 1973.
A. L.—14—Oakland vs. Detroit, 1972.
6-game Series—N. L.—14—New York vs. Houston, 1986.
7-game Series—A. L.—13—Toronto vs. Kansas City, 1985.
N. L.—12—San Francisco vs. St. Louis, 1987.

Most Times Pinch-Hitter Used, Series, Both Clubs

3-game Series—N. L.—14—Pittsburgh 9, Cincinnati 5, 1975.
A. L.—13—Oakland 8, New York 5, 1981.
4-game Series—N. L.—15—Philadelphia 8, Los Angeles 7, 1978.
A. L.—13—Baltimore 8, Chicago 5, 1983.
5-game Series—A. L.—22—Oakland 14, Detroit 8, 1972.
N. L.—20—Philadelphia 11, Houston 9, 1980.
6-game Series—N. L.—26—New York 14, Houston 12, 1986.
7-game Series—A. L.—21—Toronto 13, Kansas City 8, 1985.
N. L.—21—San Francisco 12, St. Louis 9, 1987.

Fewest Times Pinch-Hitter Used, Series

3-game Series—A. L.—0—Baltimore vs. Minnesota, 1970.
Boston vs. Oakland, 1975.
N. L.—1—Pittsburgh vs. Cincinnati, 1979.
4-game Series—A. L.—3—Oakland vs. Baltimore, 1974.
Baltimore vs. Oakland, 1974.
N. L.—5—San Francisco vs. Pittsburgh, 1971.
5-game Series—A. L.—0—Milwaukee vs. California, 1982.
N. L.—1—New York vs. Cincinnati, 1973.
6-game Series—N. L.—8—St. Louis vs. Los Angeles, 1985.
7-game Series—A. L.—2—Boston vs. California, 1986.
N. L.—9—St. Louis vs. San Francisco, 1987.

Fewest Times Pinch-Hitter Used, Series, Both Clubs

3-game Series—A. L.—4—New York 3, Kansas City 1, 1980.
N. L.—5—Atlanta 4, St. Louis 1, 1982.
4-game Series—A. L.—6—Oakland 3, Baltimore 3, 1974.
N. L.—11—Pittsburgh 6, San Francisco 5, 1971.
5-game Series—A. L.—2—California 2, Milwaukee 0, 1982.
N. L.—8—Los Angeles 5, Montreal 3, 1981.
6-game Series—N. L.—19—Los Angeles 11, St. Louis 8, 1985.
7-game Series—A. L.—7—California 5, Boston 2, 1986.
N. L.—21—San Francisco 12, St. Louis 9, 1987.

Most Pinch-Hitters, Game

A. L.—6—Oakland vs. Detroit, October 10, 1972.
N. L.—5—Los Angeles vs. Pittsburgh, October 8, 1974.
Philadelphia vs. Los Angeles, October 5, 1983.
Los Angeles vs. St. Louis, October 12, 1985.
New York vs. Houston, October 15, 1986; 16 innings.
Houston vs. New York, October 15, 1986; 16 innings.

Most Pinch-Hitters, Game, Both Clubs

N. L.—10—New York 5, Houston 5, October 15, 1986; 16 innings.
N. L.—Nine-inning record—6—Pittsburgh 3, Cincinnati 3, October 5, 1975.
San Diego 4, Chicago 2, October 6, 1984.
Los Angeles 5, St. Louis 1, October 12, 1985.
A. L.—7—Oakland 6, Detroit 1, October 10, 1972.

Most Pinch-Hitters, Inning

A. L.—4—Baltimore vs. Chicago, October 7, 1983; ninth inning.
N. L.—4—Philadelphia vs. Los Angeles, October 5, 1983; ninth inning.

Pinch-Runners

Most Pinch-Runners Used, Series

A. L.—5—Oakland vs. Baltimore, 1974; 4-game Series.
N. L.—3—New York vs. Atlanta, 1969; 3-game Series.
Cincinnati vs. Pittsburgh, 1972; 5-game Series.
Houston vs. Philadelphia, 1980; 5-game Series.
Philadelphia vs. Houston, 1980; 5-game Series.

Most Pinch-Runners Used, Series, Both Clubs

A. L.—8—Oakland 5, Baltimore 3, 1974; 4-game Series.
N. L.—6—Houston 3, Philadelphia 3, 1980; 5-game Series.

Fewest Pinch-Runners Used, Series

A. L.-N. L.—0—Held by many clubs.

Fewest Pinch-Runners Used, Series, Both Clubs

A. L.—0—Baltimore 0, Minnesota 0, 1969; 3-game Series.
Kansas City 0, New York 0, 1980; 3-game Series.
N. L.—0—Philadelphia 0, Los Angeles 0, 1978; 4-game Series.

Most Pinch-Runners Used, Game

A. L.—3—Kansas City vs. Detroit, October 3, 1984; 11 innings.
Nine-inning record—2—Detroit vs. Oakland, October 12, 1972.
Oakland vs. Baltimore, October 6, 1974.
Baltimore vs. Oakland, October 9, 1974.
Oakland vs. Boston, October 4, 1975.
N. L.—2—Cincinnati vs. Pittsburgh, October 11, 1972.
Philadelphia vs. Houston, October 12, 1980; 10 innings.
Los Angeles vs. St. Louis, October 10, 1985.

Most Pinch-Runners Used, Game, Both Clubs

A. L.—4—Boston 2, California 2, October 12 1986; 11 innings.
A. L.—Nine-inning record—3—Oakland 2, Baltimore 1, October 6, 1974.
Baltimore 2, Oakland 1, October 9, 1974.
Kansas City 3, Detroit 0, October 3, 1984; 11 innings.
N. L.—3—Philadelphia 2, Houston 1, October 12, 1980; 10 innings.
N. L.—Nine-inning record—2—Made in many games.

Most Pinch-Runners Used, Inning

A. L.—2—Oakland vs. Detroit, October 7, 1972; eleventh inning.
Baltimore vs. Oakland, October 9, 1974; ninth inning.
N. L.—1—Held by many clubs.

Series & Games

Most Series Played

A. L.—7—Baltimore, 1969, 1970, 1971, 1973, 1974, 1979, 1983; won 5, lost 2.

N. L.—6—Pittsburgh, 1970, 1971, 1972, 1974, 1975, 1979; won 2, lost 4.
Cincinnati, 1970, 1972, 1973, 1975 1976, 1979; won 4, lost 2.
Los Angeles, 1974, 1977, 1978, 1981, 1983, 1985; won 4, lost 2.

Most Games Played, Total Series
A. L.— 27—Kansas City, 6 Series; won 12, lost 15.
N. L.— 27—Los Angeles, 6 Series; won 15, lost 12.

Batting Average

Highest Batting Average, Series
3-game Series—A. L.—.336—New York vs. Oakland, 1981.
    N. L.—.330—St. Louis vs. Atlanta, 1982.
4-game Series—A. L.—.300—New York vs. Kansas City, 1978.
    N. L.—.286—Los Angeles vs. Philadelphia, 1978.
5-game Series—A. L.—.316—New York vs. Kansas City, 1976.
    N. L.—.291—Philadelphia vs. Houston, 1980.
6-game Series—N. L.—.279—St. Louis vs. Los Angeles, 1985.
7-game Series—A. L.—.277—California vs. Boston, 1986.
    N. L.—.260—St. Louis vs. San Francisco, 1987.

Highest Batting Average, Series, Both Clubs
3-game Series—N. L.—.292—New York .327, Atlanta .255, 1969.
    A. L.—.286—Baltimore .330, Minnesota .238, 1970.
4-game Series—A. L.—.282—New York .300, Kansas City .263, 1978.
    N. L.—.268—Los Angeles .286, Philadelphia .250, 1978.
5-game Series—A. L.—.283—New York .316, Kansas City .247, 1976.
    N. L.—.263—Philadelphia .291, Houston .233, 1980.
6-game Series—N. L.—.256—St. Louis .279, Los Angeles .234, 1985.
7-game Series—A. L.—.275—California .277, Boston .272, 1986.
    N. L.—.249—St. Louis .260, San Francisco .239, 1987.

Highest Batting Average, Series, Championship Series Loser
3-game Series—N. L.—.270—Philadelphia vs. Cincinnati, 1976.
    A. L.—.255—New York vs. Kansas City, 1980.
4-game Series—N. L.—.250—Philadelphia vs. Los Angeles, 1978.
    A. L.—.263—Kansas City vs. New York, 1978.
5-game Series—A. L.—.258—Kansas City vs. New York, 1977.
    N. L.—.259—Chicago vs. San Diego, 1984.
6-game Series—N. L.—.234—Los Angeles vs. St. Louis, 1985.
7-game Series—A. L.—.277—California vs. Boston, 1986.
    N. L.—.239—San Francisco vs. St. Louis, 1987.

Lowest Batting Average, Series
3-game Series—A. L.—.155—Minnesota vs. Baltimore, 1969.
    N. L.—.169—Atlanta vs. St. Louis, 1982.
4-game Series—A. L.—.177—Baltimore vs. Oakland, 1974.
    N. L.—.194—Pittsburgh vs. Los Angeles, 1974.
5-game Series—N. L.—.186—Cincinnati vs. New York, 1973.
    A. L.—.198—Detroit vs. Oakland, 1972.
6-game Series—N. L.—.189—New York vs. Houston, 1986.
7-game Series—A. L.—.225—Kansas City vs. Toronto, 1985.
    N. L.—.239—San Francisco vs. St. Louis, 1987.

Lowest Batting Average, Series, Both Clubs
3-game Series—A. L.—.202—Detroit .234, Kansas City .170, 1984.
    N. L.—.223—Pittsburgh .225, Cincinnati .220, 1970.
4-game Series—A. L.—.180—Oakland .183, Baltimore .177, 1974.
    N. L.—.232—Los Angeles .268, Pittsburgh .194, 1974.
5-game Series—A. L.—.205—Baltimore .211, Oakland .200, 1973.
    N. L.—.203—New York .220, Cincinnati .186, 1973.
6-game Series—N. L.—.204—Houston .218, New York .189, 1986.
7-game Series—A. L.—.247—Toronto .269, Kansas City .225, 1985.
    N. L.—.249—St. Louis .260, San Francisco .239, 1987.

Lowest Batting Average, Series, Championship Series Winner
3-game Series—N. L.—.220—Cincinnati vs. Pittsburgh, 1970.
    A. L.—.234—Detroit vs. Kansas City, 1984.
4-game Series—A. L.—.183—Oakland vs. Baltimore, 1974.
    N. L.—.262—Philadelphia vs. Los Angeles, 1983.
5-game Series—A. L.—.200—Oakland vs. Baltimore, 1973.
    N. L.—.220—New York vs. Cincinnati, 1973.

6-game Series—N. L.—.189—New York vs. Houston, 1986.
7-game Series—A. L.—.225—Kansas City vs. Toronto, 1985.
    N. L.—.260—St. Louis vs. San Francisco, 1987.

Slugging Average

Highest Slugging Average, Series
3-game Series—N. L.—.575 —New York vs. Atlanta, 1969.
    A. L.—.560 —Baltimore vs. Minnesota, 1970.
4-game Series—N. L.—.544 —Los Angeles vs. Philadelphia, 1978.
    A. L.—.4436—Kansas City vs. New York, 1978.
     .4428—New York vs. Kansas City, 1978.
5-game Series—A. L.—.497 —Minnesota vs. Detroit, 1987.
    A. L.—.494 —Chicago vs. San Diego, 1984.
6-game Series—N. L.—.383 —St. Louis vs. Los Angeles 1985.
7-game Series—A. L.—.4023—California vs. Boston, 1986.
     .4016—Boston vs. California, 1986.
    N. L.—.398 —San Francisco vs. St. Louis, 1987.

Highest Slugging Average, Series, Both Clubs
3-game Series—N. L.—.530—New York .575, Atlanta .481, 1969.
    A. L.—.476—Baltimore .560, Minnesota .386, 1970.
4-game Series—N. L.—.477—Los Angeles .544, Philadelphia .407, 1978.
    A. L.—.443—Kansas City .4436, New York .4428, 1978.
5-game Series—A. L.—.444—Minnesota .497, Detroit .389, 1987.
    N. L.—.423—Chicago .494, San Diego .348, 1984.
6-game Series—N. L.—.382—St. Louis .383, Los Angeles .381, 1985.
7-game Series—A. L.—.402—California .402, Boston, .402, 1986.
    N. L.—.372—San Francisco .398, St. Louis .344, 1987.

Lowest Slugging Average, Series
3-game Series—N. L.—.180—Atlanta vs. St. Louis, 1982.
    A. L.—.198—Kansas City vs. Detroit, 1984.
4-game Series—A. L.—.241—Chicago vs. Baltimore, 1983.
    N. L.—.271—Pittsburgh vs. Los Angeles, 1974.
5-game Series—A. L.—.288—Oakland vs. Detroit, 1972.
    N. L.—.278—Montreal vs. Los Angeles, 1981.
6-game Series—N. L.—.264—New York vs. Houston, 1986.
7-game Series—N. L.—.344—St. Louis vs. San Francisco, 1987.
    A. L.—.366—Kansas City vs. Toronto, 1985.

Lowest Slugging Average, Series, Both Clubs
3-game Series—A. L.—.300—Detroit .402, Kansas City .198, 1984.
    N. L.—.318—St. Louis .437, Atlanta .180, 1982.
4-game Series—A. L.—.283—Oakland .308, Baltimore .258, 1974.
    N. L.—.339—Los Angeles .391, Philadelphia .290, 1977.
5-game Series—A. L.—.304—Detroit .321, Oakland .288, 1972.
    N. L.—.307—Cincinnati .311, New York .304, 1973.
6-game Series—N. L.—.288—Houston .311, New York .264, 1986.
7-game Series—A. L.—.369—Toronto .372, Kansas City .366, 1985.
    N. L.—.372—San Francisco .398, St. Louis .344, 1987.

At-Bats & Plate Appearances

Most At-Bats, Total Series
N. L.— 907— Los Angeles; 6 Series, 27 games.
A. L.— 888— Kansas City, 6 Series, 27 games.

Most At-Bats, Series
3-game Series—A. L.—123—Baltimore vs. Minnesota, 1969.
    N. L.—113—New York vs. Atlanta, 1969.
4-game Series—N. L.—147—Los Angeles vs. Philadelphia, 1978.
    A. L.—140—New York vs. Kansas City, 1978.
5-game Series—N. L.—190—Philadelphia vs. Houston, 1980.
    A. L.—175—New York vs. Kansas City, 1977.
6-game Series—N. L.—227—New York vs. Houston, 1986.
7-game Series—A. L.—256—California vs. Boston, 1986.
    N. L.—226—San Francisco vs. St. Louis, 1987.

Most At-Bats, Series, Both Clubs
3-game Series—A. L.—233—Baltimore 123, Minnesota 110, 1969.
    N. L.—219—New York 113, Atlanta 106, 1969.
4-game Series—N. L.—287—Los Angeles 147, Philadelphia 140, 1978.
    A. L.—273—New York 140, Kansas City 133, 1978.

5-game Series—N. L.—362—Philadelphia 190, Houston 172, 1980.
           A. L.—338—New York 175, Kansas City 163, 1977.
                   Minnesota 171, Detroit 167, 1987.
6-game Series—N. L.—452—New York 227, Houston 225, 1986.
7-game Series—A. L.—510—California 256, Boston 254, 1986.
           N. L.—441—San Francisco 226, St. Louis 215, 1987.

Most At-Bats, Pinch-Hitters, Series

3-game Series—A. L.— 9—Minnesota vs. Baltimore, 1970.
           N. L.— 7—Pittsburgh vs. Cincinnati, 1975.
4-game Series—N. L.— 8—Philadelphia vs. Los Angeles, 1977, 1978.
           A. L.— 5—Chicago vs. Baltimore, 1983.
5-game Series—N. L.— 14—Cincinnati vs. New York, 1973.
           A. L.—13—Oakland vs. Detroit, 1972.
6-game Series—N. L.— 12—New York vs. Houston, 1986.
7-game Series—A. L.— 13—Toronto vs. Kansas City, 1985.
           N. L.—10—San Francisco vs. St. Louis, 1987.

Most At-Bats, Pinch-Hitters, Series, Both Clubs

3-game Series—A. L.—11—Oakland 7, New York 4, 1981.
           N. L.— 8—Atlanta 6, New York 2, 1969.
                   Pittsburgh 7, Cincinnati 1, 1975.
4-game Series—N. L.—14—Philadelphia 8, Los Angeles 6, 1978.
           A. L.— 8—New York 4, Kansas City 4, 1978.
                   Chicago 5, Baltimore 3, 1983.
5-game Series—A. L.—20—Oakland 13, Detroit 7, 1972.
           N. L.—18—Philadelphia 10, Houston 8, 1980.
6-game Series—N. L.—23—New York 12, Houston 11, 1986.
7-game Series—A. L.—19—Toronto 13, Kansas City 6, 1985.
           N. L.—19—San Francisco 10, St. Louis 9, 1987.

Most Plate Appearances, Pinch-Hitters, Series

3-game Series—A. L.— 10—Minnesota vs. Baltimore, 1970.
           N. L.— 9—Pittsburgh vs. Cincinnati, 1975.
4-game Series—N. L.— 8—Los Angeles vs. Pittsburgh, 1974.
                   Philadelphia vs. Los Angeles, 1977, 1978.
           A. L.— 7—Baltimore vs. Chicago, 1983.
5-game Series—N. L.—15—Cincinnati vs. New York, 1973.
           A. L.—14—Oakland vs. Detroit, 1972.
6-game Series—N. L.—14—New York vs. Houston, 1986.
7-game Series—A. L.—13—Toronto vs. Kansas City, 1985.
           N. L.—11—San Francisco vs. St. Louis, 1987.

Most Plate Appearances, Pinch-Hitters, Series, Both Clubs

3-game Series—A. L.—13—Oakland 8, New York 5, 1981.
           N. L.—12—Pittsburgh 9, Cincinnati 3, 1975.
4-game Series—N. L.—15—Philadelphia 8, Los Angeles 7, 1978.
           A. L.—12—Baltimore 7, Chicago 5, 1983.
5-game Series—A. L.—22—Oakland 14, Detroit 8, 1972.
           N. L.—20—Philadelphia 11, Houston 9, 1980.
6-game Series—N. L.—26—New York 14, Houston 12, 1986.
7-game Series—A. L.—21—Toronto 13, Kansas City 8, 1985.
           N. L.—20—San Francisco 11, St. Louis 9, 1987.

Fewest At-Bats, Series

3-game Series—N. L.— 89—Atlanta vs. St. Louis, 1982.
           A. L.— 95—Baltimore vs. Oakland, 1971.
4-game Series—A. L.— 120—Oakland vs. Baltimore, 1974.
           N. L.— 129—Pittsburgh vs. Los Angeles, 1974.
                   Los Angeles vs. Philadelphia, 1983.
5-game Series—A. L.— 151—Milwaukee vs. California, 1982.
           N. L.— 155—San Diego vs. Chicago, 1984.
6-game Series—N. L.— 197—Los Angeles vs. St. Louis, 1985.
7-game Series—N. L.— 215—St. Louis vs. San Francisco, 1987.
           A. L.—227—Kansas City vs. Toronto, 1985.

Fewest At-Bats, Series, Both Clubs

3-game Series—A. L.— 191—Oakland 96, Baltimore 95, 1971.
           N. L.— 192—St. Louis 103, Atlanta 89, 1982.
4-game Series—A. L.— 244—Baltimore 124, Oakland 120, 1974.
           N. L.—259—Philadelphia 130, Los Angeles 129, 1983.
5-game Series—A. L.— 308—California 157, Milwaukee 151, 1982.
           N. L.—317—Chicago 162, San Diego 155, 1984.
6-game Series—N. L.— 398—St. Louis 201, Los Angeles 197, 1985.
7-game Series—N. L.—441—San Francisco 226, St. Louis 215, 1987.
           A. L.—469—Toronto 242, Kansas City 227, 1985.

Most At-Bats, Game

N. L.— 56— Houston vs. New York, October 15, 1986; 16 innings.
N. L.—Nine-inning record—42—New York vs. Atlanta, October 5, 1969.
A. L.— 44— Baltimore vs. Minnesota, October 6, 1969.
           Kansas City vs. Detroit, October 3, 1984; 11 innings.

Most At-Bats, Game, Nine Innings, Both Clubs

A. L.— 80— Baltimore 44, Minnesota 36, October 6, 1969.
N. L.— 77— New York 42, Atlanta 35, October 5, 1969.
           Los Angeles 39, Philadelphia 38, October 4, 1978.

Most At-Bats, Extra-Inning Game, Both Clubs

N. L.— 110— Houston 56, New York 54, October 15, 1986; 16 innings.
A. L.— 85— Kansas City 44, Detroit 41, October 3, 1984; 11 innings.

Most At-Bats, Pinch-Hitters, Game

A. L.—6—Oakland vs. Detroit, October 10, 1972.
N. L.—4—Cincinnati vs. New York, October 9, 1973; 12 innings.
         Los Angeles vs. Pittsburgh, October 8, 1974.
         Philadelphia vs. Los Angeles, October 5, 1983.
         New York vs. Houston, October 15, 1986; 16 innings.
         Houston vs. New York, October 15, 1986; 16 innings.

Most At-Bats, Pinch-Hitters, Game, Both Clubs

N. L.—8—New York 4, Houston 4, October 15, 1986; 16 innings.
Nine-inning record—5—Los Angeles 3, Philadelphia 2, October 7, 1977.
         San Diego 3, Chicago 2, October 6, 1984.
         St. Louis 3, San Francisco 2, October 9, 1987.
         San Francisco 3, St. Louis 2, October 14, 1987.
A. L.—7—Oakland 6, Detroit 1, October 10, 1972.

Most Plate Appearances, Pinch-Hitters, Game

A. L.—6—Oakland vs. Detroit, October 10, 1972.
N. L.—5—Los Angeles vs. Pittsburgh, October 8, 1974.
         Philadelphia vs. Los Angeles, October 5, 1983.
         New York vs. Houston, October 15, 1986; 16 innings.
         Houston vs. New York, October 15, 1986; 16 innings.

Most Plate Appearances, Pinch-Hitters, Game, Both Clubs

N. L.— 10— New York 5, Houston 5, October 15, 1986; 16 innings.
Nine-inning record—6—San Diego 4, Chicago 2, October 6, 1984.
A. L.— 7—Oakland 6, Detroit 1, October 10, 1972.

Fewest Official At-Bats, Game

N. L.— 26— St. Louis vs. San Francisco, October 7, 1987.
A. L.—25—California vs. Milwaukee, October 6, 1982; batted 8 innings.

Fewest Official At-Bats, Game, Both Clubs

A. L.— 56— Kansas City 30, Detroit 26, October 5, 1984.
N. L.— 58— Cincinnati 30, New York 28, October 6, 1973.
         New York 31, Cincinnati 27, October 7, 1973.
         Chicago 29, San Diego 29, October 3, 1984.
         St. Louis 30, San Francisco 28, October 11, 1987.

Most At-Bats, Inning

N. L.— 12— St. Louis vs. Los Angeles, October 13, 1985; second inning.
A. L.— 10— New York vs. Oakland, October 14, 1981; fourth inning.
         Toronto vs. Kansas City, October 11, 1985; fifth inning.

Most At-Bats, Inning, Both Clubs

A. L.— 16— New York 10, Oakland 6, October 14, 1981; fourth inning.
N. L.— 15— Philadelphia 8, Houston 7, October 12, 1980; eighth inning.
         St. Louis 12, Los Angeles 3, October 13, 1985; second inning.

Most Men Facing Pitcher, Inning

N. L.— 14— St. Louis vs. Los Angeles, October 13, 1985; second inning.
A. L.— 12— New York vs. Oakland, October 14, 1981; fourth inning.

Most Men Facing Pitcher, Inning, Both Clubs

A. L.— 19— New York 12, Oakland 7, October 14, 1981; fourth inning.
N. L.— 17— Chicago 12, San Diego 5, October 2, 1984; fifth inning.
         St. Louis 14, Los Angeles 3, October 13, 1985; second inning.

Runs
Series & Game

Most Runs, Total Series

A. L.— 125— Baltimore; 7 Series, 26 games.
N. L.— 109— Los Angeles; 6 Series, 27 games.

Most Runs, Series

3-game Series—A. L.—27—Baltimore vs. Minnesota, 1970.
N. L.—27—New York vs. Atlanta, 1969.
4-game Series—A. L.—26—Baltimore vs. California, 1979.
N. L.—24—Pittsburgh vs. San Francisco, 1971.
5-game Series—A. L.—34—Minnesota vs. Detroit, 1987.
N. L.—26—Chicago vs. San Diego, 1984.
6-game Series—N. L.—29—St. Louis vs. Los Angeles, 1985.
7-game Series—A. L.—41—Boston vs. California, 1986.
N. L.—23—St. Louis vs. San Francisco, 1987.
San Francisco vs. St. Louis, 1987.

Most Runs, Series, Both Clubs

3-game Series—N. L.—42—New York 27, Atlanta 15, 1969.
A. L.—37—Baltimore 27, Minnesota 10, 1970.
4-game Series—A. L.—41—Baltimore 26, California 15, 1979.
N. L.—39—Pittsburgh 24, San Francisco 15, 1971.
5-game Series—A. L.—57—Minnesota 34, Detroit 23, 1987.
N. L.—48—Chicago 26, San Diego 22, 1984.
6-game Series—N. L.—52—St. Louis 29, Los Angeles 23, 1985.
7-game Series—A. L.—71—Boston 41, California 30, 1986.
N. L.—46—St. Louis 23, San Francisco 23, 1987.

Most Runs, Series, Championship Series Loser

3-game Series—N. L.— 15—Atlanta vs. New York, 1969.
A. L.— 10—Minnesota vs. Baltimore, 1970.
4-game Series—N. L.— 17—Philadelphia vs. Los Angeles, 1978.
A. L.— 17—Kansas City vs. New York, 1978.
5-game Series—N. L.— 26—Chicago vs. San Diego, 1984.
A. L.— 24—Kansas City vs. New York, 1976.
6-game Series—N. L.— 23—Los Angeles vs. St. Louis, 1985.
7-game Series—A. L.— 30—California vs. Boston, 1986.
N. L.— 23—San Francisco vs. St. Louis, 1987.

Fewest Runs, Series

3-game Series—N. L.— 3—Pittsburgh vs. Cincinnati, 1970.
A. L.— 4—Oakland vs. New York, 1981.
Kansas City vs. Detroit, 1984.
4-game Series—A. L.— 3—Chicago vs. Baltimore, 1983.
N. L.— 10—Pittsburgh vs. Los Angeles, 1974.
5-game Series—N. L.— 8—Cincinnati vs. New York, 1973.
A. L.— 10—Detroit vs. Oakland, 1972.
6-game Series—N. L.— 17—Houston vs. New York, 1986.
7-game Series—N. L.— 23—St. Louis vs. San Francisco, 1987.
San Francisco vs. St. Louis, 1987.
A. L.—25—Toronto vs. Kansas City, 1985.

Fewest Runs, Series, Both Clubs

3-game Series—N. L.— 12—Cincinnati 9, Pittsburgh 3, 1970.
A. L.— 18—Detroit 14, Kansas City 4, 1984.
4-game Series—A. L.— 18—Oakland 11, Baltimore 7, 1974.
N. L.— 30—Los Angeles 20, Pittsburgh 10, 1974.
5-game Series—A. L.— 23—Oakland 13, Detroit 10, 1972.
N. L.— 25—Los Angeles 15, Montreal 10, 1981.
6-game Series—N. L.— 38—New York 21, Houston 17, 1986.
7-game Series—N. L.— 46—St. Louis 23, San Francisco 23, 1987.
A. L.—51—Kansas City 26, Toronto 25, 1985.

Most Runs, Game

A. L.— 13—New York vs. Oakland, October 14, 1981.
N. L.— 13—Chicago vs. San Diego, October 2, 1984.

Most Earned Runs, Game

A. L.— 13—New York vs. Oakland, October 14, 1981.
N. L.— 12—Los Angeles vs. Pittsburgh, October 9, 1974.
Chicago vs. San Diego, October 2, 1984.

Most Runs, Game, Both Clubs

N. L.— 17—New York 11, Atlanta 6, October 5, 1969.
A. L.— 17—Baltimore 9, California 8, October 4, 1979.

Largest Score, Shutout Game

N. L.—Chicago 13, San Diego 0, October 2, 1984.
A. L.—Baltimore 8, California 0, October 6, 1979.

Most Players, One or More Runs, Game

A. L.—9—Baltimore vs. Minnesota, October 3, 1970.
New York vs. Oakland, October 14, 1981
N. L.—9—St. Louis vs. Los Angeles, October 13, 1985.

Most Players, One or More Runs, Game, Both Clubs

A. L.— 14—Baltimore 9, Minnesota 5, October 3, 1970.
Baltimore 7, California 7, October 4, 1979.
N. L.— 13—New York 8, Atlanta 5, October 5, 1969.

Inning

Most Runs, Inning

N. L.—9—St. Louis vs. Los Angeles, October 13, 1985; second inning.
A. L.—7—Baltimore vs. Minnesota, October 3, 1970; fourth inning.
Baltimore vs. Minnesota, October 4, 1970; ninth inning.
New York vs. Oakland, October 14, 1981; fourth inning.

Most Runs, Inning, Both Clubs

A. L.—9—New York 7, Oakland 2, October 14, 1981; fourth inning.
N. L.—9—St. Louis 9, Los Angeles 0, October 13, 1985; second inning.

Most Runs, Extra Inning

N. L.—4—Houston vs. Philadelphia, October 8, 1980; tenth inning.
A. L.—3—Detroit vs. Oakland, October 11, 1972; tenth inning.
Baltimore vs. California, October 3, 1979; tenth inning.
Baltimore vs. Chicago, October 8, 1983; tenth inning.

Most Runs, Extra Inning, Both Clubs

A. L.—5—Detroit 3, Oakland 2, October 11, 1972; tenth inning.
N. L.—5—Houston 4, Philadelphia 1, October 8, 1980; tenth inning.
New York 3, Houston 2, October 15, 1986; sixteenth inning.

Most Innings Scored, Game

N. L.—6—New York vs. Atlanta, October 5, 1969.
Los Angeles vs. Pittsburgh, October 9, 1974.
A. L.—6—Detroit vs. Kansas City, October 2, 1984.

Most Innings Scored, Game, Both Clubs

A. L.—8—New York 4, Kansas City 4, October 6, 1978.
California 5, Baltimore 3, October 4, 1979.
Kansas City 4, Toronto 4, October 9, 1985.
Minnesota 5, Detroit 3, October 11, 1987.
N. L.—8—New York 6, Atlanta 2, October 5, 1969.
Pittsburgh 5, San Francisco 3, October 3, 1971.
Los Angeles 5, Philadelphia 3, October 4, 1978.

Most Runs, First Inning

N. L.—5—Pittsburgh vs. Los Angeles, October 8, 1974.
A. L.—4—Baltimore vs. Oakland, October 6, 1973.
Baltimore vs. California, October 4, 1979.

Most Runs, Second Inning

N. L.—9—St. Louis vs. Los Angeles, October 13, 1985.
A. L.—4—Kansas City vs. New York, October 4, 1978.
Baltimore vs. California, October 4, 1979.
California vs. Boston, October 7, 1986.
Minnesota vs. Detroit, October 12, 1987.

Most Runs, Third Inning

A. L.—5—Boston vs. California, October 14, 1986.
Minnesota vs. Detroit, October 10, 1987.
N. L.—4—Los Angeles vs. Philadelphia, October 4, 1978.

Most Runs, Fourth Inning

A. L.—7—Baltimore vs. Minnesota, October 3, 1970.
New York vs. Oakland, October 14, 1981.
N. L.—4—Los Angeles vs. Philadelphia, October 5, 1977.
San Francisco vs. St. Louis, October 11, 1987.

Most Runs, Fifth Inning

N. L.—6—Chicago vs. San Diego, October 2, 1984.
A. L.—5—Toronto vs. Kansas City, October 11, 1985.

Most Runs, Sixth Inning

N. L.—5—St. Louis vs. Atlanta, October 7, 1982.
A. L.—4—Kansas City vs. Toronto, October 16, 1985.

Most Runs, Seventh Inning

A. L.—5—Boston vs. Oakland, October 4, 1975.
Baltimore vs. California, October 6, 1979.

N. L.—4—Pittsburgh vs. San Francisco, October 3, 1971.
    Cincinnati vs. Philadelphia, October 12, 1976.
    Los Angeles vs. Philadelphia, October 4, 1977.
    St. Louis vs. San Francisco, October 9, 1987.

Most Runs, Eighth Inning

N. L.—5—New York vs. Atlanta, October 4, 1969.
    Philadelphia vs. Houston, October 12, 1980.
A. L.—4—California vs. Milwaukee, October 9, 1982.
    Minnesota vs. Detroit, October 7, 1987.

Most Runs, Ninth Inning

A. L.—7—Baltimore vs. Minnesota, October 4, 1970.
N. L.—4—New York vs. Cincinnati, October 7, 1973.
    Los Angeles vs. Montreal, October 17, 1981.

Most Runs, Tenth Inning

N. L.—4—Houston vs. Philadelphia, October 8, 1980.
A. L.—3—Detroit vs. Oakland, October 11, 1972.
    Baltimore vs. California, October 3, 1979.
    Baltimore vs. Chicago, October 8, 1983.

Most Runs, Eleventh Inning

N. L.—3—Pittsburgh vs. Cincinnati, October 2, 1979.
A. L.—2—Oakland vs. Detroit, October 7, 1972.
    Detroit vs. Kansas City, October 3, 1984.

Most Runs, Twelfth Inning

A. L.—1—Baltimore vs. Minnesota, October 4, 1969.
N. L.—1—Cincinnati vs. New York, October 9, 1973.
    New York vs. Houston, October 14, 1986.

Most Runs, Fourteenth Inning

N. L.—1—Houston vs. New York, October 15, 1986.
    New York vs. Houston, October 15, 1986.
A. L.—Never accomplished.

Most Runs, Sixteenth Inning

N. L.—3—New York vs. Houston, October 15, 1986.
A. L.—Never accomplished.

Games Being Shut Out

Most Times Being Shut Out, Total Series

A. L.—3—Baltimore, 1973, 1974 (2).
N. L.—3—Los Angeles, 1974, 1981, 1983.

Most Consecutive Games, Total Series, Without Being Shut Out

A. L.—20—New York, October 9, 1976 through October 15, 1981.
N. L.—12—Cincinnati, October 8, 1973 through October 5, 1979.

Hits
Series

Most Hits, Total Series

N. L.— 225— Los Angeles; 6 Series, 27 games.
A. L.— 221— Baltimore; 7 Series, 26 games.

Most Hits, Series

3-game Series—N. L.—37—New York vs. Atlanta, 1969.
    A. L.—36—Baltimore vs. Minnesota, 1969, 1970.
    New York vs. Oakland, 1981.
4-game Series—N. L.—42—Los Angeles vs. Philadelphia, 1978.
    A. L.—42—New York vs. Kansas City, 1978.
5-game Series—A. L.—55—New York vs. Kansas City, 1976.
    N. L.—55—Philadelphia vs. Houston, 1980.
6-game Series—N. L.—56—St. Louis vs. Los Angeles, 1985.
7-game Series—A. L.—71—California vs. Boston, 1986.
    N. L.—56—St. Louis vs. San Francisco, 1987.

Most Hits, Series, Both Clubs

3-game Series—N. L.—64—New York 37, Atlanta 27, 1969.
    A. L.—60—Baltimore 36, Minnesota 24, 1970.
4-game Series—N. L.—77—Los Angeles 42, Philadelphia 35, 1978.
    A. L.—77—New York 42, Kansas City 35, 1978.
5-game Series—A. L.—95—New York 55, Kansas City 40, 1976.
    N. L.—95—Philadelphia 55, Houston 40, 1980.
6-game Series—N. L.—102—St. Louis 56, Los Angeles 46, 1985.
7-game Series—A. L.—140—California 71, Boston 69, 1986.
    N. L.—110—St. Louis 56, San Francisco 54, 1987.

Fewest Hits, Series

3-game Series—N. L.—15—Atlanta vs. St. Louis, 1982.
    A. L.—17—Minnesota vs. Baltimore, 1969.

4-game Series—A. L.—22—Baltimore vs. Oakland, 1974.
    Oakland vs. Baltimore, 1974.
    N. L.—25—Pittsburgh vs. Los Angeles, 1974.
5-game Series—N. L.—30—Pittsburgh vs. Cincinnati, 1972.
    A. L.—32—Detroit vs. Oakland, 1972.
    Oakland vs. Baltimore, 1973.
6-game Series—N. L.—43—New York vs. Houston, 1986.
7-game Series—A. L.—51—Kansas City vs. Toronto, 1985.
    N. L.—54—San Francisco vs. St. Louis, 1987.

Fewest Hits, Series, Both Clubs

3-game Series—A. L.—43—Detroit 25, Kansas City 18, 1984.
    N. L.—45—Pittsburgh 23, Cincinnati 22, 1970.
4-game Series—A. L.—44—Baltimore 22, Oakland 22, 1974.
    N. L.—62—Los Angeles 37, Pittsburgh 25, 1974.
5-game Series—A. L.—68—Baltimore 36, Oakland 32, 1973.
    N. L.—68—New York 37, Cincinnati 31, 1973.
6-game Series—N. L.—92—Houston 49, New York 43, 1986.
7-game Series—N. L.—110—St. Louis 56, San Francisco 54, 1987.
    A. L.—116—Toronto 65, Kansas City 51, 1985.

Most Hits, Pinch-Hitters, Series

A. L.—6—Toronto vs. Kansas City, 1985; 7-game Series.
N. L.—4—Pittsburgh vs. Los Angeles, 1974; 4-game Series.
    Los Angeles vs. Pittsburgh, 1974; 4-game Series.
    Philadelphia vs. Houston, 1980; 5-game Series.

Most Hits, Pinch-Hitters, Series, Both Clubs

N. L.—8—Pittsburgh 4, Los Angeles 4, 1974; 4-game Series.
A. L.—8—Toronto 6, Kansas City 2, 1985; 7-game Series.

Game & Inning

Most Hits, Game

A. L.—19—New York vs. Oakland, October 14, 1981.
N. L.—16—Chicago vs. San Diego, October 2, 1984.

Most Hits, Game, Both Clubs

A. L.—30—New York 19, Oakland 10, October 14, 1981.
N. L.—27—Houston 14, Philadelphia 13, October 12, 1980; 10 innings.
N. L.—Nine-inning record—25—Los Angeles 13, Philadelphia 12, October 4, 1978.

Most Hits, Pinch-Hitters, Game

A. L.—3—Kansas City vs. Detroit, October 3, 1984; 11 innings.
N. L.—2—Held by many clubs.

Most Hits, Pinch-Hitters, Game, Both Clubs

N. L.—4—Los Angeles 2, Pittsburgh 2, October 6, 1974.
A. L.—3—Kansas City 3, Detroit 0, October 3, 1984; 11 innings.
    Detroit 2, Minnesota 1, October 11, 1987.

Fewest Hits, Game

A. L.—1—Oakland vs. Baltimore, October 9, 1974.
N. L.—2—Pittsburgh vs. Cincinnati, October 10, 1972.
    Cincinnati vs. New York, October 7, 1973.
    St. Louis vs. San Francisco, October 7, 1987.

Fewest Hits, Game, Both Clubs

A. L.—6—Oakand 4, Baltimore 2, October 8, 1974.
    Baltimore 5, Oakland 1, October 9, 1974.
    Detroit 3, Kansas City 3, October 5, 1984.
N. L.—7—Houston 4, New York 3, October 12, 1986.

Most Players, One or More Hits, Game

N. L.—11—Chicago vs. San Diego, October 2, 1984.
A. L.—10—New York vs. Oakland, October 14, 1981.
    Toronto vs. Kansas City, October 11, 1985.

Most Players, One or More Hits, Game, Both Clubs

A. L.—18—New York 10, Oakland 8, October 14, 1981.
    Boston 9, California 9, October 12, 1986; 11 innings.
N. L.—16—Los Angeles 8, Philadelphia 8, October 4, 1978.
    Houston 8, Philadelphia 8, October 12, 1980; 10 innings.

Most Hits, Inning

N. L.—8—St. Louis vs. Los Angeles, October 13, 1985; second inning.
A. L.—7—Baltimore vs. Minnesota, October 3, 1970; fourth inning.
    New York vs. Oakland, October 14, 1981; fourth inning.
    Toronto vs. Kansas City, October 11, 1985; fifth inning.

Most Hits, Pinch-Hitters, Inning

A. L.-N. L.—2—Occurred many times.

Most Hits, Inning, Both Clubs

A. L.— 11— New York 7, Oakland 4, October 14, 1981; fourth inning.
N. L.— 9— Philadelphia 5, Houston 4, October 12, 1980; eighth inning.

Most Consecutive Hits, Inning (Consecutive At-Bats)

A. L.— 7— Baltimore vs. Minnesota, October 3, 1970; fourth inning; sacrifice fly during streak.
N. L.— 6— St. Louis vs. Atlanta, October 7, 1982; sixth inning; walk during streak.

Most Consecutive Hits, Inning (Consecutive Plate Appearances)

N. L.— 5— Cincinnati vs. Pittsburgh, October 8, 1972; first inning.
Los Angeles vs. Pittsburgh, October 6, 1974; eighth inning.
St. Louis vs. San Francisco, October 9, 1987; seventh inning.
A. L.— 5— New York vs. Oakland, October 14, 1981; fourth inning.

Singles

Most Singles, Total Series

N. L.— 150— Los Angeles; 6 Series, 27 games.
A. L.— 148— Baltimore; 7 Series, 26 games.

Most Singles, Series

3-game Series—A. L.— 29—New York vs. Oakland, 1981.
           N. L.— 27—St. Louis vs. Atlanta, 1982.
4-game Series—A. L.— 33—New York vs. Kansas City, 1978.
           N. L.— 27—Pittsburgh vs. San Francisco, 1971.
5-game Series—N. L.— 45—Philadelphia vs. Houston, 1980.
           A. L.— 36—New York vs. Kansas City, 1976.
6-game Series—N. L.— 42—St. Louis vs. Los Angeles, 1985.
7-game Series—A. L.— 53—California vs. Boston, 1986.
           N. L.— 46—St. Louis vs. San Francisco, 1987.

Most Singles, Series, Both Clubs

3-game Series—A. L.— 46—New York 29, Oakland 17, 1981.
           N. L.— 41—St. Louis 27, Atlanta 14, 1982.
4-game Series—A. L.— 55—New York 33, Kansas City 22, 1978.
           N. L.— 51—Philadelphia 26, Los Angeles 25, 1977.
5-game Series—N. L.— 73—Philadelphia 45, Houston 28, 1980.
           A. L.— 64—New York 36, Kansas City 28, 1976.
6-game Series—N. L.— 72—Houston 38, New York 34, 1986.
7-game Series—A. L.— 103—California 53, Boston 50, 1986.
           N. L.— 83— St. Louis 46, San Francisco 37, 1987.

Fewest Singles, Series

3-game Series—A. L.— 10—Oakand vs. Baltimore, 1971.
           N. L.— 13—Atlanta vs. New York, 1969.
4-game Series—A. L.— 14—Oakland vs. Baltimore, 1974.
           N. L.— 19—Los Angeles vs. Philadelphia, 1983.
5-game Series—N. L.— 20—Pittsburgh vs. Cincinnati, 1972.
              Cincinnati vs. New York, 1973.
           A. L.— 21—Detroit vs. Oakland, 1972.
              Oakland vs. Baltimore, 1973.
6-game Series—N. L.— 28—Los Angeles vs. St. Louis, 1985.
7-game Series—A. L.— 34—Kansas City vs. Toronto, 1985.
           N. L.— 37—San Francisco vs. St. Louis, 1987.

Fewest Singles, Series, Both Clubs

3-game Series—A. L.— 24—Baltimore 14, Oakland 10, 1971.
           N. L.— 31—Philadelphia 17, Cincinnati 14, 1976.
4-game Series—A. L.— 32—Baltimore 18, Oakland 14, 1974.
           N. L.— 44—Philadelphia 25, Los Angeles 19, 1983.
5-game Series—A. L.— 47—Baltimore 26, Oakland 21, 1973.
           N. L.— 47—Cincinnati 27, Pittsburgh 20, 1972.
6-game Series—N. L.— 70—St. Louis 42, Los Angeles 28, 1985.
7-game Series—A. L.— 78—Toronto 44, Kansas City 34, 1985.
           N. L.— 83—St. Louis 46, San Francisco 37, 1987.

Most Singles, Pinch-Hitters, Series

N. L.—4—Pittsburgh vs. Los Angeles, 1974; 4-game Series.
A. L.—4—Toronto vs. Kansas City, 1985; 7-game Series.

Most Singles, Pinch-Hitters, Series, Both Clubs

N. L.—7—Pittsburgh 4, Los Angeles 3, 1974; 4-game Series.
A. L.—4—Oakland 3, Detroit 1, 1972; 5-game Series.
      Toronto 4, Kansas City 0, 1985; 7-game Series.
      Detroit 3, Minnesota 1, 1987; 5-game Series.

Most Singles, Game

A. L.— 15— New York vs. Oakland, October 14, 1981.
N. L.— 13— St. Louis vs. Los Angeles, October 13, 1985.

Most Singles, Game, Both Clubs

A. L.— 25—Kansas City 13, New York 12, October 4, 1978.
N. L.— 18—St. Louis 10, San Francisco 8, October 14, 1987.

Fewest Singles, Game

A. L.—0—Oakland vs. Baltimore, October 9, 1974.
N. L.—1—Pittsburgh vs. Cincinnati, October 10, 1972.
      Montreal vs. Los Angeles, October 19, 1981.
      Houston vs. New York, October 12, 1986.

Fewest Singles, Game, Both Clubs

N. L.—4—New York 2, Cincinnati 2, October 6, 1973.
         New York 3, Houston 1, October 12, 1986.
A. L.—4—Toronto 2, Kansas City 2, October 12, 1985.

Most Singles, Inning

N. L.—8—St. Louis vs. Los Angeles, October 13, 1985; second inning.
A. L.—5—Kansas City vs. New York, October 4, 1978; second inning.
      New York vs. Oakland, October 14, 1981; fourth inning.
      Boston vs. California, October 14, 1986; third inning.

Most Singles, Inning, Both Clubs

A. L.—9—New York 5, Oakland 4, October 14, 1981; fourth inning.
N. L.—8—Philadelphia 4, Houston 4, October 12, 1980; eighth inning.
      St. Louis 8, Los Angeles 0, October 13, 1985, second inning.

Doubles

Most Doubles, Total Series

N. L.— 42— Los Angeles; 6 Series, 27 games.
A. L.— 40— New York; 5 Series, 20 games.

Most Doubles, Series

3-game Series—N. L.— 9—Atlanta vs. New York, 1969.
           A. L.— 8—Baltimore vs. Minnesota, 1969.
              Oakland vs. Baltimore, 1971.
              Boston vs. Oakland, 1975.
4-game Series—A. L.— 9—Baltimore vs. Chicago, 1983.
           N. L.— 8—Los Angeles vs. Pittsburgh, 1974.
              Los Angeles vs. Philadelphia, 1978.
5-game Series—A. L.— 13—New York vs. Kansas City, 1976.
              Minnesota vs. Detroit, 1987.
           N. L.— 11—Chicago vs. San Diego, 1984.
6-game Series—N. L.— 12—Los Angeles vs. St. Louis, 1985.
7-game Series—A. L.— 19—Toronto vs. Kansas City, 1985.
           N. L.— 7—San Francisco vs. St. Louis, 1987.

Most Doubles, Series, Both Clubs

3-game Series—N. L.— 17—Atlanta 9, New York 8, 1969.
           A. L.— 15—Oakland 8, Baltimore 7, 1971.
4-game Series—A. L.— 13—Baltimore 9, Chicago 4, 1983.
           N. L.— 11—Los Angeles 8, Philadelphia 3, 1978.
5-game Series—A. L.— 21—New York 12, Kansas City 9, 1977.
           N. L.— 16—Chicago 11, San Diego 5, 1984.
6-game Series—N. L.— 22—Los Angeles 12, St. Louis 10, 1985.
7-game Series—A. L.— 28—Toronto 19, Kansas City 9, 1985.
           N. L.— 11—San Francisco 7, St. Louis 4, 1987.

Fewest Doubles, Series

3-game Series—N. L.— 1—Atlanta vs. St. Louis, 1982.
           A. L.— 1—Kansas City vs. Detroit, 1984.
4-game Series—A. L.— 1—Baltimore vs. Oakland, 1974.
           N. L.— 1—Pittsburgh vs. Los Angeles, 1974.
5-game Series—N. L.— 3—Los Angeles vs. Montreal, 1981.
           A. L.— 4—Milwaukee vs. California, 1982.
              Detroit vs. Minnesota, 1987.
6-game Series—N. L.— 4—New York vs. Houston, 1986.
7-game Series—N. L.— 4—St. Louis vs. San Francisco, 1987.
           A. L.— 9—Kansas City vs. Toronto, 1985.

Fewest Doubles, Series, Both Clubs

3-game Series—N. L.— 5—St. Louis 4, Atlanta 1, 1982.
           A. L.— 5—Detroit 4, Kansas City 1, 1984.
4-game Series—A. L.— 5—Oakland 4, Baltimore 1, 1974.
           N. L.— 9—San Francisco 5, Pittsburgh 4, 1971.
              Los Angeles 8, Pittsburgh 1, 1974.
              Los Angeles 6, Philadelphia 3, 1977.
              Los Angeles 5, Philadelphia 4, 1983.
5-game Series—N. L.— 10—Montreal 7, Los Angeles 3, 1981.
           A. L.— 12—Baltimore 7, Oakland 5, 1973.
              California 8, Milwaukee 4, 1982.

6-game Series—N. L.— 10—Houston 6, New York 4, 1986.
7-game Series—N. L.— 11—San Francisco 7, St. Louis 4, 1987.
A. L.—22—Boston 11, California 11, 1986.

Most Doubles, Pinch-Hitters, Series

A. L.—2—Toronto vs. Kansas City, 1985; 7-game Series.
N. L.—1—Held by many clubs.

Most Doubles, Pinch-Hitters, Series, Both Clubs

A. L.—3—Toronto 2, Kansas City 1, 1985; 7-game Series.
N. L.—2—Los Angeles 1, Philadelphia 1, 1978; 4-game Series.

Most Doubles, Game

A. L.—6—Baltimore vs. Minnesota, October 6, 1969.
N. L.—6—Philadelphia vs. Cincinnati, October 12, 1976.

Most Doubles, Game, Both Clubs

A. L.—9—Oakland 5, Baltimore 4, October 3, 1971.
N. L.—8—Los Angeles 5, St. Louis 3, October 12, 1985.

Most Doubles, Inning

A. L.—3—Oakland vs. Baltimore, October 10, 1973; second inning.
Boston vs. Oakland, October 4, 1975; seventh inning.
Minnesota vs. Detroit, October 8, 1987; second inning.
N. L.—3—Atlanta vs. New York, October 4, 1969; third inning, consecutive.
Cincinnati vs. Pittsburgh, October 8, 1972; first inning, consecutive.
Cincinnati vs. Philadelphia, October 9, 1976; eighth inning.

Triples

Most Triples, Total Series

A. L.— 13— Kansas City; 6 Series, 27 games.
N. L.— 8— Los Angeles; 6 Series, 27 games.

Most Triples, Series

3-game Series—N. L.— 3—Cincinnati vs. Philadelphia, 1976.
A. L.— 1—Held by many clubs.
4-game Series—A. L.— 3—Kansas City vs. New York, 1978.
N. L.— 3—Los Angeles vs. Philadelphia, 1978.
5-game Series—N. L.— 5—Houston vs. Philadelphia, 1980.
A. L.— 4—Kansas City vs. New York, 1976.
6-game Series—N. L.— 2—New York vs. Houston, 1986.
7-game Series—N. L.— 4—St. Louis vs. San Francisco, 1987.
A. L.— 2—Boston vs. California, 1986.

Most Triples, Series, Both Clubs

3-game Series—N. L.— 4—Cincinnati 3, Philadelphia 1, 1976.
A. L.— 2—Baltimore 1, Minnesota 1, 1969.
Baltimore 1, Oakland 1, 1971.
Kansas City 1, New York 1, 1980.
4-game Series—N. L.— 5—Los Angeles 3, Philadelphia 2, 1978.
A. L.— 4—Kansas City 3, New York 1, 1978.
5-game Series—A. L.— 6—Kansas City 4, New York 2, 1976.
N. L.— 6—Houston 5, Philadelphia 1, 1980.
6-game Series—N. L.— 2—Los Angeles 1, St. Louis 1, 1985.
New York 2, Houston 0, 1986.
7-game Series—N. L.— 5—St. Louis 4, San Francisco 1, 1987.
A. L.— 2—Boston 2, California 0, 1986.

Fewest Triples, Series

A. L.-N. L.—0—Held by many clubs in Series of all lengths.

Fewest Triples, Series, Both Clubs

3-game Series—N. L.— 0—Cincinnati 0, Pittsburgh 0, 1975.
A. L.— 0—Boston 0, Oakland 0, 1975.
4-game Series—N. L.— 0—Pittsburgh 0, San Francisco 0, 1971.
A. L.— 0—Baltimore 0, Chicago 0, 1983.
5-game Series—N. L.— 0—Cincinnati 0, New York 0, 1973.
A. L.— 1—Detroit 1, Oakland 0, 1972.
Oakland 1, Baltimore 0, 1973.
California 1, Milwaukee 0, 1982.
Minnesota 1, Detroit 0, 1987.
6-game Series—N. L.— 2—Los Angeles 1, St. Louis 1, 1985.
7-game Series—A. L.— 1—Kansas City 1, Toronto 0, 1985.
N. L.— 5—St. Louis 4, San Francisco 1, 1987.

Most Triples, Pinch-Hitters, Series

N. L.— 1—Cincinnati vs. Pittsburgh, 1970; 3-game Series.
New York vs. Houston, 1986; 6-game Series.
A. L.—Never accomplished.

Most Triples, Game

A. L.—2—Kansas City vs. New York, October 13, 1976.
Kansas City vs. New York, October 8, 1977.
N. L.—2—Cincinnati vs. Philadelphia, October 9, 1976.
Los Angeles vs. Philadelphia, October 4, 1978.
Houston vs. Philadelphia, October 10, 1980; 11 innings.

Most Triples, Game, Both Clubs

N. L.—3—Los Angeles 2, Philadelphia 1, October 4, 1978.
A. L.—2—Baltimore 1, Minnesota 1, October 6, 1969.
Kansas City 1, New York 1, October 9, 1976.
Kansas City 2, New York 0, October 13, 1976.
Kansas City 2, New York 0, October 8, 1977.
Detroit 1, Kansas City 1, October 2, 1984.

Most Triples, Inning

A. L.—2—Kansas City vs. New York, October 8, 1977; third inning.
N. L.—1—Held by many clubs.

Home Runs
Series

Most Home Runs, Total Series

A. L.—26—Baltimore; 7 Series, 26 games.
N. L.—25— Los Angeles; 6 Series, 27 games.

Most Grand Slams, Total Series

N. L.—2—Los Angeles, 1977 (2) .
A. L.—1—Baltimore, 1970.
California, 1982.

Most Home Runs, Series

3-game Series—N. L.—6—New York vs. Atlanta, 1969.
A. L.—6—Baltimore vs. Minnesota, 1970.
4-game Series—N. L.—8—Pittsburgh vs. San Francisco, 1971.
Los Angeles vs. Philadelphia, 1978.
A. L.—5—New York vs. Kansas City, 1978.
5-game Series—N. L.—9—Chicago vs. San Diego, 1984.
A. L.—8—Minnesota vs. Detroit, 1987.
6-game Series—N. L.—5—Los Angeles vs. St. Louis, 1985.
Houston vs. New York, 1986.
7-game Series—N. L.—9—San Francisco vs. St. Louis, 1987.
A. L.—7—California 7, Boston 6, 1986.
California vs. Boston, 1986.

Most Home Runs, Series, Both Clubs

3-game Series—N. L.—11—New York 6, Atlanta 5, 1969.
A.L.— 9—Baltimore 6, Minnesota 3, 1970.
4-game Series—N. L.— 13—Pittsburgh 8, San Francisco 5, 1971.
Los Angeles 8, Philadelphia 5, 1978.
A. L.—New York 5, Kansas City 4, 1978.
5-game Series—A. L.— 15—Minnesota 8, Detroit 7, 1987.
N. L.—11—Chicago 9, San Diego 2, 1984.
6-game Series—N. L.— 8—Los Angeles 5, St. Louis 3, 1985.
Houston 5, New York 3, 1986.
7-game Series—A. L.—13—California 7, Boston 6, 1986.
N. L.—11—San Francisco 9, St. Louis 2, 1987.

Fewest Home Runs, Series

3-game Series—N. L.—0—Pittsburgh vs. Cincinnati, 1970.
Atlanta vs. St. Louis, 1982.
A. L.—0—Oakland vs. New York, 1981.
Kansas City vs. Detroit, 1984.
4-game Series—N. L.—2—Philadelphia vs. Los Angeles, 1977.
A. L.—0—Chicago vs. Baltimore, 1983.
5-game Series—N. L.—0—Houston vs. Philadelphia, 1980.
A. L.—1—Oakland vs. Detroit, 1972.
6-game Series—N. L.—3—St. Louis vs. Los Angeles, 1985.
New York vs. Houston, 1986.
7-game Series—A. L.—2—Toronto vs. Kansas City, 1985.
N. L.—2—St. Louis vs. San Francisco, 1987.

Fewest Home Runs, Series, Both Clubs

3-game Series—N. L.— 1—St. Louis 1, Atlanta 0, 1982.
A. L.— 2—New York 2, Oakland 0, 1981.
4-game Series—A. L.— 3—Baltimore 3, Chicago 0, 1983.
N. L.— 5—Los Angeles 3, Philadelphia 2, 1977.
5-game Series—N. L.— 1—Philadelphia 1, Houston 0, 1980.
A. L.— 5—Detroit 4, Oakland 1, 1972.
Kansas City 3, New York 2, 1977.
6-game Series—N. L.— 8—Los Angeles 5, St. Louis 3, 1985.
Houston 5, New York 3, 1986.
7-game Series—N. L.—11—San Francisco 9, St. Louis 2, 1987.
A. L.— 9—Kansas City 7, Toronto 2, 1985.

Most Grand Slams, Series

N. L.—2—Los Angeles vs. Philadelphia, 1977.
A. L.—1—Baltimore vs. Minnesota, 1970.
    California vs. Milwaukee, 1982.

Most Home Runs, Pinch-Hitters, Series

N. L.—2—Philadelphia vs. Los Angeles, 1978; 4-game Series.
A. L.—1—Baltimore vs. California, 1979; 4-game Series.
    Kansas City vs. Toronto, 1985; 7-game Series.

Game & Inning

Most Home Runs, Game

N. L.—5—Chicago vs. San Diego, October 2, 1984.
A. L.—4—Baltimore vs. Oakland, October 4, 1971.
    Oakland vs. Baltimore, October 7, 1973.

Most Home Runs, Game, Both Clubs

A. L.—5—Kansas City 3, New York 2, October 6, 1978.
    Kansas City 3, Toronto 2, October 11, 1985.
N. L.—5—New York 3, Atlanta 2, October 6, 1969.
    Pittsburgh 4, San Francisco 1, October 3, 1971.
    Los Angeles 4, Philadelphia 1, October 4, 1978.
    Chicago 5, San Diego 0, October 2, 1984.

Most Consecutive Games, Total Series, One or More Home Runs

N. L.—6—Los Angeles, last game vs. Philadelphia, 1977 (1 home run), all four games vs. Philadelphia, 1978 (8 home runs), first game vs. Montreal, 1981 (2 home runs).
    San Francisco, last game vs. Pittsburgh, 1971 (2 home runs), first five games vs. St. Louis, 1987 (9 home runs).
A. L.—5—New York, last three games vs. Kansas City, 1976 (4 home runs), first two games vs. Kansas City, 1977 (2 home runs).
    Milwaukee, all five games vs. California, 1982 (5 home runs).
    California, second through sixth games vs. Boston, 1986 (7 home runs).
    Minnesota, all five games vs. Detroit, 1987 (8 home runs).

Most Consecutive Games, Series, One or More Home Runs

A. L.—5—Milwaukee vs. California, October 5, 6, 8, 9, 10, 1982; 5 home runs.
    California vs. Boston, October 8, 10, 11, 12, 14, 1986; 7 home runs.
    Minnesota vs. Detroit, October 7, 8, 10, 11, 12, 1987; 8 home runs.
N. L.—5—San Francisco vs. St. Louis, October 6, 7, 9, 10, 11, 1987; 9 home runs.

Most Home Runs, Inning

A. L.—3—Baltimore vs. Minnesota, October 3, 1970; fourth inning (first 2 consecutive).
N. L.—2—Cincinnati vs. Pittsburgh, October 5, 1970; first inning (consecutive).
    San Francisco vs. Pittsburgh, October 2, 1971; fifth inning.
    San Francisco vs. Pittsburgh, October 6, 1971; second inning.
    Pittsburgh vs. Los Angeles, October 8, 1974; first inning.
    Cincinnati vs. Philadelphia, October 12, 1976; ninth inning (consecutive).
    Pittsburgh vs. Cincinnati, October 5, 1979; third inning.
    Los Angeles vs. Montreal, October 13, 1981, eighth inning (consecutive).
    Chicago vs. San Diego, October 2, 1984; first inning.
    Chicago vs. San Diego, October 6, 1984; fourth inning (consecutive).

Most Home Runs, Inning, Both Clubs

A. L.—3—Baltimore 3, Minnesota 0, October 3, 1970; fourth inning.
    Toronto 2, Kansas City 1, October 11, 1985; fifth inning.
N. L.—3—San Francisco 2, Pittsburgh 1, October 6, 1971; second inning.

Most Consecutive Home Runs, Inning

A. L.—2—Baltimore (Cuellar and Buford) vs. Minnesota, October 3, 1970; fourth inning.
    Minnesota (Killebrew and Oliva) vs. Baltimore, October 4, 1970; fourth inning.
    Oakland (Rudi and Bando) vs. Baltimore, October 7, 1973; sixth inning.
    New York (Cerone and Piniella) vs. Kansas City, October 8, 1980; second inning.

N. L.—2—Cincinnati (Perez and Bench) vs. Pittsburgh, October 5, 1970; first inning.
    Cincinnati (Foster and Bench) vs. Philadelphia, October 12, 1976; ninth inning.
    Los Angeles (Guerrero and Scioscia) vs. Montreal, October 13, 1981; eighth inning.
    Chicago (Davis and Durham) vs. San Diego, October 6, 1984; fourth inning.

Total Bases

Most Total Bases, Total Series

N. L.—358—Los Angeles; 6 Series, 27 games.
A. L.—349—Baltimore; 7 Series, 26 games.

Most Total Bases, Series

3-game Series—N. L.—65—New York vs. Atlanta, 1969.
    A. L.—61—Baltimore vs. Minnesota, 1970.
4-game Series—N. L.—80—Los Angeles vs. Philadelphia, 1978.
    A. L.—62—New York vs. Kansas City, 1978.
5-game Series—A. L.—85—Minnesota vs. Detroit, 1987.
    N. L.—80—Chicago vs. San Diego, 1984.
6-game Series—N. L.—77—St. Louis vs. Los Angeles, 1985.
7-game Series—A. L.—103—California vs. Boston, 1986.
    N. L.—90—San Francisco vs. St. Louis, 1987.

Most Total Bases, Series, Both Clubs

3-game Series—N. L.—116—New York 65, Atlanta 51, 1969.
    A. L.—100—Baltimore 61, Minnesota 39, 1970.
4-game Series—N. L.—137—Los Angeles 80, Philadelphia 57, 1978.
    A. L.—121—New York 62, Kansas City 59, 1978.
5-game Series—A. L.—150—Minnesota 85, Detroit 65, 1987.
    N. L.—134—Chicago 80, San Diego 54, 1984.
6-game Series—N. L.—152—St. Louis 77, Los Angeles 75, 1985.
7-game Series—A. L.—205—California 103, Boston 102, 1986.
    N. L.—164—San Francisco 90, St. Louis 74, 1987.

Fewest Total Bases, Series

3-game Series—N. L.—16—Atlanta vs. St. Louis, 1982.
    A. L.—21—Kansas City vs. Detroit, 1984.
4-game Series—A. L.—32—Baltimore vs. Oakland, 1974.
    Chicago vs. Baltimore, 1983.
    N. L.—35—Pittsburgh vs. Los Angeles, 1974.
5-game Series—N. L.—44—Montreal vs. Los Angeles, 1981.
    A. L.—49—Oakland vs. Detroit, 1972.
6-game Series—N. L.—60—New York vs. Houston, 1986.
7-game Series—N. L.—74—St. Louis vs. San Francisco, 1987.
    A. L.—83—Kansas City vs. Toronto, 1985.

Fewest Total Bases, Series, Both Clubs

3-game Series—N. L.—61—St. Louis 45, Atlanta 16, 1982.
    A. L.—64—Detroit 43, Kansas City 21, 1984.
4-game Series—A. L.—69—Oakland 37, Baltimore 32, 1974.
    N. L.—91—Los Angeles 56, Pittsburgh 35, 1974.
5-game Series—N. L.—99—Los Angeles 55, Montreal 44, 1981.
    A. L.—101—Detroit 52, Oakland 49, 1972.
6-game Series—N. L.—130—Houston 70, New York 60, 1986.
7-game Series—N. L.—164—San Francisco 90, St. Louis 74, 1987.
    A. L.—173—Toronto 90, Kansas City 83, 1985.

Most Total Bases, Game

N. L.—34—Chicago vs. San Diego, October 2, 1984.
A. L.—29—Baltimore vs. Minnesota, October 6, 1969.

Most Total Bases, Game, Both Clubs

N. L.—47—Los Angeles 30, Philadelphia 17, October 4, 1978.
A. L.—43—Baltimore 29, Minnesota 14, October 6, 1969.
    Toronto 22, Kansas City 21, October 11, 1985.

Fewest Total Bases, Game

N. L.—2—Cincinnati vs. New York, October 7, 1973.
    St. Louis vs. San Francisco, October 7, 1987.
A. L.—2—Baltimore vs. Oakland, October 8, 1974.
    Oakland vs. Baltimore, October 9, 1974.
    Kansas City vs. Toronto, October 12, 1985.

Fewest Total Bases, Game, Both Clubs

A. L.—6—Detroit 3, Kansas City 3, October 5, 1984.
N. L.—12—New York 10, Cincinnati 2, October 7, 1973.

Most Total Bases, Inning

A. L.—16—Baltimore vs. Minnesota, October 3, 1970; fourth inning.
N. L.—11—San Francisco vs. Pittsburgh, October 6, 1971; second inning.

Most Total Bases, Inning, Both Clubs

A. L.—18—Baltimore 16, Minnesota 2, October 3, 1970; fourth inning.

N. L.— 17—San Francisco 11, Pittsburgh 6, October 6, 1971; second inning.

Long Hits

Most Long Hits, Total Series

N. L.— 75—Los Angeles; 6 Series, 27 games.

A. L.—73—Baltimore; 7 Series, 26 games.

Most Long Hits, Series

3-game Series—N. L.— 15—New York vs. Atlanta, 1969.

A. L.—13—Baltimore vs. Minnesota, 1969, 1970.

4-game Series—N. L.— 19—Los Angeles vs. Philadelphia, 1978.

A. L.—13—Kansas City vs. New York, 1978.

5-game Series—A. L.— 22—Minnesota vs. Detroit, 1987.

N. L.—20—Chicago vs. San Diego, 1984.

6-game Series—N. L.— 18—Los Angeles vs. St. Louis, 1985.

7-game Series—A. L.— 21—Toronto vs. Kansas City, 1985.

N. L.—17—San Francisco vs. St. Louis, 1987.

Most Long Hits, Series, Both Clubs

3-game Series—N. L.—29—New York 15, Atlanta 14, 1969.

A. L.—24—Baltimore 12, Oakland 12, 1971.

4-game Series—N. L.—29—Los Angeles 19, Philadelphia 10, 1978.

A. L.—22—Kansas City 13, New York 9, 1978.

5-game Series—A. L.—33—Minnesota 22, Detroit 11, 1987.

N. L.—28—Chicago 20, San Diego 8, 1984.

6-game Series—N. L.—32—Los Angeles 18, St. Louis 14, 1985.

7-game Series—A. L.—38—Toronto 21, Kansas City 17, 1985.

N. L.—27—San Francisco 17, St. Louis 10, 1987.

Fewest Long Hits, Series

3-game Series—N. L.— 1—Atlanta vs. St. Louis, 1982.

A. L.— 2—Kansas City vs. Detroit, 1984.

4-game Series—N. L.— 4—Pittsburgh vs. Los Angeles, 1974.

A. L.— 4—Baltimore vs. Oakland, 1974.
Chicago vs. Baltimore, 1983.

5-game Series—N. L.— 8—New York vs. Cincinnati, 1973.
Los Angeles vs. Montreal, 1981.
Montreal vs. Los Angeles, 1981.
San Diego vs. Chicago, 1984.

A. L.— 9—Oakland vs. Detroit, 1972.

6-game Series—N. L.— 9—New York vs. Houston, 1986.

7-game Series—N. L.— 10—St. Louis vs. San Francisco, 1987.

A. L.—17—Kansas City vs. Toronto, 1985.

Fewest Long Hits, Series, Both Clubs

3-game Series—N. L.— 8—St. Louis 7, Atlanta 1, 1982.

A. L.—11—Detroit 9, Kansas City 2, 1984.

4-game Series—N. L.— 12—Oakland 8, Baltimore 4, 1974.

N. L.—15—Los Angeles 10, Philadelphia 5, 1977.

5-game Series—N. L.—16—Los Angeles 8, Montreal 8, 1981.

A. L.—20—Detroit 11, Oakland 9, 1972.

6-game Series—N. L.—20—Houston 11, New York 9, 1986.

7-game Series—N. L.—27—San Francisco 17, St. Louis 10, 1987.

A. L.—37—Boston 19, California 18, 1986.

Most Long Hits, Game

A. L.—8—Baltimore vs. Minnesota, October 6, 1969; 6 doubles, 1 triple, 1 home run.

N. L.—8—Cincinnati vs. Philadelphia, October 9, 1976; 5 doubles, 2 triples, 1 home run.
Chicago vs. San Diego, October 2, 1984; 3 doubles, 5 home runs.

Most Long Hits, Game, Both Clubs

A. L.—12—Oakland 6 (5 doubles, 1 home run), Boston 6 (4 doubles, 2 home runs), October 5, 1975.

N. L.—11—New York 7 (4 doubles, 3 home runs), Atlanta 4 (2 doubles, 2 home runs), October 6, 1969.

Extra Bases On Long Hits

Most Extra Bases on Long Hits, Total Series

N. L.— 133— Los Angeles; 6 Series, 27 games (42 on doubles, 16 on triples, 75 on home runs).

A. L.— 128—Baltimore; 7 Series, 26 games (44 on doubles, 6 on triples, 78 on home runs).

Most Extra Bases on Long Hits, Series

3-game Series—N. L.— 28—New York vs. Atlanta, 1969.

A. L.—25—Baltimore vs. Minnesota, 1970.

4-game Series—N. L.— 38—Los Angeles vs. Philadelphia, 1978.

A. L.—24—Kansas City vs. New York, 1978.

5-game Series—A. L.—39—Minnesota vs. Detroit, 1987.

N. L.—38—Chicago vs. San Diego, 1984.

6-game Series—N. L.—29—Los Angeles vs. St. Louis, 1985.

7-game Series—N. L.—36—San Francisco vs. St. Louis, 1987.

A. L.—33—Boston vs. California, 1986.

Most Extra Bases on Long Hits, Series, Both Clubs

3-game Series—N. L.—52—New York 28, Atlanta 24, 1969.

A. L.—40—Baltimore 25, Minnesota 15, 1970.
Baltimore 21, Oakland 19, 1971.

4-game Series—N. L.—60—Los Angeles 38, Philadelphia 22, 1978.

A. L.—44—Kansas City 24, New York 20, 1978.

5-game Series—A. L.—64—Minnesota 39, Detroit 25, 1987.

N. L.—51—Chicago 38, San Diego 13, 1984.

6-game Series—N. L.—50—Los Angeles 29, St. Louis 21, 1985.

7-game Series—A. L.—65—Boston 33, California 32, 1986.

N. L.—54—San Francisco 36, St. Louis 18, 1987.

Fewest Extra Bases on Long Hits, Series

3-game Series—N. L.— 1—Atlanta vs. St. Louis, 1982.

A. L.— 3—Kansas City vs. Detroit, 1984.

4-game Series—N. L.— 4—Chicago vs. Baltimore, 1983.

N. L.— 9—Philadelphia vs. Los Angeles, 1977.

5-game Series—N. L.— 10—Montreal vs. Los Angeles, 1981.

A. L.—11—Oakland vs. Detroit, 1972.

6-game Series—N. L.— 17—New York vs. Houston, 1986.

7-game Series—N. L.— 18—St. Louis vs. San Francisco, 1987.

A. L.—25—Toronto vs. Kansas City, 1985.

Fewest Extra Bases on Long Hits, Series, Both Clubs

3-game Series—N. L.— 12—St. Louis 11, Atlanta 1, 1982.

A. L.—17—New York 11, Oakland 6, 1981.

4-game Series—A. L.—22—Baltimore 18, Chicago 4, 1983.

N. L.—26—Los Angeles 17, Philadelphia 9, 1977.

5-game Series—N. L.—27—Los Angeles 17, Montreal 10, 1981.

A. L.—31—Detroit 20, Oakland 11, 1972.

6-game Series—N. L.—38—Houston 21, New York 17, 1986.

7-game Series—N. L.—54—San Francisco 36, St. Louis 18, 1987.

A. L.—57—Kansas City 32, Toronto 25, 1985.

Runs Batted In

Most Runs Batted In, Total Series

A. L.— 117— Baltimore; 7 Series, 26 games.

N. L.— 105— Los Angeles; 6 Series, 27 games.

Most Runs Batted In, Series

3-game Series—A. L.—24—Baltimore vs. Minnesota, 1970.

N. L.—24—New York vs. Atlanta, 1969.

4-game Series—A. L.—25—Baltimore vs. California, 1979.

N. L.—23—Pittsburgh vs. San Francisco, 1971.

5-game Series—A. L.—33—Minnesota vs. Detroit, 1987.

N. L.—25—Chicago vs. San Diego, 1984.

6-game Series—N. L.—26—St. Louis vs. Los Angeles, 1985.

7-game Series—A. L.—35—Boston vs. California, 1986.

N. L.—22—St. Louis vs. San Francisco, 1987.

Most Runs Batted In, Series, Both Clubs

3-game Series—N. L.—39—New York 24, Atlanta 15, 1969.

A. L.—34—Baltimore 24, Minnesota 10, 1970.

4-game Series—A. L.—39—Baltimore 25, California 14, 1979.

N. L.—37—Pittsburgh 23, San Francisco 14, 1971.
Los Angeles 21, Philadelphia 16, 1978.

5-game Series—A. L.—54—Minnesota 33, Detroit 21, 1987.

N. L.—45—Chicago 25, San Diego 20, 1984.

6-game Series—N. L.—49—St. Louis 26, Los Angeles 23, 1985.

7-game Series—A. L.—64—Boston 35, California 29, 1986.

N. L.—42—St. Louis 22, San Francisco 20, 1987.

Fewest Runs Batted In, Series

3-game Series—N. L.— 3—Pittsburgh vs. Cincinnati, 1970.
Atlanta vs. St. Louis, 1982.

A. L.— 4—Oakland vs. New York, 1981.
Kansas City vs. Detroit, 1984.

4-game Series—A. L.— 2—Chicago vs. Baltimore, 1983.

N. L.— 7—Los Angeles vs. Philadelphia, 1983.

5-game Series—N. L.— 8—Cincinnati vs. New York, 1973.
Montreal vs. Los Angeles, 1981.

A. L.—10—Oakland vs. Detroit, 1972.
      Detroit vs. Oakland, 1972.
6-game Series—N. L.— 17—Houston vs. New York, 1986.
7-game Series—N. L.—20—San Francisco vs. St. Louis, 1987.
      A. L.—23—Toronto vs. Kansas City, 1985.

Fewest Runs Batted In, Series, Both Clubs

3-game Series—N. L.— 11—Cincinnati 8, Pittsburgh 3, 1970.
      A. L.—18—Detroit 14, Kansas City 4, 1984.
4-game Series—A. L.—18—Oakland 11, Baltimore 7, 1974.
      N. L.—22—Philadelphia 15, Los Angeles 7, 1983.
5-game Series—A. L.—20—Oakland 10, Detroit 10, 1972.
      N. L.—23—Los Angeles 15, Montreal 8, 1981.
6-game Series—N. L.—36—New York 19, Houston 17, 1986.
7-game Series—N. L.—42—St. Louis 22, San Francisco 20, 1987.
      A. L.—49—Kansas City 26, Toronto 23, 1985.

Most Runs Batted In, Pinch-Hitters, Series

A. L.—4—Baltimore vs. California, 1979; 4-game Series.
      Toronto vs. Kansas City, 1985; 7-game Series.
      Detroit vs. Minnesota, 1987; 5-game Series.
N. L.—4—Philadelphia vs. Houston, 1980; 5-game Series.

Most Runs Batted In, Pinch-Hitters, Series, Both Clubs

A. L.—6—Detroit 4, Minnesota 2, 1987; 5-game Series.
N. L.—5—Philadelphia 4, Houston 1, 1980; 5-game Series.

Most Runs Batted In, Game

A. L.— 13—New York vs. Oakland, October 14, 1981.
N. L.— 12—Chicago vs. San Diego, October 2, 1984.

Most Runs Batted In, Game, Both Clubs

N. L.— 17—New York 11, Atlanta 6, October 5, 1969.
A. L.— 16—Baltimore 8, California 8, October 4, 1979.
      New York 13, Oakland 3, 1981.

Fewest Runs Batted In, Game, Both Clubs

A. L.— 1—Baltimore 1, Minnesota 0, October 5, 1969; 11 innings.
      Oakland 1, Baltimore 0, October 8, 1974.
      Detroit 1, Kansas City 0, October 5, 1984.
      Houston 1, New York 0, October 8, 1986.
N. L.— 1—Houston 1, Philadelphia 0, October 10, 1980; 11 innings.
      Philadelphia 1, Los Angeles 0, October 4, 1983.
      Houston 1, New York 0, October 8, 1986.

Most Runs Batted In, Inning

N. L.—8—St. Louis vs. Los Angeles, October 13, 1985; second inning.
A. L.—7—Baltimore vs. Minnesota, October 3, 1970; fourth inning.
      New York vs. Oakland, October 14, 1981; fourth inning.

Most Runs Batted In, Inning, Both Clubs

A. L.—9—New York 7, Oakland 2, October 14, 1981; fourth inning.
N. L.—8—St. Louis 8, Los Angeles 0, October 13, 1985; second inning.

Most Runs Batted In, Pinch-Hitters, Inning

A. L.—3—Baltimore vs. California, October 3, 1979; tenth inning.
N. L.—2—New York vs. Atlanta, October 4, 1969; eighth inning.
      Los Angeles vs. Pittsburgh, October 6, 1974; eighth inning.

Bases On Balls

Most Bases on Balls, Total Series

N. L.— 95—Los Angeles; 6 Series, 27 games.
A. L.— 93—Baltimore; 7 Series, 26 games.

Most Bases on Balls, Series

3-game Series—N. L.— 15—Cincinnati vs. Philadelphia, 1976.
      A. L.—13—Baltimore vs. Minnesota, 1969.
      Baltimore vs. Oakland, 1971.
4-game Series—N. L.—30—Los Angeles vs. Pittsburgh, 1974.
      A. L.—22—Oakland vs. Baltimore, 1974.
5-game Series—N. L.—31—Houston vs. Philadelphia, 1980.
      A. L.—20—Minnesota vs. Detroit, 1987.
6-game Series—N. L.—30—St. Louis vs. Los Angeles, 1985.
7-game Series—A. L.—22—Kansas City vs. Toronto, 1985.
      N. L.—17—San Francisco vs. St. Louis, 1987.

Most Bases on Balls, Series, Both Clubs

3-game Series—N. L.—27—Cincinnati 15, Philadelphia 12, 1976.
      A. L.—25—Baltimore 13, Minnesota 12, 1969.
4-game Series—N. L.—38—Los Angeles 30, Pittsburgh 8, 1974.
      A. L.—28—Baltimore 16, Chicago 12, 1983.

5-game Series—N. L.—44—Houston 31, Philadelphia 13, 1980.
      A. L.—38—Minnesota 20, Detroit 18, 1987.
6-game Series—N. L.—49—St. Louis 30, Los Angeles 19, 1985.
7-game Series—A. L.—39—California 20, Boston 19, 1986.
      N. L.—33—San Francisco 17, St. Louis 16, 1987.

Fewest Bases on Balls, Series

3-game Series—A. L.—3—Boston vs. Oakland, 1975.
      N. L.—6—Atlanta vs. St. Louis, 1982.
4-game Series—A. L.—5—Baltimore vs. Oakland, 1974.
      N. L.—5—Pittsburgh vs. San Francisco, 1971.
5-game Series—A. L.—9—New York vs. Kansas City, 1977.
      N. L.—9—Pittsburgh vs. Cincinnati, 1972.
6-game Series—N. L.—14—New York vs. Houston, 1986.
7-game Series—A. L.—16—Toronto vs. Kansas City, 1985.
      N. L.—16—St. Louis vs. San Francisco, 1987.

Fewest Bases on Balls, Series, Both Clubs

3-game Series—A. L.— 12—Oakland 9, Boston 3, 1975.
      N. L.—18—St. Louis 12, Atlanta 6, 1982.
4-game Series—N. L.—18—Los Angeles 9, Philadelphia 9, 1978.
      A. L.—21—Kansas City 14, New York 7, 1978.
5-game Series—N. L.—19—Cincinnati 10, Pittsburgh 9, 1972.
      A. L.—24—Kansas City 15, New York 9, 1977.
6-game Series—N. L.—31—Houston 17, New York 14, 1986.
7-game Series—N. L.—33—San Francisco 17, St. Louis 16, 1987.
      A. L.—38—Kansas City 22, Toronto 16, 1985.

Most Bases on Balls, Pinch-Hitters, Series

A. L.—2—Oakland vs. Boston, 1975; 3-game Series.
      California vs. Baltimore, 1979; 4-game Series.
      Baltimore vs. Chicago, 1983; 4-game Series.
      Kansas City vs. Toronto, 1985; 7-game Series.
N. L.—2—Cincinnati vs. Pittsburgh, 1972; 5-game Series.
      Pittsburgh vs. Cincinnati, 1975; 3-game Series.

Most Bases on Balls, Pinch-Hitters, Series, Both Clubs

N. L.—3—Cincinnati 2, Pittsburgh 1, 1972; 5-game Series.
      Pittsburgh 2, Cincinnati 1, 1975; 3-game Series.
A. L.—3—California 2, Baltimore 1, 1979; 4-game Series.

Most Bases on Balls, Game

A. L.— 11—Oakland vs. Baltimore, October 9, 1974.
N. L.— 11—Los Angeles vs. Pittsburgh, October 9, 1974.

Most Bases on Balls, Game, Both Clubs

A. L.— 14—Oakland 11, Baltimore 3, October 9, 1974.
N. L.— 12—Los Angeles 11, Pittsburgh 1, October 9, 1974.
      Houston 7, Philadelphia 5, October 8, 1980; 10 innings.

Fewest Bases on Balls, Game

A. L.-N. L.—0—Held by many clubs.

Fewest Bases on Balls, Game, Both Clubs

A. L.— 1—Oakland 1, Baltimore 0, October 8, 1974.
      New York 1, Kansas City 0, October 9, 1976.
N. L.—2—Cincinnati 2, Pittsburgh 0, October 10, 1972.
      Los Angeles 1, Montreal 1, October 16, 1981.
      Chicago 2, San Diego 0, October 4, 1984.
      Houston 2, New York 0, October 12, 1986.

Most Bases on Balls, Pinch-Hitters, Game

N. L.—2—Pittsburgh vs. Cincinnati, October 7, 1975; 10 innings.
A. L.—2—California vs. Baltimore, October 4, 1979.
      Baltimore vs. Chicago, October 7, 1983.

Most Bases on Balls, Pinch-Hitters, Game, Both Clubs

N. L.—3—Pittsburgh 2, Cincinnati 1, October 7, 1975; 10 innings.
A. L.—2—Detroit 1, Oakland 1, October 11, 1972; 10 innings.
      California 2, Baltimore 0, October 4, 1979.
      Baltimore 2, Chicago 0, October 7, 1983.

Most Bases on Balls, Inning

A. L.—4—Oakland vs. Baltimore, October 9, 1974; fifth inning, consecutive.
N. L.—4—Philadelphia vs. Los Angeles, October 7, 1977; second inning, consecutive.
      St. Louis vs. Los Angeles, October 12, 1985; first inning.

Most Bases on Balls, Inning, Both Clubs

N. L.—6—St. Louis 4, Los Angeles 2, October 12, 1985; first inning.
A. L.—4—Made in many innings.

Most Bases on Balls, Pinch-Hitters, Inning

N. L.—2—Pittsburgh vs. Cincinnati, October 7, 1975; ninth inning.
A. L.—2—Baltimore vs. Chicago, October 7, 1983; ninth inning.

Strikeouts

Most Strikeouts, Total Series
N. L.— 152— Cincinnati; 6 Series, 22 games.
A. L.— 148— Kansas City; 6 Series, 27 games.

Most Strikeouts, Series
3-game Series—N. L.—28—Cincinnati vs. Pittsburgh, 1975.
               A. L.—27—Minnesota vs. Baltimore, 1969.
4-game Series—N. L.—33—Pittsburgh vs. San Francisco, 1971.
               A. L.—26—Chicago vs. Baltimore, 1983.
5-game Series—N. L.—42—Cincinnati vs. New York, 1973.
               A. L.—39—Oakland vs. Baltimore, 1973.
6-game Series—N. L.—57—New York vs. Houston, 1986.
7-game Series—A. L.—51—Kansas City vs. Toronto, 1985.
               N. L.—51—San Francisco vs. St. Louis, 1987.

Most Strikeouts, Series, Both Clubs
3-game Series—N. L.—46—Cincinnati 28, Pittsburgh 18, 1975.
               A. L.—41—Minnesota 27, Baltimore 14, 1969.
                     Minnesota 22, Baltimore 19, 1970.
4-game Series—N. L.—61—Pittsburgh 33, San Francisco 28, 1971.
               A. L.—50—Chicago 26, Baltimore 24, 1983.
5-game Series—N. L.—70—Cincinnati 42, New York 28, 1973.
               A. L.—64—Oakland 39, Baltimore 25, 1973.
6-game Series—N. L.—97—New York 57, Houston 40, 1986.
7-game Series—N. L.—93—San Francisco 51, St. Louis 42, 1987.
               A. L.—88—Kansas City 51, Toronto 37, 1985.

Fewest Strikeouts, Series
3-game Series—N. L.— 9—Philadelphia vs. Cincinnati, 1976.
               A. L.—10—New York vs. Oakland, 1981.
4-game Series—A. L.—13—California vs. Baltimore, 1979.
               N. L.—16—Los Angeles vs. Pittsburgh, 1974.
5-game Series—N. L.—15—New York vs. Kansas City, 1976.
               N. L.—19—Houston vs. Philadelphia, 1980.
6-game Series—N. L.—31—Los Angeles vs. St. Louis, 1985.
7-game Series—A. L.—31—Boston vs. California, 1986.
               N. L.—42—St. Louis vs. San Francisco, 1987.

Fewest Strikeouts, Series, Both Clubs
3-game Series—N. L.—25—Cincinnati 16, Philadelphia 9, 1976.
               A. L.—26—Oakland 14, Boston 12, 1975.
4-game Series—N. L.—33—Pittsburgh 17, Los Angeles 16, 1974.
               A. L.—36—Baltimore 20, Oakland 16, 1974.
5-game Series—A. L.—33—Kansas City 18, New York 15, 1976.
               N. L.—48—Montreal 25, Los Angeles 23, 1981.
6-game Series—N. L.—65—St. Louis 34, Los Angeles 31, 1985.
7-game Series—A. L.—75—California 44, Boston 31, 1986.
               N. L.—93—San Francisco 51, St. Louis 42, 1987.

Most Strikeouts, Pinch-Hitters, Series
N. L.—7—Cincinnati vs. New York, 1973; 5-game Series.
A. L.—4—Minnesota vs. Baltimore, 1970; 3-game Series.
       Oakland vs. Detroit, 1972; 5-game Series.

Most Strikeouts, Pinch-Hitters, Series, Both Clubs
N. L.—7—Cincinnati 7, New York 0, 1973; 5-game Series.
       New York 5, Houston 2, 1986; 6-game Series.
A. L.—4—Minnesota 4, Baltimore 0, 1970; 3-game Series.
       Oakland 4, Detroit 0, 1972; 5-game Series.

Most Strikeouts, Game, Nine Innings
A. L.— 14—Oakland vs. Detroit, October 10, 1972.
         Chicago vs. Baltimore, October 6, 1983.
N. L.— 14—New York vs. Houston, October 8, 1986.

Most Strikeouts, Extra-Inning Game
N. L.— 15—Cincinnati vs. Pittsburgh, October 7, 1975; 10 innings.
         New York vs. Houston, October 14, 1986; 12 innings.
A. L.—Less than nine-inning record.

Most Strikeouts, Pinch-Hitters, Game
A. L.—4—Oakland vs. Detroit, October 10, 1972.
N. L.—3—Cincinnati vs. New York, October 7, 1973.
     Los Angeles vs. Philadelphia, October 8, 1983.

Most Strikeouts, Game, Nine Innings, Both Clubs
N. L.—20—New York 12, Atlanta 8, October 5, 1969.
       New York 14, Houston 6, October 8, 1986.
A. L.—19—Minnesota 12, Baltimore 7, October 5, 1970.
       Oakland 12, Baltimore 7, October 6, 1973.

Most Strikeouts, Extra-Inning Game, Both Clubs
N. L.—23—Cincinnati 15, Pittsburgh 8, October 7, 1975; 10 innings.
A. L.—Less than nine-inning record.

Fewest Strikeouts, Game
N. L.—0—Pittsburgh vs. Los Angeles, October 6, 1974.
A. L.—1—Baltimore vs. Oakland, October 11, 1973.
     New York vs. Kansas City, October 13, 1976.
     Kansas City vs. New York, October 4, 1978.
     Toronto vs. Kansas City, October 12, 1985.

Fewest Strikeouts, Game, Both Clubs
A. L.—3—Oakland 2, Baltimore 1, October 11, 1973.
     Kansas City 2, New York 1, October 13, 1976.
N. L.—4—Philadelphia 2, Cincinnati 2, October 12, 1976.

Most Consecutive Strikeouts, Game
A. L.—4—Oakland vs. Detroit, October 10, 1972; 1 in fourth inning, 3 in fifth inning.
     Baltimore vs. California, October 3, 1979; 3 in first inning, 1 in second inning.
     Kansas City vs. Detroit, October 5, 1984; 2 in fourth inning, 2 in fifth inning.
N. L.—4—Pittsburgh vs. Cincinnati, October 5, 1970; 2 in sixth inning, 2 in seventh inning.
     Cincinnati vs. Pittsburgh, October 7, 1975; 3 in first inning, 1 in second inning.
     Los Angeles vs. St. Louis, October 10, 1985; 2 in first inning, 2 in second inning.
     New York vs. Houston, October 8, 1986; 2 in first inning, 2 in second inning.

Most Strikeouts, Inning
A. L.-N. L.—3—Held by many clubs.

Most Strikeouts, Inning, Both Clubs
A. L.—5—Oakland 3, Baltimore 2, October 6, 1973; first inning.
     Boston 3, Oakland 2, October 4, 1975; second inning.
     Baltimore 3, Chicago 2, October 6, 1983; first inning.
     Kansas City 3, Toronto 2, October 15, 1985; eighth inning.
N. L.—5—New York 3, Atlanta 2, October 5, 1969; third inning.
     New York 3, Atlanta 2, October 6, 1969; third inning.
     Philadelphia 3, Los Angeles 2, October 4, 1977; seventh inning.

Most Strikeouts, Pinch-Hitters, Inning
A. L.—2—Oakland vs. Baltimore, October 5, 1971; ninth inning, consecutive.
N. L.—2—Cincinnati vs. New York, October 7, 1973; eighth inning, consecutive.

Sacrifice Hits

Most Sacrifice Hits, Total Series
N. L.— 15—Philadelphia; 5 Series, 20 games.
A. L.— 12—Oakland; 6 Series, 23 games.

Most Sacrifice Hits, Series
3-game Series—A. L.—5—Boston vs. Oakland, 1975.
               N. L.—5—Pittsburgh vs. Cincinnati, 1979.
                     St. Louis vs. Atlanta, 1982.
4-game Series—N. L.—4—San Francisco vs. Pittsburgh, 1971.
               A. L.—2—Baltimore vs. Oakland, 1974.
                     Oakland vs. Baltimore, 1974.
5-game Series—N. L.—7—Houston vs. Philadelphia, 1980.
               A. L.—5—California vs. Milwaukee, 1982.
6-game Series—N. L.—2—St. Louis vs. Los Angeles, 1985.
                     Houston vs. New York, 1986.
7-game Series—N. L.—5—St. Louis vs. San Francisco, 1987.
               A. L.—4—Kansas City vs. Toronto, 1985.
                     California vs. Boston, 1986.

Most Sacrifice Hits, Series, Both Clubs
3-game Series—N. L.— 7—St. Louis 5, Atlanta 2, 1982.
               A. L.— 5—Boston 5, Oakland 0, 1975.
4-game Series—N. L.— 5—San Francisco 4, Pittsburgh 1, 1971.
                     Philadelphia 3, Los Angeles 2, 1983.
               A. L.— 4—Baltimore 2, Oakland 2, 1974.
5-game Series—N. L.—12—Houston 7, Philadelphia 5, 1980.
               A. L.— 7—Oakland 4, Detroit 3, 1972.
                     California 5, Milwaukee 2, 1982.
6-game Series—N. L.— 3—St. Louis 2, Los Angeles 1, 1985.
                     Houston 2, New York 1, 1986.

7-game Series—N. L.— 8—St. Louis 5, San Francisco 3, 1987.
A. L.— 7—California 4, Boston 3, 1986.

Fewest Sacrifice Hits, Series

3-game Series—A. L.-N. L.—0—Held by many clubs.
4-game Series—A. L.— 0—New York vs. Kansas City, 1978.
California vs. Baltimore, 1979.
N. L.— 1—Pittsburgh vs. San Francisco, 1971.
Los Angeles vs. Pittsburgh, 1974.
5-game Series—A. L.— 0—Baltimore vs. Oakland, 1973.
Kansas City vs. New York, 1976.
N. L.— 1—Chicago vs. San Diego, 1984.
6-game Series—N. L.— 1—Los Angeles vs. St. Louis, 1985.
New York vs. Houston, 1986.
7-game Series—A. L.— 0—Toronto vs. Kansas City, 1985.
N. L.— 3—San Francisco vs. St. Louis, 1987.

Fewest Sacrifice Hits, Series, Both Clubs

3-game Series—N. L.— 0—Cincinnati 0, Pittsburgh 0, 1975.
A. L.— 1—New York 1, Kansas City 0, 1980.
4-game Series—A. L.— 1—Kansas City 1, New York 0, 1978.
Baltimore 1, California 0, 1979.
N. L.— 3—Pittsburgh 2, Los Angeles 1, 1974.
5-game Series—A. L.— 2—New York 2, Kansas City 0, 1976.
N. L.— 3—San Diego 2, Chicago 1, 1984.
6-game Series—N. L.— 3—St. Louis 2, Los Angeles 1, 1985.
Houston 2, New York 1, 1986.
7-game Series—A. L.— 4—Kansas City 4, Toronto 0, 1985.
N. L.— 8—St. Louis 5, San Francisco 3, 1987.

Most Sacrifice Hits, Game

N. L.— 3—Pittsburgh vs. Cincinnati, October 3, 1979; 10 innings.
Philadelphia vs. Houston, October 8, 1980; 10 innings.
Los Angeles vs. Montreal, October 17, 1981.
St. Louis vs. Atlanta, October 9, 1982.
A. L.— 3—California vs. Milwaukee, October 10, 1982.
California vs. Boston, October 12, 1986; 11 innings.

Most Sacrifice Hits, Game, Both Clubs

N. L.— 4—Pittsburgh 3, Cincinnati 1, October 3, 1979; 10 innings.
Los Angeles 3, Montreal 1, October 17, 1981.
St. Louis 2, Atlanta 2, October 9, 1982.
A. L.— 3—California 3, Milwaukee 0, October 10, 1982.
Boston 2, California 1, October 11, 1986; 11 innings.
California 3, Boston 0, October 12, 1986; 11 innings.

Most Sacrifice Hits, Inning

N. L.— 2—Philadelphia vs. Cincinnati, October 10, 1976; fourth inning.
A. L.— 1—Held by many clubs.

Sacrifice Flies

Most Sacrifice Flies, Total Series

A. L.— 10—Kansas City, 6 Series, 27 games.
N. L.— 9—Cincinnati; 6 Series, 22 games.

Most Sacrifice Flies, Series

3-game Series—N. L.— 3—Cincinnati vs. Pittsburgh, 1975.
Cincinnati vs. Philadelphia, 1976.
Pittsburgh vs. Cincinnati, 1979.
St. Louis vs. Atlanta, 1982.
A. L.— 2—Baltimore vs. Minnesota, 1970.
4-game Series—A. L.— 3—Baltimore vs. California, 1979.
Baltimore vs. Chicago, 1983.
N. L.— 1—Philadelphia vs. Los Angeles, 1978, 1983.
5-game Series—A. L.— 4—Kansas City vs. New York, 1976.
N. L.— 4—San Diego vs. Chicago, 1984.
6-game Series—N. L.— 3—New York vs. Houston, 1986.
7-game Series—N. L.— 4—St. Louis vs. San Francisco, 1987.
A. L.— 2—Toronto vs. Kansas City, 1985.
Kansas City vs. Toronto, 1985.
Boston vs. California, 1986.
California vs. Boston, 1986.

Most Sacrifice Flies, Series, Both Clubs

3-game Series—N. L.— 5—Cincinnati 3, Philadelphia 2, 1976.
A. L.— 2—Baltimore 2, Minnesota 0, 1970.

4-game Series—A. L.— 5—Baltimore 3, California 2, 1979.
N. L.— 1—Philadelphia 1, Los Angeles 0, 1978, 1983.
5-game Series—N. L.— 6—San Diego 4, Chicago 2, 1984.
A. L.— 5—Kansas City 4, New York 1, 1976.
Milwaukee 3, California 2, 1982.
6-game Series—N. L.— 3—New York 3, Houston 2, 1986.
7-game Series—N. L.— 5—St. Louis 4, San Francisco 1, 1987.
A. L.— 4—Kansas City 2, Toronto 2, 1985.
Boston 2, California 2, 1986.

Most Sacrifice Flies, Game

N. L.—3—St. Louis vs. Atlanta, October 7, 1982.
A. L.—2—Kansas City vs. New York, October 13, 1976.
California vs. Baltimore, October 4, 1979.
Milwaukee vs. California, October 8, 1982.
Baltimore vs. Chicago, October 7, 1983.
Detroit vs. Minnesota, October 7, 1987.

Most Sacrifice Flies, Game, Both Clubs

N. L.—3—St. Louis 3, Atlanta 0, October 7, 1982.
St. Louis 2, San Francisco 1, October 11, 1987.
A. L.—2—Occurred many times.

Most Sacrifice Flies, Inning

A. L.—2—Baltimore vs. Chicago, October 7, 1983; ninth inning.
Detroit vs. Minnesota, October 7, 1987; eighth inning.
N. L.—2—San Diego vs. Chicago, October 7, 1984; sixth inning.

Hit By Pitch

Most Hit by Pitch, Total Series

N. L.—7—Pittsburgh; 6 Series, 22 games.
A. L.—6—Oakland; 6 Series, 23 games.
Baltimore; 7 Series, 26 games.

Most Hit by Pitch, Series

3-game Series—A. L.— 2—New York vs. Oakland, 1981.
N. L.— 1—Atlanta vs. New York, 1969.
Pittsburgh vs. Cincinnati, 1975.
4-game Series—N. L.— 3—Philadelphia vs. Los Angeles, 1977.
A. L.— 3—Chicago vs. Baltimore, 1983.
5-game Series—A. L.— 5—Minnesota vs. Detroit, 1987.
N. L.— 2—Pittsburgh vs. Cincinnati, 1972.
Chicago vs. San Diego, 1984.
6-game Series—N. L.— 1—Houston vs. New York, 1986.
7-game Series—A. L.— 4—Toronto vs. Kansas City, 1985.
California vs. Boston, 1986.
N. L.— 2—San Francisco vs. St. Louis, 1987.

Most Hit by Pitch, Series, Both Clubs

3-game Series—A. L.— 2—New York 2, Oakland 0, 1981.
N. L.— 1—Atlanta 1, New York 0, 1969.
Pittsburgh 1, Cincinnati 0, 1975.
4-game Series—A. L.— 5—Oakland 3, Baltimore 2, 1983.
N. L.— 3—Pittsburgh 2, San Francisco 1, 1971.
Philadelphia 3, Los Angeles 0, 1977.
5-game Series—A. L.— 8—Minnesota 5, Detroit 3, 1987.
N. L.— 3—Chicago 2, San Diego 1, 1984.
6-game Series—N. L.— 1—Houston 1, New York 0, 1986.
7-game Series—A. L.— 7—California 4, Boston 3, 1986.
N. L.— 2—San Francisco 2, St. Louis 0, 1987.

Fewest Hit by Pitch, Series

A. L.-N. L.—0—Held by many clubs in Series of all lengths.

Fewest Hit by Pitch, Series, Both Clubs

A. L.-N. L.—0—Occurred in many Series.

Most Hit by Pitch, Game

A. L.—3—Minnesota vs. Detroit, October 11, 1987.
N. L.—1—Held by many clubs.

Most Hit by Pitch, Game, Both Clubs

A. L.—4—Detroit 2, Minnesota 2, October 12, 1987.
N. L.—2—Occurred in many games.

Most Hit by Pitch, Inning

A. L.-N. L.—1—Held by many clubs.

Individual Baserunning

Stolen Bases

Most Stolen Bases, Total Series

N. L.—9—Lopes, David E., Los Angeles, 1974, 1977, 1978, 1981; Chicago, 1984; Houston, 1986; 6 Series, 22 games.

A. L.—8—Otis, Amos J., Kansas City, 1976, 1977, 1978, 1980; 4 Series, 13 games.

Most Stolen Bases, Series

3-game Series—N. L.—4—Morgan, Joe L., Cincinnati, 1975.
A. L.—2—Beniquez, Juan J., Boston, 1975.
Otis, Amos J., Kansas City, 1980.
Henderson, Rickey H., Oakland, 1981.

4-game Series—A. L.—4—Otis, Amos J., Kansas City, 1978.
N. L.—3—Lopes, David E., Los Angeles, 1974.

5-game Series—N. L.—5—Lopes, David E., Los Angeles, 1981.
A. L.—3—Campaneris, Dagoberto B., Oakland, 1973.
Bush, R. Randall, Minnesota, 1987.
Gibson, Kirk H., Detroit, 1987.

6-game Series—N. L.—3—Hatcher, William A., Houston, 1986.

7-game Series—N. L.—2—Thompson, Robert R., San Francisco, 1987.
A. L.—1—Held by many players.

Most Stolen Bases, Games

N. L.—3—Morgan, Joe L., Cincinnati, October 4, 1975.
Griffey, G. Kenneth, Cincinnati, October 5, 1975.
A. L.—2—Held by many players.

Most Stolen Bases, Pinch-Runner, Game

A. L.—1—Edwards, Marshall L., Milwaukee, October 9, 1982.
N. L.—1—Johnson, K. Lance, St. Louis, October 9, 1987.

Most Times Stealing Home, Game

A. L.—1—Jackson, Reginald M., Oakland, October 12, 1972; second inning (front end of double steal).
N. L.—Never accomplished.

Most Stolen Bases, Inning

N. L.—2—Morgan, Joe L., Cincinnati, October 4, 1975; third inning.
Griffey, G. Kenneth, Cincinnati, October 5, 1975; sixth inning.
A. L.—2—Campaneris, Dagoberto B., Oakland, October 8, 1972; first inning.
Jackson, Reginald M., Oakland, October 12, 1972; second inning.
Beniquez, Juan J., Boston, October 4, 1975; seventh inning.
Bush, R. Randall, Minnesota, October 8, 1987; fourth inning.

Caught Stealing

Most Caught Stealing, Total Series

A. L.—6—McRae, Harold A., Kansas City, 1976, 1977, 1978, 1980, 1984, 1985; 6 Series, 28 games, 1 stolen base.
N. L.—4—McGee, Willie D., St. Louis, 1982, 1985, 1987; 3 Series, 16 games.
Coleman, Vincent M., St. Louis, 1985, 1987; 2 Series, 10 games.

Most Caught Stealing, Pinch-Runner, Total Series

A. L.—2—Washington, Herbert L., Oakland, 1974; 1 Series, 2 games.
N. L.—Never accomplished.

Most Caught Stealing, Series

3-game Series—A. L.—3—McRae, Harold A., Kansas City, 1980; 0 stolen bases.
N. L.—1—Held by many players.

4-game Series—A. L.—2—Blair, Paul L., Baltimore, 1974; 0 stolen bases.
Washington, Herbert L., Oakland, 1974; 0 stolen bases.
N. L.—2—Rose, Peter E., Philadelphia, 1980; 0 stolen bases.

5-game Series—A. L.—3—Patek, Freddie J., Kansas City, 1976; 0 stolen bases.
N. L.—2—Rose, Peter E., Philadelphia, 1980; 0 stolen bases.

6-game Series—N. L.—3—McGee, Willie D., St. Louis, 1985; 2 stolen bases.
Bass, Kevin C., Houston, 1986; 2 stolen bases.

7-game Series—A. L.—2—Pettis, Gary G., California, 1986; 0 stolen bases.
N. L.—2—Thompson, Robert R., San Francisco, 1987; 2 stolen bases.
Coleman, Vincent M., St. Louis, 1987; 1 stolen base.

Most Caught Stealing, Pinch-Runner, Series

A. L.—2—Washington, Herbert L., Oakland, 1974; 2 games.
N. L.—Never accomplished.

Most Caught Stealing, Game

A. L.—2—Robinson, Brooks C., Baltimore, October 4, 1969; 12 innings.
N. L.—2—Bass, Kevin C., Houston, October 15, 1986; 16 innings.
Nine-inning record—A. L.-N. L.—1—Held by many players.

Most Caught Stealing, Pinch-Runner, Game

A. L.—1—Washington, Herbert L., Oakland, October 6, 8, 1974.
Alomar, Santos, New York, October 14, 1976.
Concepcion, Onix, Kansas City, October 9, 1985.
N. L.—Never accomplished.

Most Caught Stealing, Inning

A. L.-N. L.—1—Held by many players.

Club Baserunning

Stolen Bases

Most Stolen Bases, Total Series

N. L.—25—Cincinnati; 6 Series, 22 games.
A. L.—21—Kansas City; 6 Series, 27 games.

Most Stolen Bases, Series

3-game Series—N. L.—11—Cincinnati vs. Pittsburgh, 1975.
A. L.—4—Detroit vs. Kansas City, 1984.

4-game Series—A. L.—6—Kansas City vs. New York, 1978.
N. L.—5—Los Angeles vs. Pittsburgh, 1974.

5-game Series—A. L.—7—Oakland vs. Detroit, 1972.
N. L.—7—Philadelphia vs. Houston, 1980.

6-game Series—N. L.—8—Houston vs. New York, 1986.

7-game Series—N. L.—5—San Francisco vs. St. Louis, 1987.
A. L.—2—Kansas City vs. Toronto, 1985.
Toronto vs. Kansas City, 1985.

Most Stolen Bases, Series, Both Clubs

3-game Series—N. L.—11—Cincinnati 11, Pittsburgh 0, 1975.
A. L.—4—New York 2, Oakland 2, 1981.
Detroit 4, Kansas City 0, 1984.

4-game Series—A. L.—7—Baltimore 5, California 2, 1979.
N. L.—6—Los Angeles 5, Pittsburgh 1, 1974.

5-game Series—A. L.—9—Kansas City 5, New York 4, 1976.
Detroit 5, Minnesota 4, 1987.
N. L.—11—Philadelphia 7, Houston 4, 1980.

6-game Series—N. L.—12—Houston 8, New York 4, 1986.

7-game Series—N. L.—9—San Francisco 5, St. Louis 4, 1987.
A. L.—4—Toronto 2, Kansas City 2, 1985.

Fewest Stolen Bases, Series

A. L.-N. L.—0—Held by many clubs in Series of all lengths.

Fewest Stolen Bases, Series, Both Clubs

3-game Series—A. L.—0—Baltimore 0, Oakland 0, 1971.
N. L.—1—Cincinnati 1, Pittsburgh 0, 1970.

4-game Series—N. L.— 2—Los Angeles 2, Philadelphia 0, 1978.
  A. L.— 3—Oakland 3, Baltimore 0, 1974.
5-game Series—N. L.— 0—Cincinnati 0, New York 0, 1973.
  A. L.— 3—Milwaukee 2, California 1, 1982.
6-game Series—N. L.— 10—St. Louis 6, Los Angeles 4, 1985.
7-game Series—A. L.— 2—Boston 1, California 1, 1986.
  N. L.— 9—San Francisco 5, St. Louis 4, 1987.

Most Stolen Bases, Game

N. L.—7—Cincinnati vs. Pittsburgh, October 5, 1975.
A. L.—3—Oakland vs. Detroit, October 12, 1972.
  Kansas City vs. New York, October 10, 1976.
  Detroit vs. Kansas City, October 5, 1984.

Most Stolen Bases, Game, Both Clubs

N. L.—7—Cincinnati 7, Pittsburgh 0, October 5, 1975.
A. L.—4—Detroit 2, Minnesota 2, October 8, 1987.

Longest Game, No Stolen Bases

N. L.—16 innings— New York vs. Houston, October 15, 1986.
A. L.—12 innings— Baltimore vs. Minnesota, October 4, 1969.

Longest Game, No Stolen Bases, Both Clubs

N. L.—12 innings— New York 0, Cincinnati 0, October 9, 1973.
A. L.—11 innings— Detroit 0, Oakland 0, October 7, 1972.
  Baltimore 0, Oakland 0, October 9, 1973.
  Boston 0, California 0, October 11, 1986.
  Boston 0, California 0, October 12, 1986.

Most Stolen Bases, Inning

A. L.—3—Oakland vs. Detroit, October 12, 1972; second inning.
N. L.—2—Held by many clubs.

Caught Stealing

Most Caught Stealing, Series

3-game Series—A. L.— 5—Kansas City vs. New York, 1980.
  N. L.—2—Pittsburgh vs. Cincinnati, 1970.
  Cincinnati vs. Pittsburgh, 1979.
  Atlanta vs. St. Louis, 1982.
4-game Series—A. L.— 3—Oakland vs. Baltimore, 1974.
  Baltimore vs. Oakland, 1974.
  Kansas City vs. New York, 1978.
  N. L.—2—Los Angeles vs. Philadelphia, 1983.
5-game Series—A. L.— 5—Kansas City vs. New York, 1976.
  N. L.—3—Philadelphia vs. Houston, 1980.
  Chicago vs. San Diego, 1984.
6-game Series—N. L.— 6—St. Louis vs. Los Angeles, 1985.
7-game Series—A. L.— 4—Kansas City vs. Toronto, 1985.
  California vs. Boston, 1986.
  N. L.—4—San Francisco vs. St. Louis, 1987.
  St. Louis vs. San Francisco, 1987.

Most Caught Stealing, Series, Both Clubs

3-game Series—A. L.— 5—Kansas City 5, New York 0, 1980.
  N. L.—3—Pittsburgh 2, Cincinnati 1, 1970.
4-game Series—A. L.— 6—Oakland 3, Baltimore 3, 1974.
  N. L.—3—Los Angeles 2, Philadelphia 1, 1983.
5-game Series—A. L.— 8—Kansas City 5, New York 3, 1976.
  N. L.—5—Chicago 3, San Diego 2, 1984.
6-game Series—N. L.— 7—St. Louis 6, Los Angeles 1, 1985.
7-game Series—A. L.— 8—San Francisco 4, St. Louis 4, 1987.
  A. L.—6—Kansas City 4, Toronto 2, 1985.

Fewest Caught Stealing, Series

A. L.-N. L.—0—By many clubs in Series of all lengths.

Fewest Caught Stealing, Series, Both Clubs

3-game Series—N. L.— 0—Cincinnati 0, Pittsburgh 0, 1975.
  A. L.—0—Baltimore 0, Minnesota 0, 1970.
  Boston 0, Oakland 0, 1975.
4-game Series—N. L.— 0—Los Angeles 0, Pittsburgh 0, 1974.
  A. L.—1—Chicago 1, Baltimore 0, 1983.
5-game Series—N. L.— 1—Cincinnati 1, New York 0, 1973.
  Montreal 1, Los Angeles 0, 1981.
  A. L.—1—Minnesota 1, Detroit 0, 1987.
6-game Series—N. L.— 3—Houston 3, New York 0, 1986.
7-game Series—A. L.— 4—California 4, Boston 0, 1986.
  N. L.—8—San Francisco 4, St. Louis 4, 1987.

Most Caught Stealing, Game

A. L.-N. L.—2—Held by many clubs.

Most Caught Stealing, Game, Both Clubs

A. L.—3—Baltimore 2, Oakland 1, October 10, 1973.
  Kansas City 2, New York 1, October 12, 1976.
  Milwaukee 2, California 1, October 9, 1982.
N. L.—3—Chicago 2, San Diego 1, October 7, 1984.
  St. Louis 2, Los Angeles 1, October 12, 1985.

Most Caught Stealing, Inning

N. L.—2—St. Louis vs. Los Angeles, October 10, 1985, first inning.
  St. Louis vs. Los Angeles, October 12, 1985, second inning.
A. L.— 1—Held by many clubs.

Left On Base

Most Left on Bases, Total Series

N. L.— 198— Los Angeles; 6 Series, 27 games.
A. L.— 166— Baltimore; 7 Series, 26 games.

Most Left on Bases, Series

3-game Series—N. L.—31—St. Louis vs. Atlanta, 1982.
  A. L.—30—New York vs. Oakland, 1981.
4-game Series—N. L.—44—Los Angeles vs. Pittsburgh, 1974.
  A. L.—35—Chicago vs. Baltimore, 1983.
5-game Series—N. L.—45—Houston vs. Philadelphia, 1980.
  A. L.—41—New York vs. Kansas City, 1976.
6-game Series—N. L.—51—St. Louis vs. Los Angeles, 1985.
7-game Series—A. L.—60—California vs. Boston, 1986.
  N. L.—43—San Francisco vs. St. Louis, 1987.

Most Left on Bases, Series, Both Clubs

3-game Series—A. L.— 50—Baltimore 28, Minnesota 22, 1969.
  New York 30, Oakland 20, 1981.
  N. L.— 49—Cincinnati 25, Pittsburgh 24, 1979.
4-game Series—N. L.— 68—Los Angeles 44, Pittsburgh 24, 1974.
  A. L.— 59—Chicago 35, Baltimore 24, 1983.
5-game Series—N. L.— 88—Houston 45, Philadelphia 43, 1980.
  A. L.— 74—Detroit 37, Minnesota 37, 1987.
6-game Series—N. L.— 91—St. Louis 51, Los Angeles 40, 1985.
7-game Series—A. L.— 108—California 60, Boston 48, 1986.
  N. L.— 80—San Francisco 43, St. Louis 37, 1987.

Fewest Left on Bases, Series

3-game Series—N. L.— 12—Atlanta vs. St. Louis, 1982.
  A. L.— 14—Boston vs. Oakland, 1975.
4-game Series—A. L.— 16—Baltimore vs. Oakland, 1974.
  N. L.— 22—Los Angeles vs. Philadelphia, 1977.
5-game Series—A. L.— 22—Kansas City vs. New York, 1976.
  N. L.— 24—Pittsburgh vs. Cincinnati, 1972.
6-game Series—N. L.— 36—New York vs. Houston, 1986.
7-game Series—N. L.— 37—St. Louis vs. San Francisco, 1987.
  A. L.—44—Kansas City vs. Toronto, 1985.

Fewest Left on Bases, Series, Both Clubs

3-game Series—A. L.— 33—Oakland 19, Boston 14, 1975.
  N. L.— 38—Pittsburgh 21, Cincinnati 17, 1975.
4-game Series—A. L.— 45—Baltimore 23, California 22, 1979.
  N. L.— 52—Los Angeles 28, Philadelphia 24, 1978.
5-game Series—N. L.— 54—Cincinnati 30, Pittsburgh 24, 1972.
  A. L.— 62—New York 34, Kansas City 28, 1977.
6-game Series—N. L.— 75—Houston 39, New York 36, 1986.
7-game Series—N. L.— 80—San Francisco 43, St. Louis 37, 1987.
  A. L.— 94—Toronto 50, Kansas City 44, 1985.

Most Left on Bases, Game

N. L.— 14— Philadelphia vs. Houston, October 8, 1980; 10 innings.
N. L.—Nine-inning record—13—Los Angeles vs. Pittsburgh, October 5, 1974.
A. L.— 13— Baltimore vs. Oakland, October 5, 1971.

Most Left on Bases, Game, Both Clubs

N. L.— 22— Philadelphia 14, Houston 8, October 8, 1980; 10 innings.
N. L.—Nine-inning record—20—Cincinnati 10, New York 10, October 10, 1973.
  Los Angeles 13, Pittsburgh 7, October 5, 1974.
  Los Angeles 12, Pittsburgh 8, October 6, 1974.
  St. Louis 11, Los Angeles 9, October 12, 1985.
A. L.— 21— Baltimore 12, Oakland 9, October 6, 1973.
  New York 12, Kansas City 9, October 3, 1978.
  Chicago 11, Baltimore 10, October 8, 1983; 10 innings.
  Minnesota 12, Detroit 9, October 12, 1987.

Fewest Left on Bases, Game

N. L.— 1—Pittsburgh vs. Cincinnati, October 7, 1972.
Pittsburgh vs. Los Angeles, October 9, 1974.
San Diego vs. Chicago, October 4, 1984.
A. L.— 2—Detroit vs. Oakland, October 8, 1972.
Kansas City vs. New York, October 9, 1976.
New York vs. Kansas City, October 6, 1978.

Fewest Left on Bases, Game, Both Clubs

A. L.— 6—Oakland 4, Detroit 2, October 8, 1972.
N. L.— 6—Chicago 5, San Diego 1, October 4, 1984.
Houston 3, New York 3, October 12, 1986.

Most Left on Bases, Shutout Defeat

A. L.— 11—Chicago vs. Baltimore, October 8, 1983 (lost 3-0 in 10 innings).

A. L.—Nine-inning record—10—Oakland vs. Detroit, October 10, 1972 (lost 3-0).
N. L.— 11—Philadelphia vs. Houston, October 10, 1980 (lost 1-0 in 11 innings).
N. L.—Nine-inning record—10—Los Angeles vs. Pittsburgh, October 8, 1974 (lost 7-0).
San Diego vs. Chicago, October 2, 1984 (lost 13-0).

Most Left on Bases, Two Consecutive Games

N. L.— 25—Los Angeles vs. Pittsburgh, October 5 (13), October 6 (12), 1974.
A. L.— 23—Minnesota vs. Detroit, October 11 (11), October 12 (12), 1987.

Individual Pitching

Service
Series & Games

Most Series Pitched

A. L.—6—Hunter, James, A., Oakland, 1971, 1972, 1973, 1974; New York, 1976, 1978; 10 games.
Palmer, James A., Baltimore, 1969, 1970, 1971, 1973, 1974, 1979; 8 games.
Both Leagues—6—Gullett, Donald E., Cincinnati NL, 1970, 1972, 1973, 1975, 1976, 9 games; New York AL, 1977; 1 game.
N. L.—6—McGraw, Frank E., New York, 1969, 1973; Philadelphia, 1976, 1977, 1978, 1980; 15 games.
Reed, Ronald L., Atlanta, 1969; Philadelphia, 1976, 1977, 1978, 1980, 1983; 13 games.

Most Games Pitched, Total Series

N. L.— 15—McGraw, Frank E., New York, 1969, 1973; Philadelphia, 1976, 1977, 1978, 1980; 6 Series.
A. L.— 11—Fingers, Roland G., Oakland, 1971, 1972, 1973, 1974, 1975; 5 Series.

Most Games Pitched, Series

3-game Series—N. L.—3—Upshaw, Cecil L., Atlanta, 1969.
Tomlin, David A., Cincinnati, 1979.
Hume, Thomas H., Cincinnati, 1979.
A. L.—3—Perranoski, Ronald P., Minnesota, 1969.
Todd, James, R., Oakland, 1975.
Hernandez, Guillermo, Detroit, 1984.
4-game Series—N. L.—4—Giusti, J. David, Pittsburgh, 1971.
A. L.—3—Hrabosky, Alan T., Kansas City, 1978.
Stanhouse, Donald J., Baltimore, 1979.
Lamp, Dennis P., Chicago, 1983.
5-game Series—N. L.—5—McGraw, Frank E., Philadelphia, 1980.
A. L.—4—Blue, Vida R., Oakland, 1972.
Lyle, Albert W., New York, 1977.
Berenguer, Juan B., Minnesota, 1987.
Reardon, Jeffrey J., Minnesota, 1987.
6-game Series—N. L.—5—Dayley, Kenneth G., St. Louis, 1985.
7-game Series—A. L.—4—Quisenberry, Daniel R., Kansas City, 1985.
Lucas, Gary P., California, 1986.
Schiraldi, Calvin D., Boston, 1986.
N. L.—3—Held by many pitchers.

Most Consecutive Games Pitched, Series

N. L.—5—McGraw, Frank E., Philadelphia, October 7, 8, 10, 11, 12, 1980.
A. L.—4—Berenguer, Juan B., Minnesota, October 8, 10, 11, 12, 1987.

Youngest & Oldest Pitchers

Youngest Championship Series Pitcher

A. L.—Blyleven, Rikalbert, Minnesota; 19 years, 5 months, 29 days on October 5, 1970.
N. L.—Gullett, Donald E., Cincinnati; 19 years, 8 months, 28 days on October 4, 1970.

Oldest Championship Series Pitcher

N. L.—Niekro, Philip H., Atlanta; 43 years, 6 months, 8 days on October 9, 1982.

A. L.—Sutton, Donald H., California; 41 years, 6 months, 13 days on October 15, 1986.

Games Started

Most Games Started, Total Series

A. L.— 10—Hunter, James A., Oakland, 1971, 1972, 1973, 1974; New York, 1976, 1978; 6 Series.
N. L.— 8— Carlton, Steven N., Philadelphia, 1976, 1977, 1978, 1980, 1983; 5 Series.

Most Opening Games Started, Total Series

Both Leagues—4—Gullett, Donald E., Cincinnati NL, 1972, 1975, 1976; New York AL, 1977; won 2, lost 2.
N. L.—4—Carlton, Steven N., Philadelphia, 1976, 1977, 1980, 1983; won 2, lost 1, no decision 1.
A. L.—3—Cuellar, Miguel, Baltimore, 1969, 1970, 1974; won 1 lost 0, no decision 2.
Hunter, James A., Oakland, 1972, 1974; New York, 1976; won 1, lost 1, no decision 1.

Most Games Started, Series

3-game Series—A. L.—2—Holtzman, Kenneth D., Oakland, 1975.
N. L.—1—Held by many pitchers.
4-game Series—A. L.-N. L.—2—Held by many pitchers.
5-game Series—A. L.-N. L.—2—Held by many pitchers.
6-game Series—A. L.-N. L.—2—Held by many pitchers.
7-game Series—A. L.—3—Stieb, David A., Toronto, 1985.
Clemens, W. Roger, Boston, 1986.
N. L.—2—Held by many pitchers.

Games Relieved & Finished

Most Games, Total Series, Relief Pitcher

N. L.— 15—McGraw, Frank E., New York, Philadelphia, 1969, 1973, 1976, 1977, 1978, 1980; 27 innings.
A. L.— 11—Fingers, Roland G., Oakland, 1971, 1972, 1973, 1974, 1975; 19 ⅓ innings.

Most Series, One or More Games as Relief Pitcher

N. L.—6—McGraw, Frank E., New York, Philadelphia, 1969, 1973, 1976, 1977, 1978, 1980; 15 games as relief pitcher.
A. L.—5—Fingers, Roland G., Oakland, 1971, 1972, 1973, 1974, 1975, 11 games as relief pitcher.

Most Games, Series, Relief Pitcher

3-game Series—N. L.—3—Upshaw, Cecil L., Atlana, 1969.
Tomlin, David A., Cincinnati, 1979.
Hume, Thomas H., Cincinnati, 1979.
A. L.—3—Perranoski, Ronald P., Minnesota, 1969.
Todd, James R., Oakland, 1975.
Hernandez, Guillermo, Detroit, 1984.
4-game Series—N. L.—4—Giusti, J. David, Pittsburgh, 1971.
A. L.—3—Hrabosky, Alan T., Kansas City, 1978.
Stanhouse, Donald J., Baltimore, 1979.
Lamp, Dennis P., Chicago, 1983.
5-game Series—N. L.—5—McGraw, Frank E., Philadelphia, 1980.
A. L.—4—Blue, Vida R., Oakland, 1972.
Lyle, Albert W., New York, 1977.
Berenguer, Juan B., Minnesota, 1987.
Reardon, Jeffrey J., Minnesota, 1987.
6-game Series—N. L.—5—Dayley, Kenneth G., St. Louis, 1985.

7-game Series—A. L.—4—Quisenberry, Daniel R., Kansas City, 1985.
Lucas, Gary P., California, 1986.
Schiraldi, Calvin D., Boston, 1986.
N. L.—3—Held by many pitchers.

Most Games Finished, Total Series

N. L.—9—Giusti, J. David, Pittsburgh, 1970, 1971, 1972, 1974, 1975; 5 Series, 13 games.
McGraw, Frank E., New York, Philadelphia, 1969, 1973, 1976, 1977, 1978, 1980; 6 Series, 15 games.
A. L.—8—Fingers, Roland G., Oakland, 1971, 1972, 1973, 1974, 1975; 5 Series, 11 games.

Most Games Finished, Series

3-game Series—A. L.—3—Perranoski, Ronald P., Minnesota, 1969.
N. L.—2—Held by many pitchers.
4-game Series—N. L.—4—Giusti, J. David, Pittsburgh, 1971.
A. L.—3—Stanhouse, Donald J., Baltimore, 1979.
Lamp, Dennis P., Chicago, 1983.
5-game Series—A. L.—4—Lyle, Albert W., New York, 1977.
Reardon, Jeffrey J., Minnesota, 1987.
N. L.—4—Borbon, Pedro R., Cincinnati, 1973.
6-game Series—N. L.—4—Orosco, Jesse, New York, 1986.
7-game Series—A. L.—4—Quisenberry, Daniel R., Kansas City, 1985.
Schiraldi, Calvin D., Boston, 1986.
N. L.—3—Dayley, Kenneth G., St. Louis, 1987.

Complete Games

Most Complete Games Pitched, Total Series

A. L.—5—Palmer, James A., Baltimore, 1969, 1970, 1971, 1973, 1974.
N. L.—2—Sutton, Donald H., Los Angeles, 1974, 1977.
John, Thomas E., Los Angeles, 1977, 1978.
Scott, Michael W., Houston, 1986 (2).
Cox, Danny B., St. Louis, 1987 (2).

Most Consecutive Complete Games Pitched, Total Series

A. L.—4—Palmer, James A., Baltimore, 1969 (1), 1970 (1), 1971 (1), 1973 (1); won 4, lost 0.
N. L.—2—John, Thomas E., Los Angeles, 1977 (1), 1978 (1); won 2, lost 0.
Scott, Michael W., Houston, 1986 (2); won 2, lost 0.
Cox, Danny B., St. Louis, 1987 (2); won 1, lost 1.

Most Complete Games, Series

N. L.—2—Scott, Michael W., Houston, 1986; 6-game Series.
Cox, Danny B., St. Louis, 1987; 7-game Series.
A. L.—1—Held by many pitchers.

Innings

Most Innings Pitched, Total Series

A. L.—69 ⅓—Hunter, James A., Oakland, 1971, 1972, 1973, 1974; New York, 1976, 1978; 6 Series, 10 games.
N. L.—53 ⅔—Carlton, Steven N., Philadelphia, 1976, 1977, 1978, 1980, 1983; 5 Series, 8 games.

Most Innings Pitched, Series

3-game Series—A. L.—11—McNally, David A., Baltimore, 1969.
Holtzman, Kenneth D., Oakland, 1975.
N. L.—9 ⅔—Ellis, Dock P., Pittsburgh, 1970.
4-game Series—N. L.—17—Sutton, Donald H., Los Angeles, 1974.
A. L.—12 ⅔—Cuellar, Miguel, Baltimore, 1974.
5-game Series—A. L.—19—Lolich, Michael S., Detroit, 1972.
N. L.—17—Burris, B. Ray, Montreal, 1981.
6-game Series—N.L.—18—Scott, Michael W., Houston, 1986.
7-game Series—A.L.—22 ⅔—Clemens, W. Roger, Boston, 1986.
N. L.—17—Cox, Danny B., St. Louis, 1987.

Most Innings Pitched, Game

A. L.—11—McNally, David A., Baltimore, October 5, 1969, complete game, won 1-0.
Holtzman, Kenneth D., Oakland, October 9, 1973, complete game, won 2-1.
N. L.—10—Niekro, Joseph F., Houston, October 10, 1980, incomplete game, no decision.
Gooden, Dwight E., New York, October 14, 1986, incomplete game, no decision.

Games Won

Most Games Won, Total Series

Both Leagues—4—Kison, Bruce E., Pittsburgh NL, 1971, 1972, 1974, 1975; California AL, 1982; won 4, lost 0, 5 Series, 7 games.
John, Thomas E., Los Angeles NL, 1977, 1978; New York AL, 1980, 1981; California AL, 1982; won 4, lost 1, 5 Series, 7 games.
Sutton, Donald H., Los Angeles NL, 1974, 1977, 1978; Milwaukee AL, 1982; won 4, lost 1, 4 Series, 5 games.
A. L.—4—Palmer, James A., Baltimore, 1969, 1970, 1971, 1973, 1974, 1979; won 4, lost 1, 6 Series, 8 games.
Hunter, James A., Oakland, 1971, 1972, 1973, 1974; New York 1976, 1978; won 4, lost 3, 6 Series, 10 games.
N. L.—4—Carlton, Steven N., Philadelphia, 1976, 1977, 1978, 1980, 1983; won 4, lost 2, 5 Series, 8 games.

Most Games Won, Total Series, No Defeats

Both Leagues—4—Kison, Bruce E., Pittsburgh NL, 1971, 1972, 1974, 1975; California AL, 1982.
N. L.—3—Kison, Bruce W., Pittsburgh, 1971, 1972, 1974.
Orosco, Jesse, New York, 1986 (3).
A. L.—2—Hall, Richard W., Baltimore, 1969, 1970.
Odom, Johnny L., Oakland, 1972 (2).
Splittorff, Paul W., Kansas City, 1976, 1977.
Lyle, Albert W., New York, 1977 (2).
Flanagan, Michael K., Baltimore, 1979, 1983.
Blyleven, Rikalbert, Minnesota, 1987 (2).

Most Opening Games Won, Total Series

N. L.—2—Gullett, Donald E., Cincinnati, 1975, 1976.
Carlton, Steven N., Philadelphia, 1980, 1983.
A. L.—2—Hall, Richard W., Baltimore, 1969, 1970.
John, Thomas E., New York, 1981; California, 1982.

Most Consecutive Games Won, Total Series

Both Leagues—4—Kison, Bruce E., Pittsburgh NL, October 6, 1971; October 9, 1972; October 8, 1974; California AL, October 6, 1982; one complete, three incomplete.
John, Thomas E., Los Angeles NL, October 8, 1977; October 5, 1978; New York AL, October 13, 1981; California AL, October 5, 1982; three complete, one incomplete.
A. L.—4—Palmer, James A., Baltimore, October 6, 1969; October 5, 1970; October 5, 1971; October 6, 1973; all complete.
N. L.—4—Carlton, Steven N., Philadelphia, October 6, 1978; October 7, 1980; October 4, 1983; October 8, 1983; one complete, three incomplete.

Most Consecutive Complete Games Won, Total Series

A. L.—4—Palmer, James A., Baltimore, October 6, 1969; October 5, 1970; October 5, 1971; October 6, 1973.
N. L.—2—John, Thomas E., Los Angeles, October 8, 1977; October 5, 1978.
Scott, Michael W., October 8, 12, 1986.

Most Games Won, Series

3-game Series—A. L.—N. L.—1—Held by many pitchers.
4-game Series—N. L.—2—Sutton, Donald H., Los Angeles, 1974.
Carlton, Steven N., Philadelphia, 1983.
A. L.—1—Held by many pitchers.
5-game Series—A. L.—2—Odom, Johnny L., Oakland, 1972.
Hunter, James A., Oakland, 1973.
Lyle, Albert W., New York, 1977.
N. L.—2—Hooton, Burt C., Los Angeles, 1981.
Lefferts, Craig L., San Diego, 1984.
6-game Series—N. L.—3—Orosco, Jesse, New York, 1986.
7-game Series—A. L.—2—Henke, Thomas A., Toronto, 1985.
N. L.—1—Held by many pitchers.

Most Games Won, Series, As Relief Pitcher

N. L.—3—Orosco, Jesse, New York, 1986; 6-game Series.
A. L.—2—Lyle, Albert W., New York, 1977; 5-game Series.
Henke, Thomas A., Toronto, 1985; 7-game Series.
Reardon, Jeffrey J., Minnesota, 1987; 5-game Series.

Saves

Most Saves, Total Series

N. L.—5—McGraw, Frank E., New York, 1969, 1973; Philadelphia, 1977, 1980 (2).

A. L.—2—Fingers, Roland G., Oakland, 1973, 1974.
Drago, Richard A., Boston, 1975 (2).
Gossage, Richad M., New York, 1978, 1981.
Ladd, Peter L., Milwaukee, 1982.
Quisenberry, Daniel R., Kansas City, 1985.
Reardon, Jeffrey J., Minnesota, 1987.

Most Saves, Series

3-game Series—A. L.—2—Drago, Richard A., Boston, 1975.
N. L.—2—Gullett, Donald E., Cincinnati, 1970.
4-game Series—N. L.—3—Giusti, J. David, Pittsburgh, 1971.
A. L.—1—Held by many pitchers.
5-game Series—N. L.—2—McGraw, Frank E., Philadelphia, 1980.
A. L.—2—Ladd, Peter L., Milwaukee, 1982.
Reardon, Jeffrey J., Minnesota, 1987.
6-game Series—N. L.—2—Dayley, Kenneth G., St. Louis, 1985.
7-game Series—N. L.—2—Dayley, Kenneth G., St. Louis, 1987.
A. L.—1—Held by many pitchers.

Games Lost

Most Games Lost, Total Series

N. L.—7—Reuss, Jerry, Pittsburgh, 1974, 1975; Los Angeles, 1981, 1983, 1985; won 0, 5 Series, 7 games.
A. L.—4—Alexander, Doyle L., Baltimore, 1973; Toronto, 1985; Detroit, 1987; won 0, 3 Series, 5 games.

Most Games Lost, Total Series, No Victories

N. L.—7—Reuss, Jerry, Pittsburgh, 1974 (2), 1975; Los Angeles, 1981, 1983 (2), 1985.
A. L.—4—Alexander, Doyle L., Baltimore, 1973; Toronto, 1985; Detroit, 1987 (2).

Most Consecutive Games Lost, Total Series

N. L.—7—Reuss, Jerry, Pittsburgh, 1974 (2), 1975; Los Angeles, 1981, 1983 (2), 1985.
A. L.—4—Alexander, Doyle L., Baltimore, 1973; Toronto, 1985; Detroit, 1987 (2).

Most Games Lost, Series

3-game Series—A. L.—2—Holtzman, Kenneth D., Oakland, 1975.
N. L.—1—Held by many pitchers.
4-game Series—A. L.—2—Leonard, Dennis P., Kansas City, 1978.
N. L.—2—Reuss, Jerry, Pittsburgh, 1974.
Reuss, Jerry, Los Angeles, 1983.
5-game Series—A. L.—2—Fryman, Woodrow T., Detroit, 1972.
Alexander, Doyle L., Detroit, 1987.
N. L.—2—Gullickson, William L., Montreal, 1981.
6-game Series—N. L.—2—Niedenfuer, Thomas E., Los Angeles, 1985.
7-game Series—A. L.—2—Leibrandt, Charles L., Kansas City, 1985.
McCaskill, Kirk E., California, 1986.

Runs

Most Runs Allowed, Total Series

A. L.—25—Hunter, James A., Oakland, 1971, 1972, 1973, 1974; New York, 1976, 1978; 6 Series, 10 games.
N. L.—25—Reuss, Jerry, Pittsburgh, 1974, 1975; Los Angeles, 1981, 1983, 1985; 5 Series, 7 games.

Most Runs Allowed, Series

3-game Series—A. L.—9—Perry, James E., Minnesota, 1970.
N. L.—9—Niekro, Philip H., Atlanta, 1969.
4-game Series—N. L.—11—Perry, Gaylord J., San Francisco, 1971.
A. L.—10—Frost, C. David, California, 1979.
5-game Series—A. L.—10—Alexander, Doyle L., Detroit, 1987.
N. L.—8—Gullett, Donald E., Cincinnati, 1972.
Ryan, L. Nolan, Houston, 1980.
Harris, Greg A., San Diego, 1984.
Show, Eric V., San Diego, 1984.
6-game Series—N. L.—10—Andujar, Joaquin, St. Louis, 1985.
7-game Series—A. L.—13—McCaskill, Kirk E., California, 1986.
N. L.—8—Reuschel, Ricky E., San Francisco, 1987.

Most Runs Allowed, Game

N. L.—9—Niekro, Philip H., Atlanta, October 4, 1969.
A. L.—8—Perry, James E., Minnesota, October 3, 1970.
Clemens, W. Roger, Boston, October 7, 1986.

Most Runs Allowed, Inning

N. L.—7—Reuss, Jerry, Los Angeles, October 13, 1985; second inning.

A. L.—6—Perry, James E., Minnesota, October 3, 1970; fourth inning.

Earned Runs

Most Earned Runs Allowed, Total Series

A. L.—25—Hunter, James A., Oakland, 1971, 1972, 1973, 1974; New York, 1976, 1978; 6 Series, 10 games.
N. L.—21—Carlton, Steven N., Philadelphia, 1976, 1977, 1978, 1980, 1983; 5 Series, 8 games.

Most Earned Runs Allowed, Series

3-game Series—A. L.—8—Perry, James E., Minnesota, 1970.
N. L.—6—Koosman, Jerry M., New York, 1969.
Jarvis, R. Patrick, Atlanta, 1969.
4-game Series—N. L.—10—Perry, Gaylord J., San Francisco, 1971.
A. L.—9—Frost, C. David, California, 1979.
5-game Series—A. L.—10—Alexander, Doyle L., Detroit, 1987.
N. L.—8—Gullett, Donald E., Cincinnati, 1972.
Ryan, L. Nolan, Houston, 1980.
Show, Eric V., San Diego, 1984.
6-game Series—N. L.—8—Andujar, Joaquin, St. Louis, 1985.
7-game Series—A. L.—11—Clemens, W. Roger, Boston, 1986.
N. L.—7—Reuschel, Ricky E., San Francisco, 1987.
Hammaker, C. Atlee, San Francisco, 1987.

Most Earned Runs Allowed, Game

A. L.—7—Perry, James E., Minnesota, October 3, 1970.
Clemens, W. Roger, Boston, October 7, 1986.
N. L.—7—Perry, Gaylord J., San Francisco, October 6, 1971.
Harris, Greg A., San Diego, October 2, 1984.

Most Earned Runs Allowed, Inning

A. L.—6—Perry, James E., Minnesota, October 3, 1970; fourth inning.
N. L.—6—Harris, Greg A., San Diego, October 2, 1984; fifth inning.

Shutouts & Scoreless Innings

Most Shutouts, Series

A. L.-N. L.—1—Held by many pitchers.

Most Consecutive Scoreless Innings, Total Series

A. L.—18—Holtzman, Kenneth D., Oakland, October 9, 1973 (9 innings); October 6, 1974 (9 innings).
N. L.—16—Scott, Michael W., Houston, October 8, 1986 (9 innings); October 12, 1986 (7 innings).
Dravecky, David F., San Diego, October 3, 1984 (2 innings); October 6, 1984 (2 innings); October 7, 1984 (2 innings); San Francisco, October 7, 1987 (9 innings); October 13, 1987 (1 inning).

Most Consecutive Scoreless Innings, Series

N. L.—16—Scott, Michael W., Houston, October 8, 12, 1986.
A. L.—11—McNally, David A., Baltimore, October 5, 1969.

Hits

Most Hits Allowed, Total Series

A. L.—57—Hunter, James A., Oakland, 1971, 1972, 1973, 1974; New York, 1976, 1978; 6 Series, 10 games.
N. L.—53—Carlton, Steven N., Philadelphia, 1976, 1977, 1978, 1980, 1983; 5 Series, 8 games.

Most Consecutive Hitless Innings, Total Series

A. L.—10—McNally, David A., Baltimore, October 5 (7 innings), 1969; October 4 (3 innings), 1970.
N. L.—6—Billingham, John E., Cincinnati, October 6 (6 innings), 1973.

Most Hits Allowed, Series

3-game Series—A. L.—12—Holtzman, Kenneth D., Oakland, 1975.
N. L.—10—Jarvis, R. Patrick, Atlanta, 1969.
4-game Series—N. L.—19—Perry, Gaylord J., San Francisco, 1971.
A. L.—13—Leonard, Dennis P., Kansas City, 1978.
5-game Series—A. L.—18—Gura, Lawrence C., Kansas City, 1976.
N. L.—16—Ryan, L. Nolan, Houston, 1980.
6-game Series—N. L.—17—Hershiser, Orel L., Los Angeles, 1985.
7-game Series—A. L.—22—Clemens, W. Roger, Boston, 1986.
N. L.—17—Cox, Danny B., St. Louis, 1987.

Most Hits Allowed, Game

A. L.—12—Gura, Lawrence C., Kansas City, October 9, 1976.

N. L.— 10— Jarvis, R. Patrick, Atlanta, October 6, 1969.
   Perry, Gaylord J., San Francisco, October 6, 1971.
   Hooton, Burt C., Los Angeles, October 4, 1978.
   Ojeda, Robert M., New York, October 9, 1986.
   Tudor, John T., St. Louis, October 7, 1987.

Most Consecutive Hitless Innings, Game

A. L.—7—McNally, David A., Baltimore, October 5, 1969; 11-inning
   game.
N. L.—6—Billingham, John E., Cincinnati, October 6, 1973.

Fewest Hits Allowed Game, Nine Innings

A. L.—2—Blue, Vida R., Oakland, October 8, 1974.
N. L.—2—Grimsley, Ross A., Cincinnati, October 10, 1972.
   Matlack, Jonathan T., New York, October 7, 1973.
   Dravecky, David F., San Francisco, October 7, 1987.

Most Hits Allowed, Inning

A. L.—6—Perry, James E., Minnesota, October 3, 1970; fourth inning.
   McCaskill, Kirk E., California, October 14, 1986; third in-
   ning.
N. L.—6—Harris, Greg A., San Diego, October 2, 1984; fifth inning.

Most Consecutive Hits Allowed, Inning (Consecutive At-Bats)

A. L.—6—Perry, James E., Minnesota, October 3, 1970; fourth inning
   (sacrifice fly during streak).
N. L.—5—Moose, Robert R., Pittsburgh, October 8, 1972; first inning.

Most Consecutive Hits Allowed, Inning (Cons. Plate Appearances)

N. L.—5—Moose, Robert R., Pittsburgh, October 8, 1972; first inning.
A. L.—5—Beard, C. David, Oakland, October 14, 1981; fourth inning.

Doubles, Triples & Home Runs

Most Doubles Allowed, Game

N. L.—4—Seaver, G. Thomas, New York, October 4, 1969.
A. L.—4—McNally, David A., Baltimore, October 3, 1971.
   Blue, Vida R., Oakland, October 3, 1971.

Most Triples Allowed, Game

A. L.—2—Figueroa, Eduardo, New York, October 8, 1977.
N. L.—2—Carlton, Steven N., Philadelphia, October 9, 1976.
   Christenson, Larry R., Philadelphia, October 4, 1978.

Most Home Runs Allowed, Total Series

A. L.— 12—Hunter, James A., Oakland, 1971 (4), 1972 (2), 1974
   (3), New York, 1978 (3).
N. L.— 6—Blass, Stephen R., Pittsburgh, 1971 (4), 1972 (2).

Most Home Runs Allowed, Series

3-game Series—A. L.—4—Hunter, James A., Oakland, 1971.
   N. L.—3—Jarvis, R. Patrick, Atlanta, 1969.
4-game Series—N. L.—4—Blass, Stephen R., Pittsburgh, 1971.
   A. L.—3—Hunter, James A., Oakland, 1974; New
   York, 1978.
5-game Series—N. L.—5—Show, Eric V., San Diego, 1984.
   A. L.—4—McNally, David A., Baltimore, 1973.
6-game Series—N. L.—2—Andujar, Joaquin, St. Louis, 1985.
   Niedenfuer, Thomas E., Los Angeles,
   1985.
   Fernandez, C. Sidney, New York, 1986.
7-game Series—A. L.—4—Alexander, Doyle L., Toronto, 1985.
   N. L.—3—Cox, Danny B., St. Louis, 1987.

Most Home Runs Allowed, Game

A. L.—4—Hunter, James A., Oakland, October 4, 1971.
   McNally, David A., Baltimore, October 7, 1973.
N. L.—3—Jarvis, R. Patrick, Atlanta, October 6, 1969.
   Show, Eric V., San Diego, October 2, 1984.
   Cox, Danny B., St. Louis, October 10, 1987.

Most Grand Slams Allowed, Game

A. L.—1—Perry, James E., Minnesota, October 3, 1970; fourth inning.
   Haas, Bryan E., Milwaukee, October 9, 1982; eighth inning.
N. L.—1—Carlton, Steven N., Philadelphia, October 4, 1977; seventh
   inning.
   Lonborg, James R., Philadelphia, October 5, 1977; fourth
   inning.

Most Home Runs Allowed, Inning

A. L.-N. L.—2—Held by many pitchers.

Most Consecutive Home Runs Allowed, Inning

A. L.-N. L.—2—Held by many pitchers.

Total Bases

Most Total Bases Allowed, Game

N. L.— 22—Jarvis, R. Patrick, Atlanta, October 6, 1969.
A. L.— 20—Hunter, James A., New York, October 6, 1978.

Bases On Balls

Most Bases on Balls, Total Series

N. L.— 28—Carlton, Steven N., Philadelphia, 1976, 1977, 1978, 1980,
   1983; 5 Series, 8 games.
A. L.— 19—Cuellar, Miguel, Baltimore, 1969, 1970, 1971, 1973,
   1974; 5 Series, 6 games.
   Palmer, James A., Baltimore, 1969, 1970, 1971, 1973,
   1974, 1979; 6 Series, 8 games.

Most Bases on Balls, Series

3-game Series—A. L.— 7—Boswell, David W., Minnesota, 1969.
   N. L.— 5—Norman, Fredie H., Cincinnati, 1975.
   Carlton, Steven N., Philadelphia, 1976.
4-game Series—A. L.— 13—Cuellar, Miguel, Baltimore, 1974.
   N. L.— 8—Reuss, Jerry, Pittsburgh, 1974.
   Carlton, Steven N., Philadelphia, 1977.
5-game Series—A. L.— 8—Palmer, James A., Baltimore, 1973.
   N. L.— 8—Carlton, Steven N., Philadelphia, 1980.
   Sutcliffe, Richard L., Chicago, 1984.
6-game Series—N. L.— 10—Valenzuela, Fernando, Los Angeles,
   1985.
7-game Series—A. L.— 10—Stieb, David A., Toronto, 1985.
   N. L.— 5— Tudor, John T., St. Louis, 1987.

Most Bases on Balls, Game

A. L.— 9—Cuellar, Miguel, Baltimore, October 9, 1974.
N. L.— 8—Valenzuela, Fernando, Los Angeles, October 14, 1985.

Most Bases on Balls, Inning

A. L.— 4—Cuellar, Miguel, Baltimore, October 9, 1974; fifth inning,
   consecutive.
N. L.— 4—Hooton, Burt E., Los Angeles, October 7, 1977; second
   inning, consecutive.
   Welch, Robert L., Los Angeles, October 12, 1985, first inning.

Most Consecutive Bases on Balls, Inning

A. L.— 4—Cuellar, Miguel, Baltimore, October 9, 1974; fifth inning.
N. L.— 4—Hooton, Burt E., Los Angeles, October 7, 1977; second
   inning.

Strikeouts

Most Strikeouts, Total Series

Both Leagues—46—Ryan, L. Nolan, New York NL, 1969; California
   AL, 1979; Houston NL, 1980, 1986; 4 Series,
   6 games.
A. L.— 46—Palmer, James A., Baltimore, 1969, 1970, 1971, 1973,
   1974, 1979; 8 Series, 6 games.
N. L.— 39—Carlton, Steven N., Philadelphia, 1976, 1977, 1978, 1980,
   1983; 5 Series, 8 games.

Most Strikeouts, Series

3-game Series—N. L.— 14—Candelaria, John R., Pittsburgh 1975.
   A. L.— 12—Palmer, James A., Baltimore, 1970.
4-game Series—A. L.— 14—Boddicker, Michael J., Baltimore, 1983.
   N. L.— 13—Sutton, Donald H., Los Angeles, 1974.
   Carlton, Steven N., Philadelphia, 1983.
5-game Series—N. L.— 17—Seaver, G. Thomas, New York, 1973.
   A. L.— 15—Palmer, James A., Baltimore, 1973.
6-game Series—N. L.— 19—Scott, Michael W., Houston, 1986.
7-game Series—A. L.— 18—Stieb, David A., Toronto, 1985.
   N. L.— 14—Dravecky, David F., San Francisco,
   1987.

Most Strikeouts, Game

A. L.— 14—Coleman, Joseph H., Detroit, October 10, 1972.
   Boddicker, Michael J., Baltimore, October 6, 1983.
N. L.— 14—Candelaria, John R., Pittsburgh, October 7, 1975
   (pitched first 7 ⅔ innings of 10-inning game).
   Scott, Michael W., Houston, October 8, 1986.

Most Strikeouts, Game, Relief Pitcher

N. L.— 7—Ryan, L. Nolan, New York, October 6, 1969; pitched 7 innings.
A. L.— 5—Frazier, George A., New York, October 14, 1981; pitched
   5 ⅔ innings.

Lamp, Dennis P., Toronto, October 15, 1985; pitched 3 ⅔ innings.

Leibrandt, Charles L., Kansas City, October 16, 1985; pitched 5 ⅓ innings.

Schiraldi, Calvin D., Boston, October 15, 1986; pitched 2 innings.

Schatzeder, Daniel E., Detroit, October 10, 1987; pitched 3 ⅓ innings.

Most Consecutive Strikeouts, Game

A. L.—4—Coleman, Joseph H., Detroit, October 10, 1972; 1 in fourth inning, 3 in fifth inning.

Ryan, L. Nolan, California, October 3, 1979; 3 in first inning, 1 in second inning.

Wilcox, Milton E., Detroit, October 5, 1984; 2 in fourth inning, 2 in fifth inning.

N. L.—4—Wilcox, Milton E., Cincinnati, October 5, 1970; 2 in sixth inning, 2 in seventh inning.

Candelaria, John R., Pittsburgh, October 7, 1975; 3 in first inning, 1 in second inning.

Andujar, Joaquin, St. Louis, October 10, 1985; 2 in first inning, 2 in second inning.

Scott, Michael W., Houston, October 8, 1986; 2 in first inning, 2 in second inning.

Most Consecutive Strikeouts, Start of Game

N. L.—4—Candelaria, John R., Pittsburgh, October 7, 1975.
A. L.—4—Ryan, L. Nolan, California, October 3, 1979.

Most Strikeouts, Inning

A. L.-N. L.—3—Held by many pitchers.

Hit Batsmen, Wild Pitches & Balks

Most Hit Batsmen, Total Series

A. L.—4—Tanana, Frank D., California, 1979; Detroit, 1987 (3).

N. L.—2—Seaver, G. Thomas, New York, 1969, 1973.
John, Thomas E., Los Angeles, 1977 (2).

Most Hit Batsmen, Series

A. L.—3—Tanana, Frank D., Detroit, 1987; 5-game Series.
N. L.—2—John, Thomas E., Los Angeles, 1977; 4-game Series.

Most Hit Batsmen, Game

A. L.—3—Tanana, Frank D., Detroit, October 11, 1987.
N. L.—1—Held by many pitchers.

Most Hit Batsmen, Inning

A. L.-N. L.—1—Held by many pitchers.

Most Wild Pitches, Total Series

A. L.—4—John, Thomas E., New York, 1980; California, 1982.
N. L.—3—McGraw, Frank E., New York, 1973; Philadelphia, 1976 (2).
Carlton, Steven N., Philadelphia, 1977, 1983 (2).
Valenzuela, Fernando, Los Angeles, 1981, 1983, 1985.

Most Wild Pitches, Series

A. L.—3—John, Thomas E., California, 1982; 5-game Series.
N. L.—2—Held by many pitchers.

Most Wild Pitches, Game

A. L.—3—John, Thomas E., California, October 9, 1982.
N. L.—2—Held by many pitchers.

Most Wild Pitches, Inning

A. L.—2—Zachary, W. Chris, Detroit, October 8, 1972; fifth inning.
John, Thomas E., California, October 9, 1982.
N. L.—2—Calhoun, Jeffrey W., Houston, October 15, 1986; sixteenth inning.

Most Balks, Game

A. L.-N. L.—1—Held by many pitchers.

Club Pitching

Appearances

Most Appearances by Pitchers, Series

3-game Series—A. L.—14—Minnesota vs. Baltimore, 1970.
N. L.—13—Cincinnati vs. Pittsburgh, 1979.
4-game Series—N. L.—14—Philadelphia vs. Los Angeles, 1977.
A. L.—12—California vs. Baltimore, 1979.
Chicago vs. Baltimore, 1983.
5-game Series—N. L.—21—Philadelphia vs. Houston, 1980.
A. L.—18—Kansas City vs. New York, 1976.
6-game Series—N. L.—23—St. Louis vs. Los Angeles, 1985.
7-game Series—A. L.—22—California vs. Boston, 1986.
N. L.—20—San Francisco vs. St. Louis, 1987.

Most Appearances by Pitchers, Series, Both Clubs

3-game Series—N. L.—25—Cincinnati 13, Pittsburgh 12, 1979.
A. L.—18—Minnesota 11, Baltimore 7, 1969.
Minnesota 14, Baltimore 4, 1970.
4-game Series—N. L.—26—Philadelphia 14, Los Angeles 12, 1977.
A. L.—20—Kansas City 11, New York 9, 1978.
Chicago 12, Baltimore 8, 1983.
5-game Series—N. L.—36—Philadelphia 21, Houston 15, 1980.
A. L.—30—Minnesota 16, Detroit 14, 1987.
6-game Series—N. L.—38—St. Louis 23, Los Angeles 15, 1985.
7-game Series—A. L.—40—California 22, Boston 18, 1986.
N. L.—37—San Francisco 20, St. Louis 17, 1987.

Complete Games

Most Complete Games, Series

3-game Series—A. L.—2—Baltimore vs. Minnesota, 1969, 1970.
Baltimore vs. Oakland, 1971.
N. L.—1—Cincinnati vs. Pittsburgh, 1975.
Pittsburgh vs. Cincinnati, 1979.
St. Louis vs. Atlanta, 1982.
4-game Series—A. L.—2—Oakland vs. Baltimore, 1974.
N. L.—2—San Francisco vs. Pittsburgh, 1971.
Los Angeles vs. Philadelphia, 1977.
5-game Series—N. L.—3—New York vs. Cincinnati, 1973.
A. L.—3—Oakland vs. Baltimore, 1973.
Baltimore vs. Oakland, 1973.
California vs. Milwaukee, 1982.

6-game Series—N. L.—2—Houston vs. New York, 1986.
7-game Series—N. L.—2—San Francisco vs. St. Louis, 1987.
St. Louis vs. San Francisco, 1987.
A. L.—1—Kansas City vs. Toronto, 1985.
California vs. Boston, 1986.
Boston vs. California, 1986.

Most Complete Games, Series, Both Clubs

3-game Series—A. L.—3—Baltimore 2, Oakland 1, 1971.
N. L.—1—Cincinnati 1, Pittsburgh 0, 1975.
Pittsburgh 1, Cincinnati 0, 1979.
St. Louis 1, Atlanta 0, 1982.
4-game Series—A. L.—3—Oakland 2, Baltimore 1, 1974.
N. L.—2—San Francisco 2, Pittsburgh 0, 1971.
Los Angeles 2, Philadelphia 0, 1977.
Los Angeles 1, Philadelphia 1, 1978.
5-game Series—A. L.—4—Baltimore 2, Oakland 2, 1973.
N. L.—3—New York 3, Cincinnati 0, 1973.
6-game Series—N. L.—3—Houston 2, New York 1, 1986.
7-game Series—N. L.—4—San Francisco 2, St. Louis 2, 1987.
A. L.—2—California 1, Boston 1, 1986.

Saves

Most Saves, Series

3-game Series—N. L.—3—Cincinnati vs. Pittsburgh, 1970.
A. L.—2—Boston vs. Oakland, 1975.
4-game Series—N. L.—3—Pittsburgh vs. San Francisco, 1971.
A. L.—2—New York vs. Kansas City, 1978.
5-game Series—A. L.—3—Milwaukee vs. California, 1982.
Minnesota vs. Detroit, 1987.
N. L.—2—Pittsburgh vs. Cincinnati, 1972.
Philadelphia vs. Houston, 1980.
6-game Series—N. L.—2—St. Louis vs. Los Angeles, 1985.
7-game Series—N. L.—3—St. Louis vs. San Francisco, 1987.
A. L.—1—Held by many clubs.

Most Saves, Series, Both Clubs

3-game Series—N. L.—3—Cincinnati 3, Pittsburgh 0, 1970.
A. L.—2—Boston 2, Oakland 0, 1975.
4-game Series—N. L.—3—Pittsburgh 3, San Francisco 0, 1971.
A. L.—2—New York 2, Kansas City 0, 1978.

5-game Series—N. L.—5—Houston 3, Philadelphia 2, 1980.
  A. L.—3—Milwaukee 3, California 0, 1982.
    Minnesota 3, Detroit 0, 1987.
6-game Series—N. L.—3—St. Louis 2, Los Angeles 1, 1985.
7-game Series—N. L.—3—St. Louis 3, San Francisco 0, 1987.
  A. L.—2—California 1, Boston 1, 1986.

Fewest Saves, Series, One Club and Both Clubs

A. L.-N. L.—0—Held by many clubs in Series of all lengths.

Runs, Shutouts & 1-0 Games

Most Runs Allowed, Total Series

A. L.— 108— Kansas City; 6 Series, 27 games.
N. L.— 96— Los Angeles; 6 Series, 27 games.

Most Shutouts Won, Total Series

A. L.—5—Baltimore, 1969, 1973, 1979, 1983 (2).
N. L.—3—St. Louis, 1982, 1987 (2).

Most Shutouts Won, Series

A. L.—2—Oakland vs. Baltimore, 1974; 4-game Series.
  Baltimore vs. Chicago, 1983; 4-game Series.
N. L.—2—St. Louis vs. San Francisco, 1987; 7-game Series.

Most Consecutive Shutouts Won, Series

A. L.—2—Oakland vs. Baltimore, October 6, 8, 1974.
N. L.—2—St. Louis vs. San Francisco, October 13, 14, 1987.

Most Shutouts, Series, Both Clubs

N. L.—3—St. Louis 2, San Francisco 1, 1987; 7-game Series.
A. L.—2—Oakland 1, Detroit 1, 1972; 5-game Series.
  Oakland 1, Baltimore 1, 1973; 5-game Series.
  Oakland 2, Baltimore 0, 1974; 4-game Series.
  Baltimore 2, Chicago 0, 1983; 4-game Series.

Largest Score, Shutout Game

N. L.— 13-0— Chicago 13, San Diego 0, October 2, 1984.
A. L.— 8-0— Baltimore 8, California 0, October 6, 1979.

Longest Shutout Game

A. L.—11 innings— Baltimore 1, Minnesota 0, October 5, 1969.
N. L.—11 innings— Houston 1, Philadelphia 0, October 10, 1980.

Most Consecutive Innings Shut Out Opponent, Total Series

A. L.—30—Oakland vs. Baltimore, October 5 (sixth inning) through October 9, 1974 (eighth inning).
N. L.—22—St. Louis vs. San Francisco, October 11 (fifth inning) through October 14, 1987 (ninth inning).

Most Consecutive Innings Shut Out Opponent, Series

A. L.—30—Oakland vs. Baltimore, October 5 (sixth inning) through October 9, 1974 (eighth inning).
N. L.—22—St. Louis vs. San Francisco, October 11 (fifth inning) through October 14, 1987 (ninth inning).

Championship Series 1-0 Games

A. L.—Baltimore 1, Minnesota 0, October 5, 1969; 11 innings.
  Oakland 1, Baltimore 0, October 8, 1974.
  Detroit 1, Kansas City 0, October 5, 1984.
N. L.—Houston 1, Philadelphia 0, October 10, 1980; 11 innings.
  Philadelphia 1, Los Angeles 0, October 4, 1983.
  Houston 1, New York 0, October 8, 1986.
  St. Louis 1, San Francisco 0, October 13, 1987.

Wild Pitches & Balks

Most Wild Pitches, Series

N. L.—4—Los Angeles vs. Philadelphia, 1983; 4-game Series.
A. L.—3—California vs. Baltimore, 1979; 4-game Series.
  California vs. Milwaukee, 1982; 5-game Series.
  Kansas City vs. Toronto, 1985; 7-game Series.
  Detroit vs. Minnesota, 1987; 5-game Series.

Most Wild Pitches, Series, Both Clubs

N. L.—6—Los Angeles 4, Philadelphia 2, 1983; 4-game Series.
A. L.—5—Detroit 3, Minnesota 2, 1987; 5-game Series.

Most Balks, Series

N. L.—2—Pittsburgh vs. Cincinnati, 1975; 3-game Series.
A. L.—2—Baltimore vs. Chicago, 1983; 4-game Series.

Most Balks, Series, Both Clubs

N. L.—2—Pittsburgh 2, Cincinnati 0, 1975; 3-game Series.
  Philadelphia 1, Los Angeles 1, 1977; 4-game Series.
A. L.—2—Baltimore 2, Chicago 0, 1983; 4-game Series.

Fewest Balks, Series, One Club and Both Clubs

A. L.-N. L.—0—Held by many clubs in Series of all lengths.

Individual Fielding

First Basemen
Series, Games & Average

Most Series Played

A. L.—5—Powell, John W., Baltimore, 1969, 1970, 1971, 1973, 1974; 12 games.
N. L.—5—Perez, Atanasio R., Cincinnati, 1970, 1972, 1973, 1975, 1976; 17 games.
  Robertson, Robert E., Pittsburgh, 1970, 1971, 1972, 1974, 1975; 11 games.
  Garvey, Steven P., Los Angeles, 1974, 1977, 1978, 1981; San Diego, 1984; 22 games.

Most Games Played, Total Series

N. L.—22—Garvey, Steven P., Los Angeles, 1974, 1977, 1978, 1981; San Diego, 1984; 5 Series.
A. L.—14—Chambliss, C. Christopher, New York, 1976, 1977, 1978; 3 Series.

Highest Fielding Average, Series, With Most Chances Accepted

3-game Series—N. L.—1.000—Hernandez, Keith, St. Louis, 1982; 36 chances accepted.
  A. L.—1.000—Powell, John W., Baltimore, 1969; 34 chances accepted.
4-game Series—N. L.—1.000—Garvey, Steven P., Los Angeles, 1978; 49 chances accepted.
  A. L.—1.000—Tenace, F. Gene, Oakland, 1974; 37 chances accepted.
5-game Series—N. L.—1.000—Rose, Peter E., Philadelphia, 1980; 60 chances accepted.
  A. L.—1.000—Epstein, Michael P., Oakland, 1972; 57 chances accepted.
6-game Series—N. L.—1.000—Hernandez, Keith, New York, 1986; 79 chances accepted.

7-game Series—A. L.—1.000—Buckner, William J., Boston, 1986; 54 chances accepted.
  N. L.—1.000—Lindeman, James W., St. Louis, 1987; 35 chances accepted.

Putouts, Assists & Chances Accepted

Most Putouts, Total Series

N. L.— 208— Garvey, Steven P., Los Angeles, 1974, 1977, 1978, 1981; San Diego, 1984; 5 Series, 22 games.
A. L.— 115— Powell, John W., Baltimore, 1969, 1970, 1971, 1973, 1974; 5 Series, 12 games.

Most Putouts, Series

3-game Series—N. L.—35—Hernandez, Keith, St. Louis, 1982.
  A. L.—34—Powell, John W., Baltimore, 1969.
4-game Series—N. L.—44—Garvey, Steven P., Los Angeles, 1978.
  A. L.—44—Murray, Eddie C., Baltimore, 1979.
5-game Series—A. L.—55—Epstein, Michael P., Oakland, 1972.
  N. L.—53—Rose, Peter E., Philadelphia, 1980.
6-game Series—N. L.—67—Hernandez, Keith, New York, 1986.
7-game Series—A. L.—72—Balboni, Stephen C., Kansas City, 1985.
  N. L.—63—Clark, William N., San Francisco, 1987.

Most Putouts, Game, Nine Innings

N. L.— 16— Garvey, Steven P., Los Angeles, October 5, 1978.
  Garvey, Steven P., Los Angeles, October 6, 1978.
A. L.— 15—Chambliss, C. Christopher, New York, October 14, 1976.

Most Putouts, Extra-Inning Game

N. L.— 21— Davis, Glenn E., Houston, October 15, 1986; 16 innings.
A. L.—Less than nine-inning record.

Fewest Putouts, Game, Nine Innings

N. L.—1—Robertson, Robert E., Pittsburgh, October 2, 1971.

A. L.—2—Cash, Norman, D., Detroit, October 8, 1972.
 Cooper, Cecil C., Boston, October 4, 1975.

Most Putouts, Inning

A. L.-N.L.—3—Held by many first basemen.

Most Assists, Total Series

Both Leagues—16—Chambliss, C. Christopher, New York AL, 1976,
 1977, 1978; Atlanta NL, 1982; 4 Series, 17
 games.
N. L.— 14—Perez, Atanasio R., Cincinnati, 1970, 1972, 1973, 1975,
 1976; 5 Series, 17 games.
A. L.— 11—Chambliss, C. Christopher, New York, 1976, 1977, 1978;
 3 Series, 14 games.

Most Assists, Series

3-game Series—A. L.—5—Reese, Richard B., Minnesota, 1969.
 Watson, Robert J., New York, 1980.
 N. L.—5—Perez, Atanasio R., Cincinnati, 1975.
 Chambliss, C. Christopher, Atlanta, 1982.
4-game Series—N. L.—5—Garvey, Steven P., Los Angeles, 1978.
 A. L.—3—Murray, Eddie C., Baltimore, 1979, 1983.
 Paciorek, Thomas M., Chicago, 1983.
5-game Series—A. L.—7—Chambliss, C. Christopher, New York,
 1977.
 N. L.—7—Rose, Peter E., Philadelphia, 1980.
6-game Series—N. L.—12—Hernandez, Keith, New York, 1986.
7-game Series—A. L.—7—Balboni, Stephen C., Kansas City, 1985.
 Upshaw, Willie C., Toronto, 1985.
 N. L.—7—Clark, William N., San Francisco, 1987.

Most Assists, Game, Nine Innings

A. L.—4—Balboni, Stephen C., Kansas City, October 12, 1985.
N. L.—3—Perez, Atanasio R., Cincinnati, October 4, 1975.
 Chambliss, C. Christopher, Atlanta, October 10, 1982.
 Brock, Gregory A., Los Angeles, October 16, 1985.
 Clark, William N., San Francisco, October 10, 1987.

Most Assists, Extra-Inning Game

N. L.—7—Hernandez, Keith, New York, October 15, 1986; 16 innings.
A. L.—Less than nine-inning record.

Most Assists, Inning

A. L.-N. L.—2—Held by many first basemen.

Most Chances Accepted, Total Series

N. L.— 221— Garvey, Steven P., Los Angeles, 1974, 1977, 1978,
 1981; San Diego, 1984; 5 Series, 22 games.
A. L.— 124— Chambliss, C. Christopher, New York, 1976, 1977,
 1978; 3 Series, 14 games.

Most Chances Accepted, Series

3-game Series—N. L.—36—Hernandez, Keith, St. Louis, 1982.
 A. L.—34—Powell, John W., Baltimore, 1969.
4-game Series—N. L.—49—Garvey, Steven P., Los Angeles, 1978.
 A. L.—47—Murray, Eddie C., Baltimore, 1979.
5-game Series—N. L.—60—Rose, Peter E., Philadelphia, 1980.
 A. L.—57—Epstein, Michael P., Oakland, 1972.
6-game Series—N. L.—79—Hernandez, Keith, New York, 1986.
7-game Series—A. L.—79—Balboni, Stephen C., Kansas City, 1985.
 N. L.—70—Clark, William N., San Francisco, 1987.

Most Chances Accepted, Game, Nine Innings

N. L.—18—Garvey, Steven P., Los Angeles, October 6, 1978; 16
 putouts, 2 assists, 0 errors.
A. L.—16—Balboni, Stephen C., Kansas City, October 12, 1985; 12
 putouts, 4 assists, 0 errors.
 Hendrick, George A., California, October 11, 1986; 11
 innings; 14 putouts, 2 assists, 0 errors.

Most Chances Accepted, Extra-Inning Game

N. L.—27—Hernandez, Keith, New York, October 15, 1986; 16 innings; 20 putouts, 7 assists, 0 errors.
A. L.—Less than nine-inning record.

Fewest Chances Offered, Game, Nine Innings

N. L.—2—Robertson, Robert E., Pittsburgh, October 2, 1971; 1 putout, 1 assist, 0 errors.
A. L.—3—Cooper, Cecil C., Boston, October 4, 1975; 2 putouts, 0
 assists, 1 error.

Most Chances Accepted, Inning

A. L.-N. L.—3—Held by many first basemen.

Errors & Double Plays

Most Errors, Total Series

A. L.—3—Cooper, Cecil C., Boston, 1975; Milwaukee, 1982; 2 Series,
 8 games.
 Balboni, Stephen C., Kansas City, 1984, 1985; 2 Series, 10
 games.
N. L.—2—Cepeda, Orlando M., Atlanta, 1969; 1 Series, 3 games.

Most Consecutive Errorless Games, Total Series

N. L.— 19— Garvey, Steven P., Los Angeles, San Diego, October 9,
 1974 through October 7, 1984.
A. L.— 12— Powell, John W., Baltimore, October 4, 1969 through October 9, 1974.
 Chambliss, C. Christopher, New York, October 12, 1976
 through October 7, 1978.

Most Errors, Series

3-game Series—N. L.—2—Cepeda, Orlando M., Atlanta, 1969.
 A. L.—1—Cooper, Cecil C., Boston, 1975.
 Balboni, Stephen C., Kansas City, 1984.
4-game Series—A. L.—2—Murray, Eddie C., Baltimore, 1979.
 N. L.—1—McCovey, Willie L., San Francisco, 1971.
 Garvey, Steven P., Los Angeles, 1974.
5-game Series—A. L.—2—Mayberry, John C., Kansas City, 1977.
 Cooper, Cecil C., Milwaukee, 1982.
 N. L.—1—Durham, Leon, Chicago, 1984.
6-game Series—N. L.—1—Davis, Glenn E., Houston, 1986.
7-game Series—A. L.—2—Balboni, Stephen C., Kansas City, 1985.
 N. L.—1—Driessen, Daniel, St. Louis, 1987.
 Clark, William N., San Francisco, 1987.

Most Errors, Game

A. L.-N. L.—1—Held by many first basemen.

Most Double Plays, Total Series

N. L.— 21— Garvey, Steven P., Los Angeles, 1974, 1977, 1978, 1981;
 San Diego, 1984; 5 Series, 22 games.
A. L.— 9— Powell, John W., Baltimore, 1969, 1970, 1971, 1973,
 1974; 5 Series, 12 games.

Most Double Plays, Series

3-game Series—A. L.— 6—Watson, Robert J., New York, 1981.
 N. L.— 3—Hernandez, Keith, St. Louis, 1982.
4-game Series—N. L.— 6—Garvey, Steven P., Los Angeles, 1974.
 A. L.— 6—Carew, Rodney C., California, 1979.
5-game Series—N. L.— 6—Cromartie, Warren L., Montreal, 1981.
 A. L.— 5—Epstein, Michael P., Oakland, 1972.
 Cooper, Cecil C., Milwaukee, 1982.
6-game Series—N. L.— 5—Hernandez, Keith, New York, 1986.
7-game Series—N. L.—10—Clark, William N., San Francisco, 1987.
 A. L.— 5—Balboni, Stephen C., Kansas City, 1985.

Most Double Plays Started, Series

3-game Series—A. L.— 1—Held by many players.
 N. L.—Never accomplished.
4-game Series—N. L.— 1—Garvey, Steven P., Los Angeles, 1977.
 A. L.—Never accomplished.
5-game Series—N. L.— 1—Milner, John D., New York, 1973.
 A. L.— 1—Williams, Earl C., Baltimore, 1973.
 Chambliss, C. Christopher, New York,
 1976.
6-game Series—N. L.—Never accomplished.
7-game Series—A. L.— 1—Joyner, Wallace K., California, 1986.
 N. L.— 1—Clark, William N., San Francisco, 1987.

Most Double Plays, Game

N. L.—4—Clark, William N., San Francisco, October 10, 1987.
A. L.—3—Reese, Richard B., Minnesota, October 3, 1970.
 Epstein, Michael P., Oakland, October 10, 1972.
 Tenace, F. Gene, Oakland, October 5, 1975.
 Murray, Eddie C., Baltimore, October 6, 1979.
 Grich, Robert A., California, October 14, 1986.

Most Double Plays Started, Game

A. L.-N. L.—1—Held by many first basemen.

Most Unassisted Double Plays, Game

A. L.-N. L.—1—Never accomplished.

Second Basemen
Series, Games & Average

Most Series Played

N. L.—7—Morgan, Joe L., Cincinnati, 1972, 1973, 1975, 1976, 1979;
 Houston, 1980; Philadelphia, 1983; 27 games.

A. L.—6—White, Frank, Kansas City, 1976, 1977, 1978, 1980, 1984, 1985; 26 games.

Most Games Played, Total Series
N. L.—27—Morgan, Joe L., Cincinnati, 1972, 1973, 1975, 1976, 1979; Houston, 1980; Philadelphia, 1983; 7 Series.
A. L.—26—White, Frank, Kansas City, 1976, 1977, 1978, 1980, 1984, 1985; 6 Series.

Highest Fielding Average, Series, With Most Chances Accepted
3-game Series—N. L.—1.000—Helms, Tommy V., Cincinnati, 1970; 23 chances accepted.
    Morgan, Joe L., Cincinnati, 1979; 23 chances accepted.
    A. L.—1.000—Randolph, William L., New York, 1981; 24 chances accepted.
4-game Series—A. L.—1.000—Cruz, Julio L., Chicago, 1983; 24 chances accepted.
    N. L.—1.000—Sax, Stephen L., Los Angeles, 1983; 23 chances accepted.
5-game Series—N. L.—1.000—Morgan, Joe L., Cincinnati, 1973; 39 chances accepted.
    A. L.—1.000—White, Frank, Kansas City, 1977; 29 chances accepted.
6-game Series—N. L.—1.000—Sax, Stephen L., Los Angeles, 1985; 32 chances accepted.
7-game Series—A. L.—1.000—Barrett, Martin G., Boston, 1986; 40 chances accepted.
    N. L.—.968—Thompson, Robert R., San Francisco, 1987; 30 chances accepted.

Putouts, Assists & Chances Accepted

Most Putouts, Total Series
N. L.—63—Morgan, Joe L., Cincinnati, 1972, 1973, 1975, 1976, 1979; Houston, 1980; Philadelphia, 1983; 7 Series, 27 games.
A. L.—53—White, Frank, Kansas City, 1976, 1977, 1978, 1980, 1984, 1985; 6 Series, 26 games.

Most Putouts, Series
3-game Series—N. L.—12—Morgan, Joe L., Cincinnati, 1979.
    A. L.—12—Randolph, William L., New York, 1981.
4-game Series—A. L.—13—Grich, Robert A., Baltimore, 1974.
    N. L.—11—Cash, David, Pittsburgh, 1971.
    Sax, Stephen L., Los Angeles, 1983.
5-game Series—A. L.—16—Grich, Robert A., Baltimore, 1973.
    N. L.—18—Trillo, J. Manuel, Philadelphia, 1980.
6-game Series—N. L.—13—Herr, Thomas M., St. Louis, 1985.
7-game Series—A. L.—19—Barrett, Martin G., Boston, 1986.
    N. L.—12—Herr, Thomas M., St. Louis, 1987.

Most Putouts, Game
A. L.—7—Grich, Robert A., Baltimore, October 6, 1974.
    Barrett, Martin G., Boston, October 12, 1986; 11 innings.
N. L.—6—Cash, David, Philadelphia, October 12, 1976.
    Morgan, Joe L., Cincinnati, October 3, 1979; 10 innings.
    Lopes, David E., Los Angeles, October 13, 1981.

Most Putouts, Inning
N. L.—3—Morgan, Joe L., Cincinnati, October 10, 1976; eighth inning.
    Sandberg, Ryne D., Chicago, October 4, 1984; fifth inning.
A. L.—3—Grich, Robert A., Baltimore, October 11, 1973; third inning.
    Green, Richard L., Oakland, October 8, 1974; seventh inning.

Most Assists, Total Series
N. L.—85—Morgan, Joe L., Cincinnati, 1972, 1973, 1975, 1976, 1979; Houston, 1980; Philadelphia, 1983; 7 Series, 27 games.
A. L.—80—White, Frank, Kansas City, 1976, 1977, 1978, 1980, 1984, 1985; 6 Series, 26 games.

Most Assists, Series
3-game Series—N. L.—12—Helms, Tommy V., Cincinnati, 1970.
    A. L.—12—Randolph, William L., New York, 1981.
4-game Series—N. L.—18—Lopes, David E., Los Angeles, 1974.
    A. L.—14—Cruz, Julio L., Chicago, 1983.
5-game Series—N. L.—27—Morgan, Joe L., Cincinnati, 1973.
    A. L.—17—Grich, Robert A., California, 1982.
6-game Series—N. L.—21—Sax, Stephen L., Los Angeles, 1985.
7-game Series—A. L.—28—White, Frank, Kansas City, 1985.
    N. L.—19—Thompson, Robert R., San Francisco, 1987.

Most Assists, Game, Nine Innings
N. L.—8—Trillo, J. Manuel, Philadelphia, October 7, 1980.
A. L.—7—Randolph, William L., New York, October 13, 1981.

Most Assists, Extra-Inning Game
N. L.—9—Backman, Walter W., October 14, 1986; 12 innings.
A. L.—7—Barrett, Martin G., Boston, October 12, 1986; 11 innings.

Most Assists, Inning
A. L.-N. L.—2—Held by many second basemen.

Most Chances Accepted, Total Series
N. L.—148—Morgan, Joe L., Cincinnati, 1972, 1973, 1975, 1976, 1979; Houston, 1980; Philadelphia, 1983; 7 Series, 27 games.
A. L.—133—White, Frank, Kansas City, 1976, 1977, 1978, 1980, 1984, 1985; 6 Series, 26 games.

Most Chances Accepted, Series
3-game Series—A. L.—24—Randolph, William L., New York, 1981.
    N. L.—23—Helms, Tommy V., Cincinnati, 1970.
    Morgan, Joe L., Cincinnati, 1979.
4-game Series—N. L.—27—Lopes, David E., Los Angeles, 1974.
    A. L.—25—Grich, Robert A., Baltimore, 1974.
5-game Series—N. L.—43—Trillo, J. Manuel, Philadelphia, 1980.
    A. L.—29—White, Frank, Kansas City, 1977.
6-game Series—N. L.—32—Sax, Stephen L., Los Angeles, 1985.
7-game Series—A. L.—37—White, Frank, Kansas City, 1985.
    N. L.—30—Thompson, Robert R., San Francisco, 1987.

Most Chances Accepted, Game
N. L.—13—Trillo, J. Manuel, Philadelphia, October 7, 1980; 5 putouts, 8 assists, 0 errors.
A. L.—12—Grich, Robert A., Baltimore, October 6, 1974; 7 putouts, 5 assists, 1 error.

Fewest Chances Offered, Game
A. L.—0—Thompson, Danny L., Minnesota, October 4, 1970.
    Grich, Robert A., California, October 10, 1986.
N. L.—1—Held by many second basemen.

Most Chances Accepted, Inning
A. L.-N. L.—3—Held by many second basemen.

Errors & Double Plays

Most Errors, Total Series
A. L.—4—Green, Richard L., Oakland, 1971, 1972, 1973, 1974; 4 Series, 17 games.
    Grich, Robert A., Baltimore, 1973, 1974; California, 1979, 1982, 1986; 5 Series, 21 games.
N. L.—4—Lopes, David E., Los Angeles, 1974, 1977, 1978, 1981; 4 Series, 17 games.

Most Consecutive Errorless Games, Total Series
N. L.—27—Morgan, Joe L., Cincinnati, Houston, Philadelphia, October 7, 1972 through October 8, 1983.
A. L.—16—Randolph, William L., New York, October 9, 1976 through October 15, 1981.

Most Errors, Series
3-game Series—A. L.— N. L.—1—Held by many second basemen.
4-game Series—A. L.—2—Green, Richard L., Oakland, 1974.
    N. L.—2—Sizemore, Ted C., Philadelphia, 1977.
    Lopes, David E., Los Angeles, 1978.
5-game Series—A. L.—2—Green, Richard L., Oakland, 1973.
    N. L.—1—Held by many second basemen.
6-game Series—N. L.—Never accomplished.
7-game Series—A. L.—2—Grich, Robert A., California, 1986.
    N. L.—1—Herr, Thomas M., St. Louis, 1987.
    Thompson, Robert R., San Francisco, 1987.

Most Errors, Game
A. L.—2—Green, Richard L., Oakland, October 9, 1973; 11 innings.
    Green, Richard L., Oakland, October 8, 1974.
N. L.—1—Held by many second basemen.

Most Errors, Inning
A. L.-N. L.—1—Held by many second basemen.

Most Double Plays, Total Series
N. L.—14—Morgan, Joe L., Cincinnati, 1972, 1973, 1975, 1976, 1979; Houston, 1980; Philadelphia, 1983; 7 Series, 27 games.

A. L.— 14—White, Frank, Kansas City, 1976, 1977, 1978, 1980,
1984, 1985; 6 Series, 26 games.

Most Double Plays, Series

3-game Series—A. L.— 4—Randolph, William L., New York, 1981.
N. L.— 3—Cash, David, Pittsburgh, 1970.
Herr, Thomas M., St. Louis, 1982.
4-game Series—N. L.— 4—Lopes, David E., Los Angeles, 1974.
Sizemore, Ted C., Philadelphia, 1978.
A. L.— 4—Grich, Robert A., California, 1979.
5-game Series—N. L.— 7—Scott, Rodney D., Montreal, 1981.
A. L.— 4—Green, Richard L., Oakland, 1973.
Gantner, James E., Milwaukee, 1982.
6-game Series—N. L.— 4—Backman, Walter W., New York, 1986.
7-game Series—N. L.— 6—Thompson, Robert R., San Francisco,
1987.
A. L.— 4—Barrett, Martin G., Boston, 1986.
Wilfong, Robert D., California, 1986.

Most Double Plays Started, Series

3-game Series—A. L.— 2—Johnson, David A., Baltimore, 1970.
N. L.— 2—Stennett, Renaldo A., Pittsburgh, 1975.
Herr, Thomas M., St. Louis, 1982.
4-game Series—N. L.— 3—Sizemore, Ted C., Philadelphia, 1978.
A. L.— 1—Held by many second basemen.
5-game Series—N. L.— 3—Sandberg, Ryne D., Chicago, 1984.
A. L.— 2—Gantner, James E., Milwaukee, 1982.
6-game Series—N. L.— 2—Backman, Walter W., New York, 1986.
7-game Series—N. L.— 3—Thompson, Robert R., San Francisco,
1987.
A. L.— 2—Garcia, Damaso D., Toronto, 1985.
White, Frank, Kansas City, 1985.
Barrett, Martin, G., Boston, 1986.

Most Double Plays, Game

N. L.— 4—Lopes, David E., Los Angeles, October 13, 1981.
A. L.— 3—Wilfong, Robert D., California, October 14, 1986.

Most Double Plays Started, Game

N. L.— 2—Stennett, Renaldo A., Pittsburgh, October 5, 1975.
Sizemore, Ted C., Philadelphia, October 6, 1978.
Scott, Rodney D., Montreal, October 17, 1981.
Herr, Thomas M., St. Louis, October 10, 1982.
Sandberg, Ryne D., Chicago, October 2, 1984.
Thompson, Robert R., San Francisco, October 10, 1987.
A. L.— 1—Held by many second basemen.

Most Unassisted Double Plays, Game

N. L.— 1—Morgan, Joe L., October 10, 1976.
A. L.—Never accomplished.

Third Basemen
Series, Games & Average

Most Series Played

Both Leagues—6—Nettles, Graig, New York AL, 1976, 1977, 1978,
1980, 1981; San Diego NL, 1984; 23 games.
A. L.— 6—Brett, George H., Kansas City, 1976, 1977, 1978, 1980,
1984, 1985; 27 games.
N. L.— 5—Hebner, Richard J., Pittsburgh, 1970, 1971, 1972, 1974,
1975; 18 games.
Schmidt, Michael J., Philadelphia, 1976, 1977, 1978, 1980,
1983; 20 games.
Cey, Ronald C., Los Angeles, 1974, 1977, 1978, 1981;
Chicago, 1984; 22 games.

Most Games Played, Total Series

A. L.— 27—Brett, George H., Kansas City, 1976, 1977, 1978, 1980,
1984, 1985; 6 Series.
N. L.— 22—Cey, Ronald C., Los Angeles, 1974, 1977, 1978, 1981;
Chicago, 1984; 5 Series.

Highest Fielding Average, Series, With Most Chances Accepted

3-game Series—A. L.— 1.000—Robinson, Brooks C., Baltimore,
1969; 16 chances accepted.
N. L.— 1.000—Madlock, Bill, Pittsburgh, 1979; 8
chances accepted.
4-game Series—N. L.— 1.000—Schmidt, Michael J., Philadelphia,
1977; 19 chances accepted.
A. L.— 1.000—Cruz, Todd R., Baltimore, 1983; 19
chances accepted.
5-game Series—A. L.— 1.000—Bando, Salvatore L., Oakland, 1972;
22 chances accepted.

N. L.— 1.000—Hebner, Richard J., Pittsburgh,
1972; 16 chances accepted.
6-game Series—N. L.— 1.000—Madlock, Bill, Los Angeles, 1985; 15
chances accepted.
7-game Series—A. L.— 1.000—Iorg, Garth R., Toronto, 15 chances
accepted.
N. L.— 1.000—Pendleton, Terry L., St. Louis, 14
chances accepted.

Putouts, Assists & Chances Accepted

Most Putouts, Total Series

A. L.— 25—Bando, Salvatore L., Oakland, 1971, 1972, 1973, 1974,
1975; 5 Series, 20 games.
N. L.— 20—Schmidt, Michael J., Philadelphia, 1976, 1977, 1978,
1980, 1983; 5 Series, 20 games.

Most Putouts, Series

3-game Series—A. L.— 6—Robinson, Brooks C., Baltimore, 1969.
Killebrew, Harmon C., Minnesota, 1969.
Bando, Salvatore L., Oakland, 1971.
N. L.— 5—Perez, Atanasio R., Cincinnati, 1970.
4-game Series—N. L.— 7—Cey, Ronald C., Los Angeles, 1977.
A. L.— 6—Nettles, Graig, New York, 1978.
Cruz, Todd R., Baltimore, 1983.
5-game Series—A. L.— 9—DeCinces, Douglas V., California, 1982.
N. L.— 5—Hebner, Richard J., Pittsburgh, 1972.
Cey, Ronald C., Los Angeles, 1981.
Nettles, Graig, San Diego, 1984.
6-game Series—N. L.— 6—Pendleton, Terry L., St. Louis, 1985.
Madlock, Bill, Los Angeles, 1985.
7-game Series—A. L.— 7—Brett, George H., Kansas City, 1985.
Boggs, Wade A., Boston, 1986.
N. L.— 4—Mitchell, Kevin D., San Francisco, 1987.

Most Putouts, Game

A. L.— 4—Lansford, Carney R., California, October 6, 1979.
N. L.— 3—Perez, Atanasio R., Cincinnati, October 5, 1970.
Hebner, Richard J., Pittsburgh, October 10, 1972.
Schmidt, Michael J., Philadelphia, October 9, 1976.
Schmidt, Michael J., Philadelphia, October 11, 1980; 10
innings.
Schmidt, Michael J., Philadelphia, October 7, 1983.
Nettles, Graig, San Diego, October 6, 1984.

Most Putouts, Inning

A. L.- N. L.— 2—Held by many third basemen.

Most Assists, Total Series

N. L.— 66—Schmidt, Michael J., Philadelphia, 1976, 1977, 1978,
1980, 1983; 5 Series, 20 games.
A. L.— 49—Robinson, Brooks C., Baltimore, 1969, 1970, 1971, 1973,
1974; 5 Series, 18 games.
Brett, George H., Kansas City, 1976, 1977, 1978, 1980,
1984, 1985; 6 Series, 27 games.

Most Assists, Series

3-game Series—A. L.— 11—Bando, Salvatore L., Oakland, 1975.
N. L.— 9—Schmidt, Michael J., Philadelphia, 1976.
4-game Series—N. L.— 18—Schmidt, Michael J., Philadelphia, 1978.
A. L.— 13—Robinson, Brooks C., Baltimore, 1974.
Cruz, Todd R., Baltimore, 1983.
5-game Series—N. L.— 17—Schmidt, Michael J., Philadelphia, 1980.
A. L.— 16—Bando, Salvatore L., Oakland, 1972.
6-game Series—N. L.— 19—Knight, C. Ray, New York, 1986.
7-game Series—A. L.— 18—DeCinces, Douglas V., California, 1986.
N. L.— 11—Pendleton, Terry L., St. Louis, 1987.
Mitchell, Kevin D., San Francisco, 1987.

Most Assists, Game, Nine Innings

N. L.— 8—Cey, Ronald C., Los Angeles, October 16, 1981.
A. L.— 6—Bando, Salvatore L., Oakland, October 8, 1972.
Cruz, Todd R., Baltimore, October 5, 1983.
Brookens, Thomas D., Detroit, October 11, 1987.

Most Assists, Extra-Inning Game

A. L.— 7—Rodriguez, Aurelio, Detroit, October 11, 1972; 10 innings.
N. L.—Less than nine-inning record.

Most Assists, Inning

N. L.— 3—Cey, Ronald C., Los Angeles, October 4, 1977; fourth inning.
Cey, Ronald C., Los Angeles, October 16, 1981; eighth
inning.
A. L.— 3—Cruz, Todd R., Baltimore, October 5, 1983; fifth inning.

Most Chances Accepted, Total Series

    N. L.—86—Schmidt, Michael J., Philadelphia, 1976, 1977, 1978, 1980, 1983; 5 Series, 20 games.
    A. L.—72—Bando, Salvatore L., Oakland, 1971, 1972, 1973, 1974, 1975; 5 Series, 20 games.

Most Chances Accepted, Series

    3-game Series—A. L.— 16—Robinson, Brooks C., Baltimore, 1969.
                  N. L.—13—Schmidt, Michael J., Philadelphia, 1976.
    4-game Series—N. L.—21—Cey, Ronald C., Los Angeles, 1977.
                   Schmidt, Michael J., Philadelphia, 1978.
               A. L.—19—Cruz, Todd R., Baltimore, 1983.
    5-game Series—A. L.—22—Bando, Salvatore L., Oakland, 1972.
               N. L.—21—Cey, Ronald C., Los Angeles, 1981.
    6-game Series—N. L.—24—Pendleton, Terry L., St. Louis, 1985.
                   Knight, C. Ray, New York, 1986.
    7-game Series—A. L.—24—DeCinces, Douglas V., California, 1986.
               N. L.—15—Mitchell, Kevin D., San Francisco, 1987.

Most Chances Accepted, Game

    N. L.—10—Cey, Ronald C., Los Angeles, October 16, 1981; 2 putouts, 8 assists, 0 errors.
    A. L.— 9—Cruz, Todd R., Baltimore, October 5, 1983; 3 putouts, 6 assists, 0 errors.

Fewest Chances Offered, Game

    A.L.-N.L.—0—Held by many players.

Most Chances Accepted, Inning

    A. L.-N. L.—3—Held by many third basemen.

Errors & Double Plays

Most Errors, Total Series

    A. L.—8—Brett, George H., Kansas City, 1976, 1977, 1978, 1980, 1984, 1985; 6 Series, 27 games.
    N. L.—5—Schmidt, Michael J., Philadelphia, 1976, 1977, 1978, 1980, 1983; 5 Series, 20 games.

Most Consecutive Errorless Games, Total Series

    A. L.— 17—Bando, Salvatore L., Oakland, October 3, 1971 through October 9, 1974.
    N. L.— 13—Hebner, Richard J., Pittsburgh, October 6, 1971 through October 7, 1975.

Most Errors, Series

    3-game Series—A. L.-N. L.—1—Held by many third basemen.
    4-game Series—N. L.—2—Cey, Ronald C., Los Angeles, 1974.
                   Schmidt, Michael J., Philadelphia, 1978.
               A. L.—1—Brett, George H., Kansas City, 1978.
    5-game Series—A. L.—3—Brett, George H., Kansas City, 1976.
                   DeCinces, Douglas V., California, 1982.
               N. L.—1—Held by many third basemen.
    6-game Series—N. L.—1—Pendleton, Terry L., St. Louis, 1985.
                   Knight, C. Ray, New York, 1986.
    7-game Series—A. L.—2—Brett, George H., Kansas City, 1985.
                   Boggs, Wade A., Boston, 1986.
                   DeCinces, Douglas V., California, 1986.
               N. L.—1—Mitchell, Kevin D., San Francisco, 1987.

Most Errors, Game

    A. L.—2—Brett, George H., Kansas City, October 9, 1976.
          DeCinces, Douglas V., California, October 9, 1982.
          Evans, Darrell W., Detroit, October 11, 1987.
    N. L.—2—Cey, Ronald C., Los Angeles, October 5, 1974.

Most Errors, Inning

    A. L.—2—Brett, George H., Kansas City, October 9, 1976; first inning.
    N. L.—1—Held by many third basemen.

Most Double Plays, Total Series

    A. L.—6—Nettles, Graig, New York, 1976, 1977, 1978, 1980, 1981; 5 Series, 19 games.
          DeCinces, Douglas V., Baltimore, 1979; California, 1982, 1986; 3 Series, 16 games.
    N. L.—4—Schmidt, Michael J., Philadelphia, 1976, 1977, 1978, 1980; 4 Series, 16 games.

Most Double Plays, Series

    3-game Series—A. L.—2—Bando, Salvatore L., Oakland, 1971.
                   Nettles, Graig, New York, 1981.
               N. L.—2—Schmidt, Michael J., Philadelphia, 1976.
    4-game Series—A. L.—3—Lansford, Carney R. California, 1979.
               N. L.—1—Cey, Ronald C., Los Angeles, 1974, 1978.
                   Hebner, Richard J., Pittsburgh, 1974.

Most Double Plays Started, Series

    5-game Series—N. L.—3—Parrish, Larry A., Montreal, 1981.
               A. L.—3—DeCinces, Douglas V., California, 1982.
    6-game Series—N. L.—2—Pendleton, Terry L., St. Louis, 1985.
    7-game Series—A. L.—2—DeCinces, Douglas V., California, 1986.
               N. L.—1—Mitchell, Kevin D., San Francisco, 1987.
                   Pendleton, Terry L., St. Louis, 1987.

Most Double Plays Started, Series

    3-game Series—A. L.—2—Bando, Salvatore L., Oakland, 1971.
                   Nettles, Graig, New York, 1981.
               N. L.—2—Schmidt, Michael J., Philadelphia, 1976.
    4-game Series—A. L.—3—Lansford, Carney R., California, 1979.
               N. L.—1—Cey, Ronald C., Los Angeles, 1974, 1978.
                   Hebner, Richard J., Pittsburgh, 1974.
    5-game Series—N. L.—3—Parrish, Larry A., Montreal, 1981.
               A. L.—2—Rodriguez, Aurelio, Detroit, 1972.
                   Nettles, Graig, New York, 1977.
                   DeCinces, Douglas V., California, 1982.
                   Molitor, Paul L., Milwaukee, 1982.
    6-game Series—N. L.—1—Pendleton, Terry L., St. Louis, 1985.
                   Knight, C. Ray, New York, 1986.
    7-game Series—A. L.—2—DeCinces, Douglas V., California, 1986.
               N. L.—1—Mitchell, Kevin D., San Francisco, 1987.
                   Pendleton, Terry L., St. Louis, 1987.

Most Double Plays, Game

    N. L.—2—Schmidt, Michael J., Philadelphia, October 9, 1976.
          Schmidt, Michael J., Philadelphia, October 11, 1980; 10 innings.
          Parrish, Larry A., Montreal, October 16, 1981.
    A. L.—2—DeCinces, Douglas V., California, October 14, 1986.

Most Double Plays Started, Game

    N. L.—2—Schmidt, Michael J., Philadelphia, October 9, 1976.
          Parrish, Larry A., Montreal, October 16, 1981.
    A. L.—2—DeCinces, Douglas V., California, October 14, 1986.

Most Unassisted Double Plays, Game

    N. L.—1—Schmidt, Michael J., Philadelphia, October 9, 1976.
    A. L.—Never accomplished.

Shortstops
Series, Games & Average

Most Series Played

    A. L.—6—Belanger, Mark H., Baltimore, 1969, 1970, 1971, 1973, 1974, 1979; 21 games.
          Campaneris, Dagoberto B., Oakland, 1971, 1972, 1973, 1974, 1975, California, 1979; 18 games.
    N. L.—5—Concepcion, David I., Cincinnati, 1970, 1972, 1975, 1976, 1979; 13 games.
          Russell, William E., Los Angeles, 1974, 1977, 1978, 1981, 1983; 21 games.
          Bowa, Lawrence R., Philadelphia, 1976, 1977, 1978, 1980; Chicago, 1984; 21 games.

Most Games Played, Total Series

    A. L.—21—Belanger, Mark H., Baltimore, 1969, 1970, 1971, 1973, 1974, 1979; 6 Series.
    N. L.—21—Russell, William E., Los Angeles, 1974, 1977, 1978, 1981, 1983; 5 Series.
          Bowa, Lawrence R., Philadelphia, 1976, 1977, 1978, 1980; Chicago, 1984; 5 Series.

Highest Fielding Average, Series, With Most Chances Accepted

    3-game Series—A. L.—1.000—Dent, Russell E., New York, 1980; 21 chances accepted.
               N. L.—1.000—Concepcion, David I., Cincinnati, 1979; 17 chances accepted.
    4-game Series—N. L.—1.000—Russell, William E., Los Angeles, 1974; 29 chances accepted.
               A. L.—1.000—Campaneris, Dagoberto B., Oakland, 1974; 20 chances accepted.
    5-game Series—A. L.—1.000—Patek, Freddie J., Kansas City, 1976; 31 chances accepted.
               N. L.—1.000—Harrelson, Derrel M., New York, 1973; 26 chances accepted.
    6-game Series—N. L.—1.000—Santana, Rafael F., New York, 1986; 31 chances accepted.
    7-game Series—A. L.—1.000—Biancalana, Roland A., Kansas City, 1985; 29 chances accepted.
               N. L.— .969—Uribe, Jose A., San Francisco, 31 chances accepted, 1987.

Putouts, Assists & Chances Accepted

Most Putouts, Total Series

N. L.—42—Russell, William E., Los Angeles, 1974, 1977, 1978, 1981, 1983; 5 Series, 21 games.

A. L.—31—Belanger, Mark H., Baltimore, 1969, 1970, 1971, 1973, 1974, 1979; 6 Series, 21 games.

Most Putouts, Series

3-game Series—A. L.—13—Cardenas, Leonardo A., Minnesota, 1969.

N. L.— 6—Held by many shortstops.

4-game Series—N. L.—13—Russell, William E., Los Angeles, 1974.

A. L.— 9—Patek, Freddie J., Kansas City, 1978.

5-game Series—N. L.—19—Templeton, Garry, L., San Diego, 1984.

A. L.—13—Patek, Freddie J., Kansas City, 1976.

6-game Series—N. L.—13—Santana, Rafael F., New York, 1986.

7-game Series—A. L.—13—Schofield, Richard C., California, 1986.

N. L.—11—Uribe, Jose A., San Francisco, 1987.

Most Putouts, Game

N. L.—7—Templeton, Garry L., San Diego, October 4, 1984.

A. L.—6—Belanger, Mark H., Baltimore, October 5, 1974.

Dent, Russell E., New York, October 5, 1977.

Patek, Freddie J., Kansas City, October 5, 1977.

Most Putouts, Inning

A. L.—3—Belanger, Mark H., Baltimore, October 5, 1974; third inning.

Patek, Freddie J., Kansas City, October 5, 1977; second inning.

N. L.—3—Speier, Chris E., Montreal, October 14, 1981; fifth inning.

Most Assists, Total Series

N. L.—70—Bowa, Lawrence R., Philadelphia, 1976, 1977, 1978, 1980; Chicago, 1984; 5 Series, 21 games.

A. L.—69—Belanger, Mark H., Baltimore, 1969, 1970, 1971, 1973, 1974, 1979; 6 Series, 21 games.

Most Assists, Series

3-game Series—A. L.—14—Belanger, Mark H., Baltimore, 1970.

N. L.—14—Concepcion, David I., Cincinnati, 1979.

4-game Series—A. L.—17—Campaneris, Dagoberto B., Oakland, 1974.

N. L.—17—Bowa, Lawrence R., Philadelphia, 1977.

5-game Series—A. L.—18—Patek, Freddie J., Kansas City, 1976, 1977.

N. L.—16—Chaney, Darrel L., Cincinnati, 1972.

Speier, Chris E., Montreal, 1981.

6-game Series—N. L.—18—Santana, Rafael F., New York, 1986.

7-game Series—A. L.—23—Schofield, Richard C., California, 1986.

N. L.—20—Uribe, Jose A., San Francisco, 1987.

Most Assists, Game

N. L.—9—Russell, William E., Los Angeles, October 5, 1978.

A. L.—9—Garcia, Alfonso R., Baltimore, October 4, 1979.

Most Assists, Inning

A. L.—3—Belanger, Mark H., Baltimore, October 7, 1973; seventh inning.

N. L.—3—Concepcion, David I., Cincinnati, October 3, 1979; fourth inning.

Most Chances Accepted, Total Series

N. L.— 107— Russell, William E., Los Angeles, 1974, 1977, 1978, 1981, 1983; 5 Series, 21 games.

A. L.— 100— Belanger, Mark H., Baltimore, 1969, 1970, 1971, 1973, 1974, 1979; 6 Series, 21 games.

Most Chances Accepted, Series

3-game Series—A. L.—25—Cardenas, Leonardo A., Minnesota, 1969.

N. L.—17—Concepcion, David I., Cincinnati, 1979.

4-game Series—N. L.—29—Russell, William E., Los Angeles, 1974.

A. L.—22—Garcia, Alfonso R., Baltimore, 1979.

5-game Series—A. L.—31—Patek, Freddie J., Kansas City, 1976.

N. L.—31—Speier, Chris E., Montreal, 1981.

6-game Series—N. L.—31—Santana, Rafael F., New York, 1986.

7-game Series—A. L.—36—Schofield, Richard C., California, 1986.

N. L.—31—Uribe, Jose A., San Francisco, 1987.

Most Chances Accepted, Game

N. L.—13—Russell, William E., Los Angeles, October 8, 1974; 6 putouts, 7 assists, 0 errors.

A. L.— 11— Cardenas, Leonardo A., Minnesota, October 5, 1969; 11 innings; 6 putouts, 5 assists, 1 error.

Garcia, Alfonso R., Baltimore, October 4, 1979; 2 putouts, 9 assists, 0 errors.

Fewest Chances Offered, Game

A. L.—0—Campaneris, Dagoberto B., Oakland, October 3, 1971.

Foli, Timothy J., California, October 10, 1982.

Ripken, Calvin E., Baltimore, October 6, 1983.

N. L.—0—Garrido, Gil G., Atlanta, October 5, 1969.

Bowa, Lawrence R., Philadelphia, October 11, 1980; 10 innings.

Russell, William E., Los Angeles, October 7, 1983.

Smith, Osborne E., St. Louis, October 11, 1987.

Most Chances Accepted, Inning

A. L.-N. L.—3—Held by many shortstops.

Errors & Double Plays

Most Errors, Total Series

A. L.—5—Owen, Spike D., Boston, 1986; 1 Series, 7 games.

N. L.—4—Reynolds, G. Craig, Pittsburgh, 1975; Houston, 1980, 1986; 3 Series, 9 games.

Most Consecutive Errorless Games, Total Series

A. L.— 17—Belanger, Mark H., Baltimore, October 4, 1969 through October 8, 1974.

N. L.— 13— Russell, William E., Los Angeles, October 5, 1977 through October 4, 1983.

Most Errors, Series

3-game Series—A. L.—2—Cardenas, Leonardo A., Minnesota, 1970.

N. L.— 1—Held by many shortstops.

4-game Series—A. L.—2—Patek, Freddie J., Kansas City, 1978.

Garcia, Alfonso R., Baltimore, 1979.

Gagne, Gregory C., Minnesota, 1987.

N. L.—2—Russell, William E., Los Angeles, 1977.

DeJesus, Ivan, Philadelphia, 1983.

5-game Series—A. L.—3—McAuliffe, Richard J., Detroit, 1972.

N. L.—3—Chaney, Darrel L., Cincinnati, 1972.

6-game Series—N. L.—2—Reynolds, G. Craig, Houston, 1986.

7-game Series—A. L.—5—Owen, Spike, D. Boston, 1986.

N. L.— 1—Uribe, Jose A., San Francisco, 1987.

Smith, Osborne E., St. Louis, 1987.

Most Errors, Game

A. L.—2—Cardenas, Leonardo A., Minnesota, October 4, 1970.

N. L.—2—Alley, L. Eugene, Pittsburgh, October 10, 1972.

Russell, William E., Los Angeles, October 4, 1977.

Most Errors, Inning

N. L.—2—Alley, L. Eugene, Pittsburgh, October 10, 1972; fourth inning.

A. L.—1—Held by many shortstops.

Most Double Plays, Total Series

N. L.—17—Russell, William E., Los Angeles, 1974, 1977, 1978, 1981, 1983; 5 Series, 21 games.

Bowa, Lawrence R., Philadelphia, 1976, 1977, 1978, 1980; Chicago, 1984; 5 Series, 21 games.

A. L.— 10—Belanger, Mark H., Baltimore, 1969, 1970, 1971, 1973, 1974, 1979; 6 Series, 21 games.

Most Double Plays, Series

3-game Series—N. L.—3—Garrido, Gil C., Atlanta, 1969.

Alley, L. Eugene, Pittsburgh, 1970.

A. L.—3—Held by many shortstops.

4-game Series—N. L.—6—Russell, William E., Los Angeles, 1974.

A. L.—3—Garcia, Alfonso R., Baltimore, 1979.

Ripken, Calvin E., Baltimore, 1983.

5-game Series—N. L.—6—Speier, Chris E., Montreal, 1981.

Bowa, Lawrence R., Chicago, 1984.

A. L.—4—Yount, Robin R., Milwaukee, 1982.

6-game Series—N. L.—4—Santana, Rafael F., New York, 1986.

7-game Series—N. L.—7—Uribe, Jose A., San Francisco, 1987.

A. L.—4—Biancalana, Roland A., Kansas City, 1985.

Most Double Plays Started, Series

3-game Series—N. L.—3—Alley, L. Eugene, Pittsburgh, 1970.

A. L.—2—Belanger, Mark H., Baltimore, 1971.

Campaneris, Dagoberto B., Oakland, 1975.

Milbourne, Lawrence W., New York, 1981.

4-game Series—N. L.— 3—Russell, William E., Los Angeles, 1974.
A. L.— 2—Belanger, Mark H., Baltimore, 1974.
Anderson, James L., California, 1979.
Ripken, Calvin E., Baltimore, 1983.
5-game Series—N. L.— 3—Bowa, Lawrence R., Philadelphia, 1980.
Speier, Chris E., Montreal, 1981.
Bowa, Lawrence R., Chicago, 1984.
A. L.— 2—Maxvill, C. Dallan, Oakland, 1972.
Patek, Freddie J., Kansas City, 1976.
Yount, Robin R., Milwaukee, 1982.
6-game Series—N. L.— 2—Smith, Osborne E., St. Louis, 1985.
Santana, Rafael F., New York, 1986.
Thon, Richard W., Houston, 1986.
7-game Series—N. L.— 2—Uribe, Jose A., San Francisco, 1987.
A. L.— 1—Held by many shortstops.

Most Double Plays, Game

A. L.— 3—Campaneris, Dagoberto B., Oakland, October 5, 1975.
N. L.— 3—Russell, William E., Los Angeles, October 8, 1974.
Russell, William E., Los Angeles, October 5, 1983.
Uribe, Jose A., San Francisco, October 10, 1987.
Smith, Osborne E., St. Louis, October 14, 1987.

Most Double Plays Started, Game

N. L.— 3—Russell, William E., Los Angeles, October 5, 1983.
A. L.— 2—Maxvill, C. Dallan, Oakland, October 10, 1972.
Campaneris, Dagoberto B., Oakland, October 5, 1975.
Patek, Freddie J., Kansas City, October 10, 1976.

Most Unassisted Double Plays, Game

N. L.— 1—Russell, William E., Los Angeles, October 8, 1974.
A. L.— 1—Yount, Robin R., Milwaukee, October 5, 1982.
Biancalana, Roland A., Kansas City, October 12, 1985.

Outfielders
Series, Games & Average

Most Series Played

A. L.— 10—Jackson, Reginald M., Oakland, 1971, 1972, 1973, 1974, 1975; New York, 1977, 1978, 1980, 1981; California, 1982; 32 games.
N. L.— 5—Geronimo, Cesar F., Cincinnati, 1972, 1973, 1975, 1976, 1979; 17 games.
Maddox, Garry L., Philadelphia, 1976, 1977, 1978, 1980, 1983; 17 games.

Most Games Played, Total Series

A. L.— 32—Jackson, Reginald M., Oakland, 1971, 1972, 1973, 1974, 1975; New York, 1977, 1978, 1980, 1981; California, 1982, 10 Series.
N. L.— 17—Geronimo, Cesar F., Cincinnati, 1972, 1973, 1975, 1976, 1979; 5 Series.
Maddox, Garry L., Philadelphia, 1976, 1977, 1978, 1980, 1983; 5 Series.

Highest Fielding Average, Series, With Most Chances Accepted

3-game Series—N. L.— 1.000—Parker, David G., Pittsburgh, 1975; 14 chances accepted.
A. L.— 1.000—Oliva, Antonio, Minnesota, 1970; 12 chances accepted.
4-game Series—A. L.— 1.000—Miller, Richard A., California, 1979; 16 chances accepted.
N. L.— 1.000—Stargell, Wilver D., Pittsburgh, 1974, 13 chances accepted.
5-game Series—N.L.— 1.000—Maddox, Garry L., Philadelphia, 1980; 23 chances accepted.
A. L.— 1.000—Jackson, Reginald M., Oakland, 1973; 19 chances accepted.
Rivers, John M., New York, 1977; 19 chances accepted.
6-game Series—N. L.— 1.000—McGee, Willie D., St. Louis, 1985; 18 chances accepted.
7-game Series—A. L.— 1.000—Downing, Brian J., California, 1986; 18 chances accepted.
N. L.— 1.000—McGee, Willie D., St. Louis, 1987; 16 chances accepted.

Putouts, Assists & Chances Accepted

Most Putouts, Total Series

A. L.— 69—Jackson, Reginald M., Oakland, 1971, 1972, 1973, 1974,

1975; New York, 1977, 1978, 1980, 1981; California, 1982; 10 Series, 32 games.
N. L.— 62—Maddox, Garry L., Philadelphia, 1976, 1977, 1978, 1980, 1983; 5 Series, 17 games.

Most Putouts, Series

3-game Series—N. L.— 13—Geronimo, Cesar F., Cincinnati, 1975.
Parker, David G., Pittsburgh, 1975.
A. L.— 12—Lynn, Fredric M., Boston, 1975.
4-game Series—N. L.— 16—Maddox, Garry L., Philadelphia, 1978.
A. L.— 14—North, William A., Oakland, 1974.
Miller, Richard A., California, 1979.
5-game Series—N. L.— 23—Maddox, Garry L., Philadelphia, 1980.
A. L.— 19—Jackson, Reginald M., Oakland, 1973.
Rivers, John M., New York, 1977.
6-game Series—N. L.— 18—McGee, Willie D., St. Louis, 1985.
7-game Series—A. L.— 28—Pettis, Gary G., California, 1986.
N. L.— 16—McGee, Willie D., St. Louis, 1987.

Most Putouts, Game, Left Field

A. L.— 7—White, Roy H., New York, October 13, 1976.
N. L.— 7—Stennett, Renaldo A., Pittsburgh, October 7, 1972.
Cruz, Jose, Houston, October 10, 1980; 11 innings.

Most Putouts, Game, Center Field

A. L.— 9—Pettis, Gary G., California, October 10, 1986.
N. L.— 8—Oliver, Albert, Pittsburgh, October 7, 1972.
Hahn, Donald A., New York, October 8, 1973.

Most Putouts, Game, Right Field

A. L.— 9—Barfield, Jesse L., Toronto, October 11, 1985.
N. L.— 6—Bass, Kevin C., Houston, October 14, 1986; 12 innings.
N. L.—Nine-inning record—5—Held by many right fielders.

Most Consecutive Putouts, Game

A. L.— 4—Gamble, Oscar C., New York, October 15, 1981; 3 in sixth inning, 1 in seventh inning; right field.
N. L.— 4—Dawson, Andre F., Montreal, October 19, 1981; 1 in sixth inning, 3 in seventh inning; center field.

Most Putouts, Inning

A. L.-N. L.—3—Held by many outfielders.

Most Assists, Total Series

N. L.— 5—McBride, Arnold R., Philadelphia, 1977, 1978, 1980; 3 Series, 11 games.
A. L.— 3—Oliva, Antonio, Minnesota, 1969, 1970; 2 Series, 6 games.
Jackson, Reginald M., Oakland, 1971, 1972, 1973, 1974, 1975; New York, 1977, 1978, 1980, 1981; 9 Series, 27 games.
Smith, Lonnie, Kansas City, 1985; 1 Series, 7 games.

Fewest Assists, Total Series (Most Games)

A. L.—0—Blair, Paul L., Baltimore, 1969, 1970, 1971, 1973, 1974; New York, 1977, 1978; 7 Series, 24 games.
N. L.—0—Maddox, Garry L., Philadelphia, 1976, 1977, 1978, 1980, 1983; 5 Series, 17 games.

Most Assists, Series

3-game Series—A. L.— 2—Oliva, Antonio, Minnesota, 1970.
Yastrzemski, Carl M., Boston, 1975.
Armas, Antonio R., Oakland, 1981.
N. L.— 2—Foster, George A., Cincinnati. 1979.
4-game Series—N. L.— 2—McBride, Arnold R., Philadelphia, 1977.
A. L.— 2—Miller, Richard A., California, 1979.
5-game Series—N. L.— 3—McBride, Arnold R., Philadelphia, 1980.
A. L.— 1—Held by many outfielders.
6-game Series—N. L.— 1—Wilson, William H., New York, 1986.
7-game Series—A. L.— 3—Smith, Lonnie, Kansas City, 1985.
N. L.— 1—Held by many outfielders.

Most Assists, Game

A. L.— 2—Oliva, Antonio, Minnesota, October 4, 1970.
N. L.— 2—Foster, George A., Cincinnati, October 3, 1979; 10 innings.
McBride, Arnold R., Philadelphia, October 11, 1980; 10 innings.

Most Chances Accepted, Total Series

A. L.— 72—Jackson, Reginald M., Oakland, 1971, 1972, 1973, 1974, 1975; New York, 1977, 1978, 1980, 1981; California, 1982; 10 Series, 32 games.
N. L.— 62—Maddox, Garry L., Philadelphia, 1976, 1977, 1978, 1980, 1983; 5 Series, 17 games.

Most Chances Accepted, Series

3-game Series—N. L.— 14—Parker, David G., Pittsburgh, 1975.
A. L.— 13—Lynn, Fredric M., Boston, 1975.

4-game Series—N. L.—16—Maddox, Garry L., Philadelphia, 1978.
A. L.—16—Miller, Richard A., California, 1979.
5-game Series—N. L.—23—Maddox, Garry L., Philadelphia, 1980.
A. L.—19—Jackson, Reginald M., Oakland, 1973.
Rivers, John M., New York, 1977.
6-game Series—N. L.—18—McGee, Willie D., St. Louis, 1985.
7-game Series—A. L.—28—Pettis, Gary G., California, 1986.
N. L.—16—McGee, Willie D., St. Louis, 1987.

Most Chances Accepted, Game, Left Field

A. L.—7—White, Roy H., New York, October 13, 1976; 7 putouts, 0 assists, 0 errors.
Hurdle, Clinton M., Kansas City, October 6, 1978; 6 putouts, 1 assist, 0 errors.
N. L.—7—Stennett, Renaldo A., Pittsburgh, October 7, 1972; 7 putouts, 0 assists, 0 errors.
Cruz, Jose, Houston, October 10, 1980; 7 putouts, 0 assists, 0 errors.

Most Chances Accepted, Game, Center Field

A. L.—9—Pettis, Gary G., California, October 10, 1986; 9 putouts, 0 assists, 0 errors.
N. L.—8—Oliver, Albert, Pittsburgh, October 7, 1972; 8 putouts, 0 assists, 0 errors.
Hahn, Donald A., New York, October 8, 1973; 8 putouts, 0 assists, 0 errors.

Most Chances Accepted, Game, Right Field

A. L.—9—Barfield, Jesse L., Toronto, October 11, 1985; 9 putouts, 0 assists, 0 errors.
N. L.—6—Bass, Kevin C., Houston, October 14, 1986; 12 innings; 6 putouts, 0 assists, 0 errors.
N. L.—Nine-inning record—5—Held by many right fielders.

Longest Game, No Chances Offered, Outfielder

N. L.—12 innings—Hahn, Donald A., New York, October 9, 1973.
Hatcher, William A., Houston, October 14, 1986.
A. L.—11 innings—Alou, Mateo R., Oakland, October 7, 1972.
Rice, James E., Boston, October 11, 1986.

Most Chances Accepted, Inning

A. L.-N. L.—3—Held by many players.

Errors & Double Plays

Most Errors, Total Series

N. L.—2—Smith, C. Reginald, Los Angeles, 1977, 1978; 2 Series, 8 games.
A. L.—2—Oliva, Antonio, Minnesota, 1969, 1970; 2 Series, 6 games.
Washington, Claudell, Oakland, 1974, 1975; 2 Series, 5 games.
Gamble, Oscar C., New York, 1976, 1980, 1981; 3 Series, 5 games.
Bumbry, Alonza B., Baltimore, 1973, 1979; 2 Series, 6 games.
Oglivie, Benjamin A., Milwaukee, 1982; 1 Series, 4 games.

Most Consecutive Errorless Games, Total Series

A. L.—25—Jackson, Reginald M., Oakland, New York, California, October 12, 1972 through October 10, 1982; 48 chances accepted.
N. L.—16—Oliver, Albert, Pittsburgh, October 2, 1971 through October 7, 1975; 37 chances accepted.
Geronimo, Cesar F., Cincinnati; October 7, 1972 through October 3, 1979; 50 chances accepted.

Most Errors, Series

A. L.—2—Oliva, Antonio, Minnesota, 1969; 3-game Series.
Washington, Claudell, Oakland, 1975; 3-game Series.
Gamble, Oscar C., New York, 1976; 5-game Series.
Oglivie, Benjamin A., Milwaukee, 1982; 5-game Series.
N. L.—1—Held by many outfielders.

Most Errors, Game

A. L.—2—Oliva, Antonio, Minnesota, October 6, 1969.
Oglivie, Benjamin A., Milwaukee, October 10, 1982.
N. L.—1—Held by many outfielders.

Most Errors, Inning

A. L.-N. L.—1—Held by many outfielders.

Most Double Plays, Total Series

N. L.—3—McBride, Arnold R., Philadelphia, 1977, 1978, 1980; 3 Series, 11 games.
A. L.—2—Miller, Richard A., California, 1979; 1 Series, 4 games.

Most Double Plays, Game

N. L.—2—McBride, Arnold R., Philadelphia, October 11, 1980; 10 innings.
A. L.-N. L.—Nine-inning record—1—Held by many outfielders.

Most Double Plays Started, Game

N. L.—2—McBride, Arnold R., Philadelphia, October 11, 1980; 10 innings.
A. L.-N. L.—Nine-inning record—1—Held by many outfielders.

Most Unassisted Double Plays, Game

A. L.-N. L.—Never accomplished.

Catchers
Series, Games & Average

Most Series Played

Both Leagues—6—Boone, Robert R., Philadelphia NL, 1976, 1977, 1978, 1980; California AL, 1982, 1986; 27 games.
N. L.—6—Bench, Johnny L., Cincinnati, 1970, 1972, 1973, 1975, 1976, 1979; 22 games.
Yeager, Stephen W., Los Angeles, 1974, 1977, 1978, 1981, 1983, 1985; 15 games.
A. L.—5—Etchebarren, Andrew A., Baltimore, 1969, 1970, 1971, 1973, 1974; 12 games.

Most Games Caught, Total Series

Both Leagues—27—Boone, Robert R., Philadelphia NL, 1976, 1977, 1978, 1980; California AL, 1982, 1986; 6 Series.
N. L.—22—Bench, Johnny L., Cincinnati, 1970, 1972, 1973, 1975, 1976, 1979; 6 Series.
A. L.—14—Munson, Thurman L., New York, 1976, 1977, 1978; 3 Series.

Highest Fielding Average, Series, With Most Chances Accepted

3-game Series—N. L.—1.000—Ott, N. Edward, Pittsburgh, 1979; 28 chances accepted.
A. L.—1.000—Cerone, Richard A., New York, 1981; 25 chances accepted.
4-game Series—N. L.—1.000—Dietz, Richard A., San Francisco, 1971; 36 chances accepted.
A. L.—1.000—Fisk, Carlton E., Chicago, 1983; 30 chances accepted.
5-game Series—A. L.—1.000—Simmons, Ted L., Milwaukee, 1982; 39 chances accepted.
N. L.—1.000—Bench, Johnny L., Cincinnati, 1973; 33 chances accepted.
6-game Series—N. L.—1.000—Ashby, Alan D., Houston, 1986; 60 chances accepted.
7-game Series—N. L.—1.000—Pena, Antonio F., St. Louis, 1987; 60 chances accepted.
A. L.—1.000—Whitt, L. Ernest, Toronto, 1985; 53 chances accepted.

Putouts, Assists & Chances Accepted

Most Putouts, Total Series

Both Leagues—127—Boone, Robert R., Philadelphia NL, 1976, 1977, 1978, 1980; California AL, 1982, 1986; 6 Series, 27 games.
N. L.—125—Bench, Johnny L., Cincinnati, 1970, 1972, 1973, 1975, 1976, 1979; 6 Series, 22 games.
A. L.—78—Etchebarren, Andrew A., Baltimore, 1969, 1970, 1971, 1973, 1974; 5 Series, 12 games.

Most Putouts, Series

3-game Series—N. L.—29—Sanguillen, Manuel D., Pittsburgh, 1975.
A. L.—23—Cerone, Richard A., New York, 1981.
4-game Series—N. L.—34—Dietz, Richard A., San Francisco, 1971.
A. L.—29—Dempsey, J. Rikard, Baltimore, 1983.
5-game Series—N. L.—42—Grote, Gerald W., New York, 1973.
A. L.—36—Simmons, Ted L., Milwaukee, 1982.
6-game Series—N. L.—59—Ashby, Alan D., Houston, 1986.
7-game Series—N. L.—55—Pena, Antonio F., St. Louis, 1987.
A. L.—50—Whitt, L. Ernest, Toronto, 1985.

Most Putouts, Game, Nine Innings

A. L.—15—Dempsey, J. Rikard, Baltimore, October 6, 1983.
N. L.—14—Dietz, Richard A., San Francisco, October 3, 1971.
Ashby, Alan D., Houston, October 8, 1986.

Most Putouts, Extra-Inning Game

N. L.— 15—Sanguillen, Manuel D., Pittsburgh, October 7, 1975; 10 innings.
Ashby, Alan D., Houston, October 14, 1986; 12 innings.
A. L.—Less than nine-inning record.

Fewest Putouts, Game

A. L.—1—Fosse, Raymond E., Oakland, October 11, 1973.
Martinez, J. Buck, Kansas City, October 13, 1976.
Sundberg, James H., Kansas City, October 12, 1985.
N. L.—1—Kennedy, Terrence E., San Diego, October 3, 1984.

Most Putouts, Inning

A. L.-N. L.—3—Held by many catchers.

Most Assists, Total Series

N. L.— 18—Bench, Johnny L., Cincinnati, 1970, 1972, 1973, 1975, 1976, 1979; 6 Series, 22 games.
A. L.— 14—Munson, Thurman L., New York, 1976, 1977, 1978; 3 Series, 14 games.

Most Assists, Series

3-game Series—A. L.—4—Mitterwald, George E., Minnesota, 1969.
Cerone, Richard A., New York, 1980.
N. L.—4—Bench, Johnny L., Cincinnati, 1975, 1976.
4-game Series—A. L.—5—Dempsey, J. Rikard, Baltimore, 1983.
N. L.—2—Held by many catchers.
5-game Series—A. L.—6—Munson, Thurman L., New York, 1976.
N. L.—4—Kennedy, Terrence E., San Diego, 1984.
6-game Series—N. L.—5—Carter, Gary E., New York, 1986.
7-game Series—N. L.—5—Pena, Antonio F., St. Louis, 1987.
A. L.—4—Gedman, Richard L., Boston, 1986.

Most Assists, Game

N. L.—3—Bench, Johnny L., Cincinnati, October 3, 1970; 10 innings.
Bench, Johnny L., Cincinnati, October 5, 1975.
Carter, Gary E., New York, October 15, 1986; 16 innings.
A. L.—2—Held by many catchers.

Most Assists, Inning

N. L.—2—Bench, Johnny L., Cincinnati, October 7, 1973; eighth inning.
Scioscia, Michael L., Los Angeles, October 10, 1985; first inning.
Carter, Gary E., New York, October 15, 1986; twelfth inning.
A. L.—1—Held by many catchers.

Most Chances Accepted, Total Series

N. L.— 143—Bench, Johnny L., Cincinnati, 1970, 1972, 1973, 1975, 1976, 1979; 6 Series, 22 games.
A. L.— 81—Etchebarren, Andrew A., Baltimore, 1969, 1970, 1971, 1973, 1974; 5 Series, 12 games.

Most Chances Accepted, Series

3-game Series—N. L.—30—Sanguillen, Manuel D., Pittsburgh, 1975.
A. L.—25—Cerone, Richard A., New York, 1981.
4-game Series—N. L.—36—Dietz, Richard A., San Francisco, 1971.
A. L.—34—Dempsey, J. Rikard, Baltimore, 1983.
5-game Series—N. L.—43—Grote, Gerald W., New York, 1973.
A. L.—39—Simmons, Ted L., Milwaukee, 1982.
6-game Series—N. L.—60—Ashby, Alan D., Houston, 1986.
7-game Series—N. L.—60—Pena, Antonio F., St. Louis, 1987.
A. L.—53—Whitt, L. Ernest, Toronto, 1985.

Most Chances Accepted, Game

A. L.— 16—Dempsey, J. Rikard, Baltimore, October 6, 1983; 15 putouts, 1 assist, 0 errors.
N. L.— 15—Dietz, Richard A., San Francisco, October 3, 1971; 14 putouts, 1 assist, 0 errors.
Sanguillen, Manuel D., Pittsburgh, October 7, 1975; 10 innings; 15 putouts, 0 assists, 1 error.
Ashby, Alan D., Houston, October 14, 1986; 12 innings; 15 putouts, 0 assists, 0 errors.

Fewest Chances Offered, Game

A. L.-N. L.—2—Held by many catchers.

Most Chances Accepted, Inning

A. L.-N. L.—3—Held by many catchers.

Errors & Passed Balls

Most Errors, Total Series

N. L.—5—Sanguillen, Manuel D., Pittsburgh, 1970, 1971, 1972, 1974, 1975; 5 Series, 19 games.
A. L.—3—Slaught, Donald M., Kansas City, 1984; 1 Series, 3 games.

Most Consecutive Errorless Games, Total Series

Both Leagues—18—Porter, Darrell R., Kansas City AL, October 5, 1977 through October 10, 1980 (12 games); St. Louis NL, October 7, 1982 through October 12, 1985 (6 games).
N. L.— 17—Bench, Johnny L., Cincinnati, October 9, 1972 through October 5, 1979.
A. L.— 12—Etchebarren, Andrew A., Baltimore, October 4, 1969 through October 8, 1974.
Munson, Thurman L., New York, October 12, 1976 through October 7, 1978.
Porter, Darrell R., Kansas City, October 5, 1977 through October 10, 1980.

Most Errors, Series

3-game Series—A. L.—3—Slaught, Donald M., Kansas City, 1984.
N. L.—1—Sanguillen, Manuel D., Pittsburgh, 1970, 1975.
4-game Series—N. L.—2—Sanguillen, Manuel D., Pittsburgh, 1974.
A. L.—1—Dempsey, J. Rikard, Baltimore, 1983.
5-game Series—A. L.—2—Munson, Thurman L., New York, 1976.
N. L.—1—Bench, Johnny L., Cincinnati, 1972.
Sanguillen, Manuel D., Pittsburgh, 1972.
Grote, Gerald W., New York, 1973.
6-game Series—N. L.—1—Porter, Darrell R., St. Louis, 1985.
Scioscia, Michael L., Los Angeles, 1985.
7-game Series—A. L.—1—Sundberg, James H., Kansas City, 1985.
N. L.—Never occurred.

Most Errors, Game

A. L.—2—Munson, Thurman L., New York, October 10, 1976.
Slaught, Donald M., Kansas City, October 5, 1984.
N. L.—2—Sanguillen, Manuel D., Pittsburgh, October 6, 1974.

Most Errors, Inning

A. L.-N. L.—1—Held by many catchers.

Most Passed Balls, Total Series

Both Leagues—4—Boone, Robert R., Philadelphia NL, 1976, 1977, 1978, 1980; California AL, 1982, 1986; 6 Series, 27 games.
N. L.—4—Sanguillen, Manuel D., Pittsburgh, 1970, 1971, 1972, 1974, 1975; 5 Series, 19 games.
A. L.—3—Boone, Robert R., California, 1982, 1986; 2 Series, 12 games.

Most Passed Balls, Series

N. L.—2—Sanguillen, Manuel D., Pittsburgh, 1975; 3-game Series.
Ashby, Alan D., Houston, 1986; 6-game Series.
A. L.—2—Boone, Robert R., California, 1986; 7-game Series.

Most Passed Balls, Game

N. L.—2—Sanguillen, Manuel D., Pittsburgh, October 4, 1975.
Ashby, Alan D., Houston, October 11, 1986.
A. L.—1—Held by many catchers.

Most Passed Balls, Inning

A L.-N. L.—1—Held by many catchers.

Double Plays & Runners Caught Stealing

Most Double Plays Total Series

A. L.—4—Fosse, Raymond E., Oakland, 1973, 1974, 1975; 3 Series, 10 games.
N. L.—3—Sanguillen, Manuel D., Pittsburgh, 1970, 1971, 1972, 1974, 1975; 5 Series, 19 games.

Most Double Plays, Series

A. L.—2—Mitterwald, George E., Minnesota, 1970; 3-game Series.
Fosse, Raymond E., Oakland, 1973; 5-game Series.
N. L.—1—Held by many catchers.

Most Double Plays Started, Series

A. L.—2—Fosse, Raymond E., Oakland, 1973; 5-game Series.
N. L.—1—Held by many catchers.

Most Double Plays, Game

A. L.-N. L.—1—Held by many catchers.

Most Double Plays Started, Game

A. L.-N. L.—1—Held by many catchers.

Most Unassisted Double Plays, Game

A. L.-N. L.—Never accomplished.

Most Players Caught Stealing, Total Series

A. L.— 12— Munson, Thurman L., New York, 1976, 1977, 1978; 3 Series, 14 games.

N. L.— 5— Scioscia, Michael L., Los Angeles, 1981, 1985; 2 Series, 11 games.

Most Players Caught Stealing, Series

3-game Series—A. L.— 4—Mitterwald, George E., Minnesota, 1969.
N. L.— 1—Held by many catchers.
4-game Series—A. L.— 3—Fosse, Raymond E., Oakland, 1974.
Munson, Thurman L., New York, 1978.
N. L.— 1—Held by many catchers.
5-game Series—A. L.— 5—Munson, Thurman L., New York, 1976.
N. L.— 2—Kennedy, Terrence E., San Diego, 1984.
Davis, Jody R., Chicago, 1984.
6-game Series—N. L.— 4—Scioscia, Michael L., Los Angeles, 1985.
7-game Series—A. L.— 4—Gedman, Richard L., Boston, 1986.
N. L.— 2—Brenly, Robert E., San Francisco, 1987.
Pena, Antonio F., St. Louis, 1987.

Most Players Caught Stealing, Game

A. L.-N. L.—2—Held by many catchers.

Most Players Caught Stealing, Inning

A. L.-N. L.—1—Held by many catchers.

Pitchers
Series, Games & Average

Most Series Pitched

Both Leagues—6—Gullett, Donald E., Cincinnati NL, 1970, 1972, 1973, 1975, 1976; New York AL, 1977; 10 games.
A. L.—6—Hunter, James A., Oakland, 1971, 1972, 1973, 1974; New York, 1976, 1978; 10 games.
Palmer, James A., Baltimore, 1969, 1970, 1971, 1973, 1974, 1979; 8 games.
N. L.—6—McGraw, Frank E., New York, 1969, 1973; Philadelphia, 1976, 1977, 1978, 1980; 15 games.
Reed, Ronald L., Atlanta, 1969; Philadelphia, 1976, 1977, 1978, 1980, 1983; 13 games.

Most Games Pitched, Total Series

N. L.— 15— McGraw, Frank E., New York, 1969, 1973; Philadelphia, 1976, 1977, 1978, 1980; 6 Series.
A. L.— 11— Fingers, Roland G., Oakland, 1971, 1972, 1973, 1974, 1975; 5 Series.

Most Games Pitched, Series

3-game Series—N. L.— 3—Upshaw, Cecil L., Atlanta, 1969.
Tomlin, David A., Cincinnati, 1979.
Hume, Thomas H., Cincinnati, 1979.
A. L.— 3—Perranoski, Ronald P., Minnesota, 1969.
Todd, James R., Oakland, 1975.
Hernandez, Guillermo, Detroit, 1984.
4-game Series—N. L.— 4—Giusti, J. David, Pittsburgh, 1971.
A. L.— 3—Hrabosky, Alan T., Kansas City, 1978.
Stanhouse, Donald J., Baltimore, 1979.
Lamp, Dennis P., Chicago, 1983.
5-game Series—N. L.— 5—McGraw, Frank E., Philadelphia, 1980.
A. L.— 4—Blue, Vida R., Oakland, 1972.
Lyle, Albert W., New York, 1977.
Berenguer, Juan B., Minnesota, 1987.
Reardon, Jeffrey J., Minnesota, 1987.
6-game Series—N. L.— 5—Dayley, Kenneth G., St. Louis, 1985.
7-game Series—A. L.— 4—Quisenberry, Daniel R., Kansas City, 1985.
Lucas, Gary P., California, 1986.
Schiraldi, Calvin D., Boston, 1986.
N. L.— 3—Held by many pitchers.

Highest Fielding Average, Series, With Most Chances Accepted

3-game Series—N. L.— 1.000—Gullett, Donald E., Cincinnati, 1975; 5 chances accepted.
A. L.— 1.000—Boswell, David W., Minnesota, 1969; 5 chances accepted.

Lindblad, Paul A., Oakland, 1975; 5 chances accepted.
Wise, Richard C., Boston, 1975; 5 chances accepted.
4-game Series—N. L.— 1.000—Marichal, Juan A., San Francisco, 1971; 6 chances accepted.
Carlton, Steven N., Philadelphia, 1983; 6 chances accepted.
A. L.— 1.000—Cuellar, Miguel, Baltimore, 1974; 5 chances accepted.
Hunter, James A., Oakland, 1974; 5 chances accepted.
Gura, Lawrence C., Kansas City, 1978; 5 chances accepted.
5-game Series—N. L.— 1.000—Blass, Stephen R., Pittsburgh, 1972; 4 chances accepted.
Ryan, L. Nolan, Houston, 1980; 4 chances accepted.
A. L.— 1.000—Lolich, Michael S., Detroit, 1972; 4 chances accepted.
John, Thomas E., California, 1982; 4 chances accepted.
6-game Series—N. L.— 1.000—Ojeda, Robert M., New York, 1986; 6 chances accepted.
7-game Series—A. L.— 1.000—Leibrandt, Charles L., Kansas City, 1985; 10 chances accepted.
N. L.— 1.000—Cox, Danny B., St. Louis, 1987; 9 chances accepted.

Putouts, Assists & Chances Accepted

Most Putouts, Total Series

N. L.—5—Gullett, Donald E., Cincinnati, 1970, 1972, 1973, 1975, 1976; 5 Series, 9 games.
A. L.—4—Hunter, James A., Oakland, 1971, 1972, 1973, 1974; New York, 1976, 1978; 6 Series, 10 games.
Palmer James A., Baltimore, 1969, 1970, 1971, 1973, 1974, 1979; 6 Series, 8 games.
Leibrandt, Charles L., Kansas City, 1984, 1985; 2 Series, 4 games.

Most Putouts, Series

3-game Series—N. L.— 4—Gullett, Donald E., Cincinnati, 1975.
A. L.— 2—Wise, Richard, C., Boston, 1975.
Wilcox, Milton E., Detroit, 1984.
4-game Series—A. L.— 3—Hunter, James A., Oakland, 1974.
N. L.— 2—Marichal, Juan A., San Francisco, 1971.
Sutton, Donald H., Los Angeles, 1974.
5-game Series—A. L.— 3—John, Thomas E., California, 1982.
N. L.— 2—McGraw, Frank E., New York, 1973.
Ruthven, Richard D., Philadelphia, 1980.
6-game Series—N. L.— 3—Gooden, Dwight E., New York, 1986.
McDowell, Roger A., New York, 1986.
7-game Series—N. L.— 4—Cox, Danny B., St. Louis, 1987.
A. L.— 3—Leibrandt, Charles L., Kansas City, 1985.

Most Putouts, Game

N. L.—4—Gullett, Donald E., Cincinnati, October 4, 1975.
A. L.—3—John, Thomas E., California, October 5, 1982.
Leibrandt, Charles L., Kansas City, October 12, 1985.

Most Putouts, Inning

A. L.—2—Torrez, Michael A., New York, October 7, 1977; second inning.
Leibrandt, Charles L., Kansas City, October 12, 1985; fifth inning.
Witt, Michael A., California, October 12, 1986; first inning.
N. L.—2—Gullett, Donald E., Cincinnati, October 4, 1975; third inning.
McDowell, Roger A., New York, October 15, 1986; tenth inning.

Most Assists, Total Series

A. L.— 12—Cuellar, Miguel, Baltimore, 1969, 1970, 1971, 1973, 1974; 5 Series, 6 games.
N. L.— 6—Sutton, Donald H., Los Angeles, 1974, 1977, 1978; 3 Series, 4 games.
Carlton, Steven N., Philadelphia, 1976, 1977, 1978, 1980, 1983; 5 Series, 8 games.

Most Assists, Series

3-game Series—A. L.— 4—Boswell, David W., Minnesota, 1969.
Lindblad, Paul A., Oakland, 1975.

N. L.—3—Niekro, Philip H., Atlanta, 1969.
    Ellis, Dock P., Pittsburgh, 1970.
    Zachry, Patrick P., Cincinnati, 1976.
4-game Series—A. L.—5—Cuellar, Miguel, Baltimore, 1974.
    N. L.—5—Carlton, Steven N., Philadelphia, 1983.
5-game Series—N. L.—3—Blass, Stephen R., Pittsburgh, 1972.
    Seaver, G. Thomas, New York, 1973.
    Ryan, L. Nolan, Houston, 1980.
    A. L.—3—Held by many pitchers.
6-game Series—N. L.—4—Scott, Michael W., Houston, 1986.
    Ojeda, Robert, M., New York, 1986.
7-game Series—A. L.—7—Leibrandt, Charles L., Kansas City, 1985.
    N. L.—5—Cox, Danny B., St. Louis, 1987.

Most Assists, Game

A. L.—5—Leibrandt, Charles L., Kansas City, October 12, 1985.
N. L.—4—Marichal, Juan A., San Francisco, October 5, 1971.

Most Assists, Inning

N. L.—3—Zachry, Patrick P., Cincinnati, October 10, 1976; fourth inning.
A. L.—2—Held by many pitchers.

Most Chances Accepted, Total Series

A. L.—13—Cuellar, Miguel, Baltimore, 1969, 1970, 1971, 1973, 1974; 5 Series, 6 games.
    Leibrandt, Charles L., Kansas City, 1984, 1985; 2 Series, 4 games.
N. L.—9—Cox, Danny B., St. Louis, 1985, 1987; 2 Series, 3 games.

Most Chances Accepted, Series

3-game Series—N. L.—5—Gullett, Donald E., Cincinnati, 1975.
    A. L.—5—Boswell, David W., Minnesota, 1969.
    Wise, Richard C., Boston, 1975.
    Lindblad, Paul A., Oakland, 1975.
4-game Series—N. L.—6—Marichal, Juan A., San Francisco, 1971.
    Carlton, Steven N., Philadelphia, 1983.
    A. L.—5—Hunter, James A., Oakland, 1974.
    Cuellar, Miguel, Baltimore, 1974.
    Gura, Lawrence C., Kansas City, 1978.
5-game Series—N. L.—4—Blass, Stephen R., Pittsburgh, 1972.
    Ryan, L. Nolan, Houston, 1980.
    A. L.—4—Lolich, Michael S., Detroit, 1972.
    John, Thomas E., California, 1982.

6-game Series—N. L.—6—Scott, Michael W., Houston, 1986.
    Ojeda, Robert M., New York, 1986.
7-game Series—A. L.—10—Leibrandt, Charles L., Kansas City, 1985.
    N. L.—9—Cox, Danny B., St. Louis, 1987.

Most Chances Accepted, Game

A. L.—8—Leibrandt, Charles L., Kansas City, October 12, 1985.
N. L.—6—Marichal, Juan A., San Francisco, October 5, 1971.

Most Chances Accepted, Inning

N. L.—3—Zachry, Patrick P., Cincinnati, October 10, 1976; fourth inning.
A. L.—2—Held by many pitchers.

Errors & Double Plays

Most Errors, Total Series

N. L.—2—Andujar, Joaquin, St. Louis, 1982, 1985; 2 Series, 4 games.
A. L.—1—Held by many pitchers.

Most Consecutive Errorless Games, Total Series

N. L.—13—Giusti, J. David, Pittsburgh, October 4, 1970 through October 7, 1975.
    McGraw, Frank E., New York, Philadelphia, October 10, 1973 through October 12, 1980.
    Reed, Ronald L., Atlanta, Philadelphia, October 5, 1969 through October 8, 1983.
A. L.—11—Fingers, Roland G., Oakland, October 3, 1971 through October 5, 1975.

Most Errors, Series

N. L.—2—Andujar, Joaquin, St. Louis, 1985.
A. L.—1—Held by many pitchers.

Most Errors, Game

A. L.-N. L.—1—Held by many pitchers.

Most Double Plays, Total Series

A. L.-N. L.—1—Held by many pitchers.

Most Double Plays Started, Total Series

A. L.-N. L.—1—Held by many pitchers.

Most Unassisted Double Plays, Game

A. L.-N. L.—Never accomplished.

Club Fielding

Number Of Players At Positions
First Basemen

Most First Basemen, Series

3-game Series—A. L.—3—Oakland vs. Boston, 1975.
    N. L.—2—Held by many clubs.
4-game Series—N. L.—3—Philadelphia vs. Los Angeles, 1977.
    A. L.—3—Chicago vs. Baltimore, 1983.
5-game Series—A. L.—3—Oakland vs. Baltimore, 1973.
    Kansas City vs. New York, 1977.
    N. L.—3—Houston vs. Philadelphia, 1980.
6-game Series—N. L.—3—Los Angeles vs. St. Louis, 1985.
7-game Series—A. L.—3—California vs. Boston, 1986.
    N. L.—3—St. Louis vs. San Francisco, 1987.

Most First Basemen, Series, Both Clubs

3-game Series—A. L.—4—Oakland 3, Boston 1, 1975.
    Oakland 2, New York 2, 1981.
    N. L.—4—Cincinnati 2, Pittsburgh 2, 1970.
4-game Series—A. L.—4—Baltimore 2, Oakland 2, 1974.
    Chicago 3, Baltimore 1, 1983.
    N. L.—4—Philadelphia 3, Los Angeles 1, 1977.
5-game Series—A. L.—5—Oakland 3, Baltimore 2, 1973.
    N. L.—4—Houston 3, Philadelphia 1, 1980.
6-game Series—N. L.—4—Los Angeles 3, St. Louis 1, 1985.
7-game Series—A. L.—5—California 3, Boston 2, 1986.
    N. L.—3—St. Louis 2, San Francisco 1, 1987.

Most First Basemen, Game

N. L.—3—Los Angeles vs. St. Louis, October 14, 1985.
A. L.—2—Made in many games.

Most First Basemen, Game, Both Clubs

N. L.—4—Los Angeles 3, St. Louis 1, October 14, 1985.

A. L.—3—Made in many games.

Second Basemen

Most Second Basemen, Series

3-game Series—A. L.—3—Minnesota vs. Baltimore, 1970.
    Oakland vs. Boston, 1975.
    N. L.—2—Held by many clubs.
4-game Series—A. L.—3—New York vs. Kansas City, 1978.
    N. L.—1—Held by many clubs.
5-game Series—A. L.—4—Oakland vs. Detroit, 1972.
    N. L.—2—Held by many clubs.
6-game Series—N. L.—2—New York vs. Houston, 1986.
7-game Series—A. L.—3—California vs. Boston, 1986.
    N. L.—2—San Francisco vs. St. Louis, 1987.

Most Second Basemen, Series, Both Clubs

3-game Series—A. L.—4—Minnesota 3, Baltimore 1, 1970.
    Oakland 3, Boston 1, 1975.
    N. L.—3—Made in many Series.
4-game Series—A. L.—4—New York 3, Kansas City 1, 1978.
    N. L.—2—Made in many Series.
5-game Series—A. L.—6—Oakland 4, Detroit 2, 1972.
    N. L.—3—Made in many Series.
6-game Series—N. L.—3—New York 2, Houston 1, 1986.
7-game Series—A. L.—4—California 3, Boston 1, 1986.
    N. L.—3—San Francisco 2, St. Louis 1, 1987.

Most Second Basemen, Game

A. L.—3—Minnesota vs. Baltimore, October 3, 1970.
    Oakland vs. Detroit, October 7, 1972; 11 innings.
    Oakland vs. Detroit, October 10, 1972.
    Oakland vs. Boston, October 7, 1975.
    New York vs. Kansas City, October 4, 1978.
N. L.—2—Made in many games.

Most Second Basemen, Game, Both Clubs

A. L.—4—Minnesota 3, Baltimore 1, October 3, 1970.
    Oakland 3, Detroit 1, October 7, 1972; 11 innings.
    Oakland 3, Detroit 1, October 10, 1972.
    Oakland 3, Boston 1, October 7, 1975.
    New York 3, Kansas City 1, October 4, 1978.
N. L.—3—Made in many games.

Third Basemen

Most Third Basemen, Series

3-game Series—A. L.—3—Detroit vs. Kansas City, 1984.
    N. L.—2—Held by many clubs.
4-game Series—N. L.—3—San Francisco vs. Pittsburgh, 1971.
    A. L.—2—Chicago vs. Baltimore, 1983.
5-game Series—A. L.—3—Detroit vs. Minnesota, 1987.
    N. L.—2—Held by many clubs.
6-game Series—N. L.—3—Los Angeles vs. St. Louis, 1985.
7-game Series—N. L.—3—St. Louis vs. San Francisco, 1987.
    A. L.—2—Toronto vs. Kansas City, 1985.

Most Third Basemen, Series, Both Clubs

3-game Series—A. L.—5—Detroit 3, Kansas City 2, 1984.
    N. L.—4—Cincinnati 2, Pittsburgh 2, 1970.
    San Diego 2, Chicago 2, 1984.
4-game Series—N. L.—5—San Francisco 3, Pittsburgh 2, 1971.
    A. L.—3—Chicago 2, Baltimore 1, 1983.
5-game Series—A. L.—4—Detroit 3, Minnesota 1, 1987.
    N. L.—3—Cincinnati 2, New York 1, 1973.
    Los Angeles 2, Montreal 1, 1981.
6-game Series—N. L.—4—Los Angeles 3, St. Louis 1, 1985.
7-game Series—N. L.—4—St. Louis 3, San Francisco 1, 1987.
    A. L.—3—Toronto 2, Kansas City 1, 1985.

Most Third Basemen, Game

A. L.—3—Detroit vs. Kansas City, October 3, 1984; 11 innings.
Nine-inning record—A.L.-N.L.—2—Held by many clubs.

Most Third Basemen, Game, Both Clubs

A. L.—5—Detroit 3, Kansas City 2, October 3, 1984; 11 innings.
Nine-inning record—A. L.-N. L.—3—Made in many games.

Shortstops

Most Shortstops, Series

3-game Series—N. L.—3—Pittsburgh vs. Cincinnati, 1975.
    A. L.—2—Held by many clubs.
4-game Series—N. L.—3—Pittsburgh vs. Los Angeles, 1974.
    A. L.—3—California vs. Baltimore, 1979.
5-game Series—A. L.—4—Oakland vs. Detroit, 1972.
    N. L.—3—Cincinnati vs. New York, 1973.
6-game Series—N. L.—2—Los Angeles vs. St. Louis, 1985.
7-game Series—A. L.—2—Kansas City vs. Toronto, 1985.
    Boston vs. California, 1986.
    N. L.—1—St. Louis vs. San Francisco, 1987.
    San Francisco vs. St. Louis, 1987.

Most Shortstops, Series, Both Clubs

3-game Series—N. L.—4—Cincinnati 2, Pittsburgh 2, 1970.
    Pittsburgh 3, Cincinnati 1, 1975.
    A. L.—4—Oakland 2, New York 2, 1981.
4-game Series—A. L.—5—California 3, Baltimore 2, 1979.
    N. L.—4—Pittsburgh 3, Los Angeles 1, 1974.
5-game Series—A. L.—6—Oakland 4, Detroit 2, 1972.
    N. L.—4—Cincinnati 3, New York 1, 1973.
6-game Series—N. L.—3—Los Angeles 2, St. Louis 1, 1985.
7-game Series—A. L.—3—Kansas City 2, Toronto 1, 1985.
    Boston 2, California 1, 1986.
    N. L.—2—St. Louis 1, San Francisco 1, 1987.

Most Shortstops, Game

N. L.—3—Cincinnati vs. New York, October 9, 1973; 12 innings.
    Pittsburgh vs. Los Angeles, October 6, 1974.
    Pittsburgh vs. Cincinnati, October 7, 1975; 10 innings.
A. L.—3—Oakland vs. Detroit, October 11, 1972; 10 innings.
Nine-inning record—2—Held by many clubs.

Most Shortstops, Game, Both Clubs

A. L.—4—Oakland 3, Detroit 1, October 11, 1972; 10 innings.
    Nine-inning record—3—Made in many games.
N. L.—4—Cincinnati 3, New York 1, October 9, 1973; 12 innings.
    Pittsburgh 3, Los Angeles 1, October 6, 1974.
    Pittsburgh 3, Cincinnati 1, October 7, 1975; 10 innings.

    New York 2, Houston 2, October 8, 1986.
    New York 2, Houston 2, October 14, 1986; 12 innings.
    New York 2, Houston 2, October 15, 1986; 16 innings.

Left Fielders

Most Left Fielders, Series

3-game Series—N. L.—4—Cincinnati vs. Pittsburgh, 1970.
    A. L.—3—New York vs. Kansas City, 1980.
    Detroit vs. Kansas City, 1984.
4-game Series—A. L.—3—Kansas City vs. New York, 1978.
    New York vs. Kansas City, 1978.
    Baltimore vs. California, 1979.
    California vs. Baltimore, 1979.
    Chicago vs. Baltimore, 1983.
    N. L.—3—Philadelphia vs. Los Angeles, 1983.
5-game Series—A. L.—3—Detroit vs. Oakland, 1972.
    Kansas City vs. New York, 1977.
    N. L.—5—Philadelphia vs. Houston, 1980.
6-game Series—N. L.—3—Los Angeles vs. St. Louis, 1985.
    New York vs. Houston, 1986.
7-game Series—A. L.—2—Kansas City vs. Toronto, 1985.
    N. L.—1—St. Louis vs. San Francisco, 1987.
    San Francisco vs. St. Louis, 1987.

Most Left Fielders, Series, Both Clubs

3-game Series—N. L.—6—Cincinnati 4, Pittsburgh 2, 1970.
    A. L.—4—Baltimore 2, Minnesota 2, 1970.
    Baltimore 2, Oakland 2, 1971.
    New York 3, Kansas City 1, 1980.
    Detroit 3, Kansas City 1, 1984.
4-game Series—A. L.—6—Kansas City 3, New York 3, 1978.
    Baltimore 3, California 3, 1979.
    N. L.—4—Los Angeles 2, Pittsburgh 2, 1974.
    Philadelphia 3, Los Angeles 1, 1983.
5-game Series—A. L.—5—Kansas City 3, New York 2, 1977.
    N. L.—6—Philadelphia 5, Houston 1, 1980.
6-game Series—N. L.—5—Los Angeles 3, St. Louis 2, 1985.
7-game Series—A. L.—3—Kansas City 2, Toronto 1, 1985.
    N. L.—2—St. Louis 1, San Francisco 1, 1987.

Most Left Fielders, Game

N. L.—3—Philadelphia vs. Cincinnati, October 12, 1976.
    Philadelphia vs. Houston, October 11, 1980; 10 innings.
    Philadelphia vs. Los Angeles, October 8, 1983.
A. L.—3—Detroit vs. Kansas City, October 2, 1984.

Most Left Fielders, Game, Both Clubs

A. L.—4—Kansas City 2, New York 2, October 6, 1978.
    Detroit 3, Kansas City 1, October 2, 1984.
N. L.—4—Cincinnati 2, Pittsburgh 2, October 3, 1970; 10 innings.
    Philadelphia 3, Cincinnati 1, October 12, 1976.
    Philadelphia 3, Houston 1, October 11, 1980; 10 innings.
    St. Louis 2, Atlanta 2, October 9, 1982.
    Philadelphia 3, Los Angeles 1, October 8, 1983.

Center Fielders

Most Center Fielders, Series

3-game Series—A. L.—2—Held by many clubs.
    N. L.—2—Cincinnati vs. Pittsburgh, 1979.
4-game Series—A. L.—3—New York vs. Kansas City, 1978.
    N. L.—3—Philadelphia vs. Los Angeles, 1983.
5-game Series—A. L.—3—Oakland vs. Baltimore, 1973.
    N. L.—3—San Diego vs. Chicago 1984.
6-game Series—N. L.—2—Los Angeles vs. St. Louis, 1985.
    New York vs. Houston, 1986.
7-game Series—A. L.—2—Boston vs. California, 1986.
    N. L.—2—San Francisco vs. St. Louis, 1987.

Most Center Fielders, Series, Both Clubs

3-game Series—A. L.—4—Baltimore 2, Oakland 2. 1971.
    N. L.—3—Cincinnati 2, Pittsburgh 1, 1979.
    Atlanta 2, St. Louis 1, 1982.
4-game Series—A. L.—4—New York 3, Kansas City 1, 1978.
    N. L.—4—Los Angeles 2, Philadelphia 2, 1977.
    Philadelphia 3, Los Angeles 1, 1983.
5-game Series—A. L.—5—Oakland 3, Baltimore 2, 1973.
    N. L.—4—Cincinnati 2, New York 2, 1973.
    San Diego 3, Chicago 1, 1984.
6-game Series—N. L.—3—Los Angeles 2, St. Louis 1, 1985.
    New York 2, Houston 1, 1986.
7-game Series—A. L.—3—Boston 2, California 1, 1986.
    N. L.—3—San Francisco 2, St. Louis 1, 1987.

Most Center Fielders, Game
A. L.-N. L.—2—Held by many clubs.

Most Center Fielders, Game, Both Clubs
A. L.-N. L.—3—Made in many games.

Right Fielders

Most Right Fielders, Series
3-game Series—A. L.—4—New York vs. Oakland, 1981.
  N. L.—2—New York vs. Atlanta, 1969.
    Philadelphia vs. Cincinnati, 1976.
4-game Series—N. L.—3—Held by many clubs.
  A. L.—3—Baltimore vs. Chicago, 1983.
5-game Series—N. L.—4—Houston vs. Philadelphia, 1980.
    Chicago vs. San Diego, 1984.
  A. L.—3—Baltimore vs. Oakland, 1973.
    Kansas City vs. New York, 1976.
6-game Series—N. L.—3—St. Louis vs. Los Angeles, 1985.
7-game Series—N. L.—5—St. Louis vs. San Francisco, 1987.
  A. L.—3—California vs. Boston, 1986.

Most Right Fielders, Series, Both Clubs
3-game Series—A. L.—5—New York 4, Oakland 1, 1981.
  N. L.—3—New York 2, Atlanta 1, 1969.
    Philadelphia 2, Cincinnati 1, 1976.
4-game Series—N. L.—6—Los Angeles 3, Pittsburgh 3, 1974.
  A. L.—5—Baltimore 3, Chicago 2, 1983.
5-game Series—N. L.—6—Houston 4, Philadelphia 2, 1980.
  A. L.—5—Kansas City 3, New York 2, 1976.
6-game Series—N. L.—4—St. Louis 3, Los Angeles 1, 1985.
7-game Series—N. L.—7—St. Louis 5, San Francisco 2, 1987.
  A. L.—4—California 3, Boston 1, 1986.

Most Right Fielders, Game
N. L.—4—St. Louis vs. San Francisco, October 11, 1987.
A. L.—3—New York vs. Oakland, October 14, 1981.

Most Right Fielders, Game, Both Clubs
N. L.—5—St. Louis 4, San Francisco 1, October 11, 1987.
  St. Louis 3, San Francisco 2, October 13, 1987.
A. L.—4—Kansas City 2, New York 2, October 13, 1976.
  New York 3, Oakland 1, October 14, 1981.

Catchers

Most Catchers, Series
3-game Series—N. L.—3—Philadelphia vs. Cincinnati, 1976.
  A. L.—2—Held by many clubs.
4-game Series—A. L.-N. L.—2—Held by many clubs.
5-game Series—A. L.—3—Kansas City vs. New York, 1976.
  N. L.—3—Houston vs. Philadelphia, 1980.
6-game Series—N. L.—2—St. Louis vs. Los Angeles, 1985.
7-game Series—A. L.—2—Toronto vs. Kansas City, 1985.
    California vs. Boston, 1986.
  N. L.—2—San Francisco vs. St. Louis, 1987.

Most Catchers, Series, Both Clubs
3-game Series—N. L.—4—Philadelphia 3, Cincinnati 1, 1976.
  A. L.—4—Baltimore 2, Minnesota 2, 1969, 1970.
    Baltimore 2, Oakland 2, 1971.
    New York 2, Oakland 2, 1981.
4-game Series—N. L.—4—Los Angeles 2, Philadelphia 2, 1977, 1978.
  A. L.—3—Baltimore 2, Oakland 1, 1974.
    Baltimore 2, California 1, 1979.
5-game Series—N. L.—5—Houston 3, Philadelphia 2, 1980.
  A. L.—4—Made in many Series.
6-game Series—N. L.—4—St. Louis 2, Los Angeles 2, 1985.
7-game Series—A. L.—3—Toronto 2, Kansas City 1, 1985.
    California 2, Boston 1, 1986.
  N. L.—3—San Francisco 2, St. Louis 1, 1987.

Most Catchers, Game
A. L.-N. L.—2—Held by many clubs.

Most Catchers, Game, Both Clubs
A. L.—4—Baltimore 2, Minnesota 2, October 4, 1969; 12 innings.
Nine-inning record—A. L.-N. L.—3—Made in many games.

Pitchers

Most Pitchers, Series
3-game Series—N. L.—10—Pittsburgh vs. Cincinnati, 1975.
  A. L.—9—Minnesota vs. Baltimore, 1969, 1970.

4-game Series—N. L.—9—San Francisco vs. Pittsburgh, 1971.
    Los Angeles vs. Philadelphia, 1977, 1978.
  A. L.—9—California vs. Baltimore, 1979.
    Chicago vs. Baltimore, 1983.
5-game Series—N. L.—10—Pittsburgh vs. Cincinnati, 1972.
    San Diego vs. Chicago, 1984.
  A. L.—10—Detroit vs. Minnesota, 1987.
6-game Series—N. L.—9—St. Louis vs. Los Angeles, 1985.
    Los Angeles vs. St. Louis, 1985.
7-game Series—N. L.—10—San Francisco vs. St. Louis, 1987.
  A. L.—9—California vs. Boston, 1986.

Most Pitchers, Series, Both Clubs
3-game Series—N. L.—17—Pittsburgh 10, Cincinnati 7, 1975.
    Cincinnati 9, Pittsburgh 8, 1979.
  A. L.—16—Minnesota 9, Baltimore 7, 1969.
4-game Series—N. L.—17—Los Angeles 9, Philadelphia 8, 1978.
  A. L.—15—New York 8, Kansas City 7, 1978.
    Chicago 9, Baltimore 6, 1983.
5-game Series—N. L.—18—Pittsburgh 10, Cincinnati 8, 1972.
    San Diego 10, Chicago 8, 1984.
  A. L.—17—Detroit 10, Minnesota 7, 1987.
6-game Series—N. L.—18—St. Louis 9, Los Angeles 9, 1985.
7-game Series—N. L.—18—San Francisco 10, St. Louis 8, 1987.
  A. L.—16—California 9, Boston 7, 1986.

Fewest Pitchers, Series
3-game Series—A. L.—4—Baltimore vs. Minnesota, 1970.
    Baltimore vs. Oakland, 1971.
    Kansas City vs. New York, 1980.
  N. L.—5—Pittsburgh vs. Cincinnati, 1970.
    St. Louis vs. Atlanta, 1982.
4-game Series—A. L.—5—Oakland vs. Baltimore, 1974.
    Baltimore vs. California, 1979.
  N. L.—5—Philadelphia vs. Los Angeles, 1983.
5-game Series—N. L.—6—New York vs. Cincinnati, 1973.
  A. L.—6—Oakland vs. Baltimore, 1973.
    New York vs. Kansas City, 1976, 1977.
6-game Series—N. L.—8—Houston vs. New York, 1986.
    New York vs. Houston, 1986.
7-game Series—A. L.—7—Kansas City vs. Toronto, 1985.
    Boston vs. California, 1986.
  N. L.—8—St. Louis vs. San Francisco, 1987.

Fewest Pitchers, Series, Both Clubs
3-game Series—A. L.—10—New York 6, Kansas City 4, 1980.
  N. L.—12—Cincinnati 7, Pittsburgh 5, 1970.
4-game Series—A. L.—12—Baltimore 7, Oakland 5, 1974.
  N. L.—13—Los Angeles 8, Philadelphia 5, 1983.
5-game Series—A. L.—13—Baltimore 7, Oakland 6, 1973.
  N. L.—15—Cincinnati 9, New York 6, 1973.
6-game Series—N. L.—18—St. Louis 9, Los Angeles 9, 1985.
7-game Series—A. L.—15—Toronto 8, Kansas City 7, 1985.
  N. L.—18—San Francisco 10, St. Louis 8, 1987.

Most Pitchers, Game
A. L.—7—Minnesota vs. Baltimore, October 6, 1969.
N. L.—7—San Francisco vs. St. Louis, October 14, 1987.

Most Pitchers, Game, Winning Club
N. L.—6—Los Angeles vs. Philadelphia, October 7, 1977.
  Pittsburgh vs. Cincinnati, October 3, 1979; 10 innings.
  Philadelphia vs. Houston, October 11, 1980; 10 innings.
  Philadelphia vs. Houston, October 12, 1980; 10 innings.
A. L.—5—Baltimore vs. Minnesota, October 4, 1969; 12 innings.
  California vs. Boston, October 11, 1986; 11 innings.
  Boston vs. California, October 12, 1986; 11 innings.

Most Pitchers, Game, Losing Club
A. L.—7—Minnesota vs. Baltimore, October 6, 1969.
N. L.—7—San Francisco vs. St. Louis, October 14, 1987.

Most Pitchers, Game, Both Clubs
N. L.—10—Los Angeles 6, Philadelphia 4, October 7, 1977.
  Pittsburgh 6, Cincinnati 4, October 3, 1979; 10 innings.
  Philadelphia 6, Houston 4, October 12, 1980; 10 innings.
A. L.—9—Oakland 6, Detroit 3, October 11, 1972; 10 innings.
  Kansas City 6, New York 3, October 9, 1977.
  Boston 5, California 4, October 12, 1986; 11 innings.

Most Pitchers, Inning
A. L.—5—Kansas City vs. New York, October 12, 1976; sixth inning.
N. L.—3—Made in many games.

Average

Highest Fielding Average, Series

3-game Series—A. L.— 1.000—Baltimore vs. Minnesota, 1970.
Oakland vs. Baltimore, 1971.
N. L.— 1.000—Pittsburgh vs. Cincinnati, 1979.
4-game Series—A. L.— .993—New York vs. Kansas City, 1978.
N. L.— .993—Los Angeles vs. Philadelphia, 1983.
5-game Series—N. L.— .994—San Diego vs. Chicago, 1984.
A. L.— .989—Baltimore vs. Oakland, 1973.
New York vs. Kansas City, 1977.
6-game Series—N. L.— .996—New York vs. Houston, 1986.
7-game Series—N. L.— .988—St. Louis vs. San Francisco, 1987.
A. L.— .984—Toronto vs. Kansas City, 1985.

Highest Fielding Average, Series, Both Clubs

3-game Series—N. L.—.996—Pittsburgh 1.000, Cincinnati .992, 1979.
A. L.—.995—Oakland 1.000, Baltimore .991, 1971.
4-game Series—A. L.—.982—New York .993, Kansas City .972, 1978.
N. L.—.979—Los Angeles .993, Philadelphia .966, 1983.
5-game Series—N. L.—.989—San Diego .994, Chicago .983, 1984.
A. L.—.984—Baltimore .989, Oakland .979, 1973.
6-game Series—N. L.—.985—New York .996, Houston .973, 1986.
7-game Series—N. L.—.983—St. Louis .988, San Francisco .977, 1987.
A. L.—.981—Toronto .984, Kansas City .979, 1985.

Lowest Fielding Average, Series

3-game Series—A. L.—.940—Kansas City vs. Detroit, 1984.
N. L.—.950—Atlanta vs. New York, 1969.
4-game Series—N. L.—.957—Los Angeles vs. Pittsburgh, 1974.
A. L.—.970—Baltimore vs. California, 1979.
5-game Series—A. L.—.956—Milwaukee vs. California, 1982.
N. L.—.973—Philadelphia vs. Houston, 1980.
6-game Series—N. L.—.973—Houston vs. New York, 1986.
7-game Series—A. L.—.971—California vs. Boston, 1986.
N. L.—.977—San Francisco vs. St. Louis, 1987.

Lowest Fielding Average, Series, Both Clubs

3-game Series—A. L.—.958—Boston .966, Oakland .950, 1975.
N. L.—.965—New York .981, Atlanta .950, 1969.
4-game Series—N. L.—.964—Pittsburgh .973, Los Angeles .957, 1974.
A. L.—.978—California .986, Baltimore .970, 1979.
5-game Series—A. L.—.966—California .977, Milwaukee .956, 1982.
N. L.—.978—Cincinnati .979, Pittsburgh .977, 1972.
6-game Series—N. L.—.978—St. Louis .981, Los Angeles .974, 1985.
7-game Series—N. L.—.983—St. Louis .988, San Francisco .977, 1987.
A. L.—.973—Boston .975, California .971, 1986.

Putouts

Most Putouts, Total Series

A. L.— 718— Baltimore; 7 Series, 26 games.
N. L.— 715— Los Angeles, 6 Series, 27 games.

Most Putouts, Series

3-game Series—A. L.— 96—Baltimore vs. Minnesota, 1969.
N. L.— 90—Pittsburgh vs. Cincinnati, 1979.
4-game Series—N. L.—111—Los Angeles vs. Philadelphia, 1978.
A. L.—111—Baltimore vs. Chicago, 1983.
5-game Series—N. L.—148—Philadelphia vs. Houston, 1980.
A. L.—139—Detroit vs. Oakland, 1972.
6-game Series—N. L.—189—New York vs. Houston, 1986.
7-game Series—A. L.—196—Boston vs. California, 1986.
N. L.—183—St. Louis vs. San Francisco, 1987.

Most Putouts, Series, Both Clubs

3-game Series—A. L.— 190—Baltimore 96, Minnesota 94, 1969.
N. L.—177—Pittsburgh 90, Cincinnati 87, 1979.
4-game Series—N. L.—221—Los Angeles 111, Philadelphia 110, 1978.
A. L.—219—Baltimore 111, Chicago 108, 1983.
5-game Series—N. L.—295—Philadelphia 148, Houston 147, 1980.
A. L.—277—Detroit 139, Oakland 138, 1972.

6-game Series—N. L.— 377—New York 189, Houston 188, 1986.
7-game Series—A. L.—388—Boston 196, California 192, 1986.
N. L.—363—St. Louis 183, San Francisco 180, 1987.

Fewest Putouts, Series

3-game Series—A. L.— 75—Oakland vs. Baltimore, 1971.
Oakland vs. Boston, 1975.
New York vs. Kansas City, 1980.
Oakland vs. New York, 1981.
N. L.— 76—Atlanta vs. St. Louis, 1982.
4-game Series—A. L.—102—Kansas City vs. New York, 1978.
N. L.—102—San Francisco vs. Pittsburgh, 1971.
Los Angeles vs. Philadelphia, 1983.
5-game Series—A. L.—126—California vs. Milwaukee, 1982.
N. L.—127—Chicago vs. San Diego, 1984.
6-game Series—N. L.—154—Los Angeles vs. St. Louis, 1985.
7-game Series—N. L.—180—San Francisco vs. St. Louis, 1987.
A. L.—186—Toronto vs. Kansas City, 1985.

Fewest Putouts, Series, Both Clubs

3-game Series—A. L.— 156—Baltimore 81, Oakland 75, 1971.
Boston 81, Oakland 75, 1975.
Kansas City 81, New York 75, 1980.
New York 81, Oakland 75, 1981.
N. L.—157—St. Louis 81, Atlanta 76, 1982.
4-game Series—A. L.—207—New York 105, Kansas City 102, 1978.
N. L.—207—Pittsburgh 105, San Francisco 102, 1971.
Philadelphia 105, Los Angeles 102, 1983.
5-game Series—A. L.—255—Milwaukee 129, California 126, 1982.
N. L.—256—Chicago 129, San Diego 127, 1984.
6-game Series—N. L.—310—St. Louis 156, Los Angeles 154, 1985.
7-game Series—N. L.—363—St. Louis 183, San Francisco 180, 1987.
A. L.—374—Kansas City 188, Toronto 186, 1985.

Most Players, One or More Putouts, Game

N. L.— 14— New York vs. Houston, October 15, 1986; 16 innings.
N. L.—Nine-inning record—10—Held by many clubs.
A. L.— 11— Oakland vs. New York, October 14, 1981.
Kansas City vs. Detroit, October 3, 1984; 11 innings.
California vs. Boston, October 12, 1986; 11 innings.
Boston vs. California, October 12, 1986; 11 innings.

Most Players, One or More Putouts, Game, Nine Innings, Both Clubs

N. L.— 20— Cincinnati 10, Pittsburgh 10, October 8, 1972.
A. L.— 19— Oakland 11, New York 8, October 14, 1981.

Most Players, One or More Putouts, Extra-Inning Game, Both Clubs

N. L.—23— New York 14, Houston 9, October 15, 1986; 16 innings.
A. L.—22— Boston 11, California 11, October 12, 1986; 11 innings.

Most Putouts, Outfield, Game

N. L.— 18— Pittsburgh vs. Cincinnati, October 7, 1972.
A. L.— 14— Boston vs. Oakland, October 4, 1975.
New York vs. Kansas City, October 13, 1976.

Most Putouts, Outfield, Game, Both Clubs

A. L.— 26— New York 14, Kansas City 12, October 13, 1976.
N. L.— 25— Pittsburgh 18, Cincinnati 7, October 7, 1972.

Fewest Putouts, Outfield, Game, Nine Innings

N. L.— 1—Atlanta vs. New York, October 4, 1969.
Cincinnati vs. Pittsburgh, October 5, 1970.
Montreal vs. Los Angeles, October 16, 1981.
A. L.—2—Oakland vs. Boston, October 5, 1975; fielded 8 innings.
Milwaukee vs. California, October 8, 1982.
Baltimore vs. Chicago, October 5, 1983.

Fewest Putouts, Outfield, Extra-Inning Game

N. L.—3—Cincinnati vs. Pittsburgh, October 3, 1970; 10 innings.
A. L.—4—Baltimore vs. Oakland, October 9, 1973; fielded 10 innings of 11-inning game.

Fewest Putouts, Outfield, Game, Nine Innings, Both Clubs

N. L.—5—Pittsburgh 4, Cincinnati 1, October 5, 1970.
A. L.—7—Minnesota 4, Baltimore 3, October 3, 1970.

Fewest Putouts, Outfield, Extra-Inning Game, Both Clubs

A. L.— 10— Baltimore 7, Chicago 3, October 8, 1983; 10 innings.
N. L.— 12— Cincinnati 7, Pittsburgh 5, October 2, 1979; 11 innings.
New York 6, Houston 6, October 15, 1986; 16 innings.

Most Putouts, Outfield, Inning

A. L.-N. L.—3—Held by many clubs.

Most Putouts, Outfield, Inning, Both Clubs

A. L.—6—Baltimore 3, Oakland 3, October 11, 1973; seventh inning.
N. L.—5—New York 3, Atlanta 2, October 5, 1969; seventh inning.
　　　Pittsburgh 3, Cincinnati 2, October 7, 1972; third inning.
　　　Los Angeles 3, Philadelphia 2, October 7, 1978; third inning.

Most Putouts, Catchers, Inning, Both Clubs

A. L.—5—Baltimore 3, Oakland 2, October 6, 1973; first inning.
　　　Oakland 3, Boston 2, October 4, 1975; second inning.
　　　Chicago 3, Baltimore 2, October 6, 1983; first inning.
N. L.—5—Atlanta 3, New York 2, October 5, 1969; first inning.
　　　Atlanta 3, New York 2, October 6, 1969; third inning.
　　　Los Angeles 3, Philadelphia 2, October 4, 1977; seventh inning.

Assists

Most Assists, Total Series

A. L.— 293— Baltimore; 7 Series, 26 games.
N. L.— 303— Los Angeles; 6 Series, 27 games.

Most Assists, Series

3-game Series—A. L.—41—New York vs. Kansas City, 1980.
　　　　　　N. L.—39—Cincinnati vs. Pittsburgh, 1970, 1979.
　　　　　　　　　　Atlanta vs. St. Louis, 1982.
4-game Series—A. L.—52—Baltimore vs. California, 1979.
　　　　　　N. L.—50—Los Angeles vs. Philadelphia, 1978.
5-game Series—N. L.—71—Philadelphia vs. Houston, 1980.
　　　　　　A. L.—60—New York vs. Kansas City, 1976.
6-game Series—N. L.—94—New York vs. Houston, 1986.
7-game Series—A. L.—87—Kansas City vs. Toronto, 1985.
　　　　　　N. L.—77—San Francisco vs. St. Louis, 1987.

Most Assists, Series, Both Clubs

3-game Series—N. L.— 76—Cincinnati 39, Pittsburgh 37, 1970.
　　　　　　A. L.— 73—Oakland 40, Boston 33, 1975.
4-game Series—A. L.—100—Chicago 51, Baltimore 49, 1983.
　　　　　　N. L.— 96—Los Angeles 50, Philadelphia 46, 1978.
5-game Series—A. L.—111—New York 60, Kansas City 51, 1976.
　　　　　　N. L.—123—Philadelphia 71, Houston 52, 1980.
6-game Series—N. L.—160—New York 94, Houston 66, 1986.
7-game Series—A. L.—151—California 78, Boston 73, 1986.
　　　　　　N. L.—144—San Francisco 77, St. Louis 67, 1987.

Fewest Assists, Series

3-game Series—A. L.—15—Oakland vs. Baltimore, 1971.
　　　　　　N. L.—20—Pittsburgh vs. Cincinnati, 1975.
4-game Series—N. L.—32—Pittsburgh vs. San Francisco, 1971.
　　　　　　A. L.—35—New York vs. Kansas City, 1978.
5-game Series—N. L.—38—Pittsburgh vs. Cincinnati, 1972.
　　　　　　A. L.—41—Minnesota vs. Detroit, 1987.
6-game Series—N. L.—54—St. Louis vs. Los Angeles, 1985.
7-game Series—A. L.—61—Toronto vs. Kansas City, 1985.
　　　　　　N. L.—67—St. Louis vs. San Francisco, 1987.

Fewest Assists, Series, Both Clubs

3-game Series—A. L.— 46—Baltimore 31, Oakland 15, 1971.
　　　　　　N. L.— 51—Cincinnati 31, Pittsburgh 20, 1975.
4-game Series—N. L.— 69—San Francisco 37, Pittsburgh 32, 1971.
　　　　　　A. L.— 71—Kansas City 36, New York 35, 1978.
5-game Series—N. L.— 91—Cincinnati 53, Pittsburgh 38, 1972.
　　　　　　A. L.— 91—California 46, Milwaukee 45, 1982.
6-game Series—N. L.—126—Los Angeles 72, St. Louis 54, 1985.
7-game Series—N. L.—144—San Francisco 77, St. Louis 67, 1987.
　　　　　　A. L.—148—Kansas City 87, Toronto 61, 1985.

Most Assists, Game

N. L.—31—New York vs. Houston, October 15, 1986; 16 innings.
N. L.—Nine-inning record—21—Los Angeles vs. Philadelphia, October 5, 1978.
A. L.—18—Boston vs. Oakland, October 7, 1975.

Most Assists, Game, Nine Innings, Both Clubs

A. L.—33—Boston 18, Oakland 15, October 7, 1975.
N. L.—30—Los Angeles 21, Philadelphia 9, October 5, 1978.

Most Assists, Extra-Inning Game, Both Clubs

N. L.—56—New York 31, Houston 25, October 15, 1986; 16 innings.
A. L.—Less than nine-inning record.

Most Players, One or More Assists, Game

N. L.— 10— New York vs. Houston, October 15, 1986; 16 innings.
N. L.—Nine-inning record—9—Los Angeles vs. Montreal, October 14, 1981.
A. L.— 9—Oakland vs. New York, October 14, 1981.

Most Players, One or More Assists, Game, Both Clubs

N. L.— 19— New York 10, Houston 9, October 15, 1986; 16 innings.
N. L.—Nine-inning record—13—New York 7, Atlanta 6, October 4, 1969.
　　　　　Pittsburgh 7, Cincinnati 6, October 9, 1972.
　　　　　Cincinnati 8, New York 5, October 10, 1973.
　　　　　Los Angeles 9, Montreal 4, October 14, 1981.
　　　　　Atlanta 7, St. Louis 6, October 9, 1982.
　　　　　San Francisco 7, St. Louis 6, October 14, 1987.
A. L.— 15—Oakland 9, New York 6, October 14, 1981.

Fewest Assists, Game

A. L.—2—Boston vs. Oakland, October 4, 1975.
N. L.—2—Pittsburgh vs. Cincinnati, October 7, 1972.
　　　Pittsburgh vs. Cincinnati, October 7, 1975, 10 innings.

Fewest Assists, Game, Both Clubs

N. L.— 10—Cincinnati 8, Pittsburgh 2, October 7, 1975; 10 innings.
　　　　Los Angeles 5, Philadelphia 5, October 7, 1983.
　　　　San Diego 5, Chicago 5, October 2, 1984.
A. L.— 11—Oakland 6, Baltimore 5, October 6, 1973.

Most Assists, Outfield, Game

N. L.—3—Philadelphia vs. Houston, October 11, 1980; 10 innings.
N. L.—Nine-inning record—2—Pittsburgh vs. Cincinnati, October 9, 1972.
　　　　　Cincinnati vs. New York, October 10, 1973.
　　　　　Philadelphia vs. Los Angeles, October 7, 1977.
A. L.—2—Minnesota vs. Baltimore, October 4, 1970.
　　　　Boston vs. Oakland, October 5, 1975.
　　　　Baltimore vs. California, October 5, 1979.

Most Assists, Outfield, Game, Both Clubs

N. L.—4—Philadelphia 3, Houston 1, October 11, 1980; 10 innings.
N. L.—Nine-inning record—3—Pittsburgh 2, Cincinnati 1, October 9, 1972.
A. L.—3—Minnesota 2, Baltimore 1, October 4, 1970.
　　　　Boston 2, Oakland 1, October 5, 1975.
　　　　Baltimore 2, California 1, October 5, 1979.

Most Assists, Outfield, Inning

N. L.—2—Cincinnati vs. New York, October 10, 1973; fifth inning.
A. L.—1—Held by many clubs.

Chances Offered

Fewest Chances Offered, Outfield, Game, Nine Innings

N. L.—1—Cincinnati vs. Pittsburgh, October 5, 1970.
　　　Montreal vs. Los Angeles, October 16, 1981.
A. L.—2—Kansas City vs. New York, October 7, 1978.
　　　Milwaukee vs. California, October 8, 1982.

Fewest Chances Offered, Outfield, Extra-Inning Game

N. L.—3—Cincinnati vs. Pittsburgh, October 3, 1970; 10 innings.
A. L.—4—Baltimore vs. Oakland, October 9, 1973; fielded 10 innings of 11-inning game.

Fewest Chances Offered, Outfield, Game, Nine Innings, Both Clubs

N. L.—5—Pittsburgh 4, Cincinnati 1, October 5, 1970.
A. L.—7—Minnesota 4, Baltimore 3, October 3, 1970.

Fewest Chances Offered, Outfield, Extra-Inning Game, Both Clubs

A. L.— 10—Baltimore 7, Chicago 3, October 8, 1983; 10 innings.
N. L.— 12—Cincinnati 7, Pittsburgh 5, October 2, 1979; 11 innings.

Errors

Most Errors, Total Series

A. L.— 27—Kansas City; 6 Series, 27 games.
N. L.— 24—Los Angeles; 6 Series, 27 games.

Most Errors, Series

3-game Series—A. L.—7—Kansas City vs. Detroit, 1984.
　　　　　　N. L.—6—Atlanta vs. New York, 1969.
4-game Series—N. L.—7—Los Angeles vs. Pittsburgh, 1974.
　　　　　　A. L.—5—Baltimore vs. California, 1979.
5-game Series—A. L.—8—Milwaukee vs. California, 1982.
　　　　　　N. L.—6—Philadelphia vs. Houston, 1980.

6-game Series—N. L.—7—Houston vs. New York, 1986.
7-game Series—A. L.—8—California vs. Boston, 1986.
               N. L.—6—San Francisco vs. St. Louis, 1987.

Most Errors, Series, Both Clubs

3-game Series—A. L.—10—Oakland 6, Boston 4, 1975.
               N. L.— 8—Atlanta 6, New York 2, 1969.
4-game Series—N. L.—11—Los Angeles 7, Pittsburgh 4, 1974.
               A. L.— 7—Baltimore 5, California 2, 1979.
5-game Series—A. L.—12—Milwaukee 8, California 4, 1982.
               N. L.— 9—Philadelphia 6, Houston 3, 1980.
6-game Series—N. L.—10—Los Angeles 6, St. Louis 4, 1985.
7-game Series—A. L.—15—California 8, Boston 7, 1986.
               N. L.— 9—San Francisco 6, St. Louis 3, 1987.

Fewest Errors, Series

3-game Series—A. L.—0—Baltimore vs. Minnesota, 1970.
                      Oakland vs. Baltimore, 1971.
               N. L.—0—Pittsburgh vs. Cincinnati, 1979.
4-game Series—A. L.—1—New York vs. Kansas City, 1978.
               N. L.—1—Los Angeles vs. Philadelphia, 1983.
5-game Series—N. L.—1—San Diego vs. Chicago, 1984.
               A. L.—2—Baltimore vs. Oakland, 1973.
                      New York vs. Kansas City, 1977.
6-game Series—N. L.—1—New York vs. Houston, 1986.
7-game Series—N. L.—3—St. Louis vs. San Francisco, 1987.
               A. L.—4—Toronto vs. Kansas City, 1985.

Fewest Errors, Series, Both Clubs

3-game Series—A. L.— 1—Baltimore 1, Oakland 0, 1971.
               N. L.— 1—Cincinnati 1, Pittsburgh 0, 1979.
4-game Series—A. L.— 5—Kansas City 4, New York 1, 1978.
               N. L.— 6—Philadelphia 5, Los Angeles 1, 1983.
5-game Series—N. L.— 4—Chicago 3, San Diego 1, 1984.
               A. L.— 6—Oakland 4, Baltimore 2, 1973.
6-game Series—N. L.— 1—Houston 7, New York 1, 1986.
7-game Series—N. L.— 9—San Francisco 6, St. Louis 3, 1987.
               A. L.—10—Kansas City 6, Toronto 4, 1985.

Most Errors, Game

A. L.—5—New York vs. Kansas City, October 10, 1976.
N. L.—5—Los Angeles vs. Pittsburgh, October 8, 1974.

Most Errors, Game, Both Clubs

A. L.—7—Oakland 4, Boston 3, October 4, 1975.
N. L.—5—Los Angeles 5, Pittsburgh 0, October 8, 1974.

Most Errors, Infield, Game

A. L.—3—Oakland vs. Baltimore, October 9, 1973; 11 innings.
         California vs. Boston, October 8, 1986.
N. L.—2—Held by many clubs.

Most Errors, Infield, Game, Both Clubs

A. L.—5—California 3, Boston 2, October 8, 1986.
N. L.—3—Atlanta 2, New York 1, October 5, 1969.
         Pittsburgh 2, Cincinnati 1, October 10, 1972.

Most Errors, Outfield, Game

A. L.—2—Minnesota vs. Baltimore, October 6, 1969.
         Oakland vs. Boston, October 4, 1975.
         Milwaukee vs. California, October 10, 1982.
N. L.—1—Held by many clubs.

Most Errors, Outfield, Game, Both Clubs

A. L.—3—Oakland 2, Boston 1, October 4, 1975.
N. L.—1—Made in many games.

Longest Errorless Game

N. L.—16 innings—New York vs. Houston, October 15, 1986; fielded
             16 complete innings.
A. L.—11 innings—Baltimore vs. Minnesota, October 5, 1969; fielded
             11 complete innings.
                Baltimore vs. Oakland, October 9, 1973; fielded
             10 complete innings of 11-inning game.
                California vs. Boston, October 12, 1986; fielded 11
             complete innings.
                Boston vs. California, October 12, 1986; fielded 11
             complete innings.

Longest Errorless Game, Both Clubs

N. L.—11 innings—Pittsburgh vs. Cincinnati, October 2, 1979; both
             clubs fielded 11 complete innings.
A. L.—11 innings—California vs. Boston, October 12, 1986; both
             clubs fielded 11 complete innings.

Most Errors, Inning

A. L.—3—Oakland vs. Boston, October 4, 1975; first inning.
         California vs. Boston, October 8, 1986; seventh inning.
N. L.—2—Held by many clubs.

Passed Balls

Most Passed Balls, Total Series

N. L.—4—Pittsburgh; 5 Series, 19 games.
A. L.—3—New York; 5 Series, 20 games.
       California; 3 Series, 16 games.

Most Passed Balls, Series

N. L.—2—Pittsburgh vs. Cincinnati, 1975; 3-game Series.
       Houston vs. New York, 1986; 6-game Series.
A. L.—2—California vs. Boston, 1986; 7-game Series.

Most Passed Balls, Series, Both Clubs

A. L.-N. L.—2—Made in many Series.

Most Passed Balls, Game

N. L.—2—Pittsburgh vs. Cincinnati, October 4, 1975.
       Houston vs. New York, October 11, 1986.
A. L.—1—Held by many clubs.

Most Passed Balls, Inning

A. L.-N. L.—1—Held by many clubs.

Double & Triple Plays

Most Double Plays, Total Series

A. L.—27—Oakland; 6 Series, 23 games.
N. L.—26—Los Angeles; 6 Series, 27 games.

Most Double Plays, Series

3-game Series—A. L.— 6—New York vs. Oakland, 1981.
               N. L.— 4—Atlanta vs. New York, 1969.
4-game Series—N. L.— 8—Los Angeles vs. Pittsburgh, 1974.
               A. L.— 7—California vs. Baltimore, 1979.
5-game Series—N. L.— 8—Montreal vs. Los Angeles, 1981.
               A. L.— 5—Oakland vs. Detroit, 1972.
                      Kansas City vs. New York, 1976.
                      Milwaukee vs. California, 1982.
6-game Series—N. L.— 6—New York vs. Houston, 1986.
7-game Series—N. L.—10—San Francisco vs. St. Louis, 1987.
               A. L.— 7—Kansas City vs. Toronto, 1985.

Most Double Plays, Series, Both Clubs

3-game Series—A. L.— 8—Minnesota 5, Baltimore 3, 1970.
               N. L.— 6—Atlanta 4, New York 2, 1969.
                      Cincinnati 3, Philadelphia 3, 1976.
4-game Series—A. L.—12—California 7, Baltimore 5, 1979.
               N. L.—10—Los Angeles 8, Pittsburgh 2, 1974.
5-game Series—N. L.—13—Montreal 8, Los Angeles 5, 1981.
               A. L.— 9—Oakland 5, Detroit 4, 1972.
6-game Series—N. L.— 9—New York 6, Houston 3, 1986.
7-game Series—N. L.—15—San Francisco 10, St. Louis 5, 1987.
               A. L.—11—Kansas City 7, Toronto 4, 1985.

Fewest Double Plays, Series

3-game Series—N. L.—0—Atlanta vs. St. Louis, 1982.
               A. L.—0—Detroit vs. Kansas City, 1984.
4-game Series—N. L.—0—Philadelphia vs. Los Angeles, 1983.
               A. L.—2—New York vs. Kansas City, 1978.
5-game Series—A. L.—1—Detroit vs. Minnesota, 1987.
               N. L.—3—Held by many clubs.
6-game Series—N. L.—3—Los Angeles vs. St. Louis, 1985.
7-game Series—A. L.—4—Toronto vs. Kansas City, 1985.
               N. L.—5—St. Louis vs. San Francisco, 1987.

Fewest Double Plays, Series, Both Clubs

3-game Series—A. L.— 2—Kansas City 2, Detroit 0, 1984.
               N. L.— 3—St. Louis 3, Atlanta 0, 1982.
4-game Series—N. L.— 3—Los Angeles 3, Philadelphia 0, 1983.
               A. L.— 6—Kansas City 4, New York 2, 1978.
5-game Series—A. L.— 4—Kansas City 2, New York 2, 1977.
                      Minnesota 3, Detroit 1, 1987.
               N. L.— 6—Cincinnati 3, Pittsburgh 3, 1972.
                      Cincinnati 3, New York 3, 1973.
6-game Series—N. L.— 7—St. Louis 4, Los Angeles 3, 1985.
7-game Series—A. L.—10—Boston 5, California 5, 1986.
               N. L.—15—San Francisco 10, St. Louis 5, 1987.

Most Double Plays, Game
  A. L.—4—Oakland vs. Boston, October 5, 1975.
  N. L.—4—Los Angeles vs. Montreal, October 13, 1981.
        San Francisco vs. St. Louis, October 10, 1987.

Most Double Plays, Game, Both Clubs
  A. L.—6—Oakland 4, Boston 2, October 5, 1975.

N. L.—5—Pittsburgh 3, Cincinnati 2, October 5, 1975.
        Philadelphia 3, Houston 2, October 11, 1980; 10 innings.

Most Triple Plays, Series
  A. L.-N. L.—Never accomplished.

Miscellaneous

Club & Division
One-Run Decisions

Most Games Won by One Run, Series, One Club
  3-game Series—A. L.—2—Baltimore vs. Minnesota, 1969.
             N. L.—1—Occurred often.
  4-game Series—A. L.—2—Oakland vs. Baltimore, 1974.
                New York vs. Kansas City, 1978.
             N. L.—1—Occurred often.
  5-game Series—A. L.—2—Oakland vs. Detroit, 1972.
             N. L.—2—Cincinnati vs. New York, 1973.
  6-game Series—N. L.—3—New York vs. Houston, 1986.
  7-game Series—N. L.—1—St. Louis vs. San Francisco, 1987.
             A. L.—1—Occurred often.

Most Games Decided by One Run, Series, Both Clubs
  3-game Series—A. L.—2—Baltimore (won 2) vs. Minnesota, 1969.
             N. L.—1—Occurred often.
  4-game Series—A. L.—2—Oakland (won 2) vs. Baltimore, 1974.
                New York (won 2) vs. Kansas City, 1978.
                Baltimore (won 1) vs. California (won 1), 1979.
             N. L.—2—San Francisco (won 1) vs. Pittsburgh (won 1), 1971.
  5-game Series—A. L.—3—Oakland (won 2) vs. Detroit (won 1), 1972.
             N. L.—2—Pittsburgh (won 1) vs. Cincinnati (won 1), 1972.
                Cincinnati (won 2) vs. New York, 1973.
                Philadelphia (won 1) vs. Houston (won 1), 1980.
  6-game Series—N. L.—4—New York (won 3) vs. Houston (won 1), 1986.
  7-game Series—A. L.—2—Toronto (won 1) vs. Kansas City (won 1), 1985.
                California (won 1) vs. Boston (won 1), 1986.
             N. L.—2—St. Louis (won 2) vs. San Francisco, 1987.

Length Of Games
By Innings

Longest Game
  N. L.—16 innings—New York 7, Houston 6, at Houston, October 15, 1986.
  A. L.—12 innings—Baltimore 4, Minnesota 3, at Baltimore, October 4, 1969.

Most Extra-Inning Games, Total Series
  N. L.—6—Houston, 2 Series, 11 games; won 2 lost 4.
  A. L.—5—Baltimore, 7 Series, 26 games; won 4, lost 1.

Most Extra-Inning Games Won, Total Series
  A. L.—4—Baltimore, 7 Series, 26 games; won 4, lost 1.
  N. L.—3—Cincinnati, 6 Series, 22 games; won 3, lost 1.

Most Extra-Inning Games Lost, Total Series
  N. L.—4—Houston, 4 Series, 11 games; won 2, lost 4.
  A. L.—2—Minnesota, 2 Series, 6 games; won 0, lost 2.
        Kansas City, 6 Series, 27 games; won 0, lost 2.
        California, 3 Series, 16 games; won 1, lost 2.

Most Extra-Inning Games, Series, Both Clubs
  3-game Series—A. L.—2—Baltimore vs. Minnesota, 1969.
             N. L.—2—Cincinnati vs. Pittsburgh, 1979.
  4-game Series—N. L.—1—Los Angeles vs. Philadelphia, 1978.
             A. L.—1—Baltimore vs. California, 1979.
                Baltimore vs. Chicago, 1983.

5-game Series—N. L.—4—Philadelphia vs. Houston, 1980.
           A. L.—2—Detroit vs. Oakland, 1972.
6-game Series—N. L.—2—New York vs. Houston, 1986.
7-game Series—A. L.—2—Boston vs. California, 1986.
           N. L.—Never occurred.

By Time

Longest Game by Time, Nine Innings
  N. L.—3 hours, 32 minutes—St. Louis 7, Los Angeles 5, at Los Angeles, October 16, 1985.
  A. L.—3 hours, 29 minutes—Detroit 7, Minnesota 6, at Detroit, October 10, 1987.

Longest Game by Time, Extra Innings
  N. L.—4 hours, 42 minutes—New York 7, Houston 6, at Houston, October 15, 1986, 16 innings.
  A. L.—3 hours, 54 minutes—Boston 7, California 6, at California, October 12, 1986, 11 innings.

Shortest Game by Time
  A. L.—1 hour, 57 minutes—Oakland 1, Baltimore 0, at Baltimore, October 8, 1974.
  N. L.—1 hour, 57 minutes—Pittsburgh 5, Cincinnati 1, at Pittsburgh, October 7, 1972.

Series Starting & Finishing Dates

Earliest Date for Championship Series Game
  N. L.—October 2, 1971, at San Francisco; San Francisco 5, Pittsburgh 4.
        October 2, 1979, at Cincinnati; Pittsburgh 5, Cincinnati 2; 11 innings.
        October 2, 1984, at Chicago; Chicago 13, San Diego 0.
  A. L.—October 2, 1984, at Kansas City; Detroit 8, Kansas City 1.

Earliest Date for Championship Series Final Game
  N. L.—October 5, 1970, at Cincinnati; Cincinnati 3, Pittsburgh 2; 3-game Series.
        October 5, 1979, at Pittsburgh; Pittsburgh 7, Cincinnati 1; 3-game Series.
  A. L.—October 5, 1970, at Baltimore; Baltimore 6, Minnesota 1; 3-game Series.
        October 5, 1971, at Oakland; Baltimore 5, Oakland 3; 3-game Series.
        October 5, 1984, at Detroit; Detroit 1, Kansas City 0; 3-game Series.

Latest Date for Championship Series Start
  N. L.—October 13, 1981, at Los Angeles; 5-game Series ended at Montreal on October 19, 1981.
  A. L.—October 13, 1981, at New York; 3-game Series ended at Oakland on October 15, 1981.

Latest Date for Championship Series Finish
  N. L.—October 19, 1981—Series started October 13; Los Angeles vs. Montreal; 5-game Series.
  A. L.—October 16, 1985—Series started October 8; Kansas City vs. Toronto; 7-game Series.

Series & Games Won

Most Series Won
  A. L.—5—Baltimore, 1969, 1970, 1971, 1979, 1983; lost 2.
        New York, 1976, 1977, 1978, 1981; lost 1.
  N. L.—4—Cincinnati, 1970, 1972, 1975, 1976; lost 2.
        Los Angeles, 1974, 1977, 1978, 1981; lost 2.

Most Consecutive Years Winning Series
  A. L.—3—Baltimore, 1969, 1970, 1971.
        Oakland, 1972, 1973, 1974.
        New York, 1976, 1977, 1978.

N. L.—2—Cincinnati, 1975, 1976.
Los Angeles, 1977, 1978.

Most Consecutive Series Won, Division

N. L.—5—West Division, 1974, 1975, 1976, 1977, 1978.
A. L.—5—East Division, 1975, 1976, 1977, 1978, 1979.

Most Times Winning Series in Three Consecutive Games

A. L.—3—Baltimore, 1969, 1970, 1971.
N. L.—3—Cincinnati, 1970, 1975, 1976.

Winning Series After Winning First Game

A. L.—Accomplished 12 times.
N. L.—Accomplished 12 times.

Winning Series After Losing First Game

N. L.—Accomplished 7 times.
A. L.—Accomplished 7 times.

Winning Series After Winning One Game and Losing Two

N. L.—Cincinnati vs. Pittsburgh, 1972; 5-game Series.
Philadelphia vs. Houston, 1980; 5-game Series.
Los Angeles vs. Montreal, 1981; 5-game Series.
San Diego vs. Chicago, 1984; 5-game Series.
St. Louis vs. Los Angeles, 1985; 6-game Series.
A. L.—New York vs. Kansas City, 1977; 5-game Series.
Milwaukee vs. California, 1982; 5-game Series.
Kansas City vs. Toronto, 1985; 7-game Series.
Boston vs. California, 1986; 7-game Series.

Winning Series After Winning One Game and Losing Three

A. L.—Kansas City vs. Toronto, 1985.
Boston vs. California, 1986.
N. L.—Never accomplished.

Winning Series After Losing First Two Games

A. L.—Milwaukee vs. California, 1982; 5-game Series.
Kansas City vs. Toronto, 1985; 7-game Series.
N. L.—San Diego vs. Chicago, 1984; 5-game Series.
St. Louis vs. Los Angeles, 1985; 6-game Series.

Most Games Won, Total Series

A. L.— 18— Baltimore, 7 Series; won 18, lost 8.
N. L.— 15— Los Angeles, 6 Series; won 15, lost 12.

Most Consecutive Games Won, Total Series

A. L.— 10— Baltimore, 1969 (3), 1970 (3), 1971 (3), 1973 (first 1).
N. L.— 6— Cincinnati, 1975 (3), 1976 (3).

Most Consecutive Games Won, Division

A. L.— 9— East Division, 1969 (3), 1970 (3), 1971 (3).
N. L.— 7— West Division, 1974 (last 1), 1975 (3), 1976 (3).

Series & Games Lost

Most Series Lost

N. L.—4—Pittsburgh, 1970, 1972, 1974, 1975; won 2.
A. L.—4—Kansas City, 1976, 1977, 1978, 1984; won 2.

Most Consecutive Years Losing Series

A. L.—3—Kansas City, 1976, 1977, 1978.
N. L.—3—Philadelphia, 1976, 1977, 1978.

Most Games Lost, Total Series

A. L.— 15— Kansas City, 6 Series; won 12, lost 15.
N. L.— 13— Pittsburgh, 6 Series; won 9, lost 13.

Most Consecutive Games Lost, Total Series

A. L.—6—Minnesota, 1969 (3), 1970 (3).
Oakland, 1975 (3), 1981 (3).
N. L.—6—Atlanta, 1969 (3), 1982 (3).

Attendance

Largest Attendance, Series

3-game Series—N. L.—180,338—Cincinnati vs. Philadelphia, 1976.
A. L.—151,539—Oakland vs. New York, 1981.
4-game Series—N. L.—240,584—Philadelphia vs. Los Angeles, 1977.
A. L.—195,748—Baltimore vs. Chicago, 1983.
5-game Series—A. L.—284,691—California vs. Milwaukee, 1982.
N. L.—264,950—Philadelphia vs. Houston, 1980.
6-game Series—N. L.—326,824—St. Louis vs. Los Angeles, 1985.
7-game Series—N. L.—396,597—St. Louis vs. San Francisco, 1987.
A. L.—324,430—Boston vs. California, 1986.

Smallest Attendance, Series

3-game Series—A. L.— 81,945—Baltimore vs. Minnesota, 1970.
N. L.—112,943—Pittsburgh vs. Cincinnati, 1970.
4-game Series—A. L.—144,615—Baltimore vs. Oakland, 1974.
N. L.—157,348—San Francisco vs. Pittsburgh, 1971.
5-game Series—A. L.—175,833—Baltimore vs. Oakland, 1973.
N. L.—234,814—Pittsburgh vs. Cincinnati, 1972.
6-game Series—N. L.—299,316—New York vs. Houston, 1986.
7-game Series—A. L.—264,167—Kansas City vs. Toronto, 1985.

Largest Attendance, Game

N. L.—64,924— At Philadelphia, October 8, 1977; Los Angeles 4, Philadelphia 1; fourth game.
A. L.—64,406— At California, October 5, 1982; California 8, Milwaukee 3; first game.

Smallest Attendance, Game

A. L.—24,265— At Oakland, October 11, 1973; Oakland 3, Baltimore 0; fifth game.
N. L.—33,088— At Pittsburgh, October 3, 1970; Cincinnati 3, Pittsburgh 0; first game.

Single Game Attendance, Each Club

AMERICAN LEAGUE

Club	Largest Attendance	Smallest Attendance
Baltimore	52,787 (Oct. 3, 1979)	27,608 (Oct. 5, 1970)
Boston	35,578 (Oct. 4, 1975) (Oct. 5, 1975)	32,786 (Oct. 8, 1986)
California	64,406 (Oct. 5, 1982)	43,199 (Oct. 5, 1979) (Oct. 6, 1979)
Chicago	46,635 (Oct. 7, 1983)	45,477 (Oct. 8, 1983)
Detroit	52,168 (Oct. 5, 1984)	37,615 (Oct. 11, 1972)
Kansas City	42,633 (Oct. 9, 1980)	40,046 (Oct. 13, 1985)
Milwaukee	54,968 (Oct. 10, 1982)	50,135 (Oct. 8, 1982)
Minnesota	55,245 (Oct. 8, 1987)	26,847 (Oct. 3, 1970)
New York	56,821 (Oct. 14, 1976)	48,497 (Oct. 14, 1981)
Oakland	49,358 (Oct. 7, 1975)	24,265 (Oct. 11, 1973)
Toronto	39,115 (Oct. 8, 1985)	32,084 (Oct. 16, 1985)

NATIONAL LEAGUE

Club	Largest Attendance	Smallest Attendance
Atlanta	52,173 (Oct. 10, 1982)	50,122 (Oct. 4, 1969)
Chicago	36,282 (Oct. 2, 1984) (Oct. 3, 1984)	36,282 (Oct. 2, 1984) (Oct. 3, 1984)
Cincinnati	55,047 (Oct. 12, 1976)	39,447 (Oct. 10, 1972)
Houston	45,718 (Oct. 15, 1986)	44,131 (Oct. 8, 1986)
Los Angeles	55,973 (Oct. 5, 1977)	49,963 (Oct. 4, 1983)
Montreal	54,499 (Oct. 17, 1981)	36,491 (Oct. 19, 1981)
New York	55,052 (Oct. 11, 1986)	50,323 (Oct. 10, 1973)
Philadelphia	65,476 (Oct. 8, 1980)	53,490 (Oct. 7, 1983)
Pittsburgh	50,584 (Oct. 8, 1972)	33,088 (Oct. 3, 1970)
St. Louis	55,331 (Oct. 6, 1987) (Oct. 7, 1987) (Oct. 13, 1987) (Oct. 14, 1987)	53,008 (Oct. 7, 1982)
San Diego	58,359 (Oct. 7, 1984)	58,346 (Oct. 4, 1984)
San Francisco	59,363 (Oct. 11, 1987)	40,977 (Oct. 2, 1971)

Non-Playing Personnel

Managers

Most Series, Manager

Both Leagues—7—Anderson, George L., Cincinnati N.L.; Detroit A.L.; won 5, lost 2.
A. L.—6—Weaver, Earl S., Baltimore, 1969, 1970, 1971, 1973, 1974, 1979; won 4, lost 2.

N. L.—5—Anderson, George L., Cincinnati, 1970, 1972, 1973, 1975, 1976; won 4, lost 1.
Lasorda, Thomas C., Los Angeles, 1977, 1978, 1981, 1983, 1985; won 3, lost 2.

Most Championship Series Winners Managed

Both Leagues—5—Anderson, George L., Cincinnati N.L., 1970, 1972, 1975, 1976; Detroit A.L., 1984.

N. L.—4—Anderson, George L., Cincinnati, 1970, 1972, 1975, 1976.
A. L.—4—Weaver, Earl S., Baltimore, 1969, 1970, 1971, 1979.

Most Championship Series Losers Managed

A. L.—3—Herzog, Dorrell N. E., Kansas City, 1976, 1977, 1978.
    Martin, Alfred M., Minnesota, 1969; Detroit, 1972; Oakland, 1981.
N. L.—3—Murtaugh, Daniel E., Pittsburgh, 1970, 1974, 1975.
    Ozark, Daniel L., Philadelphia, 1976, 1977, 1978.

Most Different Clubs Managed, League

A. L.—4—Martin, Alfred M., Minnesota 1970, Detroit 1972, New York 1976, 1977, Oakland 1981.

N. L.—2—Virdon, William C., Pittsburgh 1972, Houston 1980.

Umpires

Most Series Umpired

N. L.—7—Harvey, H. Douglas; 26 games.
A. L.—5—Barnett, Lawrence R.; 26 games.

Most Games Umpired

N. L.—26—Harvey, H. Douglas, 7 Series.
A. L.—26—Barnett, Lawrence R., 5 Series.

General Reference Data
Results

American League

Year-Winner	Loser
1969—Baltimore (East), 3 games;	Minnesota (West), 0 games.
1970—Baltimore (East), 3 games;	Minnesota (West), 0 games.
1971—Baltimore (East), 3 games;	Oakland (West), 0 games.
1972—Oakland (West), 3 games;	Detroit (East), 2 games.
1973—Oakland (West), 3 games;	Baltimore (East), 2 games.
1974—Oakland (West), 3 games;	Baltimore (East), 1 game.
1975—Boston (East), 3 games;	Oakland (West), 0 games.
1976—New York (East), 3 games;	Kansas City (West), 2 games.
1977—New York (East), 3 games;	Kansas City (West), 2 games.
1978—New York (East), 3 games;	Kansas City (West), 1 game.
1979—Baltimore (East), 3 games;	California (West), 1 game.
1980—Kansas City (West), 3 games;	New York (East), 0 games.
1981—New York (East), 3 games;	Oakland (West), 0 games.
1982—Milwaukee (East), 3 games;	California (West), 2 games.
1983—Baltimore (East), 3 games;	Chicago (West), 1 game.
1984—Detroit (East), 3 games;	Kansas City (West), 0 games.
1985—Kansas City (West), 4 games;	Toronto (East), 3 games.
1986—Boston (East), 4 games;	California (West), 3 games.
1987—Minnesota (West), 4 games;	Detroit (East), 1 game.

National League

Year-Winner	Loser
1969—New York (East), 3 games;	Atlanta (West), 0 games.
1970—Cincinnati (West), 3 games;	Pittsburgh (East), 0 games.
1971—Pittsburgh (East), 3 games;	San Francisco (West), 1 game.
1972—Cincinnati (West), 3 games;	Pittsburgh (East), 2 games.
1973—New York (East), 3 games;	Cincinnati (West), 2 games.
1974—Los Angeles (West), 3 games;	Pittsburgh (East), 1 game.
1975—Cincinnati (West), 3 games;	Pittsburgh (East), 0 games.
1976—Cincinnati (West), 3 games;	Philadelphia (East), 0 games.
1977—Los Angeles (West), 3 games;	Philadelphia (East), 1 game.
1978—Los Angeles (West), 3 games;	Philadelphia (East), 1 game.
1979—Pittsburgh (East), 3 games;	Cincinnati (West), 0 games.
1980—Philadelphia (East), 3 games;	Houston (West), 2 games.
1981—Los Angeles (West), 3 games;	Montreal (East), 2 games.
1982—St. Louis (East), 3 games;	Atlanta (West), 0 games.
1983—Philadelphia (East), 3 games;	Los Angeles (West), 1 game.
1984—San Diego (West), 3 games;	Chicago (East), 2 games.
1985—St. Louis (East), 4 games;	Los Angeles (West), 2 games.
1986—New York (East), 4 games;	Houston (West), 2 games.
1987—St. Louis (East), 4 games;	San Francisco (West), 3 games.

Series Won & Lost

American League—East Division

	W.	L.	Pct.
Boston	2	0	1.000
Milwaukee	1	0	1.000
New York	4	1	.800
Baltimore	5	2	.714
Detroit	1	2	.333
Toronto	0	1	.000
Totals	13	6	.684

American League—West Division

	W.	L.	Pct.
Oakland	3	3	.500
Kansas City	2	4	.333
Minnesota	1	2	.333
California	0	3	.000
Chicago	0	1	.000
Totals	6	13	.316

National League—East Division

	W.	L.	Pct.
New York	3	0	1.000
St. Louis	3	0	1.000
Philadelphia	2	3	.400
Pittsburgh	2	4	.333
Montreal	0	1	.000
Chicago	0	1	.000
Totals	10	9	.526

National League—West Division

	W.	L.	Pct.
San Diego	1	0	1.000
Los Angeles	4	2	.667
Cincinnati	4	2	.667
San Francisco	0	2	.000
Houston	0	2	.000
Atlanta	0	2	.000
Totals	9	10	.474

Games Won & Lost

American League—East Division

	W.	L.	Pct.
Boston	7	3	.700
Baltimore	18	8	.692
New York	12	8	.600
Milwaukee	3	2	.600
Detroit	6	7	.462
Toronto	3	4	.429
Totals	49	32	.605

American League—West Division

	W.	L.	Pct.
Kansas City	12	15	.444
Oakland	9	14	.391
California	6	10	.375
Minnesota	4	7	.364
Chicago	1	3	.250
Totals	32	49	.395

National League—East Division

	W.	L.	Pct.
New York	10	4	.714
St. Louis	11	5	.688
Pittsburgh	9	13	.409
Montreal	2	3	.400
Chicago	2	3	.400
Philadelphia	8	12	.400
Totals	42	40	.512

National League—West Division

	W.	L.	Pct.
Cincinnati	14	8	.636
Los Angeles	15	12	.556
San Diego	3	2	.600
Houston	4	7	.364
San Francisco	4	7	.364
Atlanta	0	6	.000
Totals	40	42	.488

Home & Road Games, Each Club

American League—East Division

	Y.	G.	H.	R.
Baltimore	7	26	13	13
New York	5	20	10	10
Detroit	3	13	7	6
Boston	2	10	6	4
Milwaukee	1	5	3	2
Toronto	1	7	4	3
Totals	19	81	43	38

American League—West Division

	Y.	G.	H.	R.
Kansas City	6	27	14	13
Oakland	6	23	10	13
California	3	16	7	9
Minnesota	3	11	5	6
Chicago	1	4	2	2
Totals	19	81	38	43

National League—East Division

	Y.	G.	H.	R.
Pittsburgh	6	22	10	12
Philadelphia	5	20	10	10
St. Louis	3	16	9	7
New York	3	14	7	7
Montreal	1	5	3	2
Chicago	1	5	2	3
Totals	19	82	41	41

National League—West Division

	Y.	G.	H.	R.
Cincinnati	6	22	11	11
Los Angeles	6	27	13	14
Houston	2	11	6	5
Atlanta	2	6	3	3
San Diego	1	5	3	2
San Francisco	2	11	5	6
Totals	19	82	41	41

Shutouts
American League (13)
Oct. 5, 1969—McNally, Baltimore 1, Minnesota 0; 3 hits (11 inn.).
Oct. 8, 1972—Odom, Oakland 5, Detroit 0; 3 hits.
Oct. 10, 1972—Coleman, Detroit 3, Oakland 0; 7 hits.
Oct. 6, 1973—Palmer, Baltimore 6, Oakland 0; 5 hits.
Oct. 11, 1973—Hunter, Oakland 3, Baltimore 0; 5 hits.
Oct. 6, 1974—Holtzman, Oakland 5, Baltimore 0; 5 hits.
Oct. 8, 1974—Blue, Oakland 1, Baltimore 0; 2 hits.
Oct. 6, 1979—McGregor, Baltimore 8, California 0; 6 hits.
Oct. 15, 1981—Righetti, Davis and Gossage, New York 4, Oak. 0; 5 hits.
Oct. 6, 1983—Boddicker, Baltimore 4, Chicago 0; 5 hits.
Oct. 8, 1983—Davis and T. Martinez, Baltimore 3, Chi. 0; 10 hits (10 inn.).
Oct. 5, 1984—Wilcox and Hernandez, Detroit 1, Kansas City 0; 3 hits.
Oct. 13, 1985—Jackson, Kansas City 2, Toronto 0; 8 hits.

National League (14)
Oct. 3, 1970—Nolan and Carroll, Cincinnati 3, Pitts. 0; 8 hits (10 inn.).
Oct. 7, 1973—Matlack, New York 5, Oakland 0; 2 hits.
Oct. 5, 1974—Sutton, Los Angeles 3, Pittsburgh 0; 4 hits.
Oct. 8, 1974—Kison and Hernandez, Pittsburgh 7, Los Angeles 0; 4 hits.
Oct. 4, 1978—John, Los Angeles 4, Philadelphia 0; 4 hits.
Oct. 10, 1980—Niekro and D. Smith, Houston 1, Phil. 0; 7 hits (11 inn.).
Oct. 14, 1981—Burris, Montreal 3, Los Angeles 0; 5 hits.
Oct. 7, 1982—Forsch, St. Louis 7, Atlanta 0; 3 hits.
Oct. 4, 1983—Carlton and Holland, Philadelphia 1, Los Angeles 0; 7 hits.
Oct. 2, 1984—Sutcliffe and Brusstar, Chicago 13, San Diego 0; 6 hits.
Oct. 8, 1986—Scott, Houston 1, New York 0; 5 hits.
Oct. 7, 1987—Dravecky, San Francisco 5, St. Louis 0; 2 hits.
Oct. 13, 1987—Tudor, Worrell and Dayley, St.L. 1, S.F. 0; 6 hits.
Oct. 14, 1987—Cox, St. Louis 6, San Francisco 0; 8 hits.

Extra-Inning Games
American League (11)
Oct. 4, 1969—12 innings, Baltimore 4, Minnesota 3.
Oct. 5, 1969—11 innings, Baltimore 1, Minnesota 0.
Oct. 7, 1972—11 innings, Oakland 3, Detroit 2.
Oct. 11, 1972—10 innings, Detroit 4, Oakland 3.
Oct. 9, 1973—11 innings, Oakland 2, Baltimore 1.
Oct. 3, 1979—11 innings, Baltimore 6, California 2.
Oct. 8, 1983—10 innings, Baltimore 3, Chicago 0.
Oct. 3, 1984—11 innings, Detroit 5, Kansas City 3.
Oct. 9, 1985—10 innings, Toronto 6, Kansas City 5.
Oct. 11, 1986—11 innings, California 4, Boston 3.
Oct. 12, 1986—11 innings, Boston 7, California 6.

National League (12)
Oct. 3, 1970—10 innings, Cincinnati 3, Pittsburgh 0.
Oct. 9, 1973—12 innings, Cincinnati 2, New York 1.
Oct. 7, 1975—10 innings, Cincinnati 5, Pittsburgh 3.
Oct. 7, 1978—10 innings, Los Angeles 4, Philadelphia 3.
Oct. 2, 1979—11 innings, Pittsburgh 5, Cincinnati 2.
Oct. 3, 1979—10 innings, Pittsburgh 3, Cincinnati 2.
Oct. 8, 1980—10 innings, Houston 7, Philadelphia 4.
Oct. 10, 1980—11 innings, Houston 1, Philadelphia 0.
Oct. 11, 1980—10 innings, Philadelphia 5, Houston 3.
Oct. 12, 1980—10 innings, Philadelphia 8, Houston 7.
Oct. 14, 1986—12 innings, New York 2, Houston 1.
Oct. 15, 1986—16 innings, New York 7, Houston 6.

Attendance

American League			National League		
Year	G.	Total	Year	G.	Total
1969	3	113,763	1969	3	153,587
1970	3	81,945	1970	3	112,943
1971	3	110,800	1971	4	157,348
1972	5	189,671	1972	5	234,814
1973	5	175,833	1973	5	262,548
1974	4	144,615	1974	4	200,262
1975	3	120,514	1975	3	155,740
1976	5	252,152	1976	3	180,338
1977	5	234,713	1977	4	240,584
1978	4	194,192	1978	4	234,269
1979	4	191,293	1979	3	152,246
1980	3	141,819	1980	5	264,950
1981	3	151,539	1981	5	250,098
1982	5	284,691	1982	3	158,589
1983	4	195,748	1983	4	223,914
1984	3	136,160	1984	5	247,623
1985	7	264,167	1985	6	326,824
1986	7	324,430	1986	6	299,316
1987	5	257,631	1987	7	396,597

Leading Batters
(Playing in all games, each Series, with four or more hits)
American League

Year	Player and Club	AB.	H.	TB.	B.A.
1969	Brooks C. Robinson, Baltimore	14	7	8	.500
1970	Brooks C. Robinson, Baltimore	12	7	9	.583
1971	Brooks C. Robinson, Baltimore	11	4	8	.364
	Salvatore L. Bando, Oakland	11	4	9	.364

Year	Player and Club	AB.	H.	TB.	B.A.
1972	Mateo R. Alou, Oakland	21	8	12	.381
1973	Dagoberto B. Campaneris, Oakland	21	7	14	.333
1974	Raymond E. Fosse, Oakland	12	4	8	.333
1975	Salvatore L. Bando, Oakland	12	6	8	.500
1976	C. Christopher Chambliss, New York	21	11	20	.524
1977	Harold A. McRae, Kansas City	18	8	14	.444
1978	Reginald M. Jackson, New York	13	6	13	.462
1979	Eddie C. Murray, Baltimore	12	5	8	.417
1980	Frank White, Kansas City	11	6	10	.545
1981	Graig Nettles, New York	12	6	11	.500
	Jerry W. Mumphrey, New York	12	6	7	.500
1982	Fredric M. Lynn, California	18	11	16	.611
1983	Calvin E. Ripken, Baltimore	15	6	8	.400
1984	Kirk H. Gibson, Detroit	12	5	9	.417
1985	Clifford Johnson, Toronto	19	7	9	.368
1986	Robert R. Boone, California	22	10	13	.455
1987	Thomas A. Brunansky, Minnesota	17	7	17	.412

National League

Year	Player and Club	AB.	H.	TB.	B.A.
1969	Arthur L. Shamsky, New York	13	7	7	.538
1970	Wilver D. Stargell, Pittsburgh	12	6	7	.500
1971	Robert E. Robertson, Pittsburgh	16	7	20	.438
1972	Peter E. Rose, Cincinnati	20	9	13	.450
1973	Peter E. Rose, Cincinnati	21	8	15	.381
1974	Wilver D. Stargell, Pittsburgh	15	6	12	.400
1975	Richard W. Zisk, Pittsburgh	10	5	6	.500
1976	John W. Johnstone, Philadelphia	9	7	10	.778
1977	Robert E. Boone, Philadelphia	10	4	4	.400
1978	Johnnie B. Baker, Los Angeles	15	7	9	.467
1979	Wilver D. Stargell, Pittsburgh	11	5	13	.455
1980	Terry S. Puhl, Houston	19	10	12	.526
1981	Gary E. Carter, Montreal	16	7	8	.438
1982	Darrell R. Porter, St. Louis	9	5	8	.556
	Osborne E. Smith, St. Louis	9	5	5	.556
1983	Michael J. Schmidt, Philadelphia	15	7	12	.467
1984	Steven P. Garvey, San Diego	20	8	12	.400
1985	Osborne E. Smith, St. Louis	23	10	16	.435
1986	Leonard K. Dykstra, New York	23	7	13	.304
1987	Jeffrey N. Leonard, San Francisco	24	10	22	.417

.400 Hitters
(Playing in all games and having 9 or more at-bats)
American League (34)

Player and Club	Year	AB.	H.	TB.	B.A.
Lynn, Fredric M., California	1982	18	11	16	.611
Robinson, Brooks C., Baltimore	1970	12	7	9	.583
White, Frank, Kansas City	1980	11	6	10	.545
Chambliss, C. Christopher, New York	1976	21	11	20	.524
Robinson, Brooks C., Baltimore	1969	14	7	8	.500
Oliva, Antonio, Minnesota	1970	12	6	11	.500
Bando, Salvatore L., Oakland	1975	12	6	8	.500
Watson, Robert J., New York	1980	12	6	11	.500
Nettles, Graig, New York	1981	12	6	11	.500
Mumphrey, Jerry W., New York	1981	12	6	7	.500
Jackson, Reginald M., New York	1978	13	6	13	.462
Milbourne, Lawrence, W., New York	1981	13	6	6	.462
Moore, Charles W., Milwaukee	1982	13	6	6	.462
Yastrzemski, Carl M., Boston	1975	11	5	9	.455
Rivers, John M., New York	1978	11	5	5	.455
Boone, Robert R., California	1986	22	10	13	.455
Burleson, Richard P., Boston	1975	9	4	6	.444
Brett, George H., Kansas City	1976	18	8	14	.444
McRae, Harold A., Kansas City	1977	18	8	14	.444
Munson, Thurman L., New York	1976	23	10	12	.435
Powell, John W., Baltimore	1970	14	6	11	.429
Otis, Amos J., Kansas City	1978	14	6	8	.429
Owen, Spike D., Boston	1986	21	9	11	.429
Fisk, Carlton E., Boston	1975	12	5	6	.417
Jackson, Reginald M., Oakland	1975	12	5	8	.417
Murray, Eddie C., Baltimore	1979	12	5	8	.417
Gibson, Kirk H., Detroit	1984	12	5	9	.417
Carew, Rodney C., California	1979	17	7	10	.412
Brunansky, Thomas A., Minnesota	1987	17	7	17	.412
Blair, Paul L., Baltimore	1969	15	6	11	.400
Johnson, Clifford, New York	1977	15	6	11	.400
Chambliss, C. Christopher, New York	1978	15	6	6	.400
Ripken, Calvin E., Baltimore	1983	15	6	8	.400
Cooper, Cecil C., Boston	1975	10	4	6	.400

National League (34)

Player and Club	Year	AB.	H.	TB.	B.A.
Johnstone, John W., Philadelphia	1976	9	7	10	.778
Porter, Darrell R., St. Louis	1982	9	5	8	.556
Smith, Osborne E., St. Louis	1982	9	5	5	.556
Shamsky, Arthur L., New York	1969	13	7	7	.538
Puhl, Terry S., Houston	1980	19	10	12	.526
Stargell, Wilver D., Pittsburgh	1970	12	6	7	.500
Zisk, Richard W., Pittsburgh	1975	10	5	6	.500
Baker, Johnnie B., Los Angeles	1978	15	7	9	.467
Schmidt, Michael J., Philadelphia	1983	15	7	12	.467
Cepeda, Orlando M., Atlanta	1969	11	5	10	.455
Concepcion, David I., Cincinnati	1975	11	5	8	.455
Stargell, Wilver D., Pittsburgh	1979	11	5	13	.455

Player and Club	Year	AB.	H.	TB.	B.A.
Rose, Peter E., Cincinnati	1972	20	9	13	.450
Thomas, Derrel O., Los Angeles	1983	9	4	5	.444
Robertson, Robert E., Pittsburgh	1971	16	7	20	.438
Carter, Gary E., Montreal	1981	16	7	8	.438
Smith, Osborne E., St. Louis	1985	23	10	16	.435
Jones, Cleon J., New York	1969	14	6	11	.429
McCovey, Willie L., San Francisco	1971	14	6	12	.429
Rose, Peter E., Cincinnati	1976	14	6	10	.429
Concepcion, David I., Cincinnati	1979	14	6	7	.429
Matthews, Gary N., Philadelphia	1983	14	6	15	.429
Landrum, Terry L., St. Louis	1985	14	6	6	.429
Cash, David, Pittsburgh	1971	19	8	10	.421
Leonard, Jeffrey N., San Francisco	1987	24	10	22	.417
Tolan, Robert, Cincinnati	1970	12	5	8	.417
Perez, Atanasio R., Cincinnati	1975	12	5	8	.417
Garner, Philip M., Pittsburgh	1979	12	5	10	.417
Russell, William E., Los Angeles	1978	17	7	8	.412
Rose, Peter E., Philadelphia	1980	20	8	8	.400
Garvey, Steven P., San Diego	1984	20	8	12	.400
Stargell, Wilver D., Pittsburgh	1974	15	6	12	.400
Cruz, Jose D., Houston	1980	15	6	9	.400
Boone, Robert R., Philadelphia	1977	10	4	4	.400

Home Runs
American League (131)

1969—4—Baltimore (East), Frank Robinson (1), Mark H. Belanger (1), John W. Powell (1), Paul L. Blair (1).
  1—Minnesota (West), Antonio Oliva (1).
1970—6—Baltimore (East), David A. Johnson (2), Miguel Cuellar (1), Donald A. Buford (1), John W. Powell (1), Frank Robinson (1).
  3—Minnesota (West), Harmon C. Killebrew (2), Antonio Oliva (1).
1971—4—Baltimore (East), John W. Powell (2), Brooks C. Robinson (1), Elrod J. Hendricks (1).
  3—Oakland (West), Reginald M. Jackson (2), Salvatore L. Bando (1).
1972—4—Detroit (East), Norman D. Cash (1), Albert W. Kaline (1), William A. Freehan (1), Richard J. McAuliffe (1).
  1—Oakland (West), Michael P. Epstein (1).
1973—5—Oakland (West), Salvatore L. Bando (2), Dagoberto B. Campaneris (2), Joseph O. Rudi (1).
  3—Baltimore (East), Earl C. Williams (1), Andrew A. Etchebarren (1), Robert A. Grich (1).
1974—3—Baltimore (East), Paul L. Blair (1), Brooks C. Robinson (1), Robert A. Grich (1).
  3—Oakland (West), Salvatore L. Bando (2), Raymond E. Fosse (1).
1975—2—Boston (East), Carl M. Yastrzemski (1), Americo P. Petrocelli (1).
  1—Oakland (West), Reginald M. Jackson (1).
1976—3—New York (East), Graig Nettles (2), C. Christopher Chambliss (2).
  2—Kansas City (West), John C. Mayberry (1), George H. Brett (1).
1977—3—Kansas City (West), Harold A. McRae (1), John C. Mayberry (1), Alfred E. Cowens (1).
  2—New York (East), Thurman L. Munson (1), Clifford Johnson (1).
1978—5—New York (East), Reginald M. Jackson (2), Thurman L. Munson (1), Graig Nettles (1), Roy H. White (1).
  4—Kansas City (West), George H. Brett (3), Freddie J. Patek (1).
1979—3—Baltimore (East), John L. Lowenstein (1), Eddie C. Murray (1), H. Patrick Kelly (1).
  3—California (West), Darnell G. Ford (2), Donald E. Baylor (1).
1980—3—New York (East), Richard A. Cerone (1), Louis V. Piniella (1), Graig Nettles (1).
  3—Kansas City (West), George H. Brett (2), Frank White (1).
1981—3—New York (East), Louis V. Piniella (1), Graig Nettles (1), William L. Randolph (1).
  0—Oakland (West).
1982—5—Milwaukee (East), Paul L. Molitor (2), J. Gorman Thomas (1), Mark S. Brouhard (1), Benjamin A. Oglivie (1).
  4—California (West), Fredric M. Lynn (1), Reginald M. Jackson (1), Robert R. Boone (1), Donald E. Baylor (1).
1983—3—Baltimore (East), Gary S. Roenicke (1), Eddie C. Murray (1), Terry L. Landrum (1).
  0—Chicago (West).
1984—4—Detroit (East), Kirk H. Gibson (1), Larry D. Herndon (1), Lance M. Parrish (1), Alan S. Trammell (1).
  0—Kansas City (West).
1985—7—Kansas City (West), George H. Brett (3), Patrick A. Sheridan (2), Willie J. Wilson (1), James H. Sundberg (1).
  2—Toronto (East), Jessie L. Barfield (1), S. Rance Mulliniks (1).
1986—7—California (West), Robert R. Boone (1), Douglas V. DeCinces (1), Brian J. Downing (1), Robert A. Grich (1), Wallace K. Joyner (1), Gary G. Pettis (1), Richard C. Schofield (1).
  6—Boston (East), James E. Rice (2), Donald E. Baylor (1), Dwight M. Evans (1), Richard C. Gedman (1), David L. Henderson (1).
1987—8—Minnesota (West), Thomas A. Brunansky (2), Gary J. Gaetti (2), Gregory C. Gagne (2), Kent M. Hrbek (1), Kirby Puckett (1).
  7—Detroit (East), Chester E. Lemon (2), Kirk H. Gibson (1), Michael T. Heath (1), Matthew D. Nokes (1), Patrick A. Sheridan (1), Louis R. Whitaker (1).

National League (133)

1969—6—New York (East), Tommie L. Agee (2), Kenneth G. Boswell (2), Cleon J. Jones (1), R. Wayne Garrett (1).
  5—Atlanta (West), Henry L. Aaron (3), A. Antonio Gonzalez (1), Orlando M. Cepeda (1).
1970—3—Cincinnati (West), Robert Tolan (1), Atanasio R. Perez (1), Johnny L. Bench (1).
  0—Pittsburgh (East).
1971—8—Pittsburgh (East), Robert E. Robertson (4), Richard J. Hebner (2), Eugene A. Clines (1), Albert Oliver (1).

  5—San Francisco (West), Willie L. McCovey (2), Rigoberto Fuentes (1), Willie H. Mays (1), Chris E. Speier (1).
1972—4—Cincinnati (West), Joe L. Morgan (2), Cesar F. Geronimo (1), Johnny L. Bench (1).
  3—Pittsburgh (East), Albert Oliver (1), Manuel D. Sanguillen (1), Roberto W. Clemente (1).
1973—5—Cincinnati (West), Peter E. Rose (2), Johnny L. Bench (1), Denis J. Menke (1), Atanasio R. Perez (1).
  3—New York (East), Daniel J. Staub (1).
1974—3—Los Angeles (West), Steven P. Garvey (2), Ronald C. Cey (1).
  3—Pittsburgh (East), Wilver D. Stargell (2), Richard J. Hebner (1).
1975—4—Cincinnati (West), Donald E. Gullett (1), Atanasio R. Perez (1), David I. Concepcion (1), Peter E. Rose (1).
  1—Pittsburgh (East), Albert Oliver (1).
1976—3—Cincinnati (West), George A. Foster (2), Johnny L. Bench (1).
  1—Philadelphia (East), Gregory M. Luzinski (1).
1977—3—Los Angeles (West), Johnnie B. Baker (2), Ronald C. Cey (1).
  2—Philadelphia (East), Gregory M. Luzinski (1), Arnold R. McBride (1).
1978—8—Los Angeles (West), Steven P. Garvey (4), David E. Lopes (2), Stephen W. Yeager (1), Ronald C. Cey (1).
  5—Philadelphia (East), Gregory M. Luzinski (2), Jerry L. Martin (1), Steven N. Carlton (1), Arnold R. McBride (1).
1979—4—Pittsburgh (East), Wilver D. Stargell (2), Philip M. Garner (1), Bill Madlock (1).
  2—Cincinnati (West), George A. Foster (1), Johnny L. Bench (1).
1980—1—Philadelphia (East), Gregory M. Luzinski (1).
  0—Houston (West).
1981—4—Los Angeles (West), Pedro Guerrero (1), Michael L. Scioscia (1), Steven P. Garvey (1), Robert J. Monday (1).
  1—Montreal (East), Jerome C. White (1).
1982—1—St. Louis (East), Willie D. McGee (1).
  0—Atlanta (West).
1983—5—Philadelphia (East), Gary N. Matthews (3), Michael J. Schmidt (1), Sixto Lezcano (1).
  2—Los Angeles (West), Michael A. Marshall (1), Johnnie B. Baker (1).
1984—9—Chicago (East), Jody R. Davis (2), Leon Durham (2), Gary N. Matthews (2), Ronald C. Cey (1), Robert E. Dernier (1), Richard L. Sutcliffe (1).
  2—San Diego (West), Steven P. Garvey (1), W. Kevin McReynolds (1).
1985—5—Los Angeles (West), Bill Madlock (3), Gregory A. Brock (1), Michael A. Marshall (1).
  3—St. Louis (East), Thomas M. Herr (1), Osborne E. Smith (1), Jack A. Clark (1).
1986—5—Houston (West), Alan D. Ashby (1), Glenn E. Davis (1), William D. Doran (1), William A. Hatcher (1), Richard W. Thon (1).
  3—New York (East), Darryl E. Strawberry (1), Leonard K. Dykstra (1).
1987—9—San Francisco (West), Jeffrey N. Leonard (4), Robert E. Brenly (1), William N. Clark (1), Kevin D. Mitchell (1), W. Harry Spilman (1), Robert R. Thompson (1).
  2—St. Louis (East), James W. Lindeman (1), Jose M. Oquendo (1).

Players With Three Homers
American League (8)

Player	Series	HR.
Brett, George H.	6	9
Jackson, Reginald M.	11	6
Bando, Salvatore L.	5	5
Nettles, Graig	6	5
Powell, John W.	5	4
Baylor, Donald E.	6	4
Grich, Robert A.	5	3
Sheridan, Patrick A.	3	3

National League (17)

Player	Series	HR.
Garvey, Steven P.	5	8
Matthews, Gary N.	2	5
Luzinski, Gregory M.	5	5
Bench, Johnny L.	6	5
Leonard, Jeffrey N.	2	4
Madlock, Bill	2	4
Robertson, Robert E.	5	4
Cey, Ronald C.	5	4
Stargell, Wilver D.	6	4
Aaron, Henry L.	1	3
Staub, Daniel J.	1	3
Baker, Johnnie B.	4	3
Foster, George A.	4	3
Oliver, Albert	5	3
Perez, Atanasio R.	6	3
Rose, Peter E.	7	3
Hebner, Richard J.	8	3

Pitchers With Three Victories
Both Leagues (4)

Pitcher and Club	Y.	W.	L.
Kison, Bruce E., Pitts. NL, Cal. AL	5	4	0
John, Thomas E., L.A. NL, N.Y. AL, Cal. AL	5	4	1
Sutton, Donald H., L.A. NL, Mil. AL, Cal. AL	5	4	1
Blyleven, Rikalbert, Minn. AL, Pitts. NL	3	3	0

American League (3)

Pitcher and Club	Y.	W.	L.
Palmer, James A., Baltimore	6	4	1
Hunter, James A., Oakland, New York	6	4	3
McNally, David A., Baltimore	5	3	2

National League (5)

Pitcher and Club	Y.	W.	L.
Carlton, Steven N., Philadelphia	5	4	2
Kison, Bruce E., Pittsburgh	4	3	2
Sutton, Donald H., Los Angeles	3	3	0
Valenzuela, Fernando, Los Angeles	3	3	1
Orosco, Jesse, New York	1	3	0

		Series		Games	
		W.	L.	W.	L.
McNamara, John F., Boston (East)		1	0	4	3
Mauch, Gene W., California (West)		0	2	5	7
Rigney, William J., Minnesota (West)		0	1	0	3
Weaver, Earl S., Baltimore (East)		4	2	15	7
Williams, Richard H., Oakland (West)		2	1	6	7

10-Strikeout Games By Pitchers

American League (6)

Date	Pitcher and Club	SO.
Oct. 5, 1969	McNally, Baltimore vs. Minnesota (11 inn.)	11
Oct. 5, 1970	Palmer, Baltimore vs. Minnesota	12
Oct. 10, 1972	Coleman, Detroit vs. Oakland	14
Oct. 6, 1973	Palmer, Baltimore vs. Oakland	12
Oct. 9, 1973	Cuellar, Baltimore vs. Oakland (10 inn.)	11
Oct. 6, 1983	Boddicker, Baltimore vs. Chicago	14

National League (4)

Date	Pitcher and Club	SO.
Oct. 6, 1973	Seaver, New York vs. Cincinnati (8⅓ inn.)	13
Oct. 7, 1975	Candelaria, Pittsburgh vs. Cincinnati (7⅔ inn.)	14
Oct. 8, 1986	Scott, Houston vs. New York	14
Oct. 14, 1986	Ryan, Houston vs. New York	12

Managerial Records

American League (19)

	Series		Games	
	W.	L.	W.	L.
Altobelli, Joseph S., Baltimore (East)	1	0	3	1
Anderson, George L., Detroit (East)	1	1	4	4
Cox, Robert J., Toronto (East)	0	1	3	4
Dark, Alvin R., Oakland (West)	1	1	3	4
Fregosi, James L., California (West)	0	1	1	3
Frey, James G., Kansas City (West)	1	0	3	0
Herzog, Dorrel N. E., Kansas City (West)	0	3	5	9
Howser, Richard D., New York (East), Kansas City (West)	1	2	4	9
Johnson, Darrell D., Boston (East)	1	0	3	0
Kelly, J. Thomas, Minnesota (West)	1	0	4	1
Kuenn, Harvey E., Milwaukee (East)	1	0	3	2
LaRussa, Anthony, Chicago (West)	0	1	1	3
Lemon, Robert G., New York (East)	2	0	6	1
Martin, Alfred M., Minn. (West), Det. (East), N.Y. (East), Oak. (West)	2	3	8	13

National League (22)

	Series		Games	
	W.	L.	W.	L.
Alston, Walter E., Los Angeles (West)	1	0	3	1
Anderson, George L., Cincinnati (West)	4	1	14	5
Berra, Lawrence P., New York (East)	1	0	3	2
Craig, Roger L., San Francisco (West)	0	1	3	4
Fanning, W. James, Montreal (East)	0	1	2	3
Frey, James G., Chicago (East)	0	1	2	3
Fox, Charles F., San Francisco (West)	0	1	1	3
Green, G. Dallas, Philadelphia (East)	1	0	3	2
Harris, C. Luman, Atlanta (West)	0	1	0	3
Herzog, Dorrel N. E., St. Louis (East)	3	0	11	5
Hodges, Gilbert R., New York (East)	1	0	3	0
Johnson, David A., New York (East)	1	0	4	2
Lanier, Harold C., Houston (West)	0	1	2	4
Lasorda, Thomas C., Los Angeles (West)	3	2	12	11
McNamara, John F., Cincinnati (West)	0	1	0	3
Murtaugh, Daniel E., Pittsburgh (East)	1	3	4	10
Owens, Paul F., Philadelphia (East)	1	0	3	1
Ozark, Daniel L., Philadelphia (East)	0	3	3	9
Tanner, Charles W., Pittsburgh (East)	1	0	3	0
Torre, Joseph P., Atlanta (West)	0	1	0	3
Virdon, William C., Pitts. (East), Hous. (West)	0	2	4	6
Williams, Richard H., San Diego (West)	1	0	3	2

Both Leagues (5)

	Series		Games	
	W.	L.	W.	L.
Combined record of Anderson, George L., Cincinnati N.L. and Detroit A.L.	5	2	18	9
Combined record of Frey, James G., Kansas City A.L. and Chicago N.L.	1	1	5	3
Combined record of Herzog, Dorrel N. E., Kansas City A.L. and St. Louis N.L.	3	3	16	14
Combined record of McNamara, John F., Cincinnati N.L. and Boston A.L.	1	1	4	6
Combined record of Williams, Richard H., Oakland A.L. and San Diego N.L.	3	1	9	9

Club Batting & Fielding

American League

Year—Club	G.	AB.	R.	H.	TB.	2B.	3B.	HR.	SH.	SF.	SB.	BB.	SO.	RBI.	B.A.	PO.	A.	E.	DP.	PB.	F.A.	LOB.	Pl.	Pi.
1969—Baltimore, East	3	123	16	36	58	8	1	4	2	0	0	13	14	15	.293	96	31	1	2	0	.992	28	20	7
Minnesota, West	3	110	5	17	25	3	1	1	0	1	2	12	27	5	.155	94	34	5	3	0	.962	22	22	9
1970—Baltimore, East	3	109	27	36	61	7	0	6	1	2	1	12	19	24	.330	81	29	0	3	0	1.000	20	14	4
Minnesota, West	3	101	10	24	39	4	1	3	1	0	0	9	22	10	.238	78	28	6	5	0	.946	20	24	9
1971—Baltimore, East	3	95	15	26	47	7	1	4	0	1	0	13	25	14	.274	81	31	1	3	0	.991	19	15	4
Oakland, West	3	96	7	22	41	8	1	3	2	0	0	5	16	7	.229	75	15	0	4	0	1.000	15	20	7
1972—Detroit, East	5	162	10	32	52	6	1	4	3	0	0	13	25	10	.198	139	48	7	4	0	.964	30	24	8
Oakland, West	5	170	13	38	49	8	0	1	4	1	7	12	35	12	.224	138	59	3	5	1	.985	38	25	8
1973—Baltimore, East	5	171	15	36	52	7	0	3	0	0	1	16	25	15	.211	135	51	2	2	1	.989	36	23	7
Oakland, West	5	160	15	32	54	5	1	5	3	0	3	17	39	15	.200	138	47	4	4	0	.979	34	22	6
1974—Baltimore, East	4	124	7	22	32	1	0	3	2	0	0	5	20	7	.177	105	50	4	4	0	.975	16	22	7
Oakland, West	4	120	11	22	37	4	1	3	2	1	3	22	16	11	.183	108	43	2	4	1	.987	30	20	5
1975—Boston, East	3	98	18	31	45	8	0	2	5	1	3	3	12	14	.316	81	34	4	3	0	.966	14	14	5
Oakland, West	3	98	7	19	28	6	0	1	0	0	0	9	14	7	.194	75	40	6	4	0	.950	19	22	7
1976—New York, East	5	174	23	55	84	13	2	4	2	1	4	16	15	21	.316	132	60	6	5	1	.970	41	22	6
Kansas City, West	5	162	24	40	60	6	4	2	0	4	5	11	18	24	.247	129	51	4	5	0	.978	22	24	9
1977—New York, East	5	175	21	46	64	12	0	2	1	2	2	9	16	17	.263	132	51	2	5	0	.989	34	18	6
Kansas City, West	5	163	22	42	66	9	3	3	2	2	5	15	22	21	.258	132	54	5	2	0	.974	28	22	8
1978—New York, East	4	140	19	42	62	3	1	5	0	1	0	7	18	18	.300	105	35	1	2	1	.993	27	21	8
Kansas City, West	4	133	17	35	59	6	3	4	1	2	6	14	21	16	.263	102	36	4	4	1	.972	28	20	7
1979—Baltimore, East	4	133	26	37	53	5	1	3	1	3	5	18	24	25	.278	109	52	5	5	1	.970	23	20	5
California, West	4	137	15	32	48	7	0	3	0	2	7	13	14	14	.234	107	37	2	7	0	.986	22	23	9
1980—New York, East	3	102	6	26	44	7	1	3	1	0	0	6	16	5	.255	75	42	1	2	0	.991	22	20	6
Kansas City, West	3	97	14	28	45	6	1	3	0	0	3	9	15	14	.289	81	29	1	3	0	.991	18	15	4
1981—New York, East	3	107	20	36	49	4	0	3	2	1	2	13	10	20	.336	81	30	1	6	1	.991	30	22	6
Oakland, West	3	99	4	22	28	4	1	0	0	0	2	6	23	4	.222	75	33	4	1	0	.964	20	24	8
1982—Milwaukee, East	5	151	23	33	52	4	0	5	2	3	2	15	28	20	.219	129	45	8	5	0	.956	24	20	7
California, West	5	157	23	40	62	8	1	4	5	2	1	16	34	23	.255	126	46	4	3	1	.977	29	20	7
1983—Baltimore, East	4	129	19	28	46	9	0	3	1	3	2	16	24	17	.217	111	49	2	4	0	.988	24	22	6
Chicago, West	4	133	3	28	32	4	0	0	1	1	0	12	26	2	.211	108	51	3	5	0	.981	35	23	9
1984—Detroit, East	3	107	14	25	43	4	1	4	2	1	4	8	17	14	.234	87	27	1	0	0	.991	20	20	5
Kansas City, West	3	106	4	18	21	1	1	0	0	0	0	6	21	4	.170	84	26	7	2	0	.940	21	22	6
1985—Toronto, East	7	242	25	65	90	19	0	2	0	2	2	16	37	23	.269	186	61	4	4	0	.984	50	24	8
Kansas City, West	7	227	26	51	83	9	1	7	4	2	2	22	51	26	.225	188	87	6	7	0	.979	44	22	7
1986—Boston, East	7	254	41	69	102	11	2	6	3	2	1	19	31	35	.272	196	73	7	5	0	.975	48	20	7
California, West	7	256	30	71	103	11	0	7	3	1	1	20	44	26	.277	192	78	8	5	2	.971	60	24	9
1987—Detroit, East	5	167	23	40	65	4	0	7	2	2	1	18	35	21	.240	129	56	5	1	1	.974	37	24	10
Minnesota, West	5	171	34	46	85	13	1	8	2	2	4	20	25	33	.269	132	41	3	5	0	.983	37	21	7

Year—Club	G.	AB.	R.	H.	TB.	2B.	3B.	HR.	SH.	SF.	SB.	BB.	SO.	RBI.	B.A.	PO.	A.	E.	DP.	PB.	F.A.	LOB.	Pl.	Pi.
1969—New York, East	3	113	27	37	65	8	1	6	1	0	5	10	25	24	.327	81	23	2	2	1	.981	19	17	6
Atlanta, West	3	106	15	27	51	9	0	5	0	1	1	11	20	15	.255	78	37	6	4	1	.950	23	23	9
1970—Pittsburgh, East	3	102	3	23	29	6	0	0	2	0	0	12	19	3	.225	81	37	2	3	0	.983	29	18	5
Cincinnati, West	3	100	9	22	36	3	1	3	0	0	1	8	12	8	.220	84	39	1	1	0	.992	18	20	7
1971—Pittsburgh, East	4	144	24	39	67	4	0	8	1	0	2	5	33	23	.271	105	32	3	3	1	.979	26	21	7
San Fran., West	4	132	25	31	51	5	0	5	4	0	2	16	28	14	.235	102	37	4	1	1	.972	33	22	9
1972—Pittsburgh, East	5	158	15	30	47	6	1	3	2	0	0	9	27	14	.190	131	38	4	3	0	.977	24	23	10
Cincinnati, West	5	166	19	42	67	9	2	4	3	1	4	10	28	16	.253	132	53	4	3	1	.979	30	21	8
1973—New York, East	5	168	23	37	51	5	0	3	3	1	0	19	28	22	.220	142	44	4	3	0	.979	30	17	6
Cincinnati, West	5	167	8	31	52	6	0	5	3	1	0	13	42	8	.186	138	59	2	3	0	.990	35	24	9
1974—Pittsburgh, East	4	129	10	25	35	1	0	3	2	0	1	8	17	10	.194	105	37	4	2	1	.973	24	22	8
Los Angeles, West	4	138	20	37	56	8	1	3	1	0	5	30	16	19	.268	108	46	7	8	1	.957	44	22	7
1975—Pittsburgh, East	3	101	7	20	26	3	0	1	0	0	0	10	18	7	.198	78	20	2	3	2	.980	21	24	10
Cincinnati, West	3	102	19	29	45	4	0	4	0	3	11	9	28	18	.284	84	31	1	2	0	.991	17	18	7
1976—Philadelphia, East	3	100	11	27	40	8	1	1	3	2	0	12	9	11	.270	79	34	2	3	0	.983	25	22	7
Cincinnati, West	3	99	19	25	45	5	3	3	1	3	5	15	16	17	.253	81	32	2	3	0	.983	20	18	6
1977—Philadelphia, East	4	138	14	31	40	3	0	2	2	0	1	11	21	12	.225	105	49	3	3	1	.981	32	21	7
Los Angeles, West	4	133	22	35	52	6	1	3	2	0	3	14	22	20	.263	108	44	5	3	0	.968	22	23	9
1978—Philadelphia, East	4	140	17	35	57	3	2	5	2	1	0	9	21	16	.250	110	46	4	4	0	.975	24	22	8
Los Angeles, West	4	147	21	42	80	8	3	8	2	0	2	9	22	21	.286	111	50	3	4	0	.982	28	22	9
1979—Pittsburgh, East	3	105	15	28	47	3	2	4	5	3	4	13	13	14	.267	90	34	0	2	0	1.000	24	20	8
Cincinnati, West	3	107	5	23	35	4	1	2	1	1	4	11	26	5	.215	87	39	1	2	0	.992	25	20	9
1980—Philadelphia, East	5	190	20	55	68	8	1	1	5	1	7	13	37	19	.291	148	71	6	7	0	.973	43	23	7
Houston, West	5	172	19	40	57	7	5	0	7	2	4	31	19	18	.233	147	52	3	4	1	.985	45	24	7
1981—Montreal, East	5	158	10	34	44	7	0	1	3	0	2	12	25	8	.215	132	52	4	8	0	.979	31	19	7
Los Angeles, West	5	163	15	38	55	3	1	4	4	0	5	12	23	15	.233	132	53	2	5	1	.989	33	23	9
1982—St. Louis, East	3	103	17	34	45	4	2	1	5	3	1	12	16	16	.330	81	35	2	3	0	.983	31	15	5
Atlanta, West	3	89	5	15	16	1	0	0	2	1	1	6	15	3	.169	76	39	1	0	1	.991	12	20	5
1983—Philadelphia, East	4	130	16	34	53	4	0	5	3	1	2	15	22	15	.262	105	36	5	0	1	.966	31	20	5
Los Angeles, West	4	129	8	27	40	5	1	2	2	0	3	11	31	7	.209	102	38	1	3	1	.993	31	22	8
1984—Chicago, East	5	162	26	42	80	11	0	9	1	2	6	20	28	25	.259	156	49	3	6	1	.983	32	23	8
San Diego, West	5	155	22	41	54	5	1	2	2	4	2	14	22	20	.265	129	43	1	4	0	.994	27	24	10
1985—St. Louis, East	6	201	29	56	77	10	1	3	2	1	6	30	34	26	.279	156	54	4	4	1	.981	51	23	9
Los Angeles, West	6	197	23	46	75	12	1	5	1	1	4	19	31	23	.234	154	72	6	3	0	.974	40	25	9
1986—New York, East	6	227	21	43	60	4	2	3	1	3	4	14	57	19	.189	189	94	1	6	0	.996	36	22	8
Houston, West	6	225	17	49	70	6	0	5	2	0	8	17	40	17	.218	188	66	7	3	2	.973	39	21	6
1987—St. Louis, East	7	215	23	56	74	4	4	2	5		4	16	42	22	.260	183	67	3	5	0	.988	37	23	8
San Fran., West	7	226	23	54	90	7	1	9	3	1	5	17	51	20	.239	180	77	6	10	1	.977	43	23	10

Minnesota third baseman Gary Gaetti (right) set a record by homering in his first two 1987 Championship Series at-bats against Detroit while San Francisco outfielder Jeffrey Leonard (above) also made Championship Series history in '87 by homering in each of the first four games of the Giants' series against St. Louis. Former Oakland and New York Yankee pitching great Catfish Hunter (left, left photo) holds Championship Series records for games started (10) and innings pitched (69⅓) while his 1972 opponent, Detroit lefthander Mickey Lolich, holds the record for most innings pitched (19) in a five-game series.

World Series

including:
- ■ Batting (Individual, Club)
- ■ Baserunning (Individual, Club)
- ■ Pitching (Individual, Club)
- ■ Fielding (Individual, Club)
- ■ Miscellaneous
- ■ Non-Playing Personnel
- ■ General Reference Data

Individual Batting

Service
Series & Clubs

Most Series Played

14—Berra, Lawrence P., New York A.L., 1947, 1949, 1950, 1951, 1952, 1953, 1955, 1956, 1957, 1958, 1960, 1961, 1962, 1963 (75 games, 65 consecutive).

Most Series Eligible, But Did Not Play

6—Silvera, Charles A., New York A.L., 1950, 1951, 1952, 1953, 1955, 1956 (37 games), played one game, 1949.

5—Jorgens, Arndt L., New York A.L., 1932, 1936, 1937, 1938, 1939 (23 games).

Most Consecutive Series Played (17 times)

5—Bauer, Henry A., New York A.L., 1949 through 1953.
Berra, Lawrence P., New York A.L., 1949 through 1953.
Lopat, Edmund W., New York A.L., 1949 through 1953.
Mize, John R., New York A.L., 1949 through 1953.
Raschi, Victor J., New York A.L., 1949 through 1953.
Reynolds, Allie P., New York A.L., 1949 through 1953.
Rizzuto, Philip R., New York A.L., 1949 through 1953.
Woodling, Eugene R., New York A.L., 1949 through 1953.
Blanchard, John E., New York A.L., 1960 through 1964.
Boyer, Cletis L., New York A.L., 1960 through 1964.
Terry, Ralph W., New York A.L., 1960 through 1964.
Ford, Edward C., New York A.L., 1960 through 1964.
Howard, Elston G., New York A.L., 1960 through 1964.
Lopez, Hector H., New York A.L., 1960 through 1964.
Mantle, Mickey C., New York A.L., 1960 through 1964.
Maris, Roger E., New York A.L., 1960 through 1964.
Richardson, Robert C., New York A.L., 1960 through 1964.

Most Series Played, One Club

14—Berra, Lawrence P., New York A.L., 1947, 1949, 1950, 1951, 1952, 1953, 1955, 1956, 1957, 1958, 1960, 1961, 1962, 1963 (75 games, 65 consecutive).

Most Series Playing in All Games

10—DiMaggio, Joseph P., New York A.L., 1936, 1937, 1938, 1939, 1941, 1942, 1947, 1949, 1950, 1951 (51 games).

Most Times Member Winning Club, As Active Player Only

10—Berra, Lawrence P., New York A.L., 1947, 1949, 1950, 1951, 1952, 1953, 1956, 1958, 1961, 1962.

Most Times on Winning Club, Playing One + Games Each Series

10—Berra, Lawrence P., New York A.L., 1947, 1949, 1950, 1951, 1952, 1953, 1956, 1958, 1961, 1962.

Most Times on Losing Club

6—Reese, Harold H., Brooklyn N.L., 1941, 1947, 1949, 1952, 1953, 1956.
Howard, Elston G., New York A.L., 1955, 1957, 1960, 1963, 1964. Boston A.L., 1967.

Most Series Played, First Four Years in Major Leagues

4—DiMaggio, Joseph P., New York A.L., 1936 through 1939.
Howard, Elston G., New York A.L., 1955 through 1958.
Kucks, John C., New York A.L., 1955 through 1958.

Most Clubs, Total Series (Playing One or More Games)

3—Schang, Walter H.; Merkle, Fred C.; Grimes, Burleigh A.; Bush, Leslie A.; Derringer, Paul; McInnis, John P.; Koenig, Mark A.; Groh, Henry K.; Smith, Earl S.; McCormick, Myron W.; Stanky, Edward R.; Pafko, Andrew; Davalillo, Victor J.; Jackson, Grant D.; Smith, Lonnie.

Most Years Between First and Second Series, Infielder

14—Maranville, Walter J., Boston N.L., 1914; St. Louis N.L., 1928.

Most Years Between First and Second Series, Pitcher

17—Kaat, James L., Minnesota A.L., 1965; St. Louis N.L., 1982.

Most Years Between First and Last Series, Outfielder

22—Mays, Willie H., New York N.L., 1951 (Giants); New York N.L., 1973 (Mets).

Most Years Between First and Last Series, Pitcher

18—Pennock, Herbert J., Philadelphia A.L., 1914; New York A.L., 1932.

Most Years Played in Majors Before Playing in World Series

21—Niekro, Joseph F., Chicago N.L., 1967; first World Series game on October 21, 1987, for Minnesota A.L. at St. Louis.

Youngest & Oldest Players

Youngest World Series Player

Lindstrom, Frederick C., New York N.L., 18 years, 10 months, 13 days, first World Series game on October 4, 1924, at Washington. Born November 21, 1905.

Oldest World Series Player (Except Pitcher)

Rose, Peter E., Philadelphia N.L., 42 years, 6 months, 2 days, last World Series game on October 16, 1983, at Philadelphia. Born April 14, 1941.

Positions

Most Positions Played, Total Series

4—Ruth, George H., Boston A.L., 1915, 1916, 1918, New York A.L., 1921, 1922, 1923, 1926, 1927, 1928, 1932, 41 games, pitcher, left field, right field, first base.
Robinson, Jack R., Brooklyn N.L., 1947, 1949, 1952, 1953, 1955, 1956, 38 games, first base, second base, left field, third base.
Howard, Elston G., New York A.L., 1955, 1956, 1957, 1958, 1960, 1961, 1962, 1963, 1964, Boston A.L., 1967, 54 games, left field, right field, first base, catcher.
Kubek, Anthony C., New York A.L., 1957, 1958, 1960, 1961, 1962, 1963, 37 games, left field, third base, center field, shortstop.
Rose, Peter E., Cincinnati N.L., 1970, 1972, 1975, 1976, Philadelphia N.L., 1980, 1983, 34 games, right field, left field, third base, first base.

Most Positions Played, Series

3—Snodgrass, Frederick C., New York N.L., 1912, center field, right field, left field, 8-game Series, 8 games.
Kelly, George L., New York N.L., 1924, center field, second base, first base, 7-game Series, 7 games.
Kubek, Anthony C., New York A.L., 1957, left field, third base, center field, 7-game Series, 7 games.
Pafko, Andrew, Milwaukee N.L., 1958, center field, left field, right field, 7-game Series, 4 games.
Moon, Wallace W., Los Angeles N.L., 1959, left field, center field, right field, 6-game Series, 6 games.
Berra, Lawrence P., New York A.L., 1960, catcher, left field, right field, 7-game Series, 7 games.
McCovey, Willie L., San Francisco N.L., 1962, first base, right field, left field, 7-game Series, 4 games.
Rettenmund, Mervin W., Baltimore A.L., 1971, center field, left field, right field, 7-game Series, 7 games.
Washington, Claudell, Oakland A.L., 1974, right field, center field, left field, 5-game Series, 5 games.
Thomas, Derrel O., Los Angeles N.L., 1981, shortstop, center field, third base.

Games

Most Games, Total Series

75—Berra, Lawrence P., New York A.L., 1947, 1949, 1950, 1951, 1952, 1953, 1955, 1956, 1957, 1958, 1960, 1961, 1962, 1963 (14 Series, 65 consecutive games).

Most Games, Total Series, One Club

75—Berra, Lawrence P., New York A.L., 1947, 1949, 1950, 1951, 1952, 1953, 1955, 1956, 1957, 1958, 1960, 1961, 1962, 1963 (14 Series, 65 consecutive games).

Most Consecutive Games Played in Consecutive Years

30—Richardson, Robert C., New York A.L., October 5, 1960 through October 15, 1964.

Most Games, Total Series, Pinch-Hitter

10—Blanchard, John E., New York A.L., 1960 (3), 1961 (2), 1962 (1), 1964 (4).

Most Games, Total Series, Pinch-Runner

9—Lewis, Allan S., Oakland A.L., 1972, 1973; 2 Series, 3 runs.

Most Games, Series, Pinch-Hitter

5—McCormick, Harry, New York N.L., 1912.
Paschal, Benjamin, New York A.L., 1926.
Secory, Frank, Chicago N.L., 1945.
Lavagetto, Harry A., Brooklyn N.L., 1947.
Warwick, Carl W., St. Louis N.L., 1964.
Shopay, Thomas M., Baltimore A.L., 1971.
Marquez, Gonzalo, Oakland A.L., 1972.
Mangual, Angel L., Oakland A.L., 1973.
Crowley, Terrence M., Baltimore A.L., 1979.
Kelly, H. Patrick, Baltimore A.L., 1979.

Most Games, Series, Pinch-Runner

6—Lewis, Allan S., Oakland A.L., 1972, 2 runs.

Batting Average

Highest Batting Average, Total Series (20 or More Games)

.391—Brock, Louis C., St. Louis N.L., 1964, 1967, 1968 (3 Series, 21 games, 87 at-bats, 34 hits).
.363—Baker, J. Franklin, Philadelphia A.L., 1910, 1911, 1913, 1914; New York A.L., 1921, 1922 (6 Series, 25 games, 91 at-bats, 33 hits).
.361—Gehrig, H. Louis, New York A.L., 1926, 1927, 1928, 1932, 1936, 1937, 1938 (7 Series, 34 games, 119 at-bats, 43 hits).

Highest Batting Average, Series

4-game Series—.625—Ruth, George H., New York A.L., 1928.
5-game Series—.500—McLean, John B., New York N.L., 1913.
Gordon, Joseph L., New York A.L., 1941.
6-game Series—.500—Robertson, Davis A., New York N.L., 1917.
Martin, Alfred M., New York A.L., 1953.
7-game Series—.500—Martin, John L., St. Louis N.L., 1931.
Lindell, John H., New York A.L., 1947 (played only six games due to broken rib).
Garner, Philip M., Pittsburgh N.L., 1979.
8-game Series—.400—Herzog, Charles L., New York N.L., 1912.

Most Series Leading Club in Batting Average

3—Baker, J. Franklin, Philadelphia A.L., 1911, 1913, 1914.
Reese, Harold H., Brooklyn, N.L., 1947, 1949, 1952 (tied).
Snider, Edwin D., Brooklyn N.L., 1952 (tied), 1955, 1956 (tied).
Hodges, Gilbert R., Brooklyn N.L., Los Angeles N.L., 1953, 1956 (tied), 1959.
Garvey, Steven P., Los Angeles N.L., 1974, 1977, 1981.

Most Series Batting .300 or Over

6—Ruth, George H., New York A.L., 1921, 1923, 1926, 1927, 1928, 1932.

Slugging Average

Highest Slugging Average, Total Series (20 or More Games)

.755—Jackson, Reginald M., Oakland A.L., 1973, 1974; New York A.L., 1977, 1978, 1981; 5 Series, 30 games, 98 at-bats, 35 hits, 7 doubles, 1 triple, 10 home runs, 74 total bases.

Highest Slugging Average, Series

4-game Series—1.727—Gehrig, H. Louis, New York A.L., 1928.
5-game Series— .929—Gordon, Joseph L., New York A.L., 1941. (Clendenon, Donn A., New York N.L., 1969, had slugging average of 1.071 but played only four games.)
6-game Series—1.250—Jackson, Reginald M., New York A.L., 1977.
7-game Series— .913—Tenace, F. Gene, Oakland A.L., 1972.
8-game Series— .600—Herzog, Charles L., New York N.L., 1912.

At-Bats & Plate Appearances

Most At-Bats, Total Series

259—Berra, Lawrence P., New York A.L., 1947, 1949, 1950, 1951, 1952, 1953, 1955, 1956, 1957, 1958, 1960, 1961, 1962, 1963 (14 Series, 75 games).

Most At-Bats, Series

4-game Series—19—Koenig, Mark A., New York A.L., 1928.
5-game Series—23—Janvrin, Harold C., Boston A.L., 1916.
Moore, Joseph G., New York N.L., 1937.
Richardson, Robert C., New York A.L., 1961.
6-game Series—28—Moore, Joseph G., New York N.L., 1936.

7-game Series—33—Harris, Stanley R., Washington A.L., 1924.
Rice, Edgar C., Washington A.L., 1925.
Moreno, Omar R., Pittsburgh N.L., 1979.
8-game Series—36—Collins, James J., Boston A.L., 1903.

Most At-Bats, Game, Nine Innings (23 times)

6—Dougherty, Patrick H., Boston A.L., October 7, 1903.
Collins, James J., Boston, A.L., October 7, 1903.
Sheckard, James T., Chicago N.L., October 10, 1908.
Groh, Henry K., Cincinnati N.L., October 9, 1919.
Burns, George J., New York N.L., October 7, 1921.
Koenig, Mark A., New York A.L., October 6, 1926.
Crosetti, Frank P., New York A.L., October 2, 1932.
Dickey, William M., New York A.L., October 2, 1932.
Sewell, Joseph W., New York A.L., October 2, 1932.
Rolfe, Robert A., New York A.L., October 6, 1936.
DiMaggio, Joseph P., New York A.L., October 6, 1936.
Brown, James R., St. Louis N.L., October 4, 1942.
Schoendienst, Albert F., St. Louis N.L., October 10, 1946.
Slaughter, Enos, St. Louis N.L., October 10, 1946.
Reese, Harold H., Brooklyn N.L., October 5, 1956.
Kubek, Anthony C., New York A.L., October 6, 1960.
Skowron, William J., New York A.L., October 6, 1960.
Boyer, Cletis L., New York A.L., October 12, 1960.
Richardson, Robert C., New York A.L., October 9, 1961.
Kubek, Anthony C., New York A.L., October 9, 1961.
Molitor, Paul L., Milwaukee A.L., October 12, 1982.
Yount, Robin R., Milwaukee A.L., October 12, 1982.
Rice, James E., Boston A.L., October 19, 1986.

Most At-Bats, Extra-Inning Game

7—Hahn, Donald A., New York N.L., October 14, 1973, 12 innings.

Most Times Faced Pitcher, Game, No Official At-Bats

5—Clarke, Fred C., Pittsburgh N.L., October 16, 1909, 4 bases on balls, one sacrifice hit.

Most At-Bats, Inning

2—Held by many players. Last players—Gagne, Gregory C. and Puckett, Kirby, Minnesota A.L., October 18, 1987, fourth inning.

Most Times Faced Pitcher, Inning

2—Held by many players. Last player—Pena, Antonio F., St. Louis N.L., October 21, 1987, fourth inning.

Most At-Bats, Inning, Pinch-Hitter

2—Burns, George H., Philadelphia A.L., October 12, 1929, seventh inning. (Flied out to shortstop and struck out.)

Most Times Faced Pitcher Twice, Inning, Total Series

3—DiMaggio, Joseph P., New York A.L., October 6, 1936, ninth inning; October 6, 1937, sixth inning; September 30, 1947, fifth inning.

Most Times Faced Pitcher Twice, Inning, Series

2—Musial, Stanley F., St. Louis N.L., September 30, ninth inning; October 4, 1942, fourth inning.

Runs

Most Runs, Total Series

42—Mantle, Mickey C., New York A.L., 1951, 1952, 1953, 1955, 1956, 1957, 1958, 1960, 1961, 1962, 1963, 1964 (12 Series, 65 games).

Most Runs, Series

4-game Series— 9—Ruth, George H., New York A.L., 1928.
Gehrig, H. Louis, New York A.L., 1932.
5-game Series— 6—Baker, J. Franklin, Philadelphia A.L., 1910.
Murphy, Daniel F., Philadelphia A.L., 1910.
Hooper, Harry B., Boston A.L., 1916.
Simmons, Aloysius H., Philadelphia A.L., 1929.
May, Lee A., Cincinnati N.L., 1970.
Powell, John W., Baltimore A.L., 1970.
Whitaker, Louis R., Detroit A.L., 1984.
6-game Series—10—Jackson, Reginald M., New York A.L., 1977.
7-game Series— 8—Leach, Thomas W., Pittsburgh N.L., 1909.
Martin, John L., St. Louis N.L., 1934.
Johnson, William R., New York A.L., 1947.
Mantle, Mickey C., New York A.L., 1960.
Richardson, Robert C., New York A.L., 1960.
Mantle, Mickey C., New York A.L., 1964.
Brock, Louis C., St. Louis N.L., 1967.
8-game Series— 8—Parent, Fred N., Boston A.L., 1903.

Most Series, One or More Runs, Total Series

12—Berra, Lawrence P., New York A.L., 1947, 1949, 1950, 1951, 1952, 1953, 1955, 1956, 1957, 1958, 1960, 1961.

Fewest Runs, Series

0—Owen, Marvin J., Detroit A.L., 7 games, 1934, 29 at-bats.
Campanella, Roy, Brooklyn N.L., 7 games, 1952, 28 at-bats.
Myers, Henry H., Brooklyn N.L., 7 games, 1920, 26 at-bats.
Thomas, J. Gorman, Milwaukee A.L., 7 games, 1982, 26 at-bats.
White, Frank, Kansas City A.L., 6 games, 1980, 25 at-bats.
Also many other players with fewer at-bats.

Most Consecutive Games, One or More Runs, Total Series

9—Ruth, George H., New York A.L., 1927, last 2 games; 1928, 4 games; 1932, first 3 games.

Most Runs, Game

4—Ruth, George H., New York A.L., October 6, 1926.
Combs, Earle B., New York A.L., October 2, 1932.
Crosetti, Frank P., New York A.L., October 2, 1936.
Slaughter, Enos B., St. Louis N.L., October 10, 1946.
Jackson, Reginald M., New York A.L., October 18, 1977.
Puckett, Kirby, Minnesota A.L., October 24, 1987.

Most Runs, Inning

2—Frisch, Frank F., New York N.L., October 7, 1921, seventh inning.
Simmons, Aloysius H., Philadelphia A.L., October 12, 1929, seventh inning.
Foxx, James E., Philadelphia A.L., October 12, 1929, seventh inning.
McAuliffe, Richard J., Detroit A.L., October 9, 1968, third inning.
Stanley, Mitchell J., Detroit A.L., October 9, 1968, third inning.
Kaline, Albert W., Detroit A.L., October 9, 1968, third inning.

Hits
Career & Series

Most Hits, Total Series

71—Berra, Lawrence P., New York A.L., 1947, 1949, 1950, 1951, 1952, 1953, 1955, 1956, 1957, 1958, 1960, 1961, 1962, 1963 (14 Series, 75 games).

Most Hits, Total Series, Pinch-Hitter

3—O'Dea, James K., Chicago N.L., 1935 (1), 1938 (0); St. Louis N.L., 1942 (1), 1943 (0), 1944 (1), 5 Series, 8 games.
Brown, Robert W., New York A.L., 1947 (3), 1949 (0), 1950 (0), 1951 (0), 4 Series, 7 games.
Mize, John R., New York A.L., 1949 (2), 1950 (0), 1951 (0), 1952 (1), 1953 (0), 5 Series, 8 games.
Rhodes, James L., New York N.L., 1954 (3), 3 games.
Furillo, Carl A., Brooklyn N.L., 1947 (2), 1949 (0); Los Angeles N.L., 1959 (1), 3 Series, 7 games.
Cerv, Robert H., New York A.L., 1955 (1), 1956 (1), 1960 (1), 3 Series, 3 games.
Blanchard, John E., New York A.L., 1960 (1), 1961 (1), 1962 (0), 1964 (1), 4 Series, 10 games.
Warwick, Carl W., St. Louis N.L., 1964 (3), 1 Series, 5 games.
Marquez, Gonzalo, Oakland A.L., 1972 (3), 1 Series, 5 games.
Boswell, Kenneth G., New York N.L., 1973 (3), 1 Series, 3 games.

Most Series, One or More Hits, Total Series

12—Berra, Lawrence P., New York A.L., 1947, 1949, 1950, 1951, 1952, 1953, 1955, 1956, 1957, 1958, 1960, 1961.
Mantle, Mickey C., New York A.L., 1951, 1952, 1953, 1955, 1956, 1957, 1958, 1960, 1961, 1962, 1963, 1964.

Most Consecutive Games, One or More Hits, Total Series

17—Bauer, Henry A., New York A.L., 1956, 7 games; 1957, 7 games; 1958, first 3 games.

Most Hits, Series

4-game Series—10—Ruth, George H., New York A.L., 1928.
5-game Series— 9—Baker, J. Franklin, Philadelphia A.L., 1910.
Collins, Edward T., Philadelphia A.L., 1910.
Baker, J. Franklin, Philadelphia A.L., 1913.
Groh, Henry K., New York N.L., 1922.
Moore, Joseph G., New York N.L., 1937.
Richardson, Robert C., New York A.L., 1961.
Blair, Paul L., Baltimore A.L., 1970.
Robinson, Brooks C., Baltimore A.L., 1970.
Trammell, Alan S., Detroit A.L., 1984.

6-game Series—12—Martin, Alfred M., New York A.L., 1953.
7-game Series—13—Richardson, Robert C., New York A.L., 1964.
Brock, Louis C., St. Louis N.L., 1968.
Barrett, Martin G., Boston A.L., 1986.
8-game Series—12—Herzog, Charles L., New York N.L., 1912.
Jackson, Joseph J., Chicago A.L., 1919.

Most Hits, Series, Pinch-Hitter

3—Brown, Robert W., New York A.L., 4 games, 1947 (consecutive; one base on balls, one single, two doubles, three runs batted in).
Rhodes, James L., New York N.L., 3 games, 1954 (consecutive; one home run, two singles, six runs batted in).
Warwick, Carl W., St. Louis N.L., 5 games, 1964 (consecutive; two singles, walk, single, one run batted in).
Marquez, Gonzalo, Oakland A.L., 5 games, 1972 (consecutive in second, third, fourth games, three singles, one run batted in).
Boswell, Kenneth G., New York N.L., 3 games, 1973 (consecutive; three singles).

Most Hits, Two Consecutive Series

25—Brock, Louis C., St. Louis N.L., 1967 (12), 1968 (13).

Most Consecutive Hits, One Series

6—Goslin, Leon A., Washington A.L., October 6 (1), October 7 (4), October 8 (1), 1924.
Munson, Thurman L., New York A.L., October 19 (2), October 21 (4), 1976.

Most Consecutive Hits, Two Consecutive Series

7—Munson, Thurman L., New York A.L., October 19 (2), October 21 (4), 1976, October 11, 1977 (1). All singles.

Most Games, Four or More Hits, Series

2—Yount, Robin R., Milwaukee A.L., October 12 (4), 16 (4), 1982.

One or More Hits Each Game, Series

Held by many players in Series of all lengths.

Fewest Hits, Series

0—Maxvill, C. Dallan, St. Louis N.L., 7 games, 1968 (22 at-bats).
Sheckard, James T., Chicago N.L., 6 games, 1906 (21 at-bats).
Sullivan, William J., Chicago A.L., 6 games, 1906 (21 at-bats).
Murray, John J., New York N.L., 6 games, 1911 (21 at-bats).
Hodges, Gilbert R., Brooklyn N.L., 7 games, 1952 (21 at-bats).
Also many other players with fewer times at bat.

Most At-Bats, Total Series, Without a Hit

22—Earnshaw, George L., Philadelphia A.L., 1929 (5), 1930 (9), 1931 (8).

Most Consecutive Hitless Times at Bat, Total Series

31—Owen, Marvin J., Detroit A.L., 1934 (last 12 times at bat), 1935 (first 19 times at bat).

Game & Inning

Most Hits, Game

5—Molitor, Paul L., Milwaukee A.L., October 12, 1982.

Most Times Reached First Base Safely, 9-Inn. Game (Batting 1.000)

5—Ruth, George H., New York A.L., October 6, 1926, three home runs, two bases on balls.
Ruth, George H., New York A.L., October 10, 1926, one home run, four bases on balls.
Brock, Louis C., St. Louis N.L., October 4, 1967, four singles, one base on balls.
Robinson, Brooks C., Baltimore A.L., October 11, 1971, three singles, two bases on balls.
Staub, Daniel J., New York N.L., October 17, 1973, three singles, one home run, one base on balls.
Garcia, Alfonso R., Baltimore A.L., October 12, 1979, two singles, one double, one triple, one base on balls.
Jackson, Reginald M., New York A.L., October 24, 1981, two singles, one home run, two bases on balls.
Brett, George H., Kansas City A.L., October 22, 1985, two singles, three bases on balls.
Puckett, Kirby, Minnesota A.L., October 24, 1987, four singles, one base on balls.

Getting All Club's Hits, Game (Most)

3—Meusel, Emil F., New York N.L., October 14, 1923, one single, one double, one triple.

Most At-Bats, Game, Nine Innings, No Hits

    5—Held by many players.

Most At-Bats, Extra-Inning Game, No Hits

    6—Jackson, Travis C., New York N.L., October 10, 1924, 12 innings.

        Critz, Hugh M., New York N.L., October 6, 1933, 11 innings.

        Millan, Felix B., New York N.L., October 14, 1973, 12 innings.

        Rivers, John M., New York A.L., October 11, 1977, 12 innings.

Most Hits, Two Consecutive Games, One Series

    7—Isbell, Frank, Chicago A.L., October 13 (4), October 14 (3), 1906.

        Lindstrom, Fred C., New York N.L., October 7 (3), October 8 (4), 1924.

        Irvin, Monford M., New York N.L., October 4 (4), October 5 (3), 1951.

        Munson, Thurman L., New York A.L., October 19 (3), October 21 (4), 1976.

        Molitor, Paul L., Milwaukee A.L., October 12 (5), October 13 (2), 1982.

Most Hits, Inning (17 times)

    2—Youngs, Ross, New York N.L., October 7, 1921, seventh inning.

        Simmons, Aloysius H., Philadelphia A.L., October 12, 1929, seventh inning.

        Foxx, James E., Philadelphia A.L., October 12, 1929, seventh inning.

        Dykes, James, Philadelphia A.L., October 12, 1929, seventh inning.

        Moore, Joseph G., New York N.L., October 4, 1933, sixth inning.

        Dean, Jerome H., St. Louis N.L., October 9, 1934, third inning.

        DiMaggio, Joseph P., New York A.L., October 6, 1936, ninth inning.

        Leiber, Henry, New York N.L., October 9, 1937, second inning.

        Musial, Stanley F., St. Louis N.L., October 4, 1942, fourth inning.

        Howard, Elston G., New York A.L., October 6, 1960, sixth inning.

        Richardson, Robert C., New York A.L., October 6, 1960, sixth inning.

        Cerv, Robert H., New York A.L., October 8, 1960, first inning.

        Quilici, Frank R., Minnesota A.L., October 6, 1965, third inning.

        Kaline, Albert W., Detroit A.L., October 9, 1968, third inning.

        Cash, Norman D., Detroit A.L., October 9, 1968, third inning.

        Rettenmund, Mervin W., Baltimore A.L., October 11, 1971, fifth inning.

        Gaetti, Gary J., Minnesota A.L., October 17, 1987, fourth inning.

Singles

Most Singles, Total Series

    49—Berra, Lawrence P., New York A.L., 1947, 1949, 1950, 1951, 1952, 1953, 1955, 1956, 1957, 1958, 1960, 1961, 1962, 1963 (14 Series, 75 games).

Most Singles, Series

    4-game Series— 9—Munson, Thurman L., New York A.L., 1976.

    5-game Series— 8—Chance, Frank L., Chicago N.L., 1908.

        Baker, J. Franklin, Philadelphia A.L., 1913.

        Groh, Henry K., New York N.L., 1922.

        Moore, Joseph G., New York N.L., 1937.

        Richardson, Robert C., New York A.L., 1961.

        Blair, Paul L., Baltimore A.L., 1970.

        Garvey, Steven P., Los Angeles N.L., 1974.

    6-game Series—10—Rolfe, Robert A., New York A.L., 1936.

        Irvin, Monford M., New York N.L., 1951.

    7-game Series—12—Rice, Edgar C., Washington A.L., 1925.

    8-game Series— 9—Sebring, James D., Pittsburgh N.L., 1903.

        Meyers, John T., New York N.L., 1912.

Most Singles, Game

    5—Molitor, Paul L., Milwaukee A.L., October 12, 1982.

Most Singles, Inning

    2—Foxx, James E., Philadelphia A.L., October 12, 1929, seventh inning.

        Moore, Joseph G., New York N.L., October 4, 1933, sixth inning.

        DiMaggio, Joseph P., New York A.L., October 6, 1936, ninth inning.

        Leiber, Henry, New York N.L., October 9, 1937, second inning.

        Cerv, Robert H., New York A.L., October 8, 1960, first inning.

        Kaline, Albert W., Detroit A.L., October 9, 1968, third inning.

        Cash, Norman D., Detroit A.L., October 9, 1968, third inning.

        Rettenmund, Mervin W., Baltimore A.L., October 11, 1971, fifth inning.

Doubles

Most Doubles, Total Series

    10—Frisch, Frank F., New York N.L. (5), 1921, 1922, 1923, 1924; St. Louis N.L. (5), 1928, 1930, 1931, 1934; 8 Series, 50 games.

        Berra, Lawrence P., New York A.L., 1947, 1949, 1950, 1951, 1952, 1953, 1955, 1956, 1957, 1958, 1960, 1961, 1962, 1963; 14 Series, 75 games.

Most Doubles, Series

    4-game Series—3—Gowdy, Henry M., Boston N.L., 1914.

        Ruth, George H., New York A.L., 1928.

    5-game Series—4—Collins, Edward T., Philadelphia A.L., 1910.

        Dempsey, J. Rikard, Baltimore A.L., 1983.

    6-game Series—5—Hafey, Charles J., St. Louis N.L., 1930.

    7-game Series—6—Fox, Ervin, Detroit A.L., 1934.

    8-game Series—4—Murray, John J., New York N.L., 1912.

        Herzog, Charles L., New York N.L., 1912.

        Weaver, George L., Chicago A.L., 1919.

        Burns, George J., New York N.L., 1921.

Most Doubles, Game

    4—Isbell, Frank, Chicago A.L., October 13, 1906.

Most Doubles, Game, Batting In Three Runs

    1—Frisch, Frank F., St. Louis N.L., October 9, 1934, third inning.

        Richards, Paul R., Detroit A.L., October 10, 1945, first inning.

        Brock, Louis C., St. Louis N.L., October 6, 1968, eighth inning.

        Pendleton, Terry L., St. Louis N.L., October 20, 1985, ninth inning.

Most Doubles, Inning

    1—Held by many players.

Triples

Most Triples, Total Series

    4—Leach, Thomas W., Pittsburgh N.L. (4), 1903, 1909; 2 Series, 15 games.

        Speaker, Tris, Boston A.L. (3), 1912, 1915; Cleveland A.L. (1), 1920; 3 Series, 20 games.

        Johnson, William R., New York A.L., 1943 (1), 1947 (3), 1949 (0), 1950 (0); 4 Series, 18 games.

Fewest Triples, Total Series (Most Games)

    0—Berra, Lawrence P., New York A.L., 14 Series, 75 games, 259 at-bats.

        DiMaggio, Joseph P., New York A.L., 10 Series, 51 games, 199 at-bats.

        Rizzuto, Philip F., New York A.L., 9 Series, 52 games, 183 at-bats.

Most Triples, Series

    4-game Series—2—Gehrig, H. Louis, New York A.L., 1927.

        Davis, H. Thomas, Los Angeles N.L., 1963.

    5-game Series—2—Collins, Edward T., Philadelphia A.L., 1913.

        Brown, Robert W., New York A.L., 1949.

    6-game Series—2—Rohe, George, Chicago A.L., 1906.

        Meusel, Robert W., New York A.L., 1923.

        Martin, Alfred M., New York A.L., 1953.

    7-game Series—3—Johnson, William R., New York A.L., 1947.

    8-game Series—4—Leach, Thomas W., Pittsburgh N.L., 1903.

Most Triples, Game

    2—Leach, Thomas W., Pittsburgh N.L., October 1, 1903.

        Dougherty, Patrick H., Boston A.L., October 7, 1903.

        Ruether, Walter H., Cincinnati N.L., October 1, 1919.

        Richardson, Robert C., New York A.L., October 12, 1960.

        Davis, H. Thomas, Los Angeles N.L., October 3, 1963.

Most Bases-Loaded Triples, Game

    1—Rohe, George, Chicago A.L., October 11, 1906, sixth inning.

        Youngs, Ross, New York N.L., October 7, 1921, seventh inning.

        Johnson, William R., New York A.L., October 7, 1943, eighth inning.

        Brown, Robert W., New York A.L., October 8, 1949, fifth inning.

        Bauer, Henry A., New York A.L., October 10, 1951, sixth inning.

        Martin, Alfred M., New York A.L., September 30, 1953, first inning.

        Garcia, Alfonso R., Baltimore A.L., October 12, 1979, fourth inning.

Most Triples, Inning

    1—Held by many players.

Home Runs

Career & Series

Most Home Runs, Total Series
18—Mantle, Mickey C., New York A.L., 1951, 1952, 1953, 1955, 1956, 1957, 1958, 1960, 1961, 1962, 1963, 1964; 12 Series, 65 games.

Most Home Runs by Pitcher, Total Series
2—Gibson, Robert, St. Louis N.L., 1964 (0), 1967 (1), 1968 (1), 3 Series, 9 games.
McNally, David A., Baltimore A.L., 1966 (0), 1969 (1), 1970 (1), 1971 (0), 4 Series, 9 games.

Fewest Home Runs, Total Series (Most Games)
0—Frisch, Frank F., New York N.L., St. Louis N.L., 8 Series, 50 games, 197 at-bats.

Most Series, One or More Home Runs, Total Series
9—Berra, Lawrence P., New York A.L., 1947 (1), 1950 (1), 1952 (2), 1953 (1), 1955 (1), 1956 (3), 1957 (1), 1960 (1), 1961 (1).
Mantle, Mickey C., New York A.L., 1952 (2), 1953 (2), 1955 (1), 1956 (3), 1957 (1), 1958 (2), 1960 (3), 1963 (1), 1964 (3).

Most HRs, 4 Consec. Games, Total Series, Homering Each Game
6—Jackson, Reginald M., New York A.L., 1977 (5), last three games; 1978 (1), first game.
5—Gehrig, H. Louis, New York A.L., 1928 (4), last three games; 1932 (1), first game.

Home Runs, Both Leagues
Skowron, William J., A.L. (7), N.L. (1).
Robinson, Frank, N.L. (1), A.L. (7).
Maris, Roger E., A.L. (5), N.L. (1).
Smith, C. Reginald, A.L. (2), N.L. (4).
Slaughter, Enos B., N.L. (2), A.L. (1).

Most Home Runs, Series
4-game Series—4—Gehrig, H. Louis, New York A.L., 1928.
5-game Series—3—Clendenon, Donn A., New York N.L., 1969.
6-game Series—5—Jackson, Reginald M., New York, 1977.
7-game Series—4—Ruth, George H., New York A.L., 1926.
　　　　　　　　Snider, Edwin D., Brooklyn N.L., 1952.
　　　　　　　　Snider, Edwin D., Brooklyn N.L., 1955.
　　　　　　　　Bauer, Henry A., New York A.L., 1958.
　　　　　　　　Tenace, F. Gene, Oakland A.L., 1972.
8-game Series—2—Dougherty, Patrick H., Boston A.L., 1903.

Most Home Runs, Series, Pinch-Hitter
2—Essegian, Charles A., Los Angeles N.L., 4 games, 1959.
Carbo, Bernardo, Boston A.L., 3 games, 1975.

Most Home Runs, Series, by Rookie
3—Keller, Charles E., New York A.L., 1939.

Most Series, Two or More Home Runs
6—Mantle, Mickey C., New York A.L., 1952 (2), 1953 (2), 1956 (3), 1956 (3), 1958 (2), 1960 (3), 1964 (3).
5—Ruth, George H., New York A.L., 1923 (3), 1926 (4), 1927 (2), 1928 (3), 1932 (2).

Most Series, Three or More Home Runs
3—Ruth, George H., New York A.L., 1923 (3), 1926 (4), 1928 (3).
Mantle, Mickey C., New York A.L., 1956 (3), 1960 (3), 1964 (3).

Most Series, Four or More Home Runs
2—Snider, Edwin D., Brooklyn N.L., 1952, 1955.

Most Home Runs, Two Consecutive Series (Two Consec. Years)
7—Jackson, Reginald M., New York A.L., 1977 (5), 1978 (2).

Most Home Runs, Three Consecutive Series (Three Consec. Years)
9—Ruth, George H., New York A.L., 1926 (4), 1927 (2), 1928 (3).

Most Home Runs, 3 Consec. Games, Series, Homering Each Game
5—Jackson, Reginald M., New York A.L., October 15 (1), 16 (1), 18 (3), 1977.
4—Gehrig, H. Louis, New York A.L., October 5, 7 (2), 9, 1928.

Most Home Runs, 2 Consec. Games, Series, Homering Each Game
4—Jackson, Reginald M., New York A.L., October 16 (1), 18 (3), 1977.

Most Consecutive Home Runs, Two Consecutive Games, Series
4—Jackson, Reginald M., New York A.L., October 16 (1), 18 (3), 1977, one base on balls included.

Most Series, Two or More Home Runs, Game
4—Ruth, George H., New York A.L., 1923, 1926, 1928, 1932 (two home runs in one game twice, three home runs in one game twice).

Game & Inning

Most Home Runs, Game (3 homers, 3 times; 2 homers, 32 times) (*Consecutive)
3—Ruth, George H., New York A.L., October 6, 1926, and October 9, 1928, (two consecutive in each game).
Jackson, Reginald M., New York A.L., October 18, 1977* (each on first pitch).
2—Dougherty, Patrick H., Boston A.L., October 2, 1903.
Hooper, Harry B. Boston A.L., October 13, 1915.
Kauff, Benjamin M., New York N.L., October 11, 1917.
Ruth, George H., New York A.L., October 11, 1923*.
Gehrig, H. Louis, New York A.L., October 7, 1928*.
Gehrig, H. Louis, New York A.L., October 1, 1932*.
Ruth, George H., New York A.L., October 1, 1932.
Lazzeri, Anthony M., New York A.L., October 2, 1932.
Keller, Charles E., New York A.L., October 7, 1939.
Elliott, Robert I., Boston N.L., October 10, 1948*.
Snider, Edwin D., Brooklyn N.L., October 6, 1952*.
Collins, Joseph E., New York A.L., September 28, 1955*.
Snider, Edwin D., Brooklyn N.L., October 2, 1955*.
Berra, Lawrence P., New York A.L., October 10, 1956*.
Kubek, Anthony C., New York A.L., October 5, 1957.
Mantle, Mickey C., New York A.L., October 2, 1958.
Kluszewski, Theodore, B., Chicago A.L., October 1, 1959*.
Neal, Charles L., Los Angeles N.L., October 2, 1959*.
Mantle, Mickey C., New York A.L., October 6, 1960.
Yastrzemski, Carl M., Boston A.L., October 5, 1967.
Petrocelli, Americo, Boston A.L., October 11, 1967*.
Tenace, F. Gene, Oakland A.L., October 14, 1972*.
Perez, Atanasio R., Cincinnati N.L., October 16, 1975*.
Bench, Johnny L., Cincinnati N.L., October 21, 1976.
Lopes, David E., Los Angeles N.L., October 10, 1978*.
Aikens, Willie M., Kansas City A.L., October 14, 1980.
Aikens, Willie M., Kansas City A.L., October 18, 1980.
McGee, Willie D., St. Louis N.L., October 15, 1982*.
Murray, Eddie C., Baltimore A.L., October 16, 1983*.
Trammell, Alan S., Detroit A.L., October 13, 1984*.
Gibson, Kirk H., Detroit A.L., October 14, 1984.
Carter, Gary E., New York N.L., October 22, 1986.

Most Home Runs, Game, by Rookie
2—Keller, Charles E., New York A.L., October 7, 1939.
Kubek, Anthony C., New York A.L., October 5, 1957.
McGee, Willie D., St. Louis N.L., October 15, 1982.

Hitting Home Runs in First Two World Series At-Bats
Tenace, F. Gene, Oakland A.L., October 14, 1972, second and fifth innings.

Hitting Home Runs in First World Series At-Bat (18 times)
Harris, Joseph, Washington A.L., vs. Pittsburgh N.L., October 7, 1925, second inning.
Watkins, George A., St. Louis N.L., vs. Philadelphia A.L., October 2, 1930, second inning.
Ott, Melvin T., New York N.L., vs. Washington A.L., October 3, 1933, first inning.
Selkirk, George A., New York A.L., vs. New York N.L., September 30, 1936, third inning.
Rhodes, James L., New York N.L., vs. Cleveland A.L., September 29, 1954, tenth inning.
Howard, Elston G., New York A.L., vs. Brooklyn N.L., September 28, 1955, second inning.
Maris, Roger E., New York A.L., vs. Pittsburgh N.L., October 5, 1960, first inning.
Mincher, Donald R., Minnesota A.L., vs. Los Angeles N.L., October 6, 1965, second inning.
Robinson, Brooks C., Baltimore A.L., vs. Los Angeles N.L., October 5, 1966, first inning.
Santiago, Jose R., Boston A.L., vs. St. Louis N.L., October 4, 1967, third inning.

Lolich, Michael S., Detroit A.L., vs. St. Louis N.L., October 3, 1968, third inning.

Buford, Donald A., Baltimore A.L., vs. New York N.L., October 11, 1969, first inning.

Tenace, F. Gene, Oakland A.L., vs. Cincinnati N.L., October 14, 1972, second inning.

Mason, James P., New York A.L., vs. Cincinnati N.L., October 19, 1976, seventh inning.

DeCinces, Douglas V., Baltimore A.L. vs. Pittsburgh N.L., October 10, 1979, first inning.

Otis, Amos J., Kansas City A.L. vs. Philadelphia N.L., October 14, 1980, second inning.

Watson, Robert J., New York A.L. vs. Los Angeles N.L., October 20, 1981, first inning.

Dwyer, James E., Baltimore A.L. vs. Philadelphia N.L., October 11, 1983, first inning.

Most Times Home Run Winning 1-0 Game

1—Stengel, Charles D., New York N.L., October 12, 1923, seventh inning.

Henrich, Thomas D., New York A.L., October 5, 1949, ninth inning.

Blair, Paul L., Baltimore A.L., October 8, 1966, fifth inning.

Robinson, Frank, Baltimore A.L., October 9, 1966, fourth inning.

Most Times Homers, Leadoff Batter Start of Game (14 times)

1—Dougherty, Patrick H., Boston A.L., October 2, 1903 (game 2)

Jones, David J., Detroit A.L., October 13, 1909 (game 5).

Rizzuto, Philip F., New York A.L., October 5, 1942 (game 5).

Mitchell, L. Dale, Cleveland A.L., October 10, 1948 (game 5).

Woodling, Eugene R., New York A.L., October 4, 1953 (game 5).

Smith, Alphonse E., Cleveland A.L., September 30, 1954 (game 2).

Bruton, William H., Milwaukee N.L., October 2, 1958 (game 2).

Brock, Louis C., St. Louis N.L., October 6, 1968 (game 4).

Buford, Donald A., Baltimore A.L., October 11, 1969 (game 1).

Agee, Tommie L., New York N.L., October 14, 1969 (game 3).

Rose, Peter E., Cincinnati N.L., October 20, 1972 (game 5).

Garrett, R. Wayne, New York N.L., October 16, 1973 (game 3).

Lopes, David E., Los Angeles N.L., October 17, 1978 (game 6).

Dykstra, Leonard K., New York, October 21, 1986 (game 3).

Most Home Runs by Pitcher, Game (14 times)

1—Bagby, James C., Cleveland A.L., October 10, 1920, 2 on base.

Ryan, Wilfred P., New York N.L., October 6, 1924, 0 on base.

Bentley, John N., New York N.L., October 8, 1924, 1 on base.

Haines, Jesse J., St. Louis N.L., October 5, 1926, 1 on base.

Walters, William H., Cincinnati N.L., October 7, 1940, 0 on base.

Burdette, S. Lewis, Milwaukee N.L., October 2, 1958, 2 on base.

Grant, James T., Minnesota A.L., October 13, 1965, 2 on base.

Santiago, Jose R., Boston A.L., October 4, 1967, 0 on base.

Gibson, Robert, St. Louis N.L., October 12, 1967, 0 on base.

Lolich, Michael S., Detroit A.L., October 3, 1968, 0 on base.

Gibson, Robert, St. Louis N.L., October 6, 1968, 0 on base.

McNally, David A., Baltimore A.L., October 16, 1969, 1 on base.

McNally, David A., Baltimore A.L., October 13, 1970, 3 on base.

Holtzman, Kenneth D., Oakland A.L., October 16, 1974, 0 on base.

Most Home Runs, Inning or Game, Pinch-Hitter (13 times)

1—Berra, Lawrence, New York A.L., October 2, 1947, seventh inning, none on base.

Mize, John R., New York A.L., October 3, 1952, ninth inning, none on base.

Shuba, George T., Brooklyn N.L., September 30, 1953, sixth inning, one on base.

Rhodes, James L., New York N.L., September 29, 1954, tenth inning, two on base.

Majeski, Henry, Cleveland A.L., October 2, 1954, fifth inning, two on base.

Cerv, Robert H., New York A.L., October 2, 1955, seventh inning, none on base.

Essegian, Charles A., Los Angeles N.L., October 2, 1959, seventh inning, none on base.

Essegian, Charles A., Los Angeles N.L., October 8, 1959, ninth inning, none on base.

Howard, Elston G., New York A.L., October 5, 1960, ninth inning, one on base.

Blanchard, John E., New York A.L., October 7, 1961, eighth inning, none on base.

Carbo, Bernardo, Boston A.L., October 14, 1975, night game, seventh inning, none on base.

Carbo, Bernardo, Boston A.L., October 21, 1975, night game, eighth inning, two on base.

Johnstone, John W., Los Angeles N.L., October 24, 1981, night game, sixth inning, one on base.

Most Grand Slams, Game (14 times)

1—Smith, Elmer J., Cleveland A.L., October 10, 1920, first inning.

Lazzeri, Anthony M., New York A.L., October 2, 1936, third inning.

McDougald, Gilbert J., New York A.L., October 9, 1951, third inning.

Mantle, Mickey C., New York A.L., October 4, 1953, third inning.

Berra, Lawrence P., New York A.L., October 5, 1956, second inning.

Skowron, William J., New York A.L., October 10, 1956, seventh inning.

Richardson, Robert C., New York A.L., October 8, 1960, first inning.

Hiller, Charles J., San Francisco N.L., October 8, 1962, seventh inning.

Boyer, Kenton L., St. Louis N.L., October 11, 1964, sixth inning.

Pepitone, Joseph A., New York A.L., October 14, 1964, eighth inning.

Northrup, James T., Detroit A.L., October 9, 1968, third inning.

McNally, David A., Baltimore A.L., October 13, 1970, sixth inning.

Gladden, C. Daniel, Minnesota A.L., October 17, 1987, fourth inning.

Hrbek, Kent A., Minnesota A.L., October 24, 1987, sixth inning.

Most Home Runs, Inning

1—Held by many players.

Most Home Runs, Two Consecutive Innings

2—Ruth, George H., New York A.L., October 11, 1923, fourth and fifth innings.

Ruth, George H., New York A.L., October 9, 1928, seventh and eighth innings.

Kluszewski, Theodore B., Chicago A.L., October 1, 1959, third and fourth innings.

Jackson, Reginald M., New York A.L., October 18, 1977, fourth and fifth innings.

Aikens, Willie M., Kansas City A.L., October 18, 1980, first and second innings.

Total Bases

Most Total Bases, Total Series

123—Mantle, Mickey C., New York A.L., 1951, 1952, 1953, 1955, 1956, 1957, 1958, 1960, 1961, 1962, 1963, 1964; 12 Series, 65 games.

Most Total Bases, Series

4-game Series—22—Ruth, George H., New York A.L., 1928.

5-game Series—17—Robinson, Brooks C., Baltimore A.L., 1970.

6-game Series—25—Jackson, Reginald M., New York A.L., 1977.

7-game Series—25—Stargell, Wilver D., Pittsburgh N.L., 1979.

8-game Series—18—Herzog, Charles L., New York N.L., 1912.

Jackson, Joseph J., Chicago A.L., 1919.

Most Total Bases, Series, Pinch-Hitter

8—Essegian, Charles A., Los Angeles N.L., 4 games, 1959; two home runs.

Carbo, Bernardo, Boston A.L., 3 games, 1975; two home runs.

Most Total Bases, Game

12—Ruth, George H., New York A.L., October 6, 1926, three home runs.

Ruth, George H., New York A.L., October 9, 1928, three home runs.

Jackson, Reginald M., New York A.L., October 18, 1977, three home runs.

Most Total Bases, Inning

5—Youngs, Ross, New York N.L., October 7, 1921, seventh inning, double and triple.

Simmons, Aloysius H., Philadelphia A.L., October 12, 1929, seventh inning, home run and single.

Long Hits

Most Long Hits, Total Series

26—Mantle, Mickey C., New York A.L., 1951, 1952, 1953, 1955, 1956, 1957, 1958, 1960, 1961, 1962, 1963, 1964; 12 Series, 65 games.

Most Long Hits, Series

4-game Series—6—Ruth, George H., New York A.L., 1928.
5-game Series—5—Dempsey, J. Rikard, Baltimore A.L., 1983.
6-game Series—6—Jackson, Reginald M., New York A.L., 1977;
one double, five home runs.
7-game Series—7—Stargell, Wilver D., Pittsburgh N.L., 1979.
8-game Series—5—Murray, John J., New York N.L., 1912.
Herzog, Charles L., New York N.L., 1912.
Weaver, George D., Chicago A.L., 1919.
Burns, George J., New York N.L., 1921.

Most Long Hits, Game

4—Isbell, Frank, Chicago A.L., October 13, 1906, four doubles.

Most Long Hits, Two Consecutive Games, One Series

5—Brock, Louis C., St. Louis N.L., October 6 (3), double, triple,
home run; October 7 (2), 2 doubles, 1968.

Most Long Hits, Inning

2—Youngs, Ross, New York N.L., October 7, 1921, seventh inning,
double and triple.

Extra Bases On Long Hits

Most Extra Bases on Long Hits, Total Series

64—Mantle, Mickey C., New York A.L., 1951, 1952, 1953, 1955,
1956, 1957, 1958, 1960, 1961, 1962, 1963, 1964; 12 Series,
65 games.

Most Extra Bases on Long Hits, Series

4-game Series—13—Gehrig, H. Louis, New York A.L., 1928; one
double, four home runs.
5-game Series—10—Clendenon, Donn A., New York N.L., 1969;
one double, three home runs.
6-game Series—16—Jackson, Reginald M., New York A.L., 1977;
one double, five home runs.
7-game Series—14—Snider, Edwin D., Brooklyn N.L., 1952; two
doubles, four home runs.
8-game Series—10—Dougherty, Patrick H., Boston A.L., 1903;
two triples, two home runs.

Runs Batted In

Most Runs Batted In, Total Series

40—Mantle, Mickey C., New York A.L., 1951, 1952, 1953, 1955,
1956, 1957, 1958, 1960, 1961, 1962, 1963, 1964 (12 Series,
65 games).

Most Series, One or More Runs Batted In

11—Berra, Lawrence P., New York A.L., 1947, 1949, 1950, 1952,
1953, 1955, 1956, 1957, 1958, 1960, 1961.

Most Consecutive Games, One or More RBIs, Total Series

8—Gehrig, H. Louis, New York A.L., 1928 (4), 1932 (4), 17 runs
batted in.
Jackson, Reginald M., New York A.L., 1977 (4), 1978 (4), 14
runs batted in.

Most Runs Batted In, Series

4-game Series— 9—Gehrig, H. Louis, New York A.L., 1928.
5-game Series— 8—Murphy, Daniel F., Philadelphia A.L. 1910.
May, Lee A., Cincinnati N.L., 1970.
6-game Series—10—Kluszewski, Theodore B., Chicago A.L.,
1959.
7-game Series—12—Richardson, Robert C., New York A.L., 1960.
8-game Series— 8—Leach, Thomas W., Pittsburgh N.L., 1903.
Duncan, Louis B., Cincinnati N.L., 1919.

Most Runs Batted In, Series, Pinch-Hitter

6—Rhodes, James L., New York N.L., 3 games, 1954.

Fewest Runs Batted In, Series

0—Clarke, Frederick C., Pittsburgh N.L., 8 games, 1903 (34 at-
bats).
Weaver, George D., Chicago A.L., 8 games, 1919 (34 at-bats).
Wagner, Charles F., Boston A.L., 8 games, 1912 (30 at-bats).
Pesky, John M., Boston A.L., 7 games, 1946 (30 at-bats).
Schoendienst, Albert F., Milwaukee N.L., 7 games, 1958 (30
at-bats).
Grote, Gerald W., New York N.L., 7 games, 1973 (30 at-bats).
Doyle, Robert D., Boston A.L., 7 games, 1975 (30 at-bats).
Also many other players with fewer at-bats.

Most Runs Batted In, Game

6—Richardson, Robert C., New York A.L., October 8, 1960.

Batting in All Club's Runs, Game (Most)

4—Bauer, Henry A., New York A.L., October 4, 1958; won, 4-0.
Boyer, Kenton L., St. Louis N.L., October 11, 1964; won 4-3.
Cey, Ronald C., Los Angeles N.L., October 11, 1978; won 4-3.
Trammell, Alan S., Detroit A.L., October 13, 1984; won 4-2.

Most Runs Batted In, Inning (14 times)

4—Smith, Elmer J., Cleveland A.L., October 10, 1920, first inning.
Lazzeri, Anthony M., New York A.L., October 2, 1936, third
inning.
McDougald, Gilbert J., New York A.L., October 9, 1951, third
inning.
Mantle, Mickey C., New York A.L., October 4, 1953, third inning.
Berra, Lawrence P., New York A.L., October 5, 1956, second
inning.
Skowron, William J., New York A.L., October 10, 1956, seventh
inning.
Richardson, Robert C., New York A.L., October 8, 1960, first
inning.
Hiller, Charles J., San Francisco, N.L., October 8, 1962, seventh
inning.
Boyer, Kenton L., St. Louis N.L., October 11, 1964, sixth inning.
Pepitone, Joseph A., New York A.L., October 14, 1964, eighth
inning.
Northrup, James T., Detroit A.L., October 9, 1968, third inning.
McNally, David A., Baltimore A.L., October 13, 1970, sixth in-
ning.
Gladden, C. Daniel, Minnesota A.L., October 17, 1987, fourth
inning.
Hrbek, Kent A., Minnesota A.L., October 24, 1987, sixth inning.

Bases On Balls

Most Bases on Balls, Total Series

43—Mantle, Mickey C., New York A.L., 1951, 1952, 1953, 1955,
1956, 1957, 1958, 1960, 1961, 1962, 1963, 1964; 12 Series,
65 games.

Most Bases on Balls, Series

4-game Series— 7—Thompson, Henry, New York N.L., 1954.
5-game Series— 7—Sheckard, James T., Chicago N.L., 1910.
Cochrane, Gordon S., Philadelphia A.L.,
1929.
Gordon, Joseph L., New York A.L., 1941.
6-game Series— 9—Randolph, William L., New York A.L., 1981.
7-game Series—11—Ruth, George H., New York A.L., 1926.
Tenace, F. Gene, Oakland A.L., 1973.
8-game Series— 7—Devore, Joshua, New York N.L., 1912.
Youngs, Ross M., New York N.L., 1921.

Most Series, One or More Bases on Balls, Total Series

13—Berra, Lawrence P., New York A.L., 1947, 1949, 1950, 1951,
1952, 1953, 1955, 1956, 1957, 1958, 1960, 1961, 1962.

Most Bases on Balls, Series, Pinch-Hitter

3—Tate, H. Bennett, Washington A.L., 3 games, 1924.

Fewest Bases on Balls, Series

0—Weaver, George D., Chicago A.L., 8 games, 1919; 34 at-bats
(also many other players with fewer at-bats).

Fewest Bases on Balls and Strikeouts, Series

0—Southworth, William H., St. Louis N.L., 7 games, 1926; 29 at-
bats (also many other players with fewer at-bats).

Most Consecutive Bases on Balls, One Series

5—Gehrig, H. Louis, New York A.L., October 7 (2), October 9 (3),
1928.

Most Bases on Balls, Game

4—Clarke, Fred C., Pittsburgh N.L., October 16, 1909.
Hoblitzel, Richard C., Boston A.L., October 9, 1916 (14 in-
nings).
Youngs, Ross, New York N.L., October 10, 1924 (12 innings).
Ruth, George H., New York A.L., October 10, 1926.
Robinson, Jack R., Brooklyn N.L., October 5, 1952 (11 in-
nings).
DeCinces, Douglas V., Baltimore A.L., October 13, 1979.

Most Bases on Balls with Bases Filled, Game

2—Palmer, James A., Baltimore A.L., October 11, 1971, consecutive, fourth and fifth innings.

Most Bases on Balls, Two Consecutive Games

6—Sheckard, James T., Chicago N.L., October 18 (3), October 20 (3), 1910.

Most Bases on Balls, Inning

2—Gomez, Vernon L., New York A.L., October 6, 1937, sixth inning.
McAuliffe, Richard J., Detroit A.L., October 9, 1968, third inning.

Strikeouts

Most Strikeouts, Total Series

54—Mantle, Mickey C., New York A.L., 1951, 1952, 1953, 1955, 1956, 1957, 1958, 1960, 1961, 1962, 1963, 1964; 12 Series, 65 games.

Most Strikeouts, Series

4-game Series— 7—Meusel, Robert W., New York A.L., 1927.
5-game Series— 9—Martinez, Carmelo, San Diego N.L., 1984.
6-game Series—12—Wilson, Willie J., Kansas City A.L., 1980.
7-game Series—11—Mathews, Edwin L., Milwaukee N.L., 1958.
Garrett, R. Wayne, New York N.L., 1973.
8-game Series—10—Kelly, George L., New York N.L., 1921.

Most Series, One or More Strikeouts

12—Mantle, Mickey C., New York A.L., 1951, 1952, 1953, 1955, 1956, 1957, 1958, 1960, 1961, 1963, 1964.

Most Consecutive Strikeouts, One Series

5—Devore, Joshua, New York N.L., October 16 (4), October 17 (1), 1911.
Mogridge, George, Washington A.L., October 7 (4), October 10 (1), 1924.
Pipgras, George W., New York A.L., October 1 (5), 1932.
Mantle, Mickey C., New York A.L., October 2 (4), October 3 (1), 1953.
Shannon, T. Michael, St. Louis N.L., October 12 (2), October 14 (3), 1964.
Jackson, Danny L., Kansas City A.L., October 19 (2), October 24 (3), 1985.

Most Strikeouts, Series, Pinch-Hitter

3—Hartnett, Charles L., Chicago N.L., 3 games, 1929.
Hemsley, Ralston B., Chicago N.L., 3 games, 1932.
Velez, Otoniel, New York A.L., 3 games, 1976.

Fewest Strikeouts, Series

0—Foli, Timothy J., Pittsburgh N.L., 7 games, 1979 (30 at-bats).
Southworth, William H., St. Louis N.L., 7 games, 1926 (29 at-bats).
Roush, Edd J., Cincinnati N.L., 8 games, 1919 (28 at-bats).
Gehringer, Charles L., Detroit A.L., 7 games, 1940 (28 at-bats).
Gilliam, James, Los Angeles N.L., 7 games, 1965 (28 at-bats).
Berra, Lawrence P., New York A.L., 7 games, 1958 (27 at-bats).
Moore, Charles W., Milwaukee A.L., 7 games, 1982 (26 at-bats).
Frisch, Frank F., New York N.L., 6 games, 1923 (25 at-bats).
Robinson, Jack R., Brooklyn N.L., 6 games, 1953 (25 at-bats).
Berra, Lawrence P., New York A.L., 7 games, 1957 (25 at-bats).
Also many other players with fewer at-bats.

Most Strikeouts, Game (*Denotes All Consecutive)

5—Pipgras, George W., New York A.L., October 1, 1932.*
4—Devore, Joshua, New York N.L., October 16, 1911.*
James, William L., Boston N.L., October 10, 1914.*
Mogridge, George, Washington A.L., October 7, 1924.*
Rowe, Lynwood T., Detroit A.L., October 4, 1934.*
Bonham, Ernest E., New York A.L., October 6, 1941.*
Collins, Joseph E., New York A.L., October 2, 1953.*
Mantle, Mickey C., New York A.L., October 2, 1953.*
Stottlemyre, Melvin L., New York A.L., October 8, 1964.

Most Strikeouts, Inning

1—Held by many players.

Sacrifice Hits & Flies

Most Sacrifices, Total Series

8—Collins, Edward T., Philadelphia A.L. (6), 1910, 1911, 1913, 1914; Chicago A.L. (2), 1917, 1919; 6 Series, 34 games.

Most Sacrifices, Series

4-game Series—3—Westrum, Wesley N., New York N.L., 195- (one sacrifice hit and two sacrifice flies).
5-game Series—4—Lewis, George E., Boston A.L., 1916.
6-game Series—3—Sheckard, James T., Chicago N.L., 1906.
Steinfeldt, Harry E., Chicago N.L., 1906.
Tinker, Joseph B., Chicago N.L., 1906.
Barry, John J., Philadelphia A.L., 1911.
Lee, William C., Chicago N.L., 1935.
7-game Series—5—Clarke, Fred C., Pittsburgh N.L., 1909.
8-game Series—5—Daubert, Jacob E., Cincinnati N.L., 1919.

Most Sacrifices, Game

3—Tinker, Joseph B., Chicago N.L., October 12, 1906 (all sacrifice hits).
Westrum, Wesley N., New York N.L. October 2, 1954 (one sacrifice hit and two sacrifice flies).

Most Sacrifice Hits, Inning

1—Held by many players.

Most Sacrifice Flies, Total Series

3—Robinson, Brooks C., Baltimore A.L., 1966 (0), 1969 (1), 1970 (0), 1971 (2); 4 Series, 21 games.
Concepcion, David I., Cincinnati N.L., 1970 (1), 1972 (1), 1975 (1); 3 Series, 16 games.

Most Sacrifice Flies, Game

2—Westrum, Wesley N., New York N.L., October 2, 1954.

Most Sacrifice Flies, Inning

1—Held by many players.

Most Runs Batted In on Sacrifice Fly

2—Herr, Thomas M., St. Louis N.L., October 16, 1982; second inning.

Hit By Pitch

Most Hit by Pitch, Total Series

3—Chance, Frank L., Chicago N.L., 1906 (2), 1907 (1).
Wagner, John P., Pittsburgh N.L., 1903 (1), 1909 (2).
Snodgrass, Frederick C., New York N.L., 1911 (2), 1912 (1).
Carey, Max, Pittsburgh N.L., 1925 (3).
Berra, Lawrence P., New York A.L., 1953 (2), 1955 (1).
Howard, Elston G., New York A.L., 1960 (1), 1962 (1), 1964 (1).
Robinson, Frank, Cincinnati N.L., 1961 (2), Baltimore A.L., 1971 (1).
Campaneris, Dagoberto B., Oakland A.L., 1973 (2), 1974 (1).
Jackson, Reginald M., New York A.L., 1977 (1), 1978 (2).

Most Hit by Pitch, Series

3—Carey, Max, Pittsburgh N.L., 7 games, 1925.

Most Hit by Pitch, Game

2—Carey, Max, Pittsburgh N.L., October 7, 1925.
Berra, Lawrence P., New York A.L., October 2, 1953.
Robinson, Frank, Cincinnati N.L., October 8, 1961.

Most Hit by Pitch, Inning

1—Held by many players.

Grounding Into Double Plays

Most Grounding Into Double Play, Total Series

7—DiMaggio, Joseph P., New York A.L., 1936, 1937, 1938, 1939, 1941, 1942, 1947, 1949, 1950, 1951; 10 Series, 51 games.

Most Grounding Into Double Play, Series

5—Noren, Irving A., New York A.L., 1955 (16 times at bat in 5 games of 7-game Series).

Most Grounding Into Double Play, Game

3—Mays, Willie H., New York N.L., October 8, 1951.

Reaching On Errors Or Interference

Most Times Reaching First Base on Error, Game

3—Clarke, Fred C., Pittsburgh N.L., October 10, 1903.

Most Times Awarded First Base On Catcher's Interference, Game

1—Peckinpaugh, Roger T., Washington A.L., October 15, 1925, first inning.

Metheny, Arthur B., New York A.L., October 6, 1943, sixth inning.

Boyer, Kenton L., St. Louis N.L., October 12, 1964, first inning.

Rose, Peter E., Cincinnati N.L., October 10, 1970, fifth inning.

Hendrick, George A., St. Louis N.L., October 15, 1982, ninth inning.

Club Batting

Service
Players Used

Most Players, Series
- 4-game Series—24—Cleveland A.L., vs. New York N.L., 1954.
- 5-game Series—25—Brooklyn N.L., vs. New York A.L., 1949.
- 6-game Series—25—Los Angeles N.L., vs. New York A.L., 1977.
- 7-game Series—26—Detroit A.L., vs. Chicago N.L., 1945.
  Boston A.L., vs. St. Louis N.L., 1946.
- 8-game Series—19—Chicago A.L., vs. Cincinnati N.L., 1919.
  New York A.L., vs. New York N.L., 1921.

Most Players, Series, Both Clubs
- 4-game Series—39—Cleveland A.L., 24, New York N.L., 15, 1954.
- 5-game Series—46—Baltimore A.L., 23, Philadelphia N.L., 23, 1983.
  San Diego N.L., 24, Detroit A.L., 22, 1984.
- 6-game Series—48—New York A.L., 24, Los Angeles N.L., 24, 1981.
- 7-game Series—51—Detroit A.L., 26, Chicago N.L., 25, 1945.
- 8-game Series—36—Chicago A.L., 19, Cincinnati N.L., 17, 1919.

Fewest Players, Series
- 4-game Series—13—Los Angeles N.L., vs. New York A.L., 1963.
  Baltimore A.L., vs. Los Angeles N.L., 1966.
- 5-game Series—12—New York N.L., vs. Philadelphia A.L., 1905.
  Philadelphia A.L., vs. Chicago N.L., 1910.
  Philadelphia A.L., vs. New York N.L., 1913.
- 6-game Series—14—Chicago N.L., vs. Chicago A.L., 1906.
  Philadelphia A.L., vs. New York N.L., 1911.
- 7-game Series—16—Detroit A.L., vs. Pittsburgh N.L., 1909.
- 8-game Series—13—Boston A.L., vs. Pittsburgh N.L., 1903.
  New York N.L., vs. New York A.L., 1921.

Fewest Players, Series, Both Clubs
- 4-game Series—31—Philadelphia A.L., 16, Boston N.L., 15, 1914.
- 5-game Series—25—Philadelphia A.L., 13, New York N.L., 12, 1905.
- 6-game Series—29—New York N.L., 15, Philadelphia A.L., 14, 1911.
- 7-game Series—33—Pittsburgh N.L., 17, Detroit A.L., 16, 1909.
- 8-game Series—27—Pittsburgh N.L., 14, Boston A.L., 13, 1903.

Most Times, One Club Using Only 9 Players in Game, Series
- 5-game Series—5—Philadelphia A.L., vs. Chicago N.L., 1910.
  Philadelphia A.L., vs. New York N.L., 1913.
- 7-game Series—5—New York A.L., vs. Brooklyn N.L., 1956.
- 8-game Series—6—Pittsburgh N.L., vs. Boston A.L., 1903.

Most Times, Both Clubs Using Only 9 Players in Game, Series
- 7-game Series— 7—New York A.L., 5, Brooklyn N.L., 2, 1956.
- 8-game Series—11—Pittsburgh N.L., 6; Boston A.L., 5, 1903.

Most Players, Game
- 21—New York A.L., vs. Brooklyn N.L., October 5, 1947.
  Cincinnati N.L., vs. New York A.L., October 9, 1961.
  Oakland A.L., vs. New York N.L., October 14, 1973, 12 innings.

Most Players, Game, Both Clubs
- 38—Chicago N.L., 19, Detroit A.L., 19, October 8, 1945, 12 innings.
  New York A.L., 21, Brooklyn N.L., 17, October 5, 1947.
  Oakland A.L., 21, New York N.L., 17, October 14, 1973, 12 innings.

Pinch-Hitters

Most Times Pinch-Hitter Used, Series
- 4-game Series—16—Cleveland A.L., vs. New York N.L., 1954.
- 5-game Series—15—Cincinnati N.L., vs. New York A.L., 1961.
- 6-game Series—13—St. Louis A.L., vs. St. Louis N.L., 1944.
  Los Angeles N.L., vs. Chicago A.L., 1959.
- 7-game Series—23—Baltimore A.L., vs. Pittsburgh N.L., 1979.
- 8-game Series— 6—Chicago A.L., vs. Cincinnati N.L., 1919.

Most Times Pinch-Hitter Used, Series, Both Clubs
- 4-game Series—19—Cleveland A.L., 16, New York N.L., 3, 1954.

- 5-game Series—25—Baltimore A.L. 13, Philadelphia N.L., 12, 1983.
- 6-game Series—22—Los Angeles N.L., 13, Chicago A.L., 9, 1959.
- 7-game Series—35—Oakland A.L., 20, New York N.L., 15, 1973.
- 8-game Series—10—New York N.L., 5, Boston A.L., 5, 1912.

Fewest Times Pinch-Hitter Used, Series
- 4-game Series—0—New York A.L., vs. Cincinnati N.L., 1939.
  Baltimore A.L., vs. Los Angeles N.L., 1966.
  Cincinnati N.L., vs. New York A.L., 1976.
- 5-game Series—0—Philadelphia A.L., vs. Chicago N.L., 1910.
  Philadelphia A.L., vs. New York N.L., 1913.
- 6-game Series—0—Philadelphia A.L., vs. New York N.L., 1911.
- 7-game Series—2—Milwaukee A.L., vs. St. Louis N.L., 1982.
- 8-game Series—1—Pittsburgh N.L., vs. Boston A.L., 1903.

Fewest Times Pinch-Hitter Used, Series, Both Clubs
- 4-game Series—3—Boston N.L., 2, Philadelphia A.L., 1, 1914.
  Cincinnati N.L., 3, New York A.L., 0, 1939.
- 5-game Series—2—New York N.L., 1, Philadelphia A.L., 1, 1905.
- 6-game Series—4—New York N.L., 4, Philadelphia A.L., 0, 1911.
- 7-game Series—8—Detroit A.L., 5, Pittsburgh N.L., 3, 1909.
- 8-game Series—5—Boston A.L., 4, Pittsburgh N.L., 1, 1903.
  New York A.L., 3, New York N.L., 2, 1921.

Most Pinch-Hitters, Game
- 6—Los Angeles N.L., vs. Chicago A.L., October 6, 1959.

Most Pinch-Hitters, Game, Both Clubs
- 8—Oakland A.L., 5, New York N.L., 3, October 14, 1973.
  Baltimore A.L.. 4, Philadelphia N.L., 4, October 15, 1983.

Most Pinch-Hitters, Inning
- 4—New York N.L., vs. Oakland A.L., October 13, 1973, ninth inning.
  Baltimore A.L., vs. Philadelphia N.L., October 15, 1983, sixth inning.
  Minnesota A.L., vs. St. Louis N.L., October 22, 1987, ninth inning.

Pinch-Runners

Most Times Pinch-Runner Used, Series
- 4-game Series—4—Philadelphia N.L., vs. New York A.L., 1950.
- 5-game Series—5—New York N.L., vs. Philadelphia A.L., 1913.
- 6-game Series—5—New York A.L., vs. Los Angeles N.L., 1981.
- 7-game Series—8—Oakland A.L., vs. Cincinnati N.L., 1972.
- 8-game Series—3—New York N.L., vs. Boston A.L., 1912.

Most Times Pinch-Runner Used, Series, Both Clubs
- 4-game Series— 6—Philadelphia N.L., 4, New York A.L., 2, 1950.
- 5-game Series— 6—Oakland A.L., 4, Los Angeles N.L., 2, 1974.
- 6-game Series— 7—New York A.L., 5, Los Angeles N.L., 2, 1981.
- 7-game Series—10—Oakland A.L., 8, Cincinnati N.L., 2, 1972.
- 8-game Series— 4—New York N.L., 3, Boston A.L., 1, 1912.

Fewest Times Pinch-Runner Used, Series
- 0—Held by many clubs in Series of all lengths.

Fewest Times Pinch-Runner Used, Series, Both Clubs
- 4-game Series—0—New York A.L., 0, Chicago N.L., 0, 1938.
  Los Angeles N.L., 0, New York A.L., 0, 1963.
  Cincinnati N.L., 0, New York A.L., 0, 1976.
- 5-game Series—0—New York N.L., 0, Philadelphia A.L., 0, 1905.
  Philadelphia A.L., 0, Chicago N.L., 0, 1929.
  New York A.L., 0, New York N.L., 0, 1937.
  Baltimore A.L., 0, Cincinnati N.L., 0, 1970.
- 6-game Series—0—Chicago A.L., 0, New York N.L., 0, 1917.
  Philadelphia A.L., 0, St. Louis N.L., 0, 1930.
  Detroit A.L., 0, Chicago N.L., 0, 1935.
  New York A.L., 0, Brooklyn N.L., 0, 1953.
- 7-game Series—0—Pittsburgh N.L., 0, Detroit A.L., 0, 1909.
  New York A.L., 0, Brooklyn N.L., 0, 1956.
  Cincinnati N.L., 0, Boston A.L., 0, 1975.
- 8-game Series—0—Boston A.L., 0, Pittsburgh N.L., 0, 1903.

Most Pinch-Runners, Game
- 2—Made in many games.

Most Pinch-Runners, Game, Both Clubs
4—St. Louis N.L. 2, Kansas City A.L. 2, October 26, 1985.

Most Pinch-Runners, Inning
2—New York N.L., vs. New York A.L., October 10, 1923, third inning.
New York A.L., vs. New York N.L., October 15, 1923, eighth inning.
Brooklyn N.L., vs. New York A.L., October 3, 1947, ninth inning.
Boston N.L., vs. Cleveland A.L., October 6, 1948, eighth inning.
Philadelphia N.L., vs. New York A.L., October 7, 1950, ninth inning.
Los Angeles N.L., vs. Chicago A.L., October 6, 1959, seventh inning.
Oakland A.L., vs. Cincinnati N.L., October 19, 1972, ninth inning.
St. Louis N.L., vs. Kansas City A.L., October 26, 1985, eighth inning.
Kansas City A.L., vs. St. Louis N.L., October 26, 1985, ninth inning.

Most Pinch-Runners, Inning, Both Clubs
2—Made in many games.

Series & Games

Most Series Played
33—New York A.L., 1921, 1922, 1923, 1926, 1927, 1928, 1932, 1936, 1937, 1938, 1939, 1941, 1942, 1943, 1947, 1949, 1950, 1951, 1952, 1953, 1955, 1956, 1957, 1958, 1960, 1961, 1962, 1963, 1964, 1976, 1977, 1978, 1981 (won 22, lost 11).
17—Brooklyn-Los Angeles N.L., 1916, 1920, 1941, 1947, 1949, 1952, 1953, 1955, 1956, 1959, 1963, 1965, 1966, 1974, 1977, 1978, 1981 (won 5, lost 12).

Most Consecutive Series, Between Same Clubs
3—New York N.L. vs. New York A.L., 1921, 1922, 1923.

Most Games Played, Total Series
187—New York A.L., 33 Series (won 109, lost 77, tied 1).

Batting Average

Highest Batting Average, Series
4-game Series—.313—New York A.L., vs. Chicago N.L., 1932. Cincinnati N.L., vs. New York A.L., 1976.
5-game Series—.316—Philadelphia A.L., vs. Chicago N.L., 1910.
6-game Series—.306—New York A.L., vs. Los Angeles N.L., 1978.
7-game Series—.338—New York A.L., vs. Pittsburgh N.L., 1960.
8-game Series—.270—New York N.L., vs. Boston A.L., 1912.

Highest Batting Average, Series, Both Clubs
4-game Series—.283—New York A.L., .313, Chicago N.L., .253, 1932.
5-game Series—.272—Philadelphia A.L., .316, Chicago N.L., .222, 1910.
6-game Series—.292—Philadelphia N.L., .294, Kansas City A.L., .290, 1980.
7-game Series—.300—New York A.L., .338, Pittsburgh N.L., .256, 1960.
8-game Series—.245—New York N.L., .270, Boston A.L., .220, 1912.

Highest Batting Average, Series, World Series Loser
4-game Series—.253—Chicago N.L., vs. New York A.L., 1932.
5-game Series—.265—San Diego N.L., vs. Detroit A.L., 1984.
6-game Series—.300—Brooklyn N.L., vs. New York A.L., 1953.
7-game Series—.338—New York A.L., vs. Pittsburgh N.L., 1960.
8-game Series—.270—New York N.L., vs. Boston A.L., 1912.

Lowest Batting Average, Series
4-game Series—.142—Los Angeles N.L., vs. Baltimore A.L., 1966.
5-game Series—.146—Baltimore A.L., vs. New York N.L., 1969.
6-game Series—.175—New York N.L., vs. Philadelphia A.L., 1911.
7-game Series—.185—St. Louis N.L., vs. Kansas City A.L., 1985.
8-game Series—.207—New York A.L., vs. New York N.L., 1921.

Lowest Batting Average, Series, Both Clubs
4-game Series—.171—Los Angeles N.L., .142, Baltimore A.L., .200, 1966.
5-game Series—.184—Baltimore A.L., .146, New York N.L., .220, 1969.
6-game Series—.197—Chicago A.L., .198, Chicago N.L., .196, 1906.

7-game Series—.209—Oakland A.L., .209, Cincinnati N.L., .209, 1972.
8-game Series—.239—Cincinnati N.L., .255, Chicago A.L., .224, 1919.

Lowest Batting Average, Series, World Series Winner
4-game Series—.200—Baltimore A.L., vs. Los Angeles N.L., 1966.
5-game Series—.209—New York N.L., vs. Philadelphia A.L., 1905.
6-game Series—.186—Boston A.L., vs. Chicago N.L., 1918.
7-game Series—.199—New York A.L., vs. San Francisco N.L., 1962.
8-game Series—.220—Boston A.L., vs. New York N.L., 1912.

Slugging Average

Highest Slugging Average, Series
4-game Series—.530—New York A.L., vs. St. Louis N.L., 1928.
5-game Series—.509—Baltimore A.L., vs. Cincinnati N.L., 1970.
6-game Series—.484—Brooklyn N.L., vs. New York A.L., 1953.
7-game Series—.528—New York A.L., vs. Pittsburgh N.L., 1960.
8-game Series—.401—Boston A.L., vs. Pittsburgh N.L., 1903.

Highest Slugging Average, Series, Both Clubs
4-game Series—.459—New York A.L., .521, Chicago N.L., .397, 1932.
5-game Series—.433—Baltimore A.L., .509, Cincinnati N.L., .354, 1970.
6-game Series—.436—Kansas City A.L., .469, Philadelphia N.L., .403, 1980.
7-game Series—.447—New York A.L., .528, Pittsburgh N.L., .355, 1960.
8-game Series—.344—New York N.L., .361, Boston A.L., .326, 1912.

Lowest Slugging Average, Series
4-game Series—.192—Los Angeles N.L., vs. Baltimore A.L., 1966.
5-game Series—.194—Philadelphia A.L., vs. New York N.L., 1905.
6-game Series—.233—Boston A.L., vs. Chicago N.L., 1918.
7-game Series—.237—Brooklyn N.L., vs. Cleveland A.L., 1920.
8-game Series—.270—New York A.L., vs. New York N.L., 1921.

Lowest Slugging Average, Series, Both Clubs
4-game Series—.267—Baltimore A.L., .342, Los Angeles N.L., .192, 1966.
5-game Series—.224—New York N.L., .255, Philadelphia A.L., .194, 1905.
6-game Series—.241—Chicago N.L., .250, Boston A.L., .233, 1918.
7-game Series—.285—Cleveland A.L., .332, Brooklyn N.L., .237, 1920.
8-game Series—.323—New York N.L., .371, New York A.L., .270, 1921.

At-Bats & Plate Appearances

Most At-Bats, Total Series
6,255—New York A.L., 33 Series, 187 games.

Most At-Bats, Series
4-game Series—146—Chicago N.L., vs. New York A.L., 1932.
5-game Series—178—New York A.L., vs. St. Louis N.L., 1942.
6-game Series—222—New York A.L., vs. Los Angeles N.L., 1978.
7-game Series—269—New York A.L., vs. Pittsburgh N.L., 1960.
8-game Series—282—Boston A.L., vs. Pittsburgh N.L., 1903.

Most At-Bats, Series, Both Clubs
4-game Series—290—Chicago N.L., 146, New York A.L., 144, 1932.
5-game Series—349—New York N.L., 176, Washington A.L., 173, 1933.
6-game Series—421—New York A.L., 222, Los Angeles N.L., 199, 1978.
7-game Series—512—St. Louis N.L., 262, Detroit A.L., 250, 1934.
8-game Series—552—Boston A.L., 282, Pittsburgh N.L., 270, 1903.

Fewest At-Bats, Series
4-game Series—117—Los Angeles N.L., vs. New York A.L., 1963.
5-game Series—142—Oakland A.L., vs. Los Angeles N.L., 1974.
6-game Series—172—Boston A.L., vs. Chicago N.L., 1918.
7-game Series—215—Brooklyn N.L., vs. Cleveland A.L., 1920.
Brooklyn N.L., vs. New York A.L., 1956.
Minnesota A.L., vs. Los Angeles N.L., 1965.
8-game Series—241—New York A.L., vs. New York N.L., 1921.

Fewest At-Bats, Series, Both Clubs

4-game Series—240—Baltimore A.L., 120, Los Angeles N.L., 120, 1966.

5-game Series—300—Los Angeles N.L., 158, Oakland A.L., 142, 1974.

6-game Series—348—Chicago N.L., 176, Boston A.L., 172, 1918.

7-game Series—432—Cleveland A.L., 217, Brooklyn N.L., 215, 1920.

8-game Series—505—New York N.L., 264, New York A.L., 241, 1921.

Most At-Bats, Game, Nine Innings

45—New York A.L., vs. Chicago N.L., October 2, 1932.
New York A.L., vs. New York N.L., October 6, 1936.
New York A.L., vs. Pittsburgh N.L., October 6, 1960.

Most At-Bats, Extra-Inning Game

54—New York N.L., vs Oakland A.L., October 14, 1973, 12 innings.

Most At-Bats, Game, Nine Innings, Both Clubs

84—New York A.L., 45, Chicago N.L., 39, October 2, 1932.
New York A.L., 45, Pittsburgh N.L., 39, October 6, 1960.

Most At-Bats, Extra-Inning Game, Both Clubs

101—New York N.L., 54, Oakland A.L., 47, October 14, 1973, 12 innings.

Fewest Official At-Bats, Game, Nine Innings

25—Philadelphia A.L., vs. Boston N.L., October 10, 1914.

Fewest Official At-Bats, Game, Nine Innings, Both Clubs

54—Chicago N.L., 27, Chicago A.L., 27, October 12, 1906.
53—Cleveland A.L., 28, Brooklyn N.L., 25, October 7, 1920 (Brooklyn N.L. batted 8 innings).
New York N.L., 27, New York A.L., 26, October 6, 1921 (New York A.L. batted 8 innings).
Brooklyn N.L., 27, New York A.L., 26, October 8, 1956 (New York A.L. batted 8 innings).
New York A.L., 29, Los Angeles N.L., 24, October 5, 1963 (Los Angeles N.L. batted 8 innings).

Most At-Bats, Inning

13—Philadelphia A.L., vs. Chicago N.L., October 12, 1929, seventh inning.

Most At-Bats, Inning, Both Clubs

17—Philadelphia A.L., 13, Chicago N.L., 4, October 12, 1929, seventh inning.

Most Men Facing Pitcher, Inning

15—Philadelphia A.L., vs. Chicago N.L., October 12, 1929, seventh inning.
Detroit A.L., vs. St. Louis N.L., October 9, 1968, third inning.

Most Men Facing Pitcher, Inning, Both Clubs

20—Philadelphia A.L., 15, Chicago N.L., 5, October 12, 1929, seventh inning.

Runs
Series & Game

Most Runs, Total Series

838—New York A.L., 33 Series, 187 games.

Most Runs, Series

4-game Series—37—New York A.L., vs. Chicago N.L., 1932.

5-game Series—35—Philadelphia A.L., vs. Chicago N.L., 1910.

6-game Series—43—New York A.L., vs. New York N.L., 1936.

7-game Series—55—New York A.L., vs. Pittsburgh N.L., 1960.

8-game Series—39—Boston A.L., vs. Pittsburgh N.L., 1903.

Most Runs, Series, Both Clubs

4-game Series—56—New York A.L., 37, Chicago N.L., 19, 1932.

5-game Series—53—Baltimore A.L., 33, Cincinnati N.L., 20, 1970.

6-game Series—66—New York A.L., 43, New York N.L., 23, 1936.

7-game Series—82—New York A.L., 55, Pittsburgh N.L., 27, 1960.

8-game Series—63—Boston A.L., 39, Pittsburgh N.L., 24, 1903.

Most Runs, Series, World Series Loser

4-game Series—19—Chicago N.L., vs. New York A.L., 1932.

5-game Series—20—Cincinnati N.L., vs. Baltimore A.L., 1970.

6-game Series—28—Los Angeles N.L., vs. New York A.L., 1977.

7-game Series—55—New York A.L., vs. Pittsburgh N.L., 1960.

8-game Series—31—New York N.L., vs. Boston A.L., 1912.

Fewest Runs, Series

4-game Series— 2—Los Angeles N.L., vs. Baltimore A.L., 1966.

5-game Series— 3—Philadelphia A.L., vs. New York N.L., 1905.

6-game Series— 9—Boston A.L., vs. Chicago N.L., 1918.

7-game Series— 8—Brooklyn N.L., vs. Cleveland A.L., 1920.

8-game Series—20—Chicago A.L., vs. Cincinnati N.L., 1919.

Fewest Runs, Series, Both Clubs

4-game Series—15—Baltimore A.L., 13, Los Angeles N.L., 2, 1966.

5-game Series—18—New York N.L., 15, Philadelphia A.L., 3, 1905.

6-game Series—19—Chicago N.L., 10, Boston A.L., 9, 1918.

7-game Series—29—Cleveland A.L., 21, Brooklyn N.L., 8, 1920.

8-game Series—51—New York N.L., 29, New York A.L., 22, 1921.

Most Runs, Game

18—New York A.L., vs. New York N.L., October 2, 1936 (Won 18-4).

Most Runs, Game, Pinch-Hitters

3—New York A.L., vs. Brooklyn N.L., October 2, 1947.

Most Earned Runs, Game

17—New York A.L., vs. New York N.L., October 2, 1936 (Won 18-4).

Most Runs, Game, Both Clubs

22—New York A.L., 18, New York N.L., 4, October 2, 1936.

Largest Score, Shutout Game

12-0—New York A.L., 12, Pittsburgh N.L., 0, October 12, 1960.

Most Players, One or More Runs, Game

9—St. Louis N.L., vs. Detroit A.L., October 9, 1934.
New York A.L., vs. New York N.L., October 2, 1936.
Milwaukee N.L., vs. New York A.L., October 2, 1958.
New York A.L., vs. Pittsburgh N.L., October 6, 1960.
Pittsburgh N.L., vs. New York A.L., October 13, 1960.

Most Players, One or More Runs, Game, Both Clubs

15—Pittsburgh N.L., 9, New York A.L., 6, October 13, 1960.

Inning

Most Runs, Inning

10—Philadelphia A.L., vs. Chicago N.L., October 12, 1929, seventh inning.
Detroit A.L., vs. St. Louis N.L., October 9, 1968, third inning.

Most Runs, Inning, Both Clubs

11—Philadelphia A.L., 10, Chicago N.L., 1, October 12, 1929, seventh inning.
Brooklyn N.L., 6, New York A.L., 5, October 5, 1956, second inning.

Most Runs, Extra Inning

4—New York N.L., vs. Oakland A.L., October 14, 1973, twelfth inning.

Most Runs, Two Consecutive Innings

12—Detroit A.L., vs. St. Louis N.L., October 9, 1968, 2 in second inning, 10 in third inning.

Most Innings Scored, Game

6—New York A.L., vs. St. Louis N.L., October 6, 1926.
New York A.L., vs. Brooklyn N.L., October 1, 1947.
New York A.L., vs. Pittsburgh N.L., October 6, 1960.

Most Innings Scored, Game, Both Clubs

9—New York A.L., 6, St. Louis N.L., 3, October 6, 1926.
New York A.L., 5, New York N.L., 4, October 6, 1936.
New York A.L., 6, Brooklyn N.L., 3, October 1, 1947.
New York A.L., 5, Brooklyn N.L., 4, October 4, 1953.
Brooklyn N.L., 5, New York A.L., 4, October 5, 1956.
Oakland A.L., 5, New York N.L., 4, October 14, 1973, 12 innings.
New York A.L., 5, Los Angeles N.L., 4, October 24, 1981.

Most Runs, First Inning

7—Milwaukee N.L., vs. New York A.L., October 2, 1958.

Most Runs, Second Inning

6—New York A.L., vs. New York N.L., October 13, 1923.
New York N.L., vs. New York A.L., October 9, 1937.
Brooklyn N.L., vs. New York A.L., October 2, 1947.
Brooklyn N.L., vs. New York A.L., October 5, 1956.

Most Runs, Third Inning

10—Detroit A.L., vs. St. Louis N.L., October 9, 1968.

Most Runs, Fourth Inning

7—Minnesota A.L., vs. St. Louis N.L., October 17, 1987.

Most Runs, Fifth Inning

6—Baltimore A.L., vs. Pittsburgh N.L., October 11, 1971.
Kansas City A.L., vs. St. Louis N.L., October 27, 1985.

Most Runs, Sixth Inning

7—New York A.L., vs. New York N.L., October 6, 1937.
New York A.L., vs. Pittsburgh N.L., October 6, 1960.

Most Runs, Seventh Inning

10—Philadelphia A.L., vs. Chicago N.L., October 12, 1929.

Most Runs, Eighth Inning

6—Chicago N.L., vs. Detroit A.L., October 11, 1908.
Baltimore A.L., vs. Pittsburgh N.L., October 13, 1979.

Most Runs, Ninth Inning

7—New York A.L., vs. New York N.L., October 6, 1936.

Most Runs, Ninth Inning, With None on Base, Two Out

4—New York A.L., vs. Brooklyn N.L., October 5, 1941.

Most Runs, Tenth Inning

3—New York N.L., vs. Philadelphia A.L., October 8, 1913.
New York A.L., vs. Cincinnati N.L., October 8, 1939.
New York N.L., vs. Cleveland A.L., September 29, 1954.
Milwaukee N.L., vs. New York A.L., October 6, 1957.
St. Louis N.L., vs. New York A.L., October 12, 1964.
New York N.L., vs. Boston A.L., October 25, 1986.

Most Runs, Eleventh Inning

2—Philadelphia A.L., vs. New York N.L., October 17, 1911.

Most Runs, Twelfth Inning

4—New York N.L., vs. Oakland A.L., October 14, 1973.

Games Being Shut Out

Most Times Shut Out, Total Series

13—New York A.L.

Most Times Shut Out, Series

4—Philadelphia A.L., vs. New York N.L., 1905.

Most Consecutive Times Shut Out, Series

3—Philadelphia A.L., vs. New York N.L., October 12, 13, 14, 1905.
Los Angeles N.L., vs. Baltimore A.L., October 6, 8, 9, 1966.

Most Consecutive Games Without Being Shut Out, Total Series

42—New York A.L., October 6, 1926, through October 1, 1942.

Hits
Series

Most Hits, Total Series

1,568—New York A.L., 33 Series, 187 games.

Most Hits, Series

4-game Series—45—New York A.L., vs. Chicago N.L., 1932.
5-game Series—56—Philadelphia A.L., vs. Chicago N.L., 1910.
6-game Series—68—New York A.L., vs. Los Angeles N.L., 1978.
7-game Series—91—New York A.L., vs. Pittsburgh N.L., 1960.
8-game Series—74—New York N.L., vs. Boston A.L., 1912.

Most Hits, Series, Both Clubs

4-game Series— 82—New York A.L., 45, Chicago N.L., 37, 1932.
5-game Series— 91—Philadelphia A.L., 56, Chicago N.L., 35, 1910.
6-game Series—120—Brooklyn N.L., 64, New York A.L., 56, 1953.
New York A.L., 68, Los Angeles N.L., 52, 1978.
7-game Series—151—New York A.L., 91, Pittsburgh N.L., 60, 1960.
8-game Series—135—Boston A.L., 71, Pittsburgh N.L., 64, 1903.

Fewest Hits, Series

4-game Series—17—Los Angeles N.L., vs. Baltimore A.L., 1966.

5-game Series—23—Baltimore A.L., vs. New York N.L., 1969.
6-game Series—32—Boston A.L., vs. Chicago N.L., 1918.
7-game Series—40—St. Louis N.L., vs. Kansas City A.L., 1985.
8-game Series—50—New York A.L., vs. New York N.L., 1921.

Fewest Hits, Series, Both Clubs

4-game Series— 41—Baltimore A.L., 24, Los Angeles N.L., 17, 1966.
5-game Series— 57—New York N.L., 32, Philadelphia A.L., 25, 1905.
6-game Series— 69—Chicago N.L., 37, Boston A.L., 32, 1918.
7-game Series— 92—Oakland A.L., 46, Cincinnati N.L., 46, 1972.
8-game Series—121—New York N.L., 71, New York A.L., 50, 1921.

Most Hits, Series, Pinch-Hitters

6—New York A.L., vs. Brooklyn N.L., 1947 (seven games).
New York A.L., vs. Pittsburgh N.L., 1960 (seven games).
Oakland A.L., vs. Cincinnati N.L., 1972 (seven games).
Baltimore A.L., vs. Pittsburgh N.L., 1979 (seven games).

Most Hits, Series, Pinch-Hitters, Both Clubs

11—New York A.L., 6, Brooklyn N.L., 5, 1947 (seven games).

Most Players One or More Hits, Each Game, Series

4—New York A.L., vs. Los Angeles N.L., 1978 (six games).

Most Consec. Hitless Innings, No Player Reaching Base, Series

9—Brooklyn N.L., vs. New York A.L., October 8, 1956 (9 innings—all 27 batters).

Game & Inning

Most Hits, Game

20—New York N.L., vs. New York A.L., October 7, 1921; St. Louis N.L., vs. Boston A.L., October 10, 1946.

Most Hits, Game, Losing Club

17—Pittsburgh N.L., vs. Baltimore A.L., October 13, 1979.

Most Hits, Game, Pinch-Hitters

3—Oakland A.L., vs. Cincinnati N.L., October 19, 1972, three singles in ninth inning.
Baltimore A.L., vs. Pittsburgh N.L., October 13, 1979, single in seventh inning, two doubles in eighth inning.

Most Hits, Game, Both Clubs

32—New York A.L., 19, Pittsburgh N.L., 13, October 6, 1960.

Fewest Hits, Game

0—Brooklyn N.L., vs. New York A.L., October 8, 1956.

Fewest Hits, Game, Both Clubs

5—New York A.L., 3, New York N.L., 2, October 6, 1921.
New York A.L., 5, Brooklyn N.L., 0, October 8, 1956.

Most Players, One or More Hits, Game

11—New York A.L., vs. St. Louis N.L., October 9, 1928.
New York A.L., vs. Pittsburgh N.L., October 6, 1960.

Most Players, One or More Hits, Game, Both Clubs

19—New York A.L., 11, Pittsburgh N.L., 8, October 6, 1960.

Most Players, One or More Hits and Runs, Game

9—New York A.L., vs. New York N.L., October 2, 1936.
New York A.L., vs. Pittsburgh N.L., October 6, 1960.

Most Hits, Inning

10—Philadelphia A.L., vs. Chicago N.L., October 12, 1929, seventh inning.

Most Hits, Inning, Pinch-Hitters

3—Oakland A.L., vs. Cincinnati N.L., October 19, 1972, ninth inning, three singles.

Most Hits, Inning, Both Clubs

12—Philadelphia A.L., 10, Chicago N.L., 2, October 12, 1929, seventh inning.

Most Consecutive Hits, Inning

8—New York N.L., vs. New York A.L., October 7, 1921, seventh inning. (Base on balls and sacrifice during streak.)

Most Consecutive Hits, Inning (Consecutive Plate Appearances)

6—Chicago N.L., vs. Detroit A.L., October 10, 1908, ninth inning, six singles.

Singles

Most Singles, Total Series

1,116—New York A.L., 33 Series, 187 games.

Most Singles, Series

4-game Series—31—New York A.L., vs. Chicago N.L., 1932.
5-game Series—46—New York N.L., vs. New York A.L., 1922.
6-game Series—57—New York A.L., vs. Los Angeles N.L., 1978.
7-game Series—64—New York A.L., vs. Pittsburgh N.L., 1960.
8-game Series—55—New York N.L., vs. Boston A.L., 1912.

Most Singles, Series, Both Clubs

4-game Series— 55—New York A.L., 31, Chicago N.L., 24, 1932.
5-game Series— 70—New York N.L., 39, Washington A.L., 31, 1933.
6-game Series— 95—New York A.L., 57, Los Angeles N.L., 38, 1978.
7-game Series—109—New York A.L., 64, Pittsburgh N.L., 45, 1960.
8-game Series— 96—Boston A.L. 49, Pittsburgh N.L., 47, 1903.

Fewest Singles, Series

4-game Series—13—Philadelphia A.L., vs. Boston N.L., 1914.
Los Angeles N.L., vs. Baltimore A.L., 1966.
5-game Series—19—Brooklyn N.L., vs. New York A.L., 1941.
Baltimore A.L., vs. New York A.L., 1969.
6-game Series—17—Philadelphia A.L., vs. St. Louis N.L., 1930.
7-game Series—27—Minnesota A.L., vs. Los Angeles N.L., 1965.
St. Louis N.L., vs. Kansas City A.L., 1985.
8-game Series—39—Boston A.L., vs. New York N.L., 1912.

Fewest Singles, Series, Both Clubs

4-game Series—29—Baltimore A.L., 16, Los Angeles N.L., 13, 1966.
5-game Series—40—New York N.L., 21, Baltimore A.L., 19, 1969.
6-game Series—42—St. Louis N.L., 25, Philadelphia A.L., 17, 1930.
7-game Series—66—St. Louis N.L., 33, Boston A.L., 33, 1967.
8-game Series—92—Cincinnati N.L., 47, Chicago A.L., 45, 1919.
New York N.L., 52, New York A.L., 40, 1921.

Most Singles, Game

16—New York A.L., vs. Los Angeles N.L., October 15, 1978.

Most Singles, Game, Both Clubs

24—New York A.L., 16, Los Angeles N.L., 8, October 15, 1978.

Fewest Singles, Game

0—Philadelphia A.L., vs. St. Louis N.L., October 1, 1930, 8 innings.
Philadelphia A.L., vs. St. Louis N.L., October 8, 1930, 8 innings.
Brooklyn N.L., vs. New York A.L., October 3, 1947, 8⅔ innings.
New York A.L., vs. Brooklyn N.L., October 4, 1952, 8 innings.
Brooklyn N.L., vs. New York A.L., October 8, 1956, 9 innings.
St. Louis N.L., vs. Boston A.L., October 5, 1967, 9 innings.

Fewest Singles, Game, Both Clubs

2—St. Louis N.L., 2, Philadelphia A.L., 0, October 8, 1930.
3—Chicago A.L., 2, Chicago N.L., 1, October 11, 1906.

Most Singles, Inning

7—Philadelphia A.L., vs. Chicago N.L., October 12, 1929, seventh inning.
New York N.L., vs. Washington A.L., October 4, 1933, sixth inning.
Brooklyn N.L., vs. New York A.L., October 8, 1949, sixth inning.

Most Singles, Inning, Both Clubs

8—Philadelphia A.L., 7, Chicago N.L., 1, October 12, 1929, seventh inning.
New York N.L., 7, Washington A.L., 1, October 4, 1933, sixth inning.
Brooklyn N.L., 7, New York A.L., 1, October 8, 1949, sixth inning.

Doubles

Most Doubles, Total Series

224—New York A.L., 33 Series, 187 games.

Most Doubles, Series

4-game Series— 9—Philadelphia A.L., vs. Boston N.L., 1914.
5-game Series—19—Philadelphia A.L., vs. Chicago N.L., 1910.
6-game Series—15—Philadelphia A.L., vs. New York N.L., 1911.
7-game Series—19—St. Louis N.L., vs. Boston A.L., 1946.
8-game Series—14—Boston A.L., vs. New York N.L., 1912.
New York N.L., vs. Boston A.L., 1912.

Most Doubles, Series, Both Clubs

4-game Series—15—Philadelphia A.L., 9, Boston N.L., 6, 1914.
5-game Series—30—Philadelphia A.L., 19, Chicago N.L., 11, 1910.
6-game Series—26—Philadelphia A.L., 15, New York N.L., 11, 1911.
7-game Series—29—Detroit A.L., 16, Pittsburgh N.L., 13, 1909.
8-game Series—28—Boston A.L., 14, New York N.L., 14, 1912.

Fewest Doubles, Series

4-game Series—3—Cincinnati N.L., vs. New York A.L., 1939.
New York A.L., vs. Philadelphia N.L., 1950.
New York N.L., vs. Cleveland A.L., 1954.
Los Angeles N.L., vs. New York A.L., 1963.
New York A.L., vs. Los Angeles N.L., 1963.
Baltimore A.L., vs. Los Angeles N.L., 1966.
Los Angeles N.L., vs. Baltimore A.L., 1966.
New York A.L., vs. Cincinnati N.L., 1976.
5-game Series—1—Detroit A.L., vs. Chicago N.L., 1907.
Baltimore A.L., vs. New York N.L., 1969.
6-game Series—2—Boston A.L., vs. Chicago N.L., 1918.
New York N.L., vs. New York A.L., 1923.
7-game Series—3—Baltimore A.L., vs. Pittsburgh N.L., 1971.
8-game Series—4—Boston A.L., vs. Pittsburgh N.L., 1903.

Fewest Doubles, Series, Both Clubs

4-game Series— 6—Los Angeles N.L., 3, New York A.L., 3, 1963.
Baltimore A.L., 3, Los Angeles N.L., 3, 1966.
5-game Series— 6—Philadelphia N.L., 4, Boston A.L., 2, 1915.
6-game Series— 7—Chicago N.L., 5, Boston A.L., 2, 1918.
7-game Series—11—St. Louis N.L., 7, Detroit A.L., 4, 1968.
8-game Series—11—Pittsburgh N.L., 7, Boston A.L., 4, 1903.

Most Doubles, Game

8—Chicago A.L., vs. Chicago N.L., October 13, 1906.
Pittsburgh N.L., vs. Washington A.L., October 15, 1925.

Most Doubles, Game, Both Clubs

11—Chicago A.L., 8, Chicago N.L., 3, October 13, 1906.

Most Doubles, Inning

3—Chicago A.L., vs. Chicago N.L., October 13, 1906, fourth inning.
Philadelphia A.L., vs. Chicago N.L., October 18, 1910, seventh inning.
Philadelphia A.L., vs. New York N.L., October 24, 1911, fourth inning, consecutive.
Pittsburgh N.L., vs. Washington A.L., October 15, 1925, eighth inning.
St. Louis N.L., vs. Detroit A.L., October 9, 1934, third inning.
Brooklyn N.L., vs. New York A.L., October 2, 1947, second inning.
Brooklyn N.L., vs. New York A.L., October 5, 1947, third inning, consecutive.
New York A.L., vs. Brooklyn N.L., October 8, 1949, fourth inning.
Chicago A.L., vs. Los Angeles N.L., October 1, 1959, third inning.

Triples

Most Triples, Total Series

47—New York A.L., 33 Series, 187 games.

Most Triples, Series

4-game Series— 3—Cincinnati N.L., vs. New York A.L., 1976.
5-game Series— 6—Boston A.L., vs. Brooklyn N.L., 1916.
6-game Series— 4—New York N.L., vs. Chicago A.L., 1917.
New York A.L., vs. New York N.L., 1923.
New York A.L., vs. Brooklyn N.L., 1953.
7-game Series— 5—St. Louis N.L., vs. Detroit A.L., 1934.
New York A.L., vs. Brooklyn N.L., 1947.
8-game Series—16—Boston A.L., vs. Pittsburgh N.L., 1903.

Most Triples, Series, Both Clubs

4-game Series— 4—Cincinnati N.L., 3, New York A.L., 1, 1976.
5-game Series—11—Boston A.L., 6, Brooklyn N.L., 5, 1916.
6-game Series— 7—New York A.L., 4, New York N.L., 3, 1923.
7-game Series— 6—St. Louis N.L., 5, Detroit A.L., 1, 1934.
New York A.L., 5, Brooklyn N.L., 1, 1947.
Detroit A.L., 3, St. Louis N.L., 3, 1968.
8-game Series—25—Boston A.L., 16, Pittsburgh N.L., 9, 1903.

Fewest Triples, Series

4-game Series—0—Held by many clubs.
5-game Series—0—Held by many clubs. Last Clubs—Detroit A.L., 1984; San Diego N.L., 1984.
6-game Series—0—Held by many clubs. Last Club—Philadelphia N.L., 1980.
7-game Series—0—Held by many clubs. Last Club—St. Louis N.L., 1987.
8-game Series—1—New York A.L., vs. New York N.L., 1921.

Fewest Triples, Series, Both Clubs

4-game Series—1—St. Louis N.L., 1, New York A.L., 0, 1928.
Cleveland A.L., 1, New York N.L., 0, 1954.
Baltimore A.L., 1, Los Angeles N.L., 0, 1966.
5-game Series—0—New York N.L., 0, Philadelphia A.L., 0, 1905.
New York N.L., 0, Washington A.L., 0, 1933.
New York N.L., 0, Baltimore, A.L., 0, 1969.
Detroit A.L., 0, San Diego N.L., 0, 1984.
6-game Series—0—Cleveland A.L., 0, Boston N.L., 0, 1948.
New York N.L., 0, Los Angeles N.L., 0, 1978.
7-game Series—0—St. Louis N.L., 0, Philadelphia A.L., 0, 1931.
8-game Series—5—New York N.L., 4, New York A.L., 1, 1921.

Most Triples, Game, Nine Innings

5—Boston A.L., vs. Pittsburgh N.L., October 7, 1903, October 10, 1903.

Most Triples, Game, Nine Innings, Both Clubs

7—Boston A.L., 5, Pittsburgh N.L., 2, October 10, 1903.

Most Triples, Inning

2—Boston A.L., vs. Pittsburgh N.L., October 7, 1903, eighth inning.
Boston A.L., vs. Pittsburgh N.L., October 10, 1903, first inning, also fourth inning.
Boston A.L., vs. New York N.L., October 12, 1912, third inning.
Philadelphia A.L., vs. New York N.L., October 7, 1913, fourth inning.
Boston A.L., vs. Chicago N.L., September 6, 1918, ninth inning.
New York A.L., vs. Brooklyn N.L., October 1, 1947, third inning.
New York A.L., vs. Brooklyn N.L., September 30, 1953, first inning.
Detroit A.L., vs. St. Louis N.L., October 7, 1968, fourth inning.

Home Runs
Series

Most Home Runs, Total Series

181—New York A.L., 33 Series, 187 games.

Most Grand Slams, Total Series

7—New York A.L., 33 Series, 187 games.

Most Home Runs, Pinch-Hitters, Total Series

5—New York A.L., 33 Series, 187 games.

Most Home Runs, Series

4-game Series— 9—New York A.L., vs. St. Louis N.L., 1928.
5-game Series—10—Baltimore A.L., vs. Cincinnati N.L., 1970.
6-game Series— 9—New York A.L., vs. Brooklyn N.L., 1953.
Los Angeles N.L., vs. New York A.L., 1977.
7-game Series—12—New York A.L., vs. Brooklyn N.L., 1956.
8-game Series— 2—Boston A.L., vs. Pittsburgh N.L., 1903.
New York A.L., vs. New York N.L., 1921.
New York N.L., vs. New York A.L., 1921.

Most Home Runs, Series, Both Clubs

4-game Series—11—New York A.L., 8, Chicago N.L., 3, 1932.
5-game Series—15—Baltimore A.L., 10, Cincinnati N.L., 5, 1970.
6-game Series—17—New York A.L., 9, Brooklyn N.L., 8, 1953.
Los Angeles N.L., 9, New York A.L., 8, 1977.
7-game Series—17—Brooklyn N.L., 9, New York A.L., 8, 1955.
8-game Series— 4—New York N.L., 2, New York A.L., 2, 1921.

Most Grand Slams, Series

2—New York A.L., vs. Brooklyn N.L., 1956.
Minnesota A.L., vs. St. Louis N.L., 1987.

Most Grand Slams, Series, Both Clubs

2—New York A.L., 2, Brooklyn N.L., 0, 1956.
St. Louis N.L., 1, New York A.L., 1, 1964.
Minnesota A.L., 2, St. Louis N.L., 0, 1987.

Most Home Runs, Pinch-Hitters, Series

2—Los Angeles N.L., vs. Chicago A.L., 1959.
Boston A.L., vs. Cincinnati N.L., 1975.

Most Home Runs, Pinch-Hitters, Series, Both Clubs

2—New York N.L., 1, Cleveland A.L., 1, 1954.
Los Angeles N.L., 2, Chicago A.L., 0, 1959.
Boston A.L., 2, Cincinnati N.L., 0, 1975.

Most Home Runs, Series, by Pitchers as Batters

2—New York N.L., vs. Washington A.L., 1924.

Most Home Runs, Series, by Pitchers as Batters, Both Clubs

2—New York N.L., 2, Washington A.L., 0, 1924.
Boston A.L., 1, St. Louis N.L., 1, 1967.
Detroit A.L., 1, St. Louis N.L., 1, 1968.

Fewest Home Runs, Series

4-game Series—0—Held by many clubs.
5-game Series—0—Held by many clubs.
6-game Series—0—Chicago N.L., vs. Chicago A.L., 1906.
Chicago A.L., vs. Chicago N.L., 1906.
New York N.L., vs. Philadelphia A.L., 1911.
Boston A.L., vs. Chicago N.L., 1918.
Chicago N.L., vs. Boston A.L., 1918.
7-game Series—0—Brooklyn N.L., vs. Cleveland A.L., 1920.
8-game Series—0—Cincinnati N.L., vs. Chicago A.L., 1919.

Fewest Home Runs, Series, Both Clubs

4-game Series—1—Boston A.L., 1, Philadelphia A.L., 0, 1914.
5-game Series—0—New York N.L., 0, Philadelphia A.L., 0, 1905.
Chicago N.L., 0, Detroit A.L., 0, 1907.
6-game Series—0—Chicago A.L., 0, Chicago N.L., 0, 1906.
Boston A.L., 0, Chicago N.L., 0, 1918.
7-game Series—2—Cleveland A.L., 2, Brooklyn N.L., 0, 1920.
8-game Series—1—Chicago A.L., 1, Cincinnati N.L., 0, 1919.

Game

Most Home Runs, Game

5—New York A.L., vs. St. Louis N.L., October 9, 1928.

Most Home Runs, Game, Both Clubs

6—New York A.L., 4, Chicago N.L., 2, October 1, 1932.
New York A.L., 4. Brooklyn N.L., 2, October 4, 1953.
Cincinnati N.L., 3, Boston A.L., 3, October 14, 1975, 10 innings.

Most Consecutive Games, Total Series, One or More Home Runs

9—New York A.L., last 2 games vs. Chicago N.L. in 1932 (7 home runs), all 6 games vs. New York N.L. in 1936 (7 home runs) and first game vs. New York N.L. in 1937 (1 home run); total 15 home runs.
New York A.L., all 7 games vs. Brooklyn N.L. in 1952 (10 home runs) and first 2 games vs. Brooklyn N.L. in 1953 (4 home runs); total 14 home runs.

Most Consecutive Games, Series, One or More Home Runs

7—Washington A.L., vs. Pittsburgh N.L., October 7 to 15, inclusive, 1925, eight home runs.
New York A.L., vs. Brooklyn N.L., October 1 to 7, inclusive, 1952, 10 home runs.

Inning

Most Home Runs, Inning (Two Home Runs, 27 times)

3—Boston A.L., vs. St. Louis N.L., October 11, 1967, fourth inning, Yastrzemski, Smith, Petrocelli, two consecutive.
2—New York N.L., vs. New York A.L., October 11, 1921, second inning.
Washington A.L., vs. Pittsburgh N.L., October 11, 1925, third inning.
New York A.L., vs. St. Louis N.L., October 9, 1928, seventh inning.
New York A.L., vs. St. Louis N.L., October 9, 1928, eighth inning.
Philadelphia A.L., vs. Chicago N.L., October 12, 1929, seventh inning.
New York A.L., vs. Chicago N.L., October 1, 1932, fifth inning.
New York A.L., vs. Chicago N.L., October 2, 1932, ninth inning.
New York A.L., vs. Cincinnati N.L., October 7, 1939, fifth inning.
New York A.L., vs. Cincinnati N.L., October 8, 1939, seventh inning.
Detroit A.L., vs. Cincinnati N.L., October 4, 1940, seventh inning.
Brooklyn N.L., vs. New York A.L., October 7, 1949, ninth inning.
Brooklyn N.L., vs. New York A.L., September 30, 1953, sixth inning.
Brooklyn N.L., vs. New York A.L., October 1, 1955, fourth inning.

Milwaukee N.L., vs. New York A.L., October 6, 1957, fourth inning.
Milwaukee N.L., vs. New York A.L., October 2, 1958, first inning.
New York A.L., vs. Milwaukee N.L., October 2, 1958, ninth inning.
Los Angeles N.L. vs. Chicago A.L., October 2, 1959, seventh inning.
New York A.L., vs. St. Louis N.L., October 14, 1964, sixth inning.
New York A.L., vs. St. Louis N.L., October 15, 1964, ninth inning.
Baltimore A.L., vs. Los Angeles N.L., October 5, 1966, first inning.
Baltimore A.L., vs. New York N.L., October 16, 1969, third inning.
Oakland A.L., vs. New York N.L., October 21, 1973, third inning.
Cincinnati N.L., vs. Boston A.L., October 14, 1975, fifth inning.
New York A.L., vs. Los Angeles N.L., October 16, 1977, eighth inning.
Los Angeles N.L., vs. New York A.L., October 10, 1978, second inning.
Los Angeles N.L., vs. New York A.L., October 25, 1981, seventh inning.
Boston A.L., vs. New York N.L., October 27, 1986, second inning.

Most Home Runs, Inning, Both Clubs
3—New York N.L., 2, New York A.L., 1, October 11, 1921, second inning.
Boston A.L., 3, St. Louis N.L. 0, October 11, 1967, fourth inning.

Most Consecutive Home Runs, Inning (10 times)
2—Washington A.L., vs. Pittsburgh N.L., October 11, 1925, third inning.
New York A.L., vs. St. Louis N.L., October 9, 1928, seventh inning.
New York A.L., vs. Chicago N.L., October 1, 1932, fifth inning.
New York A.L., vs. St. Louis N.L., October 14, 1964, sixth inning.
Baltimore A.L., vs. Los Angeles N.L., October 5, 1966, first inning.
Boston A.L., vs. St. Louis N.L., October 11, 1967, fourth inning.
Cincinnati N.L., vs. Boston A.L., October 14, 1975, fifth inning.
New York A.L., vs. Los Angeles N.L., October 16, 1977, eighth inning.
Los Angeles N.L., vs. New York A.L., October 25, 1981, seventh inning.
Boston A.L., vs. New York N.L., October 27, 1986, second inning.

Most Times Two Home Runs, Inning, Total Series
10—New York A.L., 1928 (2), 1932 (2), 1939 (2), 1958 (1), 1964 (2), 1977 (1).

Most Times Two Home Runs, Inning, Series
2—New York A.L., 1928, 1932, 1939, 1964.

Most Times Hitting Two Home Runs in Inning, Game
2—New York A.L., vs. St. Louis N.L., October 9, 1928, seventh and eighth innings.

Total Bases

Most Total Bases, Total Series
2,429—New York A.L., 33 Series, 187 games.

Most Total Bases, Series
4-game Series— 75—New York A.L., vs. Chicago N.L., 1932.
5-game Series— 87—Baltimore A.L., vs. Cincinnati N.L., 1970.
6-game Series—103—Brooklyn N.L., vs. New York A.L., 1953.
7-game Series—142—New York A.L., vs. Pittsburgh N.L., 1960.
8-game Series—113—Boston A.L., vs. Pittsburgh N.L., 1903.

Most Total Bases, Series, Both Clubs
4-game Series—133—New York A.L., 75, Chicago N.L., 58, 1932.
5-game Series—145—Baltimore A.L., 87, Cincinnati N.L., 58, 1970.
6-game Series—200—Brooklyn N.L., 103, New York A.L., 97, 1953.
7-game Series—225—New York A.L., 142, Pittsburgh N.L., 83, 1960.
8-game Series—205—Boston A.L., 113, Pittsburgh N.L., 92, 1903.

Fewest Total Bases, Series
4-game Series—23—Los Angeles N.L., vs. Baltimore A.L., 1966.
5-game Series—30—Philadelphia A.L., vs. New York N.L., 1905.
6-game Series—40—Boston A.L., vs. Chicago N.L., 1918.
7-game Series—51—Brooklyn N.L., vs. Cleveland A.L., 1920.
8-game Series—65—New York A.L., vs. New York N.L., 1921.

Fewest Total Bases, Series, Both Clubs
4-game Series— 64—Baltimore A.L., 41, Los Angeles N.L., 23, 1966.
5-game Series— 69—New York N.L., 39, Philadelphia A.L., 30, 1905.
6-game Series— 84—Chicago N.L., 44, Boston A.L., 40, 1918.
7-game Series—123—Cleveland A.L., 72, Brooklyn N.L., 51, 1920.
8-game Series—163—New York N.L., 98, New York A.L., 65, 1921.

Most Total Bases, Game
32—New York A.L., vs. St. Louis N.L., October 9, 1928.
New York A.L., vs. Chicago N.L., October 2, 1932.

Most Total Bases, Game, Both Clubs
47—New York A.L., 27, Brooklyn N.L., 20, October 4, 1953.

Fewest Total Bases, Game
0—Brooklyn N.L., vs. New York A.L., October 8, 1956.

Fewest Total Bases, Game, Both Clubs
5—New York A.L., 3, New York N.L., 2, October 6, 1921.

Most Total Bases, Inning
17—Philadelphia A.L., vs. Chicago N.L., October 12, 1929, seventh inning.

Most Total Bases, Inning, Both Clubs
21—Philadelphia A.L., 17, Chicago N.L., 4, October 12, 1929, seventh inning.

Long Hits

Most Long Hits, Total Series
452—New York A.L., 33 Series, 187 games.
(224 doubles, 47 triples, 181 homers).

Most Long Hits, Series
4-game Series—17—Cincinnati N.L., vs. New York A.L., 1976.
5-game Series—21—Philadelphia A.L., vs. Chicago N.L., 1910.
6-game Series—22—Brooklyn N.L., vs. New York A.L., 1953.
7-game Series—27—New York A.L., vs. Pittsburgh N.L., 1960.
8-game Series—22—Boston A.L., vs. Pittsburgh N.L., 1903.

Most Long Hits, Series, Both Clubs
4-game Series—27—New York A.L., 14, Chicago N.L., 13, 1932.
5-game Series—33—Philadelphia A.L., 21, Chicago N.L., 12, 1910.
6-game Series—41—Brooklyn N.L., 22, New York A.L., 19, 1953.
7-game Series—42—New York A.L., 27, Pittsburgh N.L., 15, 1960.
St. Louis N.L., 23, Milwaukee A.L., 19, 1982.
8-game Series—40—Boston A.L., 21, New York N.L., 19, 1912.

Fewest Long Hits, Series
4-game Series— 4—Cincinnati N.L., vs. New York A.L., 1939.
Los Angeles N.L., vs. Baltimore A.L., 1966.
5-game Series— 3—Detroit A.L., vs. Chicago N.L., 1907.
6-game Series— 5—Boston A.L., vs. Chicago N.L., 1918.
7-game Series— 6—Brooklyn N.L., vs. Cleveland A.L., 1920.
8-game Series—10—New York A.L., vs. New York N.L., 1921.

Fewest Long Hits, Series, Both Clubs
4-game Series—12—Baltimore A.L., 8, Los Angeles N.L., 4, 1966.
5-game Series—10—Chicago N.L., 7, Detroit A.L., 3, 1907.
6-game Series—11—Chicago N.L., 6, Boston A.L., 5, 1918.
7-game Series—19—Cleveland A.L., 13, Brooklyn N.L., 6, 1920.
8-game Series—29—New York N.L., 19, New York A.L., 10, 1921.

Most Long Hits, Game
9—Pittsburgh N.L., vs. Washington A.L., October 15, 1925; 8 doubles, one triple.

Most Long Hits, Game, Both Clubs
11—Chicago A.L., 8 (8 doubles), Chicago N.L., 3 (3 doubles), October 13, 1906.

Pittsburgh N.L., 9 (8 doubles, one triple), Washington A.L., 2 (one double, one home run), October 15, 1925.

New York A.L., 7 (4 doubles, 1 triple, 2 home runs), Cincinnati N.L., 4 (2 doubles, 2 home runs), October 9, 1961.

Longest Extra-Inning Game, Without a Long Hit

12 innings—Chicago N.L., vs. Detroit A.L., October 8, 1907.
Detroit A.L., vs. Chicago N.L., October 8, 1907.

Longest Extra-Inning Game, Without a Long Hit, Both Clubs

12 innings—Chicago N.L., 0, Detroit N.L., 0, October 8, 1907.

Extra Bases On Long Hits

Most Extra Bases on Long Hits, Total Series

861—New York A.L., 33 Series, 187 games.
(224 on doubles, 94 on triples, 543 on homers) .

Most Extra Bases on Long Hits, Series

4-game Series—34—New York A.L., vs. St. Louis N.L., 1928.
5-game Series—37—Baltimore A.L., vs. Cincinnati N.L., 1970.
6-game Series—41—New York A.L., vs. Brooklyn N.L., 1953.
7-game Series—51—New York A.L., vs. Pittsburgh N.L., 1960.
8-game Series—42—Boston A.L., vs. Pittsburgh N.L., 1903.

Most Extra Bases on Long Hits, Series, Both Clubs

4-game Series—51—New York A.L., 30, Chicago N.L., 21, 1932.
5-game Series—60—Baltimore A.L., 37, Cincinnati N.L., 23, 1970.
6-game Series—80—New York A.L., 41, Brooklyn N.L., 39, 1953.
7-game Series—74—New York A.L., 51, Pittsburgh N.L., 23, 1960.
8-game Series—70—Boston A.L., 42, Pittsburgh N.L., 28, 1903.

Fewest Extra Bases on Long Hits, Series

4-game Series— 5—Cincinnati N.L., vs. New York A.L., 1939.
5-game Series— 5—Philadelphia A.L., vs. New York N.L., 1905.
Detroit A.L., vs. Chicago N.L., 1907.
Detroit A.L., vs. Chicago N.L., 1908.
6-game Series— 7—Chicago N.L., vs. Boston A.L., 1918.
7-game Series— 7—Brooklyn N.L., vs. Cleveland A.L., 1920.
8-game Series—15—New York A.L., vs. New York N.L., 1921.

Fewest Extra Bases on Long Hits, Series, Both Clubs

4-game Series—19—New York A.L., 11, Philadelphia N.L., 8, 1950.
5-game Series—12—New York N.L., 7, Philadelphia A.L., 5, 1905.
6-game Series—15—Boston A.L., 8, Chicago N.L., 7, 1918.
7-game Series—26—Cleveland A.L., 19, Brooklyn N.L., 7, 1920.
8-game Series—42—New York N.L., 27, New York A.L., 15, 1921.

Runs Batted In

Most Runs Batted In, Total Series

791—New York, A.L., 33 Series, 187 games.

Most Runs Batted In, Series

4-game Series—36—New York A.L., vs. Chicago N.L., 1932.
5-game Series—32—Baltimore A.L., vs. Cincinnati N.L., 1970.
6-game Series—41—New York A.L., vs. New York N.L., 1936.
7-game Series—54—New York A.L., vs. Pittsburgh N.L., 1960.
8-game Series—35—Boston A.L., vs. Pittsburgh N.L., 1903.

Most Runs Batted In, Series, Both Clubs

4-game Series—52—New York A.L., 36, Chicago N.L., 16, 1932.
5-game Series—52—Baltimore A.L., 32, Cincinnati N.L., 20, 1970.
6-game Series—61—New York A.L., 41, New York N.L., 20, 1936.
7-game Series—80—New York A.L., 54, Pittsburgh N.L., 26, 1960.
8-game Series—58—Boston A.L., 35, Pittsburgh N.L., 23, 1903.

Fewest Runs Batted In, Series

4-game Series— 2—Los Angeles N.L. vs. Baltimore A.L., 1966.
5-game Series— 2—Philadelphia A.L., vs. New York N.L., 1905.
6-game Series— 6—Boston A.L., vs. Chicago N.L., 1918.
7-game Series— 8—Brooklyn N.L., vs. Cleveland A.L., 1920.
8-game Series—17—Chicago A.L., vs. Cincinnati N.L., 1919.

Fewest Runs Batted In, Series, Both Clubs

4-game Series—12—Los Angeles N.L., 2, Baltimore A.L., 10, 1966.
5-game Series—15—Philadelphia A.L., 2, New York N.L., 13, 1905.
6-game Series—16—Boston A.L., 6, Chicago N.L., 10, 1918.
7-game Series—26—Brooklyn N.L., 8, Cleveland A.L., 18, 1920.
8-game Series—46—Boston A.L., 21, New York N.L., 25, 1912.

Most Runs Batted In, Game

18—New York A.L., vs. New York N.L., October 2, 1936.

Most Runs Batted In, Game, Both Clubs

21—New York A.L., 18, New York N.L., 3, October 2, 1936.
Brooklyn N.L., 13, New York A.L., 8, October 5, 1956.

Fewest Runs Batted In, Game

0—Held by many clubs.

Most Runs Batted In, Inning

10—Philadelphia A.L., vs. Chicago N.L., October 12, 1929, seventh inning.
Detroit A.L., vs. St. Louis N.L., October 9, 1968, third inning.

Most Runs Batted In, Inning, Both Clubs

11—Philadelphia A.L., 10, Chicago N.L., 1, October 12, 1929, seventh inning.
Brooklyn N.L., 6, New York A.L., 5, October 5, 1956, second inning.

Fewest Runs Batted In, Game, Both Clubs

0—New York N.L., 0, Philadelphia A.L., 0, October 13, 1905.
New York N.L., 0, New York A.L., 0, October 13, 1921.
Chicago A.L., 0, Los Angeles N.L., 0, October 6, 1959.
New York A.L., 0, San Francisco N.L., 0, October 16, 1962.

Bases On Balls

Most Bases on Balls, Total Series

645—New York A.L., 33 Series, 187 games.

Most Bases on Balls, Series

4-game Series—23—New York A.L., vs. Chicago N.L., 1932.
5-game Series—24—New York A.L., vs. Cincinnati N.L., 1961.
6-game Series—33—New York A.L., vs. Los Angeles N.L., 1981.
7-game Series—38—New York A.L., vs. Brooklyn N.L., 1947.
8-game Series—27—New York A.L., vs. New York N.L., 1921.

Most Bases on Balls, Series, Both Clubs

4-game Series—34—New York A.L., 23, Chicago N.L., 11, 1932.
5-game Series—37—New York A.L., 23, Brooklyn N.L., 14, 1941.
6-game Series—53—New York A.L., 33, Los Angeles N.L., 20, 1981.
7-game Series—68—New York A.L., 38, Brooklyn N.L., 30, 1947.
8-game Series—49—New York A.L., 27, New York N.L., 22, 1921.

Fewest Bases on Balls, Series

4-game Series— 4—Pittsburgh N.L., vs. New York A.L., 1927.
5-game Series— 5—Philadelphia A.L., vs. New York N.L., 1905.
6-game Series— 4—Philadelphia A.L., vs. New York N.L., 1911.
7-game Series— 9—St. Louis N.L., vs. Philadelphia A.L., 1931.
8-game Series—13—Boston A.L., vs. Pittsburgh N.L., 1903.

Fewest Bases on Balls, Series, Both Clubs

4-game Series—15—New York A.L., 9, Cincinnati N.L., 6, 1939.
5-game Series—15—New York N.L., 8, Philadelphia A.L., 7, 1913.
6-game Series—17—Chicago A.L., 11, New York N.L., 6, 1917.
7-game Series—30—New York A.L., 18, Pittsburgh N.L., 12, 1960.
8-game Series—27—Pittsburgh N.L., 14, Boston A.L., 13, 1903.

Most Bases on Balls, Game

11—Brooklyn N.L., vs. New York A.L., October 5, 1956.
New York A.L., vs. Milwaukee N.L., October 5, 1957.
Detroit A.L., vs. San Diego N.L., October 12, 1984.

Most Bases on Balls, Game, Both Clubs

19—New York A.L. 11, Milwaukee N.L. 8, October 5, 1957.

Longest Game, No Bases on Balls

12 innings—St. Louis N.L. vs. Detroit A.L., October 4, 1934.

Fewest Bases on Balls, Game, Both Clubs

0—Philadelphia A.L., 0, New York N.L., 0, October 16, 1911.
New York N.L., 0, Chicago A.L., 0, October 10, 1917.
New York N.L., 0, New York A.L., 0, October 9, 1921.
Boston A.L., 0, St. Louis N.L., 0, October 7, 1967.
Philadelphia N.L., 0, Baltimore A.L., 0, October 11, 1983.

Most Bases on Balls, Inning

5—New York A.L., vs. St. Louis N.L., October 6, 1926, fifth inning.

Most Bases on Balls, Inning, Both Clubs

6—New York A.L., 3, New York N.L., 3, October 7, 1921, third inning.
New York A.L., 5, St. Louis N.L., 1, October 6, 1926, fifth inning.

Most Bases on Balls, Inning, Pinch-Hitters

2—New York A.L., vs. New York N.L., October 15, 1923, eighth inning.

Baltimore A.L. vs. Philadelphia N.L., October 15, 1983, sixth inning.

Strikeouts

Most Strikeouts, Total Series

986—New York A.L., 33 Series, 187 games.

Most Strikeouts, Series

4-game Series—37—New York A.L., vs. Los Angeles N.L., 1963.
5-game Series—50—Chicago N.L., vs. Philadelphia A.L., 1929.
6-game Series—49—St. Louis A.L., vs. St. Louis N.L., 1944.
　　　　　　　　　　Kansas City A.L., vs. Philadelphia N.L., 1980.
7-game Series—62—Oakland A.L., vs. New York N.L., 1973.
8-game Series—45—Pittsburgh N.L., vs. Boston A.L., 1903.

Most Strikeouts, Series, Both Clubs

4-game Series—62—New York A.L., 37, Los Angeles N.L., 25, 1963.
5-game Series—77—Chicago N.L., 50, Philadelphia A.L., 27, 1929.
6-game Series—92—St. Louis A.L., 49, St. Louis N.L., 43, 1944.
7-game Series—99—Detroit A.L., 59, St. Louis N.L., 40, 1968.
8-game Series—82—New York A.L., 44, New York N.L., 38, 1921.

Fewest Strikeouts, Series

4-game Series— 7—Pittsburgh N.L., vs. New York A.L., 1927.
5-game Series—15—New York N.L., vs. New York A.L., 1922.
6-game Series—14—Chicago N.L., vs. Boston A.L., 1918.
7-game Series—20—Brooklyn N.L., vs. Cleveland A.L., 1920.
8-game Series—22—Cincinnati N.L., vs. Chicago A.L., 1919.

Fewest Strikeouts, Series, Both Clubs

4-game Series—32—New York A.L., 25, Pittsburgh N.L., 7, 1927.
　　　　　　　　　　Cincinnati N.L., 16, New York A.L., 16, 1976.
5-game Series—35—New York N.L., 19, Philadelphia A.L., 16, 1913.
　　　　　　　　　　New York N.L., 20, New York A.L., 15, 1922.
6-game Series—35—Boston A.L., 21, Chicago N.L., 14, 1918.
7-game Series—41—Cleveland A.L., 21, Brooklyn N.L., 20, 1920.
8-game Series—52—Chicago A.L., 30, Cincinnati N.L., 22, 1919.

Most Strikeouts, Game

17—Detroit A.L., vs. St. Louis N.L., October 2, 1968.

Most Strikeouts, Game, Pinch-Hitters

4—St. Louis A.L., vs. St. Louis N.L., October 8, 1944, and October 9, 1944, both consecutive.

Most Consecutive Strikeouts, Game

6—Chicago A.L., vs. Cincinnati N.L., October 6, 1919; 3 in second inning; 3 in third inning.
Los Angeles N.L., vs. Baltimore A.L., October 5, 1966; 3 in fourth inning; 3 in fifth inning.
Kansas City A.L., vs. St. Louis N.L., October 24, 1985; 3 in sixth inning; 3 in seventh inning.

Most Strikeouts, Game, Nine Innings, Both Clubs

25—New York A.L., 15, Los Angeles N.L., 10, October 2, 1963.

Most Strikeouts, Extra-Inning Game, Both Clubs

25—Oakland A.L., 15, New York N.L., 10, October 14, 1973, 12 innings.

Fewest Strikeouts, Game

0—Chicago N.L., vs. Boston A.L., September 6, 1918 (did not bat in ninth inning).
Chicago N.L., vs. Boston A.L., September 9, 1918.
New York N.L., vs. New York N.L., October 6, 1921 (did not bat in ninth inning).
New York A.L., vs. Philadelphia N.L., October 4, 1950.
Brooklyn N.L., vs. New York A.L., October 3, 1952.
Pittsburgh N.L., vs. New York A.L., October 6, 1960.
Pittsburgh N.L., vs. New York A.L., October 13, 1960.
New York A.L., vs. Pittsburgh N.L., October 13, 1960.

Fewest Strikeouts, Game, Both Clubs

0—Pittsburgh N.L., 0, New York A.L., 0, October 13, 1960.

Most Consec. Strikeouts, Two Successive Games, Pinch-Hitters

8—St. Louis A.L., vs. St. Louis N.L., October 8, 1944 (4), October 9, 1944 (4).

Most Strikeouts, Inning

4—Detroit A.L., vs. Chicago N.L., October 14, 1908, first inning.

Most Strikeouts, Inning, Pinch-Hitters

3—St. Louis A.L., vs. St. Louis N.L., October 8, 1944, ninth inning.

Most Strikeouts, Inning, Both Clubs

6—Cincinnati N.L., 3, Oakland A.L., 3, October 18, 1972, fifth inning.
Kansas City A.L., 3, St. Louis N.L., 3, October 24, 1985, seventh inning.

Sacrifice Hits

Most Sacrifices, Total Series

108—New York A.L., 33 Series, 187 games.

Most Sacrifices, Series

4-game Series— 8—New York N.L., vs. Cleveland A.L., 1954.
5-game Series—12—Boston A.L., vs. Brooklyn N.L., 1916.
6-game Series—14—Chicago N.L., vs. Chicago A.L., 1906.
7-game Series—12—Pittsburgh N.L., vs. Detroit A.L., 1909.
　　　　　　　　　　St. Louis N.L., vs. New York A.L., 1926.
8-game Series—13—Cincinnati N.L., vs. Chicago A.L., 1919.

Most Sacrifices, Series, Both Clubs

4-game Series—12—New York A.L., 6, Pittsburgh N.L., 6, 1927.
5-game Series—18—Boston A.L., 12, Brooklyn N.L., 6, 1916.
6-game Series—20—Chicago N.L., 14, Chicago A.L., 6, 1906.
7-game Series—22—St. Louis N.L., 12, New York A.L., 10, 1926.
8-game Series—20—Cincinnati N.L., 13, Chicago A.L., 7, 1919.

Fewest Sacrifices, Series

4-game Series—0—Cincinnati N.L., vs. New York A.L., 1976.
　　　　　　　　　　New York A.L., vs. Cincinnati N.L., 1976.
5-game Series—0—New York N.L., vs. New York A.L., 1937.
　　　　　　　　　　Brooklyn N.L., vs. New York A.L., 1941.
　　　　　　　　　　New York A.L., vs. Brooklyn N.L., 1941.
　　　　　　　　　　Cincinnati N.L., vs. New York A.L., 1961.
　　　　　　　　　　Baltimore A.L., vs. Philadelphia N.L., 1983.
　　　　　　　　　　Philadelphia N.L., vs. Baltimore A.L., 1983.
6-game Series—0—New York N.L., vs. New York A.L., 1923.
　　　　　　　　　　New York A.L., vs. New York N.L., 1951.
　　　　　　　　　　Los Angeles N.L., vs. New York A.L., 1977.
7-game Series—1—New York A.L., vs. Brooklyn N.L., 1955.
　　　　　　　　　　St. Louis N.L., vs. Detroit A.L., 1968.
　　　　　　　　　　Baltimore A.L., vs. Pittsburgh N.L., 1979.
　　　　　　　　　　St. Louis N.L., vs. Milwaukee A.L., 1982.
　　　　　　　　　　Milwaukee A.L., vs. St. Louis N.L., 1982.
　　　　　　　　　　Minnesota A.L., vs. St. Louis N.L., 1987.
8-game Series—3—Pittsburgh N.L., vs. Boston A.L., 1903.

Fewest Sacrifices, Series, Both Clubs

4-game Series—0—Cincinnati N.L., 0, New York A.L., 0, 1976.
5-game Series—0—New York A.L., 0, Brooklyn N.L., 0, 1941.
　　　　　　　　　　Baltimore A.L., 0, Philadelphia N.L., 0, 1983.
6-game Series—2—New York N.L., 2, New York A.L., 0, 1951.
　　　　　　　　　　New York A.L., 1, Los Angeles N.L., 1, 1978.
7-game Series—2—St. Louis N.L., 1, Milwaukee A.L., 1, 1982.
8-game Series—9—Boston A.L., 6, Pittsburgh N.L., 3, 1903.

Most Sacrifices, Game

5—Chicago N.L., vs. Chicago A.L., October 12, 1906 (all sacrifice hits).
Chicago N.L., vs. Detroit A.L., October 10, 1908 (all sacrifice hits).
Pittsburgh N.L., vs. Detroit A.L., October 16, 1909 (4 sacrifice hits and 1 sacrifice fly).
New York N.L., vs. Cleveland A.L., October 2, 1954 (3 sacrifice hits and 2 sacrifice flies).

Most Sacrifices, Game, Both Clubs

7—Chicago N.L., 5, Detroit A.L., 2, October 10, 1908 (all sacrifice hits).

Most Sacrifices, Inning

3—Brooklyn N.L., vs. New York A.L., October 4, 1955, sixth inning (2 sacrifice hits, 1 sacrifice fly).

Sacrifice Flies

Most Sacrifice Flies, Total Series, Since 1955

14—New York A.L., 13 Series, 80 games.

Most Sacrifice Flies, Series

4-game Series—2—New York N.L., vs. Cleveland A.L., 1954.
Cincinnati N.L., vs. New York A.L., 1976.
5-game Series—3—Baltimore A.L., vs. Philadelphia N.L., 1983.
San Diego N.L., vs. Detroit A.L., 1984.
6-game Series—4—Philadelphia N.L., vs. Kansas City A.L., 1980.
7-game Series—5—Pittsburgh N.L., vs. Baltimore A.L., 1979.

Most Sacrifice Flies, Series, Both Clubs

4-game Series—3—Cincinnati N.L., 2, New York A.L., 1, 1976.
5-game Series—5—San Diego N.L., 3, Detroit A.L., 2, 1984.
6-game Series—7—Philadelphia N.L., 4, Kansas City A.L., 3, 1980.
7-game Series—5—Brooklyn N.L., 3, New York A.L., 2, 1956.
Milwaukee N.L., 3, New York A.L., 2, 1958.
Boston A.L., 3, Cincinnati N.L., 2, 1975.
Pittsburgh N.L., 5, Baltimore A.L., 0, 1979.

Most Sacrifice Flies, Game

2—Made in many games.

Most Sacrifice Flies, Game, Both Clubs

2—Made in many games.

Most Sacrifice Flies, Inning

2—Baltimore A.L., vs. Pittsburgh N.L., October 13, 1971, first inning.

Hit By Pitch

Most Hit by Pitch, Total Series

39—New York A.L., 33 Series, 187 games.

Most Hit by Pitch, Series

4-game Series—4—New York A.L., vs. Chicago N.L., 1932.
5-game Series—4—Chicago N.L., vs. Detroit A.L., 1907.
6-game Series—4—New York A.L., vs. Brooklyn N.L., 1953.
7-game Series—6—Pittsburgh N.L., vs. Detroit A.L., 1909.
8-game Series—5—Cincinnati N.L., vs. Chicago A.L., 1919.

Most Hit by Pitch, Series, Both Clubs

4-game Series— 4—New York A.L., 4, Chicago N.L., 0, 1932.
5-game Series— 5—Chicago N.L., 4, Detroit A.L., 1, 1907.
6-game Series— 6—New York A.L., 4, Brooklyn N.L., 2, 1953.
7-game Series—10—Pittsburgh N.L., 6, Detroit A.L., 4, 1909.
8-game Series— 8—Cincinnati N.L., 5, Chicago A.L., 3, 1919.

Fewest Hit by Pitch, Series

4-game Series—0—Held by many clubs.
5-game Series—0—Held by many clubs.
6-game Series—0—Held by many clubs.
7-game Series—0—Held by many clubs.
8-game Series—1—Held by three clubs: Boston A.L., 1912; New York A.L., 1921; New York N.L., 1921.

Fewest Hit by Pitch, Series, Both Clubs

4-game Series—0—Los Angeles N.L., 0, Baltimore A.L., 0, 1966.
5-game Series—0—Washington A.L., 0, New York N.L., 0, 1933.
New York A.L., 0, St. Louis N.L., 0, 1942.
New York A.L., 0, St. Louis N.L., 0, 1943.
6-game Series—0—St. Louis A.L., 0, St. Louis N.L., 0, 1944.
7-game Series—0—Cleveland A.L., 0, Brooklyn N.L., 0, 1920.
Detroit A.L., 0, Cincinnati N.L., 0, 1940.
New York A.L., 0, Brooklyn N.L., 0, 1956.
New York A.L., 0, Milwaukee N.L., 0, 1958.
8-game Series—2—New York A.L., 1, New York N.L., 1, 1921.

Most Hit by Pitch, Game

3—Detroit A.L., vs. St. Louis N.L., October 9, 1968.
Baltimore A.L., vs. Pittsburgh N.L., October 13, 1971.

Most Hit by Pitch, Game, Both Clubs

3—Philadelphia N.L., 2, Boston A.L., 1, October 13, 1915.
Cincinnati N.L., 2, Chicago A.L., 1, October 9, 1919.
Pittsburgh N.L., 2, Washington A.L., 1, October 7, 1925.
Detroit A.L., 3, St. Louis N.L., 0, October 9, 1968.
Baltimore A.L., 3, Pittsburgh N.L., 0, October 13, 1971.
New York N.L., 2, Oakland A.L., 1, October 14, 1973.
Minnesota A.L., 2, St. Louis N.L., 1, October 21, 1987.

Most Hit by Pitch, Inning

2—Pittsburgh N.L., vs. Detroit A.L., October 11, 1909, second inning, consecutive.
Detroit A.L., vs. St. Louis N.L., October 9, 1968, eighth inning.
Pittsburgh N.L., vs. Baltimore A.L., October 17, 1979, ninth inning, consecutive.

Reaching Base On Errors

Most First on Error, Game

5—Chicago N.L., vs. Chicago A.L., October 13, 1906.

Most First on Error, Game, Both Clubs

6—Pittsburgh N.L., 4, Boston A.L., 2, October 10, 1903.
New York N.L., 4, Philadelphia A.L., 2, October 26, 1911.
Chicago N.L., 4, Philadelphia A.L., 2, October 18, 1910.

Individual Baserunning

Stolen Bases

Most Stolen Bases, Total Series

14—Collins, Edward T., Philadelphia A.L. (10), 1910, 1911, 1913, 1914; Chicago A.L. (4), 1917, 1919; 6 Series, 34 games.
Brock, Louis C., St. Louis N.L., 1964 (0), 1967 (7), 1968 (7); 3 Series, 21 games.

Most Stolen Bases, Series

4-game Series—2—Deal, Charles A., Boston N.L., 1914.
Maranville, Walter J.V., Boston N.L., 1914.
Geronimo, Cesar F., Cincinnati N.L., 1976.
Morgan, Joe L., Cincinnati N.L., 1976.
5-game Series—6—Slagle, James F., Chicago N.L., 1907.
6-game Series—4—Lopes, David E., Los Angeles N.L., 1981.
7-game Series—7—Brock, Louis C., St. Louis N.L., 1967.
Brock, Louis C., St. Louis N.L., 1968.
8-game Series—4—Devore, Joshua D., New York N.L., 1912.

Most Stolen Bases, Game

3—Wagner, John P., Pittsburgh N.L., October 11, 1909.
Davis, William H., Los Angeles N.L., October 11, 1965.
Brock, Louis C., St. Louis N.L., October 12, 1967.
Brock, Louis C., St. Louis N.L., October 5, 1968.

Most Times Stealing Home, Game (13 times)
(*Part of Double Steal)

1—Dahlen, William F., New York N.L., October 12, 1905, fifth inning.*

Davis, George S., Chicago A.L., October 13, 1906, third inning.*
Slagle, James F., Chicago N.L., October 11, 1907, seventh inning.
Cobb, Tyrus R., Detroit A.L., October 9, 1909, third inning.
Herzog, Charles L., New York N.L., October 14, 1912, first inning.*
Schmidt, Charles J., Boston N.L., October 9, 1914, eighth inning.*
McNally, Michael J., New York A.L., October 5, 1921, fifth inning.
Meusel, Robert W., New York A.L., October 6, 1921, eighth inning.
Meusel, Robert W., New York A.L., October 7, 1928, sixth inning.*
Greenberg, Henry B., Detroit A.L., October 6, 1934, eighth inning.*
Irvin, Monford M., New York N.L., October 4, 1951, first inning.
Robinson, Jack R., Brooklyn N.L., September 28, 1955, eighth inning.
McCarver, J. Timothy, St. Louis N.L., October 15, 1964, fourth inning.*

Most Stolen Bases, Inning (7 times)

2—Slagle, James F., Chicago N.L., October 8, 1907, tenth inning.
Browne, George E., New York N.L., October 12, 1905, ninth inning.
Cobb, Tyrus R., Detroit A.L., October 12, 1908, ninth inning.
Collins, Edward T., Chicago A.L., October 7, 1917, sixth inning.

Ruth, George H., New York A.L., October 6, 1921, fifth inning.
Brock, Louis C., St. Louis N.L., October 12, 1967, fifth inning.
Lopes, David E., Los Angeles N.L., October 15, 1974, first inning.

Caught Stealing

Most Caught Stealing, Total Series

9—Schulte, Frank, Chicago N.L., 1906, 1907, 1908, 1910; 4 Series, 21 games, 3 stolen bases.

Most Caught Stealing, Series

4-game Series—2—Aparicio, Luis, Baltimore A.L., 1966, 0 stolen bases.
Foster, George A., Cincinnati N.L., 1976, 0 stolen bases.

5-game Series—5—Schulte, Frank, Chicago N.L., 1910, 0 stolen bases.

6-game Series—3—Devore, Joshua D., New York N.L., 1911, 0 stolen bases.

7-game Series—3—Brock, Louis C., St. Louis N.L., 1968, 7 stolen bases.

8-game Series—4—Neale, Alfred E., Cincinnati N.L., 1919, 1 stolen base.

Most Times Caught Stealing, Game (6 times)

2—Schulte, Frank, Chicago N.L., October 17, 1910.
Schulte, Frank, Chicago N.L., October 23, 1910.
Luderus, Fred W., Philadelphia N.L., October 8, 1915.
Johnston, James H., Brooklyn N.D., October 9, 1916.
Livingston, Thompson O., Chicago N.L., October 3, 1945.
Martin, Alfred M., New York A.L., September 28, 1955.

Most Times Caught Stealing, Inning

1—Held by many players.

Most Caught Off Base, Game

2—Flack, Max O., Chicago N.L., September 9, 1918, first base in first inning, second base in third inning.

Club Baserunning

Stolen Bases

Most Stolen Bases, Total Series

60—New York A.L., 33 Series, 187 games.

Most Stolen Bases, Series

4-game Series— 9—Boston, N.L., vs. Philadelphia A.L., 1914.
5-game Series—18—Chicago N.L., vs. Detroit A.L., 1907.
6-game Series— 8—Chicago N.L., vs. Chicago A.L., 1906.
7-game Series—18—Pittsburgh N.L., vs. Detroit A.L., 1909.
8-game Series—12—New York N.L., vs. Boston A.L., 1912.

Most Stolen Bases, Series, Both Clubs

4-game Series—11—Boston N.L., 9, Philadelphia A.L., 2, 1914.
5-game Series—25—Chicago N.L., 18, Detroit A.L., 7, 1907.
6-game Series—14—Chicago N.L., 8, Chicago A.L., 6, 1906.
7-game Series—24—Pittsburgh N.L., 18, Detroit A.L., 6, 1909.
8-game Series—18—New York N.L., 12, Boston A.L., 6, 1912.

Fewest Stolen Bases, Series

4-game Series—0—Held by many clubs.
5-game Series—0—Held by many clubs.
6-game Series—0—Held by many clubs.
7-game Series—0—Philadelphia A.L., vs. St. Louis N.L., 1931.
Detroit A.L., vs. Cincinnati N.L., 1940.
New York A.L., vs. Pittsburgh N.L., 1960.
Detroit A.L., vs. St. Louis N.L., 1968.
New York N.L., vs. Oakland A.L., 1973.
Boston A.L., vs. Cincinnati N.L., 1975.
Pittsburgh N.L., vs. Baltimore A.L., 1979.
Boston A.L., vs. New York N.L., 1986.
8-game Series—5—Boston A.L., vs. Pittsburgh N.L., 1903
Chicago A.L., vs. Cincinnati N.L., 1919.

Fewest Stolen Bases, Series, Both Clubs

4-game Series— 1—Cincinnati N.L., 1, New York A.L., 0, 1939.
New York N.L., 1, Cleveland A.L., 0, 1954.
Los Angeles N.L., 1, Baltimore A.L., 0, 1966.
5-game Series— 1—Chicago N.L., 1, Philadelphia A.L., 0, 1929.
Washington A.L., 1, New York N.L., 0, 1933.
New York N.L., 1, New York A.L., 0, 1937.
Cincinnati N.L., 1, Cincinnati N.L., 0, 1961.
Cincinnati N.L., 1, Baltimore A.L., 0, 1970.
6-game Series— 0—St. Louis N.L., 0, St. Louis A.L., 0, 1944.
7-game Series— 1—Cincinnati N.L., 1, Detroit A.L., 0, 1940.
8-game Series—12—Pittsburgh N.L., 7, Boston A.L., 5, 1903.
Cincinnati N.L., 7, Chicago A.L., 5, 1919.

Most Stolen Bases, Nine-Inning Game

5—New York N.L., vs. Philadelphia A.L., October 12, 1905.
Chicago N.L., vs. Chicago A.L., October 10, 1906.
Chicago N.L., vs. Detroit A.L., October 9, 1907.
St. Louis N.L., vs. Minnesota A.L., October 22, 1987.

Most Stolen Bases, Extra-Inning Game

7—Chicago N.L., vs. Detroit A.L., October 8, 1907, 10 innings.

Most Stolen Bases, Nine-Inning Game, Both Clubs

6—New York N.L. 5, Philadelphia A.L. 1, October 12, 1905.
Pittsburgh N.L., 4, Detroit A.L., 2, October 13, 1909.

New York N.L., 3, Philadelphia A.L., 3, October 9, 1913.
St. Louis N.L., 5, Minnesota A.L., 1, October 22, 1987.

Most Stolen Bases, Extra-Inning Game, Both Clubs

11—Chicago N.L., 7, Detroit A.L., 4, October 8, 1907, 12 innings.

Longest Extra-Inning Game No Stolen Bases

14 innings—Boston A.L., vs. Brooklyn N.L., October 9, 1916.
Brooklyn N.L., vs. Boston A.L., October 9, 1916.

Longest Extra-Inning Game No Stolen Bases, Both Clubs

14 innings—Boston A.L., vs. Brooklyn N.L., October 9, 1916.

Most Stolen Bases, Inning

3—Pittsburgh N.L., vs. Boston A.L., October 1, 1903, first inning.
New York N.L., vs. Philadelphia A.L., October 12, 1905, ninth inning.
Chicago N.L., vs. Detroit A.L., October 8, 1907, tenth inning.
Chicago N.L., vs. Detroit A.L., October 11, 1908, eighth inning.
New York N.L., vs. Boston A.L., October 14, 1912, first inning.
Chicago A.L., vs. New York N.L., October 7, 1917, sixth inning.

Caught Stealing

Most Caught Stealing, Series

4-game Series— 5—Boston N.L., vs. Philadelphia A.L., 1914.
Cincinnati N.L., vs. New York, A.L., 1976.
5-game Series— 8—Chicago N.L., vs. Philadelphia A.L., 1910.
6-game Series—13—New York N.L., vs. Philadelphia A.L., 1911.
7-game Series— 7—Cleveland A.L., vs. Brooklyn N.L., 1920.
Washington A.L., vs. Pittsburgh N.L., 1925.
St. Louis N.L., vs. Detroit A.L., 1968.
8-game Series—11—New York N.L., vs. Boston A.L., 1912.

Most Caught Stealing, Series, Both Clubs

4-game Series— 7—Cincinnati N.L., 5, New York A.L., 2, 1976.
New York A.L., 3, Chicago N.L., 3, 1938.
5-game Series—15—Chicago N.L., 8, Philadelphia A.L., 7, 1910.
6-game Series—19—New York N.L., 13, Philadelphia A.L., 6, 1911.
7-game Series—11—Pittsburgh N.L., 6, Detroit A.L., 5, 1909.
8-game Series—16—New York N.L., 11, Boston A.L., 5, 1912.

Fewest Caught Stealing, Series

4-game Series—0—Pittsburgh N.L., 1927. New York A.L., 1928, 1939.
Philadelphia N.L., 1950. Cleveland A.L., 1954.
5-game Series—0—New York N.L., 1933. New York A.L., 1937, 1942, 1943, 1949.
Brooklyn N.L., 1949. Cincinnati N.L., 1961.
Baltimore A.L.
6-game Series—0—St. Louis N.L., 1930. St. Louis A.L., 1944.
Boston N.L., 1948. New York A.L., 1977.
7-game Series—0—Philadelphia A.L., 1931. New York A.L., 1956, 1964. Boston A.L., 1986. Minnesota A.L., 1987.
Milwaukee N.L., 1958. St. Louis N.L., 1964. Pittsburgh N.L., 1972.
8-game Series—2—Boston A.L., 1903.

Fewest Caught Stealing, Series, Both Clubs

4-game Series—1—New York A.L., 1, Pittsburgh N.L. 0, 1927.
    Cincinnati N.L., 1, New York A.L., 0, 1939.
    New York A.L., 1, Philadelphia N.L., 0, 1950.
    New York A.L., 1, Cleveland A.L., 0, 1954.
5-game Series—0—New York A.L., 0, Brooklyn N.L., 0, 1949.
6-game Series—1—St. Louis N.L., 1, St. Louis A.L., 0, 1944.
    Cleveland A.L., 1, Boston N.L., 0, 1948.
7-game Series—0—St. Louis N.L., 0, New York A.L., 0, 1964.
8-game Series—6—Pittsburgh N.L., 4, Boston A.L., 2, 1903.

Most Caught Stealing, Nine-Inning Game

3—Made in many games. Last time—Chicago A.L., vs. Los Angeles, N.L., October 4, 1959.

Most Caught Stealing, Extra-Inning Game

5—New York N.L., vs. Philadelphia A.L., October 17, 1911, 11 innings, 0 stolen bases.

Most Caught Stealing, Nine-Inning Game, Both Clubs

5—Philadelphia A.L., 3, Chicago N.L., 2, October 17, 1910.

Most Caught Stealing, Inning

2—Made in many innings.

Left On Base

Most Left on Bases, Total Series

1,272—New York A.L., 33 Series, 187 games.

Most Left on Bases, Series

4-game Series—37—Cleveland A.L., vs. New York N.L., 1954.
5-game Series—42—New York A.L., vs. Brooklyn N.L., 1941.
6-game Series—55—New York A.L., vs. Los Angeles N.L., 1981.
7-game Series—72—New York N.L., vs. Oakland A.L., 1973.
8-game Series—55—Boston A.L., vs. Pittsburgh N.L., 1903.
    Boston A.L., vs. New York N.L., 1912.

Most Left on Bases, Series, Both Clubs

4-game Series— 65—Cleveland A.L., 37, New York N.L., 28, 1954.
5-game Series— 76—New York N.L., 39, Washington A.L., 37, 1933.
6-game Series—101—New York A.L., 55, Los Angeles N.L., 46, 1981.
7-game Series—130—New York N.L., 72, Oakland A.L., 58, 1973.
8-game Series—108—Boston A.L., 55, New York N.L., 53, 1912.

Fewest Left on Bases, Series

4-game Series—16—New York A.L., vs. Cincinnati N.L., 1939.
5-game Series—23—Philadelphia N.L. vs. Baltimore A.L., 1983.
6-game Series—29—Philadelphia A.L., vs. New York N.L., 1911.
7-game Series—36—Minnesota A.L., vs. Los Angeles N.L., 1965.
8-game Series—43—New York A.L., vs. New York N.L., 1921.

Fewest Left on Bases, Series, Both Clubs

4-game Series—39—Cincinnati N.L., 23, New York A.L., 16, 1939.
5-game Series—51—Baltimore A.L., 28, Philadelphia N.L., 23, 1983.
6-game Series—60—New York N.L., 31, Philadelphia A.L., 29, 1911.
7-game Series—82—Cleveland A.L., 43, Brooklyn N.L., 39, 1920.
    Brooklyn N.L., 42, New York A.L., 40, 1956.
    New York A.L., 43, San Francisco N.L., 39, 1962.
8-game Series—97—New York A.L., 54, New York N.L., 43, 1921.

Most Left on Base, Nine-Inning Game

14—Chicago N.L., vs. Philadelphia A.L., October 18, 1910.
    Milwaukee N.L., vs. New York A.L., October 5, 1957.
    Pittsburgh N.L., vs. Baltimore A.L., October 11, 1971.
    Detroit A.L., vs. San Diego N.L., October 12, 1984.

Most Left on Base, Eight-Inning Game

13—Detroit A.L., vs. Cincinnati N.L., October 6, 1940.
    St. Louis N.L., vs. Milwaukee A.L., October 20, 1982.

Most Left on Base, Extra-Inning Game

15—New York N.L., vs. Oakland A.L., October 14, 1973 (12 innings).
    Philadelphia N.L., vs. Kansas City A.L., October 17, 1980 (10 innings).

Most Left on Base, Two Consecutive Nine-Inning Games

26—Cleveland A.L., vs. New York N.L., September 29 (13), September 30 (13), 1954.

Most Left on Base, Nine-Inning Shutout Defeat

11—Philadelphia A.L., vs. St. Louis N.L., October 4, 1930, (Lost 5-0).
    St. Louis N.L., vs. New York A.L., October 11, 1943, (Lost 2-0).
    Los Angeles N.L., vs. Chicago A.L., October 6, 1959, (Lost 1-0).
    Baltimore A.L., vs. New York N.L., October 14, 1969, (Lost 5-0).

Most Left on Base, Nine-Inning Game, Both Clubs

24—Detroit A.L., 14, San Diego N.L., 10, October 12, 1984.

Most Left on Base, Extra-Inning Game, Both Clubs

27—New York N.L., 15, Oakland A.L., 12, October 14, 1973 (12 innings).

Fewest Left on Base, Game

0—Brooklyn N.L., vs. New York A.L., October 8, 1956, 9 innings.
    Los Angeles N.L., vs. New York A.L., October 6, 1963, 8 innings.

Fewest Left on Base, Game, Both Clubs

3—New York A.L., 3, Brooklyn N.L., 0, October 8, 1956.

Individual Pitching

Service
Series & Games

Most Series Played

11—Ford, Edward C., New York A.L., 1950, 1953, 1955, 1956, 1957, 1958, 1960, 1961, 1962, 1963, 1964 (22 games).

Most Games Pitched, Total Series

22—Ford, Edward C., New York A.L., 1950, 1953, 1955, 1956, 1957, 1958, 1960, 1961, 1962, 1963, 1964 (11 Series).

Most Games Pitched, Series

4-game Series—3—French, Lawrence H., Chicago N.L., 1938, 3 ⅓ innings.
    Konstanty, C. James, Philadelphia N.L., 1950, 15 innings.
    Mossi, Donald L., Cleveland A.L., 1954, 4 innings.
    Reniff, Harold E., New York A.L., 1963, 3 innings.
5-game Series—5—Marshall, Michael G., Los Angeles N.L., 1974, 9 innings.
6-game Series—6—Quisenberry, Daniel R., Kansas City A.L., 1980, 10 ⅓ innings.

7-game Series—7—Knowles, Darold D., Oakland A.L., 1973, 6 ⅓ innings.
8-game Series—5—Phillippe, Charles L., Pittsburgh N.L., 1903, 44 innings.

Most Consecutive Games Pitched, Series

7—Knowles, Darold D., Oakland A.L., October 13, 14, 16, 17, 18, 20, 21, 1973.

Youngest & Oldest Pitchers

Youngest World Series Pitcher

19 years, 20 days—Brett, Kenneth A., Boston A.L., October 8, 1967, pitched one inning in relief.

Oldest World Series Pitcher

46 years, 2 months, 29 days—Quinn, John P., Philadelphia A.L., October 4, 1930, pitched two innings, finishing game.

Games Started

Most Games Started, Total Series

22—Ford, Edward C., New York A.L., 1950, 1953, 1955, 1956, 1957, 1958, 1960, 1961, 1962, 1963, 1964 (11 Series).

Most Opening Games Started, Total Series

8—Ford, Edward C., New York A.L., 1955, 1956, 1957, 1958, 1961, 1962, 1963, 1964 (won 4, lost 3, no decision 1).

Most Consecutive Games Started, Series

2—Phillippe, Charles L., Pittsburgh N.L., October 3, 6, 1903.
Phillippe, Charles L., Pittsburgh N.L., October 10, 13, 1903.
Coombs, John W., Philadelphia A.L., October 18, 20, 1910.
Mathewson, Christopher, New York N.L., October 17, 24, 1911.
Earnshaw, George L., Philadelphia A.L., October 9, 11, 1929.
Earnshaw, George L., Philadelphia A.L., October 6, 8, 1930.

Most Series Three Games Started, Total Series

3—Gibson, Robert, St. Louis N.L., 1964, 1967, 1968.

Most Games Started, Series

4-game Series—2—Held by 12 pitchers. Last pitcher—McNally, David A., Baltimore A.L., 1966 (1 complete).
5-game Series—3—Mathewson, Christopher, New York N.L., 1905 (3 complete).
Coombs, John W., Philadelphia A.L., 1910 (3 complete).
6-game Series—3—Held by 9 pitchers. Last pitcher—Wynn, Early, Chicago A.L., 1959 (0 complete).
7-game Series—3—41 times—21 in A.L., 20 in N.L.—Held by 37 pitchers. Last pitcher—Viola, Frank J., Minnesota A.L., 1987 (0 complete).
8-game Series—5—Phillippe, Charles L., Pittsburgh N.L., 1903 (5 complete).

Oldest Pitcher to Start World Series Game

45 years, 3 months, 7 days—Quinn, John P., Philadelphia A.L., October 12, 1929, pitched 5 innings.

Games Relieved & Finished

Most Games, Total Series, Relief Pitcher

16—Fingers, Roland G., Oakland A.L., 1972 (6), 1973 (6), 1974 (4), 33 ⅓ innings.

Most Series, One or More Games as Relief Pitcher

6—Murphy, John J., New York A.L., 1936 (1), 1937 (1), 1938 (1), 1939 (1), 1941 (2), 1943 (2), 8 games as relief pitcher.

Most Games Pitched, Series, Relief Pitcher

4-game Series—3—French, Lawrence H., Chicago N.L., 1938, 3 ⅓ innings.
Mossi, Donald L., Cleveland A.L., 1954, 4 innings.
Reniff, Harold E., New York A.L., 1963, 3 innings.
5-game Series—5—Marshall, Michael G., Los Angeles N.L., 1974, 9 innings.
6-game Series—6—Quisenberry, Daniel R., Kansas City A.L., 1980, 10 ⅓ innings.
7-game Series—7—Knowles, Darold D., Oakland A.L., 1973, 6 ⅓ innings.
8-game Series—3—Barnes, Jesse L., New York N.L., 1921, 16 ⅓ innings.

Most Games Finished, Series

4-game Series—3—Reniff, Harold E., New York A.L., 1963, 3 innings.
5-game Series—5—Marshall, Michael G., Los Angeles N.L., 1974, 9 innings.
6-game Series—6—Quisenberry, Daniel R., Kansas City A.L., 1980, 10 ⅓ innings.
7-game Series—6—Casey, Hugh T., Brooklyn N.L., 1947, 10 ⅓ innings.
8-game Series—3—Barnes, Jesse L., New York N.L., 1921, 16 ⅓ innings.

Oldest Pitcher to Finish World Series Game

46 years, 2 months, 29 days—Quinn, John P., Philadelphia A.L., October 4, 1930, pitched 2 innings.

Complete Games

Most Complete Games Pitched, Total Series

10—Mathewson, Christopher, New York N.L., 1905, 1911, 1912, 1913.

Most Consecutive Complete Games Pitched, Total Series

8—Gibson, Robert, St. Louis N.L., 1964 (2), 1967 (3), 1968 (3), (won 7, lost 1).

Most Consecutive Complete Games Won, Total Series

7—Gibson, Robert, St. Louis N.L., October 12, 15, 1964; October 4, 8, 12, 1967; October 2, 6, 1968.

Most Complete Games, Series

4-game Series—2—Rudolph, Richard, Boston N.L., 1914.
Hoyt, Waite C., New York A.L., 1928.
Ruffing, Charles H., New York A.L., 1938.
Koufax, Sanford, Los Angeles N.L., 1963.
5-game Series—3—Mathewson, Christopher, New York N.L., 1905.
Coombs, John W., Philadelphia A.L., 1910.
6-game Series—3—Bender, Charles A., Philadelphia A.L., 1911.
Vaughn, James L., Chicago N.L., 1918.
7-game Series—3—Adams, Charles B., Pittsburgh N.L., 1909.
Mullin, George, Detroit A.L., 1909.
Coveleski, Stanley, Cleveland A.L., 1920.
Johnson, Walter P., Washington A.L., 1925.
Newsom, Louis N., Detroit A.L., 1940.
Burdette, S. Lewis, Milwaukee N.L., 1957.
Gibson, Robert, St. Louis N.L., 1967.
Gibson, Robert, St. Louis N.L., 1968.
Lolich, Michael S., Detroit A.L., 1968.
8-game Series—5—Phillippe, Charles L., Pittsburgh N.L., 1903.

Youngest Pitcher to Pitch Complete World Series Game

20 years, 10 months, 12 days—Bush, Leslie A., Philadelphia A.L., October 9, 1913; Philadelphia A.L. 8, New York N.L. 2.

Youngest Pitcher to Win Complete World Series Game

20 years, 10 months, 12 days—Bush, Leslie A., Philadelphia A.L., October 9, 1913; Philadelphia A.L., 8, New York N.L., 2.

Oldest Pitcher to Pitch Complete World Series Game

39 years, 7 months, 13 days—Alexander, Grover C., St. Louis N.L., October 9, 1926, St. Louis N.L., 10, New York A.L., 2.

Innings

Most Innings Pitched, Total Series

146—Ford, Edward C., New York A.L., 1950, 1953, 1955, 1956, 1957, 1958, 1960, 1961, 1962, 1963, 1964; 11 Series, 22 games.

Most Innings Pitched, Series

4-game Series—18—Rudolph, Richard, Boston N.L., 1914.
Hoyt, Waite C., New York A.L., 1928.
Ruffing, Charles H., New York A.L., 1938.
Koufax, Sanford, Los Angeles N.L., 1963.
5-game Series—27—Mathewson, Christopher, New York N.L., 1905.
Coombs, John W., Philadelphia A.L., 1910.
6-game Series—27—Mathewson, Christopher, New York N.L., 1911.
Faber, Urban C., Chicago A.L., 1917.
Vaughn, James L., Chicago N.L., 1918.
7-game Series—32—Mullin, George, Detroit A.L., 1909.
8-game Series—44—Phillippe, Charles L., Pittsburgh N.L., 1903.

Most Innings Pitched, Game

14—Ruth, George H., Boston A.L., October 9, 1916, complete game, won 2-1.

Games Won

Most Games Won, Total Series

10—Ford, Edward C., New York A.L., 1950, 1953, 1955, 1956, 1957, 1958, 1960, 1961, 1962, 1963, 1964 (won 10, lost 8), 11 Series, 22 games.

Most Consecutive Games Won, Total Series

7—Gibson, Robert, St. Louis N.L., October 12, 15, 1964; October 4, 8, 12, 1967; October 2, 6, 1968 (7 complete).

Most Games Won, Total Series, No Defeats

6—Gomez, Vernon, New York A.L., 1932, 1936, 1937, 1938.

Most Opening Games Won, Total Series

5—Ruffing, Charles H., New York A.L., 1932, 1938, 1939, 1941, 1942, four complete (lost complete game opener in 1936).

Most Games Won, Series

4-game Series—2—Rudolph, Richard, Boston N.L., 1914, (complete).
James, William L., Boston N.L., 1914, (one complete).
Hoyt, Waite C., New York A.L., 1928, (complete).
Ruffing, Charles H., New York A.L., 1938, (complete).
Koufax, Sanford, Los Angeles N.L., 1963, (complete).
5-game Series—3—Mathewson, Christopher, New York N.L., 1905, (complete).
Coombs, John W., Philadelphia A.L., 1910, (complete).
6-game Series—3—Faber, Urban C., Chicago A.L., 1917, (two complete).
7-game Series—3—Adams, Charles B., Pittsburgh N.L., 1909, (complete).
Coveleski, Stanley, Cleveland A.L., 1920, (complete).
Brecheen, Harry D., St. Louis N.L., 1946, (two complete).
Burdette, S. Lewis, Milwaukee N.L., 1957, (complete).
Gibson, Robert, St. Louis N.L., 1967, (complete).
Lolich, Michael S., Detroit A.L., 1968, (complete).
8-game Series—3—Dinneen, William H., Boston, A.L., 1903, (complete).
Phillippe, Charles L., Pittsburgh N.L., 1903, (complete).
Wood, Joseph, Boston A.L., 1912, (two complete).

Most Games Won, Series, as Relief Pitcher

2—Barnes, Jesse L., New York N.L., 1921 (8-game Series).
Casey, T. Hugh, Brooklyn N.L., 1947 (7-game Series).
Sherry, Lawrence, Los Angeles N.L., 1959 (6-game Series).
Grimsley, Ross A., Cincinnati N.L., 1972 (6-game Series).
Eastwick, Rawlins J., Cincinnati N.L., 1975 (7-game Series).

Most Games Won, Series, Losing None

4-game Series—2—Rudolph, Richard, Boston N.L., 1914.
James, William L., Boston N.L., 1914.
Hoyt, Waite C., New York N.L., 1928.
Ruffing, Charles H., New York A.L., 1938.
Koufax, Sanford, Los Angeles N.L., 1963.
5-game Series—3—Mathewson, Christopher, New York N.L., 1905.
Coombs, John W., Philadelphia A.L., 1910.
6-game Series—2—Held by many pitchers. Last pitcher—Carlton, Steven N., Philadelphia N.L., 1980.
7-game Series—3—Adams, Charles B., Pittsburgh N.L., 1909.
Coveleski, Stanley, Cleveland A.L., 1920.
Brecheen, Harry D., St. Louis N.L., 1946.
Burdette, S. Lewis, Milwaukee N.L., 1957.
Gibson, Robert, St. Louis N.L., 1967.
Lolich, Michael S., Detroit A.L., 1968.
8-game Series—2—Marquard, Richard W., New York N.L., 1912.
Eller, Horace O., Cincinnati N.L., 1919.
Kerr, Richard, Chicago A.L., 1919.
Barnes, Jesse L., New York N.L., 1921.

Saves

Most Saves, Total Series, Since 1969

6—Fingers, Roland G., Oakland A.L., 1972 (2), 1973 (2), 1974 (2).

Most Saves, Series, Since 1969

4-game Series—2—McEnaney, William H., Cincinnati N.L., 1976.
5-game Series—2—Fingers, Roland G., Oakland A.L., 1974.
Martinez, Felix A., Baltimore A.L., 1983.
Hernandez, Guillermo, Detroit A.L., 1984.
6-game Series—2—McGraw, Frank E., Philadelphia N.L., 1980.
Gossage, Richard M., New York A.L., 1981.
7-game Series—3—Tekulve, Kenton C., Pittsburgh N.L., 1979.

Games Lost

Most Games Lost, Total Series

8—Ford, Edward C., New York A.L., 1950, 1953, 1955, 1956, 1957, 1958, 1960, 1961, 1962, 1963, 1964 (won 10, lost 8), 11 Series, 22 games.

Most Consecutive Games Lost, Total Series

5—Bush, Leslie A., Philadelphia A.L., Boston A.L., New York A.L., 1914 (1), 1918 (1), 1922 (2), 1923 (1).

Most Games Lost, Total Series, No Victories

4—Summers, O. Edgar, Detroit A.L., 1908 (2), 1909 (2).
Sherdel, William H., St. Louis N.L., 1926 (2), 1928 (2).
Newcombe, Donald, Brooklyn N.L., 1949 (2), 1955 (1), 1956 (1).

Most Games Lost, Series

4-game Series—2—Sherdel, William H., St. Louis N.L., 1928.
Lee, William C., Jr., Chicago N.L., 1938.
Walters, William H., Cincinnati N.L., 1939.
Lemon, Robert G., Cleveland A.L., 1954.
Ford, Edward C., New York A.L., 1963.
Drysdale, Donald S., Los Angeles N.L., 1966.
5-game Series—2—Held by many pitchers. Last pitcher—Hudson, Charles L., Philadelphia N.L., 1983.
6-game Series—3—Frazier, George A., New York A.L., 1981.
7-game Series—2—Held by many pitchers. Last pitcher—Cox, Danny B., St. Louis N.L., 1987.
8-game Series—3—Williams, Claude P., Chicago A.L., 1919.

Runs, Earned Runs & ERA

Most Runs Allowed, Series

4-game Series—11—Alexander, Grover C., St. Louis N.L., 1928.
Lemon, Robert G., Cleveland A.L., 1954.
5-game Series—16—Brown, Mordecai P., Chicago N.L., 1910.
6-game Series—10—Sallee, Harry F., New York N.L., 1917.
Ruffing, Charles H., New York A.L., 1936.
Gullett, Donald E., New York A.L., 1977.
Sutton, Donald H., Los Angeles N.L., 1978.
7-game Series—17—Burdette, S. Lewis, Milwaukee N.L., 1958.
8-game Series—19—Phillippe, Charles L., Pittsburgh N.L., 1903.

Most Runs Allowed, Game, Nine Innings

9—Coakley, Andrew J., Philadelphia A.L., October 12, 1905.
Brown, Mordecai P., Chicago N.L., October 18, 1910.
Johnson, Walter P., Washington A.L., October 15, 1925.

Most Earned Runs Allowed, Game, Nine Innings

7—Brown, Mordecai P., Chicago N.L., October 18, 1910.
Cox, Danny B., St. Louis N.L., October 18, 1987.

Most Runs Allowed, Inning

7—Wiltse, George L., New York N.L., October 26, 1911, seventh inning.
Hubbell, Carl O., New York N.L., October 6, 1937, sixth inning.

Most Earned Runs Allowed, Inning

6—Wiltse, George L., New York N.L., October 26, 1911, seventh inning.
Cox, Danny B., St. Louis N.L., October 18, 1987, fourth inning.

Lowest Earned-Run Average, Series, 14 or More Innings

0.00—Mathewson, Christopher, New York N.L., 1905, 27 innings.
Hoyt, Waite C., New York A.L., 1921, 27 innings.
Hubbell, Carl O., New York N.L., 1933, 20 innings.
Ford, Edward C., New York A.L., 1960, 18 innings.
McGinnity, Joseph J., New York N.L., 1905, 17 innings.
Mails, J. Walter, Cleveland A.L., 1920, 15⅔ innings.
Benton, John C., New York N.L., 1917, 14 innings.
Ford, Edward C., New York A.L., 1961, 14 innings.

Shutouts & Scoreless Innings

Most Complete Shutouts Won, Total Series

4—Mathewson, Christopher, New York N.L., 1905 (3), 1913 (1).

Most Complete Shutouts Won, Series

3—Mathewson, Christopher, New York N.L., 1905 (consecutive, October 9, 12, 14).

Most Complete 1-0 Shutouts Won, Total Series

2—Nehf, Arthur N., New York N.L., October 13, 1921, October 12, 1923.

Most Shutouts Lost, Total Series

3—Plank, Edward S., Philadelphia A.L., 1905 (2), 1914 (1).

Most 1-0 Shutouts Lost, Total Series

2—Plank, Edward S., Philadelphia A.L., October 13, 1905, October 10, 1914.

Youngest Pitcher to Win Complete World Series Shutout Game

20 years, 11 months, 21 days—Palmer, James A., Baltimore A.L., October 6, 1966; Baltimore A.L., 6, Los Angeles N.L., 0.

Oldest Pitcher to Win Complete World Series Shutout Game

37 years, 11 months, 5 days—Johnson, Walter P., Washington A.L., October 11, 1925; Washington A.L., 4, Pittsburgh N.L., 0.

Most Consecutive Scoreless Innings, Total Series

33—Ford, Edward C., New York A.L., October 8, 1960, 9 innings; October 12, 1960, 9 innings; October 4, 1961, 9 innings; October 8, 1961, 5 innings; October 4, 1962, 1 inning.

Most Consecutive Scoreless Innings, Series

27—Mathewson, Christopher, New York N.L., October 9, 12, 14, 1905.

Retiring Side on Three Pitched Balls

Mathewson, Christopher, New York N.L., October 9, 1912, eleventh inning, and October 16, 1912, fifth inning.
Walberg, George E., Philadelphia A.L., October 14, 1929, seventh inning.
Bonham, Ernest E., New York A.L., October 6, 1941, seventh inning.

Hits

Most Hits Allowed, Series

4-game Series—17—Ruffing, Charles H., New York A.L., 1938.
5-game Series—23—Coombs, John W., Philadelphia A.L., 1910.
Brown, Mordecai P., Chicago N.L., 1910.
6-game Series—25—Mathewson, Christopher, New York N.L., 1911.
7-game Series—30—Johnson, Walter P., Washington A.L., 1924.
8-game Series—38—Phillippe, Charles L., Pittsburgh N.L., 1903.

Most Hits Allowed, Game, Nine Innings

15—Johnson, Walter P., Washington A.L., October 15, 1925.

Fewest Hits Allowed, Game, Nine Innings

0—Larsen, Don J., New York A.L., October 8, 1956 (perfect game).

One and Two-Hit Games, Nine Innings (Pitching Complete Game)

1—Reulbach, Edward M., Chicago N.L., October 10, 1906 (hit came with none out in seventh).
Passeau, Claude W., Chicago N.L., October 5, 1945 (hit came with two out in second).
Bevens, Floyd, New York A.L., October 3, 1947 (hit came with two out in ninth).
Lonborg, James R., Boston A.L., October 5, 1967 (hit came with two out in eighth).
2—Walsh, Edward A., Chicago A.L., October 11, 1906.
Brown, Mordecai P., Chicago N.L., October 12, 1906.
Plank, Edward S., Philadelphia A.L., October 11, 1913.
James, William L., Boston N.L., October 10, 1914.
Hoyt, Waite C., New York A.L., October 6, 1921.
Grimes, Burleigh A., St. Louis N.L., October 5, 1931.
Earnshaw, George L., Philadelphia A.L., October 6, 1931.
Pearson, Monte M., New York A.L., October 5, 1939.
Cooper, Morton C., St. Louis N.L., October 4, 1944.
Feller, Robert W., Cleveland A.L., October 6, 1948.
Reynolds, Allie, New York A.L., October 5, 1949.
Raschi, Victor A. J., New York A.L., October 4, 1950.
Spahn, Warren E., Milwaukee N.L., October 5, 1958.
Ford, Edward C., New York A.L., October 4, 1961.
Briles, Nelson K., Pittsburgh N.L., October 14, 1971.

Fewest Hits Allowed, Two Consecutive Complete Games

4—Lonborg, James R., Boston A.L., October 5 (1), October 9 (3), 1967.

Fewest Hits Allowed, Three Consecutive Complete Games

14—Mathewson, Christopher, New York N.L., October 5 (4), October 12 (4), October 14 (6), 1905.
Gibson, Robert, St. Louis N.L., October 4 (6), October 8 (5), October 12 (3), 1967.

Most Consecutive Hitless Innings, Total Series

11—Larsen, Don J., New York A.L., October 8, 1956 (9 innings), October 5, 1957 (2 innings).

Most Consecutive Hitless Innings, Game

9—Larsen, Don J., New York A.L., October 8, 1956.

Most Consec. Innings, Total Series, No Player Reaching First Base

11—Larsen, Don J., New York A.L., October 8, 1956 (9 innings), October 5, 1957 (2 innings).

Most Consecutive Innings, Series, No Player Reaching First Base

9—Larsen, Don J., New York A.L., October 8, 1956.

Most Consecutive Innings, Game, No Player Reaching First Base

9—Larsen, Don J., New York A.L., October 8, 1956 (perfect game).

Most Hits Allowed, Inning

7—Wood, Joseph, Boston A.L., October 15, 1912, first inning.

Most Consec. Hits Allowed, Inning (Consec. Plate Appearances)

6—Summers, Oren E., Detroit A.L., October 10, 1908, ninth inning, six singles.

Doubles, Triples & Home Runs

Most Doubles Allowed, Game

8—Johnson, Walter P., Washington A.L., October 15, 1925.

Most Triples Allowed, Game

5—Phillippe, Charles L., Pittsburgh N.L., October 10, 1903.

Most Home Runs Allowed, Total Series

9—Hunter, James A., Oakland A.L., New York A.L., 1972, 1973, 1974, 1976, 1977, 1978; 6 Series, 12 games.

Most Home Runs Allowed, Series

4-game Series—4—Sherdel, William H., St. Louis N.L., 1928.
Root, Charles H., Chicago N.L., 1932.
Thompson, Eugene E., Cincinnati N.L., 1939.
5-game Series—4—Nolan, Gary L., Cincinnati N.L., 1970.
Hudson, Charles L., Philadelphia N.L., 1983.
6-game Series—4—Reynolds, Allie P., New York A.L., 1953.
7-game Series—5—Burdette, S. Lewis, Milwaukee N.L., 1958.
Hughes, Richard H., St. Louis N.L., 1967.
8-game Series—2—Adams, Charles B., Pittsburgh N.L., 1909.
Harper, Harry C., New York A.L., 1921.

Most Home Runs Allowed, Game

4—Root, Charles H., Chicago N.L., October 1, 1932.
Thompson, Eugene E., Jr., Cincinnati N.L., October 7, 1939.
Hughes, Richard H., St. Louis N.L., October 11, 1967.

Most Home Runs Allowed, Inning

3—Hughes, Richard H., St. Louis N.L., October 11, 1967, fourth inning.

Most Consecutive Home Runs Allowed, Inning (9 times)

2—Yde, Emil O., Pittsburgh N.L., October 11, 1925, third inning.
Sherdel, William H., St. Louis N.L., October 9, 1928, seventh inning.
Root, Charles H., Chicago N.L., October 1, 1932, fifth inning.
Simmons, Curtis T., St. Louis N.L., October 14, 1964, sixth inning.
Drysdale, Donald S., Los Angeles N.L., October 5, 1966, first inning.
Hughes, Richard H., St. Louis N.L., October 11, 1967, fourth inning.
Wise, Richard C., Boston A.L., October 14, 1975, fifth inning.
Sutton, Donald H., Los Angeles N.L., October 16, 1977, eighth inning.
Guidry, Ronald A., New York A.L., October 25, 1981, seventh inning.
Darling, Ronald M., New York N.L., October 27, 1986, second inning.

Total Bases & Long Hits

Most Total Bases Allowed, Game

25—Johnson, Walter P., Washington A.L., October 15, 1925.

Most Long Hits Allowed, Game

9—Johnson, Walter P., Washington A.L., October 15, 1925.

Bases On Balls

Most Bases on Balls, Total Series

34—Ford, Edward C., New York A.L., 1950, 1953, 1955, 1956, 1957, 1958, 1960, 1961, 1962, 1963, 1964; 11 Series, 22 games.

Most Innings Pitched, Series, Without Allowing Base on Balls

26—Mays, Carl W., New York A.L., 1921.

Most Bases on Balls, Series

4-game Series— 8—Lemon, Robert G., Cleveland A.L., 1954.
5-game Series—14—Coombs, John W., Philadelphia A.L., 1910.
6-game Series—11—Tyler, George A., Chicago N.L., 1918.
Gomez, Vernon, New York A.L., 1936.
Reynolds, Allie P., New York A.L., 1951.
7-game Series—11—Johnson, Walter P., Washington A.L., 1924.
Bevens, Floyd C., New York A.L., 1947.
8-game Series—13—Nehf, Arthur N., New York N.L., 1921.

Most Bases on Balls, Game

10—Bevens, Floyd C., New York A.L., October 3, 1947.

Longest Game Without Allowing Base on Balls

12 innings—Rowe, Lynwood T., Detroit A.L., October 4, 1934.

Most Bases on Balls, Inning

4—Donovan, William E., Detroit A.L., October 16, 1909, second inning.
Reinhart, Arthur C., St. Louis N.L., October 6, 1926, fifth inning (3 consecutive).
Bush, Guy T., Chicago N.L., September 28, 1932, sixth inning (3 consecutive).
Gullett, Donald E., Cincinnati N.L., October 22, 1975, night game, third inning (two BB with bases full).

Most Consecutive Bases on Balls, Inning

3—Shawkey, J. Robert, New York A.L., October 7, 1921, fourth inning, (two BB with bases full).
Reinhart, Arthur C., St. Louis N.L., October 6, 1926, fifth inning, (one BB with bases full).
Bush, Guy T., Chicago N.L., September 28, 1932, sixth inning.
Hoerner, Joseph W., St. Louis N.L., October 3, 1968, ninth inning, (two BB with bases full).

Strikeouts

Most Strikeouts, Total Series

94—Ford, Edward C., New York A.L., 1950, 1953, 1955, 1956, 1957, 1958, 1960, 1961, 1962, 1963, 1964; 11 Series, 22 games.

Most Strikeouts, Series

4-game Series—23—Koufax, Sanford, Los Angeles N.L., 1963.
5-game Series—18—Mathewson, Christopher, New York N.L., 1905.
6-game Series—20—Bender, Charles A., Philadelphia A.L., 1911.
7-game Series—35—Gibson, Robert, St. Louis N.L., 1968.
8-game Series—28—Dinneen, William H., Boston A.L., 1903.

Most Strikeouts, Game

17—Gibson, Robert, St. Louis N.L., October 2, 1968.

Most Games, Ten or More Strikeouts, Total Series

5—Gibson, Robert, St. Louis N.L., 1964 (1), 1967 (2), 1968 (2).

Most Strikeouts, Game, Losing Pitcher, Nine-Inning Game

11—Bender, Charles A., Philadelphia A.L., October 14, 1911.
Newcombe, Donald, Brooklyn N.L., October 5, 1949.
Odom, Johnny L., Oakland A.L., October 18, 1972, pitched first 7 innings.

Most Strikeouts, Game, Losing Pitcher, 10-Inning Game

11—Turley, Robert L., New York A.L., October 9, 1956.

Most Strikeouts, Game, Losing Pitcher, 12-Inning Game

12—Johnson, Walter P., Washington A.L., October 4, 1924.

Most Strikeouts, Game, Relief Pitcher

11—Drabowsky, Myron W., Baltimore A.L., October 5, 1966, last six and two-thirds innings.

Most Consecutive Strikeouts, Game

6—Eller, Horace O., Cincinnati N.L., October 6, 1919; 3 in second inning, 3 in third inning.
Drabowsky, Myron W., Baltimore A.L., October 5, 1966; 3 in fourth inning, 3 in fifth inning.
Worrell, Todd R., St. Louis N.L., October 24, 1985; 3 in sixth inning, 3 in seventh inning.

Most Consecutive Strikeouts, Start of Game

5—Cooper, Morton C., St. Louis N.L., October 11, 1943.
Koufax, Sanford, Los Angeles N.L., October 2, 1963.

Most Innings, One or More Strikeouts, Nine-Inning Game

9—Walsh, Edward A., Chicago A.L., October 11, 1906 (12 strikeouts).
Gibson, Robert, St. Louis N.L., October 2, 1968 (17 strikeouts).

Most Strikeouts, Inning

4—Overall, Orval, Chicago N.L., October 14, 1908, first inning.

Hit Batsmen, Wild Pitches & Balks

Most Hit Batsmen, Total Series

4—Donovan, William E., Detroit A.L., 1907 (3), 1908 (0), 1909 (1).
Plank, Edward S., Philadelphia A.L., 1905 (1), 1911 (1), 1913 (1), 1914 (1).

Most Hit Batsmen, Series

3—Donovan, William E., Detroit A.L., 1907.
Kison, Bruce E., Pittsburgh N.L., 1971.

Most Hit Batsmen, Game

3—Kison, Bruce E., Pittsburgh N.L., October 13, 1971, 6 1/3 innings.

Most Hit Batsmen, Inning

2—Willett, Robert E., Detroit A.L., October 11, 1909, second inning (consecutive).
Granger, Wayne A., St. Louis N.L., October 9, 1968, eighth inning.

Most Wild Pitches, Total Series

5—Shumacher, Harold H., New York N.L., 1933 (2), 1936 (2), 1937 (1).

Most Wild Pitches, Series

3—Tesreau, Charles M., New York N.L., 1912.
Stuper, John A., St. Louis N.L., 1982.

Most Wild Pitches, Game

2—Tesreau, Charles M., New York N.L., October 15, 1912.
Pfeffer, Edward J., Brooklyn N.L., October 12, 1916.
Shawkey, Robert J., New York A.L., October 5, 1922.
Aldridge, Victor, Pittsburgh N.L., October 15, 1925.
Miljus, John K., Pittsburgh N.L., October 8, 1927.
Carleton, James O., Chicago N.L., October 9, 1938.
Bouton, James A., New York A.L., October 5, 1963.
Stuper, John A., St. Louis N.L., October 13, 1982.
Medich, George F., Milwaukee A.L., October 19, 1982.
Morris, John S., Detroit A.L., October 13, 1984.
Darling, Ronald M., New York N.L., October 18, 1986.

Most Wild Pitches, Inning

2—Shawkey, J. Robert, New York A.L., October 5, 1922, fifth inning.
Aldridge, Victor, Pittsburgh N.L., October 15, 1925, first inning.
Miljus, John K., Pittsburgh N.L., October 8, 1927, ninth inning.
Carleton, James O., Chicago N.L., October 9, 1938, eighth inning.
Medich, George F., Milwaukee A.L., October 19, 1982, sixth inning.

Most Balks, Inning, Game, Series or Total Series

1—Held by many pitchers.

Club Pitching

Appearances

Most Appearances by Pitchers, Series

4-game Series—13—Chicago N.L., vs. New York A.L., 1932.
Chicago N.L., vs. New York A.L., 1938.
5-game Series—18—Cincinnati N.L., vs. Baltimore A.L., 1970.
6-game Series—22—New York A.L., vs. Los Angeles N.L., 1981.
7-game Series—30—Cincinnati N.L., vs. Boston A.L., 1975.
8-game Series—14—Boston A.L., vs. New York N.L., 1912.

Most Appearances by Pitchers, Series, Both Clubs

4-game Series—21—Cleveland A.L., 12, New York N.L., 9, 1954.
5-game Series—31—San Diego N.L., 17, Detroit A.L., 14, 1984.
6-game Series—40—New York A.L., 22, Los Angeles N.L., 18, 1981.
7-game Series—52—Cincinnati N.L., 30, Boston A.L., 22, 1975.
8-game Series—25—Chicago A.L., 13, Cincinnati N.L., 12, 1919.

Complete Games

Most Complete Games, Series

4-game Series—4—New York A.L., vs. St. Louis N.L., 1928.
5-game Series—5—Philadelphia A.L., vs. New York N.L., 1905.
    Philadelphia A.L., vs. Chicago N.L., 1910.
    Philadelphia A.L., vs. New York N.L., 1913.
    Boston A.L., vs. Philadelphia N.L., 1915.
6-game Series—5—Philadelphia A.L., vs. New York N.L., 1911.
    Boston A.L., vs. Chicago N.L., 1918.
7-game Series—5—Cleveland A.L., vs. Brooklyn N.L., 1920.
    New York A.L., vs. Brooklyn N.L., 1956.
8-game Series—7—Boston A.L., vs. Pittsburgh N.L., 1903.

Most Complete Games, Series, Both Clubs

4-game Series— 5—Boston N.L., 3, Philadelphia A.L., 2, 1914.
5-game Series— 9—Philadelphia A.L., 5, New York N.L., 4, 1905.
    Boston A.L., 5, Philadelphia N.L., 4, 1915.
6-game Series— 9—Boston A.L., 5, Chicago N.L., 4, 1918.
7-game Series— 8—(Series of 1909, 1920, 1925, 1934, 1940, 1956.)
8-game Series—13—Boston A.L., 7, Pittsburgh N.L., 6, 1903.

Fewest Complete Games, Series

4-game Series—0—Pittsburgh N.L., vs. New York A.L., 1927.
    St. Louis N.L., vs. New York A.L., 1928.
    Chicago N.L., vs. New York A.L., 1938.
    New York A.L., vs. Los Angeles N.L., 1963.
    Cincinnati N.L., vs. New York A.L., 1976.
5-game Series—0—Cincinnati N.L., vs. Baltimore A.L., 1970.
    Oakland A.L., vs. Los Angeles N.L., 1974.
    Los Angeles N.L., vs. Oakland A.L., 1974.
    Philadelphia N.L., vs. Baltimore A.L., 1983.
6-game Series—0—Chicago A.L., vs. Los Angeles N.L., 1959.
    Los Angeles N.L., vs. Chicago A.L., 1959.
    Los Angeles N.L., vs. New York A.L., 1978.
    Kansas City A.L., vs. Philadelphia N.L., 1980.
    Philadelphia N.L., vs. Kansas City A.L., 1980.
    New York A.L., vs. Los Angeles N.L., 1981.
7-game Series—0—Brooklyn N.L., vs. New York A.L., 1947.
    Pittsburgh N.L., vs. New York A.L., 1960.
    Oakland A.L., vs. Cincinnati N.L., 1972.
    Cincinnati N.L., vs. Oakland A.L., 1972.
    Oakland A.L., vs. New York N.L., 1973.
    New York N.L., vs. Oakland A.L., 1973.
    Cincinnati N.L., vs. Boston A.L., 1975.
    Pittsburgh N.L., vs. Baltimore A.L., 1979.
    New York N.L., vs. Boston A.L., 1986.
    St. Louis N.L., vs. Minnesota A.L., 1987.
    Minnesota A.L., vs. St. Louis N.L., 1987.
8-game Series—3—Boston A.L., vs. New York N.L., 1912.

Fewest Complete Games, Series, Both Clubs

4-game Series—1—New York A.L., 1, Cincinnati N.L., 0, 1976.
5-game Series—0—Oakland A.L., 0, Los Angeles N.L., 0, 1974.
6-game Series—0—Chicago A.L., 0, Los Angeles N.L., 0, 1959.
    Kansas City A.L., 0, Philadelphia N.L., 0, 1980.
7-game Series—0—Oakland A.L., 0, Cincinnati N.L., 0, 1972.
    Oakland A.L., 0, New York N.L., 0, 1973.
    St. Louis N.L., 0, Minnesota A.L., 0, 1987.
8-game Series—9—New York N.L., 6, Boston A.L., 3, 1912.

Saves

Most Saves, Series (Since 1969)

4-game Series—2—Cincinnati N.L., vs. New York A.L., 1976.
5-game Series—3—Oakland A.L., vs. Los Angeles N.L., 1974.
6-game Series—3—Philadelphia N.L., vs. Kansas City A.L., 1980.
7-game Series—4—Oakland A.L., vs. New York N.L., 1973.

Most Saves, Series, Both Clubs (Since 1969)

4-game Series—2—Cincinnati N.L., 2, New York A.L., 0, 1976.
5-game Series—4—Oakland A.L., 3, Los Angeles N.L., 1, 1974.

6-game Series—4—Philadelphia N.L., 3, Kansas City A.L., 1, 1980.
7-game Series—7—Oakland A.L., 4, New York N.L., 3, 1973.

Fewest Saves, Series (Since 1969)

4-game Series—0—New York A.L., vs. Cincinnati N.L., 1976.
5-game Series—0—Baltimore A.L., vs. New York N.L., 1969.
    Cincinnati N.L., vs. Baltimore A.L., 1970.
6-game Series—0—New York A.L., vs. Los Angeles N.L., 1977, 1978.
    Los Angeles N.L., vs. New York A.L., 1977.
7-game Series—0—Boston A.L., vs. Cincinnati N.L., 1975.
    Baltimore A.L., vs. Pittsburgh N.L., 1979.
    Kansas City A.L., vs. St. Louis N.L., 1985.

Fewest Saves, Series, Both Clubs (Since 1969)

4-game Series—2—Cincinnati N.L., 2, New York A.L., 0, 1976.
5-game Series—2—New York N.L., 2, Baltimore A.L., 0, 1976.
    Baltimore A.L., 2, Cincinnati N.L., 0, 1970.
6-game Series—0—New York A.L., 0, Los Angeles N.L., 0, 1977.
7-game Series—2—Cincinnati N.L., 2, Boston A.L., 0, 1975.
    St. Louis N.L., 2, Kansas City A.L., 0, 1985.

Runs & Shutouts

Most Runs Allowed, Total Series

651—New York A.L., 33 Series, 187 games.

Most Shutouts Won, Total Series

17—New York A.L.

Most Shutouts Won, Series

4—New York N.L., vs. Philadelphia A.L., 1905.

Most Consecutive Shutouts Won, Series

3—New York N.L., vs. Philadelphia A.L., October 12, 13, 14, 1905.
    Baltimore A.L., vs. Los Angeles N.L., October 6, 8, 9, 1966.

Most Shutouts, Series, Both Clubs

5—New York N.L., 4, Philadelphia A.L., 1, 1905.

Fewest Shutouts, Series

0—Held by many clubs in Series of all lengths.

Fewest Shutouts, Series, Both Clubs

0—Held by many clubs in Series of all lengths.

Longest Shutout Game

10 innings—New York N.L., 3, Philadelphia A.L., 0, October 8, 1913.
    Brooklyn N.L., 1, New York A.L., 0, October 9, 1956.

Largest Score, Shutout Game

12-0—New York A.L., 12, Pittsburgh N.L., 0, October 12, 1960.

Most Consecutive Innings Shut Out Opponents, Total Series

39—Baltimore A.L., October 5, 1966, fourth inning, through October 11, 1969, first six innings.

Most Consecutive Innings Shut Out Opponent, Series

33—Baltimore A.L., vs. Los Angeles N.L., October 5, fourth inning, through end of game, October 6, 8, 9, 1966.

1-0 Games

Most 1-0 Games Won, Total Series

3—New York A.L.
    New York (Giants) N.L.

Most 1-0 Games Won, Series

2—Baltimore A.L., vs. Los Angeles N.L., October 8, 9, 1966.

Most 1-0 Games Won, Series, Both Clubs

2—New York A.L., 1 (October 5), Brooklyn N.L., 1 (October 6), 1949.
    Baltimore A.L., 2 (October 8, 9), Los Angeles N.L., 0, 1966.

Wild Pitches & Balks

Most Wild Pitches, Series

5—Pittsburgh N.L., vs. New York A.L., 1960.

Most Wild Pitches, Series, Both Clubs

8—New York A.L., 4, Brooklyn N.L., 4, 1947.

Fewest Wild Pitches, Series, Both Clubs

   0—Cincinnati N.L., 0, Chicago A.L., 0, 1919 (8-game Series). Also in many shorter Series.

Most Balks, Series

   2—Cleveland A.L., vs. Boston N.L., 1948.
      Minnesota A.L., vs. St. Louis N.L., 1987.

Most Balks, Series, Both Clubs

   2—Cleveland A.L., 2, Boston N.L., 0, 1948.
      Minnesota A.L., 2, St. Louis N.L., 0, 1987.

Fewest Balks, Series, Both Clubs

   0—Made in Series of all lengths.

Individual Fielding

First Basemen
Series, Games & Average

Most Series Played

   8—Skowron, William J., New York A.L., 1955, 1956, 1957, 1958, 1960, 1961, 1962; Los Angeles N.L., 1963 (37 games).

Most Games Played, Total Series

   38—Hodges, Gilbert R., Brooklyn N.L., Los Angeles N.L., 1949, 1952, 1953, 1955, 1956, 1959; (6 Series).

Highest Fielding Average, Series, With Most Chances Accepted

   4-game Series—1.000—Schmidt, Charles J., Boston N.L., 1914 (55 chances accepted).
   5-game Series—1.000—Hoblitzel, Richard C., Boston A.L., 1916 (73 chances accepted).
   6-game Series—1.000—McInnis, John P., Boston A.L., 1918 (72 chances accepted).
   7-game Series—1.000—Bottomley, James L., St. Louis N.L., 1926 (80 chances accepted).
   8-game Series—1.000—Kelly, George L., New York N.L., 1921 (93 chances accepted).
                     Pipp, Walter C., New York A.L., 1921 (93 chances accepted).

Putouts, Assists & Chances Accepted

Most Putouts, Total Series

   326—Hodges, Gilbert R., Brooklyn N.L., Los Angeles N.L., 1949, 1952, 1953, 1955, 1956, 1959; 6 Series, 38 games.

Most Putouts, Series

   4-game Series—52—Schmidt, Charles J., Boston N.L., 1914.
   5-game Series—69—Hoblitzel, Richard C., Boston A.L., 1916.
   6-game Series—79—Donahue, John A., Chicago A.L., 1906.
   7-game Series—79—Bottomley, James L., St. Louis N.L., 1926.
   8-game Series—92—Pipp, Walter C., New York A.L., 1921.

Most Putouts, Game, Nine Innings

   19—Kelly, George L., New York N.L., October 15, 1923.

Fewest Putouts, Game, Nine Innings

   1—Cepeda, Orlando M., St. Louis N.L., October 2, 1968.

Most Putouts, Inning

   3—Held by many first basemen.

Most Assists, Total Series

   29—Skowron, William J., New York A.L., 1955, 1956, 1957, 1958, 1960, 1961, 1962; Los Angeles N.L., 1963; 8 Series, 37 games.

Most Assists, Series

   4-game Series— 6—Wertz, Victor W., Cleveland A.L., 1954.
                     Pepitone, Joseph A., New York A.L., 1963.
   5-game Series— 5—Rossman, Claude, Detroit A.L., 1908.
                     Camilli, Adolph, Brooklyn N.L., 1941.
                     Sanders, Raymond F., St. Louis N.L., 1943.
                     Skowron, William J., New York A.L., 1961.
   6-game Series— 9—Merkle, Fred C., Chicago N.L., 1918.
   7-game Series—10—Cooper, Cecil C., Milwaukee A.L., 1982.
   8-game Series— 7—Kelly, George L., New York N.L., 1921.

Most Assists, Game, Nine Innings

   4—Owen, Marvin J., Detroit A.L., October 6, 1935.
      Mincher, Donald R., Minnesota A.L., October 7, 1965.

Most Assists, Inning

   2—Held by many first basemen.

Most Chances Accepted, Total Series

   350—Hodges, Gilbert R., Brooklyn N.L., Los Angeles N.L., 1949, 1952, 1953, 1955, 1956, 1959; 6 Series, 38 games.

Most Chances Accepted, Series

   4-game Series—55—Schmidt, Charles J., Boston N.L., 1914.
   5-game Series—73—Hoblitzel, Richard C., Boston A.L., 1916.
   6-game Series—87—Donahue, John A., Chicago A.L., 1906.
   7-game Series—81—Cooper, Cecil C., Milwaukee A.L., 1982.
   8-game Series—93—Kelly, George L., New York N.L., 1921.
                     Pipp, Walter C., New York A.L., 1921.

Most Chances Accepted, Game, Nine Innings

   19—Konetchy, Edward J., Brooklyn N.L., October 7, 1920; 17 putouts, 2 assists, 0 errors.
      Kelly, George L., New York N.L., October 15, 1923; 19 putouts, 0 assists, 0 errors.

Fewest Chances Offered, Game, Nine Innings

   2—Pipp, Walter C., New York A.L., October 11, 1921; 2 putouts, 0 assists.
      Cepeda, Orlando M., St. Louis N.L., October 2, 1968; 1 putout, 1 assist.

Most Chances Accepted, Inning

   3—Held by many first basemen.

Errors & Double Plays

Most Errors, Total Series

   8—Merkle, Frederick C., New York N.L., 1911, 1912, 1913 (7); Brooklyn N.L., 1916 (1), Chicago N.L., 1918 (0), 5 Series, 25 games.

Most Consecutive Errorless Games, Total Series

   31—Skowron, William J., New York A.L., Los Angeles N.L., October 10, 1956 through October 6, 1963.

Most Errors, Series

   4-game Series—1—McInnis, John P., Philadelphia A.L., 1914.
                   Gehrig, H. Louis, New York A.L., 1932.
                   Wertz, Victor W. Cleveland A.L., 1954.
                   Pepitone, Joseph A., New York A.L., 1963.
                   Chambliss, C. Christopher, New York A.L., 1976.
   5-game Series—3—Chance, Frank L., Chicago N.L., 1908.
                   Davis, Harry H., Philadelphia A.L., 1910.
   6-game Series—3—Greenberg, Henry, Detroit A.L., 1935.
   7-game Series—5—Abstein, William H., Pittsburgh N.L., 1909.
   8-game Series—3—Merkle, Fred C., New York N.L., 1912.

Most Errors, Game, Nine Innings

   2—Held by many first basemen.

Most Errors, Inning

   2—Greenberg, Henry, Detroit A.L., October 3, 1935, fifth inning.
      McCarthy, John J., New York N.L., October 8, 1937, fifth inning.
      Torre, Frank J., Milwaukee N.L., October 9, 1958, second inning.

Most Double Plays, Total Series

   31—Hodges, Gilbert R., Brooklyn N.L., Los Angeles N.L., 1949, 1952, 1953, 1955, 1956, 1959; 6 Series, 38 games.

Most Double Plays, Series

   4-game Series— 7—Pepitone, Joseph A., New York A.L., 1963.
   5-game Series— 7—Pipp, Walter C., New York A.L., 1922.
   6-game Series— 8—Robinson, W. Edward, Cleveland A.L., 1948.
                   Rose, Peter E., Philadelphia N.L., 1980.
   7-game Series—11—Hodges, Gilbert R., Brooklyn N.L., 1955.
   8-game Series— 6—Gandil, Charles A., Chicago A.L., 1919.

Most Double Plays, Started, Series

   4-game Series— 1—Held by many first basemen.
   5-game Series— 2—May, Lee A., Cincinnati N.L., 1970.
                   Garvey, Steven P., San Diego N.L., 1984.

6-game Series—1—Held by many first basemen.
7-game Series—3—Hodges, Gilbert R., Brooklyn N.L., 1955.
8-game Series—1—Stahl, J. Garland, Boston A.L., 1912.

Most Double Plays, Game, Nine Innings

4—McInnis, John P., Philadelphia A.L., October 9, 1914.
Collins, Joseph E., New York A.L., October 8, 1951.
Tenace, F. Gene, Oakland A.L., October 17, 1973.
Rose, Peter E., Philadelphia N.L., October 15, 1980.

Most Double Plays Started, Game

2—Murray, Eddie C., Baltimore A.L., October 11, 1979.

Most Unassisted Double Plays, Game

1—Grantham, George F., Pittsburgh N.L., October 7, 1925.
Judge, Joseph I., Washington A.L., October 13, 1925.
Foxx, James L., Philadelphia A.L., October 8, 1930.
Bottomley, James L., St. Louis N.L., October 1, 1931.
Gehrig, H. Louis, New York A.L., October 10, 1937.
Collins, James A., Chicago N.L., October 5, 1938.
Collins, Joseph E., New York A.L., October 7, 1956.
Coleman, Gordon C., Cincinnati, N.L., October 8, 1961.
Perez, Atanasio R., Cincinnati N.L., October 11, 1975.
Garvey, Steven P., San Diego N.L., October 9, 1984.

Second Basemen
Series, Games & Average

Most Series Played

7—Frisch, Frank F., New York N.L., 1922, 1923, 1924; St. Louis N.L., 1928, 1930, 1931, 1934 (42 games).

Most Games Played, Total Series

42—Frisch, Frank F., New York N.L. (18), 1922, 1923, 1924; St. Louis N.L. (24), 1928, 1930, 1931, 1934; 7 Series.

Highest Fielding Average, Series, With Most Chances Accepted

4-game Series—1.000—Johnson, David A., Baltimore A.L., 1966 (24 chances accepted).
5-game Series—1.000—Gordon, Joseph L., New York A.L., 1943 (43 chances accepted).
6-game Series—1.000—Gehringer, Charles L., Detroit A.L., 1935 (39 chances accepted).
7-game Series—1.000—Doerr, Robert P., Boston A.L., 1946 (49 chances accepted).
8-game Series—1.000—Ritchey, Claude C., Pittsburgh N.L., 1903 (48 chances accepted).

Putouts, Assists & Chances Accepted

Most Putouts, Total Series

104—Frisch, Frank F., New York N.L., St. Louis N.L., 1922, 1923, 1924, 1928, 1930, 1931, 1934; 7 Series, 42 games.

Most Putouts, Series

4-game Series—13—Goliat, Mike, Philadelphia N.L., 1950.
Morgan, Joe L., Cincinnati N.L., 1976.
5-game Series—20—Gordon, Joseph L., New York A.L., 1943.
6-game Series—26—Lopes, David E., Los Angeles N.L., 1981.
7-game Series—26—Harris, Stanley R., Washington A.L., 1924.
8-game Series—22—Rath, Maurice C., Cincinnati N.L., 1919.

Most Putouts, Game, Nine Innings

8—Harris, Stanley R., Washington A.L., October 8, 1924.
Lopes, David E., Los Angeles N.L., October 16, 1974.

Most Putouts, Game, Eleven Innings

9—Critz, Hugh M., New York N.L., October 6, 1933.

Most Putouts, Inning

3—Doyle, Lawrence J., New York N.L., October 9, 1913, seventh inning.
Wambsganss, William A., Cleveland A.L., October 10, 1920, fifth inning.
Rawlings, John M., New York N.L., October 11, 1921, ninth inning.
Lopes, David E., Los Angeles N.L., October 16, 1974, sixth inning.
Lopes, David E., Los Angeles N.L., October 21, 1981, fourth inning.

Most Assists, Total Series

135—Frisch, Frank F., New York N.L., St. Louis N.L., 1922, 1923, 1924, 1928, 1930, 1931, 1934; 7 Series, 42 games.

Most Assists, Series

4-game Series—18—Lazzeri, Anthony M., New York A.L., 1927.
5-game Series—23—Gordon, Joseph L., New York A.L., 1943.
6-game Series—27—Ward, Aaron L., New York A.L., 1923.
7-game Series—33—Gantner, James E., Milwaukee A.L., 1982.
8-game Series—34—Ward, Aaron L., New York A.L., 1921.

Most Assists, Game, Nine Innings

8—Ritchey, Claude C., Pittsburgh, N.L., October 10, 1903.
Schaefer, Herman, Detroit A.L., October 12, 1907.
Janvrin, Harold C., Boston A.L., October 7, 1916.
Collins, Edward T., Chicago A.L., October 15, 1917.
Harris, Stanley R., Washington A.L., October 7, 1924.
Gordon, Joseph L., New York A.L., October 5, 1943.
Doerr, Robert P., Boston A.L., October 9, 1946.

Most Assists, Inning

3—Collins, Edward T., Philadelphia A.L., October 12, 1914, fourth inning.
Kilduff, Peter J., Brooklyn N.L., October 10, 1920, third inning.
Ward, Aaron L., New York A.L., October 12, 1921, sixth inning.
Gordon, Joseph L., New York A.L., October 11, 1943, eighth inning.
Robinson, Jack R., Brooklyn N.L., October 8, 1949, seventh inning.
Garner, Philip M., Pittsburgh N.L., October 13, 1979, ninth inning.
Barrett, Martin G., Boston A.L., October 23, 1986; first inning.

Most Chances Accepted, Total Series

239—Frisch, Frank F., New York N.L., St. Louis N.L., 1922, 1923, 1924, 1928, 1930, 1931, 1934; 7 Series, 42 games.

Most Chances Accepted, Series

4-game Series—28—Lazzeri, Anthony M., New York A.L., 1927.
5-game Series—43—Gordon, Joseph L., New York A.L., 1943.
6-game Series—40—Lopes, David E., Los Angeles N.L., 1981.
7-game Series—54—Harris, Stanley R., Washington A.L., 1924.
8-game Series—52—Collins, Edward T., Chicago A.L., 1919.
Ward, Aaron L., New York A.L., 1921.

Most Chances Accepted, Game, Nine Innings

13—Ritchey, Claude C., Pittsburgh N.L., October 10, 1903; 5 putouts, 8 assists, 0 errors.
Harris, Stanley R., Washington A.L., October 11, 1925; 6 putouts, 7 assists, 0 errors.
Lopes, David E., Los Angeles N.L., October 16, 1974; 8 putouts, 5 assists, 0 errors.

Most Chances Accepted, Game, Eleven Innings

14—Critz, Hugh M., New York N.L., October 6, 1933; 9 putouts, 5 assists, 0 errors.

Fewest Chances Offered, Game, Nine Innings

0—Pick, Charles, Chicago N.L., September 7, 1918.
Bishop, Max F., Philadelphia A.L., October 6, 1931.
Coleman, Gerald F., New York A.L., October 8, 1949.
Randolph, William L., New York A.L., October 25, 1981.
White, Frank, Kansas City A.L., October 20, 1985.

Most Chances Accepted, Inning

3—Held by many second basemen.

Errors & Double Plays

Most Errors, Total Series

8—Doyle, Lawrence J., New York N.L., 1911, 1912, 1913; 3 Series, 19 games.
Collins, Edward T., Philadelphia A.L., 1910, 1911, 1913, 1914, Chicago A.L., 1917, 1919; 6 Series, 34 games.

Most Consecutive Errorless Games, Total Series

23—Martin, Alfred M., New York A.L., October 5, 1952 through October 10, 1956.

Most Errors, Series

4-game Series—2—Lazzeri, Anthony M., New York A.L., 1928.
Gordon, Joseph L., New York A.L., 1938.
Herman, William J., Chicago N.L., 1938.
Morgan, Joe L., Cincinnati N.L., 1976.
5-game Series—4—Murphy, Daniel F., Philadelphia A.L., 1905.
6-game Series—6—Lopes, David E., Los Angeles N.L., 1981.
7-game Series—5—Gantner, James E., Milwaukee A.L., 1982.
8-game Series—4—Doyle, Lawrence J., New York N.L., 1912.

Most Errors, Game, Nine Innings

3—Murphy, Daniel F., Philadelphia A.L., October 12, 1905.
Myer, Charles S., Washington A.L., October 3, 1933.
Lopes, David E., Los Angeles N.L., October 25, 1981.

Most Errors, Inning

2—Murphy, Daniel F., Philadelphia A.L., October 12, 1905, fifth inning.
Andrews, Michael J., Oakland A.L., October 14, 1973, twelfth inning.
Lopes, David E., Los Angeles N.L., October 25, 1981, fourth inning.

Most Double Plays, Total Series

24—Frisch, Frank F., New York N.L., St. Louis N.L., 1922, 1923, 1924, 1928, 1930, 1931, 1934; 7 Series, 42 games.

Most Double Plays, Series

4-game Series—6—Herman, William J., Chicago N.L., 1932.
5-game Series—6—Green, Richard L., Oakland A.L., 1974.
6-game Series—7—Frisch, Frank F., New York N.L., 1923.
Gordon, Joseph L., Cleveland A.L., 1948.
Neal, Charles L., Los Angeles N.L., 1959.
7-game Series—9—Garner, Philip M., Pittsburgh N.L., 1979.
8-game Series—7—Collins, Edward T., Chicago A.L., 1919.

Most Double Plays Started, Series

4-game Series—5—Herman, William J., Chicago N.L., 1932.
5-game Series—4—Gordon, Joseph L., New York A.L., 1941.
Green, Richard L., Oakland A.L., 1974.
6-game Series—2—Held by many second basemen.
7-game Series—4—Herr, Thomas M., St. Louis N.L., 1985.
8-game Series—4—Ritchey, Claude C., Pittsburgh N.L., 1903.

Most Double Plays, Game, Nine Innings

3—Held by many second basemen.

Most Double Plays Started, Game, Nine Innings

3—Green, Richard L., Oakland A.L., October 15, 1974.

Most Unassisted Double Plays, Game

1—Ferris, Hobart, Boston A.L., October 2, 1903.
Doyle, Lawrence J., New York N.L., October 9, 1913.
Herzog, Charles L., New York N.L., October 7, 1917.
White, Frank, Kansas City A.L., October 17, 1980.

Unassisted Triple Play

1—Wambsganss, William A., Cleveland A.L., October 10, 1920.

Third Basemen
Series, Games & Average

Most Series Played

6—Rolfe, Robert A., New York A.L., 1936, 1937, 1938, 1939, 1941, 1942 (28 games).

Most Games Played, Total Series

31—McDougald, Gilbert J., New York A.L., 1951, 1952, 1953, 1955, 1960; 5 Series.

Highest Fielding Average, Series, With Most Chances Accepted

4-game Series—1.000—Baker, J. Frank, Philadelphia A.L., 1914 (25 chances accepted).
5-game Series—1.000—Groh, Henry K., New York N.L., 1922 (20 chances accepted).
6-game Series—1.000—Nettles, Graig, New York A.L., 1978 (26 chances accepted).
7-game Series—1.000—Menke, Denis J., Cincinnati N.L., 1972 (29 chances accepted).
8-game Series—1.000—Herzog, Charles L., New York N.L., 1912 (27 chances accepted).

Putouts, Assists & Chances Accepted

Most Putouts, Total Series

37—Baker, J. Frank, Philadelphia A.L., New York A.L., 1910, 1911, 1913, 1914, 1921; 5 Series, 22 games.

Most Putouts, Series

4-game Series—10—Baker, J. Frank, Philadelphia A.L., 1914.
5-game Series—10—Steinfeldt, Harry M., Chicago N.L., 1907.
6-game Series—14—Rolfe, Robert A., New York A.L., 1936.
7-game Series—13—Kurowski, George J., St. Louis N.L., 1946.
8-game Series—13—Frisch, Frank F., New York N.L., 1921.

Most Putouts, Game, Nine Innings

4—Devlin, Arthur, New York N.L., October 13, 1905.
Coughlin, William P., Detroit A.L., October 10, 1907.
Byrne, Robert M., Pittsburgh N.L., October 9, 1909.
Leach, Thomas W., Pittsburgh N.L., October 16, 1909.
Baker, J. Frank, Philadelphia A.L., October 24, 1911.
Zimmerman, Henry, New York N.L., October 7, 1917.
Dykes, James, Philadelphia A.L., October 2, 1930.
Elliott, Robert I., Boston N.L., October 11, 1948.
Jones, Willie E., Philadelphia N.L., October 4, 1950.

Most Putouts, Inning

2—Held by many third basemen.

Most Assists, Total Series

68—Nettles, Graig, New York A.L., 1976, 1977, 1978, 1981; San Diego N.L., 1984; 5 Series, 24 games.

Most Assists, Series

4-game Series—15—Baker, J. Frank, Philadelphia A.L., 1914.
5-game Series—18—Gardner, W. Lawrence, Boston A.L., 1916.
6-game Series—20—Nettles, Graig, New York A.L., 1977.
7-game Series—30—Higgins, Michael F., Detroit A.L., 1940.
8-game Series—24—Frisch, Frank F., New York N.L., 1921.

Most Assists, Game, Nine Innings

9—Higgins, Michael F., Detroit A.L., October 5, 1940.

Most Assists, Inning

3—Pagan, Jose A., Pittsburgh N.L., October 14, 1971, ninth inning.
Bando, Salvatore L., Oakland A.L., October 16, 1974, sixth inning.
Boggs, Wade A., Boston A.L., October 19, 1986, third inning.

Most Chances Accepted, Total Series

96—Nettles, Graig, New York A.L., 1976, 1977, 1978, 1981; San Diego N.L., 1984; 5 Series, 24 games.

Most Chances Accepted, Series

4-game Series—25—Baker, J. Frank, Philadelphia A.L., 1914.
5-game Series—25—Gardner, W. Lawrence, Boston A.L., 1916.
6-game Series—27—Thomson, Robert B., New York N.L., 1951.
7-game Series—34—Higgins, Michael F., Detroit A.L., 1940.
8-game Series—37—Frisch, Frank F., New York N.L., 1921.

Most Chances Accepted, Game, Nine Innings

10—Higgins, Michael F., Detroit A.L., October 5, 1940, 1 putout, 9 assists, 1 error.

Fewest Chances Offered, Game, Nine Innings

0—Held by many third basemen.

Most Chances Accepted, Inning

4—Mathews, Edwin L., Milwaukee N.L., October 5, 1957, third inning.

Errors & Double Plays

Most Errors, Total Series

8—Gardner, W. Lawrence, Boston A.L., 1912, 1915, 1916 (6), Cleveland A.L., 1920 (2), 4 Series, 25 games.

Most Consecutive Errorless Games, Total Series

22—Cey, Ronald C., Los Angeles N.L., October 13, 1974 through October 28, 1981.

Most Errors, Series

4-game Series—2—Rolfe, Robert A., New York A.L., 1938.
5-game Series—4—Steinfeldt, Harry M., Chicago N.L., 1910.
6-game Series—3—Rohe, George, Chicago A.L., 1906.
Herzog, Charles L., New York N.L., 1911.
Jackson, Travis C., New York N.L., 1936.
Elliott, Robert I., Boston N.L., 1948.
7-game Series—4—Martin, John L., St. Louis N.L., 1934.
McDougald, Gilbert J., New York A.L., 1952.
8-game Series—4—Leach, Thomas W., Pittsburgh N.L., 1903.
Gardner, W. Lawrence, Boston A.L., 1912.

Most Errors, Game, Nine Innings

3—Martin, John L., St. Louis N.L., October 6, 1934.

Most Errors, Inning

2—Steinfeldt, Harry M., Chicago N.L., October 18, 1910, third inning.
DeCinces, Douglas V., Baltimore A.L., October 10, 1979, sixth inning.

Most Double Plays, Total Series

7—Nettles, Graig, New York A.L., 1976, 1977, 1978, 1981; San Diego N.L., 1984; 5 Series, 24 games.

Most Double Plays, Series

4-game Series—3—Nettles, Graig, New York A.L., 1976.
5-game Series—2—Jackson, Travis C., New York N.L., 1933.
Robinson, Brooks C., Baltimore A.L., 1970.
6-game Series—3—Nettles, Graig, New York A.L., 1978.
Dugan, Joseph A., New York A.L., 1923.
7-game Series—4—Davenport, James H., San Francisco N.L., 1962.
Madlock, Bill, Pittsburgh N.L., 1979.
8-game Series—3—Frisch, Frank F., New York N.L., 1921.

Most Double Plays Started, Series

4-game Series—2—Rolfe, Robert A., New York A.L., 1939.
Nettles, Graig, New York A.L., 1976.
5-game Series—2—Jackson, Travis C., New York N.L., 1933.
Robinson, Brooks C., Baltimore A.L., 1970.
6-game Series—3—Nettles, Graig, New York A.L., 1978.
7-game Series—4—Davenport, James H., San Francisco N.L., 1962.
8-game Series—2—Frisch, Frank F., New York N.L., 1921.

Most Double Plays, Game, Nine Innings

2—Held by many third basemen.

Most Double Plays Started, Game, Nine Innings

2—McMullin, Fred W., Chicago A.L., October 13, 1917.
Bluege, Oswald L., Washington A.L., October 5, 1924.
Kurowski, George J., St. Louis N.L., October 13, 1946.
Boyer, Cletis L., New York A.L., October 12, 1960.
Jones, J. Dalton, Boston A.L., October 4, 1967.
Nettles, Graig, New York A.L., October 19, 1976.

Most Unassisted Double Plays, Game

Never accomplished.

Shortstops
Series, Games & Average

Most Series Played

9—Rizzuto, Philip F., New York A.L., 1941, 1942, 1947, 1949, 1950, 1951, 1952, 1953, 1955 (52 games).

Most Games Played, Total Series

52—Rizzuto, Philip F., New York A.L., 1941, 1942, 1947, 1949, 1950, 1951, 1952, 1953, 1955; 9 Series.

Highest Fielding Average, Series, With Most Chances Accepted

4-game Series—1.000—Wills, Maurice M., Los Angeles N.L., 1966 (27 chances accepted).
5-game Series—1.000—Dahlen, William F., New York N.L., 1905 (29 chances accepted).
Scott, L. Everett, New York A.L., 1922 (29 chances accepted).
Marion, Martin W., St. Louis N.L., 1942 (29 chances accepted).
Harrelson, Derrel M., New York N.L., 1969 (29 chances accepted).
6-game Series—1.000—Scott, L. Everett, Boston A.L., 1918 (36 chances accepted).
7-game Series—1.000—Gelbert, Charles M., St. Louis N.L., 1931 (42 chances accepted).
8-game Series— .979—Peckinpaugh, Roger T., New York A.L., 1921 (46 chances accepted).

Putouts, Assists & Chances Accepted

Most Putouts, Total Series

107—Rizzuto, Philip F., New York A.L., 1941, 1942, 1947, 1949, 1950, 1951, 1952, 1953, 1955; 9 Series, 52 games.

Most Putouts, Series

4-game Series—16—Crosetti, Frank P. J., New York A.L., 1938.
5-game Series—15—Tinker, Joseph B., Chicago N.L., 1907.
Rizzuto, Philip F., New York A.L., 1942.
6-game Series—16—Jurges, William F., Chicago N.L., 1935.
7-game Series—22—Smith, Osborne E., St. Louis N.L., 1982.
8-game Series—24—Wagner, Charles, Boston A.L., 1912.

Most Putouts, Game, Nine Innings

7—Weaver, George D., Chicago A.L., October 7, 1917.
Rizzuto, Philip F., New York A.L., October 5, 1942.

Most Putouts, Inning

3—Stanley, Mitchell J., Detroit A.L., October 10, 1968, sixth inning.

Most Assists, Total Series

143—Rizzuto, Philip F., New York A.L., 1941, 1942, 1947, 1949, 1950, 1951, 1952, 1953, 1955; 9 Series, 52 games.

Most Assists, Series

4-game Series—21—Barry, John J., Philadelphia A.L., 1914.
5-game Series—25—Scott, L. Everett, Boston A.L., 1916.
6-game Series—26—Russell, William E., Los Angeles N.L., 1981.
7-game Series—32—Foli, Timothy J., Pittsburgh N.L., 1979.
8-game Series—30—Parent, Frederick A., Boston A.L., 1903.

Most Assists, Game, Nine Innings

9—Peckinpaugh, Roger T., New York A.L., October 5, 1921.

Most Assists, Extra-Inning Game

10—Logan, John, Milwaukee N.L., October 6, 1957, 10 innings.

Most Assists, Inning

3—Bancroft, David J., New York N.L., October 8, 1922, third inning.
Bluege, Oswald L., Washington, A.L., October 7, 1924, sixth inning.
Wright, F. Glenn, Pittsburgh N.L., October 8, 1927, second inning.
Ryan, John C., New York N.L., October 7, 1933, third inning.
Rizzuto, Philip F., New York A.L., October 3, 1942, second inning.
Bowman, Ernest F., San Francisco N.L., October 8, 1962, ninth inning.
Harrelson, Derrel M., New York N.L., October 14, 1969, fifth inning.
Belanger, Mark H., Baltimore A.L., October 16, 1971, seventh inning.
Harrelson, Derrel M., New York N.L., October 13, 1973, seventh inning.
Foli, Timothy J., Pittsburgh N.L., October 12, 1979, second inning.

Most Chances Accepted, Total Series

250—Rizzuto, Philip F., New York A.L., 1941, 1942, 1947, 1949, 1950, 1951, 1952, 1953, 1955; 9 Series, 52 games.

Most Chances Accepted, Series

4-game Series—27—Wills, Maurice M., Los Angeles N.L., 1966.
5-game Series—38—Tinker, Joseph B., Chicago N.L., 1907.
6-game Series—37—Rizzuto, Philip F., New York A.L., 1951.
7-game Series—42—Gelbert, Charles M., St. Louis N.L., 1931.
8-game Series—51—Risberg, Charles A., Chicago A.L., 1919.

Most Chances Accepted, Game, Nine Innings

13—Weaver, George D., Chicago A.L., October 7, 1917; 7 putouts, 6 assists, 0 errors.

Fewest Chances Offered, Game, Nine Innings

0—Boley, John P., Philadelphia A.L., October 8, 1929.
Rizzuto, Philip F., New York A.L., October 7, 1949.
Versalles, Zoilo, Minnesota A.L., October 7, 1965.
Petrocelli, Americo, Boston A.L., October 4, 1967.
Campaneris, Dagoberto B., Oakland A.L., October 18, 1972.
Concepcion, David I., Cincinnati N.L., October 16, 1975.
Smith, Osborne E., St. Louis N.L., October 23, 1985.

Fewest Chances Offered, Game, Eight Innings

0—Bancroft, David J., New York N.L., October 12, 1915.
Reese, Harold H., Brooklyn N.L., October 1, 1947.

Most Chances Accepted, Inning

3—Held by many shortstops.

Errors & Double Plays

Most Errors, Total Series

12—Fletcher, Arthur, New York N.L., 1911, 1912, 1913, 1917; 4 Series, 25 games.

Most Consecutive Errorless Games, Total Series

21—Rizzuto, Philip F., New York A.L., October 3, 1942 through October 5, 1951.

Most Errors, Series

4-game Series—4—Crosetti, Frank P. J., New York A.L., 1932.
5-game Series—4—Olson, Ivan M., Brooklyn N.L., 1916.
English, Elwood G., Chicago N.L., 1929.
6-game Series—4—Fletcher, Arthur, New York N.L., 1911.
Weaver, George D., Chicago A.L., 1917.
7-game Series—8—Peckinpaugh, Roger T., Washington A.L., 1925.
8-game Series—6—Wagner, John P., Pittsburgh N.L., 1903.

Most Errors, Game, Nine Innings

3—Barry, John J., Philadelphia A.L., October 26, 1911.
Fletcher, Arthur, New York N.L., October 9, 1912.
Weaver, George D., Chicago A.L., October 13, 1917.

Most Errors, Inning

2—Peckinpaugh, Roger T., Washington A.L., October 8, 1925, eighth inning.
English, Elwood G., Chicago N.L., October 8, 1929, ninth inning.
Bartell, Richard, New York N.L., October 9, 1937, third inning.
Reese, Harold H., Brooklyn N.L., October 2, 1941, eighth inning.

Most Double Plays, Total Series

32—Rizzuto, Philip F., New York A.L., 1941, 1942, 1947, 1949, 1950, 1951, 1952, 1953, 1955; 9 Series, 52 games.

Most Double Plays, Series

4-game Series—5—Jurges, William F., Chicago N.L., 1932.
Kubek, Anthony C., New York A.L., 1963.
5-game Series—6—Scott, L. Everett, New York A.L., 1922.
Rizzuto, Philip F., New York A.L., 1941.
6-game Series—8—Rizzuto, Philip F., New York A.L., 1951.
7-game Series—7—Reese, Harold H., Brooklyn N.L., 1955, 1956.
Foli, Timothy J., Pittsburgh N.L., 1979.
8-game Series—6—Risberg, Charles A., Chicago A.L., 1919.

Most Double Plays Started, Series

4-game Series—3—Koenig, Mark A., New York A.L., 1928.
5-game Series—4—Tinker, Joseph B., Chicago N.L., 1907.
6-game Series—7—Bowa, Lawrence R., Philadelphia N.L., 1980.
7-game Series—4—Reese, Harold H., Brooklyn N.L., 1947.
McDougald, Gilbert J., New York A.L., 1957.
Linz, Philip F., New York A.L., 1964.
Wills, Maurice M., Los Angeles N.L., 1965.
Foli, Timothy J., Pittsburgh N.L., 1979.
8-game Series—4—Risberg, Charles A., Chicago A.L., 1919.

Most Unassisted Double Plays, Series

2—Tinker, Joseph B., Chicago N.L., October 10, 11, 1907.

Most Double Plays, Game, Nine Innings

4—Rizzuto, Philip F., New York A.L., October 8, 1951.

Most Double Plays Started, Game, Nine Innings

3—Rizzuto, Philip F., New York A.L., October 10, 1951.
Wills, Maurice M., Los Angeles N.L., October 11, 1965.
Bowa, Lawrence R., Philadelphia N.L., October 15, 1980.

Most Unassisted Double Plays, Game

1—Tinker, Joseph B., Chicago N.L., October 10, 1907, and October 11, 1907.
Gelbert, Charles M., St. Louis N.L., October 2, 1930.
Kasko, Edward M., Cincinnati N.L., October 7, 1961.

Outfielders
Series, Games & Average

Most Series Played

12—Mantle, Mickey C., New York A.L., 1951, 1952, 1953, 1955, 1956, 1957, 1958, 1960, 1961, 1962, 1963, 1964 (63 games).

Most Games Played, Total Series

63—Mantle, Mickey C., New York A.L., 1951, 1952, 1953, 1955, 1956, 1957, 1958, 1960, 1961, 1962, 1963, 1964; 12 Series.

Highest Fielding Average, Series, With Most Chances Accepted

4-game Series—1.000—Combs, Earle B., New York A.L., 1927 (16 chances accepted).
5-game Series—1.000—DiMaggio, Joseph P., New York A.L., 1942 (20 chances accepted).
6-game Series—1.000—Rivers, John M., New York A.L., 1977 (25 chances accepted).
7-game Series—1.000—Evans, Dwight M., Boston A.L., 1975 (24 chances accepted).
Geronimo, Cesar F., Cincinnati N.L., 1975 (24 chances accepted).
Lynn, Fredric M., Boston A.L., 1975 (24 chances accepted).
McGee, Willie D., St. Louis N.L., 1982 (24 chances accepted).
8-game Series—1.000—Murray, John J., New York N.L., 1912 (24 chances accepted).

Putouts, Assists & Chances Accepted

Most Putouts, Total Series

150—DiMaggio, Joseph P., New York A.L., 1936, 1937, 1938, 1939, 1941, 1942, 1947, 1949, 1950, 1951; 10 Series, 51 games.

Most Putouts, Series

4-game Series—16—Combs, Earle B., New York A.L., 1927.
5-game Series—20—DiMaggio, Joseph P., New York A.L., 1942.
6-game Series—24—Rivers, John M., New York A.L., 1977.
7-game Series—24—McCormick, Myron W., Cincinnati N.L., 1940.
Pafko, Andrew, Chicago N.L., 1945.
McGee, Willie D., St. Louis N.L., 1982.
8-game Series—30—Roush, Edd J., Cincinnati N.L., 1919.

Most Putouts, Game

8—Roush, Edd J., Cincinnati N.L., October 1, 1919.
Foster, George A., Cincinnati N.L., October 21, 1976.

Most Putouts, Game, Left Field

8—Foster, George A., Cincinnati N.L., October 21, 1976.

Most Putouts, Game, Center Field

9—Otis, Amos J., Kansas City A.L., October 17, 1980, 10 innings.
8—Roush, Edd J., Cincinnati N.L., October 1, 1919.

Most Putouts, Game, Right Field

7—Murray, John J., New York N.L., October 14, 1912.
Miller, Edmund J., Philadelphia A.L., October 5, 1930.
Blades, Raymond F., St. Louis N.L., October 5, 1930.
Oliva, Pedro, Minnesota A.L., October 6, 1965.
Kaline, Albert W., Detroit A.L., October 9, 1968.
Robinson, Frank, Baltimore A.L., October 14, 1969.

Most Consecutive Putouts, Game

4—Donlin, Michael J., New York N.L., October 13, 1905 (1 in third inning, 3 in fourth inning, center field).
Paskert, George H., Philadelphia N.L., October 11, 1915 (3 in fourth inning, 1 in fifth inning, center field).
Keller, Charles E., New York A.L., October 1, 1941 (1 in second inning, 3 in third inning, left field).
Irvin, Monford M., New York N.L., September 29, 1954 (1 in eighth inning, 3 in ninth inning, left field; Irvin dropped fly for error after second putout in ninth inning).
Agee, Tommie L., New York N.L., October 14, 1969 (3 in seventh inning, 1 in eighth inning, center field).
Oglivie, Benjamin A., Milwaukee A.L., October 19, 1982 (1 in sixth inning, 3 in seventh inning, left field).

Most Putouts, Inning, Left Field

3—Keller, Charles E., New York A.L., October 1, 1941, third inning.
Irvin, Monford M., New York N.L., September 29, 1954, ninth inning.
Davis, H. Thomas, Los Angeles N.L., October 3, 1963, seventh inning.
Oglivie, Benjamin A., Milwaukee A.L., October 19, 1982, seventh inning.

Most Putouts, Inning, Center Field

3—Donlin, Michael J., New York N.L., October 13, 1905, fourth inning.
Paskert, George H., Philadelphia N.L., October 11, 1915, fourth inning.
Orsatti, Ernest R., St. Louis N.L., October 8, 1934, fifth inning.
DiMaggio, Joseph P., New York A.L., October 2, 1936, ninth inning, and October 7, 1937, sixth inning.
Maris, Roger E., New York A.L., October 11, 1964, third inning.
Smith, C. Reginald, Boston A.L., October 11, 1967, seventh inning.
Agee, Tommie L., New York N.L., October 14, 1969, seventh inning.
McGee, Willie D., St. Louis N.L., October 22, 1987, eighth inning.

Most Putouts, Inning, Right Field

3—Ott, Melvin T., New York N.L., October 4, 1933, seventh inning.
Hazle, Robert S., Milwaukee N.L., October 10, 1957, fourth inning.
Swoboda, Ronald A., New York N.L., October 15, 1969, ninth inning.
Moore, Charles W., Milwaukee A.L., October 12, 1982, eighth inning.

Most Assists, Total Series

5—Hooper, Harry B., Boston A.L., 1912, 1915, 1916, 1918; 4 Series, 24 games.
Youngs, Ross M., New York N.L., 1921, 1922, 1923, 1924; 4 Series, 26 games.

Fewest Assists, Total Series (Most Games)

0—DiMaggio, Joseph P., New York A.L., 1936, 1937, 1938, 1939, 1941, 1942, 1947, 1949, 1950, 1951; 10 Series, 51 games.

Most Assists, Series

4-game Series—2—Connally, Joseph A., Boston, N.L., 1914.
5-game Series—2—Held by many outfielders.
6-game Series—2—Held by many outfielders.
7-game Series—4—Rice, Edgar C., Washington A.L., 1924.
8-game Series—3—Dougherty, Patrick H., Boston A.L., 1903.
Hooper, Harry, Boston A.L., 1912.
Roush, Edd J., Cincinnati N.L., 1919.

Most Assists, Game

2—Held by many outfielders.

Most Chances Accepted, Total Series

150—DiMaggio, Joseph P., New York A.L., 1936, 1937, 1938, 1939, 1941, 1942, 1947, 1949, 1950, 1951; 10 Series, 51 games.

Most Chances Accepted, Series

4-game Series—16—Combs, Earle B., New York A.L., 1927.
5-game Series—20—DiMaggio, Joseph P., New York A.L., 1942.
6-game Series—25—Rivers, John M., New York A.L., 1977.
7-game Series—26—Pafko, Andrew, Chicago N.L., 1945.
8-game Series—33—Roush, Edd J., Cincinnati N.L., 1919.

Most Chances Accepted, Game, Left Field

8—Foster, George A., Cincinnati N.L., October 21, 1976 (8 putouts, 0 assists, 0 errors).

Most Chances Accepted, Game, Center Field

9—Roush, Edd J., Cincinnati N.L., October 7, 1919 (7 putouts, 2 assists, 0 errors), 10 innings.
Otis, Amos J., Kansas City A.L., October 17, 1980 (9 putouts, 0 assists, 0 errors), 10 innings.
8—Roush, Edd J., Cincinnati N.L., October 1, 1919 (8 putouts, 0 assists, 0 errors).
Leiber, Henry, New York N.L., October 2, 1926 (7 putouts, 1 assist, 0 errors).

Most Chances Accepted, Game, Right Field

7—Murray, John J., New York N.L., October 14, 1912 (7 putouts, 0 assists, 0 errors).
Miller, Edmund J., Philadelphia A.L., October 5, 1930 (7 putouts, 0 assists, 0 errors).
Blades, Raymond F., St. Louis N.L., October 5, 1930 (7 putouts, 0 assists, 0 errors).
Oliva, Pedro, Minnesota A.L., October 6, 1965 (7 putouts, 0 assists, 0 errors).
Kaline, Albert W., Detroit A.L., October 9, 1968 (7 putouts, 0 assists, 0 errors).
Robinson, Frank, Baltimore A.L., October 14, 1969 (7 putouts, 0 assists, 0 errors).

Fewest Chances Offered, Longest Extra-Inning Game

0—Cobb, Tyrus R., Detroit A.L., right field, October 8, 1907 (12 innings).
McNeeley, George E., Washington A.L., center field, October 10, 1924 (12 innings).
Medwick, Joseph M., St. Louis N.L., left field, October 4, 1934 (11⅓ innings).
Hahn, Donald A., New York N.L., center field, right field, October 14, 1973 (12 innings).
Jones, Cleon J., New York N.L., left field, October 14, 1973 (12 innings).
Griffey, G. Kenneth, Cincinnati N.L., right field, October 21, 1975, night game. (Boston A.L., won 7-6, none out in 12th inning).

Fewest Chances Offered, Three Consecutive Games

0—Browne, George E., New York N.L., right field, October 12, 1905 (9 innings); October 13, 1905 (9 innings); October 14, 1905 (9 innings).
Carey, Max, Pittsburgh N.L., center field, October 11, 1925 (8 innings); October 12, 1925 (9 innings); October 13, 1925 (9 innings).
Simmons, Aloysius N., Philadelphia A.L., left field, October 11, 1929 (9 innings); October 12, 1929 (9 innings); October 14, 1929 (9 innings).
Wilson, J. Owen, Pittsburgh N.L., right field, October 8, 1909 (9 innings); October 9, 1909 (9 innings); October 11, 1909 (9 innings).

Fewest Chances Offered, Four Consecutive Games

0—Wilson, J. Owen, Pittsburgh N.L., right field, October 8, 1909 (9 innings); October 9, 1909 (9 innings); October 11, 1909 (9 innings); October 12, 1909 (8 innings).

Most Chances Accepted, Inning

3—Held by many outfielders.

Errors & Double Plays

Most Errors, Total Series

4—Youngs, Ross, New York N.L., 1921, 1922, 1923, 1924; 4 Series, 26 games.

Most Consecutive Errorless Games, Total Series

45—DiMaggio, Joseph P., New York A.L., October 6, 1937 through October 10, 1951.

Most Errors, Series

4-game Series—3—Davis, William H., Los Angeles N.L., 1966.
5-game Series—2—Held by many outfielders.
6-game Series—3—Murray, John J., New York N.L., 1911.
Collins, John F., Chicago A.L., 1917.
7-game Series—2—Wheat, Zachary D., Brooklyn N.L., 1920.
Orsatti, Ernest R., St. Louis N.L., 1934.
Goslin, Leon A., Detroit A.L., 1934.
Mantle, Mickey C., New York A.L., 1964.
Northrup, James T., Detroit A.L., 1968.
8-game Series—2—Held by 4 outfielders (2 in 1912; 2 in 1919).

Most Errors, Game

3—Davis, William H., Los Angeles N.L., October 6, 1966.

Most Errors, Inning

3—Davis, William H., Los Angeles N.L., October 6, 1966, fifth inning.

Most Double Plays, Total Series

2—Held by many outfielders.

Most Double Plays, Series

4-game Series—0—Held by many outfielders.
5-game Series—2—Murphy, Daniel F., Philadelphia A.L., 1910.
6-game Series—1—Held by many outfielders.
7-game Series—2—Howard, Elston G., New York A.L., 1958.
8-game Series—2—Speaker, Tris, Boston A.L., 1912.
Roush, Edd J., Cincinnati N.L., 1919.

Most Double Plays Started, Series

4-game Series—0—Held by many outfielders.
5-game Series—2—Murphy, Daniel F., Philadelphia A.L., 1910.
6-game Series—1—Held by many outfielders.
7-game Series—2—Howard, Elston G., New York A.L., 1958.
8-game Series—2—Speaker, Tris, Boston A.L., 1912.
Roush, Edd J., Cincinnati N.L., 1919.

Most Double Plays, Game

2—Roush, Edd J., Cincinnati N.L., October 7, 1919 (fifth and eighth innings of 10-inning game).

Most Double Plays Started, Game

2—Roush, Edd J., Cincinnati N.L., October 7, 1919 (fifth and eighth innings of 10-inning game).

Most Unassisted Double Plays, Game

1—Speaker, Tristram, Boston A.L., October 15, 1912.

Catchers
Series, Games & Average

Most Series Played

12—Berra, Lawrence P., New York A.L., 1947, 1949, 1950, 1951,

1952, 1953, 1955, 1956, 1957, 1958, 1960, 1962 (63 games) .

Most Games Caught, Total Series

63—Berra, Lawrence P., New York A.L., 1947, 1949, 1950, 1951, 1952, 1953, 1955, 1956, 1957, 1958, 1960, 1962 (12 Series) .

Highest Fielding Average, Series, With Most Chances Accepted

4-game Series—1.000—Roseboro, John, Los Angeles N.L., 1963 (43 chances accepted) .

5-game Series—1.000—Cochrane, Gordon S., Philadelphia A.L., 1929 (61 chances accepted) .

6-game Series—1.000—Campanella, Roy, Brooklyn N.L., 1953 (56 chances accepted) .

7-game Series—1.000—Grote, Gerald W., New York N.L., 1973 (71 chances accepted) .

8-game Series—1.000—Schang, Walter H., New York A.L., 1921 (50 chances accepted) .

Putouts, Assists & Chances Accepted

Most Putouts, Total Series

421—Berra, Lawrence P., New York A.L., 1947, 1949, 1950, 1951, 1952, 1953, 1955, 1956, 1957, 1958, 1960, 1962; 12 Series, 63 games.

Most Putouts, Series

4-game Series—43—Roseboro, John, Los Angeles N.L., 1963.

5-game Series—59—Cochrane, Gordon S., Philadelphia A.L., 1929.

6-game Series—55—Cooper, W. Walker, St. Louis N.L., 1944.

7-game Series—67—Grote, Gerald W., New York N.L., 1973.

8-game Series—54—Criger, Louis, Boston A.L., 1903.

Most Putouts, Game, Nine Innings

18—Roseboro, John, Los Angeles N.L., October 2, 1963 (15 strikeouts) .

Fewest Putouts, Game, Nine Innings

1—Schang, Walter H., Philadelphia A.L., October 11, 1913.
Schalk, Raymond W., Chicago A.L., October 7, 1917.
Wingo, Ivy B., Cincinnati N.L., October 1, 1919.
Schang, Walter H., New York A.L., October 11, 1923.
Ruel, Herold D., Washington A.L., October 5, 1924.
Cochrane, Gordon S., Detroit A.L., October 6, 1934.
Hartnett, Charles L., Chicago N.L., October 2, 1935.
Seminick, Andrew W., Philadelphia N.L., October 4, 1950.
Berra, Lawrence P., New York A.L., October 3, 1952 and October 10, 1956.
Lollar, J. Sherman, Chicago A.L., October 6, 1959.
Howard, Elston G., New York A.L., October 6, 1960.
Simmons, Ted L., Milwaukee A.L., October 15, 1982.

Most Putouts, Inning

3—Held by many catchers.

Most Assists, Total Series

36—Berra, Lawrence P., New York A.L., 1947, 1949, 1950, 1951, 1952, 1953, 1955, 1956, 1957, 1958, 1960, 1962; 12 Series, 63 games.

Most Assists, Series

4-game Series— 7—Munson, Thurman L., New York A.L., 1976.

5-game Series— 9—Schmidt, Charles, Detroit A.L., 1907.
Kling, John G., Chicago N.L., 1907.
Burns, Edward, Philadelphia N.L., 1915.

6-game Series—12—Meyers, John T., New York N.L., 1911.

7-game Series—11—Schmidt, Charles, Detroit A.L., 1909.

8-game Series—15—Schalk, Raymond W., Chicago A.L., 1919.

Most Assists, Game, Nine Innings

4—Kling, John G., Chicago N.L., October 9, 1907.
Schmidt, Charles, Detroit A.L., October 11, 1907 and October 14, 1908.
Gibson, George, Pittsburgh N.L., October 12, 1909.
Rariden, William A., New York N.L., October 10, 1917.
Agnew, Samuel, Boston A.L., September 6, 1918.
Delancey, William P., St. Louis N.L., October 8, 1934.

Most Assists, Game, 11 Innings

6—Lapp, John W., Philadelphia A.L., October 17, 1911.

Most Assists, Inning

2—Held by many catchers.

Most Chances Accepted, Total Series

457—Berra, Lawrence P., New York A.L., 1947, 1949, 1950, 1951, 1952, 1953, 1955, 1956, 1957, 1958, 1960, 1962; 12 Series, 63 games.

Most Chances Accepted, Series

4-game Series—43—Roseboro, John, Los Angeles N.L., 1963.

5-game Series—61—Cochrane, Gordon S., Philadelphia A.L., 1929.

6-game Series—56—Kling, John G., Chicago N.L., 1906.
Campanella, Roy, Brooklyn N.L., 1953.

7-game Series—71—Grote, Gerald W., New York N.L., 1973.

8-game Series—62—Criger, Louis, Boston A.L., 1903.

Most Chances Accepted, Game, Nine Innings

18—Roseboro, John, Los Angeles N.L., October 2, 1963 (18 putouts, 0 assists, 0 errors, 15 strikeouts) .
McCarver, J. Timothy, St. Louis N.L., October 2, 1968 (17 putouts, 1 assist, 0 errors, 17 strikeouts) .

Fewest Chances Offered, Game, Nine Innings

1—Schang, Walter H., Philadelphia A.L., October 11, 1913 (strikeout) .
Schang, Walter H., New York A.L., October 11, 1923 (strikeout) .
Ruel, Herold D., Washington A.L., October 5, 1924 (strikeout) .
Cochrane, Gordon S., Detroit A.L., October 6, 1934 (strikeout) .
Hartnett, Charles L., Chicago N.L., October 2, 1935 (strikeout) .
Lollar, J. Sherman, Chicago A.L., October 6, 1959 (strikeout) .
Howard, Elston G., New York A.L., October 6, 1960.

Fewest Chances Offered, Game, Eight Innings

1—Killefer, William L., Chicago N.L., September 9, 1918 (strikeout) .

Most Chances Accepted, Inning

4—McCarver, J. Timothy, St. Louis N.L., October 9, 1967, ninth inning (3 putouts, 1 assist, 2 strikeouts) .

Errors & Passed Balls

Most Errors, Total Series

7—Schmidt, Charles, Detroit A.L., 1907, 1908, 1909; 3 Series, 13 games.

Most Consecutive Errorless Games, Total Series

30—Berra, Lawrence P., New York A.L., October 4, 1952 through October 9, 1957.

Most Errors, Series

4-game Series—2—Wilson, James, St. Louis N.L., 1928.

5-game Series—2—Schmidt, Charles, Detroit A.L., 1907.
Cooper, W. Walker, St. Louis N.L., 1943.
Ferguson, Joseph V., Los Angeles N.L., 1974.

6-game Series—2—Schalk, Raymond W., Chicago A.L., 1917.

7-game Series—5—Schmidt, Charles, Detroit A.L., 1909.

8-game Series—3—Criger, Louis, Boston A.L., 1909.

Most Errors, Game, Nine Innings

2—Criger, Louis, Boston A.L., October 1, 1903.
Wilson, James, St. Louis, N.L., October 7, 1928.
Ferguson, Joseph V., Los Angeles N.L., October 15, 1974.
Fisk, Carlton E., Boston A.L., October 14, 1975, night game, 9 1/3 innings.

Most Errors, Inning

2—Criger, Louis, Boston A.L., October 1, 1903, first inning.
Wilson, James, St. Louis N.L., October 7, 1928, sixth inning.

Most Passed Balls, Total Series

5—Kling, John G., Chicago N.L., 1906 (3), 1907, 1908.
4—Howard, Elston G., New York A.L., 1961 (1), 1964 (3) .

Most Passed Balls, Series

3—Kling, John G., Chicago N.L., 1906.
Burgess, Forrest H., Pittsburgh N.L., 1960.
Howard, Elston G., New York A.L., 1964.

Most Passed Balls, Game, Nine Innings

2—Kling, John G., Chicago N.L., October 9, 1906.
Killefer, William L., Chicago N.L., September 9, 1918.
Richards, Paul R., Detroit A.L., October 3, 1945.
Edwards, Bruce, Brooklyn N.L., October 4, 1947.
Burgess, Forrest H., Pittsburgh N.L., October 6, 1960.
Howard, Elston G., New York A.L., October 7, 1964.

Most Passed Balls, Inning

1—Held by many catchers.

Double Plays & Runners Caught Stealing

Most Double Plays, Total Series

6—Berra, Lawrence P., New York A.L., 1947, 1949, 1950, 1951, 1952, 1953, 1955, 1956, 1957, 1958, 1960, 1962; 12 Series, 63 games.

Bench, Johnny L., Cincinnati N.L., 1970 (1), 1972 (2), 1975 (3), 1976 (0); 4 Series, 23 games.

Most Double Plays, Series

4-game Series—2—Hartnett, Charles L., Chicago N.L., 1932.
5-game Series—2—Burns, Edward J., Philadelphia N.L., 1915.
  Mancuso, August R., New York N.L., 1933.
6-game Series—3—Kling, John G., Chicago N.L., 1906.
7-game Series—3—Schmidt, Charles, Detroit A.L., 1909.
  Bench, Johnny L., Cincinnati N.L., 1975.
8-game Series—3—Schang, Walter H., New York A.L., 1921.

Most Double Plays Started, Series

4-game Series—1—Held by many catchers.
5-game Series—1—Held by many catchers.
6-game Series—1—Held by many catchers.
7-game Series—2—Schmidt, Charles, Detroit A.L., 1909.
  Crandall, Delmar D., Milwaukee N.L., 1957 and 1958.
  Battey, Earl J., Minnesota A.L., 1965.
8-game Series—3—Schang, Walter H., New York A.L., 1921.

Most Double Plays, Game, Nine Innings

2—Schmidt, Charles, Detroit A.L., October 14, 1909.
Schang, Walter H., New York A.L., October 11, 1921.
Hartnett, Charles L., Chicago N.L., September 29, 1932.
Rice, Delbert W., Milwaukee N.L., October 9, 1957.
Gedman, Richard L., Boston A.L., October 22, 1986.

Most Double Plays Started, Game, Nine Innings

2—Schmidt, Charles, Detroit A.L., October 14, 1909.
Schang, Walter H., New York A.L., October 11, 1921.

Most Unassisted Double Plays, Game

Never accomplished.

Most Players Caught Stealing, Total Series

20—Schang, Walter H., Philadelphia A.L., 1913, 1914, Boston A.L., 1918, New York A.L., 1921, 1922, 1923. 6 Series, 32 games.

Most Players Caught Stealing, Series

4-game Series— 5—Munson, Thurman L., New York A.L., 1976.
5-game Series— 6—Kling, John G., Chicago N.L., 1910.
  Thomas, Ira F., Philadelphia A.L., 1910.
6-game Series— 8—Lapp, John W., Philadelphia A.L., 1911.
7-game Series— 5—Gibson, George, Pittsburgh N.L., 1909.
  Miller, Otto L., Brooklyn N.L., 1920.
  Battey, Earl J., Minnesota A.L., 1965.
  Freehan, William A., Detroit A.L., 1968.
8-game Series—10—Schalk, Raymond W., Chicago A.L., 1919.

Most Players Caught Stealing, Game, Nine Innings

3— (8 times)—Held by 7 catchers. Last time: Roseboro, John, Los Angeles N.L., October 4, 1959.

Most Players Caught Stealing, Extra-Inning Game

5—Lapp, John W., Philadelphia A.L., October 17, 1911, 11 innings.

Most Players Caught Stealing, Inning

2—Lapp, John W., Philadelphia A.L., October 17, 1911, tenth inning.
Robinson, Aaron A., New York A.L., October 6, 1947, first inning.
Carrigan, William F., Boston A.L., October 9, 1912, eleventh inning.
Campanella, Roy, Brooklyn N.L., October 2, 1952, first inning.

Pitchers
Series, Games & Average

Most Series Played

11—Ford, Edward C., New York A.L., 1950, 1953, 1955, 1956, 1957, 1958, 1960, 1961, 1962, 1963, 1964 (22 games).

Most Games Pitched, Total Series

22—Ford, Edward C., New York A.L., 1950, 1953, 1955, 1956, 1957, 1958, 1960, 1961, 1962, 1963, 1964 (11 Series).

Most Games, Pitched, Series

4-game Series—3—French, Lawrence H., Chicago N.L., 1938, 3 ⅓ innings.
  Konstanty, C. James, Philadelphia N.L., 1950, 15 innings.
  Mossi, Donald L., Cleveland A.L., 1954, 4 innings.
  Reniff, Harold E., New York A.L., 1963, 3 innings.
5-game Series—5—Marshall, Michael G., Los Angeles N.L., 1974, 9 innings.
6-game Series—6—Quisenberry, Daniel R., Kansas City A.L., 1980, 10 ⅓ innings.
7-game Series—7—Knowles, Darold D., Oakland A.L., 1973, 6 ⅓ innings.
8-game Series—5—Phillippe, Charles L., Pittsburgh N.L., 1903, 44 innings.

Highest Fielding Average, Series, With Most Chances Accepted

4-game Series—1.000—Tyler, George A., Boston N.L., 1914 (6 chances accepted.
  Ruffing, Charles H., New York A.L., 1938 (6 chances accepted)
5-game Series—1.000—Marquard, Richard W., New York N.L., 1913 (8 chances accepted).
  Shore, Ernest G., Boston A.L., 1916 (8 chances accepted).
  Smith, Sherrod M., Brooklyn N.L., 1916 (8 chances accepted).
6-game Series—1.000—Altrock, Nicholas, Chicago A.L., 1906 (17 chances accepted).
  Vaughn, James L., Chicago N.L., 1918 (17 chances accepted).
7-game Series—1.000—Mullin, George E., Detroit A.L., 1909 (12 chances accepted).
8-game Series—1.000—Mathewson, Christopher, New York N.L., 1912 (13 chances accepted).

Putouts, Assists & Chances Accepted

Most Putouts, Total Series

11—Ford, Edward C., New York A.L., 1950, 1953, 1955, 1956, 1957, 1958, 1960, 1961, 1962, 1963, 1964 (11 Series, 22 games).

Most Putouts, Series

4-game Series—3—Ford, Edward C., New York A.L., 1963.
5-game Series—5—Morris, John S., Detroit A.L., 1984.
6-game Series—6—Altrock, Nicholas, Chicago A.L., 1906.
  Vaughn, James L., Chicago N.L., 1918.
7-game Series—5—Kaat, James L., Minnesota A.L., 1965.
8-game Series—2—Phillippe, Charles L., Pittsburgh N.L., 1903.
  Douglas, Philip B., New York N.L., 1921.

Most Putouts, Game, Nine Innings

5—Kaat, James L., Minnesota A.L., October 7, 1965.

Most Putouts, Inning

2—Beazley, John A., St. Louis N.L., October 5, 1942 (eighth inning).
Turley, Robert L., New York A.L., October 9, 1957 (seventh inning).
Ford, Edward C., New York A.L., October 8, 1960 (ninth inning).
Purkey, Robert T., Cincinnati N.L., October 7, 1961 (ninth inning).
Denny, John A., Philadelphia N.L., October 15, 1983 (fifth inning).

Most Assists, Total Series

34—Mathewson, Christopher, New York N.L., 1905, 1911, 1912, 1913; 4 Series, 11 games.

Most Assists, Series

4-game Series— 5—Bush, Leslie A., Philadelphia A.L., 1914.
  Tyler, George, Boston N.L., 1914.
  James, William L., Boston N.L., 1914.
  Moore, Wilcey, New York A.L., 1927.
  Pearson, Monte, New York A.L., 1939.
5-game Series—10—Brown, Mordecai P., Chicago N.L., 1910.
6-game Series—12—Brown, Mordecai P., Chicago N.L., 1906.
7-game Series—12—Mullin, George, Detroit A.L., 1909.
8-game Series—12—Mathewson, Christopher, New York N.L., 1912.

Most Assists, Game, Nine Innings

8—Altrock, Nicholas, Chicago A.L., October 12, 1906.
Warneke, Lonnie, Chicago N.L., October 2, 1935.

Most Assists, Inning

3—Plank, Edward S., Philadelphia A.L., October 13, 1905, eighth inning.
Marquard, Richard W., New York N.L., October 7, 1913, fourth inning.
Warneke, Lonnie, Chicago N.L., October 2, 1935, third inning.
Murphy, John J., New York A.L., October 8, 1939, eighth inning.
Rush, Robert R., Milwaukee N.L., October 4, 1958, third inning.

Most Chances Accepted, Total Series

40—Mathewson, Christopher, New York N.L., 1905, 1911, 1912, 1913; 4 Series, 11 games.

Most Chances Accepted, Series

4-game Series— 6—Tyler, George A., Boston N.L., 1914.
Ruffing, Charles H., New York A.L., 1938.
5-game Series—10—Mathewson, Christopher, New York N.L., 1905.
Brown, Mordecai P., Chicago N.L., 1910.
6-game Series—17—Altrock, Nicholas, Chicago A.L., 1906.
Vaughn, James L., Chicago N.L., 1918.
7-game Series—12—Mullin, George, Detroit A.L., 1909.
8-game Series—13—Mathewson, Christopher, New York N.L., 1912.

Fewest Chances Offered (Most Innings), Series

0—Grove, Robert M., Philadelphia A.L., 1931; 3 games, 26 innings.

Most Chances Accepted, Game, Nine Innings

11—Altrock, Nicholas, Chicago A.L., October 12, 1906 (3 putouts, 8 assists, 0 errors).

Fewest Chances Offered, Extra-Inning Game

0—Pollet, Howard J., St. Louis N.L., October 6, 1946 (10 innings).
Roberts, Robin E., Philadelphia N.L., October 5, 1950 (10 innings).

Most Chances Accepted, Inning

3—Held by many pitchers.

Errors & Double Plays

Most Errors, Total Series

3—Phillippe, Charles, Pittsburgh N.L., 1903, 1909, 2 Series, 7 games.
Cicotte, Edward, Chicago A.L., 1917, 1919, 2 Series, 6 games.
Lanier, H. Max, St. Louis N.L., 1942, 1943, 1944, 3 Series, 7 games.

Most Errors, Series

4-game Series—1—Held by many pitchers.
5-game Series—2—Coombs, John W., Philadelphia A.L., 1910.
Lanier, H. Max, St. Louis N.L., 1942.
6-game Series—2—Potter, Nelson T., St. Louis A.L., 1944.
7-game Series—2—Phillippe, Charles L., Pittsburgh N.L., 1909.
Reynolds, Allie P., New York A.L., 1952.

8-game Series—2—Cicotte, Edward V., Chicago A.L., 1919.

Most Errors, Game, Nine Innings

2—Phillippe, Charles L., Pittsburgh N.L., October 12, 1909.
Coombs, John W., Philadelphia A.L., October 18, 1910.
Cicotte, Edward V., Chicago A.L., October 4, 1919.
Lanier, H. Max, St. Louis N.L., September 30, 1942.
Potter, Nelson T., St. Louis A.L., October 5, 1944 (starting pitcher, pitched 6 innings).

Most Errors, Inning

2—Coombs, John W., Philadelphia A.L., October 18, 1910, fifth inning.
Cicotte, Edward V., Chicago A.L., October 4, 1919, fifth inning.
Lanier, H. Max, St. Louis N.L., September 30, 1942, ninth inning.
Potter, Nelson T., St. Louis A.L., October 5, 1944, third inning.

Most Consecutive Errorless Games, Total Series

18—Ford, Edward C., New York A.L., October 7, 1950 through October 8, 1962.

Most Double Plays, Total Series

3—Bender, Charles A., Philadelphia A.L., 1905, 1910, 1911, 1913, 1914; 5 Series, 10 games.
Bush, Leslie A., Philadelphia A.L., Boston A.L., New York A.L., 1913, 1914, 1918, 1922, 1923; 5 Series, 9 games.
Reynolds, Allie P., New York A.L., 1947, 1949, 1950, 1951, 1952, 1953; 6 Series, 15 games.

Most Double Plays, Series

4-game Series—2—Bender, Charles A., Philadelphia A.L., 1914.
5-game Series—2—Bush, Leslie A., New York A.L., 1922.
6-game Series—2—Faber, Urban C., Chicago A.L., 1917.
Reynolds, Allie P., New York A.L., 1951.
Gura, Lawrence C., Kansas City A.L., 1980.
7-game Series—2—Johnson, Walter P., Washington A.L., 1924.
Stafford, William C., New York A.L., 1960.
8-game Series—1—Wood, Joseph, Boston A.L., 1912.
Cicotte, Edward V., Chicago A.L., 1919.
Quinn, John P., New York A.L., 1921.

Most Double Plays Started, Series

4-game Series—2—Bender, Charles A., Philadelphia A.L., 1914.
5-game Series—2—Bush, Leslie A., New York A.L., 1922.
6-game Series—2—Faber, Urban C., Chicago A.L., 1917.
Reynolds, Allie P., New York A.L., 1951.
7-game Series—2—Stafford, William C., New York A.L., 1960.
8-game Series—1—Cicotte, Edward V., Chicago A.L., 1919.
Quinn, John P., New York A.L., 1921.

Most Unassisted Double Plays, Game

Never accomplished.

Most Double Plays Started, Game

2—Bender, Charles A., Philadelphia A.L., October 9, 1914.
Bush, Leslie A., New York A.L., October 8, 1922.
Reynolds, Allie P., New York A.L., October 8, 1951.

Club Fielding

Number Of Players At Positions

First Basemen

Most First Basemen, Series

4-game Series—3—New York A.L., vs. Philadelphia N.L., 1950.
5-game Series—3—New York N.L., vs. Philadelphia A.L., 1913.
Oakland A.L., vs. Los Angeles N.L., 1974.
6-game Series—2—Held by many clubs.
7-game Series—4—New York A.L., vs. Milwaukee N.L., 1957.
Oakland A.L., vs. New York N.L., 1973.
8-game Series—1—Held by many clubs.

Most First Basemen, Series, Both Clubs

4-game Series—4—New York A.L., 3, Philadelphia N.L., 1, 1950.
5-game Series—4—New York N.L., 3, Philadelphia A.L., 1, 1913.
Philadelphia N.L., 2, Boston A.L., 2, 1915.
Oakland A.L., 3, Los Angeles N.L., 1, 1974.
6-game Series—3—Made in many Series.
7-game Series—6—New York A.L., 4, Milwaukee N.L., 2, 1957.

8-game Series—2—Made in many Series.

Most First Basemen, Game

3—New York A.L., vs. Milwaukee N.L., October 2, 1957.
New York A.L., vs. Milwaukee N.L., October 5, 1957.

Most First Basemen, Game, Both Clubs

5—New York A.L., 3, Milwaukee N.L., 2, October 2, 1957.
New York A.L., 3, Milwaukee N.L., 2, October 5, 1957.

Second Basemen

Most Second Basemen, Series

4-game Series—2—Pittsburgh N.L., vs. New York A.L., 1927.
New York A.L., vs. St. Louis N.L., 1928.
Philadelphia N.L., vs. New York A.L., 1950.
5-game Series—2—Held by many clubs.
6-game Series—2—Held by many clubs.
7-game Series—3—St. Louis N.L., vs. New York A.L., 1964.
Oakland A.L., vs. New York N.L., 1973.
8-game Series—1—Held by many clubs.

Most Second Basemen, Series, Both Clubs

4-game Series—3—Pittsburgh N.L., 2, New York A.L., 1, 1927.
New York A.L., 2, St. Louis N.L., 1, 1928.
Philadelphia N.L., 2, New York A.L., 1, 1950.
5-game Series—3—Made in many Series.
6-game Series—4—St. Louis N.L., 2, St. Louis A.L., 2, 1944.
7-game Series—4—Brooklyn N.L., 2, New York A.L., 2, 1956.
Milwaukee N.L., 2, New York A.L., 2, 1957.
St. Louis N.L., 3, New York A.L., 1, 1964.
Oakland A.L., 3, New York N.L., 1, 1973.
8-game Series—2—Made in four Series.

Most Second Basemen, Game

3—St. Louis N.L., vs. New York A.L., October 7, 1964.
Oakland A.L., vs. New York N.L., October 14, 1973, 12 innings.

Most Second Basemen, Game, Both Clubs

4—New York A.L., 2, Milwaukee N.L., 2, October 7, 1957.
St. Louis N.L., 3, New York A.L., 1, October 7, 1964.
Oakland A.L., 3, New York N.L., 1, October 14, 1973, 12 innings.

Third Basemen

Most Third Basemen, Series

4-game Series—3—Cleveland A.L., vs. New York N.L., 1954.
5-game Series—3—New York A.L., vs. St. Louis N.L., 1942.
Brooklyn N.L., vs. New York A.L., 1949.
Detroit A.L., vs. San Diego N.L., 1984.
6-game Series—3—Chicago A.L., vs. Los Angeles N.L., 1959.
7-game Series—3—Washington A.L., vs. New York N.L., 1924.
St. Louis N.L., vs. Philadelphia A.L., 1931.
New York A.L., vs. Milwaukee N.L., 1957.
New York A.L., vs. Milwaukee N.L., 1958.
Detroit A.L., vs. St. Louis N.L., 1968.
8-game Series—2—New York A.L., vs. New York N.L., 1921.

Most Third Basemen, Series, Both Clubs

4-game Series—4—Cleveland A.L., 3, New York N.L., 1, 1954.
5-game Series—5—Brooklyn N.L., 3, New York A.L., 2, 1949.
Detroit A.L., 3, San Diego N.L., 2, 1984.
6-game Series—4—Chicago N.L., 2, Detroit A.L., 2, 1945.
Chicago A.L., 2, Los Angeles N.L., 2, 1959.
Los Angeles N.L., 2, New York A.L., 2, 1981.
7-game Series—5—Washington A.L., 3, New York N.L., 2, 1924.
8-game Series—3—New York A.L., 2, New York N.L., 1, 1921.

Most Third Basemen, Game

2—Made in many games.

Most Third Basemen, Game, Both Clubs

4—Pittsburgh N.L., 2, Detroit A.L., 2, October 16, 1909.
New York N.L., 2, Washington A.L., 2, October 6, 1924.
Los Angeles N.L., 2, New York A.L., 2, October 28, 1981.
San Diego N.L., 2, Detroit A.L., 2, October 9, 1984.

Shortstops

Most Shortstops, Series

4-game Series—2—St. Louis N.L., vs. New York A.L., 1928.
Chicago N.L., vs. New York A.L., 1932.
Cleveland A.L., vs. New York N.L., 1954.
New York A.L., vs. Cincinnati N.L., 1976.
5-game Series—3—Cincinnati N.L., vs. Baltimore A.L., 1970.
6-game Series—2—Held by many clubs.
7-game Series—3—Chicago N.L., vs. Detroit A.L., 1945.
New York A.L., vs. Pittsburgh N.L., 1960.
8-game Series—2—New York N.L., vs. Boston A.L., 1912.

Most Shortstops, Series, Both Clubs

4-game Series—3—St. Louis N.L., 2, New York A.L., 1, 1928.
Chicago N.L., 2, New York A.L., 1, 1932.
Cleveland A.L., 2, New York N.L., 1, 1954.
New York A.L., 2, Cincinnati N.L., 1, 1976.
5-game Series—4—Cincinnati N.L., 3, Baltimore A.L., 1, 1970.
6-game Series—3—Made in many Series.
7-game Series—5—Chicago N.L., 3, Detroit A.L., 2, 1945.
New York A.L., 3, Pittsburgh N.L., 2, 1960.
8-game Series—3—New York N.L., 2, Boston A.L., 1, 1912.

Most Shortstops, Game

3—New York A.L., vs. Pittsburgh N.L., October 13, 1960.
Cincinnati N.L., vs. Baltimore A.L., October 14, 1970.

Most Shortstops, Game, Both Clubs

4—Made in many games.

Left Fielders

Most Left Fielders, Series

4-game Series—3—New York A.L., vs. Chicago N.L., 1938.
5-game Series—3—Philadelphia N.L., vs. Boston A.L., 1915.
Baltimore A.L., vs. Philadelphia N.L., 1983.
San Diego N.L., vs. Detroit A.L., 1984.
6-game Series—4—Philadelphia N.L., vs. Kansas City A.L., 1980.
7-game Series—4—Brooklyn N.L., vs. New York A.L., 1947.
New York A.L., vs. Pittsburgh N.L., 1960.
San Francisco N.L., vs. New York A.L., 1962.
Boston A.L., vs. Cincinnati N.L., 1975.
8-game Series—3—New York N.L., vs. Boston A.L., 1912.

Most Left Fielders, Series, Both Clubs

4-game Series—5—New York A.L., 3, Chicago N.L., 2, 1938.
5-game Series—5—San Diego N.L., 3, Detroit A.L., 2, 1984.
6-game Series—5—Philadelphia N.L., 4, Kansas City A.L., 1, 1980.
7-game Series—6—Brooklyn N.L., 4, New York A.L., 2, 1947.
Pittsburgh N.L., 3, Baltimore A.L., 3, 1979.
8-game Series—4—New York N.L., 3, Boston A.L., 1, 1912.

Most Left Fielders, Game

3—New York N.L., vs. Washington A.L., October 10, 1924, 12 innings.
Brooklyn N.L., vs. New York A.L., October 5, 1947.
Brooklyn N.L., vs. New York A.L., October 5, 1952, 11 innings.
Philadelphia N.L., vs. Kansas City A.L., October 19, 1980.
New York A.L., vs. Los Angeles N.L., October 24, 1981.

Most Left Fielders, Game, Both Clubs

5—Brooklyn N.L., 3, New York A.L., 2, October 5, 1947.

Center Fielders

Most Center Fielders, Series

4-game Series—2—Made by seven clubs.
5-game Series—3—Brooklyn N.L., vs. Boston A.L., 1916.
New York N.L., vs. New York A.L., 1922.
New York N.L., vs. Cincinnati N.L., 1961.
6-game Series—4—Los Angeles N.L., vs. Chicago A.L., 1959.
7-game Series—3—New York N.L., vs. Washington A.L., 1924.
New York A.L., vs. Brooklyn N.L., 1955.
Milwaukee N.L., vs. New York A.L., 1958.
8-game Series—2—New York N.L., vs. Boston A.L., 1912.
Chicago A.L., vs. Cincinnati N.L., 1919.

Most Center Fielders, Series, Both Clubs

4-game Series—4—New York A.L., 2, St. Louis N.L., 2, 1928.
5-game Series—5—New York N.L., 3, New York A.L., 2, 1922.
6-game Series—6—New York A.L., 3, Los Angeles N.L., 3, 1981.
7-game Series—5—New York N.L., 3, Washington A.L., 2, 1924.
New York A.L., 3, Brooklyn N.L., 2, 1955.
8-game Series—3—New York N.L., 2, Boston A.L., 1, 1912.
Chicago A.L., 2, Cincinnati N.L., 1, 1919.

Most Center Fielders, Game

3—New York N.L., vs. New York A.L., October 5, 1922, 10 innings.

Most Center Fielders, Game, Both Clubs

4—New York N.L., 3, New York A.L., 1, October 5, 1922.
New York A.L., 2, New York N.L., 2, October 15, 1923, 10 innings.
New York A.L., 2, Los Angeles N.L., 2, October 11, 1978.
New York A.L., 2, Los Angeles N.L., 2, October 24, 25, 1981.

Right Fielders

Most Right Fielders, Series

4-game Series—3—Cleveland A.L., vs. New York N.L., 1954.
New York A.L., vs. Los Angeles N.L., 1963.
New York A.L., vs. Cincinnati N.L., 1976.
5-game Series—4—Philadelphia N.L., vs. Baltimore A.L., 1983.
6-game Series—5—Los Angeles N.L., vs. Chicago A.L., 1959.
7-game Series—4—New York A.L., vs. Brooklyn N.L., 1955.
San Francisco N.L., vs. New York A.L., 1962.
Boston A.L., vs. St. Louis N.L., 1967.
St. Louis N.L., vs. Minnesota A.L., 1987.
8-game Series—3—Chicago A.L., vs. Cincinnati N.L., 1919.

Most Right Fielders, Series, Both Clubs

4-game Series—5—New York A.L., 3, Los Angeles N.L., 2, 1963.
5-game Series—7—Philadelphia N.L., 4, Baltimore A.L., 3, 1983.
6-game Series—9—Los Angeles N.L., 5, Chicago A.L., 4, 1959.

7-game Series—6—St. Louis N.L., 4, Minnesota A.L., 2, 1987.

8-game Series—4—Chicago A.L., 3, Cincinnati N.L., 1, 1919.

Most Right Fielders, Game

3—Held by many clubs.

Most Right Fielders, Game, Both Clubs

5—Los Angeles N.L., 3, Chicago A.L., 2, October 8, 1959.

Catchers

Most Catchers, Series

4-game Series—3—New York A.L., vs. Pittsburgh N.L., 1927.
Pittsburgh N.L., vs. New York A.L., 1927.
Philadelphia N.L., vs. New York A.L., 1950.

5-game Series—3—Detroit A.L., vs. Chicago N.L., 1908.
Boston A.L., vs. Brooklyn N.L., 1916.
New York A.L., vs. Brooklyn N.L., 1949.
Cincinnati N.L., vs. New York A.L., 1961.

6-game Series—4—Los Angeles N.L., vs. New York A.L., 1978.

7-game Series—3—Held by many clubs.

8-game Series—2—Held by many clubs.

Most Catchers, Series, Both Clubs

4-game Series—6—New York A.L., 3, Pittsburgh N.L., 3, 1927.

5-game Series—5—Boston A.L., 3, Brooklyn N.L., 2, 1916.

6-game Series—6—Los Angeles N.L., 4, New York A.L., 2, 1978.

7-game Series—6—New York A.L., 3, Pittsburgh N.L., 3, 1960.

8-game Series—4—Boston A.L., 2, New York N.L., 2, 1912.
Chicago A.L., 2, Cincinnati N.L., 2, 1919.
New York N.L., 2, New York A.L., 2, 1921.

Most Catchers, Game

3—Philadelphia N.L., vs. New York A.L., October 5, 1950, 10 innings.
Los Angeles N.L., vs. New York A.L., October 13, 1978.

Most Catchers, Game, Both Clubs

4—Detroit A.L., 2, Chicago N.L., 2, October 8, 1945, 12 innings.
Boston A.L., 2, St. Louis N.L., 2, October 15, 1946.
Philadelphia N.L., 3, New York A.L., 1, October 5, 1950, 10 innings.
Los Angeles N.L., 3, New York A.L., 1, October 13, 1978.
Los Angeles N.L., 2, New York A.L., 2, October 15, 1978.

Pitchers

Most Pitchers, Series

4-game Series— 8—Chicago N.L., vs. New York A.L., 1932.
Chicago N.L., vs. New York A.L., 1938.
Los Angeles N.L., vs. Baltimore A.L., 1966.

5-game Series—10—San Diego N.L., vs. Detroit A.L., 1984.

6-game Series—10—Brooklyn N.L., vs. New York A.L., 1953.
Philadelphia N.L., vs. Kansas City A.L., 1980.
Los Angeles N.L., vs. New York A.L., 1981.

7-game Series—11—Boston A.L., vs. St. Louis N.L., 1946.

8-game Series— 8—New York A.L., vs. New York N.L., 1921.

Most Pitchers, Series, Both Clubs

4-game Series—14—Chicago N.L., 8, New York A.L., 6, 1932.
Cincinnati N.L., 7, New York A.L., 7, 1976.

5-game Series—18—Baltimore A.L., 9, Cincinnati N.L., 9, 1970.

6-game Series—19—Brooklyn N.L., 10, New York A.L., 9, 1953.
Los Angeles N.L., 10, New York A.L., 9, 1981.

7-game Series—20—Pittsburgh N.L., 10, New York A.L., 10, 1960.
St. Louis N.L., 10, Boston A.L., 10, 1967.
Pittsburgh N.L., 10, Baltimore A.L., 10, 1971.

8-game Series—12—New York A.L., 8, New York N.L., 4, 1921.

Fewest Pitchers, Series

4-game Series—3—Boston N.L., vs. Philadelphia A.L., 1914.
New York A.L., vs. St. Louis N.L., 1928.

5-game Series—2—Philadelphia A.L., vs. Chicago N.L., 1910.

6-game Series—3—Philadelphia A.L., vs. New York N.L., 1911.

7-game Series—5—Detroit A.L., vs. Pittsburgh N.L., 1909.
Cleveland A.L., vs. Brooklyn N.L., 1920.

8-game Series—3—Boston A.L., vs. Pittsburgh N.L., 1903.

Fewest Pitchers, Series, Both Clubs

4-game Series— 9—Philadelphia A.L., 6, Boston N.L., 3, 1914.
St. Louis N.L., 6, New York A.L., 3, 1928.

5-game Series— 6—Philadelphia A.L., 3, New York N.L., 3, 1905.

6-game Series— 8—Chicago A.L., 4, Chicago N.L., 4, 1906.
New York N.L., 5, Philadelphia A.L., 3, 1911.
Boston A.L., 4, Chicago N.L., 4, 1918.

7-game Series—11—Pittsburgh N.L., 6, Detroit A.L., 5, 1909.

8-game Series— 8—Pittsburgh N.L., 5, Boston A.L., 3, 1903.

Most Different Starting Pitchers, Series

6—Brooklyn N.L., vs. New York A.L., 1947.
Brooklyn N.L., vs. New York A.L., 1955.
Pittsburgh N.L., vs. Baltimore A.L., 1971.

Most Different Starting Pitchers, Series, Both Clubs

11—Brooklyn N.L., 6, New York A.L., 5, 1955.

Most Pitchers, Game

8—Cincinnati N.L., vs. New York A.L., October 9, 1961.
St. Louis N.L., vs. Boston A.L., October 11, 1967.
Cincinnati N.L., vs. Boston A.L., October 21, 1975, 12 innings.

Most Pitchers, Game, Winning Club

6—Cincinnati N.L., vs. Oakland A.L., October 20, 1972 (Won 5-4).

Most Pitchers, Game, Losing Club

8—Cincinnati N.L., vs. New York A.L., October 9, 1961 (Lost 13-5).
St. Louis N.L., vs. Boston A.L., October 11, 1967 (Lost 8-4).
Cincinnati N.L., vs. Boston A.L., October 21, 1975, 12 innings (Lost 7-6).

Most Pitchers, Game, Nine Innings, Both Clubs

11—St. Louis N.L., 8, Boston A.L., 3, October 11, 1967.

Most Pitchers, Extra-Inning Game, Both Clubs

12—Cincinnati N.L., 8, Boston A.L., 4, October 21, 1975, 12 innings.

Most Pitchers, Inning

5—Baltimore A.L., vs. Pittsburgh N.L., October 17, 1979, ninth inning.
St. Louis N.L., vs. Kansas City A.L., October 27, 1985, fifth inning.

Average

Highest Fielding Average, Series

4-game Series—1.000—Baltimore A.L., vs. Los Angeles N.L., 1966.

5-game Series—1.000—New York A.L., vs. New York N.L., 1937.

6-game Series— .996—Boston A.L., vs. Chicago N.L., 1918.
St. Louis N.L., vs. St. Louis A.L., 1944.
Los Angeles N.L., vs. New York A.L., 1977.

7-game Series— .993—Cincinnati N.L., vs. Boston A.L., 1975.

8-game Series— .984—New York N.L., vs. New York A.L., 1921.

Highest Fielding Average, Series, Both Clubs

4-game Series—.986—New York A.L., .993, Los Angeles N.L., .979, 1963.

5-game Series—.985—New York A.L., .990, Brooklyn N.L., .980, 1941.

6-game Series—.991—Los Angeles N.L., .996, New York A.L., .987, 1977.

7-game Series—.990—St. Louis N.L., .992, Kansas City A.L., .989, 1985.

8-game Series—.983—New York N.L., .984, New York A.L., .981, 1921.

Lowest Fielding Average, Series

4-game Series—.949—New York A.L., vs. Chicago N.L., 1932.

5-game Series—.942—Brooklyn N.L., vs. Boston A.L., 1916.

6-game Series—.938—New York N.L., vs. Philadelphia A.L., 1911.

7-game Series—.934—Detroit A.L., vs. Pittsburgh N.L., 1909.

8-game Series—.944—Pittsburgh N.L., vs. Boston A.L., 1903.

Lowest Fielding Average, Series, Both Clubs

4-game Series—.954—Chicago N.L., .959, New York A.L., .949, 1932.

5-game Series—.946—Philadelphia A.L., .947, Chicago N.L., .946, 1910.

6-game Series—.947—Philadelphia A.L., .956, New York N.L., .938, 1911.

7-game Series—.941—Pittsburgh N.L., .947, Detroit A.L., .934, 1909.

8-game Series—.951—Boston A.L., .957, Pittsburgh N.L., .944, 1903.

Putouts

Most Putouts, Total Series

    4,983—New York A.L., 33 Series, 187 games.

Most Putouts, Series

    4-game Series—117—Boston N.L., vs. Philadelphia A.L., 1914.
    5-game Series—147—Boston A.L., vs. Brooklyn N.L., 1916.
    6-game Series—168—New York A.L., vs. Los Angeles N.L., 1977.
    7-game Series—201—Washington A.L., vs. New York N.L., 1924.
    8-game Series—222—Boston A.L., vs. New York N.L., 1912.

Most Putouts, Series, Both Clubs

    4-game Series—228—Boston N.L., 117, Philadelphia A.L., 111, 1914.
    5-game Series—289—Boston A.L., 147, Brooklyn N.L., 142, 1916.
    6-game Series—333—New York A.L., 168, Los Angeles N.L., 165, 1977.
    7-game Series—401—Washington A.L., 201, New York N.L., 200, 1924.
    8-game Series—443—Boston A.L., 222, New York N.L., 221, 1912.

Fewest Putouts, Series

    4-game Series—102—St. Louis N.L., vs. New York A.L., 1928.
    Chicago N.L., vs. New York A.L., 1932.
    Chicago N.L., vs. New York A.L., 1938.
    New York A.L., vs. Los Angeles N.L., 1963.
    Los Angeles N.L., vs. Baltimore A.L., 1966.
    5-game Series—126—Los Angeles N.L., vs. Oakland A.L., 1974.
    San Diego N.L., vs. Detroit A.L., 1984.
    6-game Series—153—New York N.L., vs. Chicago A.L., 1917.
    St. Louis N.L., vs. Philadelphia A.L., 1930.
    New York A.L., vs. Los Angeles N.L., 1981.
    7-game Series—177—Brooklyn N.L., vs. Cleveland A.L., 1920.
    St. Louis N.L., vs. Minnesota A.L., 1987.
    8-game Series—210—Pittsburgh N.L., vs. Boston A.L., 1903.
    New York A.L., vs. New York N.L., 1921.

Fewest Putouts, Series, Both Clubs

    4-game Series—210—New York A.L., 108, St. Louis N.L., 102, 1928.
    New York A.L., 108, Chicago N.L., 102, 1932.
    New York A.L., 108, Chicago N.L., 102, 1938.
    Los Angeles N.L., 108, New York A.L., 102, 1963.
    Baltimore A.L., 108, Los Angeles N.L., 102, 1966.
    5-game Series—258—Oakland A.L., 132, Los Angeles N.L., 126, 1974.
    Detroit A.L., 132, San Diego N.L., 126, 1984.
    6-game Series—309—Chicago A.L., 156, New York N.L., 153, 1917.
    Philadelphia A.L., 156, St. Louis N.L., 153, 1930.
    Los Angeles N.L., 156, New York A.L., 153, 1981.
    7-game Series—357—Minnesota A.L., 180, St. Louis N.L., 177, 1987.
    8-game Series—422—New York N.L., 212, New York A.L., 210, 1921.

Most Players, Nine-Inning Game, One or More Putouts

    11—New York A.L., vs. Milwaukee N.L., October 2, 1957.
    Baltimore A.L., vs. Pittsburgh N.L., October 16, 1979.

Most Players, Nine-Inning Game, Both Clubs, One or More Putouts

    19—New York A.L., 11, Milwaukee N.L., 8, October 2, 1957.
    Baltimore A.L., 10, Pittsburgh N.L., 9, October 11, 1971.

Most Players, Extra-Inning Game, Both Clubs, One or More Putouts

    20—Chicago N.L., 10, Detroit A.L., 10, October 8, 1945, 12 innings.

Most Putouts, Outfield, Game, Nine Innings

    15—New York N.L., vs. Boston A.L., October 14, 1912.
    Boston N.L., vs. Cleveland A.L., October 6, 1948.
    16—Brooklyn N.L., vs. New York A.L., October 5, 1952, 11 innings.

Most Putouts, Outfield, Game, Nine Innings, Both Clubs

    23—Pittsburgh N.L., 13, New York A.L., 10, October 6, 1927.

    Brooklyn N.L., 16, New York A.L., 7, October 5, 1952, 11 innings.

Fewest Putouts, Outfield, Game, Nine Innings

    0—New York N.L., vs. New York A.L., October 5, 1921 (1 assist).
    New York N.L., vs. New York A.L., September 30, 1936.

Fewest Putouts, Outfield, Extra-Inning Game

    1—New York N.L., vs. Oakland A.L., October 14, 1973, 12 innings.

Fewest Putouts, Outfield, Game, Nine Innings, Both Clubs

    3—New York A.L., 2, Brooklyn N.L., 1, October 10, 1956.

Most Putouts, Outfield, Inning

    3—Made in many games.

Most Putouts, Outfield, Inning, Both Clubs

    6—Kansas City A.L., 3, St. Louis N.L., 3, October 27, 1985, seventh inning.

Most Putouts, Catchers, Inning, Both Clubs

    6—Chicago A.L., 3, Cincinnati N.L., 3, October 6, 1919, second inning.
    Cincinnati N.L., 3, Oakland A.L., 3, October 18, 1972, fifth inning.
    St. Louis N.L., 3, Kansas City A.L., 3, October 24, 1985, seventh inning.

Assists

Most Assists, Total Series

    1,978—New York A.L., 33 Series, 187 games.

Most Assists, Series

    4-game Series— 67—Philadelphia A.L., vs. Boston N.L., 1914.
    5-game Series— 90—Boston A.L., vs. Brooklyn N.L., 1916.
    6-game Series— 99—Chicago A.L., vs. Chicago N.L., 1906.
    7-game Series— 99—Washington A.L., vs. New York N.L., 1924.
    St. Louis N.L., vs. New York A.L., 1926.
    8-game Series—116—Chicago A.L., vs. Cincinnati N.L., 1919.

Most Assists, Series, Both Clubs

    4-game Series—129—Philadelphia A.L., 67, Boston N.L., 62, 1914.
    5-game Series—160—Boston A.L., 90, Brooklyn N.L., 70, 1916.
    6-game Series—183—Chicago A.L., 99, Chicago N.L., 84, 1906.
    7-game Series—193—Washington A.L., 99, New York N.L., 94, 1924.
    8-game Series—212—Chicago A.L., 116, Cincinnati N.L., 96, 1919.

Fewest Assists, Series

    4-game Series— 28—New York A.L., vs. St. Louis N.L., 1928.
    5-game Series— 40—Philadelphia A.L., vs. Chicago N.L., 1929.
    Brooklyn N.L., vs. New York A.L., 1949.
    San Diego N.L., vs. Detroit A.L., 1984.
    6-game Series— 41—Philadelphia A.L., vs. St. Louis N.L., 1930.
    7-game Series— 48—St. Louis N.L., vs. Detroit A.L., 1968.
    8-game Series— 96—Pittsburgh N.L., vs. Boston A.L., 1903.
    Cincinnati N.L., vs. Chicago A.L., 1919.

Fewest Assists, Series, Both Clubs

    4-game Series— 64—St. Louis N.L., 36, New York A.L., 28, 1928.
    5-game Series— 84—New York A.L., 44, Brooklyn N.L., 40, 1949.
    6-game Series— 96—St. Louis N.L., 55, Philadelphia A.L., 41, 1930.
    7-game Series—120—Detroit A.L., 72, St. Louis N.L., 48, 1968.
    8-game Series—198—Boston A.L., 102, Pittsburgh N.L., 96, 1903.

Most Players, Nine-Inning Game, One or More Assists

    9—Chicago A.L., vs. New York N.L., October 7, 1917.
    New York A.L., vs. New York N.L., October 6, 1922.
    Chicago N.L., vs. Detroit A.L., October 8, 1945, 12 innings.
    Brooklyn N.L., vs. New York A.L., October 3, 1947.

Most Players, Nine-Inning Game, Both Clubs, One or More Assists

    15—New York A.L., 9, New York N.L., 6, October 6, 1922.
    Chicago N.L., 9, Detroit A.L., 6, October 8, 1945, 12 innings.

Most Players, Extra-Inning Game, Both Clubs, One or More Assists

    16—Los Angeles N.L., 9, New York A.L., 7, October 11, 1977, 12 innings.

Most Assists, Game, Nine Inning

21—Chicago A.L., vs. New York N.L., October 7, 1917.
Boston A.L., vs. Chicago N.L., September 9, 1918.

Most Assists, Game, Both Clubs, Nine Innings

38—Chicago A.L., 20, Chicago N.L., 18, October 12, 1906.

Fewest Assists, Game, Nine Innings

2—St. Louis N.L., vs. Detroit A.L., October 2, 1968.

Fewest Assists, Game, Both Clubs, Nine Innings

8—Philadelphia A.L., 5, St. Louis N.L., 3, October 2, 1930.
Boston A.L., 5, Cincinnati N.L., 3, October 16, 1975.

Fewest Assists, Infield, Game, Nine Innings

1—St. Louis N.L., vs. Detroit A.L., October 2, 1968.

Most Assists, Outfield, One Inning

2—Boston A.L., vs. St. Louis N.L., October 10, 1946, fifth game.

Chances Offered

Fewest Chances Offered, Outfield, Game, Nine Innings

0—New York N.L., vs. New York A.L., September 30, 1936.

Fewest Chances Offered, Outfield, Extra-Inning Game

1—New York N.L. vs. Oakland A.L., October 14, 1973, 12 innings.

Fewest Chances Offered, Outfield, Game, Nine Innings, Both Clubs

3—New York A.L., 2, Brooklyn N.L., 1, October 10, 1956.

Fewest Chances Offered, Infield, Game, Excluding First Base

2—Philadelphia A.L., vs. St. Louis N.L., October 6, 1931.

Errors

Most Errors, Total Series

140—New York A.L., 33 Series, 187 games.

Most Errors, Series

4-game Series— 8—New York A.L., vs. Chicago N.L., 1932.
5-game Series—13—Brooklyn N.L., vs. Boston A.L., 1916.
6-game Series—16—New York N.L., vs. Philadelphia A.L., 1911.
7-game Series—19—Detroit A.L., vs. Pittsburgh N.L., 1909.
8-game Series—18—Pittsburgh N.L., vs. Boston A.L., 1903.

Most Errors, Series, Both Clubs

4-game Series—14—New York A.L., 8, Chicago N.L., 6, 1932.
5-game Series—23—Chicago N.L., 12, Philadelphia A.L., 11, 1910.
6-game Series—27—New York N.L., 16, Philadelphia A.L., 11, 1911.
7-game Series—34—Detroit A.L., 19, Pittsburgh N.L., 15, 1909.
8-game Series—32—Pittsburgh N.L., 18, Boston A.L., 14, 1903.

Fewest Errors, Series

4-game Series—0—Baltimore A.L., vs. Los Angeles N.L., 1966.
5-game Series—0—New York A.L., vs. New York N.L., 1937.
6-game Series—1—Boston A.L., vs. Chicago N.L., 1918.
St. Louis N.L., vs. St. Louis A.L., 1944.
New York A.L., vs. Brooklyn N.L., 1953.
Los Angeles N.L., vs. New York A.L., 1977.
7-game Series—2—Philadelphia A.L., vs. St. Louis N.L., 1931.
New York A.L., vs. Brooklyn N.L., 1955.
Brooklyn N.L., vs. New York N.L., 1956.
St. Louis N.L., vs. Detroit A.L., 1968.
Cincinnati N.L., vs. Boston A.L., 1975.
St. Louis N.L., vs. Kansas City A.L., 1985.
8-game Series—5—New York N.L., vs. New York A.L., 1921.

Fewest Errors, Series, Both Clubs

4-game Series— 4—Los Angeles N.L., 3, vs. New York A.L., 1, 1963.
5-game Series— 6—Brooklyn N.L., 4, New York A.L., 2, 1941.
Baltimore A.L., 4, New York N.L., 2, 1969.
6-game Series— 4—New York A.L., 3, Los Angeles N.L., 1, 1977.
7-game Series— 5—Kansas City A.L., 3, St. Louis N.L., 2, 1985.
8-game Series—11—New York N.L., 6, New York A.L., 5, 1921.

Most Errors, Game, Nine Innings

6—Chicago A.L., vs. Chicago N.L., October 13, 1906.
Pittsburgh N.L., vs. Detroit A.L., October 12, 1909.
Chicago A.L., vs. New York N.L., October 13, 1917.
Los Angeles N.L., vs. Baltimore A.L., October 6, 1966.

Most Errors, Game, Both Clubs, Nine Innings

9—Chicago A.L., 6, New York N.L., 3, October 13, 1917.

Most Errors, Outfield, Game

4—Los Angeles N.L., vs. Baltimore A.L., October 6, 1966.

Most Errors, Outfield, Game, Both Clubs

4—Los Angeles N.L., 4, Baltimore A.L., 0, October 6, 1966.

Most Errors, Infield, Game

5—Chicago A.L., vs. Chicago N.L., October 13, 1906.
New York N.L., vs. Philadelphia A.L., October 17, 1911 (11 innings).
Detroit A.L., vs. St. Louis N.L., October 3, 1934.

Most Errors, Infield, Game, Both Clubs

7—New York N.L., 5, Philadelphia A.L., 2, October 17, 1911 (11 innings).
Chicago A.L., 4, New York N.L., 3, October 13, 1917.

Most Errors, Inning

3—Chicago A.L., October 13, 1917, fourth inning.
New York N.L., October 8, 1937, fifth inning.
New York N.L., October 9, 1937, third inning.
Cincinnati N.L., October 8, 1939, tenth inning.
Los Angeles N.L., October 1, 1959, third inning.
Los Angeles N.L., October 6, 1966, fifth inning.

Most Errorless Games, Total Series

89—New York A.L., 33 Series, 187 games.

Most Consecutive Errorless Games, Total Series

7—Philadelphia A.L., vs. St. Louis N.L., October 6, 7, 1930; October 1, 2, 5, 6, 7, 1931.

Most Errorless Games, Series

4-game Series—4—Baltimore A.L., vs. Los Angeles N.L., 1966.
5-game Series—5—New York A.L., vs. New York N.L., 1937.
6-game Series—5—Boston A.L., vs. Chicago N.L., 1918.
St. Louis N.L., vs. St. Louis A.L., 1944.
New York A.L., vs. Brooklyn N.L., 1953.
Los Angeles N.L., vs. New York A.L., 1977.
7-game Series—5—Philadelphia A.L., vs. St. Louis N.L., 1931.
New York A.L., vs. Brooklyn N.L., 1955.
Brooklyn N.L., vs. New York N.L., 1956.
St. Louis N.L., vs. Detroit A.L., 1968.
Cincinnati N.L., vs. Boston A.L., 1975.
St. Louis N.L., vs. Kansas City A.L., 1985.
Kansas City A.L., vs. St. Louis N.L., 1985.
Boston A.L., vs. New York N.L., 1986.
8-game Series—5—New York N.L., vs. New York A.L., 1921.

Most Consecutive Errorless Games, Series

5—Philadelphia A.L., vs. St. Louis N.L., October 1, 2, 5, 6, 7, 1931 (first 5 games).
New York A.L., vs. New York N.L., October 6, 7, 8, 9, 10, 1937 (full Series).
New York A.L., vs. Brooklyn N.L., September 29, 30, October 1, 2, 3, 1955.

Most Errorless Games, Series, Both Clubs

4-game Series— 7—Baltimore A.L., 4, Los Angeles N.L., 3, 1966.
5-game Series— 7—New York A.L., 5, New York N.L., 2, 1937.
6-game Series— 9—Los Angeles N.L., 5, New York A.L., 4, 1977.
7-game Series—10—St. Louis N.L., 5, Kansas City A.L., 5, 1985.
8-game Series— 8—New York N.L., 5, New York A.L., 3, 1921.

Fewest Errorless Games, Series

4-game Series—0—Held by many clubs.
5-game Series—0—Held by many clubs.
6-game Series—0—Held by many clubs.
7-game Series—0—St. Louis N.L., vs. Detroit A.L., 1934.
New York N.L., vs. Oakland A.L., 1973.
8-game Series—0—New York N.L., vs. Boston A.L., 1912.

Longest Errorless Game

12 innings—Detroit A.L., vs. St. Louis N.L., October 4, 1934 (fielded 12 complete innings).
New York A.L., vs. Los Angeles N.L., October 11, 1977 (fielded 12 complete innings).

Longest Errorless Game, Both Clubs

12 innings—New York A.L., vs. Los Angeles N.L., October 11, 1977 (Los Angeles only fielded 11 complete innings).
10 innings—New York A.L., vs. Philadelphia N.L., October 5, 1950.
Brooklyn N.L., vs. New York A.L., October 9, 1956 (New York fielded 9 ⅔ innings).

New York A.L., vs. Milwaukee N.L., October 6, 1957
(New York fielded 9 ⅔ innings) .
Philadelphia N.L., vs. Kansas City A.L., October 17,
1980 (Philadelphia fielded 9 ⅔ innings) .

Passed Balls

Most Passed Balls, Total Series

13—New York A.L., 33 series, 187 games.

Most Passed Balls, Series

3—Chicago N.L., vs. Chicago A.L., 1906.
Pittsburgh N.L., vs. New York A.L., 1960.
New York A.L., vs. St. Louis N.L., 1964.

Most Passed Balls, Series, Both Clubs

4—Chicago N.L., 3, Chicago A.L., 1, 1906 (6-game Series) .
New York A.L., 2, Brooklyn N.L., 2, 1947 (7-game Series) .

Fewest Passed Balls, Series

0—Held by many clubs in Series of all lengths.

Fewest Passed Balls, Series, Both Clubs

0—Held by many clubs in Series of all lengths.

Double & Triple Plays

Most Double Plays, Total Series

163—New York A.L., 33 Series, 187 games.

Most Double Plays, Series

4-game Series— 7—Chicago N.L., vs. New York A.L., 1932.
New York A.L., vs. Los Angeles N.L., 1963.
5-game Series— 7—New York A.L., vs. New York N.L., 1922.
New York A.L., vs. Brooklyn N.L., 1941.
Cincinnati N.L., vs. New York A.L., 1961.
6-game Series—10—New York A.L., vs. New York N.L., 1951.
7-game Series—12—Brooklyn N.L., vs. New York A.L., 1955.
8-game Series— 9—Chicago A.L., vs. Cincinnati N.L., 1919.

Most Double Plays, Series, Both Clubs

4-game Series—10—New York A.L., 6, Cincinnati N.L., 4, 1976.
5-game Series—12—New York A.L., 7, Brooklyn N.L., 5, 1941.
6-game Series—16—Philadelphia N.L., 8, Kansas City A.L., 8, 1980.

7-game Series—19—Brooklyn N.L., 12, New York A.L., 7, 1955.
8-game Series—16—Chicago A.L., 9, Cincinnati N.L., 7, 1919.

Fewest Double Plays, Series

4-game Series—1—New York A.L., vs. Chicago N.L., 1932.
Cincinnati N.L., vs. New York A.L., 1939.
Philadelphia N.L., vs. New York A.L., 1950.
Los Angeles N.L., vs. New York A.L., 1963.
5-game Series—0—New York N.L., vs. Baltimore A.L., 1969.
6-game Series—2—Chicago A.L., vs. Chicago N.L., 1906.
New York N.L., vs. Philadelphia A.L., 1911.
Philadelphia A.L., vs. New York N.L., 1911.
Philadelphia A.L., vs. St. Louis N.L., 1930.
New York A.L., vs. New York N.L., 1936.
Chicago A.L., vs. Los Angeles N.L., 1959.
New York A.L., vs. Los Angeles N.L., 1977, 1981.
7-game Series—2—St. Louis N.L., vs. Detroit A.L., 1934.
Baltimore A.L., vs. Pittsburgh N.L., 1971.
St. Louis N.L., vs. Minnesota A.L., 1987.
8-game Series—4—New York N.L., vs. Boston A.L., 1912.

Fewest Double Plays, Series, Both Clubs

4-game Series—4—New York N.L., 2, Cleveland A.L., 2, 1954.
5-game Series—4—New York N.L., 2, Philadelphia A.L., 2, 1905.
Baltimore A.L., 4, New York N.L., 0, 1969.
6-game Series—4—Philadelphia A.L., 2, New York N.L., 2, 1911.
7-game Series—6—Minnesota A.L., 4, St. Louis N.L., 2, 1987.
8-game Series—9—Boston A.L., 5, New York N.L., 4, 1912.

Most Double Plays, Game, Nine Innings

4—Philadelphia A.L., vs. Boston N.L., October 9, 1914.
Boston A.L., vs. Brooklyn N.L., October 7, 1916.
Chicago N.L., vs. New York A.L., September 29, 1932.
Cleveland A.L., vs. Boston N.L., October 11, 1948.
New York A.L., vs. New York N.L., October 8, 1951.
Oakland A.L., vs. New York N.L., October 17, 1973.
Philadelphia N.L., vs. Kansas City A.L., October 15, 1980.

Most Double Plays, Game, Both Clubs, Nine Innings

6—New York A.L., 3, Brooklyn N.L., 3, September 29, 1955.
Philadelphia N.L., 4, Kansas City A.L., 2, October 15, 1980.

Most Triple Plays, Series, One Club

1—Cleveland A.L., vs. Brooklyn N.L., 1920.

Miscellaneous

Club

One-Run Decisions

Most Games Decided by One Run, Total Series

54—New York A.L., 33 Series (won 26, lost 28) .

Most Games Won by One Run, Total Series

27—New York A.L., 33 Series (won 27, lost 29) .

Most Games Lost by One Run, Total Series

29—New York A.L., 33 Series (won 27, lost 29) .

Most Games Won by One Run, Series

4—Boston A.L., vs. Philadelphia N.L., 1915 (Lost 1) .
Boston A.L., vs. Chicago N.L., 1918 (Lost 0) .
Oakland A.L., vs. Cincinnati N.L., 1972 (Lost 2) .

Most Games Decided by One Run, Series, Both Clubs

4-game Series—3—New York A.L. (Won 3) , vs. Philadelphia N.L., 1950.
5-game Series—4—Boston A.L. (Won 4) , vs. Philadelphia N.L., 1915.
Oakland A.L. (Won 3) , vs. Los Angeles N.L. (Won 1) , 1974.
6-game Series—4—Boston A.L. (Won 4) , vs. Chicago N.L., 1918.
7-game Series—6—Oakland A.L. (Won 4) , vs. Cincinnati N.L. (Won 2) , 1972.
8-game Series—4—Boston A.L. (Won 3) , vs. New York N.L. (Won 1) , 1912.

Most Games Won by One Run, Series

4-game Series—3—New York A.L., vs. Philadelphia N.L., 1950.
5-game Series—4—Boston A.L., vs. Philadelphia N.L., 1915.

6-game Series—4—Boston A.L., vs. Chicago N.L., 1918.
7-game Series—4—Oakland A.L., vs. Cincinnati N.L., 1972.
8-game Series—3—Boston A.L., vs. New York N.L., 1912.

Most Consecutive Games Won by One Run, Total Series

6—Boston A.L., 1915 (last 4) , 1916 (first two) .

Most Consecutive Games Lost by One Run, Total Series

7—Philadelphia N.L., 1915 (last 4) , 1950 (first 3) .

Length Of Games

By Innings

Longest Tie Game

12 innings—Chicago N.L., 3, Detroit A.L., 3, at Chicago, October 8, 1907.

Longest Day Game

14 innings—Boston A.L., 2, Brooklyn N.L., 1, at Boston, October 9, 1916.

Longest Night Game

12 innings—Boston A.L., 7, Cincinnati N.L., 6, at Boston, October 21, 1975.
New York A.L., 4, Los Angeles N.L., 3, at New York, October 11, 1977.

Most Extra-Inning Games, Total Series

13—New York A.L., 33 Series, 187 games; Won 6, lost 6, 1 tie.

Most Extra-Inning Games Won, Total Series

7—New York N.L., 14 Series, 82 games; Won 7, lost 3, 2 ties.

Most Extra-Inning Games Lost, Total Series

6—New York A.L., 33 Series, 187 games; Won 6, lost 6, 1 tie.

Most Extra-Inning Games, Series

4-game Series—1—Boston N.L. vs. Philadelphia A.L., 1914.
  New York A.L. vs. Cincinnati N.L., 1939.
  New York A.L. vs. Philadelphia N.L., 1950.
  New York N.L. vs. Cleveland A.L., 1954.
5-game Series—2—New York N.L. vs. Washington A.L., 1933.
6-game Series—2—Philadelphia A.L. vs. New York N.L., 1911.
7-game Series—2—Washington A.L. vs. New York N.L., 1924.
  New York A.L. vs. Milwaukee N.L., 1958.
  Oakland A.L. vs. New York N.L., 1973.
  Cincinnati N.L. vs. Boston A.L., 1975.
8-game Series—2—Boston A.L. vs. New York N.L., 1912.

By Time

Longest Time Average Per Game, Series

4-game Series—Two hours, 50 minutes—New York N.L. vs. Cleveland A.L., 1954.
5-game Series—Two hours, 54 minutes—Detroit A.L. vs. San Diego N.L., 1984.
6-game Series—Two hours, 58 minutes—Kansas City A.L. vs. Philadelphia N.L., 1980.
7-game Series—Three hours, 20 minutes—New York N.L. vs. Boston A.L., 1986.
8-game Series—Two hours, 14 minutes—Boston A.L. vs. New York N.L., 1912.

Shortest Time Average Per Game, Series

4-game Series—One hour, 46 minutes—New York A.L. vs. Cincinnati N.L., 1939.
5-game Series—One hour, 46 minutes—Detroit A.L. vs. Chicago N.L., 1908.
6-game Series—One hour, 49 minutes—Philadelphia A.L. vs. St. Louis N.L., 1930.
7-game Series—One hour, 47 minutes—Cleveland A.L. vs. Brooklyn N.L., 1920.
8-game Series—One hour, 48 minutes—Boston A.L. vs. Pittsburgh N.L., 1903.

Shortest Game by Time

1 hour, 25 minutes—Chicago N.L., 2, Detroit A.L., 0, at Detroit, October 14, 1908.

Longest Day Game by Time, Nine Innings

3 hours, 48 minutes—Baltimore A.L., 9, Pittsburgh N.L., 6, October 13, 1979.

Longest Night Game by Time, Nine Innings

3 hours, 36 minutes—Boston A.L., 9, New York N.L., 3, October 19, 1986.

Longest Day Game by Time, Extra Innings

4 hours, 13 minutes—New York N.L., 10, Oakland A.L., 7, at Oakland, October 14, 1973, 12 innings.

Longest Night Game by Time, Extra Innings

4 hours, 2 minutes—New York N.L., 6, Boston A.L., 5, at New York, October 25, 1986, 10 innings.

Series Starting & Finishing Dates

Earliest Date for World Series Game, Except 1918

September 28, 1932, at New York, New York A.L., 12, Chicago N.L., 6.
September 28, 1955, at New York, New York A.L., 6, Brooklyn N.L., 5.

Earliest Date for World Series Final Game, Except 1918

October 2, 1932, at Chicago, New York A.L., 13, Chicago N.L., 6 (4-game Series).
October 2, 1954, at Cleveland, New York N.L., 7, Cleveland A.L., 4 (4-game Series).

Latest Date for World Series Start

October 20, 1981, at New York, New York A.L., 5, Los Angeles N.L., 3 (6-game Series ended at New York on October 28, 1981).

Latest Date for World Series Finish

October 28, 1981, at New York, Los Angeles N.L., 9, New York A.L., 2 (6-game Series started at New York on October 20, 1981).

Night Games

First World Series Night Game

October 13, 1971, at Pittsburgh, Pittsburgh N.L., 4, Baltimore A.L., 3.

First Year, Entire Series Played at Night

1985—October 19 through 27, St. Louis N.L. vs. Kansas City A.L., 7-game Series.

Series & Games Won

Most Series Won

22—New York A.L., 1923, 1927, 1928, 1932, 1936, 1937, 1938, 1939, 1941, 1943, 1947, 1949, 1950, 1951, 1952, 1953, 1956, 1958, 1961, 1962, 1977, 1978 (lost 11).

Most Consecutive Series Won

8—New York A.L., 1927, 1928, 1932, 1936, 1937, 1938, 1939, 1941.

Most Consecutive Years Winning Series

5—New York A.L., 1949, 1950, 1951, 1952, 1953.

Most Times Winning Series in Four Consecutive Games

6—New York A.L., 1927, 1928, 1932, 1938, 1939, 1950.

Winning Series After Winning First Game

Accomplished 47 times.

Winning Series After Losing First Game

Accomplished 36 times.

Winning Series After Winning One Game and Losing Three

Boston A.L., vs. Pittsburgh N.L., 1903 (best-out-of-nine Series).
Pittsburgh N.L., vs. Washington A.L., 1925 (best-out-of-seven Series).
New York A.L., vs. Milwaukee N.L., 1958 (best-out-of-seven Series).
Detroit A.L., vs. St. Louis N.L., 1968 (best-out-of-seven Series).
Pittsburgh N.L., vs. Baltimore A.L., 1979 (best-out-of-seven Series).
Kansas City A.L., vs. St. Louis N.L., 1985 (best-out-of-seven Series).

Winning Series After Losing First Two Games

New York N.L., vs. New York A.L., 1921 (best-out-of-nine Series).
Brooklyn N.L., vs. New York A.L., 1955 (best-out-of-seven Series).
New York A.L., vs. Brooklyn N.L., 1956 (best-out-of-seven Series).
New York A.L., vs. Milwaukee N.L., 1958 (best-out-of-seven Series).
Los Angeles N.L., vs. Minnesota A.L., 1965 (best-out-of-seven Series).
Pittsburgh N.L., vs. Baltimore A.L., 1971 (best-out-of-seven Series).
New York A.L., vs. Los Angeles N.L., 1978 (best-out-of-six Series).
Los Angeles N.L., vs. New York A.L., 1981 (best-out-of-six Series).
Kansas City A.L., vs. St. Louis N.L., 1985 (best-out-of-seven Series).
New York N.L., vs. Boston A.L., 1986 (best-out-of-seven Series).

Winning Series After Losing First Three Games

Never accomplished.

Most Games Won, Total Series

109—New York A.L., 33 Series (won 109, lost 77, tied 1).

Series & Games Lost

Most Series Lost

12—Brooklyn-Los Angeles N.L., 1916, 1920, 1941, 1947, 1949, 1952, 1953, 1956, 1966, 1974, 1977, 1978 (won 5).
11—New York A.L., 1921, 1922, 1926, 1942, 1955, 1957, 1960, 1963, 1964, 1976, 1981 (won 22).

Most Consecutive Series Lost

7—Chicago N.L., 1910, 1918, 1929, 1932, 1935, 1938, 1945.
Brooklyn N.L., 1916, 1920, 1941, 1947, 1949, 1952, 1953.

Most Consecutive Years Losing Series

3—Detroit A.L., 1907, 1908, 1909.
New York N.L., 1911, 1912, 1913.

Most Games Lost, Total Series

77—New York A.L., 33 Series (won 109, lost 77, tied 1).

Attendance

Largest Attendance, Series

4-game Series—251,507—New York N.L. vs. Cleveland A.L., 1954.

5-game Series—304,139—Baltimore A.L. vs. Philadelphia N.L., 1983.

6-game Series—420,784—Los Angeles N.L. vs. Chicago A.L., 1959.

7-game Series—394,712—Milwaukee N.L. vs. New York A.L., 1957.

8-game Series—269,976—New York N.L. vs. New York A.L., 1921.

Smallest Attendance, Series

4-game Series—111,009—Boston N.L. vs. Philadelphia A.L., 1914.

5-game Series— 62,232—Chicago N.L. vs. Detroit A.L., 1908.

6-game Series— 99,845—Chicago A.L. vs. Chicago N.L., 1906.

7-game Series—145,295—Pittsburgh N.L. vs. Detroit A.L., 1909.

8-game Series—100,429—Pittsburgh N.L. vs. Boston A.L., 1903.

Largest Attendance, Game

92,706—At Los Angeles, October 6, 1959, Chicago A.L., 1, Los Angeles N.L., 0, fifth game.

Smallest Attendance, Game

6,210—At Detroit, October 14, 1908; Chicago N.L., 2, Detroit A.L., 0, fifth game.

League

Series & Games Won & Lost

Most Consecutive Series Won, League

7—American League, 1947, 1948, 1949, 1950, 1951, 1952, 1953.

Most Consecutive Series Lost, League

7—National League, 1947, 1948, 1949, 1950, 1951, 1952, 1953.

Most Consecutive Games Won, Total Series

12—New York A.L., 1927 (4), 1928 (4), 1932 (4).

Most Consecutive Games Lost, Total Series

8—New York A.L., 1921 (last 3), 1922 (4), 1923 (first 1).
Philadelphia N.L., 1915 (last 4), 1950 (4).

Most Consecutive Games Won, League

10—American League, 1927 (4), 1928 (4), 1929 (first 2); also 1937 (last 1), 1938 (4), 1939 (4), 1940 (first 1).

Shutouts

Most Consecutive Series With Shutouts

9—1955 through 1963.

Most Consecutive Series Ending in Shutouts

3—1907, 1908, 1909.
1955, 1956, 1957.

Most Consecutive Series Without Shutouts

3—1910, 1911, 1912.
1927, 1928, 1929.
1936, 1937, 1938.
1976, 1977, 1978.

Non-Playing Personnel

Managers & Coaches

Most Series, Manager

10—Stengel, Charles D., New York A.L., 1949, 1950, 1951, 1952, 1953, 1955, 1956, 1957, 1958, 1960 (won 7, lost 3).

Most Series as Coach

15—Crosetti, Frank P., New York A.L., 1947, 1949, 1950, 1951, 1952, 1953, 1955, 1956, 1957, 1958, 1960, 1961, 1962, 1963, 1964 (10 World Series winners).

Most Series Eligible as Player and Coach

23—Crosetti, Frank P., New York A.L., 1932, 1936, 1937, 1938, 1939, 1941, 1942, 1943 (8 Series as player, 7 winners); 1947, 1949, 1950, 1951, 1952, 1953, 1955, 1956, 1957, 1958, 1960, 1961, 1962, 1963, 1964 (15 Series as coach, 10 winners).

Most World Series Winners Managed

7—McCarthy, Joseph V., New York A.L., 1932, 1936, 1937, 1938, 1939, 1941, 1943.
Stengel, Charles D., New York A.L., 1949, 1950, 1951, 1952, 1953, 1956, 1958.

Most Consecutive Years Managed World Series Winners

5—Stengel, Charles D., New York A.L., 1949, 1950, 1951, 1952, 1953 (his first five years as manager, New York A.L.).

Most Consecutive World Series Winners Managed, Total Series

6—McCarthy, Joseph V., New York A.L., 1932, 1936, 1937, 1938, 1939, 1941.

Most World Series Losers Managed

6—McGraw, John J., New York N.L., 1911, 1912, 1913, 1917, 1923, 1924.

Most Consecutive Years Managed World Series Losers

3—Jennings, Hugh A., Detroit A.L., 1907, 1908, 1909.
McGraw, John J., New York N.L., 1911, 1912, 1913.

Most Consecutive World Series Losers, Managed, Total Series

4—McGraw, John J., New York N.L., 1911, 1912, 1913, 1917.

Most Different World Series Winners Managed

2—McKechnie, William B., Pittsburgh N.L., 1925; Cincinnati N.L., 1940.
Harris, Stanley R., Washington A.L., 1924; New York A.L., 1947.
Anderson, George L., Cincinnati N.L., 1975, 1976; Detroit A.L., 1984.

Most Different Clubs Managed

3—McKechnie, William B., Pittsburgh N.L., 1925; St. Louis N.L., 1928; Cincinnati N.L., 1939, 1940.
Williams, Richard H., Boston A.L., 1967; Oakland A.L., 1972, 1973; San Diego N.L., 1984.

Most Games, Manager

63—Stengel, Charles D., New York A.L. (10 Series).

Most Games Won, Manager

37—Stengel, Charles D., New York A.L. (10 Series).

Most Games Lost, Manager

28—McGraw, John J., New York N.L. (10 Series).

Youngest Manager, World Series Club

26 years, 11 months, 21 days—Cronin, Joseph E., Washington A.L., vs. New York N.L., October 3, 1933. (Born October 12, 1906.)

Youngest Manager, World Series Winner

27 years, 11 months, 2 days—Harris, Stanley R., Washington A.L., vs. New York N.L., October 10, 1924. (Born November 8, 1896.)

Umpires

Most Series Umpired

18—Klem, William J., 1908, 1909, 1911, 1912, 1913, 1914, 1915, 1917, 1918, 1920, 1922, 1924, 1926, 1929, 1931, 1932, 1934, 1940.

Most Consecutive Series Umpired

5—Klem, William J., 1911, 1912, 1913, 1914, 1915.

Most Games Umpired

104—Klem, William J. (18 Series).

General Reference Data

Results

Year—Winner / Loser

1903—Boston A.L., 5 games; Pittsburgh N.L., 3 games.
1904—No Series.
1905—New York N.L., 4 games; Philadelphia A.L., 1 game.
1906—Chicago A.L., 4 games; Chicago N.L., 2 games.
1907—Chicago N.L., 4 games; Detroit A.L., 0 games; 1 tie.
1908—Chicago N.L., 4 games; Detroit A.L., 1 game.
1909—Pittsburgh N.L., 4 games; Detroit A.L., 3 games.
1910—Philadelphia A.L., 4 games; Chicago N.L., 1 game.
1911—Philadelphia A.L., 4 games; New York N.L., 2 games.
1912—Boston A.L., 4 games; New York N.L., 3 games; 1 tie.
1913—Philadelphia A.L., 4 games; New York N.L., 1 game.
1914—Boston N.L., 4 games; Philadelphia A.L., 0 games.
1915—Boston A.L., 4 games; Philadelphia N.L., 1 game.
1916—Boston A.L., 4 games; Brooklyn N.L., 1 game.
1917—Chicago A.L., 4 games; New York N.L., 2 games.
1918—Boston A.L., 4 games; Chicago N.L., 2 games.
1919—Cincinnati N.L., 5 games; Chicago A.L., 3 games.
1920—Cleveland A.L., 5 games; Brooklyn N.L., 2 games.
1921—New York N.L., 5 games; New York A.L., 3 games.
1922—New York N.L., 4 games; New York A.L., 0 games; 1 tie.
1923—New York A.L., 4 games; New York N.L., 2 games.
1924—Washington A.L., 4 games; New York N.L., 3 games.
1925—Pittsburgh N.L., 4 games; Washington A.L., 3 games.
1926—St. Louis N.L., 4 games; New York A.L., 3 games.
1927—New York A.L., 4 games; Pittsburgh N.L., 0 games.
1928—New York A.L., 4 games; St. Louis N.L., 0 games.
1929—Philadelphia A.L., 4 games; Chicago N.L., 1 game.
1930—Philadelphia A.L., 4 games; St. Louis N.L., 2 games.
1931—St. Louis N.L., 4 games; Philadelphia A.L., 3 games.
1932—New York A.L., 4 games; Chicago N.L., 0 games.
1933—New York N.L., 4 games; Washington A.L., 1 game.
1934—St. Louis N.L., 4 games; Detroit A.L., 3 games.
1935—Detroit A.L., 4 games; Chicago N.L., 2 games.
1936—New York A.L., 4 games; New York N.L., 2 games.
1937—New York A.L., 4 games; New York N.L., 1 game.
1938—New York A.L., 4 games; Chicago N.L., 0 games.
1939—New York A.L., 4 games; Cincinnati N.L., 0 games.
1940—Cincinnati N.L., 4 games; Detroit A.L., 3 games.
1941—New York A.L., 4 games; Brooklyn N.L., 1 game.
1942—St. Louis N.L., 4 games; New York A.L., 1 game.
1943—New York A.L., 4 games; St. Louis N.L., 1 game.
1944—St. Louis N.L., 4 games; St. Louis A.L., 2 games.
1945—Detroit A.L., 4 games; Chicago N.L., 3 games.

1946—St. Louis N.L., 4 games; Boston A.L., 3 games.
1947—New York A.L., 4 games; Brooklyn N.L., 3 games.
1948—Cleveland A.L., 4 games; Boston N.L., 2 games.
1949—New York A.L., 4 games; Brooklyn N.L., 1 game.
1950—New York A.L., 4 games; Philadelphia N.L., 0 games.
1951—New York A.L., 4 games; New York N.L., 2 games.
1952—New York A.L., 4 games; Brooklyn N.L., 3 games.
1953—New York A.L., 4 games; Brooklyn N.L., 2 games.
1954—New York N.L., 4 games; Cleveland A.L., 0 games.
1955—Brooklyn N.L., 4 games; New York A.L., 3 games.
1956—New York A.L., 4 games; Brooklyn N.L., 3 games.
1957—Milwaukee N.L., 4 games; New York A.L., 3 games.
1958—New York A.L., 4 games; Milwaukee N.L., 3 games.
1959—Los Angeles N.L., 4 games; Chicago A.L., 2 games.
1960—Pittsburgh N.L., 4 games; New York A.L., 3 games.
1961—New York A.L., 4 games; Cincinnati N.L., 1 game.
1962—New York A.L., 4 games; San Francisco N.L., 3 games.
1963—Los Angeles N.L., 4 games; New York A.L., 0 games.
1964—St. Louis N.L., 4 games; New York A.L., 3 games.
1965—Los Angeles N.L., 4 games; Minnesota A.L., 3 games.
1966—Baltimore A.L., 4 games; Los Angeles N.L., 0 games.
1967—St. Louis N.L., 4 games; Boston A.L., 3 games.
1968—Detroit A.L., 4 games; St. Louis N.L., 3 games.
1969—New York N.L., 4 games; Baltimore A.L., 1 game.
1970—Baltimore A.L., 4 games; Cincinnati N.L., 1 game.
1971—Pittsburgh N.L., 4 games; Baltimore A.L., 3 games.
1972—Oakland A.L., 4 games; Cincinnati N.L., 3 games.
1973—Oakland A.L., 4 games; New York N.L., 3 games.
1974—Oakland A.L., 4 games; Los Angeles N.L., 1 game.
1975—Cincinnati N.L., 4 games; Boston A.L., 3 games.
1976—Cincinnati N.L., 4 games; New York A.L., 0 games.
1977—New York A.L., 4 games; Los Angeles N.L., 2 games.
1978—New York A.L., 4 games; Los Angeles N.L., 2 games.
1979—Pittsburgh N.L., 4 games; Baltimore A.L., 3 games.
1980—Philadelphia N.L., 4 games; Kansas City A.L., 2 games.
1981—Los Angeles N.L., 4 games; New York A.L., 2 games.
1982—St. Louis N.L., 4 games; Milwaukee A.L., 3 games.
1983—Baltimore A.L., 4 games; Philadelphia N.L., 1 game.
1984—Detroit A.L., 4 games; San Diego N.L., 1 game.
1985—Kansas City A.L., 4 games; St. Louis N.L., 3 games.
1986—New York N.L., 4 games; Boston A.L., 3 games.
1987—Minnesota A.L., 4 games; St. Louis N.L., 3 games.

Series Won & Lost

American League

	W.	L.	Pct.
New York	22	11	.667
Cleveland	2	1	.667
⌈Oakland	3	0	1.000
⌊Philadelphia	5	3	.625
Boston	5	4	.556
Chicago	2	2	.500
⌈Baltimore	3	3	.500
⌊St. Louis	0	1	.000
Kansas City	1	1	.500
Detroit	4	5	.444
⌈Washington	1	2	.333
⌊Minnesota	1	1	.500
Milwaukee	0	1	.000
Totals	49	35	.583

National League

	W.	L.	Pct.
Pittsburgh	5	2	.714
New York Mets	2	1	.667
St. Louis	9	6	.600
⌈Boston	1	1	.500
⌊Milwaukee	1	1	.500
Cincinnati	4	4	.500
⌈New York Giants	5	9	.357
⌊San Francisco	0	1	.000
⌈Los Angeles	4	4	.500
⌊Brooklyn	1	8	.111
Philadelphia	1	3	.250
Chicago	2	8	.200
San Diego	0	1	.000
Totals	35	49	.417

Games Won & Lost

American League

	W.	L.	Tie	Pct.
New York	109	77	1	.586
⌈Baltimore	19	14		.576
⌊St. Louis	2	4		.333
⌈Philadelphia	24	19		.558
⌊Oakland	12	7		.632
Boston	33	26	1	.559
Cleveland	9	8		.529
Chicago	13	13		.500
Detroit	26	29	1	.473
Kansas City	6	7		.462
Milwaukee	3	4		.429
⌈Minnesota	7	7		.500
⌊Washington	8	11		.421
Totals	271	226	3	.545

National League

	W.	L.	Tie	Pct.
New York Mets	11	8		.579
⌈Los Angeles	21	23		.477
⌊Brooklyn	20	36		.357
⌈Boston	6	4		.600
⌊Milwaukee	7	7		.500
St. Louis	48	48		.500
⌈New York Giants	39	41	2	.488
⌊San Francisco	3	4		.429
Pittsburgh	23	24		.489
Cincinnati	22	25		.468
Chicago	19	33	1	.365
Philadelphia	6	14		.300
San Diego	1	4		.200
Totals	226	271	3	.455

Home & Road Games, Each Club

American League

	Y.	G.	H.	R.
New York	33	187	91	96
⌈Philadelphia	8	43	20	23
⌊Oakland	3	19	10	9
Detroit	9	56	28	28
Boston	9	60	31	29
⌈St. Louis	1	6	3	3
⌊Baltimore	6	33	17	16
Chicago	4	26	13	13
⌈Washington	3	19	10	9
⌊Minnesota	2	14	8	6
Cleveland	3	17	9	8
Kansas City	2	13	7	6
Milwaukee	1	7	3	4
Totals	84	500	250	250

National League

	Y.	G.	H.	R.
⌈Brooklyn	9	56	28	28
⌊Los Angeles	8	44	21	23
⌈New York Giants	14	82	41	41
⌊San Francisco	1	7	4	3
St. Louis	15	96	47	49
Chicago	10	53	27	26
Cincinnati	8	47	24	23
Pittsburgh	7	47	23	24
⌈Milwaukee	2	14	7	7
⌊Boston	2	10	5	5
Philadelphia	4	20	11	9
New York Mets	3	19	10	9
San Diego	1	5	2	3
Totals	84	500	250	250

Tie Games (3)

Oct. 8, 1907—12 innings, Chicago N.L. 3, Detroit A.L. 3.
Oct. 9, 1912—11 innings, Boston A.L. 6, New York N.L. 6.
Oct. 5, 1922—10 innings, New York A.L. 3, New York N.L. 3.

Shutouts (95)

Oct. 2, 1903—Dinneen, Boston A.L. 3, Pittsburgh N.L. 0, 3 hits.
Oct. 13, 1903—Dinneen, Boston A.L. 3, Pittsburgh N.L. 0, 4 hits.
Oct. 9, 1905—Mathewson, New York N.L. 3, Phil. A.L. 0, 4 hits.
Oct. 10, 1905—Bender, Philadelphia A.L. 3, New York N.L. 0, 4 hits.
Oct. 12, 1905—Mathewson, N.Y. N.L. 9, Phil. A.L. 0, 4 hits.
Oct. 13, 1905—McGinnity, New York N.L. 1, Phil. A.L. 0, 5 hits.
Oct. 14, 1905—Mathewson, New York N.L. 2, Phil. A.L. 0, 6 hits.
Oct. 11, 1906—Walsh, Chicago A.L. 3, Chicago N.L. 0, 2 hits.
Oct. 12, 1906—Brown, Chicago N.L. 1, Chicago A.L. 0, 2 hits.
Oct. 12, 1907—Brown, Chicago N.L. 2, Detroit A.L. 0, 7 hits.
Oct. 13, 1908—Brown, Chicago N.L. 3, Detroit A.L. 0, 4 hits.
Oct. 14, 1908—Overall, Chicago A.L. 2, Detroit A.L. 0, 3 hits.
Oct. 12, 1909—Mullin, Detroit A.L. 5, Pittsburgh N.L. 0, 5 hits.
Oct. 16, 1909—Adams, Pittsburgh N.L. 8, Detroit A.L. 0, 6 hits.
Oct. 8, 1913—Mathewson, N.Y. N.L. 3, Phil. A.L. 0, 8 hits (ten inn.).
Oct. 10, 1914—James, Boston N.L. 1, Philadelphia A.L. 0, 2 hits.
Oct. 10, 1917—Benton, New York N.L. 2, Chicago A.L. 0, 5 hits.
Oct. 11, 1917—Schupp, New York N.L. 5, Chicago A.L. 0, 7 hits.
Sept. 5, 1918—Ruth, Boston A.L. 1, Chicago N.L. 0, 6 hits.
Sept. 10, 1918—Vaughn, Chicago N.L. 3, Boston A.L. 0, 5 hits.
Oct. 3, 1919—Kerr, Chicago A.L. 3, Cincinnati N.L. 0, 3 hits.
Oct. 4, 1919—Ring, Cincinnati N.L. 2, Chicago A.L. 0, 3 hits.
Oct. 6, 1919—Eller, Cincinnati N.L. 5, Chicago A.L. 0, 3 hits.
Oct. 6, 1920—Grimes, Brooklyn N.L. 3, Cleveland A.L. 0, 7 hits.
Oct. 11, 1920—Mails, Cleveland A.L. 1, Brooklyn N.L. 0, 3 hits.
Oct. 12, 1920—Coveleski, Cleveland A.L. 3, Brooklyn N.L. 0, 5 hits.
Oct. 5, 1921—Mays, New York A.L. 3, New York N.L. 0, 5 hits.
Oct. 6, 1921—Hoyt, New York A.L. 3, New York N.L. 0, 2 hits.
Oct. 13, 1921—Nehf, New York N.L. 1, New York A.L. 0, 4 hits.
Oct. 6, 1922—Scott, New York N.L. 3, New York A.L. 0, 4 hits.
Oct. 12, 1923—Nehf, New York N.L. 1, New York A.L. 0, 6 hits.
Oct. 11, 1925—Johnson, Washington A.L. 4, Pittsburgh N.L. 0, 6 hits.
Oct. 5, 1926—Haines, St. Louis N.L. 4, New York A.L. 0, 5 hits.
Oct. 4, 1930—Hallahan, St. Louis N.L. 5, Philadelphia A.L. 0, 7 hits.
Oct. 6, 1930—Earnshaw, Grove, Phil. A.L. 2, St. L. N.L. 0, 3 hits.
Oct. 2, 1931—Hallahan, St. Louis N.L. 2, Philadelphia A.L. 0, 3 hits.
Oct. 6, 1931—Earnshaw, Philadelphia A.L. 3, St. Louis N.L. 0, 2 hits.
Oct. 5, 1933—Whitehill, Washington A.L. 4, New York N.L. 0, 5 hits.
Oct. 9, 1934—J. Dean, St. Louis N.L. 11, Detroit A.L. 0, 6 hits.
Oct. 2, 1935—Warneke, Chicago N.L. 3, Detroit A.L. 0, 4 hits.
Oct. 5, 1939—Pearson, New York A.L. 4, Cincinnati N.L. 0, 2 hits.
Oct. 6, 1940—Newsom, Detroit A.L. 8, Cincinnati N.L. 0, 3 hits.
Oct. 7, 1940—Walters, Cincinnati N.L. 4, Detroit A.L. 0, 5 hits.
Oct. 3, 1942—White, St. Louis N.L. 2, New York A.L. 0, 6 hits.
Oct. 11, 1943—Chandler, New York A.L. 2, St. Louis N.L. 0, 10 hits.
Oct. 8, 1944—Cooper, St. Louis N.L. 2, St. Louis A.L. 0, 7 hits.
Oct. 5, 1945—Borowy, Chicago N.L. 9, Detroit A.L. 0, 6 hits.
Oct. 5, 1945—Passeau, Chicago N.L. 3, Detroit A.L. 0, 1 hit.
Oct. 7, 1946—Brecheen, St. Louis N.L. 3, Boston A.L. 0, 4 hits.
Oct. 9, 1946—Ferriss, Boston A.L. 4, St. Louis N.L. 0, 6 hits.
Oct. 6, 1948—Sain, Boston N.L. 1, Cleveland A.L. 0, 4 hits.
Oct. 8, 1948—Bearden, Cleveland A.L. 2, Boston A.L. 0, 5 hits.
Oct. 5, 1949—Reynolds, New York A.L. 1, Brooklyn N.L. 0, 2 hits.
Oct. 6, 1949—Roe, Brooklyn N.L. 1, New York A.L. 0, 6 hits.
Oct. 4, 1950—Raschi, New York A.L. 1, Philadelphia N.L. 0, 2 hits.
Oct. 4, 1952—Reynolds, New York A.L. 2, Brooklyn N.L. 0, 4 hits.
Oct. 4, 1955—Podres, Brooklyn N.L. 2, New York A.L. 0, 8 hits.
Oct. 8, 1956—Larsen, New York A.L. 2, Brooklyn N.L. 0, 0 hits.
Oct. 9, 1956—Labine, Brooklyn N.L. 1, N.Y. A.L. 0, 7 hits (ten inn.).
Oct. 10, 1956—Kucks, New York A.L. 9, Brooklyn N.L. 0, 3 hits.
Oct. 7, 1957—Burdette, Milwaukee N.L. 1, New York A.L. 0, 7 hits.
Oct. 10, 1957—Burdette, Milwaukee N.L. 5, New York A.L. 0, 7 hits.
Oct. 4, 1958—Larsen, Duren, New York A.L. 4, Milw. N.L. 0, 6 hits.
Oct. 5, 1958—Spahn, Milwaukee N.L. 3, New York A.L. 0, 2 hits.
Oct. 6, 1958—Turley, New York A.L. 7, Milwaukee N.L. 0, 5 hits.
Oct. 1, 1959—Wynn, Staley, Chicago A.L. 11, L.A. N.L. 0, 8 hits.
Oct. 6, 1959—Shaw, Pierce, Donovan, Chi. A.L. 1, L.A. N.L. 0, 9 hits.
Oct. 8, 1960—Ford, New York A.L. 10, Pittsburgh N.L. 0, 4 hits.
Oct. 12, 1960—Ford, New York A.L. 12, Pittsburgh N.L. 0, 7 hits.
Oct. 4, 1961—Ford, New York A.L. 2, Cincinnati N.L. 0, 2 hits.
Oct. 8, 1961—Ford, Coates, New York A.L. 7, Cincinnati N.L. 0, 5 hits.
Oct. 5, 1962—Sanford, San Francisco N.L. 2, New York A.L. 0, 3 hits.
Oct. 16, 1962—Terry, New York A.L. 1, San Francisco N.L. 0, 4 hits.
Oct. 5, 1963—Drysdale, Los Angeles N.L. 1, New York A.L. 0, 3 hits.
Oct. 9, 1965—Osteen, Los Angeles N.L. 4, Minnesota A.L. 0, 5 hits.
Oct. 11, 1965—Koufax, Los Angeles N.L. 7, Minnesota A.L. 0, 4 hits.
Oct. 14, 1965—Koufax, Los Angeles N.L. 2, Minnesota A.L. 0, 3 hits.
Oct. 6, 1966—Palmer, Baltimore A.L. 6, Los Angeles N.L. 0, 4 hits.
Oct. 8, 1966—Bunker, Baltimore A.L. 1, Los Angeles N.L. 0, 6 hits.
Oct. 9, 1966—McNally, Baltimore A.L. 1, Los Angeles N.L. 0, 4 hits.
Oct. 5, 1967—Lonborg, Boston A.L. 5, St. Louis N.L. 0, 1 hit.
Oct. 8, 1967—Gibson, St. Louis N.L. 6, Boston A.L. 0, 5 hits.
Oct. 2, 1968—Gibson, St. Louis N.L. 4, Detroit A.L. 0, 5 hits.
Oct. 14, 1969—Gentry, Ryan, New York N.L. 5, Baltimore A.L. 0, 4 hits.
Oct. 14, 1971—Briles, Pittsburgh N.L. 4, Baltimore A.L. 0, 2 hits.
Oct. 18, 1972—Billingham, Carroll, Cin. N.L. 1, Oak. A.L. 0, 3 hits.
Oct. 18, 1973—Koosman, McGraw, N.Y. N.L. 2, Oak. A.L. 0, 3 hits.
Oct. 11, 1975—Tiant, Boston A.L. 6, Cincinnati N.L. 0, 5 hits.
Oct. 16, 1979—Candelaria, Tekulve, Pitts. N.L. 4, Balt. A.L. 0, 7 hits.
Oct. 21, 1981—John, Gossage, New York A.L. 3, L.A. N.L. 0, 4 hits.

Oct. 12, 1982—Caldwell, Milwaukee A.L. 10, St. Louis N.L. 0, 3 hits.
Oct. 16, 1983—McGregor, Baltimore A.L. 5, Philadelphia N.L. 0, 5 hits.
Oct. 23, 1985—Tudor, St. Louis N.L. 3, Kansas City A.L. 0, 5 hits.
Oct. 27, 1985—Saberhagen, Kansas City A.L. 11, St.L. N.L. 0, 5 hits.
Oct. 18, 1986—Hurst, Schiraldi, Boston A.L. 1, New York N.L. 0, 5 hits.

Attendance

Year	G.	Total	Year	G.	Total	Year	G.	Total
1903	8	100,429	1932	4	191,998	1960	7	349,813
1905	5	91,723	1933	5	163,076	1961	5	223,247
1906	5	99,845	1934	7	281,510	1962	7	376,864
1907	5	78,068	1935	6	286,672	1963	4	247,279
1908	5	62,232	1936	6	302,924	1964	7	321,807
1909	7	145,295	1937	5	238,142	1965	7	364,326
1910	5	124,222	1938	4	200,833	1966	4	220,791
1911	6	179,851	1939	4	183,849	1967	7	304,085
1912	8	252,037	1940	7	281,927	1968	7	379,670
1913	5	151,000	1941	5	235,773	1969	5	272,378
1914	4	111,009	1942	5	277,101	1970	5	253,183
1915	5	143,351	1943	5	277,312	1971	7	351,091
1916	5	162,859	1944	6	206,708	1972	7	363,149
1917	6	186,654	1945	7	333,457	1973	7	358,289
1918	6	128,483	1946	7	250,071	1974	5	260,004
1919	8	236,928	1947	7	389,763	1975	7	308,272
1920	7	178,737	1948	6	358,362	1976	4	223,009
1921	8	269,976	1949	5	236,716	1977	6	337,708
1922	5	185,947	1950	4	196,009	1978	6	337,304
1923	6	301,430	1951	6	341,977	1979	7	367,597
1924	7	283,665	1952	7	340,706	1980	6	324,516
1925	7	282,848	1953	6	307,350	1981	6	338,081
1926	7	328,051	1954	4	251,507	1982	7	384,570
1927	4	201,705	1955	7	362,310	1983	5	304,139
1928	4	199,072	1956	7	345,903	1984	5	271,820
1929	5	190,490	1957	7	394,712	1985	7	327,494
1930	6	212,619	1958	7	393,909	1986	7	321,774
1931	7	231,567	1959	6	420,784	1987	7	387,138

Extra-Inning Games (40)

Oct. 8, 1907—12 innings, Chicago N.L. 3, Detroit A.L. 3, tie.
Oct. 22, 1910—10 innings, Chicago N.L. 4, Philadelphia A.L. 3.
Oct. 17, 1911—11 innings, Philadelphia A.L. 3, New York N.L. 2.
Oct. 25, 1911—10 innings, New York N.L. 4, Philadelphia A.L. 3.
Oct. 9, 1912—11 innings, Boston A.L. 6, New York N.L. 6, tie.
Oct. 16, 1912—10 innings, Boston A.L. 3, New York N.L. 2.
Oct. 8, 1913—10 innings, New York N.L. 3, Philadelphia A.L. 0.
Oct. 12, 1914—12 innings, Boston N.L. 5, Philadelphia A.L. 4.
Oct. 9, 1916—14 innings, Boston A.L. 2, Brooklyn N.L. 1.
Oct. 7, 1919—10 innings, Chicago A.L. 5, Cincinnati N.L. 4.
Oct. 5, 1922—10 innings, New York N.L. 3, New York A.L. 3, tie.
Oct. 4, 1924—12 innings, New York N.L. 4, Washington A.L. 3.
Oct. 10, 1924—12 innings, Washington A.L. 4, New York N.L. 3.
Oct. 2, 1926—10 innings, New York A.L. 3, St. Louis N.L. 2.
Oct. 6, 1933—11 innings, New York N.L. 2, Wahington A.L. 1.
Oct. 7, 1933—10 innings, New York N.L. 4, Washington A.L. 3.
Oct. 4, 1934—12 innings, Detroit A.L. 3, St. Louis N.L. 2.
Oct. 4, 1935—11 innings, Detroit A.L. 6, Chicago N.L. 5.
Oct. 5, 1936—10 innings, New York N.L. 5, New York A.L. 4
Oct. 8, 1939—10 innings, New York N.L. 7, Cincinnati N.L. 3.
Oct. 5, 1944—11 innings, St. Louis N.L. 3, St. Louis A.L. 2.
Oct. 8, 1945—12 innings, Chicago N.L. 8, Detroit A.L. 7.
Oct. 6, 1946—10 innings, Boston A.L. 3, St. Louis N.L. 2.
Oct. 5, 1950—10 innings, New York A.L. 2, Philadelphia N.L. 1.
Oct. 5, 1952—11 innings, Brooklyn N.L. 6, New York A.L. 5.
Sept. 29, 1954—10 innings, New York N.L. 5, Cleveland A.L. 2.
Oct. 9, 1956—10 innings Brooklyn N.L. 1, New York A.L. 0.
Oct. 6, 1957—10 innings, Milwaukee N.L. 7, New York A.L. 5.
Oct. 1, 1958—10 innings, Milwaukee N.L. 4, New York A.L. 3.
Oct. 8, 1958—10 innings, New York A.L. 4, Milwaukee N.L. 3.
Oct. 12, 1964—10 innings, St. Louis N.L. 5, New York A.L. 2.
Oct. 15, 1969—10 innings, New York N.L. 2, Baltimore A.L. 1.
Oct. 16, 1971—10 innings, Baltimore N.L. 3, Pittsburgh N.L. 2.
Oct. 14, 1973—12 innings, New York N.L. 10, Oakland A.L. 7.
Oct. 16, 1973—11 innings, Oakland A.L. 3, New York N.L. 2.
Oct. 16, 1975—10 innings, Cincinnati N.L. 6, Boston A.L. 5.
Oct. 21, 1975—12 innings, Boston A.L. 7, Cincinnati N.L. 6.
Oct. 11, 1977—12 innings, New York A.L. 4, Los Angeles N.L. 3.
Oct. 14, 1978—10 innings, New York A.L. 4, Los Angeles N.L. 3.
Oct. 17, 1980—10 innings, Kansas City A.L. 4, Philadelphia N.L. 3.
Oct. 25, 1986—10 innings, New York N.L. 6, Boston A.L. 5.

Leading Batters

(Playing in all games, each Series; Capitalized name donates leader (or tied) for Series, both clubs)

American League

Year	Player and Club	AB.	H.	TB.	B.A.
1903	Charles S. Stahl, Boston	33	10	17	.303
1904	No Series				
1905	T. Frederick Hartsel, Philadelphia	17	5	6	.294
1906	GEORGE ROHE, Chicago	21	7	12	.333
	JOHN A. DONAHUE, Chicago	18	6	10	.333
1907	Claude Rossman, Detroit	20	8	10	.400
1908	Tyrus R. Cobb, Detroit	19	7	8	.368

Year	Player and Club	AB.	H.	TB.	B.A.
1909	JAMES C. DELAHANTY, Detroit	26	9	13	.346
1910	EDWARD T. COLLINS, Philadelphia	21	9	13	.429
1911	J. FRANKLIN BAKER, Philadelphia	24	9	17	.375
1912	Tris Speaker, Boston	30	9	14	.300
1913	J. Franklin Baker, Philadelphia	20	9	12	.450
1914	J. Franklin Baker, Philadelphia	16	4	6	.250
1915	GEORGE E. LEWIS, Boston	18	8	12	.444
1916	George E. Lewis, Boston	17	6	10	.353
1917	Edward T. Collins, Chicago	22	9	10	.409
1918	John P. McInnis, Boston	20	5	5	.250
	George Whiteman, Boston	20	5	7	.250
1919	JOSEPH J. JACKSON, Chicago	32	12	18	.375
1920	STEPHEN F. O'NEILL, Cleveland	21	7	10	.333
1921	Walter H. Schang, New York	21	6	9	.296
1922	Robert W. Meusel, New York	20	6	7	.300
1923	AARON L. WARD, New York	24	10	13	.417
1924	JOSEPH I. JUDGE, Washington	26	10	11	.385
1925	Joseph Harris, Washington	25	11	22	.440
1926	Earle B. Combs, New York	28	10	12	.357
1927	MARK A. KOENIG, New York	18	9	11	.500
1928	GEORGE H. RUTH, New York	16	10	22	.625
1929	James Dykes, Philadelphia	19	8	9	.421
1930	ALOYSIUS H. SIMMONS, Philadelphia	22	8	16	.364
1931	James E. Foxx, Philadelphia	23	8	11	.348
1932	H. LOUIS GEHRIG, New York	17	9	19	.529
1933	Fred W. Schulte, Washington	21	7	21	.333
1934	CHARLES L. GEHRINGER, Detroit	29	11	15	.379
1935	ERVIN FOX, Detroit	26	10	15	.385
1936	ALVIN J. POWELL, New York	22	10	14	.455
1937	ANTHONY M. LAZZERI, New York	15	6	11	.400
1938	William B. Dickey, New York	15	6	9	.400
	Joseph L. Gordon, New York	15	6	11	.400
1939	CHARLES E. KELLER, New York	16	7	19	.438
1940	Bruce D. Campbell, Detroit	25	9	13	.360
1941	JOSEPH L. GORDON, New York	14	7	13	.500
1942	PHILIP F. RIZZUTO, New York	21	8	11	.381
1943	William Johnson, New York	20	6	9	.300
1944	GEORGE H. McQUINN, St. Louis	16	7	12	.438
1945	Roger M. Cramer, Detroit	29	11	11	.379
1946	Rudolph P. York, Boston	23	6	15	.261
1947	THOMAS D. HENRICH, New York	31	10	15	.323
1948	Lawrence E. Doby, Cleveland	22	7	11	.318
1949	Thomas D. Henrich, New York	19	5	8	.263
1950	EUGENE R. WOODLING, New York	14	6	6	.429
1951	Philip F. Rizzuto, New York	25	8	11	.320
1952	EUGENE R. WOODLING, New York	23	8	14	.348
1953	ALFRED M. MARTIN, New York	24	12	23	.500
1954	VICTOR W. WERTZ, Cleveland	16	8	15	.500
1955	LAWRENCE P. BERRA, New York	24	10	14	.417
1956	LAWRENCE P. BERRA, New York	25	9	20	.360
1957	Gerald F. Coleman, New York	22	8	10	.364
1958	Henry A. Bauer, New York	31	10	22	.323
1959	THEODORE B. KLUSZEWSKI, Chicago	23	9	19	.391
1960	MICKEY C. MANTLE, New York	25	10	20	.400
1961	ROBERT C. RICHARDSON, New York	23	9	10	.391
1962	Thomas M. Tresh, New York	28	9	13	.321
1963	Elston G. Howard, New York	15	5	5	.333
1964	Robert C. Richardson, New York	32	13	15	.406
1965	Zoilo Versalles, Minnesota	28	8	14	.286
	Harmon C. Killebrew, Minnesota	21	6	9	.286
1966	JOHN W. POWELL, Baltimore	14	5	6	.357
1967	Carl M. Yastrzemski, Boston	25	10	21	.400
1968	Norman D. Cash, Detroit	26	10	13	.385
1969	John W. Powell, Baltimore	19	5	5	.263
1970	PAUL L. BLAIR, Baltimore	19	9	10	.474
1971	Brooks C. Robinson, Baltimore	22	7	7	.318
1972	F. Gene Tenace, Oakland	23	8	21	.348
1973	Joseph O. Rudi, Oakland	27	9	11	.333
1974	Dagoberto B. Campaneris, Oakland	17	6	8	.353
1975	Carl M. Yastrzemski, Boston	29	9	9	.310
1976	Thurman L. Munson, New York	17	9	9	.529
1977	REGINALD M. JACKSON, New York	20	9	25	.450
1978	BRIAN R. DOYLE, New York	16	7	8	.438
1979	Kenneth W. Singleton, Baltimore	28	10	11	.357
1980	AMOS J. OTIS, Kansas City	23	11	22	.478
1981	LOUIS V. PINIELLA, New York	16	7	8	.438
1982	ROBIN R. YOUNT, Milwaukee	29	12	18	.414
1983	JOHN T. SHELBY, Baltimore	9	4	4	.444
1984	ALAN S. TRAMMELL, Detroit	20	9	16	.450
1985	GEORGE H. BRETT, Kansas City	27	10	11	.370
1986	MARTIN G. BARRETT, Boston	30	13	15	.433
1987	Kirby Puckett, Minnesota	28	10	13	.357

National League

Year	Player and Club	AB.	H.	TB.	B.A.
1903	JAMES D. SEBRING, Pittsburgh	30	11	16	.367
1904	No Series.				
1905	MICHAEL J. DONLIN, New York	19	6	7	.316
1906	Arthur F. Hofman, Chicago	23	7	8	.304
1907	HARRY M. STEINFELDT, Chicago	17	8	11	.471
1908	FRANK L. CHANCE, Chicago	19	8	8	.421
1909	John P. Wagner, Pittsburgh	24	8	12	.333
1910	Frank M. Schulte, Chicago	17	6	9	.353
	Frank L. Chance, Chicago	17	6	9	.353
1911	Lawrence J. Doyle, New York	23	7	12	.304
1912	CHARLES L. HERZOG, New York	30	12	18	.400
1913	JOHN B. McLEAN, New York	12	6	6	.500

Year	Player and Club	AB.	H.	TB.	B.A.
1914	HENRY M. GOWDY, Boston	11	6	14	.545
1915	Fred W. Luderus, Philadelphia	16	7	12	.438
1916	Ivan M. Olson, Brooklyn	16	4	6	.250
1917	DAVIS A. ROBERTSON, New York	22	11	14	.500
1918	CHARLES PICK, Chicago	18	7	8	.389
1919	A. Earle Neale, Cincinnati	28	10	13	.357
1920	ZACHARIAH D. WHEAT, Brooklyn	27	9	11	.333
1921	EMIL F. MEUSEL, New York	29	10	17	.345
1922	HENRY K. GROH, New York	19	9	11	.474
1923	CHARLES D. STENGEL, New York	12	5	11	.417
1924	Frank F. Frisch, New York	30	10	16	.333
	Fred C. Lindstrom, New York	30	10	12	.333
1925	MAX G. CAREY, Pittsburgh	24	11	15	.458
1926	THOMAS J. THEVENOW, St. Louis	24	10	14	.417
1927	Lloyd J. Waner, Pittsburgh	15	6	9	.400
1928	Walter J. Maranville, St. Louis	13	4	5	.308
1929	Lewis R. Wilson, Chicago	17	8	8	.471
1930	Charles M. Gelbert, St. Louis	17	6	8	.353
1931	JOHN L. MARTIN, St. Louis	24	12	19	.500
1932	J. Riggs Stephenson, Chicago	18	8	9	.444
1933	MELVIN T. OTT, New York	18	7	13	.389
1934	JOSEPH M. MEDWICK, St. Louis	29	11	16	.379
1935	William Herman, Chicago	24	8	15	.333
1936	Richard Bartell, New York	21	8	14	.381
1937	Joseph G. Moore, New York	23	9	10	.391
1938	STANLEY C. HACK, Chicago	17	8	9	.471
1939	Frank A. McCormick, Cincinnati	15	6	7	.400
1940	WILLIAM M. WERBER, Cincinnati	27	10	14	.370
1941	Joseph M. Medwick, Brooklyn	17	4	5	.235
1942	James R. Brown, St. Louis	20	6	6	.300
1943	MARTIN W. MARION, St. Louis	14	5	10	.357
1944	Emil Verban, St. Louis	17	7	7	.412
1945	PHILIP J. CAVARRETTA, Chicago	26	11	16	.423
1946	HARRY W. WALKER, St. Louis	17	7	9	.412
1947	Harold H. Reese, Brooklyn	23	7	8	.304
1948	ROBERT I. ELLIOTT, Boston	21	7	13	.333
1949	HAROLD H. REESE, Brooklyn	19	6	10	.316
1950	GRANVILLE W. HAMNER, Philadelphia	14	6	10	.429
1951	MONFORD IRVIN, New York	24	11	13	.458
1952	Edwin D. Snider, Brooklyn	29	10	24	.345
	Harold H. Reese, Brooklyn	29	10	13	.345
1953	Gilbert R. Hodges, Brooklyn	22	8	11	.364
1954	Alvin R. Dark, New York	17	7	7	.412
1955	Edwin D. Snider, Brooklyn	25	8	21	.320
1956	Edwin D. Snider, Brooklyn	23	7	11	.304
	Gilbert R. Hodges, Brooklyn	23	7	12	.304
1957	HENRY AARON, Milwaukee	28	11	22	.393
1958	WILLIAM BRUTON, Milwaukee	17	7	10	.412
1959	GILBERT R. HODGES, Los Angeles	23	9	14	.391
1960	William S. Mazeroski, Pittsburgh	25	8	16	.320
1961	Walter C. Post, Cincinnati	18	6	10	.333
1962	JOSE A. PAGAN, San Francisco	19	7	10	.368
1963	H. THOMAS DAVIS, Los Angeles	15	6	10	.400
1964	J. TIMOTHY McCARVER, St. Louis	23	11	17	.478
1965	RONALD W. FAIRLY, Los Angeles	29	11	20	.379
1966	Louis B. Johnson, Los Angeles	15	4	5	.267
1967	LOUIS C. BROCK, St. Louis	29	12	19	.414
1968	LOUIS C. BROCK, St. Louis	28	13	24	.464
1969	ALBERT J. WEIS, New York	11	5	8	.455
1970	Lee A. May, Cincinnati	18	7	15	.389
1971	ROBERTO W. CLEMENTE, Pittsburgh	29	12	22	.414
1972	ATANASIO R. PEREZ, Cincinnati	23	10	12	.435
1973	DANIEL J. STAUB, New York	26	11	16	.423
1974	STEVEN P. GARVEY, Los Angeles	21	8	8	.381
1975	PETER E. ROSE, Cincinnati	27	10	13	.370
1976	JOHNNY L. BENCH, Cincinnati	15	8	17	.533
1977	Steven P. Garvey, Los Angeles	24	9	15	.375
1978	William E. Russell, Los Angeles	26	11	13	.423
1979	PHILIP M. GARNER, Pittsburgh	24	12	16	.500
1980	Robert D. Boone, Philadelphia	17	7	9	.412
1981	Steven P. Garvey, Los Angeles	24	10	11	.417
1982	George A. Hendrick, St. Louis	28	9	9	.321
	Lonnie Smith, St. Louis	28	9	15	.321
1983	Baudilio J. Diaz, Philadelphia	15	5	6	.333
1984	Kurt A. Bevacqua, San Diego	17	7	15	.412
1985	Terry L. Landrum, St. Louis	25	9	14	.360
1986	Leonard K. Dykstra, New York	27	8	14	.296
1987	ANTONIO F. PENA, St. Louis	22	9	10	.409

.400 Hitters

(Playing in all games and having 10 or more at-bats)

Player and Club	Year	AB.	H.	TB.	B.A.
Ruth, George H., New York A.L.	1928	16	10	22	.625
Gowdy, Henry M., Boston N.L.	1914	11	6	14	.545
Gehrig, H. Louis, New York A.L.	1928	11	6	19	.545
Bench, Johnny L., Cincinnati N.L.	1976	15	8	17	.533
Gehrig, H. Louis, New York A.L.	1932	17	9	19	.529
Munson, Thurman L., New York A.L.	1976	17	9	9	.529
McLean, John B., New York N.L.	1913	12	6	6	.500
Robertson, Davis A., New York N.L.	1917	22	11	14	.500
Koenig, Mark A., New York A.L.	1927	18	9	11	.500
Martin, John L., St. Louis N.L.	1931	24	12	19	.500
Gordon, Joseph L., New York A.L.	1941	14	7	13	.500
Martin, Alfred M., New York A.L.	1953	24	12	23	.500
Wertz, Victor W., Cleveland A.L.	1954	16	8	15	.500
Garner, Philip M., Pittsburgh N.L.	1979	24	12	16	.500

Player and Club	Year	AB.	H.	TB.	B.A.
McCarver, J. Timothy, St. Louis N.L.	1964	23	11	17	.478
Otis, Amos J., Kansas City A.L.	1980	23	11	22	.474
Groh, Henry K., New York N.L.	1922	19	9	11	.474
Blair, Paul L., Baltimore A.L.	1970	19	9	10	.474
Steinfeldt, Harry M., Chicago N.L.	1907	17	8	11	.471
Frisch, Frank F., New York N.L.	1922	17	8	9	.471
Wilson, Lewis R., Chicago N.L.	1929	17	8	10	.471
Hack, Stanley C., Chicago N.L.	1938	17	8	9	.471
Brock, Louis C., St. Louis N.L.	1968	28	13	24	.464
Cavarretta, Philip J., Chicago N.L.	1938	13	6	7	.462
Carey, Max, Pittsburgh N.L.	1925	24	11	15	.458
Irvin, Monford, New York N.L.	1951	24	11	13	.458
Powell, Alvin J., New York A.L.	1936	22	10	14	.455
Weis, Albert J., New York N.L.	1969	11	5	8	.455
Baker, J. Frank, Philadelphia A.L.	1913	20	9	12	.450
Jackson, Reginald M., New York A.L.	1977	20	9	25	.450
Trammell, Alan S., Detroit A.L.	1984	20	9	16	.450
Lewis, George E., Boston A.L.	1915	18	8	12	.444
Stephenson, J. Riggs, Chicago, N.L.	1932	18	8	9	.444
Harris, Joseph, Washington A.L.	1925	25	11	22	.440
Keller, Charles E., New York A.L.	1939	16	7	19	.438
Evers, John J., Boston N.L.	1914	16	7	7	.438
Luderus, Fred W., Philadelphia N.L.	1915	16	7	12	.438
Dickey, William M., New York A.L.	1932	16	7	7	.438
McQuinn, George H., St. Louis A.L.	1944	16	7	12	.438
Doyle, Brian R., New York A.L.	1978	16	7	8	.438
Piniella, Louis V., New York A.L.	1981	16	7	8	.438
Perez, Atanasio J., Cincinnati N.L.	1972	23	10	12	.435
Barrett, Martin G., Boston A.L.	1986	30	13	15	.433
Woodling, Eugene, New York A.L.	1950	14	6	6	.429
Hamner, Granville W., Phila. N.L.	1950	14	6	10	.429
Berra, Lawrence P., New York A.L.	1953	21	9	13	.429
Collins, Edward T., Philadelphia A.L.	1910	21	9	13	.429
Robinson, Brooks C., Baltimore A.L.	1970	21	9	17	.429
Cavarretta, Philip J., Chicago N.L.	1945	26	11	16	.423
Staub, Daniel J., New York N.L.	1973	26	11	16	.423
Russell, William E., Los Angeles N.L.	1978	26	11	13	.423
Chance, Frank L., Chicago N.L.	1908	19	8	8	.421
Collins, Edward T., Philadelphia A.L.	1913	19	8	12	.421
Robinson, Brooks C., Baltimore A.L.	1970	21	9	17	.429
Dykes, James J., Philadelphia A.L.	1929	19	8	9	.421
Ward, Aaron L., New York A.L.	1923	24	10	13	.417
Stengel, Charles D., New York N.L.	1923	12	5	11	.417
Thevenow, Thomas, St. Louis N.L.	1926	24	10	14	.417
Dark, Alvin R., New York N.L.	1951	24	10	16	.417
Berra, Lawrence P., New York A.L.	1955	24	10	11	.417
Dent, Russell E., New York A.L.	1978	24	10	11	.417
Garvey, Steven P., Los Angeles N.L.	1981	24	10	11	.417
Brock, Louis C., St. Louis N.L.	1967	29	12	19	.414
Clemente, Roberto W., Pittsburgh N.L.	1971	29	12	22	.414
Yount, Robin R., Milwaukee A.L.	1982	29	12	18	.414
Verban, Emil M., St. Louis N.L.	1944	17	7	7	.412
Walker, Harry W., St. Louis N.L.	1946	17	7	9	.412
Dark, Alvin R., New York N.L.	1954	17	7	7	.412
Bruton, William H., Milwaukee N.L.	1958	17	7	10	.412
Boone, Robert R., Philadelphia N.L.	1980	17	7	9	.412
Bevacqua, Kurt A., San Diego N.L.	1984	17	7	15	.412
Baker, J. Frank, Philadelphia A.L.	1910	22	9	12	.409
Collins, Edward T., Chicago A.L.	1917	22	9	10	.409
Pena, Antonio F., St. Louis	1987	22	9	10	.409
Richardson, Robert C., New York A.L.	1964	32	13	15	.406
Rossman, Claude, Detroit A.L.	1907	20	8	10	.400
Herzog, Charles L., New York N.L.	1912	30	12	18	.400
Frisch, Frank F., New York N.L.	1923	25	10	12	.400
Ruth, George H., New York A.L.	1927	15	6	12	.400
Waner, Lloyd J., Pittsburgh N.L.	1927	15	6	9	.400
Cochrane, Gordon S., Phila. A.L.	1929	15	6	7	.400
Rolfe, Robert A., New York A.L.	1936	25	10	10	.400
Lazzeri, Anthony M., New York A.L.	1937	15	6	11	.400
Gordon, Joseph L., New York A.L.	1938	15	6	11	.400
Dickey, William M., New York A.L.	1938	15	6	9	.400
McCormick, Frank A., Cinn. N.L.	1939	15	6	7	.400
Mantle, Mickey C., New York A.L.	1960	25	10	20	.400
Davis H. Thomas, Los Angeles N.L.	1963	15	6	10	.400
Yastrzemski, Carl M., Boston A.L.	1967	25	10	21	.400
Stargell, Wilver D., Pittsburgh N.L.	1979	30	12	25	.400
Aikens, Willie M., Kansas City A.L.	1980	20	8	22	.400
Henderson, David L., Boston A.L.	1986	25	10	19	.400

Home Runs
American League (361)

1903—2—Boston, Patrick H. Dougherty (2).
1904—No Series.
1905—0—Philadelphia.
1906—0—Chicago.
1907—0—Detroit.
1908—0—Detroit.
1909—2—Detroit, David J. Jones (1), Samuel Crawford (1).
1910—1—Philadelphia, Daniel F. Murphy (1).
1911—3—Philadelphia, J. Franklin Baker (2), Reuben N. Oldring (1).
1912—1—Boston, William L. Gardner (1).
1913—2—Philadelphia, J. Franklin Baker (1), Walter H. Schang (1).
1914—0—Philadelphia.
1915—3—Boston, Harry B. Hooper (2), George E. Lewis (1).
1916—2—Boston, William L. Gardner (2).
1917—1—Chicago, Oscar C. Felsch (1).
1918—0—Boston.

1919—1—Chicago, Joseph J. Jackson (1).
1920—2—Cleveland, Elmer J. Smith (1), James C. Bagby (1).
1921—2—New York, George H. Ruth (1), Wilson L. Fewster (1).
1922—2—New York, Aaron L. Ward (2).
1923—5—New York, George H. Ruth (3), Aaron L. Ward (1), Joseph A. Dugan (1).
1924—5—Washington, Leon A. Goslin (3), Stanley R. Harris (2).
1925—8—Washington, Joseph Harris (3), Leon A. Goslin (3), Joseph I. Judge (1), Roger T. Peckinpaugh (1).
1926—4—New York, George H. Ruth (4).
1927—2—New York, George H. Ruth (2).
1928—9—New York, H. Louis Gehrig (4), George H. Ruth (3), Robert W. Meusel (1), Cedric N. Durst (1).
1929—6—Philadelphia, James E. Foxx (2), Aloysius H. Simmons (2), George W. Haas (2).
1930—6—Philadelphia, Gordon S. Cochrane (2), Aloysius H. Simmons (2), James E. Foxx (1), James J. Dykes (1).
1931—3—Philadelphia, Aloysius H. Simmons (2), James E. Foxx (1).
1932—8—New York, H. Louis Gehrig (3), George H. Ruth (2), Anthony M. Lazzeri (2), Earle B. Combs (1).
1933—2—Washington, Leon A. Goslin (1), Fred W. Schulte (1).
1934—2—Detroit, Henry B. Greenberg (1), Charles L. Gehringer (1).
1935—1—Detroit, Henry B. Greenberg (1).
1936—7—New York, H. Louis Gehrig (2), George A. Selkirk (2), Anthony M. Lazzeri (1), William M. Dickey (1), Alvin J. Powell (1).
1937—4—New York, Anthony M. Lazzeri (1), H. Louis Gehrig (1), Myril O. Hoag (1), Joseph P. DiMaggio (1).
1938—5—New York, Frank P. Crosetti (1), Joseph P. DiMaggio (1), Joseph L. Gordon (1), William M. Dickey (1), Thomas D. Henrich (1).
1939—7—New York, Charles E. Keller (3), William M. Dickey (2), Ellsworth T. Dahlgren (1), Joseph P. DiMaggio (1).
1940—4—Detroit, Bruce D. Campbell (1), Rudolph P. York (1), Michael F. Higgins (1), Henry B. Greenberg (1).
1941—2—New York, Joseph L. Gordon (1), Thomas D. Henrich (1).
1942—3—New York, Charles E. Keller (2), Philip F. Rizzuto (1).
1943—2—New York, Joseph L. Gordon (1), William M. Dickey (1).
1944—1—St. Louis, George H. McQuinn (1).
1945—2—Detroit, Henry B. Greenberg (2).
1946—4—Boston, Rudolph P. York (2), Robert P. Doerr (1), D. Leon Culberson (1).
1947—4—New York, Joseph P. DiMaggio (2), Thomas D. Henrich (1), Lawrence P. Berra (1).
1948—4—Cleveland, Lawrence E. Doby (1), L. Dale Mitchell (1), James E. Hegan (1), Joseph L. Gordon (1).
1949—2—New York, Thomas D. Henrich (1), Joseph P. DiMaggio (1).
1950—2—New York, Joseph P. DiMaggio (1), Lawrence P. Berra (1).
1951—5—New York, Joseph E. Collins (1), Eugene R. Woodling (1), Joseph P. DiMaggio (1), Gilbert J. McDougald (1), Philip F. Rizzuto (1).
1952—10—New York, John R. Mize (3), Mickey C. Mantle (2), Lawrence P. Berra (2), Gilbert J. McDougald (1), Alfred M. Martin (1), Eugene R. Woodling (1).
1953—9—New York, Mickey C. Mantle (2), Gilbert J. McDougald (2), Alfred M. Martin (2), Lawrence P. Berra (1), Joseph E. Collins (1), Eugene R. Woodling (1).
1954—3—Cleveland, Alphonse E. Smith (1), Victor W. Wertz (1), Henry Majeski (1).
1955—8—New York, Joseph E. Collins (2), Lawrence P. Berra (1), Robert H. Cerv (1), Elston G. Howard (1), Mickey C. Mantle (1), Gilbert J. McDougald (1), William J. Skowron (1).
1956—12—New York, Mickey C. Mantle (3), Lawrence P. Berra (3), Alfred M. Martin (2), Enos B. Slaughter (1), Henry A. Bauer (1), Elston G. Howard (1), William J. Skowron (1).
1957—7—New York, Henry A. Bauer (2), Anthony C. Kubek (2), Mickey C. Mantle (1), Lawrence P. Berra (1), Elston G. Howard (1).
1958—10—New York, Henry A. Bauer (4), Gilbert J. McDougald (2), Mickey C. Mantle (2), William J. Skowron (2).
1959—4—Chicago, Theodore B. Kluszewski (3), J. Sherman Lollar (1).
1960—10—New York, Mickey C. Mantle (3), Roger E. Maris (2), William J. Skowron (2), Lawrence P. Berra (1), Elston G. Howard (1), Robert C. Richardson (1).
1961—7—New York, John E. Blanchard (2), Lawrence P. Berra (1), Elston G. Howard (1), Hector Lopez (1), Roger E. Maris (1), William J. Skowron (1).
1962—3—New York, Thomas M. Tresh (1), Roger E. Maris (1), Cletis L. Boyer (1).
1963—2—New York, Thomas M. Tresh (1), Mickey C. Mantle (1).
1964—10—New York, Mickey C. Mantle (3), Philip F. Linz (2), Thomas D. Tresh (2), Roger E. Maris (1), Joseph A. Pepitone (1), Cletis L. Boyer (1).
1965—6—Minnesota, Zoilo Versalles (1), Pedro Oliva (1), Harmon C. Killebrew (1), Donald R. Mincher (1), W. Robert Allison (1), James T. Grant (1).
1966—4—Baltimore, Frank Robinson (2), Brooks C. Robinson (1), Paul L. Blair (1).
1967—8—Boston, Carl Yastrzemski (3), C. Reginald Smith (2), Americo P. Petrocelli (2), Jose R. Santiago (1).
1968—8—Detroit, Albert W. Kaline (2), James T. Northrup (2), Norman D. Cash (1), William W. Horton (1), Michael S. Lolich (1), Richard J. McAuliffe (1).
1969—3—Baltimore, Donald A. Buford (1), David A. McNally (1), Frank Robinson (1).
1970—10—Baltimore, John W. Powell (2), Frank Robinson (2), Brooks C. Robinson (2), Donald A. Buford (1), Elrod J. Hendricks (1), David A. McNally (1), Mervin W. Rettenmund (1).
1971—5—Baltimore, Donald A. Buford (2), Frank Robinson (1), Mervin W. Rettenmund (1).
1972—5—Oakland, F. Gene Tenace (2), Joseph O. Rudi (1).
1973—2—Oakland, Dagoberto B. Campaneris (1), Reginald M. Jackson (1).
1974—4—Oakland, Raymond E. Fosse (1), Kenneth D. Holtzman (1), Reginald M. Jackson (1), Joseph O. Rudi (1).

1975—6—Boston, Bernardo Carbo (2), Carlton E. Fisk (2), Dwight M. Evans (1), Fredric M. Lynn (1).
1976—1—New York, James P. Mason (1).
1977—8—New York, Reginald M. Jackson (5), C. Christopher Chambliss (1), Thurman L. Munson (1), William L. Randolph (1).
1978—3—New York, Reginald M. Jackson (2), Roy H. White (1).
1979—4—Baltimore, Douglas V. DeCinces (1), Eddie C. Murray (1), Benigno Ayala (1), Richard F. Dauer (1).
1980—8—Kansas City, Willie M. Aikens (4), Amos J. Otis (3), George H. Brett (1).
1981—6—New York, William L. Randolph (2), Robert J. Watson (2), Richard A. Cerone (1), Reginald M. Jackson (1).
1982—5—Milwaukee, Ted L. Simmons (2), Cecil C. Cooper (1), Benjamin A. Oglivie (1), Robin R. Yount (1).
1983—6—Baltimore, Eddie C. Murray (2), James E. Dwyer (1), John L. Lowenstein (1), Darnell G. Ford (1), J. Rikard Dempsey (1).
1984—7—Detroit, Kirk H. Gibson (2), Alan S. Trammell (2), Martin H. Castillo (1), Larry D. Herndon (1), Lance M. Parrish (1).
1985—2—Kansas City, Frank White (1), Darryl D. Motley (1).
1986—5—Boston, Dwight M. Evans (2), David L. Henderson (2), Richard L. Gedman (1).
1987—7—Minnesota, Donald E. Baylor (1), Gary J. Gaetti (1), Gregory C. Gagne (1), C. Daniel Gladden (1), Kent A. Hrbek (1), Timothy J. Laudner (1), Stephen P. Lombardozzi (1).

National League (251)

1903—1—Pittsburgh, James D. Sebring (1).
1904—No Series.
1905—0—New York.
1906—0—Chicago.
1907—0—Chicago.
1908—1—Chicago, Joseph B. Tinker (1).
1909—2—Pittsburgh, Fred C. Clarke (2).
1910—0—Chicago.
1911—0—New York.
1912—1—New York, Lawrence J. Doyle (1).
1913—1—New York, Fred C. Merkle (1).
1914—1—Boston, Henry M. Gowdy (1).
1915—1—Philadelphia, Fred W. Luderus (1).
1916—1—Brooklyn, Henry H. Myers (1).
1917—1—New York, Benjamin M. Kauff (2).
1918—0—Chicago.
1919—0—Cincinnati.
1920—0—Brooklyn.
1921—2—New York, Frank Snyder (1), Emil F. Meusel (1).
1922—1—New York, Emil F. Meusel (1).
1923—5—New York, Charles D. Stengel (2), Emil F. Meusel (1), Ross Youngs (1), Frank Snyder (1).
1924—4—New York, George L. Kelly (1), William H. Terry (1), Wilfred D. Ryan (1), John N. Bentley (1).
1925—4—Pittsburgh, Harold J. Traynor (1), F. Glenn Wright (1), Hazen S. Cuyler (1), G. Edward Moore (1).
1926—4—St. Louis, William H. Southworth (1), Thomas J. Thevenow (1), Jesse J. Haines (1), Lester R. Bell (1).
1927—0—Pittsburgh.
1928—1—St. Louis, James L. Bottomley (1).
1929—1—Chicago, Charles J. Grimm. (1).
1930—2—St. Louis, George A. Watkins (1), Taylor L. Douthit (1).
1931—2—St. Louis, John L. Martin (1), George A. Watkins (1).
1932—3—Chicago, Hazen S. Cuyler (1), Charles L. Hartnett (1), J. Frank Demaree (1).
1933—3—New York, Melvin T. Ott (2), William H. Terry (1).
1934—2—St. Louis, Joseph M. Medwick (1), William DeLancey (1).
1935—5—Chicago, J. Frank Demaree (2), Charles L. Hartnett (1), Charles H. Klein (1), William Herman (1).
1936—4—New York, Richard Bartell (1), James A. Ripple (1), Melvin T. Ott (1), Joseph G. Moore (1).
1937—1—New York, Melvin T. Ott. (1).
1938—2—Chicago, Joseph A. Marty (1), James K. O'Dea (1).
1939—0—Cincinnati.
1940—2—Cincinnati, James A. Ripple (1), William H. Walters (1).
1941—1—Brooklyn, Harold P. Reiser (1).
1942—2—St. Louis, Enos B. Slaughter (1), George J. Kurowski (1).
1943—2—St. Louis, Martin W. Marion (1), Raymond F. Sanders (1).
1944—3—St. Louis, Stanley F. Musial (1), Raymond F. Sanders (1), Daniel W. Litwhiler (1).
1945—1—Chicago, Philip J. Cavarretta (1).
1946—1—St. Louis, Enos B. Slaughter (1).
1947—1—Brooklyn, Fred E. Walker (1).
1948—4—Boston, Robert I. Elliott (2), Marvin A. Rickert (1), William F. Salkeld (1).
1949—4—Brooklyn, Harold H. Reese (1), Luis R. Olmo (1), Roy Campanella (1), Gilbert R. Hodges (1).
1950—0—Philadelphia.
1951—2—New York, Alvin R. Dark (1), Carroll W. Lockman (1).
1952—6—Brooklyn, Edwin D. Snider (4), Jack R. Robinson (1), Harold H. Reese (1).
1953—8—Brooklyn, James Gilliam (2), Roy Campanella (1), William R. Cox (1), Carl A. Furillo (1), Gilbert R. Hodges (1), George T. Shuba (1), Edwin D. Snider (1).
1954—2—New York, James L. Rhodes (2).
1955—9—Brooklyn, Edwin D. Snider (4), Roy Campanella (2), Edmundo Amoros (1), Carl A. Furillo (1), Gilbert R. Hodges (1).
1956—3—Brooklyn, Edwin D. Snider (1), Jack R. Robinson (1), Gilbert R. Hodges (1).
1957—8—Milwaukee, Henry L. Aaron (3), Frank J. Torre (2), Edwin L. Mathews (1), John Logan (1), Delmar W. Crandall (1).

1958—3—Milwaukee, Delmar W. Crandall (1), William H. Bruton (1), S. Lew Burdette (1).
1959—7—Los Angeles, Charles L. Neal (2), Charles A. Essegian (2), Wallace W Moon (1), Edwin D. Snider (1), Gilbert R. Hodges (1).
1960—4—Pittsburgh, William S. Mazeroski (2), Glenn R. Nelson (1), Harold W Smith (1).
1961—3—Cincinnati, Gordon C. Coleman (1), Walter C. Post (1), Frank Robinso (1).
1962—5—San Francisco, Charles J. Hiller (1), Willie L. McCovey (1), Thomas F Haller (1), L. Edgar Bailey (1), Jose A. Pagan (1).
1963—3—Los Angeles, John Roseboro (1), William J. Skowron (1), Frank C Howard (1).
1964—5—St. Louis, Kenton L. Boyer (2), Louis C. Brock (1), T. Michael Shanno (1), J. Timothy McCarver (1).
1965—5—Los Angeles, Ronald R. Fairly (2), Louis B. Johnson (2), M. Wesle Parker (1).
1966—1—Los Angeles, James K. Lefebvre (1).
1967—5—St. Louis, Louis C. Brock (1), Robert Gibson (1), M. Julian Javier (1) Roger E. Maris (1), T. Michael Shannon (1).
1968—7—St. Louis, Louis C. Brock (2), Orlando Cepeda (2), Robert Gibson (1 J. Timothy McCarver (1), T. Michael Shannon (1).
1969—6—New York, Donald A. Clendenon (3), Tommie L. Agee (1), Edward E Kranepool (1), Albert J. Weis (1).
1970—5—Cincinnati, Lee A. May (2), Johnny L. Bench (1), Peter E. Rose (1), Robert Tolan (1).
1971—5—Pittsburgh, Robert E. Robertson (2), Roberto W. Clemente (2), Richard J. Hebner (1).
1972—3—Cincinnati, Johnny L. Bench (1), Denis J. Menke (1), Peter E. Rose (1)
1973—4—New York, R. Wayne Garrett (2), Cleon J. Jones (1), Daniel J. Staub (1).
1974—4—Los Angeles, William J. Buckner (1), Willie M. Crawford (1), Joseph V. Ferguson (1), James S. Wynn (1).
1975—7—Cincinnati, Atanasio R. Perez (3), Cesar F. Geronimo (2), Johnny L Bench (1), David I. Concepcion (1).
1976—4—Cincinnati, Johnny L. Bench (2), Daniel Driessen (1), Joe L. Morgan (1).
1977—9—Los Angeles, C. Reginald Smith (3), Stephen W. Yeager (2), Johnnie B. Baker (1), Ronald C. Cey (1), Steven P. Garvey (1), David E. Lopes (1).
1978—6—Los Angeles, David E. Lopes (3), Johnnie B. Baker (1), Ronald C. Cey (1), C. Reginald Smith (1).
1979—3—Pittsburgh, Wilver D. Stargell (3).
1980—3—Philadelphia, Michael J. Schmidt (2), Arnold R. McBride (1).
1981—6—Los Angeles, Pedro Guerrero (2), Stephen W. Yeager (2), Ronald C. Cey (1), John W. Johnstone (1).
1982—4—St. Louis, Willie D. McGee (2), Keith Hernandez (1), Darrell R. Porter (1).
1983—4—Philadelphia, Joe L. Morgan (2), Garry L. Maddox (1), Gary N. Matthews (1).
1984—3—San Diego, Kurt A. Bevacqua (2), Terrence E. Kennedy (1).
1985—2—St. Louis, Terry L. Landrum (1), Willie D. McGee (1).
1986—7—New York, Gary E. Carter (2), Leonard K. Dykstra (2), C. Ray Knight (1), Darryl E. Strawberry (1), Timothy S. Teufel (1).
1987—2—St. Louis, Thomas M. Herr (1), Thomas J. Lawless (1).

Players With 4 Homers (36)

Player	Series	HR.
Mantle, Mickey C.	12	18
Ruth, George H.	10	15
Berra, Lawrence P.	14	12
Snider, Edwin D.	6	11
Gehrig, H. Louis	7	10
Jackson, Reginald M.	5	10
Robinson, Frank	5	8
DiMaggio, Joseph P.	10	8
Skowron, William J.	8	8
Goslin, Leon A.	5	7
McDougald, Gilbert J.	8	7
Bauer, Henry A.	9	7
Maris, Roger E.	7	6
Simmons, Aloysius H.	4	6
Smith, C. Reginald	4	6
Keller, Charles E.	4	5
Greenberg, Henry	4	5
Bench, Johnny L.	4	5
Martin, Alfred M.	5	5
Hodges, Gilbert R.	7	5
Dickey, William M.	8	5
Howard, Elston G.	9	5
Lazzeri, Anthony M.	7	4
Foxx, James E.	3	4
Ott, Melvin T.	3	4
Henrich, Thomas D.	4	4
Gordon, Joseph L.	6	4
Campanella, Roy	5	4
Collins, Joseph	7	4
Tresh, Thomas M.	3	4
Buford, Donald A.	3	4
Brock, Louis C.	3	4
Tenace, F. Gene	3	4
Lopes, David E.	4	4
Aikens, Willie M.	1	4
Yeager, Stephen W.	4	4

Pitchers With 4 Victories (30)

Pitcher and Club	Y.	W.	L.
...ord, Edward C., New York A.L.	11	10	8
...uffing, Charles H., New York A.L.	7	7	2
...eynolds, Allie P., New York A.L.	6	7	2
...ibson, Robert, St. Louis N.L.	3	7	2
...omez, Vernon, New York A.L.	4	6	0
...ender, Charles A., Philadelphia A.L.	5	6	4
...oyt, Waite C., New York-Philadelphia A.L.	6	6	4
...oombs, John W., Phil. A.L.-Brooklyn N.L.	3	5	0
...ennock, Herbert J., New York A.L.	3	5	0
...aschi, Victor J., New York A.L.	5	5	3
...unter, James A., Oakland-New York A.L.	6	5	3
...rown, Mordecai P., Chicago N.L.	4	5	4
...athewson, Christopher, New York N.L.	4	5	5
...earson, Monte M., New York A.L.	4	4	0
...ridges, Thomas D., Detroit A.L.	3	4	1
...recheen, Harry, St.Louis N.L.	3	4	1
...opat, Edmund W., New York A.L.	4	4	1
...odres, John J., Brooklyn-Los Ang. N.L.	4	4	1
...oltzman, Kenneth D., Oakland A.L.	3	4	1
...rove, Robert M., Philadelphia A.L.	2	4	2
...ubbell, Carl O., New York N.L.	3	4	2
...urdette, S. Lewis, Milwaukee N.L.	2	4	2
...arsen, Don J., N.Y. A.L.-S.F. N.L.	5	4	2
...cNally, David A., Baltimore A.L.	6	4	2
...almer, James A., Baltimore A.L.	6	4	2
...oufax, Sanford, Los Angeles N.L.	4	4	3
...arnshaw, George L., Philadelphia A.L.	3	4	3
...pahn, Warren E., Boston N.L.-Milw. N.L.	3	4	3
...urley, Robert L., New York A.L.	5	4	3
...ehf, Arthur N., New York N.L.	4	4	4

10-Strikeout Games By Pitchers (42)

Date	Pitcher and Club	SO.
Oct. 1, 1903	Phillippe, Pittsburgh N.L., vs. Boston A.L.	10
Oct. 2, 1903	Dinneen, Boston A.L., vs. Pittsburgh N.L.	11
Oct. 11, 1906	Walsh, Chicago A.L., vs. Chicago N.L.	12
Oct. 8, 1907	Donovan, Detroit A.L., vs. Chicago N.L. (12 inn.)	12
Oct. 14, 1908	Overall, Chicago N.L., vs. Detroit A.L.	10
Oct. 12, 1909	Mullin, Detroit A.L., vs. Pittsburgh N.L.	10
Oct. 14, 1911	Bender, Phila. A.L., vs. New York N.L. (8 inn.)	11
Oct. 8, 1912	Wood, Boston A.L., vs. New York N.L.	11
Oct. 11, 1921	Barnes, New York N.L., vs. New York A.L.	10
Oct. 24, 1924	Johnson, Wash. A.L., vs. New York N.L. (12 inn.)	12
Oct. 7, 1925	Johnson, Washington A.L., vs. Pittsburgh N.L.	10
Oct. 3, 1926	Alexander, St. Louis N.L., vs. New York A.L.	10
Oct. 8, 1929	Ehmke, Philadelphia A.L., vs. Chicago N.L.	13
Oct. 11, 1929	Earnshaw, Philadelphia A.L., vs. Chicago N.L.	10
Sept. 28, 1932	Ruffing, New York A.L., vs. Chicago N.L.	10
Oct. 3, 1933	Hubbell, New York N.L., vs. Washington A.L.	10
Oct. 5, 1936	Schumacher, N.Y. N.L., vs. N.Y. A.L. (10 inn.)	10
Oct. 6, 1944	Kramer, St. Louis A.L., vs. St. Louis N.L.	10
Oct. 8, 1944	Galehouse, St. Louis A.L., vs. St. Louis N.L.	10
Oct. 8, 1944	Cooper, St. Louis N.L., vs. St. Louis A.L.	12
Oct. 10, 1945	Newhouser, Detroit A.L., vs. Chicago N.L.	10
Oct. 5, 1949	Newcombe, Brook. N.L., vs. N.Y. A.L. (8 inn.)	11
Oct. 4, 1952	Reynolds, New York A.L., vs. Brooklyn, N.L.	10
Oct. 2, 1953	Erskine, Brooklyn N.L., vs. New York A.L.	14
Oct. 3, 1956	Maglie, Brooklyn N.L., vs. New York A.L.	10
Oct. 9, 1956	Turley, New York A.L., vs. Brooklyn N.L.	11
Oct. 5, 1958	Turley, New York A.L., vs. Milwaukee N.L.	10
Oct. 10, 1962	Sanford, San Francisco N.L., vs. New York A.L.	10
Oct. 2, 1963	Koufax, Los Angeles N.L., vs. New York A.L.	15
Oct. 12, 1964	Gibson, St. Louis N.L., vs. New York A.L. (10 inn.)	13
Oct. 10, 1965	Drysdale, Los Angeles N.L., vs. Minnesota A.L.	11
Oct. 11, 1965	Koufax, Los Angeles N.L., vs. Minnesota A.L.	10
Oct. 14, 1965	Koufax, Los Angeles N.L., vs. Minnesota A.L.	10
Oct. 5, 1966	Drabowsky, Baltimore A.L., vs. Los Angeles N.L.	11
Oct. 4, 1967	Gibson, St. Louis N.L., vs. Boston A.L.	10
Oct. 12, 1967	Gibson, St. Louis N.L., vs. Boston A.L.	10
Oct. 2, 1968	Gibson, St. Louis N.L., vs. Detroit A.L.	17
Oct. 6, 1968	Gibson, St. Louis N.L., vs. Detroit A.L.	10
Oct. 11, 1971	Palmer, Baltimore A.L., vs. Pittsburgh N.L.	10
Oct. 18, 1972	Odom, Oakland A.L., vs. Cincinnati N.L. (7 inn.)	11
Oct. 16, 1973	Seaver, New York N.L., vs. Oakland A.L. (8 inn.)	12
Oct. 15, 1980	Carlton, Phila. N.L., vs. Kansas City A.L. (8 inn.)	10

Managerial Records
American League (39)

	Series		Games		
	W.	L.	W.	L.	T.
Altobelli, Joseph S., Baltimore	1	0	4	1	0
Anderson, George L., Detroit	1	0	4	1	0
Baker, Delmer D., Detroit	0	1	3	4	0
Barrow, Edward G., Boston	1	0	4	2	0
Bauer, Henry A., Baltimore	1	0	4	0	0
Berra, Lawrence P., New York	0	1	3	4	0
Boudreau, Louis, Cleveland	1	0	4	2	0
Carrigan, William F., Boston	2	0	8	2	0

	Series		Games		
	W.	L.	W.	L.	T.
Cochrane, Gordon S., Detroit	1	1	7	6	0
Collins, James J., Boston	1	0	5	3	0
Cronin, Joseph E., Washington-Boston	0	2	4	8	0
Dark, Alvin R., Oakland	1	0	4	1	0
Frey, James G., Kansas City	0	1	2	4	0
Gleason, William, Chicago	0	1	3	5	0
Harris, Stanley R., Washington-New York	2	1	11	10	0
Houk, Ralph G., New York	2	1	8	8	0
Howser, Richard D., Kansas City	1	0	4	3	0
Huggins, Miller J., New York	3	3	18	15	1
Jennings, Hugh A., Detroit	0	3	4	12	1
Johnson, Darrell D., Boston	0	1	3	4	0
Jones, Fielder A., Chicago	1	0	4	2	0
Kelly, J. Thomas, Minnesota	1	0	4	3	0
Kuenn, Harvey E., Milwaukee	0	1	3	4	0
Lemon, Robert G., New York	1	1	6	6	0
Lopez, Alfonso R., Cleveland-Chicago	0	2	2	8	0
Mack, Connie, Philadelphia	5	3	24	19	0
Martin, Alfred M., New York	1	1	4	6	0
McCarthy, Joseph V., New York	7	1	29	9	0
McNamara, John F., Boston	0	1	3	4	0
Mele, Sabath A., Minnesota	0	1	3	4	0
O'Neill, Stephen F., Detroit	1	0	4	3	0
Rowland, Clarence H., Chicago	1	0	4	2	0
Sewell, J. Luther, St. Louis	0	1	2	4	0
Smith, E. Mayo, Detroit	1	0	4	3	0
Speaker, Tris, Cleveland	1	0	5	2	0
Stahl, J. Garland, Boston	1	0	4	3	1
Stengel, Charles D., New York	7	3	37	26	0
Weaver, Earl S., Baltimore	1	3	11	13	0
Williams, Richard H., Boston-Oakland	2	1	11	10	0
	49	35	271	226	3

National League (39)

	Series		Games		
	W.	L.	W.	L.	T.
Alston, Walter E., Brooklyn-Los Angeles	4	3	20	20	0
Anderson, George L., Cincinnati	2	2	12	11	0
Berra, Lawrence P., New York	0	1	3	4	0
Bush, Owen J., Pittsburgh	0	1	0	4	0
Chance, Frank L., Chicago	2	2	11	9	1
Clarke, Fred C., Pittsburgh	1	1	7	8	0
Dark, Alvin R., San Francisco	0	1	3	4	0
Dressen, Charles W., Brooklyn	0	2	5	8	0
Durocher, Leo E., Brooklyn-New York	1	2	7	8	0
Dyer, Edwin H., St. Louis	1	0	4	3	0
Frisch, Frank F., St. Louis	1	0	4	3	0
Green, G. Dallas, Philadelphia	1	0	4	2	0
Grimm, Charles J., Chicago	0	3	5	12	0
Haney Fred G., Milwaukee	1	1	7	7	0
Hartnett, Charles L., Chicago	0	1	0	4	0
Herzog, Dorrel N.E., St. Louis	1	2	10	11	0
Hodges, Gilbert R., New York	1	0	4	1	0
Hornsby, Rogers, St. Louis	1	0	4	3	0
Hutchinson, Frederick C., Cincinnati	0	1	1	4	0
Johnson, David A., New York	1	0	4	3	0
Keane, John J., St. Louis	1	0	4	3	0
Lasorda, Thomas C., Los Angeles	1	2	8	10	0
McCarthy, Joseph V., Chicago	0	1	1	4	0
McGraw, John J., New York	3	6	26	28	2
McKechnie, William B., Pitt.-St.L.-Cin.	2	2	8	14	0
Mitchell, Fred F., Chicago	0	1	2	4	0
Moran, Patrick J., Philadelphia-Cincinnati	1	1	8	7	0
Murtaugh, Daniel E., Pittsburgh	2	0	8	6	0
Owens, Paul F., Philadelphia	0	1	1	4	0
Robinson, Wilbert, Brooklyn	0	2	3	9	0
Sawyer, Edwin M. Philadelphia	0	1	0	4	0
Schoendienst, Albert F., St. Louis	1	1	7	7	0
Shotton, Burton E., Brooklyn	0	2	4	8	0
Southworth, William H., St. Louis-Boston	2	2	11	11	0
Stallings, George T., Boston	1	0	4	0	0
Street, Charles E., St. Louis	1	1	6	7	0
Tanner, Charles W., Pittsburgh	1	0	4	3	0
Terry, William H., New York	1	2	7	9	0
Williams, Richard H., San Diego	0	1	1	4	0
	35	49	226	271	3

Both Leagues (5)

	Series		Games		
	W.	L.	W.	L.	T.
Combined record of McCarthy, Joseph V., Chicago N.L. and New York A.L.	7	2	30	13	0
Combined record of Berra, Lawrence P., New York A.L. and New York N.L.	0	2	6	8	0
Combined record of Dark, Alvin R., San Francisco N.L. and Oakland A.L.	1	1	7	5	0
Combined record of Anderson, George L., Cincinnati N.L. and Detroit A.L.	3	2	16	12	0
Combined record of Williams, Richard H., Boston A.L., Oakland A.L. and San Diego N.L.	2	2	12	14	0

Club Batting & Fielding

Year	Club	G.	AB.	R.	H.	TB.	2B.	3B.	HR.	Sac.	SB.	BB.	SO.	RBI.	B.A.	PO.	A.	E.	DP.	PB.	F.A.
1903—	Pittsburgh N.L.	8	270	24	64	92	7	9	1	3	7	14	45	23	.237	210	96	18	5	0	.944
	Boston A.L.	8	282	39	71	113	4	16	2	6	5	13	27	35	.252	213	102	14	6	2	.957
1904—	No Series.																				
1905—	New York N.L.	5	153	15	32	39	7	0	0	5	11	15	26	13	.209	135	78	6	2	0	.973
	Philadelphia A.L.	5	155	3	25	30	5	0	0	3	2	5	25	2	.161	129	56	9	2	0	.954
1906—	Chicago N.L.	6	184	18	36	45	9	0	0	13	8	18	27	11	.196	159	84	7	4	3	.972
	Chicago A.L.	6	187	22	37	53	10	3	0	6	6	18	35	19	.198	162	99	14	2	1	.949
1907—	Chicago N.L.	5	167	19	43	51	6	1	0	9	18	12	25	16	.257	144	65	10	6	1	.954
	Detroit A.L.	5	173	6	36	41	1	2	0	3	7	9	21	6	.208	138	70	9	2	1	.959
1908—	Chicago N.L.	5	164	24	48	59	4	2	1	9	13	13	26	21	.293	135	74	5	4	1	.977
	Detroit A.L.	5	158	15	32	37	5	0	0	5	5	12	26	14	.203	131	63	10	5	1	.951
1909—	Pittsburgh N.L.	7	223	34	49	70	12	1	2	12	18	20	34	26	.220	182	88	15	3	0	.947
	Detroit A.L.	7	234	28	55	77	16	0	2	4	6	20	22	26	.235	183	87	19	4	1	.934
1910—	Chicago N.L.	5	158	15	35	48	11	1	0	7	3	18	31	13	.222	132	77	12	3	0	.946
	Philadelphia A.L.	5	177	35	56	80	19	1	1	7	7	17	24	29	.316	136	59	11	6	0	.947
1911—	New York N.L.	6	189	13	33	46	11	1	0	6	4	14	44	10	.175	162	79	16	2	1	.938
	Philadelphia A.L.	6	205	27	50	74	15	0	3	9	4	4	31	21	.244	167	72	11	2	0	.956
1912—	New York N.L.	8	274	31	74	99	14	4	1	7	12	22	39	25	.270	221	108	17	4	0	.951
	Boston A.L.	8	273	25	60	89	14	6	1	8	6	19	36	21	.220	222	101	14	5	0	.958
1913—	New York N.L.	5	164	15	33	41	3	1	1	2	5	8	19	15	.201	135	67	7	1	1	.967
	Philadelphia A.L.	5	174	23	46	64	4	4	2	7	5	7	16	21	.264	138	54	5	6	0	.975
1914—	Boston N.L.	4	135	16	33	46	6	2	1	3	9	15	18	14	.244	117	62	4	4	0	.978
	Philadelphia A.L.	4	128	6	22	31	9	0	0	3	2	13	28	5	.172	111	66	3	4	1	.983
1915—	Philadelphia N.L.	5	148	10	27	36	4	1	1	5	2	10	25	9	.182	131	54	3	3	0	.984
	Boston A.L.	5	159	12	42	57	2	2	3	7	1	11	25	11	.264	132	58	4	2	0	.979
1916—	Brooklyn N.L.	5	170	13	34	49	2	5	1	6	1	14	19	11	.200	142	70	13	2	2	.942
	Boston A.L.	5	164	21	39	64	7	6	2	12	1	18	25	18	.238	147	90	6	5	1	.975
1917—	New York N.L.	6	199	17	51	70	5	4	2	3	4	6	27	16	.256	153	72	11	3	1	.953
	Chicago A.L.	6	197	21	54	63	6	0	1	3	6	11	28	18	.274	156	82	12	7	1	.952
1918—	Chicago N.L.	6	176	10	37	44	5	1	0	4	3	18	14	10	.210	156	76	5	7	2	.979
	Boston A.L.	6	217	9	32	40	2	3	0	8	3	16	21	6	.186	159	88	1	4	1	.996
1919—	Cincinnati N.L.	8	251	35	64	88	10	7	0	13	7	25	22	34	.255	216	96	12	7	0	.963
	Chicago A.L.	8	263	20	59	78	10	3	1	7	5	15	30	17	.224	213	116	12	9	1	.965
1920—	Brooklyn N.L.	7	215	8	44	51	5	1	0	5	1	10	20	8	.205	177	91	6	5	2	.978
	Cleveland A.L.	7	217	21	53	72	9	2	2	3	2	21	21	18	.244	182	89	12	8	0	.958
1921—	New York N.L.	8	264	29	71	98	13	4	2	6	7	22	38	28	.269	212	102	5	5	2	.984
	New York A.L.	8	241	22	50	65	7	2	2	9	6	27	44	20	.207	210	106	6	8	0	.981
1922—	New York N.L.	5	162	18	50	57	2	1	1	5	1	12	15	18	.309	138	70	6	4	0	.972
	New York A.L.	5	158	11	32	46	6	1	2	6	2	8	20	11	.203	129	62	1	7	1	.995
1923—	New York N.L.	6	201	17	47	70	8	2	5	0	1	12	18	17	.234	159	80	6	8	0	.976
	Washington A.L.	6	205	30	60	91	8	4	5	6	1	22	29	29	.293	162	77	3	6	1	.988
1924—	New York N.L.	7	253	27	66	91	9	2	4	7	3	25	40	22	.261	200	94	6	4	0	.980
	Washington A.L.	7	248	26	61	95	9	0	5	6	5	29	34	23	.246	201	99	12	10	1	.962
1925—	Pittsburgh N.L.	7	230	25	61	89	12	2	4	8	7	17	32	25	.265	182	89	7	4	0	.980
	Washington A.L.	7	225	26	59	91	8	0	8	10	2	17	31	25	.262	180	75	9	8	1	.966
1926—	St. Louis N.L.	7	239	31	65	91	12	1	4	12	2	11	30	30	.272	189	99	5	6	0	.983
	New York A.L.	7	223	21	54	78	10	4	4	10	1	31	31	19	.242	189	82	7	3	1	.975
1927—	Pittsburgh N.L.	4	130	10	29	37	6	1	0	6	2	4	7	10	.223	104	46	6	2	0	.962
	New York A.L.	4	136	23	38	54	6	2	2	6	2	13	25	19	.279	108	44	3	4	0	.981
1928—	St. Louis N.L.	4	131	10	27	37	5	1	1	2	3	11	29	9	.206	102	36	5	3	0	.965
	New York A.L.	4	134	27	37	71	7	0	9	5	4	13	12	25	.276	108	28	6	3	0	.958
1929—	Chicago N.L.	5	173	17	43	56	6	2	1	2	1	13	50	15	.249	131	44	7	4	0	.962
	Philadelphia A.L.	5	171	26	48	71	5	0	6	7	0	13	27	26	.281	135	40	4	2	0	.978
1930—	St. Louis N.L.	6	190	12	38	56	10	1	2	4	1	11	33	11	.200	153	55	5	4	1	.977
	Philadelphia A.L.	6	178	21	35	67	10	1	6	7	0	24	32	21	.197	156	41	3	2	0	.985
1931—	St. Louis N.L.	7	229	19	54	71	11	0	2	4	8	9	41	17	.236	186	73	4	7	0	.985
	Philadelphia A.L.	7	227	22	50	64	5	0	3	4	0	28	46	20	.220	183	69	2	4	0	.992
1932—	Chicago N.L.	4	146	19	37	58	8	2	3	1	2	11	24	16	.253	102	40	6	7	0	.959
	New York A.L.	4	144	37	45	75	6	0	8	1	0	23	26	36	.313	108	41	8	1	0	.949
1933—	New York N.L.	5	176	16	47	61	5	0	3	6	0	11	21	16	.267	141	67	4	5	0	.981
	Washington A.L.	5	173	11	37	47	4	0	2	3	1	13	25	11	.214	138	65	4	4	0	.981
1934—	St. Louis N.L.	7	262	34	73	103	14	5	2	4	2	11	31	32	.279	196	73	15	2	0	.947
	Detroit A.L.	7	250	23	56	76	12	1	2	6	4	25	43	20	.224	195	70	12	6	0	.957
1935—	Chicago N.L.	6	202	18	48	73	6	2	5	7	1	11	29	17	.238	164	74	6	5	0	.975
	Detroit A.L.	6	206	21	51	67	11	1	1	3	1	25	27	18	.248	165	72	9	7	1	.963
1936—	New York N.L.	6	203	23	50	71	9	0	4	7	0	21	33	20	.246	159	62	7	7	0	.969
	New York A.L.	6	215	43	65	96	8	1	7	3	0	26	35	41	.302	162	57	6	2	0	.973
1937—	New York N.L.	5	169	12	40	49	6	0	1	0	1	11	21	12	.237	129	46	9	5	0	.951
	New York A.L.	5	169	28	42	68	6	4	4	0	2	21	21	25	.249	132	47	0	2	0	1.000
1938—	Chicago N.L.	4	136	9	33	45	4	1	2	1	0	6	26	8	.243	102	35	3	3	0	.979
	New York A.L.	4	135	22	37	60	6	1	5	3	3	11	16	21	.274	108	39	6	4	0	.961
1939—	Cincinnati N.L.	4	133	8	27	32	3	1	0	2	1	9	22	8	.203	106	34	4	1	0	.972
	New York A.L.	4	131	20	27	54	4	1	7	2	0	9	20	18	.206	111	50	2	5	0	.988
1940—	Cincinnati N.L.	7	232	22	58	78	14	0	2	4	1	15	30	21	.250	183	67	8	9	0	.969
	Detroit A.L.	7	228	28	56	83	9	3	4	3	0	30	30	24	.246	180	80	4	4	0	.985
1941—	Brooklyn N.L.	5	159	11	29	43	7	2	1	0	0	14	21	11	.182	132	60	4	5	0	.980
	New York A.L.	5	166	17	41	54	5	1	2	0	2	23	18	16	.247	135	55	2	7	0	.990
1942—	St. Louis N.L.	5	163	23	39	53	4	2	2	7	0	17	19	23	.239	135	45	10	3	0	.947
	New York A.L.	5	178	18	44	59	6	0	3	1	3	8	22	14	.247	132	45	5	2	0	.973
1943—	St. Louis N.L.	5	165	9	37	48	5	0	2	5	1	11	26	8	.220	129	53	10	4	0	.948
	New York A.L.	5	159	17	35	50	5	2	2	4	2	12	30	14	.220	135	63	5	3	1	.975
1944—	St. Louis N.L.	6	204	16	49	69	9	1	3	7	0	19	43	15	.240	165	59	1	3	0	.996
	St. Louis A.L.	6	197	12	36	50	4	1	1	0	0	23	49	9	.183	163	60	10	4	0	.957
1945—	Chicago N.L.	7	247	29	65	90	16	3	1	10	2	19	48	27	.263	195	78	6	5	0	.978
	Detroit A.L.	7	242	32	54	70	10	0	2	8	3	33	22	32	.223	197	85	5	4	2	.983
1946—	St. Louis N.L.	7	232	28	60	86	19	2	1	8	3	19	30	27	.259	186	68	4	7	1	.984
	Boston A.L.	7	233	20	56	77	7	1	4	3	2	22	28	18	.240	183	76	10	5	0	.963
1947—	Brooklyn N.L.	7	226	29	52	70	13	1	1	3	7	30	32	26	.230	180	71	8	6	2	.969
	New York A.L.	7	238	38	67	100	11	4	4	3	2	38	37	36	.282	185	70	4	4	0	.985
1948—	Boston N.L.	6	187	17	43	61	6	0	4	7	1	16	19	16	.230	156	54	6	4	0	.972
	Cleveland A.L.	6	191	17	38	57	7	0	4	3	2	12	26	16	.199	159	72	3	9	0	.987
1949—	Brooklyn N.L.	5	162	14	34	55	7	1	4	1	2	15	38	14	.210	132	40	5	2	0	.972
	New York A.L.	5	164	21	37	57	10	2	2	2	2	18	27	20	.226	135	44	3	5	0	.984
1950—	Philadelphia N.L.	4	128	5	26	34	6	1	0	6	1	7	24	3	.203	107	35	4	1	0	.973
	New York A.L.	4	135	11	30	41	3	1	2	1	0	13	12	10	.222	111	41	2	4	0	.987
1951—	New York N.L.	6	194	18	46	61	7	1	2	1	2	25	22	15	.237	156	65	10	4	0	.957
	New York A.L.	6	199	29	49	75	7	2	5	0	0	26	23	25	.246	159	67	4	10	1	.982

Year	Club	G.	AB.	R.	H.	TB.	2B.	3B.	HR.	Sac.	SB.	BB.	SO.	RBI.	B.A.	PO.	A.	E.	DP.	PB.	F.A.
1952—	Brooklyn N.L.	7	233	20	50	75	7	0	6	6	5	24	49	18	.215	192	71	4	4	0	.985
	New York A.L.	7	232	26	50	89	5	2	10	2	1	31	32	24	.216	192	66	10	7	1	.963
1953—	Brooklyn N.L.	6	213	27	64	103	13	1	8	2	2	15	30	26	.300	154	62	7	3	0	.969
	New York A.L.	6	201	33	56	97	6	4	9	4	2	25	43	32	.279	156	60	1	5	0	.995
1954—	New York N.L.	4	130	21	33	42	3	0	2	8	1	17	24	20	.254	106	40	4	2	0	.973
	Cleveland A.L.	4	137	9	26	42	5	1	3	3	0	16	23	9	.190	111	42	4	2	0	.978
1955—	Brooklyn N.L.	7	223	31	58	95	8	1	9	8	3	33	38	30	.260	180	84	6	12	0	.978
	New York A.L.	7	222	26	55	87	4	2	8	1	3	22	39	25	.248	180	72	2	7	0	.992
1956—	Brooklyn N.L.	7	215	25	42	61	8	1	3	5	1	32	47	24	.195	183	69	2	8	0	.992
	New York A.L.	7	229	33	58	100	6	0	12	6	1	21	43	33	.253	185	66	6	7	0	.977
1957—	Milwaukee N.L.	7	225	23	47	79	6	1	8	6	1	22	40	22	.209	186	93	3	10	1	.989
	New York A.L.	7	230	25	57	87	7	1	7	4	1	22	34	25	.248	187	72	6	5	0	.977
1958—	Milwaukee N.L.	7	240	25	60	81	10	1	3	7	1	27	56	24	.250	189	78	7	5	0	.974
	New York A.L.	7	233	29	49	86	5	1	10	4	1	21	42	29	.210	191	65	3	5	0	.988
1959—	Los Angeles N.L.	6	203	21	53	79	3	1	7	4	5	12	27	19	.261	159	69	4	4	0	.983
	Chicago A.L.	6	199	23	52	74	10	0	4	4	2	20	33	19	.261	156	62	4	2	1	.982
1960—	Pittsburgh N.L.	7	234	27	60	83	11	0	4	3	2	12	26	26	.256	186	67	4	7	3	.984
	New York A.L.	7	269	55	91	142	13	4	10	3	0	18	40	54	.338	183	93	8	9	0	.972
1961—	Cincinnati N.L.	5	170	13	35	52	8	0	3	0	0	8	27	11	.206	132	42	4	7	1	.978
	New York A.L.	5	165	27	42	73	8	1	7	4	1	24	25	26	.255	135	50	5	1	1	.974
1962—	San Francisco N.L.	7	226	21	51	80	10	2	5	4	1	12	39	19	.226	183	67	8	9	1	.969
	New York A.L.	7	222	20	44	61	6	1	3	2	4	21	39	17	.199	183	67	5	5	0	.980
1963—	Los Angeles N.L.	4	117	12	25	41	3	2	3	3	2	12	25	12	.214	108	31	3	1	0	.979
	New York A.L.	4	129	4	22	31	3	0	2	1	0	5	37	4	.171	102	49	1	7	0	.993
1964—	St. Louis N.L.	7	240	32	61	90	8	3	5	6	3	18	30	29	.254	189	64	4	6	0	.984
	New York A.L.	7	239	33	60	101	21	0	10	3	2	25	54	34	.251	186	82	9	6	3	.968
1965—	Los Angeles N.L.	7	234	24	64	91	10	1	5	6	9	13	31	21	.274	180	72	6	7	0	.977
	Minnesota A.L.	7	215	20	42	71	7	2	6	2	2	19	54	19	.195	180	58	5	3	0	.979
1966—	Los Angeles N.L.	4	120	2	17	23	3	0	1	1	0	11	17	10	.142	102	44	6	4	0	.961
	Baltimore A.L.	4	120	13	24	41	3	1	4	2	0	11	30	24	.200	108	33	0	4	0	1.000
1967—	St. Louis N.L.	7	229	25	51	81	11	2	5	2	7	17	30	24	.223	183	66	4	4	1	.984
	Boston A.L.	7	222	21	48	80	6	1	8	6	1	17	49	19	.216	186	48	2	7	0	.992
1968—	St. Louis N.L.	7	239	27	61	95	7	3	7	3	11	21	40	27	.255	186	72	11	4	0	.959
	Detroit A.L.	7	231	34	56	90	4	3	8	3	0	27	59	33	.242	186	42	2	0	0	.989
1969—	New York N.L.	5	159	15	35	61	8	0	6	3	1	15	28	13	.220	135	51	4	4	0	.978
	Baltimore A.L.	5	157	9	23	33	1	0	3	1	1	15	23	9	.146	129	50	3	4	0	.984
1970—	Cincinnati N.L.	5	164	20	48	58	6	1	5	2	5	20	47	21	.213	129	43	5	3	0	.973
	Baltimore A.L.	5	171	33	50	87	7	0	10	2	0	26	33	32	.292	135	70	3	7	1	.988
1971—	Pittsburgh N.L.	7	238	23	56	84	9	2	5	4	5	26	35	22	.235	185	69	9	2	0	.966
	Baltimore A.L.	7	219	24	45	65	3	1	5	5	1	20	46	21	.205	183	89	5	5	0	.982
1972—	Cincinnati N.L.	7	220	21	46	75	8	1	3	8	12	27	37	16	.209	187	65	9	4	0	.965
	Oakland A.L.	7	220	16	46	65	4	0	5	4	1	21	36	16	.209	195	72	10	3	1	.964
1973—	New York N.L.	7	261	24	66	89	7	2	4	4	3	26	62	20	.253	198	79	9	8	1	.969
	Oakland A.L.	7	241	21	51	75	12	3	2	3	3	28	32	10	.212	126	50	6	5	0	.967
1974—	Los Angeles N.L.	5	158	11	36	54	4	1	4	4	3	16	42	14	.228	132	51	5	6	0	.973
	Oakland A.L.	5	142	16	30	46	4	0	4	8	3	25	30	29	.211	195	76	2	8	0	.993
1975—	Cincinnati N.L.	7	244	29	59	95	9	3	7	4	9	16	40	30	.242	196	72	6	6	0	.978
	Boston A.L.	7	239	30	60	89	7	2	6	7	0	12	16	21	.251	186	78	9	4	0	.966
1976—	Cincinnati N.L.	4	134	22	42	70	10	3	4	2	7	12	16	8	.313	104	41	2	6	0	.986
	New York A.L.	4	135	8	30	38	3	1	1	1	1	16	36	28	.222	105	69	1	4	0	.996
1977—	Los Angeles N.L.	6	208	28	48	86	5	3	9	2	1	37	37	25	.231	168	68	3	2	1	.987
	New York A.L.	6	205	26	50	84	10	0	8	5	1	11	31	22	.244	158	64	7	4	0	.969
1978—	Los Angeles N.L.	6	199	23	52	78	8	0	3	1	5	20	40	34	.261	159	54	2	9	1	.991
	New York A.L.	6	222	36	68	85	8	0	3	1	5	16	35	32	.306	186	79	9	11	0	.967
1979—	Pittsburgh N.L.	7	251	32	81	110	18	1	3	8	0	16	41	23	.323	186	85	9	5	0	.968
	Baltimore A.L.	7	233	26	54	78	10	1	4	1	2	26	41	23	.232	161	68	2	8	0	.991
1980—	Philadelphia N.L.	6	201	27	59	81	13	0	3	6	3	15	17	26	.294	156	72	7	8	0	.970
	Kansas City A.L.	6	207	23	60	97	9	2	8	5	6	26	44	26	.290	156	65	9	6	0	.961
1981—	Los Angeles N.L.	6	198	27	51	77	6	1	6	6	6	20	24	22	.258	153	55	4	2	1	.981
	New York A.L.	6	193	22	46	74	8	1	6	7	4	33	34	22	.238	183	74	7	9	0	.973
1982—	St. Louis N.L.	7	245	39	67	101	16	3	4	2	7	19	28	34	.273	180	81	11	3	0	.960
	Milwaukee A.L.	7	238	33	64	95	12	2	5	1	1	20	29	29	.269	132	42	3	3	0	.983
1983—	Philadelphia N.L.	5	159	9	31	49	4	1	4	1	1	7	29	9	.195	135	51	4	5	0	.979
	Baltimore A.L.	5	164	18	35	61	8	0	6	3	2	10	37	17	.213	135	40	4	5	0	.976
1984—	San Diego N.L.	5	166	15	44	60	7	0	3	4	7	11	26	14	.265	126	52	4	2	0	.979
	Detroit A.L.	5	158	23	40	65	4	0	7	4	2	24	27	23	.253	132	60	2	9	1	.992
1985—	St. Louis N.L.	7	216	13	40	58	10	1	2	3	2	18	42	13	.185	184	80	3	3	1	.989
	Kansas City A.L.	7	236	28	68	90	12	2	2	3	7	21	56	26	.288	189	63	5	4	0	.981
1986—	New York N.L.	7	240	32	65	92	6	0	7	5	8	28	43	29	.271	188	79	4	7	1	.985
	Boston A.L.	7	248	27	69	99	11	2	5	6	0	13	26	23	.278	177	69	6	2	1	.976
1987—	St. Louis N.L.	7	232	26	60	74	8	0	3	3	12	13	44	25	.259	180	74	3	4	0	.988
	Minnesota A.L.	7	238	38	64	101	10	3	7	1	6	29	36	38	.269	180	74	3	4	0	.988

St. Louis' Tim McCarver slid into the record books (above) when, in 1964, he became the last of 12 players to steal home in a World Series game. Baltimore's Dave McNally (below right) became a record-book entry in 1970 when he became the only pitcher to hit a World Series grand slam. Former Yankee slugger Mickey Mantle, shown crossing the plate (left) after a 1956 World Series home run, holds Series records for homers (18) and runs scored (42).

The Minnesota Twins put a dent in the World Series record book when they made their unlikely run to the 1987 championship. Kent Hrbek (left) and Dan Gladden (below) became the 13th and 14th players to hit grand slams in Series play and the second teammates to do it in the same Series. Pitcher Joe Niekro (above) set a record by appearing in his first World Series after playing 21 years in the major leagues. Former Oakland A's relief ace Rollie Fingers (right) holds the career Series record with six saves.

All-Star Game

including:

- ■ Batting (Individual, Club)
- ■ Baserunning
- ■ Pitching
- ■ Fielding (Individual, Club)
- ■ Miscellaneous
- ■ Non-Playing Personnel
- ■ General Reference Data

Individual Batting

Service

Games

Players Participating in All-Star Game, Each League (39)

Henry L. Aaron, National League, 1955, 1956, 1957, 1958, 1959 (2), 1960 (2), 1961 (2), 1962, 1963, 1964, 1965, 1966, 1967, 1968, 1969, 1970, 1971, 1972, 1973, 1974. American League, 1975.

Richard A. Allen, National League, 1965, 1966, 1967, 1970. American League, 1972, 1974.

Vida R. Blue, American League, 1971, 1975. National League, 1978, 1981.

Bobby L. Bonds, National League, 1971, 1973. American League, 1975.

Robert R. Boone, National League, 1976, 1978, 1979. American League, 1983.

James P. Bunning, American League, 1957, 1959, 1961 (2), 1962, 1963. National League, 1964, 1966.

Miguel Cuellar, National League, 1967. American League, 1971.

Raymond L. Culp, National League, 1963. American League, 1969.

Baudilio J. Diaz, American League, 1981. National League, 1987.

Ronald R. Fairly, National League, 1973. American League, 1977.

Roland G. Fingers, American League, 1973, 1974, 1981, 1982. National League, 1978.

Kenneth R. Forsch, National League, 1976. American League, 1981.

Philip M. Garner, American League, 1976. National League, 1980, 1981.

Richard M. Gossage, American League, 1975, 1978, 1980. National League, 1977, 1984.

George A. Hendrick, American League, 1974, 1975. National League, 1980.

David A. Johnson, American League, 1968, 1970. National League, 1973.

Ruppert S. Jones, American League, 1977. National League, 1982.

Terrence E. Kennedy, National League, 1981, 1985. American League, 1987.

John R. Mize, National League, 1937, 1939, 1940, 1941, 1942, 1946, 1947, 1948, 1949. American League, 1953.

Robert J. Monday, American League, 1968. National League, 1978.

Bobby R. Murcer, American League, 1971, 1972, 1973, 1974; National League, 1975.

Graig Nettles, American League, 1975, 1977, 1978, 1979, 1980. National League, 1985.

Albert Oliver, National League, 1972, 1975, 1976, 1982, 1983. American League, 1980, 1981.

Larry A. Parrish, National League, 1979. American League, 1987.

Gaylord J. Perry, National League, 1966, 1970, 1979. American League, 1972, 1974.

Frank Robinson, National League, 1956, 1957, 1959, 1961, 1962, 1965. American League, 1966, 1969, 1970, 1971, 1974.

Octavio V. Rojas, National League, 1965. American League, 1971, 1972, 1973.

John Roseboro, National League, 1961, 1962. American League, 1969.

Lynwood T. Rowe, American League, 1936. National League, 1947.

L. Nolan Ryan, American League, 1973, 1979. National League, 1981.

Ted L. Simmons, National League, 1973, 1977, 1978. American League, 1981, 1983.

William R. Singer, National League, 1969. American League, 1973.

C. Reginald Smith, American League, 1969, 1972. National League, 1974, 1975, 1977, 1978, 1980.

Daniel J. Staub, National League, 1967, 1968, 1970. American League, 1976.

John E. Temple, National League, 1956, 1957, 1959 (2). American League, 1961 (2).

Jason D. Thompson, American League, 1978. National League, 1982.

J. Manuel Trillo, National League, 1977, 1981, 1982. American League, 1983.

Claudell Washington, American League, 1975. National League, 1984.

David M. Winfield, National League, 1977, 1978, 1979, 1980. American League, 1981, 1982, 1983, 1984, 1985, 1986, 1987.

Most Times Playing on Winning Club

17—Willie H. Mays, N. L., 1955, 1956, 1959 first game, 1960, 1960, 1961 first game, 1962 first game, 1963, 1964, 1965, 1966, 1967, 1968, 1969, 1970, 1972, 1973 (1 tie—1961 second game). (8 consecutive).

Henry L. Aaron, N. L., 1955, 1956, 1959 first game, 1960, 1960, 1961 first game, 1963, 1964, 1965, 1966, 1967, 1968, 1969, 1970, 1972, 1973, 1974 (1 tie—1961 second game). (8 consecutive).

Most Times Playing on Losing Club

15—Brooks C. Robinson, A. L., 1960, 1960, 1961 first game, 1962 first game, 1963, 1964, 1965, 1966, 1967, 1968, 1969, 1970, 1972, 1973, 1974 (1 tie—1961 second game). (8 consecutive).

Most Games

24—Stanley F. Musial, N. L., 1943, 1944, 1946, 1947, 1948, 1949, 1950, 1951, 1952, 1953, 1954, 1955, 1956, 1957, 1958, 1959, 1959, 1960, 1960, 1961, 1961, 1962, 1962, 1963 (consecutive).

Willie H. Mays, N. L., 1954, 1955, 1956, 1957, 1958, 1959, 1959, 1960, 1960, 1961, 1961, 1962, 1962, 1963, 1964, 1965, 1966, 1967, 1968, 1969, 1970, 1971, 1972, 1973 (consecutive).

Henry L. Aaron, N. L., 1955, 1956, 1957, 1958, 1959, 1959, 1960, 1960, 1961, 1961, 1962, 1963, 1964, 1965, 1966, 1967, 1968, 1969, 1970, 1971, 1972, 1973, 1974 (23 games), A. L., 1975 (1 game).

Most Games, Pinch-Hitter

10—Stanley F. Musial, 1947, 1955, 1959, first game, 1960, 1960, 1961, 1961, 1962, 1962, 1963 10 pinch-hit at-bats.

Youngest & Oldest Players

Youngest Player to Participate in All-Star Game

Dwight E. Gooden, 1984; 19 years, 7 months, 24 days.

Oldest Player to Participate in All-Star Game

Leroy Paige, 1953; 47 years, 7 days.

Positions

Most Fielding Positions Played, Total Games

5—Peter E. Rose, N. L., Second base, left field, right field, third base, first base, 16 games.

Most Fielding Positions Played, Game

2—Held by many players.

Batting Average & At-Bats

Highest Batting Average, Five or More Games

.500—Charles L. Gehringer, A. L., 1933, 1934, 1935, 1936, 1937, 1938 (6 games, 20 at-bats).

Most At-Bats, Total Games

75—Willie H. Mays, N. L., 1954, 1955, 1956, 1957, 1958, 1959, 1959, 1960, 1960, 1961, 1961, 1962, 1962, 1963, 1964, 1965, 1966, 1967, 1968, 1969, 1970, 1971, 1972, 1973 (24 games).

Most At-Bats, Total Games, Without a Hit

10—Terry B. Moore, N. L., 1939, 1940, 1941, 1942 (4 games).

Most At-Bats, Nine-Inning Game

5—Held by many players.
Last Players—David M. Winfield, N. L., July 17, 1979.
James E. Rice, A. L., July 17, 1979.

Most At-Bats, Extra-Inning Game

7—Willie E. Jones, N. L., July 11, 1950, 14 innings.

Most Times Faced Pitcher, Inning

2—George H. Ruth, A. L., July 10, 1934, fifth inning.
H. Louis Gehrig, A. L., July 10, 1934, fifth inning.
James E. Rice, A.L., July 6, 1983, third inning.

Runs

Most Runs, Total Games

20—Willie H. Mays, N. L., 1954, 1955, 1956, 1957, 1958, 1959,

1959, 1960, 1960, 1961, 1961, 1962, 1962, 1963, 1964, 1965, 1966, 1967, 1968, 1969, 1970, 1971, 1972, 1973 (24 games).

Most Runs, Game

4—Theodore S. Williams, A. L., July 9, 1946.

Most Runs, Inning

1—Held by many players.

Hits

Most Hits, Total Games

23—Willie H. Mays, N. L., 1954, 1955, 1956, 1957, 1958, 1959, 1959, 1960, 1960, 1961, 1961, 1962, 1962, 1963, 1964, 1965, 1966, 1967, 1968, 1969, 1970, 1971, 1972, 1973 (24 games).

Most Hits, Total Games, as Pinch-Hitter

3—Stanley F. Musial, N. L., 1943, 1944, 1946, 1947, 1948, 1949, 1950, 1951, 1952, 1953, 1954, 1955, 1956, 1957, 1958, 1959, 1959, 1960, 1960, 1961, 1961, 1962, 1962, 1963 (24 games).

Most Consecutive Games Batted Safely, Total Games

7—Mickey C. Mantle, A. L., 1954, 1955, 1956, 1957, 1958, 1959 (second game), 1960 (second game). 1959, first game, pinch runner; 1960, first game, two bases on balls.
Joe L. Morgan, N. L., 1970, 1972, 1973, 1974, 1975, 1976, 1977 (was not on team in 1971).

6—Stanley F. Musial, N. L., 1953, 1954, 1955, 1956, 1957, 1958.
Willie H. Mays, N. L., 1954, 1955, 1956, 1957, 1958, 1959, first game.
Johnny L. Bench, N. L., 1971, 1972, 1973, 1974, 1975, 1976.
David M. Winfield, A. L., 1982, 1983, 1984, 1985, 1986, 1987.

Most Hits, Game

4—Joseph M. Medwick, N. L., July 7, 1937 (5 at bats, 2 singles, 2 doubles), consecutive on last four plate appearances.
Theodore S. Williams, A. L., July 9, 1946 (4 at bats, 2 singles, 2 homers, also one base on balls), consecutive on last four plate appearances.
Carl M. Yastrzemski, A. L., July 14, 1970, night game, 12 innings, (6 at bats, 3 singles, 1 double).

Most Times Reached First Base Safely, Game

5—Philip J. Cavarretta, N. L., July 11, 1944 (3 bases on balls, one single, one triple).
Theodore S. Williams, A. L., July 9, 1946 (2 singles, 2 homers, one base on balls).

Most Hits, Inning

1—Held by many players.

Singles

Most Singles, Game (8 times)

3—Charles L. Gehringer, A. L., July 7, 1937.
William J. Herman, N. L., July 9, 1940.
Stanley C. Hack, N. L., July 13, 1943.
Roberto F. Avila, A. L., July 13, 1954.
Kenton L. Boyer, N. L., July 10, 1956.
Harmon Killebrew, A. L., July 7, 1964.
Carl M. Yastrzemski, A. L., July 14, 1970, night game, 12 innings.
Rickey H. Henderson, A. L., July 13, 1982, night game.

Most Singles, Inning

1—Held by many players.

Doubles

Most Doubles, Total Games

6—David M. Winfield, N. L., 1977, 1978, 1979, 1980; A. L., 1981, 1982, 1983, 1984, 1985, 1986, 1987 (11 games).

Most Doubles, Game

2—Joseph M. Medwick, N. L., July 7, 1937.
Aloysius H. Simmons, A. L., July 10, 1934.
Theodore B. Kluszewski, N. L., July 10, 1956.
Ernest Banks, N. L., July 7, 1959.

Most Doubles, Inning

1—Held by many players.

Most Doubles Driving In Three Runs, Inning

Never accomplished.

Triples

Most Triples, Total Games

3—Willie H. Mays, N. L., 1954, 1955, 1956, 1957, 1958, 1959, 1959, 1960, 1960, 1961, 1961, 1962, 1962, 1963, 1964, 1965, 1966, 1967, 1968, 1969, 1970, 1971, 1972, 1973 (24 games).
Brooks C. Robinson, A. L., 1960, 1960, 1961, 1961, 1962, 1962, 1963, 1964, 1965, 1966, 1967, 1968, 1969, 1970, 1971, 1972, 1973, 1974 (18 games).

Most Triples, Game

2—Rodney C. Carew, A. L., July 11, 1978.

Most Triples, Inning

1—Held by many players.

Most Triples Driving In Three Runs, Inning

Never accomplished.

Home Runs

Most Home Runs, Total Games

6—Stanley F. Musial, N. L., 1943, 1944, 1946, 1947, 1948, 1949, 1950, 1951, 1952, 1953, 1954, 1955, 1956, 1957, 1958, 1959, 1959, 1960, 1960, 1961, 1961, 1962, 1962, 1963 (24 games).

Most Home Runs, Game

2—J. Floyd Vaughan, N. L., July 8, 1941 (consecutive).
Theodore S. Williams, A. L., July 9, 1946.
Albert L. Rosen, A. L., July 13, 1954 (consecutive).
Willie L. McCovey, N. L., July 23, 1969 (consecutive).
Gary E. Carter, N. L., August 9, 1981 (consecutive).

Most Home Runs, Game, Pinch-Hitter (14)

1—Arnold M. Owen, N. L., July 6, 1942, eighth inning, none on base.
David R. Bell, N. L., July 13, 1954, eighth inning, one on base.
Lawrence E. Doby, A. L., July 13, 1954, eighth inning, none on base.
Willie H. Mays, N. L., July 10, 1956, fourth inning, one on base.
Stanley F. Musial, N. L., July 13, 1960, seventh inning, none on base.
Harmon C. Killebrew, A. L., July 11, 1961, sixth inning, none on base.
George L. Altman, N. L., July 11, 1961, eighth inning, none on base.
James E. Runnels, A. L., July 30, 1962, third inning, none on base.
Reginald M. Jackson, A. L., July 13, 1971, third inning, one on base.
Octavio V. Rojas, A. L., July 25, 1972, eighth inning, one on base.
William H. Davis, N. L., July 24, 1973, sixth inning, one on base.
Carl M. Yastrzemski, A. L., July 15, 1975, sixth inning, two on base.
Lee L. Mazzilli, N. L., July 17, 1979, eighth inning, none on base.
Frank White, A. L., July 15, 1986, seventh inning, none on base.

Most Times Home Run as Leadoff Batter, Start of Game

1—Frank F. Frisch, N. L., July 10, 1934.
Louis Boudreau, A. L., July 6, 1942.
Willie H. Mays, N. L., July 13, 1965.
Joe L. Morgan, N. L., July 19, 1977.

Hitting Home Run in First At-Bat (7)

Max West, N. L., July 9, 1940, first inning, two on base.
Walter Evers, A. L., July 13, 1948, second inning, none on base.
James Gilliam, N. L., Aug. 3, 1959, seventh inning, none on base.
George Altman, N. L., July 11, 1961, eighth inning, none on base.
Johnny Bench, N. L., July 23, 1969, second inning, one on base.
Richard Dietz, N. L., July 14, 1970, ninth inning, none on base.
Lee Mazzilli, N. L., July 17, 1979, eighth inning, none on base.

Most Grand Slams, Game

1—Fredric M. Lynn, A.L., July 6, 1983, third inning.

Most Home Runs, Inning

1—Held by many players. Accomplished 125 times. 73 by N. L., 52 by A. L.

Total Bases

Most Total Bases, Total Games

40—Stanley F. Musial, N. L., 1943, 1944, 1946, 1947, 1948, 1949, 1950, 1951, 1952, 1953, 1954, 1955, 1956, 1957, 1958, 1959, 1959, 1960, 1960, 1961, 1961, 1962, 1962, 1963 (24 games).

Willie H. Mays, N. L., 1954, 1955, 1956, 1957, 1958, 1959, 1959, 1960, 1960, 1961, 1961, 1962, 1962, 1963, 1964, 1965, 1966, 1967, 1968, 1969, 1970, 1971, 1972, 1973 (24 games).

Most Total Bases, Game

10—Theodore S. Williams, A. L., July 9, 1946.

Most Total Bases, Inning

4—Held by many players.

Long Hits

Most Long Hits, Total Games

8—Stanley F. Musial, N. L., 1943, 1944, 1946, 1947, 1948, 1949, 1950, 1951, 1952, 1953, 1954, 1955, 1956, 1957, 1958, 1959, 1959, 1960, 1960, 1961, 1961, 1962, 1962, 1963 (24 games, two doubles, six home runs).

Willie H. Mays, N. L., 1954, 1955, 1956, 1957, 1958, 1959, 1959, 1960, 1960, 1961, 1961, 1962, 1962, 1963, 1964, 1965, 1966, 1967, 1968, 1969, 1970, 1971, 1972, 1973 (24 games, two doubles, three triples, three home runs.)

Most Long Hits, Game

2—Held by many players.

Most Long Hits, Inning

1—Held by many players.

Runs Batted In

Most Runs Batted In, Total Games

12—Theodore S. Williams, A. L., 1940, 1941, 1942, 1946, 1947, 1948, 1949, 1950, 1951, 1954, 1955, 1956, 1957, 1958, 1959, 1959, 1960, 1960 (18 games).

Most Runs Batted In, Game

5—Theodore S. Williams, A. L., July 9, 1946.
Albert L. Rosen, A. L., July 13, 1954.

Most Runs Batted In, Inning

4—Fredric M. Lynn, A.L., July 6, 1983, third inning.

Bases On Balls

Most Bases on Balls, Total Games

11—Theodore S. Williams, A. L., 1940, 1941, 1942, 1946, 1947, 1948, 1949, 1950, 1951, 1954, 1955, 1956, 1957, 1958, 1959, 1959, 1960, 1960 (18 games).

Most Bases on Balls, Game

3—Charles L. Gehringer, A. L., July 10, 1934.
Philip J. Cavarretta, N. L., July 11, 1944 (also one single, one triple; 5 plate appearances).

Most Bases on Balls, Inning

1—Held by many players.

Strikeouts

Most Strikeouts, Total Games

17—Mickey C. Mantle, A. L., 1953, 1954, 1955, 1956, 1957, 1958, 1959, 1959, 1960, 1960, 1961, 1961, 1962, 1964, 1967, 1968 (16 games).

Most Strikeouts, Nine-Inning Game

3—H. Louis Gehrig, A. L., July 10, 1934.
Robert L. Johnson, A. L., July 8, 1935.
Stanley C. Hack, N. L., July 11, 1939.
Joseph L. Gordon, A. L., July 6, 1942.
Kenneth F. Keltner, A. L., July 13, 1943.
James E. Hegan, A. L., July 11, 1950.
Mickey C. Mantle, A. L., July 10, 1956.
John Roseboro, N. L., July 31, 1961.
Willie L. McCovey, N. L., July 9, 1968.
Johnny L. Bench, N. L., July 14, 1970.

Most Strikeouts, Extra-Inning Game

4—Roberto W. Clemente, N. L., July 11, 1967 (consecutive).

Most Strikeouts, Inning

1—Held by many players.

Sacrifice Hits & Flies

Most Sacrifice Hits, Total Games

1—Held by many players.

Most Sacrifice Hits, Game or Inning

1—Held by many players.

Most Sacrifice Flies, Total Games

3—George H. Brett, A.L., 1976, 1977, 1978, 1979, 1981, 1982, 1983, 1984, 1985 (9 games).

Most Sacrifice Flies, Game or Inning

1—Held by many players.

HBP & GDP

Most Hit by Pitch, Total Games

1—Held by many players.

Most Times Grounding Into Double Plays, Total Games

3—Joseph P. DiMaggio, A. L., 1936, 1937, 1938, 1939, 1940, 1941, 1942, 1947, 1948, 1949, 1950 (11 games).
Peter E. Rose, N. L., 1965, 1967, 1969, 1970, 1971, 1973, 1974, 1975, 1976, 1977, 1978, 1979, 1980, 1981, 1982, 1985 (16 games).

Most Grounded Into Double Plays, Game

2—Robert C. Richardson, A. L., July 9, 1963

Club Batting

Service

Players Used

Most Players, Game

29—N. L., August 9, 1981.

Most Players, Game, Both Clubs

56—N. L. (29), A. L. (27), August 9, 1981.

Fewest Players, Game

11—A. L., July 6, 1942.

Fewest Players, Game, Both Clubs

27—A. L. (15), N. L. (12), July 1, 1938.

Pinch-Hitters

Most Pinch-Hitters, Nine-Inning Game

8—N. L., July 9, 1957.

Most Pinch-Hitters, Game, Both Clubs

11—N. L. (7), A. L. (4), July 24, 1973.
N. L. (7), A. L. (4), August 9, 1981.
N. L. (6), A. L. (5), July 11, 1967, 15 innings.

Fewest Pinch-Hitters, Game

0—A. L., July 8, 1935.
N. L., July 9, 1940.
A. L., July 8, 1980.

Fewest Pinch-Hitters, Game, Both Clubs

1—A. L., (1), N. L. (0), July 9, 1940.

Batting Average

Highest Batting Average, Game

.436—A. L., July 13, 1954, 39 at-bats, 17 hits.

Lowest Batting Average, Game

.097—N. L., July 9, 1946, 31 at-bats, 3 hits.

At-Bats & Plate Appearances

Most At-Bats, Nine-Inning Game

41—N. L., July 7, 1937.
A. L., July 12, 1949.

Most At-Bats, Nine-Inning Game, Both Clubs

79—N. L. (40), A. L. (39), July 13, 1954.

Fewest At-Bats, Nine-Inning Game

27—N. L., July 9, 1968 (8 innings).
29—N. L., July 9, 1940 (8 innings).
A. L., July 9, 1940 (9 innings).
A. L., July 13, 1943 (8 innings).
A. L., July 13, 1948 (8 innings).
A. L., July 10, 1962 (9 innings).
A. L., July 13, 1976 (9 innings).
N. L., July 13, 1982 (8 innings).

Fewest At-Bats, Nine-Inning Game, Both Clubs

57—A. L. (30), N. L. (27), July 9, 1968.

Most Consec. Batters Facing Pitcher, Game, None Reaching Base

20—A. L., July 9, 1968. (James L. Fregosi, doubled, start of game, then 20 consecutive batters were retired until Pedro (Tony) Oliva doubled in seventh inning).

Most Batters Facing Pitcher, Inning

11—A. L., July 10, 1934, fifth inning.

Most Batters Facing Pitcher, Inning, Both Clubs

19—A. L. (11), N. L. (8), July 10, 1934, fifth inning.

Runs

Most Runs, Game

13—A. L., July 6, 1983.

Most Runs, Game, Both Clubs

20—A. L. (11), N. L. (9), July 13, 1954.

Most Runs, Inning

7—A. L., July 6, 1983, third inning.

Most Runs, Inning, Both Clubs

9—A. L. (6), N. L. (3), July 10, 1934, fifth inning.

Most Innings Scored, Game

5—A. L., July 9, 1946.
N. L., July 10, 1951.
A. L., July 13, 1954.
N. L., July 10, 1956.
A. L., July 30, 1962.
N. L., July 23, 1974.
A. L., July 6, 1983.

Most Innings Scored, Game, Both Clubs

9—A. L. (5), N. L. (4), July 30, 1962.

Most Consecutive Scoreless Innings, Total Games, One League

19—American League; last 9 innings 1967; all 9 innings, 1968, first inning, 1969.

Earned Runs

Most Earned Runs, Game

12—A. L., July 9, 1946.

Most Earned Runs, Game, Both Clubs

20—A. L. (11), N. L. (9), July 13, 1954.

Fewest Earned Runs, Game

0—N. L., July 11, 1939.
A. L., July 9, 1940.
N. L., July 9, 1946.
A. L., July 13, 1960.

A. L., July 9, 1968.
N. L., July 9, 1968.
A. L., July 16, 1985.
A. L., July 14, 1987.

Fewest Earned Runs, Game, Both Clubs

0—A. L. (0), N. L. (0), July 9, 1968.

Hits

Most Hits, Game

17—A. L., July 13, 1954.

Most Hits, Game, Both Clubs

31—A. L. (17), N. L. (14), July 13, 1954.

Fewest Hits, Game

3—A. L., July 9, 1940.
N. L., July 9, 1946.
A. L., July 9, 1968.

Fewest Hits, Game, Both Clubs

8—N. L. (5), A. L. (3), July 9, 1968.

Singles

Most Singles, Game

13—A. L., July 13, 1954.

Most Singles, Game, Both Clubs

22—A. L. (13), N. L. (9), July 13, 1954.

Fewest Singles, Game

0—A. L., July 9, 1968.

Fewest Singles, Game, Both Clubs

4—N. L. (4), A. L. (0), July 9, 1968.

Doubles

Most Doubles, Game

5—A. L., July 10, 1934.
A. L., July 12, 1949.

Most Doubles, Game, Both Clubs

7—A. L. (5), N. L. (2), July 12, 1949.

Fewest Doubles, Game

0—Made in many games.

Fewest Doubles, Game, Both Clubs

0—July 6, 1942; July 9, 1946; July 13, 1948; July 8, 1958; July 13, 1976.

Triples

Most Triples, Game

2—A. L., July 10, 1934.
A. L., July 10, 1951.
N. L., July 13, 1976.
A. L., July 11, 1978.
A. L., July 6, 1983.

Most Triples, Game, Both Clubs

3—A. L. (2), N. L. (1), July 11, 1978.

Fewest Triples, Game

0—Made in many games.

Fewest Triples, Game, Both Clubs

0—Made in many games.

Home Runs

Most Home Runs, Game

4—N. L., July 10, 1951.
A. L., July 13, 1954.
N. L., July 13, 1960.
N. L., August 9, 1981.

Most Home Runs, Game, Both Clubs

6—N. L. (4), A. L. (2), July 10, 1951.
A. L. (4), N. L. (2), July 13, 1954.
A. L. (3), N. L. (3), July 13, 1971.

Most Home Runs, Extra-Inning Game, Both Clubs, No Other Runs

  3—N. L. (2), A. L. (1), July 11, 1967.

Fewest Home Runs, Game

  0—Made in many games.

Fewest Home Runs, Game, Both Clubs

  0—July 6, 1938; July 11, 1944; July 14, 1953; July 9, 1957; July 8, 1958; July 10, 1962; July 9, 1963; July 12, 1966; July 9, 1968; July 11, 1978; July 16, 1985; July 14, 1987.

Most Consecutive Games, One or More Home Runs

  9—N. L.—1969, 1970, 1971, 1972, 1973, 1974, 1975, 1976, 1977.

Most Home Runs, Inning (11 times)

  2—A. L., July 6, 1942, first inning (Boudreau, York).
    N. L., July 10, 1951, fourth inning (Musial, Elliott).
    A. L., July 13, 1954, third inning (Rosen, Boone) (consecutive).
    A. L., July 10, 1956, sixth inning (Williams, Mantle) (consecutive).
    N. L., July 7, 1964, fourth inning (Williams, Boyer).
    N. L., July 13, 1965, first inning (Mays, Torre).
    A. L., July 13, 1965, fifth inning (McAuliffe, Killebrew).
    A. L., July 13, 1971, third inning (Jackson, F. Robinson).
    N. L., July 15, 1975, second inning (Garvey, Wynn) (consecutive).
    N. L., July 19, 1977, first inning (Morgan, Luzinski).
    A. L., July 6, 1983, third inning (Rice, Lynn).

Most Home Runs, Inning, Both Clubs

  3—N. L., 2 (Musial, Elliott), A. L., 1 (Wertz), July 10, 1951, fourth inning.
    A. L., 2 (Jackson, F. Robinson), N. L., 1 (Aaron), July 13, 1971, third inning.

Total Bases

Most Total Bases, Game

  29—A. L., July 13, 1954.

Most Total Bases, Game, Both Clubs

  52—A. L. (29), N. L. (23), July 13, 1954.

Fewest Total Bases, Game

  3—N. L., July 9, 1946.

Fewest Total Bases, Game, Both Clubs

  12—A. L. (6), N. L. (6), 1968.

Long Hits

Most Long Hits, Game

  7—A. L., July 10, 1934, five doubles, two triples.
    A. L., July 6, 1983, three doubles, two triples, two home runs.

Most Long Hits, Game, Both Clubs

  10—N. L. (5), one double, four home runs; A. L. (5), one double, two triples, two home runs, July 10, 1951.

Fewest Long Hits, Game

  0—A. L., July 11, 1944.
    N. L., July 9, 1946.
    A. L., July 14, 1953.
    N. L., July 8, 1958.
    A. L., July 8, 1958.
    N. L., July 9, 1963.
    A. L., July 16, 1985.

Fewest Long Hits, Game, Both Clubs

  0—July 8, 1958.

Extra Bases On Long Hits

Most Extra Bases on Long Hits, Game

  14—N. L., August 9, 1981.

Most Extra Bases on Long Hits, Game, Both Clubs

  24—N. L. (13), A. L. (11), July 10, 1951.

Fewest Extra Bases on Long Hits, Game

  0—A. L., July 11, 1944.
    N. L., July 9, 1946.
    A. L., July 14, 1953.

  N. L., July 8, 1958.
  A. L., July 8, 1958.
  N. L., July 9, 1963.
  A. L., July 16, 1985.

Fewest Extra Bases on Long Hits, Game, Both Clubs

  0—July 8, 1958.

Runs Batted In

Most Runs Batted In, Game

  13—A. L., July 6, 1983.

Most Runs Batted In, Game, Both Clubs

  20—A. L. (11), N. L. (9), July 13, 1954.

Fewest Runs Batted in, Game

  0—A. L., July 9, 1940.
    N. L., July 9, 1946.
    A. L., July 13, 1960.
    A. L., July 12, 1966.
    A. L., July 9, 1968.
    N. L., July 9, 1968.
    A. L., July 14, 1987.

Fewest Runs Batted In, Game, Both Clubs

  0—A. L. (0), N. L. (0), July 9, 1968.

Bases On Balls

Most Bases on Balls, Game

  9—A. L., July 10, 1934.

Most Bases on Balls, Game, Both Clubs

  13—N. L. (8), A. L. (5), July 12, 1949.

Fewest Bases on Balls, Game (8 times)

  0—N. L., July 6, 1933.
    N. L., July 7, 1937.
    N. L., July 6, 1938.
    A. L., July 6, 1942.
    A. L., July 10, 1956.
    N. L., July 11, 1967, 15 innings.
    A. L., July 9, 1968.
    N. L., July 15, 1975.

Fewest Bases on Balls, Nine-Inning Game, Both Clubs

  1—A. L. (1), N. L. (0), July 15, 1975.

Fewest Bases on Balls Extra-Inning Game, Both Clubs

  2—A. L. (2), N. L. (0), July 11, 1967 (15 innings).

Strikeouts

Most Strikeouts, Game

  17—A. L., July 11, 1967 (15 innings).
  13—N. L., July 11, 1967 (15 innings).
  12—A. L., July 10, 1934.
    A. L., July 11, 1950 (14 innings).
    A. L., July 12, 1955 (12 innings).
    N. L., July 10, 1956.
    A. L., August 3, 1959.
    A. L., July 11, 1961 (ten innings).
    A. L., July 15, 1986.

Most Strikeouts, Nine-Inning Game, Both Clubs

  21—A. L. (11), N. L. (10), July 10, 1984.

Most Strikeouts, Extra-Inning Game, Both Clubs

  30—A. L. (17), N. L. (13), July 11, 1967 (15 innings).

Fewest Strikeouts, Game

  0—N. L., July 7, 1937.

Fewest Strikeouts, Game, Both Clubs

  6—A. L. (4), N. L. (2), July 8, 1958.

Sacrifice Hits

Most Sacrifice Hits, Nine-Inning Game

  3—N. L., July 11, 1944.

Most Sacrifice Hits, Nine-Inning Game, Both Clubs

  3—N. L. (3), A. L. (0), July 11, 1944.

Fewest Sacrifice Hits, Game

    0—Made in many games.

Fewest Sacrifice Hits, Game, Both Clubs

    0—Made in many games.

Hit By Pitch

Most Hit by Pitch, Game

    2—A. L., July 10, 1962.

Most Hit by Pitch, Game

    2—A. L. (2), N. L. (0), July 10, 1962.
        A. L. (1), N. L. (1), July 15, 1975.
        A. L. (1), N. L. (1), July 19, 1977.

Fewest Hit by Pitch, Game

    0—Made in many games.

Fewest Hit by Pitch, Game, Both Clubs

    0—Made in many games.

Baserunning

Individual

Most Stolen Bases, Total Games

    6—Willie H. Mays, N. L., 1954, 1955, 1956, 1957, 1958, 1959, 1959, 1960, 1960, 1961, 1961, 1962, 1962, 1963, 1964, 1965, 1966, 1967, 1968, 1969, 1970, 1971, 1972, 1973 (24 games).

Most Stolen Bases, Inning or Game

    2—Willie H. Mays, N. L., July 9, 1963.

Stealing Home, Game

    1—Harold J. Traynor, N. L., July 10, 1934, fifth inning (front end of a double steal with Mel Ott).

Most Times Caught Stealing, Nine-Inning Game

    1—Held by many players

Most Times Caught Stealing, Extra-Inning Game

    2—Pedro (Tony) Oliva, A. L., July 11, 1967, 15 innings.

Club

Most Stolen Bases, Game

    4—N. L., July 10, 1984.

Most Stolen Bases, Game, Both Clubs

    5—A. L. (3), N. L. (2), July 16, 1985.

Fewest Stolen Bases, Game

    0—Made in many games.

Fewest Stolen Bases, Game, Both Clubs

    0—Made in many games.

Most Left on Bases, Game

    12—A. L., July 10, 1934.
       N. L., July 12, 1949.
       A. L., July 13, 1960.

Most Left on Bases, Game, Both Clubs

    20—N. L. (12), A. L. (8), July 12, 1949.

Fewest Left on Bases, Game

    2—N. L., July 13, 1971 (Batted 9 innings).
      A. L., July 13, 1971 (Batted 8 innings).

Fewest Left on Bases, Game, Both Clubs

    4—N. L. (2), A. L. (2), July 13, 1971.

Pitching

Games

Most Games Pitched

    8—James P. Bunning, A. L., 1957, 1959 (first game), 1961 (2), 1962 (first game), 1963; N. L., 1964, 1966.
      Donald S. Drysdale, N. L., 1959 (2), 1962 (first game), 1963, 1964, 1965, 1967, 1968.
      Juan A. Marichal, N. L., 1962 (2), 1964, 1965, 1966, 1967, 1968, 1971.
      G. Thomas Seaver, N. L., 1967, 1968, 1970, 1973, 1975, 1976, 1977, 1981.

Most Consecutive Games Pitched

    6—Ewell Blackwell, N. L., 1946, 1947, 1948, 1949, 1950, 1951.
      Early Wynn, A. L., 1955, 1956, 1957, 1958, 1959 (2).

Games Started & Finished

Most Games Started

    5—Vernon Gomez, A. L., 1933, 1934, 1935, 1937, 1938.
      Robin E. Roberts, N. L., 1950, 1951, 1953, 1954, 1955.
      Donald S. Drysdale, N. L., 1959 (2), 1962 (first game), 1964, 1968.

Most Games Finished

    6—Richard M. Gossage, A. L., 1975, 1978, 1980; N. L., 1977, 1984, 1985.

Innings

Most Innings Pitched, Total Games

    19 ⅓—Donald S. Drysdale, N. L., 1959 (2), 1962 (first game), 1963, 1964, 1965, 1967, 1968 (8 games).

Most Innings, Game

    6—Vernon Gomez, A. L., July 8, 1935.

Games Won & Lost

Most Games Won

    3—Vernon Gomez, A. L., 1933, 1935, 1937.

Most Games Lost

    2—Morton C. Cooper, N. L., 1942, 1943.
      Claude W. Passeau, N. L., 1941, 1946.
      Edward C. Ford, A. L., 1959 (first game), 1960 (second game).
      Luis C. Tiant, A. L., 1968, 1974.
      James A. Hunter, A. L., 1967, 1975.

Runs & Earned Runs

Most Runs Allowed, Total Games

    13—Edward C. Ford, A. L., 1954, 1955, 1956, 1959, 1960, 1961.

Most Earned Runs Allowed, Total Games

    11—Edward C. Ford, A. L., 1954, 1955, 1956, 1959, 1960, 1961.

Most Runs Allowed, Game

    7—C. Atlee Hammaker, N. L., July 6, 1983.

Most Earned Runs Allowed, Game

    7—C. Atlee Hammaker, N. L., July 6, 1983.

Most Runs Allowed, Inning

    7—C. Atlee Hammaker, N. L., July 6, 1983, third inning.

Most Earned Runs Allowed, Inning

    7—C. Atlee Hammaker, N. L., July 6, 1983, third inning.

Hits

Most Hits Allowed, Total Games

19—Edward C. Ford, A. L., 1954, 1955, 1956, 1959, 1960, 1961.

Most Hits Allowed, Game

7—Thomas D. Bridges, A. L., July 7, 1937.

Most Hits Allowed, Inning

6—C. Atlee Hammaker, N.L., July 6, 1983, third inning.

Home Runs

Most Home Runs Allowed, Total Games

4—Vida Blue, A. L., 1971 (2), 1975 (2).
James A. Hunter, A. L., 1967, 1970, 1974, 1976.

Most Home Runs Allowed, Game

3—James A. Palmer, A. L., July 19, 1977.

Most Home Runs Allowed, Inning (11)

2—Morton C. Cooper, N. L., July 6, 1942, first inning.
Edmund W. Lopat, A. L., July 10, 1951, fourth inning.
Robin E. Roberts, N. L., July 13, 1954, third inning (consecutive).
Warren E. Spahn, N. L., July 10, 1956, sixth inning (consecutive).
John T. Wyatt, A. L., July 7, 1964, fourth inning.
Milton S. Pappas, A. L., July 13, 1965, first inning.
James W. Maloney, N. L., July 13, 1965, fifth inning.
Dock P. Ellis, N. L., July 13, 1971, third inning.
Vida Blue, A. L., July 15, 1975, second inning (consecutive).
James A. Palmer, A. L., July 19, 1977, first inning.
C. Atlee Hammaker, A.L., July 6, 1983, third inning.

Bases On Balls

Most Bases on Balls, Total Games

7—James A. Palmer, A. L., 1970 (1), 1972 (1), 1977 (1), 1978 (4).

Most Bases on Balls, Game

5—William A. Hallahan, N. L., July 6, 1933, 2 innings.

Strikeouts

Most Strikeouts, Total Games

19—Donald S. Drysdale, N. L., 1959, 1959, 1962, 1963, 1964, 1965, 1967, 1968 (8 games).

Most Strikeouts, Game

6—Carl O. Hubbell, N. L., July 10, 1934, 3 innings.
John S. Vander Meer, N. L., July 13, 1943, 2⅔ innings.
Lawrence J. Jansen, N. L., July 11, 1950, 5 innings.
Ferguson A. Jenkins, N. L., July 11, 1967, 3 innings.

Most Consecutive Strikeouts, Game

5—Carl O. Hubbell, N. L., July 10, 1934; 3 in first inning, 2 in second inning (Ruth, Gehrig, Foxx, Simmons, Cronin). Then Dickey singled, Gomez struck out.
Fernando Valenzuela, N. L., July 15, 1986; 3 in fourth inning, 2 in fifth inning (Mattingly, Ripken, Barfield, Whitaker, Higuera).

Hit Batsmen, Wild Pitches & Balks

Most Hit Batsmen, Inning or Game

1—Held by many pitchers.

Most Wild Pitches, Total Games

2—Ewell Blackwell, N. L., 1946, 1947, 1948, 1949, 1950, 1951.
Robin E. Roberts, N. L., 1950, 1951, 1953, 1954, 1955.
Thomas A. Brewer, A. L., 1956.
Juan A. Marichal, N. L., 1962, 1962, 1964, 1965, 1966, 1967, 1968, 1971.
David A. Stieb, A. L., 1980, 1981.
Stephen D. Rogers, N. L., 1978, 1979, 1982.

Most Wild Pitches, Game

2—Thomas A. Brewer, A. L., July 10, 1956, sixth and seventh innings.
Juan A. Marichal, N. L., July 30, 1962, ninth inning.
David A. Stieb, A. L., July 8, 1980, seventh inning.

Most Wild Pitches, Inning

2—Juan A. Marichal, N. L., July 30, 1962, ninth inning.
David A. Stieb, A. L., July 8, 1980, seventh inning.

Most Balks, Inning or Game

1—Robert B. Friend, N. L., July 11, 1960.
Stuart L. Miller, N. L., July 11, 1961.
Steven L. Busby, A. L., July 15, 1975.
James L. Kern, A. L., July 17, 1979.
Dwight E. Gooden, N.L, July 15, 1986.
Charles O. Hough, A.L., July 15, 1986.

Individual Fielding

First Basemen

Most Games Played

10—Steven P. Garvey, N. L., 1974, 1975, 1976, 1977, 1978, 1979, 1980, 1981, 1984, 1985.

Most Putouts, Total Games

53—H. Louis Gehrig, A. L., 1933, 1934, 1935, 1936, 1937, 1938.

Most Putouts, Nine-Inning Game

14—George H. McQuinn, A. L., July 13, 1948.

Most Putouts, Extra-Inning Game

15—Harmon C. Killebrew, A. L., July 11, 1967.

Most Assists, Total Games

6—Steven P. Garvey, N. L., 1974, 1975, 1976, 1977, 1978, 1979, 1980, 1981, 1984, 1985.

Most Assists, Game

3—P. Rudolph York, A. L., July 6, 1942.
William D. White, N. L., July 9, 1963.

Most Chances Accepted, Total Games

55—H. Louis Gehrig, A. L., 1933, 1934, 1935, 1936, 1937, 1938.

Steven P. Garvey, N.L., 1974, 1975, 1976, 1977, 1978, 1979, 1980, 1981, 1984, 1985.

Most Chances Accepted, Nine-Inning Game

14—P. Rudolph York, A. L., July 6, 1942, 11 putouts, 3 assists.
George H. McQuinn, A. L., July 13, 1948, 14 putouts.

Most Chances Accepted, Extra-Inning Game

16—Harmon C. Killebrew, A. L., July 11, 1967, 15 putouts, 1 assist.

Most Errors, Total Games

2—H. Louis Gehrig, A. L., 1933, 1934, 1935, 1936, 1937, 1938.

Most Errors, Game

1—Held by many players.

Most Double Plays, Total Games

6—William D. White, N. L., 1960 (2), 1961 (2), 1963.
Harmon C. Killebrew, A. L., 1965, 1967, 1968, 1971.

Most Double Plays, Game

3—Stanley F. Musial, N. L., July 8, 1958.

Most Unassisted Double Plays, Game

1—James E. Runnels, A. L., August 3, 1959, second inning.
Lee A. May, N. L., July 25, 1972, third inning.

Second Basemen

Most Games Played

13—J. Nelson Fox, A. L., 1951, 1953, 1954, 1955, 1956, 1957, 1958, 1959 (2), 1960 (2), 1961, 1963.

Most Putouts, Total Games

25—J. Nelson Fox, A. L., 1951, 1953, 1954, 1955, 1956, 1957, 1958, 1959 (2), 1960 (2), 1961, 1963.

Most Putouts, Game

7—Juan Samuel, N. L., July 14, 1987, 13 innings.

5—Frank F. Frisch, N. L., July 6, 1933.

Most Assists, Total Games

23—William J. Herman, N. L., 1934, 1935, 1936, 1937, 1938, 1940, 1941, 1942, 1943.

Most Assists, Game

6—William L. Randolph, A. L., July 19, 1977.

Most Chances Accepted, Total Games

39—J. Nelson Fox, A. L., 1951, 1953, 1954, 1955, 1956, 1957, 1958, 1959 (2), 1960 (2), 1961, 1963 (25 putouts, 14 assists).

Most Chances Accepted, Game

9—William S. Mazeroski, N. L., July 8, 1958.

Juan Samuel, N. L., July 14, 1987, 13 innings.

Most Errors, Total Games

2—William J. Herman, N. L., 1934, 1935, 1936, 1937, 1938, 1940, 1941, 1942, 1943.

J. Nelson Fox, A. L., 1951, 1953, 1954, 1955, 1956, 1957, 1958, 1959 (2), 1960 (2), 1961, 1963.

William L. Randolph, A. L., 1977, 1980, 1981.

Stephen L. Sax, N.L., 1982, 1983.

Most Errors, Game

2—William J. Herman, N. L., July 13, 1943.

William L. Randolph, A. L., July 8, 1980.

Most Double Plays, Total Games

4—William J. Herman, N. L., 1934, 1935, 1936, 1937, 1938, 1940, 1941, 1942, 1943.

William S. Mazeroski, N. L., 1958, 1959, 1960 (2).

Most Double Plays, Game

3—William J. Herman, N. L., July 13, 1943.

William S. Mazeroski, N. L., July 8, 1958.

Most Unassisted Double Plays, Game

Never accomplished.

Third Basemen

Most Games Played

18—Brooks C. Robinson, A. L., 1960, 1960, 1961, 1961, 1962, 1962, 1963, 1964, 1965, 1966, 1967, 1968, 1969, 1970, 1971, 1972, 1973, 1974 (consecutive).

Most Putouts, Total Games

11—Brooks C. Robinson, A. L., 1960, 1960, 1961, 1961, 1962, 1962, 1963, 1964, 1965, 1966, 1967, 1968, 1969, 1970, 1971, 1972, 1973, 1974 (18 games).

Most Putouts, Game

4—George C. Kell, A. L., July 10, 1951.

Brooks C. Robinson, A. L., July 12, 1966, 9 ⅓ innings.

Most Assists, Total Games

32—Brooks C. Robinson, A. L., 1960, 1960, 1961, 1961, 1962, 1962, 1963, 1964, 1965, 1966, 1967, 1968, 1969, 1970, 1971, 1972, 1973, 1974 (18 games).

Most Assists, Game

6—Kenneth F. Keltner, A. L., July 13, 1948.

Frank J. Malzone, A. L., August 3, 1959.

Most Chances Accepted, Total Games

43—Brooks C. Robinson, A. L., 1960, 1960, 1961, 1961, 1962, 1962, 1963, 1964, 1965, 1966, 1967, 1968, 1969, 1970, 1971, 1972, 1973, 1974 (18 games), 11 putouts (32 assists).

Most Chances Accepted, Nine-Inning Game

7—Kenneth F. Keltner, A. L., July 13, 1948, 1 putout, 6 assists.

Frank J. Malzone, A. L., August 3, 1959, 1 putout, 6 assists.

Most Chances Accepted, Extra-Inning Game

8—Brooks C. Robinson, A. L., July 12, 1966, 9 ⅓ innings, 4 putouts, 4 assists.

Most Errors, Total Games

6—Edwin L. Mathews, N. L., 1953, 1955, 1957, 1959, 1960, 1960, 1961, 1961, 1962 second game.

Most Errors, Game

2—Robert A. Rolfe, A. L., July 7, 1937.

Edwin L. Mathews, N. L., July 11, 1960; July 30, 1962.

Kenton L. Boyer, N. L., July 11, 1961 (ten innings).

Most Errors, Inning

2—Edwin L. Mathews, N. L., July 30, 1962, ninth inning.

Most Double Plays, Total Games

3—Frank J. Malzone, A. L., 1957, 1958, 1959, 1959, 1960, 1960, 1963.

Brooks C. Robinson, A. L., 1960, 1960, 1961, 1961, 1962, 1962, 1963, 1964, 1965, 1966, 1967, 1968, 1969, 1970, 1971, 1972, 1973, 1974 (18 games).

George H. Brett, A.L., 1976, 1977, 1978, 1979, 1981, 1982, 1983 (7 games).

Most Double Plays, Game

1—Held by many players.

Most Unassisted Double Plays, Game

Never accomplished.

Shortstops

Most Games Played

10—Luis E. Aparicio, A. L., 1958, 1959, 1959, 1960 first game, 1961 second game, 1962, 1962, 1963, 1970, 1971.

Most Putouts, Total Games

15—Luis E. Aparicio, A. L., 1958, 1959, 1959, 1960 first game, 1961 second game, 1962, 1962, 1963, 1970, 1971.

Most Putouts, Nine-Inning Game

5—Alfonso Carrasquel, A. L., July 13, 1954.

Most Assists, Total Games

24—Joseph E. Cronin, A. L., 1933, 1934, 1935, 1937, 1938, 1939, 1941.

Most Assists, Nine-Inning Game

8—Joseph E. Cronin, A. L., July 10, 1934.

Most Chances Accepted, Total Games

38—Joseph E. Cronin, A. L., 1933, 1934, 1935, 1937, 1938, 1939, 1941.

Most Chances Accepted, Nine-Inning Game

10—Joseph E. Cronin, A. L., July 10, 1934, 2 putouts, 8 assists.

Martin W. Marion, N. L., July 9, 1946, 4 putouts, 6 assists.

Most Errors, Total Games

2—Joseph E. Cronin, A. L., 1933, 1934, 1935, 1937, 1938, 1939, 1941.

Ernest Banks, N. L., 1955, 1957, 1958, 1959, 1959, 1960, 1960, 1961.

Most Errors, Game

1—Held by many players.

Most Double Plays, Total Games

6—Ernest Banks, N. L., 1955, 1957, 1958, 1959, 1959, 1960, 1960, 1961.

Most Double Plays, Game

2—Louis Boudreau, A. L., July 6, 1942.

Martin W. Marion, N. L., July 9, 1946.

Edwin J. Joost, A. L., July 12, 1949.

Ernest Banks, N. L., July 8, 1958.

Ernest Banks, N. L., July 13, 1960.

Edward Kasko, N. L., July 31, 1961.

Luis E. Aparicio, A. L., July 30, 1962.

Richard M. Groat, N. L., July 9, 1963.

Most Unassisted Double Plays, Game
  Never accomplished.

Outfielders

Most Games Played
  22—Willie H. Mays, N. L., 1954, 1955, 1956, 1957, 1958, 1959, 1959, 1960, 1960, 1961, 1961, 1962, 1962, 1963, 1964, 1965, 1966, 1967, 1968, 1970, 1971, 1972 (19 consecutive).

Most Putouts, Total Games
  55—Willie H. Mays, N. L., 1954, 1955, 1956, 1957, 1958, 1959, 1959, 1960, 1960, 1961, 1961, 1962, 1962, 1963, 1964, 1965, 1966, 1967, 1968, 1970, 1971, 1972 (22 games).

Most Putouts, Center Fielder, Nine-Inning Game
  7—Chester P. Laabs, A. L., July 13, 1943.
  Willie H. Mays, N. L., July 7, 1964.

Most Putouts, Center Fielder, Extra-Inning Game
  9—Lawrence E. Doby, A. L., July 11, 1950, 14 innings.

Most Putouts, Left Fielder, Game
  5—Samuel F. West, A. L., July 7, 1937.
  Frank Robinson, N. L., July 9, 1957.
  Joseph O. Rudi, A. L., July 15, 1975.

Most Putouts, Right Fielder, Nine-Inning Game
  4—Charles E. Keller, A. L., July 9, 1940.
  Enos Slaughter, N. L., July 14, 1953.

Most Putouts, Right Fielder, Extra-Inning Game
  6—Roberto W. Clemente, N. L., July 11, 1967 (15 innings).

Most Assists, Total Games
  3—Stanley F. Musial, N. L., 1943, 1944, 1946, 1948, 1949, 1951, 1952, 1953, 1954, 1955, 1956, 1962 second game (1947, 1959 first game, 1960 and 1961 both games, 1962 first game and 1963, pinch-hitter; 1950, 1957, 1958, 1959 second game, first base).

Most Assists, Game, Center Fielder
  1—Held by many players.

Most Assists, Game, Left Fielder
  1—Held by many players.

Most Assists, Game, Right Fielder
  2—David G. Parker, N. L., July 17, 1979.

Most Chances Accepted, Total Games
  55—Willie H. Mays, N. L., 1954, 1955, 1956, 1957, 1958, 1959, 1959, 1960, 1960, 1961, 1961, 1962, 1962, 1963, 1964, 1965, 1966, 1967, 1968, 1970, 1971, 1972 (22 games).

Most Chances Accepted, Center Fielder, Nine-Inning Game
  7—Chester P. Laabs, A. L., July 13, 1943, 7 putouts.
  Willie H. Mays, N. L., July 7, 1964, 7 putouts.

Most Chances Accepted, Center Fielder, Extra-Inning Game
  9—Lawrence E. Doby, A. L., July 11, 1950, 9 putouts, 14 innings.

Most Chances Accepted, Left Fielder, Game
  5—Samuel F. West, A. L., July 7, 1937, 5 putouts.
  Joseph O. Rudi, A. L., July 15, 1975, 5 putouts.

Most Chances Accepted, Right Fielder, Game
  4—Charles E. Keller, A. L., July 9, 1940, 4 putouts.

Most Errors, Total Games
  2—Harold H. Reiser, N. L., 1941, 1942.
  Joseph P. DiMaggio, A. L., 1936, 1937, 1938, 1939, 1940, 1941, 1942, 1947, 1949, 1950.

Most Errors, Game, Center Fielder
  2—Harold P. Reiser, N. L., July 8, 1941.

Most Errors, Game, Left Fielder
  1—Held by many players.

Most Errors, Game, Right Fielder
  1—Held by many players.

Most Double Plays, Total Games
  1—Stanley O. Spence, A. L., 1944, 1946, 1947.
  H. Thomas Davis, N. L., 1962 (2), 1963.

Most Double Plays, Game, Center Fielder
  Never accomplished.

Most Double Plays, Game, Left Fielder
  1—H. Thomas Davis, N. L., July 9, 1963.

Most Double Plays, Game, Right Fielder
  1—Stanley O. Spence, A. L., July 11, 1944.

Most Unassisted Double Plays
  Never accomplished.

Catchers

Most Games Played
  14—Lawrence P. Berra, A. L., 1949, 1950, 1951, 1952, 1953, 1954, 1955, 1956, 1957, 1958, 1959, 1960, 1960, 1961.

Most Innings Caught, Game
  15—William A. Freehan, A.L. July 11, 1967 (complete game).

Most Putouts, Total Games
  61—Lawrence P. Berra, A. L., 1949, 1950, 1951, 1952, 1953, 1954, 1955, 1956, 1957, 1958, 1959, 1960, 1960, 1961.

Most Putouts, Nine-Inning Game
  10—William M. Dickey, A. L., July 11, 1939 (9 strikeouts).
  Lawrence P. Berra, A. L., July 10, 1956 (9 strikeouts).
  Delmar W. Crandall, N. L., July 7, 1959 (9 strikeouts).
  Johnny L. Bench, N. L., July 15, 1975 (10 strikeouts).

Most Putouts, Extra-Inning Game
  13—Roy Campanella, N. L., July 11, 1950 (14 innings—12 strikeouts).
  Forrest H. Burgess, N. L., July 11, 1961 (10 innings—12 strikeouts).
  William A. Freehan, A. L., July 11, 1967 (15 innings—13 strikeouts).

Most Assists, Total Games
  7—Lawrence P. Berra, A. L., 1949, 1950, 1951, 1952, 1953, 1954, 1955, 1956, 1957, 1958, 1959, 1960, 1960, 1961.

Most Assists, Game
  3—Lance M. Parrish, A. L., July 13, 1982.

Most Chances Accepted, Total Games
  68—Lawrence P. Berra, A. L., 1949, 1950, 1951, 1952, 1953, 1954, 1955, 1956, 1957, 1958, 1959, 1960, 1960, 1961.

Most Chances Accepted, Nine-Inning Game
  11—Lawrence P. Berra, A. L., July 10, 1956 (10 putouts, 1 assist).
  Johnny L. Bench, N. L., July 15, 1975 (10 putouts, 1 assist).

Most Chances Accepted, Extra-Inning Game
  15—Roy Campanella, N. L., July 11, 1950 (14 innings—13 putouts, 2 assists).

Most Errors, Total Games
  2—Forrest H. Burgess, N. L., 1954, 1955, 1960, 1960, 1961, 1961, (pinch-hitter only in 1959, second game).

Most Errors, Game
  1—Held by many players.

Most Passed Balls, Total Games
  1—Held by many players.

Most Passed Balls, Game
  1—Held by many players.

Most Double Plays, Total Games
  1—Held by many catchers.

Most Double Plays, Game
  1—Held by many players.

Most Unassisted Double Plays, Game
  Never accomplished.

Pitchers

Most Games Played
  8—James P. Bunning, A. L., 1957, 1959 (first game), 1961 (2), 1962 (first game), 1963; N. L., 1964, 1966.
  Donald S. Drysdale, N. L., 1959 (2), 1962 (first game), 1963, 1964, 1965, 1967, 1968.

Juan A. Marichal, N. L., 1962 (2), 1964, 1965, 1966, 1967, 1968, 1971.

G. Thomas Seaver, N. L., 1967, 1968, 1970, 1973, 1975, 1976, 1977, 1981.

Most Putouts, Total Games

3—Spurgeon F. Chandler, A. L., 1942.

Most Putouts, Game

3—Spurgeon F. Chandler, A. L., July 6, 1942.

Most Assists, Total Games

5—John S. Vander Meer, N. L., 1938, 1942, 1943.

Most Assists, Game

3—John S. Vander Meer, N. L., July 6, 1938.
Donald S. Drysdale, N. L., July 7, 1964.
Michael S. Lolich, A. L., July 13, 1971.

Most Chances Accepted, Total Games

5—Melvin L. Harder, A. L., 1934, 1935, 1936, 1937 (2 putouts, 3 assists).
John S. Vander Meer, N. L., 1938, 1942, 1943 (5 assists).
Donald S. Drysdale, N. L., 1959 (2), 1962, (first game), 1963, 1964, 1965, 1967, 1968 (1 putout, 4 assists).

Most Chances Accepted, Game

4—Spurgeon F. Chandler, A. L., July 6, 1942 (3 putouts, 1 assist).

Most Errors, Total Games

1—Edgar Smith, A. L., 1941.
John F. Sain, N. L., 1947, 1948.
Samuel Jones, N. L., 1955, 1959.
Buddy L. Daley, A. L., 1960.
Roland G. Fingers, A. L., 1973, 1974, 1981; N. L., 1978.
Michael W. Scott, N. L., 1986, 1987.

Most Errors, Game

1—Held by many pitchers.

Most Double Plays, Total Games

1—Held by many pitchers.

Most Double Plays, Game

1—Held by many pitchers.

Most Unassisted Double Plays, Game

Never accomplished.

Club Fielding

Number Of Players At Positions

Infielders

Most Infielders, Game

10—N. L., July 13, 1960, second game.
N. L., July 14, 1970, 12 innings.
N. L., July 13, 1976.

Most Infielders, Game, Both Clubs

18—N. L. (10), A. L. (8), July 13, 1976.

Most First Basemen, Nine-Inning Game

3—N. L., July 9, 1946.
N. L., July 13, 1960, second game.
N. L., July 24, 1973.

Most First Basemen, Nine-Inning Game, Both Clubs

5—N. L. (3), A. L. (2), July 9, 1946.
N. L. (3), A. L. (2), July 13, 1960, second game.

Most Second Basemen, Nine-Inning Game

3—N. L., July 13, 1960, second game.
N. L., August 9, 1981.

Most Second Basemen, Nine-Inning Game, Both Clubs

5—N. L. (3), A. L. (2), July 13, 1960, second game.
N. L. (3), A. L. (2), August 9, 1981.

Most Third Basemen, Nine-Inning Game

3—A. L., July 11, 1961, first game.
A. L., July 24, 1973.
N. L., July 13, 1976.
N. L., July 6, 1983.
A. L., July 16, 1985.

Most Third Basemen, Nine-Inning Game, Both Clubs

5—A. L. (3), N. L. (2), July 11, 1961, first game.
A. L. (3), N. L. (2), July 24, 1973.
N. L. (3), A. L. (2), July 13, 1976.
A. L. (3), N. L. (2), July 16, 1985.

Most Shortstops, Nine-Inning Game

3—A. L., July 13, 1976.
N. L., July 13, 1976.
A. L., July 8, 1980.

Most Shortstops, Nine-Inning Game, Both Clubs

6—A. L. (3), N. L. (3), July 13, 1976.

Outfielders

Most Outfielders, Nine-Inning Game

8—N. L., July 24, 1973.

Most Outfielders, Game, Both Clubs

14—N. L. (7), A. L. (7), July 8, 1980.

Most Right Fielders, Nine-Inning Game

4—N. L., July 13, 1976.

Most Right Fielders, Nine-Inning Game, Both Clubs

6—N. L. (4), A. L. (2), July 13, 1976.

Most Center Fielders, Nine-Inning Game

3—Occurred many times.

Most Center Fielders, Nine-Inning Game, Both Clubs

5—Occurred many times.

Most Left Fielders, Nine-Inning Game

3—Occurred many times.

Most Left Fielders, Nine-Inning Game, Both Clubs

5—Occurred many times.

Most Left Fielders, Extra-Inning Game, Both Clubs

6—N. L. (3), A. L., (3), July 14, 1970, 12 innings.

Battery

Most Catchers, Nine-Inning Game

3—Occurred many times.

Most Catchers, Nine-Inning Game, Both Clubs

6—N. L. (3), A. L. (3), July 9, 1940.
N. L. (3), A. L. (3), July 9, 1968.
N. L. (3), A. L. (3), July 8, 1980.
N. L. (3), A. L. (3), July 16, 1985.

Most Pitchers, Game

8—N. L., August 9, 1981.
N. L., July 14, 1987, 13 innings.

Most Pitchers, Nine-Inning Game, Both Clubs

15—N. L. (8), A. L. (7), August 9, 1981.
N. L. (8), A. L. (7), July 14, 1987, 13 innings.

Fewest Pitchers, Game

2—A. L., July 8, 1935.
A. L., July 6, 1942.

Fewest Pitchers, Game, Both Clubs

6—N. L. (3), A. L. (3), July 6, 1933.
N. L. (4), A. L. (2), July 8, 1935.
N. L. (3), A. L. (3), July 6, 1938.
N. L. (3), A. L. (3), July 11, 1939.

Most Players One or More Putouts, Game, Nine Innings

14—N. L., July 13, 1976; A. L., July 6, 1983.

Most Players One or More Putouts, Game, Nine Innings, Both Clubs

25—N. L. (14), A. L. (11), July 13, 1976.
A. L. (13), N. L. (12), July 16, 1985.

Most Assists, Nine-Inning Game

16—A. L., July 6, 1942.
A. L., August 9, 1981.

Most Assists, Nine-Inning Game, Both Clubs
 26—A. L. (15), N. L. (11), July 12, 1949.
  A. L. (16), N. L. (10), August 9, 1981.

Fewest Assists, Eight-Inning Game
 4—A. L., July 9, 1940.
  N. L., July 13, 1948.

Fewest Assists, Nine-Inning Game
 5—N. L., July 10, 1934.
  N. L., July 9, 1957.
  N. L., July 23, 1969.

Fewest Assists, Nine-Inning Game, Both Clubs
 11—N. L. (6), A. L. (5), July 7, 1959.

Most Players One or More Assists, Game, Nine Innings
 10—N. L., July 24, 1973.

Most Players One or More Assists, Game, Nine Innings, Both Clubs
 19—N. L. (10), A. L. (9), July 24, 1973.

Most Errors, Game
 5—N. L., July 12, 1949.
  N. L., July 11, 1961.

Most Errors, Nine-Inning Game, Both Clubs
 6—N. L. (5), A. L. (1), July 12, 1949.

Most Errors, Extra-Inning Game, Both Clubs
 7—N. L. (5), A. L. (2), July 11, 1961 (ten innings).

Fewest Errors, Game
 0—Occurred many times.

Fewest Errors, Game, Both Clubs
 0—Occurred many times.

Most Consecutive Errorless Games
 11—1963 through 1973.

Most Double Plays, Game
 3—N. L., July 13, 1943.
  N. L., July 8, 1958.
  N. L., July 9, 1963.
  N. L., July 13, 1976.

Most Double Plays, Game, Both Clubs
 4—N. L. (3), A. L. (1), July 13, 1943.
  N. L. (3), A. L. (1), July 8, 1958.
  N. L. (2), A. L. (2), July 25, 1972, 10 innings.
  N. L. (3), A. L. (1), July 13, 1976.

Fewest Double Plays, Game
 0—Occurred many times.

Fewest Double Plays, Game, Both Clubs
 0—Occurred many times.

Miscellaneous

Earliest & Latest Game Dates

Earliest Date for All-Star Game
 July 6, 1933 at Comiskey Park, Chicago.
 July 6, 1938 at Crosley Field, Cincinnati.
 July 6, 1942 at Polo Grounds, New York.
 July 6, 1983 at Comiskey Park, Chicago.

Latest Date for All-Star Game
 August 9, 1981 at Municipal Stadium, Cleveland.

Night Games

All-Star Night Games
 July 13, 1943 at Shibe Park, Philadelphia.
 July 11, 1944 at Forbes Field, Pittsburgh.
 July 9, 1968 at The Astrodome, Houston.
 July 14, 1970 at Riverfront Stadium, Cincinnati.
 July 13, 1971 at Tiger Stadium, Detroit.
 July 25, 1972 at Atlanta Stadium, Atlanta.
 July 24, 1973 at Royals Stadium, Kansas City.
 July 23, 1974 at Three Rivers Stadium, Pittsburgh.
 July 15, 1975 at County Stadium, Milwaukee.
 July 13, 1976 at Veterans Stadium, Philadelphia.
 July 19, 1977 at Yankee Stadium, New York.
 July 11, 1978 at San Diego Stadium, San Diego.
 July 17, 1979 at The Kingdome, Seattle.
 July 8, 1980 at Dodger Stadium, Los Angeles.
 Aug. 9, 1981 at Municipal Stadium, Cleveland.
 July 13, 1982 at Olympic Stadium, Montreal.
 July 6, 1983 at Comiskey Park, Chicago.
 July 10, 1984 at Candlestick Park, San Francisco.
 July 16, 1985 at The Metrodome, Minneapolis.
 July 15, 1986 at The Astrodome, Houston.
 July 14, 1987 at Oakland Coliseum, Oakland.

Length Of Games

Longest Game, by Innings
 15 innings—at Anaheim Stadium, California, July 11, 1967. National League 2, American League 1.

Shortest Game, by Innings
 5 innings—at Shibe Park, Philadelphia, July 8, 1952 (rain). National League 3, American League 2.

Longest Nine-Inning Game, by Time
 3 hours, 10 minutes, at Municipal Stadium, Cleveland, July 13, 1954. American League 11, National League 9.

Shortest Nine-Inning Game, by Time
 1 hour, 53 minutes, at Sportsman's Park, St. Louis, July 9, 1940. National League 4, American League 0.

Longest Extra-Inning Game, by Time
 3 hours, 41 minutes, at Anaheim Stadium, California, July 11, 1967. National League 2, American League 1, 15 innings.

Games Won & Lost

All-Star Games Won
 37—National League (one tie). (Lost 20).
 20—American League (one tie). (Lost 37).

Most Consecutive All-Star Games Won
 11—National League, 1972, 1973, 1974, 1975, 1976, 1977, 1978, 1979, 1980, 1981, 1982.

Most Consecutive All-Star Games Lost
 11—American League, 1972, 1973, 1974, 1975, 1976, 1977, 1978, 1979, 1980, 1981, 1982.

Attendance

Largest Attendance, Game
 72,086 at Municipal Stadium, Cleveland, August 9, 1981.

Smallest Attendance, Game
 25,556 at Braves Field, Boston, July 7, 1936.

Non-Playing Personnel

Managers

Most All-Star Games Managed
 10—Charles D. Stengel, A. L., 1950, 1951, 1952, 1953, 1954, 1956, 1957, 1958, 1959 (2) (won 4, lost 6).

Most Consecutive All-Star Games Managed
 5—Charles D. Stengel, A. L., 1950, 1951, 1952, 1953, 1954; also 1956, 1957, 1958, 1959 (2).

Most All-Star Games Won as Manager

7—Walter E. Alston, N. L., 1956, 1960 (2), 1964, 1966, 1967, 1975, (lost 2).

Most All-Star Games Lost as Manager

6—Charles D. Stengel, A. L., 1950, 1951, 1952, 1953, 1956, 1959 first game (won 4).

Most Consecutive Defeats as All-Star Manager

5—Alfonso R. Lopez, A. L., 1955, 1960 (2), 1964, 1965.

Most Consecutive Years Managing All-Star Losers

4—Charles D. Stengel, A. L., 1950, 1951, 1952, 1953.

Umpires

Most Games Umpired

7—Albert J. Barlick, N.L., 1942, 1949, 1952, 1955, 1959, 1966, 1970.

Most Consecutive Games Umpired

2—Held by many umpires.

General Reference Data

Results

Year—Winner	Loser
1933—July 6, Comiskey Park, Chicago; A.L. 4, N.L. 2.	
1934—July 10, Polo Grounds, New York; A.L. 9, N.L. 7.	
1935—July 8, Cleveland Stadium, Cleveland; A.L. 4, N.L. 1.	
1936—July 7, Braves Field, Boston; N.L. 4, A.L. 3.	
1937—July 7, Griffith Stadium, Washington; A.L. 8, N.L. 3.	
1938—July 6, Crosley Field, Cincinnati; N.L. 4, A.L. 1.	
1939—July 11, Yankee Stadium, New York; A.L. 3, N.L. 1.	
1940—July 9, Sportsman's Park, St. Louis; N.L. 4, A.L. 0.	
1941—July 8, Briggs Stadium, Detroit; A.L. 7, N.L. 5.	
1942—July 6, Polo Grounds, New York; A.L. 3, N.L. 1.	
1943—July 13, Shibe Park, Philadelphia; A.L. 5, N.L. 3.	
1944—July 11, Forbes Field, Pittsburgh; N.L. 7, A.L. 1.	
1945—Game canceled due to wartime travel restrictions.	
1946—July 9, Fenway Park, Boston; A.L. 12, N.L. 0.	
1947—July 8, Wrigley Field, Chicago; A.L. 2, N.L. 1.	
1948—July 13, Sportsman's Park, St. Louis; A.L. 5, N.L. 2.	
1949—July 12, Ebbets Field, Brooklyn; A.L. 11, N.L. 7.	
1950—July 11, Comiskey Park, Chicago; N.L. 4, A.L. 3; 14 innings.	
1951—July 10, Briggs Stadium, Detroit; N.L. 8, A.L. 3.	
1952—July 8, Shibe Park, Philadelphia; N.L. 3, A.L. 2; 5 innings—rain.	
1953—July 14, Crosley Field, Cincinnati; N.L. 5, A.L. 1.	
1954—July 13, Cleveland Stadium, Cleveland; A.L. 11, N.L. 9.	
1955—July 12, County Stadium, Milwaukee; N.L. 6, A.L. 5; 12 innings.	
1956—July 10, Griffith Stadium, Washington; N.L. 7, A.L. 3.	
1957—July 9, Busch Stadium, St. Louis; A.L. 6, N.L. 5.	
1958—July 8, Memorial Stadium, Baltimore; A.L. 4, N.L. 3.	
1959—July 7, Forbes Field, Pittsburgh; N.L. 5, A.L. 4.	
August 3, Memorial Coliseum, Los Angeles; A.L. 5, N.L. 3.	
1960—July 11, Municipal Stadium, Kansas City; N.L. 5, A.L. 3.	
July 13, Yankee Stadium, New York; N.L. 6, A.L. 0.	
1961—July 11, Candlestick Park, San Francisco; N.L. 5, A.L. 4; 10 innings.	
July 31, Fenway Park, Boston; N.L. 1, A.L. 1 (tie).	
1962—July 10, District of Columbia Stadium, Washington; N.L. 3, A.L. 1.	
July 30, Wrigley Field, Chicago; A.L. 9, N.L. 4.	
1963—July 9, Cleveland Stadium, Cleveland; N.L. 5, A.L. 3.	
1964—July 7, Shea Stadium, New York; N.L. 7, A.L. 4.	
1965—July 13, Metropolitan Stadium, Bloomington; N.L. 6, A.L. 5.	
1966—July 12, Busch Memorial Stadium, St. Louis; N.L. 2, A.L. 1; 10 innings.	
1967—July 11, Anaheim Stadium, Anaheim; N.L. 2, A.L. 1; 15 innings.	
1968—July 9, Astrodome, Houston; N.L. 1, A.L. 0.	
1969—July 23, Robert F. Kennedy Memorial Stadium, Washington; N.L. 9, A.L. 3.	
1970—July 14, Riverfront Stadium, Cincinnati; N.L. 5, A.L. 4; 12 innings.	
1971—July 13, Tiger Stadium, Detroit; A.L. 6, N.L. 4.	
1972—July 25, Atlanta Stadium, Atlanta; N.L. 4, A.L. 3; 10 innings.	
1973—July 24, Royals Stadium, Kansas City; N.L. 7, A.L. 1.	
1974—July 23, Three Rivers Stadium, Pittsburgh; N.L. 7, A.L. 2.	
1975—July 15, County Stadium, Milwaukee; N.L. 6, A.L. 3.	
1976—July 13, Veterans Stadium, Philadelphia; N.L. 7, A.L. 1.	
1977—July 19, Yankee Stadium, New York; N.L. 7, A.L. 5.	
1978—July 11, San Diego Stadium, San Diego; N.L. 7, A.L. 3.	
1979—July 17, Kingdome, Seattle; N.L. 7, A.L. 6.	
1980—July 8, Dodger Stadium, Los Angeles; N.L. 4, A.L. 2.	
1981—August 9, Cleveland Stadium, Cleveland; N.L. 5, A.L. 4.	
1982—July 13, Olympic Stadium, Montreal; N.L. 4, A.L. 1.	
1983—July 6, Comiskey Park, Chicago; A.L. 13, N.L. 3.	
1984—July 10, Candlestick Park, San Francisco; N.L. 3, A.L. 1.	
1985—July 16, Metrodome, Minneapolis; N.L. 6, A.L. 1.	
1986—July 15, Astrodome, Houston; A.L. 3, N.L. 2.	
1987—July 14, Oakland Coliseum, Oakland; N.L. 2, A.L. 0; 13 innings.	

Home Runs (125)

Player	Date	Inning	On	Pitcher
George Ruth, A. L.	July 6, 1933	3	1	William Hallahan
Frank Frisch, N. L.	July 6, 1933	6	0	Alvin Crowder
Frank Frisch, N. L.	July 10, 1934	1	0	Vernon Gomez
Joseph Medwick, N. L.	July 10, 1934	3	2	Vernon Gomez
James Foxx, A. L.	July 8, 1935	1	1	William Walker
August Galan, N. L.	July 7, 1936	5	0	Lynwood Rowe
H. Louis Gehrig, A. L.	July 7, 1936	7	0	Curtis Davis
H. Louis Gehrig, A. L.	July 7, 1937	3	1	Jerome Dean
Joseph DiMaggio, A. L.	July 11, 1939	5	0	William Lee
Max West, N. L.	July 9, 1940	1	2	Charles Ruffing
J. Floyd Vaughan, N. L.	July 8, 1941	7	1	Sidney Hudson
J. Floyd Vaughan, N. L.	July 8, 1941	8	1	Edgar Smith
Theodore Williams, A. L.	July 8, 1941	9	2	Claude Passeau
Louis Boudreau, A. L.	July 6, 1942	1	0	Morton Cooper
Rudolph York, A. L.	July 6, 1942	1	1	Morton Cooper
Arnold Owen, N. L.	July 6, 1942	8	0	J. Alton Benton
Robert Doerr, A. L.	July 13, 1943	2	2	Morton Cooper
Vincent DiMaggio, N. L.	July 13, 1943	9	0	Cecil Hughson
Charles Keller, A. L.	July 9, 1946	1	1	Claude Passeau
Theodore Williams, A. L.	July 9, 1946	4	0	W. Kirby Higbe
Theodore Williams, A. L.	July 9, 1946	8	2	Truett Sewell
John Mize, N. L.	July 8, 1947	4	0	Francis Shea
Stanley Musial, N. L.	July 13, 1948	1	1	Walter Masterson
Walter Evers, A. L.	July 13, 1948	2	0	Ralph Branca
Stanley Musial, N. L.	July 12, 1949	1	1	Melvin Parnell
Ralph Kiner, N. L.	July 12, 1949	6	1	Louis Brissie
Ralph Kiner, N. L.	July 11, 1950	9	0	Arthur Houtteman
Albert Schoendienst, N. L.	July 11, 1950	14	0	Theodore Gray
Stanley Musial, N. L.	July 10, 1951	4	0	Edmund Lopat
Robert Elliott, N. L.	July 10, 1951	4	1	Edmund Lopat
Victor Wertz, A. L.	July 10, 1951	4	0	Salvatore Maglie
George Kell, A. L.	July 10, 1951	5	0	Salvatore Maglie
Gilbert Hodges, N. L.	July 10, 1951	6	1	Fred Hutchinson
Ralph Kiner, N. L.	July 10, 1951	8	0	Melvin Parnell
Jack Robinson, N. L.	July 8, 1952	1	0	Victor Raschi
Henry Sauer, N. L.	July 8, 1952	4	1	Robert Lemon
Albert Rosen, A. L.	July 13, 1954	3	2	Robin Roberts
Raymond Boone, A. L.	July 13, 1954	3	0	Robin Roberts
Theodore Kluszewski, N. L.	July 13, 1954	5	1	Ervin Porterfield
Albert Rosen, A. L.	July 13, 1954	5	1	John Antonelli
David (Gus) Bell, N. L.	July 13, 1954	8	1	Robert Keegan
Lawrence Doby, A. L.	July 13, 1954	8	0	D. Eugene Conley
Mickey Mantle, A. L.	July 12, 1955	1	2	Robin Roberts
Stanley Musial, N. L.	July 12, 1955	12	0	Franklin Sullivan
Willie Mays, N. L.	July 10, 1956	4	1	Edward Ford
Theodore Williams, A. L.	July 10, 1956	6	1	Warren Spahn
Mickey Mantle, A. L.	July 10, 1956	6	0	Warren Spahn
Stanley Musial, N. L.	July 10, 1956	7	0	Thomas Brewer
Edwin Mathews, N. L.	July 7, 1959	1	0	Early Wynn
Albert Kaline, A. L.	July 7, 1959	4	0	Lewis Burdette
Frank Malzone, A. L.	Aug. 3, 1959	2	0	Donald Drysdale
Lawrence Berra, A. L.	Aug. 3, 1959	3	1	Donald Drysdale
Frank Robinson, N. L.	Aug. 3, 1959	5	0	Early Wynn
James Gilliam, N. L.	Aug. 3, 1959	7	0	William O'Dell
Rocco Colavito, A. L.	Aug. 3, 1959	8	0	ElRoy Face
Ernest Banks, N. L.	July 11, 1960	1	1	Bill Monbouquette
Delmar Crandall, N. L.	July 11, 1960	2	0	Bill Monbouquette
Albert Kaline, A. L.	July 11, 1960	8	0	Robert Buhl
Edwin Mathews, N. L.	July 13, 1960	2	1	Edward Ford
Willie Mays, N. L.	July 13, 1960	3	0	Edward Ford
Stanley Musial, N. L.	July 13, 1960	7	0	Gerald Staley
Kenton Boyer, N. L.	July 13, 1960	9	1	Gary Bell
Harmon Killebrew, A. L.	July 11, 1961	6	0	Michael McCormick
George Altman, N. L.	July 11, 1961	8	0	J. Miguel Fornieles
Rocco Colavito, A. L.	July 31, 1961	1	0	Robert Purkey
James Runnels, A. L.	July 30, 1962	3	0	Arthur Mahaffey
Leon Wagner, A. L.	July 30, 1962	4	1	Arthur Mahaffey
Rocco Colavito, A. L.	July 30, 1962	7	2	Richard Farrell
John Roseboro, N. L.	July 30, 1962	9	0	Milton Pappas
Billy Williams, N. L.	July 7, 1964	4	0	Johnathan Wyatt
Kenton Boyer, N. L.	July 7, 1964	4	0	Johnathan Wyatt
John Callison, N. L.	July 7, 1964	9	2	Richard Radatz
Willie Mays, N. L.	July 13, 1965	1	0	Milton Pappas
Joseph Torre, N. L.	July 13, 1965	1	1	Milton Pappas
Wilver Stargell, N. L.	July 13, 1965	2	1	James Grant
Richard McAuliffe, A. L.	July 13, 1965	5	1	James Maloney
Harmon Killebrew, A. L.	July 13, 1965	5	1	James Maloney
Richard Allen, N. L.	July 11, 1967	2	0	Dean Chance

Player	Date	Inning	On	Pitcher
Brooks Robinson, A. L.	July 11, 1967	6	0	Ferguson Jenkins
Atanasio (Tony) Perez, N. L.	July 11, 1967	15	0	James Hunter
Johnny Bench, N. L.	July 23, 1969	2	1	Melvin Stottlemyre
Frank Howard, A. L.	July 23, 1969	2	0	Steven Carlton
Willie McCovey, N. L.	July 23, 1969	3	1	Johnny Odom
William Freehan, A. L.	July 23, 1969	3	0	Steven Carlton
Willie McCovey, N. L.	July 23, 1969	4	0	Dennis McLain
Richard Dietz, N. L.	July 14, 1970	9	0	James Hunter
Johnny Bench, N. L.	July 13, 1971	2	1	Vida Blue
Henry Aaron, N. L.	July 13, 1971	3	0	Vida Blue
Reginald Jackson, A. L.	July 13, 1971	3	1	Dock Ellis
Frank Robinson, A. L.	July 13, 1971	3	1	Dock Ellis
Harmon Killebrew, A. L.	July 13, 1971	6	1	Ferguson Jenkins
Roberto Clemente, N. L.	July 13, 1971	8	0	Michael Lolich
Henry Aaron, N. L.	July 25, 1972	6	1	Gaylord Perry
Octavio Rojas, A. L.	July 25, 1972	8	1	William Stoneman
Johnny Bench, N. L.	July 24, 1973	4	0	William Singer
Bobby Bonds, N. L.	July 24, 1973	5	1	William Singer
William Davis, N. L.	July 24, 1973	6	1	L. Nolan Ryan
C. Reginald Smith, N. L.	July 23, 1974	7	0	James Hunter
Steven Garvey, N. L.	July 15, 1975	2	0	Vida Blue
James Wynn, N. L.	July 15, 1975	2	0	Vida Blue
Carl Yastrzemski, A. L.	July 15, 1975	6	2	G. Thomas Seaver
George Foster, N. L.	July 13, 1976	3	1	James Hunter
Fredric Lynn, A. L.	July 13, 1976	4	0	G. Thomas Seaver
Cesar Cedeno, N. L.	July 13, 1976	8	1	Frank Tanana
Joe Morgan, N. L.	July 19, 1977	1	0	James Palmer
Gregory Luzinski, N. L.	July 19, 1977	1	1	James Palmer
Steven Garvey, N. L.	July 19, 1977	3	0	James Palmer
George Scott, A. L.	July 19, 1977	9	1	Richard Gossage
Fredric Lynn, A. L.	July 17, 1979	1	1	Steven Carlton
Lee Mazzilli, N. L.	July 17, 1979	8	0	James Kern
Fredric Lynn, A. L.	July 8, 1980	5	1	Robert Welch
G. Kenneth Griffey, N. L.	July 8, 1980	5	0	Thomas John
Kenneth Singleton, A. L.	Aug. 9, 1981	2	0	G. Thomas Seaver
Gary Carter, N. L.	Aug. 9, 1981	5	0	Kenneth Forsch
David Parker, N. L.	Aug. 9, 1981	6	0	Michael Norris
Gary Carter, N. L.	Aug. 9, 1981	7	0	Ronald Davis
Michael Schmidt, N. L.	Aug. 9, 1981	8	1	Roland Fingers
David Concepcion, N. L.	July 13, 1982	2	1	Dennis Eckersley
James Rice, A. L.	July 6, 1983	3	0	C. Atlee Hammaker
Fredric Lynn, A. L.	July 6, 1983	3	3	C. Atlee Hammaker
George Brett, A. L.	July 10, 1984	2	0	Charles Lea
Gary Carter, N. L.	July 10, 1984	2	0	David Stieb
Dale Murphy, N. L.	July 10, 1984	8	0	Willie Hernandez
Louis Whitaker, A. L.	July 15, 1986	2	1	Dwight Gooden
Frank White, A. L.	July 15, 1986	7	0	Michael Scott

Regular-Season Index

Batting

Category	Individual	Club	League
PLAYERS USED		35	53
Pinch-Hitters		35	
Pinch-Runners		36	
YEARS PLAYED	8	36	
20-Year Players	133		
Youngest & Oldest Players	8		
LEAGUES & CLUBS PLAYED FOR	8		
POSITIONS PLAYED	9		
GAMES PLAYED	9	36	53
2,300 or More	134		
500 or More Consecutive	135		
BATTING AVERAGE	10	36	53
Yearly Leaders	122		
Batting .300, 10 Times	134		
.300 Lifetime Average	134		
.400 Hitters	148		
Triple Crown Hitters	142		
SLUGGING AVERAGE	11	36	53
Yearly Leaders	122		
Of Players with 4,000 Total Bases	137		
AT-BATS & PLATE APPEARANCES	11	36	53
9,000 or More	135		
RUNS	12		53
Yearly Leaders	123		
1,500 or More	135		
Season & Month		37	
Game & Doubleheader, One Club		37	
Game & Doubleheader, Both Clubs		38	
Inning		39	
Most, 1st Through 26th Innings		40	
Games Being Shut Out		41	
HITS			54
Career	13		
2,500 or More	135		
Season	13	41	
Yearly Leaders	124		
200 or More, Four Times	135		
Game	14	41	
Six Hits in Game	146		
Hitting for Cycle	15		
Doubleheader	14	42	
Inning	15	43	
Batting Streaks	15	42	
30-Game Streaks	148		
DiMaggio's 56-Game Streak	147		
SINGLES	16	43	54
Yearly Leaders	124		
2,000 or More	135		
DOUBLES	16	43	54
Yearly Leaders	125		
400 or More	136		
TRIPLES	17	44	54
Yearly Leaders	126		
150 or More	136		
HOME RUNS			
Career	19		
250 or More	136		
10 or More by Pinch-Hitter	137		
Season	20	44	54
Yearly Leaders	126		
Home & Road	20		
By Clubs, Each Year		142	
50, 40, 30 & 20 in Season	21, 142		
30 Homers, 30 Stolen Bases	148		
20 Homers, 50 Stolen Bases	148		
Ruth's 60 in 1927	147		
Maris' 61 in 1961	147		
Two Consecutive Seasons	21		
Month	21	44	
Week	21		
Game	22	45	
Four & Three in Game	23, 144		
Two in Game	23		
25 Multiple-Homer Games	137		
Consecutive & in Consecutive Games	24	46	
Doubleheader	22	46	
One Day			55
Inning	22	47	
Five & Four in Inning		145	
Three Consecutive in Inning		145	
GRAND SLAMS	25	48	55
Eight or More	136		
TOTAL BASES	26	48	56
Yearly Leaders	127		
400 in Season	143		
4,000 or More	137		
LONG HITS	27	49	56
800 or More	137		
EXTRA BASES ON LONG HITS	28	49	56
1,400 or More	137		
RUNS BATTED IN	29	49	56
Yearly Leaders	128		
Game-Winning RBIs	29	49	

Category	Individual	Club	League
BASES ON BALLS	30	49	56
Yearly Leaders	129		
1,000 or More	138		
Intentional	31	50	56
STRIKEOUTS	31	50	56
Yearly Leaders	129		
1,000 or More	138		
SACRIFICE HITS	33	51	56
SACRIFICE FLIES	33	52	56
HIT BY PITCH	33	52	56
GROUNDING INTO DOUBLE PLAYS	34	52	57
REACHING BASE ON ERRORS	35	53	
REACHING BASE ON INTERFERENCE	35		

Baserunning

Category	Individual	Club	League
STOLEN BASES	57	58	60
Yearly Leaders	130		
400 or More	138		
50 Steals, 20 Homers	148		
30 Steals, 30 Homers	148		
Steals of Home	57	59	
10 or More	139		
CAUGHT STEALING	58	59	60
Caught off Base	58	59	
LEFT ON BASE		59	60

Pitching

Category	Individual	Club	League
NUMBER OF PITCHERS USED		75	78
YEARS PITCHED	61		
20-Year Pitchers	139		
LEAGUES & CLUBS	61		
GAMES PITCHED	61		
600 or More	139		
GAMES STARTED	62		
500 or More	139		
GAMES RELIEVED	62		
GAMES FINISHED	62		
COMPLETE GAMES	63	76	78
250 or More	139		
INNINGS	63	76	78
3,500 or More	139		
WINNING PERCENTAGE	64		
Yearly Leaders	130		
GAMES WON		76	79
Career	64		
200 or More	140		
Season	64		
20 & 30-Victory Seasons	64		
Complete List	148		
20 Wins, Five Times	140		
30 Wins, Two Times	141		
Month	64		
Doubleheader	65, 155		
Consecutive	65		
12 Consecutive in Season	153		
SAVES	65	76	
100 or More	141		
GAMES LOST	66	76	79
12 Consecutive in Season	153		
AT-BATS & PLATE APPEARANCES	66	76	
RUNS	67	76	79
1,500 or More	139		
EARNED RUNS	67	76	79
EARNED-RUN AVERAGE	67	76	79
Yearly Leaders	131		
3.50 or Under, Lifetime	140		
SHUTOUTS	68	76	79
Yearly Leaders	132		
40 or More	141		
CONSECUTIVE SCORELESS INNINGS	69		
1-0 GAMES	69	77	79
10 or More	141		
HITS	69	77	
4,000 or More	140		
No-Hit Games	70	77	79
Complete List	154		
One-Hit Games	70	77	79
Singles, Long Hits & Total Bases	70, 71		
Home Runs	71	77	80
Seven or More Grand Slams	140		
BASES ON BALLS	71	77	80
1,200 or More	141		
STRIKEOUTS		78	80
Career	72		
2,000 or More	141		
Season	72		
Yearly Leaders	133		
Game & Inning	73		
Consecutive	74		

Category	Individual	Club	League
HIT BATSMEN	74	78	80
WILD PITCHES	75	78	80
SACRIFICE HITS	75	78	
SACRIFICE FLIES	75	78	
BALKS	75	78	80

Fielding

Category	1B	2B	3B	SS	OF	C	P	Club	Lg
YEARS, GAMES & INNINGS	80	83	86	89	92	95	99		
AVERAGE	81	84	87	89	92	96	99	102	107
PUTOUTS	81	84	87	90	92	96	99	102	107
ASSISTS	81	84	87	90	92	96	100	103	107
CHANCES ACC. & OFF.	82	85	87	90	93	97	100	104	107
ERRORS	82	85	88	91	94	97	100	104	107
PASSED BALLS						98		105	107
DOUBLE PLAYS	83	86	88	91	95	98	101	105	107
TRIPLE PLAYS							101	106	108
Unassisted	156	156		156				156	156
BASERUNNERS VS. CATCHERS						98			
NO-HITTERS CAUGHT						99			
NUMBER OF PLAYERS AT POSITIONS	101	101	101	101	101	102	102		

Miscellaneous

Category	Individual	Club	League
HISTORIC FIRSTS	108	109	
NIGHT GAMES		111	118
POSTPONEMENTS		111	118
TIE GAMES		111	118
ONE-RUN DECISIONS		111	119

Category	Individual	Club	League
EXTRA-INNING GAMES			118
LENGTH OF GAMES			
By Innings		112	
Games of 18 or More Innings		157	
By Time		112	
GAMES WON		113	
Lifetime by Franchises		156	
90 & 100-Victory Seasons			118
Home & Road Victories			118
Consecutive		114	
13 or More in Season		158	
GAMES LOST		114	
Lifetime by Franchises		156	
90 & 100-Loss Seasons			118
Consecutive		115	
13 or More in Season		158	
WINNING PERCENTAGE			
Lifetime by Franchises		156	
Highest, Season & Month		116	
Lowest, Season & Month		116	
YEARLY PENNANT WINNERS		120	
YEARLY FINISHES, BY TEAMS		159	
CHAMPIONSHIPS & FIRST DIVISION FINISHES		116	
LAST PLACE & SECOND DIVISION FINISHES		116	
GAMES FINISHED AHEAD & BEHIND		117	
PENNANT CLINCHINGS & DAYS IN FIRST PLACE		117	
ATTENDANCE		117	119
TEAM RECORDS	159	159	

Non-Playing Personnel

Category	Individual	Club	League
MANAGERS	119	120	120
UMPIRES	120		

Championship Series Index

Batting

Category	Individual	Club
PLAYERS USED		235
Pinch-Hitters		236
Pinch-Runners		236
SERIES PLAYED	228	236
Youngest & Oldest Players	228	
CLUBS PLAYED FOR	228	
POSITIONS PLAYED	228	
GAMES PLAYED	228	236
BATTING AVERAGE	229	237
By Club, Each Series		276
Leading Batters, Each Series	274	
.400 Hitters, Each Series	274	
SLUGGING AVERAGE	229	237
AT-BATS & PLATE APPEARANCES	229	237
RUNS	230	239
Games Being Shut Out		240
HITS	230	240
SINGLES	231	241
DOUBLES	231	241
TRIPLES	232	242
HOME RUNS	232	242
Complete List	275	
Players With Three or More, Lifetime	275	
TOTAL BASES	233	243
LONG HITS	233	244
EXTRA BASES ON LONG HITS		244
RUNS BATTED IN	233	244
BASES ON BALLS	234	245
STRIKEOUTS	234	246
SACRIFICE HITS	235	246
SACRIFICE FLIES	235	247
HIT BY PITCH	235	247
GROUNDING INTO DOUBLE PLAYS	235	
REACHING BASE ON INTERFERENCE	235	

Baserunning

Category	Individual	Club
STOLEN BASES	248	248
CAUGHT STEALING	248	249
LEFT ON BASE		249

Pitching

Category	Individual	Club
SERIES PITCHED	250	
Youngest & Oldest Pitchers	250	
GAMES PITCHED	250	254
GAMES STARTED	250	
GAMES RELIEVED & FINISHED	250	
COMPLETE GAMES	251	254
INNINGS	251	
GAMES WON	251	
Pitchers With Three or More, Lifetime	275	
SAVES	251	254
GAMES LOST	252	

Category	Individual	Club
RUNS	252	255
EARNED RUNS	252	
SHUTOUTS	252	255
Complete List	274	
1-0 GAMES		255
HITS	252	
DOUBLES, TRIPLES & HOMERS	253	
TOTAL BASES	253	
BASES ON BALLS	253	
STRIKEOUTS	253	
10-Strikeout Games by Pitchers	276	
HIT BATSMEN	254	
WILD PITCHES	254	255
BALKS	254	255

Fielding

Category	1B	2B	3B	SS	OF	C	P	Club
SERIES	255	256	258	259	261	262	264	
GAMES	255	256	258	259	261	262	264	
AVERAGE	255	256	258	259	261	262	264	268
By Club, Each Series								276
PUTOUTS	255	257	258	260	261	262	264	268
ASSISTS	255	257	258	260	261	262	264	269
CHANCES ACCEPTED	255	257	258	260	261	262	264	
CHANCES OFFERED	255	257	258	260	261	262	264	269
ERRORS	256	257	259	260	262	263	265	269
PASSED BALLS						263		270
RUNNERS CAUGHT STEALING						263		
DOUBLE PLAYS	256	257	259	260	262	263	265	270
NUM. PLAYERS AT POSITIONS	265	265	266	266	266	267	267	

Miscellaneous

Category	Club
SERIES RESULTS	273
ONE-RUN DECISIONS	271
LENGTH OF GAMES	
By Innings	271
By Time	271
SERIES WON	271, 273
SERIES LOST	272, 273
GAMES WON	271, 273
GAMES LOST	272, 273
SERIES STARTING & FINISHING DATES	271
HOME & ROAD GAMES, EACH CLUB	273
EXTRA-INNING GAMES—COMPLETE LIST	274
ATTENDANCE	272
Each Series	274

Non-Playing Personnel

Category	Individual
MANAGERS	272
Complete List With Won-Lost Records	276
UMPIRES	273

World Series Index

Batting

Category	Individual	Club
PLAYERS USED		290
Pinch-Hitters		290
Pinch-Runners		290
SERIES PLAYED	282	291
Youngest & Oldest Players	282	
CLUBS PLAYED FOR	282	
POSITIONS PLAYED	282	
GAMES PLAYED	282	291
BATTING AVERAGE	283	291
By Club, Each Series		329
Leading Batters, Each Series	324	
.400 Hitters, Each Series	325	
SLUGGING AVERAGE	283	291
AT-BATS & PLATE APPEARANCES	283	291
RUNS	283	292
Games Being Shut Out		293
HITS	284	293
SINGLES	285	294
DOUBLES	285	294
TRIPLES	285	294
HOME RUNS	286	295
Complete List	326	
Players With Four or More, Lifetime	327	
TOTAL BASES	287	296
LONG HITS	287	296
EXTRA BASES ON LONG HITS	288	297
RUNS BATTED IN	288	297
BASES ON BALLS	288	297
STRIKEOUTS	289	298
SACRIFICE HITS	289	298
SACRIFICE FLIES	289	299
HIT BY PITCH	289	299
GROUNDING INTO DOUBLE PLAYS	289	
REACHING BASE ON ERRORS	289	299
REACHING BASE ON INTERFERENCE	289	

Baserunning

Category	Individual	Club
STOLEN BASES	299	300
CAUGHT STEALING	300	300
LEFT ON BASE		301

Pitching

Category	Individual	Club
SERIES PITCHED	301	
Youngest & Oldest Pitchers	301	
GAMES PITCHED	301	305
GAMES STARTED	301	
GAMES RELIEVED & FINISHED	302	
COMPLETE GAMES	302	306
INNINGS	302	
GAMES WON	302	
Pitchers With Four or More, Lifetime	328	
SAVES	303	306
GAMES LOST	303	
RUNS	303	306

Category	Individual	Club
EARNED RUNS	303	
EARNED-RUN AVERAGE	303	
SHUTOUTS & SCORELESS INNINGS	303	306
Complete List	324	
1-0 GAMES		306
HITS	304	
DOUBLES, TRIPLES & HOMERS	304	
TOTAL BASES & LONG HITS	304	
BASES ON BALLS	305	
STRIKEOUTS	305	
10-Strikeout Games by Pitchers	328	
HIT BATSMEN	305	
WILD PITCHES	305	306
BALKS	305	306

Fielding

Category	1B	2B	3B	SS	OF	C	P	Club
SERIES	307	308	309	310	311	312	314	
GAMES	307	308	309	310	311	312	314	
AVERAGE	307	308	309	310	311	312	314	317
By Club, Each Series								329
PUTOUTS	307	308	309	310	311	313	314	318
ASSISTS	307	308	309	310	311	313	314	318
CHANCES ACCEPTED	307	308	309	310	311	313	314	
CHANCES OFFERED	307	308	309	310	311	313	314	319
ERRORS	307	308	309	310	312	313	315	319
PASSED BALLS						313		320
RUNNERS CAUGHT STEALING						314		
DOUBLE PLAYS	307	308	309	310	312	314	315	320
TRIPLE PLAYS			309					320
NUM. PLAYERS AT POSITIONS	315	315	316	316	316	317	317	

Miscellaneous

Category	Club
SERIES RESULTS	323
ONE-RUN DECISIONS	320
LENGTH OF GAMES	
By Innings	320
By Time	321
SERIES STARTING & FINISHING DATES	321
SERIES WON	321, 323
SERIES LOST	321, 323
GAMES WON	321, 323
GAMES LOST	321, 323
NIGHT GAMES	321
HOME & ROAD GAMES, EACH CLUB	323
TIE GAMES	324
EXTRA-INNING GAMES—COMPLETE LIST	324
ATTENDANCE	322
Each Series	324

Non-Playing Personnel

Category	Individual
MANAGERS	322
Complete List With Won-Lost Records	328
UMPIRES	322

All-Star Game Index

Batting

Category	Individual	Club
PLAYERS USED		338
Pinch-Hitters		338
GAMES PLAYED	336	
Youngest & Oldest Players	336	
POSITIONS PLAYED	336	
BATTING AVERAGE	336	339
AT-BATS & PLATE APPEARANCES	336	339
RUNS	336	339
EARNED RUNS		339
HITS	337	339
SINGLES	337	339
DOUBLES	337	339
TRIPLES	337	339
HOME RUNS	337	339
Complete List	347	
TOTAL BASES	338	340
LONG HITS	338	340
EXTRA BASES ON LONG HITS		340
RUNS BATTED IN	338	340
BASES ON BALLS	338	340
STRIKEOUTS	338	340
SACRIFICE HITS	338	340
SACRIFICE FLIES	338	
HIT BY PITCH	338	341
GROUNDING INTO DOUBLE PLAYS	338	

Baserunning

Category	Individual	Club
STOLEN BASES	341	341
CAUGHT STEALING	341	
LEFT ON BASE		341

Pitching

Category	Individual
GAMES PITCHED	341
GAMES STARTED & FINISHED	341
GAMES WON & LOST	341
INNINGS	341
RUNS & EARNED RUNS	341
HITS	342
HOME RUNS	342
BASES ON BALLS	342
STRIKEOUTS	342
HIT BATSMEN	342
WILD PITCHES	342
BALKS	342

Fielding

Category	Individual	Club
FIRST BASEMEN	342	
SECOND BASEMEN	343	

Category	Individual	Club
THIRD BASEMEN	343	
SHORTSTOPS	343	
OUTFIELDERS	344	
CATCHERS	344	
PITCHERS	344	
NUMBER OF PLAYERS AT POSITIONS		345

Miscellaneous

Catetory	Club
EARLIEST & LATEST GAME DATES	346
NIGHT GAMES	346
LENGTH OF GAMES	346
GAMES WON & LOST	346
ATTENDANCE	346

Non-Playing Personnel

Catetory	Individual
MANAGERS	346
UMPIRES	347